# The SAGE Handbook of
# Identities

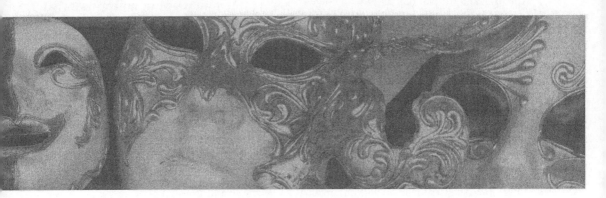

# Handbook Advisory Panel

M. Jacqui Alexander, Women's Studies and Gender Studies, University of Toronto
Tony Bennett, Social Sciences, Open University
Bronwyn Davies, Australian Youth Research Centre, University of Melbourne
Kevin Durrheim, School of Psychology, University of KwaZulu-Natal
Anthony Elliott, Sociology, Flinders University
Michael Hames-García, Ethnic Studies, University of Oregon
Dorothy Holland, Anthropology, University of North Carolina, Chapel Hill
Kim Knott, Theology and Religious Studies, University of Leeds
Gail Lewis, Social Sciences, Open University
Paula Rothenberg, The Murphy Institute, City University of New York

# The SAGE Handbook of
# Identities

Edited by
## Margaret Wetherell and
## Chandra Talpade Mohanty

Los Angeles | London | New Delhi
Singapore | Washington DC

SAGE Publications Ltd
1 Oliver's Yard
55 City Road
London EC1Y 1SP

SAGE Publications Inc.
2455 Teller Road
Thousand Oaks, California 91320

SAGE Publications India Pvt Ltd
B 1/I 1 Mohan Cooperative Industrial Area
Mathura Road
New Delhi 110 044

SAGE Publications Asia-Pacific Pte Ltd
33 Pekin Street #02-01
Far East Square
Singapore 048763

Library of Congress Control Number: 2009932172

**British Library Cataloguing in Publication data**

A catalogue record for this book is available from the British Library

ISBN 978-1-4129-3411-4

Typeset by GLYPH International Pvt. Ltd., Bangalore, India
Printed in Great Britain by MPG Books Group, Bodmin, Cornwall
Printed on paper from sustainable resources

**Mixed Sources**
Product group from well-managed
forests and other controlled sources
www.fsc.org Cert no. SA-COC-1565
© 1996 Forest Stewardship Council

FSC

# Contents

# Acknowledgements

This project owes its existence to a piece of academic match-making and we would like to thank our dear friends and colleagues Gail Lewis, Ann Phoenix and Avtar Brah for suggesting that we might collaborate on this Handbook. Despite their confidence it took a number of trans-Atlantic telephone calls talking through our histories and ways of working to establish our particular lines of difference and similarity. We needed to be sure the differences would be stimulating and the similarities sufficient. But our friends were right, and as work began and the flow of e-mails and phone calls increased, academic convenience flowered into a deep sustaining friendship. One of the great pleasures of this project (and our intellectual lives) has been the opportunity to work together.

We knew a Handbook was a big commitment but we did not realise it would take almost four years. We decided early on, however, to take our time, not to be hurried, to get the right authors, wait until they were free and had the space to discuss their chapters and their current thinking with us. We are profoundly grateful to our contributors. They have produced remarkable pieces and have remained patient, responsive and committed throughout, although they must have wondered when all their efforts might lead to some results! We are particularly grateful to our editorial team at SAGE Publications, Michael Carmichael and Sophie Hine, who philosophically accepted the delays and encouraged us to keep going for the best possible outcome. Kerry Carter prepared the manuscript for us and was remarkably efficient and positive in the face of a bewildering diversity of files and styles.

Margie would like to thank her colleagues in the UK's Economic and Social Research Council Identities and Social Action Programme for creating the kind of collective environment in which thinking differently about identities not only became possible but a pleasure (http://www.identities.org.uk). The companionship of my husband, Pete Williams, and my son, Sam Wetherell, has made it worth the effort. I would also like to thank the Open University Psychology Department secretarial team Lynda Hammond, Elaine Richardson, Gail Valentine, Sarah Pelosi and Brigid Vigrass for their help, and, most importantly, the long-term support of Wendy Hollway, my close colleague, former Head of Department and good friend.

Chandra would like to thank her colleagues and sisters in Ithaca, Syracuse, and in feminist communities around the world for their vision and commitment to struggles for social justice. It is their revolutionary collective presence in the world that keeps her going. I have been lucky to be a part of the Future of Minority Studies (FMS) project, and it is this intellectual community that has taught me to take issues of identity and social justice seriously. Satya P. Mohanty has been central to these efforts, both in terms of his own brilliant work on identity, and in his unstinting and engaged critique of my work. My daughter Uma continues to teach me that parenting is a grand adventure to be cherished always. Last but not least, Sarah Miraglia, my assistant in Women's and Gender Studies at Syracuse University was a great help in the process of preparing this manuscript. Thanks Sarah for being a truly fabulous research assistant.

# Notes on Contributors

**Linda Martín Alcoff** is Professor of Philosophy at Hunter College/CUNY Graduate Center. Recent books include *Thinking From the Underside of History* co-edited with Eduardo Mendieta (Rowman & Littlefield, 2000); *Real Knowing: New Versions of the Coherence Theory of Knowledge* (Cornell, new in paperback 2008); *Singing in the Fire: Tales of Women in Philosophy* (Rowman and Littlefield, 2003); *Visible Identities: Race, Gender and the Self* (Oxford, 2006); *The Blackwell Guide to Feminist Philosophy* co-edited with Eva Feder Kittay (Blackwell, 2006) and *Identity Politics Reconsidered* co-edited with Michael Hames-García, Satya Mohanty and Paula Moya (Palgrave, 2006).

**Moya Bailey** is a scholar of critical race, feminist, and disability studies at Emory University. Her current research examines the hidden normative and hegemonic frames that undergird the seemingly neutral category of 'health'. She looks beyond disparities in healthcare at how race, class, age, gender, sex, ability, etc. shape definitions of health and pathology. Most of her activism addresses representations of women in popular culture.

**Peter Bansel** is a researcher at the University of Western Sydney. He has worked on a number of projects that have investigated constitutive relations between neoliberalism, subjectivity and work. His doctoral work on life-history narratives articulated those practices of government through which narrating subjects are constituted as narratable, and through which subjects constitute themselves as the 'I', or embodied narrator, of their biographical accounts of experience. This work on narrative and biography emphasised a constitutive relationality between the human and the not-human, and articulated a subject who, though constituted and regulated through practices of government, is never reducible to them.

**Bethan Benwell** is Senior Lecturer in English Language and Linguistics in the Department of English Studies at the University of Stirling. Her research interests are in discourse analytical approaches to identity, gender, the media and reception studies. She is the editor of *Masculinity and Men's Lifestyle Magazines* (2003) and the co-author of *Discourse and Identity* (2006, with Elizabeth Stokoe). She is currently working with colleagues on a three year UK Arts and Humanities Research Council funded project looking at the relationship between reading, location and diaspora.

**Carole Boyce Davies** is Professor of Africana Studies and English at Cornell University. Her publications include: *Left of Karl Marx. The Political Life of Black Communist Claudia Jones* (Duke University Press, 2008); *Black Women, Writing and Identity: Migrations of the Subject*

(Routledge, 1994) and most recently she has been the general editor for the three volume *Encyclopedia of the African Diaspora* (ABC-CLIO, 2008).

**Ed Cairns** is Professor of Psychology at the University of Ulster in Coleraine, Northern Ireland where he has been on the faculty since 1972. His research focuses on the psychological aspects of political violence in relation to the conflict in Northern Ireland. He has been a visiting scholar at the Universities of Florida, Cape Town, Melbourne and Massachusetts. He is a Fellow of the British Psychological Society, a Fellow of the American Psychological Association, and Past President of the Division of Peace Psychology of the American Psychological Association. He has published extensively, his last book being: *Children and Political Violence* (Blackwell, 1996).

**Sarah E. Chinn** is an Associate Professor of English at Hunter College at the City University of New York. She is also the Executive Director of the Center for Lesbian and Gay Studies at the CUNY Graduate Center. She has published widely in American studies, queer theory, and disability studies and is the author of *Technology and Logic of American Racism: A Cultural History of the Body as Evidence* (Continuum, 2000) and *Inventing Modern Adolescence: The Children of Immigrants in Turn-of-the-Century America* (Rutgers University Press, 2008).

**Manisha Desai** is the Director of Women's Studies at the University of Connecticut. Her areas of research include gender and globalization, social movements, transnational feminisms, women's human rights and contemporary Indian society. She has published numerous articles and book chapters and is the author of *Gender and the Politics of Possibilities: Rethinking Globalization*; co-editor of *Gender, Family, and Law in a Changing Middle East and South Asia*; editor of *Women's Issues in Asia and Oceania* and co-editor of *Women's Activism and Globalization: Linking Local Struggles to Transnational Politics*.

**Saurabh Dube** is Professor of History at the Center for Asian and African Studies, El Colegio de México in Mexico City. He received a PhD from Cambridge University and previously taught at Delhi University. Dube has been a Fellow of the John Simon Guggenheim Memorial Foundation and several times visiting Professor at Cornell University. His authored books include *After Conversion* (2009); *Stitches on Time* (2004); *Untouchable Pasts* (1998) as well as a trilogy in historical anthropology in the Spanish language. Among Dube's ten edited volumes are *Enchantments of Modernity* (2009); *Historical Anthropology* (2007) and *Postcolonial Passages* (2004).

**Harry J. Elam, Jr** is the Olive H. Palmer Professor in the Humanities and Director of the Institute for Diversity in the Arts at Stanford. He is author of *Taking It to the Streets: The Social Protest Theater of Luis Valdez and Amiri Baraka; The Past as Present in the Drama of August Wilson* and co-editor of *African American Performance and Theater History: A Critical Reader; Colored Contradictions: An Anthology of Contemporary African American Drama; The Fire This Time: African American Plays for the New Millennium* and *Black Cultural Traffic: Crossroads in Performance and Popular Culture*.

**Michele Elam**, Martin Luther King, Jr. Centennial Professor, is an Associate Professor in English and Director of the Program in African and African American Studies. She is the author of *Race, Work, and Desire in American Literature, 1860–1930* (Cambridge University Press, 2003); *The Souls of Mixed Folks* (Stanford University Press, 2010) and is currently working on a book on post-race and post-apartheid performance in the US and South Africa. She has published articles in *African American Review, American Literature, Callaloo, Theatre Journal*, and *Genre*, among others. Her research interests include African American literature and theory, gender studies and mixed race studies.

**Anne Fausto-Sterling** is Professor of Biology and Gender Studies at Brown University. She has been on the Brown faculty since 1971. She began her career as a research biologist publishing on the embryology and genetics of the fruit fly, *Drosophila melanogaster*. Her work on feminist theory and science has led to the publication of two books: *Myths of Gender: Biological Theories about Women and Men* (Basic Books, 1985, 1993) and *Sexing the Body: Gender Politics and the Construction of Sexuality* (Basic Books, 2000). She is currently developing a developmental systems approach to the understanding of gender, race and sexuality that she hopes will replace the nature/nurture analytic.

**Stephen Frosh** is Pro-Vice-Master, Head of the School of Psychosocial Studies and Professor of Psychology at Birkbeck College, University of London. He is the author of many books and papers on psychosocial studies and on psychoanalysis, including *Hate and the 'Jewish Science': Anti-Semitism, Nazism and Psychoanalysis* (Palgrave, 2005) *For and Against Psychoanalysis* (Routledge, 2006); *After Words* (Palgrave, 2002) and *The Politics of Psychoanalysis* (Palgrave, 1999).

**Rosemarie Garland-Thomson** is Professor of Women's Studies at Emory University. Her fields of study are feminist theory, American literature, and disability studies. Her work develops the field of disability studies in the humanities and women's and gender studies. She is author of *Staring: How We Look* and *Extraordinary Bodies: Figuring Physical Disability in American Literature and Culture*; co-editor of *Re-Presenting Disability: Museums and the Politics of Display* and *Disability Studies: Enabling the Humanities* and editor of *Freakery: Cultural Spectacles of the Extraordinary Body*. Her current book-in-progress concerns the logic, space, and design of euthanasia in the Holocaust and American literature.

**S. Alexander Haslam** is Professor of Social and Organizational Psychology at the University of Exeter. He is former Editor of the *European Journal of Social Psychology*, and currently on the editorial board of 10 international journals including *Scientific American Mind*. His work with colleagues at Exeter and elsewhere focuses on the study of social identity in social and organizational contexts, illustrated by his most recent book *Psychology in Organizations: The Social Identity Approach* (2nd edn, Sage, 2004). He is a Fellow of the Canadian Institute of Advanced Research and a former recipient of EASP's Kurt Lewin award.

**R. Aída Hernández Castillo** earned her doctorate in anthropology from Stanford University in 1996. She is currently Professor and Senior Researcher at CIESAS, the Center for Research and Advanced Studies in Social Anthropology in Mexico City. She has worked extensively in the past on exploring gender and ethnic identities in Mesoamerica. She is the author of *Histories and Stories from Chiapas: Border Identities in Southern Mexico* (UT Press, 2001) published also in Spanish *as La Otra Frontera: Identidades Múltiples en el Chiapas Postcolonial* (2001); co-editor of *Descolonizando el Feminismo. Teorías y Prácticas desde los Márgenes* (Catedra, 2008); *Dissident Women. Gender and Cultural Politics in Chiapas* (UT Press, 2006); *Mayan Lives, Mayan Utopias: the Indigenous Peoples of Chiapas and the Zapatista Rebellion* (Rowman and Littlefield, 2003) and *The Other Word: Women and Violence in Chiapas Before and After Acteal* (IWGIA, 2001) among other books.

**Miles Hewstone** is Professor of Social Psychology at Oxford University. He has published widely in the field of general experimental social psychology including on attribution theory, social cognition, social influence, stereotyping and intergroup relations. He is a fellow of the British Academy, recipient of the British Psychological Society Presidents' Award for Distinguished Contributions to Psychological Knowledge, and a former Editor of the *British Journal of Social Psychology*. Recent books include *Applied Social Psychology* and *Self and Social Identity* (edited with Marilyn Brewer published by Blackwell) and *Causal Attribution: From Cognitive Processes to Collective Beliefs* (Blackwell).

**Wendy Hollway** is Professor of Psychology at the Open University. She is a social and qualitative psychologist whose major interests are in applying psycho-social principles to empirical research on identity. Her recent books include: *Doing Qualitative Research Differently: Free Association, Narrative and the Interview Method* (Sage, 2000) (with Tony Jefferson) and *The Capacity to Care: Gender and Ethical Subjectivity* (Routledge, 2006). She has also written on psychoanalytic epistemology, gender, sexuality and the history of work organizations. She currently holds an Economic and Social Research Council Fellowship entitled *Maternal Identity, Care and Intersubjectivity: a Psycho-social Approach*.

**Joanne Hughes** was appointed to a Chair in the School of Education, Queens University Belfast in July 2007. Her main research interests and areas of expertise are community relations and community development policy, intergroup contact theory, and the role of education in divided societies. She has published widely on these themes, with much of her work reflecting an international comparative focus.

**Monica Jardine** is Professor Emerita in Women Studies, University of Buffalo, State University of New York. She is a sociologist of colonial displacements and postcolonial transitions whose recent articles include: 'Caribbean Migrations: The Caribbean Diaspora' in *The Encyclopedia of the African Diaspora* (Vol. 1, 2008) 'Guyana' in, *The Encyclopedia of the African Diaspora* (Vol. 2, 2008) and with Carole Boyce Davies: 'Imperial Geographies and US Hegemony' in *The New Centennial Review* (Vol. 3, No. 3, 2003). Her forthcoming book is *The Subaltern Caribbean Nation: Anglophone Caribbean Nationalism and US Hegemony in the Caribbean Region*. She is a native of Guyana who became a citizen of the US in 1995.

**Richard Jenkins** is Professor of Sociology at the University of Sheffield. Trained as an anthropologist, he has done field research in Northern Ireland, England, Wales and Denmark. Among his books are *Foundations of Sociology* (2002); *Pierre Bourdieu* (2nd edn, 2002); *Rethinking Ethnicity* (2nd edn, 2008) and *Social Identity* (3rd edn, 2008).

**Bonita Lawrence** teaches Indigenous Studies at York University in Toronto. She is the author of *'Real' Indians and Others: Mixed-Blood Urban Native People and Indigenous Nationhood*, as well as co-editor (with Kim Anderson) of *Strong Women Stories: Native Vision and Community Survival*. Her research interests focus on federally unrecognized native communities, the effects of identity legislation on urban and reserve communities, and indigenous justice. She is a traditional singer, and currently volunteers with a diversion program for aboriginal offenders at Aboriginal Legal Services of Toronto.

**Helen Lucey** is a Senior Lecturer in Social Psychology at the University of Bath. She takes a psychoanalytically informed psychosocial approach to explore the ways in which psychic, emotional, social and cultural dimensions connect, intersect and overlap particularly in relation to gender, social class, families and education. Recent and forthcoming books include *Growing Up Girl: Psychosocial Explorations of Gender and Class* (2001, with June Melody and Valerie Walkerdine); *Sibling Identity and Relationships* (2006 with Ros Edwards, Lucy Hadfield and Melanie Mauthner); *Power, Knowledge and the Academy: The Institutional is Political* (2006, edited with Val Gillies) and *Psychosocial Approaches to Learning and Teaching (2010).*

**Toon van Meijl** graduated with a PhD in social anthropology from the Australian National University in 1991. Currently he is Associate Professor in the Department of Anthropology and Development Studies at the University of Nijmegen in the Netherlands. He has conducted fieldwork in Maori communities in New Zealand since 1982 and has published extensively on issues of cultural identity and the self, and on socio-political questions emerging from the debate about property rights of indigenous peoples. Major publications include the co-edited volumes *Property Rights and Economic Development; Land and Natural Resources in Southeast Asia and Oceania (1999)* and *Shifting Images of Identity in the Pacific (2004).*

**Chandra Talpade Mohanty** is Professor of Women's and Gender Studies and Dean's Professor of the Humanities at Syracuse University. Her work focuses on transnational feminist theory, postcolonial studies, and anti-racist education. She is author of *Feminism Without Borders: Decolonizing Theory, Practicing Solidarity* (2003) and co-editor of *Third World Women and the Politics of Feminism* (1991); *Feminist Genealogies, Colonial Legacies, Democratic Futures* (1997) and *Feminism and War: Confronting US Imperialism* (2008). She is series editor of *Comparative Feminist Studies* for Palgrave/Macmillan.

**Rolland Munro** is Managing Editor of *The Sociological Review* and Professor of Organisation Theory at Keele University. He has published widely on culture, power and identity and is internationally regarded for bringing new theoretical insight to the study of organisation with his ethnographies of management practice. Writings on accountability, affect, bodies, cars, class, ethics, knowledge, landscape, language, money, polyphony, reason, time, wit, and zero, among other topics, have kept him at the cutting edge of interdisciplinary collaborations and have culminated in two forthcoming books, *The Demanding Relation*, which explores our entanglement with technology and *Dividing Cultures*, which illuminates the everyday divisions through which culture works us.

**Cindy Patton** holds the Canada Research Chair in Community, Culture and Health at Simon Fraser University, British Columbia where she is also Professor of Sociology and of Women's Studies. She has written extensively on the question of gender, sexuality, and race in the context of identity, including early analysis of the politics of AIDS (*Sex and Germs*, South End Press, 1985), on the effect of the epidemic's globalization on national and personal identity (*Globalizing AIDS*, Minnesota University Press 2002), and most recently, on the construction of racial and sexual identity in post-World War II America.

**Ann Phoenix** is Professor and Co-Director of the Thomas Coram Research Unit, Institute of Education, University of London. Her research focuses on social identities and the links between psychological experiences and social processes. Her current research is on 'Transforming Experiences: Re-Conceptualising Identities and "Non-Normative" Childhoods' (as an ESRC Professorial Fellow) and (with Wendy Hollway and Heather Elliott) she recently completed an ESRC-funded project on the transition to motherhood. Her books include: *Black, White or Mixed Race?* (1993/2002 with Barbara Tizard, Routledge); *Young Masculinities*

(2002, with Stephen Frosh and Rob Pattman, Palgrave) and *Parenting and Ethnicity* (2007, with Fatima Husain, Joseph Rowntree Foundation).

**Diane Reay** is Professor of Education in the Faculty of Education, University of Cambridge with particular interests in social justice issues in education, Pierre Bourdieu's social theory, and cultural analyses of social class. Her recent books include *Degrees of Choice: Social Class, Race and Gender in Higher Education* (2005, with Stephen Ball and Miriam David) and *Activating Participation* (2005, co-edited with Gill Crozier).

**Stephen Reicher** is currently Professor of Psychology at the University of St Andrews. His interests centre on the relationship between social identity and collective action. This has involved work on such topics as crowd behaviour, leadership and political rhetoric, the construction of national identity, group solidarity, and, latterly, the mobilisation of mass hatred. At the core of all this work is a concern with the psychological group as a source of social power and of resistance to social inequality. His publications include: *Self and Nation* (with Nick Hopkins, Sage, 2001).

**Katharina Schmid** is currently a postdoctoral researcher at the University of Oxford. She previously held a position as research fellow at the Max-Planck-Institute for religious and ethnic diversity in Goettingen, Germany, after completing her PhD in Social Psychology at Queen's University Belfast. Her research interests lie in the areas of social identity and multiple categorization, as well as intergroup contact, intergroup relations and intergroup conflict. She is also interested in the effects of diversity on prejudice and social cohesion.

**Lynne Segal** is Anniversary Professor of Psychology and Gender Studies in the School of Psychosocial Studies at Birkbeck College, University of London. She has published widely in the areas of gender theory, feminist thought, identities and belongings. Her books include: *Is the Future Female? Troubled Thoughts on Contemporary Feminism; Slow Motion: Changing Masculinities, Changing Men; Straight Sex: The Politics of Pleasure; Why Feminism? Gender, Psychology and Politics; Making Trouble: Life and Politics*.

**Beverley Skeggs** is Professor of Sociology at Goldsmiths, University of London, previously at the University of Manchester, and before that Director of Women's Studies at the University of Lancaster. Her major interests are class, feminist theory, Bourdieu, sexuality and space. She has published: *Feminist Cultural Theory* (1995); *Formations of Class and Gender* (1997); *Transformations: Thinking Through Feminism* (2000, with Sara Ahmed, Jane Kilby, Celia Lury and Maureen McNeil); *Class, Self, Culture* (2004); *Sexuality and the Politics of Violence and Safety* (2004, with Les Moran, Paul Tyrer and Karen Corteen) and *Feminism After Bourdieu* (2005 with Lisa Adkins).

**Russell Spears** is Professor of Psychology at Cardiff University. He is a past editor of the *British Journal of Social Psychology*, and currently (co)editor of the *European Journal of Social Psychology*. His research interests are in social identity and intergroup relations, and cover social stereotyping, discrimination, distinctiveness and differentiation processes, group-based emotions, social influence and socio-structural variables such as power and status. He co-authored/co-edited: *The Social Psychology of Stereotyping and Group Life* (Blackwell, 1997); *Social Identity: Context, Commitment, Content* (Blackwell, 1999) and *Stereotypes as Explanations: The Formation of Meaningful Beliefs about Social Groups* (Cambridge University Press, 2002).

**Elizabeth Stokoe** is Reader in Social Interaction in the Department of Social Sciences at Loughborough University, UK. Her research interests are in conversation analysis and social interaction in various ordinary and institutional settings, including neighbour mediation, police interrogation, speed-dating and talk between friends. She is the author of *Discourse and Identity* (with Bethan Benwell, Edinburgh University Press, 2006) and is currently writing *Talking Relationships*: *Analyzing Speed-Dating Interactions* for Cambridge University Press.

**Nicole Tausch** obtained her DPhil at the University of Oxford in 2006. She is currently a British Academy Postdoctoral Fellow at Cardiff University where she is working on a project examining predictors of support for terrorism. Her research interests lie broadly in the areas of social identity, intergroup relations, prejudice, and collective action. She has published work on intergroup contact, group-based threat, and trait attribution in journals such as *Journal of Personality and Social Psychology*, *British Journal of Social Psychology*, and *Political Psychology*.

**Valerie Walkerdine** is Research Professor in the School of Social Sciences, Cardiff University. She has been researching issues of class, gender and subjectivity for many years and most recently has been working on issues of neo-liberalism, work identity and community. This has involved theoretical and methodological developments in relation to affect and to this end she was awarded an UK ESRC NCRM Network for Methodological Innovation on affect and affective communication. She is founding editor of the journal *Subjectivity* (Palgrave). Her latest book is *Children, Gender, Videogames: Towards a Relational Approach to Multimedia* (Palgrave, 2009).

**Pnina Werbner** is Professor of Social Anthropology at Keele University and author of 'The Manchester Migration Trilogy', including *The Migration Process: Capital, Gifts and Offerings among British Pakistanis* (1990/2002); *Imagined Diasporas among Manchester Muslims* (2002) and *Pilgrims of Love: the Anthropology of a Global Sufi Cult* (2003). In 2008 she edited *Anthropology and the New Cosmopolitanism: Rooted, Feminist and Vernacular Perspectives*. She has researched in Britain, Pakistan, and Botswana, and is currently director of two research projects: *New African Migrants in the Gateway City* and *In the Footsteps of Jesus and the Prophet: Sociality, Caring and the Religion Imagination in the Filipino Diaspora*.

**Margaret Wetherell** is Professor of Social Psychology at the Open University, UK and Director of the Economic and Social Research Council Programme on Identities and Social Action. She is a former Editor of the *British Journal of Social Psychology*. Her recent books include two edited collections presenting the work of the Identities and Social Action Programme *Identity in the 21st Century: New Trends in Changing Times; Theorizing Identities and Social Action* (both Palgrave). Earlier monographs include *Discourse and Social Psychology* and *Mapping the Language of Racism* (with Jonathan Potter) and *Men in Perspective*: *Practice, Power and Identity* (with Nigel Edley).

**Helen Wood** is Reader in Media and Communication at De Montfort University, Leicester, UK. Her research interests are broadly in media and social theory with a particular emphasis upon methodological innovation to capture the role of media in everyday life. She is author of *Talking With Television* (2009, University of Illinois Press) and has published a number of articles and book chapters on television, media convergence, cultural studies and audience research. She is assistant editor of the journal *Ethnography* and has co-edited the collection of the *Centre for Contemporary Cultural Studies Selected Working Papers* (2007, Routledge).

# Introduction

# The Field of Identity Studies

Margaret Wetherell

Identity entered the social sciences and humanities as a core concept in the 1950s (Gleason, 1983). Over the last 60 years it has become one of the most widely used terms in the social sciences and humanities appearing in the titles of many thousands, if not hundreds of thousands, of books and articles. Very few concepts have been as generative. In many ways, though, this success and spread are quite astonishing. Nearly every scholar who works on identity complains about its slippery, blurred and confusing nature. Identity is notoriously elusive and difficult to define and nearly every generation of scholars since the 1950s has included some keen to dismiss it as a consequence concluding it has no analytic value or purchase. Yet the study of identity persists and prospers, and the territory traced out and retraced by identity continues to be indispensable. The aim of this Handbook is to explain why. The chapters in this collection describe the field of study which has emerged over time, the ways in which it has been successively shaped, and how new generations of scholars are re-fashioning identity for the twenty-first century.

In the most basic sense, the study of identities is about what Avtar Brah (1996) calls 'names and looks', and what is done with these. But even this simple initial focus opens up a wide range of topics – orderings of 'us' versus 'them', inward–outward movements of subjectivity, narrative and memory, and political acts of intense solidarity and sometimes great violence. Like others in the field, we are reluctant to offer one overarching definition of identity. It feels important, if difficult, to resist what Amelie Rorty calls 'philosophic lust' (1976: 301) or the desire to fix meaning so the world can be neatly divided once and for all. In this Handbook, we treat identity as an open problematic – a site gathering together a wide range of concerns, tropes, curiosities, patterns of thoughts, debates around certain binaries and particular kinds of conversations.

One path through this open problematic is the study of identity as a subjective individual achievement. Here 'names and looks' translate into a felt sense of personal place, continuity and location and into accounts of 'who one is' which can be assembled and used as a guide to what should be done next. In recent years this concern with personal identity has broadened into a more general interest in social subjectivity, the social organization of memory, narrative, emotion and affect and the ways in which globalization and current 'liquid modernity' (Bauman, 2000) re-assemble and in some contexts corrode the resources people can draw upon to configure a sense of self. Researchers have become interested in how selves are assembled across the natural, the technical and the cultural to include other species (Haraway, 2007), the 'more than human', and what Bruno Latour (2002: 140) calls 'the dappled world'. Mangos, rape fields, memories, stories, genes, mirrors, passports and protest marches – the jumbled world and its affordances are figured and refigured as the meaningful connections constituting subjectively felt identity. Researchers have acquired new ways, too, for thinking about the relational, about inter-subjectivity and interaction. Personal and subjectively felt identities are no longer studied as solipsistic, solitary and static individual achievements but have become seen as mobile, flexibly negotiated, practically oriented and jointly accomplished with others.

Since the inception of identity studies, identity has been linked, too, with group membership, either ascribed by others, or avowed through sometimes passionate affiliation. This has been a second path identity studies have followed. Here the study of 'names and looks' has translated into investigations of social divisions and social solidarities and the practices of marginalization, exclusion, inclusion, resistance, segregation, denigration, etc. linked to belonging. The study of social identity has been synonymous with the study of social categories, roles and social locations such as 'woman', 'black', 'American', 'worker'. For current researchers who understand identity in this way, it remains one of the most important and significant points at which new formations of 'race', colonization and empire, ethnicities, sexuality, gender, disabilities and social class, etc. can be interrogated. But social categories, and people's stakes and interests in these, are now seen in much more complex ways. The intersections between social categories, and the subtle interweaving of forms of privilege and oppression, have become increasingly visible while postcolonial studies have given voice to a new range of standpoints.

Finally, a third path the study of identities traditionally opens up is the ethical and political. The academic study of identity began life tangled up with the civil rights movements of the 1960s and has been central to activism, to social justice campaigns and to the investigation of these. Contemporary research on identity continues to have the same compelling connections with questions of how to live and how to act. Both lay and academic answers to these questions are part of the same moral and political orders, and changes in scholarly and in everyday understandings of identity develop in relation to each other, shadowing, reflecting and commenting on broader regulatory shifts in social life. Both display the tantalizing doubled, Mobius Strip, nature of thinking in this area as socially formed minds try to reflexively grasp their conditions of formation, and where the answers found produce a next round of interpellation and political possibility. Identity continues to be the place where collective action, social movements and issues of inequality, rights and social justice come into focus and demand attention.

The variety of often contradictory directions in identity studies, the heavy-duty reflexivity identity requires, scholarly unease about the significations and etymology of 'identity', and anxieties over definition and boundaries, mean that identity studies constitute a field of great theoretical and methodological complexity – a site of continuous unsettled argument. But, truly, would we have it any other way? As this Handbook illustrates, there is a rich history, and many new theoretical developments and empirical advances to explore.

Developing the Handbook has been a highly interdisciplinary enterprise. The authors include social and developmental psychologists, sociologists, anthropologists, psychoanalysts, biologists, specialists in gender studies, media studies, religious studies, in African-American studies, etc. They are located mainly but not exclusively in the UK and the US but the content of the Handbook ranges across the globe. We have organized their contributions into four Parts. Part 1 reviews the current leading theoretical frameworks in identity studies. Part 2 then describes some of the main formative forces setting up the conditions of possibility for contemporary personhood such as biology, racialization, relational early life, culture and technology, schooling, the media and religion. Part 3 focuses on the classic social categories used to topicalize and demarcate identities such as gender, social class, ethnicities, sexualities, indigeneities and disabilities, along with the intersections between these. Part 4 then presents a range of examples of the identity dynamics found in particular sites and contexts such as in neoliberal working lives, in family life and sibling relationships, in social movements, in migration and nation-building and in specific identity conflicts such as between Protestant and Catholic in Northern Ireland and between the indigenous peoples and the settler nation-state of Canada.

Our own scene-setting for the Handbook is divided into two chapters – this introductory essay which reviews the field of identity studies and, then, at the end of the volume, a set of reflections on directions for the future in light of current political imperatives. The study of identity in the academy received a powerful impetus from civil rights movements and political struggles, it is fitting that Chandra Talpade Mohanty returns at the end of the Handbook to the questions these raised and to consider new directions. My aim in this overview introductory chapter is to try and describe (without writing an entire book …) how identity has been 'figured' in scholarship – how it has been understood, defined, framed and debated. My objective is to briefly demonstrate, first, how a field of studies stabilized in, roughly, the first 30 years of identity studies and then how identity got complicated in the last 30 years. I will make connections to individual chapters as I proceed so that the reader can better understand the background to the work presented in this volume.

## STABILIZING A FIELD OF STUDIES

According to the American historian Peter Gleason (1983), the term identity comes from the Latin *idem et idem* (the same and the same). The word 'identity' is a noun. In vernacular use, it implies an object or a distinctive fixed essence which a person, a place or a group could possess. As the term identity began to appear regularly in books and articles from the 1950s this was the meaning carried forward, flavouring the entire emerging field. The new lines of research appearing at this point built upon a long history of thought about the nature of the self and the relationship between the individual and society. Given these continuities, it is surprising to discover that social theorists such as Norbert Elias and G.H. Mead, working in the 1930s, whose thinking became so central to later studies of identity, did not in fact use the term themselves. 'Identity', in the 1950s, joined a panoply of concepts, not just 'self' and 'individual', but also 'ego', 'personhood', 'character', 'personality' and 'role'.

As Linda Alcoff lucidly and succinctly describes in Chapter 7 of this Handbook, what made a focus on identity possible was a broad set of discourses and understandings which had powerfully shaped modernity (c.f. also Burkitt, 2008; Gergen, 1991; Seigel, 2005; Taylor, 1989; for reviews). Early developments such as the Cartesian model of self as 'thinking substance' and the stress in classic liberalism on the sovereign and primordial individual combined with increased secularisation and emphases on self-realization in *this* world. Enlightenment celebrations of autonomous man (and much more rarely autonomous woman) encouraged throwing off the shackles of tradition, orthodoxy and hierarchy in favour of independent rumination on the properties of the self. These became combined with Romantic expressivist notions of the mysterious depths to be found in the wild and creative psychological interior. As Baumesiter (1986) concludes, if the self in pre-modern period had barely featured as an interesting problem, by the middle of the twentieth century it had become a site ripe for new journeys of exploration. The new field of identity was only part of the abundant guides and expert injunctions available for these new kinds of self-work.

As noted, initial studies of identity were commensurate with classic dictionary definitions of identity, the etymological roots, and everyday uses of the term. For the most part, the starting point was the active, agentic, self-producing, ego-centred, enduring and distinctive individual. Initial uses of identity took for granted continuity and persistence through time and 'entativity', or ontologies of self-contained parts in relation to other parts and to larger wholes. As Gleason describes, when identity entered the academy in the 1950s and 1960s, it immediately bifurcated and was used in two distinct senses – to describe people's personal projects of self and to describe what the members of a group or social category had in common. This splitting, and subsequent distinctions between personal and social identities, has dogged identity studies since, but both these separate lines of research stabilised their understandings of identity in very similar ways and shared an interest in 'sameness'. To find out more about how identity was figured in its first decades and, indeed, what later generations have reacted against and re-worked, I will look in this section, first, at identity as a personal project, then at how identity was configured as a property of groups and, lastly, at how the two were typically brought together. Readers who are more interested in current trends in identity studies might like to move straight to the next main section on the ways in which identity studies became complicated.

## Identity as a personal project

The most prominent identity theorist of the 1950s through to the 1970s, and the researcher who did most to popularize the new study of identity, was Erik Erikson (1950, 1968). His work is a critical reference point for a number of chapters in the Handbook, and a description of his concerns is an economic way of summarizing an entire zeitgeist and its flavour. Erikson was interested in how identity as a sense of personal coherence, manifested as an authentic and stable self, might develop across the life-cycle. His writing was highly normative, and even utopian, with a clear notion of what would count as 'good identity'. As Diane Reay notes in Chapter 14, for Erikson identity makes itself felt 'as a subjective sense of invigorating sameness and continuity' (1974: 17, cited in Reay this volume). A successful person will reach an adaptive equilibrium between personal ideals, other people's views, and their own self understandings. This person will have dealt with the challenges life presents to the sense of self and will thus have evolved through time. For Erikson, a nourishing sense of identity and personal continuity was not automatic; it was a struggle, a task and a never completed project. He thus linked identity with terms like 'anxiety' and 'crisis', describing a 'search' or 'quest' for identity. This raised the possibility that some individuals and some marginal and persecuted groups might never acquire an authentic sense of identity; and in some periods of life, such as adolescence, identity crisis might be typical.

Erikson integrated biological, social and reflexive aspects of human psychology. He was not proposing a primordial and asocial self. Identity was built out of the dialogue with social expectations. A sense of community, a realistic understanding of one's place in culture and society and what one shared with others were crucial to adjustment. Erikson understood identity as a developmental achievement which unfolded in stages. Stage theories were common-place in psychology at this period and their advantage was that they ordered change in predictable ways and explained variation. The person does not stay the same and not every individual is identical but there is some pattern to what takes place. People's responses will be shaped by the stage they have reached and, for Erikson, by the ways in which they have dealt with and resolved the problems, tasks and dilemmas posed at each different stage of childhood, adolescence and adulthood. Stephen Frosh in Chapter 1 conveys particularly well how Erikson attributed a provisional quality to identity at the same time as endorsing the possibility of achieving 'self-sameness'. Identity was not one but a sequence of tentative crystallizations and movements forward; while new challenges to the identity status quo produced new syntheses and configurations of 'constitutional givens, idiosyncratic libidinal needs, favoured capacities, significant identifications, effective defences, successful sublimations, and consistent roles' (Erikson, 1956: 71, cited in Frosh, this volume).

Research within the Eriksonian and neo-Eriksonian paradigm continues today (Schwartz, 2001). As Schwartz notes, it takes as its beginning point questions such as: 'Who am I? What are my values and goals? What is my life purpose? What makes me different from other people? Am I really the same person from one year, or decade, to the next?' (2001: 7). But, it is probably fair to say that the main interest of Erikson's work outside this area of psychology is now historical. Frosh describes, for example, how some lines of recent psychosocial and psychoanalytic thinking on identity have taken up Lacan's work instead and taken up too Lacanian suspicions of authenticity, synthesis and coherence, strivings to be 'identical with' oneself, and senses of self and identity which attempt to express its accomplished nature. Other forms of psychoanalysis and psychosocial research based on object relations theory have remained much more sympathetic to Erikson's project and his original objectives. Wendy Hollway in Chapter 11, for example, draws on the work of Winnicott and other object relations theorists to develop a psychosocial account of identity formation. Winnicott (1958) in many respects shared Erikson's utopian and humanistic thrust, expressed too by earlier social and psychoanalytic commentators on the self such as Karen Horney (1937). Like Horney, Winnicott assumed a true, creative and generative self which can become masked by a false

self-configuration as a result of bad childhood experiences. Hollway argues for the importance of maintaining approaches to identity which continue to focus on the total, substantive, acting, thinking and feeling being and on identity as a personal project.

Toon van Meijl in Chapter 3 describes how Erikson's work impacted on anthropology and the ways in which similar thinking informed the even earlier work by Ruth Benedict and others on culture and personality. He also concludes that few of these early resonances and interests in 'ego identity' and 'self-sameness' persisted or have been directly carried through into contemporary anthropological thinking. Similarly, Ann Phoenix in Chapter 15 describes how the stage theories of development which were such an influence on Erikson had a deep impact also on early empirical research on ethnicities. The self-conceptions and identities of, in particular, African Americans and black, British, young people and adults were probed to see if they had gone through the sequential path hypothesized to underpin a strong sense of ethnic identity. Phoenix notes that although this work had some progressive consequences in drawing attention to the damage inflicted by racism, later researchers have been much more sceptical about attempts to define universally experienced stages and norms in identity development. Indeed, overall, the once so influential optimistic humanistic and existential perspective characteristic of the 1960s and 1970s, so in tune with the semantic roots of 'identity', seems to be losing its force. As Beverley Skeggs describes in Chapter 17, this is, after all, a strongly classed notion of the ideal self and, historically, few have been in a position to 'possess themselves' in quite this way.

## Identity and social groups

At the same time as the study of identity as a personal project was taking off, research was burgeoning into the identities afforded by social location, by social groups and by social categories. This line of research predated civil rights movements. But, it received an extraordinary impetus from the politics of the 1960s, from feminist critiques of biological determinism and from mobilizations around racialized identities and sexualities (see the chapters in Part 3 for extensive descriptions of these influences). As Gleason (1983) notes, in the 1950s scholars began to talk, at first tentatively, and then more forcefully, for the first time about racial and ethnic identities, national identities and religious identities. Membership of a social group was taken to define a person and specify who they were in the scheme of things. To the extent that the members of groups and social categories, such as Australians, Scots, Arabs, women and men, could be assumed to share similar, essential and defining characteristics, the group as a whole could be said to have an identity. Indeed, research flourished into 'national personality' and 'national character', the traits that distinguished Americans, for instance, from citizens of other nations such as the French or the Japanese. In many ways then, this new figuring of group identity continued older vernacular concerns with identity as marking place, and marking character. Identity, however, was also thoroughly socialized and this would eventually entirely disrupt and complicate the older *idem* – the same and singular meanings of identity.

Early twentieth-century sociology had anticipated this interest in the social location of the person. Norbert Elias's work in 1939 on what he called the 'society of individuals' can be taken as a useful representative. Arguing against the psychological reductionism which explained social phenomena as aggregates of individual traits, which Durkheim (Lukes, 1985) had complained about also, and against contemporary notions of herd-like 'group minds', Elias favoured Gestalt influenced notions of individuals as parts of social wholes, notions which were also being developed in the social psychology of the period (Asch, 1952; Lewin, 1936; Sherif, 1936). In this analogical thinking, the character of the emergent whole (the social group) was seen as more than the sum of the parts

(the individual members). It was thought that the social whole acts back and defines the identity of each individual without ever being more than those individuals.

In Elias's writings a clear sense emerges of what else might be relevant to identity beyond personality and a personal sense of continuity and coherence.

> Think only of the bustle in the streets of a large city: most of the people do not know each other. They push past each other, each pursuing his or her own goals and plans. They come and go as suits them. Parts of a whole? The word 'whole' is certainly out of place, at least if its meaning is determined solely by a vision of static or spatially closed structures [...]
>
> But there is undoubtedly a different side to the picture: at work in this tumult of scurrying people, for all their individual freedom of movement, there is clearly also a hidden order, not directly perceptible to the senses. Each individual person in this turmoil belongs in a particular place. He [sic] has a table at which he [sic] eats, a bed in which he [sic] sleeps; even the hungry and homeless are both products and parts of the hidden order underlying the melee. Each of the people who pass has somewhere, at some time, a specific function, property or work, a task of some kind for others, or a lost function, lost possessions or lost work. There are shop assistants and bank clerks, cleaners and society ladies without a profession of their own; there are men who live on interest, policemen, road sweepers, ruined property speculators, pickpockets and girls with no other function than the pleasure of men; there are paper wholesalers and fitters, directors of large chemical concerns and the unemployed. As a result of his [sic] function each of these people has or had an income, high or low, from which he [sic] lives or lived; and as he [sic] passes along the street, this function and this income, more openly or more hidden, goes with him [sic]. (Elias, 1991: 13)

This understanding of identity undermined the universalism of other frames. We are forced to focus here on social differences and the ways in which people's contrasting stakes in social life, their positions of relative advantage and disadvantage, will organize their perceptions, their bodies, their appearance, their actual and imagined interests, their motivations, the knowledge they can access and their consciousness. What emerges strongly, too, is a more complex notion of the ways in identity slots might *pre-exist* the individual, so that minds, psychologies and senses of self are formed in dialogue and in conflict with what is ready-made and handed down.

In Chapter 3, Toon van Meijl describes how anthropology globalized these emphases. Anthropological work in the 1960s came to understand identity: 'mainly as the historically and culturally rooted self-image of a group of people that is predominantly shaped in contact with other groups of peoples. This meaning of identity was related to other anthropological concepts, such as worldview, value, ethos, and, last but not least, culture, all of which suggested a certain kind of homogeneity among members of a community' (Van Meijl, this volume). What was at stake here was not just a view of identity stabilized in a particular way but also the stabilization of culture and social groups as solidified, relatively determinate and relatively immutable.

Elias's words (in the extract above at least) have a functionalist flavour typical of the times, although in his later work (Mennell, 1998) he preferred to stress the network of interdependencies between people and the ways these constructed plural figurations. Others, of course, were critical of functionalist accounts of social order and divisions of labour. Theoreticians exploring identity from a Marxist perspective (Seve, 1978; see Burkitt, 2008: ch. 6 for a review, and Skeggs, Chapter 17 this volume) focused attention on social class, conflict and power. They described how consciousness and identity emerged from praxis or practical action in the world while opening up also the possibility of illusion or false perceptions of one's real social position. Eventually, this interest in ideology would encourage further, immensely important, research on cultural and social change and power/knowledge regimes, examining how social categories and social locations mutated and how their supposedly essential characteristics were continually constructed and re-constructed. This research came to include investigations of what Harry J. Elam Jr and Michele Elam describe in Chapter 9, as the lie of 'race'.

As the chapters in Part 3 of the Handbook eloquently explain, research on social identities quickly became complicated for progressive politics, generating puzzles for disability activists, indigenous people, feminists and for those engaged in civil rights movements around race and sexuality (see, also, Manisha Desai's discussion of social movements in Chapter 21 in Part 4). Rosemarie Garland-Thomson and Moya Bailey, for instance, in Chapter 20 describe how disability emerged as a politicized social identity in the spaces created by civil rights movements. This was a focus on how bodies were constructed and how people were segregated and discriminated against. Disability identity was forged in social and legal terms and developed from minority group status but also led to a rich vein of more experiential writing as those who wished to deploy disability identity began to reflect on complicated body/affect entailments.

For gender, as Lynne Segal points out in Chapter 16, linking identity to social group memberships and to social categories similarly showed up the constructed nature of the meanings and significances attributed to bodies. Early work on gender identity displaced and refuted work on psychology and biology which had been attempting to explain regularities in terms of natural differences between the sexes. It made the study of gender, in contradistinction to sex, conceivable. It supported systematic analysis of patriarchy and the social structures oppressing women. Yet the assumption that categories were stable, with clear boundaries, and that all members shared common experiences and interests came to occlude other social differences and contradictory interests. Difficult balancing acts between similarity and difference, solidarity claims and recognition of variation, along with competing grounds and methods for mobilizing opened up. For indigenous people, as R. Aída Hernández Castillo in Chapter 19 and Bonita Lawrence in Chapter 26 demonstrate, academic critiques of essentialism came into conflict with crucial prior grounds for self-understanding based on land and the people which powered fights for recognition and social justice.

The figuring of identity I am highlighting here in terms of social group membership and the social scientific research it reflected and encouraged was rich and complex. It opened up investigations not just of small, medium and large group based identities, of identities following from what were called 'cross-cultural' differences and identities derived from large-scale social categories such as gender but also investigations of identity based on the typifications of social roles. Merton (1957) developed notions of normative reference groups to encapsulate the identity dimensions of social structures and social divisions and to explain conformity. While Erving Goffman (1959), through his emphases on dramaturgy, performance, interaction, ritual and self-management, made social roles and normative reference groups mobile and brought them to life. His analyses of the presentations of self in everyday life, of stigma and 'spoiled identities', sustained interest in the active negotiation of what was shared with others through common group memberships and organized social expectations. He drew attention to the communicative and semiotic practices through which social identity was signalled and maintained.

In recent years, for a number of identity scholars (see Chapters 14 and 17 from Diane Reay and Beverley Skeggs), Pierre Bourdieu's concepts of 'field', 'capital' and 'habitus' have provided a systematic way of re-working the social bases of identity in tune with later critical analyses of the early research on identity and social location. Bourdieu (1977, 1984) explains the 'logic of practice' underpinning social life and people's positioning in social hierarchies which organize individuals' capacities and activities, including, crucially, the forms of capital, advantage and disadvantage on which they can draw. For contemporary researchers interested in the representational fields which accompany social classifications and their histories, the study of identity and social location becomes an investigation of the creation of value and

distinction, specifying the worth as well as the normative content of possible identities linked to social categories. These writers, then, come back to the study of social categories from new angles, unpacking what Diane Reay describes as the practices, affects and dispositions that bring social categories such as class to life.

## Bringing social and personal identity together

By the early 1960s identity carried both psychological and social significations. It was understood as a personal striving for coherence rooted in individual biography and was defined also by struggles within shifting fields of competing and aligning social groups. This bifurcation into the personal and the social created perhaps the most central puzzle in identity studies from the 1960s onwards – how are subjectivity and social relations yoked together? Identity became the site where questions about the relationship between the individual and society would be most extensively highlighted. The scene became set for priority disputes between sociology and psychology and for accusations of blindness on both sides. Again, this is a huge area of enquiry and my objective is not to second-guess the chapters in this Handbook which provide more extensive reviews. I aim instead, through a few examples, to show some of the typical paths the discussion took.

For many sociologists, integrating the social and the personal was uninteresting. There was no particular substance to the personal, they concluded, that was not always/ already social and research could proceed as though there was an isomorphism between the individual and their social location. The coincidence between the person and their place or social role was vaguely specified as due to 'socialization'. Many social psychologists similarly refused to find the relationship between the individual and the social interesting but for very different reasons.

Particularly in North America where social psychology followed natural science models, quantitative experimental research seemed to proceed most smoothly when premised on methodological individualism. The old Gestalt frame of parts and wholes, which suggested a mechanism relating the individual and the social, was abandoned since for many experimental social psychologists from the 1970s onwards the only obvious real and determinate entity seemed to be the individual.

For many others, as the history of the debate between structure and agency (Giddens, 1984) alone demonstrates, both of these responses were inadequate. Psychoanalytic and psychosocial researchers were especially struck by the unevenness and difficulty of socialization. Helen Lucey in Chapter 24 describes this point of view particularly well as she considers the relational matrix siblings provide for each other and the 'defended selves' produced. These insure that even experiences within the same family are very likely to result in markedly different psychologies and standpoints. This and other psychosocial research (see chapters from Frosh [1] and Hollway [11]) suggest there is no easy incorporation of the social world into the psyche, as the sociologists seemed to imply. Psychosocial analyses find instead confusion, anxiety and suffering as the self encounters others and their expectations. These researchers paint a picture of the ways in which identities are saturated with emotion and investment, full of affect, and describe the highly complex transformations which take place as new social roles clash with old narratives of the self, already existing partial and conflicted identifications, and accumulated psychosocial history. This work argues that social material is not simply 'internalized' but is transformed as it passes through the individual psyche and is worked on by psychological processes. The individual's social actions then, which create the social world for someone else, have been inflected by unconscious dynamics and this, it is argued, accounts for the many irrationalities, unpredictable enthusiasms and frequent collective hysteria of social life.

Perhaps the most developed body of work which tries to find an integrated answer to the problem of the individual and the social was social identity theory developed from the 1970s onwards in European social psychology first by Henri Tajfel (1982) and then more extensively by John Turner and his colleagues (Turner et al., 1987) working in the UK, Australia and elsewhere. This work builds on the older Gestalt traditions described above. It starts, that is, with the puzzle of how social action and group behaviour seems to be 'more than' the sum of the psychologies of the individual members. A crowd at a football match, for example, appears to have emergent properties, 'acting as one', while being nothing other than a collection of individuals.

The key insight was that the psychology of the individual might substantially change when she or he identifies with a social group. It is suggested that there are psychological processes and sequelae of group identification which made collective action possible and which lead, too, to the excesses of group conflict, such as discrimination and hostility against those defined as members of an 'outgroup'. The individual would behave in very different ways when acting in terms of social or group identity in contrast to more idiosyncratic forms of personal identity built around individual uniqueness and distinctiveness. This research tradition has now extensively explored what those processes might be and the psychology fuelling social identities and social identifications. In Chapter 2, Stephen Reicher, Russell Spears and Alexander Haslam, three leading proponents of this research, outline the arguments and review the evidence. While in Chapter 23, Katharina Schmid, Miles Hewstone, Nicole Tausch, Richard Jenkins, Joanne Hughes and Ed Cairns describe the findings from a large programme of empirical research which applies this and other theories derived from experimental social psychology to understand the conflict between Protestant and Catholic communities in Northern Ireland.

As may already be evident, probably the most dominant trope in the history of identity studies for understanding the relation between the individual and society has been, either implicitly or explicitly, the notion of a *dialectical relationship*. Berger and Luckmann (1971) working from a phenomenological sociological standpoint developed an early version of this which nicely illustrates the reasoning. They proposed two rhythms connected in a circular process – a movement of internalization where the individual took in social content from outside the self and this was then followed by social action and the moment of externalization as social material was owned and then reproduced and re-presented in new activity. Re-presented and externalized material then became objectified as collective norms, rules and roles, ready to be re-internalized, and so on in an endless spiral of thesis, antithesis and synthesis leading to a new thesis, antithesis and so on.

Debates about the individual versus the social and how to bring together personal identity and social identity tend to rest on profound binary distinctions between 'interiors' and 'exteriors' and 'in principle' splits to preserve both social determination and individual agency. Frequently, one part of the self, one aspect of consciousness, or one kind of identity is described in theory as transcendent and free, albeit at the cost of remaining undifferentiated and nebulous, while another part of the self becomes specific, accountable to the social world and formed from it. G.H. Mead famously distinguished, for example, between an 'I' which marked out agency and unique individuality, and a 'me' formed from the internalized attitudes of others. In this way people can be seen as agents, as free to change, but also as deeply exemplifying and mirroring the expectations and views of caretakers, significant others and the surrounding social world.

Richard Jenkins (2004) argues that Mead and the symbolic interactionist tradition he spawned are most persuasive when they frame the 'I/me' in dialectical terms, understanding self and identity as a never-ending synthesis and process of accommodation between internal self-definition and the external definitions of oneself offered by others. Jenkins also reminds us of the centrality of reflexivity, social interaction and language to identity and Mead's role in drawing attention to this. The I, in this sense, is the guarantor of the capacity of the self to reflect on itself and in this way self-monitor and self-realize, working over the possibilities that social interaction with specific others presents, and the regulatory and evaluative attitudes and prescriptions the self ascribes to the imagined 'generalized other' of culture.

Although, as we will see in the next section, later identity research both built on and intensely critiqued the figurings of social and personal identity which have been the focus of this section, this thread of the relationship between the psychological and the social bases of identity does not go away. In fact, it is not possible to investigate any aspect of identity without being struck by the extent to which the social is personally owned, and by the myriad of ways in which people make social locations psychological. In very many contexts, aspects of life which to the sociologist are patently socially organized and collective, and which could thus be seen as impersonal, are more commonly experienced by individuals as a matter of intense personal responsibility, as indicative of personal worth, as accountable facts of one's life, as the basis for stories and narratives, and relevant to who one is in the most strongest, motivating, ethical and moral senses.

## COMPLICATING IDENTITY

I have just described, then, the frames through which identity emerged as a field of studies in the social sciences and humanities. Scholars investigated the sense of identity afforded by 'race', social class, gender, religion, nationality, and later sexuality and disability, and provided by more localized social groups. They investigated how individuals achieved a sense of personal coherence and self-definition across the life course and they also studied the two-way traffic between psychological and social determinants of self-experience and social action. These diverse lines of work mostly took for granted, if not quite the old vernacular 'self-sameness', at least 'place' and persisting character.

Rapidly, however, and in full flow from the 1980s, social and economic change, theoretical developments across the social sciences and humanities, and developments in practical politics, tested and complicated these assumptions and led to an intriguing set of new directions in identity research. The new theoretical developments were described, inter alia, under the banners of poststructuralism, postmodernism, deconstruction, peformativity studies and queer theory, as the cultural or discursive turn, and as the moment of postcolonial theory. They led to queries, first, about whether identity and experience were in fact straightforwardly given by social location. Did class position, gender or ethnicity operate like a 'badge worn on the back' stamping out, marking and defining identities and dictating interests? Did all members of a social category share the same essential attributes? Attention turned, too, from investigating experience to investigating how accounts of experience were constructed following more sophisticated analyses of the workings of language, self-description and human meaning-making.

Further relativizing was encouraged by anthropological work on cultural difference and variation – this seemed to suggest that the focus on self, ego and the autonomous, separate, undivided social actor was a specifically western preoccupation not shared by other more collectivist cultures. As Munro (2005) describes, anthropologists contrasted more distributed, 'dividual', senses of self found in other societies and cultures with western 'individual', or 'unable to be divided', senses. But, as van Meijl notes in Chapter 3, distinctions between the west and other cultures also in turn became seen as too simplistic as greater awareness of the internal diversity of western and non-western identity narratives opened up (see also Carrithers, 1985). Furthermore, the world was rapidly changing and identity with it. Globalization appeared to be bringing about mixing and inter-connection on a scale which was becoming increasingly hard to comprehend, familiar identities were 'hybridizing' as older diasporic communities settled in and new trans-national communities emerged. In this section, I describe some of the main new lines of investigation and argument thrown up in identity studies as a consequence. I will look first at the consequences of poststructuralism and the discursive turn and then at the changes provoked by work on globalization, mixing, intersectionality, postcolonial theory and new work on 'assemblages' and 'relational materialities'.

## Fragmented discursive subjects

Arguably, the most important new complication for identity studies was the shift from examining what identity is to how identity is discursively constructed. As Bethan Benwell and Elizabeth Stokoe describe in Chapter 4, this transition was worked out on a range of scales from Foucauldian influenced genealogical studies to investigations of narratives and people's identity work in qualitative research interviews to studies of natural interaction and the fine-grain accomplishment of who one is in the interactional moment. Although these new kinds of work on identity questions shared a commitment to taking discourse seriously, they differed markedly in their assumptions about the speaking subject.

Foucauldian influenced researchers, building on Althusser's (1971) work on political and cultural ideologies, analysed the subject positions, categories and classifications evident in very broad knowledge regimes or discursive formations. These ways of making sense of and ordering persons may well have lasted generations or even centuries but could also be much more transient. Genealogical work on such formations demonstrated, as

Cindy Patton illustrates in Chapter 18, how new categories of sexual deviance and new sexual identities came into being, were solidified, measured, resisted and communicated, becoming an everyday mode of self/other reference. These investigations demonstrated how identity 'realities' were formed and were brought into being, producing subjects through their cultural and administrative power.

Other scholars, while sharing some of these interests, analysed the identity work found in smaller stretches of discourse, in the extended narratives and stories of everyday life. Rolland Munro in Chapter 10 and Valerie Walkerdine and Peter Bansel in Chapter 25, for example, take narrative sequences presented in popular cultural outputs and in interviews respectively and show how identity and 'good character' are framed, staged and formulated, creating moral orders as people reflexively orient their conduct to culturally available ways of making sense of self.

Finally, at the most micro scale, as Benwell and Stokoe illustrate (Chapter 4), conversation analysts and ethnomethodologists examined shifts in descriptions of self and others in the seconds and minutes of conversation, showing how self and identity are accomplished by speakers through the unfolding turns of interaction. Here the emphasis is on how people themselves methodically account for and bring the social world into being as an inter-subjectively available focus. Compared to Foucauldian emphases, this work typically develops a stronger sense of the active person – constructing as well as being constructed. Ethnomethodologists and conversation analysts study the activity of speaking and the concrete discursive practices neglected in genealogical work. Their focus is on participants' orientations to what is unfolding rather than specifications of subject positions in abstract 'big discourse'. What emerges from this are some important qualifications to claims that people are 'spoken' by discourse (c. f. Wetherell, 1998, for a review of these debates).

Re-reading the sociology and social psychology of identity of the 1950s, 1960s and 1970s, which I briefly summarized above, in light of these various discursive turns, what is striking is the *perceptual* model, which implicitly organized early work on identity. The individual investigated resembled the solitary introspective narrator of many humanist and realist novels – she or he seemed to stand apart, acting but mostly observing and silently thinking, independently evaluating others and their actions, and privately working out the significance of events. The predominant activities were 'recognizing', 'understanding', 'processing' and 'coming to see' who one is in the world. As research shifted from the study of experience to the study of how experience was constructed in discourse, the study of identity got noisier, more relational, less private and more dialogical (Billig, 1997). The sheer extent to which identity claims and recognitions are caught up in meaning-making of all kinds became clear. People are embedded in talk and texts, in ongoing streams of discourse, and these build social worlds.

Towards the beginning of the discursive turn, Goffman (1981) described language as like the jam of social interaction – language is sticky; like marmalade it gets everywhere, lingering on every surface. He wanted to convey by this metaphor the intrusiveness of language and its centrality to social life and the study of identity as a determinant in its own right. This and similar moves were genuinely surprising and novel. As Edwards (1997) notes, previous empirical research had more or less treated language as a 'do-nothing domain'; language was a non-intrusive servant transparently and neutrally expressing the wishes of the human master. At the end of the discursive turn, it had become clear that there was no possibility of ever wiping the world clean. Indeed, Goffman's metaphor no longer seemed apposite in light of arguments that discourse and meaning-making in the broadest senses were not additional layers but inseparably imbricated in the constitution of social and material life. Investigations of identities as a consequence would have to engage in the study of negotiation, of multiple accounts, of the hubbub and plurality of voices.

Many scholars working on identity, in social psychology and anthropology particularly, drew on the work of the Russian theorists Bakhtin, Voloshinov and Vygotsky, newly discovered in the west, to theorize this 'heteroglossia' of voices and the ways in which these shifted, changed and reflected power relations (Maybin, 2001; van Meijl, Chapter 3 this volume). This work gave a means of acknowledging that even when entirely alone, the individual is in fact always in the company of others, rehearsing past conversations, accompanied and infiltrated by communal meaning-making. These studies could return again to what in past decades of identity research had been loosely described as socialization and internalization with more purpose and investigative force as these became understood as the processes through which the developing child moves the external discursive world 'inside' to form the 'voices of the mind' (Wertsch, 1990).

It was not so much that identity became newly seen at this point in the history of the social sciences and humanities as fragmented, contradictory and multiple, earlier researchers too had appreciated the manifold possible sources of identity and the sometimes uneasy nature of people's affiliations. Now, however, the unit of analysis in identity research had decisively changed. The focus was no longer on single individuals or social groups constituting themselves 'as themselves' through time but on the multiplicity of identity possibilities in any particular situation or context. It became clear that identity positions appeared in fragments, not manifested as entire characters, and changed according to context. The discourses, too, constructing identity positions might well be contradictory with the tensions between them creating irresolvable dilemmas (Billig et al., 1988), resulting in what Judith Butler (2004) would later describe as precarious lives and potentially unliveable trajectories. Research turned to the implications of what endured among this plurality, what became invisible, what was hegemonic and with what consequences.

Benwell and Stokoe in Chapter 4 neatly sum up this transition in identity studies when they remind us of how studies of language changed over this period. Sociolinguistics, for instance, began by taking social groups and social categories as almost natural kinds, or givens, looking, for instance, at the speech markers such as accent, etc., which distinguished these groups and defined their identity. Later, however, the interest was in how a group was constituted discursively and fluidly and flexibly constructed *as though it were* a natural kind. In this spirit, Ann Phoenix in Chapter 15 notes the transition from the study of 'ethnic identities' to 'ethnicized identities' just as Harry J. Elam Jr and Michele Elam in Chapter 9 describe the move from the study of 'races' to 'racialized identities'. These moves revolutionized understandings of the operation of power, forcing attention to how power flowed through the ways people were spoken into shape, producing as well as inhibiting and repressing. Whereas previous studies of ideology had focused on what were described as false or illusory states of mind, following Foucault discourse studies highlighted how forms of intelligibility in general subjectified as they posited the conditions for being a subject. Some lament what has been lost in these moves. Linda Alcoff, for instance, in Chapter 7, develops what she describes as a post-positivist realist account of identity which attempts to rescue experience, self-knowledge and authenticity from the discursive onslaught. Certainly the focus on multiplicity and fragmentation could go too far, neglecting persistence, repetition and order over time, but Alcoff's recognition that her philosophy of identity would need to be a post-positivist account indicates just how much theory had shifted.

New discursive work on identities now particularly brought into view the centrality of *difference* to identity formation. Whereas earlier work had tried to capture as the essence of identity what was the same, what was similar and what was shared, theorists now began to highlight the ways in which acts of identity required the marking out of differences, separating self from 'other', creating hierarchies of included and excluded; where the nature of self and group came to be defined through what one was not. There was new interest in the semiotic, cultural and psychological processes involved in these markings of difference. As Avtar Brah explains:

> Power and regimes of knowledge articulate with specific socio-economic, political and cultural institutions and practices, and together they mark specific bodies, subjects, subjectivities and agencies. We are formed as subjects – American, European, South Asian, East Asian, Muslim, Christian, black, white, man, woman, hetero/gay/lesbian/trans/bisexual, and so on – in and through historically specific dynamics of power in particular contexts. [...] what is important is the way in which under given historical circumstances an arbitrary signifier – a colour, a body, a religious creed, a social arrangement/custom, or a set of cultural practices – come to be associated with particular meanings; that is, it becomes a "certain kind of difference" etched within asymmetrical power relations with specific outcomes and effects. (2007: 137–8)

Difference applies not just to the formation of large-scale social categories but, as Brah also states, makes apparent the 'impossibility' of identity at any point. Many noted the implications of the infinite slipperiness of description, drawing on Derrida's notion of 'deferral' and echoing his deconstructive arguments. Erikson had acknowledged in the 1950s that identity was always a work in progress, never finalized, but now the radical incompleteness of any description of self took centre-stage. Even heroic acts of self-rumination could not obscure that 'who one is' always seems to escape complete definition. Any act of identification, of self-summary, is a temporary and more or less arbitrary moment of closure, reliant on the

'remainder' any such act creates. Identity is endlessly accomplished and then undone, endlessly incomplete and always only 'part of the story'. As Stephen Frosh describes in Chapter 1, for Lacan, this point was elaborated in the claim that identity is 'imaginary', a mistaken, defensive and narcissistic attempt to find solidity, certainty and self-coincidence from the materials of cultural positions, narratives and possibilities on offer in the symbolic realm. Politics, however, often requires and depends on positioned action leading to the postcolonial theorist Gayatri Chakravorty Spivak's (Landry and Maclean, 1996) argument that 'strategic essentialism' was thus necessary to build alliances and to ground and bolster campaigns.

In a frequently cited essay on identity summing up and evaluating many of the theoretical shifts at stake here, Stuart Hall (1996) argued that future work might be better advised to focus on moments of identification than on describing 'identities'. Hall saw identification as the moment of encounter or meeting point between discourses/practices (and the subject positions these provide) and the processes which produce the subjectivities which construct us as subjects in the first place, as subjects who could be interpellated into discourses. It was not enough to show how people were 'spoken by' discourses we need to analyse why people invest in and take up some discursive positions rather than others.

> Identities are thus points of temporary attachment to the subject positions which discursive practices construct for us [...] They are the result of a successful articulation or "chaining" of the subject into the flow of discourse, what Stephen Heath, in his path-breaking essay on "Suture" called an "intersection" (1981, p. 106). [...] The notion that an effective suturing of the subject to a subject-position requires not only that the subject is "hailed", but that the subject invests in the position, means that suturing has to be thought of as an *articulation*, rather than a one-sided process, and that in turn places *identification*, if not identities, firmly on the theoretical agenda. (Hall, 1996: 6, original emphasis)

Other critics of Foucault such as Wendy Hollway (1984), Valerie Walkerdine, Helen

Lucey and June Melody (2001) and Anthony Elliott (2007) had made this point also. It was a reminder that with the discursive turn older questions about the relationship between the psychological and the social and what the individual brings to the social world had not gone away. As a number of chapters in this volume illustrate (see chapters from Helen Lucey [24], Stephen Frosh [1] and Wendy Hollway [11]), for many the answer was to turn back to psychoanalysis and psychosocial approaches to explain the issue of investment, finding there a variety of ways of theorizing and investigating what Hollway calls the 'hinge' between the psychological (an already constituted subjectivity and unconscious) and the social (usually understood as discursive, symbolic and material practices rather than as 'structures'). As already noted, and as Benwell and Stokoe illustrate in detail, conversation analysts, discursive psychologists and ethnomethodologists had for many years also argued that the Foucauldian position was frankly implausible in the light of the dynamic, highly reflexive, intersubjective, mobile and active discursive work revealed in the close analysis of people's actual talk and interaction (Wetherell, 1998). It is not so much that the ensemble of discourses and the play of differences create subject positions and identity slots. Rather, people do this for themselves and for each other argumentatively, collaboratively, strategically and constantly.

Other scholars interested in identity issues preferred to intensify Foucauldian arguments, following up the theoretical moves he was making before his early death. Nikolas Rose (1996), for example, followed this lead extending Foucault's genealogical methods to include contemporary 'psy' discourses and psychological expertise. Rose advocated examining all the procedures, rituals, classifications, problematizations, authorities, strategies – the technologies in other words – that form our relations to ourselves and which 'subjectify' us. Following Deleuze, Rose argued that our interior life and in fact the territory we call identity, simply

represented the 'folding' of this discursive and regulatory exteriority in on itself to form the appearance of 'inner life'. This and other work led to an explosion of interest in 'governmentality' (see Walkerdine and Bansel, Chapter 25, for a review) and in what Rose (1989) called the 'governing of the soul', the administrative, policy and institutional apparatuses which regulated human conduct and, of course, identity.

A similar, and enormously influential, approach can be found in the work of Judith Butler (1990, 1993) resting on the concept of 'performativity'. The notion of performativity is an attempt to encapsulate and maintain the radical claims at the heart of the work on the discursive constitution of subjects while making room for repetition, reiteration, durability and stability, and the psychoanalytic. It is the argument that an identity based on gender, for instance, is nothing other than persistent regulatory performances materialized over time. Gender is not biologically given. Sustained performances built around initially privileged differences, ignore and render invisible other possible differences. What is brought into being is an apparatus which is nothing other than performance but which confronts each person as always/already in place. In a sense Butler's theory explains why repetitive acts of identity occur and seem sensible and yet how reiteration alone is sufficient to instantiate identities which seem much more solid and foundational.

Butler's highly complex argument is accessibly and elegantly reviewed by Sarah E. Chinn in Chapter 5 and a number of authors in the Handbook describe the central importance of this work for theorizing gender relations (see Lynne Segal, Chapter 16) and sexualities (see Cindy Patton, Chapter 18). Although this work began with gender, it need not stop there, however, and has been applied, as Harry J. Elam Jr and Michele Elam demonstrates (Chapter 9), to racialization. Chinn describes how performativity came to sustain the emergence of queer theory and attempts to trouble and subvert identities based on the fixed binaries of sex. And, as Anne Fausto-Sterling argues in Chapter 8, it turns out that even contemporary biological studies have retreated. These also now offer no solid guarantees for foundational identities. A new politics, as well as a new mode of identity studies, is needed to think through what current biological research reveals about formative bodies.

## Intersectional, hybrid and global identities: the break-up of traditions

The theoretical shifts just described undermined any notion of identities built on naturally occurring essential differences. What was essential and what defined a person, a social group or a social category became negotiable and potentially contested. The ways in which identity was *conferred* by group membership, life experience or through belonging to a social category became not automatic but a topic of investigation. As I shall now try to trace out, these directions of travel in identity studies were fuelled by empirical and theoretical work on globalization, by postcolonial theory, work on intersectionality, by work on mobilities and diasporas, on assemblages and networks (including assemblages of human and non-human), and accounts of the decline of traditional identities along with the emergence of new mediations and modes. These further complicated identity, continuing to break up the rather simple pictures of the first wave of research which had put everyone 'in place'. This swathe of work also insisted that what needed to be explained was much more fluid, diverse and richly varied than ever previously imagined.

Perhaps the earliest and most disruptive among these new lines of study were acknowledgements of what became known as the *intersectional* nature of identity (Combahee River Collective, 1977; Crenshaw, 1991). Intersectional thinking offered a critique of monolithic analyses in terms of social categories. It was grounded in the experiences and political struggles of those whose lives were not neatly contained or defined by the singular identities provided by 'big bloc' social categories. Intersectional analyses drew attention to the 'remainder', normally bracketed out, and to the hinterland in gender studies, ethnic and racial studies, and class analyses. As Manisha Desai describes in Chapter 21, and Sarah E. Chinn in Chapter 5, black feminist groups understood early on that their experiences were multi-faceted, outside the range of convenience of much of the feminism of the day and not quite captured either by civil rights struggles over racism and homophobia. Rather, to be a black and lesbian woman was to live at the intersection of multiple axes of oppression derived from class, race, gender and sexuality with the risk of becoming invisible as scholars in the academy and some forms of identity politics constructed prototypical and excluding versions of gendered, racialized and classed life focused around the interests of straight people, white women, black men, gay men and white, working-class men.

These early realizations of identity complexity reframed identity struggles. They took a while longer to impact on research but eventually the notion of identity intersections would need to become a staple, focusing on the ways in which people articulated and instantiated multiple social categories combining them other available identity positions. Ann Phoenix in Chapter 15 describes how this opened up empirical research into ethnicity. While Diane Reay describes in Chapter 14, how understandings of identity practices broadened out bringing in as focal points new identifications such as, in schools, the identity of the 'learner', 'the nerd', 'the boffin', 'the bright one'. These identity slots were shown to intersect in complex ways with identities based on gender, 'race' and social class. Indeed, what it means to be black, working class or a boy depends on how these social categorizations are worked through some of the other dichotomous identities dominating local situations and institutions. Empirical research, then, would need to become much more sensitive to patterned ways of living across the board of salient identity positions rather than being read off in any simple way from class, ethnicity or gender.

Coming to terms with intersectionality, therefore, massively proliferated what could be relevant in any study of identity. Further proliferation occurred as researchers began to focus on social change, and as the historical specificity of modes of identification began to come into view. Researchers explored the ways in which social, cultural and technological changes produced new kinds of people, new ways of life, new social groupings and new modes of identity production. To be specific, however, about the nature of social change, and to say what was new, was immensely difficult and highly contested. Could we even be confident that the past was actually different and it was not just our theorizations which had changed?

In Chapter 24, Helen Lucey considers the import of research on social change and new forms of individualization for studies of identities and family relationships, while in Chapter 13, on media and mediated identity, Helen Wood critically reviews the evidence for some now common-place sociological narratives concerning the identity consequences of digital technology, new patterns of consumption and new forms of engagement and exposure to the media. As Wood notes, the danger is of constructing simple zero-sum contrasts – concluding either that authentic identities, face-to-face interaction, community relations and traditional ways of life are eviscerated by new technology or that new media automatically open up playful new worlds and new connected virtual communities, re-invent politics, and forms of resistance to dominant power relations.

One of the most provocative and important arguments about identity and social change is expressed in claims about 'individualization' (Bauman, 2001; Beck and Beck-Gernsheim, 2002; Giddens, 1991). As Walkerdine and

Bansel describe in Chapter 25, the argument here is that neoliberalism and globalization and the concomitant changes in the organization of working and collective lives increasingly throw individuals back on their own resources to make their own life narrative and senses of identity. Identity has become more important over time and the pressure to be 'an interesting individual' (Cronin, 2000) has intensified. Individualization theorists, and theorists extending Foucault's work into studies of governmentality (Rose, 1996, 1999), describe the emergence of a new range of technologies and imperatives for managing, narrating and working on the self. This work, as Helen Wood discusses, points to the emergence of life-style and consumption as new sources of identity, in contrast to production, work, traditional community affiliations and patterns of belonging and position in social structures. These researchers describe the psychologization of everyday life, new emphases on intimacy and intimate citizenship, the opening up of private life in public and the emergence of new economies of value around personhood (see also Beverley Skeggs, Chapter 17, in this volume).

In Chapter 10, Rolland Munro describes how new technologies 'punctualise' identity now very differently. 'Senders' of messages about identity (those who ascribe our identity) can be found in many different kinds of spaces and can operate now across very large distances. Munro argues that technology 'enframes' us so that people are 'set up to set about making and remaking their different worlds'. Some of the consequences of these new makings and discursive and material 'enframings' are outlined by Valerie Walkerdine and Peter Bansel as they examine modes of subjectivity under neoliberalism but Walkerdine and Bansel also question the spread of new patternings and draw attention back to the question of who exactly can be an individualized subject, in what contexts and on what occasions and with what consequences?

Other social changes which have decisively changed identity studies are those

associated with postcolonialism, transnationalism, the emergence of new diasporic communities, new complexities in cultural
relationships, new mobilities and migratory
flows (for a discussion of these developments
and an illustration of the effect on the making
of Caribbean identities see Chapter 22 from
Carole Boyce Davies and Monica Jardine).
But, it is not just that the staple topics of
identity studies have transmogrified, demanding that empirical work similarly expand its
reach, it is also that the range of contributing
voices to identity studies has broadened. As
Saurabh Dube describes in Chapter 6, postcolonial theory and subaltern perspectives
increased in highly fruitful and necessary
ways the range and number of standpoints
available. Postcolonial theory explores the
cultural legacies of colonialism. It examines
identities in colonized societies and processes of forging new articulations. Combined
with a subaltern standpoint it creates some
radically different spaces for academic work
on identity, as the history of colonization is
told from the perspective of those outside
hegemonic power. In this vein, Boyce Davies
and Jardine demonstrate what can be learnt
about migration, nation and identity from the
moving and evocative literary production of
diasporic Caribbean writers and theorists.

As Toon van Meijl comments in Chapter 3,
in the last 30 years, culture has become
unbounded and dynamic both in theory and
in practice. The local and the global have
become more difficult to distinguish since
investigation of any specific context or site is
likely to reveal local, national and global
networks interrelating to produce the conditions for experience and for social action, as
well as the resources available for identity
practices. The ways in which identities are
constructed across sometimes contradictory
and antagonistic discourses and cultural and
material practices with multiple origins is
now recognized.

One commentator (Harris, 2005), illustrating the strange new conjunctures emerging
from global migrations and global exposures,
asks us to think about the case of Shafik

Razul, a 24-year-old of Pakistani descent
from the West Midlands town of Tipton in
the UK. Razul had been accused of fighting
with the Taliban in Afghanistan and was
detained and interrogated by the Americans.
Two reporters from the UK *Sunday Mirror*
newspaper were invited into his family home
in 2002 in order to speak to his mother and
brothers and build up a portrait of him. Harris
picks out the key features in their report:

> Shafik was born in West Bromwich in 1977,
> attended the Roman Catholic Sacred Heart Primary
> School, has a broad Brummie accent, interested in
> girls and nightclubs, had several white girlfriends,
> often talking on his mobile phone to women.
> Once went camping in Wales, but was too scared
> to spend even one night in a tent, he wanted to go
> to bed and breakfast. Listening to gangster rap,
> following the fortunes of his favourite football
> team, Liverpool, and showing off his designer
> clothes. A small bookcase in his home containing
> books written in Punjabi and English. Played in the
> Tipton Muslim community centre football team.
> The furthest he'd travelled before was in a Club 18
> to 30 holiday to Benidorm the year before. Shafik
> Razul was wearing his favourite top, a Ralph
> Lauren American stars and stripes jumper when he
> flew into Pakistan last October, off to do a compu-
> ter programming course at University of Lahore.

To paraphrase Paul Gilroy's (2005: 439)
comments on a similar case – it is in the bat-
tered and humiliated British bodies in
Guantanamo Bay with their Brummie
accents, their nostalgia for Scottish Highland
shortbread and their interest in the football
results, in young men like Shafik with their
postcolonial lives and in the poignant detail
of Shafik's Ralph Lauren jersey, that any
over-simple notions of cultural difference, of
we and them, and any simple notion of identity categories can be laid to rest.

The danger, of course, is assuming that
everyone everywhere is engaged in mixing
highly varied cultural resources, grafting old
and new together, borrowing, appropriating
and reconfiguring to construct new, vernacular, non-foundational, 'for the moment' and
sometimes highly disjunctive identities. As
with claims about individualization, it is perhaps more productive to ask when and where
this takes place, who remains fixed in place,

in what aspects of their lives and whether 'mixing' is always politically progressive.

In Chapter 23, for example, Katharina Schmid, Miles Hewstone, Nicole Tausch, Richard Jenkins, Joanne Hughes and Ed Cairns discuss the identity dynamics found in Northern Ireland. They describe a society still deeply segregated along ethno-religious lines where older analyses of community have considerable resonance and continuing explanatory power. Similarly Bonita Lawrence in Chapter 26 writes passionately from the standpoint of indigenous people in Canada arguing that postmodern concerns with deconstruction and emphases on 'invented tradition' and playful hybridity silence indigenous people and dismember the very grounds on which their claims to legal recognition and to the nation and their fight against colonization are based. While post-positivist identity theorists, as Linda Alcoff describes in Chapter 7, want to remain open to and maintain the idea that collective and communal experiences of marginalization and discrimination, for example, are determining of social identity and have a power and authority beyond contemporary identity bricolage. Such a perspective might seek to specify, for instance, among the many mixed identity resources present in Shafik's life, the identity positions which are most strongly causally relevant to his behaviour and to his operative sense of himself at key moments of choice or across most contexts (Mohanty, 2007).

Recent identity studies have developed sophisticated ways for describing and making sense of cultural disjunctures and dynamisms. These new senses of flux must recognize and incorporate also the ways in which identities can become organized around radically different temporalities. New demands for speed can be mixed in disturbing (and potentially exciting) ways with more familiar life rhythms and inertias, combining the time of now, the temporality of popular culture and the modern workplace with what Venn (2006) describes as the slower recurrent time of tradition and generation. Pnina Werbner in Chapter 12 provides some vivid illustrations of temporal and cultural disjunctures in intersection with processes and practices of religious identity. She explores the situations in which religious affiliations become 'an identity' and thus a way of organizing difference. Her large-scale historical sweep demonstrates back and forth movements of inclusion and exclusion over time: ruptures and continuities. She describes how new distinctive religious groups form exploiting the divisions among older religions. These may draw tight boundaries around adherents, seeking new puritan beginnings. But these processes of division in religious history are offset by syncretism, hybridity and heteroglossia as diverse religious traditions meet, mingle and change each other in more gradualist fashions. Werbner reminds us, too, that what distinguishes religious identity is the claim for the transcendence. Religious identity is frequently a claim for a certain type of affective experience – ecstatic and embodied.

But bodies too, of course, are now complicated. One kind of fragmentation occurs as the whole body of old identity is replaced by the study of DNA base sequences in what Anne Fausto-Sterling in Chapter 8 describes as new genomic and post-genomic eras. She argues that current theories of identity draw on many different levels of biological knowledge (old and new). Perhaps endearingly, perhaps irritatingly, biological knowledge in the social sciences and humanities often lags behind the actual science, we are outraged by old biological nostrums long rejected by practicing biologists. Fausto-Sterling moves beyond the simplicities and orthodoxies which locate the social and the biological in competition with each other to outline a much more sophisticated biology for identity studies. This is a theory of embodiment with the kind of subtlety and complexity to match the new complexities of identity scholarship.

Fausto-Sterling's approach sits well with recognitions that the study of identity needs to spill over now to include relations with the non-human (other species and objects) and the study of bio-technical assemblages.

Donna Haraway's (2007, and see Ihde et al., 2003) work on cyborgs, on manufactured bodies, on what occurs when species meets species is exemplary in this respect. She exhorts us to forget stabilized identities and focus instead on what she calls knots of entanglement, and she studies practices of figuration and 'becoming worldly'. This entails investigating how in any particular site nature, culture, subjectivity and matter coalesce along with the divergent histories pulled together in these new figurations.

Haraway's move is equivalent, of course, to the move in discursive research on identity practices described above. In both cases the unit of analysis in research has shifted decisively from the already formulated and established individual and the group to the relational constitutive process. And this is the last point I want to pick up in this rapid review of the new intellectual territories opening up. I have described in this essay how identity studies began by assuming the self-contained identity of the solid generative individual or group member studied as 'self-sameness', as personal identity projects and as group character. In the last 30 years, identity has become disconnected from this originary image as attention turned, for example, to Foucauldian subject positions, to the slots discourses and knowledge regimes provided and to the 'making' and the 'doing' of identity. Haraway's work, research by actor-network theorists (Latour, 2005; Law, 2003, 2004) on 'relational materialities', and research on affect influenced by the philosophy of Gilles Deleuze, Spinoza, Bergson, Whitehead and William James among other sources in social psychology, geography, sociology and cultural studies (Blackman et al., 2008; Middleton and Brown, 2005; Thrift, 2008) is the latest twist in this change of focus. This work extends the decentering move to the study of affect and embodiment so that the unit of analysis becomes at the most extreme simply productive force and energy. This approach foregrounds relationality, assemblage and the connections between objects and subjects, nature and

culture, actors and networks. It is also the point at which this account must end, and we wait now to see how the questions, issues and topics studied under the banner of 'identity' will be further reincarnated in the future.

## CONCLUSION

Like many social psychologists of my academic generation in the UK, completing PhDs in the 1980s, I seem to have spent nearly all of my scholarly (and other) life engaged in debates about identity. The relationships between the individual and the social, and the connections between persons, groups and collectives were the unavoidable, defining problematic of the social psychology I studied as a student. The discursive turn complicated this in ways which marked out my own academic trajectory and now, too, recent thinking around affect, relationality, intersectionality, narrative and social subjectivity challenges my work in newly absorbing ways.

My fealty and servitude to identity extends, of course, beyond my academic interests. For my generation of white feminists growing up in Australasia and then moving out to the wider world (inspired by Lynne Segal and others) it was the prism for questioning biological determinism and rethinking socialism. Identity was also a deeply felt personal project forcing attention to questions about how to live. These were constructed for me and others in my position first, very early, through highly attractive but undoubtedly deeply problematic existentialist humanist arguments concerning what it might mean to exist and engage and then through the interest of narrating psychological 'depth' as psychoanalysis was re-worked and self-exploration became a mandatory game. Finally, and possibly more usefully, 'identity' forced recognition of the meanings of whiteness, social class, embodied privilege and the living out of intersectionality.

For a white migrant from New Zealand to the UK, identity and its formative privileges and oppressions became a way of making sense from within of the migration experience. I am a member of a group once called 'colonials', mocked for our provincial ways and our strange accents, when we returned 'home' to the UK, A grasp of positioning and the politics of identity positioning clarified but did not simplify or resolve relations between people like me and the indigenous Maori people of Aotearoa/New Zealand in the aftermath of colonialism (Wetherell and Potter, 1992; Yensen et al., 1989). It made more sense of the experience of being white 'but not quite' British in the UK. People with my particular 'name and looks' are most usually appealed to, hailed as, and included in the comfortable category of 'us' in contrast to black and brown British people, even though for most of the time I was not actually a British citizen in contrast to many black and brown citizens who had been born and raised in the UK. Belonging and inclusion based on such superficial grounds falters though and identity created the space to make sense of the differences and gaps between how one appears and what I and others carried to a country like the UK from our countries of origin.

So, after all these years and all these experiences, is this the end of identity? Some commentators have concluded that this indeed should be the end. Identity, they say, is exhausted. Du Gay (2007), for example, describes identity as a formerly generative trope which has simply now run out of steam. Some have begun to talk about scholarly and political life 'beyond identity' and 'after identity' (Rutherford, 2007), while others have argued that the term is now so ambiguous, capacious and contradictory it can no longer serve the demands of social analysis (Anthias 1998; Brubaker and Cooper, 2000). For some critics, what is dead is simply the old essentialist project of trying to describe a natural or social kind and accompanying identity politics. Their attack in other words concerns the history of identity studies and

some of the framing of identity struggles but often has little to say about the recent theoretical and empirical developments and extensions. Some critics, it seems, need identity to stay in the past, to continue as a straw concept, to keep its old connotations, so it can be attacked in ways which define the new.

Other critics (such as Anthias, 1998; Brubaker and Cooper, 2000; Yuval-Davis, 2006) have been engaged in new conceptual and definitional work, trying to reshuffle the pieces, set some boundaries on the use of linked concepts and develop some new divisions and distinctions to better enable thinking and research. Yet others responding to the Deleuzian spirit currently sweeping through European social thought turn away entirely. Their objection is that identity codifies, territorializes and closes down 'becoming' and the nomadic. The difficulty, in their view, is not the lack of a precise vocabulary but that identity freezes and obscures possible understandings of the radical openness and contingency of social life. Identity handbooks are perhaps particularly at fault because they may indicate the moment when in Deleuze and Guattari's terms (Sorenson, 2005) a 'problematic' becomes a 'solution'. 'Identity' orders, hems in, and organizes knowledge to the extent that all possibility of creative flight and expansive new perspective evaporates.

All these diagnoses of the future for identity studies have force and value, although they suggest somewhat contradictory and antagonistic ways forward. But it seems to me that whatever future work in this area looks like, it will remain for a long time yet in conversation with the histories of thought and debates which I have tried to outline in this essay. Chandra Talpade Mohanty returns to the issue of the 'staying power' of identity in her reflections at the end of this volume. She passionately and brilliantly defends the history of identity and its political and intellectual role. In my view identity continues to be good to think with precisely because of the features which some have found difficult and irritating: the long chronology, the accretion of many layers of meanings, the rich sweep, the heated debates, the constitutive ideologies, fantasies and fictions, the politics, and the very many ambiguities. In this spirit, the chapters in this Handbook provide an exceptionally rich resource for understanding the present intellectual moment. They will be a central resource for whatever comes next.

# REFERENCES

Althusser, L. (1971) *Lenin, Philosophy and Other Essays*. Trans. Ben Brewster. New York: Monthly Review Press.

Anthias, F. (1998) 'Rethinking social divisions: Some notes towards a theoretical framework', *Sociological Review*, 46 (3): 505–35.

Asch, S. (1952) *Social Psychology*. Englewood Cliffs, NJ: Prentice-Hall.

Bauman, Z. (2000) *Liquid Modernity*. Cambridge: Polity Press.

Bauman, Z. (2001) *The Individualized Society*. Cambridge: Polity Press.

Baumeister, R. (1986) *Identity: Cultural Change and the Struggle for Self*. New York: Oxford University Press.

Beck, U. and Beck-Gernsheim, E. (2002) *Individualization*. London: Sage.

Berger, P. and Luckmann, T. (1971) *The Social Construction of Reality*. Harmondsworth: Penguin.

Billig, M. (1997) 'Discursive, rhetorical and ideological messages', in C. McGarty and A. Haslam (eds), *The Message of Social Psychology*. Oxford: Blackwell.

Billig, M., Condor, S., Edwards, D., Gane, M., Middleton, D. and Radley, A. (1988) *Ideological Dilemmas*. London: Sage.

Blackman, L., Cromby, J., Hook, D., Papadopoulos, D. and Walkerdine, V. (2008) 'Creating subjectivities', *Subjectivity: International Journal of Critical Psychology*, 22: 1–27.

Bourdieu, P. (1977) *Outline of a Theory of Practice*. Cambridge: Cambridge University Press.

Bourdieu, P. (1984) *Distinction: A Social Critique of the Judgment of Taste*. London: Routledge.

Brah, A. (1996) *Cartographies of Diaspora*. London: Routledge.

Brah, A. (2007) 'Non-binarized identities of similarity and difference', in M. Wetherell, M. Lafleche and R. Berkeley (eds), *Identity, Ethnic Diversity and Community Cohesion*. London: Sage.

Brubaker, R. and Cooper, F. (2000) 'Beyond "identity"', *Theory and Society*, 29: 1–47.

Burkitt, I. (2008) *Social Selves*. 2nd edn. London: Sage.

Butler, J. (1990) *Gender Trouble*. New York: Routledge.

Butler, J. (1993) *Bodies that Matter*. London: Routledge.

Butler, J. (2004) *Undoing Gender*. New York: Routledge.

Carrithers, M. (1985) 'An alternative social history of the self', in M. Carrithers, S. Collins and S. Lukes (eds), *The Category of the Person*. Cambridge: Cambridge University Press.

Combahee River Collective (1977) *The Combahee River Collective Statement*.

Crenshaw, K. (1991) 'Mapping the margins: Intersectionality, identity politics, and violence against women of color', *Stanford Law Review*, 43 (6): 1241–99.

Cronin, A.M. (2000) 'Consumerism and "compulsory individuality": Women, will and potential', in S. Ahmed, J. Kilby, C. Lury, M. MacNeil and B. Skeggs (eds), *Transformations: Thinking Through Feminism*. London: Routledge.

Du Gay, P. (2007) *Organizing Identity*. London: Sage.

Edwards, D. (1997) *Discourse and Cognition*. London: Sage.

Elias, N. (1991) *The Society of Individuals*. M. Schroter (ed) and Translated by E. Jephcott. Oxford: Basil Blackwell.

Elliott, A. (2007) *Concepts of the Self*. 2nd edn. Cambridge: Polity.

Erikson, E. (1950) *Childhood and Society*. New York: Norton.

Erikson, E. (1956) 'The problem of ego identity', *Journal of the American Psychoanalytic Association*, 4: 56–121.

Erikson, E. (1968) *Identity, Youth and Crisis*. New York: Norton.

Gergen, K. (1991) *The Saturated Self: Dilemmas of Identity in Contemporary Life*. New York: Basic Books.

Giddens, A. (1984) *The Constitution of Society: Outline of a Theory of Structuration*. Cambridge: Polity Press.

Giddens, A. (1991) *Modernity and Self-Identity: Self and Society in the Late Modern Age*. Cambridge: Polity Press.

Gilroy, P. (2005) 'Multiculture, double consciousness and the "war on terror"', *Patterns of Prejudice*, 39 (4): 431–43.

Gleason, P. (1983) 'Identifying identity: A semantic history', *The Journal of American History*, 69 (4): 910–31.

Goffman, E. (1959) *The Presentation of Self in Everyday Life*. London: Allen Lane.

Goffman, E. (1981) *Forms of Talk*. Philadelphia, PA: University of Pennsylvania Press.

Hall, S. (1996) 'Who needs "identity"?', in S. Hall and P. Du Gay (eds), *Questions of Cultural Identity*. London: Sage.

Haraway, D. (2007) *When Species Meet*. Minneapolis, MN: University of Minnesota Press.

Harris, R. (2005) 'New ethnicities and cultural practices'. Paper presented at the ESRC Identities and Social Action Programme Launch. April, Royal Society of Arts, London.

Heath, S. (1981) *Questions of Cinema*. Basingstoke: Macmillan.

Hollway, W. (1984) 'Gender difference and the production of subjectivity', in J. Henriques, W. Hollway, C. Urwin, C. Venn and V. Walkerdine (eds), *Changing the Subject*. London: Methuen.

Horney, K. (1937) *The Neurotic Personality of Our Time*. New York: Norton.

Ihde, D., Selinger, E., Haraway, D., Pickering, A. and Latour, B. (2003) *Chasing Technoscience: Matrix for Materiality*. Bloomington, IN: Indiana University Press.

Jenkins, R. (2004) *Social Identity*. 2nd edn. London: Routledge.

Landry, D. and MacLean, G. (1996) *The Spivak Reader*. New York: Routledge.

Latour, B. (2002) 'Body, cyborgs and the politics of incarnation', in S. Sweeney and I. Hodder (eds), *The Body*. Cambridge: Cambridge University Press.

Latour, B. (2005) *Reassembling the Social: An Introduction to Actor-Network-Theory*. Oxford: Oxford University Press.

Law, J. (1993) *Organizing Modernities*. Oxford: Blackwell.

Law, J. (2004) *After Method: Mess in Social Science Research*. London: Routledge.

Lewin, K. (1936) *Principles of Topological Psychology*. New York: McGraw-Hill.

Lukes, S. (1985) *Emile Durkheim, his Life and Work: A Historical and Critical Study*. Stanford, CA: Stanford University Press.

Maybin, J. (2001) 'Language, struggle and voice: The Bakhtin/Voloshinov writings', in M. Wetherell, S. Taylor and S.J. Yates (eds), *Discourse Theory and Practice: A Reader*. London: Sage.

Mennell, S. (1998) *Norbert Elias: An Introduction*. Dublin: University College Dublin Press.

Merton, R.K. (1957) *Social Theory and Social Structure*. Glencoe: The Free Press.

Middleton, D. and Brown, S. (2005) *The Social Psychology of Experience*. London: Sage.

Mohanty, S. (2007) 'The realist theory of social identity and its implications'. Economic and Social Research Council Identities and Social Action Programme Public Lecture, 28 November, Regents College, London.

Munro, R. (2005) 'Partial organization: Marilyn Strathern and the elicitation of relations', *Sociological Review*, 53: 246–66.

Rorty, A.O. (1976) 'A literary post-script: Characters, persons, selves, individuals', in A.O. Rorty (ed.), *The Identities of Persons*. Berkeley, CA: University of California Press.

Rose, N. (1989) *Governing the Soul: Shaping the Private Self*. London: Routledge.

Rose, N. (1996) 'Identity, genealogy, history', in S. Hall and P. Du Gay (eds), *Questions of Cultural Identity*. London: Sage.

Rose, N. (1999) *Powers of Freedom: Reframing Political Thought*. Cambridge: Cambridge University Press.

Rutherford, J. (2007) *After Identity*. London: Lawrence and Wishart.

Schwartz, S.J. (2001) 'The evolution of Eriksonian and neo-Eriksonian identity theory and research: A review and integration', *Identity: An International Journal of Theory and Research*, 1 (1): 7–58.

Seve, L. (1978) *Man in Marxist Theory and the Psychology of Personality*. Brighton: Harvester Wheatsheaf.

Sherif, M. (1936) *The Psychology of Social Norms*. New York: Harper.

Seigel, J. (2005) *The Idea of the Self: Thought and Experience in Western Europe since the 17th Century*. Cambridge: Cambridge University Press.

Sorenson, B.M. (2005) 'Immaculate defecation: Gilles Deleuze and Feliz Guattari in organization theory', *Sociological Review*, 53: 120–33.

Tajfel, H. (1981) *Human Groups and Social Categories*. Cambridge: Cambridge University Press.

Turner, J., Hogg, M., Oakes, P., Reicher, S. and Wetherell, M. (1987) *Rediscovering the Social Group: A Self-Categorisation Theory*. Oxford: Blackwell.

Taylor, C. (1989) *Sources of the Self: The Making of Modern Identity*. Cambridge: Cambridge University Press.

Thrift, N. (2008) *Non-Representational Theory: Space/Politics/Affect*. London: Routledge.

Venn, C. (2006) *The Postcolonial Challenge: Towards Alternative Worlds*. London: Sage.

Walkerdine, V., Lucey, H. and Melody, J. (2001) *Growing Up Girl: Psychosocial Explorations of Gender and Class.* Basingstoke: Palgrave.

Wertsch, J. (1990) *Voices of the Mind.* London: Harvester Wheatsheaf.

Wetherell, M. (1998) 'Positioning and interpretative repertoires: Conversation analysis and post-structuralism in dialogue', *Discourse and Society*, 9: 431–56.

Wetherell, M. and Potter, J. (1992) *Mapping the Language of Racism.* London and New York: Harvester Wheatsheaf and Columbia University Press.

Winnicott, D.W. (1958) *Collected Papers. Through Paediatrics to Psychoanalysis.* New York: Basic Books.

Yensen, H., Hague, K. and McCreanor, T. (1989) *Honouring the Treaty: An Introduction for Pakeha to the Treaty of Waitangi.* Auckland, New Zealand: Penguin.

Yuval-Davis, N. (2006) 'Belonging and the politics of belonging', *Patterns of Prejudice*, 40 (3): 197–214.

# PART 1
# Frameworks

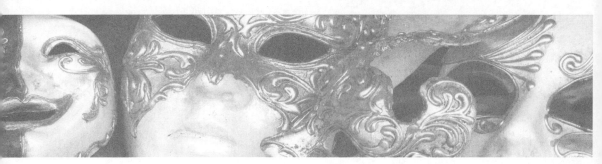

# 1

# Psychoanalytic Perspectives on Identity: From Ego to Ethics

Stephen Frosh

It is not difficult to argue that psychoanalysis is and should be a major disciplinary site through which alternative notions of identities can be explored. The psychoanalytic concept of a dynamic unconscious provides leverage on a number of central issues in the study of identities, including the tension between an understanding of identity as something fixed (repressed ideas producing stable ways of being that are resistant to change) and of identities as fluid and multiple (unconscious ideas are variable, contradictory and partial). Historically, psychoanalysis has concerned itself with issues that bear on whether identities are best thought of as primarily characterological or relational; in addition, by drawing on well-established notions such as identification, introjection and internalisation as well as more contemporary thinking on recognition, it offers routes to conceptualise the processes whereby human subjects become invested in particular identities, for example through allegiances or emotional connections with specific groups or social fractions. The key intersubjective postulate is perhaps that while the original source of identity is based on body image, identification with parents and others subsequently leads to more complex and elaborate experiences of identity in a variety of contexts. Identities are constructed through such processes of identification and recognition, and emotional investment by subjects in these processes gives identities their significance – the reason why they can be experienced as constituting psychosocial reality. Because both the constructive processes (identification, etc.) and the investment are largely or wholly unconscious, identities are lived as if they were 'given' rather than chosen; that is, they are often felt to be fundamental to the subject, as if they have been received whole and constitute the subject's essence.

This broadly psychoanalytic account has a good deal of descriptive and explanatory power. However, it does not represent the whole array of psychoanalytic thinking on identities. On the one hand, there is a strong though now dated tradition of understanding identity as a process of social adaptation, of bringing unconscious wishes into line with cultural expectations and possibilities under the guise of 'ego identity' – perhaps understandable as the capacity to know who one is in the context in which one finds oneself. More recently, this general idea has been displaced by notions of specific types of identity – particularly sexual and gender identity, ethnic and racial identity – but the sense of coming to know oneself in these more circumscribed situations still prevails. While these approaches share some of the psychoanalytic assumptions described above, it is arguable that they rely on ideas about character and selfhood that are no longer sustainable in identity studies, with its emphasis on how identities are multiple and potentially fluid, constructed through experience and linguistically coded. On the other hand, there are also alternative approaches within psychoanalysis that question the stability of identities, preferring to track them as modes of what might be thought of as 'masquerade', or as fragile and momentary assemblages of contradictory forces. In this chapter, I will explore the differing trajectories of these approaches in an attempt to offer an account of how psychoanalysis might contribute to the current project of understanding identities in the terms understood in this volume, 'as the place(s) or location(s) where social categories and social relations, symbolic representations and hierarchies of privilege and disadvantage come together and are lived out as forms of subjectivity and community'.

## CLASSICAL PSYCHOANALYTIC FORMULATIONS

Identity as a term is used only once by Freud in his writings, in a way described by some commentators as 'incidental … with a psychosocial connotation' (Grinberg and Grinberg, 1974: 499). In fact, this reference is a very interesting personal one: it is found in a letter by Freud written on the occasion of his 70th birthday in response to greetings from the Vienna Bnai Brith, the Jewish organisation with which he was deeply involved in the late 1890s, at the time when he was formulating the new psychoanalytic science (Frosh, 2005). Reflecting on the reasons that drew him to the Bnai Brith, Freud comments on how he had

neither religious nor nationalistic (i.e. Zionist) beliefs, but nevertheless,

> there remained enough to make the attraction of Judaism and the Jews irresistible, many dark emotional powers all the stronger the less they could be expressed in words, as well as the clear consciousness of an inner identity, the familiarity of the same psychological structure. (1926/1961: 368)

Erik Erikson reads this quotation as evidence that identity is necessarily tied up with the social environment, that 'It is the identity of something in the individual's core with an essential aspect of a group's inner coherence which is under consideration here' (1956: 57). Moreover, 'The term identity expresses such a mutual relation in that it connotes both a persistent sameness with oneself (self-sameness) and a persistent sharing of some kind of essential character with others' (Erikson, 1956: 57). Certainly, Freud's reference to 'the familiarity of the same psychological structure' that linked him with his Jewish peers supports the idea that he is using identity in this psychosocial sense. However, it should be noted that while 'the clear consciousness of an inner identity' is offered by Freud as one element making 'the attraction of Judaism and the Jews irresistible', it is not the one that exercises his *psychoanalytic* interest; that place is given over to the 'many dark emotional powers' to which he refers, but of which he can give no straightforward explanation. The attraction of a shared 'psychological structure' is not mysterious; it is straightforwardly observable and comes largely under the heading of what Freud calls in the same place 'ethical' demands. The other thing, however, that he calls 'dark' is described elsewhere as the 'essence' of his link with the Jewish people and its culture, and yet as currently inaccessible to science (Freud, 1930: xv); it requires more than simple reflection, more even than the psychoanalytic tools then available, to account for it. This references a debate that has surrounded the question of identity itself, and Erikson's reading of it in particular: is it really a psychoanalytic concept, or a psychosocial one that goes no further than describing predominantly conscious material? That is, what does psychoanalysis add to the debate here to what might be known from more transparent accounts?

According to Grinberg and Grinberg (1974), the term 'identity' was introduced formally into psychoanalytic literature by Victor Tausk (1933) in his classic paper, *On the Origin of the 'Influencing Machine'*, which dealt with the disintegration of self-hood and identity and the manifestation of that identity-loss in paranoia. It is in the work of Erikson, however, that the most influential account of identity can be found which can lay some claim to being psychoanalytic. Erikson understood identity to be concerned with ego functioning and to connote something like 'social character', or perhaps the relatively stable sense of oneself in a culture – an approach that was consistent with the ego psychological dominance of the American psychoanalysis of his time. For Erikson, ego analysis was laced with a commitment to a culturally or socially aware psychoanalysis, one that viewed the great task of life as bringing the individual into a constructive relationship with society. However, as was the case within the broader ego-psychological movement, the social aspects of Eriksonian theory seemed to lose their potentially critical bite and drift towards a vision of the task of development as *adapting* the individual so as to ease the potential tension with her or his social environment (Frosh, 1999). So, Erikson describes his use of the term 'identity' as 'to suggest a social function of the ego which results, in adolescence, in a relative psychosocial equilibrium essential to the tasks of young adulthood' (1956: 104). Identity is here understood as a long-lasting sense of self as something continuous, combined with a feeling of belonging in a community. Erikson comments, 'At one time […] it will appear to refer to a conscious *sense of individual identity*; at another to an unconscious striving for a continuity of personal character; and, finally, as a maintenance of an inner *solidarity* with a group's ideals and identity' (1956: 57).

Identity is, crucially and centrally, a developmental achievement of the ego, and one that is necessary for the well-being of each subject: 'I have been using the term *ego identity* to denote certain comprehensive gains which the individual, at the end of adolescence, must have derived from all of his pre-adult experiences in order to be ready for the tasks of adulthood' (Erikson, 1956: 56). For Erikson, the roots of identity 'go back all the way to the first self-recognition: in the baby's earliest exchange of smiles there is something of a *self-realization coupled with a mutual recognition*' (1956: 69). This formulation of the importance of having one's reality reflected back to one produces 'tentative crystallizations' that make the child feel known to the other and hence to the self. These crystallisations are disrupted from time to time by the actual 'discontinuities of psychosocial development', but a reasonably reliable family and a supportive community will lead to more integrated development to the degree to which they permit the child 'to orient himself toward a complete "*life plan*" with a hierarchical order of roles as represented by individuals of different age grades' (1956: 70). 'From a genetic point of view', states Erikson, 'the process of identity formation emerges as an *evolving configuration* – a configuration which is gradually established by successive ego syntheses and resyntheses throughout childhood; it is a configuration gradually integrating *constitutional givens, idiosyncratic libidinal needs, favored capacities, significant identifications, effective defences, successful sublimations, and consistent roles*' (1956: 71). It has conscious, preconscious and unconscious components, is never fully finalised (albeit largely focused on the period up to the end of adolescence, with its characteristic 'identity crisis') but is part of a lifelong developmental unfolding, and is a mixture of dynamic and psychosocial components.

In some ways, Erikson's account of identity formation, and in particular his very detailed description of the 'tasks' of adolescence, have been more influential in social psychology (particularly through their partial parroting in numerous undergraduate textbooks) than in psychoanalysis itself. This may be because of its interactionist flavour, with both sides of what that means: it is relational and links with much contemporary theory, but also has problematic psychoanalytic, as opposed to social-psychological, standing. Early on, Edith Jacobson (1964) labelled Erikson's work as not truly psychoanalytic, a description that has often been applied to potentially productive concepts that might disturb psychoanalytic orthodoxies. In Erikson's case, the disturbance may have come from the emphasis he placed on the surrounding social world, although looked at through the lens of critical social theory this does not seem particularly subversive – the community would lend its support to the process of identity formation, allowing the individual's life plans to develop and integration to occur. Wallerstein (1998), in a paper that reconsiders Erikson's legacy, suggests that his work is ever more relevant, but that this has been obscured by the language of the new theories of the 'self', which has largely replaced the ego psychological language of Erikson's time. That is, the ego psychologists rejected him because his concepts were too social, and the self-psychologists have neglected him because they regarded him as too focused on ego structures. Wallerstein comments, 'though the concept of identity, so central to Erikson's conceptualizations over a lifetime, has come in the past two decades to the forefront of psychoanalytic attention, it has done so under the rubric of the self, thereby obscuring the obvious relation of Erikson's earlier theorizing to these new emphases' (1998: 239). While the ego identity theory of Erikson became peripheral to psychoanalysis, many of the concepts deployed in contemporary intersubjectivist and self-theory have connections with it. In particular, the transactional nature of Erikson's approach, in which individual and social components of development support one another, can be traced in the sometime anodyne psychosocial elements of a fair amount of later work.

## BODIES, OBJECTS AND IDENTIFICATIONS

In their post-Eriksonian account, Grinberg and Grinberg emphasise the significance of the integrative function of the sense of identity, the way it registers 'the idea of a self which bears essentially upon the continuity and likeness of unconscious fantasies referring to bodily sensations and emotions experienced by the ego' (1974: 500) and hence has 'spatial, temporal and social' aspects. These relate to 'self-non-self differentiation', continuity of self-representations over time, and 'the relationship between aspects of the self and aspects of objects by means of the mechanisms of identification' (1974: 502). This formulation captures a good proportion of the shared ideas of psychoanalysts on this topic. Identity is a developmental notion and is formed in response to internal and external forces. It has a bodily source that grounds it in a sense of unity or unification; Grinberg and Grinberg claim that, 'The idea of the body is essential to the consolidation of the individual's identity [...] When Freud pointed out that the "ego is first and foremost a bodily ego, it is not merely a surface but is itself a projection of a surface" (1923), he was underlining one of the most important factors that form the basis of identity' (1974: 502). Revealingly, this claim has the effect of blurring the distinction between identity, self and ego, because as the quotation from Freud reveals, it is not *identity* that is classically thought of in this way, but the *ego itself*: the ego is built up out of perceptions of the body and its functions, from relationships with others that are mediated through the skin and the mouth (Greenacre, 1958), or from the kind of introjective processes based on bodily functions that are so beloved of the Kleinians, a point which will be developed below. Given that the ego is both the site of consciousness and imbued with unconscious processes (the defence mechanisms), and that identity is usually thought of as a 'sense' of being and belonging, this conflation of the two concepts begs a large number of questions. In particular, identity seems to be compressed into 'ego-identity', in the Eriksonian tradition, with attendant assumptions of integration of the ego and its absorption into notions of the 'self', setting it at odds with many contemporary formulations of the fragmentary and contingent nature of identity as a set of not necessarily reflected-upon lived experiences. Within psychoanalysis, too, the assumption of ego-integrity invites the Lacanian critique that this is a specious fantasy, an imaginary position, mistaking apparent bodily unity for psychic integrity.

Co-option of the notion of identity into that of the ego opens up another strand of psychoanalytic developmental thinking, the idea that the ego is formed through the internalisation of lost objects. As, faced with reality, the growing child has to give up desired sexual objects, so the ego takes them in, internalising them and in the process altering itself. These forsaken desires and lost objects are absorbed into the ego, along with the psychic energy invested in them, making it possible 'to suppose that the character of the ego is a precipitate of abandoned object cathexes and that it contains the history of those object choices' (Freud, 1923: 368). This notion is one Freudian basis for object relations theory and also encompasses a social account of identity formation as something founded on the fantasised relationship with real objects in the interpersonal or intersubjective world. That is, as the ego itself is formed from the internalisation of objects first experienced externally – the mother's breast predominant among them – so the formation of identity can be understood to derive from processes of internalisation and identification, in which what is 'found' externally and related to affectively, becomes taken in to provide the model, schema or template for representations of the 'inner world'. Moore and Fine, for example, draw on the concept of identification in their statement of what produces sexual identity:

Identification with both parents gives a bisexual quality to the self-representations and schemas, and self-concepts of children of both sexes. Eventually, however, an integrated self-organization is created out of the multiple former identifications contributing to its character traits. [...] The sense of identity achieves relative stability when bisexual identifications are resolved and adolescence completed. (1990: 93)

What can be seen in this is both the assumption of a normative developmental sequence leading to stable and integrated identity, and the understanding that this might result from a process whereby 'multiple former identifications' based on relationships with parents, are in some way worked on to produce this integrated self.

This type of theory reflects a widely shared perception amongst psychoanalysts that identity, selfhood and even the ego are built up, defensively or not, on the basis of taking in experiences with external 'objects' and combining them with 'internal' factors such as bodily experience or primitive phantasies to create conscious and unconscious representations. This raises the question of how 'external' things – ideas, representations of self and others – get 'into' the subject's 'inner world'. The mind is in constant dialogue with the world, putting into it some of its own contents (through projection, for example) and finding ways of producing internal representations of what it finds there. Without such engagement, it would consist only of what was produced from within; it would be a 'closed system', generating meanings on the basis perhaps of drives or in response to external stimuli, but unable to absorb features of the outside world into itself. What psychoanalysis claims is not only that external stimuli are processed by the perceptual system, but more radically that they are somehow 'internalised', taken in to become part of the mind, infecting its structure and – most importantly – its unconscious contents. That is, psychoanalysis models an 'open system' in which external experiences – encounters with 'objects', relationships, ideas – can become part of the person in a deep way. At its most sophisticated, what this produces is a theory in which 'self' and 'other' are always entwined, so that there is no way of considering any mind in isolation from any other. Thought of that way, identification is a *constructive* process, in that the internalised attributes are not destroyed but are employed in the service of some kind of development (hence, it remains distinct from incorporation in the psychoanalytic sense, which devours what it takes in), and it is likely that it is one of the most powerful methods whereby the self changes. Freud (1923) seemed to recognise this with his notion of the ego as the 'precipitate of abandoned object cathexes', even though his theory implies that the first 'thoughts' are representations of the drives, coming from within rather than without. As his work progressed, indeed, so identification became seen as more central. This is particularly the case in relation to the Oedipus complex, the outcome of which is theorised as a set of powerful identifications laying the foundations of all later personality development and specifically of sexual and gender identity. That is, as the boy, threatened with the castrating power of the father, represses his desire for the mother, so what emerges for him is a saving identification with the father that creates gender security as well as the promise of later recovery. For the girl too, even though the processes described by Freud are more confused and less potent, there is identification with the mother's position in relation to the father that leads to the gendered construction of identity alongside the channelling of desire. In addition, the construction of the superego as a response to castration anxiety is one big internalising process: what is taken in here is the fantasy of the paternal prohibition, with all its associated aggression. Hinshelwood, writing out of the Kleinian tradition in which there is an emphasis on processes of projection and introjection operating from birth, phrases this about as strongly as could ever be:

> The internal objects are phantasies, but at first phantasies are omnipotent, so through these primitive phantasies involved in identification the object is the self [...] Phantasy 'is' reality, and phantasy constructs the reality of the internal world on the basis of these primitive forms of introjective and projective identification. (1991: 320)

Because the infant is always engaged in a process of 'putting out and taking in', of projecting feelings into the external 'object' and then seeking to absorb properties of these objects, the emerging psyche is filled with representations, however crude, of the object, and it is around these object representations that it becomes structured. Hence, there is no firm division between inside and out, but rather a fluid interchange in which each penetrates the other.

Jessica Benjamin (1998) has given a subtle recent rendering of identifications in the context of gender. Holding onto the distinction between identification and incorporation, the latter being a kind of cannibalistic taking in of the other until it becomes part of the self and is no longer psychically distinct, Benjamin argues that what is precious about identification is that it allows the other to *survive* as a living and appreciated aspect of the self. Identification is consequently built out of an already-existing awareness of the other's existence *as a subject*; that is, it is a loving 'intersubjective' relationship in which aspects of otherness are accepted and used by the self, without destroying the other in the process. It is 'not merely a matter of incorporating the other as ideal, but of loving and having a relationship with the person who embodies the ideal' (Benjamin, 1998: 61). Identification can thus be seen as a form of *relationship*, not just a way in which one person acts upon another; developmentally, for example, it can be a way in which a boy aspires to be linked to his father rather than to be rivalrous with him. Indeed, in the context of gender development Benjamin claims that boys and girls both identify with the loving father, just as they do with the powerful and loving mother, making multiple identifications along the way. The effect of these multiple identifications is to produce in the child a greater range of possible gender positions, particularly enhancing 'complementarity' rather than the kind of exclusivity that results in the triumph of one gender position over another. On the basis of such complex patterns of identification in which the child incorporates aspects of all her or his loved objects into the self, it is possible to recast development as a process of making increasingly fine internal differentiations which does not necessarily (depending on the quality of actual object relationships) take place at the expense of the valuing of difference. That is, the classic view of identification, particularly in the Oedipus complex, is that it involves taking in one thing and repudiating another. Benjamin, however, outlines a more mature, post-Oedipal complementarity that brings back together the various 'elements of identification, so that they become less threatening, less diametrically opposite, no longer cancelling out one's identity' (1998: 69–70). Multiple identifications forge the basis for identities (including gender identities) which themselves are multiple and fluid, less defensive and hence less caricatured and stereotyped. *Connectedness* is emphasised here, recognising difference but not discounting the other because of it.

This rendering of identification with others as a way of taking in multiple possibilities for development is one important strand in contemporary work. However, the Lacanian critique of the ego and hence of identity applies here, with identification being understood as an 'imaginary' process of taking on an image and 'appropriating' it *as if* it represents the self. That is, identification is primarily a way of losing oneself in the other; more precisely, the fact that identification is at the root of the formation of the ego reveals that the ego is itself 'specious', a false acceptance of an image as real. Identification, psychoanalysis attests, is that process whereby the ego takes the object and makes it *subject*, incorporating each object as part of itself. According to Lacan, this is indeed a formative process, but its effect is specifically to create a kind of radical *misperception*, in which the ego is taken to be the 'truth' of the person when it is actually just 'bric-a-brac' (Lacan, 1954–5: 155), made up of bits and pieces latched onto from outside. Hence, there is a sense in which identification *falsifies*, with the subject 'using' the object to sustain a fantasy of integrity of the self. This is why Lacan was opposed to the idea that psychoanalytic psychotherapy should aim at enabling the patient to identify with the analyst; rather, he suggested, analysis should aim to show the patient how identifications are all impossibly fantastic. No one can become the model for another; instead, suggests Lacan, the 'real' of the subject lies outside what can be organised and known. Identification, therefore, may well be a major mechanism through which what is outside comes to be registered within, but this also makes it a mode of alienation, whereby the human subject is made a stranger to itself.

## POST-INTEGRATIVE IDENTITIES

The view of identities as potentially integrated, if multifarious, constructed entities formed through internalising relationships with external objects, connects with broader notions of selfhood to be found in British and more recently American psychoanalytic schools. These posit the self as arising in the crucible of caring (usually maternal) relationships that gives rise both to a set of capacities and attributes and a reflexive function that itself constitutes the 'sense of identity'. Winnicott's (1960) notions of false and true self, and in particular his ideas on the formation of secure selfhood in the context of maternal responsiveness, have been very influential in this regard, offering a precursor to contemporary theories of 'recognition' (Benjamin, 1998) that emphasise the construction of subjectivity in and through a nexus of relationships with others. Without rehearsing the details of Winnicott's account unnecessarily, it is worth recalling that the 'true self' is understood to be a *potential* for growth that will naturally unfold under the right circumstances, and that can be damaged or hidden in a hostile environment. The mother is supposed to provide her infant with the conditions under which her or his potential for selfhood can be realised. Interference with this function, for instance because of the mother's depression, is experienced by the infant as an 'impingement' on the natural organisation of experience, and leads to anxiety about total disintegration. This results in a defensive hiding away of the child's spontaneous desires in the form of a secret 'true self', which avoids expression because of the danger that it will be destroyed by the inadequate environment. To enable transactions with reality, a conformist 'false self' is formed, split off from the true self and protecting its integrity. The false self is inauthentic because it is built up on the pattern of the mother's desire, not the child's, hence its conformity: the child is formed in someone else's image of her or him, acting in line with the mother's expectations and wishes so as to win her love. In Phillips' gloss:

> It is part of Winnicott's demand on the mother that she be robust; if she is in any way rejecting, the infant has to comply with her response. It is the strategies of compliance that Winnicott calls the False Self Organization. Because of this primary and enforced attentiveness to the needs of the mother, the False Self, he writes, always 'lacks something, and that something is the *essential element of creative originality*'. (1988: 133)

The true self is the essential creativity of the human subject in action, consisting of a variety of capacities such as the ability to be alone, to be in states of 'disunity' out of which new modes of experience can emerge, to live with risk, and so on. The false self, conversely, is something close to what other psychoanalytic authors would call 'narcissistic' – a defensive shutting down, organised around close scrutiny of the other and an inability to feel real.

The impact of Winnicott's thinking on selfhood has been immense, especially when combined with his seminal notions of transitional objects and transitional spaces – those intermediate, half-imagined, half-material entities used by subjects to establish their relationship with the world, and to manifest

their creativity. At its core is, however, a set of assumptions that may be deeply evocative – as much of Winnicott's writing is – but also problematic for a poststructuralist context that refuses to take as given the idea of an easy fit between subjecthood and society. For Winnicott, everything depends on what Phillips calls 'robustness', or perhaps is better coded as 'maternal resilience'. The capacity of the mother (and in therapy, the analyst) to *survive* in the face of her infant's psychic attacks on her allows the child to absorb an experience of herself – or himself as real and legitimate, and of loved objects as also actually existing, not just as a figment of the child's imagination. This gives the child a firm sense of location in her or his own needs, which are now experienced as legitimate and acceptable, and in a setting that is not going to collapse. From this, the true self can emerge, an integrated, spontaneous, creative entity that can deal with the world on its own terms. Without such early maternal resilience, the self remains fragmentary and takes refuge behind a conforming false self striving desperately to appease a persecutory environment or – in cases where the mother is depressed and unresponsive – to bring it to life. It should be noted that this is a theory of self as an experiencing core, not of identity as a 'sense' of self – but that the latter is implicit in the former: the foundations for a clear sense of continuity, integrity and belonging lie in these early experiences of maternal holding.

In theorising clinical phenomena, many psychoanalysts operate with a loosely similar set of perceptions, understanding psychopathology as a breakdown in selfhood subsequent to failures of maternal holding and psychological recognition. This is roughly true not just of Winnicott and object relations theories, but also of followers of Klein and Bion in the British School and self-theorists and relational psychoanalysts in America. However, there is something troubling about the assumption that there is a normative progression from adequate ('good-enough') recognition of the infant's needs to a secure selfhood and an integrated self-reflexive capacity that can be called a 'sense of identity'. From outside psychoanalysis, postmodernism and poststructuralism emphasise the 'normality' of fragmentary experience; there is also a strong strand within psychoanalysis that questions the idea that psychic integration should be either a developmental or a mental health norm. This leads to a much greater interest in identity as a thing-in-process than as fixed, and also asks about the degree to which the focus on self-representation and egoic knowledge of the self (for example, as represented in integrated self-narratives) is an actively defensive process. That is, given that psychoanalysis is in many ways *deconstructive* in that it pursues the analytic decomposition of all the phenomena with which it is faced, is the search for integration, reflected in the views of self and identity to be found in much of the psychoanalytic literature, a way of avoiding psychoanalysis' own most radical insights? Does it represent an abandonment of what Laplanche refers to as 'the properly "analytic" vector, that of de-translation and the questioning of narrative structures and the ideas connected to them?' (2003: 29). In this respect, the Lacanian deconstruction of the ego is absolutely fundamental to much contemporary thought. In Lacanian terms, identity acts in the register of the imaginary, which is always over-inflated in terms of its claims to mastery and completeness; identity is thus a narcissistic entity, yet one with great power and significance. In contrast to the way much classical and object relational thinking on identity references a secure ego as the necessary underpinning of a secure sense of self, Lacan's work has as one theme the exposure of the ego as something fabricated *as a defensive structure*, hence embedding an alienation of the subject within its own psychic life. This is famously explicated in Lacan's (1949) notion of the 'mirror phase', which continues to act as a source for theorising the fragility of selfhood, despite the fact that there are many difficulties with that concept and with his paper on it, as Billig (2006) has recently demonstrated. In contrast to

Winnicott (1967), who uses the idea of mirroring to convey the importance of a developmental process in which the child sees her – or himself accurately and thoughtfully reflected back by a concerned mother (that is, who enters into her or his true self/identity through this interpersonal process), Lacan emphasises the impossibility of identity as related to a 'true' self. In his view, the ego is used to create an armour or shell supporting the psyche, which is otherwise experienced as in fragments. Lacan emphasises the *exteriority* of this process – that which appears to us as our 'self' is in fact given from the outside as a refuge, an ideal ego, a narcissistically invested image.

> The fact is that the total form of the body by which the subject anticipates in a mirage the maturation of his power is given to him only as a *Gestalt*, that is to say, in an exteriority in which this form is certainly more constituent than constituted, but in which it appears to him above all in a contrasting size that fixes it and in a symmetry that inverts it, in contrast with the turbulent movements that the subject feels are animating him. (Lacan, 1949: 2)

Here, Lacan is arguing that the subject gains relief from the intensity of fragmenting internal impulses through the boundedness and apparent stability of the mirror image – something external but connected to the subject, holding a promise of future 'power'. Whereas Winnicott portrays the mirroring function as one which allows the child actually to grow into her or his self – to genuinely find the 'maturation of his power', one might say – for Lacan this is a process in which the subject is hoodwinked into taking on the image as if it were real. Moreover, there is here an understanding of the external, social world as operating guilefully to divert the subject away from its terror of dissolution. The message given to the infant 'in the mirror' is that the ego has integrity and wholeness; but this message is a socially constructed one, legible in the reflecting surfaces and faces of an order stressing the autonomy and psychological independence of individuals. According to Lacan, the structure of human knowledge and ego functioning is therefore a delusional one, finding in the spectral image a misleading promise of integrity. This is read by Lacan as a paranoid sensation. The negativity and persecutory associations of the paranoiac are to do in part with the aggressivity of the drives, threatening to burst the image apart – a notion akin to those worked on by Klein (1946) in her description of paranoid–schizoid functioning. But it is also connected with the haunting of this satisfying image of the integrated self by the spectre or memory of something else: somewhere inside, each subject knows that it is not really whole, that this seeming-self is a cover for something disturbing. The mirror is thus a source both of reassurance and of threat, its seemingly smooth surface containing unexpected ripples caused by that which can be seen yet not quite named. Bodily unity is no guarantee of psychic unity, which in fact is disrupted continually by the play of drives.

The mirror stage reflects the impossibility of becoming a self without taking on the meanings of the other – without becoming *identified* with another's gaze, with the pre-existing desire of the other that one should be some one thing and not anything else. In Lacanian thought, the imaginary wholeness promised by the mirror is shattered by another step of alienation, the move to the Symbolic order of experience in which the structures of language interfere with the image-making process, revealing that it is already organised by a law indifferent to the emotions and desires of the individual subject. The crucial dynamic here of course is the entry of the child into language: to speak, to be part of the linguistic order, the subject has to move from the narcissism of the Imaginary to a position from which there is awareness of an outside other, something regulatory which takes the form of a law. The Symbolic order thus positions the subject as a separate, speaking entity, with her or his subjectivity organised along specifiable routes. Once again, this positioning arises from outside the subject, confirming its self-alienation: 'I identify myself in language, but only by

losing myself in it like an object' (Lacan, 1953). Thus, the positioning of the subject with respect to language requires an encounter with otherness in a way that fractures the omnipotence of the mirrored 'I' in the imaginary. If the imaginary celebrates the fictitious identity of subject and ego, it is the tearing of this identity that moves the subject into the symbolic order, and at the same time constructs the unconscious: what is 'left out' becomes repressed. This is the relevance of the familiar statement that Lacan evokes an empty subject, constituted through lack and marked by the impossibility of fulfilment or of recognition of the actuality of the other. In the Lacanian scheme, 'identity' is an aspect of the fantasy of fulfilment that is split apart by the discovery that the subject is produced by, rather than generative of, the signifying chain. When we find an identity we believe we have found something with substance, but the order of causality is the other way around: it finds us. That is, the symbolic order positions the subject in relation to other subjects, marking each as incomplete, only present through its relationship with what lies outside. Claims to identity as something fixed and legitimating become understood as defensive manoeuvres protecting the psyche against its own inherent splits.

Disruption of notions of secure identity is not confined to Lacanian theory, but is engaged in by many who try to weave a post-structuralist and postmodern sensibility into psychoanalysis. Flax, for example, also sees the defensive structures of stability and integrity at work, in her example when there are claims to stable gender identity: 'A "stable" gender identity may be partially constituted by, and may serve, multiple defensive purposes, including warding off unwanted aspects of subjectivity or affects, such as aggression' (1996: 585). The idea that identities form through identifications and introjections that may be multiple and partial is widespread, but the division between external objects and internal worlds is undermined by the way inside and out mutually construct each other – as evoked by Lacan's (1973) use of the Moebius strip and Laplanche's (1999) conceptualisation of the 'enigmatic' message, that which is implanted in each one of us as an unknown disturbance that excites and antagonises. This needs to be seen as a worm of dissent at the heart of anything that might be thought of as fixed, stable identity – we always consist of something alien at our core. 'Identity' is consequently not only always fabricated and provisional, but also it is the 'social' just as it is also the 'personal' or individual – it is not the adaptation of one to the other, but another emanation of the indissolubility of the two. This raises a set of issues that have at their core a certain kind of ethics, questions of what it might mean to live a 'good life' psychoanalytically, that might radically enlarge our current conceptualisation of 'identity politics'.

## ETHICAL IDENTITIES

Utilisation of psychoanalytic ideas in social science research has been widespread, if ambivalent. In identities work, even when employed sympathetically in contemporary psychosocial studies, it has often been used as an interpretive categorisation procedure with perhaps too firm a diagnostic subtext. That is, psychoanalysis is called on in its traditional role of making sense of apparently irrational material, or of explaining the investment that subjects might have in discursive positions that in some respects might seem to go against their own rational 'interests' (Frosh et al., 2003; Hollway and Jefferson, 2005; Roseneil, 2006). While this role is important in drawing discussions of the unconscious back into the psychological domain, it also neglects a more recent contribution of psychoanalysis to both epistemology and ethics, what Nobus and Quinn term 'making interpretation stupid' (2005: 186). The argument here is for reading against the grain, making temporary alignments with the Imaginary and tentative interpretations along the line of the symbolic in order to hold onto

the idea of a subject in process, with no fixed identity however strong the identifications might be. 'Making stupid' involves holding to the provocations of psychoanalysis as an approach that continually deconstructs, without looking out towards eventual fullness of knowledge, for example, in the form of an account or theory of identities that places them safely within the discursive sphere. Using psychoanalysis to 'explain' identities may miss the point – taken that way, psychoanalysis is just one of many vocabularies for naming the momentary stabilities of subjectivity and trying to pin them down. What psychoanalysis might offer that is other to this relates to what Nobus and Quinn (2005: 200) refer to as 'less than knowledge': the determination that subjective knowledge and knowledge of the subject is always blocked by a kind of disruptive 'thingness' which makes it the object of something else.

There is, however, an elusiveness to this kind of formulation which may or may not be necessary and which makes it hard to bring it to bear on the practical study of identities (or anything else). It is worth tracking back to see what is being evoked and what responded to in this attempt to wriggle out of too much knowledge and fixedness and instead to focus on the constant disruption that is seen both as a necessary state of knowledge (epistemology) and a paradigm for subjective encounters (ethics). In part, this is a derivative of contemporary events in the 'real' world of technological change, war and terrorism, in the rising consciousness (but neglect of action) over ecological disaster, in the dissemination of HIV/AIDS and the promises of biomedicine and the genome. One might expect that these developments will impact on people's psychological states and their senses of identity and selfhood, now perhaps more panicked than before, but also more technologically mediated through, among other things, the explosive growth of the Internet. Indeed, the argument that we are biotechnical subjects is well established in certain branches of academia, since Donna Haraway's (1991) theorisation of 'cyborgs' and Rosi Braidotti's (2006) exuberant evocation of the nomadic subject, fluidly repositioning across a multifarious terrain of non-human life, with any notion of identity well and truly dismembered as a consequence. Social and cultural theory has responded to this by seeking out models of biosocial life that emphasise multifariousness and networked connections, displacing the human subject and introducing in its place a sense of productive activity that gives rise to sensations and identities. Some of this is relevant to identity studies, including a resurgence of Deleuzian 'rhizomes' taken as models of spreading networks of articulated forces, and laying the foundations for a return to an interest in affect as that which gives rise to subjectivity, rather than following on from it. As well as being a political philosophy, this perspective addresses psychological experiences in a way that is antagonistic to the depth perspective of traditional psychoanalysis, and has resonances with Lacanian psychoanalysis' legacy of interest in the denarrativising encounter between a subject who desires and one who is 'supposed to know', an encounter that is always waiting to be punctured (for example by the famously sudden ending of a 'short' psychoanalytic session) or more soberly by the emergence into speech of something completely unexpected. These perspectives give priority to disruption over meaning making, to paradox over order, and most importantly to the crisscrossing of bodily and symbolic networks as they create points of coherence that fade away as one looks at them.

In contrast, there is a movement 'back' towards a kind of humanistic modernism that refuses the deconstructionism of some recent intellectual traditions. This can be seen in the interest in narrative that has developed in psychotherapeutic circles (Frosh, 2002) and particularly in the 'relational turn' in psychoanalysis, perhaps most strikingly in the work of Benjamin (1998, 2004) and the development of a benign conceptualisation of 'thirdness' that draws particularly strongly on Winnicott. This work is based in clinical practice, but has been extended to deal with social and political conflicts; it focuses on ways of recognising the other that can bridge without colonising, that can sustain the other's separateness and difference while allowing links to be built. In a way, perhaps what is happening here is recognition of the *difficulty* of the postmodern experience of separateness and mistranslation, and a return to an aspirational mode of writing that seeks to establish relationships, however hard that task might be. Interestingly, a similar trend can be seen to have overtaken what looked in the early 1990s like one of the most evocative responses to postmodernism, the 'performative' thinking of Judith Butler (1990), which fuelled the rise of queer theory and the more general attempt to 'queer' everything, both specifically in the realm of sexuality and generally as a disruptive, erotic, from-the-margins assault on received wisdoms. This work was phenomenally influential, yet Butler (1997) herself qualified it very quickly by drawing explicitly on psychoanalysis, referencing Freud as a way of examining the place of melancholia in the formation of gender, and moving gradually back into a space of what seems to be deeply felt identity politics, or rather in (Jewish) identity in order to do politics (Butler, 2004). Her trajectory serves well to reflect a more general retrenchment that may not be backward looking, but rather expresses a willingness to engage politically with oppression and violence with whatever tools it takes, including the tools provided by the concept of identity. One can see here a way in which Butler, perhaps the most iconic figure of queer performativity, has immersed herself in a deeply serious project to contest oppression and abuse from the perspective of ethical engagement: things matter, she says; it is not just some kind of game. (To be fair, she has always taken this position, but the exuberance of her earlier work meant that this theme was consistently overlooked.)

Butler is a key figure for discussions of the trajectories of psychoanalysis and identities for numerous reasons, not least because she is generally so influential in encouraging, post-9/11 and in the wake of HIV/AIDS, a reorientation of attention towards psychoanalytic understandings of loss and melancholy, as if it is becoming possible to consider the impact of deep relationships once again; as if, that is, feelings are being allowed back in as formative elements in the construction of personal identities. For example, in her essay 'Violence, Mourning, and Politics', Butler (2004) explores the intricate relationships between selves, communities and otherness through the lens of Freud's thinking on mourning and melancholia.

> So when one loses, one is also faced with something enigmatic: something is hiding in the loss, something is lost within the recesses of loss. If mourning involves knowing what one has lost (and melancholia, originally, means, to a certain extent, not knowing), then mourning would be maintained by its enigmatic dimension, by the experience of not knowing incited by losing what we cannot fully fathom. (2004: 21–2)

In her account, the experience of loss demonstrates just how much each of us is relationally engaged with others – it shows up the intensity of that bond, which can often be experienced as excessive and uncontrollable, as uncontained in the psychoanalytic sense. Butler emphasises here the surprising 'not-knowingness' of loss, the way it can put us in contact with an area of unexpected dependence. This is not only an *external*, relational feature of loss, but rather it is deeply *internal*, raising the spectre of the fragilities of self to which postmodernism alluded and sometimes celebrated. Deeply felt loss of the kind Butler is writing about communicates the dispersal of self, the way that with every loss something dies inside because our inner world consists of connections with others.

> What grief displays […] is the thrall in which our relations with others hold us, in ways that we cannot always recount or explain, in ways that often interrupt the self-conscious account of ourselves we might try to provide, in ways that challenge the very notion of ourselves as autonomous and in control. (Butler, 2004: 23)

The reference here is to a kind of mystery, and it is suggested that this is endemic to the way our subjectivity is premised on the link with otherness.

Working in the domain of ethics and politics, Butler utilises psychoanalytic formulations to ask how what is melancholic and mournful can be turned into an appreciation of the other, of what constitutes the essential humanity of the other person. Reflecting on the way certain others are written out of history, have their humanity decried in the interests, and as a consequence, of violence, she argues that what makes us prone to the other's violence is also what makes us involved with the other – our mutual dependence, our neediness. The 'conception of the human' that she employs here is:

> one in which we are, from the start, given over to the other, one in which we are, from the start, even prior to individuation itself, and by virtue of bodily requirements, given over to some set of primary others: this conception means that we are vulnerable to those we are too young to know and to judge and, hence, vulnerable to violence; but also vulnerable to another range of touch, a range that includes the eradication of our being at the one end, and the physical support for our lives at the other. (Butler, 2004: 31)

Bodily and psychically – the two are in an important sense one and the same here – the infant is in the hands of the other, with all the potential that situation possesses for love and care, and violence and neglect. This dependence, Butler suggests, establishes a psychic structure that lasts throughout life. It also relates to the idea of the necessary *intrusion* of the other in the formation of selfhood, an intrusion that Žižek alludes to in his formulation of 'the monstrosity of the neighbour, a monstrosity on account of which Lacan applies to the neighbour the term Thing (*das Ding*)' (2006: 43). That is, an enigmatic demand is made on the self by the other from the start of life, and this enigma resides 'in' unconscious life, or perhaps is better thought of as continually provoking it, once again destabilising identity at the same moment as it appears to give it shape.

Much of this concerns the turn to the other as central to the construction of the subject. The reason why it makes no sense to insist on a clear boundary between self and other, or indeed an autonomous personal identity, is that the other is constantly implicated in the self, not just being carried around as a set of memories and identifications, but absolutely entwined in it. What Laplanche (1999) calls the 'enigmatic signifier', the 'message' put into the infant *unknowingly* by the other/ mother, faces us with a deeply mysterious yet absolutely concrete realisation of the other's desire within us; this can be seen as *producing* the unconscious as a mode of 'outside-ness' within. Taking this argument on, the search for recognition of and by the other becomes a highly complex process in which what is being sought is a link with an other who can embody this internal strangeness and ease the subject out of it. 'Solicit[ing] a becoming', as Butler (2004: 44) puts it, is tied into the other's difference because it is in this difference that the supposed answer to the subject's question might be found; *sameness*, after all, can do no more than confirm what is already known. Žižek, briefly in Levinasian mode, similarly notes the intractability of the mystery of the other as what is essential; indeed, he argues that *not* knowing the other is crucial to intersubjectivity itself. 'If I were to "really know" the mind of my interlocutor, intersubjectivity proper would disappear; he would lose his subjective status and turn – for me – into a transparent machine. In other words, not-being-knowable to others is a crucial feature of subjectivity, of what we mean when we impute to our interlocutors a "mind": you "truly have a mind" only insofar as it is opaque to me' (2006: 178). The solidity of the other comes over in this, its absolute otherness that links both with Winnicott's (1969) ideas on how the other becomes real to the subject by surviving attack, and with the contrary Lacanian emphasis on how all psychoanalytic knowledge is constituted through language, and hence is characterised by 'mis-translation'.

Recognition of the other, in the strong sense of giving the other ascendancy, is thus a key element in the maintenance of subjecthood and identity. This Levinasian take on things contrasts with Benjamin's attempt (indexing a major relational turn in contemporary psychoanalysis) to adopt a more reciprocal understanding of how analyst and patient – self and other – construct a third position into which they can project themselves as one. Benjamin formalises her interest in connectedness and relationality through postulating a 'space' in which contact occurs, a dynamic space, a principle, relationship or function which is constantly collapsing and needing to be repaired. It has two elements (Benjamin, 2004): the 'third in the one', which is the capacity (paradigmatically of the mother or the analyst) for a subject to hold in mind what subject and other can create together, a kind of reparative capacity to believe that it is possible to comprehend the other even when the other is destructive and alien; and the 'one in the third', a pattern of being that links subject and other and produces something new, a space (for example the projected space of the analytic encounter) for meeting, reflection and newness, owned by neither party but an aspect of them both. For Benjamin, this links further with the idea of the therapist being actively present in the therapeutic encounter, ready for example to acknowledge errors, and hence very much engaged in the process of negotiating the relational dynamics of the session. Thus, Benjamin rejects the Kleinian tendency to speak from the countertransference but not to become relationally involved with it, to insist 'that the patient is ultimately helped only by understanding rather than by being understood' (2004: 35). For Benjamin, it is necessary for the analyst who is 'caught in enactment' to acknowledge it in relation to the patient, a stance or position that Benjamin refers to as the 'moral third'. Benjamin comments, 'The analyst says, in effect, "I'll go first." In orienting to the moral third of responsibility, the analyst is also demonstrating the route out of helplessness' (2004: 33).

The key move here is from playful provocativeness to ethics. Feeling has returned, but the subject has been decentred at the same time, made the product of affect and/or of wider forms of liveness. Faced with loss and violence, there has been an attempt to reconfigure otherness, either as something utterly strange towards which we nevertheless have responsibility (crudely, the vision of Levinas [1991]), or as an active subject with whom each one of us needs to forge a relationship based on mutual recognition (Benjamin's 'subject–subject' relationship). These theories have significant implications for psychotherapy, understood not as a treatment but as a mode of ethical encounter. They also return us to the question of what a psychoanalysis of identities might entail, of whether it is desirable and possible to maintain a stringent 'stupidity' that constantly enforces an austere paradigm in which identities are disrupted and degraded, or whether there comes a moment – both political and 'scientific', if these things can be separated – in which the affect that comes bubbling through as a challenge from the unconscious is also owned and humanised, and people once again are granted depth.

# REFERENCES

Benjamin, J. (1998) *Shadow of the Other: Intersubjectivity and Gender in Psychoanalysis.* New York: Routledge.

Benjamin, J. (2004) 'Beyond doer and done to: An intersubjective view of thirdness', *Psychoanalytic Quarterly*, 73: 5–46.

Billig, M. (2006) 'Lacan's misuse of psychology: Evidence, rhetoric and the mirror stage', *Theory, Culture and Society*, 23: 1–26.

Braidotti, R. (2006) *Transpositions.* Cambridge: Polity.

Butler, J. (1990) *Gender Trouble.* London: Routledge.

Butler, J. (1997) *The Psychic Life of Power.* Stanford, CA: Stanford University Press.

Butler, J. (2004) *Precarious Life.* London: Verso.

Erikon, E. (1956) 'The problem of ego identity', *Journal of the American Psychoanalytic Association*, 4: 56–121.

Flax, J. (1996) 'Taking multiplicity seriously: Some implications for psychoanalytic', *Theorizing and Practice Contemporary Psychoanalysis*, 32: 577–93.

Freud, S. (1923). The Ego and the Id. *The Standard Edition of the Complete Psychological Works of Sigmund Freud, Volume XIX (1923–1925): The Ego and the Id and Other Works*, 1–66.

Freud, S. (1930 [1955]) *Preface to the Hebrew Translation of Totem and Taboo SE13.* London: Hogarth Press.

Freud, S. (1961) *Letters of Sigmund Freud 1873–1939* (edited by E. Freud). London: Hogarth Press.

Frosh, S. (1999) *The Politics of Psychoanalysis.* London: Palgrave.

Frosh, S. (2002) *After Words: The Personal in Gender, Culture and Psychotherapy.* London: Palgrave.

Frosh, S. (2005) *Hate and the 'Jewish Science': Anti-Semitism, Nazism and Psychoanalysis.* London: Palgrave.

Frosh, S., Phoenix, A. and Pattman, R. (2003) 'Taking a stand: Using psychoanalysis to explore the positioning of subjects in discourse', *British Journal of Social Psychology*, 42: 39–53.

Geenacre, P. (1958) 'Early physical determinants in the development of the sense of identity', *Journal of the American Psychoanalytic Association*, 6: 612–27.

Grinberg, L. and Grinberg, R. (1974) 'The problem of identity and the psychoanalytical process', *International Review of Psychoanalysis*, 1: 499–507.

Haraway, D. (1991) *Simians, Cyborgs and Women: The Reinvention of Nature.* New York: Routledge.

Hinshelwood, R. (1991) *A Dictionary of Kleinian Thought.* London: Free Association Books.

Hollway, W. and Jefferson, T. (2005) 'Panic and perjury: A psychosocial exploration of agency', *British Journal of Social Psychology*, 44: 147–63.

Jacobson, E. (1964) *The Self and the Object World.* London: Hogarth Press.

Klein, M. (1946 [1975]) 'Notes on some schizoid mechanisms', in M. Klein (ed.), *Envy and Gratitude and Other Works.* New York: Delta.

Lacan, J. (1949 [1977]) 'The mirror stage as formative of the function of the I as revaled in the psychoanalytic experience', in J. Lacan (ed.), *Écrits: A Selection*, pp. 1–7. London: Tavistock.

Lacan, J. (1953 [1977]) 'The function and field of speech and language in psychoanalysis', in J. Lacan (ed.), *Ecrits: A Selection*, pp. 30–113. London: Tavistock.

Lacan, J. (1954–5) *The Seminars of Jacques Lacan, Book II: The Ego in Freud's Theory and in the Technique of Psychoanalysis.* Cambridge: Cambridge University Press.

Lacan, J. (1973 [1977]) *The Four Fundamental Concepts of Psycho-Analysis.* Harmondsworth: Penguin.

Laplanche, J. (1999) *Essays on Otherness.* London: Routledge.

Laplanche, J. (2003) 'Narrativity and hermeneutics: Some propositions', *New Formations*, 48: 26–9.

Levinas, E. (1991) *Entre Nous: On Thinking of the Other*. London: Athlone, 1998.

Moore, B. and Fine, B. (1990) *Psychoanalytic Terms and Concepts*. New Haven, CT: Yale University Press.

Nobus, D. and Quinn, M. (2005) *Knowing Nothing, Staying Stupid*. London: Routledge.

Phillips, A. (1988) *Winnicott*. London: Fontana.

Roseneil, S. (2006) 'The ambivalences of angel's "arrangement": A psycho-social lens on the contemporary condition of personal life', *The Sociological Review*, 54: 846–68.

Tausk, V. (1933) On the Origin of the 'Influencing Machine' in Schizophrenia19. *Psychoanal Q.*, 2: 519–556

Wallerstein, R. (1998) 'Erikson's concept of ego identity reconsidered', *Journal of the American Psychoanalytic Association*, 46: 229–47.

Winnicott, D. (1960 [1965]) 'Ego distortion in terms of true and false self', in D.W. Winnicott (ed.), *The Maturational Process and the Facilitating Environment*, pp. 140–152. London: Hogarth Press.

Winnicott, D. (1967 [1980]) 'The mirror-role of mother and family in child development', in D. Winnicott (ed.), *Playing and Reality*, pp. 111–118. Harmondsworth: Penguin.

Winnicott, D. (1969) 'The use of an object', *International Journal of Psychoanalysis*, 50: 711–16.

Žižek, S. (2006) *The Parallax View*. Cambridge, MA: MIT.

# 2

# The Social Identity Approach in Social Psychology

Stephen Reicher, Russell Spears and
S. Alexander Haslam

In this contribution we review a family of social psychological theories, most notably Social Identity Theory (SIT) and Self-categorization Theory (SCT), which together constitute what we refer to as the Social Identity Approach (SIA). These theories are linked by their concern with the processes that surround the way in which people define themselves as members of a social group – which, here, is the meaning of the term 'social identity'. At a conceptual level, this approach serves to transform the understanding of identity in psychology. It stresses the sociality of the construct in at least three ways. First, social identity is a relational term, defining who we are as a function of our similarities and differences with others. Second, social identity is shared with others and provides a basis for shared social action. Third, the meanings associated with any social identity are products of our collective history and present. Social identity is therefore something that links us to the social world. It provides the pivot between the individual and society.

However, the SIA should not be seen as an exercise in social theory. Within its broad framework, social identity researchers have specified detailed processes that give practical insights into the ways that groups work in society. We will address a number of these including the nature of influence and persuasion, how leadership works and the nature of group stereotypes. This work has been applied to the behaviour of many different types of groups from electorates, to crowds, to work organizations. Indeed the power of the theory is in direct relationship to its range of application.

The very richness of the theory is also a source of danger. Particular postulates can be drawn from the overall framework and developed in ways that ignore or even contradict its foundational premises. Most importantly, the SIA seeks to address how psychological processes interact with social and political processes in the explanation of human social behaviour. It seeks to work with, rather than to supplant, other disciplines and accepts that much of the explanation of action is not psychological at all. However, there are always tendencies to overstate ones contribution and to explain everything in terms of social psychology. The history of social identity research is not innocent of such tendencies. These are not only misguided, they are dangerous.

Empires generally perish by over-reaching themselves, and academic empires are no different.

For these reasons, our emphasis in this contribution is principally on the principles and tenets of the SIA. It is not meant as a comprehensive literature review. It is meant to provide a road map from which the reader can approach the social identity literature, can understand the questions and assumptions underlying it, can locate specific studies within the overall enterprise, and, occasionally, can evaluate whether these studies exemplify and expand social identity principles or violate them.

We start by putting the SIA into its historical context(s). We explain the questions and concerns that shaped its development. Next we outline the core theories themselves – SIT and SCT. We then go on to look at more recent developments of the theory, both in terms of its application to broader phenomena (such as emotions and interpersonal relations) and in terms of conceptual attempts to come to terms with the full complexity of the relationship between social identity and social reality. Finally, we explain why social identity principles fit well with other disciplines in providing a rounded explanation of human action. In sum, we seek to demonstrate that the SIA provides a social psychology for the social sciences.

## ROOTS AND INFLUENCES

The SIA in social psychology was initiated in the early 1970s by the work of Henri Tajfel and his colleagues on inter-group processes. One of the cornerstones to this approach is an insistence that the way in which psychological processes play out is dependent upon social context. Rather than using psychology to supersede other levels of explanation of human action, the aim is to account for when and how social structures and belief systems impact on what people do. To paraphrase John Turner (1999), the SIA forces

psychologists to turn their heads towards the social world. This being the case, it makes sense to start by considering how social context shaped the concerns and contours of the SIA itself.

Writing in the shadow of the Holocaust Hannah Arendt (cited by Judt, 2008, p. 33) observed that: 'the problem of evil will be the fundamental question of post-war intellectual life in Europe'. This was true both of social psychology and social psychologists, many of whom were Jewish, including Tajfel who spent his early post-war years seeking to reunite the children of the camps with their families. The question that obsessed the discipline was how could people sanction such violence to others, simply because of their group membership.

The assumption was that those who those who hate must be hateful, authoritarian personalities. Such individualism long dominated social psychology and was the foil against which SIT was developed. It assumed that any regularities of social behaviour are to be explained as either the aggregation of individual states or inter-individual interactions. However, there was an alternative. Sherif's 'boys camp studies', which spanned the years 1949–1954, demonstrated how one can induce extreme hostility by putting people in groups and then manipulating inter-group relations. Where groups exist in competition – where the one group's gain is the other's loss – members will feel and act negatively towards each other (Sherif, 1967). More graphically, Sherif showed how inter-group competition could transform the best adjusted of boys into what seemed like 'wicked, disturbed and vicious bunches of youngsters' (1966: 58) a decade before Arendt coined the term 'the banality of evil'.

However, this still left the question of precisely what conditions underlie such transformations. Inter-group competition may be sufficient to create hostility, but is it necessary? A number of studies through the 1960s suggested not. Bias against out-groups could be found even without explicit or even implicit competition. What, then, are the minimal conditions that will produce such group bias? This was the immediate question that motivated Tajfel and Turner, to develop SIT. While the Holocaust defined the broad intellectual framework within which the SIA was developed, the more immediate background was the burgeoning of social movements based on class, but also race, gender and sexuality in the upheavals of the 1960s. Suddenly, social change was back on the agenda and the role of collective processes in producing that change could not be ignored. The events of 1968 and their aftermath pointed to the group not only as a cause of social injustices but also as their solution.

At the same time, the bases of collective action were problematized. One could no longer presuppose that people would act in terms of some 'objective' aspect of their social location such as being a worker; they might equally act as a woman or as a black person. This inevitably raised questions of identity centred on actors' own understanding of themselves in their social world. Such an approach is particularly clear in Emerson's definition of national identity, endorsed by Tajfel (1978): 'the simplest statement that can be made about a nation is that it is a body of people who feel that they are a nation ...' (Emerson, 1960: 102).

These influences are clear in Israel and Tajfel's 1972 edited volume, an unofficial manifesto for an emergent European social psychology, in which Tajfel lambasted the tendency to explain social conduct as a product of individual tendencies. Social factors, to the extent that they were invoked at all, were generally seen as secondary – what Tajfel referred to ironically as 'social psychology eventually'. He then insisted that the key issue 'is that of the relations between Man [sic] and social change' (Tajfel, 1972: 108).

In the spirit of the times, Tajfel's concern with change was more than a matter of scientific concern: it was also a normative commitment. As Serge Moscovici, the other leading figure of European social psychology, put it the aim was: 'to see the development of a

science of "movement" rather than a science of "order"' (1972: 22). This normative commitment is critical to the SIA. It is precisely because collective action is the sole resource through which the powerless can challenge their subjugation that Tajfel and his successors focused on group processes. Like several others, Tajfel was interested in group-level explanations of wide-scale hostility, but, unlike the others, he remained an optimist and an activist when it came to the outcome of collective processes. This helps to explain why the concept of identity was to play such a central role in explaining the nature of these processes.

## SOCIAL IDENTITY THEORY (SIT)

### The minimal group studies

SIT developed in order to explain the findings of a series of studies designed to examine the minimal conditions that are necessary and sufficient to produce negativity towards out-groups. These 'minimal group studies' (Tajfel et al., 1971) are among the most famous in social psychology. In the initial studies, Bristol schoolboys were categorized into groups on a trivial basis (for example, their preference for painters). These were groups that had no past or future, in which there was no contact between group members. Indeed, all that participants knew was the group to which they had been assigned. Their task was then to allocate rewards between two other individuals about whom nothing was known other than the fact that one was from the 'in-group' and the other from the 'out-group' (for example, those preferring Klee over Kandinsky).

The findings were provocative and surprising: the individuals displayed high levels of in-group favouritism – tending to give more points (or money) to unidentified in-group members than to unidentified out-group members, often at the cost of maximizing absolute gains to the in-group. These findings seemed to suggest that the mere act of dividing people into groups was enough to create antagonism. As we shall see, although there is still a widespread tendency to interpret the minimal group studies in this way, it is an unwarranted and ironically decontextualized way of looking at the studies. However, it made the search for an explanation all the more urgent. Certainly the findings could not be accounted for in terms of self-interest (since people had nothing personally to gain or lose by their decisions) or by material competition between the groups. Another explanation was called for, and, over the following years, SIT came to be seen as the answer.

## From social identification to inter-group differentiation

The ideas underlying SIT bridge the gulf between Tajfel's (1969) early work on the cognitive consequences of categorization and his historical experiences of the power of group membership to define who we are, how we feel and how we see and treat others as 'other'. Tajfel reasoned that we can only understand why allocation to ostensibly meaningless groups should affect behaviour if we start by assuming that people come to define their selves in terms of group membership. His critical starting point is to break with the traditional assumption that the self should only be understood as that which defines the individual in relation to other individuals, and to acknowledge that, in some circumstances, we can define our selves through the groups to which we belong. In this way group behaviour is underpinned by social identity (Tajfel, 1978).

There are two further aspects of 'social identity' that need to be understood. The first is that it is simultaneously individual and social. First, a person's social identities – 'I am a woman', 'I am a Scot' or whatever – speak in a fundamental way to who they are in the world. However, what any of these memberships mean cannot be reduced to a person's own or indeed anybody else's

individuality. What a gender, or national identity means is a historical, cultural and contested identity, enshrined as much in museums and monuments as in debates between people. Thus social identity provides a conduit through which society inhabits the subject. In the tradition of social interactionists, such as Kurt Lewin (1952) and Solomon Asch (1952; see also Turner and Giles, 1981), it provides substance to the notion of a socially structured field within the individual. It thereby explains how large numbers of people can act in coherent and meaningful ways, by reference to shared group norms, values and understandings rather than idiosyncratic beliefs.

Second, while there are clearly psychological dynamics associated with social identification, the act of defining oneself as a group member should not be seen as arising out of some individual need. In other words, there is nothing more basic about individual identities and individual processes than about social identities and social processes. Nor is individual identity somehow more 'real' and more important to the subject than social identity. As we know all too well, people can love, hate, kill or even die for their group.

At this point, it should be clear that social identities are much more than self-perceptions: they also have value and emotional significance. To the extent that we define ourselves in terms of a group membership, our sense of esteem is attached to the fate of the group (and hence the fate of fellow group members is pertinent to our own). As English people, for instance, our sense of self-esteem is boosted when England excels. Equally, we can enhance our self-esteem by making England excel.

However, the meanings and evaluations that we attach to our group memberships are necessarily comparative. Who we are is partly defined by reference to who we are not. To excel means to do better than the others. Putting these elements together, then it follows that we will try to distinguish the groups that we belong to from other groups and we will do so in a way that is favourable to in-groups. We will seek positive group distinctiveness through differentiation between social groups along valued dimensions of comparison. This last clause is critical, but often overlooked. We shall return to it presently.

## Differentiation in the minimal group studies

The minimal group studies certainly strip away much of the usual context of group action, but they do not strip context away entirely (as if such a thing were possible). They simply render the remaining elements more powerful. Thus, whereas in the world at large there may be many ways of defining oneself, in these studies one either accepts the assigned group membership or else the task becomes meaningless. Similarly inside Tajfel's laboratory, in contrast to the world outside, only one out-group was available for comparison. Finally, whereas there are often many dimensions through which one can compare oneself to any other group (are we cleverer, stronger, kinder than them?), in the minimal group paradigm, one can only differentiate in favour of one's own group by giving a higher level of reward to in-group members than to out-group members.

So, while negative bias against out-groups in the minimal group studies can be explained as an instance of positive differentiation, one must bear in mind that the constraints within the paradigm are such that it is almost perfectly designed to produce such an outcome. In terms of the processes specified by SIT, these might better be described as *maximal*, not minimal group studies. One certainly cannot use them to suggest that discrimination against any given out-group will be universal or ubiquitous. To understand when it does happen, one must highlight the contingency of all the steps that are taken for granted in these studies. Thus, for racist hostility to occur it is necessary that racial categories are not only socially available but also that they are salient and accepted in the relevant context.

It is also necessary that racialized in-group members choose to compare themselves with the given racial other. Last, it is necessary that they seek to differentiate themselves along dimensions that lead to anti-social behaviours (for example, 'we are intelligent and hence we exclude them as stupid') as opposed to pro-social behaviours (such as, 'we are charitable and therefore help them').

It is here that it becomes critical to recall in full the claim of SIT that people seek positive differentiation *along valued dimensions of comparison*. The significance of the final clause is that, whereas the theory posits that differentiation is a generic group process, the specific behavioural outcomes of the process cannot be specified a priori, but rather require one to understand the specific belief systems (and hence the valued dimensions of comparison) associated with the specific groups of interest. That is, one must examine processes in context. Only by forgetting this core premise of the SIT can one conflate the process of differentiation (which has infinite possible outcomes) with the particular discriminatory behaviours that are found in the minimal group paradigm.

However, there is a further and more profound reason why it is wrong to think that SIT is a theory of the inevitability of discrimination. That is because, fundamentally, it is not a theory of discrimination at all. When viewed in the round, SIT is as much a theory of resistance to discrimination.

## Social identity and social change

Many accounts of SIT limit themselves to a discussion of identification, comparison and social differentiation. This leads to a focus on the internal relations between these elements as exemplified by a long-running debate on the so-called 'self-esteem hypothesis' – does differentiation indeed raise self-esteem, and do people with low self-esteem differentiate more in order to raise their self-esteem?

Quite apart from the fact that, in its bleakest form, such an approach exemplifies the individualistic reduction of group behaviour to personal motives, it misses the point that, for those who developed the theory, the process of differentiation was the starting point of this analysis, not the end point. Tajfel posited that people may have a general desire for positive self-esteem and to be positively differentiated from out-groups, but these dynamics do not operate in a social vacuum. In our unequal world, many people are consigned to groups that are negatively valued: women in a sexist world, black people in a racist world, manual labourers in a class-ridden society. How, then, do they respond to such devaluation? When do they accept and adapt to it and when do they challenge it? In other words, rather than abstract differentiation from the social context, Tajfel's concern at a conceptual level was with how psychological dynamics operate within differently structured social worlds. More substantively, he was interested in when these dynamics lead people to act together in order to change their social world. For him the concept of social identity was of interest as an intervening variable in the process of social change.

The more complete statement of SIT – as elaborated by Tajfel and Turner (1979) – therefore focuses on the psychology and strategies of low-status groups. When group boundaries are permeable (that is, so that group memberships are not fixed), one obvious solution is for members of low-status groups to disavow their current group membership and attempt to move into a higher-status group. This is referred to as a strategy of *social mobility* or 'exit'.

When boundaries are impermeable different strategies are required. One course of action is to adopt a *social creativity* strategy that involves construing the meaning of one's existing (low-status) group position. This can be done in at least three ways: either (1) by seeking to compare the in-group with other groups that are even more disadvantaged (for example, as if to say 'we may be poorer than the very rich, but at least we're better off than the very poor'), (2) by evaluating the in-group on more flattering dimensions of comparison ('we may be poor but we're friendly') or (3) by attempting to redefine the meaning of the in-group membership ('blessed are the poor').

However, none of these options changes the fundamental reality of disadvantage. Indeed, according to SIT, these social creativity strategies tend to be pursued precisely when prospects of changing one's material condition seem limited. So, when will people engage in direct group-level challenges to a high-status out-group? More specifically, when will they engage in a strategy of social competition through in-group bias (as in the minimal group studies), inter-group conflict, or collective action? According to Tajfel and Turner (1979), such solutions to the problem of low status are more likely to be pursued when members of disadvantaged groups see the inter-group status relations as illegitimate and unstable – that is, when they perceive the high-status group's position to be insecure in the dual sense of being unwarranted and potentially changeable. Such insecure social comparisons stimulate counterfactual thinking (an awareness of 'cognitive alternatives to the status quo') that provide the hope and scope for social change. They constitute the conditions under which the disadvantaged will mobilize to secure social change.

## Achievements and limitations of social identity theory

Perhaps the most important contribution of SIT lies in the concept of social identity itself. We have already stressed how this concept provides a bridge between the individual and the social and how it allows one to explain how socio-cultural realities can regulate the behaviours of individuals. In contrast to Freudian and other attempts to use identification as a means of explaining human sociality, the social nature of the bond is primary rather than secondary. That is, we do not identify with others through our common link to a leader. Rather, we are bound together through our joint sense of belonging to the same social category. Hence, what we do as group members is not constrained by the stance of a particular individual but by the socio-cultural meanings associated with the relevant social category. Put differently, social identity provides a psychological apparatus that allows humans, uniquely to be irreducibly cultural beings. In order to understand the full significance of this stance, it is necessary to be aware that social identity not only transforms our understanding of the self-concept, but also of all self-related terms. Thus, whenever we talk of self-esteem or self-efficacy or self-presentation or self-whatever, one must always ask 'what self'? That is because both the content and the dynamics of esteem, efficacy and presentation will be very different as a function of whether it relates to the personal self or to our various social identities.

Perhaps the most profound implications relate to the notion of (self-)interest, which underpins dominant conceptions of rationality. In these, the rational actor is one who effectively maximizes the utility that accrues to the individual self, where 'utility' is measured by reference to a universal standard such as monetary gain. In such conceptions, the 'self' of 'self-interest' is presupposed to be the personal self. However, where social identities are salient and constitute the self then a utility to fellow in-group members can constitute a utility to the (collective) self. Moreover, what constitutes 'utility' will vary from group to group – for some religious or ascetic groups more money may even have negative utility (it impedes entry into the afterlife). Far from rendering us irrational, groups and social identities provide us with new bases for rationality. The implications of such a position across the whole of the human sciences can hardly be overstated.

While a SIA raises a series of such issues, SIT is a long way from answering them. In order to do so, it would be necessary to be far more explicit on a series of issues on which the theory remains somewhat vague. Similar points about the relationship between defining questions and providing answers can be made when it comes to the specific contribution of SIT to an understanding of inter-group relations. As we have stressed, the most fundamental aspect of that contribution is to reinstate social change as a central issue. In a transformation that echoes Tajfel's own history, what starts in a concern with collective oppression develops into a theory of collective resistance. That said, it might be better to describe Tajfel's contribution as a matter of agenda setting rather than as the finished product. He suggests some of the ingredients that should go into such a theory: permeability, stability, legitimacy, cognitive alternatives. However, he never explicates the conditions under which these understandings arise, whether they are external to and determining of the relations between subordinate and dominant groups, or emergent products of such interactions.

There is one other aspect of Tajfel's discussion of social change that is of fundamental importance but which, again, raises more than it settles. The whole approach rests on the assumption that social change occurs when people mobilize together on the basis of shared social identity rather than act separately on the basis of their various personal identities. The unvoiced term here is power: to invoke the old trades union slogan, the power of the powerless lies in their combination *and it is social identity that makes combination possible*. However, it remains to be explained exactly how shared social identity allows people to act together purposefully and effectively. If, as we suggest, SIT is (at least in part) a theory of social power, we need to know how that power is generated.

## SELF-CATEGORIZATION THEORY (SCT)

We have noted that perhaps the greatest strength and the greatest limitations of SIT lie in the concept of social identity. SCT was developed to address these limitations (Turner et al., 1987, 1994). It seeks to clarify the distinction between social identity and other aspects of the self-concept, to explain how the self system is organized and what makes any one part of this system psychologically active in a given context. By doing this, it broadens the remit of social identity research from inter-group relations to group behaviour (and, potentially at least, social behaviour) in general.

## A cognitive definition of the social group

Formative work on SCT focused on providing a more complete explanation of the distinction between different levels of identification and the ways in which they underpin an individuals' movement along the interpersonal – inter-group continuum previously described by Tajfel (see above). Turner (1982) argues that the self is always defined in social relations (that is, in comparison to an 'other') but that this can occur at different levels of abstraction. Thus, one can define oneself as a unique individual in distinction from other individuals ('I' versus 'you') corresponding to personal identity. One can define oneself as a member of a group in distinction from other groups ('we' versus 'they') – this corresponds to social identity. One could also define oneself at higher levels of abstraction such as 'human' compared to non-human, or even as 'animate' compared to 'inanimate'.

The focus of both SIT and SCT has always been on the intermediate – social – level of identity. However, SCT goes beyond SIT in proposing that (inter)personal behaviour is not simply underpinned but also *made possible* by a salient personal identity, just as (inter)group behaviour is both underpinned and made possible by a salient social identity.

The crucial development here is that SCT, in contrast to previous models that see groups as constituted by the aggregation of interpersonal bonds between individuals, defines the group in cognitive terms. Indeed the

first embryonic outline of SCT was entitled 'towards a cognitive redefinition of the social group' (Turner, 1982). This is not to say that interpersonal bonds and interactions are irrelevant. They may act as an antecedent of self-categorization, they also change as a consequence of self-categorization, but they are not, in and of themselves, sufficient to constitute the psychological group. From this starting point, SCT addresses both the consequences and the antecedents of self-categorization as a group member. Let us consider each in turn.

## Depersonalization, self-stereotyping and social influence

Self-categorization entails a process of depersonalization. When acting in terms of individual identity, we view ourselves in terms of our individual characteristics. When acting in terms of social identity we view people in terms of their group memberships. This has a number of consequences. To start with, we will tend to see members of the same group as similar to each other (and different from members of another group). At the extremes, people will be regarded as interchangeable exemplars of the relevant social category. Moreover, insofar as this similarity with fellow group members extends to our beliefs and values, we will expect to agree with them and indeed we will strive to achieve consensus within the group (Haslam et al., 1998).

Next, we will tend to perceive the nature of individuals in terms of the characteristics we associate with the groups to which they belong. This is the process of stereotyping. While it is hardly original to claim that we stereotype individuals in terms of the groups to which they belong, more original is the claim that we will also stereotype ourselves. Thus, when we self-categorize as members of a particular group, we answer the question 'who am I'? in terms of the characteristics that we share with other group members. We also answer the question 'what should I do' with reference to the in-group stereotype.

More formally, we both self-stereotype and seek to conform to the group stereotype. This may lead us to behave differently, based on the different characteristics that are associated with the different categories that are salient at different times: as an academic in the lecture theatre I may seek to be measured, objective and dispassionate; as a sports fan on the terraces I seek to be partisan, loyal and passionate.

There will be times, however, when the nature of the in-group stereotype or when the implication of the stereotype for what we should do in the here and now will remain unclear. As a consequence, the notion of self-stereotyping becomes the basis for a model of group social influence, what Turner (1982, 1991) dubs 'referent informational influence' (RII). Members will both actively seek out and respond to information about the nature of their group stereotype and its action implications in the immediate context. Such a model has a number of important characteristics for understanding the source and the content of influence.

With regard to source, others will influence us to the extent that they are in a position to be knowledgeable about group beliefs, norms and values. That will be particularly true of individuals who are most typical (*prototypical*) of the in-group. They will therefore be best placed to guide and lead discussions about 'who we are' and hence 'what we should do'. In terms of content, suggestions and proposals must be seen to be consonant with the broad and agreed contours of the category definition. However, prototypical someone might be, they cannot get group members to do just anything, and if they were to try they would most likely lose their claim to typicality. Thus, at the same time as allowing for debate, and hence indeterminancy in the definition of social identity, RII does not allow this to overwhelm the fact that social influence takes place within a framework of cultural constraint.

This takes us to one further aspect of SCT. Traditionally, social psychologists have drawn a distinction between seeking objective information about the world (informational influence) and seeking information about the views of other group members, particularly prominent members, for the purpose of being accepted by them (normative influence). SCT rejects this distinction between informational and normative influence. Social reality testing – an understanding of who and what we are, the nature of the world in which we live and how we should act within it – is necessarily a matter of consensus. Our individual opinions about the nature of the world and of the significance of events in the world are always contingent until confirmed by others whose perspective we share and whose values we endorse – that is, by fellow group members. We therefore need information about consensual group positions in order to transform idiosyncratic opinion ('*I think* global warming is a disaster') into social fact ('global warming *is* a disaster').

SCT also rejects an underlying view that the influence of the group necessarily undermines objectivity and reason. Rooted in the distinction between informational and normative influence is an assumption that only the lone individual can be rational. Yet, as we have already intimated, social reality testing is an activity that requires others. We can only establish the validity of our collective beliefs in collaboration with others who we categorize as similar to ourselves. Hence, fellow group members serve as essential reference points for our own perception. Our reliance on them is not in conflict with our concern with reality – it is through them that individual views are co-ordinated and transformed into *shared* values, beliefs and behaviours that have an objective quality.

This challenge to the traditional equation of groups with error and irrationality is an important vein that runs through SCT. It is part of the more general defence of groups against the individualism and anti-collectivism that pervade both our culture and our discipline. This challenge is even clearer when it comes to explaining the conditions and the content of self-categorization.

## The process of categorization: category salience and category prototypes

It should be clear that self-categorization has important and wide-ranging consequences at both the individual and the societal level. It follows from this that the ways we categorize ourselves and the meanings that we attach to these categories are critical determinants of social behaviour. SCT devotes considerable attention to these two questions: what determines category salience and what determines the category prototype?

Once again, the traditional view has been to regard group-level perception as erroneous. Why do we see people (including ourselves) as group members? Because the information emanating from the social world is so complex that we have to simplify it. According to this view, the processing capacity of our brains is simply too small to see each person as an individual and so we see them as group members. It may lead to distortions, but at least it allows us to function in the world. SCT rejects this view entirely. It makes the radical claim that categorical perception reflects rather than distorts social reality (Oakes et al., 1994). We organize people into categories because this is how they are organized in the real world. To do so is not inaccurate – it is functional. For instance, in a riot, it makes no sense for demonstrators to spend time contemplating how the various riot police charging towards them are different from each other. Were they to do so, they would soon lie bloodied on the ground. What counts here is how these various individuals are equivalent in terms of their shared group membership.

Category salience is determined by two factors. One is fit, which itself has two aspects. *Comparative fit* refers to the social organization of similarities and differences between people in a given context. We apply those categories which minimize intra-class differences compared to inter-class differences. However, since social organization changes from place to place and time to time, so different categories may become salient. For example, social psychologists and sociologists together in a room may categorize themselves in terms of their respective disciplines. However, were some physicists to enter the room, then psychologists and sociologists' similarities as social scientists compared to their common differences with natural scientists would promote a shift in self-categorization. If a group of business people were to come in next, this would promote a common self-categorization as academics. *Normative fit* arises from the (expected) *content* associated with similarities and differences between people. To extend the example provided above, we will be more inclined to categorize people as 'academics' and 'businessmen' if the former are somewhat more shabby and less concerned with the profitability of their activities than the latter. Work on comparative and normative fit underscores the point that there are no inherent, stable differences between in-group and out-group, there is no pre-defined, universal identity in terms of which a person will define themselves (see Oakes et al., 1994). As the world varies so does category salience. As the 'other' with whom we compare ourselves changes so does our 'self'. Above all, categories have to be appropriate to the comparative context.

Yet it is important not to overplay the importance of fit principles in defining social categories. Individuals do not participate in social encounters by mechanically processing information from a position of detachment, deciding matter-of-factly whether or not a particular person should be seen as a member of a particular category. SCT recognizes this by proposing that the principles of fit determine category salience in interaction with a second factor: *perceiver readiness* (or *accessibility*). This means that a given category is more likely to become salient to the extent that a perceiver is psychologically predisposed to use it as a basis for perception or action because it has prior meaning and significance.

Categorization in a particular stimulus context is structured by perceivers' *prior* expectations, goals and theories – many of which derive from their group membership and group encounters. In this way experiences are given stability and predictability by personal and social *histories*. For example, the fact that racists categorize themselves and others in terms of their skin colour, depends on their being able to use skin colour as a comparatively and normatively fitting basis for categorization. It depends on the practical and ideological pre-potence of skin colour as an organizing principle. Without the latter, the stimulus array will provide noise rather than information.

## Achievements and limitations of self-categorization theory

There are those who posit a rupture between SIT and SCT, criticizing the latter as being more mechanical, abstracted and cognitivist than the former. However, as with SIT, the criticisms confuse the starting point of SCT with its end point. This starting point – underpinning group psychology with a cognitive act of self-categorization which, in turn, derives from the organization of social reality – is, in fact, critical to the advances of SCT. It provides a basis for understanding how and when specific social categories are introjected into the individual (or, to put it the other way round, how and when the individual is interpellated by specific social categories). It also provides a basis for understanding how the belief systems associated with these categories are defined, elaborated and come to shape action.

So, although SCT may have different emphases to SIT, the fundamental relationship between the two is harmonious. Indeed, one of the achievements of SCT is to develop the incipient logic of SIT. While SIT introduces the concept of social identity in the context of an analysis of inter-group relations, SCT clarifies the concept and its relationship

to other levels of identity. It explicates the processes that underlie social identification and examines the consequences for a broad range of group phenomena such as stereotyping, group judgment, group cohesion and social influence. It thereby forms the basis for a non-reductionist account of group psychology that covers intra- as well as intergroup phenomena.

While SCT makes the cognitive act of self-categorization the starting point for understanding group process it certainly does not suggest that cognition is all there is. Clearly a full understanding of the group must account for the importance that groups have for us and the passions that they invoke. Equally, group psychology must not only deal with the way we represent categories internally but also the way in which we relate to others and interact with them as a function of whether or not we categorize them as fellow group members. To reframe the same point, self-categorization theorists sometimes talk of a turn from 'the individual in the group' to 'the group in the individual'. What this means, however, is not that the one replaces the other, but rather, only if we start with an analysis of the group in the individual can we then understand the individual in the group. The reverse is impossible.

However, to argue that SCT provides a basis for understanding the quality of group interactions, the nature of lived experience in the group and the emotional intensity of collective life is not the same as saying that it has actually travelled very far down this road. The contribution of SCT can therefore only be assured by driving the research agenda onwards. As with SIT, SCT should not be reduced to a set of discrete hypotheses that can be pursued in isolation from each other – although it certainly does provide a series of powerful hypotheses notably about the effects of varying comparative contexts upon the categorization process. However, these exist within a more general framework concerning the relationship between the individual, the group and the nature of society.

## EXTENDING THE SOCIAL IDENTITY APPROACH

### *Empirical extensions*

The SIA is, by now, probably the dominant way of addressing group processes in psychology. Indeed, in Europe, it constitutes the largest tradition in all of social psychology. There are countless studies in the area and it would be impossible to summarize here all the recent extensions to SIT and SCT (for a review, see Ellemers et al., 2002). We shall limit ourselves to two areas of development that exemplify issues raised in the previous section. These concern, respectively, work on group emotionality and work on social relations between group members.

### *Group emotions*

One of the most obvious aspects of group life is its passionate nature. In groups people experience strong emotions and, classically, this has contributed to the claim that, in collective settings, affect substitutes for reason. In rebutting this claim it is important to avoid simply reversing its polarity and stressing the reasoned nature of collective action but at the expense of draining it of all passion. That is, it is necessary to deliver on the promise that the SIA, and more specifically SCT, provides a starting point from which to understand collective emotions.

In fact, from its inception, the SIA rejected the dichotomy between viewing group process as either rational (and unemotional) or emotional (and irrational). Rather, it espoused a duality between reason and emotion that was built into the original definition of social identity as our knowledge of ourselves as members of a social group along with the value and emotional significance of this membership (Tajfel, 1978). If we extend this approach and argue more generally that emotion derives from the significance of events for identities, then we have the basis for a social identity approach to emotionality (and an emotional basis for social identity). Such an approach makes three distinctive claims

that serve to develop our understanding of both emotion and social identity.

First, a series of studies in the emergent field of group emotions have shown that, when social identities are salient, we can have strong feelings about things our group has done or else things that have happened to our group, even if we have not personally participated in them. When defined at a categorical level, feelings are determined by collective histories rather than personal histories. The nature of the emotions that we feel depends upon an appraisal of the precise implications of a given circumstance for a given identity. This idea is central to the work of Eliot Smith (1993), whose Inter-group Emotion Theory (IET) kick-started the work on group emotions. Smith, like Tajfel, was initially concerned with prejudice and discrimination between groups. He sought to show that our reactions to a given out-group depend upon what we believe 'they' mean for 'us'. This will not only depend upon what we and they are like, but also upon the status and power relations between us. Thus groups with low power may *fear* powerful out-groups, whereas groups with high power will have the strength to feel *anger* if they are thwarted; groups with legitimate high-status may feel contempt, disdain or even disgust towards low-status groups, and under less threatening conditions perhaps more benevolent paternalistic emotions. Moreover, the precise emotional reaction is likely to inform and encourage the forms of action tendency directed towards the group. Anger may encourage approach towards whereas fear and disgust promote avoidance of the out-group.

There is considerable scope for extending such an appraisal approach to the study of group emotion in general. In the same way that our feelings towards out-groups depend upon a situated evaluation of the in-group, the out-group and the relations between the two, so our feelings towards anything will depend upon how we evaluate events, groups and their interrelations. Overall, the question is whether we can develop a model of different emotions within the different relations between realities and identities.

It is possible to take the argument a step further and propose that social identities should be understood less as determinants of action than as frameworks of appraisal. That is, we do not mechanically enact specific norms, values or beliefs as soon as we identify with a particular category. Rather, we consider how, as particular types of people, we should respond to a given situation. Sometimes, this may lead to paradoxes that are inexplicable if identities are seen as precise prescriptions. For instance, a group value of tolerance could lead to increased exclusion of those who are perceived as authoritarian. In other words, the process of choosing how to act proceeds by reference to identity definitions, but social identity processes are not deterministic. It is a theory of tendency and constraint with room for individual and collective agency and choice.

This argument gains added force once we start to see the terms of the appraisal process as matters of argument. Appraisal theorists have proposed that appraisals can be fast and automatic and Smith extends this to intergroup appraisals. The activation of stereotypes of self and other – and hence the meaning of the other for the self – is thus seen as almost immediate and inaccessible to consciousness. Whereas there may be times in which our understandings of the world are taken for granted, there may be others where they will be far more open to question. We must also consider how others, particularly those who want to move us to action, may construe the nature of self and other in order to create appraisals of threat and hence legitimate hostility against the out-group. The Nazi portrait of Jews as vermin, the Hutu extremist portrait of Tutsis as cockroaches, the Hindu nationalist portrait of Muslims as cow killers are all cases in point. This, however, is to stray into the area of relations among group members and of leadership in particular. We will therefore return to it in the next section.

## Intra-group relations

There are two ways of understanding the relationship between social identification and collective action. One is to suggest that, through common self-categorizations, the cognitions of a set of individuals become aligned and they therefore act in similar ways. This is a rather mechanical, lonely and silent view of social being. It suggests a world in which people act together but without ever talking to each other or impacting upon each other. A second approach is to suggest that shared social identification transforms relations between people in such a way as to enable them to act together harmoniously and productively. This approach, which more accurately reflects the perspective of SCT, is exemplified by work, already cited, on consensus formation (Haslam et al., 1998). Thus, those who identify together do not immediately and automatically achieve consensus. Rather, there is a process of consensualization by which the expectation of agreement between group members leads people to pick up on aspects of what others say with which they are in accord and, over a period of time, this shifts group discussion towards a consensus.

In recent years, there has been a growing body of research that makes similar points about the impact of social identification upon relations between group members. We are more likely to trust and respect fellow category members and more likely to cooperate with them. We are also more likely to help members of the in-group and more likely to support them even when that involves personal cost. Indeed, when social identity is salient, fellow group members are not seen as other. Even at the physical level, we desire greater proximity to in-group individuals. Their presence is an affirmation of self not an intrusion upon it.

One can sum up these various strands of work (for a review, see Reicher and Haslam, in press) by saying that intimacy is integral to identification, but as an outcome, not as a precursor. Shared social identification transforms relations between people in such a way as to enable effective co-action. Where SIT implicitly assumes that identification is the basis of collective action and social power, the work described above fills in the gaps. It details the processes that produce intra-group coordination and hence social power. But these processes have other consequences as well, on the individual as well as the collective level. One of the most interesting recent developments in social identity research concerns the impact of social identification upon mental and even physical well-being (Haslam et al., 2009). Thus, increased social support among group members makes them more able to cope with actual and anticipated difficulties and hence decreases stress and anxiety while increasing optimism and the sense of self-efficacy.

An important implication of the work we have described here is that group members are able to combine their efforts and work together in effective and socially meaningful ways even without a leader to coordinate them. All too often, observers of mass action either malign it as meaningless, or invoke a 'hidden hand' that is guiding group members. No such thing is required, since shared social identification is sufficient to explain the spontaneous sociality of group and even crowd behaviour.

That is not to say that leadership is irrelevant but, equally, leadership is not independent of social identification as a determinant of collective co-action. Over the last decade or so, research into leadership has been reinvigorated by the development of a SIA to the field. This work starts from the observation that leadership is always a group phenomenon. The analysis of leadership must therefore concern itself with the relationship between leaders and followers within a social group. Following self-categorization principles, it is proposed that this relationship is assured to the extent that both are categorized as members of the same social category.

There is a body of research that sustains the following conclusions (see van Knippenberg and Hogg, 2003):

(1) where people do not share a common social identity, leadership over them is impossible – for where there are no agreed collective norms

values and priorities that characterize the group, no-one can be entrusted to represent the group;
(2) the more a person is seen to be prototypical of the group, the more they will be seen as a leader and able to influence other group members;
(3) as the group prototype varies from one comparative context to another, so different people will come to be seen as suitable leaders.

However, it would be patently absurd to represent leadership as a passive process of assumed prototypicality. Rather, would-be leaders actively construe the nature of the shared identity and of their own selves in order to claim prototypicality – and hence the right to speak for the group. In short, successful leaders have to be skilled *entrepreneurs of identity* (Reicher et al., 2005). Moreover, as we saw in the previous section, in construing identities they also serve to construe emotions. To be consistent in terminology, we can also see skilled leaders as *entrepreneurs of emotion*.

Besides the practical implications for leadership, this perspective has more general implications for the way we conceptualize social identity processes (see below). For now, we simply want to underline the point that an analysis of leadership adds to, rather than detracts from, an understanding of the importance of social identity for social coordination.

## Conceptual extensions

### Social identity in social reality

Work in the social identity tradition has put great stress on the role of context in shaping social identity, but has paid less attention to the way in which the expression of social identity is constrained by context. The social identity model of deindividuation effects, or SIDE model (Reicher et al., 1995; Spears and Lea, 1994) makes the point that it is one thing to want to express a particular group norm, it is quite another to act in terms of a group norm where that would bring down the ire of a powerful out-group. Hence, an analysis of group behaviour requires both a cognitive analysis of the factors shaping identity salience and a strategic analysis of the factors that shape identity expression. Sometimes the same factors can operate at both levels.

This much was clear in the critique of deindividuation theories out of which (as its name suggests) SIDE was developed. These theories suggest that immersion in a group (particularly large groups such as crowds) lead to a loss of self or reduced self-awareness, eliminating the ability to regulate individual behaviour. From a social identity perspective, however, it can be shown that the lack of cues to inter-personal difference in a group increases the perception of sharing a common group membership with others ('depersonalization') and hence leads to the regulation of behaviour through social identity. This is the cognitive side of SIDE. However, such anonymity also affects the ability of out-groups to hold people to account for their actions and hence affects identity expression. This takes complex forms. Thus anonymity of the in-group to out-group members decreases the repressive power of out-groups over the in-group and hence increases the expression of group norms that would attract out-group sanction. Conversely, anonymity of group members to each other lowers their ability to elicit social support in challenging the out-group and hence lowers the expression of group norms that would attract out-group sanction. These are aspects of the strategic side of SIDE.

From these beginnings, SIDE has developed into a more general analysis of the cognitive and strategic factors governing social identity based behaviours – but with a particular emphasis on the strategic given its (relative) neglect in the past. This shows how a whole series of social identity related actions are governed by strategic concerns – from the expression of in-group bias to out-group stereotyping and including even claims to the importance of a given identity. It also shows how such strategic issues acquire particular importance when one moves from the lab to socially significant groups where actions have consequences that can include

exclusion from the group. Finally, it shows that the expression of identity is often as much an attempt to redefine group memberships as a reflection of existing memberships. One might express a particular emotion (say anger) in order to define what sorts of actions are acceptable or unacceptable to the group.

This takes us into important new territory. In most of the foregoing discussion we were considering how a predefined social identity is expressed as a function of different social realities. But, as we have just shown, identity itself is redefined in order to (re)configure social reality. Categories are more than reflections of the world. They are part and parcel of the process by which we negotiate and contest the nature of our worlds. This issue, which goes back to the central importance of change in the social identity tradition, is another key area of conceptual debate.

### Social identity and social reality

We earlier noted that one of the key contributions of SCT is to establish a link between social identities and social reality. Researchers have shown that social categories and stereotypes are not products of biases or distorted by limited information processing capacity, but reflect our social world and the reality of groups and social categories within it. This emphasis on group level social reality in the social identity tradition gives material grounding that does not completely 'psychologize' the explanation of group behaviours such as prejudice and discrimination (and provides a bridge to other social sciences that often have problems with social psychology along these lines).

We also noted there is a (parallel) danger of falling prey to a mechanical realism that takes social categories for granted, and essentializes them as fixed and determining reflections of a pre-ordained reality. There is a two-way relationship between social reality and social categories: on the one hand, social reality shapes categories; on the other, categories shape collective action that (potentially) shapes social reality. Another way of saying this is that the different sides of this relationship are, in effect, different temporal orientations: categories are both about *being* (reflecting what was and is) and about *becoming* (creating what will be). This certainly does not mean that people will accept any category construction. There may *temporarily* be a disjunction between social categories and the present organization of reality. However, unless the categories we use are seen to be in the process of becoming real (or, at least, have the prospect of becoming real) they will be discarded, not as 'wrong' but as 'useless'. To use but one example, the long history of failed nationalisms shows that the call for a state to match the nation has to be seen as practical as well as desirable. The main impediment to practicality is, of course, the refusal of powerful others to accede to demands for social reorganization.

This analysis suggests that a full understanding of the categorization process must be both historical (extended over time) and interactive (rooted in the interplay between different social groups). This is exemplified by the elaborated social identity model of crowd behaviour (ESIM) (Drury and Reicher, in press). Whereas earlier work (see above) explained the socially meaningful patterns of crowd action, it did not account for the occurrence of change during crowd events – both psychological change (the identities of participants are often altered through participation) and social (in the sense that crowd action often reconfigures social reality). ESIM was developed to fill this gap: if crowd members act on the basis of existing social identities, how come social identities change through crowd action?

ESIM suggests that the content, like the process, of self-categorization relates to the organization of social relations. Thus, to say 'I am British' is to posit a world of nations and to say where I stand and how I should/could act given my positioning in this world. On this basis, we can reframe ESIM's core question as 'how can my understanding of my social position change through acting on such an understanding'. The answer is that this will be a function of the ways in which

the other understands and reacts to my actions. Most of the time, the different groups that are involved in an interaction will share a symmetrical understanding of the nature of each party and hence each will affirm the identity of the other. However, occasionally there may be an asymmetry of understanding. Where this occurs, and where, in addition, the one party has the power to reposition the other as a function of its own understanding, then a disequilibrium will be created that initiates a process of change.

Let us provide some concrete illustrations that make the argument clearer. In a number of crowd events (see Drury and Reicher, in press) demonstrators have come to an event as liberal subjects who want to express their views and who see the police/state as a neutral guarantor of their rights (including the right to demonstrate). The police, however, often due to the presence of some radical groupings, have viewed *and treated* the crowd to be oppositional: they have been prevented from going where they wanted or voicing their demands to their intended audience. Such common repressive experience has led crowd members to become more united, to see themselves as more oppositional, to give greater heed to the voices of radical groups in their midst and the feel more empowered to challenge what they see as illegitimate police action. This, in turn, has confirmed the original police understandings and so the process of change has escalated. In short, people positioned as the opposition have become oppositional and have construed the nature of the world from that vantage point. For ESIM, self-categories are not about perception, they are both reactively and proactively about the organization of social practices.

## CONCLUSION: A SOCIAL PSYCHOLOGY FOR THE SOCIAL SCIENCES

The impact of SIT and SCT has been enormous. Seminal statements of SIT (Tajfel and

Turner, 1979) have been cited nearly 4000 times; while core statements of SCT (Turner, 1982, 1991; Turner et al., 1987, 1994) have together been cited nearly 3500 times. As the foregoing sections indicate, much of this interest has been generated among social psychologists. Nevertheless, much of it has been in social sciences other than psychology, and indeed, in total, over 2500 of the above citations have occurred in outlets beyond the realm of social psychology. The majority of these are in the domain of management and business – a fact that reflects the phenomenally successful application of social identity and self-categorization principles to the study of organizational life. This work covers a vast array of topics, but the most influential work has explored issues of leadership, motivation and communication.

It is interesting to note too, that recent growth in the impact of SIT and SCT has been as strong outside social psychology as within it. Here, as well as management and business, the fields in which growth has been most dramatic are education and political science. However, there has also been a concentrated upsurge of interest in fields of economics, public policy and environmental science.

So, why has the social identity perspective been so influential? There are at least three answers to this question. First and most straightforwardly, the core tenets of SIT and SCT have proved very helpful for researchers seeking to explain and understand a number of key features of group behaviour. In this respect, a key strength of both theories is that their defining ideas are applicable to, and testable in, a wide range of settings. Generally too, these ideas have received strong support. As a result, the perspective has simply proved very practical for researchers who are interested in 'ideas that work'.

Second, in the areas where the social identity perspective has been used as an analytic tool, it has provided a refreshing alternative to established theorizing. In this respect it has been a particularly important resource for researchers who reject the individualistic reductionism of mainstream (social) psychology and who have sought to inject a properly social sensibility into their work. Such applications also counter the general tendency for psychologists to develop highly localized 'mini-theories' that remain specific to the particular phenomenon in which they are interested. In this sense SIT and SCT together constitute a theory that is both broad and parsimonious.

The perspective also incorporates a more sophisticated political analysis of social behaviour than many alternative models. Part of the appeal of the social identity perspective is not only that it accounts for social differentiation (and its consequences), but that it does so by attending to the reality of social, material and political forces (Oakes et al., 1994). This feature has contributed to the specific impact of the perspective in political psychology and political science, but it has also proved valuable for researchers who are sensitive to the interplay between politics and psychology that is central to a number of key issues both in the social sciences (such as, geography, sociology and economics) and in the humanities (for example, linguistics, theology and history).

This sensitivity to the way in which psychology interfaces with social reality differentiates the social identity perspective from psychological theorizing that tends to reify processes and products of particular social circumstances as manifestations of psychological primitives (for example, personality, cognitive bias, evolutionary drive). Rather than pushing other disciplines aside in the rush to reductionism, the social identity perspective encourages researchers to turn *towards* the material facts of other disciplines (such as, economics, sociology, geography and history) in order to appreciate both the social structuring of the mind and the psychological structuring of the social world.

Beyond this, why is the SIA important as well as influential? It is because the approach is about both understanding the world and changing it. In a period where we are all too often told that we are at 'the end of history', social identity theories insist not only that our unequal society can be challenged but also how that can be achieved.

# REFERENCES

Asch, S.E. (1952) *Social psychology*. Engelwood Cliffs, NJ: Prentice Hall.

Drury, J. and Reicher, S.D. (in press) 'Collective psychological empowerment as a model of social change: Researching crowds and power', *Journal of Social Issues*.

Emerson, R. (1960) *From Empire to Nation*. Boston, MA: Beacon Press.

Haslam, S.A., Jetten, J., Postmes, T. and Haslam, C. (2009) 'Social identity, health and well-being: An emerging agenda for applied psychology', *Applied Psychology: An International Review*, 58: 1–23.

Haslam, S.A., Turner, J.C., Oakes, P.J., McGarty, C. and Reynolds, K.J. (1998) 'The group as a basis for emergent stereotype consensus', *European Review of Social Psychology*, 8: 203–39.

Judt, T. (2008) 'The "problem of evil" in postwar Europe', *The New York Review of Books*, 14 (2): 33–5.

Lewin, K. (1952) *Field theory in social science*. London: Tavistock.

Moscovici, S. (1972) Society and theory in social psychology. In J. Israel and H. Tajfel (Eds.). *The context of social psychology: A critical assessment* (pp. 17–68). London: Academic Press.

Oakes, P.J., Haslam, S.A. and Turner, J.C. (1994) *Stereotyping and Social Reality*. Oxford: Blackwell.

Reicher, S.D. and Haslam, S.A. (in press) 'Beyond help: A social psychology of collective solidarity and social cohesion', in M. Snyder and S. Sturmer (eds), *The Psychology of Helping*. Oxford: Blackwell.

Reicher, S.D., Haslam, S.A. and Hopkins, N. (2005) 'Social identity and the dynamics of leadership: Leaders and followers as collaborative agents in the transformation of social reality', *Leadership Quarterly*, 16: 547–68.

Reicher, S.D., Spears, R. and Postmes, T. (1995) 'A social identity model of deindividuation phenomena', *European Review of Social Psychology*, 6: 161–98.

Sherif, M. (1967) *Group Conflict and Co-operation: Their Social Psychology*. London: Routledge and Kegan Paul.

Smith, E.R. (1993) 'Social identity and social emotions: Toward a new conceptualization of prejudice', in D.M. Mackie and D.L. Hamilton (eds), *Affect, Cognition and Stereotyping*, pp. 297–315. San Diego, CA: Academic Press.

Spears, R. and Lea, M. (1994) 'Panacea or panopticon? The hidden power in computer-mediated communication', *Communication Research*, 21: 427–59.

Tajfel, H. (1972) 'Experiments in a vacuum', in J. Israel and H. Tajfel (eds), *The Context of Social Psychology*. London: Academic Press.

Tajfel, H. (ed.) (1978) *Differentiation Between Social Groups: Studies in the Social Psychology of Intergroup Relations*. London: Academic Press.

Tajfel, H. and Turner, J. (1979) 'An integrative theory of inter-group conflict', in W.G. Austin and S. Worchel (eds), *The Social Psychology of Inter-group Relations*, pp. 33–47. Monterey, CA: Brooks/Cole.

Tajfel, H., Flament, C., Billig, M.G. and Bundy, R.F. (1971) 'Social categorization and inter-group behaviour', *European Journal of Social Psychology*, 1: 149–7.

Turner, J.C. (1982) 'Towards a cognitive redefinition of the social group', in H. Tajfel (ed.), *Social Identity and Inter-group Relations*. Cambridge: Cambridge University Press.

Turner, J.C. (1991) *Social Influence*. Milton Keynes: Open University Press.

Turner, J.C. (1999) Some current issues in research on social identity and self-categorization theories, in N. Ellemers, R. Spears and B. Doosje (eds), *Social identity: Context, commitment, content* (pp. 6–34). Oxford: Blackwell.

Turner, J.C., Hogg, M.A., Oakes, P.J., Reicher, S.D. and Wetherell, M.S. (1987) *Rediscovering the Social Group: A Self-Categorization Theory*. Oxford and New York: Blackwell.

Turner, J.C., Oakes, P.J., Haslam, S.A. and McGarty, C.A. (1994) 'Self and collective: Cognition and social context', *Personality and Social Psychology Bulletin*, 20: 454–63.

van Knippenberg, D. and Hogg, M.A. (eds) (2003) *Leadership and Power: Identity Processes in Groups and Organizations*. London: Sage.

# 3

# Anthropological Perspectives on Identity: From Sameness to Difference

Toon van Meijl

For a long time the concept of identity did not belong in the toolbox of anthropologists. Traditionally identity was assumed to exist within individuals, whereas anthropology focused on the interpretation of socio-cultural relations between people. Identity was considered a psychological concept and therefore the study of identity was largely neglected by anthropologists. Over the past few decades the interest in identity has changed in anthropology, which is connected to changes in anthropology's understanding of culture, the discipline's key concept. These, in turn, follow a rather fundamental transformation of socio-cultural relations that are intertwined with the end of colonization and the beginning of globalization, and therefore also reflect on the meaning of identity. Originally identity signified a similar understanding of a person by other and self, but currently identity is basically premised on the understanding that any agreement on the identity of a person is preceded by an awareness of cultural differences. As a corollary, the study of identity is rather ambiguous. It swings between the differences and similarities in socio-cultural relations connecting individuals and groups as well as between the psychological and sociological dimensions of socio-cultural relations.

The different dimensions of identity have become particularly prominent in anthropology since the meaning of 'culture' has shifted. In the past culture referred principally to a reified essence binding a group of people together in a coherent way, but nowadays culture is more associated with heterogeneity and multivocality, with due implications for a more dynamic relationship between individual and community. A wide range of anthropological studies has demonstrated that aspects of persons, which were conventionally held as unchangeable character traits, may be considered as dynamic dimensions of symbolic, socio-cultural and political processes. Indeed, that which was formerly understood as private and fixed is now increasingly held to be public and variable. Even cross-cultural studies of emotions have shown that somehow emotions are cultural, if not political, constructions. In view of the major role that anthropological research has played in these debates it could be argued that the main contribution of anthropology to the study of identity has been to situate different senses of identity in a broader perspective by showing their cultural positioning and cultural diversity.

The debate about cultural differences in identity constructions is still one of the most dynamic fields of study in contemporary anthropology. It follows the rise of multicultural societies in the era of globalization and its associated processes of large-scale migration, which all lead to a growing complexity of cultural relationships and cultural identities. In order to grasp the increasingly dynamic nature of cultural processes and the manner in which they reflect the multiplication and hybridization of cultural identities of groups and individuals alike, anthropology and the social sciences generally are badly in need of a multidimensional concept of identity. Although some argue that the concept of identity is inadequate for the analysis of complex cultural relationships, over the years it has become part and parcel of political discourses based on, inter alia, non-western marginality, indigenousness, regional location and immigrant status. For that reason, too, the concept of identity is unlikely to disappear from popular discourses even if social scientists decide to substitute, for example, a multidimensional concept of 'self' for the allegedly outdated concept of identity. Hence it is important to scrutinize different dimensions of identity and separate analytically their shifting meanings in academic and popular discourses.

Before doing so, however, it is essential to provide a brief history of identity in anthropology, beginning with the culture and personality school. Subsequently, Erikson's notion of ego-identity will be discussed in order to understand its later extension to the social and cultural identity of groups. This shift was paralleled by the emergence of symbolic anthropology, which generated an ethnopsychological debate about intercultural notions of the self. In the 1970s, constructions of gender, ethnicity and national identity also dominated the anthropological agenda, before the rise of postmodernism and globalization led to a more dynamic

conception of culture and also of identity. Identity was gradually replaced by the notion of identifications, which never occur singularly but only in multiple form. The last part of this chapter is focussed on the new questions that are raised by the focus on multiple identifications, both in theory and in practice, illustrated with a number of case-studies from the Pacific region.

## CULTURE AND PERSONALITY: FROM MEAD TO ERIKSON

Long before the concept of identity was introduced into the discipline, anthropologists were discussing different cultural conceptions of the person, and in many ways these discussions foreshadowed the more recent identity debate. In American anthropology these interests were addressed in what was labelled the culture and personality school, which began in the 1920s. This movement proposed studying the development of personality to resolve the problems posed by functionalist assumptions of culture as a relatively closed system of behaviour. Thereby it fostered a notion of culture in which certain aspects belong only to certain individuals or categories of people.

Early analyses of the relationship between culture and personality were based on a configurational approach of culture, arguing that the cultural whole determined the nature of its parts and the relations between them. Margaret Mead (1928) and Ruth Benedict (1934), for example, contended that coherent patterns of thought and action informed and integrated all daily practices of individual persons. Later research was increasingly influenced by Freud's psychoanalysis, which resulted in the idea of a basic personality structure as developed by Abram Kardiner and Ralph Linton (1939). They argued that a causal relationship existed between culture and personality: personality was thought to result from the internalization of culture, while culture was regarded as the projection of personality.

This circular view of culture and personality is characteristic of the culture and personality school, which generated a wealth of anthropological studies in which a new emphasis emerged on the individual, thus linking anthropology and psychology (Honigmann, 1954). These analyses were innovative to the extent that they focused on the education of socio-cultural behaviour in a range of different societies, which illustrated that everywhere culture had to be learned and acquired in the course of children's development (Harris, 1969: 393–463).

The dichotomy between culture and personality, however, left advocates of the school's theory also open to criticism. The acquisition of culture and the development of personality are obviously not only one and the same process, and the important assumptions that a basic personality gave rise to a particular cultural institution and that a single personality type characterized each society were difficult to substantiate empirically (Toren, 1996). And did personality not also vary as much or more within society as it does across societies?

A detailed examination of this important tradition of research in the history of anthropology is beyond the scope of this chapter, but the culture and personality school has been important in anthropology since it extended the focus of the discipline from the group to the individual. In addition, the study of the relationship between culture and personality made many anthropologists familiar with the work of psychiatrists such as Sigmund Freud and Erik Erikson. The influence of the latter's work on the so-called 'ego-identity' of children and youngsters introduced the concept of identity to anthropology.

Erikson (1956) used the concept of ego-identity to describe the process of adjustment between the psychobiological drives of an individual's inner self with those influences on the self originating from society. It was based on the assumption that an individual always struggles to attain consistency between the self s/he would like to be and the self s/he believes is attributed to her or him

by others. Identity in this view referred primarily to a coherent sense of self or the feeling on the part of the individual of being the same as how s/he is viewed and identified by other(s). Identity was also believed to provide a sense of continuity and sameness through the individual lifecycle, in spite of developmental changes taking place.

In this view identification is the most important aspect of identity formation as identity refers to a well-adjusted personality that emerges from the same, or identical, identification of self by self and other. As a corollary, sameness and continuity are the most important characteristics of the concept of identity used by Erikson. This meaning of identity proceeds directly from the etymology of the concept, which is derived from the Latin *identitat* and/or *identitas*, which, in turn, was derived from *identidem*, a contraction of *idem et idem*, meaning 'repeatedly' (literally 'same and same'; Mackenzie, 1978: 19; see also Sökefeld, 1999).

In the 1960s, Erikson became almost a cult figure with his popular explanations of the identity crisis of troubled youth in his celebrated *Identity, Youth and Crisis* (1968). Thus, he also laid the foundation for the modern anthropological concept of identity, which is at once subjective and objective, individual and social, psychological and sociological. At the same time, however, it is not unfair to conclude that Erikson's notion of identity, with its universalist pretensions and devaluing of socio-cultural factors, later proved to be of minor relevance for comparative studies of identity in anthropology.

## SOCIAL AND CULTURAL IDENTITY: FROM GOODENOUGH TO GEERTZ

It is always difficult to establish who coined a term or introduced a new concept into an established discipline, but Ward Goodenough was probably the first who used the concept of identity in an analytical manner in his anthropological work. Goodenough's conception of identity must be understood against the background of Goffman's perception of society as a complex social situation in which individuals are linked through interdependent involvement (Goffman, 1959). Society and culture were consequently approached through the individual.

Goodenough (1963: 178–9) made a sharp distinction between personal and social identity. Those features of identity that are independent of someone's social or occupational status he saw as personal, whereas features deriving from a person's membership of a group he considered as social. A personal identity, then, represents the unique way an individual identifies him/herself, or the style with which someone engages in interaction with others. A person's social identity, on the other hand, is an aspect of self that makes a difference in how someone's rights and duties relate to other members of a group or society.

Goodenough's distinction between personal and social identity was influential in anthropology for a long time. It was developed on the basis of ethnographic field research in Micronesia, especially on Chuuk (formerly Truk), which he began in 1947. Using network analysis he mapped the different social identities of each individual in his research community by scaling and clustering the distribution of their rights and duties among their identity relationships (Goodenough, 1969). The term identity in this project was reserved for those aspects of the self that make a difference in social relationships. Accordingly, every individual has a number of different social identities. Interestingly, he discussed the simultaneous occurrence of several identities in certain interactions, when individuals would select more than one identity to deal with the situation. The composite of several identities he defined as an individual's social persona (Goodenough, 1969: 316). With this notion of a social persona Goodenough in fact anticipated the later development of the concept of hybrid or multiple identities.

Although Goodenough did not yet highlight the potential conflicts between a person's different identities, he did discuss the need to manage identity in order to make it work. Identity management entails special behaviour on the part of the individual designed to elicit information confirming a certain status belonging to a specific identity. This manipulation of identity relationships is necessary to permit or support an individual's attempts to attain consistency between a personal and a social identity.

In sum, it might be argued that, in contrast to Erikson, Goodenough emphasized the social aspects of identity, although his focus on individual strategies to achieve harmony between her/his own self-understanding and the image of her/him held by the surrounding group revealed the psychological influences on his work. In his perspective, however, individual identities were rooted primarily in the social order of the community. The assumption of sameness in the representation of self by both the individual and the group was complemented by the assumption of continuity in the individual's sense of identity. In this conception change did take place, but chiefly in situations of unstable understandings of a person's identity which necessitated a new image of a person that would restore the balance in exchanges between individual and other's representations of self. Thus, identities were believed to change largely according to predictable cultural patterns that were grounded in the stability of the community.

The connotations of sameness and stability in this early conception of identity are also apparent in the more sociological meaning of identity that was developed in the new paradigm of symbolic anthropology that emerged in the 1960s. In this tradition identity came to be understood mainly as the historically and culturally rooted self-image of a group of people that is predominantly shaped in contact with other groups of peoples. This meaning of identity was related to other anthropological concepts, such as worldview, value, ethos and, last but not least, culture, all of which suggested a certain kind of homogeneity among members of a community.

When in the 1960s, the usefulness of the culture concept was debated again in anthropology, Clifford Geertz became an influential proponent of a new trend focusing more on the symbolic dimension of culture instead of its cognitive aspects. Geertz (1973a [1966]) argued that culture is not locked inside people's heads, but is rather embedded in socio-cultural relationships and embodied in public symbols. He argued that members of a certain society communicated mainly through symbols about their culture and identity. Thus, Geertz imbued the hitherto elusive concept of culture with a relatively fixed locus, which has had an important impact on the operationalization of culture in recent decades. Symbols are widely considered as important vehicles of cultural meaning and, accordingly, symbolic anthropology brought about an epistemological shift from a focus on the function and structure of culture to the empirical question regarding the meaning of culture, of cultural symbols and of cultural identity (Ortner, 1984).

Geertz himself never elaborated the analytical advantage of the identity concept as he concentrated more on the ethos of culture than on the worldview of a society, more on the affective rather than the cognitive dimensions of a people's way of life. His new style of doing anthropology, however, parallels a new approach of identity in anthropology that emerged in the 1960s, and in which the concept was extended from the individual to the level of groups. This notion of identity was understood in analogy with worldview and emphasized culturally constituted meanings and values. It corresponded not only with the assumption of homogeneity in Goodenough's conception of social identity, but also with the prevailing view that the identity of individuals reflected the identity of their cultural group. Individual persons were regarded as having a pre-existing

identity, which was consistent with anthropological theories about the relation between person and group or community, such as in the culture and personality movement (Wallace, 1968; see also Strathern, 1994). Another important aspect of this view of identity concerned the presupposition of stability and permanence. People were regarded as sharing the same identity because they also shared the same history and culture. The community or society to which they belonged was consequently considered to be solid and immutable.

## THE EMERGENCE OF SELF

In the 1970s, identity gradually became a key concept in anthropology. This also sparked off a discussion about the theoretical terms of identity and the conditions of its use in ethnographic analyses. Before long it was disputed that individual identity could be considered a microcosm of collective identity. The incongruence between the identity of individuals and cultural groups was rather obvious, which also generated a debate about the use of an analytical concept developed for studying individuals in the study of groups. It was argued that ethnographic evidence for the construction of collective identities should be sought less from individuals and more from analyses of symbolic expressions of cultural groups (e.g. Fogelson, 1982). Methodologically, this implied the emergence of ethnographic field research by means of participant observation as the trademark of anthropology.

Although the ethnographic method became central in a variety of different trends in anthropology, the debate about the terms and conditions of identity led to two different types of thematic responses in the 1970s. First, following the culture and personality school and the early stream of cognitive anthropology, many anthropologists continued to pursue the study of the cultural constitution of the individual, but instead of using the term identity they adopted the psychological notion of self (Morris, 1994). In anthropology the self came to be understood as a process that orchestrates an individual's personal experience following which s/he becomes self-aware and self-reflective about her or his place in society (Taylor, 1989). This notion of self refers chiefly to an individual's mental representation of her or his own person, while the contrasting concept of other refers to the mental representation of other persons (Spiro, 1993). A clear separation between self and other seems to be universal, although the meaning of this distinction varies not only from person to person, but it is also an important function of culture (Shweder and Bourne, 1984).

In view of the dialectics between the self and the cultural milieu in which a person finds her/himself, which is always assumed to be different in different types of society, a dichotomy between western and non-western notions of self has been embedded in western philosophical and psychological traditions of thinking until very recently. In the west the self is routinely constructed in an essentialist way as autonomous, unitary and stable, which in itself is generally grounded in a contrasting assumption that non-western people do not possess an individuated self that is differentiated from other.

Over the past few decades the dichotomy between western and non-western notions of self has been the subject of debate in a whole range of research projects focusing on the relation between self or person and culture (e.g. Carrithers et al., 1985; Heelas and Lock, 1981; Lee, 1982; Shweder and LeVine, 1984; White and Kirkpatrick, 1985). In addition, a huge number of ethnographies have made strong cases for an interactionist and reflexive version of the self in intercultural perspective (for an overview, see Whittaker, 1992). The conclusion of these publications is that the dichotomy between western and non-western notions of the self is problematic for two reasons. First, the individualist notion of the western self must be revised since it is unquestionably more heterogeneous, contested and dialectical than is usually assumed (Murray, 1993). Second, it is currently widely accepted that a sociocentric worldview in non-western societies does not necessarily preclude the development of an individual self (Kusserow, 1999).

## GENDER, ETHNICITY AND NATIONAL IDENTITY

The second type of response to the epistemological debate about the terms and conditions of identity in the 1970s, led to an enormously diverse literature on cultural identity, more specifically on cross-cultural variations of gender, ethnic identity and national identity (e.g. Barth, 1969; De Vos and Romanucci-Ross, 1975; McCready, 1983; Rex, 1995; Robbins, 1973; Rosaldo and Lamphere, 1974; Smith, 1991, 1994). Both the extension of the concept of identity from the individual to the group level and the renewed attention to culture made anthropologists realize that the overall identity of any individual and even more of groups, invariably involves a convergence of various dimensions of identity, such as age, gender, social status, profession, ethnicity, nationality or culture. Assuming that people do not base their interactions with others on a total identity configuration, but only on that dimension that is of high saliency in a given interaction, it became therefore important to specify which dimension is given prime importance in certain interactions. In view of their professional interest in cultural differences, anthropologists began focusing on gender or on the ethnic or national dimension of identity as, in socio-cultural situations characterized by diversity or heterogeneity, gender, ethnicity or nationality usually override all other identities of an individual's repertoire from which an appropriate selection is made for a specific interaction or encounter with others. It is beyond the scope of this chapter to address the anthropological literature on gender, ethnic and national identity in any detail, but it is necessary to highlight some key points.

Although the history of anthropology had engendered influential scholars who had focused on the role of women in non-western societies, among them Margaret Mead, it was not until the early 1970s that gradually a consensus emerged about an androcentric bias in anthropology. Anthropology was largely a masculine discipline insofar as it studied the human condition of 'man'. Feminist anthropology raised the awareness of women as a separate category in anthropological approaches and analyses. Initially, this was tied up with the view that inequality between men and women was primarily a consequence of biological differences. The underlying assumption was that women are oppressed universally (Reiter, 1975). The available knowledge of cross-cultural variations in relationships between males and females, however, soon made it clear that the subordination of women was the result of socio-cultural circumstances, which also implied that they could be changed. In the 1980s, the concept of gender became increasingly important as a way of explaining the socio-cultural formation of males and females. As a corollary, feminist anthropology moved away from the notion of universal oppression to a perspective based on cultural diversity and cultural difference (Moore, 1988). The focus in feminist anthropology on differences and diversity made it no longer possible to represent women as a homogenous group, and as such this new perspective had a decisive impact on the further development of the concepts of culture and identity in the discipline at large (see below).

In the 1970s, an increased attention to ethnicity as a dominant dimension of identity in intercultural situations also emerged. This new focus generated a debate about the relative weight of primordial versus situational factors in the definition of ethnicity (Glazer and Moynihan, 1975). The primordialist position was based on the understanding that ethnicity proceeds from a primal,

psychological need to belong and should therefore be conceived of as a universal, natural fact (Geertz, 1973b [1963]). In contrast, the circumstantialist or instrumentalist perspective on ethnicity started from the position that ethnicity always contains an organizational dimension, which is activated when interest groups arise in the production and distribution of scarce resources. Viewed in this light ethnicity becomes a more dynamic process involving mainly political and economic factors (Cohen, 1978).

The perception of ethnicity as a mere function of political and economic struggles, however, disregards the fact that ethnic markers and symbols invariably precede cultural contact, even though ethnicity is not necessarily a primordial phenomenon (Barth, 1969). Eventually, therefore, a synthesis emerged in ethnicity theory, which incorporates insights from both primordialist and circumstantialist positions (Keyes, 1981). At present, there is consensus that an analysis of ethnicity must not fit the many components of inter-ethnic interaction into a single pattern based on primordial attachment, but neither should ethnicity be considered as an instrumental ideology to resist or conceal relations of political and economic dominance (Vermeulen and Govers, 1994).

The development of this view of ethnicity is paralleled by the emergence of a new approach of national identity that also emphasizes the cultural and political construction of nationalism. This notion of nationalism was developed in response to the more objectivist approach of nationalism by, among others, Ernest Gellner (1983), who argued that nationalism evolves naturally in the transition from agricultural to industrial society, in which the changing nature of production demands more homogeneity than existed in the past. Benedict Anderson (1983), in contrast, focused on the subjective imagination of the nation as a community, which in his view was made possible by the decline of religion and a growing awareness of human diversity with the rise of exploration and the development of capitalism. Although Anderson's explanation of nationalism has been criticized on empirical grounds, his focus on the subjectivist dimension of nationalism as a cultural and political construction is frequently cited, partly also since only this view explains the passions that nationalism may generate (see also Hobsbawm, 1990; Smith, 1991).

The conclusion of the debates about cultural identity, gender, ethnic identity and national identity in the anthropology of the 1970s and 1980s is again difficult to summarize, but in this context the study of identity clearly built on the new awareness in anthropology that dimensions of culture have not only form and function, but also meaning. Thus, the concept of identity (re-)introduced, at least to some extent, a psychological dimension into anthropology. And since the meaning of identity is significant for individuals and groups alike, the focus on identity also made it imperative to distinguish between individual and group motivation in ethnographic analyses, with all due consequences for anthropological interpretations of culture. Finally, it is important to conclude that the identity concept reconfirmed the importance of a historical dimension in anthropological analyses (Spicer, 1971), which became particularly evident through the rise of ethnic and national identities in the wake of the decolonization process. The end of the colonial era also constituted an important reason why culture became the subject of reflection in anthropology in the 1980s (Clifford, 1988; Clifford and Marcus, 1986; Marcus and Fischer, 1986). This debate about culture in anthropology resulted in a new understanding of the discipline's key concept, which, in turn, was related to a new understanding of the meaning of identity in contemporary, postcolonial circumstances.

## TOWARDS A NEW UNDERSTANDING OF CULTURE AND IDENTITY

In the past culture referred principally to a coherent system of shared meanings and values that were believed to bind a group of people together (Abu-Lughod, 1991). In recent decades, however, the meaning of the concept of culture has shifted to include the diversity and derivations of a variety of constructions, representations and interpretations of culture by individuals and/or subgroups in a certain society (Kuper, 1999). The differentiation of culture was first brought to light through the emergence of feminist anthropology. Later it was reinforced by the globalization process and its associated flows of transnational migration, which together have provoked the rise of multicultural societies. This, in turn, has incited a large-scale revival of cultural traditions at local levels and a growing complexity of cultural relationships. For that reason, too, a 'culture' can no longer be considered to speak with one voice, but is now understood as multi-vocal. This also entails that culture is no longer regarded as unchanging and identical for all individuals, but as an inherently dynamic process of domination and marginalization in which individuals are positioned differently. Thus, different people attempt to use the economic, political and symbolic resources that are available to them in order to try and impose their interpretation and understanding of situations on others, while at the same time attempting to prevent others from making their definition of the situation hegemonic (Wright, 1998). Finally, it is important to note that these contemporary struggles about culture and identity are taking place in situations that are characterized by unboundedness. Local, national and global networks often meet in them, and therefore the links between the various aspects of culture and identity are always historically specific and never form a closed or coherent whole.

A clarification of the new meaning of culture not only sheds light on the contemporary context in which identities are being reconstituted, but it also clarifies the need to situate the analysis of identity in different dimensions of social and cultural situations. Any contextual analysis of contemporary representations of identity will necessarily have to pay attention to the cultural complexity and inherent ambiguity of identity (Hannerz, 1992). In the global era identity implies no longer only sameness and uniqueness, since these features cannot be defined in isolation of other – cultural – identities. In increasingly multicultural contexts, identity obtains its meaning primarily from the identity of the other with whom the self is contrasted. People only know who they are by knowing who they are not. Indeed, any construction of identity is preceded by recognition of difference and an awareness of what self is not, but this psychological process is particularly prominent in intercultural situations (e.g. Woodward, 1997). Not until the difference with other individuals with a different cultural background has become apparent will the sameness and uniqueness of the cultural identity of self come to the surface. Thus, the new conception of identity refers simultaneously to the difference *and* sameness of self and other, both with psychological *and* sociological connotations.

The problem with this multidimensional view of identity, however, is its elusiveness since the precedence of difference over sameness makes it logically impossible to provide a positive perspective on what identity actually is. The absence of a 'self'-generated foundation of identity, however, seems unavoidable in the current condition of postmodernity that denies the possibility to define in positive terms the contemporary conditions of knowledge and representation, or of the subject of self and her/his identity (Jameson, 1991; Lyotard, 1984). The characterization of identity as resulting from the awareness of difference instead of sameness is to some extent also interwoven with Foucault's (1966: 398) vigorous critique of the sovereign subject that was so characteristic of the period of modernity.

As the aspect of sameness has been eclipsed by difference, so has the aspect of uniqueness been substituted by plurality in the contemporary perspective on identity. This process is likewise intertwined with the reconstitution of local identities in an increasingly global context. A paradoxical consequence of these socio-cultural and political changes associated with globalization and migration is that identities can no longer be seen as exclusive, as individual (literally 'indivisible'). Instead, it has become apparent that the local and the global are inherently connected, which causes cultural identities to be multiply constructed across different, often intersecting and antagonistic, discourses, practices and positions. As a result, the attention in anthropology and other social sciences has shifted from singular identity to multiple identities, although this emphasis is literally contradictory to the original, etymological meaning of identity in terms of sameness of self (Sökefeld, 1999: 417, 2001). Nevertheless, the idea of plural, even competing constructions of identity or conceptions of self has become rather common in social psychology and cognitive anthropology, in which it is linked to the notion of a person as a composite of many, often contradictory, self-understandings and identities (e.g. Battaglia, 1995; Holland and Lave, 2001; Holland et al., 1998; Quinn 2006; Strauss, 1997; Strauss and Quinn, 1997).

In this context it is also relevant to refer to Stuart Hall's definition of identity as 'the point of suture between, on the one hand, the discourses and practices which attempt to "interpellate", to speak to us or hail us into place as the social subjects of particular discourses, and, on the other hand, the processes which produce subjectivities, which construct us as subjects which can be "spoken"' (1996: 5–6). Identity, in other words, is increasingly regarded as a kind of nexus at which different constructions of self coincide, and sometimes also collide. Since in this view the construction of identity, or rather identities, is a never-ending process, always incomplete, unfinished and open-ended, Hall (1996: 6) also preferred the term identification to the essentialist concept of identity, an idea that has meanwhile been corroborated by the influential sociologist and philosopher Zygmunt Bauman (2001: 129).

Rather than being characterized by a singular and stable identity, in the contemporary global world the subject is constantly 'suturing' itself to different articulations between discourse and practice, which process, in turn, leads to multiple identifications at different moments in time.

## CONTEMPORARY ISSUES

The increasing recognition that identities are never singular, but always multiply constructed in different contexts, which, in turn, is intertwined with the prevalence of difference over sameness in their meaning, raises important questions that will determine the agenda of identity studies in anthropology in coming years. Formulating the parameters of the context in which the study of identity and multiple identifications is to be situated in the future, it is essential to consider recent historical changes that have had a relatively revolutionary impact on almost all societies and which have brought about a global quest for identity (Featherstone, 1995; Friedman, 1994). The paradox in the contemporary construction of identities, however, is the focus on continuity with a historical past, while identities are re-constituted in order to re-articulate the self to rapidly changing circumstances. History has, in other words, become a resource in the articulation of identifications in the present and the future: 'the so-called return to roots' is not of prime importance, argues Hall, but has been replaced by 'a coming-to-terms-with our "routes"' (1996: 4, see also Clifford, 1997).

Furthermore, it is important to establish a more intimate link between the social and the psychological in the anthropological study of identity. The new view of identity as an intersection of temporary attachments to different subject positions in various discourses and practices raises new questions for anthropology: to what extent is the differentiation of cultural conditions reflected in the emergence of multiple identifications?

How are individuals constituted in and through multiple different identities, or rather identifications? How do multiple identifications come about in individual lives? And how do multiple identifications of an individual relate to the identifications of other people in a dynamic socio-cultural context?

In addition to these questions regarding the sociological implications of changing cultures and changing identities, it is important to examine the psychological implications of contemporary cultural developments. The main question in this respect concerns the relationship between multiple identifications within individual constructions of persons (rather than between or among individuals). More specifically, how do multiple forms of difference, such as culture, space, ethnicity, class and gender intersect *within* individual actors? How are multiple identifications mediated within individual consciousness? And how do individuals relate different representations of their identifications within their experiences of themselves?

These questions were first formulated in feminist anthropology examining the dilemmas faced by women broadening their horizon beyond the traditional household (e.g. Moore, 1993, 1994). A structural difference in cultural circumstances in someone's life, however, makes the original dilemmas of women even more complicated since they add a sociological dimension to a psychological issue (Linger, 2005). They raise not only the question how people relate different representations of their identity within the self, but also the issue how in multicultural societies multiple identifications within the self may be acknowledged without representing individual subjects as negative, damaged or in crisis (Bammer, 1994).

These questions provoke the methodological problem of whether the concept of identity, or identification, is the best term available to address these issues. Some not only consider the analytical value of the concept of identity insufficient to address its entanglement with cultural complexity, but the ambiguity of identity is also compounded by the reification of identity in popular discourses, in which frequently the focus is exclusively on aspects of sameness, homogeneity and historical continuity. The confusion about the essentialization of identity in popular discourses versus the ambivalence surrounding the concept of identity in academic discourses has caused some to argue that identity has been charged with so many meanings that it has ceased to be a meaningful concept (Brubaker and Cooper, 2000).

In contrast, the German anthropologist Martin Sökefeld (2001) has argued that the ambivalence caused by the co-existence of constructivist conceptions of identity within academia and the reification of identity in popular discourse is an essential aspect in the usefulness of identity as an analytical category. He argues that the dual semantic meaning of identity can, if fully realized, offer an insurance against the conflation of categories of practice and analysis. It will remind the academy that identities, although posed by actors as singular, continuous, bounded and more or less integrated, can at the same time be considered as subject to the postmodern conditions of plurality, intersectionality and difference. Indeed, the only option may be to address identity in all its varying representations in contemporary practices. A brief ethnographic excursion into identity issues in one highly dynamic region may exemplify this.

## CHANGING IDENTIFICATIONS IN THE PACIFIC: SOME ILLUSTRATIVE CASES

Transnational migration has never been as pervasive as it is today, with unprecedented consequences for the transformation and differentiation of culture and identity. One of the most interesting regions in this context is the Asia-Pacific region since it accounts for almost 40 per cent of the millions of people who cross national borders each year (Goss and Lindquist, 2000). The Pacific region is particularly fascinating as migration in the area often leads to small island depopulation. The impact of transnational movements and shifting constructions of identity is thus magnified in small populations. In some countries, such as Niue and the Cook Islands for example, three-quarters or more of the total population now resides in New Zealand from where many have moved on to Australia. Large numbers of Tongans and Fijians are also living on the Pacific Rim. Altogether, at least half a million Polynesians are living abroad today, which is about 25 per cent of the total population.

Contemporary migration is fundamentally different from migration in the past. A search for employment no longer seems to be the main reason to cross national borders, but people migrate more and more for a whole range of other reasons, including cultural reasons associated with differences in lifestyle as disseminated by multiple global media. Transnational migration is consequently not only complicating cultural relationships within the nation-state, but the rise of the multicultural society is simultaneously having far-reaching implications for the cultural identity of individual migrants and all their relations at home and abroad.

Contemporary identity issues are also intimately connected with the consequences of globalization. Contrary to earlier expectations globalization has led to a growing cultural heterogeneity since it has incited a large-scale revival of cultural traditions at local levels. This so-called paradox of globalization is particularly evident in small-scale societies, such as those found in the Pacific, where people often believe themselves to be in danger of losing their cultural uniqueness under the impact of global influences. As a corollary, the role of tradition in contemporary discourses of culture and identity has been a topical issue in anthropology over the past two decades (e.g. Jolly and Thomas, 1992; Keesing, 1989).

The distinctive features of the intricate relationship between tradition, culture and identity in the contemporary Pacific are that culture is increasingly represented in terms of history and traditions, that it is generally reconstructed in opposition to a stereotypical representation of – former – colonial powers, which often leads to the reification and objectification of identity as a primordial feature of all Pacific peoples (Norton, 1993). Pacific identities are frequently represented as innate (Linnekin and Poyer, 1990). As such, they are regarded as unchangeable, as continuous, as timeless. In addition, representations of culture as traditional focus in particular on the expressive aspects of culture, such as language, art and ritual. These processes of essentialization both imply that discourses of culture and the discursive representation of identity become separated from identities in daily practice. In consequence, a discrepancy emerges between politicized constructions of culture and identity on the one hand, and culture and identity as lived realities on the other. Let me illustrate.

## Tonga

Tonga is one of those countries in Polynesia of which large numbers of citizens are living overseas. Over the past three decades more than half of the Tongan population has migrated to three main destinations: New Zealand, Australia and the USA (Lee, 2003; Small, 1997). Migration of Tongans to countries on the Pacific Rim is having far-reaching influences on Tongan society since expatriates send back not only money and goods, but also new ideas. Thus, the rise of remittances, which provide about half the national income of Tonga, is paralleled by the emergence of a pro-democracy movement demanding political reforms in the autocratic kingdom.

Changing attitudes towards traditional values of hierarchy in Tongan society are emerging especially among second generation Tongans who were born overseas and whose lives transgress boundaries between traditional Tongan values and the dynamic

situation in which they are living. The diversification of their lives is reinforced by the tendency of expatriate Tongan families to return to their country of origin as often as possible to meet family obligations. Regular return trips highlight the contrast between the different countries and consequently young Tongans find it increasingly difficult to remain loyal to the traditional culture of the home country of their parents. They also express more and more resistance against the pressure to speak the Tongan language and to maintain Tongan values.

Interestingly, the voice of protest is heard most often in chatrooms for Tongans overseas (Lee, 2006). Debates in the Tongan virtual community are most lively since all layers of Tongan society seem to be represented in it: aristocrats and commoners, males and females, Tongans at home and Tongans abroad. Although it is not always clear whether the role someone assumes in chatrooms corresponds with her or his position in daily life, the debates about culture and identity are revealing since they bring to the fore what Tongan-born Tongans and overseas-born Tongans are concerned about. This is not to say that overseas-born Tongans are by definition more liberal than others, since paradoxically some expatriate Tongans are more orthodox than native inhabitants of Tonga who have never left the country. Sometimes people at home are anxious not to be considered as backward which means that they faddishly follow international developments, whereas migrants in some situations adopt traditional attitudes in order to cope with a new environment which they experience as threatening

The role of the Internet in the identity debate constitutes a new and highly interesting domain of research (e.g. Franklin, 2004). The Internet is particularly important in transnational communities, in which it can make or break cultural traditions and identities. On the one hand, communication over the Internet may be a crucial resource to maintain a sense of community across boundaries

(Howard, 1999). On the other hand, however, the Internet is widely used to discuss and dispute strong and persisting cultures, such as in Tonga (Morton, 1999). The Internet provides a platform to criticize cultural traditions while it is also a means to escape from the pressure to maintain a traditional identity, which young people in particular often experience as suffocating. Some people, however, do not always have the opportunity to avoid the cultural dilemmas created by a renewed attention for cultural traditions, which leads me to a second ethnographic case-study.

## New Zealand

In New Zealand I worked with a group of young Maori people, the country's indigenous population, who had dropped out of school and who were enrolled at a special education programme in computing and manufacturing to improve their skills for the labour market. One of the assumptions of the training centre was that Maori youngsters mainly dropped out of school since the mono-cultural climate there was not amenable to children with a different cultural background. Related to this was the conviction that young Maori people would feel more at ease on a *marae*, a ceremonial centre, which is normally considered as the cultural hearth of Maori people. In the cultural practices on the *marae*, however, this was not obvious.

The cultural background of Maori trainees was characterized by a marked lack of knowledge and familiarity with *marae* protocol for ceremonial gatherings and the associated ritual speechmaking, chants and dances. Most youngsters had rarely visited *marae* and did not speak a word of Maori. Their training on the *marae* entailed their first encounter with classic Maori culture, which was reinforced by *marae* etiquette which prescribed everyone present to participate in its practices. To meet this demand the youngsters were not only trained in computing and other practical skills, but also in Maori language and 'culture', which sadly brought about strong feelings of embarrassment and of alienation from a culture which was ideologically considered to be theirs yet far removed from their personal experiences (van Meijl, 2006).

The dilemmas faced by young Maori people who are at odds with the traditional culture that is currently being revived in contemporary New Zealand, are in many ways similar to the cultural dilemmas of Tongan youngsters born overseas but raised in a Tongan family that feels obliged to stick to Tongan traditions. Both groupings are inclined to acknowledge the need to maintain cultural traditions, but they also think traditions are archaic and therefore unnecessary. Yet it would be unfair to criticize these youngsters for being contradictory or inconsistent. They are facing an irresolvable dilemma that is increasingly common in the present day since more and more people are constantly moving across cultural landscapes. People for whom multiculturalism is the order of the day have no option but to mediate their multiple identifications that can no longer be integrated into a coherent whole. The question becomes: how do they manage?

## NEW THEORETICAL DIRECTIONS

The ethnographic case-studies described above demonstrate that the increasing interdependency of societies around the world and the cultural networks transversing them not only involve an intensification of contact between different cultural groupings at social level, but also a strengthening of cultural conversations within individual identities. Increasing interculturality is reflected in the rise of multiple identifications, which in turn engenders a discussion between the various cultural positions that all have a voice within the self. And these voices are involved in complicated conversations that reflect the differentiation of culture in the global world.

Negotiations, tensions, conflicts, agreements and disagreements not only take place between different cultural groupings, but also within the selves of multicultural individuals. As mentioned above, this raises the topic of how multiple forms of difference intersect within individual actors.

In this context, two different theoretical positions come to the fore. For a long time the prevailing perspective was offered by cognitive dissonance theory as developed by Leon Festinger (1957). The central hypothesis of this approach is that any person experiences the existence of dissonance between cognitive elements as uncomfortable and therefore everyone will always try to reduce a discrepancy between conflicting cognitions and attempt to achieve consonance, consistency and coherence. In addition, people are supposed to actively avoid situations and information that might increase cognitive dissonance since these entail a form of psychological tension that any individual wishes to diminish.

In multicultural or other dynamic situations this notion of self implies that people have no choice but to accommodate diverging cultural identifications within a relatively stable and coherent self. In order to maintain a cohesive whole the self is therefore supposed to reject or suppress identifications that may conflict with other types of cognitive information and self-representations. Currently, it is widely accepted that this theoretical approach of the self is inadequate to explain the dilemmas faced by multicultural citizens in globalized circumstances (e.g. Quinn, 2006; van Meijl, 2008).

In cognitive anthropology (e.g. Holland and Lave, 2001; Holland et al., 1998) and in social psychology (e.g. Hermans and Kempen, 1993) the idea of plural, competing conceptions of identity or the self is currently related to the notion of a person as a composite of multiple, often contradictory, self-understandings and identities. This strand of analysis has been inspired mainly by the Russian literary critic Mikhael Bakhtin, and has resulted in a view of the self as a multiplicity of I-positions among which dialogical relationships are established (Hermans et al., 1992). The concept of the dialogical self is inspired not only by Bakhtin's (1984 [1929]) metaphor of the polyphonic novel, which allows for a multiplicity of positions among which dialogical relationships may emerge, but also by William James' (1890) classic distinction between I and me. The I he described as 'the self as knower', as the observing agent. The me, conversely, was portrayed as 'the self as known', as the object of self-observation and self-evaluation. On the interface between these traditions, Hermans and Kempen (1993) have argued that the I has the possibility to move from one spatial position to another in accordance with changes in situation and time. The I fluctuates among different and even opposed positions, and has the capacity imaginatively to endow each position with a voice so that dialogical relations between positions can be established.

In a sense the dialogical self is a 'society of the mind' (Hermans, 2002), because there is no essential difference between the positions a person takes as part of the self and the positions people take as members of a heterogeneous society. Both self and society function as a polyphony of consonant and dissonant voices. As such, the dialogical self is characterized by two main features that are necessary for understanding its dynamics. First, in a multivoiced self, there is constant dialogical interchange, while, second, the relationships between the several positions are characterized by relative dominance. The most important characteristic of the dialogical perspective is that the self is seen as a relational phenomenon that transcends the boundaries between the inside and the outside, between self and other. Methodologically the dialogical self has been elaborated by relating the spatialization of dialogical relations to the simultaneity of voices within a self's discourse. In Bakhtin's view individual speakers are not simply talking as individuals, but in the utterances of individual people the voices of their surrounding groups and institutions are heard, even though they may be physically absent.

The absence of the other in dialogue is closely connected with the second distinctive feature of dialogical relationships, namely relative dominance, which Hermans and Kempen (1993: 73) exemplify with reference to the relationship between self and community. If the self is defined as a multiplicity of different identities, it may be argued that the community is not only able to address the self in a variety of identities, but also to let the self know how these identities, and the way the self functions in them, are approved. An important implication of this form of cultural dominance is that some identities are strongly developed, whereas others are suppressed or even disunited from self. Indeed the prevalence of one identity implies the necessary neglect or suppression of another identity. Specific experiences, particularly negative experiences, may lead to the active suppression or even splitting of unwanted identities, which slow down the dialogical movements between different identities. But dominance of one identity over another rarely excludes dialogical exchange.

## CHALLENGES AND CONCLUSIONS

Over the past few decades the construction of identities has changed under the impact of globalization, which has transformed the core of modern society into a contact zone (Appadurai, 1991) or a network society (Castells, 1996). As a corollary, many people, adolescents in particular, now develop multiple, often multicultural identifications. Part of their identity is rooted in the culture in which they were born and raised, but another part is influenced by and oriented towards the more global situation. Some may manage to develop a hybrid identity, relatively successfully combining aspects of both local and global circumstances. Others will be involved in a never-ending struggle to work out in which situation they ideally belong. In any case, the cultural identifications of most will no longer be obvious and, as illustrated above, a great deal of confusion has emerged among young people growing up in multicultural situations. Many young people feel often alienated both from their old home and their new home. Indeed, home seems to have been lost for many, which raises the question how young people cope with the dynamics of the contemporary era.

The notion of dialogue is a main feature of contemporary constructions of the multiplication of identifications in multicultural circumstances, but the debate about the dialogical self itself raises some important questions that will determine the anthropological agenda of identity issues in the years to come. First, it is important to examine how a dialogue among a variety of different I-positions relates to the modern notion of unity as characteristic of the self. At first sight, a dialogical perspective on the self seems to contradict the idea that the self is united, but at the same time a sense of integration of the dialogical self is commonly assumed to be necessary in order to maintain a balanced personality as distinct from dissociative identity disorders. In this context, however, a remaining question concerns the experience and the portrayal of the integration of I-positions within the self. How do young Tongans born overseas and Maori youngsters not familiar with *marae* protocol experience their traversals across different cultural contact zones (see also Ibrahim, 2008; Nilan and Feixa, 2006)? To what extent are 'unity' and 'integration' still appropriate labels to characterize the dialogue among their multiple identifications?

These questions, in turn, are related to a second question regarding the assumption in the theory of the dialogical self, namely that the process of globalization arouses a great deal of uncertainty. Leading exponents of the theory of the dialogical self have recently argued that uncertainty is a sign of the present since more and more people participate simultaneously in different cultural networks which are largely disjunctive. The contradictions, ambiguities and contrasting interests that accompany the rise of the multicultural network society are assumed not just to complicate the self's attempt to attain unity among its range of I-positions, but also to confront the self with uncertainty (Hermans and Dimaggio, 2007; Hermans and Kempen, 1998).

Hermans and Dimaggio (2007) argue that multivoicedness in the global world makes a fixity of meaning no longer possible, as a result of which a universal voice for resolving contradictions and conflicting information has been silenced, which makes the future unpredictable and therefore also uncertain. The question is, however, what the implications of these global phenomena are for the self of individuals. In this respect, Hermans and Dimaggio themselves are ambiguous too, since they add to their observations that the experience of uncertainty is 'not necessarily a negative experience' since it 'may open and broaden the space for possible actions, adventures, and explorations of the unknown (e.g. travelling, international contacts, forms of international and intercultural cooperation)' (p. 34). In addition, 'uncertainty can be seen as a definitive farewell to the dogmas and ideologies of institutions that restricted and confined the self in earlier times' (*Ibid.*). But if uncertainty is not necessarily negative and even has positive connotations, is uncertainty then the most appropriate concept to describe the contemporary *condition humaine*?

In contrast with the assumptions that uncertainty characterizes the identity of individuals who are continuously moving across cultural contact zones, I would like to launch the hypothesis that the increasing interculturality of the world does not necessarily make the self increasingly uncertain at the same time. Of course, globalization challenges people to extend their selves and identities beyond the bounded domain of traditional settings, which automatically leads to a multiplication of internal positions and intensifies the multivoicedness of the self, but whether it also leads to permanent uncertainty of the self is not self-evident. The dialogical self in multicultural situations is, in my view, well aware that it will never achieve the unity that

was still the ideal of the modern self, since a differentiation in cultural dimensions is becoming a natural part of people's lives nowadays. A disjunction between different cultural perspectives is becoming an inherent aspect of the lives of an increasing number of cosmopolitan citizens. Rather than making them uncertain they take it for granted that their self is disunited and that dialogue is essential to maintain a balance between the different cultural landscapes in their lives and minds.

## ACKNOWLEDGEMENTS

I would like to thank Ward Goodenough for the inspiring conversations we had about his work on identity in the 1950s and 1960s. Hubert Hermans and Dorothy Holland both made a valuable contribution to the development of my research about the dialogical relationship between multiple identifications within the self of individuals living in multicultural societies. Henk Driessen and Michael Goldsmith made some pertinent comments on an earlier draft of this chapter, while the latter kindly also corrected my English. René van der Haar provided some useful references, but, of course, I alone bear responsibility for all remaining mistakes and deficiencies. Finally, I would like to thank my partner Ank Willems and our three wonderful daughters, Malou, Stella and Rosalie, who graciously accepted my different identity when I wrote this chapter during a protracted period of unexpected illness.

## REFERENCES

Abu-Lughod, L. (1991) 'Writing against culture', in Richard Fox (ed.), *Recapturing Anthropology: Working in the Present*. Santa Fe, NM: School of American Research Press. pp. 137–62.

Anderson, B. (1983) *Imagined Communities Reflections on the Origin and Spread of Nationalism*. London/ New York: Verso.

Bakhtin, M. (1984 [1929]) *Problems of Dostoevsky's Poetics*, ed. and trans. C. Emerson. Manchester: Manchester University Press.

Bammer, A. (1994) 'Introduction', in Angelika Bammer (ed.) *Displacements Cultural Identities in Question*. Bloomington, IN: Indiana University Press. pp. xi–xx.

Barth, Fredrik (ed.) (1969) *Ethnic Groups and Boundaries The Social Organization of Culture Difference*. Bergen/Oslo: Universitetsforlaget.

Battaglia, D. (1995) *Rhetorics of Self-Making*. Berkeley, CA: University of California Press.

Bauman, Z. (2001) 'Identity in the globalizing world', *Social Anthropology*, 9 (2): 121–9.

Benedict, R. (1934) *Patterns of Culture An Analysis of our Social Structure as Related to Primitive Civilizations*. Boston, MA: Houghton Mifflin.

Brubaker, R. and Cooper, F. (2000) 'Beyond "identity"', *Theory and Society*, 29: 1–47.

Carrithers, M., Collins, S. and Lukes, S. (eds) (1985) *The Category of the Person Anthropology, Philosophy, History*. Cambridge: Cambridge University Press.

Clifford, J. and Marcus, G.E. (eds) (1986) *Writing Culture The Poetics and Politics of Ethnography*. Berkeley, CA: University of California Press.

Clifford, J. (1988) *The Predicament of Culture Twentieth-century Ethnography, Literature and Art*. Cambridge, MA: Harvard University Press.

Clifford, J. (1997) *Routes Travel and Translation in the Late Twentieth Century*. Cambridge, MA: Harvard University Press.

Cohen, R. (1978) 'Ethnicity: Problem and focus in anthropology', *Annual Review of Anthropology*, 7: 379–403.

Erikson, E.H. (1956) 'The problem of ego identity', *Journal of the American Psychoanalytic Association*, 4: 56–121.

Erikson, E.H. (1968) *Identity, Youth and Crisis*. New York: Norton.

Featherstone, M. (1995) *Undoing Culture Globalization, Postmodernism and Identity*. London: Sage.

Festinger, L. (1957) *A Theory of Cognitive Dissonance*. Stanford, CA: Stanford University Press.

Fogelson, R.D. (1982) 'Person, self, and identity: Some anthropological retrospects, circumspects and prospects', in B. Lee (ed.), *Psychosocial Theories of the Self*. New York: Plenum. pp. 67–109.

Foucault, M. (1966) *Les mots et les choses Une Archéologie des Sciences Humaines*. Paris: Gallimard.

Franklin, M.I. (2004) *Postcolonial Politics, The Internet and Everyday Life Pacific Traversals Online*. London/New York: Routledge.

Friedman, J. (1994) *Cultural Identity and Global Process*. London: Sage.

Geertz, C. (1973a [1966]) 'Religion as a cultural system', in C. Geertz (ed.), *The Interpretation of Cultures*. New York: Basic Books. pp. 87–125.

Geertz, C. (1973b [1963]) 'The integrative revolution: Primordial sentiments and civil politics in the New States', in C. Geertz (ed.), *The Interpretation of Cultures*. New York: Basic Books. pp. 255–310.

Gellner, E. (1983) *Nations and Nationalism*. Oxford: Blackwell.

Glazer, N. and Moynihan, D.P. (eds) (1975) *Ethnicity Theory and Experience*. Cambridge, MA: Harvard University Press.

Goffman, E. (1959) *The Presentation of Self in Everyday Life*. Garden City, NY: Doubleday.

Goodenough, W.H. (1963) *Cooperation in Change An Anthropological Approach to Community Development*. New York: Russell Sage.

Goodenough, W.H. (1969) 'Rethinking "status" and "role": Toward a general model of the cultural organization of social relationships', in S.A. Tyler (ed.), *Cognitive Anthropology*. New York: Holt, Rinehart and Winston. pp. 311–30.

Goss, J. and Lindquist, B. (2000) 'Placing movers: An overview of the Asian-Pacific migration system', *The Contemporary Pacific*, 12 (2): 385–414.

Hall, S. (1996) 'Who needs identity?', in S. Hall and P. du Gay (eds), *Questions of Cultural Identity*. London: Sage. pp. 1–17.

Hannerz, U. (1992) *Cultural Complexity Studies in the Social Organization of Meaning*. New York: Columbia University Press.

Harris, M. (1969) *The Rise of Anthropological Theory A History of Theories of Culture*. London/Henley: Routledge and Kegan Paul.

Heelas, P.L.F. and Lock, A. (eds) (1981) *Indigenous Psychologies The Anthropology of the Self*. London: Academic Press.

Hermans, H.J.M. (2002) 'The dialogical self as a society of mind', *Theory and Psychology*, 12 (2): 147–60.

Hermans, H.J.M. and Dimaggio, G. (2007) 'Self, identity, and globalization in times of uncertainty: A dialogical analysis', *Review of General Psychology*, 11 (1): 31–61.

Hermans, H.J.M. and Kempen, H.J.G. (1993) *The Dialogical Self: Meaning as Movement*. San Diego, CA: Academic Press.

Hermans, H.J.M. and Kempen, H.J.G. (1998) 'Moving cultures: The perilous problems of cultural dichotomies in a globalizing society', *American Psychologist*, 53 (10): 1111–20.

Hermans, H.J.M., Kempen, H.J.G., Van Loon, L. and Rens J.P. (1992) 'The dialogical self: Beyond individualism and rationalism', *American Psychologist*, 47 (1): 23–33.

Hobsbawm, E.J. (1990) *Nations and Nationalism Since 1870: Programme, Myth, Reality*. Cambridge: Cambridge University Press.

Holland, D., Lachicotte Jr. W., Skinner, D. and Caine, C. (eds) (1998) *Identity and Agency in Cultural Worlds*. Cambridge, MA: Harvard University Press.

Holland, D. and Lave, J. (eds) (2001) *History in Person: Enduring Struggles, Contentious Practice, Intimate Identities*. Santa Fe/Oxford: School of American Research Press/James Currey.

Honigmann, J.J. (1954) *Culture and Personality*. New York: Harper and Brothers.

Howard, A. (1999) 'Pacific-based virtual communities: Rotuma on the World Wide Web', *The Contemporary Pacific*, 11 (1): 160–75.

Ibrahim, A. (2008) 'The new Flâneur: Subaltern cultural studies, African youth in Canada and the etiology of in-between', *Cultural Studies*, 22 (2): 234–53.

James, W. (1890) *The Principles of Psychology*, Vol. 1. London: Macmillan.

Jameson, F. (1991) *Postmodernism, or, the Cultural Logic of Late Capitalism*. London/New York: Verso.

Jolly, M. and Thomas, N. (eds) (1992) 'The politics of tradition in the Pacific', *Special issue of Oceania*, 62 (4).

Kardiner, A. and Linton, R. (1939) *The Individual and his Society: The Psychodynamics of Primitive Social Organization*. New York: Columbia University Press.

Keesing, R.M. (1989) 'Creating the past: custom and identity in the contemporary Pacific', *The Contemporary Pacific*, 1 (1–2): 19–42.

Keyes, C.F. (1981) 'The dialectics of ethnic change', in C.F. Keyes (ed.), *Ethnic Change*. Seattle, WA: University of Washington Press. pp. 3–30.

Kuper, A. (1999) *Culture: The Anthropologists' Account*. Cambridge, MA/London: Harvard University Press.

Kusserow, A.S. (1999) 'Crossing the great divide: Anthropological theories of the Western self', *Journal of Anthropological Research*, 55: 541–62.

Lee, B. (ed.) (1982) *Psychosocial Theories of the Self*. New York: Plenum.

Lee, H. (2006) 'Debating language and identity online: Tongans on the Net', in K. Landzelius (ed.), *Native on the Net: Indigenous and Diasporic Peoples in the Virtual Age*. London/New York: Routledge. pp. 152–68.

Lee, H.M. (2003) *Tongans Overseas: Between Two Shores*. Honolulu: University of Hawaii Press.

Linger, D.T. (2005) 'Identity', in C. Casey and R.B. Edgerton (eds), *A Companion to Psychological Anthropology: Modernity and Psychocultural Change*. Malden/Oxford: Blackwell. pp. 186–200.

Linnekin, J. and Poyer, L. (eds) (1990) *Cultural Identity and Ethnicity in the Pacific*. Honolulu: University of Hawaii Press.

Lyotard, J.F. (1984) *The Postmodern Condition: A Report on Knowledge*. Minneapolis, MN: University of Minnesota Press.

Mackenzie, W.J.M. (1978) *Political Identity*. Harmondsworth: Penguin.

Marcus, G.E. and Fischer, M.M.J. (1986) *Anthropology as Cultural Critique: An Experimental Moment in the Human Sciences*. Chicago, IL: University of Chicago Press.

McCready, W. (ed.) (1983) *Culture, Ethnicity, and Identity: Current Issues in Research*. New York/London: Academic Press.

Mead, M. (1928) *Coming of Age in Samoa: A Study of Adolescence and Sex in Primitive Societies*. New York: Morrow.

Meijl, T. van (2006) 'Multiple identifications and the dialogical self: Maori youngsters and the cultural renaissance', *Journal of the Royal Anthropological Institute*, 12 (4): 917–33.

Meijl, T. van (2008) 'Culture and identity in anthropology: Reflections on "unity" and "uncertainty" in the dialogical self', *International Journal of Dialogical Science, Target Article*, 3 (1): 165–90.

Moore, H.L. (1988) *Feminism and Anthropology*. Cambridge: Polity.

Moore, H.L. (1993) 'The differences within and the differences between', in T. del Valle (ed.), *Gendered Anthropology*. London/New York: Routledge. pp. 193–204.

Moore, H.L. (1994) *A Passion for Difference: Essays in Anthropology and Gender*. Cambridge: Polity.

Morris, B. (1994) *Anthropology of the Self: The Individual in Cultural Perspective*. London: Pluto Press.

Morton, H. (1999) 'Islanders in space: Tongans online', in R. King and J. Connell (eds) *Small Worlds, Global Lives: Islands and Migration*. London/New York: Pinter. pp. 235–53.

Murray, D.W. (1993) 'What is the Western concept of self? On forgetting David Hume', *Ethos*, 21 (1): 3–23.

Nilan, P. and Feixa, C. (eds) (2006) *Global Youth? Hybrid Identities, Plural Worlds*. London/New York: Routledge.

Norton, R. (1993) 'Culture and identity in the South Pacific: A comparative analysis', *Man* (N.S.), 28: 741–59.

Ortner, S.B. (1984) 'Theory in anthropology since the sixties', *Comparative Studies in Society and History*, 26: 126–66.

Quinn, N. (2006) 'The self', *Anthropological Theory*, 6 (3): 362–84.

Rex, J. (1995) 'Ethnic identity and the nation state: The political sociology of multi-cultural societies', *Social Identities*, 1 (1): 21–34.

Reiter, R.R. (ed.) (1975) *Towards and Anthropology of Women*. New York: Monthly Review Press.

Robbins, R.H. (1973) 'Identity, culture, and behaviour', in J.J. Honigmann (ed.), *Handbook of Social and Cultural Anthropology*. Chicago, IL: Rand McNally. pp. 1199–1222.

Rosaldo, M.Z. and Lamphere, L. (1974) *Women, Culture and Society*. Stanford, CA: Stanford University Press.

Shweder, R.A. and Bourne, E.J. (1984) 'Does the concept of person vary cross-culturally?', in R.A. Shweder and R.A. LeVine (eds) *Culture Theory: Essays on Mind, Self, and Emotion*. Cambridge: Cambridge University Press. pp. 158–99.

Shweder, R.A. and LeVine, R.A. (eds) (1984) *Culture Theory: Essays on Mind, Self and Emotion*. Cambridge: Cambridge University Press.

Small, C. (1997) *Voyages: From Tongan Villages to American Suburbs*. Ithaca, NY: Cornell University Press.

Smith, A.D. (1991) *National Identity*. Harmondsworth: Penguin.

Smith, A.D. (1994) 'The politics of culture: Ethnicity and nationalism', in T. Ingold (ed.), *Companion Encyclopedia of Anthropology*. London/New York: Routledge. pp. 706–33.

Sökefeld, M. (1999) 'Debating self, identity, and culture in anthropology', *Current Anthropology*, 40 (4): 417–47 (including 'Comments' and 'Reply').

Sökefeld, M. (2001) 'Reconsidering identity', *Anthropos*, 96: 527–44.

Spicer, E.H. (1971) 'Persistent cultural systems: A comparative study of identity systems that can adapt to contrasting environments', *Science*, 174 (4011): 795–800.

Spiro, M.E. (1993) 'Is the Western conception of the self "peculiar" within the context of the world cultures?', *Ethos*, 21 (2): 107–153.

Strathern, M. (1994) 'Parts and wholes: Refiguring relationships', in R. Borofsky (ed.), *Assessing Cultural Anthropology*. New York: McGraw-Hill. pp. 204–17.

Strauss, C. (1997) 'Partly fragmented, partly integrated: An anthropological examination of "postmodern fragmented subjects"', *Cultural Anthropology*, 12 (3): 362–404.

Strauss, C. and Quinn, N. (1997) *A Cognitive Theory of Cultural Meaning*. Cambridge: Cambridge University Press.

Taylor, C. (1989) *Sources of the Self: The Making of Modern Identity*. Cambridge, MA: Harvard University Press.

Vermeulen, H. and Govers, C. (eds) (1994) *The Anthropology of Ethnicity: Beyond 'Ethnic Groups and Boundaries'*. Amsterdam: Het Spinhuis.

Vos, G. de and Romanucci-Ross, L. (eds) (1975) *Ethnic Identity: Cultural Continuities and Change*. Palo Alto: Mayfield.

Wallace, A.F.C. (1968) 'Anthropological contributions to the theory of personality', in E. Norbeck, D. Price-Williams and W.M. McCord (eds) *The Study of Personality: An Interdisciplinary Appraisal*. New York: Rinehart and Winston. pp. 41–53.

White, G.M. and Kirkpatrick, J. (eds) (1985) *Person, Self, and Experience: Exploring Pacific Ethnopsychologies*. Berkeley, CA: University of California Press.

Whittaker, E. (1992) 'The birth of the anthropological self and its career', *Ethos*, 20 (2): 191–219.

Woodward, K. (ed.) (1997) *Identity and Difference*. London: Sage/Open University Press.

Wright, S. (1998) 'The politicization of "culture"', *Anthropology Today*, 14 (1): 7–15.

# Analysing Identity in Interaction: Contrasting Discourse, Genealogical, Narrative and Conversation Analysis

Bethan Benwell and Elizabeth Stokoe

This chapter will describe and demonstrate discourse-based approaches to the theorising and empirical analysis of identity in interaction. We start by describing the history of and context for the 'discursive turn' in identity studies. We set out two broadly competing trajectories for the study of discourse and identity: first, Foucauldian, genealogical forms of discourse analysis, encompassing critical discourse analysis, performativity theory, positioning theory, critical discursive psychology and some forms of narrative analysis; and second, ethnomethodological approaches such as conversation analysis (CA), membership categorisation and discursive psychology. We then provide two empirical case studies to contrast and evaluate these traditions. We conclude with a discussion of current debates in, and challenges for, future discourse and identity studies.

## THE ORIGINS OF A DISCURSIVE ACCOUNT

> I am a self only in relation to certain interlocutors ... a self exists only within what I call webs of interlocution. (Taylor, 1989: 36)

Discursive accounts of identity emerged during what has sometimes been described as the 'turn to discourse' in the latter half of the twentieth century. Prior to this, identity had been theorised as a self-fashioning, agentive, internal *project of the self*, whether through the rationalism of Enlightenment philosophy, the affective sensibilities of the Romantic period, or the psychodynamic theories of Freud (Benwell and Stokoe, 2006). Identity, in this paradigm, is thought to be a universal and timeless core, an 'essence' of the self that is expressed as recognisable representations. This humanist idea of identity as subjective and internally located has, however, in academic contexts, gradually been replaced with a view of identity in which 'an individual's self-consciousness never exists in isolation … it always exists in relationship to an "other" or "others" who serve to validate its existence' (Hall, 2004: 51).

This notion of identity as an *inter* subjective rather than subjective process paved the way for contemporary discursive accounts, in which identity is understood as a social phenomenon, produced and interpreted by other people, in discourse and other social and embodied conduct. Here, identity is located not in the 'private' realms of cognition, emotion and experience, but in the public realms of discourse, interaction and other semiotic systems of meaning-making. Identity is actively, ongoingly, dynamically constructed, rather than reflected, in talk and texts of all kinds. This discursive perspective also complements postmodern accounts of identity as a contingent, plural, fragmented and sometimes contradictory entity (Bauman, 2004; Laclau, 1990).

The conceptual shift brought about in the 'discursive turn' was observable in distinct academic disciplines, but united in their formulation of identity as a *product of the social*, and by extension, of discourse. For example, in psychoanalysis, the French theorist Jacques Lacan (1977) emphasised the discursive rather than the mental realm in understanding the psyche. Elsewhere in sociolinguistics, there has been a gradual shift from mapping features and patterns in language to identity variables (for example, gender, class, ethnicity) to an interactional sociolinguistics based in constructionism and performativity, whereby identity is understood as a 'dynamic and fluid process of ongoing accomplishment' (Holmes, 2007: 54–5). In social psychology, discursive psychologists rejected the notion that identity is a pre-given 'feature of the objective world' or of 'perception and cognition', arguing that it is instead a 'flexible resource in conversational interaction' (Antaki et al., 1996: 473–4).

A key figure in discourse-based approaches to identity is Michel Foucault. A fundamental premise of his work is to understand people in terms of their subject 'positions' within historical discourses. Identity is inscribed in dominant discourses, tied to social or institutional practices, such that selfhood takes on a subjected, structured quality and perpetuates existing power relations in society. Foucault's view of identity as a *description* rather than an essence affected profoundly the development of social science and humanities disciplines. In cultural studies, for instance, Hall (2000) and others use the term 'identification' to refer to the process of temporary stabilisation or 'cut' in the flow of language and meaning by which we try to fix difference, and put closure around the unstable meanings of signifiers in the discursive field. Similarly, some narrative theorists focus on the way storytellers take up subject positions in relation to 'master narratives' (Bamberg, 2004). In social psychology, Hollway and Jefferson (2005: 147) blend Foucault's notion of 'a subject located in social realities mediated ... by social discourses' with psychoanalysis in order to understand the role of psychic defences in the construction of the self. Wetherell's (1998; see also Wetherell and Edley, 1999; Reynolds, 2008) critical discursive psychological perspective is a 'two-sided approach' that combines the notion of 'subject position' with analyses of rhetoric, global patterns of sense-making and 'interpretative repertoires' to understand how identity is accomplished in 'micro-political contexts'.

In contrast to theorised accounts of discourse and identity stemming from French cultural theory, an alternative tradition based in ethnomethodology (EM) and conversation analysis developed in the social sciences during the latter part of the twentieth century. EM (literally, 'the study of people's methods') is a programme developed by the sociologist, Garfinkel (1967) who was influenced by the phenomenological philosophy of Schütz (1962) and Goffman's (1959) work on the interaction order. Garfinkel's basic idea was that people in society, or *members*, continuously engage in making sense of the world and, in doing so, methodically display their understandings of it: making their activities 'visibly-rational-and-reportable-for-all-practical-purposes' (1967: vii). Social interaction became central to EM's project of explicating members' methods for producing orderly and accountable social activities via CA which, since its inception, has developed into an empirical science for understanding everyday life. For Schegloff (1996: 4), a key figure in the development of CA, talk-in-interaction is 'the primordial scene of social life … through which the work of the constitutive institutions of societies gets done'. It is through talking that we live our lives, build and maintain relationships, and establish *'who we are to one another'* (Drew, 2005: 74, emphasis added).

EM and CA adopt an indexical, context-bound understanding of identity, in which 'the self', if it is anything, is an oriented-to, recipient-designed *accomplishment of interaction*. This means that categorical phenomena like identity are studied as phenomena of the sequential organisation of talk and other conduct in interaction. EM and CA are often aligned with constructionism and thus anti-essentialism, sharing a focus on the investigation of knowledge production (Lynch, 1993) and understanding 'the ways in which the world is *rendered* objectively available and is *maintained* as such' (Heritage, 1984: 220). Ethnomethodologists place reality temporarily in brackets, adopting the position of 'ethnomethodological indifference' (Garfinkel and Sacks, 1970: 63) in order to study how people maintain a sense of a commonly shared, objectively existing world. For EM it is a 'basic mistake' to assume that we need to 'adopt a theoretical stance on "reality" at all' (Francis, 1994: 105), partly because preoccupations about ontology inhibit close analysis of members' practices (Button and Sharrock, 2003). In everyday life, people generally treat 'identity' as a real thing that they can know about themselves and other people, and are not generally sent into a 'metaphysical spin' about their ontological status (Francis,

1994). And if people do question their own or someone else's membership of an identity category – that is, make it accountable – then this is something we can study (Stokoe, 2008).

Despite this gloss of the 'theory' of EM and CA, these traditions, and their relation in discursive psychology (Edwards, 2007; Edwards and Potter, 1992; Potter and Hepburn, 2007), are often criticised for their *atheoretical* and empirical ('empiricist') practices and lack of accountability to, and interest in, social theory. For these reasons, the keenest – often caricatured – debate about identity theory and method has been between the two 'sides' we have outlined here (Billig, 1999; Schegloff, 1997; Wetherell, 1998). However, it is in the EM/CA field that one finds a wealth of close analysis of naturally occurring materials that shows precisely *that and how* identity categories of all kinds figure systematically in, and are consequential for, social action: for example, in institutional care homes for the disabled (Antaki et al., 2007), doctor–patient consultations (Kitzinger, 2005), neighbour complaints and police interrogation (Stokoe, 2003; Stokoe and Edwards, 2007), gender identity clinics (Speer and Green, 2007) and classroom interaction (Benwell and Stokoe, 2002; Stokoe, 2006).

Having outlined the history and development of, broadly, 'macro' and 'micro' approaches to discourse and identity, we move on to now to focus on the details of these competing perspectives and their distinct warrants for analysing identity. We outline the methodological assumptions of both broad traditions and review the range of theorists, methods and approaches that are associated with each.

## DISCOURSES, GENEALOGIES, NARRATIVES AND INTERTEXTUALITY

Our first set of approaches is united by a 'macro' view of identity: subjects adopt or inhabit available *positions in*, or are *positioned by*, discourses that determine their sense of self and relationships with others. A number of principles underpin these approaches: (1) identities are objectively, historically and culturally *determined*; (2) analysts must import cultural understandings about available discourses to analyse fully the scope of identity work being done; (3) analysis attempts to connect micro (for example, the fine-grained details of talk and text) and macro contexts of discourse (the broader, social and ideological structures within which they are situated); and (4) discourse actively mediates, determines and conditions people's experiences of the world. In other words, discourse is both constitutive and reflective of social reality.

The macro view of identity is heavily influenced by two key strands in the historical development of Michel Foucault's writings. First, based on *The Archaeology of Knowledge* (1972) and *Discipline and Punish*: *The Birth of the Prison* (1975), social life and identities are understood as structured via a system of institutional, power-asymmetrical discourses. Many discourse analysts therefore examine the way public discourses are mobilised or disavowed by speakers and text producers. For instance, Sunderland (2004) draws together work that has identified various gendered discourses like 'the male sex drive discourse' (in which men have sexual wants and needs and women are the passive recipients or subjects of men's desire), and 'compulsory heterosexuality' (in which presumed sexual orientation and what counts as a normative relationship is inscribed). Second, Foucault's (1977) genealogical account of the subject represents a deconstructive mode of enquiry into formations of the self using a documentary and historiographical mode of analysis. Two main principles inform this genealogical approach: tracing the formation of discourses or identities to identify the events and circumstances by which they become arbitrarily 'fixed' and naturalised (see Carabine's [2001] documentary analysis of the discourse

of unmarried motherhood 1830–1990), and challenging the teleology and coherence of objects and identities, partly by foregrounding the possibility of alternative systems of intelligibility: '..."what we are now" is not meant as a simple description of the current state of things. Rather it is an attempt that "now" is an unstable victory won at the expense of other possible nows' (Shapiro, 1992: 12).

Foucault's notion of the 'discursively produced subject' is also reflected in 'performativity' theory developed by Judith Butler (1990). Butler suggests that identity is constructed via an available set of discourses people both inhabit and employ, but also a *performance* with all the connotations of anti-essentialism, transience, versatility and masquerade this implies. Nonetheless Butler stresses that a subject may not transcend the (gendered) discourses within which it is situated: 'there is no gender identity behind the expressions of gender; that identity is performatively constituted by the very "expressions" that are said to be its results' (1990: 33). While the constraints of these pre-constituted histories mean that identity will not necessarily be the ideal, self-determined product of a reflexive agent, at the same time the very *repetition* that inheres in its performance guarantees the *possibility* of change. Each new performance may entail the introduction of new elements: intertextual borrowings, resignification, reflexivity and disruptive tropes such as irony. In this way, Butler reconfigures Foucault's 'unnuanced' account of the subject to accommodate concepts of both structure and agency. Performativity theory has been eagerly appropriated by a number of language and gender theorists (Cameron, 1997; Coates, 1998; Hall and Livia, 1997) for whom it offers a model of gender that is emergent in discourse, versatile and adaptive to its contextual demands, but also frequently conservative or gender-normative.

Critical discourse analysis (CDA) is a Foucauldian-inspired, interdisciplinary branch of linguistics that explores the ideological workings of language in representing the world. Within CDA, identity is constituted in the grammar of language, both at the level of representation, in terms of the relationship between text and reader or conversational participants, and also in terms of the 'expressive' dimension that reveals a subject's attitudes and ideologies (Fairclough, 1989). Like Foucauldian discourse analysis, CDA identifies the discourses associated with practices or institutions that may operate 'interdiscursively' across a range of contexts (Chouliaraki and Fairclough, 1999; Wodak and Meyer, 2001). The assumption is that such discourses operate as points of identification, to be taken up, ascribed to, or inculcated by social actors. Like other approaches discussed, CDA attempts to forge links between 'micro' and 'macro' contexts, arguing that a complete analysis of discourse involves detailed engagement with a textual product ('text'), a consideration of the wider discourses in which the text is situated ('discursive practice'), and an analysis of the context of socio-cultural practice ('social practice'), such as production, transmission and consumption (Fairclough, 1995). Despite its ostensibly Foucauldian premise, CDA adopts a critical realist ontology, and its practitioners, particularly Fairclough, are clear that the Foucauldian account presents an abstracted and exaggerated version of the powerless 'subject', and fails to engage with the details of language as *situated practice* (Fairclough, 1994).

CDA is not characterised by a single methodology, but draws eclectically from a number of linguistic frameworks. One of these is *systemic functional linguistics* (SFL), a lexico-grammatical framework developed by Halliday (1995), employed by Fairclough (2001) and adapted by van Leeuwen (1996) in his taxonomy of representations of social actors in texts. The discourse-historical branch of CDA pioneered by the Vienna School, conversely favours more interdisciplinary approaches including ethnography, argumentation and rhetorical analysis (Wodak and Meyer, 2001).

Narrative analysis, positioning theory and critical discursive psychology complete this overview of Foucauldian-inspired approaches to the analysis of identity in discourse. Narrative theorists argue that we live in a 'storytelling society' through which we make sense of our lives and the events that happen in it (Denzin, 2000). Most narrative work adopts a constructionist understanding of discourse, or narrative, as constitutive of 'reality'. Selves and identities are therefore constituted in talk, and therefore in narrative as 'storied selves' (Sarbin, 1986). Narrative theorists argue that the local stories we tell about ourselves are connected in some way to wider cultural stories (or 'master narratives', 'cultural plotlines', 'discourses', 'interpretative repertoires'). This kind of inter-dependency between personal stories and culturally circulating plot lines is another common focus for narrative theorists.

The connection between 'on the ground' storytelling and wider cultural narratives is developed in a strand of narrative identity work based on 'positioning theory' (PT) (Bamberg, 2004; Davies and Harré, 1990; Harré and van Langenhove, 1991; Harré and Moghaddam, 2003). Positioning theorists examine the co-construction of identity between storyteller and audience. 'Positioning' refers to the process through which speakers adopt, resist and offer 'subject positions' (identities) that are made available in 'master narratives' or 'discourses'. For example, speakers can position themselves (and others) as victims or perpetrators, active or passive, powerful or powerless, and so on. The narrative of 'heterosexual romance' makes positions such as heroic prince/passive princess, or husband/wife available, and tells us what sorts of events do and do not belong to that narrative. People position themselves in relation to these subject positions, engaging in the 'discursive practices through which romantic love is made into a lived narrative' (Davies and Harré, 1990: 53). PT posits an intimate connection between subject positioning and social power relations; such that the analytic approach attends to identity work at the micro-conversational and macro socio-political levels. However, like CDA, positioning theorists argue against a wholly agentless sense of master discourses in which identity construction is constrained by a restrictive set of subject positions available. Instead, they claim that people may resist, negotiate, modify or refuse positions, thus preserving individual agency in identity construction (Bamberg, 2004; Sclater, 2003).

Another strand of discourse and identity work draws not just on notions of 'subject positions' but also on poststructuralism and the sociology of science. Potter and Wetherell's (1987) discourse analysis, developed as *critical discursive psychology* by Wetherell and her colleagues (Reynolds and Wetherell, 2003; Seymour-Smith et al., 2002; Wetherell and Edley, 1999), attempts to bring together, like CDA, the macro and the micro. Wetherell (1998) rejects what she sees as a purely micro-level approach, arguing that talk represents only a partial fragment of social life. Her proposed solution is a 'synthetic' approach to analysis, which combines micro-analytic attention to conversational detail with wider discourses and cultural-historical contexts. The resulting analytical approach is a 'genealogical' one which aims to trace normative practices, values and sense-making through both historical and synchronic intertextual analysis: 'The genealogical approach [...] suggests that in analysing our always partial piece of the argumentative texture we also look to the broader forms of intelligibility running through the texture more generally' (Wetherell, 1998: 403).

In Foucauldian-inspired research about the construction of masculinities in interviews with 17–18-year-old men, Wetherell (1998), and Wetherell and Edley (1997; Edley and Wetherell, 1999) adopt a grounded and indexical approach to the identification of subject positions in the young men's narratives, and then generalise the 'institutionalised forms of intelligibility' to which these subject positions are culturally attached, such as 'male sexuality as performance and achievement, a repertoire around alcohol and disinhibition, and an ethics of sexuality as legitimated by relationships and disinhibition' (1998: 400). Wetherell argues that such subject positions are not merely 'taken up' in a passive way, but do highly situated, interactional 'work'. At the same time, they are attached to prior, culturally familiar discourses situated within already-circulating, shared repertoires and thus a *resource* for the micro exigencies of identity work in talk. An example of a 'prior' subject position can be found in Wetherell's analysis of a story about one young man, Aaron, and his night out in which he 'went with' four women. At one point in the narration, one of the other participants, Phil describes Aaron as being on the 'moral low ground because he was like (.) gigolo Casanova whatever' (1998: 397). For Wetherell, the use of the term 'gigolo Casanova' is an instance of how existing narratives and discourses, richly imbued with historical and cultural meanings (a 'gigolo' is a male escort paid for his sexual favours, whilst 'Casanova' was a fictional 'great lover') are invoked as shorthand for particular kinds of ambiguous male sexual and moral behaviour. By analysing the way in which situated, local interactional identity work draws on existing interpretative repertoires, Wetherell examines the question preoccupying many discourse and identity theorists: what is the relationship between the micro and the macro in identity analysis?

### Discourses, genealogies, narratives and intertextuality: Case study

The approaches discussed above propose that identity is an expression not only of current textual or conversational contexts, but also contexts of circulating discourses, scripts and ideologies. To see such approaches might 'look like' in practice, consider the following data fragment,[1] which comes from recorded conversation between a small group of young women students in the UK who are getting ready to go out for the night. The women regularly meet in one friends' house to get dressed, do makeup, drink and chat before going out. Here, Sophie, Chloe and Emma are talking.

## 1. VH-1

| | | |
|---|---|---|
| 1 | S | An' once I left his though he was like he didn't say |
| 2 | | anything to |
| 3 | E | Oh … [sympathetically]. That's men!! That's what James |
| 4 | | was like on Sunday |
| 5 | S | But I was kinda like- cos- but that night I'd alread |
| 6 | | said boyfriends aren't worth the hassle. |
| 7 | E | [laughing] |
| 8 | S | An' then when we kinda left I was like well, I'll see |
| 9 | | ya when I see ya sometime maybe soon later I don't |
| 10 | | know. [laughs] |
| 11 | E | [laughing] Oh!! it's so compli |
| 12 | S | And when I phoned him on Saturday, an' he was just |
| 13 | | playin' it so cool on the phone I wanted to hit him. |
| 14 | E | [laughing] |

[…]

| | | |
|---|---|---|
| 15 | C | Are we thinking … Uh- do we think pink |
| 16 | S | Yes definitely yeh. |
| 17 | C | Yeh, okay I'll just dry my hair. |
| 18 | | Can I borrow your straighteners. |
| 19 | S | Yes. They're on and they should be hot. |
| 20 | C | Ooh fantastic. [leaves the room] |
| 21 | S | But um- d'you remember the eighteen |
| 22 | | year old I pulled on Wednesday? [laughing] |

[…]

| | | |
|---|---|---|
| 23 | S | When I first pulled Anthony that night I was doin' m |
| 24 | | challenge I had to pull first year, second year, an' |
| 25 | | third year an' I pulled my first year, |
| 26 | E | Yeah that was wicke |
| 27 | S | An' then I was like scourin' for my second year an' |
| 28 | | then I met Anthony an' I kinda like gave up on the |
| 29 | | challenge cos I was a bit … |
| 30 | E | I remember you tellin' me about the challenge. |
| 31 | | [laughing] |
| 32 | S | Well I gotta new one now. |
| 33 | E | Oh God!! |

[…]

| | | |
|---|---|---|
| 34 | S | But now I'm kinda like y'know I'm gonna pull anyone I |
| 35 | | want, until, y'know, he asks. |
| 36 | E | Until the- yeah exactly. |

```
37   S     Cos I've gone an' made the first move now an' asked
38         him out,
39   E     Mmm,
40   S     So now it's up to him when he's available, to ask me
41         out.
42   E     It is yeah!
43   S     Otherwise he ain't nothin' off me.
44   E     That's right yeh. It's up to him now.
45   S     Cos I've only like- cos he's the type to jus' sit down
46         and drink. So he's never gonna be on the dance floor
47         or anything so he's the type 'oh see you outside at
48         the end an' everythin' an' gonna come back with you,
49         I'll be like nuh-huh.
50   E     Oh yeah, yeah.
51   S     No. not anymore I'm not that drunk I want it that
52         much!!
53   E     Oh yeah!
```

                                [...]

```
54   E     I texted him last time, so I dunno, I hope he texts,
55         bu
56   S     The thing is, he lives in Manchester so
57   E     I know yeah.
58   S     If you wannit to work, you're gonna have to put a lot
59         of effort into it. An' he obviously hasn't got much
60         time to come down,
61   E     I know he's so busy,
62   S     So it'd have to be all you, an' that's not good.
63   E     Yeh no I'll have to see. I dunno … I do really like
64         him but-
```

                                [...]

```
65   S     D'you think hair down or hair up,
66   C     I like it down,
67   S     I better put- me hairband on I gotta do my makeu
68   C     It looks nice, your hair, y'can see the blonde now,
69         not that you couldn't see it before
70   S:    Oh!!! There's a spider!! [squealing and laughing]
71   C     Oh!! I want it out!! [squealing and laughing]
```

In the above extract we can observe two competing discourses of 'femininity'. The first is a traditional discourse: concerns with appearance and wearing pink (for example, 'do we think pink?'; 'D'you think hair down or hair up'); making supportive assessments (for example, 'I like it down'; 'It looks nice'); being afraid of insects and reacting in a stereotypically 'female' manner ('Oh!!! There's a spider!!', 'Oh!! I want it out!!'), and adherence to a traditional hetero-romantic plotline which presupposes that women will be passive and men active: ('it's up to him when he's available, to ask me out'). Additionally, the women's talk perpetuates the ideology that men and women are essentially distinct and homogenous in their behaviours and values: ('That's men!'; 'boyfriends aren't worth the hassle!'). The process of generalising about men is itself an act of identity, consciously aligning oneself with what, by default in a binary model of gender, one is not (Tajfel, 1982). This performance of familiar cultural conduct ensures that the gendered discourses are further sustained.

The second discourse is one inflected by the values of a modern form of 'laddish' masculinity. This identity has emerged and been identified in the British popular media as 'ladette', a concept defined by Ridley (2004: 6, cited in Jackson and Tinker, 2007) as someone 'mouthy and always up for a laugh [who] can smoke eight fags at once and drink all her weekly alcohol units in two hours. Likes wearing tight jeans and skimpy tops' p. 6 (see also Schippers, 2007; Whelehan, 2000). Jackson and Tinkler (2007) identify the historical forebear of 'ladette' femininity in the form of 'modern girls' represented in print media from the early twentieth century (in similarly 'moral panic' discourse). In our data, Sophie and Emma do complex and contradictory identity work that revolves around these two competing discourses of 'femininity'. The master narrative of the plot makes available the gendered subject positions of 'passive female' and 'active male', and although these positions are not taken up without resistance – the identity positions are variable and fluctuating often within one turn at talk – the trajectory of the narrative is ultimately traditional in its form.

At a gross level, Sophie is telling a number of interrelated narratives about her relationship with Anthony (lines 1–14, 21–53). Emma tells a 'second story' (Sacks, 1992) about her relationship with her own boyfriend, James

(lines 54–64). These are interspersed with short episodes about appearance as the participants get ready to go out (lines 15–20, 65–69). Within Sophie's narrative, there are two main plotlines with corresponding identities being performed and subject positions being taken up. In the first plotline, Sophie positions herself within a conventional narrative of heterosexual romance, taking up a passive position as a woman who waits for the man to make arrangements and 'take the next step': 'once I left his though he was like he didn't say anything to …' (lines 1–2). Here, the assumption is that Anthony, not Sophie, should be the one to say 'something to make arrangements'. As Allen (2003: 217) points out, 'the dominance of (hetero)sexual identity and discursive practices that support an active male and passive female sexuality are deeply embedded within social and political participation and perceived as normative'.

In reply, Emma produces a generalised assessment of Antony followed by some initial elements of a 'second story' ('That's men! That's what James was like on Sunday'). The fact that Emma makes the comment, 'That's men!', demonstrates the mundane intelligibility of Sophie's dilemma *precisely as* a situation that has a common plotline, with characters taking particular roles, beyond the immediate context of this conversation (Stokoe, 2009). This is picked up in two ways by Sophie in subsequent turns: First, in her return to narration, Sophie reports her own private reflection on her situation 'boyfriends aren't worth the hassle', again generalising about her situation via the plural category 'boyfriends' (lines 5–6). Second, she reports Anthony's response to an earlier telephone call 'an' he was just playin' it so cool on the phone I wanted to hit him!!' (lines 12–13). Here, the idiomatic phrase 'playin' it cool' is another procedure for making connections between current stories and wider circulating narratives; its very use, like categorical formulations 'That's men!', require that recipients know how to interpret current situations using familiar, iterative cultural resources.

In contrast to the traditionally passive form of femininity we see Sophie occupy here, we can observe the alternative 'ladette' form based in hegemonic masculinity, in which Sophie talks actively of 'pulling'[2] men and engaging in a 'challenge' to pull one male student from each year: 'D'you remember the eighteen year old I pulled on Wednesday?' (lines 21–22). As the story unfolds, we learn that when 'scourin' for my second year Sophie 'met Anthony'. In the first part of her story, then, Sophie positions herself agentively, as a powerful woman who takes the lead in identifying potential conquests and 'pulling' them. Note that 'to pull' is a transitive verb, with Sophie's agency built into the grammar of her story. Sophie therefore distances herself from stereotypical femininity as a way of claiming power, thus opposing 'stereotypical or normalised feminine positioning [and rejecting] the disempowerment that comes with it' (Paechter, 2006: 257).

However, this power slips away as Sophie reaches the outcome of the story: when she met Anthony she 'gave up' the challenge. This is presumably because Sophie wanted a relationship with Anthony that involved more than a one night stand. Further complexity with regards to agency, and femininity, emerges as Sophie provides the 'resolution' (Labov, 2001) to the story 'But now I'm kinda like y'know I'm gonna pull anyone I want, until, y'know, he asks' (line 34–35). Because Anthony has not been more active in

their relationship, Sophie will take an active role not by pursuing Anthony but by pursuing other men. But she will do this until Anthony 'asks'; that is, takes the active role in pursuing Sophie.

A major feature of Sophie's and Emma's narratives is about making initiating moves and reciprocity. Wowk observes that 'a conventional view of women is that they are "passive" and should "wait til asked"' (1984: 78). If women proposition men, they become accountable as a 'woman'. Despite the fact that these data were recorded in 2003/4, and despite 'radically shifting social landscapes regarding representations of gendered identities and sexuality' (Jackson and Cram, 2003: 113–14), our observations about these women's conversations suggests that little has changed with regards to normative expectations about what women and men do in sexual relations. Ideas about, for example, 'who calls who' and 'who makes the first move' in heterosexual relationships are massively pervasive in everyday and popular culture. There are thousands of books, articles and advice pages written for women about what do to 'when men don't call back' (Harmon, 2005). Such themes also litter television scripts. For example, here is a fragment of scripted dialogue from the sitcom *Friends*. One of the characters, Chandler, is reporting a date he had the previous night.

## 2. Friends Season X: 'The one with the evil orthodontist'

Chandler:     I am telling you, years from now, schoolchildren will study it as one of the greatest first dates of all time. It was unbelievable! We could totally be ourselves, we didn't have to play any games...

Monica:       So have you called her yet?

Chandler:     Let her know I like her? What are you, insane? It's the next day! How needy do I want to seem? [To the other men]

              I'm right, right?

Joey and Ross: Oh, yeah. Yeah. Let her dangle.

Monica:       I can't believe my parents are actually pressuring me to find one of you people.

Phoebe:       Oh, God, just do it! [Grabbing the phone] Call her! Stop being so testosterone-y!

Monica's reference to 'you people' indexes male gender and the activity of 'who calls who' is further gendered in Phoebe's turn: if Chandler phones his date he will not be so 'testosterone-y'. In other words, to be a man means to let women 'dangle' rather than call them immediately to make arrangements for the next date. By making intertextual connections with examples from popular culture (often exaggerated in comedy to shore up the commonplace normativeness of gender polarity, while simultaneously emphasising its absurdity) we can strengthen our warrants for arguing that these are familiar, culturally available interpretations of what constitutes normative gendered identities (Benwell, 2005).

A similar instance of intertextual allusion – this time relating to the kind of 'ladette' identity we have so far identified in our data – can be detected in the activity of these young women drinking the alcoholic drink, Lambrini as they prepare to go out (elsewhere in the conversation, they discuss getting more drink: 'I'll get the other Lambrini out the fridge as well', and assess Lambrini's qualities: 'Once you've drunk a Lambrini anything goes down.'). The activity, context and identities of the women in our data above strongly recall a series of British advertisements for Lambrini. In the advertisement below, for instance, three young women are also getting ready for a night out, and are discussing how to wear G-string underwear. 'V' is the voiceover.

Here, A is asking whether or not to wear her G-string so that it is visible or not. B turns this into a parody, hoisting the G-string up over her shoulders and dancing around with it. All the women laugh, as the voiceover joins in (also with a laugh in her voice). The women are 'Lambrini Girls', who know how to joke around and play with convention. We also have the catchphrase, 'Lambrini Girls Just Wanna Have Fun', which echoes the title of a 1980s pop song 'Girls Just Wanna Have Fun' by Cyndi Lauper. The similarities to our data extract are striking. Like the Lambrini girls, Sophie, Emma and Chloe are also preoccupied with

their appearance and solicit opinion and affirmation from one another: ('do we think pink?' 'd'you think hair down or hair up?'). They also ironically play with the excessive femininity of their behaviour and responses (laughing at the same time as squealing at a spider). And they similarly breach normative expectations of femininity by adopting a more 'masculine' approach to dating and sex ('I'm gonna pull anyone I want'). The feminine values, discourses and identities shared between this advertising campaign and our own data is highly suggestive of the way in which discourses of gender circulate endlessly throughout various contexts of popular culture, in turn influencing and being influenced by lived experience.

The observations we have made about competing and contradictory gender identities within one sequence of talk have been addressed by a number of gender theorists, suggesting that there is some kind of genealogical coherence about the state and trajectory of modern femininity: one that challenges traditional gender politics and challenges the status of hegemonic masculinity. Schippers (2007: 94) argues that:

> Practices and characteristics that are stigmatised and sanctioned if embodied by women include having sexual desire for other women, being promiscuous, 'frigid', or sexually inaccessible, and being aggressive. These are characteristics that, when embodied by women, constitute a refusal to complement hegemonic masculinity in a relation of subordination and therefore are threatening to male dominance [...] constitute a refusal to embody the relationship between masculinity and femininity demanded by gender hegemony. (2007: 95)

These intertextual connections between sites of popular culture and 'lived discourse' point to the importance for Foucauldian approaches in situating identity work within a broader texture of cultural meaning, ideology and significance, and the theoretical possibility of exploring a range of relevant sites of culture informing and being informed by the discursive moment. As Wodak suggests in her 'discourse-historical' CDA:

> A fully 'critical' account of discourse would [...] require a theorisation and description of both the

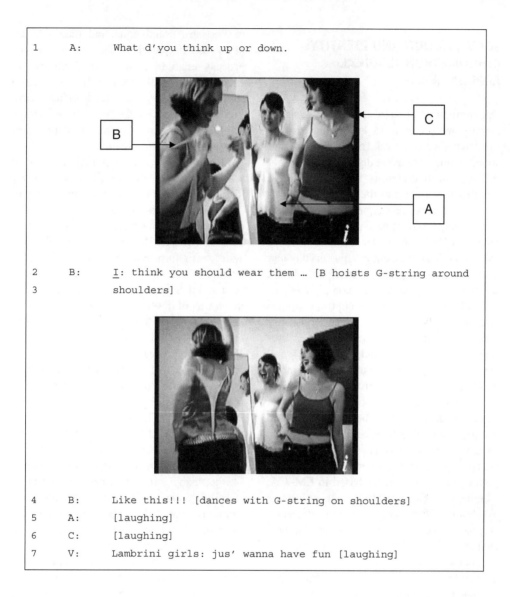

```
1      A:      What d'you think up or down.
```

```
2      B:      I: think you should wear them … [B hoists G-string around
3              shoulders]
```

```
4      B:      Like this!!! [dances with G-string on shoulders]
5      A:      [laughing]
6      C:      [laughing]
7      V:      Lambrini girls: jus' wanna have fun [laughing]
```

social processes and structures which give rise to the production of a text, and of the social structures and processes within which individuals or groups as social historical subjects, create meanings in their interactions with texts. (2001: 3)

The fact that our analysis only scratches the surface of the infinite possibilities of the 'interpenetration of communicative contexts' (Cicourel, 1992: 292) is testimony to the huge (and therefore problematic) ambitions of a potentially limitless analysis. The challenge of invoking relevant 'contexts' in an accountable,

grounded way can also lead to the term 'context' being wielded as a:

polemical, critical tool […] equivalent to 'what I noticed about your topic that you didn't write about'. With that club, I can relativise what you have to say by reference to what I have noticed or care about, potentially diminish or obliterate what you have offered and put what I have offered on center stage. (Schegloff, 1992: 214–5)

One way of avoiding these methodological conundrums is to situate analysis firmly within the bounds of the discourse data itself. It is to such analytic approaches that we now turn.

## SOCIAL ACTION AND IDENTITY: ETHNOMETHODOLOGICAL APPROACHES

One limitation of starting any analysis of identity with a view to examining *empirically* what is first and foremost *theorised* about identity – relevant discourses, multiply shifting and fluid identity 'subject positions' – is that it can obscure the fact that, in conversation at least, participants are producing *orderly* conversation, in which issues such as 'contradiction', or 'wider context' are for them to notice, and manage. In everyday and institutional conversation, participants do not see their own identities as complicated, or contradictory (notable exceptions might include Speer's studies of the gender identity clinic, in which one's own identity is precisely the issue at hand, see Speer and Parsons [2006]). This is because concerns of that kind are resolutely grounded in identity *theory*, rather than via looking to see what real life is actually like. The inter-textual and historical components of analysis are limited by what we, as analysts, already know are plausible as related components.

In contrast, approaches based in EM–CA, membership categorisation and discursive psychology – do not start with theorised notions of 'identity', 'discourses' or 'subject positions'. Instead, they start with sequences of social interaction and examine action accomplished in it. CA is a distinctive approach to the study of social life, and its aim, for founder Harvey Sacks (1984: 26), is to be an observational science of society and social action grounded in the 'details of actual events'. CA involves the study of technical transcripts of recordings of everyday and institutional talk and other conduct (such as, gesture, prosody, interaction with the material environment) in interaction. For any recording, the analytic process starts by identifying its macro-organisation and the courses of action that participants move through. Then, at a micro level, analysts identify paired turns of actions, pre-sequences,

turn-constructional units and their components and turn design. This 'slow motion' process enables conversation analysts to show how 'small' features of interaction (pauses, repairs, word selection) may have 'big' consequences for the conversation's trajectory, and hence the social relationships and lives of the participants.

In addition to the sequential analysis of talk, Sacks also developed a particularly identity-relevant theme in his work on 'membership categorisation'. This has since been developed into membership categorisation analysis (MCA) (Hester and Eglin, 1997). In addition to turn-by-turn sequencing, MCA attends to the situated use of categories in interaction. Sacks developed his ideas around the notion of the 'membership categorisation device' (MCD). MCDs comprise a collection of *categories*, and some *rules of application*. Examples of *categories* include man, anarchist, teacher, Australian, prostitute, lesbian and so on. Sacks provides an example taken from a published collection of children's written stories: 'The baby cried. The mommy picked it up' (Sacks, 1972), showing that we hear links between 'mommy' and 'baby'; specifically that the 'mommy' is the 'mommy' of the 'baby'. In this case, the MCD of 'family' collects together the categories 'mommy' and 'baby'. Categories are linked to particular actions ('category-bound activities') or characteristics ('natural predicates') such that there are conventional expectations about what constitutes a 'mommy's' or 'baby's' normative behaviour and absences are accountable. Recent developments tie membership categorisation and sequential analysis closely together (Stokoe, 2006; 2009), showing how categories and category-implicative descriptions function as constituent features in members' practices for accomplishing particular social actions.

Discursive psychology (DP) sits in the same family as CA and MCA. The term was first coined by Edwards and Potter (1992) in their book of the same title. DP's roots lie in a variety of theoretical-philosophical and empirical traditions. In addition to EM and

CA, these include the language philosophy of Wittgenstein (1958), constructivist approaches to human development (Vygotsky, 1978), and social studies of science (Gilbert and Mulkay, 1984). DP's original goal was to unpack, critique and 'respecify' (Button, 1991) the topics of social, developmental and cognitive psychology, and their methods of investigation (Edwards and Potter, 2001). It therefore aimed to challenge mainstream psychology in much the same way that EM and CA challenged mainstream sociology. DP comprises a fundamental shift from treating psychological states (for example, anger, intention, identity) as operating behind talk, causing people to say the things they do. In this way, DP challenges the traditional psychological treatment of language as a channel to underlying mental processes, and the experimental study of those processes. Instead, it studies how commonsense psychological concepts are deployed in, oriented to and handled in the talk and texts that comprise social life. Thus language is not treated as an externalisation of underlying thoughts, motivations, memories or attitudes, but as *constitutive* of them. Note that these are not *ontological* claims about the status of 'inner minds' or 'external realities': the focus is on 'how descriptions of persons and their mental states are tied to, or implied by, descriptions of actions, events, and objects in the external world' (Edwards, 2004: 186). The external world, or people's traits and dispositions, are treated by speakers as common sense evidential resources for making inferences, building descriptions, resisting accusations of interest, and so on.

From these micro perspectives, any analysis of identity categories is based in what participants do and say, rather than in what analysts take to be relevant as a function of their hypotheses, research questions, politics or theory (Antaki and Widdicombe, 1998; Kitzinger, 2005). One problem with studies that start out examining, say, how women perform femininity in discourse, is that categories are not studied 'in the activities in which they're employed' (Sacks, 1992: 27).

This means that analysts are in the business of *reproducing* rather than *studying* gendered 'facts' about the world, thereby reifying gender stereotypes and hierarchies. In contrast, the analytic task of CA is 'to analyze the workings of those categories, not to merely use them as they are used in the world' (Jefferson, 2004a: 118). To warrant an analytic claim that an identity category is relevant to any stretch of interaction, the analyst must be able to demonstrate that such identities are linked to specific actions. There are two key issues:

(1) *The problem of relevance*: Given the indefinitely extendable number of ways any person may be categorised, which, from a range of potential identities, is relevant? The answer is to go by what is demonstrably relevant to participants 'at the moment that whatever we are trying to produce an account for occurs' (Schegloff, 1991: 50).

(2) *The issue of procedural consequentiality*: If we can establish that a particular identity category is relevant, can we see that it is consequential for participants, in terms of its trajectory, content, character, or organisational procedures? Does it have 'determinate consequences for the talk?' (Heritage, 2005: 111).

In Stokoe's (2006) analysis of police interrogations, she draws on both sequential CA and Sacks's (1992) notion of 'membership categories' to demonstrate not 'just' that identity categories crop up in conversation, but that people *do things* with them: accomplish bits of interactional business by selecting particular categories, by describing people in one way rather than another way, and by formulating and reformulating categories and descriptions. In police interviews, the suspect's main business is often denying the charges put to them. One methodical use of categories comes in environments where denials get done: the suspect categorises him/herself as *someone who does not harm a particular category of persons*. In Edwards's discursive psychological analysis of the modal verb 'would' in the same interrogations, he shows how it is used by suspects 'to claim a disposition to act in ways inconsistent with whatever offence they are accused of', its value being in the way that 'its semantics provide for a sense of back-dated predictability with regard to the actions in question' (2006a: 475). In other words, because the suspect *wouldn't* (in general) do the kind of action s/he is charged with, s/he *didn't* do it (this time). Stokoe developed Edwards's observations about a particular feature of suspects' 'would-based' denials – that they regularly co-occur with a categorical reference term (for example, 'I wouldn't hit a woman'). By examining multiple instances of the same 'category-based denial' across a large corpus of data, Stokoe demonstrated how the study of identity categories can be tied to particular actions, done in particular kinds of sequential environments, as well as revealing a members' method, or interactional practice, for doing denials; in

this case, suspects' idiomatic use of self and other categorisations.

## Ethnomethodological approaches: Case study

For ethnomethodologically inspired analysis, then, it is important to show how participants' 'production of the world' is informed by particular identity categorisation devices, and 'that the parties were oriented to that categorisation device in producing and understanding – moment-by-moment – the conduct that composed its progressive realisation' (Schegloff, 2007: 475). Let us consider a final extract,[3] which comes from the same group of friends as they prepare for their night out. Sophie is talking to Chloe about her plans for the evening.

### 4:VH-1

```
1              (4.3) ((background conversation))
2    S:   Phil stoppin' in tonight. (or is he) (working).
3    C:   Um::::: (1.1) no 'he's off tomorrow but- (0.2) he's
4         not sure if he's out or not.
5              (0.4)
6    S:   ( ).
7              (0.4)
8    C:   Might be yeh but he's out with the lads.
9              (0.7)
10   S:   Yeh you won't be stuck to 'im then.=
11   C:   =No no:.
12              (0.8)
13   C:   Only like after twe[lve.
14   S:                      [Cos I hate that.
15              (0.3)
16   C:   Only after twelve.
17              (0.6)
18   C:   Cos [I miss him.
19   S:       [↑↑No:::. One. [indignant]
20   C:   Uh ↑heh ↑heh ↑heh
21              (1.0)
22   C:   One?
```

```
23   S:    One. yeah,
24   C:    All right.
25   S:    ↑↑Y'see ↑↑him ↑↑everyday?
26              (3.9)
27   S:    ↑↑Y'know??
28              (0.8)
29   S:    ↑↑Who's gonna look after all my ↑↑needs. [squeaky]
30         [( )
31   C:    [I see you everyday, I live next ↑↑door. [squeaky]
32         heh heh heh heh [heh
33   S:                        [It depends if I get myself booked up.
34   C:    If you get wha:t.
35   S:    If I get myself booked up.
36   C:    See that's the thing and there's yo(h)o hh heh heh
37                              [...]
```

After a lapse in talk, Sophie launches a new sequence with a question about what Chloe's boyfriend Phil is doing tonight. The design of this question is consequential for, and indeed hearably projects, the overall action trajectory of this sequence, which is Sophie's suspicion that Chloe might 'stick' to her boyfriend rather than spend time with her friend. Sophie's question, '[Is] Phil stoppin' in tonight.', is grammatically structured as a 'yes-no' interrogative (Raymond, 2003). A 'type-conforming' response to the question is 'yes' or 'no'; but by virtue of the question proffering a candidate answer in 'stopping in tonight', it is tilted towards a confirmatory response, 'yes [he is]'. However, what happens next is that at the end of Sophie's question, a complete 'turn constructional unit' (complete because it has completed an action; is grammatically and prosodically complete), Sophie herself takes the next TCU: Chloe does not come in at the 'transition-relevance place'.

Having issued the question, Sophie adds another TCU: '(or is he) (working)'. This provides an alternative possibility for Chloe to respond with: either 'yes [he is stopping in]' or 'yes [he is working]' and functions also to sequentially delete Chloe's lack of immediate response to Sophie's original

question. The second TCU also reduces the strength of the preference built into the first, making it easier for the next turn to be a dispreferred response. Notice that neither possibility projects a scenario in which Phil is coming out with Sophie and Chloe. This is why Sophie's first turn is hearably projecting trouble if Chloe gives a different answer, and this is what happens. Chloe's response indicates trouble: it is delayed by silence and other conduct ('um:::' (1.1)), which are typical features of dispreferred responses. She responds first to the second part of Sophie's question 'no 'he's off tomorrow' (so is not working); then to the first 'but- (0.2) he's not sure if he's out or not' (so is possibly not 'stopping in'). This is followed by a gap before Sophie says something inaudible. Chloe's next turn is an answer 'Might be yeh' plus an account 'but he's out with the lads'. This account seems still oriented to the trouble in this sequence, and the idiomatic formulation 'out with the lads' characterises a particular kind of culturally familiar activity Phil is planning to do.

Sophie formulates the upshot of Chloe's account in her next turn, 'you won't be stuck to 'im then' (line 10). This makes the kind of trouble that has been looming more explicit: Sophie wants Chloe to be *out with her*, rather than *ostensibly* so but in fact spending the night with her boyfriend. This is another 'yes-no' interrogative with a preferred answer, which Chloe supplies immediately, 'No no:.'. Stivers (2004: 260) shows how such 'multiple sayings' 'are a resource speakers have to display that their turn is addressing an in-progress course of action rather than only the just prior utterance', and function to 'communicate their stance that the prior speaker has persisted unnecessarily in the prior course of action and should properly halt their course of action'. Here, Chloe's 'No no:.' deals not only with answering Sophie's question, but also displays her understanding of the course of action that was projected at the start of the sequence: the issue of Phil's participation in their 'girls' night out'. However, after a delay, Chloe adds an 'increment' to her answer, 'Only like after twelve'. This somewhat transforms her initial answer, delimiting the boundaries of her planned actions. In overlap, and evidently not in response to this modifying increment, Sophie accounts for asking her question in the first place: 'Cos I hate that' (line 14). 'That' refers to the activity of being 'stuck' to one's boyfriend when one is meant to be out with friends. Chloe then repeats her answer 'only after twelve', which receives no immediate uptake from Sophie. Chloe provides an account for her answer, 'Cos I miss him'.

Sophie's overlapping turn (line 19) is responsive to Chloe's repetition of 'only after twelve': '↑↑No:::. One.', delivered with an 'indignant' voice quality. Chloe's initial response is laughter, rather than disagreement or confirmation of Sophie's proposal that Chloe joins Phil at one o'clock rather than twelve. At line 22, she produces a repair initiator 'one?', and Sophie confirms her proposal by repeating it and adding 'yeah,' (line 23). Chloe concedes at line 24 ('all right'). That Chloe's turn is a concession rather than enthusiastic response to Sophie's proposal is evidenced in Sophie's response, '↑↑Y'see ↑↑him ↑↑everyday?', which, along with her next two turns ('↑↑Y'know??'; '↑↑Who's gonna look after all my ↑↑needs.',

and note the lack of response from Chloe at lines 26 and 28) provide an account for why Chloe does not need to spend the evening with Phil. Chloe counters this in her eventual response 'I see you everyday, I live next ↑↑door. [squeaky] heh heh heh heh heh heh'. So here, Chloe challenges the presupposition of Sophie's account, that she sees Phil more than Sophie and 'owes' it to spend time with her friend looking after 'all her needs'. The laughter at the end of the turn works to modify the 'counter' and its dispreferred, challenging quality, thus mitigating the trouble that is emerging in the sequence. Sophie overlaps the end of this laughter saying 'It depends if I get myself booked up', which is not responsive to Chloe's previous turn but starts a new sequence about Sophie's activities when they are out. In other words, Sophie does not need Chloe if she meets a man: doing the very complainable thing she has accused Chloe of doing!

What can we say about 'identity' in this extract? The issue between the participants is to do with relationships: the appropriate activities of being a 'friend' in the context of other relationships such as romantic partnerships. In his work on membership categorisation, Sacks (1972: 37) discusses 'collection R' paired categories, including 'friend–friend', 'boyfriend–girlfriend', which are 'standardised' relational pairs that have 'a set of rights and obligations' in relation to each other. In this sequence, Sophie holds Chloe accountable for her possibly intended plans with regards to how much time she will spend with her friend or boyfriend, relevant to the normative duties and obligations of being a 'friend' (see also Land and Kitzinger's, 2007, analysis of a similar sequence in which one friend tells another 'don't blow off your girlfriends for guy:s,'). Pomerantz and Mandelbaum draw on Sacks to explain that 'people can be held accountable if they do not engage in the activities bound to whatever category they are an incumbent of. For example, if two "friends" meet each other in the street, they will normatively do what counts as appropriate greeting activities for members of that category. If they fail to engage in such conduct, they will be accountable for their missing activities' (2005: 152–3; see also Stokoe, 2003).

Here, the missing activity is a potential, rather than actual one. Sophie tells Chloe that she 'hates that'. The selection of 'that' generalises the complainable activity, and does not directly accuse Chloe of engaging in it. The sequence is saturated with moral work as Chloe's potential actions are formulated. This is because 'any consideration of the accountability of social conduct brings directly into focus moral dimensions of language use' (Drew, 1998: 295). The moral order emerges in descriptions of activities and what participants treat as legitimate warrants for certain sorts of action ascriptions (Jayyusi, 1984). It can also be displayed in category-relevant absences: if a person fails to fulfil their category-tied obligations, complaints may be relevant. In the above extract, both Sophie and Chloe are oriented to these obligations, and articulate, resist, challenge and counter them. Their conversation depends on a shared understanding of the rights and obligations that are expectable of 'friends', displaying 'the moral norms of friendship between young women' that Sophie claims Chloe may breach (Land and Kitzinger, 2007: 507).

This section has demonstrated the way identity categories are oriented to in the environment of complainability of possible conduct. The way Sophie designs her questions can be heard as preparing the grounds for a complaint, which emerges in a general rather than directly accusatory way. And the complainability and assessment of Chloe's potential conduct are grounded in the identity category 'friend'. We noted earlier that Chloe told Sophie that Phil might be having a night out 'with the lads'. The category 'lads' belongs to a collection that includes 'men', 'fellas' and so on, and these are partitions of the collection 'sex', the other major partition being 'female' (Sacks, 1992, vol. 1: 590–1). In this moment, Chloe makes relevant her membership of the 'other' partition. This logically excludes her from Phil's planned activity, and implies that she will be necessarily out with Sophie. Whether this can be called 'taking up a feminine subject position', or 'performing femininity', misses the point that the category is invoked in a specific way, to accomplish a social action, and attending to the business of her friendship with Sophie.

## CONCLUSION

This chapter has set out two broadly competing trajectories in discourse and identity research. We have shown how different theoretical and analytic lenses give a different purchase on discourse data, drawing attention to some features while obscuring others. We conclude now with some of the challenges, concerns and points of departure for future research on the ever-popular concept of 'identity', and its discursive analysis.

Throughout this chapter we have outlined two broad traditions of discourse analysis, both practically rooted in the fine-grained analysis of stretches of transcribed interaction. The differences between these two approaches are related mainly to definitions of 'context': ethnomethodological approaches rely on, and are limited to, the *local* interactional context as the site for identity analysis, whereas critical discursive, genealogical approaches are draw upon the analysts' assumptions about what aspects of the cultural and historical contexts are relevant for interpreting the data. Some commentators have criticised both traditions for their apparent 'failure' to engage with higher level theory and phenomena. For example, Hook argues that much discourse analytical work over-emphasises 'the linguistic and representational powers of language in isolation from the material arrangements of power in which they are enmeshed' (2001: 537–8). A second criticism is that micro-level analysis ignores, or does not 'access', people's 'subjectivity', 'experience' and 'unconscious'. In the new 'psychosocial' tradition, analysts 'look through' language at the 'interior' unconscious mind, to 'the divided psychosocial subject of unconscious conflict; a subject located in social realities mediated not only by social discourses but by psychic defences' (Hollway and Jefferson, 2005: 147) (a criticism also found within some forms of narrative analysts, for example, Crossley [2000]). As Sclater argues, 'it's as if there's little (if anything) more to "the self" than its multiple and shifting positionings in discourse, or language, its presentation in narrative' (2003: 324). A third, related criticism, is that an exclusive focus on the 'small' details of discourse neglects the embodied nature of social interaction.

These criticisms are united by a particular theory of language, in which any stretch of talk or text is treated as only a partial or superficial representation of what is analysable, obscuring the depth of the producer's 'experience', the unconscious motivations behind its production, the potency of its historical antecedents, the material power dynamics limiting its scope, and its embodied realisation. The solution is to import analysts' resources to 'fill out' what is inaccessible from the 'surface' of talk (Benwell and Stokoe, 2006; Edwards, 2006b, 2007). It is interesting that many who followed the 'discursive turn' in the 1970s and 1980s, and its radical re-specification of what language *is*, are now rejecting the basis on which the discursive turn was built, in which discourse is understood 'not as the product or expression of thoughts or mental states lying behind or beneath it, but as a domain of public accountability' (Edwards, 2006b: 41). Edwards has written extensively on the notion of 'the rich surface', countering the criticisms outline above:

> There is no realm of subjectivity, unconscious feelings, or objective reality, that language does not reach – indeed, the writings of those who are primarily concerned with such ostensibly language-independent and almost ineffable matters, is reflexive testimony to the adequacy of language for dealing with them. (2006b: 42)
>
> Nobody is claiming that discourse is all there is. However, the rush toward theorizing about context and subjectivity is being done without close attention to what is available on the surface. (2007: 47)

For identity researchers, then, the issues of where to look for and how to capture identity (what kinds of materials to analyse); what kinds of resources are needed to analyse it (what the analyst can bring to bear by virtue of their politics, academic position, education and training versus how participants display intersubjectivity and contextual relevance), and how to understand it ontologically (is it constructed or essential?) are the issues that are probably irresolvable. Academic arguments, like any other argument, once entrenched, become the stuff of debate, career and, eventually, history. For Hussein (2007: 821), a focus on the practical and the empirical is 'a corrective to theoretical posturing'. Likewise, we suggest that claims about ordinary people's identities should be grounded in the observable details of their lives before they are filtered through the academic machinery of theory.

## NOTES

1   This is an edited version of a longer fragment; breaks between episodes of talk are represented by […]. All names are pseudonyms.

2   In the UK context, 'to pull' refers to making a sexual conquest.

3   This sequence is transcribed using the conventions developed for CA (Jefferson, 2004b).

## REFERENCES

Allen, L. (2003) 'Girls want sex, boys want love: Resisting dominant discourses of (hetero) sexuality', *Sexualities*, 6 (2): 215–36.

Antaki, C. and Widdicombe, S. (1998) 'Identity as an achievement and as a tool', in C. Antaki and S. Widdicombe (eds), *Identities in Talk*, pp. 1–14. London: Sage.

Antaki, C., Condor, S. and Levine, M. (1996) 'Social identities in talk: Speakers' own orientations', *British Journal of Social Psychology*, 35: 473–92.

Antaki, C., Finlay, M. and Walton, C. (2007) 'How proposing an activity to a person with an intellectual disability can imply a limited identity', *Discourse and Society*, 18: 315–32.

Bamberg, M. (2004) 'Positioning with Davie Hogan: Stories, tellings, and identities', in C. Daiute and C. Lightfoot (eds), *Narrative Analysis: Studying the Development of Individuals in Society*, pp. 135–138. London: Sage.

Bauman, Z. (2004) *Identity*. Cambridge: Polity Press.

Benwell, B. (2005) '"Lucky this is anonymous". Ethnographies of reception in men's magazines: A "textual culture" approach', *Discourse and Society*, 16 (2): 147–72.

Benwell, B.M. and Stokoe, E.H. (2002) 'Constructing discussion tasks in university tutorials: Shifting dynamics and identities', *Discourse Studies*, 4 (4): 429–53.

Benwell, B. and Stokoe, E. (2006) *Discourse and Identity*. Edinburgh: Edinburgh University Press.

Billig, M. (1999) 'Whose terms? Whose ordinariness? Rhetoric and ideology in conversation analysis', *Discourse and Society*, 10 (4): 543–58.

Butler, J. (1990) *Gender Trouble: Feminism and the Subversion of Identity*. New York: Routledge.

Button, G. (1991) 'Introduction: Ethnomethodology and the foundational respecification of the human sciences', in G. Button (ed.), *Ethnomethodology and the Human Sciences*, pp. 1–9. Cambridge: Cambridge University Press.

Button, G. and Sharrock, W. (2003) 'A disagreement over agreement and consensus in constructionist sociology', in M. Lynch and W. Sharrock (eds), *Harold Garfinkel*, pp. 309–332. London: Sage.

Cameron, D. (1997) 'Performing gender identity: young men's talk and the construction of heterosexual masculinity', in S. Johnson and U.H. Meinhof (eds), *Language and Masculinity*, pp. 47–64. Oxford: Blackwell.

Carabine, J. (2001) 'Unmarried motherhood 1830–1990: A genealogical analysis', in M. Wetherell, S. Taylor and S. Yates (eds), *Discourse as Data: A Guide for Analysis*, pp. 267–310. London: Sage.

Chouliaraki, L. and Fairclough, N. (1999) *Discourse and Late Modernity*. Edinburgh: Edinburgh University Press.

Cicourel, A.V. (1992) 'The interpenetration of communicative contexts: Examples from medical encounters', in A. Duranti and C. Goodwin (eds), *Rethinking Context: Language as an Interactive Phenomenon*, pp. 291–310. Cambridge: Cambridge University Press.

Coates, J. (1998) '"Thank god I'm a woman": The construction of differing femininities', in D. Cameron (ed.), *The Feminist Critique of Language*. 2nd edn, pp. 295–320. London: Routledge.

Crossley, M. (2000) *Introducing Narrative Psychology: Self, Trauma and the Construction of Meaning*. Buckingham: Open University Press.

Davies, B. and Harré, R. (1990) 'Positioning: The discursive production of selves', *Journal for the Theory of Social Behaviour*, 20: 43–63.

Denzin, N.K. (2000) 'Foreward', in M. Andrews, S. Day Sclater, C. Squire and A. Treacher (eds), *Lines of Narrative: Psychosocial Perspectives*, pp. xi–xiii. London: Routledge.

Drew, P. (1998) 'Complaints about transgressions and misconduct', *Research on Language and Social Interaction*, 31 (3/4): 295–325.

Drew, P. (2005) 'Conversation analysis', in K. Fitch and R. Sanders (eds), *Handbook of Language and Social Interaction*, pp. 71–102. Mahwah, NJ: Lawrence Erlbaum Associates.

Edwards, D. (2004) 'Psicologia discursiva: Teoria da ligação e método com um exemplo', in L. Iñiguez (ed.), *Manual de Análise do Dircurso em Ciências Sociais*. Brazil: Editora Vozes.

Edwards, D. (2006a) 'Facts, norms and dispositions: Practical uses of the modal would in police interrogations', *Discourse Studies*, 8 (4): 475–501.

Edwards, D. (2006b) 'Discourse, cognition and social practices: The rich surface of language and social interaction', *Discourse Studies*, 8 (1): 41–49.

Edwards, D. (2007) 'Managing subjectivity in talk', in A. Hepburn and S. Wiggins (eds), *Discursive Research in Practice: New Approaches to Psychology and Interaction*, pp. 31–49. Cambridge: Cambridge University Press.

Edwards, D. and Potter, J. (1992) *Discursive Psychology*. London: Sage.

Edwards, D. and Potter, J. (2001) 'Introduction to discursive psychology', in A. McHoul and M. Rapley (eds), *How to Analyze Talk in Institutional Settings: A Casebook of Methods*, pp. 12–24. London: Continuum.

Fairclough, N. (1989). *Language and Power*. London: Longman.

Fairclough, N. (1994) 'Conversationalisation of public discourse and the authority of the consumer', in R. Keat, N. Whitely and N. Abercrombie (eds) *The Authority of the Consumer*. London: Routledge.

Fairclough, N. (1995) *Critical Discourse Analysis*. London: Longman.

Fairclough, N. (2001) *Language and Power*, 2nd edn. London: Longman.

Foucault, M. (1972) *The Archaeology of Knowledge*. London: Tavistock Publications.

Foucault, M. (1975) *Discipline and Punish: The Birth of the Prison*. New York: Random House.

Foucault, M. (1977) 'Nietzsche, genealogy, history', in D.F. Bouchard (ed.), *Language, Counter-Memory, Practice: Selected Essays and Interviews*, pp. 139–164. Ithaca, NY: Cornell University Press.

Francis, D. (1994) 'The golden dreams of the social constructionist', *Journal of Anthropological Research*, 50 (2): 1–22.

Garfinkel, H. (1967) *Studies in Ethnomethodology*. Englewood Cliffs, NJ: Prentice-Hall.

Garfinkel, H. and Sacks, H. (1970) 'On formal structures of practical actions', in J.C. McKinney and E.A. Tiryakian (eds), *Theoretical Sociology: Perspectives and Developments*, pp. 338–366. New York: Appleton-Century-Crofts.

Gilbert, G.N. and Mulkay, M. (1984) *Opening Pandora's Box: A Sociological Analysis of Scientists' Discourse*. Cambridge: Cambridge University Press.

Goffman, E. (1959) *The Presentation of Self in Everyday Life*. Harmondsworth: Penguin.

Hall, D.E. (2004) *Subjectivity*. London: Routledge.

Hall, S. (2000) 'Who needs identity?', in P. du Gay, J. Evans and P. Redman (eds), *Identity: A Reader*, pp. 15–30. London: Sage.

Hall, K. and Livia, A. (1997) '"It's a girl!" Bringing performativity back to linguistics', in K. Hall and A. Livia (eds), *Queerly Phrased: Language, Gender and Sexuality*, pp. 3–20. New York: Oxford University Press.

Harmon, S. (2005). *Why men don't call back*. Ezine@rticles, http://EzineArticles.com/?expert=Sandra_Harmon, accessed October 2009.

Harré, R. and Moghaddam, F. (eds) (2003) *The Self and Others: Positioning Individuals and Groups in Personal, Political and Cultural Contexts*. Westport, CT: Praeger.

Harre, R. and Langenhove, van L. (1991) 'Varieties of positioning'. *Journal for the Theory of Social Behaviour*, 21 (4): 393–407.

Heritage, J. (1984) *Garfinkel and Ethnomethodology*. Cambridge: Polity.

Heritage, J. (2005) 'Conversation analysis and institutional talk', in K. Fitch and R. Sanders (eds), *Handbook of Language and Social Interaction*, pp. 103–146. Mahwah, NJ: Lawrence Erlbaum Associates.

Hollway, W. and Jefferson, T. (2005) 'Panic and perjury: A psychosocial exploration of agency', *British Journal of Social Psychology*, 44 (2): 147–64.

Holmes, J. (2007) 'Social constructionism, postmodernism and feminist sociolinguistics', *Gender and Language*, 1 (1): 51–65.

Hook, D. (2001) 'Discourse, knowledge, materiality, history: Foucault and discourse analysis', *Theory and Psychology*, 11 (4): 521–47.

Hester, S. and Eglin, P. (eds) (1997) *Culture in Action: Membership Categorization Analysis*. Boston, MA: International Institute for Ethnomethodology and University Press of America.

Hussein, L. (2007) 'Book review', in B. Benwell and E. Stokoe (eds), *Discourse and Identity*. Edinburgh: Edinburgh University Press, 2006'. *Discourse and Society*, 18 (6), pp. 819–21.

Jackson, S., and Cram, F. (2003). Disrupting the sexual double standard: Young women's talk about heterosexuality. *British Journal of Social Psychology*, 42: 113–127.

Jackson, C. and Tinkler, P. (2007) '"Ladettes" and "modern girls": "Troublesome" young femininities', *Sociological Review*, 55 (2): 251–72.

Jayyusi, L. (1984) *Categorization and the Moral Order*. London: Routledge.

Jefferson, G. (2004a) 'A note on laughter in "male–female" interaction'. *Discourse Studies*, 6: 117–33.

Jefferson, G. (2004b) 'Glossary of transcript symbols with an introduction', in G. Lerner (ed.), *Conversation Analysis: Studies from the First Generation*. Amsterdam: John Benjamins.

Kitzinger, C. (2005) 'Speaking as a heterosexual: (How) does sexuality matter for talk-in-interaction?', *Research on Language and Social Interaction*, 38 (3): 221–65.

Labov, W. (2001). Uncovering the event structure of narrative. In *Georgetown University Round Table 2001*. Georgetown University Press.

Land, V. and Kitzinger, C. (2007) 'Third-person reference forms in self-reference', *Discourse Studies*, 9 (4): 493–525.

Lacan, J. (1977) *Ecrits: A Selection*. New York: W.W. Norton.

Laclau, E. (1990) *New Reflections on the Revolution of our Time*. London: Verso.

Lynch, M. (1993) *Scientific Practice and Ordinary Action: Ethnomethodology and Social Studies of Science*. Cambridge: Cambridge University Press.

Paechter, C. (2006) 'Masculine femininities/feminine masculinities: Power, identities and gender', *Gender and Education*, 18 (3): 253–63.

Pomerantz, A. and Mandelbaum, J. (2005) 'Conversation analytic approaches to the relevance and uses of relationship categories in interaction', in K.L. Fitch and R.E. Sanders (eds), *Handbook of Language and Social Interaction*, pp. 149–171. Mahwah, NJ: Lawrence Erlbaum Associates.

Potter, J. and Hepburn, A. (2007) 'Discursive psychology: Mind and reality in practice', in A. Weatherall, B. Watson and C. Gallois (eds), *Language and Social Psychology Handbook*, pp. 160–181. London: Palgrave.

Potter, J. and Wetherell, M. (1987) *Discourse and Social Psychology: Beyond Attitudes and Behaviour*. London: Sage.

Raymond, G. (2003) 'Grammar and social organization: Yes/No interrogatives and the structure of responding', *American Sociological Review*, 68: 939–67.

Reisigl, M. and Wodak, R. (2001) *Discourse and Discrimination*. London: Routledge.

Reynolds, J. (2008) *The Single Woman: A Discursive Investigation*. London: Routledge.

Reynolds, J. and Wetherell, M. (2003) 'The discursive climate of singleness: The consequences for women's negotiation of a single identity', *Feminism and Psychology*, 13 (4): 489–510.

Sacks, H. (1992) *Lectures on Conversation*. Vols I and II, edited by G. Jefferson. Oxford: Blackwell.

Sacks, H. (1972) 'On the analysability of stories by children', in J.J. Gumperz and D. Hymes (eds), *Directions in Sociolinguistics: The Ethnography of Communication*, pp. 325–345. New York: Rinehart and Winston.

Sarbin, T. (Ed.) (1986). *Narrative Psychology: The Storied Nature of Human Conduct*. New York: Praeger.

Schegloff, E.A. (1991) 'Reflections on talk and social structure', in D. Boden and D. Zimmerman (eds), *Talk and Social Structure*, pp. 44–71. Berkeley, CA: University of California Press.

Schegloff, E.A. (1992) 'In another context', in A. Duranti and C. Goodwin (eds), *Rethinking Context: Language as an Interactive Phenomenon*, pp. 191–228. Cambridge: Cambridge University Press.

Schegloff, E.A. (1996) 'Issues of relevance for discourse analysis: Contingency in action, interaction and co-participant context', in E.H. Hovy and D.R. Scott (eds), *Computational and Conversational Discourse: Burning Issues – an Interdisciplinary Account*, pp. 3–38. New York: Springer.

Schegloff, E.A. (1997) 'Whose text? Whose context?', *Discourse and Society*, 8 (2): 165–87.

Schippers, M. (2007) 'Recovering the feminine other: Masculinity, femininity, and gender hegemony', *Theoretical Sociology*, 36: 85–102.

Schutz, A. (1962) *Collected Papers, Volume I: The Problem of Social Reality*. The Hague: Martinus Nijhoff.

Sclater, S. Day (2003) 'What is the subject?' *Narrative Inquiry*, 13 (2): 317–30.

Seymour-Smith, S., Wetherell, M. and Phoenix, A. (2002) '"My wife ordered me to come!": A discursive analysis of doctors' and nurses' accounts of men's use of general practitioners', *Journal of Health Psychology*, 7: 253–67.

Shapiro, M.J. (1992) *The Postmodern Polity*. Minneapolis, MN: Minnesota University.

Speer, S. and Green, R. (2007) 'On passing: The interactional organization of appearance attributions in the psychiatric assessment of transsexual patients',

in V. Clarke and E. Peel (eds), *Out in Psychology: Lesbian, Gay, Bisexual, Trans and Queer Perspectives*, pp. 335–368. Chichester: John Wiley.

Stivers, T. (2004) '"No no no" and other types of multiple sayings in social interaction', *Human Communication Research*, 30 (2): 260–93.

Stokoe, E.H. (2003) 'Mothers, single women and sluts: Gender, morality and membership categorization in neighbour disputes', *Feminism and Psychology*, 13 (3): 317–44.

Stokoe, E. (2006) 'On ethnomethodology, feminism, and the analysis of categorial reference to gender in talk-in-interaction', *Sociological Review*, 54 (3): 467–94.

Stokoe, E. (2008) 'Categories, actions and sequences: Formulating gender in talk-in-interaction', in L. Litosseliti, H. Saunston, K. Segall, and J. Sunderland (eds) *Language and Gender Research Methodologies*. London: Palgrave Macmillan.

Stokoe, E. (2009) Doing actions with identity categories: Complaints and denials in neighbour disputes. *Text and Talk*, 29 (1), 75–97.

Stokoe, E. and Edwards, D. (2007) '"Black this, black that": Racial insults and reported speech in neighbour complaints and police interrogations', *Discourse and Society*, 18 (3): 337–72.

Sunderland, J. (2004) *Gendered Discourses*. London: Palgrave Macmillan.

Tajfel, H. (1982) *Social Identity and Intergroup Relations*. Cambridge: Cambridge University Press.

Taylor, C. (1989) *Sources of the Self: The Making of Modern Identity*. Cambridge, MA: Harvard University Press.

Van Leeuwen, T. (1996) 'The representation of social actors', in C. Rosa Caldas-Coulthard and M. Coulthard (eds), *Texts and Practices: Readings in Critical Discourse Analysis*, pp. 32–70. London: Routledge.

Vygotsky, L.S. (1978) *Mind in Society: The Development of Higher Psychological Processes*. London: Harvard University Press.

Wetherell, M. (1998) 'Positioning and interpretative repertoires: Conversation analysis and post-structuralism in dialogue', *Discourse and Society*, 9 (3): 431–56.

Wetherell, M. and Edley, N. (1999) 'Negotiating hegemonic masculinity: Imaginary positions and psycho-discursive practices', *Feminism and Psychology*, 9: 335–56.

Whelehan, I. (2000) *Overloaded: Popular Culture and the Future of Feminism*. London: The Women's Press.

Wodak, R. (2001). The discourse-historical approach. In R. Wodak and M. Meyer (Eds.), *Methods of Critical Discourse Analysis*. London: Sage.

Wodak, R. and Meyer, M. (eds) (2001) *Methods of Critical Discourse Analysis*. London: Sage.

5

# Performative Identities:
# From Identity Politics to
# Queer Theory

Sarah E. Chinn

In this chapter I hope to trace the ways in which feminist understandings of the category of 'identity' changed with the growth of theories of performativity over the course of the 1990s and into the twenty-first century. Of course 'identity' had for more than a decade played an immense role in the ways in which feminists had thought about gender, particularly in terms of race and class, particularly in the United States. The ground breaking and hugely influential statement issued in 1977 by the Combahee River Collective, a group of US women of color, put 'identity' at the core of black feminist practice, and 'identity politics', a political practice that, in their words, 'evolve[d] from a healthy love for ourselves, our sisters and our community, which allows us to continue our struggle and our work' (1977: 275). For the Collective, 'identity' in many ways spoke for itself – its mission was to identify black feminist issues and empower black feminists, particularly lesbians, to find the resources, space, and political support to work on those issues. Where the identities 'black', 'lesbian', or 'woman' came from, what social or cultural forces produced them, seemed less

urgent than the fact of their being and the ramifications of their operations.

This focus on identity and identity politics was enormously influential in progressive political circles, and had unusual resonance for lesbian and gay politics, people, and scholarship. The expropriation of scholarly and political talk around homosexuality by social scientists, doctors, psychoanalysts, and researchers who rarely had gay people's interests as their primary motivation (and whose impetus was most often to diagnose, analyze, and 'cure' sexual and gender non-conformity) led queer people to carve out and insist upon a distinct identity that combined valorization of homosexual desire and claims to unalterable identity. As Diana Fuss observed, '"gay pride", "gay culture", "gay sensibility" are all summoned as cornerstones of the gay community, indices of the emergence of a long-repressed collective identity' (1989: 97).

At the same time, however, poststructuralist theorists, most notably Michel Foucault, had found their way into US academia, profoundly undermining any unitary sense of what constituted that collective identity and repudiating any claim to sexuality and sexual desires as untouched by history. Denise Riley's (1988) contribution to this discussion even challenged the universality of the term 'women', which, she argued, has historically been used to exclude marginalized female subjects from the collectivity of womanhood. Rather, 'women' as a group have always been identified through historically specific ideas of personhood and subjectivity. Similarly, as Chandra Talpade Mohanty pointed out, women in colonized nations were too often represented as wholly victimized and dehumanized, in contrast to their Western counterparts who were 'secular, liberated, and [in] control of their own lives' (1997: 273). The shorthand name for this debate, 'essentialism versus social construction' spiraled into heated disagreement between those who insisted on the contingency and national/geopolitical specificity of identity and those who believed in a stable, trans-historical self. In 1990, however, with the publication of Judith Butler's watershed book, *Gender Trouble*, the terms of this debate changed dramatically, shifting the focus from identity and history to performativity.

Of course, like all changes, this one was actually quite a long time coming. Butler, trained as a philosopher and versed equally thoroughly in Hegelian idealism, Derridean deconstruction, and French feminism, reached back into a rich storehouse of post-1945 philosophy and feminist theorizing to synthesize her central concept of gender performativity. Indeed, much of *Gender Trouble* comprises her answers to (and eventual dismissal of) her predecessors, a typical gambit for academic philosophy. In what follows, I trace where the idea of gender performativity came from, the effects it had on feminist, queer, and other theorizing, and where those ideas find us at the beginning of the twenty-first century.

As we will see, Butler actively (one might even say strenuously) worked, both in *Gender Trouble* and her later book *Bodies that Matter: on the Discursive Limits of Sex* (1993) to disarticulate her theory of performativity from ideas of performance and

theatricality. For Butler, the notion of performance entails a desire for a certain level of knowingness and agency: the belief that whatever I am representing is just playacting, and that I can locate the 'real' me underneath the representation. However, at the same time that Butler was developing and refining the concept of gender performativity, other theorists, in both queer and transgender studies, were looking closely at the phenomena of theatricality and gendered performance, while at the same time drawing upon the idea of non-voluntary performativity. Kate Bornstein, Eve Kosofsky Sedgwick, Sue-Ellen Case, and Michael Moon, for example, have remarked upon a close connection between outrageous, self-conscious theatrics of gender and the too-often unchallenged performances of gendered identity that we go through every day.

One of the most impassioned debates that emerged, albeit unintentionally, from *Gender Trouble*, was between people who were strongly invested in theories of gender performativity and those who felt a powerful connection to what Kath Weston (1991) has called 'street theory', which comes out of the ways queer people have imagined the spaces their own gendered identities – of queen, dyke, butch, transsexual, nelly, femme – occupy. While this debate was often reduced to an opposition between 'academia' on the one hand and 'activism' on the other, I'd argue that it was more complex than this. First, many of the mostly young scholars who embraced Butler's ideas were themselves activists, who had cut their teeth on a variety of political movements in the 1980s: anti-apartheid, pro-choice, anti-US intervention in Central America, AIDS activism, queer activism, and so on. But what was at stake was a sea change in understanding how sexuality and sexual desire operate. At the bottom of this debate was a range of interconnected questions: where does gender come from? How much choice do we have over our genders? Are there inevitable links between sex, gender, and sexuality? Could we have a world, or even a person, without gender?

For gay men and lesbians who had courageously held onto their sexual autonomy despite a crushing psychiatric and social consensus that condemned them as sick and perverse, the idea that their deeply felt desires were 'no more' than discursive formations struck them as a diminution of their core selves. For theorists of performativity, by contrast, Butler's book seemed like a way out of dead-end arguments about what 'made' people gay: indeed, her acknowledgment that *all* identities were constructed and could, however subtly, change over time was taken as a sign that things do not have to be the way they are, that there is the possibility of a more flexible, varied, and just way (or ways) that gender and sexuality can be expressed.

In this chapter I will be laying out where ideas about gender performativity come from, how they intersect, and how we can use them. This question of 'use' is possibly the most controversial element of performativity theory, and the place where the different camps of theorists get into the most passionate disagreement. Since queer theory has its roots in political movements for liberation, we need to ask, how can a theory of performativity help us change currently repressive structures of sexuality, that depend on the assumption and enforcement of binary, heterosexist gender? I will also be tracing the development of Butler's own uses of performativity from her earlier work in *Gender Trouble* and *Bodies that Matter* to her newer exploration of gender and, I would argue, a deeper investment not just in the mechanics but the ethics of gender and gender expression in a more recent book, *Undoing Gender* (2004).

## PERFORMATIVITY AND PHILOSOPHY

Given her training as a philosopher and her engagement with theories of language, it is not surprising that Butler found her way to thinking about gender in terms of performativity, a concept that emerged from philosophical inquiry. The first person to use the term 'performativity' in a sustained study was the philosopher of language J.L. Austin. In a series of Harvard lectures later collected into the book *How to Do Things With Words* (1962), Austin explored the role of what he called 'performative language'. He initially divided language into two kinds: constative and performative. Constative language is merely descriptive; it tells us about the world around us – 'the grass is green' or 'my name is Sarah' – but does not affect the world or the things it describes. Performative language, on the other hand, is language that makes something happen – just by saying something we do something.

For Austin the paradigmatic example is 'I pronounce you husband and wife'. This sentence does not simply describe a state of affairs: it is performing an act that can be enacted only by words. Before the words were said, the two people they embrace had no more legal relationship than any two people unrelated by blood; afterwards their relationship has changed into 'married couple'. Other kinds of performative language are bets, vows and acts of naming. To say 'I bet' or 'I promise' or 'I name this baby Sarah' or 'I sentence you to five years in prison' is not just saying, it is doing. Certainly, all these acts of performative language might require other proofs – a handshake, a contract, a marriage license, to name a few – but those texts all require, or at the very least imply, the moment of performativity that brings the act into being.

As a philosopher, Austin was especially concerned with ways in which these 'speech acts', as he called them, could go wrong. Of course, the worst case scenario is that the person saying the performative words does not mean them and is offering a false promise. Alternatively, it could be that the person does not have the authority to perform the words – there is no money to back up the bet, the baby belongs to someone else or already has a name or is just a doll, the person handing down the sentence is only masquerading as a judge. It is also possible things might go wrong along the way or that there is no one to hear the performance and validate it. Austin called these exceptions 'infelicities', arguing that while constative language can be incorrect or false ('the earth is flat', 'my bed is floating in mid-air'), performative language can only be misapplied or inappropriate. In philosophical terms, these problems are not falsehoods, but simply 'unhappy'.[1]

Although Austin's primary concern here was the structural functioning of language, he acknowledged that speech, particularly in the form of speech acts, is a social phenomenon and that speech acts are tied up in social conventions and rituals that seem self-evident but in fact are quite minutely choreographed. A lot of things have to go right in order for a bet to go through, not least of which is that all parties have to agree what a bet means, what the terms are and the obligations a bet entails. But it is rare that the parties involved have to explain what betting itself means; it is assumed that everyone knows. Indeed, the conventions of betting, promising, swearing and so on are a major part of human interaction from early childhood on – they may become more complex in adulthood, but the basic structure does not change.[2] Since his main concern was *how* performative language worked, he did not stop to ask *why* it worked. What is it that makes us all agree without realizing that we agree that bets are bets, that marriage is a meaningful institution, that parents have the right to name their own children?

This question was partially answered by another philosopher, Jacques Derrida, in his discussion of performativity in the essay *Signature, Event, Context*, collected in the volume *Limited, Inc.* (1972, trans. 1988). Using Austin as springboard (a line from *How to Do Things With Words* serves as the epigraph for the essay), Derrida questioned the transparency and determinacy of context, and Austin's argument that speech acts have no referents outside themselves (that is, that they are only about the action they perform rather than descriptive of a thing or action beyond the utterance).

By contrast, Derrida claimed that performatives seem self-evident and self-referential because speech acts are by nature reiterative. That is, they conform to a pre-existing model that can, in fact *must*, be cited in order to make sense, and that exists outside of its performers and witnesses. (Derrida claims that this iterable citation is, in fact, the defining characteristic of all language, but that's a whole other story.) More importantly, these conventions have no origin except in themselves; the citation of performative speech, rather than being the result of commonly held understandings of what speech acts do, in fact *produce* those understandings. Ultimately, then, when we utter performative speech acts we are not acting with full or even conscious intention within a given context, but instead constructing the context through our citation of the utterance.

What was most interesting to Derrida about this theoretical development was the idea that speech acts, as citations of themselves, always threatened to fall apart even as they reinforced their power. Understanding speech acts as citational rather than originary reverses how we understand intentionality, context, and consciousness in relation to performative language; as he put it, their performative effects 'do not exclude what is generally opposed to them, term by term [that is, contingency, undecidability, the absence of intention]; on the contrary, they presuppose it, in an asymmetrical way, as the general space of their possibility' (p. 19). But what Derrida does not explain is what these iterable events actually mean in terms of cultural practice: who says them, and about whom, with what results. While he takes for granted that language is citational – and performative language plays out that citationality in particularly sharp relief – he does not explore where the assumption of the models to be cited comes from, or why people feel so unselfconscious performing them. Why do we cite some utterances and not others? Why are some contexts produced by the practice of reiteration rather than other contexts?

## ITERATION, IDEOLOGY, DISCOURSE

Derrida's older contemporary, Louis Althusser, provides some answers to these questions. Despite their significant ideological, methodological, and temperamental differences, and an age difference of 12 years, Althusser and Derrida had much in common. Both were products of French colonial Algeria, although Derrida's experience as a Jew during the Vichy regime intensified the sense of dislocation and divided loyalties experienced by the *pieds-noirs*, as French colonials in Algeria were known. Both were educated at the *École normale superieure* (ENS), a hotbed of philosophical and political activity in the years after the Second World War, where they both also later taught (in fact, Althusser was instrumental in hiring Derrida at the ENS). And both were deeply interested in how we are products of the social and linguistic structures we believe we produce: language, culture, power.

As a Marxist, however, Althusser was most concerned with material and economic relations, with the explicit workings of power, and why, to put it bluntly, since Marx had exposed the exploitative mechanisms of capitalism, workers all over the industrial world had not risen up against the bourgeoisie. For Althusser, the answer lay in the phenomenon of ideology, which shapes every thought, every belief and every action in capitalist society. In part people's inaction is due to fear of the power and violence of the state, which could easily crush resistance. But fear cannot explain people's enthusiasm for the perpetuation of their own oppression. Althusser theorized that there must be social mechanisms that teach everyone to agree to their own domination by capitalism, to consider it not just acceptable or even a virtue, but self-evident and inevitable, something that one would have to be crazy or evil not to accept as true. Those mechanisms operate through ideology.

Ideology's power lies in its ubiquity. For Althusser 'children at school learn the rules of good behaviour ... rules of morality, civic,

and professional conscience' (1971: 132), but these rules, while masquerading as universal, are actually created by and intrinsic to bourgeois hegemony. On a larger scale, the spoken and unspoken rules of society provide the ways in which we understand our place in the world and without which we cannot function as subjects. Althusser calls these mechanisms Ideological State Apparatuses (ISAs) – they are political structures that are produced by and uphold the state but that feel private, individualized, and normal. But the concepts of 'public' and 'private' are themselves constructed by the bourgeois state and underpin it; recognizing ISAs as functions of the state, rather than public institutions or private feelings, allows us to see how the ruling class exercises its control.

For Althusser the most important part of ISAs is that they feel so natural. They are not just obvious, but exist as what he calls 'obviousnesses' – self-evident 'facts of life'. In fact, he suggests that a defining characteristic of ideology that 'it imposes (without seeming to do so, since these are "obviousnesses") obviousnesses as obviousnesses, which we cannot *fail to recognize* and before which we have the inevitable and natural reaction of crying out.... "That's obvious! That's right! That's real!"' (Althusser, 1971: 172). He maintained that this happened through a process of 'interpellation' or hailing. Interpellation works like this: through ISAs we understand our world and thereby ourselves. In fact, we can only understand ourselves as subjects in the world through the mediation of ISAs like education, religion, the family, the legal system. Althusser argued that subjects do not create ISAs: quite the opposite. In fact, ISAs interpellate us or call us into being, literally giving us (legal) names, constructing family relationships and so on, even as they make seem self-evident the fact of having a name, or an aunt, or a legal system that has the power to establish and maintain both of those facts. In Austin's terms, then, interpellation is the definitive performative speech act: when the doctor says 'it's a girl', or a parent says 'that's my child' or a judge says 'I sentence you' (or 'I marry you') they are all reiterating ideology saying 'you are a subject'. Moreover, despite their significant differences, Althusser imagined ideology functioning much like the way Derrida described the process of citation and iteration in performative speech acts: a performance that produces itself as an effect.

Part of Althusser's discussion of ideology is an analysis of the punitive and policing elements of interpellation's performativity. There is a constant threat of not being a subject, or of having one's subjectivity severely compromised. As we'll see, this kind of policing is particularly effective in the realm of gender – people who do not conform to expectations of gender are accused of not being 'real women' or 'real men'. Since so much of our sense of self depends upon fitting into the appropriate gender, to fail in being a 'real woman', for example, is to be an incomplete subject. Of course, the worst fate is falling off the ideological map and being a non-person. It is hard to imagine what a non-subject could be; something we do not have a name for or cannot recognize as even human, perhaps. Those are the people we call 'unnatural', as though their inability to conform to ideological – that is to say social – structures divorces them from the *natural* order of things.

Althusser's concept of a subject created by ideology was taken up by his student at the ENS, Michel Foucault. After a brief flirtation with communism, Foucault rejected the historical materialism that informed Althusser's work. Central to Foucault's ideas was the notion that systems of power such as the family or the legal system produce subjects, not vice versa. For Foucault, power is a kind of historical actor itself, not always or necessarily at the service of a ruling class. In a decisive break with the Marxism of Althusser and many of his own colleagues, Foucault argued that power is not just 'a general system of domination exerted by one group over another, a system whose effects, through successive derivations, pervade the entire social body' (1977: 92). Power does not exist

at a single point or even series of points, but is omnipresent, the sum of 'force relations' at work in any historical moment. 'Power is everywhere', Foucault famously claimed, 'not because it embraces everything, but because it comes from everywhere. And "Power", insofar as it is permanent, repetitious, inert, and self-producing, is simply the overall effect that emerges from all these mobilities ... it is the name that one attributes to a complex strategical situation in a particular society' (1977: 93).

For Foucault, relations of power were intimately interconnected with all kinds of social relationships: top-down, bottom-up, horizontally, diagonally, and so on. These power relations are produced and perpetuated, as well as resisted and changed, through 'discourse', that is, the various ways a culture defines, understands, and talks about itself. The most powerful characteristic of discourse is that the effects it produces seem self-evident, inevitable, even a product of natural rather than social and cultural phenomena. His work traced the historical development – what he called 'genealogies' – of seemingly unchanging discursive formations such as madness, criminality, justice, sexuality, and medicine: ideas that are formed through the articulation of power relations and shape the ways in which people understand themselves as subjects.

One of Foucault's most influential works is *The History of Sexuality*, a projected three volume study that traced the genealogy of 'sexuality' as an identity from the eighteenth century to the current era (Foucault died before completing this project beyond the first introductory volume). Foucault believed that sexual identities as we inhabit them today – 'gay', 'heterosexual', 'bisexual', 'homosexual', 'lesbian', and so on – are not fixed or 'natural', but rather are a product of the interlocking systems of power that form subjectivity. In other words, in order to be a subject one has to 'have' a sexuality, something that makes an specific set of identities out of a collection of sexual practices, desires, and partnerings. After all, only some practices get attached to identities, mostly in connection to the gender of the partners; other practices are just 'preferences'. Part of the work of these discourses of sexuality is to seem self-evident and natural as well as compulsory.

Discourse is in many ways like a menu in a restaurant: there may be a lot of choices within it, but you can only order from the menu, and you have to pay the price indicated. The menu circumscribes what choices you can make, or, more importantly, can even consider making. The same goes for sexuality. That is, not only do you have to inhabit a sexuality in order to understand yourself as a subject, you cannot imagine not doing so in the terms set up by discourse. The menu may broaden, it may offer increasing numbers of options, but it still delimits what choices a person can make. As Foucault forcefully showed, under the current discursive regime, one cannot *not* have a sexuality; one cannot *not* have a gender. These are the structures within which we understand ourselves not just as sexed and desiring, but as human. Bluntly put: a person without a gender is not a person.

## Reading gender trouble

Looking at the development of the concept of performativity, and its emergence out of these several strands of philosophy in the years after the Second World War, it is hardly surprising that Judith Butler is philosopher by training. At the same time, Butler was immersed in the feminist theorizing of the 1970s and particularly the 1980s, which (despite stereotypes to the contrary) often focused on debunking gender and sexual norms. In her astute analysis of Butler's work, Moya Lloyd (2007) works through Butler's relationship to the 'diversity feminists' who dominated much US feminist thinking, and French feminists such as Luce Irigaray and Hélène Cixous, whose work was rooted in philosophical tradition and post-structuralist thought. While her training in Continental philosophy certainly meant that

the French feminists constituted a crucial influence, and her determined opposition to the kind of identity politics that she saw as ultimately destructive and divisive owes a large debt to Denise Riley's work, it is worth considering the role of the feminist and gay activism of the 1980s, particularly the anti-censorship, pro-choice, and AIDS activist movements, as a more subtle but no less valuable influence on Butler's theory of performativity.

The crux of Butler's argument is her critique of feminism's attachment to identity, since identity requires that we agree on 'a single or abiding ground, which is invariably contested by those identity positions or anti-identity positions that it invariably excludes' (1990: 5). But if gender is not an identity – that is, a set of attributes and behaviors that belong to a certain kind of person, whether by nature or by training – what is it? Drawing explicitly on the groundwork laid down by Austin and Derrida, Butler claimed that gender was an embodied act in the same way that performative language is a speech act. Gender is performative. Moreover, gender is not naturally or inevitably attached to specific anatomically shaped bodies; indeed 'bodies' themselves are made comprehensible by the discursive formations that co-construct 'sex' and 'gender' (that is, what we see as biological and what we believe is socially or culturally conditioned).[3]

In *Gender Trouble*, Butler took on two basic but not quite identical issues. The first was the relationship, foundational to much second-wave feminist theorizing, of what came to be known as the 'sex/gender divide': roughly speaking, the assumption that biological sex is the pre-discursive raw material that social forces shape into 'gender'. The second was how 'gender', which for Butler meant everything produced by discourse under the binarized, opposed pairs of signs 'man', 'woman', 'masculine', 'feminine', and so on, operates at all. At the foundation of her discussion is the claim that 'there is no gender identity behind the expressions of gender; that identity is performatively constituted by the very "expressions" that are said to be its results' (1990: 25).

From the very beginning of *Gender Trouble*, Butler challenged the assumption that sex was, in the words of Ellen Ross and Rayna Rapp, 'bare biological facts' that are 'experienced culturally' and 'expressed socially' through gender (1983: 51). Of course, this assumption was itself a major departure from conventional beliefs that the identities and behaviors attached to gender were inevitable outgrowths of biological sex. Feminist scholars of the 1980s broke significant new ground in insisting that gender was not transparent or trans-cultural, but instead the result of complex social relations that rested upon structures of male dominance.

Butler pushed the argument that gender was produced by social relations into a new arena, claiming that gender 'ought not to be conceived merely as the cultural inscription of meaning on a pregiven sex (…) gender must also designate the very apparatus of production whereby the sexes themselves are established. As a result, gender is not to culture as sex is to nature; gender is the discursive/cultural means by which "sexed nature" or "a natural sex" is produced and established as "prediscursive"' (1990: 7). Our bodies are not beings in and of themselves. A body is 'a variable boundary, a surface whose permeability is politically regulated, a signifying practice within a cultural field of gender hierarchy and compulsory heterosexuality' (1990: 138).

In *Bodies That Matter* Butler amplified this claim, working through the idea that 'sexual difference is often invoked as an issue of material differences' – that is, the supposed irreducibility of the sexed body. Summoning the concept of abjection, the psychic casting out of the part of the self that normativity cannot abide, she argued that the formation of the self itself 'requires an identification with the normative phantasm of "sex", and this identification takes place through a repudiation which produces a domain of abjection of all the ways the body *must not* be – not sexed, sexed "wrong", not

mapped onto the binary model of male/female, and so on' (1993: 3). For Butler, biological sex is not only not a fact of nature, its production through discourse is coercive and prescriptive. 'Sex' itself is 'a regulatory ideal, a forcible and differential materialization of bodies' (1993: 22), not a self-evident explanation for why various bodies look certain ways. 'Sex' makes sense of bodies through a regime of binarized difference, and any bodies that do not exactly fit into the binary are denied, abjected, surgically altered, or reassigned. Butler talks about issues of nonconforming, unsexed, resexed, and unsexable bodies in *Undoing Gender*, about which I'll talk a little later.

In Butler's view, sex and gender are produced by and perpetuate norms of behavior, feeling, action, and psyche. That is, 'the regulatory norms of "sex" work in a performative fashion to constitute the materiality of bodies and, more specifically, to materialize the body's sex, to materialize sexual difference in the service of the consolidation of the heterosexual imperative' (1993: 2). Part of this process is to repudiate everything that does not conform to this compulsory heterosexuality; however, as we will see, this repudiation of the abject, incomplete, or unsuccessful part of the sexed self is rarely if ever fully achieved and occurs, as Butler puts it, with 'consequences [we] cannot fully control' (1993: 3).

At this point, then, Butler makes her most radical move, an analysis that distances her from previous US feminist scholars. Rather than seeing gender as extending from sex, Butler argues that sex is produced by gender. That is, the discursive formations of masculinity and femininity require the belief in a naturally bifurcated structure of biological sex. In order for gender to seem inevitable, sex (that is, the ways in which are bodies are made intelligible to us by being assigned as male or female, never neither, never both, and never just something else) must appear self-evident, must be, in Althusser's words, an 'obviousness'. *Of course* everyone is biologically either male or female. *Of course* anatomy, sex, and gender are mapped directly onto each other. And *of course* sexuality is motivated by gendered desires.

For Butler, there is no 'of course' about it. We are conscripted – press-ganged – into gender even before we are conscious of it. We are interpellated into gender from birth: the words 'it's a girl', are in fact a command and a threat: 'be a girl; if you want to be a real subject with a real identity, act out girl-ness'. Most of the ways to 'be a girl' are implicit within discourse, and others must be explicitly enforced by parents, educational institutions, magazines, and so on. And of course, the most effective way in which gender is enforced is the fact that it just feels natural to behave in certain ways, 'as a girl'. Girlness is, in Althusser's terms, the obvious-ness of obviousness. It speaks for itself and through us.

Butler's central point is that gender perfor-mativity is neither optional nor natural. Once a child has been 'girled', for example, with the words 'it's a girl', she is compelled to perform girlness and (or perhaps *because*) she does not even recognize this compulsion. Gender is performed reiteratively through an array of 'acts, gestures and desires' (the girl really *wants* to be a girl) that imply an essen-tial gendered self. But, for Butler, these 'acts and gestures, articulated and enacted desires create the *illusion* of an interior and organiz-ing gender core' (1990: 136, emphasis added). There is no subject underneath the gender, no universal self. Rather, the self is constructed through its strenuous perfor-mance of gender.

Many people feel that their gender is the most intrinsic part of them, deeply rooted in their beings. According to Butler, though, nothing could be further from the truth. Gender is 'a construction that conceals its genesis; the tacit collective agreement to per-form, produce, and sustain discrete and polar genders as cultural fictions is obscured by the credibility of those productions – and the punishments that attend to not agreeing to believe in them' (1990: 140). We produce gender through processes of citation, through

the '*stylized repetition of acts*. The effect of gender is produced through the stylization of the body and, hence, must be understood as the mundane way in which bodily gestures, movements, and styles of various kinds con-stitute the illusion of an abiding gendered self' (1990: 140, original emphasis). We feel our genders because we have learned to per-form them again and again, however incom-pletely we manage to embody the norm of gender itself.

Ultimately, there is no real or true gender. It is an imitation without an original, a cita-tion without a source, as all discursive forma-tions are. As Derrida argued, signification itself '*is not a founding act but rather a regu-lated process of repetition* that both conceals itself and enforces its rules precisely through the production of substantializing effects' (Butler, 1990: 145, original emphasis). Of course, the question all this brings us to is 'why'? Butler's answer is simple: to repro-duce normative heterosexuality, which requires that everyone is either male or female, with no gaps and no exceptions. According to the dominant discourse of het-erosexuality, everyone is a boy or a girl, and combines accordingly. This is all very well, but as we know there are exceptions: people who desire members of their own sex, people who change gender, people whose physical sexual characteristics (penis, vagina, ovaries) are multiple or partial and cannot be easily attached to a gender, and so on. There is also always the fear that one is not getting it right by being feminine or masculine 'enough'. Surely these exceptions, failures and doubts would weaken the discourse of gender.

Well, says Butler, maybe and maybe not. In many cases, failure and incoherence strengthen the power of discourse, either through a fear that one's subjectivity is being compromised (the embarrassment of being called 'Sir' instead of 'Miss', for instance) or through active punishment of inappropriate behaviors (queer bashing, rape, commitment to a mental institution being among the more violent examples). Too often, subjects blame the inevitable gaps in their successful gender performances on their own inability to live up to the standard; a process that polices the subject through mechanisms of shame and embarrassment.

The greatest irony inherent to this insight is that built into this process of citation and reiteration is the continual threat – indeed, the ongoing reality – of our failure to fully and completely achieve what gender demands. In large part, this is intrinsic to performativity itself: if we are endlessly copying something that has no original, no wonder we feel insecure about the authenticity of our performance. But another element is that gender's failure is inscribed into its performance, very much as for Foucault resistance is a constitutive and inevitable part of the exercise of power.

In fact, there can be times when incoherent gender performativity can expose the constructedness of gender and (hetero)sexuality. Butler lands on drag as a possible place this can happen. Drag is a self-conscious, larger-than-life reiteration of heterosexual normativity that 'fully subverts the distinction between inner and outer psychic space and effectively mocks both the expressive model of gender and the notion of a true gender identity' (Butler, 1990: 137). By performing gender in a hyperbolic, stylized way, drag queens do not simply imitate femininity, they reveal how women perform (which is to say, imitate) femininity as well, and what hard work it is. Through parody, drag can expose the seeming naturalness and effortlessness of gender itself; it does not imitate an original, but reveals that there is no original, only layers of performance. Drag says, 'if you think my pretending to be a woman is hard, think what an effort it must be for a woman to do'.

This is not to say that drag is inherently subversive. In fact, it can reinforce heteronormativity in several ways. First it can burlesque the idea of successful imitation by the 'inappropriate' gender, by appearing ridiculous. A mainstream reading of stereotype of the swaggering butch or effeminate queen does not expose gender as much as it restates the lines between identity and behavior: men and women are not supposed to act that way. Similarly, comedic half-baked drag by 'obvious' men – a popular trope that reaches from Milton Berle through to the Kids in the Hall and the British comedy show *Little Britain* – tells us 'real men can't help but be masculine, even in women's clothes'.

On the opposite end of the spectrum, drag can also obscure gender's constructedness by focusing on the supposed 'original' and fetishizing it. A man performing 'woman' can romanticize and naturalize 'womanhood' as much as 'real' women can.

But, says, Butler, drag can get us out of the sense of inevitability that surrounds gender performativity. As she argues, '*in imitating gender, drag implicitly reveals the imitative structure of gender itself – as well as its contingency* [...] In the place of the law of heterosexual coherence, we see sex and gender denaturalized by means of a performance which avows their distinctness and dramatizes the cultural mechanism of their fabricated unity' (1990: 138, original emphasis). This kind of parody can show that even though our gendered options might be limited, we can apply and combine them in a wide variety of ways, attaching behaviors to discordant bodies. Drag is about repeating heterosexual constructs in non- (or anti-)heterosexual contexts, challenging the primacy of the supposed heterosexual 'original'. It can also point out the intimate links between gender, race and class, and that certain gendered performatives require specific racial or class identities to go along with them.

These connections between gender, sexuality, race, and class were not a major part of Butler's analysis in *Gender Trouble*, though. Indeed, one of the most significant critiques is centered on Butler's almost complete omission in that book of the role of race and racial difference in constructing gender. After all, as any number of feminist scholars, both of color and white, have long pointed out, while binarized gender is enforced in any number of arenas, what those genders mean, particularly in the context of histories of white supremacy and European and US colonization and imperialism, varies significantly depending upon the context (Anzaldúa, 1987; Carby, 1987; Frankenberg, 1993; Harper, 1996).

Butler has certainly been alert to these critiques, and in *Bodies That Matter* she explicitly addressed how racial and class differences in particular are co-articulated with the discursive formations of gender. In her analysis of Nella Larsen's 1929 novel *Passing*, Butler explores the connections between the heterosexual imperative and the prohibition on miscegenation in the United States, wondering what it would mean to imagine 'the disjunctive ordering of the human as 'masculine' or 'feminine' as taking place not only through a heterosexualizing symbolic with its taboo on homosexuality, but through a complex set of racial injunctions which operate in part through the taboo on miscegenation' (1993: 166). Black women, in this reading, are interpellated not just as female but as black/female, an identity that is defined in opposition to 'white female' and in a complex relation with 'white male'. Butler's conclusion, clearly informed by feminist scholars of color such as Barbara Christian, Norma Alarcón, Claudia Tate, and Deborah MacDowell (who formulated the first explicitly lesbian reading of *Passing*) – scholars Butler mentions by name in this discussion – is that 'the symbolic domain, the domain of socially instituted norms, is composed of *racializing norms*, and that they exist not merely alongside gender norms, but are articulated through one another. Hence, it is no longer possible to make sexual difference prior to racial difference or, for that matter, to make them into fully separable axes of social regulation' (Butler, 1993: 182).

Ultimately, though, it has been scholars of color who have produced many of the most compelling discussions of race, gender, and sexuality through the analytic of performativity. Unlike Butler, who had to rethink gender performativity in order understand how racialization was an integral part of gender, these scholars take for granted

the multiple ways in which non-white subjects, particularly queer subjects of color, are interpellated, whose identities, in Kimberlé Crenshaw's (1993) influential phrase, are 'intersectional'. After all, marginalization can be a useful analytic tool in recognizing the discursive constructions of norms, a realization that may require more effort from those whom the norm putatively embraces. As José Esteban Muñoz puts it in *Disidentifications: Queers of Color and the Performance of Politics*, 'the fiction of identity is one that is accessed with relative ease by most majoritarian subjects [...] [minoritarian subjects] are formed in response to the cultural logics of heteronormativity, white supremacy, and misogyny' (1999: 5), quite a different dynamic for those whose subjectivity is often demonized by those logics.

In *Disidentifications*, Muñoz combines Butler's theory of performativity with the field of Performance Studies, examining how self-conscious performances work through the compulsory performances of race, sexuality, and gender. In his reading of Vaginal Creme Davis, a black drag queen/performance artist based in Los Angeles, he argues that Davis's 'uses of humor and parody function as disidentificatory strategies whose effect on the dominant public sphere is that of a counterpublic terrorism. At the center of all of Davis's cultural productions is a radical impulse towards cultural critique' (Muñoz, 1999: 100). As Muñoz's work suggests, a self-conscious deployment of norms of gender, race, and class, for example, can generate a meaningful political critique beyond the realm of academic theorizing.

## PERFORMANCE, PERFORMATIVITY, EXCESS, AND SHAME

Vaginal Davis's parodic drag is in some ways a direct descendent of J.L. Austin's theories of performative language. One infelicity that Austin dismissed early on in *How to Do Things with Words*, but that has important applications for the theories of gender performativity that grew out of his work, is the possibility that the performative is being performed for performance's sake, on a stage or as part of a conscious masquerade. An example of infelicity he gives is the 'mockery' in which 'there is no accepted conventional procedure; it is a mockery, like marriage with a monkey' (1962: 24).[4] Contemporary lesbians and gay men have performed mockeries of marriage, both as a joke and in earnest, between two or more women or men for a variety of reasons. One has been to highlight the fact that marriage is a convention, not a natural fact: that it is one of the building blocks of heterosexism and enforces specific oppressive positions for women and men. This kind of mockery is aggressive and self-consciously comic, often involving hairy-chested men in elaborate wedding gowns, burlesqued religious rituals, and broad sexual humor. This is somewhat akin to the Yippie nomination of a pig for US President in 1968 – not only did it call into question the whole US political process, it also cast some serious doubts on the calibre of the 'real' candidates and asked how different they were from the admittedly adorable pig nominee.

Not all mockeries are jokes, however. In most parts of the world and (as the repudiation of gay marriage in California with the passage of Proposition 8 in November 2008 shows) for many people, marriage between two women or two men is 'a mockery'. It falls outside the realm of convention; it is a legal impossibility except in those places in which it is specifically included in or has been added to the definition of marriage. Austin's example of marriage to a monkey is telling, since within the heterosexual matrix, marriage between two members of the same sex has the same performative values: not simply none, but a negative value. It is not just unhappy, it is a travesty.

Misperforming gender (that is, being on the receiving end of that judgment of travesty) whether on purpose – in a conscious mockery – or by mistake can be humiliating. In a culture in which heteronormativity rules

with stern resolve, and staying within gender norms is a central element of the heterosexual matrix, being mistaken for the 'wrong' gender is an embarrassment. This is particularly true for men, since to be identified with femaleness is by definition a step down, for women or for men. The words 'sissy', 'nelly', 'effeminate', all have a harsher sting than their equivalents 'butch' or 'mannish'. In many ways, formative learning experiences about gender have shame attached to them: parents or peers saying 'don't do that, it's not for girls/boys'.

Several theorists of gender performativity see shame as a focal point for understanding how gender works. Eve Kosofsky Sedgwick has speculated that experiencing shame has a foundational role in subject formation: In her essay *Queer Performativity* she argues that: 'Shame is a bad feeling attached to what one is: one therefore is *something*, in experiencing shame. The place of identity, the structure "identity".... may be established and naturalized in the first instance *through shame*' (1993: 12). For Sedgwick, then, shame is a constitutive element of all the things that make up identity, most centrally gender and sexuality; it is woven into the parts of ourselves that feel the most personal and the most important

In a more recent version of this essay, Sedgwick explores in detail not just how shame feels but what it *does* – that is, she theorizes it as a performative rather than as (just) an expression of an interior state. She draws on the psychologist Silvan Tomkins' work in affect theory, arguing that shame makes a double move 'toward painful individuation, toward uncontrollable relationality' (2003: 37). The prototype of shame is the parent who refuses to mirror back an infant's gaze or smile; it is 'a disruptive moment in a circuit of identity-constructing identificatory communication' (2003: 36) that makes the child feel simultaneously wholly alone and in need of connection. Shame constructs identity by interrupting relationality – either the refused connection of others who reject us, or dis/identification with the shameful behavior of others.

No wonder, then, that shame is such a rich topic for theories of sexuality, gender, and performativity. Like gender itself, shame plays out on the exterior of the body through averted eyes, ducked head, sometimes blushes, while being felt as an interior state (not to mention the desire to be interiorized, the desire to be swallowed up by the earth). And little is more shameful than being rendered either invisible or distasteful by others. The long focus in gay activism on visibility speaks precisely to the need to ward off the shame of not being seen or being misrecognized. And the psychoanalytic diagnosis of homosexuality as a disorder of paranoia and/or narcissism ('everyone's out to get me/the world revolves around me') is, ultimately, the inverse of the queer experience of shame in which one feels both invisible and hyperconspicuous in one's difference.

And no wonder that liberation movements are so often about pride, since they represent an attempt to root out that shame. However, Sedgwick argues, 'to view performativity in terms of habitual shame and its transformations opens a lot of new doors for thinking about identity politics' (2003: 62). Since the experience of shame is a vital part of the experience of being/becoming queer, 'the forms taken by shame are not distinct "toxic" parts of a group or individual identity that can be excised; they are instead integral to and residual in the processes by which identity itself is formed' (2003: 63). The performance of shame – the averted eyes, the hot face, and so on – are part of the accreted performance of difference itself. Drag, Butler's paradigm for the parody of heteronormativity, skates along the surface of shame and depends in very large part on context for its coherence – drag queens in a gay bar are not the same people as drag queens in a police van, for example.[5]

Sedgwick hardly sentimentalizes shame, but she does see shame as a pivotal tool in the struggle to rethink the coercive power of gender. What if the things we are supposed to be the most ashamed of, the things we are supposed to hide (our failed, or perverse, or incomplete, or mismanaged gender performances) are thrust front and center? Can there be liberation in shamelessness, which does not mean a neutralization of shame (as pride tries to do), but a celebration of the things we're supposed to be ashamed of? Sedgwick picks up on Butler's suggestion that a way out of gender performativity might be an exaggerated performance of the norm when, in a now classic essay co-written with Michael Moon (1993), she picks her ideal gender performer, the drag movie star Divine.

Divine was the alter ego of Baltimore actor Glenn Milstead, brought to life by director John Waters. She was not just enormously fat (over 300 pounds), she was deliciously trashy, starring in films such as *Mondo Trasho*, *Female Trouble*, *Pink Flamingos*, and, more respectably, *Hairspray*. Divine's characters were invariably tacky in fluffy high-heeled shoes and garish makeup, doing revolting things (things she should have been ashamed of ...) like cannibalism, incest, and, less dramatically, like being a big queen, being fat, being vulgar. Divine performs extravagantly all the shameful things about bodies that we're taught to eradicate or at least cover up from sight. Divine is sleazy, 'too much', a hyperbole of womanhood even as she is impossible to believe as the way we imagine 'real' women. But Divine's performance is as believable as the gender performances of any woman. On her they are as 'natural' as the performance of normative womanhood (which is to say, not at all) and as seemingly moored to her body. As Sedgwick and her co-writer Michael Moon point out, 'Divine's performances forcibly remind us [...] that "drag" [...] is inscribed not just in dress and its associated gender codes but in the body itself: in habitual and largely unconscious physical and psychological attitudes, poses, and styles of bodily relation and response' (1993: 220).

Here Sedgwick and Moon manage a kind of alliance between the coercive aspects of gender performativity and the extreme theatricality possible in drag. Divine's genius is in bridging the gap. She thinks she is just citing the performative rules of gender, and she acts 'natural' doing it, but to us it is so far from normative gender that it is grotesque (or delightful, depending on your taste). Divine makes a virtue out of her shame, shaking her viewers out of their acceptance of similar feelings. We cannot not choose shame, just as we cannot not choose our gender, but Divine transforms that coercion into an embrace.

## PERFORMATIVITY/THEATRICALITY

In their essay on Divine, Moon, and Sedgwick blur the line between performativity and theatricality, between heteronormativity and agency. By contrast, in all her work on gender performativity, Judith Butler sounds one chord over and over: gender may be performative but it is not (unless in the context of parody) theatrical. Gender is not constructed by a single act, but by a *process* that only seems stable, a process of reiteration that produces the effect of identity. As she maintains in *Bodies that Matter*, 'gender performativity cannot be theorized apart from the forcible and reiterative practice of regulatory sexual regimes [...] and in no way presupposes a choosing subject' (Butler, 1993: 15). In part this is because it is so hard to see outside gender performativity. After all, how can we know what alternative options might be if we could choose them? If our subjectivity – our sense of ourselves in every way – is constructed through the process of citing gender norms, and the attendant fears of failure, how could we possibly imagine life outside those norms? But even if we could, it is almost impossible to separate and choose individual gender behaviors from the larger system of gender performativity, or to separate them from an oppressive regime of heteronormativity.

But what about those people who change sex? Would not going through the process of having to unlearn one set of performances and pick up a whole new set provide adequate

space in between to see the gaps and fissures in gender? Not to say that such insight is inevitable – plenty of energy has been spent so that transsexuals can feel unselfconscious about performing their new genders, so they can feel like 'real' women and men. But there is a portion of the transsexual/transgender community that has tried to use that in between space as a place to undo gender.

Kate Bornstein has been a major voice in this movement. As a man, and later as a woman, Bornstein was painfully conscious of the coercive elements of gender performativity: 'I was always acting out something that everyone assumed I was' (1995: 8–9). In her discomfort with being a man and identifying as a woman, she underwent genital surgery and hormone treatments, going from Al to Kate. Ironically, under the pressure of having to perform femininity, she went through another profound transformation into a lesbian-identified feminist. Having had to unlearn masculinity and learn femininity, Bornstein embarked on the project of unlearning femininity as a woman. For Bornstein, feminism provided the place to look at gender critically; finally she could recognize the ways in which she had had to exert a huge amount of effort to acquire and maintain her gender identities in order to be a meaningful subject in her own eyes as well as the eyes of others.

In her writing and performance art, Bornstein has tried to imagine ways to re-imagine the terms along which we cite gender. Unlike Butler, Bornstein feels quite comfortable with the language of choice and affiliation – she believes it is possible to see outside the binary of heteronormativity, even if we do not know what is there. The metaphors that Bornstein uses for binary gender – a cult and a class system – are telling. While cults enforce membership by a delicate combination of coercion, threats and rewards, they are, at least at the beginning, voluntary. On the other hand, class may be something one is born into, but it is not biologically bounded in the same way we think of gender.

Bornstein asks, what would it be like to belong to a gender in the same way one might belong to a sports team, or a religion, or a fan club, or a political party, or a fraternal organization? Each of these modes of 'belonging' bring with them slightly different levels of choice, faith, activity, and enjoyment: most people join a religion for a set of reasons quite unlike the reasons others join an amateur soccer club. But all those memberships require a certain set of behaviors and performances that are both conventional *and* at least in part voluntary. After all, joining a sports team requires that you play by the rules, but does not force you to carry those rules into all elements of your life – only when you are playing. Bornstein does not deny the conventional and ritual elements of gender. Rather, she wants to refocus gender performativity as pure ritual. In a perfect world, being a woman would be about performing womanness rather than having to accept an ideological package along with it.

Perhaps the central phrase here is 'in a perfect world'. Bornstein is unembarrassed about the utopian quality of her theory. After all, she acknowledges that she still feels coerced by gender to perform her womanhood adequately, to be a convincing 'she'. Like Sedgwick and Moon, she does not underestimate the role of shame in the regime of heterocentric gender. Misperforming or being misperceived in her gender can still humiliate. More importantly, it is not clear from her writing how we could even achieve her goal of 'gender fluidity'. Accepting that gender is an imitation of a copy of an act *ad infinitum* is not necessarily the same as extricating oneself from its regulatory grip.

Susan Stryker, another transgender activist and scholar, takes on performativity in a very different way in her influential essay *My Words To Victor Frankenstein Above the Village of Chamounix – Performing Transgender Rage* (1994). Stryker's embrace of the term 'monster' to describe transgendered and transsexual people acknowledges that people can be remade, reshaped, re-gendered, put together out of spare parts – anything but organically and self-evidently, 'naturally' whole. As Stryker argues:

> though medical techniques for sex reassignment are capable of crafting bodies that satisfy the visual and morphological criteria that generate naturalness as their effect, engaging with those very techniques produces a subjective experience that belies the naturalistic effect biomedical technology can achieve. Transsexual embodiment, like the embodiment of the monster, places its subject in an unassimilable, antagonistic, queer relationship to a Nature in which it must nevertheless exist. (1994: 250)

Rather than reinforcing binary sex, Stryker suggests that sex reassignment reveals how constructed biological sex is. The transgendered postoperative body exists in opposition to the fantasy of nature, and through its performance of maleness or femaleness, gives us a sense of the ways in which sex is always a scrim through which bodies are understood, not a natural language bodies effortlessly speak. Interestingly, unlike Sedgwick, Moon, or Bornstein, Stryker is less interested in the potential of sexed and gendered bodies to self-consciously undo the mandates of heteronormativity and more invested in how, as drag does for Butler, transsexuality can widen the gaps in how sex and gender are reiterated. It is worth remarking upon, too, that Stryker's meditation and rage are occasioned by the birth of her lover's daughter, and the effortlessness with which the child is enlisted into sex with the performative utterance 'it's a girl', a phrase that transforms an ungendered, undefined newborn into a female subject. Certainly Butler points out the coercion of this phrase, but for Stryker, who was impressed into boy-and manhood at birth and consciously moved over into femaleness, this moment feels especially, bitter – she is forced to witness the moment at which sex is imposed, a moment that caused her so much pain from childhood into her adult life. As Stryker shows, thinking about gender assignment from a transgender lens intensifies the meaning of what heteronormativity does and dramatizes how biological sex itself is discursively imposed again and again.

## GENDER, ETHICS, AND THE LIVABLE LIFE

Stryker's reminder of the effects of performative utterances in coercing newborn children into gender extends discussions of performativity beyond the theoretical and into the realm of lived experience. How we actually experience our bodies, how we live in them, not just how we theorize them, has been a vexed subject for Butler; as she says, ventriloquizing her critics in Bodies that Matter, 'surely bodies live and die, eat and sleep; feel pain, pleasure; endure illness and violence; and these "facts", one might skeptically proclaim, cannot be dismissed as mere construction. Surely there must be some kind of necessity that accompanies these primary and irrefutable experiences' (1993: xi). Butler comes at this challenge from a few different directions. First, she argues that because something is discursively constructed does not mean it is not deeply felt and authentically experienced; the power of discourse is to invest its formations with profound emotional content (one might argue, somewhat counter-intuitively, that the more natural and inevitable something feels, the more complexly it is implicated in discourse – as Butler says, 'if certain constructions appear constitutive, that is, have this character of being that "without which" we could not think at all, we might suggest that bodies only appear, only endure, only live within the productive constraints of certain highly gendered regulatory schemas' [1993: xi]).

This, however, is only part of the answer. In a line of thought that finds its beginnings in Bodies that Matter and, I would argue, its apex in her 2004 book Undoing Gender, Butler engages in an ongoing meditation on what it might mean to occupy a body that does not have the imprimatur of gender in one way or another; that is, to live a life that discourse makes no room for. For Butler, this is the conundrum of 'livability'.

Much of Butler's focus on livability intersects with her interest in mourning, melancholia, and grief.[6] This is hardly surprising: Butler's entrance into academic life overlapped with the first years of the HIV/AIDS epidemic in the United States, and her writing is suffused with discussions of the threat of homophobic violence and the psychic costs of grief, particularly grief that cannot be spoken publicly or fully and adequately mourned.

In her 1997 book, Excitable Speech: A Politics of the Performative, Butler takes up other ways in which one can do things with words, particularly the concept of hate speech, speech that is imagined to be analogous to physical or psychic violence (and that intensifies the kind of interpellation that she worked through in Gender Trouble). And the foundational idea of performative gender and its difficult relationship to the political wends its way through all her work. But it is in her most recent book, Undoing Gender, that Butler extends her thinking about performative identity in profound new directions, expanding far deeper into the realm of ethics and the possibility of living what she calls a 'livable life' within the current regimes of gender and sexuality.

Undoing Gender moves far beyond Butler's earlier work of analyzing how gender operates and moves in the direction of thinking about how we might undo it or help it come undone. It is, I would argue, a profoundly ethical book, engaged with questions of how one should treat others, how lives might (rather than should) be lived, and how it might be possible to make currently unlivable lives feel more livable. Certainly, it is rooted in theories of performativity, but its focus is on the process of interpellation as much as or more than the citation of the performative. For, as Althusser showed, we cannot exist as subjects without being called into subjectivity. But for Butler interpellation is not just being called; it is being recognized as a person, being able to see oneself as part of a community, a polity, a family, or any other kind of human group. That is to say, we are not simply called into subjecthood by impersonal forces of ideology or discourse.

We are also called into ourselves by those closest to us – those who have the most power to make us feel loved or unlovable.

This raises a significant dilemma: 'I may feel that without some recognizability I cannot live. But I may also feel that the terms by which I am recognized make life unlivable' (Butler, 2004: 4). Susan Stryker, movingly encapsulates this dilemma in her essay 'My Words to Victor Frankenstein': 'A gendering violence is the founding condition of human subjectivity; having a gender is the tribal tattoo that makes one's personhood cognizable. I stood for a moment between the pains of two violations, the mark of gender and the unlivability of its absence. Could I say which one was worse? Or could I only say which one I felt could best be survived?' (1994: 252) Livability requires some level of loss – the question is what kind of loss is least damaging?

*Undoing Gender* recognizes that gender is, in the final analysis, a relational act, a performative organized around and filtered through desire: through (in Lacanian terms) those things we most want and cannot – perhaps should not – have. This seems to me its greatest achievement. While *Gender Trouble* is a tour de force of philosophical argument, it is, in the final analysis, bloodless. The battles it fights are theoretical and seem oddly untouched by the bodies it analyzes. In *Undoing Gender*, by contrast, Butler puts her cards on the table: 'Let's face it', she writes, 'we're undone by each other. And if we're not we're missing something. If this seems so clearly the case with grief, it is only because it was already the case with desire' (2004: 19).

We may perform gender within ourselves, but within gender we are 'given to the other'; although we are bound by the language of individuality, that discourse 'fails to do justice to passion, grief, and rage, all of which tear us from ourselves, bind us to others, transport us, undo us, and implicate us in lives that are not our own, sometimes fatally, irreversibly' (Butler, 2004: 20). A struggle for rights, then, is not just a fight for individual freedoms, but for the possibility '*to be*

*conceived as persons*' (2004: 32), even as the process of interpellation forces us into performing identities that shut down other ways we might be or want to be.

In *Undoing Gender*, Butler is particularly interested in exploring the work that norms do. On the one hand, norms are not free-standing, they do not exist outside their discursive contexts. Norms exist to the extent that they are performed, insofar as people enact and re-enact them. As Butler argued for drag in *Gender Trouble*, this opens a window of opportunity, since 'to the extent that gender norms are *reproduced*, they are invoked and cited by bodily practices that also have the capacity to alter norms in the course of their citation' (2004: 52, original emphasis). Much of Butler's work in *Undoing Gender*, then, is to explore those moments in which citationality might be disrupted, either consciously or unconsciously, to undo gender (or, perhaps in a more deconstructive vein, to show how gender is undoing itself).

The most poignant example of this is the story of David/Brenda. In infancy, David's penis was severely injured, and his parents, with the encouragement of doctors and psychologists, decided to raise him as a girl – 'Brenda' (this was further complicated by the fact that David had an identical twin brother). Butler's analysis here is fascinating. She both interrogates explanations of this story that would insist on the essential nature of David's maleness while at the same time taking seriously David's own narrative of trauma at being coerced into girlhood. Her larger concern is that the process by which David was Brenda and then became David (again) proceeded against the insistence that Brenda fulfill certain gendered mandates or risk being unlovable. David's achievement, in Butler's analysis, is not that he (re)claimed maleness, but that despite the hostility of doctors to any deviation from femininity on Brenda's part, s/he decided that s/he was worth loving, that her/his life was worth living.

David/Brenda's radical act was to claim a right to selfhood, to insist on inclusion in 'universal' values of intrinsic human worth. While this might seem to run counter to Butler's strictly anti-foundationalist claim that subjectivity is a set of effects produced by reiterated acts, towards the end of *Undoing Gender* she stakes a claim to the 'universal' in explicitly nonessentialist terms. The 'universal' has, after all, always existed as a way to exclude exceptions – women, queers, the colonized, the disabled, to name a few – who then could not lay claim to the rights, responsibilities, and privileges membership in universal humanity provides; moreover, the 'universal' depends upon those exclusions for its definitional integrity.[7]

For Butler, this double move of claiming universality while limiting 'the universal' to a specific group of people is the source of possible challenges to the claim itself. As she observes, 'to be excluded from the universal, and yet to make a claim within its terms, is to utter a performative contradiction of a certain kind [...] To claim that the universal has not yet been articulated is to insist that the "not yet" is proper to an understanding of the universal itself: that which remains "unrealized" by the universal constitutes it essentially' (2004: 191). At this moment, Butler reverses the process of interpellation, breaks open the routine of performativity. To bestow upon oneself the name that is defined through one's exclusion, to perform an identity that pushes to the margins the identity with which one is brought into being, to insist on livability, on lovability in the face of hostility and violence is, ultimately, the reparative work that not just troubling but *undoing* gender can do.

## PERFORMING THE UNIVERSAL

For me, Butler's radical reworking of the concept of the universal through the mechanism of performativity is the most valuable contribution her recent work has made. The language of 'sexual rights' has increasingly taken hold in transnational sexuality studies

and particularly in the world of the United Nations and non-governmental organizations, but there has been surprisingly little discussion of how we might understand human rights outside of a Eurocentric/colonialist context without simply rejecting 'human rights' as a valuable concept. Butler's commitment to contingency, to not knowing where we might end up, could be seen as an impediment to the discourse of universal rights, which depends so heavily on unanimity and certitude. However, her focus on what we need to feel loved, that our lives should not just proceed, but flourish, seems to me exactly the right formula for thinking about human rights in general and sexual rights in particular.

This insight intersects powerfully with the assumptions behind disability studies, which insists that the able bodied should not simply help people with disabilities adjust to the world as it is, but rather recognize that the ethos that disabled communities embrace – values of interdependence, accommodation, and the contingency of human bodies – can benefit everyone, and would create a more just and equitable world for everyone. My own work on Audre Lorde's *Zami* and its uses of blindness tries to exemplify this rethinking of universal assumptions about sexuality and vision (Chinn, 2003). For Lorde, near-blindness provides 'Audre', *Zami*'s protagonist, with alternative models of sexual desire and pleasure that do not lament the lack of visuality but instead create generative ways of wholly rethinking sexual connection between people along the registers of touch, smell, and taste.

In this context, then, sexual desire, sexual self-determination, and sexual pleasure are profoundly shaped by the circumstances that produce them, but not in the usual way: that is, not in a way that attempts to regulate and normalize them. In *Zami*, circumstances that some readers might interpret as limiting sexual pleasure – the inability to see the object of one's desire crisply and clearly, for example – actually make possible a rich and rewarding register of sexual practices and perceptions. Visuality is not done away with, and Lorde in no way argues that enjoying desire through looking cannot provide a whole host of pleasures. But she bypasses the old arguments about the power of the gaze by imagining sexualities that do not *need* vision to be fully inhabited. Looking becomes one strategy among others – and in many ways a pretty poor strategy at that – to experience sex, sexual desire, and sexual identity.

In *Undoing Gender*, Butler quotes Cheryl Chase's central critique of doctors who deal with babies who are intersexed or have ambiguous or nonspecific genitalia: 'They can't conceive of leaving someone alone' (2004: 64).[8] Leaving an intersexed person alone is deeply challenging to dimorphic ideas about sex and gender and raises any number of possibly disturbing questions: what might it mean for someone to figure out their gender as they went along? How might an un-, partially, or multiply gendered person exist in the world? What kind of world would we need to make that existence not just livable but actually pleasurable? And, finally, what might the experience of intersexuality be able to teach those of us who are more invested in our genders about the structures of gender, genital anatomy, sexual pleasure, fashion choices, children's toys, to name just a few intersecting phenomena? The tendency towards a kind of imperialism within discursive structures about cultural and sexual difference fosters the belief in the mainstream that the dominant group knows more about marginalized people than they know about themselves, that they know what's best for them, and that of course those on the margins are yearning to be just like those at the center. The impulse to leave people alone does not necessarily have to operate as libertarianism, or result in their loneliness: for Chase it seems much more to be part of a collaborative project in which parents, doctors, friends, communities, other children, teachers, and so on can be involved to help create a loving world for intersexed people.[9]

Towards the end of *Undoing Gender*, Butler argues that 'the thought of a possible life is only an indulgence for those who already know themselves to be possible. For those who are still looking to become possible, possibility is a necessity' (2004: 219). The ethical challenge, then, is to create the conditions of possibility for *more*: more possibility, more kinds of subjectivity, more genders, more sexualities, more justice, more self-consciousness and reflexivity, more pleasure, more care for others, more love for ourselves and the ones we love, more relationality. Certainly, there will always be loss and grief and pain. But those experiences should be lived through with dignity rather than humiliation (a lesson that HIV/AIDS and AIDS phobia has taught us with terrible clarity). To experience ourselves as fully human in relation to ourselves and other people is perhaps our greatest challenge, and our most important task.

## NOTES

1   In fact, by the end of the lecture series, Austin had thoroughly undone the opposition between performative and constative language, arguing, in essence, that all language both describes and does. But for our purposes, this opposition functions.

2   Indeed, by the age of four or five, my own children were constructing complex methods of promising and betting, and expressed deep outrage at the possibility of broken promises and bets placed in bad faith.

3   This was not an entirely new idea. Inspired largely by Foucault, scholars in the 1980s, particularly those associated with the journal *Representations*, argued that 'the human body itself has a history' aside from, and even in opposition to, scientific discoveries about bodily function (Gallagher and Laqueur, p. vii). For example, in his groundbreaking essay 'Orgasm, generation, and the politics of reproductive biology', Thomas Laqueur showed how up until the beginning of the nineteenth century, Western anatomy conceived of male and female bodies were structurally the same, and that female reproductive organs were simply male anatomy tucked inside women's bodies because of women's 'insufficient heat to extrude the organs of reproduction' (1987: 5). Female orgasm warmed up women's reproductive organs sufficiently to allow for conception, so orgasm was, in this view, essential to successful reproduction. This idea, what Laqueur calls

the 'one sex model', had almost wholly evaporated by the nineteenth century, amid an insistence of women's lack of sexual desire. Laqueur argues that 'neither advances in reproductive biology nor anatomical discoveries seem sufficient to explain the dramatic revaluation of female orgasm that occurred in the late eighteenth century and the even more dramatic reinterpretation of the female body' as opposite to the male, what he calls the 'two sex model' (1987: 17).

Laqueur comes to the conclusion that 'the political, economic, and cultural transformations of the eighteenth century created the context in which the articulation of radical differences between the sexes became culturally imperative' (1987: 35). Unlike Butler a few years later, however, he does not question the transparency of 'the sexes'; that is, while he shows how understandings of anatomical differences between men and women changed radically in less than a century, he takes for granted that certain anatomical arrangements inevitably and naturally represent sexed selves, something Butler works to undermine.

4   In her essay 'Around the performative', Eve Kosofsky Sedgwick jokes that Austin's repeated recursion to marriage as the definitive performative act, 'a more accurate name for *How to Do Things with Words* might have been *How to say (or write) 'I do' hundreds of times without winding up any more married than you started out*' (p. 70).

5   More recently, Kathryn Bond Stockton has analyzed the interconnections of shame around the axes of sexuality and race. Stockton argues that 'we cannot grasp certain complicated cultural, historical entanglements between 'black' and 'queer' without, at the same time, interrogating shame – its beautiful, generative, sorrowful debasements that make bottom pleasures so dark and so strange' (2006: 8).

6   One of Butler's most provocative theories about heteronormativity is that it is formed in part through melancholy, that is, through unresolved grief at the enforced foreclosure of the possibility of same-sex desire and love. Within this theory, 'drag exposes or allegorizes the mundane psychic and performative practices by which heterosexualized genders form themselves through the renunciation of the *possibility* of homosexuality, a foreclosure that produces a field of heterosexual objects at the same time that it produces a domain of those whom it would be impossible to love' (1993: 235).

7   A well-known example of this phenomenon is Saul Bellow's claim that European literary production is transparently great, and that other cultures' artistic production can only be judged by those 'universal standards'. This unself-conscious assumption of universal artistic value produced by a very limited demographic group of people that explicitly excludes other forms of art is best encapsulated by his question in

7 March 1988 *New Yorker*, 'Who is the Tolstoy of the Zulus? The Proust of the Papuans? I'd be glad to read him.'

8   For a fascinating example of this inability on the part of surgeons, see Paula Machado (2008). Machado was present during a debate among doctors about 'what to do with' a child who was born with ambiguous sex chromosomes and genitalia. In Machado's telling, the question by one of the doctors 'but why operate?' was met with 'a degree of shock and even impatience. Laughter and mutters could also be heard. After all, the team's concern was how best to intervene, which required the unequivocal definition of the baby's sex' (2008: 238).

9   My own experience of having children has both sharpened my commitment to leaving intersexed babies alone and the immense challenges such a decision entails. When I was pregnant, I thought a great deal about what I would do if one of my children (I was carrying twins) were born intersexed and felt strongly that I would not intervene surgically. Now raising a boy and a girl I am very aware of how gender is policed both for and by young children. My own desire to let my children make their own gendered decisions is far more complicated than I had imagined, given the welter of other pressures from every other part of their lives: school, friends, television, books, extended family, and their own efforts to work out what gender means and how it operates.

# REFERENCES

Althusser, L. (1971) 'Ideology and ideological state apparatuses', in *Lenin and Philosophy and Other Essays*. Trans. Ben Brewster, pp: 170–86. London: NLB.

Anzaldúa, G. (1987) *Borderlands/La Frontera: The New Mestiza*. San Francisco, CA: Spinsters/Aunt Lute Books.

Austin, J.L. (1962) *How to Do Things With Words: The William James Lectures Delivered at Harvard University in 1955*. Cambridge, MA: Harvard University Press.

Bornstein, K. (1995) *Gender Outlaw: On Men, Women, and the Rest of Us*. New York: Vintage Books.

Butler, J. (1990) *Gender Trouble: Feminism and the Subversion of Identity*. New York: Routledge.

Butler, J. (1993) *Bodies that Matter: On the Discursive Limits of 'Sex'*. New York: Routledge.

Butler, J. (1997) *Excitable Speech: A Politics of the Performative*. New York: Routledge.

Butler, J. (2004) *Undoing Gender*. New York: Routledge.

Carby, H. (1987) *Reconstructing Womanhood: The Emergence of the Afro-American Woman Novelist*. New York: Oxford University Press.

Case, S.-E. (1993) 'Toward a butch-femme aesthetic', in H. Abelove et al. (eds), *The Lesbian and Gay Studies Reader*, pp: 294–306. New York: Routledge.

Chinn, S.E. (2003) 'Feeling her way: Audre Lorde and the power of touch', in R. McRuer and A. Wilkerson (eds), *Desiring Disability: Queer Studies Meets Disability Studies. GLQ*, 9: 1–2.

Combahee River Collective (1983) 'The Combahee River Collective Statement', in B. Smith (ed.), *Home Girls: A Black Feminist Anthology*, pp: 272–81. New York: Kitchen Table, Women of Color Press.

Crenshaw, K.W. (1993) 'Beyond racism and misogyny: Black feminism and 2 Live Crew', in M.J. Matsuda et al. (eds), *Words That Wound: Critical Race Theory, Assaultive Speech and the First Amendment*, pp: 111–32. Boulder, CO: Westview Press.

Derrida, J. (1972) *Limited, Inc.* Trans. Alan Bass. Evanston, IL: Northwestern University Press.

Foucault, M. (1977) *The History of Sexuality: an Introduction*. Trans. Alan Hurley. New York: Vintage.

Frankenberg, R. (1993) *White Women, Race Matters: The Social Construction of Whiteness*. Minneapolis, MN: University of Minnesota Press.

Fuss, D. (1993) *Essentially Speaking: Feminism, Nature, and Difference*. New York: Routledge.

Gallagher, C. and Thomas L. (eds) (1987) *The Making of the Modern Body: Sexuality and Society in the Nineteenth Century*. Berkeley, CA: University of California Press.

Harper, P.B. (1996) *Are We Not Men? Masculine Anxiety and the Problem of African-American Identity*. New York: Oxford University Press.

Laqueur, T. (1987) 'Orgasm, generation, and the politics of reproductive biology', in Gallagher, C. and Laqueur, T. (eds), 1–41.

Lloyd, M. (2007) *Judith Butler: From Norms to Politics*. Cambridge: Polity Press.

Machado, P. (2008) 'Intersexuality and sexual rights in Southern Brazil', *Culture, Health and Society*, 11: 237–50.

McClintock, A., Mufti, A. and Shohat, E. (eds) (1997) *Dangerous Liaisons: Gender, Nation and Postcolonial Perspectives*. Minneapolis, MN: University of Minnesota Press.

Mohanty, C.T. (1997) 'Under Western eyes: Feminist scholarship and colonial discourses', in A. McClintock, A. Mufti and E. Shohat (eds), *Dangerous Liaisons: Gender, Nation and Postcolonial Perspectives*. Minneapolis, MN: University of Minnesota Press.

Muñoz, J.E. (1999) *Disidentifications: Queers of Color and the Performance of Politics*. Minneapolis, MN: University of Minnesota Press.

Riley, D. (1988) *'Am I That Name?': Feminism and the Category of 'Women' in History*. London: Macmillan.

Ross, E. and Rapp, R. (1983) 'Sex and society: A research note from social history and anthropology', in A. Snitow, C. Stansell and S. Thompson (eds), *Powers of Desire: The Politics of Sexuality*, pp: 51–73. New York: Monthly Review Press.

Sedgwick, E.K. (2003) *Touching Feeling: Affect, Pedagogy, Performativity*. Durham, NC: Duke University Press.

Sedgwick, E.K. and Moon, M. (1993) 'Divinity: A dossier, a performance piece, a little-understood emotion', in *Tendencies*, pp: 215–51. Durham: Duke University Press.

Stockton, K.B. (2006) *Beautiful Bottom, Beautiful Shame: Where 'Black' Meets 'Queer'…* Durham, NC: Duke University Press.

Stryker, S. (1994) 'My words to Victor Frankenstein above the village of Chamounix: Performing transgender rage', *GLQ*, 1: 237–54.

Waters, J. *Female Trouble* (1974), *Multiple Maniacs* (1970), *Pink Flamingos* (1972) *and Other Films* (widely available on video).

# 6

# Critical Crossovers: Postcolonial Perspectives, Subaltern Studies and Cultural Identities

Saurabh Dube

This chapter discusses issues of identity as embedded in and articulated by postcolonial perspectives and subaltern studies. In speaking of identities, my reference is to wide-ranging processes of formations of subjects, expressing not only particular personhoods but also collective groupings. Upon such an understanding, identities comprise a crucial means through which social processes are perceived, experienced and articulated. Indeed, defined within historical relationships of production and reproduction, appropriation and approbation, and power and difference, cultural identities (and their mutations) are essential elements in the quotidian constitution (and pervasive transformations) of social worlds. This chapter explores the ways in which postcolonial and subaltern approaches have considered cultural and historical identities as part of critical elaborations, at once theoretical and empirical, of colony and empire, history and community, and nation and modernity.

## UNRAVELLING ORIENTATIONS

Around three decades ago, Edward Said's seminal study, *Orientalism* (1978) crucially underscored the mutual entailments of European colonialism and empire with western knowledge and power. Of course, long before the appearance of this work there existed several studies of European images of non-European peoples, which identified various stereotypes, especially surrounding the identities of the self and the other. However, such work tended to be 'documentary rather than critical or analytical', so that an intriguing array of examples of European representations was presented, but their 'discursive affiliations and underlying epistemologies' were frequently underplayed (Thomas, 1994: 22–3). Intervening in this field, *Orientalism* made a persuasive case for the discursive fabrication – at once, ideological and material – of the Orient as an object and identity through the profound dynamic of knowledge and power constitutive of western empires.

Now, it is not only that anti-colonial thinking has a longer past than Said's study – a question to which I will return – but that, exactly at the time of the first publication and early receptions of *Orientalism*, there were other writings expressing related concerns (Abdel-Malek, 1963; Fabian, 1983; Grosrichard, 1998 [1979]; JanMohamed, 1983; Nandy, 1982). At the same time, it is equally the case that Said's arguments had an unprecedented, ripple effect on scholarship. On the one hand, *Orientalism* had shifted the terms of debate and discussion on metropolitan representations of non-European peoples and their cultural identities. Here was a shift from uncovering the singular biases of determinate depictions to unravelling the deeper domains of discursive domination, a move that further highlighted the complicity between earlier imperial imaginings and contemporary academic renderings of the Orient. On the other hand, Said's work came to crystallize the key emphases – and critical tensions – of an emergent academic arena, one entailing explorations of colonial discourses and imperial representations.

In this terrain, the implications and weaknesses of prior critical work on colonial writing, including *Orientalism*, were elaborated, extended, and exceeded by studies bearing distinct orientations. Especially important were Homi Bhabha's (1994) explorations of the inherent 'ambivalence' of colonial discourse – as well as the disruptive, 'hybrid' identities of colonized subjects – in order to challenge singular conceptions of colonial cultural writings.[1] Such endeavours further intersected with other ongoing struggles around issues of identities, especially those undertaken by minorities and feminists (JanMohamed and Lloyd, 1990; Spivak, 1985). They also acutely elaborated poststructuralist theory, expressly endorsing anti-humanist perspectives (Bhabha, 1994; Spivak, 1988). Taken together, from the early 1980s, discussions and debates on western representations of non-western worlds and

non-European identities, as part of the wider elaboration of critical theories of colonial discourse, led to the gradual emergence of the field (now even considered a discipline) of postcolonial studies – not solely in metropolitan academic arenas but gradually also in provincial scholarly terrains.[2]

Over the past two decades, important interventions by postcolonial critics – as well as by scholars of anthropology, history and religion – have gone on to access yet exceed colonial discourse theory. Exploring the 'idea', 'invention' and 'imagination' of diverse subordinate, geo-political terrains and identities across the globe (Inden, 1990; Mudimbe, 1988, 1994; Rabasa, 1993), such endeavours have further seized upon the contradictory, contingent and contested dynamics of empire and nation. These dynamics were driven by interlocking identities of class and gender and race and sexuality. As we shall see, such writings have focussed on projects of power as shaped by the acute entanglements of the dominant and the subaltern, the colonizer and the colonized, and the metropolis and the margins. They have variously questioned thereby the unchallenged efficacy accorded to authoritative agendas of empire, nation, modernity and globalization. Indeed, such scholarship has drawn upon historical, ethnographic and literary materials to trace the interplay between the construction and institutionalisation of emergent identities – entailing key conjunctions of racial and sexual boundaries and gender and class divisions as constitutive of colonial cultures, postcolonial locations and western orders (see Dube, 2004a, b, 2007a for wider discussions). Unsurprisingly, postcolonial studies constitute today a vibrant field of debate and discussion.

Accompanying these developments, from the end of the 1970s, critical departures were afoot in the history writing of the Indian subcontinent. Reassessments of nationalism in South Asia were often central to such endeavours (Chakrabarty, 2002; Sarkar, 1983). Here, an important role was played by the formation of the subaltern studies endeavour, based on meetings between a small set of enthusiastic younger historians of India, most of them then in England, with a distinguished senior scholar of colonial India, Ranajit Guha, who taught History at the University of Sussex. The protagonist were separated by a generation yet shared a mutual political and ethical sensibility (Prakash, 1994). The purpose of their discussions in England and India was to thrash out a new agenda for the historiography of the subcontinent, an agenda that recognized the centrality of subordinate groups – rightful but disinherited protagonists – in the making of the past, and thereby redressed the elitist imbalance of much of the writing on the subject. Thus, the subaltern studies project was born (for details see Dube, 2004a).

Drawing on yet departing from wider traditions of 'histories from below', especially its British variants, an opening programmatic statement defined the aim of the endeavour as an effort 'to promote a systematic and informed discussion of subaltern themes in the field of South Asian Studies to rectify the elitist bias of much research and academic work' (Guha, 1982: viii). Here, the category of the subaltern, derived from the writings of the Italian socialist Antonio Gramsci, was used as a metaphor for the general attribute of subordination in South Asia – whether such subordination was expressed in terms of class, caste, age, gender, race or office.

Clearly, questions of identity were central to the project. Thus, the earlier exercises within the endeavour exactly articulated subaltern identities, reconstructing the varied trajectories and the modes of consciousness of the movements of subordinate groups in India in order to emphasize the autonomy and agency of these communities (Guha, 1982–89). Such articulations of historical identities within subaltern studies had a dual dimensions: for one part, the notion of subaltern could acquire the attributes of a singular and homogeneous entity; at the same time, expressed as a critical category the subaltern held possibilities of sustaining analyses that elaborated the articulation of distinct

identities – of community and class, caste and race, and gender and nation.

Not surprisingly, as part of the extended development of the subaltern studies endeavour the identities of the subaltern – as a category and an entity – have found ever varied and even wider manifestations. On the one hand, more recent writings within the project have discussed the multiple mediations and diverse modalities – social and epistemic in nature, cultural and discursive in character – that shore up the production of subaltern subjects and their mutating identities. Here, the writings of Shahid Amin (1995), Partha Chatterjee (1993, 2004), Dipesh Chakrabarty (2000, 2002), Gyanendra Pandey (2001, 2006) and Gyan Prakash (1999) in particular have variously utilized the notion of the subaltern in order to interrogate dominant knowledge(s) of empire and nation, state and modernity. On the other hand, with the original impulse of subaltern studies finding varied appropriations and extensions across different continents from at least the 1990s, there have arisen debates and discussions that have been animated by broader considerations of colonial knowledge and postcolonial difference, multicultural politics and cultural identities.[3] Especially influential in these arenas have been Gayatri Spivak's writings that harness 'deconstructionist' readings and 'strategic' sensibilities to fashion against-the-grain readings of subaltern subjects (Guha and Spivak, 1988; Spivak, 1987, 1988).[4] All of this has further underscored the question of the convergences between subaltern and postcolonial studies.

Now, it warrants emphasis that postcolonial and subaltern approaches are often elided with each other. Yet, as the discussion so far would have indicated, the two should not be simply collapsed together. Thus, while postcolonial orientations emerged under the sign of the colony, the subaltern studies project was born under the mark of the nation. This is to say that whereas postcolonial understandings privileged colonialism as a historical departure in the making of the modern world, the subaltern studies project took as its starting point the requirements of examining 'the failure of the nation to come into its own' (Guha, 1982: ix).

It is also the case, however, that from the beginning critical engagements both with colony and nation have characterized these two approaches, at the very least implicitly. This should not be surprising. To start off, the ideological antecedents not only of postcolonial perspectives but of subaltern studies lay in long and critical traditions of anti-colonial thought and decolonizing practice. Here, the writings and politics of Frantz Fanon, Amílcar Cabral and Aimé Césaire could acutely influence the very formations of postcolonial scholarship. At the same time, the terms and textures of subaltern studies – in a manner convergent with postcolonial perspectives – emerged equally informed by wider anti-imperial sensibilities. Such sensibilities extended from the diverse politics of counter-colonialism and decolonization that began in 1940s through to events of the 1960s entailing critiques of imperialism and racism – embodied, for example, in the dramatic moment of 1968 – and the continuation of these struggles into the 1970s across different parts of the world. Together, postcolonial and subaltern studies were preceded and shaped by these wider developments and the extension of their spirit into academic arenas, especially the emergent critiques of reigning paradigms within the disciplines as well as formations of new perspectives on the left, including 'world-systems' theory, radical peasant studies and critical revisions of Marxism (Asad, 1973; Vincent, 1990: 225–9, 308–14; Wolfe, 1997).

Indeed, having registered the limitations of readily collapsing subaltern and postcolonial perspectives, in what follows I elaborate the key developments that have emerged from the intersections between these enquiries. It follows, too, that instead of attending to momentarily significant yet ultimately narrow academic controversies that have surrounded these approaches, my focus is on the place of these perspectives in articulating wider worlds of identity and alterity, and meaning

and power. Together, throughout the chapter my attempt would be to eschew the tendency towards comfortably foreclosing postcolonial and subaltern studies as bounded arenas in order to open up instead the possibilities they hold as intellectual enquiries.

## CONTENTIOUS QUESTIONS

From their beginnings, postcolonial criticism and subaltern studies have been characterized by intellectual silences and theoretical tensions, issues that I have discussed elsewhere (Dube, 2004a, b). The point now is that to approach these scholarly tendencies as shaped by key contentions is to acknowledge at once their limitations *and* possibilities. Such a task further requires considering these knowledge formations in the manner of critical rubrics – rather than hypostatizing them as fully finished knowledge(s) – that emerge intimately linked to other theoretical orientations.

On the one hand, the crucial difficulties that beset the postcolonial and the subaltern as categories and perspectives derive from the fact that their many meanings and persistent contentions register unproductive ambiguity. Thus, as has been repeatedly emphasized, among others by prominent postcolonial critics such as Anne McClintock (1995) and Ella Shohat (1996), the concept of the postcolonial has rested upon the divide between the colonial and the postcolonial. Here, following an apparently historical but in fact acutely ideological insinuation, one totalized terrain (the colonial) leads to another undifferentiated arena (the postcolonial). This serves to homogenize history and to sanitize politics. Not surprisingly, the notion of the subaltern has been equally dogged with accusations of empirical imprecision, analytical aggrandizement and epistemological obfuscation. The charges stick when postcolonial and subaltern studies are treated as privileged perspectives and exclusive enquiries.

On the other hand, across different scholarly disciplines and diverse academic contexts, abiding endeavours engaging and articulating postcolonial and subaltern perspectives have undertaken salient tasks, each carrying acute implications for understandings of identities. To begin with, such efforts have rethought empire, including by pointing to the prior and persistent play of colonial schemes in contemporary worlds. They have highlighted thereby the immense import and ongoing influence of the interplay between enlightenment and empire, race and reason, the metropolis and the margins, and religion and politics. Moreover, writings in this terrain have severally questioned the place of an imaginary yet palpable 'west' as history, modernity and destiny – for each culture and every identity. Especially important here have been newer understandings of communities, histories and modernities, which have challenged prior, modular conceptions of these categories-entities. Furthermore, endeavours elaborating subaltern and postcolonial identities have unravelled the terms and limits of state, nation and citizen in western and non-western worlds, prudently underscoring the significance of critical difference in such distinct yet entangled terrain. Finally, in taking up such tasks, the most prescient efforts have pointed to the critical place and presence not only of elite and heroic protagonists but of marginal and subaltern subjects – simultaneously shaped by the crisscrossing identities of gender and race, caste and class, age and office, community and sexuality – in the making of colony and modernity, empire and nation, religion and politics, and state and citizen. To register such critical developments is to cast postcolonial propositions and subaltern studies as participant-interlocutors in wider, ongoing debates rethinking the nation-state and the west, the colony and the post-colony, and history and modernity (for a wider discussion, see Dube, 2004a). Clearly, issues of identity have played a crucial role here.

When I write of identity the reference is to processes of formations of subjects –

processes, formations, and subjects that militate against persistent projections of sovereign 'individuals' and primordial 'communities'. Instead, as indicated earlier, identities entail at once collective groupings and particular personhoods, where the one betokens the other. This is to say that as critical attributes of the constitution of subjects, identities form essential elements in the everyday production and reproduction of social life. They turn on simultaneously symbolic and substantive – and structured yet fluid – attitudes and imaginings, norms and practices, and rituals and dispositions. Here are to be found the resources through which social relationships within and between groups, classes, communities and genders are perceived, experienced and articulated.

Moreover, in the perspective that I am sketching, identities are defined within historical relationships of production and reproduction, appropriation and consumption, empire and modernity, and nation and globalization. They emerge critically mediated by shifting configurations of gender and caste, race and age, office and sexuality. Such relationships and configurations, predicated upon power, involve diverse renderings of domination and subordination – as well as negotiations and contestations of authority – in distinct arenas. Constitutive of dominant and subaltern identities, here are to be found contradictory processes that are simultaneously characterized by the work of hegemony and the reworking of power, which form part of the same logic.[5]

Lastly, in such an orientation, identity neither spells a priori sameness, nor indicates unchanging inventories of exclusive beliefs, bounded traditions and distinct customs of particular communities. Rather, identities entail at once assertions of sameness and practices of difference. They turn upon the ways in which symbolic imaginaries and meaningful practices are implicated in and lived within human worlds, insinuated at the core of the entangled relationships and contentious processes of these terrains. Since these relationships, processes and worlds change, transformation and difference are at the heart of identities.

It bears emphasis that underscoring the intersections between overlapping yet distinct processes of power, technologies of representation, relationships of production and modes of reproduction as critical to the articulation of identities – themselves rendered as an integral part of historical practices – has important consequences. Challenging pervasive, commonplace, reductive projections of identity, it clears the ground for explorations of the substantive, mutual contributions of subaltern studies and postcolonial perspectives in understandings of identities.[6] It is to such critical contributions that I now turn.

## COLONY AND EMPIRE

Influential tendencies within postcolonial perspectives and subaltern studies have tended to treat colony and empire as totalized formations (Dube, 2004b, 2007a). At the same time, important writings within these fields, broadly understood, have also thought through postulates of overarching colonial structures and overriding imperial systems. Such rethinking has been led by seminal scholarship in historical anthropology – for example, the work of Jean and John Comaroff (1991, 1992, 1997) and Ann Stoler (1995, 2002, 2008), among others. Studies in this new genre have explored the contradictory location and contending agendas of distinct colonizing peoples and diverse colonized groups in the creation of colonial cultures of rule. This has involved discussions of the representations and practices and the boundaries and the contradictions of imperial agents, settler communities and evangelizing missionaries in colonial locations. In brief, there have been critical examinations not only of colonized populations but also of colonizing peoples, even if the programmatic desire toward treating the colonizer and the colonized as part of a single analytical field has sometimes receded into the background here.

At any rate, such studies have revealed the persistent fault lines and the critical divisions between different agents of colonialism, diverse agendas of empire (for wider discussions see, Comaroff and Comaroff, 1991; Dube, 2004a; Stoler, 1989; also see, Guha, 2004; Wolfe, 1999). On the one hand, the racial mythologies and the 'home-spun' life styles of colonizers sought to blur such faultlines. On the other, divisions between different colonialist groups also stood highlighted within everyday representations and quotidian practices in distinct contexts.

It follows that the view of colonialism as a monolithic venture, a seamless and homogeneous project stands severely tested today. At issue here are not only the variations in the colonial endeavours and imperial exertions of different nations and separate epochs, featuring diverse forms of production and exchange, all important distinctions recognized in earlier scholarship. Rather, recent ethnographies and histories have revealed that the conflicting interests and the contending visions of empire of differentially located interests and actors several times drove a single colonial project. At the same time, distinct colonial projects could draw upon each other's models and metaphors, while imbuing them with varied and contrary salience (Stoler, 1989, 2002; Stoler and Cooper, 1997; Thomas, 1994).

Three examples should suffice. In the case of colonial South Africa, John Comaroff (1989) has shown that the exact divisions and conflicts between British administrators, evangelical missionaries and Dutch settlers led to the elaboration of apartheid and empire. My own work on the evangelical enterprise in central India underscores that American missionaries in the region borrowed from the governmental modalities and cartographic practices of her majesty's imperial administration in order to elaborate a rather distinct vision and practice of 'the Empire of Christ' (Dube, 2004a, 2009). Finally, K. Sivaramakrishnan's (1999) study of the construal of the colonial state, the shaping of forests, and the making of 'tribal' places in nineteenth-century woodland

Bengal, eastern India brings together several of the concerns outlined above. Imaginatively intervening in debates in recent environmental studies and colonial discourse theory, he brings to bear on postcolonial and subaltern studies the perspectives of a critical historical geography, itself shoring up an innovative environmental history. On the one hand, Sivaramakrishnan attends to the construction of space as part of historical practice, transcending, too, facile distinctions between 'metaphorical' and 'material' spaces. On the other hand, his emphases further suggest the importance of tracking how the conflicting interests and the contending visions of empire of differentially located actors could coalesce in a single colonial project.

All this has underwritten close analyses of the relationship between the metropolis and the colony. It has become increasingly clear that there were conjunctions and connections – and contentions and contradictions – between efforts to discipline and normalize subject groups at home and attempts to civilize and control subject populations in the colonies (Comaroff and Comaroff, 1992: 265–95; Davin, 1978; also see, Keane, 2007). Such explorations have carried forward earlier examinations and contemporary discussions of imperial histories and colonial cultures as deriving from interactions between the colonizer and the colonized. They have crucially considered the mutual shaping of European processes and colonial practices in order to imaginatively analyse how developments in distant margins could influence metropolitan transformations, how the impulses of empire and their reworking in the colonies brought about changes at the heart of western orders (Burton, 1998; Cohn, 1996; Collingham, 2001; Mignolo, 1995; Said, 1994; Stoler, 1995; also see Chatterjee, 2001; Cohn, 1987; Gikandi, 1996). The deliberations have included the imaginative excursus by Peter van der Veer (2001) into the interplay between religion and politics in the common constitution of empire and nation in Britain and India, which further highlights the differences of the modern state in these terrains,

while also questioning the binary of a secular west and a religious east. They have extended to the incisive examination by Uday Mehta (1999) of the focal presence of the Indian colony in the shaping of the very premises of dominant political thought in nineteenth-century Britain, revealing the significance of empire in structuring the 'anthropological' propensities of liberal theory, its fundamental 'strategies of exclusion'.

Such recognition has further led to varied analyses of the many modes and diverse forms entailed by colonial processes. There have been remarkable studies of the colonisation of space, language, and the body (Arnold, 1993; Collingham, 2001; Goswami, 2004; Fabian, 1986; Hunt, 1999; Mignolo 1995; Mitchell, 1988; Vaughan, 1991); critical discussions of imperial travel, exhibitory orders and museum collections (Fabian, 2000; Grewal, 1996; Pratt, 1992); deft analyses of colonial representations (Guha, 1983; Rafael, 1988; Scott, 1994; Wolfe, 1999); astute probing of the politics under empire of art, literature, culture and consumption (Gikandi, 1996; Guha-Thakurta, 2004; Mathur, 2007; Pinney, 1998, 2004; Tarlo, 1996); and striking work on sexuality, race and desire as shaping the metropolis and the margins (Chatterjee, 1999; Mani, 1998; Manderson and Jolly, 1997; Sinha, 1995, 2006; Stoler, 2002). The cultures spawned by colonialism have made a striking appearance on the stage of the humanities and the social sciences.

In several ways, this emphasis has provided a valuable corrective to the reification of an impersonal world capitalist system and the privileging of abstract colonial structures, each with their own subterranean dynamic and irrevocable logic, which characterized several influential writings in the past (see Dube, 2004b for a wider discussion). At the same time, the concerns of culture here do not necessarily discount considerations of political economy and aspects of state power. Rather, several significant studies in this new genre – for example, the writings of Frederick Cooper (1996) on Africa; Fernando Coronil

(1997) on Latin America; and Ritu Birla (2009) on South Asia – suggest the importance of tracking the interplay between forms of representation, processes of political economy and imperatives of state formation in expressions of identity. Here, there is no a priori privilege accorded to any one of these heuristic domains on the grounds of meta-theory. Instead, the mutual determinations of these analytical arenas appear better articulated through histories and ethnographies that eschew rigorously formal frameworks and avoid resolutely abstract blueprints.

Such nuanced understandings of culture and power have emerged bound to powerful reminders that gender and sexuality crucially inflected the formations of identity under colony and empire.[7] Salient scholarship has underscored that the profound importance of gender identities for imperial formations extended very widely: from the life-styles of Euro-American peoples in the colony to the politics of colonial representations; from the tensions of empire to the implications of colonial civility; and from the divisions among the colonialists to varieties of material exchanges, museum collections and exhibitory orders. Similarly, the key influence of sexual subjectivities cut across truly broad, criss-crossing terrain: from the mutual entailments of the metropolis and the margins to the colonization of languages and bodies; from the contradictory location of colonial agents to the complex fabrication of imperial cartographies; and from definitions of space(s) of wilderness to delineations of time(s) of modernity. On the one hand, in each case, the critical force of gender and sexuality shaped and structured the different dynamics and diverse dimensions of colonialism's cultures and the identities these spawned. On the other, as Anne McClintock's (1995) incisive explorations drawing together developments in metropolitan Britain and South Africa highlight, the intersections between the race, class and gender – as imaginaries and institutions – in the construal of identities have acquired new meanings

through their elaboration within colonial fields and imperial terrains.

The critical spirit of such work has been extended by two other developments. First, key discussions within postcolonial and subaltern studies have rethought the past and the present of the disciplines, especially keeping in view their linkages with determinations of colony and nation and race and gender. Of special significance here have been forceful considerations offered by Chandra Talpade Mohanty (2003) and Dipesh Chakrabarty (2000), for instance, concerning the inequalities and inequities of knowledge and power between the west and the rest, dominant visions and minority voices, and metropolitan histories and provincial pasts. Second, the corpus of writings that has stressed the critical place of the colonial experience in the making of the modern world, emphases that have reached beyond analyses of the shaping of Europe by empire. Extremely important here have been discussions of the 'coloniality of power' by scholars of Latin America such as Enrique Dussel (1995) and Walter Mignolo (1995, 2000) as well as other, distinct studies focusing on the linkages of Enlightenment and empire and race and reason (Baucom, 2005, Berman, 2004, Fischer, 2004; also see, Muthu, 2003; Scott, 2005).

## PASTS AND COMMUNITIES

All of this is equally indicative of the manner in which the critical rethinking of history, identity, and historical identities has been at the core of subaltern and postcolonial perspectives. On the one hand, members of the South Asian subaltern studies collective such as Ranajit Guha (1983, 1997), Dipesh Chakrabarty (2000) and Gyanendra Pandey (2001) – alongside other intellectuals (Cohen, 1994; Klein, 1997; Trouillot, 1995; also see, Hartman, 1997, 2007), focusing on diverse geo-political areas – have pointed to the place of power in the production of the past.

This has served to underscore the inherently political character of history-writing while putting a question mark on the very nature of the academic-historical archive. On the other, scholars of anthropology, history and other disciplines have emphasized the precise plurality of cultural pasts, the manner in which history and temporality are differently approached and understood and seized upon and set to work by distinct social groups in conversation with their identities (Cohen and Odhiambo, 1989; Florida, 1995, Price, 1983, 1990; Rappaport, 1994; Rosaldo, 1980; White, 2000).

Three overlaying emphases have played a salient part in such considerations (Dube, 2007a). To begin with, it has been diversely admitted that forms of historical consciousness vary in their degree of symbolic elaboration, their ability to pervade multiple contexts, and their capacity to capture people's imaginations – between and across cultural groups and their identities. Second, it has been increasingly noted that history does not just refer to events and processes out there, but that it exists as a negotiated resource at the core of shifting configurations of historical worlds and social identities. Third and finally, as was indicated earlier, there has been an opening up of critical questions considering the coupling of history writing with the modern nation and of the haunting presence of a reified 'west' in widespread beliefs in historical progress.

Together, in approaching the past and the present, such efforts towards critical history-writing have often bound the impulse to cautiously probe and affirm social worlds with the desire to carefully narrate and describe them. The endeavours have taken truly seriously requirements of evidence and fidelity to facts. Yet they have also sieved historical evidence through critical filters and construed facts unexpected, facts that speak in the uneasy echoes of limiting doubt rather than deal in dead certainties (Dube, 2004a; Redfield, 2000). It only follows that the emphases outlined above have not resorted to

oppositions involving cyclical notions of the past as characteristic of the east and linear conceptions of history as constitutive of the west. Nor have they approached the assertive appropriations and enunciations of the past in historical and contemporary worlds by submitting to views that each of these visions is equally true. Rather, they have precisely probed such overwrought blueprints and solipsistic schemes by tracking expressions of history as made up of interleaving, conflict-ridden processes of meaning and authority, ever entailing identity and alterity (Chaturvedi, 2007; Deshpande, 2007; Dube, 1998; Gold and Gujar, 2002; Mayaram, 2004; Price, 1998; Trouillot, 1995).

In this terrain, the explorations have extended from tracing the variability and mutability that can inhere in the perceptions and practices of the past of historical communities through to tracking the uses of the past and their contending validities in the making of identities, especially the play of power in the production of history. In elaborations of these conjoint emphases, particularly pertinent are Shahid Amin's (1996) innovative account of the interplay between governmental demands and subaltern desires in the remembering and monumentalizing of a critical event of Indian nationalism in north India across the twentieth century; Ajay Skaria's (1999) thickly textured study of wildness, environment, gender and politics among the Dangis of western India, especially as based on these people's historical narratives of 'colonial' and 'extra-colonial' times; and Ishita Banerjee-Dube's (2007) imaginative enquiry into the unfolding of oral and written histories and sectarian and ascetic formations – each inflected by the presence of the law and the state – within a popular religious formation in eastern India from the mid-nineteenth century through to the present.

All of these writings have variously combined historical fieldwork and ethnographic archival research. Unsurprisingly, they have been accompanied by analyses that have not

only unravelled the persistence of oppositions between myth and history in authoritative projections but precisely placed question
marks on pervasive projections of the west
and nation as history, modernity and destiny
– for all people and every identity, as was
noted earlier. Important examples of such
work reside in the challenges posed by
Dipesh Chakrabarty's (2000, 2002) forceful,
philosophical critique of the developmental
premises of 'historicist' thinking as well as
by Gyanenendra Pandey's (2001, 2005)
recent, critical considerations of the formidable violence that is at once embodied and
ignored, made routine and glossed over, by
the modern coupling of nation and history
(also see Nandy, 1995).

No less than in relation to history, the
acute rethinking of identity in connection
with community has been at the core of postcolonial and subaltern endeavours. Here, too,
there has been a braiding of two apparently
incommensurable yet actually complementary emphases. On the one hand, several
scholars associated with subaltern studies,
particularly Partha Chatterjee (1993), have
underscored the key role of the community as
an ethical formation in questioning and challenging projects of power – of colony and
empire and nation and history. On the other
hand, distinct strands of critical scholarship
have queried persistent portrayals of the community as an ineluctably anachronistic, tightly
bounded entity, one tending towards consensus in its expression, entailing allegiance to
primordial tradition, and as broadly opposed
to modernity. Together, communities have
come to be understood as active participants
in wider processes of colonialism and empire,
nation and nationalism, state and citizen, and
modernity and globalization, participants that
imbue such processes – themselves made up
of diverse relationships of meaning and power
– with their own terms and textures (for a
wider discussion, see Dube, 2007a).

Subaltern and postcolonial approaches have
explored the many meanings of community
construed by its members, especially their
symbolization and elaboration of boundaries

as providing substance to their differences
and identities. This has involved examinations of the constitutive location of community within wide-ranging processes
of power as well as of its internal divisions
as expressed in terms of property, gender,
law and office (Chowdhry, 1994; Das, 1995;
Dube, 2004a; Gupta, 2002; Kasturi, 2002;
also see Puri, 2004). Moreover, such efforts
have been fortified by incisive accounts of
communities as questioning and contesting
dominant projects of meaning and power,
including those turning on empire and nation
and religion and race, unravelling their
challenge to authority in a historically and
ethnographically layered manner (Guha,
1983; Hardiman, 1987; Mayaram, 1997; Rao,
2009). Finally, there have been diverse endeavours to write greater heterogeneity into the
concept of community. Indeed, recent recon-
figurations of the category have derived
further support from the thinking through of
the antinomy between community and state,
moves that have queried the analytical binaries of modern disciplines, which are closely
tied to totalizing templates of a universal
history and exclusive blueprints of a western
modernity.

Some studies have combined these overlapping emphases. In addition to the work of
Skaria (1999) on the Dangs in western India
and of Banerjee-Dube (2007) on Orissa in
eastern India that has been referred to above,
this is evident in a historical and anthropological exploration of an untouchable and
heretical caste-sect formation of Chhattisgarh
in central India over the past two centuries
(Dube, 1998). The account focuses on a
large, internally differentiated community
in order to: trace the endeavours of its members within changing relations of power and
property under precolonial regimes and colonial rule in the region; explore the group's
negotiation and reproduction of ritual authority and gender hierarchies; and track its
articulations of caste and Hinduism, evange-
lism and empire, and state and nation, especially as these were played out in everyday
arenas. These writings suggest that prudent

procedures in postcolonial perspectives and subaltern studies are afoot in the rethinking not only of community and history but also of nation-state, nationalism and modernity.

## NATION AND MODERNITY

Key departures in subaltern studies and postcolonial understandings have played an important role in reformulations of approaches to nation and nationalism. Beginning with the critical rethinking of these concepts-entities within subaltern studies by scholars such as Ranajit Guha, Partha Chatterjee, Shahid Amin and Gyanendra Pandey, the endeavours have extended in postcolonial scholarship to Homi Bhabha's (1990) highlighting of the pedagogical performances of the nation and Rajeswari Sunderrajan's (2003) unravelling of the scandal of the state.

Together, the writings in these arenas have thought through pervasive projections of nations, nationalisms and national identities as expressing innate ideas, primordial patterns and timeless designs. They have interrogated also the ways in which wide varieties of renderings of historical identities can be differently yet intimately bound to authoritative – indeed, biographical – portraits of nation-states and nationalist endeavours, each understood as image and practice. In such questioning, a key role has been played by the acute recognition that nations, nationalisms and national identities are historically and socially constructed artefacts and processes. This is to say that although nations, nationalisms and the identities they spawn are among the most consequential features of modern times, they nonetheless display attributes of what Benedict Anderson (1982) has called 'imagined communities'. Following such recognition, there have been astute studies of the historical construction of nations, nationalisms and national cultures/identities as projects and processes of power. Here, ethnographies and histories have come together with sociological discussions and

literary explorations not only to query familiar understandings of these categories and entities but to do this by tracking their varied creations and formidable fabrications (Amin, 1995; Chatterjee, 1993; Guha, 1997; Pandey, 2001; van der Veer, 1994; see Dube, 2004b, for a wider discussion). At the same time, other related endeavours have focused on how the ideological frames, pedagogical performances and narrative techniques that assiduously construe nation, nationalism and nationalist identities acquire a forceful presence in the world, assuming pervasive worldly attributes (Alonso, 1994; Amin, 1995; Butalia, 1998; Pinney, 2004; Tarlo, 1996).

These emphases have been accompanied by analyses stressing the distinctions and differences at the core of nation, nationalism and the identities they engender, particularly considering the subaltern expressions, anticolonial manifestations and gendered dimensions of these ensembles. The subaltern studies project and associated scholarly developments have led to rich explorations of the idioms and trajectories of wide varieties of subaltern endeavours. Against the grain of nationalist propositions and instrumentalist projections concerning the politics and identities of the lower-orders, these analyses have shown that in the broader terrain of anticolonial politics subaltern ventures followed a creative process of straddling and subverting the ideas, symbols and practices defining dominant nationalism. Such initiatives articulated thereby supplementary politics and accompanying identities with distinct visions of the nation and particular expressions of nationalism that accessed and exceeded the aims and strategies of a generally middle-class leadership (Dube, 2004a, b, contain a broader discussion).

Unsurprisingly, extending the terms of these deliberations, it has been emphasized that expressions of middle-class anti-colonial nationalisms and nationalist identities embodied their own attributes of difference and distinction, ahead of likenesses of the nation in the looking-glass of Europe. In particular, Partha Chatterjee (1993) has shown that by drawing on yet reworking European democratic and republican traditions and Enlightenment and post-Enlightenment principles, middle-class nationalist endeavours and identities translated and transformed the ideals of the sovereign nation and the images of the free citizen through forceful filters of the subjugated homeland and the colonized subject (also see, Prakash, 1999). With distinct accents, other critical writings have unravelled issues of the presence of gender and the place of women in formations of modern nations and articulations of nationalist identities. In place here have been astute explorations of the mapping of the nation through identifications of domesticity; the gendered construal of the homeland as a feminine figure; women's participation and presence in nationalist endeavours and identities; and the ambiguous, ambivalent identifications of gender that attend their definition as citizen-subjects. In this way, the analytic of gender has incisively interrogated the attributes of authority and alterity at the heart of nations and nationalisms in their dominant and subaltern incarnations (Menon and Bhasin, 1998; Roy, 2005; Sarkar, 2001; Sinha, 2006).

All of this has further meant that salient work within subaltern and postcolonial studies has probed the identities and differences embodied by nation and state, examining especially their intimate associations as well as contending connections with modern power and global transactions. Rather than accepting the spatial and temporal identifications of the nation as settled analytical co-ordinates, recent writings have explored the interplay of imperatives of nation and nationalism with trans-national processes, critically examining how the one can be inextricably embedded in the other. Brian Axel's (2001) study of historical representations among Sikhs and the making of the 'diaspora' of the 'community' as well as Manu Goswami's (2004) work questioning the limitations of 'methodological nationalism' are important examples. Still other studies have focused on the nation-state as entailing sets of frequently conflicting disciplines to normalize and order

society and identity, bringing to fore what Hansen and Stepputat (2001) have summarized as three 'practical' languages of governance and three 'symbolic' languages of authority, which are together crucial for understanding state, nation and identity. The pedagogies, performances and practices of state and nation – and the identities they engender – have been critically unravelled through scholarship that has focused on the quotidian configurations and everyday identifications of these concepts and entities. Such different yet interconnected emphases have clarified that across shifting contexts and terrains, propelled by distinct agendas and aspirations, nationalisms and nation-states have articulated wide varieties of historical practice, disciplinary power and cultural identity (Bénéï, 2008; Gupta, 1998; Hansen, 2001; Tarlo, 2003)

At the same time, incisive discussions in postcolonial and subaltern scholarship have pointed toward the need for critical considerations of modernity and modern-identity, their processes and persuasions. There has been prescient probing in this terrain of the analytical abstractions and the formalist frames that often attend understandings of these categories. It has become clear that ahead of their exclusive images, the divergent articulations of modernity and contending identifications of the modern have been linked to particular processes of history, identity and difference (Comaroff and Comaroff, 1997; Dube, 2004a; Gilroy, 1993; Mbembe, 2001; also see Appadurai, 1996). Equally, such work has highlighted that the diverse manifestations of modernity and modern-identity have been frequently influenced by singular likenesses of 'western modernity', where the singularity and universal cast of the latter are differently engaged by the plural and vernacular attributes of the former (Coronil, 1997; Dube 2009b; Dube and Banerjee-Dube, 2006; Ferguson, 1999; see also Mitchell, 2000). Precisely, these distinct procedures shape, structure and suture the terms and textures of empire, nation and globalization. Unsurprisingly, formations and elaborations of modernity and modern-identity are increasingly discussed and debated today as contradictory and contingent processes of culture and power, as chequered and contested histories of meaning and mastery (Dube, 2009a; Fischer, 2004; Meyer and Pels, 2003; Saler, 2006).

Several of the emphases outlined above come together in Laura Bear's (2007) remarkable historical anthropology of the Indian railways and the Anglo-Indian community, a pre-eminent 'railway caste'. She explores worlds of modernity and identity by considering questions of empire and intimacy, nation and difference, race and sexuality, citizenship and kinship, and subject and self-making. Bear's proposition is to detail and describe the generative practices and constitutive meanings of these intermeshed processes by thinking them down to their expressions on the ground. Ever attentive to the exact specificity and tangibility, concrete contention and contradiction, and immense ambiguity and murkiness of modernity and identity, her work also imaginatively interweaves the cautious querying, careful unravelling and prudent affirmation of social worlds.

## EMERGENT POSTERITIES

At the end, in lieu of a conclusion, let me consider some of the directions in which work on identities in postcolonial and subaltern scholarship might proceed in the future. Far from merely listing subjects that should be studied and methodologies that ought to be adopted, my aim is to underscore the importance of inculcating certain key dispositions towards intellectual endeavour.[8] At stake are bids that critically query the privileging of theory as the primary object of enquiry.

To start off, it is salient to think through projections that render identities as mere objects of knowledge, awaiting their ineluctable endorsement, inevitable refinement or irrevocable exorcism at the hands of prescient knowledge(s). Instead, it is crucial to approach identities as acutely intimating *conditions of knowing*: to explore identities as entities, concepts and coordinates that shore up our worlds, demanding critical articulation *and* careful affirmation. It follows that such procedures – of the simultaneous querying and affirmation of identities – can be usefully understood as entwining hermeneutic impulses and critical considerations. This is to say as protocols entailing the interplay of prudent questionings of social identities and their academic apprehensions *with* intimate accounts of the diversity and distinction of these terrains. Here, there is neither the excision of the details of identities by their being assimilated to the endless analytics of unpicking and unmasking nor is there the privileging of the particulars of identities by their being presented as innate embodiments of alterity and difference.

Indeed, in enquiring into identities, it is critical to query the pervasive antinomies between the universal and the particular and power and difference. After all, it is much too easy to rail against the claims of universality and power in order to simply celebrate the particularity and alterity of identities. Instead, the more challenging task involves exploring the articulation of identities as expressing the shared entailments and mutual productions of power and difference, as interleaving the founding exclusions and constitutive contradictions of authority and alterity. This means, finally, that the productive possibilities of postcolonial emphases and subaltern studies inhere in constant vigilance against their self-projections as always subversive, already known modes of scholarly knowledge and political criticism. Rather, it is through the self-questioning of their formative presumptions and formidable limitations that these approaches can more adequately explore cultural identities and social processes – as shaped by the concatenations of distinct yet coeval temporalities and of overlapping yet heterogeneous histories – in past and present worlds.

## NOTES

1 Other critical assessments of Said's text within cultural-literary studies include Bart Moore-Gilbert (1997: 34–73; Young, 1990: 119–40, see also, Yegenoglu, 1998). Constructive-critical engagements with Orientalism within anthropology and history include Clifford (1988); and Thomas (1994: 5–7, 21–27). See also, Breckenridge and van der Veer (1993).

2 Writings introducing postcolonial theory are academic industry. Here, following my own preferences, I refer the interested reader to the texts by Young (1990, 2001, 2003), McLeod (2000), Gandhi (1998), Loomba (1998), Moore-Gilbert (1997), Mongia (1996) and Lazarus (2004).

3 A single example should suffice, concerning the impact of the (South Asian) subaltern studies project on writings on Latin America. Not only has there been the formation of a wide-ranging Latin American subaltern studies project in the US, but the work of the South Asian collective has found wide discussion in Latin America itself. For the former tendency see, Rabasa et al. (1994 [published 1996]), Rodriguez (2001) and Beverley (1999). On the latter initiatives see Cusicanqui and Barragan (1997), Kraniauskas and Zermeño (1999) and Dube (1999). Consider also, Mallon (1994); and my own trilogy in historical anthropology in the Spanish language (Dube 2001, 2003, 2007).

4 Arguably, two crucial moments in the conflation of postcolonial and subaltern studies were: first, the volume on *Selected Subaltern Studies* that Gayatri Spivak co-edited with Ranajit Guha, a volume that carried a Foreword by Edward Said and used Spivak's (1985) prior deconstructive reading of the project as its Introduction (Guha and Spivak, 1988); and, next, the rendering by Gyan Prakash (1994) of subaltern studies as a form of postcolonial criticism.

5 This is to say that just as analytically fatal mistakes surround understandings of hegemony as a closed system of cultural and ideological control by dominant groups so also theoretically grave errors attend the reification of subaltern autonomy and agency (Dube, 2004a).

6 To take such steps is to simultaneously register that ready presumptions regarding the 'identities' (narrowly conceived) of the scholarly protagonists of subaltern and postcolonial perspectives have led to the two enquiries being collapsed together.

7 As already indicated, the reminders have flowed from important interventions of scholars such as Ann McClintock, Lata Mani, Mrinalini Sinha and Ann Stoler. At the same time, the implications of such studies have equally acquired formative force in critical conjunction with the writings of other feminist critics of colour such as Gayatri Spivak, Trinh T. Minh-Ha (1989), Chandra Talpade Mohanty (2003) and bell hooks (1999).

8 The proposals in this section derive from the protocols and procedures of what I have called a history without warranty (Dube 2004a, 2009b).

## REFERENCES

Abdel-Malek, A. (1963) 'Orientalism in crisis', *Diogenes*, 44: 104–12.

Alonso, A.M. (1994) 'The politics of space, time and substance: State formation, nationalism and ethnicity', *Annual Review of Anthropology*, 23: 379–400.

Amin, S. (1995) *Event, Metaphor, Memory: Chauri Chaura (1922–1992)*. Berkeley, CA: University of California Press.

Appadurai, A. (1996) *Modernity at Large: Cultural Dimensions of Globalization*. Minneapolis, MN: University of Minnesota Press.

Arnold, D. (1993) *Colonizing the Body: State Medicine and Epidemic Disease in Nineteenth-Century India*. Berkeley, CA: University of California Press.

Asad, T. (ed.) (1973) *Anthropology and the Colonial Encounter*. London: Ithaca Press.

Axel, B.K. (2001) *The Nation's Tortured Body: Violence, Representation, and the Formation of the Sikh 'Diaspora'*. Durham, NC: Duke University Press.

Banerjee-Dube, I. (2007) *Religion, Law and Power: Tales of Time in Eastern India, 1860–2000*. London: Anthem Press.

Baucom, I. (2005) *Specters of the Atlantic: Finance Capital, Slavery and the Philosophy of History*. Durham NC: Duke University Press.

Bear, L. (2007) *Lines of the Nation: Indian Railway Workers, Bureaucracy, and the Intimate Historical Self*. New York: Columbia University Press.

Bénéï, V. (2008) *Schooling Passions: Nation, History and Language in Contemporary Western India*. Stanford, CA: Stanford University Press.

Berman, R.A. (2004) *Enlightenment or Empire: Colonial Discourse in German Culture*. Lincoln, NE: University of Nebraska Press.

Beverley, J. (1999) *Subalternity and Representation: Arguments in Cultural Theory*. Durham, NC: Duke University Press.

Bhabha, H.K. (1994) *Location of Culture*. London: Routledge.

Birla, R. (2009) *Stages of Capital: Law, Culture and Market Governance in Late Colonial India*. Durham, NC: Duke University Press.

Breckenridge, C. and Van der Veer, P. (eds) (1993) *Orientalism and the Postcolonial Predicament: Perspectives on South Asia*. Philadelphia, PA: University of Pennsylvania Press.

Burton, A.M. (1998) *At the Heart of the Empire: Indians and the Colonial Encounter in Late-Victorian Britain.* Berkeley, CA: University of California Press.

Butalia, U. (1998) *The Other Side of Silence: Voices from the Partition of India.* New Delhi: Viking Penguin.

Chakrabarty, D. (2000) *Provincializing Europe: Postcolonial Thought and Historical Difference.* Princeton, NJ: Princeton University Press.

Chakrabarty, D. (2002) *Habitations of Modernity: Essays in the Wake of Subaltern Studies.* Chicago, IL: University of Chicago Press.

Chatterjee, I. (1999) *Gender, Slavery and Law in Colonial India.* Delhi: Oxford University Press.

Chatterjee, P. (1993) *The Nation and its Fragments: Colonial and Postcolonial Histories.* Princeton, NJ: Princeton University Press.

Chatterjee, P. (2004) *The Politics of the Governed: Reflections on Popular Politics in Most of the World.* New York: Columbia University Press.

Chatterjee, Piya. (2001) *A Time for Tea: Women, Labor and Post/Colonial Politics on an Indian Plantation.* Durham NC: Duke University Press.

Chaturvedi, V. (2007) *Peasant Pasts: History and Memory in Western India.* Berkeley, CA: University of California Press.

Chowdhry, P. (1994) *The Veiled Woman: Shifting Gender Equations in Rural Haryana 1880–1980.* Delhi: Oxford University Press.

Clifford, J. (1988) 'On orientalism', in J. Clifford (ed.), *The Predicament of Culture: Twentieth-Century Ethnography, Literature and Art.* Cambridge, MA: Harvard University Press. 255–76.

Cohen, D.W. (1994) *The Combing of History.* Chicago, IL: University of Chicago Press.

Cohen, D.W. and Odhiambo, E.S.A. (1989) *Siaya: Historical Anthropology.* Cleveland, OH: Ohio University Press.

Cohn, B.S. (1987) *An Anthropologist among the Historians and Other Essays.* Delhi: Oxford University Press.

Cohn, B.S. (1996) *Colonialism and Its Forms of Knowledge: The British in India.* Princeton, NJ: Princeton University Press.

Collingham, E.M. (2001) *Imperial Bodies: The Physical Experience of the Raj, c.1800–1947.* Cambridge: Polity Press.

Comaroff, J.L. (1989) 'Images of Empire, contests of conscience: Models of colonial domination in South Africa', *American Ethnologist*, 16: 661–85.

Comaroff, J. and Comaroff, J.L. (1991) *Of Revelation and Revolution: Christianity, Colonialism and Consciousness in South Africa*, Vol. 1. Chicago, IL: Chicago University Press.

Comaroff, J. and Comaroff, J.L. (1992) *Ethnography and the Historical Imagination.* Boulder, CO: Westview Press.

Comaroff, J. and Comaroff, J.L. (1997) *Of Revelation and Revolution: The Dialectics of Modernity on the South African Frontier*, Vol. 2. Chicago, IL: Chicago University Press.

Cooper, F. (1996) *Decolonization and African Society: The Labour Question in French and British Africa.* Cambridge: Cambridge University Press.

Cooper, F. and Stoler, A.L. (eds) (1997) *Tensions of Empire: Colonial Cultures in a Bourgeois World.* Berkeley, CA: University of California Press.

Coronil, F. (1997) *The Magical State: Nature, Money and Modernity in Venezuela.* Chicago, IL: University of Chicago Press.

Cusicanqui, S.R. and Barragan, R. (eds) (1997) *Debates Post Coloniales: Una Introducción a los Estudios de la Subalternidad.* La Paz, Bolivia: Sierpe.

Das, V. (1995) *Critical Events: An Anthropological Perspective on Contemporary India.* Delhi: Oxford University Press.

Davin, A. (1978) 'Imperialism and motherhood', *History Workshop*, 5: 9–65.

Deshpande, P. (2007) *Creative Pasts: Historical Memory and Identity in Western India, 1700–1960.* New York: Columbia University Press.

Dube, S. (1998) *Untouchable Pasts: Religion, Identity and Power among a Central Indian Community, 1780–1950.* Albany, NY: State University of New York Press.

Dube, S. (ed.) (1999) *Pasados Poscoloniales: Colección de Ensayos sobre la Nueva Historia y Etnografía de la India.* Mexico City: El Colegio de México.

Dube, S. (2001) *Sujetos Subalternos: Capítulos de una Historia Antropológica.* Mexico City: El Colegio de México.

Dube, S. (2003) *Genealogías del Presente: Conversión, Colonialismo, Cultura.* Mexico City: El Colegio de México.

Dube, S. (2004a) *Stitches on Time: Colonial Textures and Postcolonial Tangles.* Durham, NC: Duke University Press.

Dube, S. (2004b) 'Terms that bind: Colony, nation, modernity', in S. Dube (ed.), *Postcolonial Passages: Contemporary History-Writing on India.* New Delhi: Oxford University Press. 1–37.

Dube, S. (2007a) 'Anthropology, history, historical anthropology', in S. Dube (ed.), *Historical Anthropology: Oxford in India Readings in Sociology and Social Anthropology.* New Delhi: Oxford University Press. 1–73.

Dube, S. (2007b) *Historias Esparcidas.* Mexico City: El Colegio de Mexico.

Dube, S. (ed.) (2009a) *Enchantments of Modernity: Empire, Nation, Globalization.* London: Routledge.

Dube, S. (2009b) *After Conversion: Cultural Histories of Modern India.* New Delhi: Yoda Press.

Dube, S. and Banerjee-Dube, I. (eds) (2006) *Unbecoming Modern: Colonialism, Modernity, Colonial Modernities.* New Delhi: Social Science Press and Berghahn Books.

Dussel, E. (1995) *The Invention of the Americas: Eclipse of 'the Other' and the Myth of Modernity.* New York: Continuum.

Fabian, J. (1983) *Time and the Other: How Anthropology makes Its Object.* New York: Columbia University Press.

Fabian, J. (1986) *Language and Colonial Power: The Appropriation of Swahili in the Former Belgian Congo.* Cambridge: Cambridge University Press.

Fabian, J. (2000) *Out of Our Minds: Reason and Madness in the Exploration of Central Africa.* Berkeley, CA: University of California Press.

Ferguson, J. (1999) *Expectations of Modernity: Myths and Meanings of Urban Life on the Zambian Copperbelt.* Berkeley, CA: University of California Press.

Fischer, S. (2004) *Modernity Disavowed: Haiti and the Cultures of Slavery in the Age of Revolution.* Durham, NC: Duke University Press.

Florida, N. (1995) *Writing the Past, Inscribing the Future: History as Prophecy in Colonial Java.* Durham, NC: Duke University Press.

Gandhi, L. (1998) *Postcolonial Theory: A Critical Introduction.* New York: Columbia University Press.

Gikandi, S. (1996) *Maps of Englishness: Writing Identity in the Culture of Colonialism.* New York: Columbia University Press.

Gilroy, P. (1993) *Black Atlantic: Modernity and Double-Consciousness.* Cambridge, MA: Harvard University Press.

Gold, A. and Bhoju Ram, G. (2002) *In the Time of Trees and Sorrows: Nature, Power and Memory in Rajasthan.* Durham, NC: Duke University Press.

Goswami, M. (2004) *Producing India: From Colonial Economy to National Space.* Chicago, IL: University of Chicago Press.

Grewal, I. (1996) *Home and Harem: Nation, Gender, Empire and the Cultures of Travel.* Durham, NC: Duke University Press.

Grosrichard, A. (1998 [1979]) *The Sultan's Court: European Fantasies of the East.* Trans. L. Heron. London: Verso.

Guha, R. (1982) 'Preface', in R. Guha (ed.), *Subaltern Studies I: Writings on South Asian History and Society.* Delhi: Oxford University Press. vii–viii.

Guha, R. (ed.) (1982–89) *Subaltern Studies I–VI: Writings on South Asian History and Society.* Delhi: Oxford University Press.

Guha, R. (1983) *Elementary Aspects of Peasant Insurgency in Colonial India.* Delhi: Oxford University Press.

Guha, R. (1997) *Dominance without Hegemony: History and Power in Colonial India.* Cambridge, MA: Harvard University Press.

Guha, R. (2004) 'Not at Home in Empire', in S. Dube (ed.), *Postcolonial Passages: Contemporary History-Writing on India.* New Delhi: Oxford University Press 38–46.

Guha, R. and Spivak, G.C. (1988) *Selected Subaltern Studies.* New York: Oxford University Press.

Guha-Thakurta, T. (2004) *Monuments, Objects, Histories: Art in Colonial and Post-Colonial India.* New York: Columbia University Press.

Gupta, A. (1998) *Postcolonial Developments: Agriculture in the Making of Modern India.* Durham, NC: Duke University Press.

Gupta, C. (2002) *Sexuality, Obscenity and Community: Women, Muslims, and the Hindu Public in Colonial India.* Delhi: Permanent Black.

Hansen, T.B. (2001) *Wages of Violence: Naming and Identity in Postcolonial Bombay.* Princeton, NJ: Princeton University Press.

Hansen, T.B. and Stepputat, F. (2001) 'Introduction: States of imagination', in Thomas Blom Hansen and Finn Stepputat. (eds), *States of Imagination: Ethnographic Explorations of the Postcolonial State.* Durham, NC: Duke University Press. 1–38.

Hardiman, D. (1987) *The Coming of the Devi: Adivasi Assertion in Western India.* Delhi: Oxford University Press.

Hartman, S.H. (1997) *Scenes of Subjection: Terror, Slavery and Self-Making in Nineteenth-Century America.* New York: Oxford University Press.

Hartman, S.H. (2007) *Lose Your Mother: A Journey Along the Atlantic Slave Route.* New York: Farrar, Straus and Giroux.

hooks, b. (1999) *Ain't I a Woman: Black Women and Feminism.* Cambridge, MA: South End Press.

Hunt, N.R. (1999) *A Colonial Lexicon of Birth Ritual, Medicalization and Mobility in the Congo.* Durham, NC: Duke University Press.

Inden, R.B. (1990) *Imagining India.* Cambridge, MA: Basil Blackwell.

JanMohamed, A.R. (1983) *Manichean Aesthetics: The Politics of Literature in Colonial Africa.* Amherst, MA: University of Massachusetts Press.

JanMohamed, A.R. and Llyod, D. (eds) (1990) *The Nature and Context of Minority Discourse.* New York: Oxford University Press.

Kasturi, M. (2002) *Embattled Identities: Rajput Lineages and the Colonial State in Nineteenth-Century North India.* New Delhi: Oxford University Press.

Keane, W. (2007) *Christian Moderns: Freedom and Fetish in the Mission Encounter.* Berkeley, CA: University of California Press.

Klein, K.L. (1997) *Frontiers of Historical Imagination: Narrating the European Conquest of Native America, 1890–1990.* Berkeley, CA: University Of California Press.

Kraniauskas, J. and Guillermo, Z. (eds) (1999) 'Historia y subalternidad', *Historia y Grafia,* 12. (Special issue.)

Lazarus, N. (ed.) (2004) *The Cambridge Companion to Postcolonial Literary Studies.* New York: Cambridge University Press.

Loomba, A. (1998) *Colonialism/Postcolonialism.* London: Routledge.

Mallon, F.E. (1994) 'The Promise and dilemma of subaltern studies: Perspectives from Latin American histories', *American Historical Review,* 99: 1491–515.

Manderson, L. and Jolly, M. (eds) (1997) *Sites of Desire, Economies of Pleasure: Sexualities in Asia and the Pacific.* Chicago, IL: University of Chicago Press.

Mani, L. (1998) *Contentious Traditions: The Debate on Sati in Colonial India.* Berkeley, CA: University of California Press.

Mathur, S. (2007) *India by Design: Colonial History and Cultural Display.* Berkeley, CA: University of California Press.

Mayaram, S. (1997) *Resisting Regimes: Myth, Memory and the Shaping of a Muslim Identity.* Delhi: Oxford University Press.

Mayaram, S. (2004) *Against History, Against State: Counterperspectives from the Margins.* Delhi: Permanent Black.

Mbembe, A. (2001) *On the Postcolony.* Berkeley, CA: University of California Press.

McClintock, A. (1995) *Imperial Leather: Race, Gender and Sexuality in the Colonial Contest.* New York: Routledge.

McLeod, J. (2000) *Beginning Postcolonialism.* Manchester: Manchester University Press.

Mehta, U.S. (1999) *Liberalism and Empire: A Study in Nineteenth-Century British Liberal Thought.* Chicago, IL: University of Chicago Press.

Menon, R. and Bhasin, K. (1998) *Borders and Boundaries: Women in India's Partition.* New Delhi: Kali for Women.

Meyer, B. and Pels, P. (eds) (2003) *Magic and Modernity: Interfaces of Revelation and Concealment.* Stanford, CA: Stanford University Press.

Mignolo, W. (1995) *The Darker Side of the Renaissance: Literacy, Territoriality, and Colonization.* Ann Arbor, MI: University of Michigan Press.

Mignolo, W. (2000) *Local Histories/Global Designs: Coloniality, Subaltern Knowledges and Border Thinking.* Princeton, NJ: Princeton University Press.

Minh-Ha, T.T. (1989) *Woman, Native, Other: Writing Postcoloniality and Feminism.* Bloomington, IN: Indiana University Press.

Mitchell, T. (1988) *Colonizing Egypt.* Berkeley, CA: University of California Press.

Mitchell, T. (2000) 'The Stage of Modernity', in T. Mitchell (ed.), *Questions of Modernity.* Minneapolis, MN: University of Minnesota Press. 1–34.

Mohanty, C.T. (2003) *Feminism without Borders: Decolonizing Theory, Practicing Solidarity.* Durham, NC: Duke University Press.

Mongia, P. (ed.) (1996) *Contemporary Postcolonial Theory: A Reader.* London: Hodder Arnold.

Moore-Gilbert, B. (1997) *Postcolonial Theory: Contexts, Practices, Politics.* London: Verso.

Mudimbe, V.Y. (1988) *The Invention of Africa: Gnosis, Philosophy and the Order of Knowledge.* Bloomington, IN: Indiana University Press.

Mudimbe, V.Y. (1994) *The Idea of Africa.* Bloomington, IN: Indiana University Press.

Muthu, S. (2003) *Enlightenment against Empire.* Princeton, NJ: Princeton University Press.

Nandy, A. (1982) *The Intimate Enemy: Loss and Recovery of the Self Under Colonialism.* Delhi: Oxford University Press.

Nandy, A. (1995) 'History's forgotten doubles', *History and Theory,* 34 (1): 44–66.

Pandey, G. (2001) *Remembering Partition: Violence, Nationalism and History in India.* Cambridge: Cambridge University Press.

Pandey, G. (2006) *Routine Violence: Nations, Fragments, Histories.* Stanford, CA: Stanford University Press.

Pinney, C. (1998) *Camera Indica: The Social Life of Indian Photographs.* Chicago, IL: University of Chicago Press.

Pinney, C. (2004) *Photos of the Gods: The Printed Image and Political Struggle in India.* London: Reaktion Books.

Prakash, G. (1994) 'Subaltern studies as postcolonial criticism', *American Historical Review,* 99: 1475–94.

Prakash, G. (1999) *Another Reason: Science and the Imagination of Modern India.* Princeton, NJ: Princeton University Press.

Pratt, M.L. (1992) *Imperial Eyes: Travel Writing and Transculturation.* London: Routledge.

Price, R. (1983) *First-Time: The Historical Vision of an Afro-American People*. Baltimore, MD: Johns Hopkins University Press.

Price, R. (1990) *Alabi's World*. Baltimore, MD: Johns Hopkins University Press.

Price, R. (1998) *The Convict and the Colonel: A Story of Colonialism and Resistance in the Caribbean*. Boston, MA: Beacon Press.

Puri, S. (2004) *The Caribbean Postcolonial: Social Equality, Post-Nationalism, and Cultural Hybridity*. New York: Palgrave Macmillan.

Rabasa, J., Sanjines, J. and Carr, R. (eds) (1994). *Subaltern Studies in the Americas*, a special issue of *dispositio/n: American Journal of Cultural Histories and Theories*, 46. (Published 1996.)

Rabasa, J. (1993) *Inventing America: Spanish Historiography and the Formation of Eurocentrism*. Oklahoma, OK: University of Oklahoma Press.

Rafael, V. (1988) *Contracting Colonialism: Translation and Christian Conversion in Tagalog Society under Early Spanish Rule*. Ithaca, NY: Cornell University Press.

Rao, A. (2009) *The Caste Question: Untouchable Struggles for Rights and Recognition*. Berkeley, CA: University of California Press.

Rappaport, J. (1994) *Cumbe Reborn: An Andean Ethnography of History*. Chicago, IL: University of Chicago Press.

Redfield, P. (2000) *Space in the Tropics: From Convicts to Rockets in French Guiana*. Berkeley, CA: University of California Press.

Rodriguez, I. (ed.) (2001) *A Latin American Subaltern Studies Reader*. Durham, NC: Duke University Press.

Rosaldo, R. (1980) *Ilongot Headhunting 1883–1974: A Study in Society and History*. Stanford, CA: Stanford University Press.

Roy, A. (2005) *Gendered Citizenship: Historical and Conceptual Explorations*. Hyderabad: Orient Longman.

Said, E.W. (1978) *Orientalism*. New York: Pantheon Books.

Said, E.W. (1994) *Culture and Imperialism*. New York: Vintage.

Saler, M. (2006) 'Modernity and enchantment: A historiographic review', *American Historical Review*, 111: 692–716.

Sarkar, S. (1983) *Modern India: 1885–1947*. Delhi: Macmillan.

Sarkar, T. (2001) *Hindu Wife, Hindu Nation: Community, Religion and Cultural Nationalism*. Delhi: Permanent Black.

Scott, D. (1994) *Formations of Ritual: Colonial and Anthropological Discourses on the Sinhala Yaktovil*. Minneapolis, MN: University of Minnesota Press.

Scott, D. (2005) *Conscripts of Modernity: The Tragedy of Colonial Enlightenment*. Durham, NC: Duke University Press.

Shohat, E. (1996) 'Notes on the post-colonial', in P. Mongia (ed.), *Contemporary Postcolonial Theory: A Reader*. London: Hodder Arnold. 321–34

Sinha, M. (1995) *Colonial Masculinity: The 'Manly Englishman' and the 'Effeminate Bengali' in the Late Nineteenth Century*. Manchester: Manchester University Press.

Sinha, M. (2006) *Specters of Mother India: The Global Restructuring of an Empire*. Durham, NC: Duke University Press.

Sivaramakrishnan, K. (1999) *Modern Forests: State-making and Environmental Change in Colonial Eastern India*. New Delhi: Oxford University Press.

Skaria, A. (1999) *Hybrid Histories: Forest, Frontiers and Wildness in Western India*. New Delhi: Oxford University Press.

Spivak, G.C. (1985) 'Subaltern studies: Deconstructing historiography', in R. Guha (ed.), *Subaltern Studies IV: Writings on South Asian History and Society*. Delhi: Oxford University Press. 330–63.

Spivak, G.C. (1987) *In Other Worlds: Essays in Cultural Politics*. Foreword by Colin McCabe. London: Methuen.

Spivak, G.C. (1988) 'Can the subaltern speak?', in C. Nelson and L. Grossberg (eds), *Marxism and the Interpretation of Culture*. Urbana, IL: University of Illinois Press. 271–313.

Stoler, A.L. (1989) 'Rethinking colonial categories: European communities and the boundaries of rule', *Comparative Studies in Society and History*, 13: 134–61.

Stoler, A.L. (1995) *Race and the Education of Desire: Foucault's History of Sexuality and the Colonial Order of Things*. Durham, NC: Duke University Press.

Stoler, A.L. (2002) *Carnal Knowledge and Imperial Power: Race and the Intimate in Colonial Rule*. Berkeley, CA: University of California Press.

Stoler, A.L. (2008) *Along the Archival Grain: Epistemic Anxieties and Colonial Common Sense*. Princeton, NJ: Princeton University Press.

Sunder, R.R. (2003) *Scandal of the State: Women, Law, and Citizenship in Postcolonial India*. Durham, NC: Duke University Press.

Tarlo, E. (1996) *Clothing Matters: Dress and Identity in India*. Chicago, IL: University of Chicago Press.

Tarlo, E. (2003) *Unsettling Memories: Narratives of India's 'Emergency'*. Delhi: Permanent Black.

Thomas, N. (1994) *Colonialism's Culture: Anthropology, Travel and Government*. Princeton, NJ: Princeton University Press.

Trouillot, M.R. (1995) *Silencing the Past: Power and the Production of History*. Boston, MA: Beacon Press.

Van der Veer, P. (1994) *Religious Nationalism: Hindus and Muslims in India*. Berkeley, CA: University of California Press.

Van der Veer, P. (2001) *Imperial Encounters: Religion and Modernity in India and Britain*. Princeton, NJ: Princeton University Press.

Vaughan, M. (1991) *Curing their Ills: Colonial Power and African Illness*. Stanford, CA: Stanford University Press.

Vincent, J. (1990) *Anthropology and Politics: Visions, Traditions and Trends*. Tuscon, AZ: University of Arizona Press.

White, L. (2000) *Speaking with Vampires: Rumor and History in Colonial Africa*. Berkeley, CA: University of California Press.

Wolfe, P. (1997) 'History and imperialism: A century of theory, from marx to postcolonialism', *American Historical Review*, 102: 380–420.

Wolfe, P. (1999) *Settler Colonialism and the Transformation of Anthropology: The Politics and Poetics of an Ethnographic Event*. London: Cassell.

Yegenoglu, M. (1998) *Colonial Fantasies: Towards a Feminist Reading of Orientalism*. Cambridge: Cambridge University Press.

Young, R. (1990) *White Mythologies: Writing History and the West*. London: Routledge.

Young, R. (2001) *Postcolonialism: An Historical Introduction*. Cambridge, MA: Wiley-Blackwell.

Young, R. (2003) *Postcolonialism: A Very Short Introduction*. Oxford: Oxford University Press.

# 7

# New Epistemologies: Post-Positivist Accounts of Identity

Linda Martín Alcoff

Post-positivist approaches to the formulation of social identities are relatively new developments that were formed in reaction to the inadequacy of poststructuralist and postmodern deconstructions of identity, on the one hand, and the implausibility of Cartesian based modernist accounts of the self, on the other (Moya and Hames-García, 2000). Neither the modernist nor the postmodernist theoretical traditions gives sufficient scope for the role that an individual's particular social identity plays in shaping their subjectivity, experience, or knowledge (Alcoff, 2006; Siebers, 2008). To remedy this, the metaphysics of post-positivist realism has been applied to the realm of identity theory in order to provide a mediated approach to experience and knowledge combined with a modified realism about identity (Mohanty, 1997; Moya, 2002).

This introduction will provide a sketch of the three theoretical traditions that have motivated the development of a post-positivist account of identity. I will refer to these traditions by the following shorthand: modernist accounts of the self, postmodernist accounts of identity, and post-positivist approaches to

realism. I will then turn in the following sections to an exploration of the five topics of central concern in this debate: self-knowledge, experience, social location, group identity, and epistemic salience. Each of these topics will be discussed in relation to the three positions, so that the motivations and plausibility of the post-positivist approach can be made clear.

A note of warning about the generality of this discussion is perhaps too obvious to be necessary but nonetheless feels important to include here. In an essay of this type and size, one cannot be attentive to the many differences and variegations within intellectual traditions, or the real complexity of even a single strand. Nonetheless, despite the internal heterogeneity in every theoretical tradition, there are shared elements that are discernible, especially with the benefit of hindsight.

Modernist approaches to the self, dating back to Descartes in the western philosophical canon, have grounded many of the key features in contemporary discussions of social identity, especially in relation to the privilege of first person self-knowledge and the normative ideals of autonomy and individuality. Descartes argued that reliable knowledge is that which can be traced to some clear and distinct ideas, such as clear perceptions of objects or interior mental states and an intuitive grasp of logical relations. These became the cornerstone elements of the trend known as Rationalism, which viewed human beings as essentially rational beings who can discern the truth about both themselves and the world around them. Rationalism provided powerful anti-authoritarian arguments that were later taken up by Enlightenment radicals who sought to overturn the epistemic hierarchies of both the church and the aristocracy. Kant presented this in the slogan "think for yourself," rather than relying on others to do your thinking for you. Yet this liberatory epistemology was based on a notion of individual autonomy that was itself dependent on a particular account of the self as capable of transparent self-understanding. Without a robust self-knowledge, autonomy would be meaningless. To maintain self-knowledge, the modern European philosophers imagined subject formation as a bootstrap affair decontextualized from one's social location. Such notions became increasingly implausible when structural social theories developed from the nineteenth century and onward that offered better explanations for belief and action, relying more on cultural context and background structures than individual intent. Because the modernist account of the self is so completely decontextualized, social identity continues to have little relevance for those working in this tradition, and group-based identities are generally viewed as oppressive impositions that threaten individual autonomy.

Structural social theories began to erode reliance on the modernist account of the self, with its focus on the first person point of view, by approaching individuals as embedded within varying social and cultural systems. These structured systems pre-determined the conditions of individual agency, including moral, practical, and doxastic agency,

which in turn had significant effects on the individual's experience, attitudes, and general subject formation. No longer could the first person point of view be taken as foundational. This also meant that each individual's own perception of their self-interest should not be taken as the basis for their action. Rather, how an individual acts, and reasons, was to be understood via the perspective engendered from their social location. In *On the Jewish Question* Marx developed an account, building in part from Hegel, that religious, ethnic, and class identities affect public deliberation, not as insurmountable determinations but as interests – whether or not they are perspicuous to individuals – that construct oppositional relations between groups (Alcoff and Mendieta, 2003). The solution to public disputes, then, cannot come from rational debate alone but from a political transformation of the conditions in which individuals become social subjects with conflicting perspectives and interests. Freud's structural approach to the formation of the self was similar to Marx's in positing deep structures relatively invisible from the first person point of view that were causally efficacious in the formation of an individual's goals and values. Both Marx and Freud accepted the Enlightenment goal of enhanced freedom through enhanced self-knowledge, but both believed that enhanced self-knowledge required theoretical mediation (i.e., therapy) and collective action (i.e., political parties) rather than simple introspection.

This emerging structuralism primarily concerned the formation of interests and values – the building blocks of modernist political theory – but with Nietzsche and Heidegger it took an even more radical turn to incorporate beliefs, the sphere of meaning and intelligibility, and emotions. Heidegger (1962) adapted Husserl's phenomenological concept of "world" as an always already meaningful or meaning-laden constitution of our environment into a culturally and socially specific world. In a further departure from the early modern tradition, Heidegger argued that we do not in reality encounter a world devoid of meanings and values, or experience ourselves as projecting values or being the source of all value. Rather, we typically encounter a world already overlaid with meaningfulness and affectivity. Consider, for example, the way we experience time. Modern science tells us that time is divisible into equal and uniform units, but this is not how we experience the units of time while waiting for a loved one, or sitting through a tedious lecture, or enjoying an exciting movie. The temporal dimensions of time – or time as it is directly lived and experienced by us – are neither uniform nor equal. Heidegger argues that this experience – experience as actually lived directly in the first person – is the foundational basis of all knowledge, rather than the abstractions of the theoretical sciences that render temporal units as uniform and maintain that solid substances actually contain more space than matter. Yet, because it is our human experience that is foundational to theory, we actually have no foundations, because these experiences are relative to life worlds of variegated meanings and values; for some, an action movie goes by very quickly while for others it might be quite tedious to sit through. To base knowledge on immediate experiences remains, for Heidegger, the most reliable method because it is less theoretically mediated and more direct than scientific abstractions from experience. And yet this reliance on experience calls into question both foundationalism and universalism because experiences themselves are neither universal nor decontextual.

From this and other sorts of criticisms of the modernist accounts of the self, poststructuralist and postmodernist accounts of the self emerged that eventually led to a deconstruction of the social identities that Marx began to make visible. The meaningful and evaluative dimension of an experience, such as an experience of collectivity or an experience of freedom, began to look more and more like the end-product of a large and complex process of social construction. The innovations of poststructuralism were to argue that

the solid structures Marx and Freud and other structuralists such as Levi–Strauss put forward as universal deep structures of all societies or all human psyches were not universal at all. Rather, there might be multiple structures at play in a given context, or there might be both diachronic and synchronic structural change. All of this changeability and variability to structures led theorists to change their understanding of structures themselves, as less like closed, rigid systems and more like open, internally fractious systems with permeable boundaries and permanent contradictions and instability. Social identities such as class then lost their predictive and explanatory capacity, since they could not be relied upon to remain stable or basic to self-formation, nor could the social system of class itself be relied on as having a stable form or set of predictable outcomes. Just as the foundationalism of the self had given way, so too did the foundationalism of social structures based on group identity and social position.

Although this theoretical trajectory of developments in regard to the self, the individual, and the society primarily concerned the metaphysics and the political implications of subjective formation, a parallel development in the theoretical analysis of reality developed a concordance with the same major trends. Modernist confidence in the human ability to know its world, to discern its deep structures and to develop ontologies that "carve nature at its joints," to use Plato's famous phrase, gave way in the nineteenth century as the theoretical sciences developed ever more arcane and indirect models of reality that were often in conflict with other models and were regularly replaced (Shapin, 1994). Science thus began to look more like a mediated human activity and less like an observation of reality. And if science is only capable of developing partially correct models of the nature of reality, how can any other domain of inquiry make realist claims?

Realism is roughly the view that there is a truth about the way the world is and that human beings can achieve knowledge of this truth. Many variations of realism have developed in the past century to accommodate the complexity and fallibility of human knowledge, as well as variations of anti-realism that claim it is best to forego the realist aspiration and settle with instrumental and practical utility. The latter is all human beings actually need science or philosophy for, after all. Yet many others have preferred to complicate realism rather than forego it entirely on the grounds that the anti-realist is implausibly assuming that we can never know anything about the real nature of the universe. Surely, the realist argues, given how many bridges, and bombs, we manage to build, we must be getting something right, even though our ontological models are surely imperfect and partial and we will probably never achieve a perfect correspondence.

Post-positivist approaches to realism would include all of those approaches that reject transparency, infallibility, foundationalism, and characterizations of observation as unmediated and pre-theoretical. Post-positivist approaches today make up a long list, and include critical realism, contextual realism, constructivist realism, internal realism, pragmatic realism, and immanent realism, just to name a few. Social theories that offer explanations of social phenomena are just as much in need of post-positivist realism as are scientific theories of natural processes at the subatomic level. Consider how many new developments in social theory have emerged, such as concerns with gender, race, and class, and with intersectionality, which correct previously incomplete theories and deficient methodologies. Thus, we should assume that such corrections will continue, new and more plausible theories will develop, thus rendering our best current analyses fallible.

With this brief foray into modernist accounts of the self, postmodernist accounts of identity, and post-positivist approaches to realism, we can now turn to an analysis of post-positivist accounts of identity proper, to see how these theoretical debates and developments have merged into this recent innovative approach. As we'll see, the post-positivist approach to identity does not repudiate all aspects of any of these traditions, but like them, develops its own arguments substantively out of what has come before.

## SELF-KNOWLEDGE

The importance of self-knowledge for identity, as this section will show, concerns our understanding of the basic nature of the self and its relationship to externalized social categories as well as historical events. The question of whether we can develop a theory of the self that is essentially independent of the categories of social identity hinges on whether we can plausibly maintain an individualized and effective self-knowledge unmediated by our social location.

One might well ask, following Descartes, what can possibly have more justification than claims we make about our own internal states, our conscious motivations, or our emotional states? The intuition that no knowledge claim will be as reliable or resistant to doubt as self-knowledge lies behind the method proposed by Descartes to ground our beliefs on a firm foundation and thus thwart skepticism. If all of the general beliefs we hold can be traced back in some logical or causal sequence to our internal states, then we can achieve certainty as well as distinguish justified from unjustified beliefs, and effectively rid ourselves of dogma. Scholasticist approaches to knowledge dominant in Europe prior to the Renaissance could not be further from this idea, given their reliance on received and revealed wisdom – primarily that found in religious texts or from religious authorities – to serve as the starting points for all knowledge. Direct perceptual experience that contradicted revealed wisdom could never carry the day, and women who initially denied being witches were sometimes later convinced that they were so by the argumentative strategies of a priestly caste trained in Scholastic methods. The Cartesian reliance on self-knowledge was a powerful tool to overturn authoritarian epistemologies of all sorts.

The belief in self-knowledge as the most direct and reliable form of knowledge led to epistemologies based on individual processes of belief formation. Since there are no collective or group *selves* (modernists assumed, anyway), or collective conscious states, then if the ground of knowledge is in one's own direct awareness of internal states the ground of knowledge will always ultimately be assessed by individuals. The requirement of public confirmation and repeated testability that Bacon wrote into his formulation of the scientific method worked one scientist or laboratory at a time.

Descartes's initial faith in the infallibility of self-knowledge, however, was quickly eroded. Descartes himself developed thought-experiments to contradict his absolute faith in self-knowledge, hypothesizing that an evil god or demon might implant experiences in his mind that were only apparently real, or that a dream might appear so real that it would be indistinguishable from a wakeful state. However, Descartes managed to justify the infallibility of self-knowledge by arguing that an all-benevolent God (that is, the God whom he believed to exist) would neither mislead us nor allow us to be structurally misled in a global fashion, as would be the case if we were brains in a vat or lived a Matrix-like existence. But Descartes's need to rely on God's epistemic benevolence was only a harbinger of the problems self-knowledge would encounter throughout the modern period as it became key to the debates between empiricists and rationalists, who disagreed about whether and how the individual self could discern truths. The empiricists saw the self as discerning truth through empirical or perceptual experience and the rationalists saw the self as discerning truth through direct intuitions of universals. But for both, the process of discernment engaged in by individuals was imagined to be unmediated, transparent, and direct.

Kant is often credited with making a break from the rationalist/empiricist debates precisely through his imaginative reconstruction of the role of the self in knowledge. For Kant, there is no unmediated knowledge, even self-knowledge of internal states, because experience is always the product of perceptual content together with extra-perceptual concepts, such as causation, that are more imposed on the world than they are derived from it. This account substantially increased the human contribution to knowledge and thus the role of the self in not only perceiving but also constituting the true. Hegel then radicalized this idea further by a historicist unmooring of the concepts that Kant envisioned as hard wired and universal (at least for white European males).

For Hegel the self continued to mediate all knowledge but it was a contextualized, historically embedded self that played a substantive and particularized role in the constitution of knowledge. Given their agreement that concepts are constituted by human beings rather than mere reflections of reality, for both Hegel and Kant all knowledge must begin with self-knowledge in order to assess the self's mediating influence on knowledge. Hegel, however, was less optimistic than Kant about the possibility of achieving complete self-knowledge, given that every self is historically and culturally embedded. The owl of Minerva flies at dusk, he wrote, to signal the idea that from within the midst of the play of historical forces we are unable to assess the contours of our own historical subjectivity. Only from an external vantage point can those contours be observed in full relief. Hegel imagined this external vantage point to be primarily temporal but one might also imagine it to be geographical and cultural.

Hence from Hegel forward self-knowledge played only a structural or background role in the justification of knowledge, since individuals could not claim any absolute privilege to knowing all the elements that influence their perceptions and judgments. Both the hermeneutic and phenomenological traditions take this as their starting point, including both Kant's claim that all knowledge is mediated by the self and Hegel's additional claim that complete self-knowledge is ultimately elusive.

Social theories in the Marxist tradition and the social psychological theories that began with George Herbert Mead also started from a reduced hubris about self-knowledge. Mead's account brings groups into the question of self-knowledge in a particularly striking manner. For Mead, individual experience, even interior emotional experiences in large part, cannot be understood or explained without recourse to collective processes of meaning making, just as the emotional reactions one can observe in the audience at a football game would make no sense unless one knew the rules of the game. Pure athletic ability is not what garners the most applause and admiration but acts that advance a team toward winning. Experiences and behavior thus require contextual analysis to be understood; they are not spontaneous eruptions at the individual level, but responses to contextually meaningful prompts.

There have been a number of poststructuralist critiques of self-knowledge, some of which are continuous with aspects of Kant, Hegel, Marx, and Mead, but taking a more thorough-going eliminativist position on the self in general. Foucault's (1978) account is perhaps the most widely influential and also the most damning of the possibility of self-knowledge. For Foucault, discursive formations construct selves through conventions of practice; thus there is no natural self. Foucault suggests, following Nietzsche, that in the modern west Christian practices of the confessional created the very possibility of having a relation with one's self, that is, an interrogative, exploratory, sometimes accusatory relation, through which one pursues self-knowledge. Thus he claims not only that self-knowledge is elusive, but that the project of pursuing self-knowledge is historically and culturally contingent. Christianity plays the key role in his (and Nietzsche's) account because it is not merely concerned with one's behavior but also with one's desires, thoughts,

and fantasies, all of which were made subject by the Council of Trent to confessional penance. In this way the modern self – highly self-conscious, self-aware, and even self-obsessed – was born.

Moreover, on Foucault's account, the practices of the Christian confessional not only turned our attention toward our desires, thoughts, and fantasies, but assisted in producing desires, thoughts, and fantasies that we did not have before we went to confession. Prohibitions produce anxious and excited affective responses to acts or thoughts that might otherwise pass without perturbation. The requirement of the confessional process to recite and remember led to an intensity of affect, a development of desire, and thus in some cases an incitement to act. Perverts, in Foucault's famous claim, were thus born, not in the sense that for the first time persons engaged in acts that later were categorized as perversions, but in the sense that person's developed selves with a rich interior life of affect and thought patterns that constituted "the pervert" in subjective form. Just as perverts were created, so too were "normal" sexual subjectivities, such as the "normal heterosexual couple," through similar practices of self-inspection and judgment. Subject-formation is in this way, he claimed, constitutively linked to processes of subjectivation.

Foucault's account adds an evaluative aspect to the kinds of contextual-based analysis done in the tradition of Mead. That is, Foucault is not simply saying that we need contexts to understand individual behavior and beliefs, but that the contexts within which selves are formed are themselves formed in the nexus of power/knowledges that are linked to disciplinary strategies. These are not like the rules of football but more like the socialization processes used in the military to create completely new selves with automatic responses and inactive critical faculties.

The role of self-knowledge on such an account devolves from providing the grounds of knowledge to being a symptomatic effect of discourse and culture. Even basic perception is seen as discursively constituted, a claim that gains credence from the racist perceptual judgments of police officers who routinely murder African American and Latino men who they perceive incorrectly as armed and dangerous.

Thus, Foucault's critique of self-knowledge has a lot of plausibility, especially in societies where individuals are so dominated by a mass culture with little space or time in their lives in which they are not plugged in, in one way or another, to social outlets that are generating a constant barrage of information, analysis, and visual imagery, and which also have implicit guides for thought and action and strong prompts for desires and fantasies. Nonetheless, the claim that self-knowledge plays no epistemic role at all in achieving reliable knowledge is also implausible. One recurrent problem of both structuralist and poststructuralist approaches to social theory is that they make it difficult to explain resistance. If every individual action is a response to a social prompt, from where do new challenges and new critiques of oppression emerge, such as Foucault's? This common charge against structuralism was partially addressed by poststructuralists who argued that structures are neither uniform nor impermeable but always harbor latent contradictions that can be operationalized by social movements (Halperin, 1995). Marxist dialectics also viewed structures as harboring contradictions, but Marxists thought there would always be a central conflict with a predictable resolution. In contrast, for poststructuralists, the contradictions are not centrally organized, and neither is resistance predictable.

By eclipsing all possible causal explanations for human behavior that might refer to natural selves or natural dispositions, poststructuralists have to explain all resistance via the immanent processes made possible within the contradictions inherent to a discursive formation. Yet there are a number of powerful historical examples that seem to defy this explanation. It is apparent from slave narratives that some slaves experienced themselves differently than the masters' representations of them, even when they lacked community or a substantive link to their ancestors' cultures. Women's movements for equality also developed out of very unformed and under-articulated feelings of dissatisfaction (the 'problem that had no name', as Betty Friedan called it) that had little to no cultural purchase in the discourses of the day. Subaltern groups often report a disconnect between the dominant representations accepted in their society and their own sense of who they are. All of these examples add support to the idea that self-knowledge is not socially constructed all the way down, and that we may have a reserve of autonomous experience from which to take issue with oppressive stereotypes (Combahee River Collective, 1979). How, then, might we formulate an account of identity that would sanction self-knowledge as a potential source of insight without naively characterizing experience as unmediated? This is the question post-positivists address.

## EXPERIENCE

The issue of experience is central to the argument that social identities have epistemic and political salience, since that salience follows from the fact that identities are the repository of, and thus a sign of, certain kinds of experiences. The identity "woman," for example, may be assumed to correlate to experiences of feminine socialization, to threats if not acts of sexual violence and harassment, to service work at home and in the public sphere, and/or to reproductive labor. Because identity is generally assumed to correlate to such a list of experiences, some argue that male-to-female transsexuals are not "women," despite their anatomical concordance. Identity is also taken as politically relevant in electoral politics, eliciting trust, and solidarity because of the assumption that a shared identity means a shared set of experiences. Obviously, such assumptions of common experiences based on common identities are not always justified, but there is enough justification that the assumptions are continually reproduced.

But what can identity actually indicate about an individual's experience? As the transsexual example might indicate, is the linkage between identity and experience unnecessarily reductive? And even if the broad majority of a social group does share certain sorts of experiences, can we assume that those experiences will be interpreted in the same way, or will result in shared values or political dispositions?

Modern western philosophy has little to say about the nature of group experience, since this tradition was focused instead on experience in its most general and minimalist form, such as observations of color or intuitions about abstract relations. Although Kant has a more substantive account of the nature of experience, an account that viewed experience as always mediated by concepts, he too took these mediation processes to be universal. Thus Kant assumed that individual experience could be analyzed as a universal. Not until the development of interpretive traditions in the human and social sciences, and hermeneutics in particular, was experience theoretically analyzed for its substantive cultural and historical content. Experience then began to be understood as at least partly constituted within specific domains of discourse, cultural sign systems, textual traditions, and social values.

Consider, for example, the highly variant ways in which a work of art might be experienced (Gadamer, 1991). Iconic religious art of past centuries was embedded within a set of ritual practices, making possible, for example, a believer's communication with the supernatural realm. The formal features of the artwork were designed to be of service to this transcendental role, and could be read by those knowledgeable about the tradition to get information about the nature of the otherworldly realm, the relations between its protagonists, and the measures one should take to reach them. An individual's ecstatic experience of such art would be quite different than contemporary art students, for example, who may be interested primarily in the production technique, the formal features, or the historical influence of the work in the development of artistic traditions.

Our experience of everyday events – including our perceptions and emotional reactions – are similarly variegated by our social identities, traditions, and cultures. The logical positivists of the early twentieth century attempted to secure a method whereby one could reach below the level of mediation to pure data reports, and a similar effort was pursued by Husserl, so that one could get "to the things themselves." The dream of the early positivists, such as Moritz Schlick, was to base science on this firm foundation of pure observations reports, which were to be expressed in linguistically spare and unmediated form such as "red patch here now." By using linguistic minimalism Schlick hoped that cultural differences, and differences of tradition or creed, could be cleared away from the business of science. Only the sciences that could ground their theories on such minimal observation reports would be deemed knowledge; all other human inquiry – including all of the social or human sciences – was merely expressive.

This dream died a famously quick and decisive death, as it became clear that the natural sciences themselves had to rely on unconfirmed working assumptions, that data bits could serve no inferential role without theoretical commitments, nor could individual scientific claims be validated except in clusters. But the positivist idea that mediated experiences compromise procedures and have reduced epistemic worth, continues to linger. And if scientific judgment itself is compromised, what of our everyday judgments?

For poststructuralists, the lesson of the fall of positivism is to curtail our reliance on observation and experience, rather than to reframe the epistemic assumptions behind the positivist account (Butler, 1990, 1993). In other words, poststructuralists dismiss the epistemic reliability of experience just as the early logical positivists did, and for the same reason, because experience is replete with historically and culturally specific mediations. Experience is taken to be that which is in need of explanation, rather than that which can provide explanation. Thus, it is the end-point of a causal sequence about which the individual has little awareness. This causal sequence includes discursive formations, social practices, and so forth, such as those elements that engender such different affective as well as cognitive experiences of works of art.

Post-positivist accounts of realism, by contrast, have challenged and reframed the positivist characterization of mediated experiences as epistemically compromised. Post-positivists such as Quine and Putnam pointed out that even in its compromised state science provides reliable knowledge with practical utility and sometimes alarming success (Alcoff, 1996). If theoretical assumptions cannot be confirmed, and all judgments are mediated, we may need to revise our ontological characterization of the truth content of science, but we do not need to deny that science has any truth content at all. In other words, we need to hold back from asserting a simple correspondence between the theoretical posits and ontological models of the sciences on the one hand and the world "as it is in itself," but this does not mean that those theoretical posits are mere fictions or, worse, illusions. They are human-made models whose practical efficacy indicates some purchase on the real.

What this implies for experience is that we need not take the inevitability of mediation as dooming experience to epistemic vacuity. Mediations can actually enhance our ability to grasp the nature of the world, just as scientific models do. Mediating elements can be comparatively evaluated for their epistemic effects. Values may be unavoidable, but all values do not have the same effects on knowing. Assumptions about the necessity of hierarchy, for example, may inhibit the development of models for cellular organisms, just as assumptions about the naturalness of

gender-based divisions of labor inhibited knowledges in the social sciences. Moreover, these unhelpful assumptions and values may be related to certain group experiences and not others.

Adopting the lessons of post-positivist realism changes the way we think about the role of experience in relation to knowledge as well as to identity (Moya, 2002). One need not be a positivist who believes that experience is unmediated to accept the validity of experience as a source of knowledge. When I visually judge the adequacy of a particular carbon target for its utility in a particle accelerator, or when I make a prediction of voting patterns based on data from a questionnaire about party affiliations, I am bringing to bear a wealth of theoretical commitments embedded within a set of technical procedures. I am also engaging in a judgment call rather than a deduction, and in some cases, with regard to certain kinds of topics, my judgment calls may be mediated by a group-related experience I have.

Post-positivist accounts of identity have made significant arguments about how to understand the mediated character of experience within a realism that validates the epistemic role of experience. This means that we need a more sophisticated account of what experience consists in and how it works in the production of knowledge, in order to account for the variable mediations of experience. Post-positivism rejects the post-structuralist and positivist view that all mediations are epistemically the same, or will have the same effect on the epistemic outcome of inquiry and how reliable it is. These points will be developed in the final section of this essay.

## GROUP IDENTITY

The question of identity is really a question about groups. To say that I have a Latina identity is to say that I belong in some sense to the group "Latinas" and this in turn implies that such a group exists. But in what sense do such groups exist, and in what sense can individuals be said to have a necessary, non-volitional relationship to such groups so that they can be identified as such?

Much of the skepticism and political concern about the use of identity categories results from the concern about groups and the relation of groups to individuals. For much of the modern western tradition, individuals are the sole loci of agency, rationality, and moral culpability. To the extent it is useful to refer to groups, it is understood that groups are aggregates of individuals, and for the purposes of explanation, should be reduced to their individual parts. Thus for the great liberal contract theorists, the development of theories of justice and the legitimacy of the state can be reduced to the question of individual interests; groups need not enter into the equation at all.

This modern predilection toward individuals is based fundamentally on a metaphysical account of selves, from which political implications follow. Groups do not really exist, in a metaphysical sense. Rather, the term "group" is seen as simply a way of describing similarities among individuals. From seventeenth-century liberalism to twentieth-century existentialism, groups are ontologically derivative upon individuals.

If individuals are all that truly exist, then we cannot speak (or can only speak metaphorically) about group interests, group rights, group trauma, or even, some argue, group history. To do so is not only metaphysically inaccurate, but it also oppresses individuals within groups who might be unfairly and inaccurately characterized, spoken for, or presumptively "known." So not only are groups unreal, they are dangerous. Given this philosophical legacy, western democratic theory has had a predictably difficult time with groups, and only recently have issues such as group rights been seriously debated in the mainstream. Democratic theory generally addresses only the relation of the state to the individual, and often considers group political behavior (e.g., "interest group politics") suspect. Again, such skepticism makes sense

given the view that groups are essentially aggregates of individuals. It is no wonder, then, that the ideal goal is to have the state treat everyone as individuals, without any separate treatment for groups such as racial minorities or women. Many governments have, of course, discriminated against individuals on the basis of their group membership, denying them suffrage as well as equal rights and protections. So the assumption is that individuals will want to be free of this group designation and be allowed to operate within the state as free individualized persons.

Poststructuralist approaches to groups start from an eliminativist orientation to selves, as we've seen, which are diametrically opposed to the modern notion of the self as the unique locus of agency, rights, and morality, all robustly conceived. So one might imagine that poststructuralists would be more open to the possibility that groups have a real existence. Yet this is not the case, since poststructuralists take a similarly eliminativist position toward groups. The concept of a group is an objective characterization that treats human beings as reified things, as if they could be described and predicted and analyzed as natural or found objects (Brown, 1995). For theorists such as Deleuze, this is a kind of category mistake that is a form of territorialization akin to colonialism. Deleuze's metaphysics does not incline him toward ontological individualism but to reject preset relations between persons or distinct boundaries of any sort. The fluid nature of human, as well as animal, existence precludes artificial boundary setting that would attempt to control my constitutive relatedness to others or my opening onto multiple planes of experience.

Foucault offers further reasons to be skeptical about the ontological status of groups, and his reasons are again both metaphysical and political. Group identities are in some cases at least, he suggests, false reifications of indeterminate experiences that work to coercively coordinate behavior through hegemonic cultural discourses. Thus, for example, some have argued that homosexuality as an *identity*, rather than as just a practice or form of desire, only came into existence after the state made sexuality its concern and after discourses of power/knowledge began to objectify sexual practices and define them as essential entities with moral implications and therapeutic needs. The arena of sexual activity itself does not necessarily entail any identity categories at all being attached to specific practices, and certainly without an emphasis on the object (i.e., gendered object) of desire rather than its manner of expression or level of intensity. Foucault does not imagine such processes occurring only or even primarily from the top down in a society, and yet he retains a critical suspicion toward the subjectification of practices which would tell us a purported deep truth about "what we are" (Halperin, 1995).

One immediate question here is whether Foucault's or Deleuze's analysis would apply across the board to all group concepts. Poststructuralism tends, like western modernism, toward sweepingly general analyses at the micro level that are then applied to widely divergent phenomena. Examples of this sort would include the Freudian-inspired analyses of group attachments as delusional attempts to secure stable egos under a condition of lack and constant disintegration, or Nietzschean-inspired analyses of identity-based social movements as grounded in *ressentiment*. The great diversity in the historical formations of group identity concepts such as race, ethnicity, gender, sexuality, and disability would seem to mitigate the possibility of a single evaluative analysis.

Post-positivist approaches to realism are useful here once again by allowing for a more modest, and mediated, understanding of how group concepts refer (Mohanty, 1993). One of the main bases for skepticism against group identities made by both modernists and poststructuralists is that groups cannot exhaust individuals, that there is something fluid and varied and changeable about individuals that group concepts elide. But this is to assume that when group concepts are used, there is a perfect correspondence between the group and the person, as if all that is true of the group "Latina" will also be true of me. Poststructuralists are constantly pointing to the "remainder" or "excess" beyond the content of social identity categories, and often are, like the existentialists, locating agency and freedom only in this remainder or excess, that is, in the way in which I escape the essence of *latinidad*. But from a post-positivist view, neither group concepts nor identity concepts are perfect representations that capture the essence of the individual, or all aspects – past, future, and present – of their selves. They are like models, or theories, that have limited merit based on their explanatory value. And the persistent fact that many individuals use group concepts to describe themselves indicates, not false consciousness or territorialized subjectivity, but their practical and political utility to name social experiences (Castells, 1997; Cruz, 1998; Dawson, 1994). A more serious challenge to the concept of group identity comes from the fact that groups are always heterogeneous and every individual is a member of multiple groups, some of which may have a very different social status and different political interests (Hames-García, 2000). This challenge will be addressed in the last section.

## SOCIAL LOCATION

The concept of social location has developed only in recent decades as a way to conceptualize the socially and epistemically relevant aspects of one's identity that are objective in the sense of arising out of the objective structures of society. The idea of social location is not exhaustive of identity, but is put forward as one element or aspect of identity. The concept of social location is especially relevant for the concept of group identity, since social location is a central way that groups are identified and differentiated. However, there have been some specific elements to the debate over the concept of social location that need to be mentioned here.

The concept of social location, as stated above, refers primarily to the objective aspect of one's identity, rather than to the subjective aspect. The subjective aspect includes the person's own lived sense of self, or their first person experience of who they are in the world. That is, the subjective aspect is the way one sees one's self, whereas the objective aspect concerns the way a person is identified by others, such as in socially recognized and official categories, in government or employment forms, or just in the conventional patterns of recognition in their particular social milieu. The separation made here between subjective and objective aspects is more heuristic than real, since there is an obvious relationship between one's internal sense of self and how one is viewed. The relation is mutually influencing – meaning that either the subjective or the objective side can have an effect on the other – or less minimally, we might say the relation is mutually constitutive. Yet the point of making the separation is to be able to articulate the way in which we sometimes find our subjective and objective identities at odds with one another. For example, we might not recognize our lived sense of self in derogatory, low-status objective interpellations. This is often the experience of persons who face identity-based discriminations or oppression based on fallacious representations. There can also be resistance among identity groups that enjoy social domination and who reject the idea that they have substantial social identities that impact their lives and fortunes. For such persons, their own lived sense of self is individual and personal and has no constitutive relation to the social privileges accorded their group identity.

Both the relevance and the objectivity of the concept of social location have been contested. For the modern tradition, social location was invisible or left untheorized even while it was the implicit correlate of a person's epistemic trustworthiness, degree of rationality, likelihood of morality, and so on. Many ancient and modern western philosophers from Aristotle to Kant did actually address social location in the sense of objective identity to explain why slaves were slavish, women irrational, peasants untrustworthy, and dark peoples incapable of self-government. All one needed to know about a person was this objective social location to be justified in a host of presumptions about them, according to these arguments. Yet at the same time that such views about identity were espoused in the context of philosophical theories about the self, democracy, and knowledge, these same theories neglected to analyze the ways in which social location might make a difference in what one believed or what one knew. The development of the concept of social location was meant to be a corrective to this hypocritical approach, so as to make visible the theories of diverse social location and make possible a more reflective theoretical analysis.

For much of contemporary liberalism, social location is still something one can wholly transcend in a volitional manner. The objectivist determinations of one's identity via categories of race or gender need only affect one's life if one lets them. To the extent that state and social practices enforce the relevance of social location, such practices should be overturned. So, either social location is already irrelevant (at least potentially if people will only stop using the "race card" or "gender card"), or it should be made irrelevant. In neither case does it merit much philosophical attention.

Poststructuralists have primarily contested the objectivity of claims about social location, and have been worried about essentialist and reductive approaches that would assume sharing a social location implies that individuals share political perspectives and experiences. A further worry has been an essentializing of the political and epistemic salience of social location, as for example in versions of Marxism that privileged the proletariat social location for leading human history toward progress. Feminist standpoint theory was similarly criticized initially as essentialist for proposing that women's social location gave us a shared insight and political stance.

Clearly, the various histories of social movements have borne out these concerns about essentialism, and the mistake of assuming overly homogenized effects of social location. There is no uniform politics across individuals who share a social location. Furthermore, social locations themselves are not uniform: the social location inhabited by women is cut across by other social locations involving race, class, sexuality, disability, ethnicity, religion, citizenship status, nationality, and age. Given this complexity, on some poststructuralist accounts social location has no relevance to a given individual's political commitments. Which one of the many dimensions of an individual's social location will be operationalized in a given moment is subject to both contextual conditions and volition. The implication of this view is that one cannot characterize the aspects of a given social location that have more epistemic or political salience than others, and therefore one's social location drops out from being able to play a predictive or explanatory role in social theory.

The concept of a standpoint was developed by Sandra Harding as different from social location in order to address some of these concerns about essentialism. A standpoint is achieved, it is self-conscious and politically reflexive, and thus is not merely a feature of one's objective status apart from one's subjective identity. Not all women have a feminist standpoint, and men too can develop a feminist standpoint. And standpoints are conceptualized by Harding more like methodological orientations than sets of unchanging political commitments. In this way, standpoints are rendered free of the charge of essentialism. Standpoints remain connected to social location in that the standpoint tries to ask questions and develop theory from the point of view of particular social locations and their attendant common practices (Wylie, 2004).

Post-positivist approaches to identity have generally considered both the concept of social location and the related concept of standpoints as useful elements for a theory

of identity, and even vitally necessary ones. How can the very concept of "studying up" or "shifting the geography of reason" or attending to the "locus of enunciation" work without the concepts of both social location and standpoint? One need not take a simplistic approach to the idea of social location for it to have some explanatory value in understanding such phenomena as the development of women's and ethnic studies, or diversified voting patterns, or the emergence of new social movements. We need to retain both of these concepts with attention to what they can and cannot explain, and how they operate in relation to selves.

## EPISTEMIC SALIENCE

Finally, we come to the topic of epistemic salience, or the question of how identities matter in practices of knowing. This section will simply draw out the epistemic implications of the previous sections, both on the question of how identities are epistemically salient today and how they should be salient in a normative account that aims to optimize reliable knowing.

As we have seen, both modern and postmodern philosophies have largely repudiated the epistemic salience of identity, though for differing reasons and, in the case of the modern tradition, simultaneous with a hypocritical acceptance of epistemic hierarchies between social identities. But there are legitimate concerns about the dangers of positing a privileged, infallible standpoint, a homogenized experience and interpretation of oppression across marginalized groups, or a unified, transparent self that can achieve complete or nearly complete self-knowledge. Yet the epistemic salience of identities can be maintained if we develop a more complicated, and realistic, picture of how it works. The point of importing the lessons of post-positivist realism into an account of identity is precisely to avoid the overly homogenized notions of experience and assumptions of infallibility, problems that follow from unmediated approaches to knowledge.

One way to consider the question of epistemic salience in very concrete terms is to ask whether it makes a difference that those engaged in academic research are a diversified group or not. If one truly believes that identity has no epistemic salience, then one must allow that academic research on any topic could flourish even if the researchers had uniform identities: that whites could study non-whites and men could study women with no discernible adverse effect. This is technically possible, one might concede, perhaps in the future with very different social conditions, but the past and present of academic research stands as a strong indicator that identities do make a difference.

The controversy over Edward Said's (2004) critical evaluation of Orientalism is an instructive example here, since the controversy at bottom concerned the epistemic implications of Said's critique. Said argued that part of the doctrine of Orientalism, which he defined (with a creative use of Foucault) as a kind of broad and politicized epistemological field, involved the claim that "Orientals" cannot study themselves, since they lacked both objective distance and the knowledge and habits of western rational methods. In developing his critique of Orientalism, Said had to take issue with this epistemic assessment of "Oriental" identity, and he did so in part by making an assessment of western identities in relation to the possibility of developing adequate knowledge. Said pointed out that westerners operating in the midst of colonialism were hardly objective, and the claim that they were epistemically privileged over the scholarly sources inside the Orient, because the latter were insufficiently objective, was a bogus claim. Said did not argue for the absolute privilege of either insider or outsider, nor did he homogenize either side, and in fact, he argued against the very binary of west–east as one of the problematic constructions of Orientalism. Nonetheless, both his critique

of Orientalism and his proposals for correction started from a general understanding that identities in the form of social location, group identity, and experience have potential epistemic implications that warrant analysis. It was no coincidence that western colonialist scholars developed a limited conceptualization of their object of study.

Said generalized his own experience of the debate over his work to other identity based scholarship in the following remark: "feminism or women's studies, black or ethnic studies, socialist and anti-imperialist studies, all … take for their point of departure the right of formerly un– or mis-represented human groups to speak for and represent themselves in domains defined, politically and intellectually, as normally excluding them, usurping their signifying and representing functions, overriding their historical reality" (2004: 200). The correction of cognitive distortions and omissions produced by conditions of colonialism or social oppression need the participation of those whose "historical reality" has been overridden.

A post-positivist approach to the question of the epistemic salience of identity responds to the intuitive pull of such examples that indicate that identities do indeed have epistemic salience. Yet a post-positivist approach would not take identities as reliable in themselves to justify claims nor assume that the relationship between identity and knowledge is the same under any set of circumstances. Rather, it retains the starting assumption that identities might be relevant in any context, but holds that the question of their relevance needs to be asked and evaluated in each context rather than theoretically and methodologically foreclosed.

Alison Wylie (2004) has recently articulated a reasonable formulation of epistemic standpoints and their relevance to inquiry, and her account exemplifies a post-positivist approach. Wylie begins with the plausible claim that "[…] what we know is structured by the social and material conditions of our lives" (2004: 341) The variable social and material conditions experienced by varying groups can yield advantages in research, including "access to evidence (sometimes including background or collateral evidence); inferential heuristics that confer particular skill in disembedding empirical patterns; an expanded range of interpretive and explanatory hypotheses for making sense of evidence; and, often a condition of the rest, critical disassociation from the taken-for-granteds that underpin authoritative forms of knowledge" (Wylie, 2004: 346). Note that for Wylie, these accrue to standpoints, or achieved analytical and critical perspectives, rather than social locations per se, but social location plays a part in the ability to achieve a standpoint because of the variable "social and material conditions of our lives".

Wylie concludes that we can claim a "contingent epistemic advantage to subdominant standpoints" (2004: 349). There is no automatic, decontextualized privilege here, and the emphasis on standpoints counters an assumption about transparent experience or complete self-knowledge. The stuff of social location and experience is more like the untheorized raw material that needs to be shaped and reflected upon to yield theoretical advantage, though that raw material has epistemic salience in and of itself. Wylie takes a strongly contextualist position on when such advantages actually accrue, and argues that under some conditions, being an outsider or having an emotional distance from a topic might actually be advantageous. We must always retain an openness to the possibility of learning from others. This sort of moderated approach that forecloses the epistemic utility of neither interest nor disinterest by theoretical fiat, and denies absolute validity to any particular social position, is typical of a post-positivist approach.

## A POST-POSITIVIST ACCOUNT OF IDENTITY

The intuition behind the development of post-positivist approaches to identity is that,

while it is implausible to deny the political relevance and epistemic salience of identity, the concerns about identity developed within the poststructuralist and postmodern traditions in the past few decades warrant a serious reconsideration of how we think about what identities are and how they operate. Modernist approaches can in the main be left behind as too unreflective on the topic of identity, and generally too simplistic in their accounts of selves, knowledge, and rationality. This lack of reflexivity about identity left modern traditions largely incapable of understanding their own cognitive shortcomings, as in the case of Orientalism, as well as incapable of adequately understanding the epistemic implications of new social movements and new identity-based scholarship.

Poststructuralism emerged as a critical engagement with the modern philosophical traditions of thinking about the self. But poststructuralism also parted company with the liberatory discourses of anti-colonialist and new social movements in the mid-twentieth century that couched their demands in humanist and universalist terms. The demand for the rights of sexually stigmatized groups, to take one example, to freely express their "authentic" desires made naturalistic assumptions about sexual desire and the stability of sexual identities. The very concept of liberation had to be rethought, in so far as its aim was to liberate identities that in reality were formed within discourses of domination. Moreover, the assumption that marginalized groups had uniform political aims and that these aims were certain to be equally liberatory for all within the group had been shown to be false. Poststructuralism viewed these sorts of problems as caused by inadequate notions of how meaning works, as if the meaning of identities or political values can be determined in advance.

However, poststructuralism has created a great deal of confusion about what can be claimed in the way of values, politics, and reliable knowledge (Mohanty, 1993). And it has lost any ability to explain the role that identities play in academic research and social movements. In regard to the movements against identity based forms of oppression, poststructuralism has only strategic essentialism to propose as a way to understand how identities are operating in the political domain. However, strategic essentialism maintains without redressing the theoretical incoherence between analytical viewpoint and social action, and in so doing it lends itself to a problematic elitism of theorists who "know" the truth about identity and activists who, presumably, do not.

In contrast to poststructuralism, the post-positivist approach seeks to revise and reconstruct, rather than simply deconstruct, the way in which social identities are understood. It makes four proposals toward such revisionary work.

First, as Satya Mohanty (1993, 1997) has argued, identities should be seen as more like explanatory theories than as fundamental metaphysical posits. This would make identities open to empirical testing to see whether they are adequate conceptions of social reality. It also renders identity concepts as revisable, fallible constructions that help us to make sense of historical events as well as personal experiences. The principal reason to hold onto the concept of social identities is not because they are strategically useful for the purposes of political mobilization, or because they comprise such a powerful part of the dominant discourse that we cannot dislodge them, but because they have great explanatory value. The category "Latino" is an obvious social construction, for example, with a dubious political genealogy, and yet it remains critically important as a way to understand not only the political debates in the United States today but also the current lived experience of millions whose daily experience is in environments that are majority-Anglo. This situation is obviously changeable, and it should also be obvious that the term "Latino" does not correspond to any unchanging essence. To assert a term's explanatory value is not to say that the explanation will persist across historical changes or that it will work the same across the many racial and national and sexual differences, among others, within Latino communities. But it is to say that there is an empirical basis for the use of the term "Latino" that cannot be dismissed as a theoretical error or political mistake.

Second, a helpful way to conceptualize identities without losing sight of these complexities, or so I have argued, is along the lines of the concept of the hermeneutic horizon (Alcoff, 2006). Horizons consist in one's tradition, which the classic hermeneuticists imagined to be mono-cultural but which can also be imagined as the heterogeneous amalgam of one's affective relations to macro historical events (such as slavery, genocide) along with the cultural discourses, both textual and visual, to which one has access, as well as one's own individual and personal history and set of experiences. There are individual but also group-related aspects to everyone's horizon, although the latter are always subject to an interpretive process in which individuals interpret the meanings, moral and political implications of their group-related experiences. The concept of the horizon thus provides a way to explain the mediated nature of interpretation such that one carries forth one's tradition into the process of interpreting new claims, new events, and new experiences. In this way, as Hames-García (2000) has argued, we can explain the existence of differences within groups and the lack of political uniformity as due to the multiplicity within horizons and their mediated character. But we can also maintain that identity has epistemic salience because there are group-related and group-generated differences between affective relationships and experiences. Group identity determines some of the content of one's horizon, but does not determine what we make of it or how we react to it.

Third, as Moya (2002) has emphasized, identities are relevant because they are the rough correlates of experience, and because experience is a critically important touchstone for the adequacy of theories. Experience need not be transparent or unmediated, wearing its meaning on its sleeve, so to speak, for it to have theoretical importance. A good example here used by Satya Mohanty is the feminist consciousness-raising group, which took experiences as the raw material for a collective and democratic process of analysis in order precisely to reflect critically on the ways in which we had previously understood our experiences in the past and the ways in which we might develop new analyses. The use of experience in such formats was not presumed to be a clear or simple way to develop political insight; if experience were susceptible to simple analysis or had a transparent meaning, it would not have required such extended collective sharing and unpacking. Yet if participants had not had the experiences of rape, sexual harassment, wife-battering, sexual dissatisfaction, or of having illegal abortions, and so on, the analysis in consciousness-raising groups would not have been able to proceed as productively as it clearly did.

Fourth, as Siebers (2008) and Alcoff (2006) have emphasized, identities need to be understood phenomenologically as embodied and corporeal, rather than as discursive overlays on a bodily experience imagined to be inert and open to any meaning whatsoever laid on top of it. We need to remain attentive to the corporeal aspects of anti-black racism or of disabled identities or of the markedly different ways human beings participate in biological reproduction. To stress such differences does not require an essentializing but it does emphasize the need to attend to the body and not merely to language or cultural representations. The body is not, after all, infinitely plastic, amenable to a plethora of meanings and interpretations, or analogous to the open-ended nature of language. We might dramatically re-signify the word "black," "bitch," or "queer"; we cannot dramatically re-signify death, torture, or rape. We need an account of identity that will retain this material consciousness of the limits of human embodied experience.

Together, these four proposals suggest a concept of identity that is indeed complex, yet salient and meaningful. On a post-positivist approach, there is no way to predetermine the political meanings of various identities, but there is legitimacy to insisting that the question of the relevance of identity needs always to be on the table in assessing both research methods and results. Although any realistic approach to identities must acknowledge their fluidity and thus the revisability of current formulations, still, if we accept the likelihood that group differences will persist into the future, this reconstructed approach to identity might engender a similarly reconstructed, and decolonized, humanism.

# REFERENCES

Alcoff, L.M. (1996) *Real Knowing: New Versions of the Coherence Theory.* Ithaca, NY: Cornell University Press.

Alcoff, L.M. (2006) *Visible Identities: Race, Gender and the Self.* New York: Oxford University Press.

Alcoff, L.M. and Mendieta, E. (eds) (2003) *Identities: A Reader.* New York: Blackwell.

Butler, J. (1993) *Bodies That Matter: On the Discursive Limits of 'Sex'.* New York: Routledge.

Butler, J. (1990) *Gender Trouble: Feminism and the Subversion of Identity.* New York: Routledge.

Brown, W. (1995) *States of Injury: Power and Freedom in Late Modernity.* Princeton, NJ: Princeton University Press.

Castells, M. (1997) *The Power of Identity, Vol. II of The Information Age: Economy, Society and Culture.* Oxford: Blackwell.

Combahee River Collective. (1979) 'A black feminist statement', in Z.R. Eisenstein (ed.), *Capitalist Patriarchy and the Case for Socialist Feminism,* pp. 362–372. New York: Monthly Review Press.

Cruz, J.E. (1998) *Identity and Power: Puerto Rican Politics and the Challenge of Ethnicity.* Philadelphia, PA: Temple University Press.

Dawson, M.C. (1994) *Behind the Mule: Race and Class in African-American Politics.* Princeton, NJ: Princeton University Press.

Foucault, M. (1978) *The History of Sexuality.* Vol. 1. Trans. Robert Hurley. New York: Random House.

Gadamer, H-G. (1991) *Truth and Method.* 2nd edn. Trans. Joel Weinsheimer and Donald G. Marshall. New York: Crossroad Press.

Halperin, D. (1995) *Saint Foucault: Toward a Gay Hagiography.* New York: Oxford University Press.

Hames-García, M. (2000) '"Who are our own people?" Challenges for a theory of social identity', in P.M.L. Moya and M.R. Hames-García (eds), *Reclaiming Identity: Realist Theory and the Predicament of Postmodernism*, pp. 102–129. Berkeley, CA: University of California Press.

Heidegger, M. (1962) *Being and Time*. Trans. John Macquarrie and Edward Robinson. New York: Harper and Row.

Mohanty, S. (Spring 1993) 'The epistemic status of cultural identity', *Cultural Critique*, 24: 41–80.

Mohanty, S. (1997) *Literary Theory and the Claims of History*. Ithaca, NY: Cornell University Press.

Moya, P.M.L. (2002) *Learning From Experience: Minority Identities, Multicultural Struggles*. Berkeley, CA: University of California Press.

Moya, P.M.L. and Hames-García, M.R. (eds) (2000) *Reclaiming Identity: Realist Theory and the Predicament of Postmodernism*. Berkeley, CA: University of California Press.

Said, E. (2004) *Humanism and Democratic Criticism*. New York: Columbia University Press.

Shapin, S. (1994) *A Social History of Truth: Civility and Science in Seventeenth Century England*. Chicago, IL: University of Chicago Press.

Siebers, T. (2008) *Disability Theory*. Ann Arbor, MI: University of Michigan Press.

Wylie, A. (2004) 'Why standpoint matters', in S. Harding (ed.), *The Feminist Standpoint Theory Reader*, pp. 339–351. New York: Routledge.

# PART 2

# Formations

# 8

# Biology and Identity

Anne Fausto-Sterling

In the late twentieth century, we entered the era of the genome. Biomedical researchers rapidly conceptualized individual identities in terms of DNA base sequences. Racial identity has become discernable in terms of DNA markers, tiny alterations in the sequence of letters which underlie genetic structure. Geneticists rush to identify special chromosome regions affiliated with (gay male) homosexuality and new discoveries, however tentative, become part of a social and legal discourse about what it means to be gay. In an attempt to ferret out the molecules that contribute to gender identity formation, laboratories move beyond the study of hormones into the expression of gene sequences in the embryonic brain.

Yet, even as the genomic era blossoms, a post genomic period dawns. Indeed, temporally, we inhabit a hybrid era in which theories of identity draw on many levels of biological knowledge. In this essay we look at what biologists, and to some extent psychologists, think about the contribution of biology to racial, gendered and sexual identity formation. To the extent that biological knowledge circulates openly in the realm of culture (the newspapers, television, courts of law, blogs and informal conversations) researchers' beliefs about the biological roots of identity become as well, a cultural and

sociological contribution to individual identity formation. In other words, while individual biology may contribute to identity formation through the activities of genes, hormones and the like, knowledge of scientific beliefs about biology circulates as a cultural effect that shapes identity via the social world.

## RACE AND ETHNICITY

In the United States, a critical examination of health disparities provides one entry point to unravel the bio-social skein of racial and ethnic identities. Statistically, health outcomes differ depending upon ethnic or racial group. Thus one reads of exceptionally high levels of type two diabetes among Native Americans and African Americans, higher frequency (compared to European Americans) of dangerously high blood pressure among African Americans, greater susceptibility to bone disease in Asian American women, and severe asthma in Hispanic Americans. There are two points to be drawn out here. First, the mere act of gathering the data requires sampling discrete populations in which individuals claim particular racial or ethnic membership (Fullwiley, 2007). As has been well documented (Epstein, 2007; Nobles, 2000) the very drawing of the categories for medical research depends on the political process of census taking. The health disparities are real enough, and, by definition, map onto the categories defined by the US census.

But, and this is the second point, are racial and ethnic categories useful for seeking biological explanations of disease formation? This question has generated enormous debate within the biomedical research community (Braun, 2002; Braun et al., 2007; Fausto-Sterling, 2004; Rebbeck et al., 2006). Simple international comparisons suggest that the racial categories used for US health statistics do not provide a good foundation for understanding health disparities. One example will make the point.

It is widely understood among medical practitioners that African Americans more frequently have chronic hypertension compared with European Americans. The medical results of high blood pressure can include kidney disease, stroke and a variety of heart conditions (Cooper and Kaufman, 1998; Cooper and Rotimi, 1994; Krieger and Sidney, 1996). Although many social and epidemiological explanations of increased high blood pressure have been offered, the dominant paradigm in US medicine is genetic. The belief is that blacks must have genes that make them susceptible to this medical condition. Cooper, however, has examined the rates of hypertension in blacks and whites of differing nationalities. In comparing rates of hypertension in black populations sampled from Nigeria, Jamaica and the United States, Cooper and his colleagues found frequencies of 13.5%, 28.6%, and 44%, respectively. For European origin populations from the United States, England and Germany, the prevalence was 26.8%, 41.7%, and 55.3%, respectively (Cooper et al., 2005). This simple international comparison is sufficient to disconnect race from hypertension prevalence. These authors suggest that "the impact of environmental factors may have been under-appreciated" (2005: 1).

Despite evidence of important environmental contributions, medical researchers continue to hunt for racially or ethnically associated genetic underpinnings to explain health disparities. Identity politics shape researchers' approaches to understanding the biology of disease formation, making it less likely that they will pursue certain approaches that might be more fruitful in the clinic than hunting for genes. Indeed, such non-genetic approaches might erode the strength of racial and ethnic identity formation including individual scientists' self-concept. Below, I explore one example that illustrates these claims.

When scientists completed the first draft of the linear base sequence of the human genome project, they declared that race had become passé (Schwartz, 2001). For a moment, geneticists seemed to join forces with social scientists who had earlier proclaimed that race was a social, not a biological category (American Anthropological Association, 1996). However, in what seems like mere nano-seconds, the genome sequence as a confirmation of a unified human identity, transformed through the actions of biomedical researchers into a data bank to be plumbed for evidence of racial and ethnic differences. The sequenced genome opened wide the genomic era in which scientists had at their fingertips astonishing tools with which to identify minute – single base pair – variations between the genetic codes of individuals and groups of individuals (Gura, 2001; Reich et al., 2003; The International HapMap Consortium, 2003; Weiss and Terwilliger, 2000; Whitehead Institute, 2004). The new debate about race has brought new terminology; scientists now prefer to write about groups that share a common ancestry. One manifestation of this linguistic transition is the development of groups of DNA sequences called Ancestry Information Markers (AIMS), currently available as a patented commercial product for use in genealogical research, forensics and biomedical research (http://www.dnaprint.com/welcome/home/index.php). The forensic use of these markers is of great social importance, contributing to the high incarceration rate of black males in the US (Duster, 2006), but here we focus on their use in biomedical research.

The company website describes AIMS in the following fashion:

About 0.1% of the 3 billion bases of our DNA are different from person to person and these locations are called polymorphisms. Of all polymorphisms, only a few percent are different as a function of ancestry. AIMs carry information about population structure, inter- and intra-individual diversity and our history as a species. Our scientists have authored and filed patent applications covering the human genomes best AIMs and key methods for using them to assist with designing clinical trials, epidemiology studies, or inferring elements of certain physical or clinical traits such as skin colour or drug response. AIM-based methods are important because our links to human disease, drug response and elements of our physical appearance are best identified through a detailed understanding of human heredity and identity. (DNA Print Genomics, 2008a)

The genomic era scientists who track racial and ethnic contributions to health disparities realize that their categories are based on the frequency of particular DNA sequences in different populations. Furthermore, they are quite aware of the fact that the populations of interest to health policy advisors are historically mixed. An Hispanic of Mexican descent, for example, has European and Amer-Indian ancestors. An Hispanic of Puerto Rican origin is likely to have had European and African ancestry. Because there are no racially pure populations, genomic researchers track what they call admixture[1]: they developed tools to estimate what percentage of an individual's genome sequence comes from particular ancestral populations. Thus one research group used AIMS to calculate that Mexican ancestry averaged 3.4% African, 45% European, and 52% Native American (Fullwiley, 2008). Fullwiley also notes that the category European itself hides ancestral diversity – fifteenth-century Spain being populated by Greeks, Jews, Arabs, gypsies, etc. But in the context of race in twenty-first century American medical genetics "European" has consolidated into a single identity.

Consider now the findings that asthma prevalence is highest for Puerto Rican Americans (13.1%), followed by Native Americans (9.9%) and non-Hispanic blacks (9.5%). Asthma mortality for whites increased from 2.1 to 2.6 deaths per million population over the 1980–1984 to 2000–2001 time period; during the same period, the mortality rate for African Americans increased from 9.9 to 13.2 deaths per million population (American Academy of Allergy, 2006). Fullwiley (2008) follows the thought processes and laboratory practices of a genome researcher, Esteban Burchard, as he searches the genome, using AIMS and admixture tools to identify population (read racial and ethnic) specific gene sequences that can explain these disparities. This researcher, himself "Hispanic" recounts growing up in an "Hispanic ghetto" and being "keenly aware of race" since childhood (p. 707 Fullwiley, 2008). He picked his laboratory research team for their "diverse backgrounds" (p. 707), is committed to training future minority scientists and through the decorations and pictures hung in his office emphasizes his Mexican roots.

At times his identity allegiances clash with his identity as a scientist to let the data drive his conclusions. Fullwiley dramatically describes an effort to square data suggesting that genetic variation does NOT account for variability in asthma severity with his deep belief that genetic variation in racially or ethnically identified populations *must* be at the root of differences in health outcomes. One aspect of a belief in biological race stands out in her analysis, that of European ancestry as the invisible norm. Admixture studies often try to correlate the percent of "other" genes, with the degree of disease expression. But in some of Burchard's (and other) work they anomalously found instead a correlation of severity with the percentage of European heritage. After struggling with his findings, Burchard starts to shift his explanatory framework, but clings to his belief in race as a biological phenomenon.

In the previous example, then, we see that socially provided ethnic/racial identities have profoundly affected the production of scientifically based analyses of race and ethnicity within the field of medicine. But the genomic era's contribution to the construction of racial identity stretches beyond the medical. One remarkable phenomenon is the rise of private companies that offer genetic ancestry tests. At least two dozen companies sold over half a million genetic ancestry tests in the last seven years (Bolnick et al., 2007). One of these companies, Ancestry by DNA (DNA Print Genomics, 2008), is a consumer arm of the DNA Print Genomics, which markets the previously discussed AIMs, used in medically relevant admixture tests. The same company also sells a forensic product, DNAWitness™ that "will provide the percentage of genetic make up amongst the four possible groups of Sub-Saharan African, Native American, East Asian, and European. When appropriate, DNAWitness™ allows for a breakdown of the European ancestry into four components: North-western European, South-eastern European, Middle Eastern and South Asian." The website boasts that "customers include medical examiner's offices, special task forces, sheriffs' departments, and district attorney's offices from various cities. These cities include the three largest US metropolitan areas of New York City, Los Angeles, and Chicago" (DNA Print Genomics, 2008b, c).

So-called "recreational genomics" companies sometimes specialize in specific constituencies. For example http://www.african ancestry.com/index.html asks African Americans to consider their real origins, "Before the Middle Passage and the time of slavery in the Americas"; they promise purchasers of their DNA tracing service the chance to "redefine who you are," to "find your identity." In a sales video they feature a young African American man lamenting that at school events he cannot bring in a food offering from his parents' or grandparents' home country, or participate in a special school day devoted to the history of his country, because

he does not know what country he came from. But by tracing his DNA he hopes to remedy that problem. A similar claim is made by Professor Henry Louis Gates, founder of another commercial ancestry venture, AfricanDNA.com. Gates (2008) writes that the lack of ancestral information for the descendents of former US slaves cripples "our ability to know ourselves by connecting with our family's past." This lack of knowledge, he argues, has limited "what we can achieve." But DNA can, according to Gates, unlock this hidden past, and by implication, aid the continued advancement of African Americans.

Fascinatingly, Gates sees the biological marker as a means to verify a cultural heritage. He writes that African slaves brought with them "their music, dances, religious beliefs" and much else. Yet, as Alondra Nelson (2008) writes, when faced with contradictions, the DNA evidence can outweigh contradictory historical or cultural evidence. She recounts interviews with an African American woman who had used conventional genealogical evidence to trace her lineage to southern Africa. But a DNA Ancestry test placed her roots in modern day Ghana. At first willing to acknowledge the scientific limitations of this placement, the woman slowly gave her identity over to the DNA, with its greater claim to specificity. It seems that in the genomic era biological information holds greater power over identity development than genealogical and historical documentation, or oral and cultural tradition.

In the face of the possibility, still on the horizon, of affordable sequencing of every gene in an individual's DNA, the use of a few critical DNA tracers to map ancestry seems like a crude approximation to a potentially complex story. Harvard researcher George Church (2008) hopes to reduce the cost of sequencing an entire individual human genome from its current US$350,000, making it a luxury purchase of the highest degree (Harmon, 2008). Church's aim is to develop a method inexpensive enough to permit the mapping of 100,000 personal genomes

(Lauerman, 2008). Church touts this project as an exciting venture that can engage research subjects in the project of scientific knowledge production. As displayed in a logo on the personal genomics website, personal genomics provides a link between individual knowledge, personal identity, health and science. In this ultimate rendering of DNA identity we see the connections between individual identity (for example, as a person who has a gene for protein variant X) and group membership (protein variant X can be found in people of North African descent).

Notably, an emphasis on DNA as a source of identification reinforces a static picture of human existence. We are born with the same DNA with which we die. It makes us a member of some group(s) or not. We have identities which lead us to ally with others of similar identity, or not. A genomic stance of this sort is profoundly non-developmental. There is no account of changing identities, no discussion of human growth and development, and certainly no account of how culture and history changes identity categories. As we will discuss in the sections on gender and sexuality, the lack of a developmental perspective severely limits our understanding of identity formation. In the case of race, the static, genomics view of racial or ethnic identity is peculiar as well, in that it ignores a directly relevant, extensive area of scientific inquiry and current interest. I refer to what Nadia Abu El-Haj (2007) calls postgenomics. She defines postgenomics as "a network of epistemologies, practices and technologies" that examine gene expression (2007: 284). I will return to a discussion of post genomic biology and practices in the final section of this chapter.

## GENDER IDENTITY

Psychologist John Money developed the phrase "gender identity" in the 1960s to connote an individual's internal sense of self as either a man or woman (or boy or girl).

The origins or causes of this self belief is a topic of considerable debate, of which more in a moment. But self-identification as either a male or female has implications for a second, more political, group identification. In discussions of gender identity, the distinctions between individual identity and group affiliation sometimes lack clarity. Here, we focus primarily on biological theories of gender identity and only more briefly treat the existence of political or medical activism based on individual gender identity. Such activism includes feminism, transsexual and transgender activism and intersex activism. The question of whether gay or homosexual activism can be considered as a gender-based activism requiring a commitment to a particular individual psychic gender identity is vexed and deserving of an essay of its own.

In the 1950s John Money and colleagues, using data from pioneering studies of patients with ambiguous sexual development, developed a layered model of sex and gender. Beginning from the chromosomal make-up of the fertilized egg (chromosomal sex), they outlined a developmental sequence which progressed from the chromosomal level to the formation of either embryonic testes or ovaries in the developing fetus (fetal gonadal sex) and then to the production of hormones by the fetal gonad (fetal hormonal sex). Fetal hormonal sex was understood to contribute to the formation of the internal reproductive system (uterus, vas deferens, etc.) and external genitalia (genital sex). At birth, Money and his colleagues argued that the adults surrounding the newborn identified sex based on their perception of external genital anatomy (genital dimorphism); this identification initiated a social response that began the gender socialization of the newborn. Money and his colleagues believed that a child's gender identity appeared during the first three years of life as a response to the influences of adult socialization. Initially, Money and colleagues wrote about this identity formation as completely malleable, without biological influence. By 1972, in their classic work *Man and Woman, Boy and Girl*, Money and his colleague Anke Ehrhardt seemed less certain of the idea of total plasticity, but still emphasized the high degree of malleability in gender identity formation in the first two years of life (Money and Ehrhardt, 1972). Regardless of whether they thought that biological components contributed to gender identity formation, they were clear that gender identity became fixed at some point around two years of age. Their concept of early identity fixation became the underpinning for the view that "corrective" surgery for children born with ambiguous genitalia needed to be done early and swiftly. For critical discussions of these ideas see (Dreger, 1998, 1998; Fausto-Sterling, 2000; Kessler, 1998).

Money's beliefs about the social influences in gender identity formation held remarkable sway for several decades. One scientist who consistently challenged his point of view was Milton Diamond. He emphasized the idea that fetal gonadal hormones influenced the fetal brain to produce "brain sex"; in a manner that is even today unspecified, brain sex pushed male and female development into divergent developmental pathways (Diamond, 1965). As development proceeded into the postnatal period, the child starts to manifest his or her gender identity. For decades Diamond could not obtain a wide hearing for his ideas, but all that changed when (due to Diamond's efforts) it became clear that Money had cooked the books on

one of his key pieces of evidence – the claim that a normally formed XY boy had been successfully transformed into a girl with a female gender identity following reconstructive surgery and careful instructions to the parents to rear "him" as a girl. This complex set of steps was necessitated by a botched circumcision that destroyed the infant boy's penis (Colapinto, 2001; Diamond and Sigmundson, 1997). This is, of course, the famous Joan/John case, filled with personal tragedy and high drama and sensationalized in popular books (Colapinto, 2001).

John Money's downfall ushered in an almost complete swing of the nature–nurture pendulum. Claims of biological determination of gender identity formation ascended while the idea that socialization contributed importantly to gender identity formation became subject to ridicule. How, then, does the evidence stack up today? In their prescient 1978 book, Kessler and McKenna developed a table to assess the relationship between often-accepted biological factors and the development of gender. Here I acknowledge their influence as I redraw the table (Table 8.1) to focus on gender identity and incorporate more recent biological and medical findings.

First, there is broad agreement that Money was right that chromosomal sex, gonadal sex, internal reproductive organs, external genitalia and pubertal hormones are not, in and of

**Table 8.1    Biological factors and gender identity development: What do we know?**

| Biologists' criteria for gender I.D. determination | Relationship | Evidence |
|---|---|---|
| Chromosomes | No | Androgen insensitivity syndrome |
| Gonads | No | Turner's syndrome |
| Internal reproductive organs | No | Turner's syndrome |
| Prenatal hormones | Possible | No direct evidence |
| External genitalia | No | Transsexuals |
| Pubertal hormones | No | CAH assigned as male at birth |
| Other | Under debate | Cloacal exstrophy |
| | | Childhood gender identity disorder |
| | | Adult transsexual narratives |
| | | Brain studies of adult transsexuals |
| | | Finger length ratios |

themselves, direct determinants of gender identity. The extensive study of individuals for whom gender identity and one or more of these biological formations is discordant makes this quite clear. Thus, most XY individuals (who also have testes) who are completely insensitive to their own androgens develop a female gender identity. Similarly, in extreme cases of congenital adrenal hyperplasia (androgen overproduction *in utero*), XX individuals develop a male gender identity despite having ovaries and a uterus. The idea that prenatal hormones affect brain development in some manner that influences gender identity formation remains a favorite hypothesis despite a lack of direct evidence or the elucidation of a specific developmental pathway to support it. Nevertheless, biologists and biological psychologists remain quite committed to either a prenatal hormone or a brain sex hypothesis.

In the absence of direct evidence (and the unlikelihood of ever obtaining it given the fact that we cannot experiment with human development), the prenatal hormone hypothesis takes the following form: the fetal gonad produces hormones that affect brain development in some unspecified manner. The assumption is that the brain produces gender identity. In the most extreme version, there are no social influences on brain identity development. On other renderings, the hormones are understood to "predispose" the brain to develop a particular gender identity, although what the nature of such a predisposition might be is never explicit. Those who believe strongly in a hormone–brain–identity nexus use indirect evidence to support their case. I will briefly discuss two of these arenas – the study of gender assignment and acceptance in children born with various disorders of sexual development and the study of childhood gender dysphoria.

Sexologists have begun to develop some consensus that gender identity development is not tightly linked to prenatal hormones. Recently, Meyer-Bahlburg (2005) reviewed the results of medical intervention in three rare conditions, cloacal exstrophy of the

bladder, penile agenesis (failure of the penis to develop) and traumatic loss of the penis at a very young age. Cloacal exstrophy is a rare birth defect in which infants are born without external genitalia and with other malformations of the bladder and surrounding tissue. Historically this was a lethal condition, but in recent years surgeons have successfully reconstructed such children, usually shaping them as females. For 46,XY patients this has meant surgical feminization, removal of the testes, and assigning the infants as females. How successful have these reassignments been? The assumption is that these XY children were exposed to androgens prenatally. If this exposure somehow determines gender identity, then assigning them to be raised as girls should not work. If other factors (social and/or biological) contribute importantly to gender identity formation then such children can succeed in developing a female gender identity.

Meyer-Bahlburg reviewed the cases of 46,XY children with cloacal extrosphy who had been assigned and raised as either girls or boys. Of 51 patients with early female gender assignment, 33 were still living as females, 11 were living as males, and 7 had expressed wishes to become male. Male-assigned and raised patients (279 to date) all were still living as males at the time of publication. One was starting to express a desire to become female. Many of these patients are still young, and their choices may well change as they progress through adulthood.

The sample sizes for cases with penile agenesis or traumatic loss are small. But when Meyer-Bahlburg adds these results to the cloacal exstrophy studies, the following picture emerges: Sixty-nine percent of the female-assigned XY children of childhood age (including 7% who expressed desires to change sex) lived as females; 91% of the adolescent aged children (including 23% who wished to change sex) lived as females; in adulthood fewer – 65% (including 18% who wished to transition to male) lived as women. By contrast all of the male-raised 46,XY patients, in all age groups, lived as males.

Meyer-Bahlburg concludes that the data do not indicate full biological determination of gender identity, either by prenatal hormones or genetic or other factors – "gender assignment and the concomitant social factors have a major influence on gender outcome" (2005: 432).

By the age of two to three years children learn to correctly identify the sex of others (Martin et al., 2002, 2004) but have begun to develop an awareness of gender appropriate roles as early as 18 months (Serbin et al., 2002). In contrast to those who believe that gender identity formation results from prior biological differences (discussed above), many cognitive-social psychologists understand gender identity formation to result from a process of learning, cognitive development and social reinforcement (Bandura and Bussey, 2004; Martin et al., 2002). Individuals with clinically defined gender identity disorders have been the subject of much clinical study, which in turn, provides fodder for arguments concerning the role of biology in gender identity formation. A rich literature exists concerning adults with gender identity variance – sometimes called transsexual, sometimes transgender (Meyerowitz, 2002; Stryker and Whittle, 2006); however, the transgender movements (Feinberg, 1996, 1998) and various positive presentations of the self as gender outlaws (Bornstein, 1994) is complex and somewhat outside the purview of this essay.[2] In the discussion that follows I focus on how the emergence of gender identity variability in very young children intersects with biological arguments concerning the foundations of gender identity.

The popular press and many adult transsexuals themselves define a transsexual as a genetically and developmental normal (in the anatomical sense) person who believes him or herself to be trapped in the "wrong" body. Thus by definition the phenomenon involves a sense of self (identity) that is invisible and seems to have no origins in anatomical measures of intersexuality. The commonly sought treatment, however, is to "correct" the anatomy to conform to the identity. Such anatomical change is accompanied by hormonal treatments to bring the body's biochemistry into line as well. Because of the strength of their desire to synchronize anatomy and identity, and because often they recall wanting since childhood to be the other sex, many adult transsexuals believe their condition to have a biological origin. Many suspect that there is something unusual about their own brain development. Indeed, a few postmortem studies of brains of male to female transsexuals (MtF) claim to prove that a region of the hypothalamus in the brain is "female-like" in MtFs, a finding which they take as evidence of a biological cause for this unusual gender identity (Kruijver et al., 2000; Zhou et al., 1995). Others, however, provide evidence that the cross hormone therapy undergone by the MtFs in these earlier studies produced the brain differences found (see Lawrence, 2007). At this time, then there is little substantive evidence to support the idea that adult MtFs have feminized brains, which cause their desire to change their anatomy to fit their identity (Lawrence, 2007). (For further information on definitions of and research on adult transsexuals see Lawrence, 2008.)

If studies of adult transsexuals fail to offer evidence of a biological origin of the phenomenon, then the existence of gender variant children, some as young as two years of age seems to many to prove a biological origin. The argument in general is that only biology could explain such an early origin of gender variance. The American Psychiatric Association first listed a mental illness called Gender Identity Disorder of Childhood (GIDC) in its Diagnostic and Statistical Manual (DSM) in 1980 (Martin, 2008). Since then the diagnostic criteria have undergone a variety of modifications. DSM-IV states that GIDC children display a constellation of behaviors: "(1) a strong and persistent cross-gender identification ... (2) persistent discomfort with his or her sex ... (3) disturbance not concurrent with a physical intersex condition and (4) disturbance causes clinically significant distress or impairment in social, occupational or other important areas of functioning" (quoted in Zucker and Cohen-Kettenis, 2008: 384). The actual prevalence of children with the above constellation of behaviors is difficult to assess, especially because of the range of variability in gender non-conforming behaviors in children who, in the end, do not have identity issues. Nevertheless, some estimate that between 0.9% and 1.7% of boys and girls in a general North American population wish to be a member of the opposite sex (Zucker and Cohen-Kettenis, 2008).

Gender non-conformance rises to the level of mental illness when children are referred to mental health clinics for treatment. About five times as many boys as girls are referred to one well-known Canadian clinic while the ratio is about 3:1 boys: girls in a well-known Dutch clinic. At these clinics, gender non-conforming children are referred between the ages of three and six years (Zucker and Cohen-Kettenis, 2008). In one recent case, publicized on US television, the child in question began exhibiting gender non-conforming behavior by his/her second year of age (Goldberg, 2007). Experts and lay people alike disagree deeply about the proper course to follow with such children – intervene to make them more comfortable with their physical sex, or work with family and school systems to accommodate the gender non-conformity (Langer and Martin, 2004; Martin, 2008; Menvielle and Tuerk, 2002; Menvielle et al., 2005; Spiegel, 2008; Zucker and Cohen-Kettenis, 2008). These vexed questions lie outside the purview of this essay. Here I examine whether the existence of gender identity variance in such young children provides evidence of a biological contribution to gender identity formation.

There is only one twin study that estimates the heritability of Childhood Gender Identity Disorder to be 0.62. While this suggests the possibility of a genetic component to the emergence of GIDC, the study only involves a small number of twin pairs. Thus at this writing there is very little evidence to support a genetic basis for GIDC and virtually no speculation as to a possible genetic mechanism by which gender identity variance might be produced. Although strictly speaking, hormonal theories are a subset of genetic theories, the sexology literature often treats hormonal theories as a distinct mode of explanation. The prenatal hormonal hypothesis holds that gender identity variance results from an altered prenatal hormone environment that somehow influences brain development. We have already reviewed some of the evidence for hormonal influences in gender identity development that derives from the study of physical disorders of sexual development. As discussed by Martin (2008) there is little in the way of additional evidence to suggest that prenatal hormone variability contributes to childhood gender variance.

Martin (2008) reviews several competing psychodynamic explanations of early childhood gender variance. However, to structure the debate in terms of biology versus psychology misses some essential features of human development. In recent years dynamic systems theorists have made a compelling case for accounts of human development that emphasize how behavior becomes embodied (Fausto-Sterling, 2000; Hayles, 1993; Thelen, 1995, 2000; Thelen and Smith, 1994). In the case of gender variant children, it is significant that the variation becomes visible in a developmental window when gender identity and a sense of gender permanence usually establish themselves (Fagot and Leinbach, 1989, 1993; Fagot et al., 1986, 1992; Ruble and Martin, 1998; Martin et al., 2002). It is possible to imagine any number of contexts or constellations of circumstances that might lead to minority identity expressions. With repetition, these could become quite literally embodied, that is a persistent feature of an individual's identity and personality. At the level of neurophysiology, we presume that these features function via neural networks within the brain. Developing more dynamic hypotheses and new experimental paradigms, ones in which neural development (and thus behaviors, identities and preferences) *result from* initial behavioral exploration should be on the agenda of the next generation of researchers.

Much of the controversy over early treatment of GIDC children and later outcomes concerns the idea that gender variant children become homosexual adults (Bem, 2008; Corbett, 1993, 1996; Green, 2008; Martin, 2008; Zucker, 2008). The idea that such early emerging behaviors must be "biological" is used to support the idea that adult homosexuality has a biological cause. There is one important bit of slippage in this argument; GIDC is an example of extreme gender variance. Gender non-conforming behaviors, however are quite common, and while many adult homosexuals retrospectively associate them with a later emergence of homosexual desire, they are a far less striking form of behavior than GIDC.

The relationships between gender, anatomical sex and sexuality are complex. Theo Sandfort (2005) attributes the origin in American psychology of the idea that homosexual men are feminine and lesbians are masculine to the 1936 work of Lewis M. Terman and Catherine C. Miles. Although Terman and Miles identified homosexual men who did not fit these patterns of opposites, they failed to theorize about masculine gay men. Subsequent citations of their work also ignored this theoretical complication, giving birth to the unquestioned link between male homosexuality and femininity. Practicing psychoanalyst Ken Corbett writes that "calling gay men feminine neither sufficiently problematizes their experience of gender nor adequately captures the vicissitudes of gender" (1993): 345). He argues that "male homosexuality is a differently structured masculinity, not a simulated femininity" (1993: 345). Despite these complexities, arguments about the biological basis of homosexuality lean heavily on the relationship between GIDC and later homosexuality. Nevertheless, in recent years biological theories have come to rest as well on somewhat more direct evidence, which we address next.

## BORN GAY?

Discussions of homosexuality in the popular media usually frame matters in terms of two mutually exclusive possibilities: genes versus choice (Fausto-Sterling, 2007). In the first event a person is born with a genetic constitution that, through manner unknown, leads them to develop an adult same sex sexual orientation; in the second "things happen" during childhood and adolescence to produce homosexuality. In the most extreme rendering of this latter possibility, individuals are supposedly able to choose consciously between being gay or being straight. This debate frames arguments in the social arena. On the one hand, religious fundamentalists argue that if homosexuals can choose to be straight, then they have no basis on which to claim legal protections or equal civil status on matters pertaining to marriage and shared property rights. On the other, gay activists base their claims for civil rights on the idea that homosexuality is inborn, and in this sense no different than sex or race (Lutes, 2008).

How *does* sexual orientation develop? Careful study of the question starts by distinguishing between three aspects of sexual orientation – behavior, desire and identity. In a large, survey of sexuality (both hetero and homo) in the United States sociologist Edward O. Laumann and his colleagues estimated the frequencies for men and women of these three components among those who indicated some aspects of homosexuality (Laumann et al., 1994). Table 8.2 lists their findings. A few things stand out. First, the largest subset for both men (44%) and women (59%) consisted of individuals who indicated to survey takers that they found the idea of sex with a person of the same sex very or somewhat appealing, or were attracted to persons of the same sex but did not engage in same sex behaviors, or identify as homosexual (feelings or thoughts but no action). The second largest grouping for those indicating some component of homosexuality were men (24%) and women (15%) who exhibited all three components, that is desire, behavior and identity (feelings, actions and self-labeling concur). A smaller number of men (6%) and women (13%) indicated same sex desire and behavior but did not identify as gay or lesbian.

**Table 8.2 Results of Laumann et al. sexuality survey**

| Percent of same-sex sample | Desire only | Behavior only | Identity only | Desire & behavior | Desire & identity | Desire, behavior & identity | Identity & behavior |
|---|---|---|---|---|---|---|---|
| Men | 44 | 22 | 2 | 6 | 1 | 24 | 0 |
| Women | 59 | 13 | 0 | 13 | 1 | 15 | 0 |

If one wants to study the biological basis of sexual orientation, the fact that the word *homosexuality* disaggregates into several combinations of behaviors and desires makes for some big methodological problems. Attempts to link particular gene loci to sexual orientation (Hamer et al., 1993; Mustanski et al., 2005) have the same general approach. They recruit subjects based on identity via gay newspapers, bars, leaflets at gay pride parades, etc. They compare DNA sequences in suspect chromosome regions to control chromosomes – usually from heterosexual siblings. In the case of twin studies, they compare the frequency of concordance (if one twin has a trait, then does the other one also have that trait?) for sexual orientation in identical and thus supposedly genetically identical twins to fraternal twins, who like any sibling, only share 50% of DNA sequences on average (Bailey et al., 2000; Kendler et al., 2000; Kirk et al., 2000). Most researchers using this approach expect to gain insight into only one component of sexual orientation – the biological basis of sexual attraction. Assuming that the numbers in Table 8.2 have some generality, this approach, which relies on individuals with a formed gay identity leaves out 21% of the males 45% of the females who have homosexual desire but not a gay identity. Additionally, this type of study does not address those who have same sex encounters (22% of the men and 13% of the women) but who do not indicate same sex desire (i.e. the idea of having same-sex sex does not appeal to them) and do not have a gay identity.

Cornell psychologist Ritch Savin-Williams advocates studying same sex attraction without starting with a preselected, self-identified population. He argues that this can

be accomplished by focusing on biological measures of sexual arousal. These include measuring genital arousal following erotic stimuli, using brain scans, eye tracking or pupil dilation in response to visual stimuli. While the strength of such an approach lies in avoiding preselection, the weakness is that it is not developmental. That is, we still cannot learn how particular stimuli become eroticized or how a body's sensory systems become trained to respond to particular stimuli (Savin-Williams, 2006; Savin-Williams and Ream, 2007).

With the limitations of genetic and twin studies addressed, what is the weight of evidence to date that links particular genetic compositions to the development of gay identity and desire? Further understanding of the development of sexual attraction is certainly of interest, even if it does not tell us about all types of behavior and does not explain sexual identity formation. It is a fair guess that physical attraction or desire is one component of identity formation and that at the same time the existence of particular, culturally defined categories of identity might contribute to the mental training and perhaps physiological entrainment of physical attraction or desire.

The "standard" story is that prenatal hormones differ in male and female fetal development and that these differences affect brain development in some way that preconditions future development. It is, however, becoming clear, that if the hormone–brain route is explanatory for human development, it is not the only possible explanatory route. Scientists have now begun to study the direct effects of genes on brain development. In this case, there are no postulated hormonal intermediates (Bocklandt and Vilain, 2007; Fausto-Sterling, 2000). In a recent review of the genetic literature on sexual orientation Bocklandt and Vilain (2007) argue that sexual orientation is a sexually dimorphic (either/or) trait and that the link between childhood gender expression and later sexuality suggests biological influences. They review the hormonal evidence and conclude that "although there is no convincing evidence linking differences in sexual orientation to variations in prenatal androgens, there is abundant evidence for a strong genetic component" (2007: 256). On what does this evidence consist?

We have already briefly mentioned twin studies. In such studies researchers ask: if one member of a pair of identical twins has a homosexual identity, what is the likelihood that the other twin will also report in as gay? They compare this frequency to that found in fraternal twins, who are, genetically speaking, no less different. All of the twin studies cited earlier find higher concordance rates for identical compared to fraternal twins. Although there are serious methodological caveats to such studies, they are nevertheless cited extensively as evidence for a genetic contribution to the developmental of homosexual orientation in men.

At the level of molecular genetics, we find that solid data becomes increasingly sparse. Fifteen years after the initial report from geneticist Dean Hamer's research lab of a factor on the X-chromosome relating to homosexuality, indisputable independent confirmation is still lacking (Bocklandt and Vilain, 2007; Hamer et al., 1993). Geneticists who acknowledge the complexity of sexual orientation think that several genes are likely to be involved and that these may be located on the autosomes as well as the sex chromosomes. One study has attempted to locate these other genes, with mixed success (Fausto-Sterling, 2007; Mustanski et al., 2005). One last idea for molecular influences on the development of sexual orientation floated by Bocklandt and Hamer (2003) is that it is gene *expression* rather than gene differences that can explain different developmental patterns in sexual orientation. I return

to this idea in the final section of this essay, because it provides an important opening for environmental and experiential events to influencethe development of sexual identity. In this case, such influences are understood to exert an effect on gene activity; thus, the molecular basis of difference can be seen as an effect of environment, rather than a first cause. Such effects are often referred to as "epigenetic effects" and are a topic of great interest within the field of molecular biology (NOVA, 2007).

## THINKING NONESSENTIALLY ABOUT THE BODY: THE END OF NATURE VERSUS NURTURE

Turning to genes, or hormones, or some other pure biological difference cannot offer a convincing story about biology and identity. Neither, I think, does social or cultural theory stand successfully on its own foundation without reference to biological formation. The body (including the brain) forms a dynamic site of assembly. The social, the cultural and individual experience all combine in the body, shaping biological structure to produce new biosocial formations. Cutting edge animal research is starting to show, at the level of particular nerve cells, how this works. For example, in a songbird called the zebra finch, newly divided nerve cells survive best in animals exposed to a diverse social network of both male and female birds. In contrast, older neurons survived best in individuals housed with only one cage mate (Adar et al., 2008). In this example, we see exactly how the social shapes the biological, at the level of individual brain cells. We cannot achieve this level of explanation for human development now. But we need to prepare the ground by developing theoretical approaches that combine nature and nurture rather than pitting them as opposites. We can gain insight into the broad brush outlines of a more dynamic theory by returning to studies of early childhood gender nonconformity.

Although the link to biology is indirect, early childhood gender nonconformity is frequently cited to prove that sexual orientation and homosexual identity is innate. The chain of evidence starts with surveying adults with well-formed gay or lesbian identities to discover if they remember childhood gender nonconforming behaviors. The line of argument is twofold. First, if gender identity is inborn, and if homosexuality can be understood as a kind of gender reversal (of which more presently), then perhaps homosexuality can be understood as a variant of gender identity formation. In this view, lesbian women would be more masculine while gay men would be more feminine. If this gendered valence reached far back into early childhood, that might in itself be evidence of innateness. A trait that appears early is less likely, in this view, to have been shaped by experience and socialization than one that appears later.

Zucker (2008) provides an extensive review of studies demonstrating a correlation between adult homosexuality and memories of childhood gender nonconformity. In his metanalysis (a compilation of smaller studies) he found that strikingly more homosexual men remembered being gender nonconformists as children compared with heterosexual men, although there was overlap between the distributions (i.e. some straight men reported gender nonconforming childhoods). A similar, but less extreme result was found for women, that is there was quite a bit more overlap in remembered childhood gender nonconformity between heterosexual and homosexual women (Bailey and Zucker, 1995).

Although the above findings are strong, the direct link to biology is tenuous. Indeed, they also provide the basis for other, more developmental interpretations. Developmental interpretations provide a number of advantages over static biology.[3] First, developmental accounts construct a life cycle view of identity. Self-understandings of sexual orientation change during the life course, and longitudinal studies are especially able to reveal the nuances of such change. Second, they

permit the possibility that biological change in sensory and affective systems result from experience and culturally specific input. Thus, dynamic developmental theories integrate the physiology and neurology of sex itself, sexual attraction and sexual ideation with the processes of identity formation, cultural shaping of gender and sexual orientation and the politics of gender that plays out at the level of political and economic institutions. Below I consider three lines of scholarship that emphasize this more dynamic approach.

Psychologist Daryl Bem (2008) argues that there is a causal link between childhood gender expression and sexual orientation. His theory – the Exotic becomes Erotic (EBE) – offers an explanation for both opposite sex and same-sex desire. He does not intend his model as an absolute prescription for all individuals, but rather as a modal or average explanation. He suggests that biological variables (these could be genetic, and/or development) affect early temperament, which in turn influence the development of preferences for sex typical or atypical play. Such preferences lead in turn to feeling different from opposite or same-sex peers. He further postulates that individuals develop attractions to those from whom they feel different during childhood. Thus, early gender interests lead to later physiological or sexual attractions.

Bem emphasizes a somewhat open-ended developmental trajectory in which individual biological features affecting temperament contribute to life paths that eventually lead to the development of same-sex or opposite sex desire. Clinical psychologist Susan Coates, who has treated young boys with CGID, also considers that early individual temperamental differences contribute to extreme childhood gender nonconformity. Setting aside for the moment the question of whether CGID and less extreme forms of gender non-conformity are all part of a single spectrum of behaviors, it is worth considering how Coates weaves together individual temperament (which probably results from individual differences in neurological development), family dynamics and the normal developmental processes of acquiring gender knowledge (Coates, 1992; Coates and Wolfe, 1995).

Coates distilled several important characteristics from a study of over 130 CGID boys. First, cross gendered behaviors emerge during a critical period of development (two to four years), a period when children are acquiring gender knowledge and identity; understanding gender as a permanent and unchangeable feature is the last component to emerge at ages three to five years of age (Martin et al., 2002). Second, CGID often appears and consolidates quite suddenly, and, according to Coates, frequently (but not always) in the context of some kind of psychic trauma. The boys who enter her practice often have extreme separation anxiety, depression or other behaviors that might lead parents to seek psychological treatment. Furthermore, other family members, or the family dynamic itself, can be psychopathological. Finally, Coates argues that individual temperament may be understood as a biological predisposition that makes some children more vulnerable to the other components that sometimes contribute to producing CGID. In her study, Coates associates several biopsychological markers with gender identity disorder in young boys. These include a sense of physical fragility, the avoidance of highly physical play, anxiety in new situations, intense attention to others, high sensitivity to others' emotional states, high vulnerability to separation or loss, an unusually acute ability to imitate others, and extraordinary sensory sensitivity to sound, color, texture, smell and pain (Coates 1992; Coates and Wolfe, 1995).

From a psychoanalytic perspective, Coates understands a child's cross gender behavior as an attempt to manage overwhelming anxiety and to cope with complex family trauma. The behaviors are thus a symptom of a complex dynamic rather than the result of an inborn variation in some part of the brain thought to somehow directly control gender development. Analyst Kenneth Corbett (1996) states matters more positively. He argues that boyhood GID and less extreme gender nonconformity do not represent a continuum of femininity, so much as "a continuum of ego integration and psychic structure" in which GID and gender-nonconforming boys may be equally feminine, but in the latter group "the femininity is contained within a more stable psychic structure" (1996: 438).

Corbett writes that the very category of gender identity disorder demands that we develop theoretical approaches that explain how the psyche, the soma and the social build one another. He agrees that Coates' work moves us in this direction, showing how gender and psychic growth are woven together. Corbett complains, however, that Coates does not pay proper theoretical attention to the social components of gender. Specifically, he finds that she does not investigate the idea of effeminacy "as a contested realm of human experience" (1996: 443). This fact leads her towards a kind of clinical ambivalence toward cross-gendered behaviors in her young patients. It thus remains unclear, to the present day, when gender nonconformity in childhood might be considered a sign of mental ill health and when not. Corbett argues that by not examining boyhood femininity in the context of mental health, we maintain gender "as a system of conformity as opposed to a system of variation" (1996: 444).

Most theories that link biology to the development of gender identity or sexual orientation focus on boys and men. Many researchers find that girls and women are "messy" and "more complex" and thus more difficult to study using simple, linear theories of causation (Pattatucci, 1998; Pattatucci and Hamer, 1995). However, some theorists have devoted serious attention to gender differentiation and the development of sexual orientation in women. Peplau and Huppin (2008), for example, believe that childhood gender (non) conformity does not hold the key to understanding female sexual orientation. First, they argue that the evidence that lesbians are in some fashion physically and physiologically masculinized is weak at best. Furthermore, while the memory of childhood gender non-conformity is elevated among lesbian compared to heterosexual women, there are many more tomboys in childhood than there are lesbians in adulthood. In other words, childhood gender nonconformity in girls is not a particularly good predictor of adult sexual orientation.

Peplau and Huppin also note that female sexuality and an individual woman's interpretation of her experiences, predispositions and personality vary across time (both historical and developmental) and place. They point to a growing view that compared to males, female sexuality is more changeable over time. If this is, indeed the case, then careful study of female development may produce rather different theories of the development of desire than have those which have focused on men and boys. In turn, new ideas based on female development may provide a different lens through which to re-examine male development. One important case in point involves the work of psychologist Lisa M. Diamond.

In a considerable body of work (Diamond, 1998, 2000a, b, 2005a, b, c, 2006, 2008a, b), Diamond takes issue with the typical assumption that individuals with stable, exclusive and early appearing same-sex attractions comprise "the most common and representative 'types' of sexual minorities" (Diamond, 2005c: 119). At this writing, Diamond is a decade into a longitudinal study that started with 100 sexual minority women in their late teens and early 20s. She reinterviews "her" women every two years. Diamond quickly found that the either/or categories of homo vs. heterosexual did not fit the behaviors and identities of the women she studied. Even adding in a third category – that of bisexual – did not account for her findings. Essentialist models that favor a biological "cause" of homosexuality understand individuals to develop fixed sexual predispositions. The (social) scientific literature usually considers bisexuality either as a third permanent type or as a transitional stage in the development of homosexual identity.

Diamond (2008a) proposed and tested a third model – that of bisexuality as a heightened capacity for fluidity. The women in her sample identified themselves as lesbian, bisexual or unlabeled. During the 10 years of her study the lesbian women started as 29% of her sample and ended as 21%. The bisexual-identified women started as 19% of the sample and gradually declined to 12%, while the unlabeled women started as 7%, increased to 13% by year 8 and then decreased to 6%. Furthermore, the women switched back and forth in correlation with the gender of the person with whom they were having a relationship. For example, 31% of women who identified as lesbians during the first two years of the study later had full relationships with men; these women changed their identity to bisexual or unlabeled. Furthermore, when the women in Diamond's study were younger the correlation between behavior and felt attraction was high. Ten years into the study, however, most of the women were behaviorally monogamous, but still reported same or other-sex attraction.

By looking at the dynamics of identity and behavioral change over longer periods, Diamond has identified the need for a new paradigm for understanding possible relationships between sexual identity and biology, at least for women. She questions what she calls the "master narrative" of sexual identity development – a narrative that features stability or type, early recognition of or retrospectively identifiable signs of sexual variance and a coming out story in which a fixed identity is assumed. She further emphasizes the cultural and environmental components that influence sexual identity formation. She does not understand these to be in opposition to biology. Instead, a dynamic developmental approach seeks to show change over time, with the understanding that the biology of desire can be influenced by sexual practice at the same time that the sexual expression of desire is at one level fundamentally a physiological expression (Diamond, 2007, 2008b).

## CONCLUSION: BODIES INCORPORATE EXPERIENCE

Consider the fact, discussed in the first section of this essay, that American blacks have higher rates of hypertension than whites. If a gene for hypertension does not cause this difference, then how are we to understand it? The dynamic and social framework to answer this question has been laid out by Krieger and by Sterling. In a now classic study, Krieger and Sidney demonstrated that racial discrimination itself produced increased blood pressure in young, black adults (Krieger and Sidney, 1996). She and her colleagues focus especially on the impact of economic deprivation and racism on differential gene expression (Krieger, 2005). In this model people with the same genetic make-up have different physical outcomes because different sets of genes are active or silent at critical periods in their lifetimes. Thus biological (in this case medical) difference is produced over time in response to different social and environmental experiences.

Neurophysiologist Peter Sterling reaches a similar overall conclusion by referring to a biological mechanism called allostasis, which involves the regulation of physiological systems that control blood pressure. In this example, which is compatible with Krieger's approach, the guiding molecules are hormones. Although the concept has a longer history, the word, first coined in 1988 (Schulkin, 2003; Sterling and Eyer, 1988) has gained in popularity among physiologists concerned with animals' physiological function in complex, often dangerous environments (McEwen and Lasley, 2002; Schulkin, 2003). Allostasis depends on communication between so-called low level feedback systems that locally regulate physiological responses and higher order mechanisms in the brain. The brain learns, often using the emotional responses of fear, joy, pleasure and desire, to anticipate future events and to up (or down) regulate physiological responses in advance of such expectations.

The allostasis model proposes that hypertension is an orchestrated response to a predicted need to remain vigilant to a variety of insults and danger – be they racial hostility, enraging acts of discrimination or living in the shadow of violence. Over time, all of the components that regulate blood pressure adapt to life under stress. The framework of allostasis, in which pathologically high blood pressure emerges as a step-wise, cumulative and predictable response to life stress provides a very different way to investigate the relationship between race and hypertension. It suggests developmental research, for example, starting with studies of the relationships between important childhood stressors and incremental hypertensive responses (see also Fausto-Sterling, 2004).

Concepts such as allostasis, which involve physiological responses modified by experience have potential application to the development of sexual physiology and response. But what of the development of gendered behavior, identity and sexual orientation? Here, we need to overlay the question of sexual physiology with one of desire, which I assume is produced by neurological connections that develop in the brain. The principles on which to build such theory derive from contemporary understandings of neuroplasticity.

The human brain has $10^{11}$ neurons connected by $10^{15}$ synapses. How do these connections become established during development in such a way that each of us makes sense out of the world and on the whole functions successfully within it (Chklovskii et al., 2004)? Part of the answer is that sensory inputs barrage babies in the womb and after birth and influence the anatomy and specific connectivity of neural circuits. During the first six months after birth, for example, the total length of dendrites in cells in the prefrontal cortex increases more than 200-fold (Quartz, 2003). Quartz writes that "neural development during the acquisition of major cognitive skills is best characterized as a progressive construction of neural structures, in which environmentally derived activity plays a role in the construction of neural circuits" (2003: 292). To connect these ideas to the emergence of gender and sexuality it will be important to attend to the shaping of early emotional and affective development. Some information about these processes already exists but they have yet to be investigated and theorized in the context of gender development (Fausto-Sterling et al., 2009; Schore, 1994, 2001).

Academic work linking race, gender and sexual identities to biology has produced important results. But attempts to use biological difference as an explanatory force in the study of identity are hampered by a theoretical framework that pits biology against culture. In this chapter, I call for a rethinking of biology in terms of dynamical systems. Behaviors, desires and identities are embodied via specific biological systems. Critically, however, the forces influencing embodiment are social; further, we can imagine – at least in principle – how certain basic biological mechanisms such as control of gene expression, allostasis and neural plasticity process social inputs to play a role in identity formation and expression. We know enough to devise research programs that will investigate more intelligently than in the past the interdependencies of the biological and the social. Now all that remains is to get to work.

## NOTES

1   The very notion of admixture, of course, presumes that some pure racial or ethnic category once existed; thus even though admixture studies are more scientifically sophisticated they still rely, finally, on 19th Century racial categories. see Abu-El-Haj (2007).

2   For an insightful discussion of how the categories of transsexuality and homosexuality *result from* our contemporary distinctions between gender and sexuality see: Valentine (2007).

3   As opposed to dynamic biology with is not easily separated from social experience.

## REFERENCES

Abu El-Haj, N. (2007) 'The genetic reinscription of race', *Annual Review of Anthropology*, 36: 283–300.

Adar, E., Nottebohm, F. and Barnea, A. (2008) 'The relationship between nature of social change, age, and position of new neurons and their survival in adult zebra finch brain', *Journal of Neuroscience* 28 (20): 5394–400.

American Academy of Allergy, Asthma and Immunology. (2006) Health Disparities in Asthma, Retrieved May 29, 2008, from http://www.aaaai.org/media/news_releases/2006/02/021606.stm

American Anthropological Association (1998) *Statement on 'race'*, American Anthropological Association. http://www.aaanet.org/stmts/racepp.htm Last accessed 10/25/2009

Bailey, J.M., Dunne, M.P. et al. (2000) 'Genetic and environmental influences on sexual orientation and its correlates in an Australian twin sample', *Journal of Peronality and Social Psychol*, 78 (3): 524–36.

Bailey, J.M. and Zucker, K.J. (1995) 'Childhood sex-typed behaviour and sexual orientation: A conceptual analysis and quantitative review', *Developmental Psychology*, 31: 43–55.

Bandura, A. and Bussey, K. (2004) 'On broadening the cognitive, motivational and sociostructural scope of theorizing about gender development and functioning: Comment on Martin, Ruble, and Szkrybalo (2002)', *Psychological Bulletin*, 130 (5): 691–701.

Bem, D.J. (2008) 'Is there a causal link between childhood gender nonconformity and adult homosexuality?', *Journal of Gay and Lesbian Mental Health*, 12 (1/2): 61–80.

Bocklandt, S. and Hamer, D.H. (2003) 'Beyond hormones: A novel hypothesis for the biological basis of male sexual orientation', *Journal of Endocrinological Investigation*, 26 (3 Suppl): 8–12.

Bocklandt, S. and Vilain, E. (2007) 'Sex differences in brain and behaviour: Hormones versus genes', *Advances in Genetics*, 59: 245–66.

Bolnick, D.A., Fullwiley, D., Fullwiley, D., Duster, T.,Cooper, R. S., Fujimura, J. H., Kahn, J., Kaufman, J. S., Marks, J., Morning, A., Nelson, A., Ossorio, P.,Reardon, J., Reverby, S. M., TallBear, K. (2007) 'Genetics. The science and business of genetic ancestry testing', *Science*, 318 (5849): 399–400.

Bornstein, K. (1994) *Gender Outlaw: On Men, Women and the Rest of Us*. London: Routledge.

Braun, L. (2002) 'Race, ethnicity and health: Can genetics explain disparities?', *Perspectives in Biology and Medicine*, 45 (2): 159–74.

Braun, L., Fausto-Sterling, A., Fullwiley, Duana, Hammonds, Evelynn M., Nelson, Alondra, Quivers, Williams, Reverby, Susan M.,Shields, Alexandra E. (2007) 'Racial categories in medical practice: How useful are they?', *Public Library of Science Medicine*, 4 (9): 271.

Chklovskii, D.B., Mel, B.W., Svoboda, K. (2004) 'Cortical rewiring and information storage', *Nature*, 431 (7010): 782–8.

Church, G. (2008) *Personal Genome Project*. Available at: http://www.personalgenomes.org/. 2008.

Coates, S. (1992) 'The etiology of boyhood gender identity disorder: An integrative model', in J.W. Barron (ed.), *The Interface of Psychoanalysis and Psychology*.

Coates, S.W. and Wolfe, S.M. (1995) 'Gender identity disorder in boys: The interface of constitution and early experience', *Psychoanalytic Inquiry*, 15: 6–38.

Colapinto, J. (2001) *As Nature Made Him: The Boy Who Was Raised as a Girl*. New York: Harper.

Cooper, R.S. and Kaufman, J.S. (1998) 'Race and hypertension: Science and nescience', *Hypertension*, 32 (5): 813–6.

Cooper, R. and Rotimi, C. (1994) 'Hypertension in populations of West African origin: Is there a genetic predisposition?', *Journal of Hypertension*, 12 (3): 215–27.

Cooper, R.S., Wolf-Maier, K., Luke, A., Adeyemo, A., Banegas, J. R., Forrester, T., Giampaoli, S., Joffres, M., Kastarinen, M., Primatesta, P., Stegmayr, B., Thamm, M. (2005) 'An international comparative study of blood pressure in populations of European vs. African descent', *BMC Med*, 3: 2.

Corbett, K. (1993) 'The mystery of homosexuality', *Psychoanalytic Psychology*, 10 (3): 345–57.

Corbett, K. (1996) 'Homosexual boyhood: Notes on girlyboys', *Gender and Psychoanalysis*, 1: 429–61.

Diamond, L.M. (1998) 'Development of sexual orientation among adolescent and young adult women', *Developmental Psychology*, 34 (5): 1085–95.

Diamond, L.M. (2000a) 'Passionate friendships among adolescent sexual-minority women', *Journal of Research on Adolescence*, 10 (2): 191–209.

Diamond, L.M. (2000b) 'Sexual identity, attractions and behaviour among young sexual-minority women over a 2-year period', *Developmental Psychology*, 36 (2): 241–50.

Diamond, L.M. (2005a) 'From the heart or the gut? Sexual-minority women's experiences of desire for same-sex and other-sex partners', *Feminism and Psychology*, 15 (1): 10–14.

Diamond, L.M. (2005b) '"I'm straight, but I kissed a girl": The trouble with American media representations of female-female sexuality', *Feminism and Psychology*, 15 (1): 104–10.

Diamond, L.M. (2005c) 'A new view of lesbian sub-types: Stable versus fluid identity trajectories over an 8-year period', *Psychology of Women Quarterly*, 29 (2): 119–28.

Diamond, L.M. (2005) 'Toward greater specificity in modeling the ecological context of desire', *Human Development*, 48 (5): 291–7.

Diamond, L.M. (2006) 'Careful what you ask for: Reconsidering feminist epistemology and autobiographical narrative in research on sexual identity development', *Signs*, 31 (2): 471–91.

Diamond, L.M. (2007) 'A dynamical systems approach to the development and expression of female same-sex sexuality', *Perspectives in Psychological Science*, 2 (2): 142–61.

Diamond, L.M. (2008a) 'Female bisexuality', *Developmental Psychology*, 44 (1): 5–14.

Diamond, L.M. (2008b) *Sexual Fluidity: Understanding Women's Love and Desire*. Cambridge, MA: Harvard University Press.

Diamond, M. (1965) 'A critical evaluation of the ontogeny of human sexual behaviour', *Quarterly Review of Biology*, 40: 147–75.

Diamond, M. and Sigmundson, K. (1997) 'Sex reassignment at birth: Long-term review and clinical implications', *Archives of Pediatric and Adolescent Medicine*, 151 (3): 298–304.

DNA Print Genomics (2008a) *AIMS* (Ancestry Informative Markers). Available at: http://www.dnaprint.com/welcome/science/2008.

DNA Print Genomics (2008b) *Forensic*. Available at: http://www.dnaprint.com/welcome/products andservices/forensics/. 2008.

DNA Print Genomics (2008c) *Geneology*. Available at: http://www.ancestrybydna.com/welcome/home/. 2008.

Dreger, A.D. (1998) '"Ambiguous sex" – or ambivalent medicine? Ethical issues in the treatment of intersexuality', *Hastings Center Report* (May–June): 24–35.

Dreger, A.D. (1998) *Hermaphrodites and the Medical Invention of Sex*. Cambridge, MA: Harvard University press.

Duster, T. (2006) 'Comparative perspectives and competing explanations: Taking on the newly configured reductionist challenge to sociology', *American Sociological Review*, 71: 1–15.

Epstein, S. (2007) *Inclusion: The Politics of Difference in Medical Research*. Chicago, IL: Chicago University Press.

Fagot, B.I. and Leinbach, M.D. (1989) 'The young child's gender schema: environmental input, internal organization', *Child Development*, 60: 663–72.

Fagot, B.I. and Leinbach, M.D. (1993) 'Gender-role development in young children: from discrimination to labeling', *Developmental Review*, 13: 205–24.

Fagot, B.I., Leinbach, M.D., Hagan, Richard (1986) 'Gender labeling and the adoption of sex-typed behaviours', *Developmental Psychology*, 22 (4): 440–3.

Fagot, B.I., Leinbach, M.D., O'Boyle, C. (1992) 'Gender labeling, gender stereotyping and parenting behaviours', *Developmental Psychology*, 28 (2): 225–30.

Fausto-Sterling, A. (2000) *Sexing the Body: Gender Politics and the Construction of Sexuality*. New York: Basic Books.

Fausto-Sterling, A. (2004) 'Refashioning race: DNA and the politics of health care', *Differences: A Journal of Feminist Cultural Studies*, 15 (3): 1–37.

Fausto-Sterling, A. (2007) 'Frameworks of desire', *Daedalus*, 136 (2): 47–57.

Fausto-Sterling, A., Garcia Coll, C., Lamarre, Megan. (2009) *Sexing the Baby: A Dynamic Approach to the Emergence of Sex-Related Differences in Infants and Toddlers*. Submitted for publication

Feinberg, L. (1996) *Transgender Warriors*. Boston, MA: Beacon Press.

Feinberg, L. (1998) *Trans Liberation: Beyond Pink or Blue*. Boston, MA: Beacon Press.

Fullwiley, D. (2007) 'The molecularization of race: Institutionalizing human difference in pharmacogenetics practice', *Science as Culture*, 16 (1): 1–30.

Fullwiley, D. (2008) 'The biologistical construction of race: Admixture and the new genetic medicine', *Social Studies of Science*, 38 (5): 695-735.

Gates, H.L. (2008) African DNA. Available at: http://www.africandna.com/. 2008.

Goldberg, A.B. (2007) *Born With the Wrong Body: Transgender 10-Year-Old Girl and Her Family Talk to Barbara Walters* ABC News: 20/20. USA: 20 minutes.

Green, R. (2008) 'Childhood cross-gender behaviour and adult homosexuality: Why the link?', *Journal of Gay and Lesbian Mental Health*, 12 (1/2): 17–28.

Gura, T. (2001) 'Can SNPs deliver on susceptibility genes?', *Science*, 293: 593–5.

Hamer, D., Hu, S. et al. (1993) 'Linkage between DNA markers on the X chromosome and male sexual orientation', *Science*, 261: 321–5.

Harmon, A. (2008) 'Gene map becomes a luxury item', *The New York Times*. New York: The New York Times Company.

Hayles, N.K. (1993) 'The materiality of informatics', *Configurations*, 1 (1): 147–70.

Kendler, K.S., Thornton, L.M., Gilman, S. E., Kessler, R. C. (2000) 'Sexual orientation in a U.S. national sample of twin and nontwin sibling pairs', *Am J Psychiatry*, 157 (11): 1843–6.

Kessler, S. (1998) *Lessons from the Intersexed*. New Brunswick, NJ: Rutgers University Press.

Kirk, K.M., Bailey, J.M., Dunne, M. P., Martin, N. G. (2000) 'Measurement models for sexual orientation in a community twin sample', *Behavioral Genetics*, 30 (4): 345–56.

Krieger, N. (2005) 'Stormy weather: Race, gene expression and the science of health disparities', *American Journal of Public Health*, 95 (12): 2155–60.

Krieger, N. and Sidney, S. (1996) 'Racial discrimination and blood pressure: The CARDIA study of young black and white adults', *American Journal of Public Health*, 86 (10): 1370–78.

Kruijver, F.P., Zhou, J.N., Pool, C. W., Hofman, M. A., Gooren, L. J., Swaab, D. F. (2000) 'Male-to-female transsexuals have female neuron numbers in a limbic nucleus', *Journal of Clinical Endocrinology and Metabolism*, 85 (5): 2034–41.

Langer, S.J. and Martin, J.I. (2004) 'How dresses can make you mentally ill: Examining gender identity disorder in children', *Child and Adolescent Social Work Journal*, 21: 5–23.

Lauerman, J. (2008) *Google backs Harvard Scientist's 100,000 Genome Quest* (Update 2). Bloomberg. com: Bloomberg L.P.

Laumann, E.O., Gagnon, J.H. et al. (1994) *The Social Organization of Sexuality: Sexual Practices in the United States*. Chicago, IL: University of Chicago Press.

Lawrence, A.A (2007) *A Critique of the Brain-Sex Theory of Transsexualism.*

Lawrence, A.A. (2008) 'Gender identity disorders in adults: Diagnosis and treatment', in D.L. Rowland and L. Incrocci (eds), *Handbook of Sexual and Gender Identity*. New York: John Wiley and Sons.

Lutes, J. (2008) 'What the Science Says and Doesn't Say about Homosexuality'. Available at: http//www.soulforce.org.

Martin, C.L., Ruble, D.N. Szkrybalo, J. (2002) 'Cognitive theories of early gender development', *Psychological Bulletin*, 128 (6): 903–33.

Martin, C.L., Ruble, D.N., Szkrybalo, J. (2004) 'Recognizing the centrality of gender identity and stereotype knowledge in gender development and moving toward theoretical integration: Reply to Bandura and Bussey (2004).' *Psychological Bulletin*, 130 (5): 702–10.

Martin, J.I. (2008) 'Nosology, etiology and course of gender identity disorder', *Journal of Gay and Lesbian Mental Health*, 12 (1/2): 81–94.

McEwen, B. and E. Lasley (2002) *The End of Stress as we know it*. Washington, DC: Joseph Henry Press.

Menvielle, E. and C. Tuerk (2002) 'A support group for parents of gender-nonconforming boys', *Journal of the American Academy of Child and Adolescent Psychiatry*, 41 (8): 1010–13.

Menvielle, E.J., Tuerk, C., Perrin, E.C. (2005) 'To the Beat of a Different drummer: the gender variant child',' *Contemporary Pediatrics*, 22 (2): 38–39 &ff.

Meyer-Bahlburg, H.F. (2005) 'Gender identity outcome in female-raised 46,XY persons with penile agenesis, cloacal exstrophy of the bladder, or penile ablation', *Archives of Sexual Behaviour*, 34 (4): 423–38.

Meyerowitz, J. (2002) *How Sex Changed: A History of Transsexuality in the United States*. Cambridge, MA: Harvard University Press.

Money, J. and A.A. Ehrhardt (1972) *Man and Woman, Boy and Girl*. Baltimore, MD: John's Hopkins University Press.

Mustanski, B.S., Dupree, M.G., Nievergelt, C. M., Bocklandt, S., Schork, N. J., Hamer, D. H. (2005) 'A genomewide scan of male sexual orientation', *Human Genetics*, 116 (4): 272–8.

Nelson, A. (2008) 'Bio science: Genetic geneology testing and the pursuit of African ancestry', *Social Studies of Science*, 38 (5), 759–783.

Nobles, M. (2000) *Shades of Citizenship: Race and the Census in Modern Politics*. Palo Alto, CA: Stanford University Press.

NOVA (2007) *Ghost in your Genes: Epigenetic therapy.*

Pattatucci, Á.M. (1998) 'Molecular investigation into complex behaviour: Lessons from sexual orientation studies', *Human Biology*, 70 (2). 367–86.

Pattatucci, A.M.L. and Hamer, D.H. (1995) 'Development and familiarity of sexual orientation in females', *Behaviour Genetics*, 25 (5): 407–20.

Peplau, L.A. and Huppin, M. (2008) 'Masculinity, femininity and the development of sexual orientation in women', *Journal of Gay and Lesbian Mental Health*, 12 (1–2): 145–65.

Quartz, S.R. (2003) 'Learning and brain development: A neural constructivist perspective', in P.T. Quinlan (ed.), *Connectionist Models of Development: Developmental Processes in Real and Artificial Networks*. New York, Taylor and Francis: Psychology Press. pp. 279–309.

Rebbeck, T.R., Halbert, C.H, Sankar, P. (2006) 'Genetics, epidemiology and cancer disparities: is it black and white?', *Journal of Clinical Oncology*, 24 (14): 2164–9.

Reich, D.E., Gabriel, S.B., Altshuler, D. (2003) 'Quality and completeness of SNP databases', *Nature Genetics*, 33: 457–8.

Ruble, D. and Martin, C.L. (1998) 'Gender development', in N. Eisenberg (ed.), *Social, Emotional and Personality Development*. New York: Wiley. pp. 933–1016.

Sandfort, T.G.M. (2005) 'Sexual orientation and gender: Stereotypes and beyond', *Archives of Sexual Behavior*, 34 (6): 595–611.

Savin-Williams, R.C. (2006) 'Who's gay? does it matter?', *Current Directions in Psychological Science*, 15 (1): 40–44.

Savin-Williams, R.C. and Ream, G.L. (2007) 'Prevalence and stability of sexual orientation components during adolescence and young adulthood', *Archives of Sexual Behavior*, 36 (3): 385–94.

Schore, A.N. (1994) *Affect Regulation and the Origin of the Self: The Neurobiology of Emotional Development*. Hillsdale, NJ: Lawrence Erlbaum Associates.

Schore, A.N. (2001) 'Effects of a secure attachment relationship on right brain development, affect regulation and infant mental health', *Infant Mental Health Journal*, 22 (1–2): 7–66.

Schulkin, J. (2003) *Rethinking Homeostasis: Allostatic Regulation in Physiology and Pathophysiology*. Cambridge, MA: MIT Press.

Schwartz, R.S. (2001) 'Racial profiling in medical research', *New England Journal of Medicine*, 344 (18): 1392–3.

Serbin, L.A., Poulin Dubois, D., Eichstedt, J. (2002) 'Infants' response to gender-inconsistent events', *Infancy*, 3 (4): 531–42.

Spiegel, A. (2008) 'Parents consider treatment to delay son's puberty: New therapy would buy time to resolve gender crisis', *All Things Considered*. USA, National Public Radio: 20 minutes and 12 seconds. May 8, 2008.

Spiegel, A. (2008) 'Two families grapple with sons', *Gender Preferences: Psychologists Take Radically Different Approaches in Therapy. All Things Considered*. USA, National Public Radio: 22 minutes and 45 seconds. May 8, 2008.

Sterling, P. and Eyer, J. (1988) 'Allostasis: A new paradigm to explain arousal pathology', in S. Fisher and J. Reason (eds), *Handbook of life stress, Cognition and Health*. New York: John Wiley and Sons.

Stryker, S. and Whittle, S. (eds) (2006) *The Transgender Studies Reader*. New York: Routledge.

The International HapMap Consortium (2003) 'The international hapmap project', *Nature*, 426: 789–96.

Thelen, E. (1995) 'Motor development: A new synthesis', *American Psychologist*, 50 (2): 79–95.

Thelen, E. (2000) 'Grounded in the world: Developmental origins of the embodied mind', *Infancy*, 1 (1): 3–28.

Thelen, E. and Smith, L.B. (1994) *A Dynamic Systems Approach to the Development of Cognition and Action*. Cambridge, MA: MIT Press.

Valentine, D. (2007) *Imagining Transgender: An Ethnography of a Category*. Durham, NC: Duke University Press.

Weiss, K.M. and Terwilliger, J.D. (2000) 'How many diseases does it take to map a gene with SNPs?', *Nature Genetics*, 26: 151–7.

Whitehead Institute (2004) *Human SNP Database*. http://www.wi.mit.edu/news/archives/2001/el_0212a.html

Zhou, J.N., Hofman, M.A. et al. (1995) 'A sex difference in the human brain and its relation to transsexuality', *Nature*, 378 (6552): 68–70.

Zucker, K.J. (2008) 'Reflections of the relation between sex-typed behaviour in childhood and sexual orientation in adulthood', *Journal of Gay and Lesbian Mental Health*, 12 (1/2): 29–59.

Zucker, K.J. and Cohen-Kettenis, P.T. (2008) 'Gender identity disorder in children and adolescents', in D. L. Rowland and L. Incrocci (eds), *Handbook of Sexual and Gender Identity Disorders*. New York: John Wiley and Sons. pp. 376–422.

# 9

# Race and Racial Formations

## Harry J. Elam, Jr and Michele Elam

Race – racism – is a device. No More. No less. It explains nothing at all …. It is simply a means. An invention to justify the rule of some men over others. [But] it also has consequences; once invented it takes on a life, a reality of its own …. And it is pointless to pretend that it doesn't *exist* – merely because it is a *lie*! (Tshembe in Hansberry, 1994: 92)

We should see race as an element of social structure rather than an irregularity within it; we should see race as a dimension of human representation rather than an illusion. These perspectives inform the theoretical approach we call racial formation. (Omi and Winant, 1994: 55)

## RACE AND RACIAL FORMATIONS: THE TRUTH OF THE LIE

As our epigraphs suggest, most contemporary scholars, from playwrights to academics, recognize the fact that 'race' is not a biological fact but, rather, a social construction and politicized accounting of both real and imagined differences. 'Race' is, as Mark Twain put it, a 'legal fiction'. But as both Hansberry, and Omi and Winant point out, this illusion has had, and continues to have, very powerful material consequences in the modern world. The fraud of race informs the realities of daily lives, social organizations, religious rituals, and political institutions.

Thus, we begin – rather than end – this discussion of race and racial formations with the recognition that 'race' as we know it as both a lie and a truth.

Many have offered cogent critiques of race as a self-evident and politically innocent verity; they document the ways in which religion, philosophy, history, government institutions, juridical systems, and the biological and social sciences participate in – indeed, were invested in – discourses that created a racist cosmology, a world order which ranked people of color as atavistic, backward in every evaluative category, from intelligence to hygiene (Fredrickson, 2002; Goldberg, 1993; Gossett, 1963; Gresson III, 1995). Others offer an excellent accounting of the misuses of scientific claims of race (Gould, 1992; Weinbaum, 2004).[1] Stephen Jay Gould was pivotal in providing a history and critique of the methods and motivations underlying the popularity of nineteenth-century biological determinism, in particular – the belief that the social and economic differences between human groups from inherited, inborn distinctions and that society, in this sense, is an accurate reflection of biology.

Despite this and many other critiques, in the last 15 years there has been a slow re-biologizing of race. The development of the

Human Genome Project, which for many implied a genetic basis for race; the rising popularity of companies providing swab and blood tests that putatively serve up accountings of racial genealogies; and the marketing of pharmaceuticals targeted at certain races, even though they are for medical conditions associated with demographic populations, all have led to an increasing popular tendency to believe again that race is simply biological fact. Further, this re-biologizing tends to reintroduce, as well, the idea that genetics (versus power relations, discrimination practices, or governmental policies, for instance) has near-full explanatory force for social arrangements and inequities, past and present. Richard Herrnstein and Charles Murray's highly controversial and much-contested *Bell Curve: Intelligence and Class Structure in American Life* (1996), which argues that inborn intelligence accounts for nearly all social differences, and thus programs for ameliorative social change or racial reform are pointless endeavors, is representative of this kind of argument and its disturbing policy implications. This book sparked a firestorm of debate but also gave license and intellectual legitimation to many more similar arguments (Levin, 2005; Lynn and Vanhanen, 2006; Sarich and Miele, 2005). All see race as 'real' but its reality, as they see it, is fixed, inhering, and inexorably supports the status quo because that they all conclude that inequities are genetic inevitabilities and thus, social injustice is merely an unfortunate but unavoidable consequence. The potent resurgence of biological discourses about race reminds us that attitudes about what race is and what it means are cyclical and not necessarily progressive – though we often speak of the historical advances against racism, race itself is dynamically usable. Some of the ideas from the nineteenth century are rehearsed and refashioned to fit contemporary political desires and national agenda, though always in the name of disinterested science. Given such shape-shifting, it is not always clear whether such steps take us forward or backward except perhaps in retrospect.

## POST-RACE DEBATES: NEW AND OLD DEFINITIONS OF RACE

So what does race mean in the twenty-first century? Our discussion of race and racial formation occurs in this context: how to talk about race when many contemporary popular and scholarly discourses either insist that 'race' no longer exist and therefore does not/should not matter – or say it matters, but only in ways that smack of nineteenth-century positivism that that provide the underwriting rationale for racist social structures.

The idea that the time of race is past – that we have arrived at the so-called 'post-race' moment – is often associated with progress and enlightenment. We can and should move beyond Civil Rights era definitions of race, the argument goes, in which historical models and ways of thinking about race no longer apply. From Todd Boyd's (2002) claim that we are now in the 'post-civil rights' period, or Mark Anthony Neal's (2002) 'post soul'[2] era, many scholars and intellectual pundits echo Stanley Crouch claim that 'race is over' (1996: 170).[3] Associated with that claim is the idea that to move beyond race is to move into modernity, to go beyond time and time-bound notions of race. But this appeal to historylessness is, in fact deceptive, since 'black', 'brown', 'yellow', 'white', and every variation of mixed race, have all been and continue to be raced in and through time. As Ira Berlin argues in *Many Thousand Gone*, race 'is a particular kind of social construction – a historical construction [...] it cannot exist outside of time and place' (1998: 1). Accordingly, how race has evolved as a concept has been inextricably linked to its historic contexts of its use with its meanings dependent upon these specific historic circumstances.

Perhaps from the earliest moments of one civilization's encounter with other peoples, humans have sought to understand and to offer explanations for their differences, to theorize and classify the divergence in appearance of peoples. Motivating such definitions are matters of politics, religion, economic power relations. As Berlin notes, race 'is the product of history and it only exists on the contested social terrain in which men and women struggle to control their destinies' (1998: 1). Through history, people have defined race in terms of their own interests, circumstances and desire to 'control their destinies'. But controlling one's destiny inevitably means controlling others' destinies, since all our destinies are intertwined and interdependent. After all, the US's ideal of 'manifest destiny' wreaked havoc on the destinies of the indigenous. And, as Mary Louise Pratt (1992) has argued, British and Belgian colonialism and imperialism exploited and then merged religious missionary, economic interests, and civilizing 'uplift' projects. All European contacts with Africa and Asia were, therefore, interested speculations. In the sixteenth century, white Europeans attributed black difference to classical or biblical sources. Christianity associated blackness with evil and disease, allying whiteness with goodness and purity. Eventually, the mere presence of blackness, construed a threat to Englishness in the 1500s. In 1596, blacks were numerous enough in England that Queen Elizabeth had numbers of them deported to Spain and Portugal and then five years later repeated this act. In Elizabethan England, black constituted not only difference but deviance.[4]

White superiority became tied to a notion of permanent racial hierarchy that impacted the development and divisions of labor, class, and privilege across the modern world. In the case of the slave trade, black inferiority became a justification for the condition of slavery. European expansion, the impulse to realize the nation's higher destiny, in the seventeenth and eighteenth centuries depended upon the conquest and enslavement of other nations and its peoples. Enlightenment philosopher, David Hume,

wrote in an infamous footnote to his essay, *Of National Character*:

I am apt to suspect the Negroes and in general all the other species of men (for there are four or five different kinds) to be naturally inferior to the whites. There never was a civilized nation of any other complexion than white, nor even any individual eminent either in action or speculation. No ingenious manufactures amongst them, no arts, no sciences. Such a uniform and constant difference could not happen, in so many countries and ages, if nature had not made an original distinction betwixt these breeds of men. Not to mention our colonies, there are Negroe slaves dispersed all over EUROPE, of which none ever discovered any symptoms of ingenuity. (1987: 236)

Hume voices here the perspective that profoundly influenced the construction of race in slavery even as he himself opposed it: that black's native disposition justified the 'Peculiar Institution' of slavery and the resultant separation of the races.

These early notions of white superiority became scientifically linked to biological inheritance in the mid-nineteenth century. Scientists such as the Frenchman, George Cuvier – who would dissect Saartje Baartman, the so-called 'Hottentot Venus', upon her death – began in the 1800s to classify the races as types of or a varieties of a human evolution with blacks at the bottom and whites on the top. Other scientists such as the American, Samuel George Morton, maintained that cranial measurements indicated racial difference – according to his data, whites had larger brains and thus, it was argued, larger heads. J.C. Nott and G.R. Glidden in their 1854 book, *Types of Mankind*, proposed that the divergences in racial types permanently and naturally influenced the constitution and behavior of peoples and provided for the separation of the races. The negro, they maintained constituted a biologically inferior type (Banton, 1998: 56). Looking back on this era, sociologist Michael Banton argues in *Racial Theories* that in the United States, the 'conception of race as type developed most systematically' rather than accidentally or arbitrarily, and slavery provided not so much a laboratory for, but evidence of, the racial theories of scientific racism (Banton,1998: 48). These notions of racial typology served to legitimize slavery and vice versa. Up to the American Civil War and following, a racial caste system developed in the America supported by discriminatory laws and reinforced by white control of labor resources.

With the turn of the century, emancipation and reconstruction, the racial climate in America changed, and with it the ever-adaptable definitions of race. The work of Charles Darwin moved conceptions of race away from permanent typologies by noting that human species were constantly evolving. Other theories arose, as we suggested at the outset of this essay, that attributed racial difference to genetics. Yet, prompted by the threat of black economic and social advancement, the association of race with privilege became even more tightly knit and tightly guarded. Whiteness connoted status and access. New legal sanctions reinforced this privilege and signaled the abrupt end to black voting rights. In 1896, with *Plessy* v. *Ferguson*, the Supreme Court upheld the notion of 'separate but equal' as constitutional.[5] A sustained eruption of racial violence further separated the races and kept blacks on the bottom rung of the economic, social and political hierarchy. Between 1880 and 1950, over 4000 African Americans were lynched with little effort made by the authorities to stop or prosecute the perpetrators. Racialized practices of segregation and discrimination limited black access to education, employment, and housing, and the annexing of Hawaii and the Philippines, the subordination of Puerto Rico, the removals of Native Americans and various exclusions acts similarly prevented people of Native, Asian, and South and Latin American descent from full enfranchisement.

Importantly, the racism animating these practices was and is not merely a function of personal ill-will, but rather is structurally imbricated in all institutions. As Omi and Winant put it in the epigraph, racism is not anomalous but fundamental to the formation of a national identity in which enfranchised

citizens were necessarily white and propertied. Out of this recognition developed the field of 'whiteness studies', which explores the development and maintenance of whiteness as a racial formation in relation to other races, and which defines whiteness as it operates as a default, unmarked race with special and tacit privileges (Fiske, 1996).[6] Whiteness – like all racial categorizations – is a fluid designation: in the early twentieth century, Jews and Catholics in the United States were branded as 'black', and in a move which points up the political utility of race, South African citizens of Chinese descent recently successfully petitioned to be legally designated as 'black' so they could achieve full rights under the post-apartheid government.[7]

Critical to the theorizing of race, racism and racialization is the work of Algerian psychiatrist/philosopher Frantz Fanon in the 1950s, who responded to the colonial hierarchy which enfranchised whites and psychically and socially enslaved blacks. Working in Tunisia after he was expelled from Algeria in 1947, Fanon grounded his psychiatric practice in the conjunction of psychoanalytic approaches with social therapy. For Fanon, the psychological condition of his black subjects was a product of their interaction with colonialism and the social forces that surrounded them. As Francois Verges argues, Fanon's 'psychology was a sociology of mental disorder' that linked the symptoms of madness to the cause of freedom (1996: 52). This struggle for freedom under the colonial project produced among both blacks and whites particular socio-psychological responses to and resultant understandings of race. His first book, *Black Skins, White Masks* – originally published in 1952 became a manifesto for black revolution change in the 1960s and 1970s and has re-emerged at the forefront on postcolonial studies in the 1990s:

> The Negro enslaved by his inferiority, the white man enslaved by his superiority alike behave in accordance with a neurotic orientation [...] The Negro's behavior makes him akin to an

obsessive neurotic type or if one prefers, he puts himself into a complete situational neurosis. In the man of color there is a constant effort to run away from his own individuality, to annihilate his own presence. (Fanon, 1967: 60)

As Fanon argues, the madness and melancholy of race is situational, inextricably connected to the abuses of racism and the colonial society. As Shu-mei Shih notes in her analysis of Fanon, 'race is a psychological experience because it is a social one' (2008: 1351). Specifically, Fanon theorizes race functions relationally under colonialism, 'for not only must the black man be black he must be black in relation to the white man' (1967: 110). This relationality establishes racial difference and positions blacks as inferior and whites as superior. Moreover, as blacks learn that white is associated with good and black with evil, they come to loath blackness and to desire instead with whiteness. It is this 'will to whiteness', as Langston Hughes puts it in *The Racial Mountain*, that Fanon finds both socially and psychologically problematic. His black Antillean kinsmen, Fanon maintains, saw themselves as French not as Negro, and identified the Negro as primitive other. Locating blackness in relation to whiteness, the colonized Negro imagines him – or herself through a white gaze and accordingly endures and participates in the socio-psychic strains of racialization under colonialism.

Fanon makes clear that race under colonialism is not a biological reality but, rather, a product of lived experience within historical, cultural, and social circumstances. The visibility of blackness has a significant impact on how black subjects are interpellated and how they in turn understand themselves. Fanon writes, 'I am overdetermined from without. I am a slave not to the "idea" that others have of me but of my own appearance' (1967: 116). Visibly marked as black, Fanon points out, means that he is racialized not as an individual but as a collective subject, 'the Negro'. The Negro, he points out, historically stands 'for Evil […][and by contrast] is not whiteness in symbols always

ascribed in French to Justice, Truth, Virginity? The black man is the symbol of Evil and ugliness' (1967: 180). Fanon argues that what whites perceive as 'the Negro' is a construction, a product of their fears, their unconscious, and their racialized projections, and as such, it conditions the lives of both whites and blacks.

Fanon acknowledges that moving against the negative perceptions of blackness by whites requires black self-definition and the assertion of positive associations with blackness. He critiques the *Negritude* movement as articulated by former Senegalese President, Leopold Senghor, Martinique poet, Aimé Césaire, and others. *Negritude*, a literary and political movement of 1930s, rejected white French colonial racism and promoted black identity and a black literary aesthetic. And yet, the politics of *Negritude*, as Fanon reveals, imagine Africa as one homogeneous whole and thus ignores the permutations of blackness within its different countries and regions. Moreover, Fanon finds *Negritude* still operates as a relational racial paradigm that inverts rather than destroys the conventional black–white binary. Problematically *Negritude*, he asserts associates blackness with expressiveness, creativity and ingenuity, while whiteness through history is still cast as the site of rationalism, industry and progress. Thus, Fanon is particularly cautious about the utility of race and in his critique of *Negritude* points to problems of essentialization that scholars in the 1990s would later identify within the racial identity politics of the 1960s and 1970s.

## THE USEFULNESS OF RACE

Because of the long history of oppression of non-white races, race is often equated with racism. Hence the frequent call to go beyond the 'group think' of racial or cultural nationalism, which is sometimes cast as a threat to national unity or humanist universalism.

But as scholars such as Linda Martín Alcoff, Satya P. Mohanty, Michael Hames-García and others cogently argue, racialized experiences are not all negative. Not only can they be the crucible for cherished traditions and heritages, but as importantly, can also afford invaluable critical insight into social structures. As Alcoff argues in *Visible Identities: Race, Gender and the Self*, race often lets us see more about society than the body that is raced.[8] Understanding fully, as she does, the limitations of a 'vision-centric approach' (2006: 197) and the privileging of sight as vehicle of knowledge or litmus test for race (2006: 198), she argues that although the visible does not reveal biologic or metaphysical truths, it most certainly indexes social realities. As she puts it, 'the practices of visibility are indeed revealing of significant facts about our cultural ideology, but what the visible reveals is not the ultimate truth; rather it often reveals self-projection, identity anxieties and the material inscription of social violence'(2006: 8).

Race has the potential to be employed productively: it is a mistake to equate it with merely destructive impulses and effects. Kimberlé Crenshaw's important concept of 'intersectionality' and Aída Hurtado's concept of 'relational privilege' capitalize on this notion, for it reminds us that to understand the uses and misuses of race, it must always be considered as a shifting variable among many, that race is salient at different moments in relation to class privilege, social position, gender, sexual orientation, nation, and so on (Crenshaw, 1996; Hurtado, 2006). Chandra Talpade Mohanty (1991, 1996, 2003), for example, has reshaped the paradigms of both race studies and social justice with transnational analyses that always implicate the complex ways in which gender as well as state apparatuses and colonization inform particular racialized social practices and individual experiences. The transnational turn in race studies recognizes the global nature of intersectionality as well as the politics of 'cultural traffic' (Elam and Jackson, 2005) even in this 'post-race'

moment. Thus, the riots in the suburbs of Paris France in October and November 2005, carried out largely by youth of African and North African decent, spoke not only to the particular conditions of immigrants and people of color within France but to wider questions of how race continues to operate within matters of labor, education and housing in Europe and beyond.

## NEW THEORETICAL PERSPECTIVES: RACE AS PERFORMANCE

Omi and Winant refer to 'racial formation' as a way of historicizing the practices and circumstances that generate and renew racial categories and racialized structures:

> We define *racial formation* as the sociohistorical process by which racial categories are created, inhabited, transformed, and destroyed ... racial formation is a process of historically situated *projects* in which human bodies and social structures are represented and organized. Next we link racial formation to the evolution of hegemony, the way in which society is organized and ruled ... From a racial formation perspective, race is a matter of both social structure and cultural representation' (1994: 55–6).

The expression, racial formation, therefore is a reminder that race is formed, made; it is a doing, a process, a daily performance that is constantly changing and replenished. The model of race as performance similarly involves a recognition of the doing required of racial formations. The performative dimension of racial formation involves considering always not just the bodies 'doing' race but also the representational context in which this occurs – if you will, the cultural staging and social witnessing required to make race meaningful and powerful.

A full accounting of race therefore should involve attention to the social stage, the play-script, the direction, and the audience – the metaphors here help us ask different kinds of questions about race: Not what is race, but when and where does race emerge? To what effects and ends is it put? In whose interest is it that a people are racialized in any given moment in time and space? What narrative does it enable or disable? In short, what does it *do*? As Toni Morrison asks in *Playing the Dark*: *Whiteness and the Literary Imagination* (1993), the question should not be simply 'is it racist', but rather what does race – its presence or its conspicuous absence – make possible in any work of literature?

Thinking of race as performance also requires a challenge to the idea of racial identity as fixed or inhering. Deepening and extending Judith Butler's notion of racial performativity, Elin Diamond argues, performance has a more complex social context and function. As an interaction between audience, performer and context:

> Every performance … embeds features of previous performances: gender conventions, racial histories, aesthetic traditions – political and cultural pressures that are consciously and unconsciously acknowledged. (1996: 1–2)

The meaning of racial performance, like the staging of identity, can only really be understood through its emergence within interpretive rubrics and socially situated contexts, both past and the present. Racial performance is in continuous negotiation with social practices, social relations, social norms – it is an encounter with an Other. Analyzing race as a type of performance helps determine the social politics and cultural dynamics of the concept of race as well as more carefully explain in what ways and to what ends racialization processes occur.

The 2008 United States electoral campaign that ultimately resulted in the election of the first African American President, serves as potent example of how race might be understood as performed. Repeatedly along the campaign trail, Barack Obama, the son of a black Kenyan father and white Kansas mother faced questions about his blackness. At an early point in the 2008 presidential campaign before Obama had secured the Democratic nomination and after the incendiary racial claims made by the

African American pastor of Obama's Chicago church home, the Reverend Jeremiah Wright, had gained national attention, conservative critics on Fox News argued that Obama was too black, too partisan to be America's president. Jesse Jackson and other older black politicians objected that upstart, precocious Obama had not properly risen through the ranks and followed the protocol expected of black politicians. Contested throughout was how Obama 'performed' blackness: whether he 'properly' employed the tropes, history, behaviors, and attitudes associated with blackness.

To be sure, what Obama in his campaign and subsequent election has ushered in is a new age of black politics that have deliberately looked back to and yet moved beyond earlier paradigms of raced-based political patronage and previously conventional performances of blackness (Elam, 2008). Analyzing race as a type of performance can help make sense of the social politics and cultural dynamics emerging in the new millennium and gets at the higher stakes of race in the post-race moment: how and in what circumstances do we see race (the anxiety about its visibility, after all, made most acute on stage which must make visible race and thus must take up self-consciously the problem that race is not writ on the body); how does the performance of race on stage not just reflect but inform the everyday performances of race offstage – even more specifically, how are political racialized identities and political constituencies formed in theatre for the 'real world' in this historical moment?

## NEW DIRECTIONS: MIXED RACE AND COMPARATIVE RACIALIZATIONS

Famously, scholar W.E.B. Du Bois (1903) remarked that the critical problem of the twentieth century is the color line. But any critical understanding of the dynamics of race in the twenty-first century needs to account for the emerging politics of mixed-race.

Part of this involves examining not only interracial and intraracial relations – *Afro Asian Encounters*: *Culture, History, Politics*, edited by Heike Raphael-Hernandez and Shannon Steen (2006), *Afro-Orientalism* by Bill Mullen (2004), *Everybody Was Kung Fu Fighting*: *Afro-Asian Connections and the Myth of Cultural Purity* by Vijay Prashad (2002), or *Yellow*: *Race in America Beyond Black and White* by Frank H. Wu (2003) all go beyond black and white relations. But there is another phenomenon emerging in race studies related to but also quite distinct from intraracial analyses: mixed-race identification. Peoples of mixed-race descent are both a colonial and diasporic phenomenon, the result of immigration, conquest, and historically, sexual violence – from Brazil to South Africa to the Philippines.[9] Laura E. Gomez (2007) in *Manifest Destinies*: *The Making of the Mexican American Race* analyzes the ways in which Mexican Americans and mestizos were characterized as both white and non-white according to political interests, and G. Reginald Daniel (2006) in *Race and Multiraciality in Brazil and the United States*: *Converging Paths?* notes how miscegenation gave the appearance of a 'racial democracy' in both countries while still upholding racialist hierarchies based on blood and color. A new mixed-race political identification has emerged at the turn of the twenty first century in the US and elsewhere that attempts to establish an identity that is not derivative of this history, though it remains fraught with the legacy of colorism and privilege. Comparative race study offers windows onto the processes of race and the political competition between racial paradigms and works against claims of exceptionalism – the idea that a particular racial paradigm is so distinct that it can only be understand as an exception, incomparable, impervious to analysis. While, of course, it is important not to make global claims or to conflate regional or historical differences, comparisons can yield perspective and insight into respective cultures. For instance, legislative and juridical efforts to regulate race in all countries in response to race mixing in the US, Africa, Brazil, and South Africa similarly reflect the acute national anxiety over race, which are always keyed to economic and political interests (Johnson, 2003; Young, 1995). In that sense, the shared and variable efforts to legislate and police race mixing – that is, the boundaries of race itself – serve as case studies into the production and maintenance of race.

Recent political claims to a mixed-race race identity in the US (further enabled and legitimized by the 'mark all that apply' racial option in the 2000 census) are examples of the performance of race – for these what Omi and Winant call 'race projects' are also always political initiatives, and illustrate suggest the ways in which racial designations are never neutral descriptions, but rather always prioritize and distribute resources, in which state often plays a significant role (1994: 55).[10] The notion of mixed race complicating contemporary constructions of race in the new millennium is neither new nor simply a North American phenomenon. In South Africa's new Rainbow Nation – as Desmond Tutu has termed it, foregrounding South Africa's racial diversity and a corresponding national politics that has overturned the past policies of apartheid, those classified as Coloured find themselves at a particularly critical juncture in relation to the new government's efforts at racial reform and its programs of affirmative action intended to redress the wrongs of the past. South African Coloureds[11] are legally positioned under apartheid between racial regimes – what Werner Sollors has called 'neither/nor', (Sollors, 1995) and what Mohamed Adhikari terms 'not white enough, not black enough' (Adhikari, 2005) – have had similarly charged and ambivalent political alliances, first with Afrikaner accommodationism, then with Black Consciousness 'rejectionism' of the 1970s, the 'nonracialism' of the 1980s, and Coloured cultural nationalism in the 1990s (Dalmage, 2004; Ifekwunigwe, 2004; Williams, 2006).[12]

Questions of Coloured oppression, privilege, and marginalization have always been highly contested matters in South Africa. In 1994, the first free elections not only ushered in the post-apartheid state, but also signaled a watershed moment for the Coloured community. The wide majority of Coloureds in South Africa's western Cape – the place where the majority of Coloureds live due to a variety of historical, cultural, and political factors including governmentally imposed racial segregation – voted against the ANC's Nelson Mandela and for National Party, the party that practiced the brutalities of apartheid. This much publicized and much debated act of electoral racial politics brought to crisis the Coloured's 'problematic of the middle', its troubled negotiation between progressive ideals and conservative impulses (Farred, 1981: 1).[13]

Most recently, Cape Coloureds have made concrete efforts – aided by local arts, literature, and theatre festivals – to redefine and re-assert a distinctive cultural identity that is not simply a structural effect of apartheid racialism nor complicit with its legacy. 'Colouredness', these activists suggest, exist on a continuum of color, cultural practices, and political commitment, one that cannot be fully conflated any longer with either white privilege or black solidarity. Colouredness potentially interrupts, then, both the political momentum of the Black majority and the new racial paradigms of post-apartheid South Africa. The effort to locate a progressive identity within the post-Civil Rights and post-apartheid moment, to posit a productive rather than merely reactive identity that resists both the traps of victimage, privilege, and biologic essentialization: 'Coloured identities are not based on "race mixture" but on cultural creativity, creolized formations, shaped by South Africa's history of colonization, slavery, segregation and apartheid' (Eramus, 2001: 14).[14]

As in the US, the development of race as a concept in South Africa has been equally impacted by black and Indian servitude and laws used to maintain racial separation.

The Dutch colonials in the Cape of Good Hope in the mid-1600s needed a labor force for the Dutch East India Company's operation and looked to enlist the native people. Finding, however, the indigenous Khoikhoi people little inclined to heavy labor, the Dutch imported slaves from neighboring tribes and regions. Thus, in a pattern different from that in the United States, until the late eighteenth and early nineteenth centuries, as noted by George Fredrickson, on the Cape of Good Hope, race mattered in the determination of status but was not all-important. The social hierarchy was composed of white upper class company officials and prosperous wine and grain farmers; an intermediate group of freemen, mostly white in ancestry, but including (for most purposes) some free people of color; and a servile class, entirely non white but by this time subdivided into chattel slaves and Khoikhoi servants. (1981: 88)

In part because of this, Coloured people have never been fully enfranchised: 'There is no doubt that the Coloureds are citizens of this country. There is just as little doubt that they are not part of this homogenous identity that can be described as the nation' (H.F. Verwoerd, quoted in the South African play, *A Coloured Place*, by Malika Ndlovu, 1998).[15] However, the narrative that mixed race people are 'excesses' to history, to use that provocative phrase, is deceptive since as Betsy Erkkila (2004), in *Mixed Bloods And Other Crosses: Rethinking American Literature From The Revolution To The Culture Wars* has powerfully demonstrated, they are absolutely fundamental to earliest processes of history and nation-making. As Thiven Reddy (2001) in 'The politics of naming; The constitution of Coloured subjects' argues, during apartheid, the category Coloured functioned to hold the whole system of classification in South African together. 'The stability of the main racial categories, by which I mean that these categories assume an unquestioned and taken for granted status, rely on some notion of a category denoting mixed and Other' (Reddy, 2001: 64–5)

As Reddy maintains, the category of in-betweeness helps to fix the categories of blackness and whiteness and in fact to 'give the classificatory system is very meaning' (2001: 68). Hence it is the highest irony that they are absent from a history that requires their absenting, their forgetting, for its own narratives of purity. Literature and theatre of mixed race in the US and South Africa increasingly invoke this self-reflexive dimension, so that the specimen requiring scrutiny is not simply the mixed race figure but the nation itself.

But despite the greater interest in mixed race people, many continue to see themselves as, according to one critic, 'residual, in-between, or lesser identity characterized as "lacking", supplementary, excessive, inferior or simply non-existent' (Attridge and Jolly 1998:15–16). As Homba Ntaoska puts it, 'Coloureds don't know where they come from. We know where we come from. Whites know where they come from. But these coloureds don't know whether they are white or black' (Attridge and Jolly, 1998: 18). Or more damningly, as Marike de Klerk (FW De Klerk's ex-spouse) crudely characterized it, Coloured people are a 'negative group, the leftovers' and 'as a people that we left after the nations were sorted out' (Attridge and Jolly, 1998: 18).[16]

In short, 'mixed race' and 'Coloured' are not merely demographic facts but as races in the making – racial performances. The fraught epistemological condition and social location of mixed-race and Coloured peoples urges us to question both the thresholds of racial identity (where does 'black' begin or end?) and the limits of intra – and inter-racial political mobilization (how and on what terms can internally diverse communities ally with or subvert political hegemonies?). With what implications do Coloured and mixed race people assert a politics that hails identity as an act of will triumphing above time, space, place, nation, race? Such questions at the center of debates about the possibilities and thresholds of this post-race Geist.

In the US, the proposition that colored people are mongrels without culture, national, or political coherence has led to compensatory celebratory representations of mixed race people. As writer Danzy Senna humorously puts it in her essay, *The Mulatto Millennium*:

> Strange to wake up and realize you're in style [...] It was the first day of the new millennium and I woke to find that mulattos had taken over [...] According to the racial zodiac, 2000 is the official Year of the Mulatto. Pure breeds (at least the black ones) are out and hybridity is in. America loves us in all our half-caste glory. (1998: 12)

Understanding race as performance means considering that the meanings and matter of race are actively constructed in the moment even as they are dependent on historical associations and established markers Performances of Coloured and mixed-race identities in every day life often engage and seek to deconstruct racial borders and the apparatuses that police them. In the U.S. this has led to is a fetishizing of the ubiquitous box on public forms, and has its parallel in South Africa: the passbook designating racial identity. In both cases, the forms and their checking by self or another function as ritual performances of race in which identity is validated or revoked. But in the social dramas playing out in the aftermath of the Census and of apartheid, new performances of mixed race and Colouredness have emerged as ways to address the crisis of how to identify when the legal strictures governing racial classification are no longer in place but the racialization processes informing them continue, arguably, uninterrupted or at least marginally transformed. In this new time, some Coloured artists and scholars have agitated for a recognition of the African roots of Coloured identities and have argued that it is possible to be both Coloured and African (Black), where before these categories where understood under apartheid as antithetical. Zimitri Erasmus asks that Coloured identity be understood 'as part of the shifting texture of a broader black experience' (2001: 14).

Yet, as we have suggested the move to construct both Coloured or mixed race identities is not necessarily progressive, as such constructions are often haunted and even shaped by racial practices of the past, perhaps more poignantly and less visibly, because of advocates' insistence that they do not. For in seeking to celebrate their difference and indigeneity under the new South Africa, Coloured advocates have in many ways reinscribed the very racial stratification found under apartheid, as Jon Michael Spencer (2000) has so passionately argued. The Vote for the National Party by Cape Coloureds in 1994 can be read as a powerful performance of a Coloured identity that in its enactment initiated other performative responses with divisive consequences – greater separation between blacks and Coloured groups, more internal tensions between working class and 'elite' Coloureds, and a new anti-affirmative action stance embraced by Coloureds who aligned themselves with the 'victim minority' stance of National Party whites. As Zoë Wicomb laments:

> And the shame of it lies not only in what we have voted against – citizenship within a democratic constitution that ensures the protection of individual rights, the enshrinement of gay and lesbian rights, the abolition of censorship and blasphemy laws – but in the amnesia with regard to the National Party's atrocities in maintaining apartheid. (1998: 99)

In defining themselves as a new people liberated from the historic necessity of selecting a singular racial designation, mixed race advocates in the U.S. might be also accused of a similar historical amnesia for failing to recognize the high political cost of such a stance, not least of which, as Wicomb suggests, similarly includes a missed chance for coalitional alliances with other minoritized groups. And certainly, in 2000, conscious of the impact of racial designations on federal resources, African American, Latino, and Asian American activists feared, with some justification, that the mixed-race designation would dilute the total numbers of their

respective constituencies, and therefore agitated against coloring in more boxes. The strained relations with traditional communities of color put the lie to proclamations of mixed race people as natural bridges, individuals somehow born into and specially gifted in affiliative work. Even more problematically, Coloured and mixed race advocates potentially risk creating by implication and default a new ethnic monolith that consolidates difference, a new tradition of identity politics of the very kind that they suggest that they oppose. In fact by valorizing the percentages of mixedness within an individual – as a character in the play by Lisa Jones, *Combination Skin*, puts it, 'But I'm half French, German, Caribbean, Venezualan, and half 100% Irish' (1991: 223) – mixed race devotees have in fact re-associated and sometimes ludicrously race with blood and biology, implying a homogeneity in monoracial groups that never existed (few black people are unmixed) and been called out by many as using their racial mix for what Carl Degler calls an 'escape hatch' from blackness.

A transnational study of US mixed-race and Coloured comparative racializations through performance in the 'post-race' and post-apartheid periods may get at some of the larger issues surrounding new millennial race and racial formation. Theorizing the specific dynamics of mixed-race representation and advocacy in not only the US and South Africa, particularly at this time in their respective histories, provides unique insight into pivotal global shifts in race politics, social realities, and claims to identity in the new millennium. The new movement in transnational, intraracial and comparative racial projects helps clarify the profound impact of these emergent and wedge movements on contemporary race politics. As Shu-mei Shih argues, racialization is 'inherently comparative' (p. 1350). Here, Shih and we again return to and invoke Fanon because of his particular focus on the relationality of blackness and whiteness. As Shih reiterates, quoting from *Black Skin, White Masks*, 'the black man is comparison'. Comparative racialization, then, relies on a relationality beyond the similarities and differences between two different racial contexts or races; rather, as Shih maintains, it involves *bringing 'submerged or displaced relationalities into view'* (2008: 1349–50).

Significantly, the interdisciplinary lens that we have selected for this examination is performance, which, as Jon McKenzie (2001) argues, is a transformative force for institutional and social change. The dynamics of the performance encounter – the productive interaction between audience and performer that has a potentially transformative impact on both – can function as a critical site to examine the practices, behaviors, cultural codes that produce racial difference and meanings. For it is not simply a matter of how race is done, but how this doing is received and who sanctions its performance. Power, privilege, and agency are critical to the performance encounter, as they are crucial to racial formation. Saidiya Hartman in her important study, *Scenes of Subjection*, uses the phrase 'performing blackness' to facilitate her theorization of 'displays of power, the punitive and theatrical embodiment of racial norms, the discursive reelaboration of blackness and the affirmative deployment and negation of blackness in the focus on redress' (1997: 57). Following Hartman, analyzing performances of race can illuminate divergent enunciations of race and the struggles that produce them.

And so we offer this engagement with performance not as singular theoretical answer to racial analysis, but as a force for recognizing the continually evolving process of racial formation. For race is constantly made and remade over time. Cultivating the field of comparative racialization enables us to understand that this evolution does not happen in vacuum – it brings these global changes into relation. We can observe not only how race has been produced but the consequences of its utility. In addition, such processes of comparative racialization can ironically reveal the provocative irony

that as we supposedly move beyond race we remain ensnared by particular patterns of racialization.

## NOTES

1   In the latest edition of this book, Gould offers a scathing indictment of Richard Hernstein and Charles Murray's *Bell Curve: Intelligence and Class Structure in American Life*.

2   Mark Anthony Neal argues that 'post soul babies' represent that generation of people who have no 'nostalgic allegiance to the past (back in the days of Harlem, or the thirteenth-century motherland, for that matter) but firmly in the grasp of the existential corners of this brave new world' (2002, p. 5).

3   Others who advance similar ideas, though from different disciplinary perspectives, include Anthony Appiah, Naomi Zack, Ellis Cose, Dinesh D'Souza, Paul Gilroy, and Walter Benn Michaels.

4   Many excellent anthologies examine the way national identity and racism were inextricably intwined. See Kaplan and Pease (1993).

5   See the excellent book on whiteness and the construction and naturalization of it and other races by Lopez (2006). As one reviewer – Matthew Frye Jacobson, author of *Roots Too: White Ethnic Revival in Post-Civil Rights America* – puts it, '*White by Law* remains one of the most significant and generative entries in the crowded field of 'whiteness studies'. Ian Haney López has crafted a brilliant study, not merely of how 'race' figures in the juridical logic of U.S. citizenship, but of the ways in which law fully participates in the wholesale manufacture of those naturalized groupings we know as 'races'. A terribly important work.'

6   John Fiske's definition of whiteness is frequently cited. See also David R. Roediger's (2006, 2007) field-defining work on whiteness.

7   Zoë Wicomb writes: 'The Pretoria High Court issued a landmark ruling on Wednesday classifying Chinese South Africans as black, making them eligible for benefits for those who suffered under aparthid. The Chinese Association of South Africa had challenged their exclusion from laws aimed at redressing economic imbalances under white-minority rule, which ended in 1994. The association contended that Chinese citizens continued to be marginalized under the country's black economic empowerment and affirmative action legislation. Both laws benefit the country's black, Indian and mixed-race populations. Patrick Chong, the group's leader, said "Under the apartheid rule we were classified as colored – a term used to describe a mixture

of black and white. After the democratic government came into power, our status was no longer recognized as coloured, so we were in-between"' (1998: A9).

8   See also the excellent foundational collection on the saliency of racial identity edited by S. P. Mohanty, P.M.L. Moya, L. Martín-Alcoff and M. Hames-García (2005).

9   For excellent discussions of race and diasporic identities, see: James, (1963), Hall, (1980) and Hayes (2003).

10   See Michele Elam (2010) for an analysis of the cultural and literary politics of mixed race identification in the U.S.

11   We use the term advisedly and without capitalizations, as many scholars do, to signal a self-conscious shift from the apartheid classification, though still preserving what is for many the continued saliency, if ongoing redefinition, of the racial self-identification.

12   For a history of Census designations of 'mulattos', see Morning (2003) and Perlmann, (2000).

13   See also Goldin (1987).

14   'To be sure, the emergence of a distinct coloured identity is the outcome of a complicated series of events and negatives rather than simply a result of the divide and rule manipulation by the white supremacists state. For over a century, coloniz-ers in South African made consistent efforts to manipulate coloured identity and to engineer a political alliance among coloured and whites as a way of forestalling any alliances between coloured people and other oppressed peoples in SA' (Colleran, p. 210).

15   *A Coloured Place* premiered in 1996 at the Southern Life Playhouse Company Women's Arts Festival at the Playhouse in Durban, with Chantal Snyman and directed by Lueen Conning.Quoted in Malika Ndlovu (Lueen Conning), *A Coloured Place* in *Black South African Women: An Anthology of Plays*, ed. Kathy A. Perkins, (New York: Routledge, 1998). Pp. 13–42.

16   The idea of leftovers of history resonates with Ralph Ellison's narrator in *Invisible Man*, who similarly says black people are left out of history, not agents of and in history.

# REFERENCES

Adhikari, M. (2005) *Not White Enough, Not Black Enough: Racial Identity in the South African Coloured Community*. Athens, OH: Ohio University Press.

Attridge, Derek and Rosemary Jolly (1998) *Writing South Africa: Literature, Apartheid and Democracy,* *1970–1999*. Cambridge: Cambridge University Press.

Berlin, I. (1998) *Many Thousands Gone: The First Two Centuries of Slavery in North America*. Cambridge, MA: Harvard University Press.

Banton, M. (1998) *Racial Theories*. Cambridge: Cambridge University Press.

Boyd, T. (2002) *The New H.N.I.C.: The Death of Civil Rights and the Regin of Hip Hop*. New York: New York University Press.

Crenshaw, K. (1996) *Critical Race Theory: The Key Writings That Formed the Movement*. New York: New Press.

Crouch, S. (1996) 'Race is over', *New York Times*, 26 September: 170.

Dalmage, H.M. (ed.) (2004) *The Politics of Multiracialism*. Albany, NY: State University of New York Press.

Daniel, G.R. (2006) *Race and Multiraciality in Brazil and the United States: Converging Paths?*. University Park, PA: Penn State University Press.

Diamond, E. (1996) 'Introduction', in E. Diamond (ed.), *Performance and Cultural Politics*. New York: Routledge. Pp. 1–14

Du Bois, W.E.B. (1903) 'Of our spiritual strivings', *In The Souls of Black Folk*. New York: N.H. Norton.

Elam, H.J. Jr. and Jackson, K. (eds) (2005) *Black Cultural Traffic: Crossroads in Global Performance and Popular Culture*. Ann Arbor, MI: University of Michigan Press.

Elam, M. (2008) 'Obama's mixology', *in The Root*. Available at: http://www.theroot.com/views/obamas-mixology.

Elam, M. (2010) *The Souls of Mixed Folks*. Stanford, CA: Stanford University Press.

Erasmus, Z. (2001) 'Introduction', *Coloured by History, Shaped by Place: New Perspectives on Coloured Identities in Cape Town*. Cape Town: Kwela Books. Pp. 13–28.

Erkkila, B. (2004) *Mixed Blood and Other Crosses: Rethinking American Literature from the Revolution to the Culture Wars*. Philadelphia, PA: University of Pennsylvania Press.

Fanon, F. (1967) *Black Skins, White Masks*. New York: Grove Press.

Farred, G. (1981) *Midfielder's Moment: Coloured Literature and Culture in Contemporary South Africa*. Boulder, CO: Westview Press.

Fiske, J. (1996) *Media Matters: Race and Gender in U.S. Politics*. Minneapolis, MN: University of Minnesota Press.

France-Presse, A. (2008) 'South Africa: Chinese gain right to benefits for the discriminated', *The New York Times*, 20 June: A9.

Fredrickson, G. (1981) *White Supremacy: A Comparative Study of American and South African History*. Oxford: Oxford University Press.

Fredrickson, G. (2002) *Racism: A Short History*. Princeton, NJ: Princeton University Press.

Goldberg, D.T. (1993) *Racist Culture: Philosophy and the Politics of Meaning*. London: Wiley-Blackwell.

Goldin, I. (1987) *Making Race: The Politics and Economics of Coloured Identity in South Africa*. London: Longman.

Gomez, L.E. (2007) *Manifest Destinies: The Making of the Mexican American Race*. New York: New York University Press.

Gould, S.J. (1992) *The Mismeasure of Man*. New York: W.W. Norton & Compnay, Inc. (1st edn, 1981.)

Gossett, T. (1963) *Race: The History of an Idea in America*. New York: Oxford University Press.

Gresson III, A.D. (1995) *The Recovery of Race in America*. Minneapolis, MN: University of Minnesota Press.

Hall, S. (1996) 'Race, articulation, and societies structured in dominance', Reprinted in A. Houston, M.D. Baker and R.H. Lindeborg (eds) *Black British Cultural Studies: A Reader*. Chicago, IL: Chicago University Press. (1st edn, 1980). Pp. 16–6.

Hansberry, L. (1994) *Les Blancs: The Collected Last Plays*. New York: Vintage. Pp. .37–125.

Hartman, S. (1997) *Scenes of Subjection: Terror, Slavery and Self-Making in Nineteenth Century America*. New York: Oxford University Press.

Hayes, B.E. (2003) *The Practice of Diaspora: Literature, Translation and the Rise of Black Internationalism*. Cambridge: Cambridge University Press.

Herrnstein, R. and Murray, C. (1996) *Bell Curve: Intelligence and Class Structure in American Life*. New York: Free Press.

Hume, D. (1987) 'Of national character', *In Essays Moral Political and Literary*. Indianapolis: Liberty Fund, Inc.

Hurtado, A. (2006) *The Color of Privilege: Three Blasphemies on Race and Feminism*. Ann Arbor, MI: University of Michigan Press.

Ifekwunigwe, J.O. (ed.) (2004) *'Mixed Race' Studies: A Reader*. London: Routledge.

James, C.L.R. (1963) *The Black Jacobins: Touissant L'Ouve'erture and the San Domingo Revolution*. New York: Vintage Press.

Johnson, K. (ed.) (2003) *Mixed Race America and the Law: A Reader*. New York: New York University Press.

Jones, L. (1991) 'Combination Skin', in K. Perkins and R. Uno (eds) (1996), *Contemporary Plays by Women of Color*. New York: Routledge Press.

Kaplan, A. and Pease, D. (eds) (1993) *The Cultures of United States Imperialism*. Durham, NC: Duke University Press.

Levin, M. (2005) *Why Race Matters*. New York: Praeger Publishers.

Lopez, I. (2006) *White By Law*. New York: New York University Press.

Lynn, R. and Vanhanen, T. (2006) *IQ and Global Inequality*. Seattle, WA: Washington Summit Publishers.

Martín-Alcoff, L. (2006) *Visible Identities: Race, Gender and the Self*. New York: Oxford University Press.

McKenzie, J. (2001) *Perform or Else*. London: Routledge.

Mohanty, C.T and Alexander, M.J. (1996) *Feminist Genealogies, Colonial Legacies, Democratic Futures*. New York: Routledge.

Mohanty, C.T. and Russo, A. (eds) (2003) *Feminism Without Borders: Decolonizing Theory, Practicing Solidarity*. Durham, NC: Duke University Press.

Mohanty, C.T., Russo, A. and Torres, L. (eds) (1991) *Third World Women and the Politics of Feminism*. Indianapolis, IN: Indiana University Press.

Mohanty, S.P., Moya, P.M.L., Martín-Alcoff, L. and Hames-García, M. (eds) (2005) *Identity Politics Reconsidered*. New York: Palgrave.

Morning, A. (2003) 'New faces, old faces: Counting the multiracial population past and present', in L.I. Winters and H.L. DeBose (eds) *New Faces in a Changing America: Multiracial Identity in the 21st Century*. Thousand Oaks, CA: Sage. Pp. 41–67.

Mullen, B. (2004) *Afro-Orientalism*. Minneapolis, MN: University of Minnesota Press.

Neal, M.A. (2002) *Post-Soul Babies: Black Popular Culture and the Post-Soul Aesthetic*. New York: Routledge.

Ndlovu, M. (1998) 'A Coloured place', in K. Perkins (ed.), *Black South African Women: An Anthology of Plays*. New York. Pp. 13–42

Omi, M. and Winant, H. (eds) (1994) *Race and Racial Formation*. New York: Routledge.

Perlmann, J. (2000) 'Reflecting the changing face of America: Multiracials, racial classifications and American intermarriage', in W. Sollors (ed.), *Interracialism: Black-White Intermarriage in American History, Literature and Law*. New York: Oxford University Press. Pp. 506–534.

Prashad, V. (2002) *Everybody Was Kung Fu Fighting: Afro-Asian Connections and the Myth of Cultural Purity*. Boston, MA: Beacon Press.

Pratt, M.L. (1992) *Imperial Eyes: Studies in Travel Writing and Transculturation*. New York: Routledge.

Raphael-Hernandez, H. and Steen, S. (ed.) (2006) *AfroAsian Encounters: Culture, History, Politics.* New York: New York University Press.

Reddy, T. (2001) 'The politics of naming; The constitution of Coloured Subjects', in Z. Erasmus (ed.), *Coloured by History, Shaped by Place: New Perspectives on Coloured Identities in Cape Town.* Cape Town: Kwela Books. Pp. 64–79.

Roediger, D.R. (2006) *Working Towards Whiteness.* New York: Basic Books.

Roediger, D.R. (2007) *The Wages of Whiteness.* London: Verso.

Sarich, V. and Miele, F. (2005) *Race and the Reality of Human Differences.* Boulder, CO: Westview Press.

Senna, D. (1998) 'The mulatto millennium', in C. Chiawei O'Hearn (ed.), *Half and Half: Writers Growing Up Biracial and Bicultural.* New York: Pantheon Books. Pp. 12–27.

Shi, S. (2008) 'Comparative racialization: An introduction', *PMLA,* 123 (5): 1347–1362.

Sollors, W. (1995) *Neither Black nor White yet Both: Thematic Explorations of Interracial Literature.* Cambridge, MA: Harvard University Press.

Spencer, J.M. (2000) *The New Colored People: The Mixed Race Movement in America.* New York: New York University Press.

Verges, F. (1996) 'Chains of madness, chains of colonialism: Fanon and freedom', in A. Read (ed.) *The Fact of Blackness: Frantz Fanon and Visual Representation.* Seattle, WA: Bay Press. Pp. 46–75.

Wicomb, Z. (1998) 'Shame and identity: The case of the Coloured in South Africa', in D. Attridge and R. Jolly (eds) *Writing South Africa: Literature, Apartheid and Democracy, 1970–1995.* Cambridge: Cambridge University Press.

Weinbaum, A.E. (2004) *Wayward Reproductions: Genealogies of Race and Nation in Transatlantic Modern Thought.* Durham, NC: Duke University Press.

Williams, K.M. (2006) *Mark One or More: Civil Rights in Multiracial America.* Ann Arbor, MI: University of Michigan Press.

Wu, F.H. (2003) *Yellow: Race in America Beyond Black and White.* New York: Basic Books.

Young, R.J.C. (1995) *Colonial Desire: Hybridity in Theory, Culture and Race.* New York: Routledge.

# 10

# Identity: Culture and Technology

Rolland Munro

What kind of culture incites people to think about each other in terms of identities? This is the question I explore in this chapter. What interests me is why the topic of identity, formerly a focus for academic research, is bursting the banks of theory and burgeoning into daily conversation and chitchat? Transgressing the mainstays of class, gender, age and ethnicity, identity mushrooms into a myriad of everyday matters such as taste, desire, or lifestyle on one hand, and issues of opportunity, success, and expertise on the other. Specifically, I am asking what is it about Euro-American culture that is making people discriminate so finely between different identities; and, moreover, has us doing this from moment to moment?

For this chapter, I define identity in terms of accounts that mark someone as belonging to a category or class of being. Such orderings are two sided. First, there are the many ways in which we are *dressed* by others; the cultural forms and discursive structures that mint the coin of identity. Many of the typifications that circulate here are ordered hierarchically (Derrida, 1982), with terms such as rich, white and male being privileged over others such as poor, black and female (Strathern, 1997). Although such readings of

identity are deemed 'cultural', they also greatly affect the distribution of power. The main point here is that each of us is 'situated' (Goffman, 1964) by other people's readings of who or what we are. For example, Barack Obama being marked 'black' is a matter that precedes the presidential candidate making his African-American roots 'visible' and 'available' (Munro, 1999a).

The ramifications on identity of these typifications are more latent and pervasive than might first appear. Given mud sticks, people work hard to avoid accounts that label them negatively. For example, although attempts to smear her fellow-Democrat back-fired on Hilary Clinton during the 2008 US primaries, Obama still had to take great care to avoid the more denigrated aspects of his ethnicity:

> The Obama camp has sometimes been slow, and even reluctant, to respond, because if he attacks her [Clinton] personally (which the Clinton campaign would like him to do), he's not Barack Obama anymore. Moreover, Obama takes care not to come across as the 'angry black' – a stereotype he does not fit, but that could be imposed upon him by others. (Drew, 2008)

For all the talk of people making their own destiny, identity is thus seldom a matter of choice but lies rather in the hands of others.

It is others, such as colleagues, friends, family, pundits, rivals and bosses, who affirm or deny identities and so 'pass' them into circulation (Garfinkel, 1967).

Second, there is the multiplicity of occasions in which we find ourselves *addressed;* the spin by which 'calls' are issued for this rather than that identity. These calls tend to address each of us like an instruction: black *or* white? Christian *or* Muslim? Hawk *or* dove? One of us *or* The Enemy? Where such calls successfully 'punctualize' identity within the here and now (Munro, 2004), we find ourselves 'enframed' as Heidegger (1978) has it in his rethinking of technology. People are *set-up* to set about making and re-making their different 'worlds'. Inasmuch as certain identities and not others can be understood as being *ordered* and *re-ordered* by these calls, from moment to moment, it is these differences in 'worlds' that are sustained and reproduced to order.

An intensification in these processes of 'ordering and reordering' is masked by the degree to which identities take the form of information in the face of global technologies. Transmitted onwards by unknown or 'absent senders' across a plethora of media, rather than merely created and consumed locally, *readings* of identity can make any response to a 'call to arms' today unpredictable, as witnessed by Hilary Clinton's innuendo on *60 Minutes* that Obama was not a Muslim 'as far as I know'. This was picked up and reiterated by the Republican Sarah Palin in the 2008 presidential campaign. In both cases, however, Obama's restraint – as a black who had already come out on *record* as 'Christian' – let him appear noble and long-suffering. So rather than his 'slowness' making Clinton or McCain look more of the statesman, the majority of voters looked on these smears on his identity as tawdry, exactly the kind of stuff any marginalized group has to put up with.

In reflecting upon the question of formations, which is the subject of this part of the Handbook, I trace the consumption and reproduction of identities through examining, in turn, these dual processes of 'dressing'

and 'addressing'. What I want to unpick with this approach is an uncritical historicizing of 'solid' identities as melting into air; as if Euro-Americans have shifted from being the 'bearer of cultures' instantiating identities that were once authentic and real to become mere reflections, shadowy signifiers of the smoke and mirrors of technology. Against the postmodern idea of self as able to choose among multiple identities, I trace ways in which the diversity of 'calls' upon identity heightens, instead, an *intermittency* in their production. As I now illustrate, far from identities being produced permanently due to the demographics of origin, they frequently appear in 'spurts' (Geertz, 1993) as part of the democratics of choice.

## RELATIONS ON THE MOVE

As witnessed by the sheer number of recent films that take identity as their motif, questions of 'Who we are?' are much in fashion. Last night, for example, I watched back-to-back two new British Broadcasting Corporation (BBC) dramas, *Lark Rise to Candleford* and *The Last Enemy*, both of which capture issues of identity. As their titles indicate, each serial circulates a very different myth. The rural idyll *Lark Rise to Candleford* evokes a golden age in which, once upon a time, communities were all of a piece. As a re-make of Orwell's *1984*, *The Last Enemy* projects Britain as a future dystopia, a police state in which the movements of individuals, and their purchases, are tracked minutely through the intense use of identity cards and massive banks of biometric information. I will use these two very different productions to orient my discussion.

*Lark Rise* takes its name from a rustic hamlet, set in a bucolic landscape in Oxfordshire in the late nineteenth century. Adapted for the BBC from three autobiographical novels by Flora Thompson, and originally staged as a National Theatre production, the first episode was quipped by the UK newspaper the *Guardian* as an 'extended Hovis advert', picking up on the bread-makers who advertise their wholemeal loaf as if it was still baked in idyllic rustic settings. As scripted by Bill Gallagher, the inhabitants are portrayed as living in tumbledown cottages that face each other, with all sharing the work on the land and all joining in on the weekly festivities. As a consequence, everyone on the screen projects what were once taken to be 'real identities': solid, three-dimensional depths of character that everyone else in the hamlet is familiar with. Each knows their own strengths and the other's weaknesses. So far, so good.

These down-to-earth relations contrast sharply with the ambitions and pretensions of the rising bourgeoisie in nearby Candleford. As the series progresses, it becomes clear people in the nearby market town are not always what they seem. Candleford folk can be secretive about their past; hiding from the gaze of others either their histories, or kin who have fallen by the wayside. This is as true for the (quiet and deserving) postwoman, Mrs Macey, whose husband is in prison for having killed a man, as it is for the owners of the draper's shop, the two (obnoxiously nosey) Pratt sisters, Ruby and Pearl, who have changed their names in order to disown their reprobate father. Even the (upright and respectable) postmistress, Dorcas Lane, harbours a secret in that she still loves her friend and childhood sweetheart, the local squire.

Time itself forms part of this contrast. In Candleford prosperity is linked to progress. Time's arrow is moving forward in ways that has people looking onwards and upwards. In the small market town, people have a future. Like the novelist herself, also the daughter of a stonemason, Laura, the daughter of a Lark Rise family, has moved to Candleford to take up employment in the Post Office. The quiet hero of the piece, often using her eyes more than her mouth, she is bright and educated. And unlike her father, Robert Timmins, a gifted stonemason, who is as set in his ways as he is in his liberal opinions, Laura is looking to better herself. So it is no surprise that the amiable but illiterate Alf, her childhood friend in Lark Rise, is all but forgotten as she falls in with an upwardly mobile under-gamekeeper, Philip. And no surprise either to the weekly audience of almost seven million that, when walking out with Philip, she ducks and hides from her father on one of his rare visits to Candleford.

The mundane goings-on in Lark Rise, by contrast to Candleford, portray time as circular. In the hamlet people fall in and out of the workhouse, as they fall in and out of bad times. Occasionally someone goes off to sea, or a debtor or poacher (anachronistically) is taken off to prison. But the dominant motif is that of *return*. Just as the seasons come and go, so the inhabitants of Lark Rise are in and out of each other's houses. This is how they 'occupy' each other; and fill up each other's lives. As such, the idea of his daughter disowning him in the street – of being absent when present – is beyond Robert Timmins's comprehension. Even when the truth of this disjunction is pointed out to him, the stonemason cannot imagine such a possibility: 'Laura's not like that'. And so her new identity remains, for the moment, hidden from him.

This historicising of identity as made transient by town life masks other issues, such as the way lives become prospective as much as retrospective. For the moment, it is worth noting that there seems little use for a *concept* such as identities within a place like Lark Rise. As depicted in films such as *The Bridges of Madison County* (starring Clint Eastwood and Meryl Streep), the issue of who people are, and what they are likely to do, is so established in certain rural areas, and so well understood between inhabitants, that the term identity seems better reserved for the work of understanding strangers (Bauman, 1995). So 'figuring' people out, say, in terms of the place they come from, the class they inhabit, or the work they do, appears more relevant to life in the city where people are on the make and hence socially mobile in respect of their relations and relationships (Simmel, 1971). Indeed, in prospering Candleford, it is not only histories that can be hidden. In that people can also make themselves appear and disappear when they will, as just noted in the case of Laura, an intermittency in the *performance* of identity is now possible.

## CULTURE AND 'ATTACHMENT'

Although frequently deployed to distinguish relations among the living, culture is yet strewn with paths and routes from those 'who have gone before'. As suggested by anthropology's most potent pieces of writing, cultural performances thus connect the quick to the dead. For example, drawing on Schmitz's (1963) ethnography of Wantoat, Strathern tells how the 'first people' are made present:

> Performers literally magnify themselves. They wear barkcloth and bamboo extensions ... carried by being tied onto the body of the dancer ... In some cases, such figures triple the dancer's height ... the whole edifice gives the appearance of a tree with a man at its base. (1991: 63)

In their dressing this way, Strathern's point is that the performers create a 'doubling' of parts. The audience moves, back and forth, from a focus on the 'dancer' at the base of the bamboo extensions to seeing the figure of 'towering trees'.

As I have elaborated elsewhere Strathern is making a crucial turn here on the matter of 'adding' parts (Munro, 1996). Her play on the idea of *attachment* suggests both the adding on of a material prosthetic, like that of a wooden leg, and the elicitation of a dramatic 'part' in which relations of 'belonging' are also exchanged. In the movement of the dancers, the initiates ambulate between the frisson of the dance, one moment, and the birth of mankind, the next. Sitting uncomfortably close to the heat of a huge fire, they move back and forth between the here and now and the birth of their ancestors. Knowing the creation story, in which huge lengths of bamboo are filled with the blood of an old man after a boy wounds him as a bird, they all await the explosion that will burst afresh the first man and woman from the towering bamboo.

What I want to stress here is the *motility* of relations (Munro, 1996). In my interpretation we are always in *extension*, always in relations that demand an adding on of 'parts'. And extension is all that we are ever 'in', as we move *across* from one set of relations being performed to another. For example, in the story of *Lark Rise* which I have been re-telling, the prosthetics of Laura's 'attachment' to her new beau, Philip, are made all too vibrantly 'visible' by her walking out arm in arm with him. This adding on of parts, in both senses, makes manifest her involvement with someone, albeit this engagement is unbeknown to her father. The surprise of seeing Robert in Candleford thus not only has her hiding her new engagement from him; what she masks is also a new 'detachment' from her father. She feels the parental call, but in absenting herself from her father's presence, she hopes to avoid having to make herself 'available' to him on this occasion.

The nub of identity, ... is thus an ability to alter 'parts', in both senses. It is more than a putative capacity to move ... across social spaces, altering roles as we go. One minute, at work, the dutiful employee or whiz kid, the next moment, at home, the loving daughter or caring spouse. Yes, stabilities in the presentation of self are discernible (Goffman, 1971), but this should not be confused merely with the taking up and casting off of 'roles'. ('Bonds' also sediment over time creating vessels usefully called relationships, like that of father and daughter, or employer and worker. As that which 'ships' and sustains relations, relation-ships help privilege and reproduce specific modes of commerce and exchange as much as each helps ensure certain forms of relations are created and nurtured over others.)

What abstractions such as roles omit are the conditions that are made possible by these displays of motility. For instance, the materials of world-making that help establish some connections over others includes the very materials for that particular relationship we address as 'self'. What is so beguiling about modern notions of self is that the myth of choice perpetuates a misleading idea that self travels first 'outwards' into a 'dyadic' relationship, like that of father and daughter. This overlooks the intricacies of kith and kin. So that when in turn this involvement is over, each sees themselves as returning inwards, if momentarily, to their 'core' self. Once this re-turn is sufficiently *routed* in its own right to take on the mantle of choice, the phenomenology of securing a safe home-coming to self becomes familiar and predicates an introversion of 'self accounting to the self, for the self' ( Roberts, 1991). All this privileges self-surveillance *as* a form of being at home (Latimer and Munro, 2009), with the rider that such detachment can also lead self to treat the other part of the dyad *as* Other.

In such ways Laura's refusal to recognize her father in the street is already having its effects. Making herself 'invisible' looks temporary; a momentary disconnection from Robert, as no doubt Laura herself thinks. However, when father and daughter quarrel later over her choice of Philip as beau, she reveals to the stonemason that Robert's identity is that of a man 'who walks down the street as if he owned one half and was about to buy the other'. A most unkind account in which to dress someone as moneyless as her father, especially since Robert's stand against private property often gets him into trouble. A nice jibe, all the same, in respect of how accounts can both hit the mark and yet be so profoundly wrong! For, although Laura's father takes pride in the idea that he cannot be bought, his warrant to this identity is based on the fact that he, unlike others, speaks his mind. So much so that even the local squire envies Robert his freedom with opinions, explaining that he feels too bound by his position to be so free himself.

## TECHNOLOGY AND IDENTITY

As noted matters stretching well beyond the environs of the town are affecting those living in Candleford. Which brings me to the vexed matter of identity seemingly being 'decided' by what Law (1986) and Latour (1987) have called *centres of calculation*. Fashion, for example, is dictated in the late nineteenth century by Paris in the form of the patterns and silks imported by the nosey sisters in the draper's shop, Pearl and Ruby. So, too, the post office, on which the sisters' business depends, is run by Miss Lane in accordance with regulations devised by officials in far-off London. This is no mere convention. All those joining the Post Office are bound to honour the regulations by virtue of swearing a solemn oath.

The villain of the 'social drama' (Turner, 1986) that disturbs the rural peace in *Lark Rise* arrives in the form of a new technology (Turner, 1986). The first part of the nineteenth century in England has seen major postal reforms, which add up to the institution of sending letters being thoroughly absorbed culturally. For example, the invention of stamps permits pre-payment; and the introduction of postmarks enables delays to be monitored; whereas the business of sending telegrams is entirely novel. So when Thomas, the postman, sets off from Candleford to Lark Rise with its first ever telegram, he discovers its intended recipient, Queenie, cannot pay the extra cost for delivery – the extra cost being due to the hamlet lying outside the statutory mileage limit. Thus the information it contains remains sealed up, the news that her brother is gravely ill delayed until the angry inhabitants of Lark Rise gather together enough money for Queenie to purchase this knowledge.

In breaking a rule 'in a public setting' (Turner, 1986: 39), the finicky postman thus finds himself caught between different *calls* on his identity. To pass as a 'good' person in the eyes of all those living at Lark Rise, Thomas is being called on to prioritize the needs of the community he serves and overlook the negligible excess in distance. As a 'trustworthy' employee of Candleford Post Office, however, he is bound to be scrupulous in exacting the charge that is due. The tension that arises in this episode is thus a classic illustration of Durkheim's argument that changes to the *moral order* lag behind the structural changes being wrought by the division of labour. Identity has come to mean not only the different 'cultures' people stand for; as a consequence of an on-going division of labour, identity is also a matter of the different 'technologies' that people come to represent.

As Thomas cannot accommodate both of these very different 'calls' at the one and same time, readings of his identity are about to be *punctualized* (Munro, 2004). While familiar to us all, this kind of dilemma is sometimes squared, in theory, by recourse to distinctions between 'social' and 'personal' identities. Indeed, Thomas may well be trying to square things for himself by arguing that, as the 'representative' of a major public institution, he has no alternative but to uphold the regulations to the letter. So that in his own eyes, his 'attachment' to the Post Office need cause only a momentary disconnection from his continued existence as a human being. It is unlikely, however, that such theoretical niceties wash with the outraged villagers. In choosing to protect the probity of the Post Office, and ignore the will of their community, it is inevitable that Thomas loses 'face' in the eyes of those living in Lark Rise (Goffman, 1955).

Indeed, the consequences of this infraction by Thomas go well beyond him (Goffman, 1963). On the one side are those in Lark Rise, who feel the injustice perpetrated on them by over-zealous officials. On the other is the whole township of Candleford, branded by Queenie's loyal neighbours as 'having got above and beyond themselves'. As Turner suggests:

> Conflicts between individuals, sections, and factions follow the original breach, revealing hidden clashes of character, interest, and ambition. These mount towards crisis of the group's unity and continuity unless rapidly sealed off by redressive public action, consensually taken by the group's leaders, elders and guardians. (1986: 39)

Fortunately the ever-astute Miss Lane, as postmistress, can mediate between these warring sides by translating the regulations for herself. So when the next telegram arrives, before the first is delivered, to announce the death of Queenie's brother, she argues that no regulation can hold up such serious news and sets out herself to deliver the later telegram without charge.

In resolving, at least for the moment, these conflicting moral orders, Miss Lane's prompt action prevents open warfare from breaking out between Lark Rise and 'hoity-toity' Candleford. But further intervention is necessary to mollify those in the hamlet and so, in line with Turner's (1986) point that redressive action is often ritualized, the actual distance between the two places is solemnly measured with virtually everyone in attendance. Which result bodes badly for Lark Rise until Miss Lane makes another interpretation of the regulations, ruling that the distance measured should not be by the main road but by the most direct route; a matter of yards as it happens but just enough to place Lark Rise within the circuit of Candleford. The irony here is delicious; as clearly, for all other territorial purposes, no-one in Lark Rise would willingly admit to such an identity!

Things come to a head for Thomas nonetheless, when Miss Lane's reading of Post Office regulations clashes with their more narrow interpretation by a new inspector based in Oxford. Local discretion has its limits, as those inside Candleford are about to find out. When the new inspector exercises his higher authority over the matter of Sunday collections, Thomas is hoisted on his own petard. This is not a 'call' on which he can enjoy any role distance (Goffman, 1971). As a devout Christian, the postman, who previously performed himself as such an ardent follower of rules, is suddenly faced with a new dilemma over identity. Should he conform to the regulations, as his oath demands, and collect the post on Sunday? Or should he follow his conscience and lose his position?

## ADDRESSING IDENTITIES

The concept of information technologies creating 'centres of calculation' in which one world vision is privileged over another brings me next to the serendipity of the costume drama *Lark Rise* being scheduled on Sunday evening immediately ahead of a futuristic thriller, *The Last Enemy*. As a cautionary tale about a surveillance-led society, this remake of *1984* is about to send a 'call' to viewers to think more seriously about their increasing reliance on technology. Framings of time are thus reversed. From quietly enjoying customs and rituals in which people are 'dressed' in funny clothes, albeit with hat and gown rather than barkcloth and bamboo, Euro-American viewers are suddenly being 'addressed' by the politics of the near future.

The synopsis of this second BBC television series offers its hero, Stephen Ezard, a very different set-up to George Orwell's classic:

Stephen Ezard is a brilliant but reclusive mathematician with obsessive-compulsive disorder who lives in peace and seclusion somewhere in China to escape the rush and disorder of today's society. When he returns to Britain in order to bury his estranged brother, killed in a mysterious explosion in the Middle East, it is to find that it is an ID-demanding, card-swiping, body-searching nation where surveillance is omnipresent.

Strict identity with *1984* is thus incidental. Yes, the main actor Benedict Cumberbatch brings verve and originality to Stephen, the Winston Smith character (Gill, 2008), but more telling are the differences in substance and plot.

To create its Orwellian nightmare, *The Last Enemy* extrapolates current developments in information technologies. So the familiar faces of surveillance – identity cards, CCTV cameras, unmanned satellites, gigantic databases – are brought together to form the 'Total Information Awareness' (TIA) system. Although intended to be the real star of the show, TIA lacks however the impact of the *telescreens* of its antecedent, 'Big Brother is watching you'. Instead the all-pervasive nature of TIA is simulated merely by viewers accessing all manner of information through the eyes of those authorized to use the system. Even less successfully, the opening and closing sequences are made as if we, the audience enter or leave *the* system for each episode.

As in *1984*, what are highlighted are the perils immanent in such technologies. At least for those who have access to it, TIA becomes the solution to everything that is going on. For surprisingly, given poor UK experience in the government commissioning of large IT systems, TIA works and so those who use it rely on TIA absolutely. Indeed, in the absence of any sense of community, discussed below, the technology (which received grumblings on the web over its lack of authenticity) is the only thing that binds everyone together. As the 'centre of calculation', TIA turns out to be the only constant to which people in power can 'attach'.

## BLANK FIGURES

From early on in *The Last Enemy* it is clear that Stephen Ezard, the unlikely hero, has few attachments outside his mathematics and has returned home from China simply, and only, to bury his estranged brother. As it happens, none of the other characters has any affiliation inside this security-transformed Britain either. Yes, his brother Michael is incredibly popular, as witnessed by the sheer number that turn up for his funeral, but these links all stem from a knack of making instant friends in his work abroad. And one has to ask here why his wife, Yasim, is so immediately, and inescapably, drawn to Stephen, the 'accidental man', who appears to have nothing to offer beyond what looks like a boyish crush? What is it about Michael that makes intimacy with him so impossible for his wife and his brother? Other than they serve to form the three corners of the time-honoured love triangle, each appears to have no British connections and no lasting commitments.

So the fast-moving plot follows the movements of these 'blank' figures as they transfigure themselves through a series of different identities (Lee and Hetherington, 2000).

Like the figure of the joker, Stephen Ezard starts out as a political 'innocent', a naïve and reclusive mathematician (Serres, 2007). But in chasing his brother's wife, Stephen finds himself, unexpectedly, fronting the government's campaign to persuade the public of the merits of their totalitarian approach to information. So too, like Harry Lime in Graham Greene's *Third Man,* his brother turns out not to be dead. Having evaded the explosion intended for him, the question arises whether Michael is another joker in the pack, involved as he is in a much more mysterious mission than being a UN aid-worker might suggest? Similarly, Michael's wife is an unknown quantity. We first meet Yasim as a doctor looking after an unknown and dying Arab girl, but who is she really? Who does she love? What is she after? And everywhere and nowhere at once is the cipher known simply as 'Russell'. Played effortlessly by Robert Carlyle, Russell morphs from being a renegade MI5 officer to being the 'father' of the dying Arab girl and onwards, in the end, to appearing as the 'sweeper' who cleans up on behalf of the government.

This all-pervading occlusion over identity gives zip to an atmosphere in which any one character might join up with any other. *At any time.* Unlike slow-moving dramas like *Lark Rise,* there is no settled 'perspective' within which identity can take shape. As the identities of the actors alter, so do the 'worlds' each is enacting change:

> Stephen Ezard is an awkward, accidental hero, but he is also running around handling guns, coming across bodies, escaping bullets and policemen, living underground, being tortured, being driven around in the boot of a car and having a passionate sexual affair with his brother's widow. (Kinnes, 2008)

Picking up on the pace and energy of the award-winning US series 24, the quasi real-time format thus gives 'motility' to identity as well as to the action. Gone is the 'solidity' of *Lark Rise* characters like the postmistress Dorcas Lane and the stonemason Robert Timmins. In their place, we are watching

people who might turn out to be *anyone.* Not anyone, that is, in terms of questions about who people really are. That is not the issue. The more pressing question, from the point of view of each of the main characters, is 'Who are you to me?' Might you, in fact, be working for 'the other side'?

## MAKING ALLIES

Enter the usual suspects: the spooks, government ministers, bent businessmen and mad scientists. In various permutations these all combine forces to create a totalitarian state, the kind of dystopia made familiar to us by Hollywood in a long line of futuristic thrillers. And just as those watching television an hour before have been treated to a division in identities between the communities of Lark Rise and Candleford, so now there is a great moral divide in *The Last Enemy.* On the one side, as described above, are the rag-bag of jokers who find themselves being tracked by the surveillance devices. On 'other side' are the thinking forces of bureaucracy and progress.

Played with utter conviction, the spooks and elected politicians represent the 'networks' of power. Rather than forge relationships among their own groups, these make *alliances,* which stretch from the government working hand in hand with senior security figures to the politicians themselves being in bed with enterprises able to deliver the necessary information technology. This last includes, for instance, two shameless entrepreneurs to whom delivery of the TIA system has been 'outsourced' on the basis of their willingness to do the politicians' bidding and use any means to deliver the product.

These alliances last for at least as long as anyone's strategies and goals align. For at the core of this making and unmaking of alliances is a complete absence of loyalties. What matters within networks are no longer matters of belonging, the backward-looking stuff of history, but the future-oriented realpolitik of working towards common goals.

And this is precisely how one of the no-hopers and jokers happens to get involved. Being 'visible' for his path-breaking research, Stephen Ezard is also about to be made 'available' to help. Already 'dressed' as *the* expert on the mathematics underwriting super-fast computing, he is now being 'addressed' as having the expertise, and cachet, to *re-present* the system to Parliament. And in being so 'called', Stephen is expected to make the system's security enhancements 'visible' to the general public; enhancements that the system, in turn, is about to make 'available' to those who think total surveillance is the best way of running the country.

Key to the forging of these exotic alliances, as they shift from moment to moment, is the enigmatic Barbara Turney, whose ambiguous role at the centre of government holds the dark secret at the heart of the story, the involvement of a large pharmaceutical company engaged in a 'blood' project. As one critic reports a conversation with Gub Neal, the producer of *The Last Enemy,* on a unit bus during filming:

> Identity cards will work up to a point, but they will get lost or forged. The next step up is an intravenous tag, which people carry around from birth, and which can't be removed unless we take off a limb. (Kinnes, 2008)

This is the dream of an information society, the ability to implant a unique marker, a rigid designator, in the body and so stabilize the possibilities of machine-recognition. This particular frightening scenario has already happened. Unknown to Michael and his wife Yasim, the blood they were using in their UN aid programme had rigid designators implanted in it in order to make each person's identity unique. But the experiment has gone badly wrong and this is what has led to Yasim's patients dying as if struck down by a mysterious virus.

It is just this disaster that has led the spooks to come together with one of the rising stars of the government. This junior minister is a sort of Blair-babe who says all the right things about providing people with the right amount of security. And just as dangerously, she carries a naïve belief in the idea that the end justifies the means. Fortunately the series ends before the next logical progression takes place. As the producer of the series continues:

> Or, even better, there's a pathogen that attaches itself to your DNA. What if you can then introduce an ID tag that has a corrective effect on individuals, or that reacts in different ways depending on your ethnicity? The possibilities are endless. (Kinnes, 2008)

But perhaps not altogether unlikely when the buying of various types of expertise includes biochemists, whose 'visibility' as experts is also making themselves 'available' to such projects in the name of science and research?

## RIGID DESIGNATORS

That the security of a society is essentially about information is the main trope explored in *The Last Enemy.* As in *Gattaca,* as in much else of this particular film genre, the social trope of 'passing' has itself been passed over to machines. Machines are depicted as having taken over the membership work of affirming identity (Garfinkel, 1967; Goffman, 1971) with fingerprint scans used to grant access to buildings and iris scans for more secure rooms. However, on the back of an estimated five million CCTV cameras in the UK, what is being monitored most intensively is the *circulation* of people.

Critically, for all its focus on total surveillance, *The Last Enemy* eschews the notion of 'thought control', Orwell's major trope. Most surveillance in *The Last Enemy* takes place instead over movement on the street, not as in *1984* in the home. Every journey outside, whether by car or by foot, is being recorded and ready for instant replay. What those keeping watch are after is a moment-to-moment record of where everyone *is* – the concatenation of calculative devices making each person's physical location 'visible' and 'available' to the security forces in real time. This is not to say there are not also cameras hidden inside people's homes; but this remains an optional extra, something to be used as and when needed. Contrast this reliance on total information with another futuristic thriller *Minority Report*, the Philip K. Dick story in which a psychic technology is used to arrest and convict killers before they commit murder.

*The Last Enemy* explores a more behaviourist position in social science by sticking to what can be done with information that is already available. Eschewing the fantasy of state power being based on its knowledge of our inner thoughts, the focus is instead on the ability to work out who, and what, people 'are' through the data banks that store the details of every individual's purchases, down to the minutiae of each single item. On analogy with a forensic identification of criminals with their *modus operandi*, what 'preferences' these reveal about people can be collated for every individual resident. All that needs to be added in order to totalise control is for the state to make the ID card, with its unique identifiers, mandatory to any purchase. With the added refinement of it being made illegal to buy goods without a card, all possible points of sale are then covered.

So why bother to control people's thoughts when you already control their biomass? This is the key question addressed by the drama *The Last Enemy*. And the veracity of this proposition is what Stephen Ezard is slowly to experience. For as soon as he is deemed no longer useful to the TIA project, Stephen's ID card is cancelled. At which point he can no longer travel or eat. Any attempt to enter the transport system, or buy food, and there is a SWAT team of security police all too ready to jump on him. In this version of Britain in the near future, the person known as Stephen Ezard has suddenly been denied identity. Or at least the rigid designator (Kripke, 1980) that collates all information into his 'identity' has now been inverted in ways that denies him any existence.

## INFORMATION AND IDENTITY

Whereas costume dramas such as *Pride and Prejudice* and *Lark Rise* tend to attract older audiences, conspiracy thrillers such as *The Bourne Identity* and *The Enemy of the State* are typically aimed at the young. And rather than play with identities generally, wherein the question of 'Who we are?' is answered in terms of universals, such as class, ethnicity, age and gender, the action typically takes place along its more individuated correlate. So far from working with ideas of 'otherness' more generally, with all their problems of inclusion and exclusion, the main actors in *The Last Enemy* seem endlessly absorbed instead with working out for themselves the pressing question: 'Are you Other to me?'

The perversities of this perspective are multiple. This is not simply because the identity work made familiar to the Sunday night audience by *Lark Rise,* with all its emphasis on loyalty and local ties, has disappeared from the screen. What is fascinating is that those in control in *The Last Enemy*, those on the receiving end of information, always want more! A fetish for information that is easily justified and circulated as 'a need to know', as witnessed in the following text by a top spook in Ian Rankin's early spy thriller *Watchman*:

> We must know everything, or else how can we protect you? If we don't know who your enemies are, we can't hope to protect you against them. Bear that in mind. (Rankin, 2003/1988: 102)

Yet far from elaborating the familiar theme that knowledge is power, *The Last Enemy* ultimately proves to be an exercise in 'occlusion'. It is set in a world in which no one, including government ministers, really knows anything. Despite knowledge being everywhere, on a scale and precision undreamed of before, the vital links are always missing.

Elsewhere I have suggested how the split in accounts between *records* and *readings* is endemic to all forms of inscription (Munro, 1999b). This split helps manufacture a displacement in interaction, which in turn creates a fissure within interpretation into which the uncertainty of other possibilities can creep. The felt lack in information sets up a scenario of 'endless deferral' (Munro, 2005) in which there is always more to know. However, many bodies the security forces in *The Last Enemy* have already taken out, their bosses find they do not want to kill Stephen or his brother's wife – at least until they can be sure they know what these others know. In other words the whole path of totalising information leads nowhere. In assuming that either Stephen or Michael's wife must be working for someone, the rationally paranoid can never get the final information they assume they need. Far from 'filling out' identity, information creates and even magnifies doubt.

It is these unintended consequences of the links forever being forged between knowledge and security that bring us close to the Orwellian nightmare. Perversely, the vast information collected on 'individuals' in *The Last Enemy* has the effect of *occluding* the very relations and bonds that people, in their occasional and everyday interaction, help to form. As such, the absence of everyday conduct on screen represents not so much the death of those communities that have 'gone before' as it notates how people can become so 'individuated' that their ambit no longer stretches beyond bare existence. This brings me to consider a difficult truth: that 'attachment' to information, both as a society and as an individual, can itself be destructive to any sense of belonging.

## RECAPITULATION

My concern in this chapter has been to show how two myths of identity link more generally to understandings of culture and technology. First, the location of culture within the habitus of a certain time and place gives emphasis to persons as 'bearers of culture', especially insofar as their everyday interaction helps keep each other collectively in line. Yet stories of collectivities as formed through social sanctions (Douglas, 1966; Garfinkel, 1967) also suggest forms of belonging that make persons out to be little more than victims of sedimented customs, rituals that 'root' them within the past. Second, the locution of individuals as 'mastering' technology (Heidegger, 1978; Munro, 2004b) creates an equally false impression of relations being picked up and dropped at will. The discourses that circulate among Euro-Americans today deny the many ways that self is 'routed' towards the future and mask the 'emplacement' that is a consequence of the systems that engross us, such as information, money and cars (Latimer and Munro, 2006).

Informed by these theoretical debates on identity, I have chosen to illustrate the myths that accompany them by way of two television dramas that happened to appear back to back on the BBC at the time of writing. The first of these, *Lark Rise to Candleford*, recycles popular ideas about identity, especially those that link it with themes of belonging. As a costume drama, the visuals highlight for example the different ways in which the characters are *dressed* to represent their different territories and belongings. And literally so. For those in the hamlet Lark Rise are clad in rustic attire, symbolic of the hold time has on them in terms of the seasons, whereas those in Candleford tend to be dressed to impress, as suits those for whom progress 'calls'. Similarly, while the ways of those in Lark Rise do not lack character, their repertoires and habits for the most part are portrayed as stuck in the past, whereas those in Candleford by contrast find themselves looking forwards into the future.

For all this there is still a subtlety about what is happening to identity in these dramas that goes beyond myth and legend. For example, as information technologies emerge in ways that start to unpick the 'solidity' of day-to-day relations in rural England in the latter part of the nineteenth century, their effects can be seen to be already working the trope of identity by way of the detour of persons exercising what they (mis)take to be their 'individual' choice. Yes, Paris may be dictating what to wear more generally, but Adeline, the squire's wife in *Lark Rise,* is no simple slave to fashion as this presents itself in Candleford. In picking which particular kind of 'dress' suits her in Ruby and Pearl's shop, she continues to exercise her discretion over what *she* takes to be good taste. Similarly, in picking which way to go over the institutional rules about the collection of Sunday post, Thomas is exercising discretion over how *he* finds himself addressed by God's will.

The second drama, *The Last Enemy*, offers a different take, conjuring up a 'system' that is so totalitarian that the figure of 'self' comes to stand in direct opposition – as the human face of humanism. Yet with each trope, self and system, taking up what the other leaves out, I hope to have shown how the cacophony of 'calls' by which each of us are *addresse*d today reflects the mesh of dualisms, such as that of self and system, through which identities are both distributed and designated. For example, even the unwitting hero of the piece, the isolate Stephen Ezard, is beset by 'calls' upon him: to do his duty by burying his estranged brother and look after his brother's widow; to appear as the expert in mathematical computing and sell TIA to the public and parliament; to prove his manhood by jumping into bed with the Blair-babe junior minister; and to risk his life tracking down the biological pathogens that have been introduced into the blood programmes run by UN Aids charities.

Striking too is the way in which Stephen has returned to a world in which there is a near absence of everyday relations. An unexpected consequence of this information society' is a radical individuation, which results in those mob-like gatherings that Bauman (2001) has named 'peg communities'. Consequently, these serial events aside, there is no longer any such thing as community; and hence no prospect of belonging to anything other than the networks along which information can be exchanged. So life is portrayed in *The Last Enemy* as a world emptied out of belonging. Society, as in Nancy's (1990) analysis, has become the 'inoperative community'. Decent, if politically naïve members, in their conspicuous absence, *are* 'the disappeared'. Communities have simply 'gone'. And 'disappeared' not through diabolical acts, as in the case of the Argentine (see Bell, 2008), but more through processes of disciplining and management that have come to be known to scholars as 'governmentality' (Foucault, 1991).

We are left to presume that the British are leading a life *as* individuals, with no identity other than that provided by work and shopping. So as befits a futuristic thriller, the dramatic prospect in *The Last Enemy* is about the *loss* of identity in a security-conscious state. As I have tried to illustrate, the issue of identity here is never just one of a shift from hegemony to multiplicity, the myth that you can now be whoever you like. It is also a matter of understanding first *how* 'calls' to be this person (rather than that person) are issued. The moral orders flow from the information needs of 'the system' and thus focus on the imperatives of 'transparency' and of selves having nothing to hide, themes that ultimately – however much that rhetoric seduces initially – sit badly with the democratics of choice. Yes resistance, in the form of whatever it takes to preserve your individuality, is to be expected, even desired, but it is important to see that resistance often manifests itself in ways that merely reincarnate security agendas. In a state heading towards totalitarian forms of control, the questions that beset its citizens are not simply about whether one gives up in order to fit in, or fights for freedoms previously taken for granted as rights. It is about understanding just how difficult it is to avoid becoming complicit, one way or another with the prevailing regimes.

Nothing of this analysis is to suggest that there is any truth to the idea that we are 'free' to choose. Or that we can really be 'who we wanna be' in ways that let us take charge of our own destiny. As I have illustrated, what helps perpetuate these illusions of democracy and freedom, oddly enough, is a preference displayed by film and television producers for exploring 'total' systems of surveillance. Counter-pointing these all-enveloping regimes with the lone hero, ready to overcome all odds, elides other forms of assemblage, such as the power of what Mann (2002) has called sousveillance. As for instance Dennis (2008) picks up in the case of the 'dog-shit' girl, where the combination of hand-held cameras from mobile phone technology has combined with bloggers on the World Wide Web to provide 'virtual communities' that exercise sanctions every bit as pervasive and devastating as those associated with more 'traditional' locations.

## CONCLUSION

The aim in this chapter has been to open up the topic of identity by comparing two key myths that circulate among Euro-Americans. The first of these refers to what I call the *demographics of origin,* the idea that forms of culture are formatively induced from people dwelling in a particular place or locale. Here social dramas are typically played out in terms of the contesting loyalties between different territorial groups ( Rosaldo, 1980; Whyte, 1949). The second myth refers to what I call the *democratics of choice.* Here the major trope is the way in which technology has been made so widely available as to facilitate a centred image of self as moving at will in and out of a range of 'multiple identities' (Giddens, 1991; Schutz, 1972).

In taking up these themes I have sought to expose how each of these perspectives, culture and technology, obscures how identities are formulated and acted upon within the everyday exercise of power. Yes, 'divisions' such as class, gender, age and ethnicity contribute to how each of us is *dressed*; they play their part in the formation of mundane territories and locales. Yet in creating

typifications and negative identities, these major distinctions remain emblematic of the more fine-grained resources by which powers of inclusion and exclusion are made pervasive and mundane in all walks of life. So, too, the asymmetries that radiate from western technologies tend to be glossed over by a technocratic ideology that invariably dematerializes culture. The difficulty then is not simply that culture and technology are treated as if they existed separately in their own domains. The issue is that the myriad of cultural divisions that are fabricated, such as that between 'self' on the one hand and 'system' on the other, are re-enacted as if there is an on-going battle between technology and culture, with the former equated with the future and the latter mistaken for the past (Strathern, 1993).

In linking these themes of identity and power, I have tried more generally to trace how we (and, yes, this *is* the problematic term) have come to be *addressed* today. Calls, I suggest, are issued, one way or another, in terms of a specific mode of being in the world (see also Munro, 2001). Specific modes that are always *partial*, in both senses of the word, in terms of the connections they ask us to make: say *as* 'individuals', the 'self-starters' who are to find their own destiny. Or *as* 'team players', colleagues who know how to 'pull together' in a crisis. Or *as* 'citizens', persons who are 'responsiblized' in terms of duties towards their communities. Or *as* 'human beings', activists who come to the aid of those 'brothers or sisters' being denied their human rights. Or even *as* 'best customers', consumers whose 'loyalty' has earned a few bonus points on this or that credit card. And of course much, much more.

The result is an *intermittency* in the circulation of identities; the way in which we seem seamlessly to shift from being hard-hearted one minute to being kind the next, or say the moment of 'classlessness' in which a wealthy male entrepreneur finds it convenient to pass himself off as an 'ordinary Joe' (Pascale, 2008). These moments, in which the making of oneself 'visible' *as* this (rather than that), not only takes place in 'spurts' (Geertz, 1993). As importantly, they are often to be found standing in advance of 'calls' for this (or that) to be made 'visible' as well as 'available' (Munro, 1999a). So that, for example, to appear as an individual today, each of us has to be seen to exercise 'our' choice. To appear, say, as a citizen, each of us has to make visible how we are carrying out 'our' duties. To be modern and up-to-date each of us has to display 'our' belongings, the goods ( Douglas and Isherwood, 1980) we have purchased with 'our' own money. To be expert, each has to show how she or he has mastered 'our' technologies and is in control of 'our' resources. And so on.

Here I want to stress that it also matters *when* identities are 'read' as answered. To be *addressed* usually requires more than being *dressed* for the 'part' each is being called upon to play. It also requires self to be standing in advance, ready to answer a 'call' for this or that identity. This is because the power of affirmation, presence and absence, always lies in the hands of others. Here is the sticking point at which power gains purchase. And from which identity always operates on exclusion as much as it may also, momentarily, seem to act as a form of inclusion. For, as we already know, *their* fashion need not be *our* fashion. *Their* choice is not necessarily *our* choice. *Their* sense of duty is not always that which *we* would have them do. Well, of course. Yet however much each of us might stand against something we dislike, or abhor, it remains the case that identity itself lies in the gift of others. And this is why power is distributed not only with matters like information, but remains intricately tied to matters that endlessly affect the interplay we like to call identity.

# REFERENCES

*60 Minutes*, 2 March 2008.

Bauman, Z. (1995) 'The stranger revisited – and revisiting', *In Life in Fragments*. Oxford: Blackwell.

Bauman, Z. (2001) 'On mass, individuals and peg communities', in N. Lee and R. Munro (eds), *The Consumption of Mass, Sociological Review Monograph*, pp: 102–113. Oxford: Blackwell.

Bell, V. (2008) 'On Fernando's photograph: The potential of the ghost and the politics of (re)appearance', *Mobilising the Imaginary: The 'Unreal' in Law, Gender and Sexuality Research*. Keele University, 1 May.

Callon, M. (1980) 'Struggles and negociations to define what is problematic and what is not: The sociologic of translation', in K.D. Knorr, R. Krohn and R.D. Whitley (eds), *The Social Processes of Scientific Innovation*, pp: 197–211. Dordrecht : Reidel.

Derrida, J. (1982) *Margins of Philosophy*. Trans. A. Bass. Chicago, IL: Chicago University Press.

Douglas, M. (1966) *Purity and Danger: An Analysis of the Concepts of Pollution and Taboo*. London: Routledge.

Douglas, M. and Isherwood, B. (1980) *The World of Goods: Towards an Anthropology of Consumption*. Harmondsworth: Penguin.

Drew, E. (2008) 'Molehill politics', *The New York Review of Books*, 55 (6): 17 April.

Foucault, M. (1991) 'Governmentality', trans. Rosi Braidotti, in G. Burchell, C. Gordon and P. Miller (eds), *The Foucault Effect: Studies in Governmentality*. Hemel Hempstead: Harvester Wheatsheaf.

Garfinkel, H. (1967) *Studies in Ethnomethodology*. Englewood Cliffs, NJ: Prentice-Hall.

Geertz, C. (1993) 'Deep Play: Notes on the Balinese cockfight' in *The Interpretation of Cultures*, pp: 412–53. London: Fontana.

Gill, A.A. (2008) 'The last enemy was 1984 remade by Médecins sans frontieres', *The Sunday Times*, 24 February.

Giddens, A. (1991) *Modernity and Self-Identity: Self and Society in the Late Modern Age*. Cambridge: Polity Press.

Goffman, E. (1955) 'On face-work: An analysis of ritual elements in social interaction', *Psychiatry*, 18: 213–31.

Goffman, E. (1971) *The Presentation of Self in Everyday Life*. Harmondsworth: Pelican.

Goffman, E. (1963) *Behavior in Public Places*. New York: The Free Press.

Goffman, E. (1964) 'The neglected situation', *American Anthropologist* NS, 66 (2): 133–6.

Heidegger, M. (1959) *An Introduction to Metaphysics*. Trans. R. Manheim. New Haven, CT: Yale University Press.

Heidegger, M. (1962) *Being and Time*. Trans. J. Macquarrie and E. Robinson. Oxford: Basil Blackwell.

Heidegger, M. (1978) 'The question concerning technology', in D.F. Krell (ed.), *Basic Writings*. London: Routledge.

Hetherington, K. and N. Lee (2000) 'Social order and the blank figure', *Society and Space*, 18 (2): 169–84.

Kingsley, D. (2008) 'Keeping a close watch: The rise of self-surveillance and the threat of digital exposure', *The Sociological Review*, 56 (3): 347–57.

Kinnes, S. (2008) 'The last enemy turns eyes on the spies', *The Sunday Times*, 10 February.

Kripke, S. (1980) *Naming and Necessity*. Cambridge, MA: Harvard University Press.

Latimer, J. (2004) 'Commanding materials: (Re)-legitimating authority in the context of multi-disciplinary work', *Sociology*, 38 (4): 757–75.

Latimer, J. and Munro, R. (2006) 'Driving the social', in S. Bohm, C. Land and M. Patterson (eds), *Against Automobility*, *Sociological Review Monograph*, pp: 32–53. Oxford: Blackwell.

Latimer, J. and Munro, R. (2009) 'Keeping and dwelling: Relational extension and the idea of home and otherness', *Culture*, 12: 317–31.

Latour, B. (1987) *Science in Action: How to Follow Scientists and Engineers through Society*. Milton Keynes: Open University Press.

Munro, R. (1996) 'A consumption view of self: Extension, exchange and identity', in S. Edgell, K. Hetherington and A. Warde (eds), *Consumption Matters: The Production and Experience of Consumption*. Oxford: Blackwell.

Munro, R. (1999a) 'The cultural performance of control', *Organization Studies*, 20 (4): 619–39.

Munro, R. (1999b) 'Power and discretion: Membership work in the time of technology', *Organization*, 6 (3): 429–50.

Munro, R. (2004) 'Punctualising identity: Time and the demanding relation', *Sociology*, 38 (2): 293–311.

Munro, R. (2004) 'The remains of the say: Zero, double-crossing and the landscaping of language', *Journal for Cultural Research*, 8 (2): 183–200.

Munro, R. (2005) 'Just waiting: The social injustice of suspending participants between bidding and deferral', in R. Lippens (ed.), *Imaginary Boundaries: Social Justice across Disciplines*, pp: 51–67. Oxford and Portland Oregon: Hart.

Nancy, J.-L. (1991) 'The inoperative community', Trans. Peter Conner, in P. Connor (ed.), *The Inoperative Community*. Minneapolis, MN: University of Minnesota Press.

Orwell, G. (1954) *1984*. Harmondsworth: Penguin.

Pascale, C-M. (2008) 'Common Sense and the Collaborative Production of Class.' *Cultural Sociology*, 2(3): 345–67.

Rankin, I. (2003/1988) *Watchman*. London: Orcon.

Roberts, J. (1991) 'The possibilities of accountability'. *Accounting, Organizations and Society*, 16: 355–68.

Rosaldo, M. (1980) *Knowledge and Passion: Llongot Notions of Self and Social Life*. Cambridge: Cambridge University Press

Schutz, A. (1972) *The Phenomenology of the Social World*. London: Heinemann.

Serres, M. (2007) *The Parasite*. Trans. Lawrence R. Schehr. Minneapolis, MN: University of Minnesota Press.

Simmel, G. (1971) *Georg Simmel on Individuality and Social Forms*. Ed. D. Levine. Chicago, IL: University of Chicago Press.

Schmitz, C.A. (1963) *Wantoat: Art and Religion of the North-East New Guinea Papuans*. The Hague: Mouton and Co.

Strathern, M. (1991) *Partial Connections*. Savage, MD: Rowman and Littlefield.

Strathern, M. (1993) 'Culture is a drag', *THES*.

Strathern, M. (1996) 'The concept of society is theoretically obsolete: For the motion', in T. Ingold (ed.), *Key Debates in Anthropology*. London: Routledge.

Strathern, M. (1997) 'Gender: division or comparison', in K. Hetherington and R. Munro (eds), *Ideas of Difference: Social Spaces and the Labour of Division*, *Sociological Review Monograph*, pp: 42–63. Oxford: Blackwell.

Turner, V. (1986) 'Dewey, dilthey and drama: An essay in the anthropology of experience', in V. Turner and E. Bruner (eds), *The Anthropology of Experience*. Urbana, IL: University of Illinois Press.

Whyte, W.F. (1949) *Street Corner Society*.

# 11

# Relationality:
# The Intersubjective
# Foundations of Identity

Wendy Hollway

In this section of the Handbook, most of the formative forces explored for identities have been social: in terms of theoretical resources for understanding identities, the current conjuncture highlights social groups, power relations, disciplinary practices, discourses and narratives. In this chapter, I am going to take relations as the core formative principle, not social relations but rather relationality (specifically unconscious intersubjective dynamics) as a founding principle for identity formation and transition. I want to show not only *that* relationality is fundamental to identity but *how* it is.

In other contexts I would use the term subjectivity or self instead of identity to describe the achievement of a self or personal identity, but here I purposely use 'identity' to cover the whole ground, in an attempt not to reproduce individual–social dualism. Cromby for example defines 'mere identities' as 'ideal types of subject to which we must pay lip service in order to avoid censure' (2007: 94). Conversely, he identifies forces that 'get inscribed on the soul', such as disciplinary practices of subjectification and power

relationships that 'affect the very fabric of our being'. Venn (2006), also references two traditions, Foucauldian and social group differences, in distinguishing between subjectivity and identity. The first addresses singularity; the second group categories of belonging:

> the term subjectivity refers to the entity constituted as a position with regard to real processes and mechanisms of constitution of subjects generally (...) the substantive acting, thinking and feeling being often does not conform to these norms or to all of them; it is a self, the product of an interiorization of attitudes, values, expectations, memories, dispositions, instantiated in intersubjective relations and activities that, through historically specific self-reflective practices of recognition, constitute a particular named person, a singularity (...) Identity, on the other hand, refers to the relational aspects that qualify subjects in terms of categories such as race, gender, class, nation, sexuality, work and occupation, and thus in terms of acknowledged social relations and affiliations to groups. (...) Identity as a concept thus always directs attention to the relational aspect of subjectivity. (Venn, 2006: 79–80)

The literatures to which Cromby and Venn refer split identity and subjectivity in unacceptable ways and leave out what I regard as a necessary psychological approach to identity formation: an explanation of *how* (by what processes) social forces become embedded in the person. This omission figures in the continued lack of an explanation of agency within theoretical accounts that err on the side of social determinism. What is actually involved in the 'interiorisation' to which Venn refers and what difference do such processes make to the consequent identity, including the 'substantive acting, thinking and feeling being'?

Even in Venn's careful definition, in which subjectivity references interiorisation, self-reflective practices and singularity, the 'processes and mechanisms' appear one-way, from the social to the constitution of subjectivity. My goal is to provide an account of identity formation that provides a corrective by exploring the psychological processes, so that the result is a genuinely psycho-social analysis, in which internal and external processes are co-constitutive; that is they have effects both ways. As the question is framed in the object relations tradition of psychoanalysis: 'We are constructed of dynamic, internalised relationships between self and object. In turn we externalize our inner worlds onto our outside relationships, which turn again to influence our inner organisation throughout our development as children and adults' (Scharff, 1992: xviii).

The idea of unconscious intersubjective dynamics is central to this endeavour and this entails working with a basic principle of all psychoanalysis, namely the essentially conflictual nature of experience. So when I use the term conflict, I am meaning something ordinary, inevitable and an underlying principle of life and change. Venn points out that 'the relational aspect of subjectivity' has been favoured in the concept of identity so perhaps this term can act as a bridge, given my emphasis on relationality. However, a great deal of theoretical work is required to transform his use of relational so that it can accomplish my psycho-social goal.

To explore these themes and investigate the relational core of identity, this chapter will draw in particular on research on mothering and the transition to first-time motherhood as it is a prime site in which questions of relationality, identity and unconscious subjectivity arise. The chapter unfolds in six sections. The first section sets the scene and introduces relevant framing perspectives from feminist theory, psychoanalysis and developmental psychology. The second section then discusses the concept of objects and relations in psychoanalytic theorising before moving on to consider transitional objects in the third section and identification in the fourth section. Section five of the chapter then presents some empirical material and an extended case study from research on the transition to motherhood while the final section then summarises the main conclusions of the chapter.

## SETTING THE SCENE

A major influential strand of feminist writing in the last 25 years has been the attempt to redefine theories of identity to support a feminine, rather than a masculine, norm. In philosophy, this has entailed a critique of the Kantian, Enlightenment principle of the autonomous, independent, self-interested, individualistic subject in favour of a connected, relational, caring subject who is formed and embedded in social relationships and whose ethics are defined by care for others (Mackenzie and Stoljar, 2000). Critical psychology, in a parallel critique, focussed on how twentieth-century psychology espoused a similar model of the individual and aimed 'to demonstrate that the individual is not a fixed or given entity but rather a particular product of historically specific practices of social regulation' (Henriques et al., 1984/1998: 12). The literature on mothering and the ethics of care has had difficulty not falling into a gendered dualism where the principle of relationality defines women's (caring) identities and the principle of autonomy defines men's (Hollway, 2006a: ch. 2). It is feminist psychoanalysis that has made the most progress in explaining how, psycho-socially, this comes about (Hollway, 2006a: ch. 2). However, most writings – in a more philosophical and social theory vein – have not directly addressed the formation of identity and few have lingered on the detailed questions of how to theorise identity once the notion of the autonomous individual subject is called into question. Jessica Benjamin (1990, 1995, 1998, 1999) is prominent among the writers who ask how relationality (in her terms, intersubjectivity[1]) actually works. This is required, I believe, to unpick the binary thinking that sees relationality and connectedness as the opposite of autonomy and separateness. In what senses are they both always at play and in conflict?

An important recent tradition of sociological theory – individualisation theory – is based on the argument that macro-social forces, developing over a long modern and late modern period of western history, are producing more individualised individuals and this applies to women as well as men (Beck and Beck Gernsheim, 1983/2002). At the rather general level at which this kind of theorising takes place, there is no attempt to inquire into the psychological processes whereby this might be achieved (but see Roseneil, in press). Hence, as in so many areas of social theory, there is a tendency for the resultant account of identity formation to be socially determinist and not address how agency is accomplished. I have argued elsewhere that a psycho-social analysis based on the psychoanalytic principle of unconscious conflict can achieve this (Hollway and Jefferson, 2005). It is to this I now turn.

I shall be drawing on two interlinked traditions of psychoanalysis – British object relations and American relational psychoanalysis – that understand identity formation as radically relational (representing a move away from Freudian drive theory). Both share the psychoanalytic premise of conflictual

unconscious dynamics that do not observe the boundaries of the physical individual but move between and among people without their intention or awareness. This is the nub of the idea of unconscious intersubjective dynamics. Developmental principles are also fundamental to their accounts of the baby's acquisition of a self (or identity) within the primary relationship with a mother or substitute. The theme of formations in this section of the Handbook encourages a life-historical time perspective, which is essential in treating identities as always in process of becoming. Developmental approaches to identity have been largely ignored by social scientists or critiqued in a way that risked throwing the baby of development out with the bathwater of developmentalism[2] (for example, Smart et al., 2001). Rather, in thinking developmentally I aim to focus on the 'dynamics of becoming' (Loewald, 1980: 6), which continue throughout life. My account examines two time points therefore: infancy and the adult state involved in becoming a mother. These are intricately connected.

Winnicott encapsulated the radically relational nature of self in his famous aphorism, quoted by Masud Khan in the introduction to Winnicott's collected papers, 'there is no such thing as an infant, meaning of course that whenever one finds an infant one finds maternal care, and without maternal care there would be no infant' (1975/1984: xxxvii). While physical care is basic to this proposition, it is the psychological care that accompanies it that Winnicott understood so insightfully, drawing on his long years of paediatric practice. Loewald, an early thinker in what became the relational tradition, puts the same point as follows: 'mother and baby do not get together and develop a relationship, but the baby is born, becomes detached from the mother, and thus a relatedness between two parts that originally were one becomes possible' (1951/1980: 11). He extends this principle to the relationship between selves (at any age) and the objects that make up reality, a relatedness that does not start with 'two separate entities that come into contact with each other, but on the contrary from a unitary whole that differentiates into distinct parts' (1951/1980: 11). The idea of intersubjectivity thus means more than people being 'in interpersonal relation', which presupposes two people, always already separate, who relate. Winnicott's account of breastfeeding infants provides an example: 'Psychologically the infant takes from a breast that is part of the infant, and the mother gives milk to an infant that is part of herself' (1971: 16). In this light relationality is the originary core of personal identity and it is the processes of detachment and differentiation that require explanation.

The premise of radical intersubjectivity at the core of the self is contested by other developmental theorists, notably Stern (2000: 88) who argues that infants already have access to an experience of separateness from birth onwards. I do not find a problem in accepting that the seeds of both individuality and intersubjectivity exist from the beginning. My position (Hollway, 2006a) is to posit both individuality and intersubjectivity in the make-up of the self and to explore the tensions and conflicts between and among these that eventuate in the many and changing expressions of identity that are evident across time, space, social differences and individuals. The case for individuality has its origins in the separateness of the infant's bodily sensations and drives (see Frosh, Chapter 1 this volume), such as pain and hunger, which while they may be communicated successfully, originate in the infant. This reality lays the foundation for individuality, but unconscious intersubjective communication means that individuality is never uncontested, always in tension with relationality, in the way in which external objects are related to. This is the terrain of British object relations theory.

## OBJECTS AND RELATIONS IN PSYCHOANALYTIC THEORY

In the UK, object relations psychoanalysis, originating in the work of Melanie Klein

in the first half of the twentieth century, established relations with 'objects' as the central principle in identity formation, agency and interaction with the external world. Events in the external world are not just mediated by language or discourse but, importantly, by people's states of mind or 'internal worlds' where desire and anxiety act creatively on experience and transform it, so that its relation to reality can never be simply assumed or dismissed. The idea of an internal world refers, in object relations theory, to a world of unconscious fantasy made up of the self and other internal objects such as people, things, ideas and values (Fakhry Davids, 2002: 67). This world 'provides a template for our interactions with the outside world, is itself shaped by these, and is the wellspring of our psychic well-being and of creativity itself' (Fakhry Davids, 2002: 67). This general principle provides an analytic bridge to understand the relation between internal and external objects and worlds and between agency and social formations of identity. In different ways, the external world – and people's complex relations with its various aspects – is an integral part of this account of identity formation and change.

Winnicott's influence on theories of self development has been huge (see Frosh, Chapter 1 this volume) and through the take-up of his work by American theorists such as Jessica Benjamin and Thomas Ogden has shaped US relational psychoanalysis in no small degree. Ogden (cited in Gentile, 2007: 555) characterises Winnicott's paradoxical conception as representing 'a quiet revolution in analytic thinking … The analytic conception of the subject has increasingly become a theory of the interdependence of subjectivity and intersubjectivity. The subject cannot create itself' (Ogden, 1994: 59–60). I shall return to the centrality of paradox when I introduce Winnicott's account of transitional phenomena.

In the US, 'relational psychoanalysis'[3] has taken a similar, although later, turn (see for example Mitchell and Aron, 1999).

Benjamin's account (1999) of the development of subject–object and subject–subject relations is an important illustration of how contemporary psychoanalysis takes as its main focus the often unconscious intersubjective dynamics that move between people, such that the notion of an essentially boundaried, psychologically impermeable, individual can be seen, not just as a historical product of Enlightenment thinking but as an ontological distortion. Her developmental account of 'how domination is anchored in the hearts of the dominated' (Benjamin, 1990: 5) is a vital insight into the Foucauldian claim that power relations get inscribed upon the soul. In Winnicott's account, on which Benjamin's is based, a child's development is a challenge to transform 'doer-done to' relations (where mothers are 'done to', or as Winnicott put it 'ruthlessly used') into subject–subject relations where a mother can be a subject in her own right.

Because of the hegemony of the autonomous, bounded self-centred subject in western thinking, concepts of relationality and intersubjectivity have too readily been reclaimed into a paradigm in which self-contained individuals relate with each other (for example, see my critique of Joan Tronto's treatment of care ethics, Hollway, 2006a, Ch. 1). Melanie Klein's formulation 'we are members one of another' points to an intersubjectivity that is far more radical than that. However, this idea of others being inside us and vice versa does not exclude psychological differentiation and separation: individuality. It does, however, raise important questions of how this is achieved.

Although unconscious intersubjectivity is an important principle in making psychological processes psycho-social, it is not sufficient. The external world consists of matter (Gentile, 2007), groups and institutions, language and discourses as well as relationships. Object relations theory problematises relationships with this external world; relations with external objects that include other people as well as what we normally think of as objects (things).[4] It gives an account of the challenges of relating to reality, how it is distorted, denied, projected, introjected and also accepted. It is encounters with ever-changing reality that ensure that identity is always in process. For psychoanalysis, these encounters are inevitably conflictual, and conflict – deriving from both external and internal worlds – precipitates ongoing formation and reformation of identity. The inevitability of unconscious conflict and the paths into which consequent defences flow, provide a densely textured account of how reality is 'created' as well as 'found' (Winnicott 1963: 181). This is a constructionist account that has an agentic identity at its core.

The other side of the coin of infant intersubjectivity is maternal subjectivity.

Becoming a mother sets in motion a particular dynamic in women that starkly exemplifies 'the dialectic between individuality and intersubjectivity' (Ogden, 2001: 20); one that characterises adult identity more generally. This is because intersubjectivity is the new infant's only viable option. Margot Waddell presents this plainly:

> At its simplest, there is, for the baby, one life-saving presence. The lack of that presence is experienced as a pain and possibly a trauma, arousing feelings which he will not willingly suffer. (1998: 62)

The baby's consequent demands are likely to precipitate the new mother into a preoccupation, if she is psychologically available. They ensure that a mother is challenged to re-experience the intersubjective state of her baby in an intensified way, along with whatever state of differentiation she has achieved as an adult. Winnicott, in coining the term 'primary maternal preoccupation', regards it as necessary for the new mother to be able to reach a state of 'heightened sensitivity, almost an illness, and to recover from it' (1956: 302). The infant's development of a self has to be paralleled by maternal development (Parker, 1995), involving recognition of its need to differentiate:

There is no possibility whatever for an infant to proceed [...] towards and beyond primary identification [...] unless there is a good-enough mother [...] one who makes active adaptation to the infant's needs, an active adaptation that gradually lessens, according to the infant's growing ability to account for failure of adaptation and to tolerate the results of frustration. (Winnicott, 1971/2005: 13–14)

All this adds up to a picture of maternal identity as an important site for exploring identity through the idea of identity transitions generated by conflict.

Sylvia, for example, a white English mother in her mid-20s, had thought for years that she was unable to conceive and her work identity was very central for her. When she did become pregnant and her baby survived some dangerous foetal conditions, she conveyed the new place of intersubjectivity in her experience as follows:

I didn't think it would be this great [...] I didn't realise how much I could *love* someone. And I didn't realise how much you love a child (pause) *at all*, I didn't get that.

While I have phrased these processes of identity formation in terms of general psychodynamic principles, they can also be situated societally by referring to individualisation theory. Historical developments in western cultures – captured (if overstated) in the label 'individualisation' – have nurtured the capacities for identities to be autonomous and separated. Based on a masculine 'Europhallogocentric' norm (Venn, 2000: 84), this traditionally has split off women and treated them as other. However recent changes in gender relations have enabled many women to occupy these same 'masculine' identity positions, especially within the world of work. Lynne Layton argues that 'it is possible that one psychic result of women's liberation is the kind of female psyche best suited to a male work environment, the kind based in defensive autonomy' (2004: 35). This identity development is presumably produced by an array of social factors including educational and work institutions, the discourses available in which women can position themselves, the workplace (and other) practices required of them, and the way they are recognised by those around them. Becoming mothers precipitates conflicts between this individuality and the radical relationality that infants unselfconsciously demand in their primary relationships. It is evident from our research data that this conflict, often referred to by new mothers as needing to 'get my own life back' in the context of 'putting the baby first', is a primary motor for identity change.

The capacity for intersubjectivity exists in everyone, because it provides the floor, the 'unthought known' (Bollas, 1987: 3), of everyone's early experience which may be suppressed and repressed but is never erased. To this extent everyone is open to interpellation at the level of unconscious intersubjective communication. Ogden captures the radical nature of intersubjective dynamics in his concept of the 'third'. By this he means 'the dialectical movement of subjectivity and intersubjectivity' (Ogden 1994/1999: 462), a meeting of two people at a psychic level. The third is 'a creation of the first two who are also created by it'. Ogden (1994/1999: 462) says that in his concept of the third, he is indebted to Winnicott's famous claim 'there is no such thing as a baby (apart from maternal provision)'. Although there exist a mother and an infant in their physical separability, these 'coexist in dynamic tension with the mother-infant unity' (1994/1999: 463). This idea of a third space in a dyadic relationship that belongs to neither of the two embodied participants has radical implications for the idea of relationality because in this third space (also referred to by Ogden as an intersubjectivity) the separate subjectivities of two participants are indistinguishable. Therefore the concept of the third is useful here to try to convey the idea of an area of experience that does not reduce to the individuals involved. Below, I shall pursue it further through Winnicott's understanding of transitional phenomena, where it originated. It helps me to hold the idea of intersubjectivity and individuality in dynamic tension as I attempt to describe the psychological processes that are involved in the ongoing formation and change of identity.

When this dialectic is applied to understanding identity, it is possible to imagine how one or other of these two terms will dominate at different times of a person's life and in different circumstances and social positions, as I do with regard to becoming a mother.

## TRANSITIONAL OBJECTS

For Winnicott, the task of reality acceptance is central to the understanding of that aspect of identity formation requiring babies to differentiate from maternal care and increasingly experience a separate self. Following Freud, he saw the infant as necessarily caught up in an illusion of omnipotence (a defence against extreme vulnerability), from which he or she gradually has to accomplish disillusion by relinquishing control and magical thinking when faced with the obduracy of reality. It is important for a more general theorising of identity transition that Winnicott believed that 'the task of reality acceptance is never completed, that no human being is free from the strain of relating inner and outer reality, and that relief from this strain is provided by an intermediate area of experience which is not challenged' (1971/2005: 18). He theorises 'an intermediate area of experiencing, to which inner reality and external life both contribute' (1971/2005: 3) through his concept of transitional objects. It is of considerable importance for psycho-social theorising because it is also the area of play and creativity as manifest in cultural life.

Before proceeding, let me comment on Winnicott's unapologetic use of the idea of reality because this idea has become unacceptable to many social scientists following the post-structuralist turn. The principle that the external world is never directly accessible, always multiply mediated (for example, by

power relations and discourses) resulted in the treatment of reality as a dangerous concept, best avoided (see Hollway, 2006b). This line of critique was of considerable importance given the naïve realism that it addressed. But Winnicott's use of the concept of reality was not naïve. He explored the mediations of reality – of the external world – in terms of inner world dynamics. This inner world was not reduced to any assumption of a unitary individual, but rather was always, incessantly, in a state of tension, or conflict with the external world (including people and things). This psycho-social account of how reality is mediated is notable by its absence in contemporary social theory. To face external reality is always a strain because it does not conform to our wishes; it is outside our omnipotent control and giving up the illusion of omnipotence is hard. Benjamin (1999) refers to the same crucial developmental shift towards the achievement of an autonomous identity when she talks about the move from doer–done to relations to subject–subject relations. It can immediately be seen how often the ideal of subject–subject relations breaks down. It is during this process of coming to terms with the illusion of control not working that transitional objects are important. Between the undifferentiated experience of the newborn infant and the relatively stable experience of a separate identity, Winnicott places an intermediate area that he calls transitional space. Here objects are experienced by the baby as neither external nor internal. Their very nature is paradoxical: the transitional object 'is not an internal object (which is a mental concept) – it is a possession. Yet it is not (for the infant) an external object either' (Winnicott, 1971/2005: 13). It is 'a neutral area of experience' (1971/2005: 17) between the infant's needed illusion of omnipotence and the acknowledgement of a reality where objects, including importantly the mother, are not under his or her control: 'It is not the object, of course, that is transitional. The object represents the infant's transition from a state of being merged with the mother to a state of being in relation to the mother as something outside and separate' (Winnicott 1971/2005: 19). When infants can treat external objects as external, they will also be experiencing a self, because these are two sides of the same achievement.

Jill Gentile regards this 'encounter with matter' as 'a triumph of personal agency over a brute inanimate reality, a triumph of the infant in becoming an author of, rather than a mere reactor to, his experience' (2007: 547). She goes on to argue that 'the material world is critical to our constitution of subjectivity and that we simultaneously impose our weight upon it and surrender to its unyielding aspects' (2007: 547). These dynamics, incessantly experienced, generate 'a subject who comes into being between desire and limit' (2007: 548). External reality is, in this light, an essential term in theorising identity, because it provides limit. As Gentile indicates, an emphasis on the material world suggests limitations in Ogden's idea of thirdness. For Ogden and Benjamin, intersubjectivity 'is predicated upon a symbolic space between mother and infant. Symbolic space, or the symbolic use of the material world, stands as a third to the dyad' (Gentile, 2007: 549). For Gentile, the problem with this is that 'the explicit "third" of matter is often obscured in favour of a depiction of meaning creation at the intersection of subjectivities' (2007: 549). Such meaning creation is at the heart of the creation of identity and it should, following Gentile, take into account the limiting function of matter.

In the following section, I want to focus even more specifically on the processes whereby objects move between the external and inner world and how they come to make up identity. The concept of identification, as elaborated in psychoanalysis, provides a theorisation of these processes.

## IDENTIFICATION

The psychoanalytic concept of identification provides a theoretically powerful resource

for understanding the two-way traffic between internal and external worlds, as Frosh (Chapter 1 this volume) points out. Freud said that 'identification is known to psychoanalysis as the earliest expression of an emotional tie with another person' (1921: 105). So here we have a concept that can provide insight into relationality and has emotional life at its core. The radical implication of the concept is that there is no firmly established boundary separating one person from another where emotional life is concerned (which means every aspect of mental life):

> Freud's development of a theory of identification was a momentous step in understanding how the apparent boundaries of the self are actually permeable, how the apparently isolated subject constantly assimilates what is outside itself … the ego is not really independent and self-constituting, but is actually made up of the objects it assimilates. (Benjamin, 1998: 79)

The elaboration of identification has been central to an object relations psychoanalytic account of what I call identity formation and identity transition. Ralph Hinshelwood, in a core definition of identification, captures the way both individuality and intersubjectivity are engaged in this process: 'identification concerns the relating to an object on the basis of perceived similarities with the ego' (1991: 319) (for 'ego', one can read self or identity in this context). He goes on to stipulate just how difficult it is to achieve the kind of object relating that is capable of acknowledging the separateness of identity: 'the simple recognition of a similarity with some other external object that is recognised as having its own separate existence is a sophisticated achievement' (1991: 319). We have seen how, in object relations theory, this achievement and its vicissitudes are understood as a central part of infant and child development and that recognition of separateness remains a precarious and intermittent achievement.

Adult to adult intersubjectivity is different in degree but not in kind from infant–mother intersubjectivity because it is still based on the unconscious flowing of mental states between one person and another that constantly modifies them. The subjective experience of these dynamics has been a central feature of the clinical repertoire, where they are understood as transference and countertransference. These provide psychoanalytic psychotherapists with ways of understanding based on their own subjective and embodied experiences that do not rely on what patients say. Ogden, Bion and Winnicott all learned something about infant–mother dynamics through the transference and countertransference in their work as analysts. Winnicott claimed that such patients can 'teach the analyst more about early infancy than can be learned from direct observation of infants [...] since what happens in the transference is a form of infant-mother relationship' (Winnicott, 1965, cited in Rayner, 1991: 131). Clearly then, these dynamics are not confined to the infant – mother relationship.

Unconscious intersubjectivity moves in two directions and these are complementary parts of identification; projective and introjective identification. Their more simple variants, projection and introjection are based, according to Klein, on the earliest experience of matter in and out of the infant's body, ingestion and expulsion or evacuation. The equivalent processes serve to take in and get rid of any psychological objects that are needed or causing discomfort (good or bad objects).

Introjection has a physical, undigested quality to it, yet it is the source from which selves are made up, in the sense that it is through taking in objects (parts of people, things and meanings) that the self is furnished with content. But this does raise the question of how these external objects are transformed into aspects that belong to the self. Freud described identification as something whose result was a change in identity: 'a process by which an object was relocated within the ego boundaries that had once been experienced as external' and 'causes an alteration of the ego' (Hinshelwood, 1991: 332). Not all external objects that become

internal objects are identified with, but if so they cause an alteration of the ego; that is – in our terms – they change identity. Indeed identification with loved objects is the way that people acquire a personality, a basic, normal process in human relations. Projection, by contrast, depletes the self, being the mechanism whereby objects that could enlarge the self are prohibited because they are anxiety provoking. The conceptual move from projection and introjection to projective and introjective identification extends the theoretical leverage to intersubjectivity proper because it refers to how objects, basically bad and good, are related to once they are moved in or out.

Bion's concept of projective identification was influential in the move in this direction, exploring it as a two-way loop, a truly intersubjective process. His concept of containment, based on the process of projective identification, theorises what he regarded as the most primitive unconscious modes of communication (outside an awareness of time and outside thought) originating in the mother (container)–infant (contained) relationship. According to Bion, projective identification is the normal model of communication between infants and adult caretakers. Infants, still without the mental capacities to contain their own anxieties, rely on the containment of adults for psychological survival. However, he first described containment through a clinical example involving two adults:

> When the patient strove to rid himself of fears of death which were felt to be too powerful for his personality to contain he split off his fears and put them into me, the idea apparently being that if they were allowed to repose there long enough they would undergo modification by my psyche and could then be safely reintrojected. (Bion, 1959: 103, quoted in Hinshelwood, 1991: 247)

Bion contrasts this 'modification' with what happens when the other – mother or analyst – fails to contain the subject's fears:

> On the occasion I have in mind the patient felt [...] that I evacuated them so quickly that the feelings

were not modified but had become more painful [...] he strove to force them into me with increased desperation and violence. (Bion, 1959: 103, quoted in Hinshelwood, 1991: 247)

This example provides an illustration of projective identification as a mode of unconscious communication. Kleinian theory of self-formation is sometimes accused of being too intraspychic, too preoccupied with internal objects. In Bion's hands, however, 'the external object is an integral part of the system [...] Bion's formulation (of the container/contained model) shows not just *that* the environment is important but *how* it is important' (Spillius, 1988: 156).

Successful containment – at first in the container of the mother or other carer – is significant because it attenuates the splitting of good and bad. All external objects contain both good and bad and it is a basic principle for all those who came after Klein that healthy development and the formation of an integrated self depends on becoming able to tolerate the reality that good and bad exist in the same object. Containment helps to achieve this, thus making a crucial difference in the capacity of the self to identify with external objects rather than become depleted through splitting and projection.

Here we have an account of integration that transcends postmodern debate about the multiplicity of identity and then conflates this with a claim about identity's fragmentary character. Integration is not a given (as in essentialist paradigms of the individual) but neither is fragmentation inevitable. The multiple objects which are available to be identified with as parts of the self precipitate conflictual unconscious intersubjective dynamics in the strain to face the reality of good and bad in the same object. Klein, Bion and Winnicott are in agreement that modes of experiencing will always oscillate between acceptance of brute reality and the kinds of illusion that chafe against it and sometimes refuse it. As Gentile points out (above), this is a source of agency and creativity.

## INDIVIDUALITY AND INTERSUBJECTIVITY IN THE IDENTITY TRANSITION TO BECOMING A MOTHER

Identity transition was the topic of a recent research project[5] in which 19 mothers of different class and ethnicities, all living in the same area of London, participated from late pregnancy to when their first babies were one-year-old. The psychoanalytically informed interview and observation methods used to generate data were designed to shed light on the overarching question 'how do women's identities change in the process of becoming mothers for the first time?'.

### *Justine*

Justine, a 24-year-old, working-class, black woman of African Caribbean heritage, illustrates the conflict between individuality and intersubjectivity as follows: 'Everything I think of from the time I wake up to the time I go to sleep is Aisha first. Everything. I can't just get up and go out any more. I can't just think of myself any more.' She referred to how much becoming a mother had unsettled her former identity too: 'I like being a Mum, I love it (...) I've noticed my whole persona slowly started to change. (...) I feel a bit topsy turvy.'

At the third and final interview, when her daughter Aisha was 13-months-old, Justine is experiencing conflicts concerning Aisha's 'clinginess'. She cannot leave Aisha with anyone and many people, including her partner, are critical of her for this problem in a picture of otherwise successful mothering:

Because he does think that I smother her [baby mutters] and maybe in a way I do, but like I said it's just because it's just the two of us the majority of the time so there's no one else to smother apart from her really (...) [Int: and the arguments are about how you're looking after her] Yeah and not so much how I look after her just why she's so clingy and I can't expect anything less because of the way she is [6]and all the rest of it but er [baby moans] um I don't just get it just from him either, everyone says the same thing and I am starting [baby moans] to scratch my head a bit and okay maybe I am smothering her a bit too much.

It would be easy to draw the conflict as being between Aisha and Justine; that is between the (intersubjectively based) demands of her baby and Justine's (individuality-based) wishes for some time and space of her own. No doubt this is part of the picture. But the above extract suggests Justine's active, if unintentional part in Aisha's clinginess. First she acknowledges how close the two of them are and have been, as a result of the considerable periods of time they spend alone together ('there's no one else to smother'). This history, since Aisha's birth, has been shaped by social and material circumstances: the relative absence of Aisha's non-live-in father and the cramped flat in which Justine and Aisha share a bed (Aisha will not go to sleep unless Justine lies down beside her). Further, a story that Justine tells the interviewer suggests her active, if unconscious collaboration in this state of affairs. She is bemoaning (not for the first time) how impossible it is to go out on her own and instances an event which she badly wanted to attend at which a cousin is giving a poetry reading. Michael was actually in the flat, so it might seem possible to have arranged that he stay with his daughter. But he was asleep and she uses this fact without questioning it as a reason for staying with Aisha. Here we see, in addition to the recursive negotiation of a gendered division of childcare, her inter-subjective involvement with her baby daughter that produces an ambivalence in her about going out, even though Aisha would be OK with her Dad: it is not just Aisha who is 'clingy'.

Justine had given up work before becoming pregnant, unsatisfied with a series of clerical jobs and not knowing how to get started on a proper career. Now Justine identifies in Aisha aspects of herself that she feels she failed to accomplish. These are objects that she internalised from her mother, who projected those same hopes into her; namely to use the fact that she was clever to get a good

education and establish a career before she had a family. Like Justine, her mother became pregnant early and suspended her career. Justine illustrates her dual identifications with her mother and daughter when she says 'I'm bringing her up the way my Mum brought us up (…) *introducing* her to a lot of things early because apparently I was a smart and quick child, just quick to catch on and Aisha's exactly the same'. Likewise, talking of her future hopes for Aisha, she hopes that she will:

just focus on a career base, you know, afford to, you know, be able to afford your house and that kind of thing. I don't want her to ever live like how I am now because I feel like I had the opportunity to go out there and just not be like under the Tower Hamlets[7] section and have to go homeless and that palaver, but if I had stayed at work when, when I should have, then I wouldn't be like this. I would probably be on a mortgage thing and so I'd like her to just go that way, just different from what I did.

Elsewhere, she makes it clear that career success is just what her mother had hoped for her. This provides an illustration of unconscious intergenerational transmission of identities and shows how multiple this transmission is, encompassing material circumstances, practices and relationships, all articulated in a network of conflicts, both conscious and unconscious, both interpersonal and intra-psychic.

### Liyanna

Liyanna provides a further example of inter-generational identifications. She is a 30-year-old, Bangladeshi-origin mother. At the second interview, when her daughter was around four-months-old, Liyanna had prepared some family photos to show the interviewer. One photo is of her mother with her older sister, Amina. She and Amina, who she describes as having 'always been pretty close', have a difficult relationship with their mother who has been chronically depressed throughout their lives. She says:

It's this picture, it's so strange. [baby cries]. I was showing it to my sister the other day, and I said to her that when I used to look at this before it was like 'oh there's Mum and Amina' ... and you just sort of flick through it, you know, and I never really stopped to analyse it. But I said to her, since I've had Maryam, I look at that picture and I know exactly what my Mum was feeling when she was looking down at my sister. [Int: Really?] 'Cos I know how I feel when I look down at her, and when I play with her, and it's just taken on a whole new meaning, you know, it's like there's my Mum and that's her first-born child, it's a little girl, same as me, you know, and I can just see the love and the emotion that she's feeling when she – when she – when that picture was taken.

There is a lot at stake here for Liyanna because she is now able to recognise that she was loved by her mother; a recognition that has become possible because she has experienced how she loves her own daughter. She regards this access to a new emotional understanding as 'strange' because the same photo before she became a mother would have held no such significance. If we phrase this in terms of identification, we can say that becoming a mother has enabled her to identify with her mother at the same time as identifying with her daughter through her identity as the daughter of her mother. The bond with her own daughter, through this double identification, then produces a recognition of how her mother felt for her own baby daughter. However, the generational identification is not quite as direct as she implies because she is not her mother's first-born, so Liyanna's identification as her mother's baby ('same as me') passes through her close older sister, to enable the parallel with her first-born daughter. Through this she acquires an emotional understanding of loving and being loved that was not accessible before she became a mother herself. It depends, object relationally speaking, on being able to access simultaneously her internalised mother and daughter and to identify both of these as parts of herself.

What this adds, theoretically, to my account, is the intergenerational transmission of maternal identifications, largely becoming active when one becomes a mother oneself.

When these identifications coincide with the way that new mothers are repositioned by those around them and the way that they are required to engage in a whole new set of daily practices that reflect the overriding dependency of a vulnerable new infant, whose life they feel responsible for, we have a powerful cluster of influences precipitating identity transition (Elliott et al., 2009).

## Sylvia

Sylvia is a white, English woman in her mid-20s, who suffered from epilepsy and other illnesses. The following example provides an insight into identity as positioning in expert discourses. In hospital for 10 days after the birth, Sylvia was having great difficulties breastfeeding. She was visited by a 'nightmare' breastfeeding counsellor who she experienced as putting pressure on her. The counsellor's claim that breastfeeding would give her a strong bond with her daughter upset her and she was 'so close to snapping'. In the interview she elaborates at length what she felt like saying back, which was an argument about how a strong bond was not exclusively dependent on breastfeeding. This story illustrates Sylvia's almost uncontrollably difficult feelings about breastfeeding, which she tried and failed to provide for her baby. In the context of her body's inadequacies in providing nourishment for her baby prior to birth, it is likely that breastfeeding took on special significance – unique to Sylvia – of her body's capacity to nurture. Therefore it was quite traumatic when she failed to do this. It was because she felt bad about this failure that the expert's comments about bonding were so unbearable to hear that she almost 'snapped': she needed to believe that her bond with Rosemary would not be compromised by her failure to breast feed. For other mothers in our group, failure to breastfeed did not hold this set of meanings. We can see the power of experts to impose on a person's identity, in this example being influential in Sylvia's feeling of being a failure for not breastfeeding. However, the personal significance for Sylvia of this failure, revealed by understanding her history, adds a psychological dimension. Both the external influence and the consequences of her earlier life on her internal world contribute to the meanings of a practice, namely breastfeeding. Later on she comments that 'I beat myself up about that [not breastfeeding] for a long time' and cites her partner as telling her 'you really did try to do it and it just didn't work'. Probably her partner's alternative positioning of her – one based on the reality rather than the ideal – helped her gradually to get over this feeling of failure.

After a history of difficulties (which I have not the space to go into here) Sylvia has created an idealised good object of her relationship with her precious baby. Inevitably the reality will not live up to this and her failure to breastfeed is an early instance. She projects the bad on to the 'nightmare' breastfeeding counsellor and feels temporarily free to 'hate' it there (Klein, 1946/1988). Over time, however, she comes to face the reality that there is both good and bad in the relationship with her baby and becomes more accepting – not without considerable difficulty and with her partner's help – of her failure to breastfeed.

## Silma

Silma, 25-years-old and of Bengali heritage, had worked as a retail assistant in a department store. Since she was a teenager, Silma had a 'phobia' about giving birth, fearing that she could never accomplish it. She accounted for this by her very small size. However, she also had set herself the goal of having a baby before she was 25. The birth, which was not as bad as she had feared, was thus a particularly momentous occasion: 'When I heard the crying, I thought "Oh my God I did it" [laughs]' and "Oh thank God, I've, I've made it"'. This background knowledge adds extra meaning to Silma's pride at being

recognised as having a baby when she returns home from hospital and adds unique meaning to her exclamation 'Hey, I've got a baby.' The local community, predominantly of Bangladeshi origin, acts towards Silma's new – maternal – identity by positioning her as a new mother. One perhaps obvious point should not be forgotten here: Silma actually has a baby. The positioning and recognition are based on the material reality, an example of the 'third' of matter, something that has often been marginalised in positioning and identity theory, as Gentile argued (see above).

Getting home from hospital is one early transitional moment in Silma's identity positioning. After a while, as she tells the interviewer, she feels treated with more 'respect' by her aunties: 'official phone calls, dates being fixed and the food being cooked'. Before she wouldn't stay around in the room listening but now finds 'it's quite interesting how they talk'. Her young sister gives her 'dirty looks' and says:

> 'oh my God, you're talking like Mum … you're not my Mum. You used to be like this. You used to be worse than me' [laughs]. But now … because I've changed, and I don't want my little sister to be in that state … she goes 'oh what about when you used to stay out late, did anyone hurt you?' And I was like, 'Yeah that was *me*' [laughs].

This is a good example of the joint action of practices and relational positioning in Silma's identity transition. She starts by noticing her different treatment by the women of her mother's generation. It is not just their positioning of her (for example, the formal invitations), but how her own preferred practices have changed too: she likes to stay around with these Aunts listening to 'how they talk', something she did not do before she had a baby. The contrast between her new identity as a mother and her old one is drawn through how she experiences her sister as still positioning her as she used to be – giving her dirty looks that she prefers the aunts' company and that she is now talking just like their Mum. Her little sister accuses her with the charge 'you used to be worse than me' and it becomes clear that she is referring to Silma's old practices of staying out late. When she worries about her little sister doing just the kind of thing she did until not so long ago herself, Silma identifies as a mother rather than a daughter. Silma recognises her inconsistency (produced out of the ordinary conflict within the multiplicity of identity) but puts it down to being 'because I've changed' (a change that does not bar her access to daughterly identification at other times and in other relationships).

The roles of the aunts and the little sister in this account illustrate that Silma is undergoing changes in generational identification that involve identifying in a maternal position not only with her new baby. It means that she finds more in common with her aunts and less in common with her younger sister. These aunts are simultaneously carriers of a generational identity, to which she now has access as a mother, and an ethnic identity that derives from the Indian subcontinent. Yet Silma was born and brought up in London and has had access to westernised ways of dressing and socialising as an English teenager, as we see next.

In the same section of the interview, Silma reflects on such features of her current changes. She described her old self as 'so wild', out with friends all the time, staying out late. Now, she says, 'I've gone a bit mature, more understanding, like a more motherly type'. She is 'around family more'. 'Strangely', she says, this has affected her clothes-wise: from being a 'jeans maniac' (tight jeans 'my bum would stick out'), she does not feel comfortable in them any more. Now she refers to shalwar kameezes as 'normal clothes' and 'the ones I really like' (she received four as birthday gifts). She finds this change 'strange', which suggests that it is not something that she has consciously chosen but that she has discovered in her changed preferences. Her free association moves from turning into a 'motherly type' to her new discomfort in wearing jeans. The reason, she implies – suggested by a

further free association to the idea that her bum stuck out in tight jeans – is that she is not currently comfortable with exposing her body in tight clothes. Her preference now, the clothes 'I really like', which now are referred to as 'normal', is for the shalwar kameez, which contrasts to jeans by its looseness and the way it conceals the body shape.

Here is an example of an identity practice that reflects the ordinary conflicts set in motion by new identifications with an older generation of women in her family whose primary identities are defined by being mothers. The practices and the positioning in her relationships with significant others are bound up together in the same experience. The example also illustrates how the dynamics involved in identity – the forces that propel the identity change – are based on ordinary conflict. We saw it in the opposing influences of Silma's aunts and her little sister. In this situation, the aunts represent what she is in the process of becoming and the sister what she is in the process of leaving behind; she is not either one or the other, but a mobile mixture of both as she re-experiences herself from moment to moment in the course of different events and practices. The wider process of becoming will probably continue in similar vein and will never arrive at a fixed point. Her changing preference in clothes illustrates this conflict, suggested in the statement 'I don't feel comfortable wearing jeans' but leaves open both future changes and her clothes preferences in different situations. The principle of underlying normal conflict in identity dynamics provides a space for understanding agency. It means that Silma's changes of dress are not determined by social forces such as the practice of Islam represented by some of those around her.

## CONCLUSION

I have argued that relationality is a foundational principle of identity, but also that the person in their singularity (what I have referred to as individuality) is consistent with this principle as long as, first, there are concepts that enable an explanation of how identity is formed (the psycho-social principles that enable relational transactions between external and internal worlds) and, second, an account of how these two principles coexist in experience and across time (ordinary conflict acting as a dynamic principle). The concept of identification is central to my explanation and my illustrations suggest how multiple and dynamic identifications operate to furnish and change identity not just moment by moment but across generations.

If intersubjectivity is foundational because of the early developmental processes involved in creating identity, starting with the infant-mother unit, individuality is also inalienable, based on the body's singularity. Enlightenment thinking took the individual as an unproblematic starting point, based on the notion of an autonomous mind. The object relations and relational traditions in psychoanalysis have given a nuanced account of psychological separateness never fully or finally achieved; an account based at the same time on relationality and on embodiment. One important strand of thinking derives from Esther Bick's (1986) work in theorising the skin as a boundary that defines the limits of the individual. How this boundary (definitionally relating inside and outside) is experienced and psychologically made meaningful is a fundamental issue in understanding identity (Anzieu, 1989; Ogden, 1994). Skin is therefore also helpful in conceptualising 'internal' and 'external' worlds and the transactions between them. Such psychoanalytic theorising is a rich source of understanding embodiment in a way that is not biologically reductionist but understands the psychological and intersubjective processes expressed and experienced in modes of embodiment. A theoretical focus on embodiment also provides a link to the role of practices in identity formation, for example providing subjectivity where Bourdieu draws attention

to repeated everyday embodied routines and unconscious practices (Bourdieu, 1977, 1990; see also Elliott et al., 2009).

Finally, I would like to pick up the role of 'reality' in identity processes. In a post-constructionist paradigm, matter and other obdurate examples of reality (mediated of course, but still obdurate), can be theorised for their effectivity in providing limit, which conflicts with a wish for omnipotent control that is characteristic of the emergence of identity and never finally resolved. Winnicott's account of transitional objects and that intermediate area of experience that is a relief from the strain of relating inner and external life inscribes creativity (and with it agency) in the making of identity and rescues it from being either simply a product of social forces or of autonomous minds.

## NOTES

1   The terms relationality and intersubjectivity have converged in the work of Benjamin and Ogden, both recognised as within the American relational psychoanalysis tradition, but both privileging the term intersubjectivity to refer to the unconscious dynamics that govern interpersonal relationships.

2   Developmentalism views child development as fixed, staged and normative (Burman, 2008).

3   Relational psychoanalysis 'began to accrue to itself […] later advances of self psychology, particularly intersubjectivity theory; social constructivism in its various forms; certain currents within contemporary psychoanalytic hermeneutics, more recent developments in gender theorising … the centrality of transference-countertransference interaction and […] the legacy of Sandor Ferenczi' (Mitchell and Aron, 1999: xi–ii)

4   This usage is intended to reflect the focus on the early infantile state where these different kinds of objects are undifferentiated. It also enables a theoretical focus on how babies achieve (and to some extent fail to achieve) selves for which 'subject–subject' relations are possible.

5   The empirical material in this section is taken from 'Identities in process: becoming mothers for the first time in Tower Hamlets' a UK Economic and Social Research Council funded project, award number RES148-25-0058. Tower Hamlets is a borough within London with high indices of deprivation, a history and present of new immigrant populations

and a concentration of initiatives supporting parents with young children. All participants were given pseudonyms.

6   'The way she is' is tautologous; 'the way I am' would make the most sense. This slip of the tongue suggests how easy it is for Justine to move into an identification with Aisha, evidence of the strong intersubjective unity that she still experiences with her daughter.

7   Tower Hamlets' housing policy was that if pregnant women became homeless, they were entitled to get emergency council accommodation.

# REFERENCES

Anzieu, D. (1989) *The Skin Ego*. London: Yale.

Beck-Gernsheim, E. (1983/ 2002) 'From "living for others" to "a life of one's own"', in U. Beck and E. Beck-Gernsheim, *Individualization*. London: Sage. Chapter 5: 54–84.

Benjamin, J. (1990) *The Bonds of Love*. London: Virago.

Benjamin, J. (1995) *Like Subjects, Love Objects – Essays on Recognition and Sexual Difference*. New Haven, VT: Yale University Press.

Benjamin, J. (1998) *Shadow of the Other: Intersubjectivity and Gender in Psychoanalysis*. New York: Routledge.

Benjamin, J. (1990/1999) 'Recognition and destruction: An outline of intersubjectivity', in S. Mitchell and L. Aron (eds), *Relational Psychoanalysis: The Emergence of a Tradition*. pp. 181–210 Hillsdale, NJ: Analytic Press.

Bick, E. (1986) 'Further considerations of the function of the skin in early object relations: Findings from infant observation integrated into child and adult analysis'. *British Journal of Psychotherapy*, 2 (4): 292–301.

Bion, W.R. (1959) 'Attacks on linking', *International Journal of Psycho-Analysis*, 40: 308–15.

Bollas, C. (1987) *Shadow of the Object*. New York: Columbia Press.

Bourdieu, P. (1977) *Outline of a Theory of Practice*. Cambridge: Cambridge University Press.

Bourdieu, P. (1990) *The Logic of Practice*. Cambridge: Polity Press.

Burman, E. (2008) *Deconstructing Devlopmental Psychology*. 2nd edn. London: Routledge.

Cromby, J. (2007) 'Towards a psychology of feeling', *Critical Psychology*, 21: 94–118.

Elliott, H., Gunaratnam, Y., Hollway, W. and Phoenix, A. (2009) 'Meaning, practices and identity change in the transition to becoming a mother', in M. Wetherell (ed.), *Theorising Identities and Social Action*, pp. 19-37. Basingstoke: Palgrave.

Fakhry Davids, M. (2002) 'Fathers in the internal world: From boy to man to father', in J. Trowell and A. Etchegoyen (eds), *The Importance of Fathers, a Psychoanalytic Re-evaluation*. pp. 67–92. New York: Brunner-Routledge.

Freud, S. (1921) *Group Psychology and the Analysis of the Ego*. Standard Edition, 18. London: Hogarth.

Gentile, J. (2007) 'Wrestling with matter: Origins of intersubjectivity', *Psychoanalytic Quarterly*, LXXVI: 547–81.

Henriques, J., Hollway, W., Urwin, C., Venn, C. and Walkerdine, V. (1984) *Changing the Subject*. London: Methuen.

Hinshelwood, R.D (1991) *Dictionary of Kleinian Thought*. London: Free Association Books.

Hollway, W. (2006a) *The Capacity to Care: Gender and Ethical Subjectivity*. London: Routledge.

Hollway, W. (2006b) 'Towards a psycho-social account of self in family relationships: The legacy of 20th Century discourses', *Theory and Psychology*, 16 (4): 465–82.

Hollway, W. and Jefferson, T. (2005) 'Panic and perjury: A psycho-social exploration of agency', *British Journal of Social Psychology*, 44 (2): 147–63.

Khan, M. 'Introduction' in Winnicott, D.W. (1958/1984) *Collected Papers. Through Paediatrics to Psychoanalysis xi-xlviii*. London: Karnac.

Klein, M. (1946/1988) 'Notes on some schizoid mechanisms', in M. Klein (ed.), *Envy and Gratitude and Other Works*. pp. 1–24. London: Virago.

Layton, L. (2004) 'Relational no more', in J.A. Winer, J.W. Anderson and C.C. Kieffer (eds), *The Annual of Psychoanalysis, Volume XXXII, Psychoanalysis and Women*. pp. 29–42. Hillsdale, NJ: Analytic Press.

Loewald, H. (1951/1980) 'Ego and reality', in Loewald, H. (ed.), *Papers on Psychoanalysis*. pp. 3–20. New Haven, CT: Yale University Press.

MacKenzie, C. and Stoljar, N. (eds) (2000) *Relational Autonomy: Feminist Perspectives on Autonomy, Agency and the Social Self*. New York and Oxford: Oxford University Press.

Mitchell, S and Aron, L. (1999) *Relational Psychoanalysis: The Emergence of a Tradition*. Hillsdale, NJ: Analytic Press.

Ogden, T. (1994) *Subject of Analysis*. London: Karnac Books.

Ogden, T. (1994/1999) 'The analytic third: working with intersubjective clinical facts' in S. Mitchell and L. Aron, (eds), *Relational Psychoanalysis: The Emergence of a Tradition*. pp. 459–592. Hillsdale, NJ: The Analytic Press.

Ogden, T. (2001) *Conversations at the Frontier of Dreaming*. Hillsdale, NJ: The Analytic Press.

Parker, R. (1995) *Torn in Two: The Experience of Maternal Ambivalence*. London: Virago.

Rayner, E. (1991) *The Independent Mind in British Psychoanalysis*. London: Free Association Books.

Roseneil, S. (forthcoming) *Sociability, Sexuality, Self: Relationality and Individualization*.

Scharff, D. (1992) *Refinding the Object and Reclaiming the Self*. Northdale, NJ: Jason Aronson.

Smart, C., Neale, B. and Wade, A. (2001) *The Changing Experience of Childhood*. Cambridge: Polity.

Spillius, E. Bott, (ed.) (1988*)* *Melanie Klein Today. vol 1: Mainly Theory*. London: Routledge.

Stern, D. (2000) 'The relevance of empirical infant research to psychoanalytic theory and practice', in J. Sandler, A-M. Sandler and R. Davies (eds), *Clinical and Observational Psychoanalytic Research: Roots of a Controversy. André Green and Daniel Stern*. pp. 73–90. London: Karnac.

Venn, C. (2000) *Occidentalism*. London: Sage.

Venn, C. (2006) *The Postcolonial Challenge: Towards Alternative Worlds*. London: Sage.

Waddell, M. (1998) *Inside Lives*. London: Tavistock.

Winnicott, D.W. (1956/1984) 'Primary maternal preoccupation', in Winnicott (ed.), *Collected Papers. Through Paediatrics to Psychoanalysis*. pp. 300–305. London: Karnac.

Winnicott, D.W. (1958/1984) *Collected Papers. Through Paediatrics to Psychoanalysis*. London: Karnac.

Winnicott, D.W. (1963/1990) 'Communicating and not communicating leading to a study of certain opposites', in Winnicott, *The Maturational Processes and the Facilitating Environment*. London: Karnac.

Winnicott, D.W. (1965/1990) *The Maturational Processes and the Facilitating Environment*. London: Karnac.

Winnicott, D.W. (1971/2005) *Playing and Reality*. London: Routledge.

# 12

# Religious Identity

## Pnina Werbner

To speak of religious identity is to refer to a particular way of approaching 'difference'. Religious identity is, above all, a discourse of boundaries, relatedness and otherness, on the one hand, and encompassment and inclusiveness, on the other – and of the powerful forces that are perceived to challenge, contest and preserve these distinctions and unities. In this sense the conjunction of religion and identity is both more, and less, than religion, seen broadly as a world-encompassing way of life relating to the sacred, and identity, as the locus of self and subjectivity. Religious identity may be invoked to explain or legitimise conflicts between and within religious groups. It emerges whenever groups are torn apart by schismatic or sectarian divisions, or engage among themselves in arguments of identity, often passionate and sometimes violent, even where doctrinal differences appear to be minimal.

Religious identity also surfaces discursively when settled religions are challenged by encounters with neighbouring or invading groups. It is a trope foregrounded whenever religion is politicised in new ways; when, for example, a self-identifying group threatens to encompass or dominate the state, to reform subjects' modes of living and thinking, or to transform civil society, in the name of transcendental moral precepts. On such occasions religious identity becomes in public discourse an essential truth, the mysterious

locus of axiomatic value, an explanation for mobilisation and a source of inexplicable passion. These turbulent times of resurgence or conflict contrast with others when religions, however defined, come to be taken for granted, when boundaries between religious groups are frequently blurred and co-existence often unmarked, so that a commerce in symbols and ritual modes of worship leads unreflectively to syncretic amalgams.

For believers, religious identity marks, above all, the division between human and sacred worlds, person and God, sacred and profane. It conceptualises and embodies cosmologies of difference between the living and the dead. In this respect, religious identity points to the experience of transcendence and divinity both for individuals and collectivities.

In this chapter, I begin by examining the theoretical foundations of religious identity in the study of totemism, outlined in the early works of Fustel de Coulanges, Durkheim and Levi-Strauss. These inaugural works theorise, I argue, the marking and transcending of religious boundaries and the embodied, embedded, aesthetic and ritual dimensions of religious practice. Following this, I survey briefly the limitations of current definitions of religion in relation to critical debates on the emergence of 'World Religions'. These debates raise issues of religious *process*: of rupture and continuity, which are addressed by recent theories of the politics of syncretism, heteroglossia and hybridity versus anti-syncretism and puritanism. The convivial participation of different religious groups at pilgrimage centres, in ritual processions or in other communal arenas enables the incorporation and movement of strangers across territorial boundaries. Against this, frontier encounters or reformist movements give rise to a sharpening of religious identities and with it to communal conflicts, a topic the paper addresses by exploring scholarly debates on the rise of communalism on the Indian subcontinent.

In the light of these debates I turn in part three of the chapter to some contemporary explorations of religious resurgence or 'fundamentalism' and the saliency of religious identity as exemplified in the emergence of political Islam and Islamic neo-fundamentalism, the global spread of Christian missionising, evangelical and Pentecostal movements, and the rise of Jewish, Hindu and Buddhist nationalisms. Such conjunctural movements challenge, of course, simplistic ideas of the Enlightenment or modernity as leading inexorably to secularisation, the disenchantment of the world or the death of religion. They raise novel questions about the conservative or democratising role of religion in the public sphere. But religious identity is also a matter of individual subjectivity. Hence, in the final part of this chapter I explore the emergence of complex religious identities as dimensions of personhood and personal experience. Given the breadth and complexity of the issues surveyed here, my discussion of each will necessarily be sketchy and brief, and is intended to point the reader to key debates and issues and to major scholarly texts, rather than provide a comprehensive account of each topic.

## TOTEMISM

In *The Elementary Forms of Religious Life* Durkheim (1964[1915]) defines religion as

> [...] a unified system of beliefs and practices relative to sacred things, that is to say, things set apart

and prohibited – beliefs and practices which unite into one moral community called a Church, all those who adhere to them. (1964[1915]: 47)

While any fixed distinction between the sacred and profane has been much disputed by later theorists (for a subtle discussion see Asad, 2003; Morris, 1987: 121–2), it forms the basis of Durkheim's theory of religion as identity. Rather than privileging the idea of gods or spirits, the stress is on the *unity* of morality, belief and practice, underpinned by institutionalised organisation and collective consciousness and solidarity.

Durkheim describes the Australian Aboriginal *Corrobori*, the periodic meeting of the clan at sacred sites for ritual celebration in which sacred ritual totemic emblems are displayed and manipulated, as a period of intense emotion and action, of running, jumping, shrieking and rolling in the dust to which are added the beating of boomerangs and the whirling of bull roarers. This 'collective effervescence' in which passions are released is experienced as intensely powerful. Participants feel they are being dominated and carried away by a power external to themselves that makes them into new beings (Durkehim, 1964[1915]: 218). This is the moral power of society, which dominates individuals and is imbued in their consciousnesses. Hence, the totem is not a mere representation of the physical world. On the contrary, it is powerfully imbued with the collective sentiments and passions associated with ritual participation. So powerful are these that the totem seems like an external force, transcendent to the individual, to be venerated, having sentimental force (Durkehim, 1964[1915]: 230). Such religious emblems perpetuate society beyond the life of any specific individual; they are hereditary, having a continuity of their own.

In this formulation, Durkheim appears to be proposing a simple correspondence theory. He famously argued that 'the totemic principle, [...] [is] nothing else than the clan itself, personified and represented to the imagination under the visible form of the animal or vegetable which serves as totem'

(1964[1915]: 206). Society, in other words, being immanent in each of its members, worships itself. In sharing substance with the totemic object, man recognises himself as a social being. Social time is cyclical: everyday life, the profane, marked by individual pursuits and petty conflicts, is periodically interrupted by intense bursts of collective effervescence.

But on closer inspection it emerges that the sacred effervescent moments generated during the *Corrobori* are not merely epiphenomenal reflections of material, territorial or political interests. On the contrary: religious identities are boundary-crossing, transcending the local and creating the grounds for more universal, inclusive identities. The totemic clan, as Durkheim himself repeatedly admits, is *not in any way a corporate, territorial or interest group* (1964[1915]: 167), an argument for which he was later castigated for inconsistency (Evans Pritchard, 1965; Lukes, 1973a).

How are we to understand the paradoxical statement that the totem is both a 'flag' of the group and yet not constitutive of pre-existing economic or social groups? The answer to this puzzle highlights the originality of Durkheim's thought. First, at a higher level of semiotic abstraction, totemic clans form a complex system of named groups classified according to a cosmological order that encompasses the whole natural universe, from the sun, moon and stars to animals and plants. Second, clan exogamy generates networks of affinity across the whole tribe. But above all, in stressing the non-correspondence between territorial or interest groups and totems, Durkheim wished to stress the transcendent abstract power of sociality or group morality, irrespective of *specific* social interests. The individual experience of participating in the Corrobori is not simply of solidarity within a bounded interest group (economic, territorial) but of the power of the social as a principle above the individual, a power that both dominates and protects. This is the 'totemic principle', the mysterious force, we may say, of religious

identity; a deeply moral power, embodied materially and symbolically; neither a mask of utilitarian interests nor a marker of territorial groups; neither the discursive product of literate elites nor a disguised expression of the political community. Ritual observance in moral harmony with others strengthens the individual, emboldens him and gives him courage; it re-energes and liberates a person (Durkheim, 1964[1915]: 209, 211), while the reach of religious identities extends beyond any bounded group.

This focus on clan morality merely hints at Durkheim's later development of his theory of totemism in the final chapter of *Elementary Forms* – namely, that beyond each totemic clan's confined 'church', totemism opens up the possibility of a 'religious cosmopolitanism', the vision of a transcendent globalising world – a movement in which Durkheim arguably pays homage to his teacher, Fustel de Coulanges (Inglis and Robertson, 2008: 17). For Fustel de Coulanges religion both marked and transgressed boundaries, and existed at different social scales. Historically Fustel traces an evolution from the religion of the domestic hearth to the gods of the city to unbounded religious universalism (1956 [1984]).

These insights drawn from Durkheim's theory of totemism and its development, form the starting point for this essay. Religious identities are imbued with power, continuity and sentimental force. Like other identities, they do not exist in isolation but are located within generative, open, 'totemic' systems. Writing about totemism as a cosmological system representing a social world of friendship and enmity, resemblance and difference, Levi Strauss has argued that it is 'a vision of humanity without frontiers' (1966: 166).

Drawing on Levi-Strauss and Fustel de Coulanges to analyse the movement of strangers in West Africa, Richard Werbner argues that '[r]eligion and strangerhood transform together' (1989: 224). He makes the further point, critical to my discussion below, that against nineteenth-century evolutionary theories that posit an expansion of religious identities towards increasing universalisation, there may equally be a reverse move towards 'retribalisation'; indeed, he says, 'movements have to be explained in either direction, towards *societas* or towards *civitas*, from boundary maintenance or from boundary transcendence' (1989: 224). In other words, just as religious identities can be opened up to become more cosmopolitan or inclusive, so too they can be parochialised. The relationship is dialectical and dynamic. The Mwali cult studied by Werbner, a 'cult of the macrocosm, must continually 'resolve opposite tendencies, towards inclusiveness and universalism, on the one hand, and towards exclusiveness and particularism on the other' (1989: 247). Rather than universalism, 'dynamic tension' is thus a key feature of the religious identities produced at pilgrimage centres and sacred shrines. They are 'cults of the middle range, [...] more far-reaching than any parochial cult of the little community, yet less inclusive in belief and membership than any world religion in its most inclusive form' (1989: 247).

It is significant, as Werbner notes, that pilgrimage centres are key ritual sites for encounter between strangers from different ethnic and religious groups. In South Asia Muslims and Hindus historically mingled at saints' shrines and lodges or participated together in processions on ritual occasions. But as I argue below, relations between the same religious groups have also been marked by periodical outbursts of communal violence in which the lines between religious groups have been sharply drawn.

## DEFINITIONAL CONUNDRUMS AND THE WORLD RELIGIONS DEBATE

If totemism theorised the principle of religious identity, the rise of world religions has generated definitional conundrums. In particular, the inability to define religion as

the locus of internal conflict, division and diversity, of difference within transcendent unity, appears to plague most definitions of religion. In his celebrated essay, *Religion as a Cultural System*, Clifford Geertz defines religion as:

(1) a system of symbols which acts to (2) embellish powerful, pervasive, and long lasting moods and motivations in men by (3) formulating conceptions of a general order of existence and (4) clothing these conceptions with such an aura of factuality that (5) the moods and motivations seem uniquely realistic. (1973a: 90)

Geertz's phenomenological stress is on the seeking of (unified) meaning in the face of perceived uncertainty and chaos. There is no hint in the essay that the Islam which he studied in Java was, by his own account, divided and divisive; that its 'moods and motivations' differed radically among different and sometimes opposed Muslim Javanese social segments, each with its own publicly recognised religious identity, 'symbolic acts' and 'conceptions of a general order of existence' (Geertz, 1973b).

Geertz carefully distinguishes in this definitional essay (though perhaps not elsewhere) among religion, science, aesthetics (a mere matter of the 'visual'), and common sense, the latter somewhat akin to the Durkheimian notion of the profane. For Asad, the assumption that religion is an analytically identifiable categorical domain across different societies and historical epochs essentialises religion and posits an unwarranted separation from politics and 'power' (1993: 28). In a far-reaching critique of Geertz's essay, Asad insists, drawing on Foucauldian notions of discourse as power/knowledge that:

[...] there cannot be a universal definition of religion, not only because its constituent elements and relationships are historically specific, but because that definition is itself the historical product of discursive processes. (1993: 29)

A discursive approach to religion, Asad argues, cannot accommodate Geertz's phenomenological quest for *sui generic* 'meaning'. Meaning is itself a construction, a truth regime authorised by a religious establishment.

Terms like 'religion' are always the specific product of particular discursive formations at particular moments in history. It was the medieval Christian church, Asad proposes, which, once it had established its sole authority as a source of authentic discourse (1993: 38), drew and redrew the boundary between the religious and secular (1993: 39). In the normalising discourse of the church, Islam's conflation of religion and politics was defined as an aberration. He thus disagrees not only with Geertz's definition but also with Dumont's historical view that Christianity gave way 'by scissiparity, as it were, to an autonomous world of political institutions and speculations' – once 'the great cloak' of medieval religion lost its 'all embracing capacity,' to become an individual affair (1971: 32).

Following Asad, some have argued that:

> [...] the category of religion has quite a specific history embedded deeply in the development of modern European public culture and the increasingly intense interactions between Europe and the wider world ... over the past 500 years or so. (Hirst and Zavos, 2005: 4)

Echoing this critique, Green and Searle-Chatterjee propose that the world religion model is a recent one that

> [...] implicitly assumes that religious activity and belief can be understood independently of the contexts in which they appear. Religion is taken to be a separable and definable phenomenon that has crystallised into about six distinct major faiths with specific institutions and literatures. (Green and Searle-Chatterjee, 2008: 2)

Although it might seem that Asad's discursive-specific approach would lead to the view that since there is no universal object of study we might call 'religion', there are no grounds for a comparative religious approach, Asad himself draws back from the brink, arguing for the possibility in anthropology of studying particular 'religions'. How such religions may be identified remains, however, obscure. Equally problematic is the absence of a theoretical conceptualisation of internal contestation, heterodoxy and dissent, despite the fact that fissiparous tendencies appear to be a pervasive feature of many

religions, however defined. An alternative is to regard religion as merely a discursive field of competitive power, in which protagonists have no shared sentiments in common, no rituals or collective values one might call religious. The theoretical danger of such an approach is, of course, as Clifford Geertz might say, of throwing the religious baby out with the bathwater, a danger averted by Eisenstadt's Weberian theorisation of world religions. This has the merit also of recognising the relative antiquity of religion, against its construction as a recent European 'modern' invention.

According to Eisenstadt, Judaism and Islam were discursively recognised as discrete and separate well before the advent of modernity. As early as the eighth century AD, not only Jews and Christians but Hindus and Zoroastrians were defined by Muhammad bin Qasim, conqueror of Sind, as *ahl al-Dhimma*, 'People of the Book', although, as Friedman says, this 'expansion of the concept entailed a compromise with idolatry' (Friedmann, 2003: 52). Hinduism was a term coined by Persians to refer to the people of South Asia well before the arrival of the British. By the late thirteenth century, the term Hindu was routinely used as a religious designation (Talbot, 2003: 90). Indeed, Eisenstadt has suggested that the crystallisation of 'Axiel-Age civilisations' occurred in the first millennium BC. It arose, he argues, from a revolution typified by the 'emergence and institutionalisation of [a] new basic ontological conception of the *chasm between the transcendental and mundane orders*' (Eisenstadt, 1999: 4, emphasis added), which entailed the perception that the mundane order was 'incomplete', and thus both human personality and socio-political and economic orders were in need of reconstruction 'according to the precepts of a higher ethical or metaphysical order or vision'. Eisenstadt proposes that 'this reconstruction suggests a movement toward "salvation"', a Christian term which had its equivalents in all these civilisations (1999: 4). Such transcendental ontological visions and tensions were institutionalised in centres of elite intellectual learning and 'distinct symbolic organisational arena(s)', which attempted, often with limited success, to 'permeate' and 'absorb' their peripheries (1999: 4). Rulers, the political order, were held accountable to a higher authority, whether God or Divine Law, while new political elites appeared in dynamic tension with the religious ones.

The expansion of a self-consciously self-defining Islam from the seventh century AD onwards, and the subsequent violence generated in Europe and the Near East by the medieval Crusades in a Christian movement to purify the Holy Land and Jerusalem for Christendom – a movement associated along its path as Norman Cohn reminds us (1957: 49–51 *passim*) with repeated pogroms against the Jewish population – both attest to the existence of religion as a concept and a mobilising banner well before the European Enlightenment and Age of Exploration. Nor is this surprising. Religious encounters generate discourses of religious identity, in the same way that ethnic or national encounters do. Identities, whatever the historical period, are always located within a shifting social field of difference and differentiation. In 'frontier settings', as Talbot argues, 'prolonged confrontation between different groups intensifies self-identity' (2003: 52). But, equally, *internal* religious divisions are often the most fierce and even murderous; one cannot overlook the centrifugal processes of 'antagonisation' and 'heterogenisation' that crystallise in response to the forging of unified national or religious identities, as van der Veer reminds us (1994a: 14–5).

Religious polemics emerged well before the European Enlightenment. Yehuda HaLevi wrote the *Kuzari*, an imaginary polemical dialogue between Judaism and Greek philosophy, Christianity, Islam and Karaism, in 1140, while living in exile in medieval Spain. Another poetical polemics was written in India, by Eknath, in the sixteenth century as a Hindu–Muslim ('Turk') dialogue, in which the differences between the two religions are spelled out sharply in a discourse that has, strikingly, barely changed since, though this particular poem ends in rapprochement (Zelliot, 2003). As Levi-Strauss reminds us (1966), ordering and classifying activities are in no way exclusively modern. They were the distinctive hallmark of Neolithic man. Totemism, we have seen, is itself a way of deploying a classification of natural species to create conceptually a homologous human world of difference and resemblance.

Eisenstadt's essentially dialectical approach allows, unlike Asad's, for the emergence of heterodoxies and schismatic or dissenting groups and tendencies. The centre's power is always tentative, since 'alternative, competing transcendental visions' constantly develop within it. These, Eisenstadt suggests, crystallise around three basic 'antinomies inherent in the very premise of these civilisations': the tension between reason and revelation, the range of possible transcendental visions and their methods of implementation, and the desirability of institutionalising these visions, an issue at the heart of discussions of religious fundamentalism.

Such an approach enables a broad understanding of what religion is while escaping the straightjacket of decontextualised entitification or essentialism that Asad rightly warns against, of spurious typological comparisons between apparently fixed, discrete unities endowed artificially with agency typifying the World Religions approach. It highlights the fact that anthropological and sociological analyses must shift their gaze away from such constructed entities to a comparative analysis of *processes*, in this case of religious boundary-making, unmaking and remaking, and the discourses that generate, inform or reflect on these. When and why do religious groups who for centuries have shared public spaces of convivial celebration and syncretic ritual decide to actively and sometimes violently deny shared participation? This question has led to a debate among South Asian scholars regarding the limits of religions and of religious identities in South Asia.

## PILGRIMAGE, RELIGIOUS CONVIVIALITY AND SACRED PERIPHERALITY

Shared shrines, processions and religious festivals have been analysed as sacred sites in which different ethnic and religious groups have historically participated side by side. According to Victor Turner, a defining feature of pilgrimage centres is their sacred peripherality. As 'centres out there', *beyond* the territorial political community, they erase differences between groups so that ritual journeys come to be transformative movements of amity (Turner, 1974: ch. 5). Pilgrimage centres are thus alternative loci of value centred on religious identity rather than territorially defined political communities. Like the rites of passage of tribal societies, the ritual movement in pilgrimage culminates in a liminal (or liminoid) moment of '*communitas*', which is anti-structural and anti-hierarchical, releasing an egalitarian sociality among pilgrims. Like totemism, pilgrimage creates an alternative ethical order, one uncircumscribed by territorially defined relations of power and authority.

While Turner's optimistic vision has been criticised (Werbner, 1977: xii *passim*; see also Eade and Sallnow, 1991), there is evidence that Sufi pilgrimage shrines in South Asia often transcend the boundaries between Hindus and Muslims, while simultaneously recognising difference and hierarchy (Rehman, 2007; Saheb, 1998; Werbner, 2003; Werbner and Basu, 1998). This marking of both equality and difference points to the fact that rather than total 'religious synthesis', the amity at these shrines is better described as a moment of heteroglossia, (Bakhtin, 1981: 368): like urban processions and carnivals, worship at these shrines is open to multiple interpretations by different cohorts of participants who nevertheless share a joint project of shared communication and devotional performance. Religious identity is anchored in these moments of communitas and dialogism without negating diversity.

Invoking this conviviality, the 'rupture' view of South Asian religion(s) contends that before British colonialism, Muslim and Hindu elites had shared interests, while the masses participated in a shared syncretistic culture (Saiyed, 1989: 242; but see Van der Veer, 1994: 29, for a critique of Nandy, 1990). The evidence for a prior dialogical co-existence and blurred religious boundaries between Hindus and Muslims draws on ethnographic studies of sites of shared religious participation – shrines and religious processions – and on evidence of the lengthy process of Islamic conversion. These were disrupted, it is argued, by the British colonial state's bureaucratic ordering activities of classification, enumeration and legislation, and above all by electoral politics, coupled with modernising religious reform, leading inexorably to the new phenomenon of religious communal violence.

Talbot, however, critiques the view that, 'Communal violence was itself a British construct,' making it 'questionable whether Hindu or Muslim identity existed prior to the nineteenth century in any meaningful sense' (2003: 84). Against this, she points out that from the very start, 'Hindu and Muslim identities were not formed in isolation. The reflexive impact of the other's presence moulded the self-definition of both groups' and this created a clear sense of identity during 'frontier' encounters.

Eaton's work (1993) on Islamic conversion clarifies the proposition that Islamicisation processes in South Asia occurred very gradually, in the form of embodied ideas, not reducible to the effects of Muslim reformists' missionary zeal; a process which, according to Robinson (1983), is still continuing. Against that, Ahmad (1981) theorises the localisation or 'indigenisation of Islam'. The need is, however, as Basu (1998) has argued, to recognise the reverse process as well: of an 'Islamicisation of the indigenous' in South Asia, as local myths are purified and given an Islamic gloss when Islam comes to be embedded in different geographical and cultural settings (Eaton, 1993: 284).

As elsewhere, the politics of syncretism in South Asia define religious 'purity' and 'hybridity' in political terms (Stewart and Shaw, 1994). Against the syncretic amity at Sufi shrines, Islamicisation processes in contemporary South Asia are influenced by the mutual hostilities, antagonisms and wars between Hindus and Muslims. Since Partition, and in the face of more recent Hindu nationalist religious discourses and communal violence, culminating in the destruction of the Babri mosque in Ayodhya, religion has become more intensely politicised than ever, shaping theories of both syncretism and anti-syncretism (van der Veer, 1994a).

## COMMUNAL ARENAS AND THE SYNCRETISM ANTI-SYNCRETISM DEBATE

Religious syncretism belongs to a lexical family that includes terms such as hybridity, creolism or cultural bricolage. Such terms are open to the accusations that they imply prior bounded 'wholes', and are thus misleading. In an historical review, Shaw and Stewart argue against this view, and against the linked idea that syncretism denotes the inauthentic and deviant. Instead, they propose that our scholarly interest should focus upon *processes* of religious synthesis and *discourses* of syncretism (1994: 7), since syncretism is integrally bound up with anti-syncretism, 'the antagonism to religious synthesis shown by agents concerned with the defence of religious boundaries.' The politics of syncretism, as Richard Werbner argues in his afterword to the volume, is a 'politics of interpretation and re-interpretation' (1994: 212). Anti-syncretism, Shaw and Stewart perceptively note, 'is frequently bound up with the construction of "authenticity"', which is in turned often linked to notions of "purity" (1994: 212). By contrast, syncretism is often thought to be peaceful, tolerant and inclusive.

Hence, against Geertz's (1968) proposal that Islam is plural and embedded in commonsense, taken-for-granted, historically and culturally specific locales, it may be argued that in theory, and often in practice, when a world religion encroaches into an already charged social field, as in South Asia, both religious practice and scriptural exegesis are likely to be politicised and to *lose* the taken-for-granted, doxic transparency that they once possessed. Instead, in such frontier encounters, as Talbot (2003: 52) calls them, religions become highly self-conscious, reflexive ideologies. Intertextuality, in other words, relativises all knowledge (see Werbner, 2003: 289–91).

In a groundbreaking study Sandria Freitag (1989) traces the rise of religious communalism in South Asia to events at the end of the nineteenth century. A basic distinction Freitag makes is between the 'relational' community, on the one hand, produced locally through shared celebration of religious festivals, ceremonies and processions in urban public arenas, and, on the other hand, ideological constructions of community that invoke a much wider pan-India nationality. Popular public arena celebrations in eighteenth- and nineteenth-century North India were multicultural. They ranged from colourful Hindu processions like *Ramnaumi*, in which the god Ram and effigies of other gods were paraded through the streets, to *Muharram* processions in which flags and *tazias*, replicas of the tombs of the martyred grandsons of the Prophet, Ali and Hussein, were removed from their storage in *imambara* buildings, processed through the streets, and ultimately buried in an area defined as *karbala* (Korom, 2003). There were also processions to saints' shrines, and a multiplicity of seasonal festivals such as Holi and Diwali, while popular dramas such as *Ramlila* enacted the Ramayana, the battle of good and evil, over a period of at least 10 days. Celebrated in carnivalesque style, with folk music, food, dance and drink available in abundance, most years these public events were open to the whole population, irrespective of religious identity, living in the town or neighbourhood.

The intimate relationship between the pre-colonial rulers and this public culture was disrupted by the advent of colonialism. The colonial authorities, who remained remote from these local public arenas, could prosecute disturbers of the peace in the courts but were unable to stem hostilities when they erupted periodically on the ground. Muslims felt increasingly beleaguered as the majority Hindu population's sheer numbers influenced administrative decisions. In the twentieth century, violent divisions among Muslims themselves arose, reflecting rising sectarianism and the growing influence of Islamic reform movements in British India (on this see Metcalf, 1982). Yet shared Muslim processions continued to be held in Pakistan in the 1970s, and were witnessed in the 1990s in India by Pinault. Nevertheless, reformist debates about proper conduct of self-flagellation during Muharram were part of growing sectarian violence (Abou Zahab, 2008).

The pulsating rhythms of religious festivals in India, with their periodical moments of liminal, multivocal or heteroglossic collective effervescence, were a metaphor for community throughout the eighteenth and nineteenth centuries. But because public culture and identity were articulated in a religious vocabulary, this meant that whatever the causes of communal clashes – and these were not always religious – conflicts were constructed in religious terms. By the end of the nineteenth century new actors had entered the public arena – including modern political parties. The period since then came to be marked by an increasing intensity of communal rioting, which culminated ultimately in the death of hundreds of thousands of Hindus, Muslims and Sikhs during the aftermath of the Partition of India and Pakistan in 1947.

Through all this, religious identities continued to be generated and embedded in performance. This did not cease with the rise of the Hindutva religious nationalist movement, though its move was towards new, invented traditions. Nevertheless, these mimicked familiar popular culture forms, in particular processions and pilgrimages, as we shall see below, and drew on myths of origin to legitimise nationalist ideologies.

## THE RISE OF FUNDAMENTALISM AND THE TOTALISING OF RELIGIOUS IDENTITY

If religious identities are produced through border encounters and internal power struggles, and are embedded in ritual performance and in religious festivals, these vary in scale, from the most intimate and exclusive – offerings or domestic sacrifice to the ancestors – to the widest and most inclusive congregation at a distant pilgrimage site, beyond the little community or any territorial group. In such celebrations of identity, sacred moments alternate with profane, and the boundaries of ritual communities are not sharply policed.

The challenge is to explain when and under what circumstances do religious boundaries come to be sharply, and often violently, drawn. Fustel de Coulanges, it will be recalled, argued that when city-states waged wars, they carried their gods with them. The expansion of Islam and the Crusades, like the imperial wars that preceded them, were cast in this way in a religious idiom. But it was the seventeenth-century Thirty Years' War between European states aligned with Catholic, Lutheran and other Protestant sects – the last major religious war in Europe, leaving in its trail bloodshed and devastation – that marked the rise of the reformist Puritans and other Protestant sects with their proto-fundamentalist tendencies. In South Asia during the same period Shaykh Ahmed Sirhindi, an early reformist Naqshbandi Sufi, denounced the Mughal Emperor Akbar for his open tolerance of

Hindu traditions and discourses, and attacked Sufi 'syncretic' customs as *bida*, unlawful innovation, arguing that 'Islam and infidelity are two irreconcilable opposites' (Friedmann, 2003: 55–6, 61). These were the precursors of modern-day fundamentalist movements.

Eisenstadt, whose argument once again I find compelling in enabling us to theorise the underlying structural and intellectual commonalities between apparently quite different fundamentalist movements, typifies these early proto-fundamentalist movements as 'utopian heterodoxies', which 'promulgated eschatological visions' aiming at a 'total reconstruction of the mundane order according to sharply articulated transcendental visions' (1999: 25). The movements stressed the need 'to purify existing social and political reality in the name of a pristine vision' – a sacred text, exemplary person or exemplary period (Eisenstadt, 1999: 26). Hence, also, they stressed the construction of 'sharp symbolic and institutional boundaries, and the distinction between purity and pollution, […] the purity of the internal fundamentalist community as against the pollution of the outside world' (Eisenstadt, 1999: 26). They 'evinced strong ideological totalistic tendencies', a weak tolerance of ambiguity, and a tendency to 'ritualise' behaviour. Hence, they defined all external enemies as the 'epitome of pollution'. Finally, they 'denied the autonomy of reason as against revelation or faith' (Eisenstadt, 1999: 26).

This cluster of features points also to a trend in these movements towards the totalising of religious identity, both collective and individual. It is a tendency that came to be fully expressed later, in religious fundamentalist movements that arose in the early twentieth century in North America, Europe and the Middle East, following the 'great revolutions' of the eighteenth century (Eisenstadt, 1999: 39–40) with their vision of a new political order based on a utopian reformist (secular) ethics of social and individual reconstruction and progress. These secular revolutions wished to bring the 'City of God' closer to the 'City of Man', though

in this case, their universalist Gods were Reason, Egalitarianism, Social Justice and Popular Sovereignty. One tendency evident in these revolutions, which may be termed the pluralist or procedural, was the path taken by the Founding Fathers of the American Revolution; the other, the French and, particularly, the Jacobin – promoted a totalising conception of the common good, achievable through 'totalistic political action; a belief in the ability of politics to reconstitute society', and an overarching totalitarian, all-encompassing ideology (Eisenstadt, 1999: 72–3).

Modern religious fundamentalist movements were shaped by this Jacobin project. They are 'modern' in rejecting tradition, i.e., the continuous historical evolution of religious discourse and practice, and in their faith in the possibility of social and personal moral reconstruction. They are, at least in principle, universalist, egalitarian and voluntary. They endorse collective political mobilisation and activism. But they are anti-modern in their utopian orientation to an eschatological vision of a pristine *past* moment, rather than 'progress' to a utopian future, as envisioned by the secular democratic revolutions. They differ also from pluralist democratic visions in their qualification of the Enlightenment's foundational premise of autonomous individual reason, their invasive control of the private sphere and their tendency to conflate the civil and political spheres (Eisenstadt, 1999: 92). Their xenophobic and Manichean ideological division of the world into good and evil, inside and outside, pure and polluted, are central to their definition of religious identities and political activism, all of which are based around strong notions of purity and danger (Douglas, 1966). Most movements that arose included an almost obsessive marking of gender divisions, represented in diacritica such as the veil in Islam or (in the case of men) the beard, symbolising the defence of women's 'purity' (especially sexual) and of the boundaries of women's engagement with the outside world (see, for example,

Yuval-Davis, 1992), although some movements were more egalitarian in gender terms, allowing women an active role and a place in the public sphere.

This, in broad strokes, is the blueprint for fundamentalism outlined by Eisenstadt. It is evidently Weberian in its approach, starting from the intellectual antinomies of modernity (Eisenstadt, 1999: 62–4) and tracing the contradictory trends these generate, which ultimately shape subjects' different life projects, identities and subjective insertion into society. Like most scholars of utopian and millenarian movements, Eisenstadt stresses that they occur during periods of transition, change and uncertainty, or, more specifically, among persons 'dislocated' or 'banned' from the cultural or political centre and positioned on the periphery.

In reality, however, fundamentalist movements are not so much, or not only, endogenous intellectual solutions to the predicaments of modernity but a political response to specific national and international geopolitical circumstances and power struggles. Their trajectories depend on the extent to which they capture the political centre or are peripheralised, and, more broadly, the dissenting or critical role they play vis-à-vis the centre. The impact of an increasingly international media, enabling the transmission of images of global theatres of violence and terror to a worldwide audience is critical to these trajectories. In reality also, despite their declared egalitarianism, most fundamentalist movements focus on charismatic leaders who hold complete sway over followers, much as Sufi masters do, and develop rather similar hierarchical organisational structure.

The fundamentalism blueprint outlined above must therefore be regarded more as a generative model for comparative analysis than an accurate description of any particular movement's genesis. This is evident, for example, even in the most cursory comparison of radical Islamist movements such as the Iranian revolution, the Taliban and al-Qaeda, and among all these movements

and various other more conservative or feminist so-called fundamentalist groups. The Iranian revolution, for example, was fuelled by resentment to the Shah of Iran's authoritarian, highly repressive regime's aggressive secularisation and modernisation programme, supported by a multitude of American advisors and entrepreneurs, which led to an alliance between Shi'a clerics, a powerfully autonomous and economically secure group in Iran, and other economic groups in the society. The complex constitutional theocratic democracy that has evolved in Iran since 1978 has witnessed the clerics cede some of their power only to claw it back since the elections in 2006 and 2009. In the case of the Taliban, American support for Islamist guerrilla groups fighting the Communist regime in Afghanistan during the Cold War era, and the period of anarchy and chaos following the Soviet withdrawal, led to the transformation of the Taliban, formed in madrassahs in the North West Frontier Province among Afghan refugees, into an activist militant neo-fundamentalist force. Despite their origins in the relatively apolitical Deobandi reform movement that emerged in India at the end of the eighteenth century (Metcalf, 1982), the Taliban's totalitarian stress on personal morality and purity led, in the absence of any coherent theory of the state, to a reign of terror, in which women were forbidden to work or girls to study, even in primary schools, and all traces of popular culture were violently banished. Even kite flying or owning singing birds were banned.

Al-Qaeda first emerged among returnee Saudi Afghan war veterans, suppressed by the Saudi regime, and was fuelled by resentment towards the authoritarianism and elitism of the House of Saud, propped up by its American patrons (Al-Rasheed, 2007). It recruited from among an international cohort of young Islamists trained in the Afghan jihadist camps. One might go on in the same fashion to trace the rise of Hamas or Hizbullah, and to contrast these movements with Jamaat-i-Islami, an early fundamentalist group in India and Pakistan that engages unofficially in violence against other sectarian groups through its student wing, but is neither jihadist nor a mass movement. Instead, it espouses Islamicisation through the ballot box. Another quite different example is of feminist Islamic groups in Malaysia and Indonesia who seek to return to the early Islamic scriptures in order to promote a programme of gender equality (Robinson, 2008; Stivens, 2008); yet another is the more puritanical pietist women's movement in Pakistan or Egypt affiliated to the Muslim Brotherhood (Mahmood, 2005).

Such comparisons do not so much negate the fundamentalism blueprint outlined above but highlight the fact stressed by most oriental scholars of Islamism that even when they invoke a global ideology, Islamic movements are first and foremost responses to national political failures. Among these may be included the inefficiency, corruption and authoritarianism of many imperfectly modernised postcolonial Muslim states, allied with the growing importance of civil society in the Muslim world; this is signalled by the efflorescence of independent local mosques and local preachers beyond the control of authoritarian regimes. Such mosques are funded by labour migrants working in the Gulf or by the Saudi regime, which has used its petro-dollars to support Islamists for a long time. Despite claims to global universalism, then, most Islamist movements are embedded in projects of national identity in the postcolonial era and are thus in many respects not so different from the religious nationalist movements discussed below. This conjunctural aspect of world religious identities is evident also in the case of Christianity as a global movement.

## RUPTURE OR EMBEDDEDNESS? CONJUNCTURAL IDENTITIES AND THE GLOBAL SPREAD OF CHRISTIANITY

Islamist Reformists have condemned the annual Muslim carnivalesque celebration of *Muharram* in Trinidad (Korom, 2003) and the Berber annual masquerade ritual of *Bilmawn* celebrated after the Eid in the Atlas mountains, (Hammoudi, 1993), festivals which renew and purify the community, on the grounds that these rituals are traditional accretions from a pre-Muslim past. These hardliners prohibit – often very aggressively – music, dance, singing, drama, masquerade, the public exposure of the female body and any overt sexual play. They create barriers to communication by marking themselves as beyond the boundary through dress, veiling, beards and so forth.

But against this impetus to uniformity, just as Islam in Trinidad, Morocco, Indonesia or Pakistan has been for centuries both one and many, embedded in a relatively taken-for-granted way in widely separated localities, so that doctrinal and symbolic continuities are buried beneath superficial differences, so too is Christianity observed in an enormous variety of local and invented traditions in different parts of the world.

The spread of world Christianity began in the sixteenth century, somewhat later than Islam, and followed the routes of European Imperial conquest and colonisation. Thus Latin America became almost universally Catholic, the United States was dominated by the early Puritans who had escaped European persecution, and Africa was initially carved up between colonising nations, with French, Belgian and Portuguese territories primarily Catholic, Lutherans dominant in Namibia and Ghana, and the other British colonies 'split into discrete packages of missionary territory', even within a single colony (Maxwell, 1999: 256). In these the main mission churches – Anglican, Protestant, Catholic, Methodist or Baptist – respected and agreed not to transgress into each other's sacred domains. Nevertheless, even within a single Christian denomination, traditions have varied so that, for example, the passion and resurrection of Christ are allegorised and ritually embodied quite differently in different parts of the world, depending on the circumstances of their introduction. The agony of the crucifixion is ritualised in Latin America and to a lesser extent, Melanesia, whereas in Africa the stress has been, with the notable exception of the Black Jesus cult in Malawi, on the promise of redemption and Jesus the healer. In the Iberian case, the story is of 'cosmic martyrdom', the 'terrifying violation of the person', by barbaric conquerors (Werbner, 1997: 320–1), vicarious suffering through 'flagellation, the manifestation of stigmata, the shedding of human blood, the full imitation of Christ's embodied agony', but these have been notably absent in Africa (1997: 324). This points to the *conjunctural* nature of all religious identities, responsive to their provenance, the time they were introduced and different receptive environment, a feature particularly marked in the case of Christianity because of its schismatic and sectarian tendencies. In speaking of conjuncture I am not referring here to the 'intersection' of identities (of religion with gender, ethnicity, class and so forth), but to religious identities that carry, as Geertz suggested, an 'aura of factuality' that makes their 'moods and motivations seem uniquely realistic', a rooted tradition, when they come to be embedded in different places.

The early Protestant Pentecostals who entered Southern Africa from the USA, Scotland and Scandinavia at the turn of twentieth century were followed, since the 1970s, by an increasingly massive movement that has swept throughout Latin America, Africa, Asia and Papua New Guinea. This new Christian global expansion illustrates clearly the conjunctural quality of religious identity. Pentescostal churches have historically tended to fissure and effloresce into new churches – Zionist, Apostolic, Spiritual, and so forth are all collective rubrics for this enormous efflorescence (Maxwell, 1999; Robbins, 2004: 122). Richard Werbner has characterised this variation as an 'argument of images': different Pentecostal churches in Zimbabwe led by different 'Prophets', who all have built transnational religious organisations, differ in their constructions of microcosm versus macrosm, of sacred centrality or

peripherality and of personhood, while at the same time, believers retain their sense of belonging to a global community (1989: ch. 8). Churches vary in their embodied aesthetics of worship and appearance. Comaroff (1985), in particular, notes the 'subversive bricolage' of sartorial and other signifying practices adopted by the Southern African ZCC, the Zionist church she studied, who enact through symbolic inversion, she argues, a magical resistance to hegemonic representations. The schismatic tendencies in Pentecostalim lead over time to a wide variety of churches, each with its own prophets and church hierarchies, aesthetic and ritual style and doctrinal idiosyncrasies. As research in Botswana shows, whatever their origins many churches accommodate with traditional beliefs and ritual practices – with ideas about ancestral wrath, the efficacy of animal sacrifice, spirit possession, divination, initiation ritual and other local cults of affliction (see, for example, Klaits, 2008). We may speak, following Bourdieu's (1984) analysis of class in *Distinction*, of an emergent semiotic of difference generated by church schisms and splinters, each of which claims and elaborates distinction in uniquely fashioned religious identities within the broader Pentecostal movement.

Pentecostals are not merely – like other evangelicals – born again self-confessed sinners seeking redemption through re-baptism into the church; they are baptised in the Holy Spirit, and the Spirit endows them with the mystical capacity to speak with tongues, heal, exorcise (witches and other demonic or evil spirits) and prophesy. These spiritual gifts are shared with Catholic charismatics and, since the 1960s, with other Protestants (Robbins, 2004: 121). Pentecostalism is an 'experiential' religion. In this sense it cannot be said to be 'fundamentalist'. Christian fundamentalists believe that the gifts of the Spirit ceased to be available to people once they were given to the apostles (Robbins, 2004: 122–3). Fundamentalism's 'chief ritual', according to Ninian Smart, 'is preaching, for which it feels the need of a certainty and an authority flowing from an inerrant Bible' (1987: 227). The mass enthusiastic singing, clapping, music and ecstatic collective effervescence of Pentecostal meetings separates them sharply from the soberness of the fundamentalists. Second, Pentecostal sects and movements are mostly apolitical, and in this too they differ from fundamentalists whose utopian aim is to reconstruct the mundane social and political order according to a 'sharply articulated transcendental vision', to borrow Eisenstadt's phrase above (see also Martin, 1990; Robbins, 2004: 123). Most commentators agree that Pentecostal churches' primary stress is on purity, personal security, work and family responsibility, along with strong condemnation of adultery, alcohol drinking and wasteful spending (Kiernan, 1994: 77–9; Martin, 1998: 127–8). This makes them attractive, commentators argue, to deprived, alienated urban migrants, 'mobile subjects' living in postmodern uncertainty (Bauman, 1998; for a critique see Martin, 1998). Such deprivation, failure-of-modernity theories miss, however, a key feature of all independent churches early on identified for Methodism by Edward P. Thompson (1963): namely, that they provide spaces for leadership; roles, activities and organisational outlets for women as well as men, and a global network for aspiring subaltern groups (Martin, 1998). The same is true for Muslim migrants (Werbner, 2002).

Evangelicals are egalitarian; their ideological stress is on personal moral reconstruction, asceticism and a strict ethical code. Pentecostals rely on ecstatic experience, the power of prayer and millennial notions of the imminence of the Second Coming, rather than a literal reading of the biblical text. They commonly depict the world beyond the church as dangerous and satanic, made up of sinners, witches and traditional spirits (Meyer, 1999). The reality on the ground is, however, more often of tolerance of pluralism and acceptance of difference, of mingling or shared participation with members of other churches whom most

Pentecostals must interact with in their everyday lives, in the sinful world beyond the church. The exception to this are some world renouncing millennial movements who go into 'the wilderness' (see Werbner, 1989). It would also seem that the new Pentecostal 'prosperity' gospel churches making inroads throughout the world since the 1990s make nonsense of any claims to asceticism (on Sweden see Coleman, 2000; on Ghana Gifford, 2004). Their media preachers reach vast audiences.

Much of the debate on Pentecostal-charismatic (P/c) Christianity has been cast, as Joel Robbins notes (2004), in terms either of global western cultural homogenisation or indigenising local adaptability, in which independent churches are '*the bridge over which Africans are brought back to heathenism*' (Sundkler, 1961: 297, original emphasis, quoted in Stewart and Shaw, 1994: 14). The conversion experience for Pentecostals begins with rituals of *rupture*, both from their past and 'traditional' religion, and from their social surroundings, especially because their time is heavily monopolised by church activities (Robbins, 2004: 127–8, 131). Perhaps paradoxically, defining a previous world of spirits as satanic sustains the belief in witchcraft and spirits, even as it tends to demonise them (Meyer, 1999). Over time, however, this initial rupture often comes to be attenuated by the efflorescence of new churches focused on a wide range of prophets and charismatics, carving out distinctive spiritual niches (Comaroff, 1985; Maxwell, 1999; Werbner, 1989: ch. 9). Nevertheless, Christian converts, whether in mission churches or independent new churches, often resist syncretic mixtures in church worship. They separate them from traditional ritual observances and insist on preserving what they perceive to be authentic Christian belief and practice, which define them as members of a world religion. They thus reject the Second Ecumenical Council of the Vatican's new inculturationist policy according to which 'the language and mode of manifesting [faith] may be manifold' (Stewart and

Shaw, 1994: 11), and see themselves as 'modern' religious subjects, a subject to which I turn next.

## MODERN ENCOUNTERS: NATIONALISM, SECULARISM AND PUBLIC RELIGIOUS IDENTITIES

The totemic principle that animates religious identities, this chapter has argued so far, may not correspond to any territorial or interest group; it is a force sustained through intense, liminal moments of affective, embodied performance, which alternate with mundane or profane everyday life. The fluidity of religious identities is reflected in the fact that they both transgress and transcend fixed boundaries, to encompasses strangers in religious cosmopolitanism. At the same time, the totemic principle is constantly contested and recuperated in the fissiparous, schismatic and sectarian impulses of the axial religions. The force of religious identity thus rarely reflects or corresponds to a single unified, bounded, discrete 'religion'.

It is not sufficient, however, to conclude from this that religious identities are merely fluid and 'performative' in the individual sense. Ritual performances are highly complex, *staged* symbolic and aesthetic *collective* events. They may or may not transcend the local; when they do, they bring together different ethnic and religious communities for shared worship in a spirit of conviviality, without necessarily erasing their differences. Ritual carnivalesque festivals and celebrations are thus often heteroglossic, interpreted from quite different perspectives. They can, however, also erupt into violence. The longer they persist the more frequently they come to be contested (Eade and Sallnow, 1991; Hayden, 2002). Nevertheless, public celebrations often sustain the porousness of religious boundaries and hence of religious identities, while doctrinally and ethically, they may promote toleration, transcendence, encompassment and peaceful co-existence.

Against that, we have seen, a salient feature of frontier encounters and even more so of modern religious reform or fundamentalist movements has been their drive to demarcate boundaries sharply by purifying religion of 'inauthentic' practices. While historically, frontier encounters are not new, I want to conclude this chapter by considering, first, the ways in which religious identities have liberalised, intensified or been reified in response to the ruptures and new dogmas of modernity – secularism, liberalism, modern racism, nationalism and the rise of the nation-state. Second, in response to these opposed trends, I want to consider to what extent contemporary religious identities are inflected by other identities, especially gender, ethnicity, electoral politics and citizenship.

Contemporary politics of religious identity in the public sphere can be seen as constituting a broad continuum, from liberal and humanist religious tendencies, on one side, to fascist and xenophobic religious nationalisms, on the other. Jose Casanova (1994), for example, has urged us to recognise that modernity has not resulted, *pace* Weber, in the relegation of religion to the private sphere. Catholicism, which long buttressed authoritarian regimes in fascist Spain or South America, he argues, was transformed in the 1990s into a democratising and liberalising force – in Poland, Spain and Latin America. If the Spanish Christian expansion into the colonies was often violent and they continued to bolster authoritarian, elitist regimes, late twentieth-century missionaries brought with them the message of 'liberation theology', insisting that faith cannot be sustained unless poverty is alleviated and human rights observed.

Missionaries often formed the ideological vanguard of colonialism's expansion in the name of Europe's modernist civilising mission. Wherever they went, they built schools, churches and hospitals, introduced new technologies such as the plough, documented the flora and fauna, wrote dictionaries, translated the Bible into vernacular languages and promoted new material life styles and modern

Christian ideas about personal prayer, work as a calling, personal hygiene and sexual morality. Initially they converted only a tiny minority gathered at mission stations, but their schools frequently educated the future nationalist elites of the colonies.

Despite the spread of independent churches since independence, established mission activities have not ceased even in the post-colonial era. Maxwell (2006a, b) has reviewed the wide range of scholarship on missionaries in Africa. For the postcolonial era, he argues, their role has been both dissenting and repressive, sometimes both in the same country. While the Anglican Bishop of Harare in Zimbabwe declared Robert Mugabe to be 'more Christian than himself', Maxwell observes ironically, '[i]t was left to the Catholic Church to fulfil the prophetic role and speak up for the victims of violence and repression as it had done against the racist settler regime of Ian Smith' (2006b: 417). The same Catholic church, showing 'its capacity for both good and evil', supported the genocide of Tutsis in Ruanda, luring them into churches and actively participating in death squads. '[K]illers paused during massacres to pray at the alter' (Maxwell, 2006b: 417).

The conjunctural politics arising from the religious encounter with European Herder-inspired cultural nationalism, and right-wing, modern (secular) nationalist tendencies has created the strange hybrid of millennial religious nationalism – among Hindus in India, Sinhalese in Sri Lanka and Jews in Israel/Palestine. Like fundamentalists, the nationalists' message is Jacobin: totalistic, transcendental, eschatological and purificatory, drawing sharp boundaries around the religious community that exclude the polluting and dangerous Other; the difference being that, unlike the fundamentalists, religious nationalists' claims for renewal are territorially as well as communally focused.

Religious nationalist movements in both India and Sri Lanka drew on German supremacist Aryan ideas conjoined with notions of heredity and caste to create a comprehensive xenophobic nationalist ideology, which was transcendental, ontological, organicist and redemptive (Bhatt, 2001: 104–8, 132–5; Jaffrelot, 1996). The 'Aryan myth' built on Orientalist philological discoveries that Sanscrit was an Indo-European language and the view that the original Vedic religion had been corrupted, and hence that *Hindutva*, the Hindu nation, had degenerated from its former glory. Scholars have traced the origins of *Hindutva* in the nineteenth century and demonstrate its real connection to European Nazism and fascism (Bhatt 2001: 120, 123–4; see also Jaffrelot, 1996: 53–8). The high value placed on militarism, violence and supremacy in the movement came along with a thrust to define a Hindu 'civilisation', primordially rooted in worship of the god Ram and the 'goddess' *bharat-mata*, 'mother India' (Bhatt, 2001: 187), a land conceived to stretch well beyond India's political borders. In the Hindutva racist imagination, Muslims and Christians are defined as dangerous outsiders, both within and beyond the boundaries, to be expelled from the body politic.

Recognising the power of the past, like most religious nationalist movements, *Hindutva* invented a religio-nationalist performative tradition surrounding the myth and cult of the god Ram, raised to the stature of supreme God, in what some regard as a 'semitising' tendency to emulate monotheistic religions. Rather than the Vedas, the movement elevated the later, more accessible *Bhagavad Gita* and *Ramayana* epics to be its central sacred texts (Bhatt, 2001: 185–6), and drew on devotional *Bhakti* ritual traditions to stage spectacular all-India sacrifices (*yagna*) and religious processions (*yatra*) in order to mobilise the masses and intimidate Muslims and secular Indians (Bhatt, 2001: 171–2). These mass rituals were invented and led by the VHS, a Hindu nationalist movement of orthodox Hindus, monks and priests within the broader *Hindutva* 'family', the *Sangh parivar*. This consisted of a vast network of named organisations, institutions and a political party, the BJP. In one invented tradition based on the *Ramayana*, in 1983 the VHS organised the first of a series of mass processions across India, following the travels of the god Vishnu incarnated as Rama, son of the Ayodhya king, to save the world from the growing powers of the demons. The processions moved from the far corners of India in opposed directions, their paths crossing at VHS headquarters. In each sacred place they visited the pilgrims were blessed by local religious leaders, while a multitude of smaller, five-day processions, which the VHS claimed reached 60 million people, met the processions as they followed 'well-known pilgrimage routes that link major religious centres, suggesting the geographical unity of India as a sacred area of Hindus. In this way, pilgrimage was effectively transformed into a ritual of national integration' (van der Veer, 1994: 123–4). Since 1984, when the Hindutva began a campaign to 'liberate' the 'birthplace' of Lord Rama at Ayodhya, redefined as the sacred centre of the Hindu cosmos (Brass, 2003: 12–5; Jaffrelot, 1996: 399–403), thousands of people have died in mass pogroms. The Babri mosque, built allegedly by Muslim invaders above Ram's temple that marked the place of his birth, was destroyed by a mob in 1992 in a signal political event which was followed by violent rioting. The riots inflicted heavy losses of life and property, especially among Indian Muslims, in many parts of the country (Bhatt, 2001: 195–6; Jaffrelot, 1996: 455–64 *passim*).

The RSS and VHS's violent mob politics has gone along with their political party's involvement in democratic coalition electoral politics, but despite the BJP's attempts to appeal to lower castes, to *dalits* and even Muslims, scholars agree that the Hindu nationalist movement has remained upper caste and middle class; an elitist response to the growing involvement of mass lower caste groups in an increasingly pluralised Indian democratic politics (Hansen, 1999). This implies that the apparent spontaneity of its religious identitarian politics is merely a facade.

In a major critique based on detailed empirical research, Paul Brass has refuted a hegemonic discourse of religious communalism in India that explains religious riots as the spontaneous eruption of populist, primordialist religious and caste sentiments or 'identities' (Brass, 1997, 2003: 369, 377–9). Instead, he locates the violence in the near Hobbesian Indian context of endemic rural violence and distrust (1997: 273), widespread police mendacity and corruption and highly competitive national and local politics. He demonstrates that riots are produced in certain, select locations by political actors representing a wide range of constituencies and able to access criminal and armed elements along with a 'lumpen proletariat' mob. These select places develop an 'institutionalised riot system', in which 'riot specialists' 'convert' local incidents that occur during deliberately provocative religious processions (2003: 364–6; 2003: 378) into violent pogroms, through a 'game of brinksmanship' and 'dramatization' (Brass, 1997: 285–8). A critical backdrop to these dramas is the pervasive, taken for granted 'rhetoric of community', enunciated by secular and Hindu politicians alike in their attempts to mobilise votes, and the absence in these places of an accountable, neutral and disciplined police force (1997, 2003: 379). Brass describes the new Hindutva-inspired, post-1980s riots as 'dramatic productions with large casts of extras' (1997: 282; 2003: 364), following predictable plots in 'theatres' of violence.

Similar processes of violent, xenophobic religious nationalism in the conflict between the majority Sinhalese and the minority Tamil can be found in modern postcolonial Sri Lanka. There too the Sinhalese have adopted the Aryan racist myth (Tambiah 1986: 5–6, 58–9; 1992: 131) and, in an 'invention of tradition', the cult of Kataragama has emerged as their 'preeminent guardian god' with its central shrine becoming the site of 'massive pilgrimages and ecstatic festivals' (1986: 59–63). In Sri Lanka too, an origin myth, the *Mahavamsa* (sixth century AD), which tells the tale of the virtuous king who unified the island against demonic Tamil invaders, has been literally applied as historical truth in postcolonial politics. Kapferer (1988) has argued that the legitimacy and ontological reality of the myth for ordinary Sinhalese derives its authenticity from its embeddedness in everyday Sinhalese exorcism rituals. Finally, as in India, in Sri Lanka too theatres of violence are orchestrated productions by religious monks and right wing politicians deploying criminal elements to create riots and massacres.

We find similar themes elsewhere, as in *Gush Emunim* ('Block of the Faithful'), the Jewish nationalist religious settlement movement in the occupied territories of Judea and Samaria, rooted in a mystical relation to the land that draws its legitimacy from God's biblical covenant with Abraham. The Gush is moved by the millennial belief that reclaiming the land of their forefathers from its current Arab inhabitants, defined as *Amalek*, the unassimilable gentile 'other', will hasten the arrival of the Messiah – a redemptive, eschatological view which, like its Hindu and Buddhist counterparts, begins from a sense of national trauma and loss and looks to a glorious, mythic past. As in other religious nationalisms, here too a revisionist, racist, right-wing European ideology has fused Jewish religiosity with a distorted secular-liberal pioneering Zionist nationalism, itself rooted in nineteenth Russian *Narodnik* return-to-the-soil ideals. As elsewhere, so too in Israel, coalition electoral politics have magnified the influence of an activist religious minority and its politicians, and ultimately shaped the fate of the nation and of the whole Middle East. As in India and Sri Lanka, Jewish religious nationalists have been violent not only in committing atrocities against Muslims and Arabs; they also sanctioned the assassination of a Jewish Prime Minister, invoking the Talmudic law of *rodef* (pursuer) and *moser* (turncoat, traitor), epithets for a Jew who has betrayed the Jewish people by abandoning his or her birthright, following the signing by Prime Minister Yitzak Rabin of the Oslo Accords.

Religious nationalists and 'Jacobin' fundamentalists who advocate the political replacement of the state by utopian theocracies in the name of a transcendental god, can be seen as one polar response to the rise of the modern nation-state. For them religious identity is pure, all-encompassing and exclusionary. But by the same token, modern religious identities can be democratic, liberal, tolerant, peaceful and humanist, as in Gandhian, nonviolent, Hindu humanism, Buddhist monks' struggle for democracy in Burma, peaceful Islamic Sufi mysticism or Jewish peace movements in Israel.

Democratic states allow religious pluralism in the private domain and, increasingly, in a multicultural move, are being challenged to grant recognition to minority religious identities in public, though not without a good deal of agonising. In the post Second World War era, and especially in the late twentieth century, large diasporas of pious Muslims from South Asia, North Africa and Turkey have begun to challenge taken-for-granted public norms. In Britain following the Rushdie affair, in France and elsewhere in Europe with the 'scarf affair', in Denmark with the 'cartoon affair,' and in the US after the September 11 bombing of the World Trade Center twin towers, well-established democracies have had to debate the limits of toleration, free speech, free attire or even the rights of religious communities to live encapsulated lives without constant surveillance. 'Multiculturalism' in Europe has thus become in certain contexts a euphemism for the need to resolve the challenges posed by diasporic religious identitarian passionate commitments, which seem to reveal intractable political dilemmas in different countries (on the UK see Modood, 2007; Werbner, 2002). I have called this process 'multiculturalism in history', to convey these affairs' historical impact on expanding notions of citizenship in the West (Werbner, 2005).

The move in democratic nation-states towards so-called 'identity politics' (of religion, gender, sexuality, disability or age) is critiqued by many as challenging the still all too real, encompassing inequalities of class and poverty. Against that one can argue that these new citizenship movements wish to highlight the fact that resolving inequalities is more than just a matter of wealth redistribution: it involves a politics of *recognition*, as Charles Taylor (1994) famously argued. According to this argument religious identity, the force of the 'totemic principle', is not merely collective – although it is that too – but individually experienced, a matter of subjectivity, agency and selfhood. Hence, the denial of identity is tantamount to an effacement of the person.

I want to turn now thus, in conclusion, to the question of religious identity as personal experience and knowledge, constitutive of subject and subjectivity.

## COMPLEX RELIGIOUS IDENTITIES, PERSONHOOD AND EXPERIENCE

For individual subjects, their religious identity is grounded in cosmologies of difference: between the sacred and the profane, the living and the dead, person and God, self and other, men and women, priests and followers, divine kings and their subjects. Most centrally, modes of transcending the ontological division between the sacred and the profane in a religious tradition also define degrees of preferred individual closeness to or distance from divinities and sacred objects. The passion vested in the religious imagination with its distinctive ethos, ideas and ritual practices, also shape individual notions of personhood and experience. These configure a personal ethics of right and wrong, self and other, illness and well-being, as they are embedded in moral universes of significant social relations, and in ritual devotional practices and modes of occult healing.

A focus on religious subjects makes evident the extent to which religious identities are complex, differentiated, intersected and hierarchical even within a single religious tendency. Hence, for example, world renouncers, imbued with divine grace or incarnating the divine, are familiar figures in the religious landscape of many traditions. In these, a separation is posited between ordinary devotees and exceptional figures believed to possess extraordinary ethical and charismatic powers of healing, blessing and knowing. Such figures often follow extreme ascetic practices of bodily self-denial and prayer regimes or, alternatively, of antinomian transgression, trance and ecstatic possession. These practices set them apart. Their closeness or embodiment of divinity is regarded as extremely dangerous for ordinary believers. In Sufi mystical Islam, for example, disciples who wish to achieve gnosis, divine knowledge, must be guided on the Sufi path by a Sufi master, if they are not to go mad or lose themselves in divine ecstasy (see Werbner, 2003). The moral lives and codes of conduct of such figures – shamans, prophets, saints, gurus or priests – often form ideal templates to be emulated by devotees.

Not all religious traditions seek communion between person and God or divinity. Throughout much of Africa, the condition of being too close to ancestral divinities or God above is regarded as extremely dangerous and 'hot', causing affliction among the living and signalling a moral malaise in their social universe which has aroused or angered the dead, so that the aim of both personal and communal sacrificial offerings is to distance gods and spirits to their appropriate place of rest, where they form a cooling, protective canopy – *not* to reach a state of communion as in Catholicism (Evans-Pritchard, 1956; Werbner, 1989: ch. 3).

While Protestantism introduced notions of a direct, unmediated relationship through prayer between potentially all individuals and God, and, indeed, as we have seen, being possessed by the Holy Spirit is an ideal of

Pentecostal Christianity, such possession is nevertheless regarded as imbued with danger. The possessed are held and supported by fellow congregants, and possession is episodic and experiential rather than permanent (see Csordas, 2002).

Much of the comparative debate on religious personhood has tended to focus on the marginalised or oppressed status of women in Catholicism, Judaism, Islam, Hinduism and other religious traditions. A particular instance of this debate has surrounded the predominance of women in cults of demonic affliction or spirit possession in Africa and elsewhere. Grounded initially in reductive feminist approaches, a key issue has been whether spirit possession by boundary-crossing, capricious or demonic spirits of the wild is merely a form of religious blackmail by oppressed women demanding consumer goods from their men. Against this manipulative view are counter examples, as among Kalanga in Botswana and Zimbabwe, where the possessed are elite women, and the ritual associated with demonic expulsion mobilises a wide range of kin and neighbours, purifies the homestead and converts consumer goods acquired through labour migration into a 'good faith economy' (Werbner, 1989: ch. 2). This example points to the fact that cults of affliction, as Victor Turner (1968) aptly called them in his extensive oeuvre on the Ndembu of Zambia, create social solidarity among persons (not only women) suffering illness, sterility and bereavement, cutting across other social divisions within a broader social field. A more subtle feminist counter-hegemonic, 'resistance' approach is by Janice Boddy in her analysis of the Zar cult of the Northern Sudan. Boddy (1989) argues that demonic possession among childless Muslim women enables them to overcome an overdetermined 'closure' – of the womb enclosed by pharonic circumcision and infibulation, of confinement to the walled house, and marriage within the socially enclosed village. Demonic possession frees women, she proposes, to experience themselves as less constrained and more sensual Others, by

adopting a range of persona, among them many real historical figures, who invade the community from beyond its boundaries (Boddy, 1989). It is thus, she believes, a mode of emotional as well as physical healing. Spirit possession can also enable communication of unspoken feelings across gendered divisions (Lambek, 1981). It is often an elaborate aesthetic and experiential performance that serves to purify and renew the cosmos, as in Sinhalese exorcism rituals for young teenage girls approaching puberty (Kapferer, 1983).

Writing against both resistance and identitarian feminist discursive traditions, Saba Mahmood analyses the women's Islamic pietist *da'wa* mosque movement in Egypt in terms of an 'Aristotelian formulation of *habitus*, which is concerned with ethical formation and presupposes a specific pedagogical process by which a moral character is secured' (2005: 135) through repeated bodily practices such as prayer or the Muslim scarf in such a way that 'outward' behaviour and 'inward dispositions' are merged into a single unity that takes permanent 'root in one's character' (2005: 136). Pietist women in Egypt, many of them middle class, the majority workers in the Egyptian economy, adopt *voluntarily* this strict Islamic bodily regime, often regarded as a sign of Muslim women's oppression, in order to inculcate in themselves virtues of modesty, humility, patience and closeness to God, expressed when they cry during supplicatory prayer (Mahmood, 2005: 129–30). The point is that bodily acts or performances, like wearing the veil, 'do not serve as a game of presentation, detachable from an essential, interiorized self' (Mahmood, 2005: 158). They are thus not a 'flag' or totem of Islamic identity played in the charged political arena of secular and Islamist contestation in Egypt. Clearly, also, they are not subversive of patriarchal domination in an obvious way, and hence cannot be neatly fitted into feminist 'resistive' approaches (Mahmood, 2005: 158). Instead of being the subjected or abject objects of the male gaze, by intentionally cultivating their modesty, piety and closeness to God, the women assert their autonomy and agency beyond any exterior gaze.

Mahmood draws on a wide range of philosophical texts, starting from Foucault's interrogation of ascetic ethical self-fashioning as bodily practice in ancient Greece, to Judith Butler's theorisation of the feminist subject, in order to crystallise her own approach to the paradoxical possibility of 'docile' agency. Her analysis misses, however, in my view, the fact that like other proselytising fundamentalist movements, in this one too self-fashioned virtue is ultimately activist and *other* oriented, above all towards God and his mission on earth, to bring Muslims back to the true faith and engage in good works. Much of the pedagogical effort women invest in regular mosque lessons and courses is devoted to the acquisition of literacy in classical Islamic texts and hermeneutical traditions which, over time, qualifies them to act as instructors of other women, to lead the prayers and claim the right to act in public, even against their husbands' wishes. The impact of this activist proselytising impulse is, of course, what worries the Egyptian government, not the personal piety of the women, despite the apparently apolitical agenda of the women's piety movement.

These features of the Egyptian mosque movement reveal its crucially *modern* grounding: it parallels similar religious movements in Judaism and Christianity, in which women claim the equal right to pursue religious scholarship, literacy and positions of leadership. Hence, Jewish orthodox women in Israel and the United States claim the right to study the *Talmud* and lead the prayers (El-Or, 2002). Anglican women have achieved the right to be ordained as Bishops. This expansion of women's rights *within* religious movements is modern in the sense that it posits a change in the very definition of women not merely as virtuous but as scholars and intellectuals with leadership capacities. At the same time some of these movements (though not all) draw strict,

impermeable boundaries around the faithful. Seen in terms of wider historical processes, it may be argued that it is the mass expansion of print capitalism and literacy in the twentieth century, and hence also of *religious* literacy, that has challenged the exclusive authority of a caste of male priests and religious experts, and led to the global spread of reformist and fundamentalist movements (Robinson, 1996).

## CONCLUSION

This essay has crossed many boundaries in its attempt to convey the richness and complexity of religious identities. Starting with classical texts, I have argued that religious identities, like other identities, do not exist in isolation but are located within generative, open, totemic systems. Sacred effervescent moments of totemic celebration highlight the fact that even local religious identities are not just epiphenomenal reflections of material, territorial or political interests. Religions are, fundamentally, boundary-crossing social formations. Their transcendence of the local creates the grounds for more universal, inclusive identities, but these in turn generate new schismatic, sectarian and fissiparous tendencies. I began the essay with definitions and classifications in order to challenge a prevalent view that only in the modern era have religions and religious identities become bounded and discrete. Rather than colonialism or modernity, the boundaries of religious identities have historically been sharply marked, I demonstrate, in frontier encounters, and blurred in processes of conversion and shared celebration in religious festivals, shrines and processions. But such hybridisation processes also generate, dialectically, counter-movements of reform and purification in which syncretic tendencies come to be highly politicised and religious boundaries sharply demarcated. Reformist fundamentalist movements have responded to secular liberalism's utopian aim of reconstructing society by formulating totalising religious alternatives to this vision which, depending on geopolitical circumstances, sometimes become intolerant, revolutionary or anti-democratic. Religious nationalism with its invented rituals draws even sharper and more xenophobic boundaries around identity, as it posits a sacred mythical relationship between worshipers, the past and a territorially demar-cated land. To achieve its ends, such move-ments may resort to deliberatively provoking communal violence within nation-states.

Throughout the essay I have stressed the embodied, performative and politicised features of religious identity, as well as its eschatological, utopian dimensions. The multifarious ways in which the ontological chasm between person and god, the sacred and the profane, is experienced, embodied, transcended and ritualised, is reflected in the continuous efflorescence of religious identi-ties. Rather than being relegated to the pri-vate sphere, the encounter with modernity, extreme nationalism, the nation-state, elec-toral politics and women's liberation has generated a wide range of public political identities in world religions, ranging from liberal democratic humanism to authoritarian and even genocidal racism. Alongside these collective responses have also come new definitions of the person and her relation to the sacred. These modern religious tenden-cies and passionate convictions have coin-cided with the creation of new religious minorities in the West through international migration, which have challenged western democratic nation-states to engage anew with the problem of religious pluralism, free speech, toleration and 'multiculturalism'.

# REFERENCES

Abou Zahab, M. (2008) '"Yeh matam kayse ruk jae?" ("How could this *matam* ever cease?"): Muharram processions in Pakistani Punjab', in K.A. Jacobson (ed.), *South Asian Religions on Display*. London: Routlege. pp. 104–114.

Ahmad, I. (1981) 'Introduction', in I. Ahmad (ed.), *Ritual and Religion Among Muslims in India*. Delhi: Manohar. pp. 1–20.

Al-Rasheed, M. (2007) *Contesting the Saudi State: Islamic Voices from a New Generation*. Cambridge: Cambridge University Press.

Asad, T. (1993) *Genealogies of Religion*. Baltimore, MD: John Hopkins University Press.

Asad, T. (2003) *Formations of the Secular: Christianity, Islam, Modernity*. Standford, CA: Standford University Press.

Bakhtin, M. (1981) *The Dialogic Imagination*. Trans. C. Emerson and M. Holquist). Austin, TX: University of Texas Press.

Basu, H. (1998) 'Hierarchy and emotion: love, joy and sorrow in a cult of black saints in Gujarat, India', in P. Werbner and H. Basu (eds), *Embodying Charisma: Modernity, Locality and the Performance of Emotion in Sufi Cults*. London: Routledge. pp. 117–139.

Bhatt, C. (2001) *Hindu Nationalism: Origins, Ideologies and Modern Myths*. Oxford: Berg.

Bauman, Z. (1998) 'Postmodern religion?', in P. Heelas (ed.), *Religion, Modernity and Postmodernity*. Oxford: Blackwell Publishers. pp. 55–78.

Boddy, J. (1989) *Wombs and Alien Spirits*. Madison, WI: Wisconsin University Press.

Bourdieu, P. (1984) *Distinction: A Social Critique of the Judgement of Taste*. London: Routledge.

Brass, P.R. (1997) *Theft of an Idol: Text and Context in the Representation of Collective Violence*. Princeton, NJ: Princeton University Press.

Brass, P.R. (2003) *The Production of Hindu-Muslim Violence in Contemporary India*. New Delhi: Oxford University Press.

Cohn, N. (1957) *The Pursuit of the Millennium*. London: Mercury Books.

Coleman, S. (2000) *The Globalisation of Charismatic Christianity: Spreading the Gospel of Prosperity*. Cambridge: Cambridge University Press.

Comaroff, J. (1985) *Body of Power, Spirit of Resistance*. Chicago, IL: University of Chicago Press.

Csordas, T.J. (2002) *Body/ Meaning/Healing*. New York: Palgrave

Douglas, M. (1966) *Purity and Danger*. London: Routledge and Kegan Paul.

Dumont, L. (1972) *Homo Hierarchicus*. London: Paladin.

Durkheim, E. (1964[1915]) *The Elementary Forms of the Religious Life*. London: George Allen and Unwin.

Eade, J. and Sallnow, M.J. (eds) (1991) *Contesting the Sacred: the Anthropology of Christian Pilgrimage*. London: Routledge.

Eaton, R.M (1993) *The Rise of Islam and the Bengal Frontier 1204–1760*. Berkeley, CA: University of California Press.

Eaton, R.M (ed.) (2003) *India's Islamic Traditions, 711–1750*. New Delhi: Oxford University Press.

Eisenstadt, S.N. (1999) *Fundamentalism, Sectarianism and Revolution: The Jacobin Dimension of Modernity*. Cambridge: Cambridge University Press.

El-Or, T. (2002) *Next Year I will Know More: Literacy and Identity among Young Orthodox Women in Israel*. Trans. Haim Watzman. Detroit, MI: Wayne University Press.

Evans-Pritchard, E.E. (1956) *Nuer Religion*. Oxford: Clarendon Press.

Evans-Pritchard, E.E. (1965) *Theories of Primitive Religion*. Oxford: Clarendon Press.

Freitag, S.B. (1989) *Collective Action and Community: Public Arenas and the Emergence of Communalism in North India*. Berkeley, CA: University of California Press.

Friedmann, Y. (2003) 'Islamic thought in relation to the Indian context', in R.M, Eaton (ed.), *India's Islamic Traditions, 711–1750*. New Delhi: Oxford University Press. pp. 50–63.

Fustel de Coulanges, N.D. (1956)[1864]) *The Ancient City*. New York: Doubleday/Anchor Books.

Gifford, P. (2004) *Ghana's New Christianity: Pentecostalism in a Globalising African Economy*. London: Hurst and Company.

Green, N. and Searle-Chatterjee, M. (2008) 'Religion, language and power: An introductory essay', in N. Green and M. Searle-Chatterjee (eds), *Religion, Language and Power*. London: Routledge. pp. 1–25.

Geertz, C. (1968) *Islam Observed: Religious Development in Morocco and Indonesia*. New Haven, CT: Yale University Press.

Geertz, C. (1973a) 'Religion as a cultural system', in *The Interpretation of Cultures*. London: Hutchinson and Co. Chapter 4.

Geertz, C. (1973b) 'Ritual and social change: A javanese example', in *The Interpretation of Cultures*. London: Hutchinson and Co. Chapter 6.

Geertz, C. (1973c) 'Deep Play: Notes on the Balinese Cockfight', in *The Interpretation of Cultures*. London: Hutchinson and Co. Chapter 15.

Hammoudi, A. (1993) *The Victim and Its Masks: An Essay on Sacrifice and Masquerade in the Maghreb*. Chicago: University of Chicago Press.

Hansen, T.B. (1999) *The Saffron Wave: Democracy and Hindu Nationalism in Modern India*. Princeton, NJ: Princeton University Press.

Hayden, R. (2002) 'Antagonistic tolerance: Competitive sharing of religious sites in South Asia and the Balkans', *Current Anthropology*, 43 (2): 205–31.

Hirst, J.S. and John Zavos, J. (2005) 'Riding a tiger? South Asia and the problem of "religion"', *Contemporary South Asia*, 14 (1): 3–20.

Inglis, D. and Robertson, R. (2008) 'The elementary forms of globality: durkheim and the emergence and nature of global life', *Journal of Classical Sociology*, 8 (1): 5–25.

Jaffrelot, C. (1996) *The Hindu Nationalist Movement and Indian Politics, 1925 to the 1990s*. London: Hurst Company.

Kapferer, B. (1983) *A Celebration of Demons: Exorcism and the Aesthetics of Healing in Sri Lanka*. Bloomington, IN: Bloomington University Press.

Kapferer, B. (1988) *Legends of People, Myths of State: Violence, Intolerance and Political Culture in Sri Lanka and Australia*. Washington, DC: Smithsonian Press.

Kiernan, J. (1994) 'Variation on a Christian theme: The healing synthesis of Zulu Zionism', in C. Stewart and R. Shaw (eds), *Syncretism/Anti-Syncretism: The Politics of Religious Synthesis*. London: Routledge., pp. 65–78.

Klaits, F. (2010) *Death in a Church of Life: Moral Passion During Botswana's Time of AIDS*. Berkeley, CA: University of California Press.

Korom, F.J. (2003) *Hosay Trinidad: Muharram Performances in an Indo-Caribbean Diaspora*. Philadelphia, PA: University of Pennsylvania Press.

Lambek, M. (1981) *Human Spirits: A Cultural Account of Trance in Mayotte*. Cambridge: Cambridge University Press.

Levi-Strauss, C. (1966) *The Savage Mind*. London: Weidenfeld and Nicholson.

Lukes, S. (1973) *Emile Durkheim: His Life and Work*. Harmondsworth: Penguin.

Mahmood, S. (2005) *Politics of Piety: The Islamic Revival and the Feminist Subject*. Princeton, NJ: Princeton University Press.

Martin, B. (1998) 'From pre- to postmodernity in Latin America: The case of Pentecostalism', in P. Heelas (ed.), *Religion, Modernity and Postmodernity*. Oxford: Blackwell Publishers. pp. 102–146.

Martin, D.A. (1990) *Tongues of Fire*. Oxford: Blackwell.

Maxwell, D. (1999) 'Historicizing Christian independency: The Southern African pentecostal movement 1908–60', *Journal of African History*, 40: 243–64.

Maxwell, D. (2006a) 'Writing the history of African Christianity: Reflections of an editor', *Journal of Religion in Africa*, 36 (3–4): 379–99.

Maxwell, D. (2006b) 'Post-colonial Christianity in Africa', in H. McLeod (ed.), *World Christianities 1914–2000, The Cambridge History of Christianity* Vol. 9. Cambridge: Cambridge University Press. pp. 401–421.

Metcalf, B.D. (1982) *Islamic Revival in British India: Deoband, 1860–1900*. Princeton, NJ: Princeton University Press.

Meyer, B. (1999) *Translating the Devil*. Trenton, NJ: African World Press.

Modood, T. (2007) *Multiculturalism*. Cambridge: Polity Press.

Morris, B. (1987) *Anthropological Studies of Religion*. Cambridge: Cambridge University Press.

Nandy, A. (1990) 'The politics of secularism and the recovery of religious tolerance', in V. Das (ed.), *Mirror of Violence: Communities, Riots and Survivors in South Asia*. New Delhi: Oxford University Press. pp. 69–93.

Rehman, U. (2007) 'Sufi shrines and identity-construction in Pakistan', PhD thesis, University of Copenhagen.

Robbins, J. (2004) 'The globalization of Pentecostal and charismatic Christianity', *Annual Review of Anthropology*, 33: 117–43.

Robinson, F. (1983) 'Islam and Muslim Society in South Asia', *Contributions to Indian Sociology* (N.S.), 17 (2): 185–203.

Robinson, F. (1996) 'Islam and the impact of print in South Asia', in N. Crook (ed.), *The Transmission of Knowledge in South Asia: Essays on Education, Religion, History and Politics*. New Delhi., pp. 62–97.

Robinson, K. (2008) 'Islamic cosmopolitics, human rights and anti-violence strategies in Indonesia', in P. Werbner (ed.), *Anthropology and the New Cosmopolitan; Rooted, Feminist and Vernacular Perspectives*. Oxford: Berg Publishers. pp. 111–134.

Saheb, S.A.A. (1998) 'A "festival of flags": Hindu-Muslim devotion and the sacralising of localism at the shrine of Nagore-e-sharif', in P. Werbner and H. Basu (eds). *Embodying Charisma: Modernity, Locality and the Performance of Emotion in Sufi Cults*. London: Routledge. pp. 55–76.

Saiyed, A.R. (1989) 'Saints and Dargahs in the Indian subcontinent: A review', in C.W. Troll (ed.), *Muslim Shrines in India: Their Character, History and Significance*. New Delhi: Oxford University Press. pp. 240–256.

Stewart, C. and Shaw, R. (1994) 'Introduction: Problematising syncretism', in Charles Stewart and Rosalind Shaw (eds), *Syncretism/Anti-Syncretism: the Politics of Religious Synthesis*. London: Routledge. pp. 1–24.

Stivens, M. (2008) 'Gender, rights and cosmopolitan-isms', in P. Werbner (ed.), *Anthropology and the New Cosmopolitanism: Rooted, Feminist and Vernacular Perspectives*. Oxford: Berg Publishers. pp. 87–110.

Talbot, C. (2003) 'Inscribing the other, inscribing the self: Hindu-Muslim identities in pre-colonial India', in Richard M. Eaton (ed.). *India's Islamic Traditions, 711–1750*. New Delhi: Oxford University Press. pp. 83–119.

Tambiah, S.J. (1986) *Sri Lanka: Ethnic Fratricide and the Dismantling of Democracy*. London: I.B. Taurus.

Tambiah, S.J. (1992) *Buddhism Betrayed: Religious, Politics and Violence in Sri Lanka*. Chicago, IL: University of Chicago Press.

Taylor, C. (1994) 'Multiculturalism and "the politics of recognition"', in A. Gutmann (ed.), *Multiculturalism and the Politics of Recognition*. Princeton, NJ: Princeton University Press. pp. 25–74.

Thompson, E.P. (1963) *The Making of the English Working Class*. London: Penguin.

Turner, V. (1968) *The Drums of Affliction*. Oxford: Clarendon Press for the International African Institute.

Turner, V. (1974) *Dramas, Fields and Metaphors: Symbolic Action in Human Society*. Ithaca, NY: Cornell University Press.

Van der Veer, P. (1994a) *Religious Nationalism: Hindus and Muslims in India*. Berkeley, CA: University of California Press.

Van der Veer, P. (1994b) 'Syncretism, multiculturalism and the discourse of tolerance', in Charles Stewart and Rosalind Shaw (eds), *Syncretism/Anti-Syncretism: The Politics of Religious Synthesis*. London: Routledge., pp. 185–200.

Werbner, P. (2002) *Imagined Diasporas among Manchester Muslims*. Oxford: James Curry.

Werbner, P. (2003) *Pilgrims of Love: The Social Anthropology of a Global Sufi Cult*. London: Hurst Publishers.

Werbner, P. (2005) 'The translocation of culture: Migration, community and the force of multicultural-ism in history', *Sociological Review*, 53 (4): 745–68.

Werbner, P. and Basu, H. (1998) 'Introduction: The embodiment of charisma', in P. Werbner and H. Basu (eds) *Embodying Charisma: Modernity, Locality and the Performance of Emotion in Sufi Cults*. London: Routledge. pp. 3–27.

Werbner, R. (1977) 'Introduction', in R. Werbner (ed.) *Regional Cults*. ASA Monographs No. 16. London and New York: Academic Press.

Werbner, R. (1989) *Ritual Passage, Sacred Journey: The Process and Organisation of Religious Movement*. Manchester: Manchester University Press.

Werbner, R. (1994) 'Afterword' in Charles Stewart and Rosalind Shaw (eds), *Syncretism/Anti-Syncretism:* *the Politics of Religious Synthesis*. London: Routledge. pp. 201–204.

Werbner, R. (1997) 'The suffering body: Passion and ritual allegory in christian encounters', *Journal of Southern African Studies*, 23 (2): 311–24.

Zelliot, E. (2003) 'A medieval encounter between Hindu and Muslim', in R. M. Eaton (ed.). *India's Islamic Traditions, 711–1750*. New Delhi: Oxford University Press. pp. 64–82.

# 13

# From Media and Identity to Mediated Identity

Helen Wood

## 'THE MEDIA ARE LIKE THE AIR THAT WE BREATHE'

It is now received common sense that mediated and symbolic forms play a significant role in the construction of identity in the contemporary era. So ubiquitous are media in everyday life that we can receive information, access forms of pleasure and entertainment, communicate with proximate and distanced others, as well as increasingly *produce* as well as consume our own media forms. In John Thompson's (1995: 24) phrase 'the media are like the air that we breathe'. From the macro staging of world politics to the micro enabling of intimate forms of connection, much of human communication is now, in some form or other, mediated by technology. For some that raises questions tinged with nostalgia and regret about the disappearance of authenticity and 'real' human qualities of identity. For others there is utopian potential for the human transcendence of physical limitations. Albeit at the risk of reduction, to simplify things here, we can employ metaphors of profit or loss:

- Global media forms offer resources which enable both the visibility of difference and maintenance of distinction (profit)/global media forms erode

local cultural practices in a general trend towards cultural imperialism (loss).
- New forms of access to information enable more liberated forms of gendered identity construction (profit)/the prevalence of gendered media forms and heterosexual fantasies reaffirm ideologies of gender in relatively conservative ways (loss).
- An increased range of choice in the adoption of 'lifestyles' from media and cultural resources enable us to more freely construct our identity practices (profit)/the growing individualization of identity pursuits uproots traditional forms of community and collectivity (loss).
- The inhabitation of virtual on-line worlds frees up identity from material and physical constraints and offers new forms of identity construction and senses of community (profit)/escaping into virtual worlds detracts from face-to-face communication eroding truly human identity and social connection (loss).

The problem is that over-generalizing these debates, as I have done here, produces 'the media' as a monolith: a homogenous entity invidiously either interrupting or enhancing human experience. I have used the economic metaphor of profit and loss deliberately, not because it can encompass the breadth of research on media and identity (much of which of course is much more sophisticated) but because it encapsulates the essential character of the logic governing the way media research gets abstracted: a zero-sum calculation of media influence. If we take up an invitation to engage with a media form here then we must be declining a more social/human invitation elsewhere. This tends to weigh mediated communication against face-to-face communication: Energy in one (mediated) direction must draw energy away from seemingly more certain forms of (non-mediated) identity construction, usually supported by a humanist emphasis upon community, family, locality, etc.

In this chapter I will examine some of the trends in work on media and identity (many of which address the question of identity in relatively implicit ways) through a set of interrelated dichotomies. The first represents how we might see identity as located between *texts and audiences* through which media studies have been concerned with the power of the media and the relative agency of consumers. The second and related pair involves the sketching of ideas about how the media impact upon the individual in terms of either *isolation or connection*. And finally I look at the tension between *reason and emotion* in more dynamic accounts of mediated identity. Reverberating within these pairs are other sets of dichotomous relationships, between models of media as *transmission or ritual*, and discussions about the differences between *old and new* media.

Simplifying the debates in terms of profit and loss scenarios as outlined above, even if unwittingly, construes identity as an already-formed Cartesian whole from which media can only add or subtract, rather than seeing both subjectivity and media as co-constitutive agents in the formation of contemporary identity. It is this possibility that I take up and develop in the third of the dichotomies above. Following on from Stuart Hall's cue, derived from Foucault, identities are constructed in relational interactions: 'Identities are thus points of temporary attachment to the subject positions which discursive practices construct for us' (2000: 19). I want to develop this point by suggesting that we should understand media both in terms of how products invite subjective *attachments*, but also in terms of how texts and technologies involve us in identity *practices*. This means we need to think through identity both in terms of subject-positioning and in terms of social action, because we need both if we are to overcome the tendency towards zero-sum thinking in evaluative debates. By transcending static dichotomies we can move towards a more embedded and wide-ranging understanding of media as plural and as constitutive of identity within broader sets of communicative social relations.

## TEXTS AND AUDIENCES

One overarching framework for these debates is the evaluation of the balance of power between media and their audiences. To what extent is identity subject to the media's messages or is the consumer in control of how they choose to receive and adopt media forms? Concern with media power is often characterized as a 'transmission' model where the sending of messages from relatively few places to dispersed receivers operates through a linear, hierarchical model of power in which concentration of media ownership is key to understanding the media's hegemonic power. On the other hand recognizing the agency of the audience (consider the fact that many media products fail in the market place) has often accounted for how audiences 'resist' or reconstruct media messages in localized forms of identity practices.

### Mass media and mass consumption

The concept of identity has not always been addressed explicitly in the analysis of the media power. However, it is never implicitly far away from the earliest debates about the mass media and questions of ideology. The work of the Frankfurt School, beginning in the 1940s, was concerned with the development of the culture industries, the production of mass culture and its stultifying effects on the standardization of art and culture. For Adorno and Horkheimer mass production and mass consumption have a negative impact upon the individual: 'In the Culture Industry the individual is an illusion not merely because of the standardization of the means of production. He is tolerated only so long as his complete identification with the generality is unquestioned' ([1944]1999: 40). Here commercial culture offers pseudo-individuality, fake routes to experiences of human experience which only damage rather than enrich the human spirit. These and related arguments, such as Herbert Marcuse's (1964) *One Dimensional Man*, help to explain how capitalism establishes and maintains its grip on power as the 'masses' are distracted from the 'real' questions of their existence by the hedonistic pleasures of popular entertainment and consumption.

Since, the development of the field of 'mass communications' has continued by analysing the media's influence over consumers and has tended to take issue with media's 'messages'. As James Carey sketches, the traditions of the 'mass communications' schools of thought have emerged through a 'transmission' view of communication, 'strongly related to the nineteenth century desire to use communication and transportation to extend influence, control, and power over wider distances and greater populations' (1989: 43). Thus the study of mass communications has involved analysing polemic, rhetoric and the art of persuasion in an attempt to understand how the media's (ideological) messages can powerfully influence belief and culture. Among these arguments have been concerns about media imperialism: that western media function with a colonizing mission, exerting power in different parts of the world. Thus connections are made between foreign policy and commercial interests as western media transmit their own capitalist ideologies, creating gross inequalities in media flows, and impacting greatly upon indigenous markets imposing cultural homogeneity (Mattelart et al., 1984).

An over-riding concern with 'message' has tended to see the consumer straightforwardly as the 'receiver' and sometimes as an empty book upon which new frameworks for identity can be written. However, developments from this Marxist emphasis upon evaluating the significance of mass media's influence over the individual have helped to develop theories of media and subjectivity. The dual figures of the 'mass' and the 'individual' have been central to Marxist thinking. On the one hand the mass media help to constitute the population into a standardized body largely by sapping agency, while at the same time this is only achieved by the way the products of the mass media work on the individual psyche. In an attempt to explain this phenomenon Louis Althusser's classic essay on 'Ideology and state apparatus' (1971) attempts to overcome the economically reductive theory of Marxist ideology in order to explain the connection between ideology and subjectivity. Althusser's main contention is that state apparatus 'interpellate', call upon, individuals as subjects of their ideologies. He incorporates Lacanian psychoanalysis to explain how individuals recognize themselves as being addressed and implicated within ideological structures: 'all ideology hails or interpellates concrete individuals as concrete subjects' 1971: 115).

Whilst in Althusser's work the dual processes of what is social and what is psychic can be seen as somewhat contradictory (see Hall's, 1996 critique), Althusser's formulation has been readily applied to the media. In film theory analyses of film texts have often involved a search for the implied subject-position available within the narratives, *mise-en-scène* and symbolic structures of the form. Feminist theory in particular has pointed out the predominance of a masculine subject position in Hollywood film where the viewer is called to identify with the male protagonist and to objectify the largely non-diegetic appearances of women (Mulvey, 1975), and has considered how daytime television pre-figures the ideal-consumer as ideal mother (Modleski, 1983). In these models the turn towards subjectivity has been subsequently developed through psychoanalytic theories of pleasure and identification.

In another direction, an overriding concern with 'messages' and the drive to demystify them, drew strength from structuralist models to account for the way in which media texts might 'address' their consumers. Roland Barthes (1973) and the text *Myth Today* is largely credited with offering media studies a science of signs to deconstruct media texts. His structuralist explication of the orders of denotation and connotation allow us to identify how images are juxtaposed against one another (syntagmatic relations) or selected from a range of choices (paradigmatic relations) in order to generate a particular cultural meaning, which in turn is revealing of the myths of any particular society.

These positions as outlined so far concentrate on the products of the media: film, advertising, news, etc. in order to estimate their impact upon the *implied* reader or consumer. The identity of the consumer is generic as either, 'the mass', or constituted at the level of the individual, 'the subject'. Although I am oversimplifying these large areas of theory (since they are all mostly theoretical expositions) when concerned with the 'mass consumer' they tend to fall into Carey's categorization of 'transmission' models in that they are all concerned with media content, writing at a time when there were fairly limited modes of media production distributing to an increasing number of individuals. Many of the theoretical positions outlined so far make sense from within their historical contexts of the early development of mass media and its use as propaganda by the state or by capitalist enterprise. None of these models are too concerned with the notion of 'real' audiences as they are situated in lived contexts of consumption.

## The social subject

The influence of cultural studies and its refusal of some of the assumptions of the 'mass communications' tradition played a significant role in moving on our understanding of media's role in identity practices. As early as 1958 the cultural historian Raymond Williams argued that 'there are no masses, only ways of seeing people as masses', a sentiment which began to characterize some of the empirical work undertaken at the Centre for Contemporary Cultural Studies (CCCS) in Birmingham. Dominated by a concern to register distinctions between media power and agency in lived contexts, Stuart Hall's (1980) 'encoding/decoding' model set out the terms for debate around which processes of 'decoding' the media's messages are as formative in meaning making as the processes of 'encoding'. In that sense identity, as it is formed within the social, is fundamentally influential to how forms of media come to generate different sets of understandings for consumers.

Hall's theoretical framework was pitched as a direct challenge to the linear models of communication as transmission from within the 'mass communications' tradition, and enabled David Morley to test out the hypothesis on different social groups. Morley's (1980) study *The Nationwide Audience* proved that groups from different class backgrounds interpreted the message of a particular television news magazine programme in alternative ways. Some, he suggested, took up the dominant message, assuming the preferred reading of the text, some offered negotiated readings, and others entirely oppositional readings to those 'encoded' with the programme. This work pointed to the fact that to understand the role of the media in identity formation it was not enough to rely on the role of the media analyst in interpreting texts, since interpretations at the level of lived culture could be surprising and differentiated once located within social dynamics. This allowed for the 'ethnographic turn' in media studies where it became generally accepted that meaning is ultimately contingent on contexts of consumption. Rather than assuming one message and one effect, the work of the CCCS enabled us to grasp the polysemic nature of media and their attachments in interpretive communities.

Once empirical audience research based on these principles was underway, the findings tended to challenge the dominant hypothesis about media transmission and indoctrination. Although some research has tended to overplay the notion of the 'active audience' (Fiske, 1987), a label that has largely been misappropriated in summaries of the field (Gray, 1999), on the whole this work has enriched our understanding of the way in which media are embedded into distinct forms of identity production. Work on global exports of soap opera found that readers incorporated the dominant meanings of soap opera in ways dependant upon their own localized meaning systems, rather than adopting the text as 'straight'. Middle Eastern viewers of the television programme *Dallas*[1] for example saw the show as evidence that capitalist ideology is morally corrupt, rather than as a celebration of American culture (Liebes and Katz, 1990). Similarly Daniel Miller, in his work on the soap opera *The Young and the Restless* in Trinidad, found that despite fears over growing Americanization on the island, the large numbers of viewers used the soap in order to think through local issues (Miller, 1993). Thus, rather than confirming the media imperialism thesis, empirical work on the ground tended to find that even imported media forms were used to confirm localized senses of meaning and identity.

Thus the ethnographic turn in media analysis has secured a concern for a more richly textured and locally contingent notion of cultural identity, whereby media forms are understood as offering modes of ontological security in the globalized epoch. Other studies have suggested that class plays a significant role in modes of interpretation as well as taste in relation to media forms (Gray, 1992; Press, 1991; Thomas, 1995), while bodies of feminist work have established how forms of pleasure and aesthetics have been tied to feminine pursuits and cultural competences (e.g. Brunsdon, 1981; Hermes, 1995; Hobson,

1980, 1982, 1991; Moseley, 2002). Indeed, the work of feminist scholarship has been central to the development of work of media reception, not least because of a commitment to challenging the ways women in particular have been characterized as the naïve dupes of mass-produced fantasies. Popular media fictions have been seen to both reinforce, as well as allow space to expose, the often contradictory discourses of femininity.

Other recent work of this ilk has emerged from anthropology, considering how contemporary cultural identities are constructed through particular global and local media. Marie Gillespie's (1995) work on young Asians living in Southall in London considered how both Western media and Indian religious films were important mediators in the negotiation of diasporic identity. Other ethnographic work shows how national texts help constitute forms of discussion and orientation around national and gendered identities, entering into debates about processes of cultural citizenship (Abu-Lughod, 2005; Mankekar, 1999; Tufte, 2000). Rather than seeing 'mass media' as having a direct 'effect' on identity a number of audience studies registered the active and culturally specific ways in which media are adopted in localized contexts of consumption. Here grounded studies of media consumption evoke the very boundlessness of media processes and the impossibility of constructing a rigid frame around text and audience (Gray, 1999).

## ISOLATION AND CONNECTION

The second conceptual pair that I will use to organize this mapping of the field is the tension over whether media forms encourage us to spend more time alone, or whether they facilitate new forms of collective identity. Of course these discussions can be traced in the outlines above too as concepts of 'mass media' have tended to assume a direct 'effect' on isolated individuals. Caricatures abound about those who have succumb to the plug in drug of television, or the Internet, sitting alone as couch potatoes and interacting with television personalities, or with distant Internet 'friends', rather than engaging in meaningful social relationships. This is despite the fact that on the whole empirical research on audiences suggests that television and popular media tend to be used as 'social glue' and as ways to make new forms of connection. Here I want to focus upon how there has been a renewed interest in questions of isolation or connection in contemporary social theory that makes assumptions about the workings of media in stages of advanced capitalism.

## Individualization and lifestyle

In the earliest theories of the mass media, worrying over the media's power lends itself to identifying the consumer as a powerless (and largely faceless) individual, unified only by their atomized relations to forms of labour. Traces of these earlier assumptions can be found through a newer lens of theories of 'individualization' in contemporary culture. The apparent triumph of capitalism and the re-organization of labour relations away from material production towards service economies have brought a shift in the organization of community which impacts upon identity. One consequence, apparently, has been the move away from older forms of collective identity practices towards the foregrounding individual life narratives. Globalized forms of 'life politics', potentially assisted by the media and self-help industries contributes to uprooting individuals from their more localized contexts of identity, particularly in relation to identity categories such as class and gender.

Social theorists Giddens (1991) and Beck (1992) suggest that in a post-industrial society individuals are now compelled to make life plans, conduct and their own subjectivities the centre of their concerns. For Beck this is seen in the fact that every individual is forced to consider their worth in relation to the competitive labour market which rearranges

their relationship to the class structures of the industrial society and throws into tension traditional roles within the industrial nuclear family. In this way self work and the narrative of selfhood takes over traditional affiliations; class, for example, as a significant category disappears. The thesis suggests that any secure sense of identity is thrown into question while an individual struggles instead to re-orient themselves to the personal risk relations, or trust relations, with which they are faced. Beck remarks, 'community has been dissolved in the acid bath of competition' (1992: 94).

Neither Beck nor Giddens give us much empirical detail, particularly on the media here, but in both accounts the media seem to hover, as one of the most determinate specters in this re-organization of society. Giddens refers to the increasing 'mediation' of experience in trust relations, while Beck blames television directly for playing a role in the 'isolation and standardization of experience'. The implication for Beck is that the media help to configure the disassociation of individuals, whilst at the same time as offering compensatory resources through processes of self-reflexivity. According to Giddens, a retreat from older forms of structural relations makes the focus upon 'intimate relationships' all the more significant, and for Beck this throws greater emphasis upon the private sphere – what he refers to as 'political privatism'. He says of the private sphere, that it is not what it appears to be:

> It is the outside turned inside and made private, of conditions and decisions made elsewhere, in the television networks, the educational system, in firms or the labour market [...] with general disregard of their private biographical consequences. (1992: 133).

What were once understood as structural inequalities become redefined in terms of the individualization of social risks: social problems become psychological dispositions. So we might be able to see the increased opening out of intimacy in various media with their emphasis on self-management and self-improvement in this regard. The work of

Nick Rose (1984) has been taken up in media studies, as a renewed interest in media ideologies has emerged, making it possible to analyse contemporary media forms in terms of their role in broader neo-liberal projects of governmentality. For instance, accounts of the changes in news, documentary forms, lifestyle and factual programming outline the ways in which individual dilemmas become the central (and dramatic) focus instead of the structural contexts in which they are framed (Andrejevik, 2004; Ouellette and Hay, 2008; Palmer, 2003). In conditions of considerable flux and change media encourage individuals to engage in identity self-work while under constant forms of governmental and commercial surveillance.

These arguments chime with Putnam's (2000) 'bowling alone' position (based on evidence from the US) that there exists a decline in civic engagement and senses of belonging in relation to community networks. (While more people engage in bowling as an activity, club memberships are in rapid decline.) Communities, social networks and localized forms of identity are eroded by the desire, mostly generated through forms of consumption, to focus on the individual. Developments in media technologies have fuelled this type of argument: the increase in personalized media, the Sony Walkman®, Apple iPod®, PC and personalized TV, encourage isolation even in public spaces. For Putnam developed democracies suffer greatly from such a rapid decline in social capital as people engage more concertedly in practices that involve symbolic resources and symbolic capital.

Collected together in this way, ideas about individualization can present a rather bleak account of the function of the media in modes of identity formation. But of course the use of symbolic resources in identity projects is an ambiguous phenomenon. These arguments are also surrounded by discussions of the phenomenon of 'lifestyling' as a product of the development of mass consumption and an inherent part of consumer culture. Our practices of consumption are

now more central to us than our roles associated with production in processes of identity: what we buy is more significant than what we do. Consumption increasingly offers more choice. With intensified market segmentation, affiliations of taste and markers of style become more salient to forms of identification than previously possible (Featherstone, 1987). The products of media, stars, personalities and brands become significant symbols in the orientation of identity around modes of consumption. While for some this might be interpreted as the marketization of identity, the branding of oneself as capital extends its line of flight (Klein, 1999), others locate resistance in all acts of consumption (de Certeau, 1984).

Of course the media afford *both* opportunities. There are gains as well as losses afforded through the rise of lifestyling. The rise of identity politics through the social movements of the 1970s and 1980s were given visibility not only through news media, but also through popular culture. For example, bell hooks (1991) discusses the way black popular culture (music and film) enabled 'talking back' and assisted black political action through public culture, whilst Bonnie Dow (1996) charts the role of television in the mainstreaming of feminism. It is not the case that the extension of mass consumption and popular culture has a wholly one-sided effect on the formation of identity – the developments that encouraged individual identity-play also enabled political identity practices.

## Community and connectivity

While, on the one hand there is a relatively convincing narrative about the media's role in encouraging individualized identity practices and forms of *dis*connection, on the other, one can construct the converse point of view by taking a different route through the literature. The development of media technologies have of course contributed to how we currently experience time/space relations, the uncoupling of space and time enables us to simultaneously witness events from far flung distances. In one narrative framework this poses negative cultural imperialism and isolation but in another it poses the potential for unity. It is possible to see the erosion of distinctions between public and private, through new forms of spatial arrangements, in a different light to that presented by Beck. In processes of de-territorialization, where the global meets the local in the sitting room (Morley, 2000), there lies the possibility for new forms of connectivity which transcend space and time. For McLuhan and Powers (1989), who famously describe such conditions as moving towards a 'global village', this is suggestive of global forms of *connection* more than individuation. For Meyrowitz (1985), though with much more concern, the removal of a sense of place re-organizes the potential for group identity.

Media can therefore serve to erode the distinctions that have traditionally kept cultures apart. For example, commentators have charted the rise of the nation state and its dependence upon the development of modern media systems. Media, particularly broadcasting have been fundamental to nationalizing projects where the spread of mass communication and rising levels of literacy have enabled newer bonds which transcend immediate locations (Scannell and Cardiff, 1991). What Benedict Anderson (1991) famously charted as 'imagined community', which obviously generates its own rights of exclusion as well as inclusion, pertains to a mediated and symbolic sense of 'community' nonetheless. Put this way, media can undermine rather than create isolation as they break down physical and material barriers of time and place.

## Virtual networks

This position on mediated connection has gained pace through developments in new media. Where traditionally media studies have observed a concern with audiences, the language now is registered as a concern with 'networks'. In other words while we were once involved in debates about the weighting of power between text and audience – between power and resistance in the transmission of messages – we are now also concerned with how media generate webs of connection, which is seen to be characteristic of broader global social change (Castells, 2000). This is sometimes referred to as a shift between the broadcast model of communication to the Internet model of communication, to which we will return.

For now, let us consider what is at stake in some of the discussions about these newer forms of connectivity. Reverberating within the old, as well as some of the more recent pessimistic debates, is a nostalgic yearning for a loss of 'real' community through which it is assumed that a more authentic, not faked or simulated, form of identity is available. For example, consider the implication within descriptors like 'prosthetic self' (Lury, 1998), which now abound in contemporary social theory. These ideas are tinged with a sense that media offer 'simulated' relationships (to deploy Baudrillard's [1994] phrase) which cannot live up to 'real' face-to-face forms of communication. Robert Putnam's version of social capital relies on the assumption that co-presence and co-temporality define (truly human) aspects of social identity. But of course new media forms brought about through high speed connections such as the Internet mean 'connectivity' no longer requires those conditions, and we might have to rethink what it means to be social in a wired world.

There is a body of work in which, particularly new media, affords the constitution of new *virtual* identities and communities which, rather than being construed as negative distractions from the real, offer spaces to be creative with, and to positively steer, our identity constructions (Beniger, 1987; O'Brian, 1997; Rheingold, 1993; Turkle, 1997). Using postmodern theories of identity construction, the fragmented and mutable aspects of identity formation are in keeping with the Microsoft® Windows®-based metaphor in which RL (real life) is just one more window (Turkle, 1997). In this way the potential of the virtual offers us ways of transcending physical constraints as we engage in multiple user domains (MUDs and MOOs [MUD, object oriented]) and inhabit 'second life' worlds, where we can generate new identities entirely based on forms of connection with distanced others. So, for example, take Donna Haraway's (1990) now famous declaration, 'I would rather be a cyborg than a goddess', which lauds the potential of digital culture to transcend gender divisions. It is not so much that traditional identities are in decline through forms of individualized identity practices, but that older forms of inclusion and exclusion based upon material and physical conditions can be shed entirely in favour of generating a new map of identity with liberating potential. The most optimistic spin on this potential suggests that the virtual world has the ability to be accessible to all (the digital divide notwithstanding), which enables a more democratic and flexible space with which to construct and rebuild forms of identity beyond physical boundaries.

Added to this is the possibility that new forms of community are enabled that are free from some of the divisive and hierarchical power dynamics inherent in the politics of physical communities. Baym (1998) argues that community values can be enhanced in electronically mediated relationships, a position which is largely accompanied by a utopian rhetoric of possibility. The work of Howard Rheingold is seen as typical of this position: 'virtual communities are social aggregations that emerge from the Net when enough people carry on those public discussions long enough, with sufficient human feeling, to form webs of personal relationships in cyberspace' (1993: 5). This registers a language of connection, rather than of isolation. Because digital culture enables us to participate in media practices rather than be passive consumers of the media already produced for us, its capacities for connection, and the sharing of ideas, experiences and

files, have already been applauded for the facilities they offer to democratic participation. Recent large-scale organizations of political demonstrations have generally been attributed to the possibilities engendered through the web. Virtual online activities therefore offer the ability to 'practice' identity and generate 'new' communities in multiple spaces.

For many, the development of ideas of virtual identity represent the ultimate extension of postmodern theories of identity where the self is always in progress and mutable. Although questioning the interiority of identity as an already fixed whole has been the focus of much of the work on identity in the humanities and social sciences, one might see virtual identity to represent the ultimate exteriorisation of identity. Mark Poster (2007) draws our attention to that fact that our engagements with technological forms of life have increasingly externalized and materialized identity to the extent that 'identity theft' is a real offence, constructing identity as an asset, as an object, rather than as subject. 'What is stolen is not one's consciousness but one's self as it is embedded in (increasingly digital) databases. The self constituted in these databases, beyond the ken of individuals, may be considered the digital unconscious' (2007: 129). The discourses that surround identity theft according to Poster draw upon both the exteriorizing of identity that technological conditions create, but also on the insecurities generated through liberal ideas of individualization in which the search for one's true self has been commodified and rendered unsafe. For some the exteriorization of the self through modern technology can only ultimately involve us in commodifying identity, as in Alison Hearn's (2008) discussion of the 'branding' of identity through Internet sites such as YouTube.

The first wave of theories of the new media tended towards either utopian or apocalyptic claims around the future of human identity in a virtual world. Some of the potential for creative identity construction embedded here offers a technocentric vision in which new media forms offer us control of the switches in a 'second media age' (Poster, 1995). Through a networked and non-linear many-to-many model of communication forms of subjectivity engendered by 'old media' become open to transgression. Here the increased ability to *produce* as well as consume our own media (for example, the phenomenon of citizen journalism) forge new ways in which contemporary identity can be practiced through greater access to public culture (Jenkins, 2004).

## New media/old media

However, the technocentrism evident in some of the utopian discourses outlined above offers us an uneasy alliance between choice and control. Many of the models concerning media and identity tend towards technological determinism: where media drive particular social changes. In the case of older effects theories the media is an external catalyst impacting upon individuals, and in the case of the first wave of 'new media' studies technophilia tends to overplay the media's liberating potential. Because new media has the potential to be more 'interactive' does it necessarily have the ability to allow us to be more pro-active in our mediated forms of identity construction?

More recent analyses have offered studies of the way in which very real and lived inequalities and distinctions get transferred onto virtual terrain. So for instance take the much discussed conversation around 'can there be a rape in cyberspace?' (Dibble, 2001), or the fact that most email traffic moves around within the same building, and the fact that half of the world has no digital access at all which has been termed 'the digital divide' (Morley, 2000). In Wittel et al.'s (2002) study of the new media sector in London, they find that processes going on in virtual society are usually extensions of what is happening in 'real' society. Using Woolgar's (2002) fourth rule of virtuality, 'the more virtual, the more real,' virtual processes can simply work to

extend similar patterns in the real world. Empirical research on the use of social networking sites suggests that they do offer teens new spaces to work out identity and status, potentially helping them cope with the stresses of contemporary insecurities (Boyd, 2007a). However, rather than the technology effacing traditional social distinctions (an ability that may well be embedded in the capability of the technology) its actual use serves only to reinforce class distinctions. Danah Boyd's (2007b) study of teen use of the sites shows a distinction between users of Facebook and users of MySpace™: she describes Facebook as more 'preppy' (having started at Harvard) while MySpace™ is more 'fringe' being used more by lower classes and ethnic minorities.

Many arguments are concerned with how senses of belonging and collectivity can either be transferred to, or re-written for, new virtual environments. But these shifts from old to new media, from forms of transmission to network, apparently affect a shift in the way in which subjectivity can be constituted in the contemporary age. In the networked model of 'new media' the production of subjectivity in relation to the object of media is re-constituted. This is mostly because there is new potential for 'users' (and not readers) to become message makers too in the re-distributive 'network' of production. Some commentators such as Scott Lash (2002) suggest that we need to re-orient our thinking around 'information flows' where we have moved from a media culture into a technological culture. In the older era of representation there is a clear distance between the cultural representation, the object it represents, and the subject, setting up a particular set of relations (we might see these in Althusserian terms as processes of interpellation), whereas the information order is characterized by immanence where subjects become interfaces *within* the network of communication. Users are therefore located in relation to their connectivity, rather than subject to texts' subject-positionings that are relatively fixed. The Internet age is thus characterized by a new proximate aura where subjects are implicated in the making of communication flows so that they no longer have any distance with which to reflect upon the 'meaning' of particular types of information. In the contemporary age the logic of information 'flow' produces instability in any structure of meaning thereby dissolving any systematic relationship between the signifier and signified, rendering the tools of semiotics, which were fundamental to the formation of media analysis, rather redundant to the analysis of the politics of the (new) media. There has been a tendency to think that the new media era charges us to start thinking from scratch about the relationships between media and identity, but I would argue that is largely because we have oversimplified the distinctions between old/ new media in the first place.

## BEYOND DICHOTOMIES: THE CENTRALITY OF MEDIA

Two-way media and interactivity offered through new media forms therefore suggest action and connectivity while old media forms only permit us to be passive and disconnected (Lash, 2002). However, again there are problems associated with such a clear dichotomy which do not take into account the ways in which supposedly old media have embedded themselves in daily social interaction, or the ways in which they serve particular functions of social integration, and collective forms of belonging, evidence of which abounds in some of media reception research described above. (Take for example work on the role of television consumption in the formation women's friendship groups where soap opera helps establish the grounds for talk about oneself and forms of friendship [Brown, 1994; Hobson, 1991].) I have argued elsewhere that understanding media in terms of forms of connectivity is not a process that should be actioned *only* on the basis of new media technology, but that all media have always been integrated into social forms of communication (Wood, 2009). What I hope is emerging, despite the best efforts of some social theorists, is that the relationship between media and identity cannot be wholly straightjacketed into evaluative debates. It is impossible to draw a totalising account or 'measure' of what 'the media' does.

Despite the public thrashing and denigrating of media studies courses, any first-year media student will tell you that the word 'media' is plural. While there are different forms, genres and different types of technologies, there are also different institutions and organizations that construct our experience of media in surprisingly diffuse ways. (Take for example the decisions over broadcasting regulation made between the differences in political organizations in Europe and the US.) While the current push towards the convergence of media (the move towards personalized downloadable media as telecommunications and broadcast technology merge) might suggest an edge towards homogeneity, the picture is more complex. As the search for niche audiences and niche markets becomes more and more significant it potentially opens up the space for different types of cultural distinction (single language or culture channels, for example). At the same time there is also a push in another direction, as competition often means meeting mainstream needs where the search for a guaranteed hit can produce more of the same: the sale and resale of television formats for example (Moran, 1998).

What we *do* know for sure is that media are now constitutive of identity practices; so much so that we can now produce and perform ourselves 'through' media. This is where we can concur with the propositions of the individualization thesis, despite the fact that they give us very little insight into how the mediation of identity might work. Nick Couldry (2003) in his discussion of media rituals gives us the concept of 'media selves' to help explain selfhood *as* a mediated phenomenon, one in which most of us habitually engage. This reaffirms the media's power in that it ritualizes a 'myth of the mediated centre'. I have briefly mentioned earlier the expansion of selfhood and identity work as central themes in much media production (see Dovey, 2000). What is significant here is the way in which the 'mediation' of self-disclosure is taken for granted, and yet this is what Couldry discusses as '[...] the most puzzling aspect of this whole landscape: its links to the ritually reinforced notion that the media provide a "central" space where it makes sense to disclose publicly aspects of one's life that one might otherwise not disclose to *anyone*' (2003: 116 original emphasis). To be able to perform well at mediated selfhood is applauded in contemporary culture. This begins to make sense of the way celebrity – being someone through the media – has become so central to contemporary popular culture. Graeme Turner (2004) suggests that celebrity has become a reference point for new kinds of identity formation that are evident in some young people's 'life plans'. In this sense it no longer makes sense (if it ever did) to see 'media' and 'identity' as distinct and coherent organs, which has been the implication in concerns over profit and loss. We should not, as Waisbord (1998) argues, put the 'cart of media before the horse of identity' in a technocentric view of global change, but we must fill in the gaps left by the individualization thesis in terms of the diffuse processes of mediation at work in contemporary identity formations.

Roger Silverstone (1993) for example, refers to idea that media communication (in particular television) can be understood in terms of 'object-relations' theory in that media form transitional objects for the comprehension of 'me' and 'not me' (see Moores, 2005). Understanding media and identity formation as co-constitutive and context-dependant I want to argue demands that we have to avoid thinking with over-generalized dichotomies. James Carey's (1989) work proposed that we need to think less about the transmission mode of media and more about the 'ritual' mode of media: that is the media's role in the maintenance of societies in time, a call taken up convincingly in the work of

Nick Couldry. While Carey refuses an entirely functionalist account of the media, we might see his version of 'ritual' in terms of the way in which media are implicated in social bonds, rather than just in the sending of messages. Similarly, in my work I have argued that we need to incorporate an understanding of the way in which media is embedded into socio-communicative spheres of everyday life and to see continuities between interpersonal and mediated communication (Wood, 2009).

If we take on board the notion of the self as a symbolic project in which individuals are involved in using the media as resources, not just as 'subject' to their messages, then empirical work can account for how engagements with media help us to rehearse and formulate identities. This requires a fine-grained level of analysis between technologies, forms and genres. In my own work, using a method I call 'text-in-action', I discuss how when women conversationally 'interact' with daytime talk television, they produce rather complex narratives of themselves within the contexts of what they are hearing on talk shows (Wood, 2005, 2006). Rather than understanding television talk in terms of the straightforward interpretation of messages which provides a relatively stable notion of meaning and de-construction, my work enables me to see what the women *do* as identity practice with television. In the extract below Alice is watching *Kilroy* (a BBC discussion programme similar in style to the US programme *Donahue*). The topic under discussion is whether the elderly should pay for their own care and until now Alice has agreed with some of the discussion that wealthy people should pay using the profits from the sale of their houses. As the programme unfolds she begins to question this principle, thinking about her own home and then finally about her responsibilities as a mother: 'I'm more concerned that there's a home here to come to–'. To understand interactions like these in terms of whether audiences receive a dominant message seems to evade the point. Alice is working through her

**Alice/Kilroy discussion program on 'should the elderly pay for their own care?'**

|   |   | Studio | | Home |
|---|---|---|---|---|
| 1 | Kilroy | … Let us say it was me and I've got | Alice | That's the other side of the |
| 2 |  | this expensive house and I now |  | argument, of course. |
| 3 |  | need nursing care – not National |  |  |
| 4 |  | Health Service treatment but |  |  |
| 5 |  | nursing care. I have to sell my |  |  |
| 6 |  | house in order to get that care. I |  |  |
| 7 |  | have to sell my house in order to |  |  |
| 8 |  | pay for it. hh Are you saying that I |  |  |
| 9 |  | shouldn't have to sell my expensive |  |  |
| 10 |  | house, that I should be able to give |  |  |
| 11 |  | it to my children and your low paid |  |  |
| 12 |  | constituents who are in work now |  |  |
| 13 |  | paying taxes should pay to keep me |  |  |
| 14 |  | in care while I give my expensive |  |  |
| 15 |  | house to my children? Is that fair? |  |  |
| 16 | Expert | Hang on |  |  |
| 17 |  | [audience noise] |  |  |
| 18 | Woman | He is not saying that at all |  | When you put it like that yes, |
|  | Expert | Can I just- |  | Yes, |
| 19 | Audience | Heh, heh, heh, heh |  |  |
| 20 | Woman | No, he is NOT |  |  |
| 21 | Kilroy | I'm asking HIM |  |  |
| 22 | Woman | Go on then |  |  |
| 23 | Kilroy | Go on then she said, go on then Alf | Alice | But, you see a modest home |
| 24 | Expert | Right, now I'm saying a number of |  | wouldn't last very long would it? |
| 25 |  | things. I'm saying that it was not |  | I'm on about our sort of |
| 26 |  | their expectation that they would |  | [gestures around the room] |
| 27 |  | have to dispossess er mainly |  | I'm more concerned that |
| 28 |  | daughters, caring relatives, many |  | there's always a home here to |
| 29 |  | who have given up the prospect of |  | come to if things go wrong |
| 30 |  | marriage, of a career to look after |  | that was my concern. |
| 31 |  | an elderly mother or father or both |  |  |
| 32 |  | and whose reward for that is now to |  |  |
| 33 |  | be told that they've lost the home |  |  |
| 34 |  | they expected to inherit. |  |  |

own position as a mother, in a mediated performance of identity.

My work is based upon principles from pragmatics – that meaning is generated as much in interaction in terms of what words *do*, as much as what they semantically *mean*. In media studies an overemphasis upon semiotics (media as signs) has stood in the way of developing a pragmatics of mediated communication (Wood, 2009). As the extract above demonstrates the women in my study move through discursive positions as they

engage with a text that does not necessarily have a rigid meaning system. Talk television encourages them to engage in social forms of connection with and against others in the studio as they engage in a ritualized form of gendered communication similar to gossip. Here we can see that subjectivity and textuality are complexly imbricated (Wood, 2005). This seems to reinforce Giddens (1991) theorisation that contemporary society involves the dis-embedding and the re-embedding of social relationships. But it also challenges his conclusion that dis-embedding necessarily 'propels social life away from the hold of pre-established precepts or practices' (1991b: 20). My work shows how this genre encourages women to rehearse their gendered selves as wives, mothers, and carers: in short re-embedding can mean the mediation of relatively fixed notions of womanhood. Similarly, Lisa Adkins (2003) has questioned an inevitable link between self-reflexivity and individualization, and others have argued that processes of individualization have tended to re-make, rather than undo, classed and gendered distinctions.

Therefore, there is considerable work to be done on exploring the relationship between the increasing mediation of selfhood and contemporary identity practice. Work on the self does not in itself mean work on the individual (the very gendering of the self-help industry indexes the complicated relationship between ideologies of self and gender). In John Thompson's (1995) critique of the relatively impoverished notions of selfhood available in early structuralist work on the media, he also points out that simply replacing interpellation with theories of self-reflexivity is not enough, since the resources one can access to construct a self are 'distributed unevenly'. Thus social inequalities and their relations with group identities are very much part of the workings of mediated self-reflexivity.

## Reason and emotion: Audiences of reality television

In drawing this chapter to a conclusion I want to finish with one last organizational pair. That is the distinction between reason and emotion. Early work on television consumption, stemming from a Marxist concern with the ideological interpretation of meaning took social class as its bases in the assumption that social location would effect the deconstruction of meaning (Hall 1980; Morley 1980). However, since post-structuralist discontent about taking particular groups as a priori categories of gender and class

(Ang and Hermes, 1996), there has been little recent work which has categorically thought about the explicit role media forms might play in formations of classed identities.

However, this chapter takes its lead from Morley (2006) and suggests that questions of the relationship between traditional identity markers such as class and the role of the media still remain, even if they have been marginalized by some trends in theoretical and methodological problematics – most notably, post-structuralism and the individualization thesis. If theories of individualization actually reproduce social distinctions and 're-make' class in new ways (Skeggs, 2004, and see Skeggs, Chapter 17 this volume) then we must also begin to understand how that process is also mediated.

While the early work on class was concerned with meaning systems and the deconstruction of meaning based upon social experience, recent work I have conducted with Beverley Skeggs has drawn upon the idea that media are ubiquitous in their embedding of identity practices and therefore might also work in more socially ritualized ways. Focusing on the contemporary push towards self-telling and display in the contemporary explosion of 'reality' television (characterized by the increasing use of non-actors in television programmes) our work is concerned with how the self mediates class and gender identities (Skeggs and Wood, 2008; Wood and Skeggs, 2004, 2008; Wood et al., 2008). We have become used to the 'ordinary' person on television so much so that the distance between those on television and audiences is increasingly eroded – part of the ongoing re-drawing of distinctions between the private and the public in processes of mediation. Therefore, we consider the 'ritual' role of reality television in terms of a 'mediated social/public realm' (Biressi and Nunn, 2005).

As Blackman and Walkerdine (2001) discuss, the media's incitement of public emotion has for too long been ignored in the discussion of media and cultural identity, while Sarah Ahmed's (2004) work

| Audio marker Visual Image | Programme audio extract Wife Swap | Brockley Viewers' comments |
|---|---|---|
| 18.50 Kate driving home from work | Kate: "I can't believe it's eight o'clock and I left home 13 hours ago no wonder I've got a headache its just ridiculous" | |
| Kate pulling onto drive | Voice over: By the time Kate gets home its eight thirty. | **Sally**: Nightmare, absolute nightmare in it? |
| Kate enters the house | Kate: 'How's Lottie' | **Sonia**: I had to leave home at seven with (?child's name) to get to work and drop them off I had to leave at seven |
| | Mark: She's fast asleep | **Sally**: Oh no she's crying, she had a mare of a day. |
| | Kate: Ah | **All**: Yeah. |
| | Mark: She was shattered | **Sonia**: She's not had her all day has she? I suppose with all them children ((? )) |
| Kate to Camera Shot of Lottie sleeping | I'm quite disappointed that Lottie was in bed and I didn't get to bath her I'm so tired | Sal: But that's not fair on that child! Sonia: Exactly and that's what she's feelin' |
| Kate and Mark in the living room | My body feels realty alive but my head feels dead quite often at home it's the other way round. Mark: Do you think Tracy would be feeling like that now? | **Sal**: ((?)) **Sonia**: mmm I'm taking the mother's role [performs] and when I woke you up and dragged you out of bed at six o'clock in the morning [and dropped you off at seven o'clock **Sal**: [to have you out by seven **Sonia**: and now its eight thirty at night and you ain't seen me all day. (2) The kid's in bed. **Sal**: How you gonna make up for that? **Sonia**: You can't |

(Brockley is a ward of Lewisham in South London that is characterized by a larger than average African and Caribbean populations and social housing.[2])

on 'affective economies' suggests that processes of social and cultural distinction operate through affective sensibilities. Our work considered how 40 women from different social locations, working and middle class, white, black and Asian, respond and react to the forms of self-telling and display on television. Analysis of the texts of reality television (on the messages) suggested that reality television remakes notions of working-class identity through a framework of removing social distinctions from their historical and material contexts and 'spectacularising' aspects of behaviour as individual modes of failure. We argue that this mirrors how class is being re-conceptualized in contemporary neo-liberal politics and that the process of individualizing does not remove class but reworks it into a discourse of personal psychology (Wood and Skeggs, 2008, also see Walkerdine, 2003).

When we conducted audience reception work, watching programmes with participants and conducting interviews and focus groups, we found that emotional reactions to the moral positions on display were encountered in ways which mapped onto classed, raced and gendered dispositions. Most participants were drawn into a relationship with participants on television where both empathy and moral judgement could be deployed simultaneously (Wood et al., 2008). Often empathy was evoked through making connections with the self on the grounds of an affinity with the pressures of gender, femininity or motherhood. Like my previous work mediated self-reflexivity involved narratives of gendered lives. But there were also distinctions in the ways the women approached identifying and dis-identifying with those on television. Our middle-class participants were more likely to resource their positions on moral authority through discourses of education and taste, while our working-class groups were more likely to claim their authority through notions of authenticity and often moral discourses of motherhood. And our Asian participants from Clapham resourced their moral authority through making cultural distinctions of difference. In the extract above black, working-class viewers from Brockley react strongly to an aspirational working mother on the UK reality television programme *Wife Swap*[3]. That working-class mothers tended to take the high moral ground on mothering in a cultural climate where the working-class (usually single) mother bears the brunt of much public scorn for bad 'parenting skills' should come as no surprise.

Significant to this discussion is that group identities in the project emerged in terms of the differentiated access to resources that our participants had to display their own 'value' in relation to the televised others. It was not the case that the mediated self-reflexivity here meant that each audience member judged the televised others in a straightforward process of individualization. Rather, using the television as a resource in this way worked in combination with other material resources, some of them dependent upon social structure and cultural difference, in which our participants were implicated. We refer to this process as 'circuits of value', where the women connected to or detached from others depending upon the value they attached to identity practices, rather than to identity *categories* (Skeggs and Wood, 2008).

Television here plays an affective role in recognition of the self patterned by class, race and gender. We suggest that the textual form of reality television creates a 'structure of immanence' for viewers through which there is rarely a singular stable reading of the programme, but rather a set of immediate reactive moments through which our audiences experience and locate themselves within the unfolding drama. In that sense we show how mediated worlds and lived worlds are simultaneously experienced in significant reactive

moments of connection and disconnection. What is at work here, in engagements with a particular technology (television), and with a particular genre (reality television) is evidence both of how the immediacy of the text incorporates the viewer into the action (subject positioning), but also how that process involves viewers in ritual actions of connection and disconnection (identity practice).

## CONCLUSION

In this chapter I have argued for a more dialectical approach to replace apparent polarities of text–audience, isolation–connection and reason–emotion to begin to locate a more precise politics of how a diffuse set of media objects work, and are un-worked, within a diffuse set of identity practices. In so doing we must see how media have become ritually involved in processes of identity, both in terms of how media address audiences, but also in terms of how they engage us in activities of identity, whether that is through watching television or blogging on the Internet. We need to see mediations as complex negotiations involving institutions and cultural practices, as well as texts and technologies, instead of indulging in some of the evaluative debates that can be a distraction from entering into discussions about how self and identity are now precisely 'mediated'.

## NOTES

1   ***Dallas*** is an American prime-time television soap opera that originally ran from 1978 to 1991. It revolved around the Ewings, a wealthy Texan family in the oil and cattle-ranching industries and was a global export.

2   Area Profile Summary

Our four groups of ten women were recruited from friendship networks from four areas of south London.

The **New Addington** group is all white and working class. Five mothers, five non-mothers, ages 18–72. Occupations mainly centre on care work and full-time mothering. New Addington is a ward of

Croydon, an outer London Borough, and is noted for its physical isolation, with a population of 10,351. Nearly one-half of the accommodation of the area is social council rented housing, with an unemployment rate of 4%. It is mostly white (88%) and most of the population, nearly 90%, is born in the UK.

The **Forest Hill** group is middle class working in arts and education, mostly white and mixed race. seven white, three self-defined as mixed race, all self defined as middle-class (three mothers, seven non-mothers), ages 30–57. Occupations centre on public sector educational, art and psy-drama work. Forest Hill is a ward of Lewisham, an inner London Borough, with a population of 14,000. Over one-half of the accommodation in the area is owner occupied (Victorian housing) and approximately 23% is council housing with 9% unemployment. It has a 30% population of black or minority ethnic residents, lower than the average for inner London, and just over 70% of its population were born in the UK.

The **Brockley** group is racially mixed, white and Caribbean, and all working class. Six black British, three white, one Maltese (only one not a mother), ages 26–68. Occupations in public sector and service sector administrative, caring and secretarial work. Brockley is another ward of Lewisham in inner London with a population of 13,697. Of the housing in this area 37% is owner occupied and 26% council rented, with 8% unemployment. Brockley has a lower percentage of British residents (48.8%) than the London average (59.8%), nearly 30% identify themselves as black or black British, mostly Caribbean or African.

The **Clapham** group are Southern and British Asian, Asian, Pakistani, Bangladeshi, settled and recently arrived; there are transnational class differences, (seven mothers, two non-mothers) ages 18–45. Two are highly educated professional women, one student, the rest are full-time mothers or part-time helpers with husband's work. Clapham is a ward of Lambeth in inner London with a population of 13,332. Most accommodation in Clapham consists of flats of which approximately 35% are owner occupied, 62% are rented (30% rented from the council), with 4.7% unemployment. Clapham is known to be a rather diverse area in terms of affluence and ethnicity, 38% of the population are from ethnic minorities.

(Area information compiled from 2001 Census: http://neighbourhood.statistics.gov.uk and http://www.ideal-homes.org.uk.)

3  *Wife Swap* is a documentary style programme originally produced by British independent television production company RDF Media and first broadcast in 2003 on the UK's Channel 4. Two families, usually from vastly different social classes and lifestyles, swap wives/mothers (and sometimes husbands) for two weeks.

# REFERENCES

Abu-Lughod, L. (2005) *Dramas of Nationhood: The Politics of Television in Egypt.* Chicago, IL: University of Chicago Press.

Adkins, L. (2003) 'Reflexivity: Freedom or habit of gender', *Theory, Culture and Society*, 20 (6): 21–42.

Adorno, T. and Horkheimer, M (1999) 'The culture industry: Enlightenment as mass deception', in S. During (ed.), *The Cultural Studies Reader*. 2nd edn. London: Routledge. pp. 31–41.

Ahmed, S. (2004) *The Cultural Politics of Emotion.* London: Routledge.

Anderson, B. (1991) *Imagined Communities: Reflections on the Origin and Spread of Nationalism.* Revised ed. London: Verso.

Andrejevik, M. (2004) *Reality TV: The Work of Being Watched.* London: Rowman and Littlefield.

Ang, I. and Hermes, J. (1996) 'Gender and/in media consumption', in Curran, James and Gurevitch(eds) *Mass Media and Society*, London: Edward, pp. 307–329.

Althusser, L. (1971) 'Ideology and ideological state apparatus', in Lenin (ed.), *Philosophy and Other Essays*. London: New Left Books, pp. 127–186.

Baudrillard, J.C. (1994) *Simulacra and Simulation.* Ann Arbor, MI: University of Michigan Press.

Barthes, R. (1973) *Mythologies.* London: Paladin.

Baym, N. (1998) 'The emergence of on-line community', in S.G. Jones (ed.), *Cybersociety.2.0: Re-visiting Computer Mediated Communication and Community.* London: Sage, pp. 35–68.

Beck, U. (1992) *Risk Society: Towards a New Modernity.* London: Sage.

Beniger, J.R. (1987) 'Personalisation of mass media and the growth of pseudo-community', *Communication Research*, 14 (3): 252–371.

Biressi, A. and Nunn, H. (2005) *Reality TV: Realism and Revelation.* London: Wallflower.

Blackman, L. and Walkderine, V. (2001) *Mass Hysteria: Critical Psychology and Media Studies.* Basingstoke: Palgrave.

Boyd, D (2007a) 'Why youth heart social network sites: The role of networked publics in teenage social life', in D. Buckingham (ed.), *MacArthur Foundation Series on Digital Learning – Youth, Identity and Digital Media Volume.* Cambridge, MA: MIT Press, pp. 119–142.

Boyd, D. (2007b) 'Viewing American class divisions through Facebook and myspace', *Apophena Blog Essay.* 24 June. Available at: http://www.danah.org/papers/essyas/ClassDivisions.html (accessed 25 September 2008).

Brown, M.E. (1994) *Soap Opera and Women's Talk*. London: Sage.

Brunsdon, C. (1981) 'Crossroads: notes on soap opera', *Screen*, 22 (4): 32–7.

Carey, J. (1989) *Communication as Culture*. London: Routledge.

Castells, M. (2000) *The Rise of the Network Society*, 2nd edn. Oxford: Blackwell.

Couldry, N. (2003) *Media Rituals: A Critical Approach*. London: Routledge.

De Certeau, Michel (1984) *The Practice of Everyday Life* Berkeley: University of California Press.

Dibble, J. (2001) 'A rape in cyberspace; or how an evil clown, a Haitian trickster spirit, two wizards and a cast of dozens turned a database into a society', in D. Trend (ed.), *Reading Digital Culture*. Oxford: Blackwell, pp. 199–213.

Dovey, J. (2000) *Freakshow: First Person Media and Factual Television*. London: Pluto Press.

Dow, B. (1996) *Prime-time Feminism: Television, Media Culture and the Women's Movement since 1970*. Philadelphia, PA: University of Pennsylvania Press.

Giddens, A. (1991) *Modernity and Self-identity*. Cambridge: Polity.

Gillespie, M. (1995) *Television, Ethnicity and Cultural Change*. London: Routledge.

Fiske, J. (1987) *Television Culture* London and New York: Routledge.

Featherstone, M. (1987) 'Lifestyle and consumer culture'. *Theory Culture and Society*, 4 (1): 55–70.

Gray, A. (1992) *Video Playtime: The Gendering of a Leisure Technology*. London: Routledge.

Gray, A. (1999) 'Audience and Reception Research in Retrospect: the trouble with audiences'' In Alasuutari, P. (ed) *Rethinking the Media Audience*, London: Sage.

Hall, S. (1980) 'Encoding/decoding', in S. Hall et. al. (eds), *Culture, Media, Language: Working Papers in Cultural Studies*. London: Hutchinson, pp. 128–138.

Hall, S. (1996) 'Who needs "identity"?', in S. Hall and P. Du Gay (eds), *Questions of Cultural Identity*. London: Sage, pp. 1–17.

Haraway, D. (1990) 'A manifesto for cyborgs: Science technology and socialist feminism in the 1980s', in L. Nicholson (ed.), *Feminism/Postmodernism*. London: Routledge, pp. 190–223.

Hearn, A. (2008) 'Variations on the branded Self: Theme, invention, improvisation and inventory', in D. Hesmondhalgh and J. Toynbee (eds), *The Media and Social Theory*. London: Routledge, pp.194–210.

Hermes, J. (1995) *Reading Women's Magazines: An Analysis of Everyday Media Use*. Cambridge: Polity Press.

Hobson, D. (1980) 'Housewives and the mass media', in S. Hall et al. (eds), *Culture, Media, Language*. London: Hutchinson, pp. 105–114.

Hobson, D. (1982) *Crossroads – The Drama of a Soap Opera*. London: Methuen.

Hobson, D. (1991) 'Soap operas at work', in E. Seiter et al. (eds), *Remote Control: Television, Audiences and Cultural Power*. London: Routledge, pp. 150–67.

hooks, b. (1991) 'Talking back', in F. Russell et al. (eds), *Out There: Marginalisation and Contemporary Culture*. Cambridge: MIT Press, pp. 337–344.

Jenkins, H. (2004) 'Taking media in our own hands', *Technology Review*, November 4. http://www.technologyreview.com/biomedicine/13905/. Last accessed on 17/11/09.

Klein, N. (1999) *No Logo*. Canada: Knopf.

Lash, S. (2002) *Critique of Information*. London: Sage.

Liebes, T. and Katz, E. (1990) *The Export of Meaning*. Oxford: Oxford University Press.

Lury, C. (1998) *Prosthetic Culture: Photography, Memory and Identity*. London: Routledge.

Mankekar, P. (1999) *Screening Culture: Viewing Politics*. Durham, NC: Duke University Press.

Marcuse, H. (1964) *One Dimensional Man*. Boston, MA: Beacon Press.

Mattelart, A., Delcourt, X. and Mattelart, M. (1984) *International Image Markets*. London: Comedia.

McLuhan, M. and Powers, B.R. (1989) *The Global Village: Transformations in World Life and Media in the 21st Century*. New York: Oxford University Press.

Miller, D. (1993) 'The young and the restless in Trinidad: A case study of the local and the global in media consumption', in R. Silverstone and E. Hirsch (eds), *Consuming Technologies*. London: Routledge, pp. 163–182.

Modleski, T. (1983) 'The rhythm of reception: Daytime television and women's work', in E. A. Kaplan (ed.), *Regarding Television: Critical Approaches an Anthology*. Los Angeles, CA: American Film Institute, pp. 67–75.

Moores, S. (2005) *Media/Theory: Thinking about Media and Communications* Comedia, London and New York: Routledge.

Moran, A. (1998) *Copycat TV: Globalisation, Program Formats and Cultural Identity*. Luton: University of Luton Press.

Morley, D. (1980) *The Nationwide Audience*. London: BFI.

Morley, D. (2000) *Home Territories: Media, Mobility and Identity*. London: Routledge.

Morley, D. (2006) 'Unanswered questions in audience research', *The Communication Review*, 9: 101–21.

Moseley, R. (2002) *Growing Up with Audrey Hepburn: Text, Audience, Resonance*. Manchester: Manchester University Press.

Mulvey, L. (1975) 'Visual pleasure and narrative cinema', *Screen*, 16 (3): 6–18.

O'Brien, J. (1997) 'Gender on (the) line: An erasable institution? In P.Kollock and M. Smith (eds.) *Communities in Cyberspace*. Berkeley, CA: University of California Press, pp. 177–193.

Ouellette, L. and Hay, J. (2008) *Better Living Through Reality TV: Television and Post-welfare Citizenship*. Oxford: Blackwell.

Palmer, G. (2003) *Discipline and Liberty: Television and Governance*. Manchester: Manchester University Press.

Poster, M. (1995) *The Second Media Age*. Cambridge: Polity.

Poster, M. (2007) 'The secret self: The case of identity theft', *Cultural Studies*, 21 (1): 118–40.

Putnam, R. (2000) *Bowling Alone: The Collapse and Revival of American Community*. New York: Simon and Schuster.

Press, A. (1991) *Women Watching Television*. Philadelphia, PA: University of Pennsylvania Press.

Rheingold, H. (1993) *The Virtual Community: Homesteading on the Electronic Frontier*. Reading, MA: Addison Wesley.

Rose, N. (1984) *Governing the Soul: The Shaping of the Private Self*. London: Routledge.

Scannell, P. and Cardiff, D. (1991) *A Social History of British Broadcasting*. Vol 1. Oxford: Blackwell.

Silverstone, R. (1993) 'Television, ontological security and the transitional object', *Media, Culture and Society*, 15: 573–98.

Skeggs, B (2004) *Class, Self, Culture*. London: Sage.

Skeggs, B. and Wood, H. (2008) 'The labour of transformation and circuits of value around reality TV', *Continuum*, 22 (4): 559–572.

Thomas, L. (1995) 'In love with inspector morse: Feminist subculture and quality television', *Feminist Review*, 51: 1–25.

Thompson, J. (1994) 'Social theory and the media', in D. Crowley and D. Mitchell (eds), *Communication Theory Today*. Cambridge: Polity, pp. 27–49.

Thompson, J. (1995) *The Media and Modernity* Cambridge: Polity.

Turner, G. (2004) *Understanding Celebrity*. London: Sage.

Tufte, T. (2000) *Living With the Rubbish Queen*. Luton: University of Luton Press.

Turkle, S (1997) *Life on the Screen: Identity in the Age of the Internet*. New York: Touchstone Press.

Waisbord, S. (1998) 'When the cart of media is before the horse of identity: A critique of technology-centred views on globalisation', *Communication Research*, 25 (4): 377–98.

Walkerdine, V. (2003) 'Re-classifying upward mobility: Femininity and the neo-liberal subject', *Gender and Education*, 15 (3): 237–48.

Wood, H. and Skeggs, B. (2004) 'Notes on ethical scenarios of self on British reality TV', *Feminist Media Studies*, 4 (2): 205–208.

Wood, H. (2005) 'Texting the subject: Women, television and modern self-reflexivity', *Communication Review*, 8 (2): 115–35.

Wood, H. (2007) 'The mediated conversational floor: An interactive approach to audience reception analysis', *Media, Culture and Society*. 29 (1): 75–103.

Wood, H. (2009) *Talking With Television: Women, Talk Shows and Modern Self-Reflexivity*. Chicago, IL: University of Illinois Press.

Wood, H., Skeggs, B. and Thumim, N. (2008) 'It's just sad: Affect, judgement and emotional labour in reality TV viewing', in J. Hollows and S. Gillis (eds), *Homefires: Domesticity, Feminism and Popular Culture*. London: Routledge, pp. 135–150.

Wood, H. and Skeggs, B. (2008) 'Spectacular morality: Reality television, individualisation and the re-making of the working class', in D. Hesmondhalgh and J. Toynbee (eds), *The Media and Social Theory*. London: Routledge, pp. 177–193.

# 14

# Identity Making in Schools and Classrooms

Diane Reay

Individuals construct their identities in relation to others, and, in particular, in relation to understandings of 'the other'. So for Lois Weis (1990: 3) identity can be defined as a sense of self in relation to others. As Bourdieu (2002) asserts, identity is all about difference. David Sibley describes how individuals engage in processes of boundary construction that generate 'stereotypical representations of others which inform social practices of exclusion and inclusion but which, at the same time, define the self' (1995: 5). This relational aspect of identities is particularly key in the context of schools and classrooms. Students' identities are constructed as much through a sense of 'what we are not' and notions of how others see us as conceptions of who 'we' are.

The contemporary emphasis is on the shifting and fluid nature of social identities. There has been a move within educational research towards more contingent, hybrid fluid understandings of identity. Key examples of such ideas include Foucault's (1978) notions of 'technologies of the self' and discursive positioning, Butler's (1990) work on performativity and Beck's (1992) thesis of individualization. Particularly influential in

the UK context has been the work of Stuart Hall on new ethnicities. For Hall, identities are about processes of becoming rather than being: 'not "who we are" or "where we came from", so much as what we might become, how we have been represented, and how that bears on how we might represent ourselves' (1996: 4). Within such constantly changing understandings of identity what has remained constant is the critical role schooling plays in identity formation. No other public institution is as crucial for the development of the identities children and young people will carry into adulthood. School norms, practices and expectations provide key symbolic materials that students draw on to make sense of their experiences and define themselves (Perry, 2002):

Perhaps it is the singular nature of the modernist school, where people of the same age are forced into a common arena, that compels individuals and groups to find a place and identity within a single complex matrix. No matter how heterogeneous their backgrounds or how differently their cultural destinies would have been played out without the unnatural social atmosphere of the school, it is within the constraints of this institution that young people negotiate their identities. (Willis, 2006: 518–19)

While Willis may be overstating the primacy of schooling in the identities of children and young people, it is uncontestable that as children move through middle childhood towards adolescence, the peer group begins to replace the family as the primary context within which identity and identification occurs and develops (Jenkins, 2004). Jenkins asserts that 'for some organizations "people-production" is their core business' p. 23. This is especially true of the educational system. But even more crucially schools are where children and young people engage with difference. Although school experiences are to varying degrees segregated by gender, ethnicity and social class, for most children and young people school remains the primary arena for engaging and dealing with a whole array of differences. Schools then are crucial sites of identity work and identity making. One key implication of the importance of process and change when studying identities is that the interest should shift from looking at 'the result' – the outcome of the identity formation process, and move to interrogating the process itself; to look at how identity shifts and changes in different contexts, spaces and times. In 1974, Erik Erikson was writing that identity makes itself felt 'as a subjective sense of invigorating sameness and continuity' (1974: 17). In the twenty-first century sameness and continuity have been replaced by provisionality and contingency. Furthermore, we have moved a long way from the period when identities were simply understood as categories or labels. If we take the example of social class, identity research often worked with static notions, individuals were either working or middle class, or on rare occasions upper class, but there was little interrogation of the practice and processes, affects and dispositions that lay beneath such identity categories and brought them to life. In contrast, class identity in Stephen Ball's recent work is 'a set of perspectives on the social world and relationships in it, marked by varying degrees of reflexivity' (2003: 6).

Connell (2001) has observed that such approaches to identity theory lead in some instances to assumptions that we can all be whatever we strive to be. Yet, while identities can both be constructed through and within discourses and are often performed, they are also constrained by material and structural inequalities. As Connell points out, 'fluidity may be a great deal less fluid when examined in the institutional contexts of everyday lives' (2001: 8). Similarly, Jenkins cautions that 'fluidity may be the exception rather than the rule' (2004: 19). Notions of the individual as a 'free agent' have become particularly pervasive within many of our assumptions about education (du Gay, 2007). As a consequence it is important in relation to issues of social inclusion and social exclusion in schools and classrooms to ensure there is also a focus on the 'fixing' mechanisms that limit the fluidity of identities and mitigate against individuals overcoming disadvantage (Skeggs, 2005a). The most obvious of these are the inequalities that arise from differences of race, ethnicity, sexuality, dis/ability, social class and gender. But there are further confounding factors based on, for example, locality, institutional ethos, levels of academic attainment, and crucially the attitudes and practices of more advantaged others (Butler, 2003; Butler with Robson, 2003).

To further complicate and compound the ways in which identities are played out in classrooms, as Louise Archer points out, 'identities are not just consciously articulated, argued and asserted – they have an unconscious, emotional and psychic dimension' (2003: 158). There is a growing body of empirical work that uses psychoanalytical concepts to explore and theorize individual and collective patterns of investment and disavowal that enter in the formation of identities (Reay, 2005; Roseneil, 2006; Shaw, 1995). Individuals make powerful emotional and psychic investments in certain subject positions available to them in particular contexts (Frosh et al., 2002). And such psychic investments are sustained and defended by projecting anxieties, fears and desires onto others. According to Hollway and Jefferson 'the idea of a defended subject shows how subjects invest in discourses when these offer positions which provide protection against anxiety and therefore supports to identity' (2000: 23).

A further challenge within educational contexts lies in the frequent conflation of learner identities with social identities grounded in categories of race, ethnicity, dis/ability, social class and gender. Learner identities refer specifically to the conceptualizations children have of themselves as learners, but as with social identities, these are relational and pupils construct themselves and are constructed by others as particular types of learners in relation to both other pupils and their teachers. Sociologists have tended to assume that social identities are always dominant in the classroom, often eliding learner with social identities. So, for example, white working-class boys are homogeneously perceived to have poor learner identities, while disruptive anti-school positions are seen to be the preserve of both black and white working-class boys. Similarly, British Chinese students are viewed as industrious diligent pupils, identified as 'boffins' (Archer and Francis, 2005), while white middle-class students are seen to be universally 'bright'. However, social identities cannot be transposed onto learner identities, there is no neat fit but rather varying degrees of overlap and synergy in which the development of a sense of self as a learner is crucial to the shaping of a coherent and viable wider identity (Pollard and Filer, 2007: 447). As Pollard and Filer (2007) argue, many students develop differentiated learner and social identities across both school and out-of-school contexts.

How these complexities, the messiness, of identities are played out in educational settings will be explored through the theoretical work of Pierre Bourdieu and Basil Bernstein and more empirically driven work within sociology of education. I will be drawing on empirical studies of identity work in classrooms, including my own in order to achieve two aims. First, I hope to indicate the current state of theoretical play in relation to how we understand identities in educational settings. Second, I intend to illustrate how contemporary identity theories are utilized to elucidate the multiplicity of social interactions in schools, and demonstrate how inclusion, exclusion, social conflicts and solidarities, defences and desires are key to the formation of both social and learner identities.

## IDENTITIES IN SCHOOLS AND CLASSROOMS

The meaning of identity within education has shifted across time, disciplines and epistemological frameworks but there are a number of enduring themes. Whereas social class once had primacy (Lacey, 1970) most contemporary educational research focuses across an array of identity categories, including race, ethnicity, sex, gender, sexuality, culture, ability and disability. In fact the current concern with multiple identity categories has eclipsed the previous dominance of social class. This growing concern with multiple identities was initially viewed in additive terms and contemporary educational research still has a strong focus on intersectionality, a more nuanced and sophisticated development of the additive approach (Brah and Phoenix, 2004). However, more recently emphasis has shifted to underscore the complex range of limits and possibilities made available by particular constellations of identity categories (Archer, 2003; Youdell, 2006). Youdell argues that identity categories – of 'race', ethnicity, disability, class, gender, sexuality – become meaningful through interaction with other categories, and that these 'constellations of categorizations' may be seen as shifting and non-necessary. Students are constituted through constellations, particularly through 'dichotomies of *good/bad students and acceptable/unacceptable and even ideal/impossible learners*' (Youdell, 2006: 30, original emphasis).

Similarly Pamela Perry's (2002) research in the US found striking differences in how white students interpreted and performed whiteness as a cultural identity, depending on the constellation of identity categories available to them. She also reveals the ways in which such differences are powerfully shaped by both the ethnic composition of the peer group and the institutional practices of the school.

In the UK context there has been a growing salience of schooling in identity formation since the introduction of compulsory schooling for all in 1870. Currently, there are plans to raise the compulsory school leaving age to 18, while nursery provision continues to grow apace. The consequences are that more and more children are spending a minimum of 15 years in classrooms of one kind or another. However, if we are to see the real power of schooling on identity and identification we need to consider the development over the last 20 years of increasingly pervasive systems of educational assessment both here in the UK and in the US (Broadfoot and Pollard, 2006). Recent research has estimated that the typical pupil sits over thirty tests before the age of 11 (Hackett, 2001), while research commissioned by one of the UK's teaching unions, the National Union of Teachers, calculated that the more educationally successful students can now expect to take more than 75 external tests and exams during their school careers (Smithers, 2000). This all consuming focus on testing and measuring has served to re-emphasize and valorize ability as measured on test scores as the 'be-all and end-all' of education (Gillborn and Youdell, 2000). But a further consequence is the power of categories of ability for identity and identification. Ellen Brantlinger found that middle class parents and their children in her US study 'constructed intelligence as the essence of positive identity' and saw themselves as substantially brighter than the working classes (2003: 40). Similarly, in my ESRC research project on the white middle classes choosing multiethnic urban comprehensives, across 95 interviews with middle-class parents they used the term bright 251 times to describe their children (Reay et al., 2007). In contrast, black and white, working-class primary school girls (Reay, 2005) used terms like 'rubbish' and 'I'll be a nothing' to describe how they see themselves in relation to the testing regime. Below is just one small snippet of data to illustrate the power of testing and assessment for children's identities not just as learners but more broadly:

Sharon:  I think I'll get a two, only Stuart will get a six.

Diane:   So if Stuart gets a six, what will that say about him?

Sharon:  He's heading for a good job and a good life, and it shows he's not gonna be living on the streets and stuff like that.

Diane:   And if you get a level two, what will that say about you?

Sharon:  Um, I might not have a good life in front of me, and I might grow up and do something naughty or something like that.

The system of educational value that produces the middle classes as valuable, academic stars such as Stuart or even relatively successful levels 3 and 4 pupils simultaneously judges girls such as Sharon as valueless, without worth. And it is clear that Sharon has internalized this judgement with implications not only for her learner identity but her sense of self more widely.

As is evident in the example above, the key issues of agency and structure that were explored in the introduction are powerfully salient in the context of schooling. Children even more than adults are seen as in a process of becoming. Fluidity and flux are particularly important given their young age and so student identities within schools and classrooms are often seen as in process:

> Struggling to acquire the means to represent themselves to self and others is part of growing up. However, this active work always occurs under socially given conditions which include structures of power and social relations, institutional constraints and possibilities but also available cultural repertoires. (Epstein and Johnson, 1998: 116)

As is clear in the case of Sharon, the addendum to any emphasis on change and dynamism is the extent to which children are able to shape their own identities and how far they can negotiate the symbolic systems through which they represent themselves and are represented by others. Within schooling hierarchies both official school knowledge and the peer group must be negotiated. Reputation, status and public image in the eyes of both peers and teachers becomes important but to differing degrees for different groups of students.

There has been an apparent 'makeover' of social and learner identities within the prevailing individualized conceptual framework (Beck, 1992; Giddens, 2000). So whereas 30 years ago resistance to schooling was seen in terms of class consciousness (Willis, 1977), contemporary theorizations would understand both resistance and conformity as identity work that to varying degrees is contextualized within broader notions of the social. So Bottrell (2008, forthcoming) argues that young people's management of constraints and opportunities both informs and is informed by identity work and that both resistance and conformity are necessary aspects of identity work according to the relations of specific contexts.

However, social identities of class, race, gender and sexuality continue to rub up uncomfortably against learner identities within much educational research. At one extreme some research primarily from a psychological perspective ignores social categories in a narrow focus on student learning attitudes, dispositions and practices that sees the classroom as a space sealed off from the social. Constructs of 'the pupil' are represented like those of 'the child' as socially neutral and unitary. At the other extreme some sociological research views the classroom as a social arena dominated by a cacophony of classed, gendered and raced voices almost disconnected from learning. More reflexive research increasingly attempts to work at and across the interface between social and learner identities in schools to explore the relationships between the two and recognize both the regular convergences but also significant divergences.

Most of this work continues to focus at the level of the classroom and staffroom but in the next section I draw on the work of Basil Bernstein in order to take in the broader picture of educational policy making and its contribution to identity formation within schooling. The quandary for research on identities within education is how to maintain a reflexive and critical lens on identities and identifications within any one of the influential contexts for identity making without losing sight of the impact of other, often broader contexts such as the policy field, the nation-state and even the global arena. Both Bernstein and Pierre Bourdieu, whose work and its application to educational research is discussed later, have attempted to keep the links and concomitant tensions between the individual and the collective, agency and structure, micro and macro contexts in play in their work. So the next two sections explore in detail how identities can be theorized in illuminating but very different ways. First, I look at Bernstein's theory of pedagogic identities as an exemplar of identity formation at the macro level, and what it tells us not only about temporal shifts in social and learner identities but also about the key role of the nation-state through the workings of government and its political elites. Second, I utilize Bourdieu's conceptual framework to focus down at the micro level of the classroom and to demonstrate that even when the focus is on the individual student important insights about collective identities remain integral to the analysis. In exploring these approaches to identity formation I am going to focus on the UK education system as my main case but it is important to point to key work in the US and Australian contexts that focus on identity formation within education (Lareau, 2003; McLeod, 2000; Weis, 2006; Wexler et al., 1992; Yates, 2006).

## BERNSTEIN'S THEORY OF PEDAGOGIC IDENTITIES

Throughout his academic career Basil Bernstein (1996, 2000) was preoccupied with the way in which forms of pedagogic transmission and the ordering of knowledge influenced identities and identity change. For Bernstein understanding the relationship between the formation of a specifically pedagogic identity and social identities is crucial if we are to capture the complexities of identity formation in classrooms. His work highlights the need to distinguish between the social identity shaped within the external fields, and the pedagogic identities generated within the classificatory relations of schooling.

A distinctive feature of Bernstein's theory of pedagogic identities is its attempt 'to connect macrolevel class and power relations to the microlevel educational processes of the school' (Sadnovnik, 1991: 48). In many applications of Bernsteinian theory we see clearly the agentic dimensions of identity (Bourne, 2003; Daniels et al., 2004) but Bernstein's (2000) most recent and speculative work underscores the power of structure, and in particular, the state in identity formation. However, Bernstein is not arguing for a return to conventional 'ascribed' cultural markers such as age and gender, or achieved positions such as class and occupation. Rather, he outlines four identity constructions: retrospective and prospective identities are generated through resources managed by the state while de-centred and therapeutic identities are

generated from local community based resources. It is the former two, retrospective and prospective identities that are of particular interest in relation to the educational field as they constitute a model of identity formed through the pedagogic practices of schooling.

According to Bernstein, key to the British state's reassertion of control over education since the 1970s is the projection of new student, teacher, and consequently new citizen identities. For Bernstein the centralizing state is attempting to manage educational change in a context of new economic, cultural and moral challenges, by reasserting much stronger centralized control, with the explicit aim of reshaping the identities of pupils and teachers, and of future citizens, in determinate ways (Beck, 2008). Certainly, we can see evidence of the far greater control and regulation in the vast assessment system I talked about earlier but it is also present in the prescriptive National Curriculum and the tight monitoring, regulation of teachers' work and students' learning, and the constant rhetoric around standards and discipline (Ball, 2007).

Bernstein argues that the prospective pedagogic identity projected under Thatcherism[1] was designed to shape 'what were considered to be appropriate attitudes, dispositions and performances relevant to a market culture and reduced state welfare' (Bernstein, 2000: 68), and while obviously, there is enormous heterogeneity among the cohort of students going through school over this period, we can glimpse some of the impact on identities and identification in the frequent references to 'Thatcher's children' (Wagg, 1996). As Bernstein pointed out, 'the emphasis on the performance of students, the steps taken to increase and maintain performance, for the survival of the institution, is likely to facilitate state-promoted instrumentality' (2000: 61). Thatcherism as a political philosophy sought to project and underscore what Beck (2007: 185) labels 'a new-old British identity' grounded in self-made and self-supporting identities with a strong sense of self-reliance and individualism.

It is too soon to state authoritatively the ways in which neo-liberal and new managerialist influences in education are shaping student identities. However, more individualistic, entreprenuerial and aspirational conceptions of the self have been promoted by both Conservative and Labour governments over the last 30 years, and there is increasing evidence of both instrumentalism and pragmatism within education. Knowledge acquired through both schooling and higher education is too readily assumed to be objective and value-free. Bernstein's work shows us that that clearly is not the case. Like the young women on child care courses at the further education college in Beverley Skeggs' (1997) study, students throughout the educational system are being taught historically specific, culturally biased and value-laden knowledge that impacts powerfully on identity formation.

For Bernstein accelerating processes of privatization, individualization, marketization and managerialism are resulting in identities:

> based on a new concept of 'work' and 'life' which might be called 'short-termism'. This is where a skill, area of work, undergoes continuous development, disappearance or replacement, where life experiences cannot be based on stable expectations of the future and one's location within it. (2000: 59)

Although this new concept and understanding of life and work clearly has applicability across the labour market, Bernstein's focus is the educational system and shifts in teacher and student identities.

As Bernstein cogently argues, such processes conspire to valorize and promote a new kind of ability –'trainability'– the propensity to accept, even welcome, continuous pedagogic reforms. Bernstein also emphasizes the social emptiness of 'trainability'. As such, John Beck points out, trainability 'denotes a vacant space waiting to be filled with whatever temporary contents market, or institutional, or government imperatives may dictate' (2008: 193). There is little academic work on the sorts of subjects schooling is producing. There is a current outcry about over-stressed and anxious students. There has also been a strong media focus on the unhappiness that continuous testing, and the reassertion of ability hierarchies in schools through setting and streaming, have generated, but very little on the kinds of citizens school students are educated to be. However, Bernstein's work is an important, if speculative, corrective to this lacuna in contemporary academic work, locating the educational system at the centre of identity formation.

At one level Bernstein's is very much a social constructionist model of identities in which identities can be seen to be constituted through discourse. However, Bernstein's model also signals the importance of both notions of collective identity and the key role of the state and government policy in identity formation within education. Contemporary emphases on agency at the level of the individual have tended to eclipse notions of both collective identities and the contribution of the state and wider structural forces in identity formation within the educational field. Bernstein's concepts of centrally formed pedagogic identities redress these omissions by reintroducing the role of the state in developing what Bernstein (1996, 2000) calls new 'official' student, citizen and teacher identities. Although speculative, Bernstein's focus on collective identities and the power of dominant government discourses and policies to shape identities provides a helpful foil to the increasing emphasis on individual agency in identity formation in schooling. His theories remind us that identity making in schools and classrooms is the work of policy and political elites as much as it is the individual agency of the student and teacher. Rather, the two can reinforce and synchronize but also clash and collide. To take license with Marx's dictum 'we make ourselves but in conditions that are strongly influenced by more powerful others'. And this is especially true when we are talking about a group, children and young people, with little institutional and social power. So, Bernstein's theorizing proves to be a powerful antidote to the contemporary emphasis on flux and fluidity in much educational research on identities. Identities may be made and remade in schools and classrooms but according to Bernstein they are not made in conditions of our own choosing. Rather government policies in the shape of the National Curriculum, Ofsted inspections, and national assessment testing are setting the boundaries within which student and teacher identities are formed. In the next section I draw on the concepts of another key sociologist of education, Pierre Bourdieu, whose research is also centrally concerned with the tensions between agency and structure in the formation of identities within education. While Bourdieu has not engaged as directly with identity or identity formation in schools as Bernstein has done, his theories do have strong implications for identity research. There has been a proliferation of educational research that utilizes his concepts in order to understand identities both in the schooling context (Lareau, 2004) and in higher education (Reay et al., 2005).

## BOURDIEU AND CLASSROOM IDENTITES

In this section, I draw on my own empirical work on primary classrooms to illustrate how Bourdieu's concepts of field, habitus and capitals provide an analytic lens for understanding identities. Space is too limited to provide a detailed account of Bourdieu's conceptual framework (although see Reay, 2004, 2006) but I will provide a brief synopsis. Bourdieu sees habitus as a system of dispositions that potentially generate a wide repertoire of possible actions, simultaneously enabling the individual to draw on transformative and constraining courses of action (1990c: 87). However, the addendum in Bourdieu's work is always an emphasis on the constraints and demands that impose themselves on people.

Yet, despite this implicit tendency to behave in ways that are expected of 'people like us', for Bourdieu there are no explicit rules or principles that dictate behaviour. The practical logic which defines habitus is not one of the predictable regularity of modes of behaviour, but instead 'that of vagueness, of the more-or-less, which defines one's ordinary relation to the world' (Bourdieu, 1990b: 78).

Bourdieu's related concept of field adds to the possibilities of his conceptual framework and gives habitus a dynamic quality. Field for Bourdieu is the context in which practices take place. It is important to emphasize the relational aspects of habitus and field. As Bourdieu himself points out:

> The relation between habitus and field operates in two ways. On one side, it is a relation of conditioning: the field structures the habitus, which is the product of the embodiment of the immanent necessity of the field (or of a hierarchy of intersecting fields). On the other side, it is a relation of knowledge or cognitive construction: habitus contributes to constituting the field as a meaningful world, a world endowed with sense or with value, in which it is worth investing one's energy. (Bourdieu in Wacquant, 1989: 44)

This dynamic relationship between habitus and field allows us to understand identity as always in process, influenced by context but simultaneously influencing and having an impact on that context. But also habitus as 'the product of the embodiment of the immanent necessity of field (or of a hierarchy of intersecting fields)' points to notions of identity in which some aspects are foregrounded in certain contexts while other aspects become far more salient when that context changes. And the array of capitals, cultural, social, economic and symbolic, individuals have access to make a difference to the choices and options available to them. We see this very forcefully in the data I draw on below where class, gender and ethnic resources mean that some students can move powerfully across a variety of different educational fields, their identities have a degree of fluidity, while other students are fixed within these same fields (Skeggs, 2004).

## The tensions and synergies between social and learner identities in primary classrooms

Classroom life in schools is extremely complex and multifaceted and in order to understand identities and identifications in anything other than an over-simplified way it is helpful to view them through the prism of a number of overlapping fields of power and influence. In my ESRC research project with Madeleine Arnot on consulting students about their teaching and learning we explored the complex relationships between social and learner identities (Arnot and Reay, 2006; Reay and Arnot, 2004).

The extracts I draw on below focus on social and learner identities in a primary classroom in a multiethnic urban primary school. In particular, the data challenges the conflation of social and learner identities that I argued earlier has been common in educational research. In class 4W, as in all the other classes in the school, the pupils are predominantly working class. This is key when we examine the relationship of the field of official school knowledge with those of other salient fields for these children. For some children in 4W, especially the quiet well behaved girls, to be positioned centrally within the field of official school knowledge accrues no profit in other fields such as those of the peer group culture and its sub-fields of gender and social class. They may be good learners but their orientation to learning, which was one of diligence, conformity and relative passivity, translates into low status within the pupil peer group hierarchy (Walkerdine, 1989). These girls have status and standing which comes through their middle-class cultural capital within official/teacher discourses of teaching and learning. Yet, they are often marginalized within the field of the working-class, male peer group culture where neither their middle class-cultural capital nor their femininity held value:

Diane:   Which children are doing best at learning?

Martin:  Navid, he's good.

Diane:   And Yussef and Melanie

Jamie:   Navid, Melanie and Yussef.

Yet there are actually five children in the top set in the class. Stephanie and Nancy, due to a combination of their undisguised middle-classness, conventional femininity and enthusiastic attitude to schoolwork, are rendered insignificant. As a consequence the profits they might have expected from being clever and high achieving are rarely realized within the wider peer group (Archer and Francis, 2005; Reay, 2001). This marginalization was evident throughout the data. Whenever children, across gender, class and ability gave examples of good learners, the refrain was always 'Navid, Melanie and Yussef' – usually in that order:

Jason:   Some people are quicker than others

Jordan:  Like Navid and Melanie and Yussef

Ricky:   Melanie and Navid and that.

When Nancy is recognized as doing well in the class there is often a qualification or reservation. As in the last two examples, there are times when Nancy's good behaviour and learning are used as a reproach against her. I would argue that visible in this

DR:       Which children in your class get the most positive
          attention?

Danielle: Melanie

```
Myra:      Melanie
Susie:     Nancy
Danielle:  No, Nancy's just being good
DR:        So who gets the most positive feedback from the teacher?
Myra:      Melanie
Danielle:  Yeah, definitely Melanie
```

And:

```
Del:       They always say that girls are better than boys but I don't
           agree
Martin:    Except for Nancy, she's just perfect. Yuk (all the group
           giggle)
Marvin:    She's a pain
```

collective view of Nancy and Stephanie is a disparagement of high ability and academic success when it is vested in conventional femininity (Francis and Skelton, 2005; Skelton and Francis, 2003). This collective view was impacting on Nancy's learner identity. In the individual interview she asserted:

> I know I'm in the top group but I'm not seen as one of the clever children. I'm not really clever. I'm in the top group because I work hard.

Here we can see clearly 'the internal–external dialectic of identification' (Jenkins, 2004: 24) through which Nancy's learner identity is being constituted.

In contrast to the denigration of Nancy and Stephanie, a central thread running through all of the focus groups is a respect and admiration for Melanie, Yussef and Navid. All the focus groups when asked which children got the most positive attention from teachers cited Melanie, Yussef and Navid. These three manage to straddle the apex of two hierarchies of esteem, both that of official knowledge and learning and the peer group. Exceptionally, Melanie has manoeuvred herself into a unique position for a white, middle-class girl in a working-class ethnically diverse, inner-city primary school. As is evident in later quotes, she appears to have 'the power of naming' (Bourdieu, 1990a), at least in relation to other girls, usually reserved for boys. We catch glimpses of how Melanie

as a girl has managed to negotiate this unique position for herself. Unlike the other girls she has worked extremely hard at being central within the field of the peer group culture. This is evident in her self-designation and performance as a tom-boy. This includes a hard won aptitude at football ('I've done loads of practice'), which means that she, alongside only two other girls in the year, is allowed to play football with the boys in the playground. It is also evident in her bravado and, at times, professed 'live and let live' approach to school work:

> You can't just say 'Oh, I don't care about what was on TV last night, let me get on with my writing' because everyone would think you were a saddo.

Both Stephanie and Nancy's conformity with conventional gender regimes and Melanie's resistance to and flaunting of them constitute powerful identity work. However, while Stephanie and Nancy are relatively fixed by their traditional femininity, Melanie demonstrates a cultural repertoire that allows her to move across the different fields of peer group and mainstream schooling without losing status in either one. We can see the fluidity of identity as Melanie moves across the fields of pupil peer group culture and the more mainstream fields of classroom teaching and learning. At times, in more classic 'female' mode (Francis and Skelton, 2005), like the other girls in the top set, she is keen to please the teacher:

> I think sometimes when I'm doing my work, I usually … usually I try to do it well to please Mrs Wilson because I usually want to please her. I don't really want to disappoint her. So I'm trying to do my best.

In spite of occupying the same position in the field of the peer group culture, we can see here how different her learning orientation is to that of Navid and Yussef both of whom focus as much on pleasing themselves as on pleasing the teacher. In the interview with the class teacher, Mrs Wilson commented:

> Some of the top group, especially Stephanie and Melanie often ask my opinion about their work. They ask what they need to do to improve it especially in literature.

When asked if the boys ask as well, she laughs and says: 'It's a kind of girl thing'.

## High status masculinities and femininities: Achieving desired learner identities

But Navid and Yussef are not straightforwardly 'doing a boy thing'. In fact there is nothing straightforward about Navid and Yussef's positioning. Navid, Iranian and Yussef, Somalian were both born in their countries of origin but moved to the UK with their families when they were babies. Both families are now poor and subsisting on state benefits. They also live on one of the most demonized council estates in the area. Although both Navid and Yussef are described as working class by school staff and are able to perform 'working-class lad' (Willis, 1977) very well their class positioning is more complex and ambiguous. All four parents are university educated and are clearly working with very different educational horizons for their children than the working-class parents living in the area. Yussef and Navid may have access to little economic capital but they maintain a strong sense of entitlement and academic confidence, the legacy, I suggest, of their parents' cultural capital. Both Yussef and Navid are part of the school's gifted and talented cohort and while none of the working-class boys originally assigned to the group have managed to survive the designation of being 'gifted and talented', Navid and Yussef are both thriving in the group apparently without having to pay the costs in terms of wider male peer group reprobation. As may be becoming clearer, in order to understand both dynamics of power and influence and processes of inclusion and exclusion in the class, the fields of social class, official learning and the peer group need to be overlaid with further fields of gender and ethnicity, together with an analysis of the different capitals that are valued and esteemed in each of those fields. Only then can the complex and contradictory positionings of Melanie, Navid and Yussef be understood. I want to go back to re-examine high status femininities in this classroom and how they are performed. In the excerpt below Melanie both stakes out her own position on the gender continuum and makes very clear the distinction between herself and Stephanie:

Melanie:    If you're a girlie you won't get accepted at all. Because if you go around wearing little dresses and everything, everybody will more or less think you're a weirdo.

Diane:    And you were saying in the playground that you don't have to come across as too clever because that's difficult too.

Melanie:    Yeah you need to look cool but it's difficult if you're too clever.

Diane:    So what's best for being popular?

Melanie:    If you're clever, but not too clever and if you're really cool you are popular. But if you are like really clever

and geeky and always talk about science then you're unpopular. If you're a girlie like Stephanie you're unpopular
and if you're an airhead then you're unpopular as well.

And:

Melanie:    If we talked about work we'd be known as the saddos of the
            class. Talking about your work is really sad.
Carly:      Stephanie loves talking about her work
Melanie:    She's really sad.

We can see here the hazards of being positioned as clever and conventionally feminine for girls like Stephanie, and the active constitution of her social and learner identities by more powerful others. Those, like Melanie, with more of the cultural capital valued within the peer group have the power to actively position Stephanie as a 'sad' 'geeky' learner and a despised unpopular 'girlie'.

In contrast, part of Melanie's bid for distinction in 4W comes through playing down her academic ability and stressing the difference between herself and girls who occupy more conventional femininities. Unlike Stephanie and Nancy, Melanie has developed habitus as 'an art of invention and reinvention' (Bourdieu, 1990a). Melanie can be seen to fit Wilkinson's description of 'a masculinized new woman at ease with male attributes' (1999: 162). She recognizes and responds to prevailing gender hierarchies which situate being male with having more power and status, and is 'active at the edges of the boundaries of masculinity and femininity' (Thorne, 1993). Yet for Melanie classroom life is full of possible hazards and potential falls from grace. She has to work extremely hard at her centrality. Her class position here is both an asset and a handicap and yet another aspect of identity she has to work hard at. Melanie comes from probably the most economically and culturally privileged family in 4W. Her parents are both academics and she talks about the extra work both parents set her and is the only child in the class to assert the superior knowledge of her parents over that of the school and

its teachers. Her resources of cultural capital are evident in the quotation here:

> All the things our teachers tell us, I don't usually do. I do it in the way my Mum or Dad tells me because they're university lecturers so they know better.

But at the same time she emphasizes separating the two spheres and that is clearly what she succeeds in doing in her own practice:

> When you go home people don't know and don't care if you're doing homework or if you've got a tutor as long as you don't boast about it. But like if you're really posh and you act posh in the classroom, showing off then all the other kids hate you.

The children, including Melanie, talk scornfully about posh children but the category never includes Melanie herself. Melanie constantly utilizes her cultural capital – it is evident in her confident dialogue with teachers, her assertiveness and ability to challenge teachers' knowledge. Yet she is also engaging in a strategic deployment that entails what is in effect a partial masking of both her femininity and her middle-classness. Unlike Navid and Yussef with whom she shares 'the best learner' status, Melanie has had to mask aspects of identity that accrue social and cultural profits in social fields other than the predominantly working-class, inner-city primary school in which she is struggling for ascendancy. The chief contrast between herself and the two boys is her high level of awareness and self-consciousness – a hyper-reflexivity in relation to her positioning in these myriad overlapping fields. Her habitus has had to evolve and change in the unfamiliar field of the predominantly working-class pupil peer group, and this she has managed extremely successfully, developing new dispositions that accord with the field. While it appears that Navid and Yussef only have to follow their natural inclinations to achieve distinction, Melanie has had to calculate and strategize; to develop a socio-analysis of her positioning within schooling (Bourdieu 1990a). While Navid and Yussef are Bourdieu's 'fish in water' (Bourdieu, 1990a: 108; Bourdieu and Wacquant, 1992: 127) within a peer group that is predominantly working class and male dominated, Melanie has to engage in a complex re-invention in order to be dominant within the field. Yet, there remain similarities. In addition to their evident high ability what Melanie, Yussef and Navid share across differences of gender, ethnicity and social class positioning are key aspects of dominant cultural capital, namely a sense of entitlement and the confidence to challenge (Lareau and Weininger, 2003; Reay, 1998). All three display high visibility within both the classroom and the playground, and an investment in attention-seeking behaviour. Like Daniella in Parlo Singh's research on learning in primary classrooms, Melanie has managed to subvert symbolic boundaries so 'she can speak from positions which were perceived to be traditionally male domains' (1990: 47). In contrast, Nancy and Stephanie are clever but not in the best way. The trick, which they have not learnt, is to negotiate the many dimensions of identity in the school setting without relinquishing too much status and standing in any one.

## Marginalized learner identities: Feminized masculinities in working-class classrooms

The repercussions for the well behaved middle-class girls, Nancy and Stephanie were less apparent than the consequences of the peer group hierarchy for two of the well behaved boys. The two children in 4W who were most defeated by the invidious hierarchy that operates in the classroom were two minority ethnic, working-class boys, Ong who is Vietnamese and Ali who is Bangladeshi. These boys stood out or, more accurately, paled into insignificance because unlike the other working-class boys in the class they were both quiet, well behaved and tried hard with their school work. Benjamin et al. (2003: 551) argue that historical legacies, current economic conditions and the concern over boys' underachievement make it extremely difficult to construct an identity as an academically successful working-class boy. While boys like Navid and Yussef are sufficiently rich in resources of hegemonic masculinity (Connell, 1995) to negotiate the position of academically successful, working-class boy without incurring social costs (Thorne, 1993), Ali and Ong have little choice. Both are subjected to social marginality and invidious judgements on the basis that they are not important enough to matter:

Here we can see a combination of low economic and cultural capital and a very

| Diane: | So does anyone get left out? |
| Joseph: | Ong and Ali. |
| Del: | Yeah, Ong and Ali |
| Matty: | Cos they're sad |
| Diane: | Why are they sad? |
| Matty: | Cos they don't say anything and no-one wants to play with them |

And:

| Stephanie: | I think Ong gets left out a lot |
| Nancy: | Yes, Ong and Ali |

| Diane: | Why's that? |
|---|---|
| Stephanie: | The other boys are a bit unkind to them cos they don't wear trendy clothes. |
| Nancy: | It's not their fault. I don't think their families have got much money. |
| Stephanie: | Ong's very quiet but he's nice though. |

different type of masculinity to that valorized in the class, acting to conspire against Ong and Ali and contribute to their social marginalization. As Emma Renold asserts, 'being academically orientated for a boy is often devalued and denigrated because of its equation with femininity' (2001: 375). It is also likely, as Archer and Francis (2005) found in relation to the Chinese boys in their study, that their minority ethnic status as Vietnamese and Bangladeshi was also a factor. While Navid and Yussef manage to avoid connotations of femininity despite their high achievement by investing heavily in laddish behaviour (Francis, 2001), Ong and Ali are 'feminized' within the classroom context because of their diligence, conformity and relative passivity (see also Archer and Francis, 2007) – the very qualities that have also led to Nancy and Stephanie's social marginalization. The boundaries of Ong and Ali's identities are policed by more powerful others, forcing them to construct narrow boundaries for themselves that limit the possibilities for positive social and learner identities. They come to see themselves as they are seen by others – as neither popular nor good learners. Listening to what the other children in the classroom said it became clear that learning for Ali and Ong was a fraught process despite their efforts to work hard. It was also evident in what Ali and Ong themselves say. They had

a strong sense of unfairness in relation to both the classroom and the playground.

In 4W we can see vividly the different identities and identifications and the extent to which they shift both across and within different groups of pupils, and in particular, the complex dialectic between class, gender, ethnicity and perceived academic ability in which generalization on the basis of different categories fails to capture the messiness of the identity work at play. We can also see clearly from the interactions in 4W how researching classroom life provides a powerful lens on a range of identity dilemmas and how children and young people negotiate these. The children's experiences illustrate regular conflicts and tensions across masculinities, femininities, academic performance, social class, ethnicity and peer group popularity, and the ways in which access and possession of various capitals can lead to positive or negative resolution that can enhance or diminish children's sense of self. Some children, like Melanie, Yussef and Navid for whom identity is a mobile resource, have the power to shift in and out of different identities, while others like Nancy, Stephanie, Ong and Ali are fixed in and through the representations of more powerful others. In all this movement and messiness Bourdieu's concepts of field, capitals and habitus can be productively deployed to show how identities

| Diane: | How do you feel when you are learning in school, Ali? |
|---|---|
| Ali: | I find it a bit hard. I get worried, but … it's … does anyone else get worried? |
| Ong: | Yeah, I do |
| Diane: | You get worried Ong? |
| Ong: | Yeah, sometimes I nearly cry |
| Diane: | You nearly cry? |

| Ong: | Yeah, because your head gets all muddled up and you eyes get hot and sweating and all sweat comes out and people think you are crying. |
| Ong: | Its not fair they say we're rubbish footballers so they wont let us play at lunch time. |
| Ali: | And they keep us out of their teams in PE because they say we're not good enough when we are. |
| Ong: | It's not fair but when we complain the teachers do nothing. |

are reproduced, defended, challenged and reconstituted, and the ways in which key aspects of identity such as class, race and gender are affirmed and dismissed at different times and in different contexts within educational settings. It is in such seemingly mundane interactions within classrooms, and between students who identify and are identified according to a variety of social categories, that the active construction of inclusion and exclusion within school settings becomes apparent.

Beverley Skegg's (2005b) in a powerful critique of identity argues that contemporary political theorists including Nancy Fraser assume that everyone simply has or owns an identity. In contrast, she asserts that there are many in society, such as significant numbers of black people and the white, working class, who are subject to forced identification where negative identities are imposed. In the context of this classroom Nancy and Stephanie have little room for manoeuvre within the predominantly working class male peer group culture and are forced to accept the negative attributions of the peer group, but within the official field of teaching and learning they have more power. Ong and Ali are not so fortunate and, across both fields, are represented through inferior social and learner identities that they lack the cultural and social capital to reconstruct in more favourable ways.

## CONCLUSION

In the last two sections I have drawn on Bernstein's theories to examine macro understandings of educational identities, while using Bourdieuian concepts to look at identity at the micro level. But, as the research of Daniels et al. (2004) and Bourne (2003) demonstrate, Bernstein can be utilized to examine micro aspects of identity. Similarly, Bourdieu's work can be deployed to explore macro dimensions of identity formation in schooling. In particular, his work with Passeron (1977) on the reproduction of classed identities within the French educational system is a powerful analysis of structural and individual inequalities in schooling. What is important is for educational research and theory to engage with both the macro and the micro level of identity formation, to examine identity work as an ongoing accomplishment within the spheres of the local, the nation-state and the global.

Castells (2004) asserts that it is easy to agree on the fact that identities are constructed. Rather, he argues the real issue is 'how, from what, by whom and for what' (2004: 7). In this chapter I have explored some of 'how, from what, by whom and for what' of identities in schools and classrooms. Underpinning all these questions of identity is the extent to which the educational system is a key site of the formation not only of pedagogic/learner identities but also of wider social identities. I have drawn on theories and concepts from both Basil Bernstein and Pierre Bourdieu to illustrate processes of identity making in schools and classrooms. Schooling can both interfere with positive identity formation as in the case of Ong, Sharon and Ali or promote it as was the case for Navid, Yussef and Mel. Their narratives demonstrate some of the ways in which school micro-politics and peer group power dynamics work to construct student identities, and how institutional processes can elevate and centre, or deflate and marginalize, students' sense of self. Beyond the micro level, reverberations from state and government policy have powerful 'after-shocks' on children and young people in classrooms, labelling and constructing some as 'good, ideal learners' but also resulting, for others, in 'a "false" (imposed, rejected, inferior) self (identity) that is personally dislocating and fragmenting' (Hudak, 2001: 21).

## NOTE

1   Thatcherism is the term used to describe the right-wing, neo-liberal free market policies introduced under the term of the conservative Prime Minister Margaret Thatcher.

## REFERENCES

Archer, L. (2003) *Race, Masculinity and Schooling: Muslim Boys and Education*. Buckingham: Open University Press.

Archer, L. and Francis, B. (2005) '"They never go off the rails like other ethnic groups": Teachers' constructions of british chinese pupils' gender identities and approaches to learning', *British Journal of Sociology of Education*, 26 (2): 165–82.

Archer, L. and Francis, B. (2007) *Understanding Minority Ethnic Achievement: Race, Gender, Class and Success*. London: Routledge.

Arnot, M. and Reay, D. (2006) 'Power, pedagogic voices and pupil talk: The implications for pupil consultation as transformative practice', in R. Moore, M. Arnot, J. Beck and H. Daniels (eds), *Knowledge, Power and Social Change*. London: Routledge. pp. 75–93.

Ball, S.J. (2003) *Class Strategies and the Educational Market: The Middle Classes and Social Advantage*. London: RoutledgeFalmer.

Ball, S.J. (2007) *Education plc: Understanding Private Sector Participation in Public Sector Education*. London: RoutledgeFalmer.

Beck, J. (2007) 'Directed time: Identity and time in new right and new labour policy discourse', in R. Moore et al. (eds), *Knowledge, Power and Educational Reform: Applying the Sociology of Basil Bernstein*. London: Routledge. pp. 181–95.

Beck, J. (2008) *Meritocracy, Citizenship and Education*. London: Continuum Books.

Beck, U. (1992) *Risk Society: Towards a New Modernity*. Newbury Park, CA: Sage.

Benjamin, S., Nind, M., Hall, K., Collins, J. and Sheehy, K. (2003) 'Moments of inclusion and exclusion: Pupils negotiating classroom contexts', *British Journal of Sociology of Education*, 24 (5): 547–58.

Bernstein, B. (1996) *Pedagogy, Symbolic Control and Identity. Theory, Research, Critique*. 1st edn. London: Taylor & Francis.

Bernstein, B. (2000) *Pedagogy, Symbolic Control and Identity. Theory, Research, Critique*. Rev. edn. Oxford: Rowman and Littlefield.

Bottrell, D. (2008) 'Resistance, resilience and social identities: Reframing "problem youth" and the problem of schooling', *Journal of Youth Studies*, 10 (5): 597–616.

Bourdieu, P. (1990a) *The Logic of Practice*. Cambridge: Polity Press.

Bourdieu, P. (1990b) *In Other Words: Essays Towards a Reflexive Sociology*. Cambridge: Polity Press.

Bourdieu, P. (1990c) *Sociology in Question*. Cambridge: Polity Press.

Bourdieu, P (2002) 'The progressive restoration', *New Left Review*, 14: 2–12.

Bourdieu, P. and Passeron, J.C. (1977) *Reproduction in Education, Society and Culture*. London: Sage.

Bourdieu, P. and Wacquant, L. (1992) *An Invitation to Reflexive Sociology*. Chicago, IL: University of Chicago Press.

Bourne, J. (2003) 'Vertical discourse: The role of the teacher in the transmission and acquisition of decontextualised language', *European Educational Research Journal*, 2 (4): 496–520.

Brah, A. and Phoenix, A. (2004) 'Ain't I a woman? Revisting intersectionality', *Journal of International Women's Studies*, 5 (30): 75–86.

Brantlinger, E. (2003) *Dividing Classes*. New York: Routledgefalmer.

Broadfoot, P. and Pollard, A. (2006) 'The changing discourse of assessment policy: The case of english primary education', in H. Lauder, P. Brown, J. Dillabough and A.H. Halsey (eds), *Education, Globalisation and Social Change*. Oxford: Oxford University Press. pp. 760–765.

Butler, J. (1990) *Gender Trouble*. London: Taylor & Francis.

Butler T. (2003) 'The middle class and the future of london', in M. Parkinson and M. Boddy (eds), *Cities: Competitiveness and Cohesion* 269–84. Bristol: Policy Press.

Butler, T. with Robson, G. (2003) *London Calling: The Middle Classes and the Re-Making of Inner London.* Oxford: Berg.

Castells, M. (2004) *The Information Age. Volume 11: The Power of Identity.* Oxford: Blackwell.

Connell, R. (1995) *Masculinities.* Cambridge: Polity Press.

Connell, R. (2001) 'Introduction and overview', *Feminism and Psychology: Special Issue: Men and Masculinities,* 5–10.

Daniels, H. Creese, A Hey, V, Fielding, S, Leonard, D and M Smith (2004) 'Gendered learning in two modalities of pedagogic discourse', in J. Muller, B. Davies and A. Morais (eds), *Reading Bernstein, Researching Bernstein 141–59.* London: RoutledgeFalmer.

Du Gay, P. (2007) *Organising Identity.* London: Sage.

Epstein, D. and Johnson, R. (1998) *Schooling Sexualities.* Buckingham: Open University Press.

Erikson, E. (1974) *Identity: Youth and Crisis.* London: Faber and Faber.

Foucault, M. (1978) *The History of Sexuality. Vol. 1: An Introduction.* Trans. R. Hurley. New York: Pantheon.

Francis, B. (2001) *Boys, Girls and Achievement: Addressing the Classroom Issues.* London: Routledge.

Francis, B. and Skelton, C. (2005) *Reassessing Gender and Achievement.* London: Routledge.

Frosh, S., Phoenix, A. and Pattman, R. (2002) *Young Masculinities.* London: Palgrave.

Hackett, G. (2001) 'The most over-tested nation in the world', *The Times Educational Supplement,* 27 April: 14.

Hall, S. (1996) 'Introduction: Who needs "identity?"', in S. Hall and P. du Gay (eds), *Questions of Cultural Identity,* pp. 1–10. London: Sage.

Hollway, W. and Jefferson, T. (2000) *Doing Qualitative Research Differently.* Buckingham: Open University Press.

Hudak, G. (2001) 'On what is labelled "playing": Locating the "true" in education', in G. Hudak and P. Kihn (eds), *Labelling: Pedagogy and Politics.* New York: RoutledgeFalmer.

Giddens, A. (2000) *The Third Way and Its Critics.* Cambridge: Polity Press.

Gillborn, D. and Youdell, D. (2000) *Rationing Education: Policy, Practice, Reform and Equity.* Buckingham: Open University Press.

Jenkins, R. (2004) *Social Identity.* 2nd edn. London: Routledge.

Lacey, C. (1970) *Hightown Grammar: The School as a Social System.* Manchester: Manchester University Press.

Lareau, A. (2004) *Unequal Childhoods: Class, Race and Family Life.* Berkeley CA: University of California Press.

Lareau, A. and Weininger, E. (2003) 'Cultural capital in educational research: A critical assessment', *Theory and Society,* 32 (5–6): 567–606.

McCleod, J. (2000) 'Subjectivity and schooling in a longitudinal study of secondary students', *British Journal of Sociology of Education,* 21 (4): 501–21.

Perry, P. (2002) *Shades of White: White Kids and Racial Identities in High School.* Durham, NC: Duke University Press.

Pollard, A. and Filer, A. (2007) 'Learning, differentiation and strategic action in secondary education: Analyses from the identity and learning programme', *British Journal of Sociology of Education,* 28 (4): 441–58.

Reay, D. (1998) *Class Work: Mothers' Involvement in Children's Schooling.* London: University College Press.

Reay, D. (2001) 'Spice girls, "nice girls", "girlies" and tomboys: Gender discourses, girls' cultures and femininities in the primary classroom', *Gender and Education,* 13 (2): 153–66.

Reay, D. (2004) '"It's all becoming a habitus": Beyond the habitual use of Pierre Bourdieu's concept of habitus in educational research', *Special Issue of British Journal of Sociology of Education on Pierre Bourdieu,* 25 (4): 431–44.

Reay, D. (2005) 'Beyond consciousness?: The psychic landscape of social class', *Sociology Special Issue on Social Class,* 39 (5): 911–28.

Reay, D. (2006) 'Cultural capital theories', in B. Banks, S. Delamont and C. Marshall (eds), *Gender and Education: An Encyclopedia.* New York: Greenwood Press.

Reay, D. and Arnot, M. (2004) 'Participation and control in learning: A pedagogic democratic right?', in L. Poulson and M.Wallace (eds), *Learning to Read Critically in Teaching and Learning,* pp. 151–72. London: Sage.

Reay, D., David, M.E. and Ball, S. (2005) *Degrees of Choice: Social Class, Race and Gender in Higher Education.* Stoke-on-Trent: Trentham Books.

Reay, D. et al. (2007) 'A darker shade of pale: Whiteness, the middle classes and multi-ethnic inner city schooling', *Sociology,* 41 (60): 1041–60.

Renold, E. (2001) 'Learning the "hard" way: boys, hegemonic masculinity and the negotiation of learner identities in the primary school', *British Journal of Sociology of Education,* 22 (3): 369–84.

Roseneil, S. (2006) 'The ambivalences of angel's "arrangement": A psycho-social lens on the contemporary condition of personal life', *The Sociological Review*, 54: 846–68.

Sadnovnik, A. (1991) 'Basil bernstein's theory of pedagogic practice: A structuralist approach', *Sociology of Education*, 64 (1): 48–63.

Shaw, J. (1995) *Education, Gender and Anxiety*. London: Taylor & Francis.

Sibley, D. (1995) *Geographies of Exclusion: Society and Difference in the West*. London: Routledge.

Singh, P. (1990) 'Institutional discourse and practice: A case study of the social construction of technological competence in the primary classroom', *British Journal of Sociology of Education*, 14 (1): 39–58.

Skeggs, B. (1997) *Formations of Class and Gender*. London: Sage.

Skeggs, B. (2004) *Class, Self, Culture*. London: Routledge.

Skeggs, B. (2005a) 'Exchange, value and affect: Bourdieu and "the self"', in L. Adkins and B. Skeggs (eds), *Feminism after Bourdieu*. Oxford: Blackwell. pp. 75–96.

Skeggs, B. (2005b) 'The problem with identity', in A. Lin (ed.), *Knowledge and Discourse* 11–35. New York: Lawrence Erlbaum Associates.

Skelton, C. and Francis, B. (eds) (2003) *Boys and Girls in the Primary Classroom*. Buckingham: Open University Press.

Smithers, R. (2000) 'Exam regime harms pupils', *Guardian*, 4 August.

Thorne, B. (1993) *Gender Play: Girls and Boys in School*. Buckingham: Open University Press.

Wacquant, L. (1989) 'Towards a reflexive sociology: A workshop with Pierre Bourdieu', *Sociological Theory*, 7: 26–63.

Wagg, S. (1996) 'Don't try to understand them: politics, childhood and the new education market', in J. Pilcher and S. Wagg (eds), *Thatcher's Children? Politics, Childhood and Society in the 1980s and 1990s* 8–28. London: Falmer Press.

Walkerdine, V. (1989) *Counting Girls Out*. London: Virago.

Weis, L. (1990) *Working Class Without Work: High School Students in an Urban Community College*. Boston, MA: Routledge and Kegan Paul.

Weis, L. (2006) 'Masculinity, whiteness, and the new economy – An exploration of privilege and loss', *Men and Masculinities*, 8 (3): 262–72.

Wexler, P. Wexler with the assistance of W Crichlow, J Kern and R Martusewicz (1992) *Becoming Somebody: Towards a Social Psychology of Schooling*. Washington: Falmer Press.

Wilkinson, H. (1999) 'The Thatcher legacy: Power feminism and the birth of girl power', in N. Walters (ed.), *On the Move – Feminism for a New Generation* 27–47. London: Virago.

Willis, P. (1977) *Learning to Labour*. Farnborough: Saxon House.

Willis, P. (2006) 'Foot soldiers of modernity: The dialectics of cultural consumption and the twenty-first century school', in H. Lauder, P. Brown, J. Dillabough and A.H. Halsey (eds), *Education, Globalisation and Social Change*. Oxford: Oxford University Press. pp. 507–523.

Yates, L. (2006) 'Vocational subject-making and the work of schools: A case study', *Australian Journal of Education*, 50 (3): 281–96.

Youdell, D. (2006) *Impossible Bodies, Impossible Selves: Exclusions and Student Subjectivities*. Dortrecht: Springer.

# PART 3

# Social Categories

# 15

# Ethnicities

Ann Phoenix

Ethnic riots have broken out in Nairobi, Kisumu, Eldoret, and numerous other places in Kenya. People have been pulled from their cars and their identification cards checked for their names, which symbolize their ethnic identity, and then killed if they belong to groups being targeted. (Genocide, 2008)

The repeated global eruption of 'ethnic conflicts' indicate that, in particular contexts, ethnicities and the identities associated with them can readily be evoked as sources of concerted action. Given its global significance, it is not surprising that ethnic identities are studied and debated in many disciplines. In particular, the 'problematic conflation of ethnicity with conflict' has frequently been challenged (Karner, 2007: 16). Brubaker (2004) argues that ethnic groups are often reified in ways that routinely treat ethnicised and national conflicts as struggles between bounded and internally homogeneous groups. It is now generally accepted that there is no one-to-one correspondence between ethnicity and culture; that ethnic groups are internally differentiated (Anthias and Yuval-Davis, 1992) and that ethnic identities are based on socially constructed cultural differences – rather than definite, fixed differences (Eriksen, 2001). Ethnicity has instead been conceptualised as an emergent property of

processes of claims making (Watson, 1981) and as processes of categorisation and group-making projects. In other words, ethnicity is what people do, rather than what they are (Brubaker, 2004).

The terminology of 'race' and ethnicity is in continual flux, largely because it is not entirely satisfactory. 'Race' is often used in ways that overlap with 'ethnicity' because both are about processes of boundary maintenance (Anthias and Yuval-Davis, 1992). However, ethnicity refers to a collectivity or community that makes assumptions about common attributes related to cultural practices and shared history. Thus religion, language and territory are all included in the term ethnicity. It is, to an extent, insider defined. However, it is a contentious term that is hard to define with multiple, contested interpretations (Cohen, 1999a). While ethnic group is sometimes used to refer to those in less powerful social positions, who are often subjected to racism, ethnicity refers to everybody. Thus the term 'majority ethnic group' is sometimes used to refer to ethnic groups which have relatively more power, often because their cultural practices and presence are taken for granted as natural in a society. In Britain and the US majority ethnic groups are white, but there are also white (as well as black) 'minority ethnic groups'. The majority/minority distinction has been much criticised for its pejorative overtones and the ways in which many people confuse them with numerical proportions, rather than power relations. As a result 'majoritised' and 'minoritised' have gained currency (see Brah, 1996).

Since the middle of the 1980s, the term 'racialisation' has gained popularity as a way to signal that 'race' is a socially constructed process (Lewis and Phoenix, 2004; Murji and Solomos, 2005, and see H.J. Elam Jr and M. Elam's discussion, Chapter 9 this volume). While conceptually more productive than 'race', 'racialisation' is sometimes employed in ways that ignore the plurality of contexts and processes through which it is expressed (Goldberg, 2005). It continues to be used, however, since it avoids the 'raciology' and 'compulsory raciality' that Gilroy (2000) has challenged and yet engages with the ubiquity and durability of racisms in ways that notions of 'post-race' do not (Ali, 2003; Rattansi, 1992). For parallel reasons, the concept of ethnicisation has also gained prominence as a way to indicate the socially constructed nature of ethnicities. The two terms are interlinked in that ethnicised groups also have racialised positions and racialised identities (Restrepo, 2004).

The title of this chapter 'Ethnicities' is intended to disrupt essentialist assumptions that, for example, blackness and whiteness (as racialised positionings) are internally coherent, with no commonalities between them. At the same time it signals that racisms take many different forms and are plural since groups racialised differently (often on the basis of ethnicisation) are subjected to different forms of racism (Brah, 1996). It also acknowledges the more common use of ethnicity than 'race' in most of Europe (Rathzel, 1994). Although ethnicity has often been used to avoid consideration of racism (Essed, 1991; Omi and Winant, 1986; Rattansi, 2007), this is not the case here.

The theorisation of identities is also contested (Moya, 2000). Not surprisingly then, any (necessarily partial) overview of identities and ethnicities has to capture theoretical and empirical diversity as well as highlighting what appear to be promising contemporary trends. In the closing decades of the twentieth century two main currents were apparent in research on ethnicised identities. One was influenced by post-Eriksonian notions of identity development and examined research evidence designed to position minoritised ethnic groups on a hierarchy of ethnic development. These approaches used standardised tests to measure ethnic identities and assumed that people from minority ethnic groups have to take pride in their ethnic identity to reach the apex of identity development. Such approaches run counter to those that focus on ethnicised, rather then ethnic identities. These take as their starting point that identities are socially constructed, multiple, potentially contradictory and situationally variable and that ethnicities are part of the process of boundary maintenance and so of border negotiations and contestations.

The study of ethnic identities has changed markedly over the last two decades. In particular, minoritised ethnic people's resistance to negative interpretations of their identities and behaviour (CCCS, 1982; Gilroy, 1987) led to a shift in research focus away from outsider-imposed assumptions about 'the racially oppressed' to more sympathetic attempts to understand relational positioning (Bulmer and Solomos, 2004; Solomos and Back, 2000).This chapter considers the main debates on ethnicities and identities. It takes a developmental and social perspective and focuses not just on adult ethnicised identities but also children and young people's experiences, drawing on material from a range of disciplines and methodologies. It looks first at some of the more traditional research on the stages of ethnic identity development, and work in social psychology, before describing the development of more dynamic and intersectional approaches focusing on the negotiation of identities, including whiteness.

## STAGING ETHNIC IDENTITY DEVELOPMENT

Ethnic identity development consists of an individual's movement toward a highly conscious identification with their own cultural values, behaviors, beliefs, and traditions. Ethnic and racial identity models provide a theoretical structure for understanding individuals' negotiation of their own and other cultures. (Chávez and Guido-DiBrito, 1999: 41)

Over the last 40 years, studies of ethnic identity development have proliferated. These tend to treat ethnic identity development as part of a broader process of linear development where people come to identify with the values and behaviours that are accepted by researchers or clinicians as belonging to their ethnic group. Ethnic identity models (referred to hereafter as stage models) tend to be neo-Eriksonian in that they are underpinned by Erik Erikson's psychosocial approach. Such approaches generally assume that psychological health is contingent on 'secure' commitments to ethnicity.

William Cross (1971) was one of the first to produce a stage model of racial identity. Cross developed his model in the US during the period of black consciousness and Black Power. His model describes black people as initially lacking a proud, racialised identity, and eventually identifying as black and being proud to do so. For Cross, racial identity is constructed as responsive to, and contingent on, social context. Cross argued that experience of racism encourages development of what he called the 'encounter stage' of racial identity, where individuals are conceptualised as being both angry and puzzled about how they have been treated. In Cross's model of psychological nigrescence, racial identity is a 'resocialization experience'. Individuals pass through four stages of development – pre-encounter, encounter,

emersion–immersion and internalization-commitment at their own pace and, as in Erikson's model, can revisit earlier stages in their adult life. Optimal racial identity is a process that develops from non-Afrocentrism through Afrocentrism to multicultural nigrescence as people shift from being completely unaware of race to being centred on black culture then finally being able to ally with members of other groups. Racial identity is measured by the Cross Racial Identity Scales (CRIS – Vandiver et al., 2001). In later refinements of his model, Cross drew on Social Identity Theory (see Chapter 2) in order to develop 'Nigrescence Theory' (Cross, 1995), but argues that his latest approach shares and takes forward earlier understandings of the relationship between social identities and mental health.

Cross's model has been very influential in work on racial and ethnic identity (Banks, 1996) for Berry's acculturation model (Georgas et al., 2006) and for Helms and Parham's (1996) Racial Identity Attitude Scale, which measures white and black racial identity. Perhaps the most widely cited stage model, however, is that developed in the US by Jean Phinney (1992), the Multi-Ethnic Identity Model (MEIM) which, unlike many standardised instruments, has been made freely available on the Internet. This may be why it has been tested and employed by many researchers in many countries. Phinney has obtained continuous funding from the US National Institute for Health since 1984 and, with her colleagues, has conducted research on ethnic identity in various groups of minority ethnic and white young people (Phinney, 1990, 1992, 1995, 2003).

Phinney's model addresses ethnic identity as a social identity (following Tajfel, 1974) with four dimensions: self identification; affirmation/belonging; identity achievement; ethnic behaviours and practices, plus other orientation. She draws on Erik Erikson's ego identity approach with its focus on exploration and commitment as central to identity development in adolescence. Phinney defines ethnic identity as a dynamic and multidimensional construct that is ascribed and results from shared background and powerful bonds. In recent years she has critiqued the tendency for researchers to assign ethnic group labels to their participants, which may or may not match the person's own evaluation of their racial/ethnic identity. Phinney argues that people often have choices between labels (e.g. Mexican American, Chicano or Latino), each of which has particular connotations that cannot be correctly designated by others. She finds that people from similar ethnic backgrounds show similar patterns in their values, beliefs and behaviours that differentiate them from people in other ethnic or cultural groups.

There are many advantages of stage theories such as those developed by William Cross and Jean Phinney. For example, they have consistently paid attention to ethnic and cultural diversity and contributed to keeping these issues visible in psychological literature in non-pathologising ways. They also enable relatively quick and easy collection of data from large numbers of people. Conceptually, they are dynamic in that they recognise development across stages (and for Phinney over the life course) as well as potential movement back to stages that have apparently been passed. In addition, they attempt to address theoretical changes in the literature, such as recognising plural identities and taking note of people's self identifications. They are multifaceted, including affective, behavioural and cognitive components, sometimes focussing on white majoritised as well as minoritised ethnic group identities and on ethnic identities in a range of countries (Berry et al., 2006).

However, there are a number of difficulties with the measures on which these theories are based. Their very convenience of administration makes them necessarily reductionist of complexity. There are a limited number of ways in which people constructed as being within the same racial/ethnic group are represented. Researchers frequently analyse racial/ethnic identities by the group to which they assign participants, rather than relying on self identification. They tend not to take an intersectional approach and so pay limited attention to the ways in which, for example, gender and social class intersect with ethnicity to produce different identifications. Furthermore, the hierarchical structure of the models suggest an ideal of progress toward an achieved ethnic identity and limits the types of ethnic identities that are viewed as positive, apparently with little recognition that constructions of racial/ethnic identities change over time in any society. In stage models, psychological health is assumed to follow from making commitments to an identity in the way the analyst considers healthy, not how research participants choose. Phinney says: 'Our research shows that adolescents who have made a commitment to their group and have a secure understanding of their group membership show more positive psychological profiles than those who are unclear about the meaning of their ethnicity or dissatisfied with their group membership' (2005a: 190). This assertion seems somewhat essentialist in imposing notions of what ought to be the case on identities that demonstrably have been in flux over the last 50 years. A further problem is that, according to this conceptualisation, fundamentalist identities would be the most 'healthy' since they require strong commitments to group identities (Phoenix and Rattansi, 2005).

The terminology used by stage theorists is potentially revealing. Phinney (2005b), for example, talks of an 'integrated profile', (drawing on old notions of integration and/or current concerns with integration to prevent terrorism in northern countries); an 'ethnic profile', which seems to reduce ethnic identities to the fixed and singular; and 'high' and 'low' ethnic identity, which enshrines fixed hierarchy. It is striking that the numerous studies drawing on stage models tend to test the models or apply them to additional groups, rather than questioning their underlying conceptualisation (Quintana et al., 2006; Worrell, 2006). Yet, the dynamism and utility of stage models is limited by their fixed and pre-delineated notions of what constitutes racial/ethnic identity. As a result they implicitly reproduce a view of ethnic identity as static, coherent and often unitary, even though they explicitly aim to represent dynamism and plurality.

## SELF-CATEGORISING SOCIAL IDENTITIES

'Who the person is' is seen as an outcome of self-categorisation-in-context, and through different categorisations and associated processes of social influence future 'selves' can be made more or less likely to emerge. Of course, our enduring knowledge affects the way we see ourselves, how others see us, and how we make sense of social reality, but it is also the case that these knowledge resources can be transformed, updated, and re-interpreted in light of the current circumstances that come to define the person as an individual or group member. (Reynolds and Turner, 2006: 263)

Social identity theory (SIT) has already been mentioned in the previous section as one of the theories on which both CRIS and MEIM are based. It has been highly influential and generated hundreds of studies within psychology, but has had more limited impact in other disciplines (see Reicher et al., Chapter 2 this volume, for an extended description of the theory and Schmid et al., Chapter 23 this volume for an application to group conflict in Northern Ireland). This section briefly discusses the relevance of SIT to ethnicised identities noting work on stereotype threat and self-categorisation and ending with some comments evaluating the overall contribution of this tradition of work.

One implication of SIT's focus on how social identities evoke emotions is that it is threatening to self-esteem for people to belong to socially subordinate groups. In different fields of research, it has become clear that people defend themselves from psychological threats (Hollway and Jefferson, 2000; Major and O'Brien, 2005; Wilson and Gilbert, 2005). Claude Steele developed a theory he called 'stereotype threat'. In a range of studies, Steele and his colleagues find that when people's social identity is attached to a negative stereotype, they will tend to under-perform in ways consistent with the stereotype (Steele and Aronson, 1995). Steele (1997) suggests that this is because they will be anxious in case they conform to that negative stereotype and so will have various anxiety symptoms that impair their performance, such as being distracted and/or hotter and more uncomfortable than usual. Davis and Silver (2003) suggest that, rather than black participants giving socially desirable answers to white researchers (as has often been argued), their survey research indicates that black research participants suffer from stereotype threat when asked research questions by white researchers. Marx and Goff (2005) found that black testers who do not confirm stereotypes can eliminate threat from the testing situation and increase black participants' test scores. This suggests that black researchers would not necessarily overcome stereotype threat simply by being black. This happens only if they are viewed by black participants as countering negative stereotypes.

Shelton et al. (2006) considered how social identity threat can affect inter-ethnic interactions and friendships. They focused on individuals' concerns that they will be judged on the basis of group stereotypes and found that these meta-stereotypes can be a source of social identity threat during inter-ethnic interactions. The impacts of inter-ethnic interactions are not straightforward. Positive interaction dynamics can, however, foster the development of inter-ethnic friendships and reduce prejudice (Shelton et al., 2006). However, while avoidance is unlikely to foster intergroup friendship development, it can sometimes lead ethnic minorities to have more positive attitudes towards whites. The strategies that 'threatened' individuals use for coping with meta-stereotyping can have different effects on the partners in the interaction, leading one (particularly the non-threatened individual) to want to pursue a friendship and the other to be less interested. Alternatively, the person who feels threatened may avoid inter-ethnic contact without any change in their feelings about the group that is potentially threatening. At the same time, the avoidance may leave the potential outgroup interaction partner feeling more negative. There are many possibilities for 'larger-scale misunderstandings between members of different social identity groups' (Shelton et al., 2006: 353). Perceived threats to identity are thus a primary source of intergroup tension, prejudice, and hostility. The fact that Shelton et al., treat as equivalent the threat to white people fearing attributions of prejudice and unfairness and threats to minoritised ethnic groups about racist stereotypes perhaps limits its utility in that the equivalence of these 'threats' has not been established and the groups are not socioeconomically equal.

The psychological consequences of self-categorisation have been a major theme developing from SIT research. It is argued that in any situation individuals will have a range of possible ways of describing themselves extending from group identities to more personal idiosyncratic senses of identity. These various possibilities for self-categorisation have been shown to have a moderating impact on ethnic identity. For example, Verkuyten and Nekuee (2001) found that if Iranian refugees living in the Netherlands saw themselves in group terms as 'typical Iranians', their personal and ethnic self-esteem were interlinked and they were more likely to perceive greater group discrimination than personal discrimination. They also preferred problem-focused coping strategies for dealing with racism than emotion-focused coping. Verkuyten et al. (1999) similarly found that ethnic Dutch participants who were most likely to have high social self-categorisations reported more negative emotions to minority ethnic groups than those with low social self-categorisations. Reynolds and Turner (2006) argue that work in the field of self-categorisation demonstrates that any analysis of prejudice must simultaneously address collective as well as individual psychological processes. In this, self-categorisation theory fits with the current

zeitgeist on identities, which recognises that prejudice, for example, is not formed and fixed in the past and a fixed characteristic of individuals, but arises from the contemporary, creative negotiation of social practices.

Other social psychologists, such as Michael Billig, originally involved in developing this line of work, have been critical of SIT analyses of ethnic and national identities. Billig (1995) argues that this approach treats groups as if they are interchangeable. As a result, no difference is made between groups artificially constructed in laboratories on the basis of minimal differences and categories such as gender, ethnicity or nationality that have meaning outside the laboratory. In other words, Billig is suggesting that the meanings associated with social groups may be more important for people's social identities than how an individual categorises themselves. The notion that people self-stereotype in order to act in concert with group identities is too static to account for fast-changing social identities. A further danger is that theories of this sort treat prejudice and oppression as natural results of general cognitive processes and motivation – that is, as if prejudiced identities are natural and inevitable. This is both unwarranted and serves to maintain the status quo in power relations (Reicher, 2004). Despite these criticisms, this field has been one in which some researchers have consistently addressed ethnicised identities. Furthermore, developments in this area demonstrate the convergence in cross-disciplinary understandings about the main issues to be addressed and accounted for in the field of identities (for example, theorising individuals and groups simultaneously, change, plurality and essentialism).

## THEORISING INTERSECTIONAL PLURALITY

Growing up in India, I was Indian; teaching high school in Nigeria, I was a foreigner [...] Doing research in London, I was black. As a professor at an American university, I am an Asian woman [...]

In North America I was also a 'resident alien' with an Indian passport – I am now a U.S. citizen whose racialization has shifted dramatically (and negatively) since the attacks on the World Trade Center and the Pentagon on 11 September 2001. (Mohanty, 2003: 190)

The above extract illustrates two insights from work on ethnicity. First, that ethnicity is differentiated by social class as well as by gender, sexuality, and so forth (Rattansi, 1994). Second, that differences between members of the same socially constructed groups (intra-categorical differences) can be turned against those defined as outgroups.

Intersectionality is the term that has come to represent the fact that people are always simultaneously positioned in many categories so that there is no essence to any category. Intersectionality is one of the fastest-growing areas of the human sciences. Its popularity has partly resulted because Kimberlé Crenshaw (1989) put a name to ways of theorising that black feminists had long advocated and that working class and lesbian feminists had promoted (Combahee River Collective, 1977). As Crenshaw (1994) recognises, intersectional analyses had been conducted long before the term was coined. Black women, in particular, had argued that it is important to deconstruct the category 'women' and to recognise that social class and 'race' produce both commonalities and differences between women. The Combahee River Collective (1977) of black lesbians was groundbreaking, for example, in arguing for strategic alliances across various categories of difference:

Although we are feminists and lesbians, we feel solidarity with black men and do not advocate the fractionalization that white women who are separatists demand. Our situation as black people necessitates that we have solidarity around the fact of race, which white women of course do not need to have with white men, unless it is their negative solidarity as racial oppressors. We struggle together with black men against racism, while we also struggle with black men about sexism. (reprinted in Nicholson, 1997: 65)

Intersectionality thus indicates that a focus on any one social category can only be understood in the context of other categories and of differences, as well as commonalities, within groups. Feminist researchers have shown how women's experiences and life chances differ according to their 'race', ethnicity, sexuality and social class – that is, gender and sexuality are class-based and racialised social relations (Anthias and Yuval-Davis, 1983; Brah, 1996; Lewis, 2000; Lykke, 2003). It was for this reason that Crenshaw coined the term intersectionality since she found that in US juridical studies of violence against women, black women were continually rendered invisible and, indeed, often still are (Crenshaw, 2009). In a similar way, Lutz's (2008) research on migrant women domestic workers in German households necessarily leads to the interrogation of the category 'woman' in that women may be interlinked in complementary everyday practices while their varied social class, ethnicised, national and motherhood positionings differentiate their interests and the power relations between them.

Intersectionality thus makes clear that all categories are associated with power relations and cannot be neutral (Brah and Phoenix, 2004; Collins, 1998; Thornton and Nettles, 2001). Hence, it allows the interrogation of 'unmarked' positions such as 'whiteness' and 'masculinity' as well as of 'marked' positions such as 'blackness' and 'femininity'. As is evident from the example of the Combahee River Collective above, the intersection of categories can generate political solidarity. For example, Alexander (2006) suggests that the radical project of de-colonization requires moving across boundaries (for example, of nation-state, social class, race, gender, sexuality and nationality). The boundary crossing she advocates is designed to acknowledge inequalities while recognising the relationships between categories. Intersectionality thus destabilises the notion of speaking as black, working class or a woman and of claiming fixed identities based on these categories. This eschews the legitimacy of identity politics, which involves groups using particular identities associated with social categories in order to resist oppression and produce social change. Intersectionality fits better with a notion of strategic alliances, where people make temporary alliances for particular purposes. Yet, while intersectionality makes clear that claims to identities (for example, as black or as a woman) are always open to challenge and change, some versions of it can allow multiple identities (for example, as black, working-class lesbians) to be treated as if they are fixed and so reproduce identity politics and ignore agency (Prins, 2006).

An example from Dhamoon (2006) illustrates more concretely how intersectionality can also be used to further political projects while simultaneously recognising shifting identities and allowing strategic alliances. Analysing the Aboriginal Women's Roundtable Report on Gender Equality (2000), she shows how Canadian Aboriginal women used their intersecting identities as women and Aboriginal as 'oppositional consciousness against colonial and imperial processes' and the state. However, they did not do this in strategic essentialist ways. They rejected the Canadian government's attempts to homogenise them on the grounds that their identities were diverse.

Stuart Hall provides a further example of the utility of intersectional analyses and how everyday intersectionality produces shifting, unpredictable and unstable identifications that decentre some identities and foreground others in relation to particular issues at particular times.

In 1991, President Bush [Senior], anxious to restore a conservative majority to the US Supreme Court, nominated Clarence Thomas, a black judge of conservative political views. In Bush's judgement, white voters (who may have been prejudiced about a black judge) were likely to support Thomas because he was conservative on equal-rights legislation, and black voters (who support liberal policies on race) would support Thomas because he was black. In short, the President was 'playing the identities game'.

During the Senate 'hearings' on the appointment, a black woman, Anita Hill, a former junior colleague of Thomas's, accused Judge Thomas of sexual harassment. The hearings caused a public scandal and polarised American society. Some blacks supported Thomas on racial grounds; others opposed him on sexual grounds.

Black women were divided, depending on whether their 'identities' as blacks or as women prevailed. Black men were also divided, depending on whether their sexism overrode their liberalism. White men were divided, depending, not only on their politics, but on how they identified themselves with respect to racism and sexism. White conservative women supported Thomas, not only on political grounds, but because of their opposition to feminism. White feminists, often liberal on race, opposed Thomas on sexual grounds. And because Judge Thomas is a member of the judicial elite and Anita Hill, at the time of the alleged incident, a junior employee, there were issues of social class position at work in these arguments too. (Hall, 1992: 279–80)

Intersectionality is arguably apposite for the theorising and researching of identities in that it conceptualises ontology (Prins, 2006). There are numerous research examples of the intersection of ethnicities with, for example, gender and social class that demonstrate the complexities of commonalities and differences in ethnicised identities (see, for example, Alexander and Mohanty, 1997; Back, 2007; Cohen, 1997; Frankenberg, 1993; Lewis, 2000; Räthzel, 2008; Staunæs, 2005; Yuval-Davis, 2006a). One of the advantages of intersectionality as a theory is that it facilitates multi-level analyses ranging from statistical to single-case analyses (McCall, 2005). Buitelaar uses a single case approach and draws on a Bakhtinian-inspired narrative approach to analyse the ways in which a Dutch politician of Moroccan background orchestrates 'voices within the self that speak from different I-positions' (2006: 259). This analysis demonstrates that the politician's identities are dialogical, constructed and emergent in relation to gender, ethnicity, religion and career.

While the use of the concept of intersectionality is burgeoning, there has been a proliferation of ways in which it is used and some dissatisfaction with the tendency for it to be conceptualised as intersecting roads (see, for example, Yuval-Davis, 2006a). Some theorists have suggested new terms to encompass intersectionality. Bhavnani for example, suggests the term 'configurations' 'to examine the manner in which power inequalities, shifting meanings and common sense frames are condensed in social issues' (1993: 58). Anthias (2007) proposes the concept of translocational positionality to avoid presupposing that groups pre-exist their social circumstances and so masking commonalities across constructed boundaries. According to a translocational framework, identity claims and attributions are always situated and produced in complex locations that shift as much as categories and identities do. These ideas are in concert with those proposed by Jacqui Alexander and Chandra Talpade Mohanty (1997) who have taken forward intersectional understandings, but argue for clarity in thinking about the interconnections between location, identity and the construction of knowledge, rather than dismissing them as essentialist as postmodernist theory does (c.f. Sudbury, 1998).

A rather different critique is proposed by Skeggs (2006a) who argues that social divisions have different organizing logics. 'Race', therefore, cannot be treated in the same way as social class. Skeggs' critique does not mean that she does not simultaneously consider, for example, ethnicity, gender and social class, since these have been major aspects of her work (Skeggs, 2006b). Instead, she rejects the treating of all categories as if they operate in the same way. Verloo (2006) agrees with Skegg's critique, but suggests that this does not necessitate the eschewing of intersectionality since inequalities are not independent of each other. Overall, most critics of intersectionality argue for complex, nuanced treatments, rather than the abandoning of the concept (Grabham et al., 2008; Nash, 2008).

## DOING ETHNICISED POSITIONING IN CHILDREN AND YOUNG PEOPLE

The long tradition of research in this area has yielded important – sometimes surprising – findings, many of which run counter to popular beliefs. For example, children who have been racially stigmatized do not, contrary to widespread belief, experience low levels of personal self-esteem [...] popular notions that children are naturally naïve to race and that they are taught to be racist by parents turns out to be simply wrong [...] Unlike many areas of scholarship that involve uneven development, there has been sustained academic interest over more than 50 years into topics associated with race, racism, and the developing child. This body of work has been consistently responsive to social movements that span historical periods (e.g., the civil rights movement in the U.S.) [...] [T]he field represents an interesting nexus between developmental and social psychological theories. (Quintana and McKown, 2008: 1–2)

From the beginning of the 1970s, developmental psychology made an important shift from conceptualising human development as a decontextualised and individual process to theorising it as necessarily social. In sociology, anthropology and other human sciences, childhood became a major field of study from the 1980s. As a result, there is now a substantial body of published work on the ways in which children negotiate ethnicised positioning. Work on adult ethnic identities frequently ignores the fact that adults have long experience of negotiating these issues and treats the history of these negotiations in childhood as an empty box. Yet few people would deny that issues of 'race' and ethnicity are central to the lives of many children and young people living in northern societies and hence constitute an integral part of social development and of the context in which adults negotiate their identities.

Research in the UK, the US and Canada generally finds that 'race' and ethnicity are inscribed in children's lives and are often salient from about two or three years of age. The trajectory mapped by such research is one in which consciousness of colour and ethnicity is evident in the early school years, increases through the middle school years (Boulton and Smith, 1992; Milner, 1983) and continues in secondary school (Gillborn, 2008; Griffin, 1985; Tizard and Phoenix, 2002). 'Race', racism and ethnicity have mostly been demonstrated to have a direct impact on the ways in which children define themselves and others, on their experiences and the ways in which they act towards people of other colours or ethnicities. It has also been shown to affect the ways in which other people think about and act towards them (Ogilvy et al., 1990, 1992; Sonuga-Barke, 1993; Van Ausdale and Feagin, 2001; Wright, 1992). Not surprisingly, black and Asian children and those of mixed black–white and Asian–white parentage are subject to most racial discrimination and hence have most easily accessible discourses about 'race' and racism.

## Doll/photograph studies and self-esteem

Two black psychologists, Kenneth and Mamie Clark (1939, 1947) conducted the now classic 'doll' studies. They studied 253 'Negro' children; 134 in segregated southern schools and 119 in integrated northern schools. The tests consisted of four elements: children's 'racial awareness' through recognition of dolls' skin colour; black children's 'ability to identify themselves in racial terms' (Clark, 1963); 'racial preferences'; and a 'coloring test'. Clark and Clark concluded that many black children want to be white because they have internalised society's negative views of their 'race' and experience self-rejection and low self-esteem. The Clarks' findings were used (successfully) to argue for the desegregation of US schools in the 1954 case of *Brown* v. *Board of Education* on the grounds that segregation damaged the racial identity of Negro children. However, their interpretation of their findings have since been challenged (for example, including by Bruno Bettelheim, see Clark, 1963: 199 and Harold Garfinkel, see Murphy et al., 1984). Clark and Clark's research ushered in a paradigm of work on children and 'race' which still continues partly, no doubt, because the methods that have been developed are easy to use with young children and take little time to administer so that large samples

can be recruited. These issues received renewed attention in the US, when a 17-year-old, black, young woman filmed a replication of the original study in 2005 with similar results (Davis, 2005; Edney, 2006).

Many studies have focused on low self-esteem and psychic damage in black children (Hutnik, 1991) and the fact that young children tend to choose friends of the same colour as themselves (Boulton and Smith, 1992). In the 'first generation' of studies on minority ethnic groups and self-esteem, it was assumed that black children and those from other minoritised ethnic groups would necessarily suffer low self-esteem as a result of racism and their tendency to 'misidentify' (Verkuyten, 2008). However, the 'second-generation' of studies (which used standardised scales) and directly assessed (rather than inferred) self-esteem, found no evidence of the expected correspondence between self esteem and 'positive black identity' (Jackson et al., 1986). This fits with work on self esteem more generally, which suggests that putting too much emphasis on fostering children's self-esteem can be detrimental to their development (Seligman, 2004).

A 'third-generation' of studies is currently attempting to investigate, and account for, the contradictions between the expectations produced by 'first generation' studies and the findings of 'second generation' studies (Allen et al., 2005). Verkuyten (2008) suggests that there are both methodological and theoretical explanations for the failure to find differences in self-esteem between majority and minority ethnic groups. Methodologically, the reliance on self-report measures and on trait-like, rather than state-dependent self-esteem may partly explain contemporary findings. Theoretically, distinctions between personal and ethnic identity and between implicit and explicit self have been largely neglected so that it is the conscious elements of self-esteem that are tapped in most studies, when implicit self-esteem may be less positive. As Verkuyten acknowledges, little is known about what works to improve self-esteem and why it works.

## Negotiating everyday racialised/ ethnicised practices

Research on children's 'racial preferences' indicate that racialisation and ethnicisation have an impact on children's identities and, to some extent, how they feel about themselves and their social world. There is also evidence that children have some understanding of national differences from early in their lives (Barrett, 2007). Yet, despite evidence to the contrary, there are still pervasive discourses that maintain that young children are 'colour blind' (Williams, 1997). According to this argument, not only are children colourblind, but those who care for young children also tend not to notice colour differences between them (Carrington and Short, 1989). The denial that 'race' is an issue for young children is particularly prevalent in schools which are predominantly composed of white children (Gaine, 2006), although racism and racist discourses do have an impact in such settings (Troyna and Hatcher, 1992). Children in mainly white schools can also be sophisticated in their understanding of racism and aware of the fact that they should conceal it from their teachers (Short, 1991). This 'colour blind' approach is arguably pervasive because discourses of 'race' and racism intersect with other, equally prevalent discourses about childhood which suggest that it is a haven of innocence where children need to be protected from the nastier realities of adult life (Van Ausdale and Feagin, 2001).

While much of the work on children, ethnicity and development is done in psychology, work on how children negotiate racialised and ethnicised identities in their everyday practices comes from a range of disciplines and have been much influenced by the burgeoning of the sociology of childhood, much of which makes central children's own accounts. This section considers examples of important new lines of research which explore some common themes: racialisation and ethnicisation as an interactional resource for children, children's ethnicised friendships and intersectional identities.

There is now a small body of studies that indicate the complex ways in which children use racialisation and ethnicisation as interactional resources. Van Ausdale and Feagin (2001) conducted a study of how children aged three to six years 'do race' that remains unique. Debra van Ausdale spent 11 months doing ethnography in a US preschool, where she acted as a sympathetic, but non-authority adult figure. As a result, the children behaved in her presence in ways they did not with their teachers. A striking finding is that the parents and teachers who looked after the children were frequently unaware of, or in denial of, children's ethnicised understandings, taking a color-blind approach (c.f. Rothenberg, 2000). Teachers can be very surprised when they discover that racist discourses are part of children's everyday practices and identities – as an action research study in three Scottish primary schools found (Donald et al., 1995). Marie Louise Seeberg (2003) found a similar picture in her ethnographic study of primary schools in Oslo and Amsterdam. Norwegian children were 'race cognisant' and sometimes played with essentialist racism, but were 'race evasive' with teachers.

Van Ausdale and Feagin found that young, white children use racial and national terms, focus on racialised features such as skin colour and facial features and are sometimes discriminatory. Black and mixed-parentage children employed different ways of identifying themselves and dealing with their white peers' positioning of them. The following two examples illustrate this.

> Like most of the children we observed, Carla is not the unsophisticated, innocent child of many adult imaginations. This three-year-old knows how to use racial material, such as the hurtful epithet, which she has learned from other sources. But she is not just imitating what she might have heard in some other social setting. She applies this particular bit of racial knowledge to a distinctive and personal interactive encounter. The range of concepts she has linked together are remarkable, she has not acted indiscriminately, using an ugly name only to foster a reaction in the other child. Instead, Carla uses 'nigger' to explain and justify her action to an interested onlooker, the teacher. (Van Ausdale and Feagin, 2002: 1–2).

> (E)ven at three and a half years of age Taleshia had already developed a wide variety of coping techniques for dealing with the racial categorizing and discrimination imposed on her by her non-Black peers. She selected her countering strategies, from active resistance to passive withdrawal, based in part on the context of her interactions. How she managed her life was inextricably bound to how racism shapes the social character of her world, and she managed with extraordinary intelligence and sophistication'. (Van Ausdale and Feagin, 2002: 191–2)

Van Ausdale and Feagin demonstrated that the three-year-olds they studied identified themselves and others in racialised, ethnicised, linguistic and national terms and negotiated these identities, sometimes using them as interactional resources to include and exclude other children. They argue that children as social actors are capable of reproducing and contesting social systems of inequality that predate them and creating new ways of negotiating their ethnicised identities. Since the children were not consistently excluding or resistant in negotiating ethnicisation, it may be that they were too young to have ethnicised understandings or consistent ways of viewing the world and are innocent about racialisation and ethnicity. Such contradictions are, however, also common in older age groups.

> Immediately after the interview [...] this young supporter of a racist party, and of compelling all of 'them' to leave 'our country', was to be seen walking arm in arm with a young Asian girl, chatting and laughing in easy friendship. (Billig et al., 1988: 106)

Adults have also been found to express contradictory ideas about people from other ethnicised groups (Billig, 1991; Bonilla-Silva, 2002; van Dijk, 1993).

Van Ausdale and Feagin's research was ground breaking, observing children as young as three-years-old in detail. Their findings provide support to aspects of other research in this area. For example, although she made little of this, Robyn Holmes (1995) found that five-year-old US children differ by ethnicity in the likelihood of identifying themselves by ethnicity (with black children being more likely to describe themselves in colour terms) and that they could also sometimes refuse to accept that mixed-parentage children had white parents. Ruth Woods (2007) found that 9–10-year-old British children are creative in their understandings of identities and racisms, including discriminatory practices as well as racist name-calling and discrimination on grounds of religion. Connolly (1998) found that five- and six-year-old children at an inner-city, multi-ethnic primary school in England also negotiate racism. Slightly older children have been found to be more sophisticated in their racialised/ethnicised interactions. Troyna and Hatcher (1992) studied 8–11-year-olds in a mainly white primary school in the UK and found that they employed racism instrumentally in the service of psychosocial goals so that racist name calling was 'performative'; used as a resource to 'do' various identities and gain advantage in power relations. It was, therefore, sometimes used by children who identified as strongly anti-racist.

The negotiation of outsider ascriptions of ethnicity and insider identifications continue for older children in schools. From an ethnographic study in three US schools Amanda Lewis (2003) concludes that 'race' is ubiquitous both inside and outside schools and is part of many daily interpersonal interactions and is one way in which young people understand the world and make decisions about how to behave. Her analyses suggest that processes of racialization work through interpersonal interactions in which people attempt to assess other people by reading and interpreting visible cues such as skin colour, facial features, accent or neighbourhood. They use this information to map systems of meaning, and so of inclusions or exclusions, onto individuals. Racial categorization cannot merely be imposed from above, and some of the young people Lewis studied resisted and/or were enraged at how they were categorised (for example, as white, rather than Latino, or as Chinese, rather than mixed parentage). However, racial categories and the meanings associated with them cannot entirely be rejected. Insider claims and identifications are limited by the social context and the categories available. Lewis gives the example of the champion golfer Tiger Woods, who coined the neologism Cabalaisian to claim a new racialised/ethnicised identity, but was still mostly read as black. Nonetheless, the resistance of some of the young people did sometimes allow new ethnicised identifications.

Such complex negotiations of ethnicised identities are also demonstrated in European research. For example, Staunaes (2005) used a case study of a white, ethnic Dane to demonstrate how the intersections of ethnicity, gender, age and sexuality complicate her relationships with Arab boys in ways that produce troubled subject positions and render her 'other' in the school setting. Staunaes demonstrates that whiteness has to be understood as situated in specific contexts and that ethnicised identities are negotiated in shifting constellations of heteronormative power relations. In the Australian context, Youdell (2006) analysed the relational negotiations, contradictions and tensions between the performance of 'white supremacy-masculine authority/entitlement' on the part of teachers and boys who are simultaneously good 'ethnic' students and 'bad' academic students. Both Staunaes and Youdell suggest that the cost of being subjected in these ways produces tensions for the white, ethnic Danish young woman (Staunaes) and for both teachers and students (Youdell).

All these studies indicate that children are not only 'race-cognisant' early in their lives, but are able to use ethnicised identities as interactional resources and that ethnicisation is central to the negotiation of their identities. In a US study, Laura Abrams (2003) found that 15–18-year-old, young women were acutely aware of women's subordinate social position, but their experiences and their strategies for dealing with this varied according to whether they went to a wealthy, suburban school in a white community or a working-class, urban, ethnically mixed school. In a study of young people living in Brixton, London (an area that is marginalised and stigmatised as being full of drugs and violence because it has a visible black population), Caroline Howarth (2002) found that 12–16-year-olds from a range of ethnic groups recognise how they are stereotyped because of the area from which they come and develop a range of strategies to deal with this. The following unpublished example, from research on the social identities of 14–18-year-old Londoners (see, for example, Phoenix and Tizard, 1996; Tizard and Phoenix, 2002), highlights some of the ways in which 'race', class and gender intersect in everyday life, for an 18-year-old, middle-class, black man from an affluent family.

Q:  Do you ever think that you're treated differently or discriminated against?

A:  [...] I think it might have been a possibility at some point, but going to be served in a restaurant, I'll leave no doubt in the waiter or waitress's mind that quite frankly I'll not put up with nonsense, so if I tell them that I want a good table I will look at them hard and say I would like a good table and same sort of way as I let them know exactly what food, you know, what kind of a person they would be messing with. It doesn't really – it doesn't send me on an ego trip. It's just something that I feel I have to do, you know, it's a sort of preliminary action that sort of says, automatic as getting up in the morning, or you know – if I am going out in the evening, these are one of the things that I will remember, you know, tie, wallet, handkerchief and to be forthright when asking for a table. That's something built in.

The young man quoted above naturalises social positioning in the identity he claims and warrants this in his account. He explains how he negotiates and pre-empts racist discrimination because I have asked him specifically about that and he has a conscious account about defending himself from the potential disadvantage it produces. However, he takes for granted two other, intersecting, sets of social position that confer privilege on him: gender and social class position. The certainties conferred by social class position, male private school education and having sufficient money enabled the above young man to develop the strategy of 'not putting up with (racist) nonsense' in 'good restaurants'. This strategy would not have been as open to an impoverished, working-class, black, young man or as available to a middle-class, black, young woman. Okeley (1987), for example, discusses the ways in which (white) public school girls have been prepared for a different life from their male peers.

Such complex negotiations also pertain to young people's ethnicised friendships. Ethnographic studies increasingly demonstrate that children and young people are not preoccupied with ethnicisation and racism, but frequently interact in culturally syncretic ways consistent with Paul Gilroy's (2004a) conceptualization of 'convivial multicultures' (Rampton et al., 2008). They also, however, engage in ethnicised separation (Back, 1996; Boulton and Smith, 1992; Hewitt, 1986, 1996). Tatum (2003) suggests that informal ethnicised segregation may not necessarily be problematic in that different groups have different needs and 'people of color' have a strong need for connection and empowerment. 'Affinity groups', she argues, need separate 'spaces' that facilitate positive identity exploration, where people can pose questions, process issues and perhaps interrupt the cycle of racism. For 'adolescents of color', affinity groups provide support for identity, while young, white people also benefit from separate spaces for discussing race and processing their reactions to racism. Overall then, these various lines of research

suggest that young people are not only positioned in societal structures, but are aware of how they are positioned and account for themselves in ways that demonstrate that they have to negotiate often difficult, intersecting, social relations.

## DYNAMIC DIFFERENCES AND NEGOTIATED CONTEXTS: 'NEW ETHNICITIES' AND THE PSYCHOSOCIAL

[…] one can only think identity through difference. To think is to construct that inevitable distance between the subject that is thinking and the subject that is being thought about […] It is one of Michel Foucault's greatest insights that in order to become 'subjects' we must be 'subjected' to discourses which speak us, and without which we cannot speak […] I always refused the notion that a whole politics could be identified with any single identity position […] (Hall, 2007: 270, 274, 281)

Stuart Hall has undoubtedly been the most influential theorist in the rethinking of racialised and ethnicised identities and the epigraph that introduces this section summarises his theoretical position. Hall (1992) coined the term 'new ethnicities' to signal that everybody has multiple, decentred identities that are complex and situated in particular historical periods and geographical locations. He argues that cultural and ethnic identities are not free floating. They have histories, but change over time so that they are not grounded in the recovery of the past. Hall's focus on multiplicity, complexity, contradiction, transformation and situatedness has generated both theoretical debate, empirical work and challenge (see, for example, Linda Alcoff's Chapter 7, this volume, which compares poststructural approaches such as Hall's with the approach that has come to be known as 'post-positivist realism'). In recent years, researchers within the new ethnicities tradition have become interested in exploring further the psychosocial dimensions of ethnicised identities elaborating and enhancing the dynamic and conetxtualised emphases characteristic of this work.

Ali Rattansi's (2007) work owes much to Stuart Hall's theorisation and can be characterised as postmodern and psychoanalytic. His analysis of a controversial episode in the UK triggered by the football commentator, Ron Atkins, indicates his approach.

At a point when Atkins believed that the microphone was switched off he described a black footballer as a 'f—ing lazy black nigger'. On the face of it [...] the remarks have obvious racist connotations. [...]

Atkins promptly apologized for the remarks, claimed that he was not a racist, but resigned. This was not the end of the matter. Atkins was also reputed to be someone who had been a pioneer in promoting black football talent and some black footballers came out publicly in support of Atkins. Other black footballers, however, said that Atkins was well known for racially abusing black footballers, and they claimed to have personal experiences of such abuse.

What is one to make of Atkins's alleged racism? Did the unguarded comments reveal his real views, camouflaged by support for black players which could be seen simply as a cynical strategy for opportunistically taking advantage of potential skills?

On the basis of what I have said about the nature of personal and social identities in general, and judging on the basis of limited information about him we would be justified in concluding that Atkins, like many others, has contradictory and ambivalent responses to black people. He is neither really only a racist nor really a non-racist. Like most white people in Britain, he has culturally absorbed both sorts of views, and his response to any particular black person depends on the context and circumstances in which he is interacting with the black individuals.

Atkins-type responses can be better understood in the light of [...] the multiplicity of identities of individuals as well as the resulting de-centredness of their subjectivity such that individuals are not always fully knowledgeable about the layers of identification in their makeup, nor in control of their responses, so that they may end up behaving in a manner they abhor and have long tried to avoid. (Rattansi, 2007: 120–1)

Rattansi's analysis makes clear the complexity, contradiction, inconcludability and cultural embedding of racialised identities. Atkins is not categorised as a racist, but as producing both racist and non-racist practices in specific contexts. Rattansi argues that the unconscious decentres identities so that

people may produce behaviour that surprises and even appals them. The advantage of this approach is that it allows a focus on process and a move beyond the impasse produced by denials of racism to focus on how people juggle with a variety of identities and narratives. It accounts for differences in racist identities; varied responses to different racialised groups; rational argument sometimes dispelling racism (although it often does not) and that people change over time. Rattansi's analysis takes seriously the multiple viewpoints of those subject to, and those producing, racism and is committed to value judgements that can point the way forward to political action and recognise the plurality, contingency, ambivalence and contradiction of racisms and racialised identities.

The utility of this approach is also exemplified by Gunaratnam and Lewis (2001), who use interviews with social workers to expand theorisation of Hochschild's (1983) notion of emotional labour to racialisation as well as gender. Gunaratnam and Lewis argue that 'emotions are an integral part of how "race" is produced and experienced in social care organisations' (2001: 134). They demonstrate that the everyday work practices of black, Asian and white social workers are imbued with defensive unconscious processes that involve suppression, repression and splitting of emotions around racism, as in the quotation below from a white hospice social worker:

Jo: I don't actually think it is just a literal fear of being accused of being racist, I actually think it is a fear of triggering (...) the rage and fury. Maybe I should speak for myself (...) about white people's history of treatment of black people. That it is not just a 'You're a racist'. I mean ... I know ... it is devastating to be criticised. But ... for me, it's like, it's not just that is it? It's like the whole history behind the kind of (...) I don't know, how much ... does that immobilise us? Does that stop ... me taking risks with families? (Extract from group interview with white hospice social workers.) (Gunaratnam and Lewis, 2001: 132)

Gunaratnam and Lewis also analyse their own racialised emotional labour as researchers negotiating identifications of commonality and difference and defensiveness about emotions of anger and fear in the interviews. Gunaratnam and Lewis's analysis helps to clarify how identities are situated and changing, rather than fixed. Emotion and imagination (including unconscious identities) are both central to what can be difficult negotiations, pushing people into troubled subject positions (Wetherell, 1998) in the course of everyday work practices.

The unconscious is also central to Paul Gilroy's argument that British attitudes to race are patterned by ambivalence between 'postcolonial melancholia' and an emergent 'unruly and unplanned multiculture' (2004a: xiv). The identities of postcolonial countries, he suggests, are marked by their colonial history and are deeply melancholic because they refuse to face up to the loss of empire. According to Gilroy, contemporary melancholia is marked by a 'signature combination of manic elation with misery, self-loathing and ambivalence, as analysed by Sigmund Freud' (2004b). At the same time, there is a 'spontaneous tolerance and openness evident in the underworld of Britain's convivial multiculture' (Gilroy, 2004a: 131). Unconscious processes are equally part of Appadurai's (1996) notion that ethnoscapes are part of the social imaginary and Fanon's (1967a) notion that the minoritised are 'victims of essence'. For Fanon, essentialist othering has a marked impact on blackness because racialised identities are necessarily relational, contingent and ambivalent processes.

There is less work on how minoritised groups construct majority ethnic groups. However, hooks (1992) and Raylene Lewis (2007) have provided insider insights for blacks Americans and South African, 'coloured' women, respectively. In a unique, innovative study, Lewis conducted interviews with 22 expatriate 'coloured' South African women living in Western Australia. The women drew on multiple categories for identification, including black or 'mixed race' for some. They were keenly aware that white Australians did not accept them as Australian and so were constrained in how

they could identify. They often took care to differentiate themselves from Aborigines who they recognised were most despised in the white Australian racialised hierarchy. At the same time, they struggled with the recognition that they were not considered different from black people, although in South Africa they had been accorded higher status than the black population. Lewis' study demonstrates how the women managed and re-negotiated complex ethnicised identities in the context of their families, their South African histories and their location in Western Australian society.

Amina Mama (1995) similarly found that black British women needed to negotiate the tensions they experienced from being constructed as behaving in ways that are 'not black enough'. Gail Lewis's (2000) study of black women social workers and Lutz's (1993) study of Turkish women social workers in the Netherlands and in Germany also show the tensions involved in black and Turkish women's negotiation of their racialised and gendered identities with minoritised and majoritised clients and often managers from the white majority ethnic group. All these issues – negotiations; emotional implications, the unconscious and the discursive construction of ethnicised identities – are accepted across a wide spectrum of theoretical positions as important to the framing of ethnicised identities.


## WHITENESS

[...] In attacking the notion that whiteness and Blackness are 'the same', we specifically undermine what has become, [...] via the notion of 'reverse racism', a major prop underpinning the popular refusal among whites to face both racism and themselves. [...]Whiteness is now a particularly brittle and fragile form of social identity and it can be fought. (Roediger, 1994: 12)

A major development in considerations of ethnicised identities has been acceptance that whiteness should not remain an unmarked term, but should be interrogated as an identity position. It was only at the beginning of the 1990s that a steady trickle of work on whiteness began to appear (Dyer, 1997; Fine et al., 1997; Gallagher, 1995; Hage, 1998; Hall, 1992; hooks, 1992; Ware, 1992). Such work made it clear that it was no longer acceptable for whiteness to be taken for granted as normative and unremarkable. Hooks (1992), for example, pointed out that black people living in the US have a history of habitually looking at white people since their safety depends on being able to read white people's actions and intentions. Relationality is thus consciously implicated in their identities.

By way of contrast, most white people have not been conscious of their whiteness. Frankenberg (1993) interviewed 30 white women in the US and found that many were 'race and power evasive'. Their narratives indicated that they made enormous efforts not to see 'race' and would sometimes deny having met any black people until relatively late in their lives, until they remembered black nannies or black neighbourhoods they knew in childhood. Many of Frankenberg's sample did not identify as white – considering that to do so would be racist (Billig, 1991). Instead, some employed humanist discourses in saying that they did not care whether someone was 'green, striped or purple', because we are all 'human'. This rendered their privileged position invisible in comparison to the problem of 'people of colour', leaving whiteness unexamined (Rothenberg, 2000; Wetherell and Potter, 1992). Part of the power imbued in whiteness arises from its taken-for-granted unmarkedness (Youdell, 2006).

This white exceptionalism makes the occasions when it becomes conscious, anxiety-provoking, ambivalent and discomfiting (Cohen, 1999a, 1999b; MacDonald et al., 1989; Perry, 2002; Winant, 2001). In an ethnographic study of a secondary school in the UK, Alice Pettigrew (2007) argues that white students have a limited understanding of their heritage that leads them to adopt temporally and spatially foreshortened frameworks for locating themselves and others in

their social world. This leads them to reject black students' claims to collective identities and to experience dilemmas and discomfiture about 'race', 'ethnicity' and nation. Pettigrew suggests that the notion of complicity is helpful in understanding white British subjectivities in that it emphasises differentiated experiences and the mutual constitution of relational identities. This empirically informed analysis fits with Gilroy's (2004a, b) theorisation of melancholia as part of contemporary white British identities noted above. Winant (2001) suggests that new anxieties about whiteness have emerged so that those who wish to transcend, forget or abolish it are as anxious as those who wish to preserve it. Whiteness, however, is no more homogeneous than any other racialised/ethnicised identity. Frankenberg (1993), for example, found that some of the white women she interviewed were 'race cognisant' and put effort into understanding how structural and institutional racial inequities operate.

A major site of differentiation in whiteness relates to its intersections with social class. Bev Skeggs' (1997) in-depth interview study of 83 young, white, working-class women makes clear some of the ways in which social class and gender pattern whiteness. Skeggs found that the women characteristically saw themselves through other people's eyes as 'less than' and 'not right' in contradistinction from the white middle classes, who they considered to embody value. In consequence, they focused on respectablility as central to their identities and identity projects.

The fact that whiteness constitutes a source of insecurity – particularly for the working classes – has led to some resentment against minority ethnic groups who are frequently constructed as responsible for the economic problems of the white working classes (Hewitt, 1996, 2005). Such discourses not only demonstrate the relationality and associated emotional marking of ethnicised identities, but paradoxically, can be argued to show identification with constructed aspects of blackness as well as desire for the other. In particular, they show identification with a position of non-responsibility for devalued status (since there is a racialised other to blame) while maintaining identification with whiteness as the more powerful racialised position. For some white young men, desire for the ethnicised other involves emulation of black boys in attempts to approximate hegemonic masculinity (Back, 1996; Frosh et al., 2002). Initiatives such as the British Broadcasting Corporation's *White Season* (BBC 2, March 2008) are no doubt in recognition of what has been called 'fragile white identities' (Giroux, 1998) by aiming to redress the invisibility of the white working classes. However, such initiatives potentially demonstrate the relevance of Gilroy's notion of melancholia in that they dehistoricisze white, working-class disadvantage and portray white, working-class identities as necessarily oppositional to migrants and constructed around racism.

Autobiographies of white identities contribute a more subtle view of whiteness that, for example, shows its intersections with gender, social class and religion (Caraway, 1991; Rothenberg, 2000). Dalton Conley's (2001) memoir *Honky* is unusual in documenting a white childhood spent in the predominantly black and Latino projects of New York's Lower East Side. His parents were artists who were from affluent, middle-class families, but were themselves economically impoverished. His story revolves around the experience of being almost the only white boy (he had a sister) in the housing complex. As a Yale sociologist, he suggests that his childhood constituted a sort of social science experiment on the meaning of being middle class 'by raising a kid from a so-called good family in a so-called bad neighborhood' (2001: xiii). The intersection of whiteness, masculinity and middle-class resources produced a complex mix of commonalities and differences with the black children in the neighbourhood, but provided him with educational and social advantages that his black peers did not have. While *Honky* has been critiqued for reproducing stereotypes of black families as all unsuccessful and all the same,

it does illuminate how historically and geographically located and relational are ethnicised identities and desires.

## CONCLUSION

Any consideration of ethnicities and identities is necessarily a story of change, contestation and debate. Such considerations are, however, arguably also exciting in illuminating the state-of-the-art in contemporary theorising. In different areas and from different theoretical frameworks, this chapter has documented a history of shifts in ethnicised identities, often from essentialised, fixed understandings of ethnicities and identities to more open theorisations and empirical analyses of multiplicity, dynamism, decentring and unconscious processes. In many ways it is a story of contrasting possibilities in that racisms remain current and are also mutable. Whiteness has been destabilised by being made visible and there are increasing reports of everyday practices of 'convivial multicultures' (Gilroy, 2004a).

The huge wave of hope and enthusiasm that greeted the election and inauguration of Barack Obama spells new possibilities for ethnicised identities to be lived as 'ordinary'. This is one way in which ethnicised identities can constitute epistemic resources (Moya, 2006). Ethnicised identities continue to be employed to justify violent conflicts and racialising cultures continue to be ordinary (Lewis, G. 2007). Perhaps for such reasons, the theoretical repudiation of fixed, bounded, ethnic identities often falls on deaf ears. It is, therefore, important that academic work continues to engage with the power differentials associated with 'the politics of belonging' (Yuval-Davis, 2006b). It also needs to analyse the banality and constructedness of ethnicised identities in an aspirational and future-oriented vision. Such a vision would necessarily foreground considerations of why ethnicities matter, why they should not and of how the ways in which we analyse them have consequences for social action (Anthias, 2001; Papadopoulos and Sharma, 2008).

# REFERENCES

Abrams, L.S. (2003) 'Contextual variations in young women's gender identity negotiations', *Psychology of Women Quarterly*, 27 (1): 64–74.

Alexander, J. (2006) 'Colonialism and its contemporaries: Feminist reflections on the state of war and the meaning of solidarity', *Rethinking Nordic Colonialism*. Greenland.

Alexander, J. and Mohanty, C.T. (1997) *Feminist Genealogies, Colonial Legacies, Democratic Futures*. New York: Routledge.

Ali, S. (2003) *Mixed-Race, Post-Race. Gender, New Ethnicities and Cultural Practices*. Oxford: Berg.

Allen, L., Bat-Chava, Y., Aber, J. and Seidman, E. (2005) 'Adolescent racial and ethnic identity in context', in G. Downey, J. Eccles and C. Chatman (eds), *Navigating the Future:Social Identity, Coping and Life Tasks* (pp. 143–66). New York: Russell Sage Foundation.

Anthias, F. (2007) 'Boundaries of "race" and ethnicity and questions about cultural belongings', in N. Gopalkrishnan and H. Babacan (eds), *Racisms in the New World Order: Realities of Cultures, Colours and Identity* (pp. 12–21). Newcastle: Cambridge Scholars Publishing.

Anthias, F. and Yuval-Davis, N. (1992) *Racialized Boundaries: Race, Nation, Gender, Colour and Class and the Anti-Racist Struggle*. London: Routledge.

Anthias, F. and Yuval-Davis, N. (1983) 'Contextualising feminism: Gender, ethnic and class divisions', *Feminist Review*, 15: 62–75.

Appadurai, A. (1996) *Modernity At Large: Cultural Dimensions of Globalization*. Minneapolis, MN: University of Minnesota Press.

Back, L. (1996) *New Ethnicities and Urban Culture: Racisms and Multiculture in Young Lives*. London: UCL Press.

Back, L. (2007) *The Art of Listening*. Oxford: Berg.

Banks, J. (1996) 'Measures of assimilation, pluralism, and marginality', in R.L. Jones (ed.), *Handbook of Tests and Measurements for Black Populations Vol. 2* (pp. 269–82). Hampton, VA: Cobb and Henry.

Barrett, M. (2007) *Children's Knowledge, Beliefs and Feelings about Nations and National Groups*. Hove: Psychology Press.

Barth, F. (1969) *Ethnic Groups and Boundaries*. Oslo: Scandinavian University Press.

BBC (2008) *White Season*. Available at: http://news.bbc.co.uk/1/hi/programmes/newsnight/7279997.stm (accessed 6 March 2008).

Berry, J.W., Phinney, J., Sam, D. and Vedder, P. (2006) *Immigrant Youth in Cultural Transition: Acculturation, Identity and Adaptations Across National Contexts*. New York: Psychology Press.

Bhavnani, K.-K. (1993) 'Comments on M.J.Spink's paper: Qualitative research on social representations', *Papers on Social Representations*, 2 (1): 55–60. Available at: http://www.psr.jku.at/PSR1993/2_1993Bhavn.pdf (accessed 23 December 2009).

Billig, M. (1995) *Banal Nationalism*. London: Sage.

Billig, M. (1991) *Ideology and Opinions:* Studies in Rhetorical Psychology. London: Sage.

Billig, M., Condor, S., Edwards, D., Gane, M., Middleton, D. and Radley, A.R. (1988) *Ideological Dilemmas*. London: Sage.

Bonilla-Silva, E. (2002) 'The linguistics of color blind Racism: How to talk nasty about blacks without sounding "racist"', *Critical Sociology*, 28 (1–2): 41–64.

Boulton, M. and Smith, P.K. (1992) 'Racial preferences and perceptions among Asian and European British middle school children', *Social Development*, 1: 55–65.

Brah, A. (1996) *Cartographies of Diaspora*. London: Routledge.

Brah, A. and Phoenix, A. (2004) 'Ain't I A woman? Revisiting intersectionality', *Journal of International Women's Studies*, 5 (3): 75–86.

Brubaker, R. (2004) *Ethnicity Without Groups*. Harvard, MA: Harvard University Press.

Buitelaar, M. (2006) '"I am the ultimate challenge": Accounts of intersectionality in the life-story of a well-known daughter of moroccan migrant workers in the Netherlands', *European Journal of Women's Studies*, 13: 259–76.

Bulmer, M. and Solomos, J. (eds) (2004) *Researching Race and Racism*. London: Routledge.

Caraway, N. (1991) *Segregated Sisterhood: Racism and the Politics of American Feminism*. Knoxville, TN: University of Tennessee Press.

Carrington, B. and Short, G. (1989) *Race and the Primary School*. Windsor: NFER-Nelson.

Centre for Contemporary Cultural Studies (1982) *The Empire Strikes Back: Race and Racism in 70s Britain*. London: Hutchinson.

Chávez, A.F. and Guido-DiBrito, F. (1999) 'Racial and ethnic identity and development', *New Directions for Adult and Continuing Education*, 84: 39–47.

Clark, K.B. (1963) *Prejudice and Your Child*. 2nd edn. Boston, MA: Beacon Press.

Clark, K.B. and Clark, M.P. (1939) 'The development of consciousness of self and the emergence of racial identification in negro preschool children', *Journal of Social Psychology*, 10: 591–9.

Clark, K.B. and Clark, M.P. (1947) 'Racial identification and preference in negro children', in T.M. Newcomb and E.L. Hartley (eds), *Readings in Social Psychology*. Pp. 169–78. New York: Holt, Rinehart and Winston.

Cohen, P. (1997) *Rethinking The Youth Question: Education, Labour and Cultural Studies*. London: Routledge.

Cohen, P. (1999a) *New Ethnicities, Old Racisms*. London: Zed Books.

Cohen, P. (1999b) 'Labouring under whiteness', in R. Frankenberg (ed.), *Displacing Whiteness: Essays in Social and Cultural Criticism*. Pp. 244–82. Durham, NC: Duke University Press.

Collins, P.H. (1998) 'It's all in the family: Intersections of gender, race and nation', *Hypatia*, 13 (3): 62–82.

Combahee River Collective (1977) *The Combahee River Collective Statement*. Available at: http://circuitous.org/scraps/combahee.html (accessed 23 December 2009).

Conley, D. (2001) *Honky*. USA: Vintage Books.

Connolly, P. (1998) *Racism, Gender Identities and Young Children: Social Relations in a Multi-Ethnic, Inner-City Primary School*. London: Routledge.

Crenshaw, K. (1989) 'Demarginalizing the intersection of race and sex: A black feminist critique of antidiscrimination doctrine, feminist theory and antiracist politics', *University of Chicago Legal Forum*, Volume 1989 pp. 139–67.

Crenshaw, K. (2009) 'Intersectionality – reflections on a twenty year old concept', Keynote address to Celebrating Intersectionality? Debates on a Multi-Faceted Concept in Gender Studies. International Conference Goethe-University January 23, Frankfurt.

Cross, W. (1971) 'Toward a psychology of black liberation: The negro-to-black convergence', *Black World*, 20: 13–27.

Cross, W. (1995) 'The psychology of nigrescence: Revising the cross model', in G. Ponterotto, J. Casas, L. Suzuki and C. Alexander (eds), *Handbook of Multi-cultural Counseling*, Pp. 93–122. Thousand Oaks, CA: Sage.

Davis, D. and Silver, B. (2003) 'Stereotype threat and race of interviewer effects in a survey on political knowledge', *American Journal of Political Science*, 47: 33–45.

Davis, K. (Director). (2005) *A Girl Like Me*. [Motion picture.]

Dhamoon, R. (2009) *Identity/Difference Politics: How difference is produced, and why it matters*, Vancouver: University of British Columbia.

Dixon, J. (2007) 'Prejudice, conflict and conflict reduction', in W. Hollway, H. Lucey and A. Phoenix (eds), Pp. 145–72. Buckingham: Open University Press.

Donald, P., Gosling, S., Hamilton, J., Hawkes, N., McKenzie, D. and Stronach, I. (1995) '"No problem here": Action research against racism in a mainly white area', *British Educational Research Journal*, 21 (3): 263–75.

Dyer, R. (1997) *White*. London and New York: Routledge.

Edney, H.T. (2006) 'New "doll test" produces ugly results by Hazel Trice Edney'. Available at: http://www.finalcall.com/artman/publish/article_2919.shtml#top (accessed 9 March 2008).

Eriksen, T.H. (2001) 'Ethnic identity, national identity and intergroup conflict: The significance of personal experiences', in L.A. Jussim (ed.), *Social Identity, Intergroup Conflict and Conflict Reduction*. Pp. 42–70. Oxford: Oxford University Press.

Essed, P. (1991) *Understanding Everyday Racism: An Interdisciplinary Theory*. London: Sage.

Fanon, F. (1967a) *Black Skin, White Masks*. New York: Grove.

Fanon, F. (1967b) *The Wretched of the Earth*. Harmonsdworth: Penguin.

Fine, M., Weis, L., Powell, L. C. and Mun Wong, L. (eds) (1997) *Off White: Readings on Race, Power and Society*. London: Routledge.

Frankenberg, R. (1993) *White Women, Race Matters: The Social Construction of Whiteness*. London: Routledge.

Frosh, S., Phoenix, A. and Pattman, R. (2002) *Young Masculinities*. London: MacMillan.

Gaine, C. (2006) *We're All White Thanks: The Persisting Myth About 'White' Schools*. Stoke-on-Trent: Trentham Books.

Gallagher, C.A. (1995) 'White reconstruction in the university', *Socialist Review*, 24 (1/2): 165–87.

Genocide, I.f. (2008) 'Genocide watch: Kenya', International Association of Genocide Scholars. Available at: http://www.isg-iags.org/actionalerts/20080101.html

Georgas, J., Berry, J., van de Vijver, F., Kagitçibasi, Ç. and Poortinga, Y. (2006) *Families Across Cultures: A 30 Nation Psychological Study*. Cambridge: Cambridge University Press.

Gillborn, D. (2008) *Racism and Education: Coincidence or Conspiracy?* London: Routledge.

Gilroy, P. (1987) *There Ain't No Black in the Union Jack*. London: Routledge.

Gilroy, P. (2000) *Against Race: Imagining Political Culture Beyond the Color Line*. Cambridge, MA: Harvard University Press.

Gilroy, P. (2004a) *After Empire: Multiculture or Postcolonial Melancholia*. London: Routledge.

Gilroy, P. (2004b) *Melancholia and Multiculture*. Available at: http://www.opendemocracy.net/arts-multiculturalism/article_2035.jsp (accessed 13 March 2008).

Giroux, H. (1998) 'White noise: Toward a pedagogy of whiteness', in K. Myrsiades and L. Myrsiades (eds), *Race-ing Representation: Voice, History and Sexuality*. Pp. 42–76. London: Rowman and Littlefield.

Goldberg, T. (2005) 'Racial Americanization', in K. Murji and J. Solomos (eds), *Racialization: Studies in Theory*. Pp. 87–102. Oxford: Oxford University Press.

Grabham, E.,Cooper, D., Krishnadas, J. and Herman, D. (2008) *Intersectionality and Beyond: Law, Power and the Politics of Location*. London: Routledge-Cavendish.

Griffin, C. (1985) *Typical Girls? Young Women from School to the Job Market*. London: Routledge and Kegan Paul.

Gunaratnam, Y. and Lewis, G. (2001) 'Racialising emotional labour and emotionalising racialised labour: Anger, fear and shame in social welfare', *Journal of Social Work Practice*, 15 (2): 131–48.

Hage, G. (1998) *White Nation: Fantasies of White Supremacy in a Multicultural Society*. Annandale, VA: Pluto Press.

Hall, C. (1992) *White, Male and Middle Class*. Cambridge: Polity.

Hall, S. (2007) 'Epilogue: Through the prism of an intellectual life', in B. Meeks (ed.), *Culture, Politics, Race and Diaspora*, Pp. 269–91. London: Lawrence and Wishart.

Hall, S. (1992) 'Questions of cultural identity', in S. Hall, D. Held and T. McGrew (eds), *Modernity and its Futures*, Pp. 274–316. Cambridge: Polity.

Helms, J.E. and Parham, T.A. (1996) 'The racial identity attitude scale', in R.L. Jones (ed.), *The Handbook of Tests and Measures for Black Populations*, Pp. 167–72. Oakland, CA: Cobb and Henry.

Hewitt, R. (2005) *White Backlash and the Politics of Multiculturalism*. Cambridge: Cambridge University Press.

Hewitt, R. (1996) *Routes of Racism: The Social Basis of Racist Action*. Stoke-on-Trent: Trentham Books.

Hewitt, R. (1986) *White Talk, Black Talk: Inter-racial Friendship and Communication amongst Adolescents*. Cambridge: Cambridge University Press.

Hochschild, A. (1983) *The Managed Heart: Commercialization of Human Feeling*. Berkeley, CA: University of California Press.

Hollway, W. and Jefferson, T. (2000) *Doing Qualitative Research Differently*. London: Sage.

Holmes, R. (1995) *How Young Children Perceive Race*. Thousand Oaks, CA: Sage.

hooks, b. (1992) *Black Looks: Race and Representation*. Boston: South End Press.

Howarth, C. (2002) '"So, you're from Brixton?": The struggle for recognition and esteem in a multicultural community', *Ethnicities*, 2 (2): 237–60.

Hutnik, N. (1991) *Ethnic Minority Identity: A Social Psychological Perspective*. Oxford: Clarendon Press.

Karner, C. (2007) *Ethnicity and Everyday Life*. London: Routledge.

Lewis, A.E. (2003) 'Everyday race-making: Navigating racial boundaries in schools', *American Behavioral Scientist*, 47 (3): 283–305.

Lewis, G. (2000) *'Race', Gender and Social Welfare*. Cambridge: Polity.

Lewis, G. (2007) 'Racializing culture is ordinary', *Cultural Studies*, 21 (6): 866–86.

Lewis, G. and Phoenix, A. (2004) 'Racialisation and ethnicisation', in K. Woodward (ed.), *Questioning Identity*, Pp. 115–50. London: Routledge.

Lewis, R. (2007) 'The construction of identity through race and ethnicity: Coloured South African women in Western Australia'. PhD thesis, Edith Cowan University.

Lutz, H. (1993) 'In between or bridging cultural gaps? Migrant women from turkey as mediators', *New Community*, 19 (3): 485–92.

Lutz, H. (2008) *Migration and Domestic Work: A European Perspective on a Global Theme*. London: Ashgate.

MacDonald, I., Bhavnani, R., Khan, L. and John, G. (1989) *Murder in the Playground: The Report of the MacDonald Inquiry into Racism and Racial Violence in Manchester Schools*. London: Longsight Press.

Major, B. and O'Brien, L.T. (2005) The social psychology of stigma. *Annual Review of Psychology*, 56: 393–421.

Mama, A. (1995) *Beyond the Masks: Race, Gender and Subjectivity*. London: Routledge.

Marx, D.M. and Goff, P.A. (2005) 'Clearing the air: The effect of experimenter race on targets, test performance and subjective experience', *British Journal of Social Psychology*, 44: 645–57.

McCall, L. (2005) 'The complexity of intersectionality', *Signs: Journal of Women's Studies*, 30 (31): 1771–802.

Milner, D. (1983) *Children and Race Ten Years On*. London: Ward Lock Educational.

Mohanty, C.T. (2003) *Feminism without Borders: Decolonizing Theory, Practicing Solidarity*. Durham, NC: Duke University Press.

Moya, P. (2000) 'Introduction: reclaiming identity', in P. Moya and M. Hames-Garcia (eds), *Reclaiming Identity: Realist Theory and the Predicament of Postmodernism*, Pp. 1–28. Berkeley, CA: University of California Press.

Moya, P. (2006) 'What's Identity Got to do With It? Mobilizing Identities in the Multicultural Classroom', in L. M. Alcoff, M. Hames-García, S. P. Mohanty, and P. M. L. Moya (eds) *Identity Politics Reconsidered*. pp. 96-117, New York: Palgrave MacMillan.

Murphy, J., Brown, H. and John, M. (eds) (1984) *Dialogues and Debates in Social Psychology*. Hove: Lawrence Erlbaum Associates.

Murji, K. and Solomos, J. (eds) (2005) *Racialization: Studies in Theory and Practice*. Oxford: Oxford University Press.

Nash, J.C. (2008) 'Re-thinking intersectionality', *Feminist Review*, 89 (1): 1–15.

Nicholson, L. (ed.) (1997) *The Second Wave: A Reader in Feminist Theory*. New York: Routledge.

Ogilvy, C., Boath, E., Cheyne, W.M., Jahoda, G. and Schaffer, H.R. (1990) 'Staff attitudes and perceptions in multi-cultural nursery schools', *Early Child Development and Care*, pp. 1–13.

Ogilvy, C., Boath, E., Cheyne, W.M., Jahoda, G. and Schaffer, H.R. (1992) 'Staff-child interaction styles in multi-ethnic nursery schools', *British Journal of Developmental Psychology*, 10: 85–97.

Okeley, J. (1987) 'Privileged, schooled and finished: Boarding school education for girls', in G. Weiner and M. Arnot (eds), *Gender Under Scrutiny*, Pp. 101–13. London: Hutchinson.

Omi, M. and Winant, H. (1986) *Racial Formation in the United States: From the 1960s to the 1980s*. New York: Routledge.

Papadopoulos, D. and Sharma, S. (2008) 'Race/matter – materialism and the politics of racialization'. Available at: http://www.darkmatter101.org/site/wp-content/uploads/2008/02/Race-Materiality-Issue2-Feb08-darkmatter.pdf (accessed 13 March 2008).

Perry, P. (2002) *Shades of White: White Kids and Racial Identities in High School*. Durham, NC: Duke University Press.

Pettigrew, A. (2007) 'Complexity, complicity and community in the classroom and curriculum: identifications with "ethnicity", "race" and "nation" in a British secondary school', PhD thesis, University of the West of England.

Phinney, J. (1990) 'Ethnic identity in adolescents and adults: A review of research', *Psychological Bulletin*, 108: 499–514.

Phinney, J. (1992) 'The multi-group ethnic identity measure: A new scale for use with adolescents and young adults from diverse groups', *Journal of Adolescent Research*, 7: 156–76.

Phinney, J. (1995) 'Ethnic identity and self-esteem: A review and integration', in A. Padilla (ed.), *Hispanic Psychology: Critical Issues in Theory and Research*, Pp. 57–70. Thousand Oaks: Sage.

Phinney, J. (2003) 'Ethnic identity and acculturation', in K. Chun, P. Ball and G. Marin (eds), *Acculturation: Advances in Theory, Measurement and Applied Research*. Washington, DC: American Psychological Association.

Phinney, J. (2005a) 'Ethnic identity in late modern times: A response to rattansi and phoenix', *Identity: An International Journal of Research and Theory*, 5 (2): 187–94.

Phinney, J. (2005b) 'Ethnic identity among immigrant youth: A cross national perspective', Talk to UCLA Center for Research, Education, Training, and Strategic Communication on Minority Health Disparities. Available at: www.lsic.ucla.edu/classes/psych/mays/phinney.html

Phoenix, A. and Rattansi, A. (2005) 'Proliferating theories: Self and identity in post-eriksonian contexy: A rejoinder to Berzonsky, Kroger, Levine, Phinney, Schachter, and Weigert and Gecas', *Identity: An International Journal of Theory and Research*, 5 (2): 205–25.

Phoenix, A. and Tizard, B. (1996) 'Thinking through class: The place of social class in the lives of young londoners', *Feminism and Psychology*, 6: 427–42.

Prins, B. (2006) 'Narrative accounts of origins: A blind spot in the intersectional approach?', *European Journal of Women's Studies*, 13: 277–90.

Quintana, S. and McKown, C. (2008) 'Introduction: Race, racism and the developing child', in S. Quintana and C. McKown (eds), *Handbook of Race, Racism and the Developing Child*. Pp. 1–16. Hoboken, NJ: John Wiley.

Quintana, S., Aboud, F., Chao, R., Contreras-Grau, J., Cross, W., Hudley, C., et al. (2006) 'Race, ethnicity, and culture in child development: Contemporary research and future directions', *Child Development*, 77 (5): 1129.

Rampton, B., Dover, C., Harris, R., Georgakopolou, A. and Leung, C. (2008) *Urban Classroom Culture and Interaction*. London: Identities and Social Action, ESRC.

Räthzel, N. (2008) *Finding the Way Home: Young People's Stories of Gender, Ethnicity, Class and*

*Places in Hamburg and London.* Göttingen: V&R Unipress.

Rathzel, N. (1994) 'Harmonious "heimat" and disturbing "auslander"', *Feminism and Psychology.* Reprinted in K.-K. Bhavnani and A. Phoenix (eds), *Shifting Identities Shifting Racisms*, 4: 81–98. London: Sage.

Rattansi, A. (1992) 'Changing the subject? racism, culture and education', in J. Donald and A. Rattansi (eds), Pp. 11–48. *'Race', Culture and Difference.* London: Sage.

Rattansi, A. (1994) ' "Western" racisms, ethnicities and identities', in A. Rattansi and S. Westwood (eds), *Racism, Modernity and Identity: On the Western Front*, Pp. 15–86. Cambridge: Polity Press.

Rattansi, A. (2007) *Racism: A Very Short Introduction.* Oxford: Oxford University Press.

Reicher, S. (2004) 'The context of social identity: Domination, resistance and change', *Political Psychology*, 25: 921–45.

Restrepo, E. (2004) 'Ethnicization of blackness in colombia', *Cultural Studies*, 18 (5): 698–753.

Reynolds, K.J. and Turner, J.C. (2006) 'Individuality', *European Review of Social Psychology*, pp. 233–70.

Roediger, D. (1994) *Towards the Abolition of Whiteness.* London: Verso.

Rothenberg, P. (2000) *Invisible Privilege: A Memoir About Race, Class and Gender.* Lawrence, Kansas: University of Kansas Press.

Seeberg, M.L. (2003) *Dealing with Difference: Two Classrooms, Two Countries. A Comparative Study of Norwegian and Dutch Processes of Alterity and Identity, Drawn from Three Points of View.* Bergen: University of Bergen.

Seligman, M.E.P. (2004) *Authentic Happiness: Using the New Positive Psychology to Realize Your Potential for Lasting Fulfillment.* New York: Free Press.

Shelton, J.N., Richeson, J.A. and Vorauer, J.D. (2006) 'Threatened identities and interethnic interactions', *European Review of Social Psychology*, 17 (1): 321–58.

Short, G. (1991) 'Prejudice, power and racism: Some reflections on the anti-racist critique of multi-cultural education', *Journal of Philosophy of Education*, 25 (1): 5–16.

Skeggs, B. (1997) *Formations of Class and Gender: Becoming Respectable.* London: Sage.

Skeggs, B. (2006a) 'Which bits to exploit? Making value from emotional telling on reality TV', *PhD Course on Intersectional Analysis*, 18–20. January. Aalborg, Denmark.

Skeggs, B. (2006b) 'Respectability – becoming a proper person', *Inaugural Professorial Lecture.* London: University of London.

Solomos, J. and Back, L. (eds) (2000) *Theories of Race and Racism: A Reader.* London: Routledge.

Sonuga-Barke, E.J.S., Minocha, K., Taylor, E. and Sandberg, S. (1993) 'Inter-ethnic bias in teacher's ratings of hyperactivity', *British Journal of Developmental Psychology*, 11: 187–200.

Staunaes, D. (2005) 'From culturally avant-garde to sexually promiscuous: Troubling subjectivities and intersections in the social transition from childhood into youth', *Feminism and Psychology*, 15 (2): 149–67.

Steele, C. (1997) 'A threat in the air: How stereotypes shape intellectual identity and performance. *American Psychologist*, 52: 613–29.

Steele, C. and Aronson, J. (1995) 'Stereotype threat and the intellectual test performance of african-americans', *Journal of Personality and Social Psychology*, 69 (5): 797–811.

Sudbury, J. (1998) *Other Kinds of Dreams: Black Women's Organizations and the Politics of Transformation.* London: Routledge.

Tajfel, H. (1974) 'Social identity and intergroup behavior', *Social Science Information*, 13: 65–93.

Tatum, B. (2003) *'Why Are All The Black Kids Sitting Together in the Cafeteria?': A Psychologist Explains the Development of Racial Identity.* New York: Basic Books.

Thornton, Dill, B. and Nettles, S.M. (2001) 'What do we mean by intersections?' *Connections.* Available at: http://www.crge.umd.edu/pdf/RC2001 spring.pdf

Tizard, B. and Phoenix, A. (2002) *Black, White or Mixed Race? Race and Racism in the Lives of Young People of Mixed Parentage.* 2nd edn. London: Routledge.

Troyna, B. and Hatcher, R. (1992) *Racism in Children's Lives: A Study of Mainly White Primary Schools.* London: Routledge.

Van Ausdale, D. and Feagin, J. (2001) *The First R: How Children Learn Race and Racism.* Lanham, MD: Rowman and Littlefield.

Van Dijk, T. (1993) *Elite Discourse and Racism.* Newbury Park, CA: Sage.

Vandiver, B., Fhagen-Smith, P., Cokley, K. and Cross, W. (2001) 'Cross's nigrescence model: From theory to scale to theory', *Journal of Multicultural Counseling and Development*, 29 (3): 174–200.

Verkuyten, M. (2008) 'Perceived discrimination, ethnic minority identity and self-esteem', in S. Quintana and C. McKown (eds), *Handbook of Race, Racism and the Developing Child*, Pp. 339–65. Hoboken, NJ: John Wiley.

Verkuyten, M. and Nekuee, S. (2001) 'Self-esteem, discrimination and coping among refugees: The moderating role of self-categorization', *Journal of Applied Social Psychology*, 31 (5): 1058–75.

Verkuyten, M., Drabbles, M. and Nieuwenhuijzen, K.V. (1999) 'Self-categorisation and emotional reactions to ethnic minorities', *European Journal of Social Psychology*, 29 (5–6): 605–19.

Verloo, M. (2006) 'Multiple inequalities, intersectionality and the european union', *European Journal of Women's Studies*, 13 (3): 211–28.

Ware, V. (1992) *Beyond the Pale*. London: Verso.

Watson, G. (1981) 'The reification of ethnicity and its political consequence in the north', *Canadian Review of Sociology and Anthropology*, 18 (4): 453–69.

Wetherell, M. (1998) 'Positioning and interpretative repertoires: Conversation analysis and post-structuralism in dialogue', *Discourse and Society*, 9: 387–412.

Wetherell, M. and Potter, J. (1992) *Mapping the Language of Racism: Discourse and the Legitimation of Exploitation*. London: Sage.

Williams, P. (1997) *Seeing a Color-Blind Future: The Paradox of Race (Reith Lectures, 1997)*. New York: Noonday Press.

Wilson, T.D. and Gilbert, D.T. (2005) 'Affective forecasting: Knowing what to want', *Current Directions in Psychological Science*, pp. 131–34.

Winant, H. (2001) 'White racial projects', in B. Rasmussen, I. Nexica and M. Wray (eds), *The Making and Unmaking of Whiteness*, Pp. 97–112. Durham, NC: Duke University Press.

Woods, R. (2007) 'Children defining and experiencing racism in 21st century Britain', *Cronem*. Surrey.

Worrell, F. (2006) 'The relationship between racial and ethnic identity in black adolescents: The cross racial identity scale and the multigroup ethnic identity measure', *Identity*, 6 (4): 293–315.

Wright, C. (1992) *Race Relations in the Primary School*. London: David Fulton Publishers.

Youdell, D. (2006) 'Subjectivation and performative politics–butler thinking althusser and foucault: Intelligibility, agency and the raced-nationed-religioned subjects of education', *British Journal of the Sociology of Education*, pp. 511–28.

Yuval-Davis, N. (2006a) 'Intersectionality and feminist Politics', *European Journal of Women Studies*, 13 (3): 193–210.

Yuval-Davis, N. (2006b) 'Belonging and the politics of belonging', *Patterns of Prejudice*, 40 (3): 197–214.

# 16

# Genders: Deconstructed, Reconstructed, Still on the Move

## Lynne Segal

If the study of identities is a key nodal point for interdisciplinary research in the social sciences and humanities, 'gender' remains *a*, if not *the*, pivotal point in the study of identities, with their continuously shifting frameworks, formations, sites and categories. Conversely, shifting understandings of the frameworks, formations, sites and categories of identity impact upon and become part of what constitutes our notions of gender, sex and sexuality, whether seen as our inescapable predicament, notions we would like to subvert or dispose of, incentives for voluntary self-fashioning. This is just one of the reasons why, as Dave Glover and Cora Kaplan note: 'Gender is now one of the most restless terms in the English language, a word that crops up everywhere, yet whose uses seem to be forever changing, always on the move, producing new and often surprising inflections of meaning' (2000: ix). Such discursive prolixity has grown around what was, in English, once merely a grammatical term relating to the assumed biological sex of a person, as male or female (Scott, 1988: 29).

That 'gender' is now ubiquitous as a topic for debate in disciplines across the Humanities and Social Sciences, and has even become an interdisciplinary field in its own right, is itself evidence of the highly diverse and contested nature of the issues it addresses. It is also a testament to the impact and authority of feminist thought and research across differing scholarly domains, as well as to the numerous confrontations with feminist epistemologies, from both within and without. Gender today remains as controversial as it is inescapable, controversial *because* it still seems inescapable, despite all the differing attempts to displace or diversify it as a core site of identity. The theorising, situating, performing, refashioning or undoing of 'gender' (more recently of genders), always shadowed by apprehensions around sexuality, has from the beginning aroused unease, ambiguity and resistance. To understand the perpetual return of old anxieties around sex, gender and sexuality, we need to rehearse some of them, as they have differing implications for analysing identities.

## SEX BEFORE GENDER

The late nineteenth century is generally regarded as the crucible for the gender patterns of western modernity. It consolidated the notion, if never the actualities, of separate spheres for men and women, with their associated presumptive/prescriptive mentalities: man's independence, toil and leadership outside the home establishing his authority within the family; the bourgeois wife's gentle, nurturing, spiritual ways exemplifying woman's estate. As historian Thomas Laqueur argues, prior to the nineteenth century sexual differences were seen to vary as 'matters of degree rather than in kind' (Laqueur, 1990: 125). However, in the very instant of the consolidation of sexual difference there were already rising anxieties over the place and nature of men and women. From the second half of the nineteenth century the rise of first wave feminism was seen as putting manhood in danger, wherever it arose: the 'masculine woman' (those seeking education or the right to vote) undermined the 'natural' demarcations of sexed difference. The impact of Darwin on the medical sciences, alongside the newly emerging field of sexology, was mostly understood as entailing 'the divergent evolution of the sexes', as the influential British biologists Geddes and Thompson argued in 1899: males are more 'active, passionate and variable'; females 'more passive, conservative, sluggish and stable' (Geddes and Thompson, 1998: 16). Furthermore, the Darwinian significance accorded sexual differentiation merged with racist views of the day to declare African, Asian and Jewish bodies less sexually segregated than that of the Aryan, and hence more degenerate. Before committing suicide in 1903, at the age of 23, the Jewish writer Otto Weininger mirrored the escalating European anti-Semitism of the early twentieth century in his book *Sex and Character*, insisting that Jewish man was saturated with femininity, making him more sexually obsessed and devoid of any form of manly heroism or greatness (Weininger, 2005). Male and female identities were one's biological fate, as was racial hierarchy.

Again, no sooner were sexologists and other researchers scrutinising and classifying these proper contrasts between men and women (physical, sexual, psychological) than sexual variations, or 'aberrations' leapt out at every turn. In Britain in 1904, Havelock Ellis (2006) was detailing the primordial contrasts between men and women, while simultaneously documenting the multiple variations within the sexes. With no notion of gender separate from biological sex, and with sex in its natural manifestation directed towards reproductive goals, the existence of sexual variations, especially homosexuality, was attributed by Karl Ulrichs in Germany, and Edward Carpenter in Britain, to the existence of a 'third' or 'intermediate sex'. However, it was soon clear that observing and quantifying the possible variations in sex related activities produced biological mayhem. That exuberant recorder of sexual diversity, the German sexologist Magnus Hirschfeld, suggested that there were almost infinite forms of 'sexual intermediaries', as everybody was to some degree biologically transgendered or bisexual. This led him to argue that not only were there no pure forms of masculinity or femininity, but that counting up all the possible variations in sexual organs, physical characteristics, sex drive and emotional characteristics – ranging from the 'womanly woman' to the 'manly man' – produced over 43 million specific variations in sexual proclivities (Hirschfeld in Bland and Doan, 1998: 103). As we will see, Hirschfeld's theoretical outlook at the opening of the twentieth century would only be fully resumed and differently materialised at its closing, in contemporary discourses and practices of transgender politics.

The instability of the psychic installation of sexual difference quickly proved a prominent feature in Freud's writing, as psychoanalysis crept into western thinking from the closing decades of the nineteenth century, soon vying with social Darwinism and sexology. Freud too was diligently recording the existence of identity problems and perverse sexualities; indeed, in his *Three Essays on Sexuality* (1977), adult heterosexuality was seen as emerging only out of earlier forms of polymorphous perversity, and never truly transcending it. Relatedly, and crucially, Freud suggested that there was no basic psychic sexual difference at birth (1979: 141). He saw the psychic consequences of sexual difference as the bedrock of identity, yet its foundations were always precarious (see Frosh, Chapter 1 this volume). From 1905 onwards, Freud's ideas became increasingly more sophisticated, highlighting the psychic ambivalence shadowing all the presumed biological certainties of his day around 'masculinity' and 'femininity', 'activity' and 'passivity'. Like Hirschfeld, Freud was anticipating trends that would re-appear (through a somewhat different philosophical lens) only at the end of the century, this time in the Derridean deconstructive turn, where hierarchical binaries are always unstable and contradictory, haunted by all they attempt to exclude. In a footnote added to his *Three Essays* in 1915 Freud tried to clarify the matter:

> It is essential to understand clearly that the concepts of 'masculine' and 'feminine', whose meaning seems so unambiguous to ordinary people, are among the most confused that occur in science [...] in human beings pure masculinity or femininity is not to be found either in a biological or a psychological sense. Every individual displays a mixture of the character-traits belonging to his own and the opposite sex; and he shows a combination of activity and passivity whether or not these [...] tally with his biological ones. (1979: 142–3)

However, despite Freud's best efforts, confused these concepts would remain, not least in his own writing, which retained the essential polarity of sexual difference even as he questioned it: 'A woman who has loved in the masculine way will hardly let herself be forced into playing the part of a woman', he writes in 1920, concluding the case study of his briefly analysed young lesbian patient' (Freud, 1979: 400). Freud did not speak of gender identities, but rather of psychic structures formed through identifications, most often with the parent of the same sex as the child. Nevertheless, in charting the vicissitudes of psychosexual development on the pathway towards 'mature' heterosexual manhood or womanhood (a state he thought may indeed never materialise), Freud began the displacement of the Darwinian installation of biology, alone, as the key to human identity, that is, he began the move from biology to

culture. The move to culture would only be consolidated once 'gender' came to be used as an analytic tool half a century later, although the job of untangling the confusions surrounding what exactly gender signifies is far from concluded.

Varied as its usages would quickly become, the first significant attempt to employ the concept of gender, independently from that of biological sex, only emerges in the late 1960s. It is most often associated with the writing of the psychoanalytically trained Californian psychiatrist, Robert Stoller. In *Sex and Gender* Stoller (1968) drew upon his work with transsexuals to argue the importance of distinguishing 'sex', in the biological sense of anatomical difference, from 'gender identity', as a psychological category, and from 'gender role', as an expected form of social behaviour. Disagreeing with Freud, who saw the psychical consequences of anatomical difference emerging later, Stoller suggested that children acquire a strong sense of their gender identity in the first few years of life. However, this notion of 'core-gender identity' trails disorder in its wake: 'the two realms (sex and gender) are not inevitably bound in anything like a one-to-one relationship, but may go into quite independent ways' (Stoller, 1968: 29). Nevertheless, even Stoller could not have foreseen quite how intrepid the independent voyages of these differing notions of sex, gender identities, and gender roles, were to become. This is because the academic delineations and research agendas addressing 'gender' were soon variously entangled both within and between competing disciplinary frameworks, as well as within and between the shifting outlook and goals of different movements for liberation.

## WOMEN'S LIBERATION AND THE RISE OF GENDER THEORY

The explosion of interest in gender and its multiple manifestations occurred along with the birth of second wave feminism, also at the close of the 1960s. Thus for many years, at least in the Anglophone world, thinking about gender was all but synonymous with thinking about women and their secondary place in the world. Furthermore, for a while, exploring the social, cultural and psychological configurations of gender primarily involved confronting the authoritative voice of a biological determinism that had been used, hitherto, to position women overall as belonging to the subordinate sex: establishing them as weaker, subordinate, servicing, passive, submissive creatures in comparison with the men. 'Gender' was, then, first of all, the name English-speaking feminists began to use for the acquired, culturally diverse, hence mutable ways of becoming a woman – or a man. However, with manhood already the designation for humanity, it was women, rather than men, who were the sex apparently marked out by their gender, their 'femininity' differentiating them from the basic model. From the beginning, also, in ways that would only gradually be refined, 'gender' was used in at least four overlapping ways: to refer to distinctive *personal attributes*, especially those associated with women and 'femininity'; to *cultural processes* operating in the acquisition of such attributes; to *language* and the differential symbolic value of gender-related terms and discourses; to the hierarchical *power relations* maintaining men overall as the dominant sex.

Within the feminist milieu first instigating the research on gender in the 1970s, Simone de Beavoir's (1949) *The Second Sex* was a guiding light. Published over two decades earlier, Beauvoir had not herself used the notion of gender, but had undertaken the broadest possible sweep across scholarly domains to describe what it meant to be situated, and identified, *as* a woman: 'One is not born, but rather becomes a woman'. In that becoming, readers would learn, woman is installed in her condition as 'object and prey' for man, never as 'sovereign subject'. Women had yet to be recognised by men as 'free and autonomous' beings, just like them. Beauvoir's goal was to establish that a woman's behaviour is not dictated by her physiology, but shaped by her situation: her grasp upon the world, the world's grasp upon her. Beauvoir did notice the age-old dilemma confronting 'an emancipated woman', who must refuse 'to confine herself to her role as female, because she will not accept mutilation', though aware that 'it would also be a mutilation to repudiate her sex' (Beauvoir, 1973: 295, 29, 328). It was this dilemma that, as we shall see, provided the first wave of contention within gender theories.

Aware of the way in which the belief in natural sex differences had served to constrain and marginalise women, social scientists in the 1970s tended to look for gender *similarities*, suggesting, along the lines of Ann Oakley, that the apparently stable differences between men and women were 'ineradicably over-ridden by cultural learning' (1972: 170). Within psychology, sex-difference research increased a thousand-fold from the late 1960s (Spence, 1993: 5). Following Maccoby and Jacklin's classic survey in 1974, indicating that psychologists hitherto had actually found, though failed to highlight, more similarities than differences between the sexes, it became customary to overview the research literature on sex differences every 10 years. As distinct from the few that would grab media headlines, the general findings of this research over the decades continued to emphasise 'gender similarities', pointing to the importance of social context whenever differences were found (Deaux, 1984; Hyde, 2005). However, other psychologists argued that even highlighting sex-similarities still endorsed a way of looking at the world generated within polarised gender categories, and one reducing gender itself to individual attributes (c.f. see articles in Kitzinger, 1994). Most feminist psychologists therefore turned away from the mainstream preoccupation with individual attributes, introducing instead a theoretical literature that incorporated a broader 'social construction' framework. Social constructionism explained the distinctiveness of women's lives in terms of their specific social context, and the meanings assigned to activities or experiences conventionally performed by, or attributed to, women. Here, gender attributes were no longer reduced to stable individual abilities or traits, but were nevertheless still seen as the culturally induced incorporation of central and abiding patterns of activities and outlooks typifying 'femininity', which also served to install and entrench women's subordinate social position compared to men.

As with the 'mismeasure' or misreporting of individual attributes, new research across the social sciences and humanities emphasised the disparagement shadowing discourses addressing the feminine, alongside the hurdles women faced compared to men throughout all phases of their lives. Within the diversity of approaches to gender research, the text most often cited to clarify the notion of gender as a product of culture was that of the American anthropologist, Gayle Rubin's (1975) essay *The Traffic in Women: Notes on the Political Economy of Sex*. Here she argued that anatomical markers of difference were used to construct a 'sex-gender system' that incorporates the ways in which any particular society conceives and organises kinship, reproduction, sexuality, including all the institutional practices and divisions of labour governing relations between the sexes, which confined women and men to separate and opposed groups and confirmed men as the dominant sex. Although universal, the diversity of sex-gender systems made it evident that there was nothing either biological or inevitable about this process: 'Far from being an expression of natural differences, exclusive gender identity is the suppression of natural similarities' (Rubin, 1975: 179–80).

It was the persistence of women's subordination to men, throughout all historical periods and differing economic and political structures, which led many feminists at this time to refer to 'patriarchy' as a universal structure for ensuring male domination over women. Radical feminists, in particular, saw patriarchy as fundamental to all social hierarchies, deriving from the power of the father

in the family, giving men control over women's sexuality and fertility (Delphy, 1977). Socialist feminists, in contrast, tended to emphasise that women's subordination had no single cause. They analysed the complex and contradictory ways in which production processes and the family are related to each other, making the maintenance or undermining of gender hierarchies inseparable from addressing all other forms of social domination and cultural oppression (Beechey, 1979). Meanwhile, liberal feminists, originally most evident in organisations such as NOW (National Organization of Women) in the USA, believed that gender hierarchy could be overcome by reforms in existing social arrangements, encouraging women's equal participation in all areas of public life (Friedan, 1978). Whatever their precise political orientation, however, all feminists in the 1970s were primarily preoccupied with demonstrating women's institutional marginalisation and cultural denigrations.

The search for symbolic and material sites, practices and discourses of gender would dispatch armies of researchers. Summarising decades of gender publications in the early 1990s, psychologists Rhoda Unger and Mary Crawford concluded: 'Boys have no difficulty becoming "men", but girls become "women" reluctantly and at a later age. Maturity does not confer status on women' (1992: 170). Beyond the academy, at its crucial interface with the media, it was the psychologist Carol Gilligan's studies of adolescent girls in the US which had provided the best known qualitative research, suggesting that girls lose out on reaching puberty by pressures to abandon their autonomy and become acceptable to men (Brown and Gilligan, 1992). In the gender theory consolidated in the 1980s, no cultural site was seen as outside the formation and maintenance of hierarchical gender relations, from the apparently most personal realm of sexual intimacies, to familial structures, the workplace, ruling elites, or any other sphere of human activity (Connell, 1987). Inevitably, trying to theorise the complex usages of gender as an analytic tool, from attending to gender's complex modes of production to its outcome as a form of identity, however conceived or misconceived, was bound to produce significant contention. Despite, and because of, so much research on gender, it remained unclear just what gender identity was, indeed, whether it was something women wanted to affirm, or to question and transcend.

## IDENTITY INVESTMENT vs PROLIFERATIONS OF DIFFERENCE

Gender theory enabled feminists to highlight the ways in which anatomical differences were culturally encoded to produce and inflate gender disparities. However, from the mid-1970s, there was always a parallel process of asserting the potential of 'feminine' difference, as women's bodies, minds and varied but distinct identities were to be reclaimed from the ideological disparagements and institutionalised disadvantages hitherto attending them. Adrienne Rich's (1976) *Of Women Born* serves as a landmark text in this move, celebrating the revolutionary potential of women's life-giving bodies and maternal experiences. Though erased in the ubiquitous hegemonic regime of 'compulsory heterosexuality', Rich would later relocate female nurturing along a subterranean 'lesbian continuum', which she saw existing in all 'women-identified' women, those attentively caring for each other from cradle to grave. Mirrored in subsequent feminist appropriations of psychoanalytic object-relations theory, especially in the wake of Nancy Chodorow (1978), this writing on difference would soon lead many feminist scholars to distance themselves from and belittle their early mentor, Simone de Beauvoir, nowhere more so than in France (Segal, 2007: 164–72).

Paradoxically, the appeal of what became known as 'difference-theory', prioritising gender contrasts in many of the most influential scholarly and popular forums of

Anglo-American feminism, occurred alongside a parallel but potentially problematic interest in the divisions between women themselves. Thus the 1980s also saw anger directed at the false universalising of 'gender' analysis, and any accompanying claim to women's shared identities and values (whether as wives, mothers, daughters or anything else) coming, for instance, in black, feminist challenges criticising earlier failures to prioritise racism, poverty, or ethnic specificities, when addressing women's lives (Anzaldua, 1987; Lorde, 1981). The centrality and significance of attending to gender difference was thus always threatened by the proliferation of other differences, which might well place women and men together in more similar contexts of power, or vulnerability (Mohanty, 1991). These dilemmas surrounding the multiplicity of identities in the houses of difference, at its height in what has often been described as the battles over 'identity politics' of the 1980s, were only further compounded with the impact of poststructuralism and deconstruction on feminist and gender scholarship from the close of the decade.

Poststructuralism questioned the category of personal experience, while emphasising the complexity and volatility of all discursive positions. The French philosopher Jacques Derrida's 'deconstructive' method of studying texts was used by feminists such as Gayatri Spivak, in postcolonial criticism, and Judith Butler, in feminist reappraisals, to uncover the metaphysical error of assuming that knowledge is grounded in any foundational experience, rather than in the shifting heterogeneity of discourses that serve to produce meaning (Butler, 1990; Spivak, 1987). Although hostile to sociological theories of gender, feminist psychoanalytic literature influenced by Jacques Lacan similarly eschewed notions of gender identities, or experience, to address the pivotal place of sexual difference at the heart of the Symbolic order. From this perspective, gender theorists had mistakenly focused on social and material aspects of women's subordination, ignoring the deeper *linguistic asymmetry* between the sexes: the semiotic and symbolic structures that place women outside its categories of representation, irrespective of specific social and political arrangements. In significant contrast with the object-relations views mentioned above, stressing the contrasting gender identities flowing from female mothering, Lacanian interpretations suggest that 'femininity' is never securely acquired, but rather that 'the unconscious constantly reveals the failure of identity', in the words of Jacqueline Rose (1986: 91). Even so, although sexual difference is seen here as a site of instability and failure, at the individual unconscious level it is nevertheless presented as a permanent structure in the timeless Symbolic. Inescapable antagonism between the sexes is thus inscribed within the Lacanian formation of subjectivity, despite the impossibility of any positive articulation of the 'feminine', or any eradication of women's negative entry into culture through the transformation of differing practices in specific institutional sites.

Given the foreclosure of any affirmation of the feminine within the Lacanian Symbolic, for many the most puzzling, yet seductively challenging, of all theorists of difference were those who used Lacan's erasure of the 'feminine' to invent their own alternative dissident poetics of the 'feminine feminine'. Thus Hélène Cixous and Luce Irigaray alongside, if somewhat distinct from, Julia Kristeva, celebrated the subversive potential of the tactile, rhythmic semiosis of the pre-Oedipal, pre-symbolic, maternal murmurings and communications, to subvert and disorder the Symbolic order. This particular troubling of the phallocentric symbolic order, however, could be thought of as challenging traditional ways of thinking only to the extent that the notion of feminine 'difference' remained forever on the move, something that seemed to arise from no existing categories but rather always stretching what is conceivable, as the US feminist scholar Drucilla Cornell suggested, remaining free from 'any of the identifications we know and imagine as Woman' (1995: 147). However, such avant-garde

feminist aesthetics, aiming to speak the silenced or unspeakable, describe the unnoticed or unreadable, was criticised by prominent postcolonial feminist critics, including Gayatri Spivak (1987), for its continued privileging of *sexual* difference over all other forms of difference. Other critics, myself included, worried that the new interest in difference, including developing a vision of the feminine to empower women, whether defined in terms its nurturing or corporeal specificities, or its disruptive 'otherness', now threatened to downplay not only the multiplicity of differences, but to displace the original point of historicising gender. That original goal was a sweeping if often chaotic attempt to promote women's self-affirmation alongside a feminist politics of gender equality, whether in the public sphere or personal life, to enable the development of the diverse skills, talents and potential of women everywhere (Felski, 1997; Fraser, 2007; Segal, 1999).

Looking back, these feminist battles over the minimising or maximising of gender or sexual difference, added to all the contention that arose over gender's intersection with other axes of oppression and disadvantage, seem largely inevitable. Both yesterday and today women have oscillated between passionate identification with women are supposed to be and the desire to escape the constraining shackles of the feminine. As British, feminist theorist and poet Denise Riley suggests, feminism will always have to 'negotiate the quicksands of "women" which will not allow it to settle on either identities or counter-identities, but which condemn it to an incessant striving for a brief foothold' (1988: 5). Nevertheless, by the 1990s the differing battles over difference, parity, otherness, and poststructuralism's questioning of all identity categories, led some feminist scholars to conclude that gender theory, if not feminist scholarship itself, was exhausted, as American philosopher Linda Alcoff (1988) worried at the close of the 1980s, in an essay addressing 'the identity crisis in feminist theory.' This anxiety around gender categories has continued up to the present, as

Kath Weston (2002) noted in her book *Gender in Real Time*. Yet feminists have been neither able to retreat from nor resolve the many questions gender raises.

## GENDERING MEN

Just when feminists were most embattled over how best to theorise women's distinct gender identity, or diverse differences, a new recognition that men might have gender troubles of their own was consolidated in writing and research undertaken by men developing an interest in gender. It took over a decade to mature, but in the mid-to-late-1980s 'Men's Studies' was launched in the US (see the chapters in Brod, 1987). In the 1990s the abundance of books and articles addressing men and masculinity grew rapidly, with research on the difficulties facing boys on their pathway to adulthood catching up with the attention hitherto directed at girls and women (Edley and Wetherell, 1995). Setting the scene, one of the early researchers in the US, Joseph Pleck (1981), produced several studies suggesting that gender expectations regulating men's expression of acceptable masculine identities were restrictive, contradictory and confusing, promoting dysfunctional behaviour in many boys and men. Using a different theoretical framework, Chodorow's work on the lasting effects of girls' early identification with nurturing mothers (implanting women's greater relational capacities at the expense of any firm sense of autonomy) was reversed by some male clinicians, such as William Pollack, to highlight the greater pitfalls boys faced in becoming men: boys having to 'disidentify' from mother and all things seen as tender or dependent, creating lasting trauma (Levant and Pollock, 1995).

Such unprecedented interest in men and masculinity occurred at a time when rising unemployment and other economic shifts were beginning to have an increasing effect on the lives of disadvantaged groups of men,

even though, popular lament notwithstanding, the new hazards uncovered in men's lives were rarely the direct effect of changes underway in the world of women (Segal, 2007: xx–xxiii). As with women, the growing research on men's lives, conduct and self-perceptions quickly revealed evidence of ambiguity, complexity and mutability in notions of 'masculinity'. Attempting to stabilise the concept, R.W. Connell (1995), for instance, wrote of the notion of 'hegemonic masculinity', not to refer to normative notions of masculinity (in terms of toughness, independence, assertiveness) as any stable set of acquired attributes, but rather as socio-historical configurations of multiple gender practices that together work to legitimate male dominance. Similarly, in my own writing I used existing research and theorising to suggest that 'masculinity' is an abstraction, condensing notions of power and authority, which required us to speak of multiple masculinities to encompass the position of those groups of men who are definitively situated *outside* the western masculine ideal of straight, white, heterosexual manhood (Segal, 2007).

Hegemonic or normative masculinity, therefore, was not seen here as reducible to the specific identities or behaviour of particular men, but rather to a set of assumptions and expectations produced within institutional sites of men's power, from family lives, schoolrooms, workplaces, sporting rituals to ruling political and cultural elites. Masculinity theorists who remained sympathetic to the feminist goal of eliminating traditional patterns of gender hierarchy not only highlighted the need to recognise diversities of masculinities, but also, in differing ways, drew attention to the instabilities and fraudulence of masculinity's dominant ideals. Historians of manhood, such as George Mosse (1996), pointed out that normative masculinity was regularly seen as undermined in panics over effeminacy, its survival threatened by the presence of sexual deviancy (especially homosexuality) or other threats from those it positioned as inferior.

The 'proofs' of masculinity always relied upon upholding its timeless contrasts with, and dominance over, some other subordinate term that was perpetually threatening to escape from its inferior place – such as 'femininity' (Kimme, 1996l; Segal, (1990).

## QUEER CHALLENGES: SUBVERSIONS VERSUS RECUPERATIONS

Men and women were now jointly engaged in studying the diversities of gender identities when a new challenge to any form of identity theorising arose in academic forums, known as 'queer theory'. Queer agendas first appeared as a type of political activism in the US in the late 1980s, with gays, lesbians and other sexual dissidents organising against social and cultural discrimination and abuse, against obscenity laws (including feminist campaigns to criminalise pornography) and, above all, against the lack of adequate official response to the crisis of HIV/AIDS, then decimating the male gay community. In the absence of universal healthcare and the presence of homophobic panic around HIV/AIDS, the AIDS Coalition to Unleash Power (ACT UP) was formed as a new liberation movement in the US. Almost immediately, earlier forms of identity politics and community activism, whether feminist, gay or lesbian, were declared redundant, especially with the growing awareness that the AIDS threat was not confined to clearly identified sexual groups. Queer's criticism of former identity positions was heightened by the fact that its activism appeared just when the rapid absorption of poststructuralist ideas and deconstruction was making its mark on academic theorising. With both 'femininity' and then 'masculinity' already seen by gender theorists as culturally contingent, queer theory was soon broadcasting the possibilities for further subversion or playful reversals of gender and sexual categories as 'queer methodology' stood out in cutting-edge scholarship on certain academic platforms throughout the 1990s.

Judith Butler's *Gender Trouble*, with its distinctive appropriations of philosophical poststructuralism, provided the founding text for most queer theorists, eager to expose the linguistic mobility, or performativity, of both sexed bodies and gender categories: 'There is no gender identity behind the expressions of gender [...] Identity is performatively constituted by the very "expressions" that are said to be its results' (Butler, 1990: 29). In Butler's work, the human body was seen as acquiring its sexed markings through the range of discourses available for assigning significance to a definitive range of bodily activities, leaving unmarked or unmentionable other possibilities inherent in those same bodies. On this perspective, the very category of sex itself was no longer seen as existing outside culture and prior to gender, but rather the significance given to certain anatomical markings, in particular the body parts identified with and incited to perform within the active/passive binary (or 'heterosexual matrix') for distinguishing male from female performance: assigning 'phallic' activity to male bodies; receptive passivity to female bodies. Within such constraining linguistic binaries, the only ones available for giving an account of ourselves, Butler argues that the assertion of a heterosexual identity necessarily entails the suppression of the possibility of homoerotic desire. Identity-formation thus foregrounds only certain differences, negating others, while also encouraging individuals to project inner conflicts and inconsistencies outwards into differences between themselves and other types of people. Here also, the earlier stress placed on the significance of the sex/gender distinction is itself seen as firming up rather than loosening the separation between biology and culture, as well as making gender rather than sex pivotal in differentiating women from men. Butler would later reflect that some of the theorising in *Gender Trouble* had seemed most clearly instantiated as she pondered the gendered performance of drag queens in gay bars, when she realised that some men could do femininity much better she could, or wanted to: 'And so I was confronted by the transferability of the attribute' (2004: 213).

The transferability of the attribute, including that most privileged signifier disguised as all-powerful, the phallus, was in a sense at the heart of Queer's rethinking of genders. A diverse array of queer theorists were soon celebrating the subversive possibilities for exposing the artificiality or constructedness of oppositional gender markings and thereby undermining the 'heteronormative' universe, as Michael Warner (1993) designated the old sex/gender order in his *Fear of a Queer Planet*. Spelling out some of queer's repercussions for the transferability of gender signifiers, Eve Sedgwick suggested that 'masculinity did not necessarily belong to men, nor femininity to women' (1995: 13). Elaborating this point at the close of the 1990s, Judith Halberstam's (1998) *Female Masculinity* traced the notion back to the 'female husband' and the 'androgyne' of earlier times through to the more familiar 'tomboy', 'butch dyke' or 'lesbian boy' today. Detached from actual men, queer theorists saw such hybrid identities as a significant way of undermining the oppressive aspects of normative masculinity, with its apparent 'naturalised relation between maleness and power' (Halberstam, 1998: 2). 'The marvellous revival of butch-femme erotics reminded us that we knew how to turn masculinity on its head [...] macho dykes in leather [...] have undone the phallus with their collection of dildos', Cindy Patton agreed (1994: 239). Drawing on his reformulations of psychoanalytic thinking, gay cultural theorist Leo Bersani (1987) had earlier made a parallel if slightly different point. Gay men may 'gnaw at the roots of male heterosexual identity', but this is not so much in their exposure or parody of masculinity's constructedness, but rather that, despite their 'nearly mad identification with it, *they never cease to feel the appeal of it being violated*' (Bersani, 1987: 209).

As we saw above, it was Robert Stoller's account of the pathological plight of transsexuals, those desiring bodily transformations in line with their sense of self, which launched the contemporary notion of 'gender' in the social sciences. Neatly inverting this history, those proudly proclaiming that they are 'transsexual by choice, not by pathology', see themselves as undermining, perhaps fatally, the existing notion of gender: the cultural imperative to be either a man or a woman (Bornstein, 1994: 118; Wilchins, 1997). Although far from speaking for all transsexuals, those who like to see themselves as 'gender outlaws' argue that the greater availability of transsexual technologies, hormone replacement therapies, assisted reproductive technologies, together contribute to a continuing push for the legal recognition of recombined or hybrid genderings that will, one day, spell out the end of gender (Carver, 2007; Herdt, 1994). Arguments for the recognition of a multiplicity of genders has also come from biological knowledge about the existence of the 'intersexed'. In her book, *Sexing the Body*, the North American biologist, Anne Fausto-Sterling, argues that human sexuality is best understood not as a dichotomy but as a continuum, because 1.7 per cent of human births are born with irregularities that mean they cannot be not firmly located within either the male or the female sex: 'If nature really offers us more than two sexes then it follows that our current notions of masculinity and femininity are cultural conceits' (2000: 31).

Proclaiming the potential indeterminacy of gender via collective enactments of diverse trans-gender crossings, dissident sexualities or the biological variations of the intersexed, has been crucial in providing places for many people to speak from, belong to, or use as a basis for advocacy, demanding equal treatment in law. These are people whose non-heteronormative existence, if not hidden, had hitherto made them targets for abuse, their lives often barely liveable. Yet, as I have suggested elsewhere, in its celebration of the endless permutations of the staging of the self, whether as bulldagger, lipstick lesbian, drag queen, leather clone, metamorph, or whatever, there is a danger of queer celebrations becoming more, rather than less, obsessed with gender: foregrounding its pluralistic performativities, without necessarily escaping the long shadow of its coercive symbolic, structural and discursive histories (Segal, 1999: 60–6). We are still left needing to know *why* it is that gendered markings and sexual preferences remain such key site of identity, despite the visibility of their diversities. As Marge Garber (1992) points out, it should never have been hard to notice the transgressive allure of the less firmly gendered, especially when Freud long ago emphasised the perverse dynamics underpinning presumptions of innate sexual difference and adult heterosexual adjustment (Freud, 1905). Yet, as I explored in *Straight Sex* and *Why Feminism*, to date, both sexual and gender hierarchies have shown a remarkable capacity to thrive *despite* the evidence of their obvious inconsistencies, instabilities and knowledge of the work that goes into maintaining them; indeed, *despite* the attraction, repulsion, tolerance, anxiety, disdain or violence others may express when confronting those violating normative mandates, as in queer's theatres of subversion (Segal, 1994, 1999: ch. 5). Furthermore, the radical surgical invasiveness accompanying transsexual shifts seem to confirm the continuing inescapable grip of gender binaries, quite as much as any dismantling of them.

As if in confirmation of gender's still ruling hegemony over conceivable biological, or evolutionary, mandates, it is gender, rather than sex, which is seen as the fixed and fundamental category in transsexual crossings, the body merely its mismatched facade. Indeed, female to male transsexual Jay Prosser argues that if we listen carefully to transsexual and transgendered narratives, they suggest 'not the revelation of the fictionality of gendered categories but [rather] the sobering realisation of their ongoing foundational power', fictional or not (1998: 11). Additionally, the 'postmodern' attention to bodily markers of these leading queer theorists (mostly situated within the US academy) can be seen as entirely in tune with, rather than confronting, capitalism's restless

strivings for the commodification of almost anything, seen especially in the soaring expansion of cosmetic surgeries and pharmaceutical marketings. Furthermore, Butler herself was always more sceptical than some of her followers about claims that the exposure of gender fictions and performativities could easily disrupt or undo their coercive implanting. In an early interview she explained:

> What's interesting is that this voluntarist interpretation, this desire for a kind of radical theatrical remaking of the body, is obviously out there in the public sphere. There's a desire for a fully phantasmatic transfiguration of the body. But no, I don't think that drag is a paradigm for the subversion of gender. I don't think that if we were all more dragged out gender life would become more expansive and less restrictive [...] drag has its own melancholia. (Osborne and Segal, 1994: 35)

From the beginning, Butler emphasised as well that one could not anticipate exactly how queer might continue its task of challenging normative gender structures and discourses, if it did, since it must remain itself always flexible, even open to yielding 'in favour of terms that do [its] political work more effectively' (Butler, 1993: 230).

Interestingly, despite stressing the continuing significance of placing identities (of any sort) under erasure, including their own identities, today it is sometimes queer scholars themselves who have begun examining the limits of their queer epistemology, stressing the dangers of what they call 'queer liberalism' (see chapters in Eng et al., 2005; Morland and Wilcox, 2005). In my view, it is important to welcome, not dismiss, this fraught dialogue between questioning all identity categories (applauding the spaces where gender flexibilities and sexual ambiguities flourish), even as we also notice the significance of, even necessity for, the psychological assurances and political efficacy that identity categories can offer. It seems clear enough that the questioning of gendered identities and the disclosure of the fraudulence of binary thinking does not on its own undo the diverse economic and political structures, which often themselves prove remarkably flexible. It is the concatenation of discursive, economic and political structures that together work to maintain, undermine or rebuild identity positions, in the case of gender so often managing to shore up or refashion the symbolic entitlements of the 'masculine' (perhaps nowadays even when seemingly embodied or enacted by a woman), thereby still entailing the relative insignificance and vulnerability of the 'feminine' (even when seemingly embodied or enacted by a man).

## GLOBALISING GENDERS

Whatever our fondness or disdain for the assertion of traditional gender identities, there is some scholarly consensus today that gender markings, insofar as they apply to individuals, are best seen as over-determined, conflicting, always ongoing processes of *becoming*, in which 'gendering' practices shift over a life time. This helps us understand the apparent inconsistencies in ongoing research on expressions of metropolitan western gendered identities, whether of men or women. Researching men, Margaret Wetherell and Nigel Edley (1999), for instance, have stressed the ironic, playful, often detached attitudes many men express in relation to dominant ideals of heroic masculinity. In partial agreement, cultural researchers, such as Bethan Benwell (2004), highlight the persistently self-mocking and evasive images of masculinity in the men's life-style magazines, such as *FHM* or *Loaded*, which flourished from the 1990s. However, parallel research, emphasising the power of dominant ideals of masculinity, finds London schoolboys still fearful of not being thought adequately tough, cool, interested in sport, and more, in ways that both control and restrict the range of behaviour permissible in boys (Frosh et al., 2002). Such ambiguities, coupling apparent sexual confidence in young people with extensive anxieties over the possession of appropriate and acceptable

gendered bodies and behaviour, persist ubiquitously in research on both women and men in the affluent world.

Researching gender and the media more broadly, British researcher Ros Gill (2006) notes that the idea of 'girl power', for instance, sits uncomfortably alongside reports of epidemic levels of anorexia among young women. Meanwhile, studies of young men's sense of well-being increasingly report that the continuing objectification of the men's bodies, and the rising consumption of steroid supplements, have combined with media celebration of the muscular 'six-pack' male torso, generating negative body images and lowered self-acceptance in boys, even rising rates of anorexia (Tager et al., 2006). Everywhere, it seems, aspects of traditional sexism are being reworked, encouraging people's attempts to exhibit acceptable gendered bodies, though operating in new, sometimes heightened if more ingenious, ways than before. Pondering such ambiguities in women's lives, Angela McRobbie (2008), who studied the culture and conduct of young women in the UK for over 30 years, argues that gender relations are currently being re-stabilised in western democracies by falsely assuming the existence of sexual equality, with women exhorted to discard any lessons from feminism. In her view, the media's meretricious promotion of female freedom exhorts 'top girls' to become champions of their own lives through the tireless consumption of fashion, beauty and possibilities for career success, even celebrity, while simultaneously delighting in the sexist humiliation and harsh denigration of any famous woman at the least sign of her failing.

Such treacherous promotion of female 'celebrity' in a supposedly post-feminist world also works to separate images of the affluent western woman from the unseen existence of other female folk, whose lives in the factory treadmills of the so-called Third World, or struggling to survive as immigrant workers elsewhere, are airbrushed away. From the US, veteran feminists, Barbara Ehrenreich and Arlie Hochschild (2003), have been recording the voices of those they call 'global woman', noting the distinctly gendered experiences of immigrant domestic labourers, nannies and childminders, forced by economic necessity to abandon their own homes and children to service the personal needs of others in richer countries. These women are nowadays indispensable to meet the 'care deficit' in the 'over-developed' world, where women, much like men, are trying to manage the ever-lengthening working day in more competitive and insecure sites of paid labour. What is new about today's domestic worker, who bares certain similarities to the live-in maids or even wet-nurses of old, is the vast distance separating them from the world and family they have left. Surveying Britain, Rosie Cox (2006) asserts that there are well over two million domestic servants today, more than there were in Victorian times. Moreover, many of those domestic workers are trapped by immigration rules that allow them to enter and remain in the UK only so long as they stay with the particular families that engaged their services. Paid little above meagre board and lodgings, and with no regulation of their working conditions, many of these women end up as lonely au pairs, having little social contact with those around them and, all too often, scant protection from the serious exploitation of their labour. In Cox's view, this results in the virtual slavery of some undocumented servants. Many factors combine to produce the situation of these new domestic workers, including the high levels of global inequality, women's place working the long hours required of today's job market, together with the inadequacies of public childcare provision. However, it is also a product of the continuing lack of equal participation by men in childcare and domestic tasks. Overall, as surveys across Europe and in North America testify, although men overall have increased their participation in such activities, the average wife or female partner still does over twice as much housework and childcare as the average man each day, and even more in times of domestic crisis, as when children are sick (Burchell et al., 2007; Sayer, 2005).

Although significantly updated to meet the demands of the contemporary global economy, traditional gender practices thus continue to determine many aspects of the lives of both men and women worldwide. This suggests that whatever the potential flexibility and volatility of our conceptions of both genders and sexualities, everyday practices continue to rub up against the gendered actualities of lived experience, and the cultural resources available for making sense of them. As we have seen, traditional images of women as second-class and vulnerable are reinforced by postcolonial labour flows treating armies of women from poorer women as a uniquely servicing class of nannies, cleaners and sexual-servicers. At the very same time, professional armies of men, equipped with high-tech tools of destruction, are moving from richer to poorer countries, increasingly deployed in military actions in regions strategically important for the economic interests of the current world superpower, the US, and its minions (Venn, 2006: 157–8). Any optimism surrounding the proliferation of more egalitarian and compassionate images of masculine identities in western discourses, therefore, is currently being undermined by the intensified growth of militaristic embodiments of masculinity around the globe, especially after the Al-Qaeda orchestrated destruction of the World Trade Center in Manhattan, on September 11, 2001. Moreover, it is such regressive gender dynamics that help explain the recent rise of religious fundamentalism. As some commentators from the Islamic world noted at the time, the spectacular 'triumph' of 9/11 was adroitly staged both to assuage the sense of inferiority and injustice of a deeply divided Muslim world and then to ignite its anger against the western military onslaught certain to follow (Belge, 2001). In virile mimicry, western hawks become fundamentalism's willing allies, as the US, supported by the UK, launched its own deliberately awesome military invasions, followed by occupation, in Afghanistan and Iraq.

Inevitably, in warfare we see the wholesale refurbishment of 'masculinist' postures and practices, with the long-term effects of armed conflict and displaced populations that follow from it everywhere giving rise to dramatic leaps in violence against women, and increased sexual trafficking of women (Cockburn, 2007; Enloe, 2004). It is also notable that women now make up 15 per cent of the ranks of these new warriors, but they must find a niche within the virile cultures of bantering brutality and boredom that typify army life, as former US sergeant Kayla Williams (2006) epitomises when recording her contempt for any women soldiers showing signs of weakness in this macho world. In Israel, now one of the most militarised societies in the developed world, some feminists have spent at least a decade researching and publicising the effects this has on their society. As Rela Mazali (2003) notes, militarism generates its own regressive gender dynamics, with its potent hierarchies and bullying machismo, solidified around notions of conquest, duty and service. Feminist research has indicated that as many as 80 per cent of Israeli women soldiers say they have experienced some form of sexual harassment, while also highlighting the permeable boundaries between the military and the civil society, revealing significantly higher percentages of women murdered or beaten by male partners serving in the Israeli Defence Force (Adelman, 2003).

The effect of militarism in securing traditional notions of masculinity is thus one side of the current global conjuncture. There is another side, as Mazali has also highlighted, detailing the high rates of suicide and stress experienced by Israeli men in the Israeli Defence Force, which go almost completely unreported (Mazali, 1995). Looking closely at the effects of warfare on gender identities and practices elsewhere, we need to heed the secrets veiled behind military machismo. We hear little of the long-term effects of armed combat in shattering men's identities, with male soldiers and civilians caught up in war zones not only facing death and physical

dismemberment, but also possible experiences of sexual humiliation, rape and other forms of bodily abuse at the hands of 'the enemy' (Bourke, 1996; Jones, 2004). Moreover, men's symbolic 'unmanning' in bodily degradations on battlefields, or captivity, so appallingly evident in the recent revelations of torture and sexual humiliation of prisoners in Abu-Graub, is only the most extreme version of ways in which men can be made to feel helpless, passive and victimised throughout their lives, whether in schoolyards, workplaces, wherever. Revealing men's bodily vulnerabilities, including their susceptibility to rape, is another way of undermining gender polarities. It is not one, however, that either men themselves or women have till recently been prepared to admit. Focusing on the nuances of men's actual suffering could also serve to undermine dominant the myths of 'masculinity', those repudiating the vulnerabilities men share with women. As Judith Butler (2004) argues in *Precarious Life*, were we to begin from the understanding that all human bodies are fundamentally dependent and vulnerable, we might find new grounds for stressing gender similarities. Our common condition as individuals, she stresses, is precisely this shared helplessness, as evident in the susceptibility of our desires and attachments to rejection and loss, as in our enduring physical vulnerability.

Taking on board the intersections of gender with ethnicity and conflict in the global arena also raises other conceptual problems for gender and feminist scholars. As western feminisms have struggled for release from the residues of patriarchal control over female bodies and sexualities, quite different choices have emerged from some women claiming they are seeking alternatives to the imperiousness of western modernity. Facing current forms of western economic and military belligerence, the wearing of the veil has been claimed as a defiant and empowering personal choice by some Islamic women, especially within western contexts where they are freer to reject such veiling practices.

Researching contemporary Islam, Turkish scholar Nilüfer Göle (2002) suggests it is precisely in their proximity to rather than their distance from modern life that has triggered a return to religious identity among migrant Muslims in Europe. Referring to women who once embraced wholly secular, western ways, Göle notes the emergence of a contradictory stance today. The Islamic headscarf is deliberately appropriated rather than passively worn, claimed by a new generation of women who have had access to higher education but chosen to reject assimilation to western regimes of emancipation to assert instead their public visibility and embodied difference through an affirmation of Islamic identity. Here, we find women returning to claiming difference as an empowering identity, this time in the face of what they see as an often-hostile west. Referring to the fierce debate within French feminism over the wearing of the veil in the classroom, Göle (2007) confidently critiques those feminists who sided with the authorities trying to ban the veil, claiming that migrant girls adopting the Islamic headscarf in French and German schools today are closer in many respects to their classmates than to their first-generation, homebound, uneducated mothers. Difficult as it may seem to translate, it is surely clear that there are new ways of challenging traditionally conceived notions of gender when they intersect with challenges to westernised notions of modernity and globalisation.

## CONCLUSION: GENDERS AND GENDERING

As I indicated at the opening of this chapter, gender is one of the most elusive of topics to isolate and analyse. This is all the more difficult if we think of genders not so much as a form of social organisation or a cultural semiotics for mapping the body, but in terms of identities: whether these are seen as attributes of individuals, layerings of personality, structures of consciousness, or the

diverse performativities that have been variously used to theorise sexed subjectivities. In much of the new theorising of gender it is clear that its meanings are always on the move, with gender shifting from a primarily biological category to a near exclusively cultural process. Moreover, the particular fears, anxieties and desires associated with gender identities clearly change over a life time, sometimes appearing very much to the fore, a key focus of interest, at other times seeming to retreat into the background of a life. Still nurturing seeds that were implanted by Freud's first descriptions of the polymorphous perverse infant just over a century ago, some recent psychoanalytic framings, describing themselves as 'postmodern', argue that the best way of viewing ourselves is always through a lens of irony or scepticism, one that enables us to tolerate, if not embrace, ambiguities and change in our gendered self-perceptions (Dimen and Goldner, 2002). In thereby calling into question the fixity of gender binarism, it becomes possible to pluralise the notion of gender. The possibility of there being more than two genders was eagerly embraced by those influenced by queer epistemology or claims about the intersexed. Here, from a place where some felt that how the world situated them was at odds with how they experienced themselves, it could be argued that gender should refer to however people 'choose' to position themselves. On this view, then, we should think not of gender but of genders, allowing for the possibility of multiple genders to encompass those who see themselves as neither purely masculine nor feminine, but combinations of the two, or anything in between, which is sometimes the goal of those eager for the end of gender altogether.

Yet, for all its multiplicities of meaning and fluidities of enactment, many of the old polarities between women and men, femininity and masculinity, continue to embed themselves anew. This volatile mixture, of course, is hardly unique to gender, at least when viewed as a form of identity. Identities in general always tend to be on the move.

Yet we cannot manage without them. It's not just, as James Baldwin once said, that identities form 'the garment with which one covers the nakedness of the self', but that we lack recognisable selves at all, without such garments (1976: 77). Identities, as we now know, are indeed best seen as unstable, contingent, and always in need of re-affirmation through the performative work (to use Butler's language) we must do to stabilise them as safe and secure marks of our existence. Nevertheless, our descriptive markings, whether seen as freely chosen or else thrust upon us, may still not be quite as fluid as some recent theorising has been suggesting. Moreover, in her recent writing, and against the thrust of her earlier critics, the Butler of today always insists rather forcefully: 'What operates at the level of cultural fantasy is not finally dissociable from the ways in which material life is organised' (2004: 214). The way in which material life is being organised, as we saw above, has far from eliminated the warp and weave of old gender patterns, which is just what the new world of shifting labour migrations, intensified warfare and other gendered imprints of the global contemporary force us to acknowledge.

## REFERENCES

Adelman, M. (2003) 'The military, militarism and the militarization of domestic violence', *Violence Against Women*, 9 (9): 1118–52.

Alcoff, L. (1988) 'Cultural feminism versus post-structuralism: The identity crisis in feminist theory', *Signs*, Spring, 13 (3): 33–50.

Anzaldua, G. (1987) *Borderlands/La Frontera: The New Mestiza*. San Francisco, CA: Spinsters, Aunt Lute.

Baldwin, J. (1976) *The Devil Finds Work*. New York: Dial Press.

De Beauvoir, S. (1973) *The Second Sex*. 1st edn 1949. New York: Vintage Press.

Beechey, V. (1979) 'On patriarchy', *Feminist Review*, 3: 66–82.

Belge, M. (2001) 'Inside the fundamentalist mind'. Available at: http://www.openDemocracy (last accessed on 4 October, 2001).

Benwell, B. (2004) 'Ironic discourse: Evasive masculinity in men's lifestyle magazines', *Men and Masculinities*, 7 (1): 3–21.

Bornstein, K. (1994) *Gender Outlaw: On Men, Women, and the Rest of Us*. London: Routledge.

Bourke, J. (1996) *Dismembering the Male: Men's Bodies, Britain, and the Great War*. Chicago, IL: University of Chicago Press.

Brod, H. (ed.) (1987) *The Making of Masculinities: The New Men's Studies*. Boston, MA: Allen and Unwin.

Brown, L.M. and Gilligan, C. (1992) *Meeting at the Crossroads*. Cambridge, MA: Harvard University Press.

Burchell, B. Fagian, C. and O'Brie Materialist Feminismn, C. Smith, M (2007) *Gender and Working Conditions in the European Union*. Available at: http://www.eurofound.europa.eu/ publications/htmlfiles. Last accessed in 2008.

Butler, J. (1990) *Gender Trouble: Feminism and the Subversion of Identity*. London and New York: Routledge.

Butler, J. (1993) *Bodies That Matter*. London and New York: Routledge.

Butler, J. (2004) *Precarious Life: The Power of Mourning and Violence*. London: Verso.

Carver, T. (2007) 'Trans'-trouble: Trans-sexuality and the end of GENDER', in J. Browne (ed.), *The Future of Gender*. Cambridge: Cambridge University Press, pp. 116–135.

Chodorow, N. (1978) *The Reproduction of Motherhood: Psychoanalysis and the Sociology of Gender*. London: University of California Press.

Cockburn, C. (2007) *From Where We Stand: War, Women's Activism and Feminist Analysis* London and New York: Zed Books.

Connell, R.W. (1987) *Gender and Power: Society, the Person and Sexual Politics*. Cambridge: Polity Press.

R.W. Connell (1995), *Masculinities*, Cambridge: Polity Press.

Cornell, D. (1995) 'Rethinking the time of feminism', in S. Benhabib et al. (eds), *Feminist Contentions: A Philosophical Exchange*. London: Routledge, pp. 17–43.

Cox, R. (2006) *The Servant Problem: Paid Domestic Work in a Global Economy*. London: I.B. Taurus.

Deaux, K. (1984) 'From individual differences to social categories: Analysis of a decade's research on gender', *American Psychologist*, February: 105–116.

Delphy, C. (1977) *The Main Enemy: Materialist Analysis of Women's Oppression*. London: Women's Research and Resources Centre.

Dimen, M. and Goldner, V. (2002) *Gender in Psychoanalytic Space*. New York: Other Press.

Edley, N. and Wetherell, M. (1995) *Men in Perspective: Practice Power and Identity*. Hemel Hampstead: Harvester Wheatsheaf.

Ehrenreich, B. and Hochschild, A. (eds) (2003) *Global Woman: Nannies, Maids and Sex Workers in the New Economy*. London: Granta Books.

Ellis, H. (2006) *Man and Woman: A Study of Human Secondary Sexual Characters*. Kila, Montana: Kessinger Publishing Co. [1st edn 1904.]

Eng, D.L., Halberstam, J. and Munoz, J.E. (2005) 'What's queer about queer studies now?', *Special Issue of Social Text*, 84–85.

Enloe, C. (2004), *The Curious Feminist: Searching for Women in a New Age of Empire* L. Berkeley, CA: University of California Press.

Fausto-Sterling, A. (2000) S*exing the Body: Gender Politics and the Construction of Sexuality*. New York: Basic Books.

Felski, R. (1997) 'The doxa of difference', *Signs*, 23 (1): 41–56.

Fraser, N. (2007) 'Mapping the feminist imagination: From redistribution to recognition to representation', in J. Browne (ed.), *The Future of Gender*. Cambridge: Cambridge University Press, pp. 6–39.

Freud, S. (1977) *Three Essays on Sexuality*. The Pelican Freud Library, Vol 7. Harmondsworth: Penguin.

Freud, S. (1979) 'The psychogenesis of a case of homosexuality in a woman', 'Female Sexuality', in *Case Histories*, The Pelican Freud Library, Vol. 9. Harmondsworth: Penguin. [1st edn 1920.]

Friedan, B. (1978) *It Changed My Life: Writings on the Women's Movement*. New York: Random House.

Frosh, S, Phoenix, A. and Pattman, R. (2002) *Young Masculinities*. London: Palgrave.

Garber, M. (1992) *Vested Interests: Cross Dressing and Cultural Anxiety*. London: Routledge.

Geddes, P. and Thompson, J.A. (1998) *The Evolution of Sex* [1899] excerpted, in Bland, L. and Doan, L. (eds), *Sexology Uncensored: The Documents of Sexual Science*. Cambridge: Polity Press, pp. 14–16.

Gill, R. (2006) *Gender and the Media*. Cambridge: Polity Press.

Göle, N. (2002) 'Islam in public, New visibilities and new imaginaries' *Public Culture*, 14 (1): 173–90.

Göle, N. (2007) 'Islam, European public space and civility', *Eurozine*. Available at: http://www.eurozine.com/articles/2007-05-03-gole-en.html, Last accessed in 2008.

Halberstam, J. (1998) *Female Masculinity*. Durham, NC: Duke University Press.

Herdt, G. (ed.) (1994) *Third Sex, Third Gender: Beyond Sexual Dimorpism in Culture and History*. York: Zone Books.

Hirschfeld, M. ([1998] Tranvestities [1910] excerpted in Bland, L. and Doan, L. [eds]), *Sexology Uncensored: The Documents of Sexual Science*, Part 1, 'Gender and Sexual Difference', Cambridge: Polity Press, pp. 97–104.

Ones, A. 2004) *Men of the Global South: A Reader*. London: Zed Books.

Kimmel, M (1996) *Manhood in America: A Cultural History*. New Jersey: Free Press, 1996.

Kitzinger, C. (ed.) (1994) 'Special feature: Should psychologists study sex differences?', *Feminism and Psychology*, 4 (4): 501–46.

Laqueur, T. (1990) *Making Sex: Body and Genders from the Greeks to Freud*. Cambridge, MA: Harvard University Press.

Levant, R. and Pollock, R. (eds) (1995) *A New Psychology of Men*. New York: Basic Books.

Lorde, A. (1981) 'An open letter to Mary daly', in C. Moraga and G. Anzaldua (eds), *This Bridge Called My Back: Writings by Radical Women of Color*. Watertown, MA: Persephone Press, pp. 63–98.

Oakley, A. (1972) *Sex, Gender and Society*. London: Temple Smith.

Osborne, P. and Segal, L. (1994) 'Gender as performance: An interview with Judith Butler', *Radical Philosophy*, 67: 32–9.

Martin, B. (1994) 'Extraordinary homosexuals and the fear of being ordinary'. *Differences*, 24 (2–3): 101–25.

Mazali, R. (1995) 'Raising boys to maintain armies', *BMJ*, 311: 694, 9 September.

Mazali, R (2003) 'And what about the girls?': What a culture of war genders out of view', *Nashim: A Journal of Jewish Women's Gender Issues*, 6.

McRobbie, A. (2008) *Gender Culture and Social Change: In the Aftermath of Feminism*. London: Sage.

Mohanty, C. T. (1991) 'Cartographies of Struggle: Third World Women and the Politics of Feminism', in C. T. Mohanty, A. Russo, and L. Torres (eds.), *Third World Women and the Politics of Feminism*. Bloomington, IN: Indiana University Press, pp. 2–47.

Mohanty, C.T. (2003) *Feminism Without Borders: Decolonizing Theory, Practicing Solidarity*. Durham, NC: Duke University Press.

Mosse, G.L. (1996) *The Image of Man: The Creation of Modern Masculinity*. Oxford: Oxford University Press.

New Profile (2006) 'Annual report'. Available at: http://coalitionofwomen.org, /home/organizations/new_profile/new_profile_annual_report, Last accessed in 2008.

Patton, C. (1994) 'Unmediated lust', in T. Boffin and J. Fraser (eds), *Stolen Glances: Lesbians Take Photographs*. London: Pandora Press, pp. 233–240.

Pleck, J. (1981) *The Myth of Masculinity*. Cambridge, MA: MIT Press.

Prosser, J. (1998) *Second Skins: The Body Narratives of Transsexuality*. New York: Columbia University Press.

Rich, A. (1980) 'Compulsory heterosexuality and lesbian existence', *Signs*, 5 (4).

Rubin, G. (1975) 'The traffic in women: Notes on the "political economy" of sex', in R. Reiter (ed.), *Towards an Anthropology of Women*. New York: Monthly Review Press, pp. 157–210.

Sayer, L.C. (2005) 'Gender, time and inequality: Trends in women's and men's paid work, Unpaid work and free time', *Social Forces*, 84 (1): 285–303.

Scott, J.W. (1988) 'Gender: A useful category of historical analysis', in *Gender and the Politics of History*. New York: Columbia University Press, pp. 28–50.

Sedgwick, E.K. (1995) 'Gosh Boy George, You must be awfully secure in your masculinity', in M. Berger, B.Wallis and and S. Watson (eds), *Constructing Masculinity*. London: Routledge, pp. 16–20.

Segal, L. (1990) *Slow Motion: Changing Masculinities, Changing Men*, London: Virago Segal, L. (1994) *Straight Sex: The Politics of Pleasure*. London: Virago.

Segal, L. (1999) *Why Feminism: Gender, Psychology, Politics*. Cambridge: Polity.

Segal, L. (2007) 'Men after feminism: What's left to say?', Intro. to 3rd edn. *Slow Motion: Changing Masculinities, Changing Men*. London: Palgrave. [1st edn 1990.]

Spence, J. (1993) *Gender Issues in Contemporary Psychology*. London: Sage.

Spivak, G.C. (1987) 'French feminism in an international frame', in G. Spivak *Other Words*. London: Routledge, pp. 133–153.

Stoller, R. (1968) *Sex and Gender: On the Development of Masculinity and Femininity*. New York: Science House.

Tager, D., Good, G. and Morrison, J. (2006) 'Our bodies, ourselves revisited: Male body image and psychological well-being', *International Journal of Men's Health*, 5 (3): 109–223.

Unger R. and Crawford, M. (1992) *Women and Gender: A Feminist Psychology*. New York: McGraw-Hill.

Venn, C. (2006) *The Postcolonial Challenge: Towards Alternative Worlds*. London: Sage.

Warner, M. (1993) *Fear of a Queer Planet: Queer Politics and Social Theory*. Minneapolis, MN: University of Minnesota Press.

Weininger, O. (2005) *Sex and Character: An Investigation of Fundamental Principles*. Trans. Ladislaus Löb. Bloomington, IN: Indiana University Press. [1st edn 1903.]

Weston, K. (2002) *Gender in Real Time: Power and Transience in a Visual Age*. London: Routledge.

Wetherell, M. and Edley, N. (1999) 'Negotiating hegemonic masculinity: Imaginary positions and psycho-discursive practices', *Feminism and Psychology*, 9 (3): 335–56.

Wilchins, R.A. (1997) *Read My Lips: Sexual Subversion and the End of Gender*. Ithaca, NY: Firebrand Books.

Williams, K. (2006) *Love My Rifle More Than You: Young, Female and in the Army*. London: Weidenfeld and Nicolson.

# 17

# Class, Culture and Morality: Legacies and Logics in the Space for Identification

Beverley Skeggs

The conditions of possibility for class identity are always shaped by forms of capital, types of governance and claims for legitimacy. Identity always includes processes of identification and recognition (or dis-identification and mis-recognition), and identity is located within a symbolic system of value attribution; that is, some identities are considered worth having and others not. The concept identity also invokes assumptions about social compositions and how we value and 'count' people, individual or group identity, and assumptions about consciousness and property ownership of oneself: we 'have' an identity, it is something with which that we own in ourselves, or it is something we make an identification. These assumptions: recognition, value, social composition, counting and consciousness all have their routes in debates about the concept of class, which produce interesting configurations for identity and how it can be known. All these conceptualisations exist within capitalism, the system for extracting value and making profit from labour and commodities.

When we examine the historical production of the concept class what we see is how it has operated to conceptualise inequalities of different kinds, of which identity is only one aspect. For instance, it has been convincingly argued from a range of disciplines that the working class had to learn to recognise themselves as such. The concept working class was initially developed through terms of exclusion – that which was not middle class – and the term middle class was made from the distance drawn from the aristocracy and the urban mass. The term class has always been loaded with moral-value, with long historical legacies (stretching back to the Ancient Greeks, as Ste Croix [1981] notes). As a term, like all other terms, it codifies histories and interests within its definition. This is not to say that it is purely discursive, for it is a term that has very powerful material effects. As Mary Poovey notes:

The reified abstractions that standardized modes of knowing generate then produce effects that are simultaneously symbolic and material- as we see, for example, in the case of the census, where abstractions like 'minorities' (however defined) receive differential symbolic and material treatment according to prevailing assumptions about their relative value to society as a whole. (Poovey 1995: 5)

Some theorists maintain that definitions of class are strictly restricted to the economic, but British Imperialism, for instance, was not just an economic system, it was legitimated through a moral project: 'the civilising mission'. Capital rarely cares who it extracts value from, but nation-states and forms of governance enable moral values to be attributed to different classes through the binary oppositions of good–bad citizen, respectable–unrespectable, deserving–undeserving. Class-ifications are never neutral terms, but emerge as the result of interests that can be consolidated in abstract explanations, not only shaped by interest groups in the conditions of their emergence, but also by their citation, their performative function, and the struggles for legitimation that take place across different sites of institutionalisation such as welfare, law, education and the media. Social theorists are part of this legitimation/institutionalisation process, and the current state of debates about class in social and cultural theory show the range of interests and perspectives at stake between those who want to use and organise around the category for purposes of social justice and those who want to deny the existence of class to hide and legitimate their own privilege. What is significant is the longevity of the term, the way it is used as means for explaining all social organisation, how it is almost impossible to extract it from the entwined condition of its utterance, how it is so intimately tied up to nation, sexuality, race and gender, how it has been known through proximity to labour, and how it is mostly disconnected from matters of identity.

For the purposes of this chapter I will begin with the historical legacies that inform the use of the concept class, examining what was at stake in the development of particular definitions, moving on to look at how class has a long and partially hidden history (although depending on who does the looking) in the idea of self, which has significance for how identity can be know, recognised and performed. I will then explore in detail, through reference to ethnographic research, how relationships to class are shaped by morality, culture and affect and lived by a group of white, working-class women; then extending the argument into other research to examine the relationship between value and identity.

## THE EMERGENCE OF THE CONCEPT 'CLASS': TRAJECTORIES AND LEGACIES

There are two major theoretical/political trajectories to the development of class as a concept. The first, Marxist, prioritises the role of exploitation and struggle in the making of classes and hence social relations more generally; the second focuses on class hierarchies and status without reference to struggle and exploitation (Cannadine, 1988). For Marxists, class has a number of distinctive features: class is a *relationship* always relative to other groups; the relationship is *antagonistic* because it is based on exploitation and control. Therefore class is about the struggle between groups over control, in which exploiters and exploited fight it out. The antagonism is formed in the process of *production*; *and* class is an *objective* relationship. It does not matter what people think about their location (subjective class position, identity), rather, it is about the location of people according to economic relationships (Callinicos and Harman, 1987) or ideological positioning (Althusser, 1971). And just because somebody believes they are middle class does not mean that they stop being exploited by the capitalist class. For Marx, however, coming into consciousness about class exploitation, becoming aware of one's positioning, and challenging the standpoints of the ruling ideas of the ruling class, would lead to a *collective* recognition of a 'class for itself' (the proletariat) that could effectively oppose and overthrow the bourgeoisie. Coming into consciousness, which could be seen as recognising a class identity, entails an understanding of position, capitalism and ideology. More generally, for Marx and Engels consciousness was not an individual matter, rather a 'mode of life':

> As individuals express their life, so they are. What they are, therefore, coincides with what they produce and *how* they produce. The nature of individuals thus depends on the material conditions which determine their production. (1968[1848]: 108)

Individuals identify as a class in so far as they have to battle against another class, making class identity into a temporal/spatial strategic matter formed through conflict, exploitation and unequal relations of power. For Marx it is the bourgeoisie that calls into existence the modern working-class – the proletarians – 'who live only so long as they find work and who find work only so long as their labour increases capital' (Marx and Engels, 1968[1848]: 51). The proletariat is 'the special and essential product of the bourgeoisie'. It is only when workers form unions, or what he calls 'combinations' can the precarious nature of their existence be made more secure, but only temporarily. So, class is not an identity for Marx and Engels, instead a description of the conditions of existence of labour under capitalism, and consciousness is not about taking up an identity or making an identification with a category but of recognising the exploitative conditions of one's existence.

This perspective could not be more different to the other major trajectory that forms the etymology of the concept class. With no need for a revolution to overthrow the bourgeoisie, this perspective concerns itself with the precise nature of classification, employment 'aggregates', status and how to best conceptualise occupational groups in a hierarchical order. It began in 1665 with William Petty, who set out to calculate the value of the 'people' of England for taxation purposes. Petty is attributed with devising what is now known as the 'political arithmetic' tradition of class analysis (associated with the hierarchy rather than the class struggle tradition) in order to enumerate what was otherwise un-measurable (Poovey, 1995). The person was conceptualised as a quantifiable, knowable, hence *governable object* tightly linked to national concerns and formation. James Thompson documents how, throughout the eighteenth century, there was a 'drive toward an abstract and consistent and therefore predictable representation of exchange, that is, toward (new) scientific, quantitative, and mathematical modelling' (1996: 28). These processes involved the calculation and quantification of labour, making the person an object of calculation, subject to domination and impersonal forces beyond their control. These processes of calculation became institutionalised in the eighteenth century through the machinery of the *New Poor Law*, which generated an avalanche of new information and mandated more and more far-reaching, fact-gathering, inspection and legislation.

The continued emphasis on measurement and calculation deflects attention away from the reasons for inequality into a methodological debate about how best to measure, into scientific calculus, as if divisions were the result of mathematical formulae. The significant difference between the two main perspectives is cause and effect: one attempts to explain why classes come into effect, while the other measures the end product of historical social relations. But central to both is work: labour as a force that shapes all relations and the potential for subjectivity (selling one's labour) and work organised into occupations for measurement. Work also becomes central to working-class organisations such as trade unions as a source of potential identification. Hence also feminist critiques which showed, firstly via Marxism, that paid labour was only one way in which capitalism operates, pointing to the significance of domestic labour for social reproduction thus sustaining exploitation and secondly via feminist stratification critiques which argue that measuring women's social class on husband's and father's occupation was inadequate (Crompton, 1993; Stanworth, 1984).

Yet, as Mike Savage (2003) notes, class-consciousness was also central to traditions in British sociology and anthropology between 1950s–mid-1970s that focused on stratification. In the mid-1970s he identifies a shift to the structural aspects of inequality, within this non-Marxist tradition. For instance, John Goldthorpe (1996) identified with the move to structural measurement, after much debate within sociology and political science refined the British Government's traditional five Registrar General's categories of social class into seven new categorizations, all based on the collation of occupational groups: for example, professional/managerial to unskilled, to take into account economic changes, such as the decline of the manufacturing industry and the rise of the service industry.

There is however one element still missing from the historical epistemology of class, and that is morality and how it was articulated culturally. Definitions of class often encode ideas of a person's moral worth, and it is in the attribution of morality that the link is made to 'living' class and possibilities for identification. There have been certain periods when class was definable *primarily* by economic, monetary and market value; at others it was defined in relation to moral behaviour. During the 1850s and 1860s, for instance, there is less talk of working class and middle class, and more of deserving and undeserving poor, of 'respectable artisans and "gentlemen", as emphasis was placed on moral rather than economic criteria' (Crossick, 1991: 61). It was in the play for legitimation that morality became central to defining class. Adam Smith, the proponent of political economy, for instance, advanced the concept of self-interest (and its according

accrual of wealth) as a moral imperative, and the emergent bourgeoisie were concerned to legitimate their mercantile interests by differentiating themselves from the degenerate behaviour of aristocrats via the use of religious justification.[1]

However, it was not until the early nineteenth century that the term 'class' regularly appears in discourse and is consolidated in descriptions of society. Some theorists argue that the term class emerged to coincide with the rise of the 'middle sort' (Williams, 1988). Dror Wahrman (1995) maintains that the crucial moment for fixing the idea of the middle class was around the time of the Reform Act 1832 where the need for political representation allowed the middle class to be consolidated as a group. A central issue is who had access to the symbolic means to legitimate themselves in particular ways, and what resources they used to conceptualise themselves. Terry Eagleton notes how the middle class used the expression of 'taste' and the generation of distinctive cultures: 'the ultimate binding force of the bourgeois social order [were] habits, pieties, sentiments and affections' (1989: 22) by which they attributed higher moral value to themselves. The claims to high culture and taste continue to be a mechanism for promoting distinction and enabling the recognition of class positions (Bourdieu, 1984[1979]).

The emergence of the term working class is subject to a similarly contested debate. Lynette Finch (1993) documents how, in Australia, class emerged from the middle-class colonial welfare administrators as a category to define the urban poor. Carrying with them British definitions, she illustrates how they developed their own interpretations and categorisations that were particularly gendered, conceived through the interpretation of the behaviour of women of urban slums:

> The range of chosen concerns through which middle-class observers made sense of the observed, included references to: living room conditions [...] drinking behaviour [...] language (including both the type of things which were spoken about,

and the manner in which they were referred to – literally the types of words used); and children's behaviour [....] (1993: 10)

As she notes, these were *moral*, gendered, references. In an equally detailed historical analysis of British imperial discourse, Ann McClintock suggests that the concept of class has an historical link to more generalisable 'others', who were known through the concept of degeneracy, a term applied as much to classifying racial 'types' as to the urban poor:

> The degenerate classes, defined as departures from the normal human type, were as necessary to the self-definition of the middle-class as the idea of degeneration was to the idea of progress, for the distance along the path of progress travelled by some portions of humanity could be measured only by the distance others lagged behind. (1995: 46)

Domestic servants, for instance, were often depicted by the racialised imagery of degradation – of contagion, promiscuity and savagery. As Fredrick Engels notes of the working class: 'a physically degenerate race, robbed of all humanity, degraded, reduced morally and intellectually to bestiality' (1958[1844]: 33). What we see in Engels' comment is how a description, used in his case to advocate for social justice, is limited by the prevailing discourses of his time, which semiotically attach degeneracy to the working classes. In the bourgeois claim for moral legitimacy, domestic servants, in particular, became the projected object for dirt, and more explicitly were associated with the care of back passages[2] and the generalised poor came to be represented as excrement. Osbourne's pamphlet on *Excremental Sewage* in 1852 represents the working-class as a problem for civilisation, as sewerage that contaminates and drains the nation (Yeo, 1993). However, hygiene became one of the first discourses to connect to marketing and commodities as a solution to the threat to the nation by those figured as decadent, degenerate and unhygienic: washing the nation clean offered a defence to the threatening pollution of race, class, gender and sexuality. Dirt and waste, sexuality and contagion, danger and disorder, degeneracy and pathology, became the moral evaluations by which the working-class were coded and recorded in the representations of the day (Nead, 1988), not dissimilar to those reproduced today: Chris Haylett (2001) for instance notes how in the 1990s in the UK the white, working class were increasingly coloured, coded as 'dirty white' in government rhetoric; as degenerate, atavistic and abject, surplus to the requirement of a vanguard bourgeois cosmopolitan nation.

Gender, race and sexuality amalgamate in all class definitions. As McClintock puts it, 'the invention of racial fetishism became central to the regime of sexual fetishism became central to the policing of the "dangerous classes"' (1995: 182). In most debates about the formation of class aristocratic women are seen to signal constitutive negative limits, particularly despised for their excessive and lascivious sexuality. Foucault argues that the middle-class, struggling to find the means to define themselves, used reference to commodification to regulate sexuality as a means of social identification:

> The middle-class thus defined itself as different from the aristocracy and the working-classes who spent, sexually and economically, without moderation [...] It differed by virtue of its sexual restraint, its monogamy and its economic restraint or thrift'. (1979: 100)

When Foucault identifies the four discourses that came to produce sexuality (the Malthusian couple, the masturbating child, the hysterical woman, the perverse adult) we can see a similar process occurring with class. The discourses and figures of the dangerous outcast, the urban mass, the revolutionary alien, the contagious woman and the dirty degenerate came to produce what was known as working classness. The category of the contagious woman, figured through the prostitute, presented specific definitional problems. The paradox of needing to name, identify, quantify and know, also produced the possibility of breathing life into the figure, making it a lived possibility, and thereby provoking a range of questions about why and for whom the prostitute exists. The sexuality of working-class women became a source of desire and 'scientific' observation for the Victorian male reformers such as Malthus and Mumby, who tried to apply 'scientific methods' to the study of their objects of fascination. The association with sexuality did not offer any potential for identity; rather it was the absolute limit to it, to moral value. However, the outcome of this projected exclusion was to make the limit the site of all that was interesting and potentially desirable. Hence the long obsession with black and white, working-class danger and sexuality when the middle class engage in class-tourism, 'poorism' or affect-stripping.[3]

These perspectives on race and sexuality produced in the interests of consolidating the legitimation of powerful groups via quantification, empirical observation and moral attribution, came to institutionalise class in very specific ways associated with governance and economy. Vron Ware (1992), for instance, shows how British abolition struggles cannot be understood without connecting sexuality, race and class with their national formation, which then takes on a transnational significance. The entwining of race and class was particularly central to the shaping of contemporary racial politics in the UK (and Angela Davis would argue, the US). Take Hall et al.'s comment:

> It is through the modality of race that blacks comprehend, handle and then begin to resist the exploitation which is an objective feature of their class situation. Race is therefore not only an element of the 'structures'; it is a key element of the class struggle – and thus in the *cultures* of black labour. (Hall, Critcher et al. 1978: 347)

The processes of historical de-legitimation and de-subjectification work across different forms of categorisation to de/attach value to subjects. Yet the connections made through categorical relations are not ones of equivalence. They operate with very different logics. Connected constitution does not mean

that there is a correspondence between categories.[4] Neither does 'being classed' (being classified and positioned by others) equate with taking up an identity. Zizek (2004) notes that there is a fundamental difference between the goals of identity groups (those who willingly make an identification that can be recognised to make public claims for legitimacy) and class struggle. The goal of identity groups is to translate antagonism into difference, whilst the goal of class struggle is precisely the opposite: to aggravate class difference into class antagonism. To set up a series of equivalences between race, gender and class is to obscure the peculiar logic of class struggle, which aims at overcoming, subduing, even *annihilating* the other.[5] In one case, we have a horizontal logic involving mutual recognition among different identities; in the other we have the logic of struggle with an antagonist. A similar division exists between the assimilationist aspirations of multiculturalists and the vertical logic of anti-racism. Zizek notes that the contemporary paradox is that populist fundamentalists (he refers specifically to the conservative fundamentalists in the US whose rhetoric was widely deployed by the Republican party in the GW Bush election campaign) retain this logic of antagonism while the liberal left persists with the logic of the recognition of differences (see later).

## RECOGNITION AND PERFORMATIVITY

Drawing on the work of Austin (1962) and making an argument similar to that of Judith Butler (1999), Bourdieu (1992)[6] argues that theory is performative, bringing into effect that which it names. He aims to challenge descriptions that consist in treating classes on paper as real classes, which he identifies as a 'theoreticist error'.[7] Metaphors, he argues, allows us to move beyond the alternatives of realism and nominalism, enabling us to make abstractions about social relations and to think about how they are 'made'. He notes:

> The title of E.P. Thompson's book *The Making of the English Working Class* must be taken quite literally; the working class such as it appears to us today through the words meant to designate it, 'working class', 'proletariat', 'workers', 'labour movement', and so on, through the organisations that are supposed to express its will, through the logos, bureaus, locals, flags, etc., is a well founded historical artefact. (Bourdieu, 1989: 18)

Class as a performative classification brings the perspective of the classifier into effect in two ways: first, to confirm the perspective of the classifier; and, second, to capture the classified within discourse. As Bourdieu notes 'nothing classifies somebody more than the way he or she classifies' (1989: 19). Whether we opt to understand class as a symptom of exploitation and political struggle or as a matter of hierarchy and classification says more about us (the classifier and our identifications) than those who may be subject to the very material effects of the classification.

However, in all of these debates over definition, as Finch (1993) documents, the working class (the classified) did not identify with the value-laden content of the classification, as degenerate, dangerous, lascivious and/or contagious. Rather, they operated with different value systems (as E.P. Thompson [1966] and Martha Vicinus [1974] demonstrate). Yet not having access to the symbolic systems of representation they were unable to directly challenge the negative classifications and positioning of themselves. So while huge amounts of energy were put into defining, knowing, classifying, recognising and moralising the working class, they went about their business using their own evaluations and deriding displays of moral authority that condemned them.[8] That is, until, as E.P Thompson notes, they learnt to politically organise around the term. The term working class came to have increasing significance for trade union organising (Marx's combination groups, such as the Chartists) and the formation of political parties (the British Labour Party), offering a space for identification for those who could join, and there are substantive debates about the exclusion of women from trade union campaigns through the rhetorical gendered claims of the 'male breadwinner' (Brenner and Ramas, 1984). But another way in which the working class 'combined', which is often overlooked, is through their demands for decadence, for fun and pleasure; a necessary defence, Zizek (2000) argues, against the grim conditions endured. Through fun and pleasure they also found alternative ways of challenging the legitimacy of the classifiers. Vicinus reveals how the working class reversed moral judgements by heaping scorn on those with pretensions to gentility, by laughing at those who restrained their own pleasure and by deriding those who tried to occupy the moral high ground: 'Putting on airs was the greatest sin anyone could commit' (1974: 262–3). A statement still found in contemporary research on class relations (Walkerdine and Lucey, 1989). Music hall and contemporary entertainment dramatise a class struggle in which the working class challenge the moral authority that seeks to condemn them.

The attempts to make the working class recognise their classification is also noted by Carolyn Steedman (1999, 2000) who introduces an important factor into the performative emergence of the category class. She traces how a working-class self as a moral categorisation, came into existence through the religious discourse of redemption, a self that had to be respectable and prove itself to be capable of narrating itself in the ways established by the state-legal interlocutor systems of poor relief. If the *Reform Law* (political representation structured through property ownership) was key to the formation of the middle class, the *Poor Law* (basic economic subsistence) was significant to the establishment of the working class. In these differentially invested and incited formations: one that makes political claims for legitimated legal property ownership and one that is forced to perform a category in order to stay alive, class difference is historically shaped. In all of these classification processes, as we have seen, class is in continual constitution, not just through other classifications but also through the concepts we use, which appear as neutral.

This is particularly pertinent in relation to how debates about personhood develop into ideas about the individual, the self and identity. It is very difficult to speak about 'the self' without introducing the whole historical baggage of classed history that enabled the concept of the self to come into existence in the conceptual shape that is used today. And because of the close link between identity and self – where identity is seen to be central to self-formation, it is worth discussing how class relations shape the self. Briefly, the idea of the self developed from the discourse of possessive individualism, the cornerstone of seventeenth-century political theory (Macpherson, 1962). Marilyn Strathern (1992) documents how the concept of the 'possessive individual' (that is a person who is defined through *his* capacity to own property in *his* person) developed from the perspective of an elite property holding small group, with access to circuits of symbolic distribution who were able to legitimate their own interests and establish their own authority by defining themselves against the 'mass', as the constitutive limit for what an individual could be. The perspective of the 'possessive individual' was replicated in various different ways and institutionalized in law, via property relations and the development of concepts of rights-bearing individuals (this is, of course, a very shorthand and reductive story, see (Skeggs, 2004) [2004] for a book-length account). What was central to the reproduction of the possessive individual was how particular techniques such as narrative, biography and scientific discourse, were used to legitimate interest: the heroic individual and the civilised person were consolidated as identity spaces through the promotion of the rhetoric of advanced civilisation established by eugenics. By institutionalising themselves, not just

through law, but through different systems of knowledge, the middle class were able to consolidate their interests across a variety of fields. These different relationships to property and their legitimation leave long legacies for understanding who is classified as having the potential to become an individual, a civilised person, a valued national citizen, and who can defend these positions in law and hence who can make recognition claims through identity on the nation-state and beyond.[9]

## CONTEMPORARY CLASS FORMATIONS

The study of class always takes a particularly national formation, which as Philip Kelly (2007) argues is one of its limits. In Britain, Mike Savage (2000) illustrates how analysis of class worked as a means by which British social scientists identified their distinctive expertise vis-à-vis other national traditions. Drawing on long historical traditions for studying the social and deploying established techniques (such as measurement, hierarchy and labour, as described above) Savage identifies how debates in the UK and US revolved around how to conceptualise the 'social', for example, as conglomerates of individuals or as structures of power, which usually conflated with 'social class'. He shows how the 'political arithmetic technique' diversified into new fields, such as social policy, welfare and education, which were all nationally specific. Also, the conflict identified in class relations took specific forms, with a strong Marxist line in the UK, and a functionalist one in the US. As a concept class also took on a national tone that traversed academic boundaries and entered the popular becoming a site of wider political debate. Class relations also became the foundation by which national social change was measured, often through comparative studies where comparison was used to highlight the specificities of the nation (Wright, 1985).

We can see this in contemporary debates about post-Fordism, de-traditionalisation and disorganised capital, where in an attempt to understand social formation and social change, class becomes a structuring absence, that which is being moved from and thus is the baseline of the movement, hence terms such as post-, de- and dis- mark the movement from a focus on class formations, while echoing their presence.

As a concept class is, therefore, being used to do many things: classify and legitimate inequalities, provide academic legitimacy, frame an academic discipline, speak to 'the people', measure social change, explain national formation and stand in for the social itself. It is hardly surprising then, that it stubbornly remains as a concept after all the attempts to retreat from it, deny it, refigure it, dismiss it, trivialise it and de-centre it. For, as Cannadine notes, 'the history of class is as much about the history of *ideas* about society as it is about society itself' (1998: 171).

Within ideas about society are contained ideas about the possibility of identity and identification. As we have seen, a category has to exist for an identification to be made, for an identity to be created and inhabited. One important recent development in class analysis has been the work of Pierre Bourdieu, who brings together elements of the trajectories identified: exploitation, measurement and morality to understand how class is shaped by access to different capitals which over time become literally embodied as a class habitus.

Bourdieu (1979, 1985 and 1987) develops a model of social topography to demonstrate how relative positions and the *relations* between these positions constitute forms of power, enabling bodies to move in social space. Bourdieu identifies four main types of capital: economic, cultural, social, and symbolic:

- *Economic capital* – includes income, wealth, financial inheritances, and monetary assets: what you own.

- *Cultural capital* – this can exist in three forms: in an embodied state, that is, in the form of long lasting dispositions of the mind and the body; in the objectified state, in the form of cultural goods; and in the institutionalized state, resulting in such things as educational qualifications. Bourdieu defines cultural capital as high culture.
- *Social capital* – resources based on connection, networks and group membership: who you know, used in pursuit of favour and advancement.
- *Symbolic capital* – the form the different types of capital take once they are perceived and recognised as legitimate. Legitimation is the key mechanism in the conversion to power. Cultural capital has to be legitimated before it can have symbolic power. Capital has to be regarded as legitimate before it can be capitalised upon, before its value is realisable.

People are distributed in social space according to: the global *volume* of capital they posses; the *composition* of their capital, *evolution* of the volume and composition according to their *trajectory* in social space. It is not just the volume and composition of the right sort of cultural capital (for national belonging), but it is also *how* one accumulates it that makes an important difference to its capacity to be converted. Bourdieu distinguishes between those who only have to *be what they are* as opposed to those who *are what they do* and, therefore, have to constantly prove that they are capable of carrying symbolic value.

Taste is the most obvious manifestation of this process, whereby access to high culture enables people to develop dispositions and knowledge over time (refined and distanced contemplation for instance as opposed to expressions of direct hedonism). The ability to accrue high culture dispositions depends on exposure to social spaces, what he calls 'fields', abstract spaces in which the forces of history cohere, where battles for value and legitimacy are fought and where different forms of capital are converted (or not) into value over time. The symbolic system creates, circulates and maintains distinctions from the perspective and interest of those with power (symbolic capital), enabling them to accrue value to themselves whilst keeping others contained in social spaces with little prospect of conversion, unable to access the capitals that have value to enable social movement to occur. I will now develop this analysis through some ethnographic research I conducted over a period of 11 years to show how the possibilities for identification work through the different legacies and logics, shaped by gender and class.

## AFFECTIVE MORAL CLASS ANTAGONISMS

My research showed how, for a group of white, working-class women from the north of England, processes of mis-recognition shape their responses to identity formation; they dis-identify from the term working class, which only offers the possibility of pathology. They literally stand in discomfort under a sign that has no meaning for them; instead positioning themselves with value. The women were identified sociologically as working class, that is, by a range of different social measures and cultural practices (see Formations of Class and Gender [Skeggs, 1997]). They did not want to be identified as working class, and certainly did not occupy a working-class identity, a reaction whose logic became apparent during the course of the longitudinal research, and enabled me to think through the usefulness of the term identity when put together with class.

Immersed in the lives and spaces of these women over time I became highly conscious of the numerous ways in which they were constantly subject to negative value judgements, about their futures and pasts, behaviour, intelligence, taste, bodies and sexuality, to such an extent that it shaped their spatial sense of entitlement, engagement and limit: where they did or did not want to go. The women were not strongly visibly marked as excessive, loud, dirty or dangerous, yet 'being looked down on' was their description of a process to which they were continually

subject, a visual assessment by others that repeatedly positioned them as lacking value. For instance, when they entered 'posh shops' Wendy notes how they were acutely aware of being read and judged by others:

> We'd all gone up to Manchester the other Saturday, you know for a day out, the three of us … We were in Kendals during the day, you know where the really posh food is, and we were laughing about all the chocolates and how many we could eat – if we could afford them- and this woman she just looked at us. If looks could kill. Like we were only standing there. We weren't doing anything wrong. We weren't scruffy or anything. She just looked. It was like it was her place and we didn't belong there. And you know what? We just all walked away. We should have punched her in the face. We didn't say anything until about half an hour later. Can you imagine? Well and truly put in our place … It's things like that that put you off going. You feel better staying around here. (Wendy, 1986)

The gaze that embodies the symbolic reading of the women makes them feel 'out of place', thereby generating a sense of where their 'place' should be. Here they are not called directly into effect, a performative interpellation into identity, but indirectly, through a defensive reaction to the judgement. This makes the classification of class operate as a negative structuring absence, not a positive source of identification.

The shop assistants gaze is a judgement of taste,[10] with spatial consequences, which classifies the classifier as much as the classified. It displays the repetition of the 'hidden injury' identified by Richard Sennett (1977). However, even though this gaze resulted in a desire to return to the safety of 'one's place', such readings were not always accepted:

> That's like when you're walking through the perfume bit of Owen and Owen [department store] and they're spraying perfume all over the posh ones and you know you're not going to get any. Me and Jane, we used to stand there till she sprayed us. (Morag, 1986)[11]

This defensive response displays a refusal to stay in, or be put in, place by others. But it is a constant struggle to continually deflect the negative connotations. For Morag, Yvonne, Ann and Wendy, working class is not an identity that is taken up in relation to a positive recognition, but an awareness of negative judgements. As Yvonne notes:

> All my life I've wanted to say 'look I'm as good as you', well now I think this house says it. It says 'I've made it, I'm respectable and you can't put me down'. (1992)

And Anne talks of how every decision is a matter of assessment in trying to deflect the negative evaluations of others:

> All the time you've got to weigh everything up: is it too tarty? Will I look like a right slag in it? What will people think? It drives me mad that every time you go to put your clothes on you have to think: do I look dead common? Is it rough? Do I look like a dog?

When I grew up my mother was (and even now in her eighties, still is) obsessed with the fear of 'looking common'. To be identified as common was one of the worst things that could happen to her: 'mortifying' she would say in a very visible rendition of spatial containment. Re-signification of the term was attempted so that 'common tart' became a humorous amelioration, but only if spoken by those subject to similar judgements. For the term common was (and still is), shorthand for a middle-class taste judgement that says 'worthless', without directly betraying the perspective and position of the judger as a privileged snob.

As Andrew Sayer (2005) notes, moral boundary drawing and value attribution treats the merits claimed for the judging group as if universally valid. He describes how the middle class rarely want to acknowledge the privileged social and economic position from which they speak, displaying embarrassment and evasion, often denying the significance of class, or individualising difference, responses which he suggests indicate an awareness that class differences lack moral justification. Sayer points to the moral significance of class, precisely because it cannot be divorced from attributions of worth and person-value, creating unequal possibilities for flourishing and suffering. This is more than identity; it is ontology, the conditions for the possibilities for living.

If we add Spinoza's (1996) theory of affect to Bourdieu's spatial metaphors, we can see how what he terms 'the force of existing' is in a continuous variation. Spinoza, writing in the sixteenth century, maintains that when we come across somebody good, if they make us joyful, they increase our capacity/ability to act, whereas if we meet sadness inhibition increases and decreases our capacity to act. Spinoza was concerned to understand how people with power use sadness to affect us to increase their power and decrease the power of others (he studied priests). This continual variation experienced through social encounters: increase–diminution–increase–diminution, Spinoza defines as affective movement. I would argue that the repeated attachment of negative value to the working class intensifies and increases diminution. This is not limited to individualised social encounters but how our total social relations are shaped through this process; affects arise from within the system of social relationships, institutions and practices that exceed individuals. When one enters a social encounter with an awareness of the possibilities for denigration, a defensive response to the potential negative evaluation is prepared.

Spinoza also notes how continuous variation in the force of existing is determined by the ideas one gives to the affects we feel. So if we feel diminished we may look for an idea to explain our detumescence. If we look to the category of working class to explain our negative evaluation, we may either be able to convert it into something positive, such as trade union activity, or may generate distance from it in order to protect ourselves from its negative effects (feeling, sad, diminished and out of place). Likewise, if diminished by class we may be able to protect our value through other classificatory systems such as sexuality, gender or race which have different potentials for re-signification and value attachment (for example, 'black and proud' or 'queer and here'). Thus the encounter is a dialectical movement of value, whereby one may establish value at the cost of another; hence why judgements of taste and classification are considered by Bourdieu to be acts of symbolic violence:

> If there is any terrorism it is in the peremptory verdicts which, in the name of taste, condemn to ridicule, indignity, shame, silence [...] men and women who simply fall short, in the eyes of their judges, of the right way of being and doing. (1986: 511)

The women's responses above demonstrate a clear understanding of the ideas by which they are positioned: 'they think we're shit', a point on which the majority of teachers agreed expressing: 'there's no point educating them, they'll only have hundreds of babies'. The women's responses are an understanding of person-value. They know that being recognised as working-class has led to their devaluation, which is too negatively loaded for re-signification. This is why these understandings rarely produce a consciousness that leads to positive collective class identification, but instead to the desire to have and be seen to have value, constantly morally mediated.

The fear of being judged shaped how the women, literally and metaphorically, moved through social space: they apologised for failure at school, for not having immaculately clean houses (which they did have), not having brand new furniture, for the wrong bodies, living in the wrong area, liking the wrong music, wearing the wrong clothes (see *Formations*). As Annette Kuhn notes:

> Class is not just about the way you talk, or dress, or furnish your home; it is not just about the job you do or how much money you make doing it; nor is it merely about whether or not you have A levels or went to university, nor which university you went to. Class is something beneath your clothes, under your skin, in your reflexes, in your psyche, at the very core of your being. In the all-encompassing English class system, if you know that you are in the 'wrong' class, you know that therefore you are a valueless person. (1995: 98)

Kuhn clearly identifies the way repeated negative evaluations become lived 'at the very core of being' as a form of ontological insecurity which produced in the women of my research constant surveillance of themselves and the development of strategies to gain value. By condemning people for not being able to 'look right', 'do it right' or 'be right', responsibility is attributed to them for something which is determined by 'an accident of birth', their inheritance of and exposure to economic, cultural, symbolic and social capital *and* also for the negative affect they encounter.

I argued, as a result of the research findings that this group of working-class women *dis-identified* from class positioning and class identity; ideas which only attached negative value to them. They did not want to be recognized as working-class because for them that recognition always involved *mis-recognition*; that is, they were read constantly as something they were not (worthless) and accordingly diminished.

However, the ideas they attach to their experience of diminution are the result of class relations, about unfairness and injustice, the difficulty of challenging negative value and the attempt to gain moral high ground. Julie outlines her ideas in a discussion of 'dressing down':

> Yea, I've seen that in Alderly Edge with the younger ones. I guess it's because they're students and they are trying to show how clever and bohemian they are. But it is really clever because like if you were poor or at least not very well off you wouldn't dare look that scruffy because everybody would know just how little money you had so it's really only the very rich who can get away with it. What I mean is *it's just like another way of maintaining differences between groups*. You have to be really rich to be really scruffy or else you'd feel *really bad and be dead ashamed of yourself* but they're not, they get away with it. (1992)

Or when directly speaking about the middle class:

> When I first went to work as a nanny I couldn't stand it. They really think they're something else. They treat you like shit. What I've noticed is they never look at you. Well they do at first they look you all over and make you feel like a door rag, but then they just tell you what to do. Some of them want you to know you're shit in comparison to them. I jacked it in shit money, being made to feel like shit. Even the kids. They learn really early that

you're not worth the ground they walk on. They're bastards. (Cynthia, 1992)

They always assume they have a right to anything and everything. It's like whatever they are doing that's their right. They just think the world is made for them. (Angela, 1989)

Julie, Cynthia and Angela have a strong sense of class positioning and how they are positioned without worth *and* how others position themselves with entitlement. And whilst the women desperately desire to gain respect, have value and be taken seriously this *does not* mean that they aspire to be middle class. As Cynthia and Angela articulate, the middle class behaves in ways of which Cynthia and Angela do not approve. The research was suffused with comments of awareness, affects of resentment and derision: class antagonism expressed loudly:

It's the way they think they know about things all the time. Sue's (her sister) brother in law is a scream. He sits there pontificating. Talking absolute shite about everything. I just think he's a dickhead. We all do. Everyone takes the piss out of him. (Cindy, 1989)

They come into the restaurant ordering things in a hoity toity manner. They're really ignorant. It's fucking pizzas for Christ sakes. We'd put snot on their pizzas – you can never tell, and they're usually dead stingy with the tips. You can always tell the rich ones, they keep hold of their money. (Rachel, 1986)

What gets me about these people with loads of money is they look crap. They haven't a clue about style, about what to wear, about how to put things together. If I had that much money I'd look fucking brilliant. (Cynthia, 1992)

These are strong statements of anger, of moral indignation. Other research shows these feelings are mutual with the middle classes making equally derisory comments (Frazer, 1992; Lawler, 2002; Ortner, 1991; Walkerdine et al., 2001). Yet there is a difference in *the intensity* and *type* of the affects expressed, with anger, frustration, resentment and indignation appearing as more vehement expressions than the derision, disgust and contempt of the middle class. The proximity to legitimacy (what Bourdieu calls symbolic capital) defines which affects are represented as a legitimate response, while others are represented as irrational and/or excessive. Affects exist within a circuit of symbolic value that legitimates their expression: for instance, Steph Lawler (2002) notes how two protests in the UK, both against registered sex-offenders living in a community (similar to Megan's Law in the US), were attributed with a different legitimacy depending on who performed the protest. The middle-class mothers were presented in the national press as devoted and vigilant, as a worried 'we' who were right to be concerned about 'our' (the nation's) children, enabling a general moral identification to be made, unlike the working-class women (known as the Paulsgrove protesters) who were vilified as a mob, ignorant, threatening, repulsive and horrific, vigilante rather than vigilant.

The negative value and affects attached to the Paulsgrove women, however tells us more about the journalists' class-based obsessions and fears than those of the protestors. Elsewhere I have mapped the extraordinary fascination with and hatred of working-class culture by middle-class commentators, resulting in terms such as 'chav' in the UK (the *Oxford English Dictionary* 2004 word of the year[12]), visualised on the Chavscum.com website. A site where 'the hatred almost explodes off the computer screen', a comment made by the ex-Conservative party advisor, Ferdinand Mount who describes its content as 'weird loathing' and 'vile caricatures' (2004: 90). In his most recent book, on class, he remarks:

What I do not think many people have yet woken up to is that the working class has been subjected to a sustained programme of social contempt and institutional erosion which has persisted through many different governments and several political fashions. (2004: 273)

As ex-head of Margaret Thatcher's Number Ten Policy Unit (responsible for creating class inequalities), he charts, but expresses surprise at, the 'bad manners' and vulgarity of the middle classes who now feel it is legitimate to display their hatred of the working class so blatantly. Legal theorist,

David Garland demonstrates how it is not just institutional erosion but the institutionalisation of hate in criminal law that since the 1980s punishes a working class that is seen to be beyond redemption, without the possibility of rehabilitation (Ruddick, 2006).

Even if the working class feel anger, resentment and hate, it is unlikely that their expression of these emotions will be given legitimacy – they are more likely to be criminalised for their expression. Yet the same expressions by the middle class may be institutionalised. Sara Ahmed (2004) suggests that we inhabit an affective economy where hate is economic; that is hate circulates between signifiers in relationships of difference and displacement and is distributed across a variety of figures where through the process of what she calls 'metonymic slide' figures such as 'chavs' (and in her example of 'asylum seekers', a highly racialised negative term in the UK) become readable as nationally cancerous, as rotting the moral fabric of the nation. Hate, she maintains, cannot be found just in one figure, but works to create the very outline of different figures or objects of hate, a creation that crucially aligns the figures together and constitutes them as a 'common' threat, but with different intensities (for example, the female and male 'chav'). In such affective economies, she argues, emotions *do things*, they align individuals with communities – or bodily space with social space – through the very intensity of their attachments. What we see in the UK through the expression of such unadulterated contempt is a public alignment of middle-class values *against* working-class lifestyles. The affects of antagonism become central to how people express their social relations and to how people are recognised, evaluated and legitimated. The circulation of negative affects, just like the values they accompany are deflected by the working class through the reversal of the judgement: they define the middle class as ignorant, clueless, stupid, tight and badly dressed. This reversal

becomes particularly acute around issues of childcare:

> Don't they like their own kids? Is that why they give them away all the time? (Cynthia, 1992)
>
> Of course I'll bring up my children by myself, you can't go shopping them out, you shouldn't have them if that's what you'll do. (Ann, 1990)
>
> I think it's awful how rich women who should know better shop out their children, I just can't see the point in having them if you don't want to care for them, that's what it's all about, I think it's really awful, what are the kids going to grow up like knowing their mothers don't really care about them, it's like those who send their kids off to paying schools, they never see them. I don't reckon that sort should be allowed to have children. (Sally, 1990)

By claiming themselves to be the real and proper mothers they invert class divisions and claim *moral superiority* over the middle-class women, who by 'shopping out' their children reveal themselves to be uncaring, unnatural, irresponsible and ultimately immoral. This inversion of value has also been documented in other research on motherhood (Duncan, 2005; Lawler, 2000; Reay, 1998) and child development (Walkerdine and Lucey, 1989). What we see is a continual struggle over legitimacy to judge value, experienced affectively and expressed here through the moral discourse of eugenics.

## MOBILISING MORAL VALUE

Moral legitimacy pervades not just everyday experience but also theoretical descriptions. John Kirk (2007) investigates those who make strong claims for the cultural significance of English, northern, working-class cultures, but who paradoxically proceed to map this culture's disappearance; a paradox he suggests produced by a nostalgic belief in the 'then' of industrialism and the 'now' of consumerism, where the past is described as a moral economy of solidarity and collective care. Kirk carefully interrogates two texts which make this textual move of past/present: Richard Hoggart (1957) and

Simon Charlesworth (2000), noting how Hoggart's period of cultural deficit and the decline of collective class culture from the late 1950s to the 1970s represents the golden years for Charlesworth's past/present, a time before the onslaught of Thatcherism and industrial decline. Charlesworth vividly describes a tragic structure of feeling of the dispossessed, where being in the world is a matter of lack, deprivation and loss, compensated for by the useless consolations of commodity desire, a similar description to Hoggart's 1950s 'candy floss world' in which mass entertainments are full of corrupt brightness, improper appeals and moral evasions. As Kirk points out, both offer two victims in the present: the working-class and its self-identity. Both identify the inadequacies of the people to generate meaning beyond commodity driven pleasure. He notes how for both Hoggart and Charlesworth: 'the sense of no longer holding a coherent narrative of one's being in the world, of not possessing the symbolic freight or the cultural capital to compete or to participate in social life, render these working-class people mute' (2007: 35), lacking in personal resources colonised by the commodity form in which commodity desire replaces common identity.

These representations of the working class as tragically mute, or commodity dupes, contrasts with not only the loud antagonisms expressed above but also with the studies of working-class boys as infinitely creative within their cramped spaces. Paul Willis (1977) notes the hedonism, excitement and defiance of authority achieved by inverting the school's core values. Drawing on American sub-culture theory from the 1950s (Cohen, 1955) he shows how boys disengage themselves from the schools rituals and values and re-orientate themselves instead around leisure activities. Walter Miller (1958) suggests that their behaviour is not an inversion as such, but represents the focal concerns of masculine working-class culture – excitement, toughness and luck. Values, which David Matza (1964) suggests, are also one part of the dominant culture and

other class factions. This 'creative' analysis shows how dominant values are inverted but very differently in terms of gender, If we apply Bourdieu's multiple capitals theory we can see how gender cuts through this re-valuation process: irresponsibility for young men, responsibility for young women. (Although I'd argue that excitement, recreation and hedonism have also been part of young women's culture, often but not always, curtailed by family responsibilities.)

The displays of working-class, masculine identity premised on irreverence, ultimately fitted Willis's 'lads' back into the world of industrial labour via gender by inverting the binary of mental and manual to reposition themselves as the ones with hard masculine value; yet hard masculinity is precisely what the hard industrial factory required (the research was in the mid 1970s). But Willis's research is a study of challenges to authority via culture rather than challenges to capitalism. A point amplified by contemporary research, which examines what happens to the working class when traditional work conditions are destroyed and gender becomes detached from the traditional sexual division of labour. Lois Weis's (2004) longitudinal ethnography of the transition of 'Freeway' from an industrial steel town to a restructured service economy, demonstrates how a considerable amount of class, race and gender re-embedding occurs, with redundant men no longer able to fulfil their 'hard work' ethos or deal with domesticity. The women become more resourceful and creative in dealing with the new conditions, suggesting that irreverence and inversion are highly specific responses to the conditions of their own creation; creation within changing capitalist relations.

The search for dignity beyond work, for value in conditions of devaluation, by both men and women, black and white, has also been charted by Mitch Duneier (1992) who illustrated how a group of black men in Chicago desired to be recognised as respectable *not* as dangerous, criminal or pathological, which (like the women of the

Formations research) was often how they were misrecognised and diminished in social encounters.[13] Likewise, Michelle Lamont (2000) identifies a distinct moral code focusing on personal integrity and the quality of interpersonal relationships[14] among both white and black, working-class men to whom she spoke; they too did *not* want to become middle class. These were not responses of radical creativity (Willis) or antagonistic moral inversion (Skeggs) but straightforward attempts to claim worth and value for themselves. These studies, however, also point to the lack of antagonism present in generalised American class discourse and American cultural theory, what bell hooks calls 'the elephant in the room' – the unnamed subject that everybody knows is central to their lives but cannot be named as such; instead: 'Race and gender are used as screens to deflect attention away from the harsh realities that class politics exposes' (2000: 7).

Mobilisation of moral value as part of a class struggle is not straightforward. Tom Frank (2004) notes how in the US in the 1990s a disaffected, unemployed, male, working class were persuaded through anti-liberal populist public outrage rhetoric to elevate 'morality' via the protection of the family and the foetus, and in so doing align themselves with a Republican Right that promoted the interests of the super-rich.[15] Part of the Republicans' rhetorical appeal was its ability to detach already formed moral values such as unpretentiousness, authenticity, hard work and loyalty from the conditions of their original production (working-class life), a space which was increasingly entrenched, and re-attach them to the interests of an imaginary safe and secure prosperous right-wing nation through the promise of respect and respectability. That the rhetorical struggle was able to insert middle-class pretentiousness – a bilingual, French-speaking liberal elite with French culinary taste came under particular attack – as an already established yet unspoken source of antagonism, what Frank calls class animus, gave space to that which could not previously be spoken,

class war and the 'elephant in the room' was split into two figures: the liberal middle class versus the moral working class.

Affect is put to powerful effect in the right-wing rhetoric describing liberals as arrogant, despicable, self-important show-offs, in short, 'snobs', who:

> [...] [p]romote immoral destructive behaviour because they are snobs, they embrace criminals because they are snobs, they oppose tax cuts because they are snobs, they adore the environment because they are snobs. (Coulter, 2002: 27–9)

The aim of such rhetoric, Frank maintains, was to generate indignation by voicing the fury of the imposed upon, enabling diminished subjects to voice their indignation, not just through claims to respectability but by revenge: deriding the denigrators. Contempt returns to contempt. Cultural grievances and the challenges to authority are given national space and credibility, but the projected target has moved. It is class war of a kind but the alliance is not made with members of the same class, those of the same social position, but the powerful, those who put the grieved into the cramped spaces in the first place, from where they now speak back. This, I would argue, is not about identity, although the mobilisation occurs through its terms against a figure of identity (the liberal middle class), but about projected fantasies where inequalities disappear and justice is achieved.

What we see from these different political mobilisations is how they are premised on *already structured* class relations by which class antagonism can be activated. The working-class men identified by Frank in Kansas were ripe for recruitment to moral causes, such as protecting the foetus, because if offered them moral value while visualising and naming an enemy that fitted their already existing class antagonisms based on their experience of inequality, injustice and experience of diminishing value. Their grievances were detached from source and they were offered an affective fantasy of revenge to which they attached themselves, for a time.

The moral struggles of the women of my ethnography are like microcosm of this process; they live the antagonism and the diminishing, struggling to gain moral value through motherhood and respectability in an attempt to make their lives bearable and value-full. Unlike the Kansas men they have not been mobilised around the visualisation of an enemy, instead they engage in minor battles in cramped spaces on a daily basis. In 2009 Barak Obama also mobilised affect but this time of a positive kind – hope. In the midst of national negativity he was able to propose the potential of a better future. In this political imaginary grievance take a different shape, attached to the positive future rather than the negative past. Local and national affects are the ways in which the experience of structural inequality attach to mechanisms for the creation of person-value.

What we see in all the working-class ethnographies (from early sub-culture theory to the contemporary, through race and gender) is a desire to be recognised as having value, and thereby not denigrated, when one is repeatedly symbolically positioned as value-less. As respondents from another research project kept repeating to me 'it's so unfair to be punished for something which is an accident of birth'.[16] Inequality and injustice is felt more intensely when people are blamed or cast as immoral for that into which they were born.

That a logic of antagonism underpins all class relations makes sense when we see how people have to live the devaluation process on a daily basis, not just through unequal access to resources, but also through diminishing and humiliation. What the antagonism displays is a resentment against unequal and unjust power structures and those who put them into effect. This is why identity does not offer enough explanatory power for the way class shapes lives: class is a product of capitalism, an archaeological structure of inequalities and antagonisms that can be hailed and lived in different ways (but always as forms of inequality distributing different

types of unequal value). It is difficult for the working-class to gain economic equality (as history shows), but the claim to moral value is one way in which inequalities can be partially assuaged, in which value can be gained and judgement challenged.

## CONCLUSION

Different discourses have defined class: socialism, moral reform, taxation, political representation and individualism, all representing different interests over time and space, and performatively bringing into effect different figures such as the degenerate, contagious, dangerous and, rarely, heroic. Moreover, the inheritance of class relations shapes the likelihood of entry into positive–negative value economies, into the possibilities for accruing and converting different forms of capital. The complexity of this process cannot be accounted for by the term 'identity'. Just as Butler notes in relation to the category 'woman':

> If 'women' within political discourse can never fully describe that which it names, that is neither because the category simply refers without describing nor because 'women' are the lost referent, that which 'does not exist', but because the term marks a dense intersection of social relations that cannot be summarised through the terms of identity. (1993: 218)

Exactly the same process applies for class. Class is a relationship between people who inherit not just different categories, but also who inherit the values of those categories, the inequalities and injustices. To inherit inequalities which are then symbolically repeated as if a measure of a person leads to justifiable resentments.

If Wendy Brown is correct in her observation that 'the political purchase of contemporary American identity politics would seem to be achieved in part through a certain re-naturalisation of capitalism' (1995: 60) then it makes total sense that those who are subject to the ravages and most brutal forms of exploitation by capitalism cannot make identity work for them. If identity politics works through making 'claims' on capitalism and the state for recognition, how can recognition be mobilised by those who are continually misrecognised and do not have access to circuits of symbolic value in order to socially adjust their value attribution. Those who have been most successful in the deployment of identity claims are those who have the highest consumer potential for capital, for example, women and gay men, as Rosemary Hennesey (2000) and Denis Altman (2001) show, or in the opening out of new markets through the branding of a bland multi-culturalism (that stands in opposition to antagonistic anti-racism) and extends the reach of late capitalism, as Zizek (1997) demonstrates. Brown asks:

> To what extent do identity politics require a standard internal to existing society against which to pitch their claims, a standard that not only preserves capitalism from critique, but sustains the invisibility and inarticulateness of class – not incidentally, but endemically? Could we have stumbled upon one reason why class is invariably named but rarely theorised or developed in the multi-culturalist mantra, 'race, class, gender, sexuality? (1995: 61)

Zizek suggests that the almost impossibility of deploying identity politics anymore to class is not just about making-claims but is a much more powerful example of the political occlusion of class (in which social theorists are complicit when suggesting class decline): 'when class antagonism is disavowed, when its key structuring role is suspended, we are dealing with an exemplary case of the mechanism of ideological displacement' (2000: 97). A process we saw explicitly through the different ways in which affects can be mobilized with the 'right' fantasy of revenge and hope.

When class antagonism goes unremarked 'other markers of social difference may come to bear an inordinate weight; indeed, they may bear all the weight of the sufferings produced by capitalism in addition to that attributable to the explicitly politicized

marking' (Brown, 1995: 60). Other identities have to bear the surplus-investment from the class struggle whose extent is not acknowledged. Capitalism is not just a phenomenon limited to the domain of economics but the structuring principle that over-determines the social totality. To place class as an equivalent identity, Zizek contends, is to depoliticise the economy.

Capitalist dynamics infuse and traverse all struggles (such as sexuality, race and gender) operating as the very background and terrain for their emergence of minority subjectivities. Class is not a category of identity but a perspective for approaching the continuous combat to configure life in the value-form against that which would resist it, and the forms of subjectivity that arises from class struggle (Zizek, 2000: 87). Class relations still determine life chances, health and wealth regardless of how people speak their relationship to them. Class relations are dynamic forces that underwrite all social encounters. Capitalism is the inequality generator shaping how people live, what they inherit and how they move through social space. To understand this process fully we need an analysis of an 'economy of personhood' within capitalism which can explain how different values – economic, cultural, symbolic, social, moral, can be accessed, attached and utilised and how they work through encounters that repeatedly enhance or diminish value in the person.

## NOTES

1  We just need to turn to the literature of Jane Austen to see how this process between the upper and middle class is enacted through property relations and gender.

2  Yeo (1993) shows how middle-class women used working-class women to clean the dirty bits, enabling the middle class to appear as hygienic.

3  See Skeggs (2004) for an elaboration of this process.

4  See Yvette Taylor (2005) on how sexuality and class do and do not intersect.

5   Although both race and gender identity politics have at different historical moments advocated antagonistic annihilation.

6   See (Butler, 1999).

7   Jacque Ranciere (1983) however, accuses Bourdieu of reproducing exactly that which he sets out to critique by 'measuring' homologies between class and taste and by quantifying the French education system in terms of class privilege.

8   This became highly apparent in a recent research project I conducted (for CRESC, Manchester University 2006) on the British government's 'Respect Agenda' (see http//:www.gov.org/respect). When a group of 10 ex-offenders now in higher education were given the agenda to discuss they melodramatically ripped it up, and put it in the bin, with shouts of 'respect, what respect, they've got no respect for us'.

9   The European Commission for Human Rights has been the major site for rights based claims .

10   Some would identify this judgement as the narcissism of small difference for it is likely that the shop assistants could be sociologically identified  as working class, but as Robbins observes, many servants in Victorian England took on the judgements of their employers against each other in order to generate a modicum of value for themselves. The significance of this move is that the judgement is repeated continually across a range of sites, so it is the recurring effect of the negative judgement, rather than the small difference that is significant.

11   During the writing of this chapter I went to have my hair cut. The hairdresser told me a joke about two Essex girls (the geographical euphemism for London working-class) at the perfume counter. What is it about perfume counters?

12   Referring to excessive Burberry clad, gold wearing, loud, white, working-class youth. Bogan (in Australia) and White Trash and/or Hillbilly are similar figures of fear and loathing. The women receive extreme vilification through association with reproduction: 'pram face' (personified in British 'alternative' comedy – *The Catherine Tate Show*)

13   See Rahjan Khanna (2007) for a brilliant discussion of the problems with the concept of dignity.

14   Qualities also identified by Eva Illouz (1997) in her research on class differences in attitudes to romance.

15   Although see Larry M. Bartels (2005) who challenges Frank's general argument with specific statistical analysis of voting habits, showing that it is the middle-class that have moved further right in moral voting issues. In the US the book is called 'What's wrong with Kansas'. In the UK, 'What's wrong with America'.

16   CRESC (Manchester) 2007 'Contingencies of Value'.

# REFERENCES

Ahmed, S. (2004) 'Affective economies', *Social Text*, 22 (2): 117–39.

Althusser, L. (1971) *Lenin and Philosophy and Other Essays*. London: New Left Books.

Altman, D. (2001) *Global Sex*. Chicago, IL: Chicago University Press.

Austin, J. (1962) *How to Do Things With Words*. Oxford: Clarendon.

Bartels, L.M. (2005) *'What's the Matter With What's the Matter With Kansas?'*. Washington, DC: American Political Science Association.

Bourdieu, P. (1979) 'Symbolic power', *Critique of Anthropology*, 4: 77–85.

Bourdieu, P. (1984)[1979] *Distinction: A Social Critique of the Judgement of Taste*. London: Routledge and Kegan Paul.

Bourdieu, P. (1985) 'The social space and the genesis of groups', *Theory and Society*, 14: 723–44.

Bourdieu, P. (1987) 'What makes a social class? On the theoretical and practical existence of groups', *Berkeley Journal of Sociology*, pp. 1–17.

Bourdieu, P. (1989) 'Social space and symbolic power', *Sociological Theory*, 7: 14–25.

Bourdieu, P. (1992) *Language and Symbolic Power*. Cambridge: Polity Press.

Brenner, J. and Ramas, M. (1984) 'Rethinking women's oppression', *New Left Review*, 144: 33–72.

Brown, W. (1995) *States of Injury*. Princeton, NJ: Princeton University Press.

Butler, J. (1993) *Bodies That Matter: On the Discursive Limits of 'Sex'*. London: Routledge.

Butler, J. (1999) 'Performativity's social magic', in R. Shusterman (ed.), *Bourdieu: A Critical Reader*, pp. 113–129. Oxford: Blackwell.

Callinicos, A. and Harman, C. (1987) *The Changing Working-Class: Essays on Class Structure Today*. London: Bookmarks.

Cannadine, D. (1988) *Class in Britain*. New Haven, CT: Yale University Press.

Charlesworth, S. (2000) *A Phenomenology of Working Class Experience*. Cambridge: Cambridge University Press.

Cohen, A.K. (1955) *Delinquent Boys: The Culture of the Gang*. Chicago, IL: Free Press.

Coulter, A. and Gurley, G. (2002) 'Coultergeist', *New York Observer*, Newssheet, pp. 27–29. New York.

Crompton, R. (1993) *Class and Stratification: An Introduction to Current Debates*. Cambridge: Polity.

Crossick, G. (1991) 'From gentlemen to the residuum: Languages of social description', in Victorian Britain, in P.J. Corfield (ed.), *Language, History and Class*, pp. 150–178. Oxford: Blackwell.

Duncan, S. (2005) 'Mothering, class, rationality', *Sociological Review*, 53 (1): 50–76.

Duneier, M. (1992) *Slim's Table: Race, Respectability and Masculinity*. Chicago, IL: University of Chicago Press.

Eagleton, T. (1989) 'The ideology of the aesthetic', in P. Hernadi (ed.), *The Rhetoric of Interpretation and the Interpretation of Rhetoric*, pp. 79–87. Durham, NC: Duke University Press.

Engels, F. (1958[1844]) *The Condition of the Working-Class in England*. St Albans: Panther.

Finch, L. (1993) *The Classing Gaze: Sexuality, Class and Surveillance*. New South Wales Sydney: Allen and Unwin.

Foucault, M. (1979) *The History of Sexuality: Volume One, an Introduction*. London: Penguin.

Frank, T. (2004) *What's the Matter with America: The Resistable Rise of the American Right*. London: Secker and Warburg.

Frazer, E. (1992) 'Talking about gender, race and class', in D. Cameron, E. Frazer, P. Harvey, M.B.H. Rampton and K. Richardson (eds), *Researching Language: Issues on Power and Method*, pp. 281–290. London: Routledge.

Goldthorpe, J. (1996) 'Class analysis and the re-orientation of class theory: The case of persisting differentials in educational attainment', *British Journal of Sociology*, 45: 211–33.

Haylett, C. (2001) 'Illegitimate subjects? Abject whites, neoliberal modernisation and middle class multiculturalism', *Environment and Planning D: Society and Space*, 19: 351–70.

Hennessy, R. (2000) *Profit and Pleasure: Sexual Identities in Late Capitalism*. London and New York: Routledge.

Hoggart, R. (1957) *The Uses of Literacy*. London: Penguin.

hooks, b. (2000) *Where We Stand: Class Matters*. London: Routledge.

Illouz, E. (1997) *Consuming the Romantic Utopia: Love and the Cultural Contradictions of Capitalism*. Berkeley, CA: University of California Press.

Kelly, P. (2007) '*Filipino Migration, Transnationalism and Class Identity' WPS 90*. Singapore: Asia Research Institute, National University Singapore.

Khanna, R. (2007) 'Indignity', *Ethnic and Racial Studies*, 30 (2): 257–81.

Kirk, J. (2007) *Class, Culture and Social Change: On the Trail of the Working-Class*. Basingstoke: Palgrave Macmillan.

Kuhn, A. (1995) *Family Secrets: Acts of Memory and Imagination*. London: Verso.

Lamont, M. (2000) *The Dignity of Working Men: Morality and the Boundaries of Gender, Race and Class*. Cambridge, MA: Harvard University Press.

Lawler, S. (2000) *Mothering the Self: Mothers, Daughters, Subjects*. London: Routledge.

Lawler, S. (2002) 'Mobs and monsters: Independent man meets Paulsgrove woman', *Feminist Theory*, 3 (1): 103–13.

Macpherson, C.B. (1962) *The Political Theory of Possessive Individualism*. Oxford: Oxford University Press.

Marx, K. and Engels, F. (1968[1848]) *Manifesto of the Communist Party*. London: Lawrence and Wishart.

Matza, D. (1964) *Delinquency and Drift*. New York: Wiley.

McClintock, A. (1995) *Imperial Leather: Race, Gender and Sexuality in the Colonial Context*. London: Routledge.

Miller, W.B. (1958) 'Lower class culture as a generating milieu of gang delinquency', *Journal of Social Issues*, 15: 5–19.

Mount, F. (2004) *Mind the Gap: Class in Britain Now*. London: Short Books.

Nead, L. (1988) *Myths of Sexuality: Representations of Women in Victorian Britain*. Oxford: Blackwell.

Ortner, S. (1991) 'Reading America: Preliminary notes on class and culture', in G.R. Fox (ed.), *Recapturing Anthropology: Working in the Present*, pp. 163–191. Santa Fe, NM: School of American Research Press.

Ranciere, J. (1983) *The Philosopher and His Poor*. Durham, NC: Duke University Press.

Reay, D. (1998) *Class Work: Mother's Involvement in their Children's Primary Schooling*. London: UCL Press.

Ruddick, S. (2006) 'Abnormal, the 'new normal' and destabilizing discourses of rights', *Public Culture*, 18 (1): 53–77.

Savage, M. (2000) *Class Analysis and Social Transformation*. Buckingham: Open University Press.

Savage, M. (2003) 'A new class paradigm? Review article', *British Journal of Sociology of Education*, 24 (4): 535–41.

Sayer, A. (2005) *The Moral Significance of Class*. Cambridge: Cambridge University Press.

Sennett, R. and Cobb, J. (1977) *The Hidden Injuries of Class*. Cambridge: Cambridge University Press.

Skeggs, B. (1997) *Formations of Class and Gender: Becoming Respectable*. London: Sage.

Skeggs, B. (2004) *Class, Self, Culture*. London: Routledge.

Spinoza, B., de (1996) *Ethics*. London: Penguin.

Stanworth, M. (1984) 'Women and class analysis: A reply to Goldthorpe', *Sociology*, 18 (2): 153–71.

Ste. Croix, G., de. (1981) *The Class Struggle in the Ancient Greek World*. London: Duckworth.

Steedman, C. (1999) 'State sponsored autobiography', in B. Conekin, F. Mort and C. Waters (eds), *Movements of Modernity: Reconstructing Britain 1945–1964*, pp. 103–122. London: Rivers Oram.

Steedman, C. (2000) 'Enforced narratives: Stories of another self', in T. Cosslett, C. Lury and P. Summerfield (eds), *Feminism and Autobiography: Texts, Theories, Methods*, pp. 25–40. London: Routledge.

Strathern, M. (1992) *After Nature: English Kinship in the Late Twentieth Century*. Cambridge: Cambridge University Press.

Thompson, E.P. (1966) *The Making of the English Working Class*. Harmondsworth: Penguin.

Thompson, J. (1996) *Models of Value: Eighteenth Century Political Economy and the Novel*. Durham, NC: Duke University Press.

Vicinus, M. (1974) *The Industrial Muse: A Study of Nineteenth Century British Working Class Literature*. London: Croom Helm.

Wahrman, D. (1995) *Imagining the Middle-Class: The Political Representation of Class in Britain, c. 1780–1840*. Cambridge: Cambridge University Press.

Walkerdine, V. and Lucey, H. (1989) *Democracy in the Kitchen: Regulating Mothers and Socialising Daughters*. London: Virago.

Walkerdine, V., Lucey, H. and Melody, J. (2001) *Growing up Girl: Psychosocial Explorations of Gender and Class*. Basingstoke: Palgrave.

Ware, V. (1992) *Beyond the Pale: White Women, Racism and History*. London: Verso.

Weis, L. (2004) *Class Reunion: The Remaking of the American White Working Class*. New York: Routledge.

Williams, R. (1988) *Keywords: A Vocabulary of Culture and Society*. London: Fontana.

Willis, P. (1977) *Learning to Labour: How Working Class Kids Get Working Class Jobs*. Farnborough: Saxon House.

Wright, E. (1985) *Classes*. London: Verso.

Yeo, E. (1993) *The Contest of Social Science in Britain: Relations and Representations of Gender and Class*. Lancaster: Lancaster University.

Zizek, S. (1997) 'Multiculturalism, or, the cultural logic of multinational capitalism', *New Left Review*, 225: 28–52.

Zizek, S.(2000) 'Class struggle or postmodernism: Yes, please!', in J. Butler, E. Laclau and S. Zizek (eds), *Contingency, Hegemony, Universality: Contemporary Dialogues on the Left*, pp. 90–136. London: Verso.

Zizek, S. (2004) 'Over the rainbow', *London Review of Books*, 4 (11): 20.

# 18

# Sexualities

Cindy Patton

## A FASHION FOR SELF-FASHIONING

Most everyone in the Commonwealth, Europe, or North America can tell you what they are – gay, straight, bisexual, bicurious. The categories of sexual identity subdivide as their capacity to designate fails some individuals. In our current context, it seems natural that everyone has a sexual identity; indeed, we feel a certain amount of pity toward those who disclaim a sexual identity, and relieved when those who held one at odds with our own perception of them finally 'come out' as whatever they have determined themselves truly to be. But how did it happen that something so clearly variable across cultures, places, times, and even individual life spans should be taken as not only a natural possession of each individual psyche but also universal?

Sexual identity may be the example *par excellence* of the research object constituted by its own investigation, or in this case, doubly constituted; it is almost impossible to talk about sexual identity without also talking about sexuality, an object of study necessitated by investigation of the elusive category, desire, and its tawdry side kick, practice. To understand the trajectory of research on sexual identity, it is important to recognize that the past century of work that is plainly 'about' sexual identity – that is, about the rise, nature, and use of sex, as opposed to research or philosophizing about,

say, eros – tracks alongside, and is often contingent on, shifting definitions of what counts as a sexual act, ideas about the source of sexual desire, and theories about the place of social structure in the production, recognition, and regulation of bodies, acts, and desires. Because its object is so uncertain (more likely a series of different objects), research on sexuality and sexual identity is uniquely interdisciplinary, conjoining work on art and literature, history, sociology, anthropology, philosophy, psychology, biology, and genetics. This work is also uniquely political: from Hirschfeld and Freud to Kinsey to current queer theorists and somatechnicians, leading researchers, clinicians, and educators have conducted their work largely with the aim of reducing the suffering of people they believed to be unfairly burdened (personally or socially) by the composition or direction of their erotic feelings. Because research on sexuality is so regularly at odds with the social, cultural, and legal structures that govern personal conduct, those who engage in this research have often been accused of being 'perverts' themselves. To a degree unknown in other academic specialties, research on sexuality (in the inaugural years, and, still foremost, *deviant* sexualities) is haunted by the demand to justify the study of its object: 'the love that dare not speak its name' is thought capable of contaminating those who study it.

It is tempting to think of sexual identity as something of a postscript to the bigger and bolder forms of identity (e.g., cultural, national, racial); indeed, many people consider sexual identity to be the most recent, 'personal', and least important parsing of the aspects of human diversity around which one might form a sense of self. However, historian and philosopher Michel Foucault suggested that the now widely held conviction that identity lies within is the historical culmination of the west's long and circuitous contemplation of the flesh. In his *Introduction to a History of Sexuality* (1990[1977]) and *The Uses of Pleasure* (1990[1985]), Foucault argues against the idea that there is a bedrock sexuality that an individual uncovers and then embraces as their sexual identity. Instead, in those volumes, and in the earlier *Discipline and Punish* (1977) and the later *Care of the Self* (1990[1986]), Foucault demonstrates the incremental shift in the west from overt mechanisms of control toward practices of self-regulation. This shift from power to knowledge/power necessitated the constitution of a 'self', complete with subjectivity capable of inner dialogue ('I searched my soul', 'I asked myself'), which could serve as the locus for organizing and cultivating practices of self-regulation. Because (sexual) reproduction and sexual play cross paths with population control and the political consolidation it allows, we should not be surprised that sexual desire and sexual alterity were invented, then recursively linked.

As I hope to chronicle here, sexual identity remains an ontologically contentious category, which means I necessarily occupy a position in the debate once framed as essentialism versus social construction. Although this framing gradually disappeared (not least because 'essentialist' became a nasty epithet), the fundamental issues remain and in polarized form: what is the ontological status of any or all of the cascade of potentially linked objects – the desiring body (potentially intrinsic), sexual acts (almost necessarily extrinsic, except, perhaps as unspoken sexual fantasy or sexual memory), and sexual

identity (argued to be intrinsic, but as Janet Halley (1993, 1999) shows in her research on homosexuality and employment law, communicated extrinsically, except in the case of 'coming out to oneself', an act that requires the form of interiority whose genealogy Foucault traced)? It is no doubt already obvious that I adopt Foucault's position as I side step the question of what sexual identity is in favor considering how the concept arose and has been worked out within western research. I first lay out the early murmurings of the research object 'sexual identity', work which struggles with the moral and biological nature of 'sexuality'. I then identify the successors whose mid-twentieth-century work in the social sciences enabled the emergence of sexual identity in parallel with the other identities in the political agon of identity politics. I move on quickly to the historical research that the social science projects enabled, focusing on the political context that made particular styles of research on sexual identity – the so-called essentialist work – seem so urgent and plausible. This approach to the history of sexual identity should go some distance in explaining why the seemingly 'essentialist' identity related to the gay civil rights movements of the 1970s and 1980s lost its shock value, opening up the space for queer and performative sexual identities. This style of linking an interiority with practices and calling it 'identity' is what I believe most people mean when they speak of 'sexual identity'. While apparently stable, it rests on an ongoing and uneasy compromise between opposing ontologies of sexuality: the 'sexual identity' that becomes globalized, significantly through the activism in relation to and management of the HIV/AIDS pandemic, is simultaneously conceived of as the product of fixed drives and as a social construction. This identity arose as the most personal complement of and in parallel with other now well accepted identities (black, Chicano, disabled, etc.) that were part of the larger rainbow of progressive identity-based social movements, a history well-documented in John D'Emilio's (1983) *Sexual Politics/Sexual Communities*. In the final section of this chapter, I consider how the historically and culturally circumscribed notion of sexual identity that was forged in the crucible of identity politics, by the 1990s, under the pressure of late modern globalization, especially in the vehicle of the HIV/AIDS epidemic, became recognizably international, even as it marked divergent people and practices.

There are so many works from which to select, and such charged academic and political debates about sexuality and sexual identity that it is almost impossible not to fling myself into these debates. Instead, I trace particular academic and activist uses of the idea of sexual identity. It is not, contra the ongoing claim of most social researchers, that we do not understand sexuality very well, but rather, that we have so many uses for the idea of sexual identity that avenues of research continually open up. For example, in the 1980s US, changes in the law made it seem possible for homosexuals to be recognized as a type of citizen in a plurality of differences. Lesbian and gay historians took up the political task of finding not only homosexual forebearers, but also homosexual communities, the evidence necessary to prove that lesbians and gay men had always been part of America, and, because they were oppressed for their sexuality, should find their place alongside groups who were to attain civil rights and protections. Is this work an example of intellectually bankrupt essentialism, or of historically bound interpretations of complicated evidence in a politically charged context? To undercut the ontological status of one's difference was risky business in the civil rights era.

These activist-academics are but one chapter in an incoherent story of research on sexual identity in the sometimes autonomous, sometimes mutually antagonistic trajectories of the social science and humanities disciplines that have had the most to say about sexual identity: psychology, sociology, anthropology, history, and literature. (I leave literature aside in this account because its contribution, though monumental, was primarily on the side of destabilizing fixed notions of identity in favor of what would become 'queer' identities and queer theory, a topic covered in Chapter 5. Why literary theory was able to take the lead in deconstructing the sexual identity of identity politics has to do both with its freedom from the empirical demands of the scientific methods to which even qualitative research nods, and because the work that would become most influential after identity politics was written in French and imported through literature departments before becoming widely read in the social sciences.) In the earliest time period I will discuss – the turn of the twentieth century – psychology, sociology, and anthropology had not fully differentiated. Researchers in each of these three disciplines shared a conviction that sexuality was poorly understood, and that existing forms of moral and/or legal regulation of sexuality, and especially, of deviancy, were immoral or, for conservatives, ineffective. But their approach to the study of sex, sexuality, and sexual identity increasingly diverged until it seemed that they were studying different objects. For all of their intentions to improve the lot of the sexually peculiar, the effect of the early twentieth century research endeavors, paradoxically, was to increase scrutiny of deviants, who were encouraged to align their self-conception with researchers' definitions and present themselves for study. Research needs an object.

## CONSTITUTING A SPEAKABLE (AND SPEAKING) SUBJECT

### *Psychoanalysis and psychology*

The history of psychology is complex and contentious (Danziger, 1990), however, in general, the field, heavily indebted to philosophy of mind, has been primarily interested in the individual and even the infra-individual – behavior, affect, and mind – including a clinical focus on diagnosis and treatment of disorders of any or all of these. The analytic disagreements within psychology have long centered on the nature of human consciousness and selfhood (Teo, 2005), and ongoing disputes over the status of sexual identity – in particular, non-heterosexual identities – rely on arguments about the location of sexual desire in the mind or mental processes; is sexuality 'hard wired' into the brain? If so, how? Can sexual desire, sexual practice, and/ or sexual identity be modified? Even before psychology emerged as a scientific discipline, nineteenth-century, proto-psychologists had linked gender and brain, arguing that the female and male brains produced thought differently, a small step on the longer path to debates about sexuality as a property of persons (Malane, 2005). Twentieth-century psychology seemed to provide a scientific basis for the Enlightenment claim that a universal humanity lay beneath superficial differences in temperament and behavior, an argument critical to resituating the question of sexuality from legal and moral regulation of behavior to a concern with the nature of sexual desire and its power to motivate a range of intentions and actions. By the turn of the twentieth century, psychology was squarely aligned with the proposition that sexuality is an individual property.

The dominant method of early research in psychology was the case study, a strategy suited to the work of clinician-researchers – often physicians – who wanted to use science to challenge social and religious norms that stigmatized or policed non-dominant sexual activities (including the full gamut: sex before or outside marriage, sex in improper positions or with improper persons or things). Early clinician–researchers developed three main theories to explain 'sex variants', eventually focusing most closely on what emerged as the category 'homosexual', research that would soon be criticized as positivism swept through all academic disciplines. Case studies would be dismissed as insufficiently scientific because they lacked controls ('normal subjects') and instead focused on

people who had sought help to resolve a disjuncture between their somatic experiences or desires and the social definitions of sexual practice and, later, sexual identity.

Karl Ulrich (1825–1895), himself a 'homosexual' and a dedicated campaigner against Germany's law against sex between men ('Paragraph 175'), developed a theory that homosexuals – or in his nomenclature, urnings – were a form of hermaphrodite, with a sexual disjuncture between body (male) and brain (female). Positing (predominantly, male) homosexual desire as innate to this physical duality, Ulrich argued for the repeal of anti-homosexual laws and argued for tolerance for those who, in the major cities of Europe, were fashioning subcultures hospitable to a range of sex variants (Kennedy, 1988). Many subsequent sex theorists adopted Ulrich's definition, but not always his politics; morally conservative researchers and clinicians understood such persons – eventually renamed 'inverts' – to be medically diseased and in need of treatment – forced if necessary – to prevent further development of the newly visible sex variant subcultures in Europe.

The second main argument about homosexuality focused on the physical aspects of sodomy and pederasty. Ambrose Tardieu (1818–1879), argued that 'active' pederasts had a unique shape to their penises, while 'passive' pederasts had funnel shaped anuses, making sex between them more graceful and pleasurable – natural – than the heterosexual alternative (Rosario, 1996). Although this theory attracted few adherents, the fascination with the anatomy of the sex variant body extends into the present. Early to mid-twentieth-century research described lesbians as suffering from enlarged clitori, and in the early years of the HIV/AIDS epidemic (1980–present) right-wing literature was full of descriptions of homosexual men's anuses as 'loose', and potentially dribbling 'AIDS germs'. Contemporary discussions about inter-sexed and transgendered bodies and trans-sexuality revived an interest in the significance of variant anatomical configuration, especially discrepancies between sex and gender role, producing a complex identity movement and counter-movement discussed elsewhere in this volume (see Chapter 8). Tardieu was also one of the first to argue for a distinction between men who had sex with men for money or power, and those who engaged in such sex because of the demands of their differently structured bodies, an idea that reverberates in the distinction between 'situational' versus 'real' homosexuality as an explanation of bisexuality in both women (Rust, 2000) and men (Stewart, 2007), a concept that underwrites some apparently progressive HIV policy (Brooks et al., 2003; May et al., 2002; Silenzio, 2003).

A third argument, and perhaps the most groundbreaking because it sought explicitly to undercut the grounds for pathologizing sex variation, came from Sigmund Freud (1962, 1963), who argued that while there is an ideal developmental trajectory to mature sexuality and sexual identity development, in practice, it is almost never achieved. The vast majority of individuals experience some kind of 'deviation', either in object (e.g., failure to reliably settle on an appropriate person – not only homosexuals, who chose the same sex, but also pedophiles, who chose non-adults, and those who want to have sex with animals or objects) or in aim (e.g., failure to reliably desire penetrative sex, including fixation on oral sex, masturbation, voyeurism, etc.). For Freud, each deviation was the result of an underlying pathology (e.g., melancholy or mania), itself a result of incomplete expression of the life drive ('libido', often incorrectly reduced to sex), but these could be alleviated through psychoanalysis. Freud was not interested in changing sexual behavior, since sexual deviation was the result, not the cause of pathology.

By the 1930s, psychology came under pressure from scientific positivism and, like virtually all academic disciplines in the western academy, was swept up in the frenzy to apply to their research objects the new scientific method developed in the physical sciences (Pickren, 1997). Psychological research

shifted toward experimental design, which required clear measures of pathology. At the same time, nation states intensified their efforts to decide who was and was not fit for military service. After World War I, the League of Nations created the first version of the *International Statistical Classification of Diseases* (ICD), which did not include mental disorders. The US Army developed a screening system to weed out mentally defective (including homosexual) recruits in the years leading up to World War II. At the end of World War II, with the formation of the United Nations (UN), the newly created (1947) health branch – the World Health Organization (WHO) – revised the ICD to include mental disorders for the first time (Charles, 1968). The American Psychiatric Association entered this positivistic frenzy and asserted its superiority as the adjudicator of diagnoses – including homosexuality – when it created the first version of the 1952 Diagnostic and Statistical Manual (DSM), a document that is substantially based on the US Army's World War II screening schema (Houts, 2000).

Efforts to devise a clinically reliable definition of homosexuality were contested by psychologists and homosexuals, who disagreed among themselves about the relationship between desire, practices, and what was beginning to be understood as identity. Gay activists and progressive psychologists in the 1970s took aim at the DSM, viewed as a lynchpin in the state repression of lesbians and gay men because defining homosexuality as a pathology enabled legal discrimination against lesbians and gay men in employment (especially the military, government, and teaching) and allowed immigration officials to exclude foreigners based on sexuality. Although the exclusion of gay foreigners was officially dropped in 1990, subsequent legal activism was required to include homosexual persecution as a rationale for asylum, and the definitions of partner and spouse cannot change as long as 'defense of marriage' domestic legislation remains. Nevertheless, consuls have been instructed since 2001 to allow homosexual partners of US citizens to accompany them (Romero, 2006).

After the heated debates about changing the definition of pathological sexuality or removing homosexuality altogether, the American Psychiatric Association (1974), finally unable to stop talking about sexual deviancy once and for all, adopted the logic of civil rights: it was the *pathologization* of homosexuality that causes problems for individuals, not homosexuality *per se* (Conrad and Schneider, 1992; Marotta, 1981). Although homosexuality was removed from the DSM-IV, various forms of 'dystonia' remained (e.g., the feeling that one is at odds with oneself, including with internalized social norms), echoing early invert theories that posit a split between body and mind.

Clinicians were left with few guidelines for what to do with the people who came in with unhappiness about their homosexuality. While the majority of counseling professionals incrementally shifted toward helping their clients 'come out' and 'adjust' to what was increasingly thought of as a subculture or lifestyle (a framework that was directly dependent on parallel research in sociology and anthropology, as I will discuss next), a solid minority of practitioners continue to develop reorientation therapies aligned with the Christian New Right evangelical conviction that it matters little whether an individual became homosexual or was 'born that way', they must learn to resist living a life of sin and become heterosexual. For both gay-positive and reorientationist clinicians, the goal of counseling intensified around the idea of a sexual identity – positing either two types of identity (gay/lesbian or straight – bisexuality was soon pathologized by progressives as an inability to accept one's intrinsic homosexuality), which the counselor carefully helped a client integrate as a full sense of self, or positing one identity – heterosexual – from which other sexual identities were sinful diversions. It is important to note that, historically and logically speaking, homosexual identity was defined

first – initially as 'not-the-norm', and, in the 1980s as a 'healthy homosexual' – and heterosexual identity only much later, arguably, as a reaction against the clear articulation of a positive homosexual identity.

Interestingly, gay-positive counselors, apparently 'essentialist' in their understanding of identity began to move away from the ego-psychology understanding of sexual identity as a culmination in favor of an understanding of identity as a process of ongoing self-representation. The advent of neuropsychology enabled a new round of research on whether there is a 'gay brain', but this work only briefly reignited the essentialism versus social construction debates; work by LeVay (1991, 1993) in particular detaches sexual orientation from sexual identity by remaining agnostic on the social processes by which an intrinsically homosexual body would become gay or lesbian. There is a lively body of research on the bio-/physio-neurology of sexual desire/sexual orientation; however this is largely ignored now by social constructionist and Foucaultian social scientists and historians, who remain agnostic about the biological origins of the sexual desire/orientation that may underpin the social worlds of those whom they study.

## Eros around the world

If psychology offered three different theories of sexuality and sexual identity, then anthropology contributed a shift in focus and a new sobriety to the study of non-western sexual cultures, validating and dignifying the study of sexuality, and at the same time, bringing empirical evidence of forms of sexual identity quite different than those psychologists encountered in their clinical and research activities. Anthropologists were not the first intellectuals to bring tales of the Other back to the centers of the empire. Travel writers had shocked their ostensibly straight-laced Victorian audience with exotic tales about the sexual customs they found abroad. As anthropologists would later point out, clergy were the cultural handmaiden to the colonial economic enterprise; by focusing on the alien sexual organization of the colonial subjects, clergy could easily justify their 'civilizing' projects framed in the language of Victorian Christian morality. Anthropologists organized these opposing rationales for examining other peoples' sex lives into the study of the culture, taking the family (and kinship) rather than the individual (and mind) as the fundamental building block. This shifted the focus of inquiry from sexuality as a property of persons to sexual *roles* – and thus sexual identities – as a social relationship, and laid the groundwork for importing ideas like sexual culture and (queer) kinship into later research on urban, western sexual identities.

Unlike psychology, which from the outset yoked basic research to clinical application, anthropology in general, with the exception of brief war-time stints during World War II and the Vietnam War, did not develop primarily as an applied discipline (Silliltoe, 2006). This early lack of clear academic identity and relationship to the state enabled anthropologists to function as broader critics of their contemporaneous norms. Without a formal platform for demonstrating its broad social value, anthropologists were often as ostentatious as their adventurer predecessors. Proto-feminist anthropologist Margaret Mead (1961[1930]) was well-known for her lectures, films, and popular magazine articles on the sexual development of girls in Samoa, which she cited to argue against the Victorian sexual order and in favor, by the 1960s, of the sexual revolution. Mead's exceptionally close relationship with two female colleagues has lead biographers and commentators to suggest that she was bisexual. Although Mead never claimed a particular sexual identity, she used her anthropological research to argue that an individuals' sexuality is not fixed but changes over the life course.

Anthropology eventually came to reflect upon its colonialist roots, and turned the evidence it once used to argue for Spenserian cultural Darwinism to instead demonstrate that any apparent moral universality across 'modern' and 'primitive' was a result of the colonial period and especially, Christianization (Comaroff, 1991). This was an especially important insight as sexual identity was internationalized through HIV/AIDS discourse; in 1987 the US Senate was unable to pass its first major HIV/AIDS funding bill without the so-called 'Helms Amendment', which limited funding to organizations which did not 'promote homosexuality and promiscuity'. Linking right-wing ideas about sexuality and sexual identity to funding was globalized by the George W. Bush administration which in 2003, placed restrictions on international HIV/AIDS funding to exclude groups that helped sex trade workers, and required that a percentage of the funding be used for 'abstinence only' safe sex education, formalizing what had been clear from the colonial era forward: adopting 'Christian' norms and values marked states as 'modern', and resulted in the emergence of state-sponsored homophobia and repression of people with non-dominant sexual identities or practices where only cultural norms had shaped these before colonialism (Stoler 1995). But by 1988, the World Health Organization, using anthropological data on sexual diversity argued for including anti-homophobia, improvement of women's capacity to make decisions about sex, and decriminalization of sex work as part of the health/human rights formula, and states liberalized their approach to homosexuality in order to find favor with a different set of global funders (Uganda, see Patton, 1999) or state legitimators (Taiwan, see Patton, 1998).

Anthropological research challenged the universality of any particular form of sexual expression, in some spectacular cases demonstrating that activities perceived as sex in some cultures are not so perceived in others. For example, Gilbert Herdt's (1981) work on the Sambia extended earlier work on 'ritual homosexuality', which had already demonstrated a range of male–male sexual practices to be important within 'primitive' cultures. Herdt's work shows that in Sambian culture, semen is perceived to be the most critical life fluid and must be carefully distributed to both men and women. In order for Sambian boys to become men capable both of defending the clan and contributing to the creation of babies, they had to fellate adult males, thereby consuming the precious fluid they would need as men. Significantly, Herdt shows, this male–male act was not only not seen as 'sex' by the Sambia, but it conveyed a masculine and not a homosexual identity.

Many scholars detailed cases in which kinship structures included important same-sex bonds that implicitly allowed either for homosexual sexual relationship or permitted social identities beyond whatever stood as normatively male and female. For example, Moodie's (1994) work on South Africa shows that in the mid-twentieth century, men who migrated to work in the mines often engaged in homosexual sex, but not only that, developed long-term relationships with male 'town wives' parallel to the bigamous heterosexual relationships of other miners. While most of the men who took male 'town wives' expressed a preference for relationships with women, Moodie finds cases of men who increased the amount of time they spent at the mine, essentially maintaining their same-sex relationship in preference to their heterosexual relationship in their home village.

Formalized female same-sex relationships have long played an important organizational role in sub-Saharan Africa. Cadigan (1998) reviews the extensive literature on locally specific structures of 'female husbands' in a range of different cultural groups. While anthropologists go to some length to offer functionalist rationales (building wealth, end-running kinship strategies that favor men), the erotic content of such relationships is hard to dismiss. Indeed, Njambi and O'Brien (2000), reviewing their own interviews in the context of existing literature, suggest that the wives are reticent to explicitly discuss homosexual sex, but the female husbands happily detail their pursuit of sexual pleasure. Although much of the permissible promiscuity is with men, female husbands note that they grow tired of men (who are, it must be noted, their social and economic competition). This work suggests that while gendered social roles with sexual expectations (men sleep around, women do not) strongly govern individual sexual behavior, female husbands – who are socially male – develop a strong identity that includes the cultivation of their sexual freedom, even if this is not allowed to take a public homoerotic form with female partners. (Anthropologists seem to lapse into biological essentialism in order to avoid the question of the social meaning of sexual relations between female and a male 'husbands'. Do female husbands revert to being females – who are not supposed to be having sex outside marriage – when they exercise their socially male sexual identity to have sex as they please? Surely this is some form of homoerotics.)

Jennifer Robertson's (1998) historical anthropological work suggests another compromise within an apparently uniform sexual identity structure. The female cross-dressing and stage relationships in the all-female Takarazuka Japanese theatre create the opportunity for something like a lesbian identity at the margins of apparently intransigent sex roles. The women who took male lead roles often carried these personas and desires off-stage, playing the dashing sex magnet to swooning female fans, and sometimes forming sexual relationships with other actresses.

## Urban life, deviance, and sex

Sociology made further contributions to the study of sexual identity, focused on social structures in the developed world, especially in the modern metropolis. Almost from the beginning as a recognizably distinct academic discipline, sociology was directly linked with the modern state, engaging in theory-building and policy intervention that offered some direction on how to manage the state's increasing role in what had once been the private and religious domains. In particular, early sociologists weighed in on how to expand educational systems, how to manage the poor, how to understand religion in a secularizing context, and how to build the bureaucracies required of the more interventionist state. The dominant theoretical model of early sociology was structural functionalism (a framework also developed by Malinowski), which argued that each component of a society played a specific role that allowed the society as a whole to achieve stability and reproduce itself, with a teleological eye toward a more democratic and prosperous future. Norms were the theoretical lynchpin of structural–functional theories of society: society had to enforce norms in order to progress, and the family was understood as a locus for, in particular, the enforcement of how sex roles functioned. But norms were invisible except through the study of deviations from them. Arguably, the intensification of interest in norms actually produced the perceptual apparatus to both research and, as an object of such research, experience 'sexual deviancy' as a condition or person-type rather than a form of criminality. Sociologists became interested in how deviant individuals negotiated the social structures they found themselves in, re-embracing the individual but not in order to understand the contribution of interiority to normativity, but rather to explore the 'presentation of self' (Goffman, 1959) and the 'management of stigma' (Goffman, 1963). Although this important work of Erving Goffman (and social interaction theory more generally) was eclipsed in the late 1970s when Foucault's translated works became widely available on the American academic scene, the idea that individual deviancy led to patterned styles of negotiating dominant norms laid the intellectual groundwork (along with Franz Fanon's concept of shifting dual identity, as in *Black Skins/White Masks* [1965], an enormously popular read for 1970s gay liberationists) for the gay rights movement. Splitting the difference between claims to a special point of view on the world ('gay is good!') and claims to be 'just like you', the gay rights movement would argue that 'gay' identity was not necessarily born of a common essence but rather – or

equally – of a shared history of oppression. This understanding of gay identity enabled activists to link to the broader 'Rainbow Coalition'; gay oppression was a specific instance of the broader oppression – variously, patriarchy, capitalism, or colonial status – that affected other groups in their own specific way.

## From a homosexual nosology to the history of the homosexual

If the early twentieth century contemplations of sexuality concerned definition of who would count as what, and why, the post-Word War II years where characterized by a bracketing of definition in favor of creating a broad public face for whoever cared to stand up and be counted within the category of 'homosexual' and, by the 1970s, 'gay'. The minor but significant body of works on 'the homosexual' in psychology and sociology, and important anthropological works that questioned the universality of modes of 'being straight', laid the groundwork for future research. In the US context, and perhaps most famously, the activities of sexologists continued to explore the variety of sexual experience across different classes, regions, and with attention to male and female differences, including male and females practices and experiences of same sex desires (Irvine, 2005; Weeks, 1985).

Probably the most significant academic research on the sex lives of ordinary people was the massive Kinsey project, popularized then through trade paperbacks, magazine and newspaper coverage, and incorporation as a pop culture reference (Kinsey et al., 1948). Kinsey was a fly biologist whose training and disposition as a researcher was nosological, and whose personal interests were evolving and persistent. (Kinsey had relationships with men and women and had no clear name for himself beyond a kind of libertine person with a scientific quest to say aloud what had remained unspoken in post-World War II American life.) Psychology was partially transformed by the hard-to-dismiss mapping out of the American sexual landscape, nevertheless, the explosive discovery of the pervasiveness of American sexual curiosity was largely translated back into clinicians' still pathologizing diagnostic framework.

Three other more or less widely known and sensational work influenced the conceptualization of sexual identity in the research that occurred on the cusp of the gay liberation movement, affecting both activists and social scientists. Occupying rather different political positions, all sympathetic to homosexuals, the Kinsey reports and these works were the first widely accessible and popularly available research on homosexuality, and almost certainly helped frame the sense of identity that emerged among first 'homophile' movement participants and later, gay liberationists.

In the 1950s through 1970s, Evelyn Hooker conducted standardized psychological tests on self-identified (and not through clinical channels) homosexual and heterosexual men, and found no difference between the groups. Her work suggested that while the homosexual was clearly a social category, it had no place as a clinical category, an argument parallel to Kinsey's, but established from within psychology (Hooker, 1957). This work was critical to efforts in the 1970s to have homosexuality removed from the list of disorders canonized in the DSM.

Donald Webster Cory (actually Edward Sagarin, who would return to school in the 1950s and become a sociology and criminology professor in the 1960s, though still using his pseudonym for his popular works) published a popular, pocket-sized paperback called *The Homosexual in America: A Subjective Approach* (1951). The wildly popular book was completely independent of the Kinsey project, but was read against the same context, although with rather different politics. Sagarin did not reject the 'sickness' thesis of homosexuality, but he did argue that homosexuals were for that very reason a substantial and misunderstood minority (figures provided by Kinsey!) deserving of protection from discrimination and persecution. As Sagarin acquired his academic credentials he began to publish sociological articles supportive of the conservative approach to homosexual rights. He nevertheless continued his homophile movement activities as Cory, including active involvement in early gay publishing that was important to the development of a sense of group identity among homophile activists and other readers. This included a collection of homosexual short stories by famous authors and editorship of the major homophile movement magazine, *ONE*. He opposed the emerging work of Hooker and Laud Humphreys (below) and other sociologists who were arguing for the normalcy of gay life. The dual life of Sagarin/Cory eventually became known when Laud Humphreys subtly but quite publicly 'outed' him at a sociology conference after he delivered a public attack on the new scholarship. It was unclear whether his biggest crime was to stay closeted, to publish similar works under two different names, or to attack the liberationist sociologists. Sagarin disappeared from the intellectual and activist scene in 1974, nevertheless, his early works were influential both for the more apologetic part of the gay movement and within sociology.

Laud Humphreys was deeply influenced by the two decades of Evelyn Hooker's work and published an important interview with her in 1978. His *Tearoom Trade: Impersonal Sex in Public Places* (1975) conducted as dissertation research in the 1960s, was a study of anonymous male–male sex in public washrooms. Humphreys found that half the men who regularly participated in fellatio with men did not consider themselves homosexuals, establishing the importance of considering sexual identity and sexual practice different aspects of individual experience interrelated in complex ways. This work also became controversial, in part for its content but in part for its methods. Long before ethics standards were fully codified, the University of Washington attempted unsuccessfully to strip Humphreys of his Ph.D., publicly arguing that his method of public observation posing as a voyeur was unethical and that his use of license plates to track down subjects was a violation of their privacy. (It is likely that the underlying reason was the chancellor's distress at the attempt to normalize what he viewed as criminal behavior.) After this episode, sociologists began to debate research methods and research ethics more explicitly, including considering where to draw the line with covert research, that is, is the information gleaned great enough and the consequences for research subjects small enough that some 'covert' research is ethical?

These last researchers' work spanned the shift from the 'homophile' movement, which largely sought accommodation for homosexuals, who could achieve a coherent sexual identity in the psychological sense (self-acceptance as sexually deviant, whether 'sick' or 'healthy' according to different models), and the gay liberation movement, which cultivated and politicized the form of identity that I think is the reference today of the phrase 'sexual identity'. Two different political contexts in the 1960s and 1970s shaped the evolution of Hooker's and Humphreys' work toward the gay liberation position, and directly affected the push to develop not only a social science of sexuality, but also a history of homosexuals, homophobia, and eventually, sexuality.

I emphasize the American context because while there were important homophile and gay movements in the UK and Europe, World War II constituted a breach in European movements (the Nazi's had put homosexuals in concentration camps), while the US was experiencing the dramatic development of a new form of civil identity in the form of the black civil rights movement. Over time, the nationally specific gay identities of the post-World War II era would interact with the American version, I want to suggest that the influence of these emergent sexual identities (and concepts of sexual identity) were more unilateral. For all the challenges to and modifications of the American version of gay identity, the civil rights-based notion of public sexual presence remained largely unscathed as it was globalized through the 1990s. As I hope to show quickly in the final section, globalized gay identity's capacity to accept social construction worked with its capacity to convey rights for a minority fixed by some essence or shared experience, pointing to its origins in the American version of 'identity politics'.

## THE SUBJECTS SPEAKS: THE SOCIAL FORMATION OF THE STUDY OF 'SEXUAL IDENTITY'

While the emergent human sciences grappled with finding or constituting a research object – first sexuality, and by the mid-twentieth century, sexual identity – countless people lived lives against the sexual norms of their places and times. I have tried to indicate some of the investments in discovering in sexualities particular ways of being, and indicate some of the pressure that these investments created for individuals and groups who were undergoing study and naming. Historians of sexuality and of homophobia played an important role in both establishing the historical continuities in sexual difference, but also in uncovering the variety of sexualities. The social structures of sexual alterity that these researchers found give us a rich sense of what was happening 'on the ground' as the human sciences, using a range of different disciplinary strategies, began to create a scientific language and conceptual framework into which individuals began to fit themselves. Following Foucault, we must read the evidence of sexual alterity through two lenses: first, as subjective effects that were sometimes lived *within* otherwise (and shifting) heteronormative structures and sometimes lived across the grain of such structures; and second, as the product of the human sciences that helped constitute the unruly objects of their study.

Historians had a somewhat easier time legitimating the study of sexuality than their peers in the social sciences. While many of the important historians of sexuality were themselves 'gay' or 'lesbian', the fact that historians study the past tended to diminish (though not eliminate) the criticism of self-justification or bias: historians were simply uncovering the facts of lives now past. Second, and perhaps more importantly, in the mid-twentieth century, historians shifted away from political histories of great actors and watershed moments and began studying the everyday life of ordinary people. This opened up the study of the past to include new research methods (from quantitative analysis to oral history) and new topics, including sexuality. Finally, the public history movement engendered a wide range of local projects in which members of a community collected their own life-materials and created their own history, one of the most enduring legacies of the lesbian and gay movement of the 1970s–1990s has been to gather and preserve a wide range of ephemera in lesbian and gay history archives.

The public history movement took on special importance for lesbians and gay men haunted by images of the Nazis burning Hirschfeld's archive of materials related to nineteenth-and early twentieth-century sexual minorities. Although activists in the mid-twentieth-century homophile movement had identified important homosexual forbearers, the increasing emphasis on demonstrating both 'positive' gay and lesbian role models, and demonstrating the oppression and resilience of lesbian and gay communities intensified the search for a past. 'Outing' the famous – living and dead – was a popular activity before the Internet accelerated the transit speed of gossip and raised questions about the political utility of devoting 'movement' energies to identifying people who might not embrace movement politics. Nevertheless, there was a certain amount of glee in discovering queer roots in one's own city. Several of these projects resulted in

publications, notably the Boston Lesbian and Gay History Project (Kane, 1999), the Chicago Gay History Project (Baim, 2008), Seattle's Northwest Lesbian and Gay History Museum Project (2004), and the San Francisco Lesbian and Gay History Project which started in 1978. Other public historians spent less time writing up their discoveries, and primarily collected and catalogued collections for other's use, for example, the unique and important, Lesbian Herstory Archive. In addition, academic historians sometimes worked closely with community groups and institutions to produce oral histories of communities, notably *Boots of Leather* (1993), a result of Liz Kennedy and Madeline Davis' collaboration with the Buffalo (New York) Women's Oral History Project.

Historical research on sexual alterity tended toward two poles: the history of sexual regulation and social homophobia, and the history of contingent constructions of sexuality, sexual identity, and sexual community. For historians of regulation or homophobia, homosexuality was ahistorical, a relatively unchanging property of persons; what changed were the social, religious, and legal reactions to 'it'. Gay activists found this research extremely helpful when they sought to establish the long-term persecution and oppression of homosexuals, but right wing homophobes used their evidence against proposed sexuality-related civil rights; for them, the persistence of moral judgment against and persecution of homosexuality showed that it was fundamentally wrong. John Boswell's (1980) sentinel *Christianity, Social Tolerance and Homosexuality* demonstrated on the contrary that homosexuality was not widely regulated until the modern period, a powerful argument that nevertheless read the archive assuming a continuous homosexuality.

Probably the most important and popular history of homosexual oppression and resistance, continuously in print through multiple editions for 20 years, is *Sexual Politics/Sexual Communities* (1983) in which John D'Emilio applies a New Left understanding of the transformation of false consciousness into political mobilization to chronicle the rise of homosexual resistance in the face of ongoing social and legal repression. Although a moving and historically rigorous account of the rise of homosexual activists in urban enclaves, D'Emilio tacitly assumes that a common experience rooted both in homosexual desire and in social rejection of homosexuality finally propels an invisible community into political action. Because of its transformative effect on activists (who read their copies until they fell apart), it is easy to miss the fact that D'Emilio assumes as a constant the very sexual identity that the historical period produced. D'Emilio's widely read and acclaimed book launched what is probably still the dominant form of historical research. While these works serve as a counterweight to the popular idea that gay liberation started in New York, the researchers famous and obscure who detailed the local rise of gay liberation across North America, and indeed, anywhere around the world where gay liberation has arisen, rely on the idea of sexual identity forged by the gay liberation movement, and writ large the individual coming out teleology: out of myriad forms of same sex desire and its oppression arise a unified international gay liberation movement. However impressive and even inspirational the gains of global gay liberation have been, the global gay movement is as much an effect of the writing of its history as it is a product of history itself.

The second type of work includes Foucault's *Introduction to a History of Sexuality* (translated into English in 1978) and work inspired by his genealogical approach to history, and social constructionist work, probably most significantly, Jeffrey Weeks' (1977) *Coming Out: Homosexual Politics in Britain, from the Nineteenth Century to the Present*. It is important not to confuse social constructionist and Foucauldian work. Social constructionist work in history is heavily indebted to the sociological work of Berger and Luckmann (1966), and is well aligned with the sociological work on sexuality that was occurring at the same time. Britain's Mary MacIntosh (1968) called for historical work to employ the concepts developed by the new gay liberationist sociology, and the move toward social history in general blurred the distinction between the two formerly distinct disciplines.

In both its sociological and historical forms, social construction theory argues that individuals interact and represent themselves to each other in ways that become conventional, and thus, offer roles that can be occupied by others. These roles become institutionalized, and the aggregate of these institutionalized roles is social reality. Although there is debate among philosophers about the ontological status of the socially constructed reality, in most of the versions adopted within the study of sexuality, social construction theory remains a realist theory; there is a 'real' 'sexuality' upon which are built the various self conceptions of individuals and groups and which limits the range of possible self conceptions. At the height of the essentialism/social construction debates, radical anti-essentialists viewed realist social construction theories to be tantamount to essentialist theories.

This is in sharp contrast to the Foucault-inspired historical research. Here, historians argue that sexuality is itself a construct, no matter how attached individuals may become to their identity. Foucault argues that particular discursive and institutional configurations produce a 'reality effect' – that is, they are experienced as real by social subjects. It is important to conduct archeological and genealogical research on reality effects (for example, sexuality), but the researcher must be careful not to conclude that there is a real object of study that merely undergoes renaming over time. Rather, this line of work (especially in the archeological form) argues that the historian's task is to identify what can be said and by whom, a position sometimes called historical nominalism (Flynn, 1989).

After the community and city studies in the mold of D'Emilio's sentinel work, the next largest body of research is social constructionist research that remains more or less agnostic about the facticity of sexual identities in favor of focusing on forms of homosexuality embedded in dominant culture. This research shows an impressive range of same-sex affectational, erotic, and social bonds. Importantly, apparently identical relationships are often conceptualized – and arguably experienced – quite differently, that is, the social categories of sexual alterity often include sexual practices that are identical to those in the normative category.

One important step in broadening and complicating the idea of what a sexual identity might have been (or might be) was the early 1980s work on cults of friendship. Psychologists had been inclined to view same-sex friendships as a sublimation of homosexual sex, sometimes viewing this as positive (e.g., a way of avoiding improper sex) and sometimes negative (e.g., a disruption in the process of developing a full and healthy homosexual identity). At a moment in history when it was advantageous to be able to show the frequency and diversity of homosexuality, influenced by Second Wave and cultural feminist claims that women's erotic bonds are less 'phallic' and certainly incorporating Kinsey's enormous popular scale for ranking homosexual tendencies ('1–6'), gay and lesbian historians suggested that 'non-genital' manifestations of erotic imagination should also count more as 'gay and lesbian' than not. In her popular *Surpassing the Love of Men* (1981) Lillian Faderman argued that distinct and well-developed cultures of female friendship have existed at least since the Renaissance. Practices such as early twentieth-century 'smashing', structured and public crushes between students at women's colleges, entailed specific identities – the smasher and her object of attention. These works simultaneously suggested that female–female eroticism had always found a form, and that women's

self-conception of these relationships amounted to various forms of identity – whether other scholars, many of whom criticized Faderman for reading contemporary definitions into the past, were comfortable grouping these women together as lesbian or not. If such research on one hand muddied the question of what kind of self-claim was required to have a lesbian identity and irritated sex radical feminists who saw such work as accepting the dictum that sex between women is not 'real sex', documenting structured and role-bound female friendship, it made it plausible to count as 'lesbians' important women such as Eleanor Roosevelt or Margaret Mead, who each had 'special friendships', but who lacked or concealed their place in a public lesbian culture. Similar work on nineteenth-century male friendship identified not only specific crytohomosexuals but also identified distinctive self-understandings of those male–male desires. Michael Lynch's (1985) beautiful and influential essay on phrenology associated intensive male–male friendship with a special place on the side of the skull.

Somatizing male friendship away from the phallus enabled the homosexuals who gravitated to phrenology to justify their attachments to men as a higher order of relationship than that in which they were supposed to engage with women. The democratic and utopian possibilities of men's bonds were also explicitly theorized by Edward Carpenter (1912) in his *The Intermediate Sex*, and poetically valorized by Walt Whitman. Of course, such cults of friendship may have been populated by sexual fellow travelers, but their form of identity was utopian rather than indexical (e.g., pointing to a sexuality) as were the identities of those who wrote about them a century later. Once the doors were open to expanding not just the bounds of lesbian identity (after all, as Queen Victoria is reputed to have been shocked that such a thing was possible), but homosexual male identity, historians felt freed from the requirement to find plausible evidence that historical figures were gay and shifted instead to identifying homosexual structures within apparently hegemonic straight culture. Significantly, this reinvigorated the idea of 'real' and 'situational' homosexuality, since the one partner to the homosexual act seemed not to understand themselves as such; in this research it was possible to see a variety of sexual identities that co-existed with the normative identities or normative practices.

Readers may ask why this story of sexual identity is so heavily populated with deviants, homosexuals, and gay men. As I suggested in the beginning, following Foucault, sexual identity is a late chapter in a longer tale of the flesh. In fact, even a cursory search for recent social science works on heterosexual identity reveals that while many researchers use the category 'heterosexual' to refer to males and females for the purposes of distinguishing their attitudes toward sexuality and modes of sexual practice, it is far from clear that many people actually 'have' a heterosexual identity. Psychologists seem to assume that it is critical to develop (any) sexual identity in order to have a fully-formed personal identity (but not asexual, as in the new Asexuality Visibility and Education Network, which promotes dialog between 'sexual and asexual people' – DSM-IV includes 'Hypoactive Sexual Desire Disorder'). Theoretical frameworks that point to the enmeshment of gender (and gender identity) and sexuality (and sexual identity) make it clear that to be a (western) man requires having sex with a woman, but this is a fragile ground upon which to assert or research a heterosexual identity. When researchers take up as their object claims to heterosexuality, they almost inevitably discover that 'heterosexual identity' does not contain the parallel (if ontologically problematic) experiential element of gay identity: heterosexuals do not seem to identify as such, but mostly as 'not gay'. Unlike gay or lesbian (or now, transgender and asexual) identity-holders, heterosexuals rarely say 'I always knew I was different/gay/lesbian/ etc.' They do not, as Simoni (2001) argues,

because they are not different – they are part of the oppressing hegemony (like whites in the Euro-American contexts) and hence, are not forced to claim (or hide) a despised sexual identity. But this incorporation of the research on racial identity, while illuminating of the power of heterosexism and homophobia to shape identity, is inexact: there are clear pathways to male and female identity development (however precarious), and these are intended to run in parallel in such a way as to culminate in a sexual act between the two, even if this is more identity-conveying for men than for women. How is it possible that the many years of careful research in so many disciplines has failed to yield either a coherent idea of sexual identity or the discarding of the project of finding such idea?

## GLOBAL GAY: THE HIV/AIDS EPIDEMIC AND THE NECESSITY OF IDENTITY

Activists and researchers of the 1970s and early 1980s were engaged in lively, if, as I have suggested, necessarily contextually-bound articulations of identities complexly related, as I have tried to show, to sexuality. However vital their definitional battles, in terms of decreasing social harms of discrimination and stigma, and in terms of improving the life changes of lesbians and gay men, they remained primarily local engagements with specific legal, medical or policy bodies and mainly within the power centers of the West. To a great extent, gay liberationists and lesbian/gay civil rights activists fought directly on their own behalf. But with the advent of the HIV epidemic, which quickly took on global proportions, these political players incrementally lost control over self-definitions (however strategic were these uses of sexual identity), and the very same power brokers from which they had liberated their names took control once again, often speaking on their behalf.

The mysterious and apparently fatal illness that would come to be called 'AIDS' came to epidemiologists and physicians in 1980, resulting in the first published report in 1981. (US Centers for Disease Control, 1981). This account noted that the six men who had died of the rare pneumonia were known to their doctors to be gay. The gay liberation movement had existed for a decade, and the gay civil rights movement had just begun to replace the apologetics of the early homophile civil rights movement, which did not wholly contest the 'homosexuality as illness' position with the assimilationist healthy homosexual/except for the sex of our partner 'we're (more or less) just like you' approach to sexual identity, both supported by the research of activist academics working from the range of positions I have outlined above. Neither groups approach to sexual identity prepared them for the encounter with the public health enterprise that the HIV/AIDS epidemic would represent. Both liberationists and civil rights activists began to grapple with HIV/AIDS, although perhaps not quickly enough. Although there were some gay men's health groups in the major metropolitan areas, which had carefully cultivated relationships with, usually, the public health nurses who diagnosed and treated sexually transmitted diseases, there was little movement infrastructure around health issues. (The notable exception, in these pre-Internet days, was the National Gay STD Service Newsletter, which was the first vehicle for circulating reasonable information about the emerging disease.) The lack of recognition of health as a gay civil rights agenda item, and a certain level of antagonism between movement leaders and those they perceived to be bar attendees and insufficiently political (wrongly also stereotyped as the first people with AIDS, although this was entirely misinformation, since important gay liberation activists were prominent among the first diagnosed and the first to make public their diagnosis), resulted in a momentary gap between what had been sexual-identity-based political organizing and what became disease-based organizing.

Newly-on-the-scene newspapers such as the *New York Native* took aim at the long-term activists too quickly to realize the extent of the epidemic and its capacity to trigger long-standing forms of homophobia, sex-phobia, and discrimination. In the early years of the epidemic, a third sexual-identity force quickly emerged, one that essentialized the physicality of gay male sex as the genesis of gay identity (as opposed to the more public/political shared history of oppression position of the gay civil rights movement or the gay ethos as a more democratic and life affirming approach of the gay liberation movement).

Public health officials and doctors – some gay, some sympathetic to claims about homophobia – and gay activists and researchers quickly reconfigured themselves to consolidate versions of gay identity. Suddenly, after a century of fighting for the legitimacy of their research, sociologists, anthropologists, and psychologists of sexuality were called to the table. Early safe sex campaigns were heavily influenced by a combination of community self-knowledge and the lines of sociological research that insisted that sexual behavior and sexual identity were not necessarily well-aligned – as epidemiologic data would soon show, there were significant numbers of men who had sex with men, but did not identify as gay, even violently contested this idea. In addition, sociologists were able to point to the places where 'men who have sex with men' might congregate, and they had some ideas about how to communicate to them about safe sex. Sociologists and social psychologists who were interested in the management of stigma and its effects on individuals quickly entered the conversation to argue, making good on the APA's 1974 statement, that it was homophobia and not homosexuality that created the 'low self-esteem' that seemed to drive a lack of commitment to shifting toward safe sex practices.

Anthropologists played a very special role in describing and sculpting the emerging epidemic. Urban anthropologists were heavily involved in studying both sexual minority cultures, sex trade cultures, and the drug culture that often bound these together. Their work shed light on the apparently inexplicable early distribution of cases among apparently socially unlinked four Hs: 'homosexuals', 'heroine users', '(w)hores', and 'Haitians'. The last confused race, immigration status, and country, a conflation never completely sorted out, but forgotten once 'African AIDS' arrived on the nomenclature board – attributed to exotic sexual practices, a colonialist reprise that the anthropologists went to great lengths to debunk with their research on 'heterosexuals' and 'men who have sex with men' on that continent. Anthropologists were also extremely important in underscoring the diversity of sexual bargains in cultures that had differently structured sex and gender roles (e.g., cultures with intermediate sexes – berdache, hijra, fa'ahfafine, kathoey, Mashoga, Mangaiko, etc. – each with its own self-understanding and social role) which witnessed tragically high case loads that suddenly transformed more or less accepted forms of gender (and hence, sexual practice) alterity into an identifiable class of people with the dreaded disease.

The Global Programme on AIDS under Jonathan Mann (1984–1990, when he was ousted in favor of a more by-the-book tropical medicine expert from another WHO division) hired an interesting list of gay and feminist researcher-activists to advise on how to work with communities to create good AIDS education campaigns, including safe sex campaigns. The consultants pointed to the longstanding legal and social homophobia in the west and argued that while western gays might nevertheless be positioned to promote safe sex, their analogs around the world were not. The GPA adopted an anti-homophobia and anti-discrimination position, in support of 'men who have sex with men' (soon called MSMs and at one point called 'homosexually active men', or HAMs) in other parts of the world, and began to send consultants to help them organize. There were already fledgling gay movements

in some major cities in the developing world, however, their constituencies were more likely postmodern and well-plugged into the global images of, among other exotic western exports, gay men. Much like in the west, the men who participated in same sex (and now 'high risk') sex often denied that they were 'gay'. Thus, while the GPA took a huge step in an apparently progressive direction by initiating a human-rights rationale for health (hence, affirming positive gay identity, supporting sex trade workers in making life choices, supporting women's independence from men), their work, while utilizing the widest range of research from anthropology and sociology, relied upon the now very conventional equation of:

positive (gay) sexual identity = positive sense of self = rational decision-making (in sex)

Consolidated through international AIDS activism and global health public discourse, this notion of sexual identity was easy to detach from its complex origins in the study of sexual alterity, and apply to members of the dominant culture. The term 'heterosexual community' had emerged by the late 1980s as if the unmarked and largely non-experience category of 'heterosexual identity' also had a special culture unto itself, as opposed to merely being the dominant culture. At this point in the staggering two-step dance was the simultaneous triumph of the most notable sexual alterity (gay men receiving endorsement and support for non-discrimination by the most global health organization!) and the sign of near-complete loss of control of the meaning and requirements of 'having' a sexual identity. While sexual identity agnostics and skeptics continue to have an indirect influence on both social science and medical research on sexual identity and on activist endeavors, the large body of research that hopes to parse sexual identity (now gay and non-gay) in order to find the small variable that will enable educators to design more and more targeted education exerts a huge gravitational force on not only research, but on the very capacity to have or resist 'sexual identity'.

# REFERENCES

American Psychiatric Association (1974) 'Position statement on homosexuality and civil rights', *American Journal of Psychiatry*, 131 (4): 497.

Baim, T. (ed.) (2008) *Out and Proud in Chicago: An Overview of the City's Gay Movement*. Chicago, IL: Agate Surrey Publishing.

Berger, P.L. and Luckmann, T. (1966) *The Social Construction of Reality: A Treatise in the Sociology of Knowledge*. New York: Anchor Books.

Boswell, J. (1980) *Christianity, Social Tolerance and Homosexuality: Gay People in Western Europe from the Beginning of the Christian Era to the Fourteenth Century*. Chicago, IL: University of Chicago Press.

Brooks, R., Rotherman-Borus, M.J., Bing, E.G., George, A. and Henry, C.L. (2003) 'HIV and AIDS among Men of Color who have Sex with Men and Men of Color who have Sex with Men and Women', *AIDS Education and Prevention*, 15: 1–7.

Cadigan, R.J. (1998) 'Woman-to-woman marriage: Practices and benefits in sub-Saharan Africa', *Journal of Comparative Family Studies*, 29 (1): 89–98.

Carpenter, E. (1921) *The Intermediate Sex: A Study of Some Transitional Types of Men and Women*. London: Allen and Unwin.

Charles, J. (1968) 'Medical history origins: History and achievements of the world health organization', *British Medical Journal*, 2: 293–6.

Comaroff, J. (1991) *Of Revelation and Revolution: Christianity, Colonialism and Consciousness in South Africa*. Chicago, IL: University of Chicago Press.

Conrad, P. and Schneider, J.W. (1992) *Deviance and Medicalization: From Badness to Sickness*. Philadelphia, PA: Temple University Press.

Cory, D.W. (1951) *The Homosexual in America: A Subjective Approach*. New York: Greenberg.

Danziger, K. (1990) *Constructing the Subject: Historical Origins of Psychological Research*. Cambridge: Cambridge University Press.

D'Emilio, J. (1983) *Sexual Politics, Sexual Communities: The Making of a Homosexual Minority in the United States*. Chicago, IL: Chicago University Press.

Faderman, L. (1981) *Surpassing the Love of Men: Romantic Friendship and Love Between Women from the Renaissance to the Present*. New York: HarperCollins.

Fanon, F. (1965) *Black Skin, White Masks*. New York: Gove Press.

Flynn, T.R. (1989) 'Foucault and historical nominalism', in H.A. Durfee and D.F. T. Rodier (eds), *Phenomenology and Beyond: The Self and Its Language*. New York: Springer.

Foucault, M. (1977) *Discipline and Punish: The Birth of the Prison*. Trans. Alan Sheridan. New York: Pantheon Books.

Foucault, M. (1990) *The History of Sexuality, Vol. 1: An Introduction*. Trans. Robert Hurley. New York: Vintage Books. [Originally published in English 1978.]

Foucault, M. (1990) *The History of Sexuality, Vol. 2: The Use of Pleasure*. Trans. Robert Hurley. New York: Vintage Books. [Originally published in English 1985.]

Foucault, M. (1990) *The History of Sexuality, Vol. 3: The Care of the Self*. Trans. Robert Hurley. New York: Vintage Books. [Originally published in English 1986.]

Freud, S. (1962) *Three Essays on the Theory of Sexuality* (1901–1905). Trans. James Strachey. New York: Basic Books.

Freud, S. (1963) *Sexuality and the Psychology of Love* (1905–1938). Trans. Philip Rieff. New York: Collier Books.

Goffman, E. (1959) *Presentation of Self in Everyday Life*. New York: Doubleday Anchor Books.

Goffman, E. (1963) *Stigma: Notes on the Management of Spoiled Identity*. New York: Simon and Schuster.

Halley, J. (1993) 'Reasoning about sodomy: Act and identity in and after Bowers *vs.* Hardwick', *Virginia Law Review*, 79 (7): 1721–80.

Halley, J. (1998) 'Gay rights and identity imitation: Issues in the ethics of representation', in D. Kairys (ed.), *The Politics of Law*. 3rd edn. Philadelphia, PA: Temple University Press.

Halley, J. (1999) *Don't: A Reader's Guide to the Military's Anti-Gay Policy*. Durham, NC: Duke University Press.

Herdt, G. (1981) *Guardians of the Flute*. Chicago, IL: University of Chicago Press.

Kane, N. (ed.) (1999) *Improper Bostonians: Lesbian and Gay History from the Puritans to Playland*. Boston, MA: Beacon Press.

Hooker, E. (1957) 'The adjustment of the male overt homosexual', *Journal of Projective Techniques*, 21: 18–31.

Houts, A.C. (2000) 'Fifty years of psychiatric nomenclature: Reflections on the 1943 war department technical', *Journal of Clinical Psychology*, 56 (7): 935–67.

Humphreys, L. (1975) *Tearoom Trade: Impersonal Sex in Public Places*. New York: Aldine.

Humphreys, L. (1978) 'An interview with Evelyn Hooker', *Journal of Family and Economic Issues*, 1 (2): 191–206.

Irvine, J. (2005) *Disorders of Desire: Sexuality and Gender in Modern American Sexology*. Philadelphia: Temple University Press. [1st edn 1990.]

Kennedy, E.L. and Davis, Madeline D. (1993) *Boots of Leather, Slippers of Gold: The History of a Lesbian Community*. New York: Routledge.

Kennedy, H. (1988) *The Life and Work of Karl Heinrich Ulrichs: Pioneer of the Modern Gay Movement.* Boston, MA: Alyson.

Kinsey, A.C., Pomeroy, W.B. and Martin, C.E. (1948) *Sexual Behaviour in the Human Male.* Philadelphia, PA: Saunders.

LeVay, S. (1991) 'A difference in hypothalamic structure between homosexual and heterosexual men', *Science*, 253: 1034–7.

LeVay, S. (1993) *The Sexual Brain.* Cambridge, MA: MIT Press.

Lynch, M. (1985) '"Here is adhesiveness": From friendship to homosexuality', *Victorian Studies*, 29 (1): 67–97.

MacIntosh, M. (1968) 'The homosexual role', *Social Problems*, 16: 182–92.

Malane, R. (2005) *Sex in Mind: The Gendered Brain in Nineteenth-Century Literature and Mental Sciences.* New York: Peter Lang Publishing, Inc.

Marotta, T. (1981) *The Politics of Homosexuality.* Boston: Houghton Miffin.

May, J.P. and Williams Jr, Ernest L. (2002) 'Acceptability of condom availability in a U.S. jail', *AIDS Education and Prevention*, 14: 85–92.

Mead, M. (1961) *Coming of Age in Samoa: A Psychological Study of Primitive Youth for Western Civilization.* New York: William Morrow. [Originally published 1930.]

Moodie, D.T. (1994) *Going for Gold: Men, Mines and Migration.* Berkeley, CA: University of California Press.

Njambi, W.N. and O'Brien, W.E. (2000) 'Revisiting "woman-woman marriage": notes on gikuyu women', *National Women's Studies Association Journal*, 12 (1): 1–23.

Northwest Lesbian and Gay History Museum Project (2004) *Claiming Spaces.* Seattle, WA: Girlie Press.

Patton, C. (1996) *Fatal Advice: How Safe-Sex Education Went Wrong.* Durham, NC Duke University Press.

Patton, C. (1998) 'Stealth bombers of desire: The globalization of "alterity" in emerging democracies', *Working Papers in Gender/Sexuality Studies*, 3/4: 301–23.

Patton, C. (1999) 'From nation to family: Containing "African AIDS"', in S.J. Hesse-Biber, C.K. Gilmartin and R. Lydenberg (eds), *Feminist Approaches to Theory and Methodology: An Interdisciplinary Reader.* New York: Oxford University Press.

Patton, C. (2002) 'Globalizing AIDS', *Theory Out of Bounds.* Vol. 22. Minneapolis, MA: University of Minnesota Press.

Pickren, W. (1997) 'History of psychology: Robert Yerkes, Calvin Stone, and the beginning of programmatic sex research by psychologists, 1921–1930', *The American Journal of Psychology*, 110 (4): 603–19.

Robertson, J.E. (1998) *Takarazuka: Sexual Politics and Popular Culture in Modern Japan.* Berkeley, CA: University of California Press.

Robertson, P.K. (2004) 'The historical effects of depathologizing homosexuality on the practice of counseling', *The Family Journal: Counseling and Therapy for Couples and Families*, 12 (2): 163–9.

Romero, V. (2006) 'Homosexuality and immigration', in P. Finkelman (ed.), *Encyclopedia of American Civil Liberties.* New York: Routledge.

Rosario, V. (1996) 'Pointy penises, fashion crimes, and hysterical mollies: The pederasts inversions', in J. Merrick and B.T. Ragan (eds), *Homosexuality in Modern France.* New York: Oxford University Press.

Rust, P.C.R. (2000) 'Bisexuality: A contemporary paradox for women', *Journal of Social Issues*, 56 (2): 205–21.

Sillitoe, P. (2006) 'The search for relevance: A brief history of applied anthropology', *History and Anthropology*, 17 (1): 1–19.

Silenzio, V.M. B. (2003) 'Anthropological assessment for culturally appropriate interventions targeting men who have sex with men', *American Journal of Public Health*, 93 (6): 867–71.

Simoni, J.M. and Walters, K.L. (2001) 'Heterosexual identity and heterosexism: Recognizing privilege to reduce prejudice', *Journal of Homosexuality*, 41 (1): 157–73.

Spitzer, R.L. (1981) 'The diagnostic status of homosexuality in DSM-III: A reformulation of the issues', *American Journal of Psychiatry*, 138: 210–15.

Stewart, E.C. (2007) 'The sexual health and behaviour of male prisoners: The need for research', *The Howard Journal*, 46 (1): 43–59.

Stoler, A.L. (1995) *Race and the Education of Desire: Foucault's History of Sexuality and the Colonial Order of Things.* Durham, NC: Duke University Press.

Teo, T. (2005) *The Critique of Psychology: From Kant to Postcolonial Theory.* New York: Springer.

Weeks, J. (1977) *Coming Out: Homosexual Politics in Britain from the Nineteenth Century to the Present.* New York: Quartet Books.

Weeks, J. (1985) *Sexuality and Its Discontents: Meanings, Myths and Modern Sexualities.* New York: Routledge and Kegan Paul.

# 19

# Indigeneity as a Field of Power: Multiculturalism and Indigenous Identities in Political Struggles[1]

R. Aída Hernández Castillo

> Group's self-identification as tribal or indigenous is not natural or inevitable, but neither is it simply invented, adopted, or imposed. It is, rather, a positioning that draws upon historically sedimented practices, landscapes, and repertoires of meaning, and emerges through particular patterns of engagement and struggle. (Tania Li)[2]

Writing this chapter has represented a genuine challenge for me, as I have worked to construct a dialogue between theoretical debates in the 'north' and theoretical and political concerns in the Latin American academic community.[3] It has been a labour of translation – both literally and conceptually. Translating debates and placing them in the framework of the political contexts in which they have emerged is fundamental to understanding the relevance of certain analytical perspectives in particular countries, and their lack of relevance in other geopolitical realities. Even the term 'indigeneity,' which I was asked to address for this Handbook, has no literal translation in Spanish. While some authors have chosen to use the Anglicism *indigeneidad* (see Arias, 2006; Canessa, 2006), this term is not commonly used in Latin American social sciences, and does not appear in the dictionary of the Royal Spanish Academy.[4]

In the Spanish version of this chapter I opted to use the analytical description 'social construction of indigenous identities' to refer to the social, cultural and political processes through which the meaning of being indigenous has been constructed. In line with the argument I will develop here, these processes have involved various dialogues of power with national and global discourses.

In the Latin American context, the historical constructivist perspective of identities has been analytically acknowledged by various scholars of ethnicity and nationalism (Chávez and Hoffman, 2004; Gutiérrez Chong, 2004; Hernández Castillo, 2001; Zarate, 1994), however it has received little attention in debates taking place in the political arena. Political mobilizations in favour of indigenous rights and the alliances between academics and organizations have prioritized other types of debates, such as those focused on indigenous autonomy, multicultural reforms and the tension between the collective rights of peoples and individual rights. The concept of *indigenous* has not been questioned and instead, it has been taken for granted, and from that conceptualization, the political struggles of those previously referred to as 'native peoples' have been initiated and given momentum.

The political discourses of indigenous organizations with respect to their ancient cultures and their different cultural logics based on a collective sense, have been responded to or criticized more from liberal universalist perspectives, than from post-structuralist perspectives questioning the exclusions implied by these subaltern identities. Part of the challenge faced by those of us who defend the pertinence of a constructivist perspective is that our analytical arguments can be easily used by those opposed to the political demands of indigenous movements. At the same time, for some sectors of the Latin American indigenous movement, the concepts of 'constructed identities' or the 'invention of tradition' could even be offensive, viewed as a critique of the genuine or legitimate nature of their identities (MacLeod, 2008). In the framework of this *cultural climate*[5] it has been important to clarify that acknowledging the way in which power relations influence our subjectivities and define our collective identities does not signify a denial of the possibilities for building political projects – on the basis of these contradictory consciousnesses – aimed at working toward social justice (Hernández Castillo, 2001).

The political discourses and practices of organized indigenous women have begun to separate the utopian impulse that sometimes characterizes the essentialist representations of indigenous cultures, from the limitations implied in the construction of an alternative national project – when these representations serve as an excuse for not confronting power relations and inequality *among* indigenous peoples (Alvarez C. 2005; Cumes, 2007; Cumbre de Mujeres Indígenas, 2003; Gutíerrez and Palomo, 1999; Sánchez, 2005; Velásquez 2003).

In this sense the political concerns of indigenous women are echoed in other voices which, emanating from the black diaspora or transnational migration, have pointed to the limitations of identitary constructions that are based on authenticity discourses, or that deny the possibilities of border identities in which various cultural repertoires converge. In the context of migration to the north and the deterritorialization of thousands of the planet's inhabitants, it becomes politically relevant to discuss the process in which what is *indigenous* is socially constructed, and the way it is linked with community and with territory. This explains why critical reflections of this identitary space are more common in this part of the world.

The purpose of this chapter is to build a bridge between various theoretical and political debates around indigenous identities, and this involves crossing national and conceptual borders. It is hoped that these theoretical reflections contribute to a critical re-thinking of some constructions of 'being indigenous' that may lead to new exclusions.

In the sections that follow I will first discuss the origin and the concepts 'indigeneity/ indigenous', historizing the transnational processes of the last five decades through which the concepts have been appropriated to create spaces of political organization in anti-colonial struggles. Second, I will locate these processes in the context of the political debates on multicultural reforms and indigenous rights in Latin America. Third, I will approach the debates on neoliberal multiculturalism, emphasizing the way in which organized indigenous peoples have confronted this new form of governance in the Latin American nation-states. Finally, I will discuss the criticisms of 'indigeneity' that have developed from the study and politics of other subaltern identities: Diaspora and Transnational Studies, Afro Latino and Mestizo Studies and Feminist Studies, to call for a formulation of a more inclusive definition of indigenous identity. To conclude, I suggest that it is our, those of us who from our position in the academic world support the recognition of what are referred to as indigenous rights, political responsibility to listen to the diversity of voices speaking from their identity as indigenous people.

## THE CONSTRUCTION OF INDIGENEITY

On 13 September 2007, the United Nations General Assembly approved the UN Declaration on the Rights of Indigenous Peoples. A total of 143 countries voted in favour, 1 country abstained, and the US, Australia, Canada and New Zealand were in opposition. The new UN Declaration signalled the end of a cycle of struggle that began 22 years earlier and involved the active participation and lobbying of indigenous leaders and intellectuals across five continents. The new Declaration has 46 articles, and recognizes the right of indigenous peoples to self-determination, control over their lands and natural resources, and the preservation of their culture and traditions.

As with many tools of international law, the Convention's effectiveness will depend on the degree to which indigenous peoples, organizations and social movements appropriate these laws, and whether the existing social fabric has the potential to exert political pressure to achieve their effective enforcement. This Declaration is only the tip of the iceberg, however, in relation to broader political-organizational processes that have transformed the concept of *indigenous* from a legal, analytical term to a concept of self-identification, creating a new collective imaginary and a transnational space (Warren, 1998; Warren K. and Jackson J. (eds), 2002). This has made it possible to share experiences and develop joint strategies, and establish links among groups as different as the Maori of New Zealand, the Adivasi of India and the Mayans of Guatemala.

While indigenous representatives were lobbying at the United Nations, seeking support from member states for the Declaration, the *indigeneity* discourse was travelling along rural roads through the five continents. It reached the most isolated villages through workshops, marches and meetings in which community leaders, NGO members and promoters of liberation theology began to popularize the concept for referring to 'native peoples' and to denounce the effects from colonialism on their lives and territories. Thus, in addition to local terms of self-identification such as Zapoteco, Mixe, Aymara, Navajo and Evenki, there was a new identitary sense of being *indigenous*. This had the effect of constructing a new *imaginary community* (Anderson, 1983) with other oppressed peoples around the world. Various analysts have pointed out that the movement for indigenous rights was 'born transnational' (Brysk, 2000; Tilley, 2002), since from its very beginnings it extended beyond local struggles and self-identifications.

Unlike the analytical concept of 'ethnic groups,' the concept of 'indigenous' crossed the limited borders of academia and encompassed the formulation of a new political agenda extending beyond the immediate, local problems confronted by the peoples identified with this new concept. The degree to which indigenous people appropriated this new transnational identity depended largely on the organizational processes in each region and on their access to these global discourses. In many regions the local terms of self-identification, such as Quechua, Acateco, Chamula and Popti, continue to be more important than their indigenous identity (Canessa, 2006; Cumes, 2007). In other regions, identities as *campesinos* (peasants) or mestizos continue to be the terms of self-identification used by the population, which viewed from the outside, might be classified as indigenous, due to their linguistic specificity and cultural features. For a variety of historic reasons, however, they have not appropriated this concept (De la Cadena, 2000; Mattiace, 2007).

According to authors who have reconstructed the history of this concept, the word *indigenous* appears in some colonial documents from the fourteenth century, and is defined as 'people bred upon that very soyle [sic]', to distinguish the inhabitants of the Americas from those brought over as slaves by the Spanish and Portuguese (De la Cadena and Starn, 2007). Nevertheless, before the 1950s the concept of *indigenous* was used primarily in botanical works to refer to the native origin of plants. The term appeared for the first time in an international document in 1957 in Convention 107 of the International Labour Organization (ILO), in reference to the 'Protection and Integration of Indigenous and other Tribal and Semi-Tribal Populations in Independent Countries' (Niezen, 2000). At that time the population referred to in the Convention did not participate in its formulation, and was probably unaware of the significance of the term that was intended to encompass its identities.

If we review academic and political texts from that time period, we find continued reference in world anthropology to 'primitive cultures', and in Latin America, social scientists and the state referred to these human collectives as *campesinos* (peasants). This does not mean there was a lack of cultural identity shared at the community or regional level, or a lack of a particular history transmitted through oral traditions and visions of the world that contrasted with and sometimes confronted western conceptions of the individual and nature. However, this knowledge and these practices were not conceptualized as being 'indigenous', and in most cases the necessary link was not made with the knowledge of other human collectives that had similar colonization experiences.

Thirty years later the development of new communication technologies has created new possibilities for people to imagine themselves as part of the same community, even when they have not met face-to-face. This is what Lyotard (1984) and Harvey (1990) have called *time space compression*. These new technologies have made it possible for native peoples who have experienced colonialism, racism and exclusion to come into contact with others with similar experiences and to build a shared sense of identity as indigenous people.

From this perspective we could say that the practices, institutions and artistic production of these peoples have become *indigenous* over the course of the last three or four decades – however this would always be defined in terms of alterity, or in other words, according to what is *not indigenous*. This led Mary Louise Pratt (2007) to propose that the term *indigenous* has been based from its very beginnings on a conception of time and space linked to the colonial encounter, since it refers to those who were 'already there' when the colonizers arrived.[6]

This relational nature of the indigenous identity is even more evident in contexts of non-European colonization, where we find a broader political debate between various cultural communities focused on who is indigenous and who is not. A clear example of these disputes, that denaturalize indigenous identity, is the analysis conducted by Amita Baviskar (2007) on the way that indigeneity discourses are used by the right-wing in India to exclude religious minorities such as Muslims – in contrast to the struggle in this same country by Adivasi tribal groups to make use of international instruments on indigenous rights, in order to avoid being forcibly displaced from their homes so that a dam can be built.

If we situate the emergence of these identities historically and if we denaturalize the definition of *being indigenous*, we find that this social construction has taken place in the framework of dialogues of power in which the hegemonic discourses of nation-states, of international entities and social scientists have been used, resisted, re-elaborated or rejected by the social actors who have begun to identify themselves as indigenous, and have used this definition to establish a position from which they can take political action. It is in this sense that I am referring to *indigeneity* as a field of power in which various social actors participate in a struggle for the construction of meaning, in the framework of systems of economic, racial and gender inequality that determine the legitimization and de-legitimization of the various definitions.

From this perspective, this chapter and my previous writings on the indigenous movement in Mexico are part – although marginally – of this field of power in which different definitions of what it is to be indigenous are confronted. By acknowledging my participation in these dialogues and the productive capacity of academic knowledge, I am positioning myself politically as one of the voices defending a broad, non-exclusionary definition of the indigenous identity, which acknowledges the multiplicity of political genealogies and experiences characterizing the sense of belonging to this imagined community. I therefore reject the temptation to reify indigenous identities on the basis of authenticity criteria, whether involuntarily or strategically, since in my opinion this can contribute to creating new exclusions.

## DEBATES ON EQUALITY AND DIFFERENCE IN LATIN AMERICA

There is a fairly generalized tendency among anthropologists in Latin America to support demands for recognition of indigenous rights. In the political arena, many of us have debated against liberal perspectives that, in the name of equal rights discourse, reject all policies that would grant cultural recognition.[7] Such liberal perspectives continue to defend the formation of a monocultural state, while failing to recognize the long history of exclusion implicated in the developmentalist integrationism of Latin American states (Aguilar, 2004; Viqueira, 1999). These monocultural nationalisms flourished throughout all of Latin America during the nineteenth century and managed to permeate the collective imaginary around national identity.[8]

In exchange for belonging to the nation, it was necessary only to renounce 'backward' customs and identify with the national identity (assumed to be mestizo, Spanish-speaking and modern). This policy of 'equality' was the basis for a national identity that was implemented in many Latin American countries through physical and symbolic violence aimed at 'integrating Indians into the nation'.

For decades these experiences affected thousands of peasants from various regions of Latin America, and as a result, they rejected any identity other than a national identity.

This history of the imposition of monocultural national citizenship – with different degrees of violence – can be found in various indigenous regions of the Americas. And ironically, the equality discourse generated an intensification of inequality. To paraphrase Iris Marion Young, we can say that achieving formal equality did not eliminate social differences, and to the contrary, the rhetorical commitment to the equality of individuals made it impossible to even mention how these differences are structuring privilege and oppression (2000: 276).

A critical analysis of universal citizenship and of the failure of *indigenista* policies emphasizing integration and acculturation has led an entire generation of Latin American anthropologists to work together in solidarity with the struggles for the rights of indigenous peoples. This link between academia and indigenous movements has, since the 1970s, generated critical reflections by anthropologists such as Guillermo Bonfil Batalla, Rodolfo Stavenhagen, Mercedes Olivera, Carlos Guzmán Bockler, Roberto Cardoso de Oliveira and Héctor Díaz Polanco. Their reflections have been appropriated and discussed by indigenous leaders who have resisted *indigenista* projects promoting acculturation in the name of development (Bonfil Batalla 1981). From sometimes contrasting perspectives – however, all influenced by Marxism and by theories of internal colonialism – this generation of critical anthropologists challenged the functionalist representations that some US anthropologists had developed for Latin American indigenous peoples as inhabitants of isolated, harmonious communities arising from ancient cultures. In contrast to these representations, the analysis by Latin American anthropologists emphasized the insertion of indigenous peoples in systems of inequality, and denounced the racism and economic marginalization concealed behind the rhetoric of national integration.[9]

It was under the influence of this cultural climate and partly in response to the demands of indigenous organizations that a process of legislative reforms was initiated in the 1980s in a number of Latin American countries. These reforms were aimed at recognizing the multicultural nature of states, and replaced the discourse on equality with new rhetoric on cultural diversity and on the need to develop multicultural public policies. These reforms varied greatly from one country to another, however, most recognized the multicultural nature of the state and the collective rights of indigenous peoples, their normative systems and forms of self-government, and their right to use and preserve their own indigenous languages.[10] Since these reforms, government censuses report the existence of 40 million men and women who identify themselves as being indigenous, representing approximately 10 per cent of the inhabitants of Latin America.[11]

In this new political context, those who defend universal citizenship have raised their voices to reject or limit the scope of multicultural reforms attempting to isolate the cultural dimension from territorial or political dimensions. Separating policies of recognition from policies of redistribution has been a strategy of Latin American neoliberal states, aimed at making indigenous demands less radical. Many academics committed to the struggles of indigenous peoples have written about and denounced the new limitations placed on indigenous autonomy by these reforms (Hernández et al., 2004).

Nevertheless, other voices have questioned the 'indigenous resurgence' from other political positions and have pointed out the limitations of the indigenous identity as a space for political mobilization, or have denounced the way in which indigeneity has been used by neoliberal governments in the new strategy of control and regulation.

These perspectives suggest that multicultural reforms – by placing responsibilities in the hands of indigenous peoples and communities

that were previously state responsibilities – respond to the neoliberal agenda's decentralization and promotion of a more participative civil society, subscribing to the construction of what have been defined as *neoliberal citizenship regimes* (Yashar, 2005) or *neoliberal multiculturalism* (Hale, 2005). The social adjustment required in the neoliberal model includes the construction of a pluralist state in which everyone participates – and this may coincide with the political agenda of indigenous peoples demanding greater autonomy and greater possibilities for participation.

Although later works have attempted to demonstrate that countries making fewer structural reforms have adopted the multicultural agenda and vice versa – suggesting a weaker link between neoliberalism and multiculturalism (Van Cott, 2005) – these critical perspectives in relation to the multiculturalization of Latin American states have allowed us to reassess the successes of indigenous movements and to reconsider the focus on legislative reforms as the movement's main political strategy.

## INDIGENOUS SOCIAL AGENCY IN RELATION TO NEOLIBERAL MULTICULTURALISM

In Mexico, multicultural reforms have been carried out nearly contemporaneously with constitutional reforms facilitating the restructuring of the economy in line with International Monetary Fund guidelines. These restructuring policies have included the privatization of semi-official companies, the removal of guaranteed prices for agricultural products, the elimination of subsidies and the opening of markets to import products. Economists describe these changes as a transition from the import substitution industrialization model, which prevailed in Mexico from 1940 to 1980, to an export oriented industrialization model. This new model prioritizes the opening up of markets, leaving local producers to 'freely' confront the global market (Alvarez Bejar, 1992).

These economic reforms have been analysed in a context that explains the emergence of the Zapatista National Liberation Army (Collier, 1999; Harvey, 1998; Rus et al., 2003). This indigenous uprising, which began in January 1994 in the Mexican state of Chiapas, revealed the exclusions inherent in the neoliberal model, and contributed an alternative concept of cultural rights to the debate – in which the right to land, control over territory and self-determination were fundamental elements.

During the last 10 years, we have witnessed the consolidation of a politics of representation in which the slogan 'a world in which many worlds fit' has prompted the re-thinking of political alliances from a non-exclusionary indigenous identity. The point here is not to assess the political achievements of Zapatism. However, beyond the difficulties this movement has experienced in building national alliances, it is important to recognize the impact of its cultural politics in destabilizing hegemonic visions of *indigeneity*. In other work I have argued that, at the level of politics of representation, Zapatism has provoked points of rupture in the state's hegemony, demanding the power to 'name' and establish the terms of dialogue, by reorienting the debate on multiculturalism to a discussion on the autonomy and self-determination of indigenous peoples (Hernández Castillo, 2001). At the same time, this indigenous movement has responded to hegemonic representation in relation to indigenous culture by defending non-essentialist perspectives that include reformulating traditions, indigenous law and forms of local government, from perspectives that are more inclusive of men and women (Speed et al., 2006).

The Zapatism experience is not an isolated one. In a collective study in 10 indigenous regions in Mexico, Guatemala and Colombia, we have found that in contexts where indigenous women are organizing around political and/or productive objectives, they are theorizing on their culture from perspectives that reject the hegemonic definitions of tradition and culture imposed by official *indigenism* and by the most conservative sectors of national indigenous organizations. They point to the need to change the elements in 'customs' that exclude and marginalize women (Hernández Castillo et al., 2008).

These counter-hegemonic constructions of indigenous identities take place even in institutional contexts produced by multicultural reforms. A case in point is the Indigenous Tribunal of Cuetzalan, in the Nahuat region of the Sierra Norte in the Mexican state of Puebla. The experience of this Tribunal in reconstituting community law has been analysed by Adriana Terven (2005). The Tribunal was created in May 2002, based on an agreement by the Plenary Court of Justice in the framework of a series of reforms in state-level legislature for incorporating the recognition of cultural diversity. This space has been appropriated by the region's indigenous organizations, which have decided to 'reactivate' their normative systems and reproduce their own cultural logic. Women have actively participated in this re-invention of indigenous law – after having organized for years around gender equity through a craftswomen's organization called Maseualsiuamej (Mejía, 2008). The participation of some of these indigenous women leaders in the Advisory Council for the Indigenous Tribunal and the links between this Council and the local Indigenous Women's Center (which has worked to support victims of sexual and domestic violence) have facilitated a process of reflection on the most inclusive forms of indigenous justice, including the experiences and reflections arising from the struggles for women's rights at the regional level.

If we consider the state's hegemony as an unfinished process, we can understand that the agenda of neoliberal multiculturalism has not been completely successful, and that because of its need to reinforce civil society and promote decentralization, it has also opened up new opportunities for indigenous peoples to work toward expanding their possibilities for autonomy and self-determination.

Based on the analysis of these experiences and other similar ones in other geographic and cultural contexts (Hodgson, 2002, Tuhiwai Smith, 2007), I have reservations regarding the analytical perspectives that emphasize the productive capacity of state discourses on indigeneity, without acknowledging the capacity of social actors to respond to or reject these constructions.

Some of these analysts have pointed to the close links between the multiculturalization of Latin American states and neoliberal structural reforms (Hale, 2005). They have also referred to the way in which neoliberal governments have – instead of acknowledging the cultural practices and identities of indigenous peoples – dedicated their efforts to constructing identities that new legislative frameworks claim to represent. These analysts have argued that the state imposition of definitions of 'indigenous cultures' as 'pre-modern' and linked to poverty, have allowed neoliberal governments to justify economic exclusions in the name of culture (Escobar, 1997; Martínez Novo, 2006, 2007).

While these perspectives draw attention to the way these cultural differences are used politically by nation-states and capital, they offer us very little on the responses and resistance by the social actors defined as 'indigenous' to these policies of representation. The construction of indigeneity is not a process that moves in a single direction. The hegemony of government definitions is being fragmented by discourses and representations constructed through the daily life and political practices of the social movements that these policies are intended to regulate.

## INDIGENOUS IDENTITIES: CHALLENGES FROM OTHER SUBALTERN IDENTITIES

Not only have those defending liberalism and universal citizenship criticized identity politics in a broader sense and more specifically in relation to the politicization of indigenous identities, but also left-oriented sectors that continue to prioritize a class-based perspective and the anti-capitalist struggle as the primary strategies for building social justice and proposing political strategies. Tensions, differences and confrontations between the Marxist left and indigenous movements have characterized national liberation struggles in Central America. And they continue to affect political life in countries such as Guatemala and Nicaragua, where the building of political alliances has been hindered by resistance on the part of the Marxist left to acknowledge their racism and ethnocentrism.[12]

These perspectives insist that the left's political project must be universalist in nature: intended for all human beings regardless of their cultural, ethnic or gender identities. This is based on the premise of 'common interest', which is placed above and beyond the specific interests of identitary groups (Hobsbawm, 1996). From these political perspectives, gender or anti-racist demands must be framed within the anti-capitalist struggle. Nevertheless, the history of socialism has demonstrated that sexism and racism are not rooted in the capital–labour contradiction, and that woman, indigenous and other excluded groups have not always found social justice in the political projects professing to be universal in nature.

The need to build political alliances between different struggles continues to be one of the primary concerns of the democratic left in Latin America. It is important to reflect upon the criticisms made of indigenous identities by other subaltern identitary spaces not included within the field of power corresponding to indigeneity. In particular, I would like to respond to some of the criticisms made of the concept of indigenous identities based on the perspectives of diaspora theory and transnationalism; the experiences of Afro-Latinos and mestizos in Latin America; and feminist analyses.

### Diasporic and transnational identities

One of the important criticisms made of the indigenous political agenda is that it is based on identitary definitions that refer to historic connections with a specific territory ('people bred upon that very soyle [sic]', 'native peoples') and to an alterity clearly defined on the basis of differentiated cultural logics ('alternative epistemologies' and 'holistic cosmovisions'). These definitions exclude human collectives that, while they share the experience of racism and colonialism, have been characterized by territorial mobility and cultural hybridity. Various 'deterritorialized' intellectuals have questioned the political effectiveness of indigeneity discourses that vindicate ancestral roots in specific territories, precisely at a moment in history when 170 million people around the world are not living in the countries in which they were born. The so-called diaspora theory has represented an analytical alternative for those interested in reflecting upon dispersed communities whose origins are linked to colonialism and imperialism.

These analytical perspectives, developed most notably in the fields of cultural studies (Gilroy, 1987; Hall, 1993) and postcolonial studies, borrow the concept of diaspora from analyses of Jewish history, and apply it to other displacement experiences. They use the historical reference points of colonialism and the various forms of power that have forced people to move from metropolitan centres to colonial peripheries – in the case of colonizers, slaves, migrant workers – and in the opposite direction, after the decolonization processes of the twentieth century. Diasporic identities characterize the communities that reside outside their 'territories of origin' or outside those territories that are imagined to be their 'native land' and that maintain the cultural features of their native communities. Generally, these cultures have been analyzed from perspectives that emphasize cultural hybridity and porous cultural borders, and that question ethnic absolutisms and nativisms that claim decolonization can be achieved by returning to native territories (see Gilroy, 1993).

The deterritorialized Jewish community has been the case *par excellence* in diaspora

studies, however this same perspective has been used to analyse the African diaspora (Gilroy, 1993; Jalloh and Maizlish, 1996; Lemelle and Kelley, 1994), Irish diaspora (Akenson, 1993; Bielenberg, 2000), Cuban diaspora (Bonnin and Brown, 2002), Mexican diaspora (Rouse, 1991) and Indian diaspora (Shukla, 2001), to mention only some of the examples.

If studies of indigenous identities have tended to emphasize their cultural integrity, alternative epistemologies, connections to the earth and to territory, and historic continuity, then in contrast, studies of diasporic identities have pointed to porous borders, deterritorialization, cultural fragmentation and historic discontinuity. There has been a tendency to contrast these two theoretical perspectives, without recognizing the analytical and political bridges being built by the social actors – of flesh and bones – who are described by these conceptual apparatuses.

The migration of indigenous Latin Americans to the US and Europe has created a point of convergence between the struggles for cultural recognition and the struggles for migrant rights, redefining indigenous identities in transnational contexts (Besserer, 2006; Kearney, 1996). Patricia Artía (2008), in her work on the Indigenous Front of Binational Organizations (*Frente Indígena de Organizaciones Bi-Nacionales*), analyses the experiences of Mixtec women who have built political alliances with Laotian, Hmong and El Salvadoran women, in the framework of an oral history workshop designed to recapture their experiences as indigenous, as women and as migrants. The result of this experience is a collective book entitled *Immigrant Women: A Road to the Future*, in which these women from different cultural communities unite their voices to denounce the racism and sexism of US society. From these perspectives, diasporic identities and indigenous identities are not viewed as contrasting, but rather as complementary, in their struggle for citizen rights.

Although Latin American indigenous migration has been analysed from the theoretical framework of transnationalism, there are currently proposals to begin to create bridges between diaspora theory and transnational indigenous studies, with the aim of understanding how being indigenous is given a new meaning when the link between identity and territory no longer exists (Clifford, 2007). One of the fundamental differences established between diaspora experiences and transnational identities is that it is assumed in the first case that returning to the community of origin is not possible and/or desirable for the social actors involved and therefore the community of origin becomes a mythical place of reference in the reconstitution of diasporic cultures. Meanwhile, transnational identities are assumed to be closely linked to the community of origin, with multi-local affiliations.

Studies conducted in various indigenous regions of Mexico, although primarily among Mixtecs in the state of Oaxaca (Besserer, 2006; Kearney, 1996), have revealed fallacies in the modernization paradigm used to analyse migration from a bipolar perspective that emphasized the tendency of migrants to lose their connection with their regions of origin and to begin to integrate into the receiving society. The studies of the communities referred to as 'deterritorialized' (Glick Schiller et al., 1992) analyse the bonds that migrants have with their families, communities and traditions, beyond the nation-states to which they have migrated. These changes in the perspectives used to analyse migration – which began particularly in the early 1990s – invite us to broaden our own perspectives on indigeneity and community, and to break away from the connection between identity and territory, in order to explore the way in which a deterritorialized sense of belonging is constructed, often through multi-local affiliations (Bash et al., 1994; Glick Schiller et al., 1992; Rouse, 1992).

It is important to recognize that even before the intensification of migratory processes in indigenous regions toward urban areas within the same countries and toward more industrialized countries (particularly the US, Canada and Spain), territorial mobility was already part of the experiences constituting the indigenous identity in various regions of Latin America. A case in point is the Mam population in Chiapas with which I have been working for the past 15 years. When analysing the historic construction of their indigenous identities, it is especially helpful to make use of the methodological approach of transnationalism, since the cultural identities of Mams have been affected by migratory experiences: from Guatemala to Mexico at the end of the nineteenth century and to various regions in the state of Chiapas throughout the twentieth century. The sense of belonging to an *imagined community* has been linked to a historic memory more than to territory. Therefore, their recent migrations to the east coast of the US (Hernández Castillo, in press) may be one more story to tell in the reconstruction of narratives of belonging that continue to be socialized in family get-togethers or in the *Palabra* and *Música Mam* radio programs broadcast weekly on the *Voz de la Frontera Sur*. At the same time Mam peasants may be developing multi-local affiliations, as they maintain their family and social bonds with their communities of origin through new communication technologies, and as they build new communities in the space they share with Guatemalan workers in the US. These multi-local affiliations were preceded by the formation of multiple identities – which allow them to make demands as peasants, indigenous, Mams or Jehovah's Witnesses at any time, depending on the context.

Perhaps recent advances in communication technologies allow the connections between different localities to be more intense than in the past between the Sierra Madre of Chiapas and the Cuchumatan region of Guatemala. However, the experiences of territorial mobility and transnational community are not new for indigenous Mams. And despite the violence associated with the integrationist programs of the Mexican state, their *imagined community* has even included Mam-speakers who remained on the other side of the border. Ironically, economic globalization processes instead of wiping out their indigenous identities – have led them to re-discover their 'Guatemalan indigenous brothers and sisters' thousands of kilometres from their communities of origin. For some of them, this has represented a return to their indigenous identity, and a return of their native language – which the integrationist programmes of the Mexican state attempted to destroy.[13]

Innovative multi-local ethnographies indicate how these new networks have formed 'transnational communities' in which people have essentially dual lives (Portes, 1995: 812). The extent to which second and third generation indigenous inhabitants of Chiapas will be able to maintain these dual lives is not yet clear. We do know, however, that the process of cultural homogenization anticipated by the most apocalyptic perspectives on globalization does not appear to be an immediate reality for 'border crossers' *par excellence*.

The persistence of indigenous identities within the globalization process does not, however, necessarily involve anti-systemic, contesting identities. Some authors such as Zygmunt Bauman (2001) propose that the regeneration of identities is linked to the current phase in the globalization of capital, and that this phenomenon is a response to the exacerbated individualization suffered by industrialized societies. In this regard he indicates that these new identities being reinvented in the framework of the globalization process are not contrary to the globalizing tendency, nor do they get in its way, but rather, constitute a legitimate offshoot and natural companion of globalization. Far from detaining globalization, according to Bauman, these identities 'grease the wheels' of globalization (Bauman, 2001: 174).

It is difficult to predict the future of indigenous identities in the new transnational context, and specifically in the case of the Pan-Mayan identities taking shape from Los Angeles to Guatemala, passing through Chiapas and Yucatan. However, other experiences in indigenous migration indicate that these identities do not always 'grease the wheels of capital', and in fact often obstruct the capacity to extract profit and to promote homogenized forms of consumption. The experiences of transnational organizations of indigenous migrants, as described by Jonathan Fox and Gaspar Rivera-Salgado (2004), and those of indigenous women in the oral history workshop (Artía, 2008), describe a rather encouraging scenario in which the globalization of grassroots solidarity has made it possible for indigenous people from various regions of Mexico and around the world to build common fronts for demanding labour rights, to struggle for better working conditions and to demand migration reforms that will allow them full citizenship.

In the new transnational context, indigenous Latin Americans are establishing alliances and coordinating actions with the Native American population and with migrants from various countries. They identify themselves as indigenous in certain contexts, as Mexican migrants in others, and as agricultural workers when they are mobilizing around labour demands. The tensions and contradictions evident in theoretical debates between diasporic identities and indigenous identities do not appear to present a problem for the political actions of these human collectives.

The way that social actors imagine their identities and defend them as spaces for political action, depends a great deal on their personal and organizational histories. If in our academic work we reify some identities as more authentic or more emancipative than others, we may actually encourage new exclusions. Some imagine and defend these identities as ancient identities linked to the earth and to territory, while others reconstruct them as hybrid identities open to change and characterized by different affiliations. If as academics, we make either of these perspectives appear to be the norm, we will be silencing and colonizing the experiences of both those defending indigeneity and those defending diaspora identities.

## Revisiting mestizaje and Afro-Latin identities

Other important criticisms that should be taken into account, as we re-think the conceptualization of indigenous identities and the construction of political alliances, are those made by scholars investigating mestizaje as the cultural identity of subaltern sectors. Many of these works have served to challenge the analysis of mestizaje exclusively as the dominant ideology in national projects in Latin America. The abundant Latin American literature on mestizaje, nationalism and racism produced in recent decades has failed to consider an analysis of processes in which a portion of the considerable marginalized sectors are appropriating mestizaje as their cultural identity.[14] In other words, we are referring here to the construction of mestizaje at the grassroots level – which has not always coincided with the developments and representations in official discourse.

Anthropological studies on the construction of Mestizo identities, which have proliferated in recent years, have used two important theoretical works as their analytical point of reference.[15] From different textual strategies and perspectives, these two works have confronted ethnic essentialisms, pointing to the need for re-thinking the matter of mestizaje and recognizing the existence of fluid cultural borders in an increasingly globalized world. Reflections on the *Nueva Mestiza* by Chicana writer and literary critic Gloria Anzaldúa, published in 1987, and the conceptualization of hybrid cultures proposed by Mexican–Argentinian anthropologist Néstor García Canclini in 1989, confronted the essentialist discourses defended by both the Chicano movement in the US and the indigenous movement in Latin America.

In the US at the end of the 1980s, *Borderlands/La Frontera: The New Mestiza*, a book of poetry, literary essays and social analysis written in *Spanglish* by Gloria Anzaldúa (1987), became a fundamental book for political analysts and activists who defended the emergence of new hybrid cultures, and for various reasons, did not identify with those who – from feminist or nationalist postures – promoted a type of identity politics based on an essentialist conception of identities. With her own experience, she demonstrates the limitations of identity policies based on criteria of authenticity and exclusion. Anzaldúa´s work did not intended to establish a general theory of identity, or claim that identities were always experienced as multiple and contradictory, but rather to simply acknowledge that in the new global context there are many individuals like her, who experience a complex mixture of identities that keep their head 'buzzing' with all the contradictions.

In 1989 Néstor García Canclini published his book *Culturas Híbridas. Estrategias para Entrar y Salir de la Modernidad* (later published in English in 1995, with the title *Hybrid Cultures: Strategies for Entering and Leaving Modernity*) at a time when most Latin American anthropologists had united around support for the demands of Latin American indigenous movements. The book *México Profundo. Civilización Negada* by Guillermo Bonfil Batalla, was being discussed and cited not only in academic classrooms, but also in the meetings and workshops of indigenous organizations. The distinction between *México Profundo*, based on the ethical-political values of the indigenous world, and *México Imaginario*, emerging from the individualist values of western society, became an analytical scheme for understanding not only the reality in Mexico, but in all of Latin America. Confronting these dichotomous visions of Latin American reality, Néstor García Canclini borrowed the concept of hybridation from natural sciences, to refer to sociocultural processes in which discrete practices or structures, existing separately, are combined to generate new structures, objects and practices. It is nearly impossible, he said, in an increasingly globalized world to continue to speak of 'pure' or 'authentic' cultures, and he rejected the existence of identities characterized by self-contained, ahistorical essences.

His radical criticism of identities contrasts with the analytical perspectives that continue to defend the existence of different – and in many ways, opposing – cultural logics between indigenous and non-indigenous individuals. Not only does he reject the importance, at the political level, of the indigenous identity as an organizational space, but he relativizes the notion of identity and at the methodological level, he proposes replacing identity as an object of study with intercultural heterogeneity and hybridation. Leaning toward postmodern scepticism of identity politics, Néstor García Canclini theorizes and goes about his academic work without taking the indigenous movement into consideration. He focuses his attention on cultural industries and on urban-popular cultures – and this allows him to explore with precision the hybridation processes that interest him. He never concerns himself with explaining why – despite the existence of 'porous' cultural borders and permanent hybrid and mixed processes – indigenous identities continue to be imagined as solid identities that have inherited ancient cultures and therefore the articulation of regional and local struggles continues throughout the American continent.

While these two works cannot be considered anthropological studies in the strictest sense, both contributed to reformulating the terms of the discussion on mestizaje and creating the cultural climate for the academic legitimization of mestizo identities as subaltern identities, and for some authors, emancipatory identities.

A pioneering work in ethnographic research of this topic is the study conducted by Marisol de la Cadena (2005) on the 'indigenous mestizos' in Peru. She demonstrates that the term 'mestizo' – unlike the term 'hybrid cultures' – is not only an analytical concept and an ideology of domination, but it has become a term of self-identification for poor peasants who view the mestizo identity as a way to move up the social scale and more easily access benefits as a Peruvian

citizen – without necessarily losing the features of the indigenous culture that are significant in their lives. Marisol de la Cadena, like Gloria Anzaldúa, does not so much defend the transforming potential of the mestizo identity, but rather, describes it as a reality in which thousands of Peruvians live, and recognizes that, on the one hand, the 'de-Indianization' aspect of mestizaje can legitimize the discrimination against those considered to be Indian, however at the same time, it can open up possibilities for a better life, without the need to renounce indigenous ways, styles and beliefs (2000: 6).

Along the same line of analysis, Jan French points out that renewed interest on the part of academics and activists in the concept of mestizaje can be explained by the fact that it opens up some possibilities in relation to the dilemmas presented by neoliberal multiculturalism. Specifically, it resolves the problem of deciding who is indigenous and who is not, it does not exclude other subaltern groups that cannot claim to be culturally different, and it avoids the formation of new ethnic barriers and new exclusions (French, 2007: 6).

Without failing to recognize the importance of these criticisms of identitary purisms, the problem with some of these analytical perspectives is that, once again, they appear to present mestizaje as an identity of a prescriptive nature more than as an experienced reality. A new type of universalism seems to be hidden behind these demands of hibridity and mestizaje as spaces *par excellence* for imagining the alternative modernities of the globalized world.

From other political positionings, a number of scholars of Afro-Latino cultures have also pointed to the way in which imaginaries around indigeneity have contributed toward strengthening the connection between the recognition of collective rights and the existence of differentiated cultural features in subaltern groups, making the political struggles of Afro-descendents difficult. These perspectives have indicated that in the struggle for the recognition of communal lands, there has been a tendency to defend the existence of a special spiritual relationship between indigenous peoples and 'Mother Earth'. This places black communities at a disadvantage when it comes to demanding this type of right, since they are not imagined to possess this kind of connection (Hooker, 2005; Ng'weno, 2007). The influence of the indigeneity discourse in the legitimization of communal lands is reflected in the fact that the Afro-descendent communities that have gained recognition of their collective rights are those who have managed to make their demands from the position of having cultural identities presented as indigenous.[16] This has led some authors to speak of the 'indigenization' of Afro-descendent identities (Wade, 2006).

While this process could be interpreted as Afro-Latinos appropriating the strategies used in the struggles waged by indigenous movements, it is not without its contradictions, since many black populations that have not managed to present themselves as 'culturally different' have not enjoyed the benefits of the redistribution processes accompanying some of the multicultural reforms in Latin America. In addition to this example of political exclusion, the most important criticism made by these authors in relation to the rhetoric of indigeneity is the tendency to replace struggles against racial discrimination with struggles for cultural recognition. The neoliberal regimes of multicultural citizenship are more open to listening and responding to demands made on the basis of cultural or ethnic differences than those made on the basis of a claim of racial discrimination (Anderson, 2007; Hooker, 2005; Wade, 2006). In the first case, the need for transformations in racialized structures of inequality can be avoided or silenced, since it is possible to speak of culture without speaking of power, while it is impossible to speak of racism and exclusion without denouncing the perpetuation of systems of inequality and internal colonialism.

According to these authors, the imaginaries mobilized around indigeneity have diminished the possibilities for anti-racist political alliances between indigenous and Afro-descendent movements. In the examples of the 'indigeneization' of black struggles, such as the case of the Garifunas of Honduras (analysed by Mark Anderson [2007]), a specific type of collective subject with differentiated cultural characteristics has been prioritized. The struggles of the Garifunas have been subordinated to discourse on indigenous rights, and this has signified that their demands in relation to racism and economic exclusion have been displaced.

From a perspective that emphasizes the productive capacity of state discourses, these critics of indigeneity point out that the way in which indigenous subjectivities and the subjectivities of Afro-descendents are imagined and mobilized in the framework of the new Latin American multiculturalism is not only a reflection of essential identities, but it is also a result of the differentiated way in which these two subaltern groups have been historically racialized.

In an effort to denaturalize the differences between black cultures and indigenous cultures in Latin America, Peter Wade (1997), has historicized the way in which indigenous have been 'constructed' – characterized as premodern and profoundly different culturally, however also as raw material in the construction of Latin American mestizo nations. Blacks, for their part, have been 'constructed' as being from outside the nation and 'deculturated'. This has meant that the black population has tended to propose their demands more in terms of anti-racist struggles and struggles for civil rights that will allow them to be included in the national project through full citizenship, and not in terms of differentiated cultural rights.

These demands from the perspective of historic constructivism, aimed at understanding the way in which the cultural differences of Afro-descendent and indigenous populations have been impacted by discourses of power, allow us to denaturalize and re-think these differences from more inclusive perspectives that open the way to political alliances. This is precisely what has been taking place in various parts of the continent, where struggles for the recognition of cultural rights have been waged alongside anti-racism struggles. The Zapatista movement is one example that has placed the problem of racism in Mexico on the political debate agenda. It has also waged a political struggle for the recognition of the collective rights of indigenous peoples. Alliances between Afro-descendents and indigenous are also being established in Ecuador, Brazil and Colombia, on the basis of an anti-racist political platform.

There are other experiences characterized by the resurgence of Afro-descendent identities, and the articulation of their struggles with those of the indigenous movement, however there is little analysis on these phenomena. The *moreno* populations inhabiting the Costa de Guerrero coastal region in Mexico provide one example. These groups have historically identified themselves as *costeños* (people from the Coast) and have begun to build alliances with the indigenous movement in the same Mexican state, on the basis of their identities as Afro-Mexicans. An autonomous inter-cultural university project Universidad del Sur (UNISUR), without state support and without official recognition, is currently being developed. Mestizo, indigenous and Afro-Mexican communities have come together to initiate an educational project based on their cultural and social specificities. In this case the official constructions of 'alterity' have been answered with the emergence of more open perspectives on indigenous identities that include mestizo and *moreno* peasants. Beyond the specific terms of self-identification, this political project has appropriated the international tools for indigenous rights to use them in their demands for the right to self-government and to multilingual, intercultural education.

## FEMINIST CRITICISMS OF INDIGENEITY

Finally, I would like to address the criticisms of indigeneity on the part of feminist analyses of cultural identities and ethnic nationalisms. There is considerable literature on feminist theory that asserts that both official and ethnic nationalisms have tended to use women's bodies as raw material in the construction of their political projects (Gutiérrez Chong, 2004; Yuval Davis, 1997).

These perspectives have pointed out that the emphasis on the multicultural policies has led to the strengthening of cultural essentialisms that often serve patriarchal interests within identitary collectives. The ahistorical representations of cultures as homogenous entities of shared values and customs, existing on the margin of power relations, lead to cultural fundamentalisms that view any attempt by women to transform practices negatively affecting their lives as a threat to the group's collective identity. By historicizing cultural practices, such as sati (widows being burned alive in the funeral pyres of their husbands) (Mani, 1998; Oldenburg Veena, 1994) and infibulation or genital mutilation (Koso-Tomas, 1987; Mama, 1995; Mari Tripp, 2002), these feminists have been able to demonstrate that many of the 'traditional' practices negatively affecting and attacking the lives of women have changed over time, that they often originated in colonial contexts, and that when they are modified or done away with, this does not affect the group's identitary continuity.

These studies have shown us that when the transformation of certain traditions affect the interests of the sectors in power, then arguments are raised with regard to the dangers to cultural integrity. A case in point is the debate around the agricultural rights of women in Africa and in various countries in South Asia, where the argument of 'defending traditions' has been used to delegitimize women's demands for land (Mari Tripp, 2002). These reflections by postcolonial feminisms assist us to re-think indigenous cultures from analytical perspectives that include the dialogues of power on which they were constituted. By deconstructing the way in which certain features are selected (and others are not) as representative of a culture or as vital to an identity, we can reveal the networks of power hiding behind the representation of difference.

In the Latin American context, some academics who defend indigenous rights have contributed to developing idealized representations of these peoples, without leaving any room for the voices and challenges of women within those very groups. These representations have been used by groups in these collectives who possess power, in order legitimize their privileges. The other extreme of this perspective has been represented by those who disqualify all the institutions and practices of indigenous peoples on the basis of their colonial origin, and who stereotype their cultures – also on the basis of 'selective labelling'.

This is a debate in which I have been politically involved in Mexico. Over a number of decades mine has been among the voices critical of the essentialism in the Mexican indigenous movement, which has refused to address the issue of gender-based exclusions and domestic violence within indigenous communities.

Because of my double identity as an academic and as an activist in a feminist organization working against sexual and domestic violence through a support centre for women and children (in which a high percentage of women seeking help were indigenous), I have had to confront both discourses idealizing the indigenous culture, elaborated by a significant sector of Mexican anthropologists, and the ethnocentrism of a major sector of liberal feminism. In a polarized context in which women's rights have been presented as opposed to the collective rights of peoples, it has been difficult to defend less extreme perspectives on indigenous cultures that recognize the power dialogues through which they are constituted, and at the same time, to defend the right to one's own culture and the self-determination of indigenous peoples.

This polarization of feminists and Indianist postures intensified during the last decade, after the Zapatista movement proposed the need to reform the constitution so that the autonomous rights of indigenous peoples would be recognized (Hernández Castillo, 2002). In this context, a major sector of Mexico's liberal feminists developed alliances with liberal anti-autonomous sectors, in order to emphasize the dangers that recognizing the collective rights of indigenous peoples would represent for indigenous women. Suddenly, a number of academics who had never written a single line in favour of indigenous women began to express their 'concern' for their rights, and even to cite – out of context – the works of some feminist academics, myself included, who had written on domestic violence in indigenous regions. This particular situation changed the context for framing our academic work, indicating the need to contextualize our reflections on domestic violence beyond cultural analyses, to include an analysis of state violence and to emphasize the importance of the structural context in which this violence occurs (Hernández Castillo, 2006).

At this political crossroads, organized indigenous women were the ones who gave us some clues on how to re-think indigenous demands from a non-essentialist perspective. Their theorizations on culture, tradition and gender equity were expressed in political documents, the minutes of meetings and public discourses.[17] Indigenous women never asked for this 'protection' from liberal intellectuals or from the state, which would only limit the autonomy of their people. To the contrary, they have defended their right to self-determination and to their own culture, while fighting within the indigenous movement to redefine the terms in which tradition and custom are understood and to actively participate in building autonomous projects.

A significant sector of Mexico's hegemonic feminists have raised their voices to defend the liberal rights of equality without analysing the relationship between liberalism and feminism, and while assuming, on principle, that liberalism has given greater equity to women,[18] than the indigenous cultures in which women continue to be victim to forced marriage, polygamy, segregation and political exclusion, to name some of the 'backward' practices mentioned as part of 'indigenous cultures'. Feminists from India, such as Chandra Talpade Mohanty (1991) and Lata Mani (1999), have responded to representations such as those from Mexican critics of the recognition of indigenous rights by pointing out that presenting the women of the 'Third World' (in our case, indigenous women) as simply victims of patriarchy is a form of discursive colonialism that denies the spaces that women have opened up in the framework of their own cultural dynamics.[19]

In Mexico, a response to these representations is being offered by an indigenous women's movement, which appeared under the influence of the Zapatista uprising. This movement has focused efforts on reformulating the demands for national multicultural recognition based on a broader definition of culture that includes not only the hegemonic voices and representations, but also the diversity of voices and contradictory processes that lend meaning to the life of a human collective.

However, this reformulation of indigenous identities by women is not exclusive to the Mexican process. During the last decade we have seen organizational processes of indigenous women emerging in various regions of Latin America. In these processes the collective demands of their peoples are conjugated with their specific gender-related demands. We might point out that we have been witnesses to the emergence of a new political identity that cannot be absorbed within the political identities of indigenous movements or within the gender identities of feminist movements.

The different political genealogies and personal histories of organized indigenous women in Latin America have defined the way in which these women and their organizations prioritize or do not prioritize the gender-related demands and/or the collective demands of their peoples. The significant degree of internal diversity in the continental movement of indigenous women is both its strength and its weakness. Reaching consensuses or proposing general demands has involved negotiating political perspectives around how culture is experienced and conceptualized, and around the rights and relationships between men and women. These tensions are especially evident within the Guatemalan Mayan movement in which indigenous women have broadly debated the tensions between gender and culture, and are the continent's pioneers in systematizing their reflections on these issues.[20]

Given the diversity of voices emerging from organizations of indigenous women, it is easy to be tempted to legitimize some and silence others, considering those who defend the indigenous cosmovision as a space of resistance to be 'authentic', and discrediting those who propose the existence of an indigenous feminism as 'acculturated'. Or at the other extreme, labelling those in ethnic-political movements who reject feminisms as 'essentialist and conservative', or as opening up space in political and academic debates only to those who have the most in common with the agenda of urban, western feminism. Both perspectives can result in new strategies of discursive colonialism that deny the richness and complexity of these new political identities.

Acknowledging and recapturing these multiple voices is fundamental in order to assess the different contributions from women toward the construction of an inclusive, democratizing indigenous agenda.

## FINAL REFLECTIONS

The purpose of this review of theoretical and political debates on indigeneity was not to seek the 'correct' perspective for understanding the reconfiguration of indigenous identities in Latin America. Rather, my aim has been to attempt to understand the political context in which analytical proposals have been made, with the objective of building bridges between different intellectual traditions.

The reservations expressed – from transnational perspectives, diaspora theory, Afro-Latin studies and feminist theory – with regard to the indigenous identity as a space for political mobilization are not exclusively analytical exercises carried out in the academic world. In most cases they have been written from political positions characterized by concern for building social justice from the perspective of an inclusive political agenda.

As I have attempted to demonstrate through concrete examples, the fears existent around exclusions and cultural fundamentalisms have not always been well substantiated. The analytical constructions of what is *indigenous*, as elaborated in discourses of power, have been responded to in diverse and contradictory ways by indigenous migrants in the US, indigenous Zapatistas in Chiapas, coalitions of indigenous, mestizos and Afro-Mexicans in Guerrero, and by the continental movement of indigenous women – and in all these cases we find examples of non-essentialist, inclusive definitions of what is understood as 'to be indigenous'. The phantom of 'cultural fundamentalism' should not cause us to discredit a priori the political struggles of those social actors who have found a point of support in the indigenous identity that allows them to imagine themselves in the world and to confront the homogenizing tendency in economic globalization.

Many of these voices are indicating that modernity as a cultural system – which has left a significant portion of humanity behind, including women and indigenous, and which has constructed a system of values and powers by denying all that is not masculine and western – is in crisis and should be replaced with some type of alternative project. And many of these same voices – as they work to construct this new alternative project – have turned their focus to the knowledge that they are constructing as 'ancestral', and that allows them to think that other possible futures do indeed exist.

Some of the elements in epistemological and political proposals from the various subaltern identities that I have addressed in this chapter could be useful in reformulating the academic definitions of *indigenous*, from the perspective of non-prescriptive visions.

The criticisms generated by transnational theory, by diaspora theory, by 'feminists of colour' (to use a concept of self-definition) and by postcolonial feminists point to the need to profoundly re-think the construction of *indigenous* – not to discard the concept as an analytical tool, not to delegitimize the struggles of indigenous organizations, but to contribute, from our work as academics, to the construction of more inclusive definitions of culture and identity.

## NOTES

1  Translation by Jana Schroeder.
2  In De la Cadena, Marisol and Orin Starn 2007: 11.
3  I am using the concept 'North' from a geo-political perspective, making use of the colloquial concept that we use in Latin America to refer basically to the US and Europe – where the majority of the literature on 'indigeneity' has originated. The dialogues I have narrated here have been established fundamentally in English-speaking academia, which include the diaspora of intellectuals from the 'South' who have migrated to the 'North'.
4  In some cases translations have generated conceptual confusion, as in the case of 'indigenism', used in English by authors such as Ronald Niezen (2000) to refer to the transnational movement that has appropriated indigenous identity. In Spanish, however, *indigenismo* refers to state policies toward indigenous peoples, and in Latin America these policies have been characterized by their focus on integration.
5  I am borrowing the concept of *cultural climate* to refer to the expression of a specific configuration of worldviews in a given period of time, that generates a particular sensitivity to one problem or another, or that narrows or broadens the horizon for what seems socially and politically possible' (Werner Brand, 1992: 2).
6  This argument differs from one of the positions taken in the political-academic debate in Latin America that also emphasizes the colonial nature of indigenous cultures, in order to discredit their 'authenticity' and to defend acculturation policies (Martínez Peláez, 1970; Aguirre Beltrán, 1970). Mary Louise Pratt does not refer to the colonial nature of cultural practices of the indigenous population, but instead, the relational nature of the origin of this self-definition.
7  There is a considerable amount of anthropological production in Latin America that defends the recognition of indigenous rights (Bengoa, 2000; Díaz

Polanco, 1998, 2006; Hernández Castillo et al., 2004; López Barcenas, 2000a, b, 2004; Stavenhagen and Iturralde, 1990; Sierra and Chenaut, 1995; and many others). There is also more recent production around multicultural reforms in Latin America and their impact on the lives of indigenous peoples, as presented at various conferences of the Latin American Network of Legal Anthropology (*Red Latinoamericana de Antropología Jurídica* – RELAJU). See http://www.relaju.com.

8   There are a number of works that analyse the formation of nationalist discourse, and the way in which such discourse was appropriated at the local level by subaltern classes (Gall, 2004; Mallón 1995).

9   In other writings I have analysed the importance of what has been referred to as co-participative research and/or action research, as methodological contributions of Latin American social sciences to the decolonization of knowledge (Hernández Castillo, 2007). It was based on these methodologies that alliances were constructed between critical anthropologists and indigenous movements. In the framework of these dialogues, an expanded reflection was generated of the colonial uses of anthropology, as expressed at the Barbados I and II meetings (see: abyayala.nativeweb.org/declarations.barbados.1.html).

10   Various authors have analysed these legislative reforms and the multicultural public policies promoted by Latin American states (see Assies et al., 2000; Sieder, 2002; Van Cott, 2000).

11   This data is not very precise, since the criteria for defining who is indigenous and who is not vary greatly among different countries.

12   A political history of these tensions in the case of Guatemala can be found in MacLeod (2008). And see Hale (1994), regarding the conflict between Miskitos and Sandinistas in Nicaragua.

13   Many Mexican Mam migrants, who no longer spoke their native language due to the campaigns initiated by post-revolutionary governments to oblige them to speak Spanish, recuperated their language when they met Mam-speaking indigenous Guatemalans in the US. A Mam migrant from the municipality of Mazapa de Madero describes his migration experience, commenting: 'When I got there, I was surprised there were so many *idiomistas* (indigenous language speakers). Lots of *chapines* (Guatemalans) from over here in San Marcos and from Huehue (Guatemalan departments). But over there, we were all the same – there weren't any differences. They immediately explained to me where to buy food, and how to make cheaper calls to Mexico, with some phone cards that you could talk up to two hours for only five dollars. At first, when they talked among themselves, they spoke in Mam, and I didn't say anything and they thought I didn't understand. I was embarrassed by my pronunciation.

But I gradually tried harder, and it was as if the words of my grandfather came back to me, from when we were little and they spoke to us in *Tokiol* (Mam). What I didn't do with my Uncle Petronilo, I did on the other side [of the border], with my Guatemalan *compadres*. Now I joke with them in *Tokiol*, and nobody says whether I'm Guatemalan or Mexican – we're the same people and we help each other out'. (Interview with G. C., at the *Horizontes Ejido*, Mazapa de Madero, May, 1993).

14   My own work on the construction of a nation at the Mexico–Guatemala border analyses the use of the 'Myth of Mestizaje' as the justification for submitting the Mam population to campaigns of forced integration (Hernández Castillo, 2001). The pioneering work of Olivia Gall (2004) and Alicia Castellanos (1994) on racism in Mexico also addresses mestizaje as the ideology of power. Other analyses on the mestizaje-integrationism-racism connection can be found in Basave (1992), and Bastide (1970).

15   See Audinet (2004), De la Cadena (2000, 2005), Field (2002), French, (2004), Klor de Alva (1995) and Wade (2006).

16   Some examples are the Garifunas in Guatemala and Honduras, and the Sumos and Miskitos in Nicaragua.

17   Some of these documents, such as the Revolutionary Law on Women in the Zapatista Army of National Liberation (*Ley Revolucionaria de Mujeres del Ejército Zapatista de Liberación Nacional*) and the speech by Zapatista *Comandante Esther* before the national Congress, defending indigenous law as a political construction that is being reconstituted by organized women, can be found in Speed et al. (2006).

18   I use the term 'hegemonic feminism' to refer to the feminism that has emerged in the country's central region and theorized in academia, and in which the struggle against abortion and in favour of reproductive rights has been the focus. Since the Coalition of Feminist Women was formed in 1976 and later the National Front for Women's Liberation and Rights (FNALIDM) in 1979, the legalization of abortion and the fight against domestic violence were the demands that kept this sector of feminists together. This sector of feminism dominated other popular and rural feminisms in which class demands were closely linked with gender demands. For a history of hegemonic feminism, see Tuñón (1997). For a history of popular feminism and the class-related nature of their demands, see Masolo (1992).

19   Other criticisms of the ethnocentrism of liberal feminism can be found in Alarcón (1990) and Trinh (1988).

20   See Alvarez (2005), Cumes (2007a), Chirix (2003), Gabriel (2004), Grupo de Mujeres Mayas Kaqla (2002, 2004), MacLeod and Cabrera (2000), Velásquez Nimantuj (2003).

# REFERENCES

Aguilar Rivera, J.A. (2004) *El Sonido y la Furia: La Persuasión Multicultural en México y Estados Unidos.* México: Santillana Ediciones Generales.

Aguirre Beltrán, G. (1967) *Regiones de Refugio.* México City: Instituto Indigenista Interamericano.

Akenson, D.H. (1993) *The Irish Diaspora: A Primer.* Toronto: P.D. Meany Co.

Alarcón, N. (1990) "The Theoretical Subjects of This Bridge Called My Back and Anglo-American Feminism" in *Making Faces/Making Soul: Haciendo caras*, ed. Gloria Anzaldúa, pp. 30–59. San Francisco: Aunt Lute.

Álvarez Béjar, A. (1992) 'Industrial restructuring and the role of Mexican labor in NAFTA', *U.C. Davis Law Review*, 27 (4): 897–915.

Álvarez, C. (2005) 'Cosmovisión maya y feminismo ¿Caminos que se unen?'. Paper presented in the Panel 'Mayanismos y Feminismos' del Congreso de Estudios Mayas, August, Guatemala.

Anderson, B. (1983) *Imagined Communities: Reflection on the Origin and Spread of Nationalism.* London: Verso.

Anderson, M. (2007) 'When Afro becomes (like) indigenous: Garifuna and Afro-indigenous politics in Honduras', *Journal of Latin American and Caribbean Anthropology*, 12 (2): 384–413.

Anzaldúa, G. (1987) *Borderlands/La Frontera: The New Mestiza.* San Francisco, CA: Spinters/Aunt Lute.

Arias, A. (2006) 'Enterrando el Mito del primitivismo, redescubriendo a un autor eminentemente contemporáneo', in J.C. Escobedo (ed.), *Página de la Literatura Guatemalteca.* Available at: http://www.literaturaguatemalteca.org.

Artía, P. (2008) 'Prácticas políticas transnacionales: Las mujeres del frente indígena de organizaciones binacionales', in R.A. Hernández Castillo (ed.), *Etnografías e Historias de Resistencia. Mujeres Indígenas, Procesos Organizativos y Nuevas Identidades Políticas.* México: CIESAS/PUEG-UNAM. Pp. 331–361.

Assies, W., van der Haar, G. and Hoekema, A. (eds) (2000) *The Challenge of Diversity: Indigenous Peoples and Reform of the State in Latin America.* Amsterdam: Thela Thesis.

Audinet, J. (2004) *The Human Face of Globalization: From Multicultural to Mestizaje.* Lanham, MD: Rowman and Littlefield.

Basave (1992)*México Mestizo: Análisis del Nacionalismo Mexicano en torno a la Mestizofilia de Andrés Molina Enríquez*, México D.F.:Fondo de Cultura Económica, Bastide, Roger, (1970), *El prómixo y el extraño*, Buenos Aires: Amorrortu,

Bash, L., Glick Schiller, N. and Szantopn Blanc, C. (1994) *Nations Unbound: Transnational Projects, Poscolonial Predicaments and Deterritorialized Nation-States.* Amsterdam: Gordon and Breach Publishers.

Bastide, R. (1970) *El proximo y el extraño.* Buenos Aires: Amorrortu.

Bauman, Z. (2001) *La Sociedad Individualizada.* Madrid: Editorial Cátedra.

Baviskar, A. (2007) 'Indian indigeneities: Adivasi engagements with Hindu nationalism in India', in M. De la Cadena and O. Starn (eds), *Indigenous Experience Today.* Oxford: Berg. Pp. 275–305.

Bengoa, J. (2000) *La Emergencia Indígena en América Latina.* México: FCE.

Besserer, F. (2006) *Topografías Transnacionales. Hacia una Geografía de la Vida Transnacional.* México: Plaza y Valdez.

Bielenberg, A. (2000) *The Irish Diaspora.* Harlow: Pearson Education Limited.

Bonfil Batalla, G. (ed.) (1981) *Utopía y Revolución: El Pensamiento Político Contemporáneo de los Indios en América Latina.* México City: Editorial Nueva Imagen.

Bonnin, R. and Brown, C. (2002) 'The cuban diaspora: A comparative analysis of the search for meaning among recent cuban exiles and cuban Americans', *Hispanic Journal of Behavioral Sciences*, 24 (4): 465–78.

Brysk, A. (2000) *From Tribal Village to Global Village: Indian Rights and International Relations in Latin America.* Stanford, CA: Stanford University Press.

Canessa, A. (2006) *Minas, Mote y Muñecas: Identidades e Indigeneidades en Larecaja.* La Paz, Bolivia: Mama Huaco.

Castellanos Guerrero, A. (1994) 'Asimilación y diferenciación de los indios de México', in A. Castellanos Guerrero (ed.), *Revista de Centro de Estudios Sociológicos*, No. 35. México: El Colegio de México. Pp. 32–56.

Chavez, M. and Hoffman, O. (2004) 'Movilidad identitaria y reconfiguración de espacios y territorios en Putumayo, Colombia y la Costa Chica, México', Ponencia presentada en el Seminario *Más allá de la Identidad: Perspectivas Contemporáneas Comparativas sobre Lugar, Espacio y Movilidad en América Latina*. 9 Noviembre. Departamento de Antropología de la Facultad de Ciencias Humanas, Universidad Nacional de Colombia.

Chirix García, E.D. (2003) *Alas y Raíces, Afectividad de las Mujeres Mayas. Rik'in ruxik' y ruxe'il, ronojel kajowab'al ri mayab' taq ixoqi'.* Ciudad de Guatemala: Grupo de Mujeres Mayas Kaqla, Nawal Wuj.

Clifford, J. (2007) 'Varieties of indigenous experience: Diasporas, homelands, sovereignties', in M. De la Cadena and O. Starn (eds), *Indigenous Experience Today.* Oxford: Berg. Pp. 197–225.

Collier, G. (1999) *Basta! Land and the Zapatista Rebellion in Chiapas*. Berkeley, CA: Institute Food First.

Collier, J. (1999) 'Liberalismo y Racismo, Dos Caras de la Misma Moneda', in M.T. Sierra Camacho (ed.), *Racismos y Derechos, Dimensión Antropológica*, Año 6 (15): January–April, 11–26.

Cumbre de Mujeres Indígenas de América (2003) *Memoria de la Primera Cumbre de Mujeres Indígenas de América*. México City: Fundación Rigoberta Menchú Tum.

Cumes, A. (2007a) 'Las Mujeres son 'más indias': Género, multticulturalismo y mayanización. ¿esquivando o retando opresiones?' (ms).

Cumes, A. (2007b) 'Multiculturalismo y unidad nacional en guatemala: Dinámicas de mayanización en un contexto turbulento e ideologizado'. Paper presented in the International Coloquium '*Ciudades Multiculturales de América. Migraciones, Relaciones Interétnicas y Etnicidad*', Monterrey, Nuevo León, México, 29–31 October.

De la Cadena, M. (2000) *Indigenous Mestizos: The Politics of Race and Culture in Cuzco, Peru*, 1919–1991. Durham, NC: Duke University Press.

De la Cadena, M. (2005) 'Are mestizos hybrids? The conceptual politics of andean identities', *Journal of Latin American Studies*, 37 (2): 259–84.

De la Cadena, M. and Starn, O. (eds) (2007) *Indigenous Experience Today*. Oxford: Berg.

Díaz Polanco, H. (1998) *La Rebelión Zapatista y la Autonomía*. México City: Siglo XXI.

Díaz Polanco, H. (2006) *Elogio a la Diversidad*. México City: Siglo XXI.

Escobar, A. (1997) *El Final del Salvaje: Naturaleza, Cultura y Política en la Antropología Contemporánea*. Bogotá: Instituto Colombiano de Antropología.

Field, L.W. (2002) 'Blood and traits: Preliminary observations on the analysis of mestizo and indigenous identities in Latin America vs. The U.S.', *Journal of Latin American Anthropology*, 7 (1): 2–33.

Fox, J. and Rivera Salgado, G. (eds) (2004) *Indígenas Mexicanos Migrantes en los Estados Unidos*. México City: Editorial Miguel Ángel Porrúa/Universidad Autónoma de Zacatecas.

French, J.H. (2004) 'Mestizaje and law making in indigenous identity formation in Northeastern Brazil: After the conflict came the history', *American Anthropologist*, 106 (4): 663–74.

Gabriel Xiquín, C. (2004) 'Liderazgo de las mujeres mayas en las leyendas y mitologías según su cosmovisión', (ms) Ciudad de Guatemala.

Gall, O. (2004) 'Identidad, exclusión y racismo: Reflexiones teóricas y sobre México', *Revista Mexicana de Sociología*, 66 (2): 221–259.

García Canclini, N. (1989) *Culturas Híbridas. Estrategias para Entrar y Salir de la Modernidad*. México City: Grijalbo/ CONACULTA.

Gilbert, M.J. and Nugent, D. (eds) (1994) *Every Day Forms of State Formation: Revolution and the Negotiation of Rule in Modern México*. London: Duke University Press.

Gilroy, P. (1987) '*There Ain't No Black in the Union Jack*': The Cultural Politics of Race and Nation. London: Hutchinson.

Gilroy, P. (1993) *The Black Atlantic. Modernity and Double Consciousness*. Cambridge, MA: Harvard University Press.

Glick Schiller, N., Bash, L. and Szantopn Blanc, C. (eds) (1992) *Towards a Transnational Perspective on Migration: Race, Class, Ethnicity and Nationalism Reconsidered*. New York: New York Academy of Science.

Grupo de Mujeres Mayas Kaqla' (2000) 'Algunos Colores del Arco Iris, Realidad de las Mujeres Mayas'. Documento de debate, Ciudad de Guatemala.

Grupo de Mujeres Mayas Kaqla' (2004) *La Palabra y el Sentir de las Mujeres Mayas de Kaqla*. Ciudad de Guatemala: Ediciones Kaqla

Gutiérrez, M. and Palomo, N. (1999) 'Autonomía con mirada de mujer', in A. Burguete (ed.), *México: Experiencias de Autonomía Indígena*. Copenhagen: IWGIA.

Gutiérrez Chong, N. (ed.) (2004) *Mujeres y Nacionalismos en América Latina. De la Independencia a la Nación del Nuevo Milenio*. México: Universidad Nacional Autónoma de México.

Hale, C. (1994) *Resistance and Contradiction: Miskitu Indians and the Nicaraguan State 1894–1987*. Stanford, California: Stanford University Press.

Hale, C. (2002) 'Does multiculturalism menace? Governance, cultural rights and the politics of identity in Guatemala', *Journal of Latin American Studies*, 34: 485–524.

Hale, C. (2005) 'Neoliberal multiculturalism: The remaking of cultural rights and racial dominance in central America', *Political and Legal Anthropology Review*, 28 (1): 10–28.

Hall, S. (1993) 'Cultural identity and diaspora', in P. Williams and L. Chrisman (eds), *Colonial Discourse and Postcolonial Theory: A Reader*. Hemel Hempstead: Harvester Wheatsheaf.

Harvey, D. (1989) *The Condition of Postmodernity. An Enquiry into the Origins of Cultural Change*. New York: Blackwell Press.

Harvey, N. (1998) *The Chiapas Rebellion: The Struggle for Land and Democracy*. Durham, NC: Duke University Press.

Hernández Castillo, R.A. (2001) *Histories and Stories from Chiapas. Border Identities in Southern Mexico*. Austin, TX: University of Texas Press. [Published in Spanish as *La Otra Frontera: Identidades Múltiples en el Chiapas Postcolonial*. México: CIESAS y Ed. Porrua.]

Hernández Castillo, R.A. (2002) 'Indigenous law and identity politics in México: Indigenous men's and women's perspective for a multicultural nation', *Political and Legal Anthropology Review*, 25 (1): 90–110.

Hernández Castillo, R.A. (2006) 'Fratricidal war or ethnocidal strategy: Women's experience with political violence in Chiapas', in V. Sanford and A.-A. Asale (eds), *Engaged Observer Anthropology, Advocacy and Activism*. New Jersey: Rutgers University Press. Pp. 149–70.

Hernández Castillo, R.A. (2007) 'Socially committed anthropology from a dialogical feminist perspective'. Paper presented in the *Panel Critically Engaged Collaborative Research: Remaking Anthropological Practice*, Annual Meeting of the American Anthropological Association (AAA), San José, California. November 24, 2007.

Hernández Castillo, R. A. (2008) *Etnografías e Historias de Resistencia. Mujeres Indígenas, Procesos Organizativos y Nuevas Identidades Políticas*. México: CIESAS/PUEG UNAM.

Hernández Castillo, R.A. (In press) 'Movilidades transfronterizas, Identidades transnacionales: Nuevos cruces de fronteras entre los indígenas mames Mexicanos', in M. Chavez (ed.), *Identidades y Movilidades en México y Colombia*.

Hernández Castillo, R.A., Sierra, T. and Paz, S. (eds) (2004) *El Estado y los Indígenas en Tiempos del PAN*. Mexico City: CIESAS-Porrúa.

Hobsbawm, E. (1996) 'La política de la identidad y la Izquierda', *Debate Feminista*, 7 (14): 86–101.

Hodgson, D. (2002) 'Precarious alliances: The cultural politics and structural predicaments of the indigenous rights movement in Tanzania', *American Anthropology*, 104 (4): 1086–97.

Hooker, J. (2005) 'Indigenous inclusion/black exclusion: Race, ethnicity and multicultural citizenship in Latin America', *Journal of Latin American Studies*, 37 (2): 285–310.

Jalloh, A. and Maizlish, S. (eds) (1996) *The African Diaspora*. College Station, TX: Texas A & M University Press.

Kearney, M. (1996) *Reconceptualizing the Peasantry*. Boulder, CO: Westview Press.

Klor de Alva, J. (1995) 'The postcolonialization of the (Latin) American experience: A reconsideration of "colonialism", "postcolonialism", and "mestizaje"',

in G. Prakash (ed.), *After Colonialism: Imperial Histories and Postcolonial Displacements*. Princeton, NJ: Princeton University Press. Pp. 65–79.

Koso-Thomas, O. (1987) *The Circumcision of Women. A Strategy for Eradication*. London: Zed Books.

Lemelle, S.J. and Kelley, R.D. G. (eds) (1994) *Imagining Home: Class, Culture and Nationalism in the African Diaspora*. London: Verso.

López Bárcenas, F. (2000a) 'La diversidad negada. Los derechos indígenas en la propuesta gubernamental de reforma constitucional', in G. García Colorado and I.E. Sandoval (eds), *Autonomía y Derechos de los Pueblos Indígenas*. México City: Cámara de Diputados–Instituto de Investigaciones Legislativas. Pp. 30–53

López Bárcenas, F. (2000b) 'La diversidad mutilada. Los derechos indígenas en la constitución de oaxaca', in G. García Colorado and I.E. Sandoval (eds) *Autonomía y Derechos de los Pueblos Indígenas*. México City: Cámara de Diputados–Instituto de Investigaciones Legislativas. Pp. 125–147.

López Bárcenas, F. (2004) 'La Lucha por la autonomía indígena en México. Un reto al pluralismo', In R.A. Hernández Castillo, M.T. Sierra Camacho and S. Paz, (eds), *El Estado y los indígenas en tiempos del PAN*. Mexico City: CIESAS-Porrúa. Pp. 207–230.

Lyotard, J.-F. (1993[1984]) *La Condición Postmoderna*. Trans. Mariano Antolín Rato. México: Red Editorial Iberoamericana.

Macleod, M. (2008) 'Luchas Político-Culturales y Auto-representación Maya'. PhD Dissertation in Latin American Studies, Facultad de Ciencias Políticas y Sociales, Universidad Nacional Autónoma de México.

Macleod, M. and Cabrera, M.L. (eds) (2000) *Identidad: Rostros sin Máscara (Reflexiones sobre Cosmovisión, Género y Etnicidad)*. Ciudad de Guatemala: Oxfam Australia.

Mallon, Florencia E. (1995) *Peasant and Nation. The Making of Postcolonial México and Peru*, Berkeley, Los Angeles: University of California Press.

Mama, A. (1995) 'Sheroes and villains: Conceptualizing colonial and contemporary violence against women in Africa', in M.J. Alexander and C.T. Mohanty (eds), *Feminist Genealogies, Colonial Legacies and Democratic Futures*. New York: Routledge Press. Pp. 46–63.

Mani, L. (1998) *Contentious Traditions: The debate on Sati in Colonial India*. Berkeley, CA: University of California Press.

Martínez Novo, C. (2006) *Who Defines Indigenous?: Identities, Development, Intellectuals and the State in Northern Mexico*. London: Rutgers University Press.

Martínez Novo, C. (2007) 'Multiculturalismo oficial y cohesión social en América Latina: Una Reflexión desde la etnografía sobre los casos de México y ecuador'. Paper presented to the 2007 Congress of the Latin American Studies Association, Montreal, 5–8 September.

Massolo, A. (1992) *Por amor y coraje. Mujeres en movimientos urbanos de la ciudad de México.* Mexico City: El Colegio de México.

Martínez Peláez, S. (1970) *La Patria del Criollo.* Ciudad de Guatemala: Universitaria.

Mattiace, S. (2007) '"We are like the wind". Ethnic mobilization among the maya of yucatán'. Paper presented at the XXVII Latin American Studies Association Meetings in Montreal, Canada, 5–6 September.

Maybury-Lewis, D. (ed.) (2002) *The Politics of Ethnicity. Indigenous Peoples in Latin American States.* Cambridge, MA: David Rockefeller, Harvard University Press.

Mejía, S. (2008) 'Los derechos de las mujeres nahuas de cuetzalan. la construcción de un feminismo indígena, desde la necesidad', in R.A. Hernández Castillo (ed.), *Etnografías e Historias de Resistencia. Mujeres Indígenas, Procesos Organizativos y Nuevas Identidades Políticas.* México: CIESAS/PUEG-UNAM. Pp. 453–503.

Moller Okin, S. (1999) *Is Multiculturalism Bad For Women?* Princeton, NJ: Princeton University Press.

Narayan, U. (2000) 'Essence of culture and a sense of history: A feminist critique to cultural essentialism', in U. Narayan and S. Harding (eds), *Decentering the Center. Philosophy for a Multicultural, Postcolonial and Feminist World.* Bloomington, IN: Indiana University Press. Pp. 60–84.

Niezen, R. (2000) *The Origins of Indigenism: Human Rights and the Politics of Identity.* Berkeley, CA: University of California Press.

N'gweno, B. (2007) 'Can ethnicity replace race? Afro-Colombians, indigeneity and the Colombian multicultural state', *Journal of Latin American and Caribbean Anthropology*, 12 (2): 414–40.

Oldenburg, V.T. (1994) 'The continuing invention of the sati tradition', in J. Stratton Hawley (ed.), *Sati, the Blessing and the Curse. The Burning of Wives in India.* New York: Oxford University Press. Pp. 50–89.

Parker, A., Russo, M., Sommer, D. and Yaeger, P. (eds) (1992) *Nationalisms and Sexualities.* London: Routledge.

Pratt, M.L. (2007) 'Afterword: Indigeneity today', in M. De la Cadena and O. Starn (eds), *Indigenous Experience Today.* Oxford: Berg Publishers. Pp. 397–405.

Portes, A. (1995) 'Transnational communities: Their emergence and significance in the contemporary world system'. Working Papers Series, No. 16. Program in Comparative and International Development, Department of Sociology, Johns Hopkins University.

Primera Cumbre de Mujeres Indígenas de América (2003) *Memoria.* CNI: México.

Rouse, R. (1991) 'Mexican migration and the social space of post-modernism', *Diaspora*, 1 (1): 8–23.

Rus, J., Hernández, R.A. and Shannan, M. (eds) (2003) *Mayan Lives, Mayan Utopias: The Indigenous Peoples of Chiapas and the Zapatista Rebellion.* Lanham, MD: Rowman and Littlefield.

Sánchez, M. (2005) *La Doble Mirada: Luchas y Experiencias de las Mujeres Indígenas de América Latina.* México City: UNIFEM/ILSB.

Shukla, S. (2001) 'Locations for South Asian diasporas', *Annual Review of Anthropology*, 30: 551–72.

Sieder, R. (ed.) (2002) *Multiculturalism in Latin America: Indigenous Rights, Diversity and Democracy.* London: Palgrave.

Sierra, M. T. (1997) 'Esencialismo y autonomía: Paradojas de la reivindicaciones indígenas', *Alteridades*, 7 (14): 131–43.

Sierra, M.T. (2004) 'Diálogos y prácticas interculturales. Derechos humanos, derechos de las mujeres y políticas de identidad', *Desacatos*, 15–16: 126–48.

Sierra, M.T. and Chenaut, V. (1995) *Pueblos Indígenas ante el Derecho.* México City: CIESAS.

Smith, M.M. and Guarnizo, L.E. (eds) (1998) *Transnationalism from Below.* London: Transaction Publishers.

Speed, S., Hernández Castillo, R.A. and Lynn, S. (eds) (2006) *Dissident Women: Gender and Cultural Politics in Chiapas.* Austin, TX: University of Texas Press.

Stavenhagen, R. (2000) *Conflictos Étnicos y Estado Nacional.* México: Editorial Siglo XXI.

Stavenhagen, R. (2001) *La Cuestión Étnica.* México: El Colegio de México.

Stavenhagen, R. and Iturralde, D. (1990) *Entre la ley y la Costumbre: El Derecho Consuetudinario Indígena en América Latina.* México: Instituto Indigenista Interamericano de Derechos Humanos.

Terven, A. (2005) 'Revitalización de la Costumbre Jurídica en el Juzgado Indígena de Cuetzalan. Retos desde el Estado'. Master thesis, CIESAS, México City.

Tilley, V.Q. (2002) 'New help or new hegemony? The transnational indigenous peoples' movement and "being Indian"', *Journal of Latin American Studies*, 34 (3): 525–54.

Trinh, M. (1988) *Woman, Native, Other: Writing Postcoloniality and Feminism*, Indiana: Indiana University Press.

Tripp, A.M. (2002) 'The politics of women's rights and cultural diversity in Uganda', in M. Molyneux and S. Razavi (eds), *Gender, Justice, Development and Rights.* Oxford: Oxford University Press. Pp. 413–441.

Tuhiwai Smith, L. (2007) 'The native and the neoliberal down under: Neoliberalism and endangered authenticities', in M. De la Cadena and O. Starn (eds), *Indigenous Experience Today.* Oxford: Berg. Pp. 333–355.

Tuñón, E. (1997) *Mujeres en escena: de la tramoya al protagonismo (1982-1994).* Mexico City: Programa Universitario de Estudios de Género PURG/UNAM.

Van Cott, D. (2000) *The Friendly Liquidation of the Past: The Politics of Diversity in Latin America.* Pittsburgh, PA: University of Pittsburgh Press.

Van Cott, D. (2005) *From Movements to Parties in Latin America: The Evolution of Ethnic Politics.* Cambridge: Cambridge University Press.

Velásquez Nimatuj, I.A. (2003) *La Pequeña Burguesía Indígena Comercial de Guatemala: Desigualdades de Clase, Raza y Género.* Ciudad de Guatemala: SERJUS y CEDPA.

Viqueira, J.P. (1999) 'Los peligros del chiapas imaginario', *Letras Libres,* 1 (1): 20–8.

Wade, P. (1997) *Race and Ethnicity in Latin America.* London: Pluto Press.

Wade, P. (2005) 'Rethinking mestizaje: Ideology and lived experience', *Journal of Latin American Studies,* 37 (2): 239–57.

Wade, P. (2006) 'Etnicidad, multiculturalismo y políticas sociales en latinoamérica: Poblaciones afrolatinas (e indígenas)', *Tabula Rasa,* 4: 59–81, enero-junio. Universidad Colegio Mayor de Cundinamarca, Bogotá, Colombia.

Warren, K.B. (1998) *Indigenous Movements and their Critics: Pan-Maya Activism in Guatemala.* Princeton, NJ: Princeton University Press.

Warren K. and Jackson J. (eds) (2002) *Indigenous Movements, Self-Representation and the State in Latin America.* Austin, TX: University Press.

Werner Brand, K. (1990) 'Aspectos cíclicos de los nuevos movimientos sociales', in R. Dalton and M. Kuechler (eds), *Los Nuevos Movimientos Sociales.* Valencia: Edicions Afons el Magnanim. Pp. 110–134.

Yashar D. (2005) *Contesting Citizenship in Latin America: The Rise of Indigenous Movements and the Postliberal Challenge.* New York: Cambridge University Press.

Young, I. M. (2000) *La Justicia y la Política de la Diferencia.* Valencia: Ediciones Cátedra.

Yuval Davis, N. (1997) *Gender and Nation.* London: Sage.

Zarate Hernández, E. (1994) *Los Señores de Utopía. La Etnicidad Política en una Comunidad Purépecha.* Guadalajara: El Colegio de Michoacan/CIESAS.

# 20

# Never Fixed: Modernity and Disability Identities

Rosemarie Garland-Thomson and Moya Bailey

Contemporary disability identity has emerged in the US and western world in concert with institutional, legislative, and material changes that have defined disability as a civil rights issue and have mandated integration of people with disabilities into previously segregated spaces. In contrast, our collective understanding of disability has been that it is a pathological condition to be addressed by medical treatment. These transformations in thinking and practice wrought by the larger civil rights movement, which includes the disability rights movement, reframed disability as a politicized social identity and people with disabilities as a minority group that has been subjected to discrimination and exclusion from full rights (Shapiro, 1993).

The concept of disability as a social identity – as opposed to simply an historical group or medical designation – has thus emerged as part of the identity politics movement in a post-civil rights era in the US, western, and the developing world. One might say that the concept of civil and human rights which has emerged as a sociopolitical agenda internationally over the last 40 years has invented disability identity in order to further social justice, access to the privileges and rights of democratic societies, and recognition of cultural diversity. Considering

disability as a distinctive social identity reveals several significant points. First, the identity category of people with disabilities is a cross-gender, race, ethnic, sexual, and class social group into which all people will enter if they live long enough. People with disabilities, defined broadly, are the largest minority group in the US, constituting an estimated 20–30 percent of the US population, which is increasing dramatically as baby boomers age (Disability, 2009) and at least 12 percent worldwide, which the World Bank and the United Nations consider an underreported measurement. Second, disability equity is part of a national and international rights agenda, which includes laws and policies such as the Americans with Disabilities Act of 1990 (ADA) and the United Nations Convention on the Rights of Persons with Disabilities and its Optional Protocol of 2006 and 2007 that define disability as a civil and human rights issue. These initiatives prohibit discrimination, mandate full integration, and assure reasonable accommodation as well as equity in education, employment, and housing. Understanding people with disabilities as members of a social identity category subject to discrimination and needing legal protection has yielded a group identity forged in social and legal terms. In conjunction with this elaboration of the sociopolitical group, disability has emerged as a diversity issue and a constituency to be served within public and private institutions.

Drawing on the particular, geographically focused literature of the Anglo-European and US contexts, this chapter reviews the development of disability identity within the modern understanding of the individualistic citizen subject endowed with natural and civil rights accruing from egalitarian political status in late capitalist democracies. Within this framework, disability identity is called into being through the conflicting discourses of modern medicalization and social equality. This chapter reviews the social and political history of that identity group development, lays out a post-civil rights conception of disability identity, details the specificity of disability identity within a comparative identity mode, and sketches the development of critical disability studies within academia.

## HISTORY

The US civil rights movement of the 1950s and 1960s prompted a myriad of marginalized groups to examine the systemic nature of their oppression. Among these groups were people with disabilities. As blacks articulated their oppression in the language of identity politics, others began to theorize oppression in a similar way. This was a critical moment. Working against assumptions that disability is deviant and abnormal, activists in the disability rights movement began to identify as people with disabilities, members of a social class oppressed by institutional and structural elements in society. This important conceptual reframing opened the door to reconceptualizing disability as a stigmatized social identity (Riddell and Watson, 2003). The Civil Rights Act of 1964 would serve as a model for important disability legislation such as the Americans with Disabilities Act of 1990.

Disability, like other identities, intersects with all aspects of self. As awareness of disability identity has developed, issues of race, sexuality, class, age, type of impairment, etc. have come to complicate identity politics.

Many of the early disability rights activists drew directly from the civil rights struggle in the forms of protests they launched. For example, Ed Roberts, one founder of the modern disability rights movement, began his activism by suing the University of California school system for denying him admission because of his disability (Johnson, 2005; Longmore and Umansky, 2001). His challenge to the school made way for four other people with quadriplegia to be admitted. They named themselves the Rolling Quads and continued to challenge the University of California schools' discrimination against people with disabilities. Activist organizations such as the Mental Patients' Liberation Front began to form as well, raising consciousness and pursuing direct action to change societal stigma against people with disabilities (Longmore and Umansky, 2001).

Some of the protests at the time addressed inaccessible federal buildings. To expose inaccessibility, activists hurled themselves from their wheelchairs and attempted to crawl up the steps to gain entry. People with disabilities organized to create independent living centers and lobbied for deinstitutionalization. Publications for different disabled communities emerged as well as increased state and federal programs that managed resources for those with disabilities. These actions directly challenged traditional cultural depictions of people with disabilities. Disability activists countered representations of themselves as in need of rescue by able-bodied benevolence. One of the longest lasting protests has challenged Jerry Lewis' annual Labor Day telethon, which raises money for the Muscular Dystrophy Association through characterizing disability as 'being half a person' (Longmore, 2003).

Signed in the summer of 1990, The Americans with Disabilities Act outlines nondiscriminatory practices much like the

Civil Rights Act of 1964 on which it is modeled. The ADA is charged with defining disability on a case by case basis and assuring that people who meet the criteria are afforded rights and services denied due to prejudice and discrimination (Longmore and Umansky, 2001). The act has been useful in helping ensure that people with disabilities receive the services they need but also functions as a gate-keeping mechanism that limits the number of people who can claim disability. A 2008 amendment to the law seeks to clarify and expand what counts as a disability while also acknowledging that discrimination may occur when people are perceived to have impairments.

Disability rights activist Harriet McBryde Johnson was a lawyer who frequently argued cases involving the ADA. A wheelchair user and person with a congenital neuromuscular disease, Johnson spent much of her adult life opposing the Muscular Dystrophy Association's annual telethon that raised money for the organization by depicting people with MD as suffering and in need of pity and charity from able-bodied people. Her book *Too Late to Die Young* is an important treatise on disability identity which chronicles her perspectives and politics as a woman with significant disabilities. Notably, Johnson (2005) debated with Peter Singer a proponent of euthanasia who suggests that parents should be able to euthanize their disabled children. Essays detailing her positions on disability were published in a series of issues of the *New York Times Magazine* (Johnson, 2003).

## DISABILITY IDENTITY FORMATION

This contemporary, post-civil rights conception of disability identity informs how people with the human variations we think of as disability can conceptualize themselves and how citizens who identify as nondisabled think of people stigmatized by conditions and differences traditionally understood as forms of inferiority or effects of misfortune. Interactions between bodies and the world make disability from the raw material of human variation and precariousness. This framing of disability identity as a social construction rather than inherent physical inadequacy draws from and complements contemporary critical theories of gender and race. Such a constructivist notion of disability identity contributes to comparative identity theories by developing a narrative of disability that complicates our understanding of identity formation (Gill, 2001). Disability as a social identity group designation brings forward several issues specific to disability that help us forge a more capacious and complex understanding of identity formations and how they operate both for individuals and groups and in relation to both achieved and described identities.

## Social and political issue

First, framing disability as a social and political issue rather than embodied essence offers an opportunity to theorize how a particularly large and varied set of human particularities come to be grouped together under the logic of an identity category. Disability includes ideological categories as varied as sick, deformed, ugly, old, maimed, afflicted, retarded, insane, mad, abnormal, or debilitated – all of which disadvantage people who fall into this identity category by devaluing ways of being that don't conform to culturally standard form and function. The discredited identity of disability privileges and establishes the borders of designations such as normal, healthy, beautiful, fit, competent, or intelligent, which provide social capital to those who can claim such status or subject positions. Because the characteristics gathered under the rubric disability are sensory, perceptual, psychological, emotional, cognitive, and/or physical, the designation provides a particular challenge in conceptualizing a cohesive group identity, shared experience upon which to build identity, and identity community formation across individuals.

Identity groups often develop and cohere through family and community proximity, common cultural traditions, cross-generational inculcation, or identification based on shared similar traits and social practices. Race and gender solidify in part through these circumstances and practices; for example, people often learn to be raced and are raced socially by being born into families who in large part identify themselves as belonging to a certain race or ethnic group; females often learn to be women within families. Women share for the most part similar aspects of female embodiment, and people are raced in part according to specific physiological similarities based on genotype. Disability identity is complicated and emerges in patterns often distinct from identities such as race, ethnicity, gender, and class. The variety of disabilities, along with age of onset, can make creating or finding a disabled community difficult. Societal assumptions about what is normal discourage people from claiming disability identity as well. Human variations labeled as abnormal are highly stigmatized. Mobilizing identity politics around stigmatized identity categories is challenging. People with disabilities can be isolated from one another and feel inferior. Thus, disability identity confronts common understandings of embodiment and interiority. Some people are born with impairments that inform their negotiation of the world around them while others acquire their impairments over time. It is arguably more difficult for people with disabilities to find a sense of community and pride which are essential components of identity formation.

The phenotypical or physiologically idiosyncratic traits that mark disability vary widely. Institutions or communities based on racial or gender identification are robust and recognized. In contrast, people whose human particularities invite disability identity are usually raised in families which identified as nondisabled and often do not have access to cultural institutions or social groups that provide a structure for disability identity. Institutions which solidify disability identity are primarily medical facilities or segregated schools. The contemporary tendency toward integrating people with disabilities into mainstream institutions and public spaces has reduced access to identity communities that segregated spaces such as special education settings or medical institutionalization provided in a pre-civil rights era. Nevertheless, disability identity is forged through political alliances now in a way that was conceptually and geographically limited before the disability rights and integration movement. In contrast to gender or race identity in the contemporary era in the developed west, disability experience upon which identity can be based occurs primarily through the common cultural experience of medicalization of one's bodily particularities, stigmatizing of devalued physical, psychic, and cognitive characteristics, and exclusion through architectural and attitudinal barriers. These potentially shared experiences upon which disability identification or consciousness can be built are specific to the concept and material circumstances of disability and generally differ from patterns of racial and gender identity formation. Thus, considering disability as a vector of analysis in comparative identity studies illuminates in new ways larger process of identity formation.

Having to negotiate medical care can reinforce perceptions of inferiority or marginal status because medical professionals have been trained to fix and cure disease according to a medical model of disability. Fix and cure can be conflated with aesthetic therapies such as braces or prosthesis that can comfort the able-bodied more than the person with a disability. Audre Lorde, for example, discusses the insistence by hospital staff that she wear a prosthetic breast after a mastectomy. Lorde's caregivers (1980) argued that wearing a prosthesis was necessary and an issue of morale for female patiens. The medical model has been useful in helping to develop rehabilitation and assistive technology, but it also underwrites disability stigma.

Normalization and the elimination of all signs of disability are preferred, rather than creating space for multiple ways of being in society.

## Fluid category

Second, the identity category *disabled* operates as a particularly fluid identity in comparison with racial, ethnic, and gender identities. Whereas these latter identity categories are certainly not stable nor essential, most people are assigned and accede to – with various degrees of comfort or fit, to be sure – a relatively constant racial, ethnic, or gender identity over a lifetime, at least relatively definitively at a given time.

Anyone can willingly or unwillingly enter into disability identity at any time, and status along with its material markers can be transitory. The move between nondisabled and disabled status can occur dramatically and instantaneously, as we saw for example in the very public identity narrative of Christopher Reeve, who was Superman one moment and quadriplegic the next. Moving in and out of disability status to so-called temporary disabilities is also quite common, as we saw when President Bill Clinton was a temporary wheelchair user in the White House, which developed in him a politicized awareness about disability access. In one sense, disability identity is, then, the social manifestation of two fundamental facts of our shared humanity: that our bodies are always in transition in response to a perpetual interaction with our environment and that humans are enormously varied in every facet of their being over a lifetime. What we think of as disability admits to a wider range of human variation, then, both diachronically and synchronically than what we think of as gender or race, which is not to overstate differences among people with disabilities in comparison to men and women or black or white people as such, but rather to note that the idea of disability itself is an enormous tent, admission to which one must pay with a chunk of social capital called normal or nondisabled. Forfeiting that advantageous and often unremarked piece of social privilege is one of the major adjustments in transitioning to disabled identity (Linton, 2005; Murphy, 1987).

Disability identity like most identity formation necessitates the presence of three components: role models, history, and community. Having access to other people who have disabilities and also identify their disability as playing a significant role in their conceptions of self can be difficult to find. Some disabilities are hereditary and people may have family members that can serve in this role but this is not often the case. People with disabilities are often in predominantly able-bodied families which can lead to feelings of isolation and pressure to downplay their disabilities. Access to disability history is even more difficult to acquire. Only recently are women's history and racial history being taught in schools. Disability history is even less accessible. This makes it difficult to see oneself as a member of a group that has a historical presence in society.

Like people who identify as lesbian, gay, bisexual, transgender, and queer, people with disabilities do not generally grow up with role models or people within the family who share their identity. Creating community presents unique challenges as there are so many ways that people come to identify as disabled. Finding role models and community can be difficult with such a dispersed population.

Institutions have been instrumental in helping forge disability identity. Initially designed to uphold segregation between people with physical and cognitive disabilities and the able-bodied, institutions became places where people with disabilities could interact with each other and begin to form a group identity. Similar to historically black colleges and universities, institutions were constant reminders of the prejudices of society while simultaneously creating space that fostered a sense of community. Most notably people who are hard of hearing and who identify as deaf have used this segregation to their benefit (Davis, 1997).

Deaf people have forged an identity that sometimes comes into conflict with people who identify as disabled. Those who identify as 'deaf' reject the phonocentric representation of themselves as hearing impaired (Riddell and Watson, 2003). They argue that sign language and deaf identity mark another culture that is not based in disability. Some within the disability community struggle with this conception as it seems deaf people are attempting to distance themselves from the stigma of disability by saying they are not disabled (Davis, 1997). While in the minds of many disability activists, disability is large enough to include deafness, many deaf people read it's preoccupation with societal structures as a disregard for a minority culture. The minority language of sign speaks to its own culture and world, which is not necessarily evident in many people's understanding of what disability culture could be.

Similarly wheelchair users speak of a hierarchy among chairs where those who use manual chairs are subtly encouraged to keep their distance from those who use power chairs because of the perceived level of functioning interpreted by the able-bodied (Intersection, 2008). Creating community across a spectrum of identities that differ in terms of their origin, duration, difficulty, mobility, sensory perception, etc., is quite challenging. Physical disabilities are often privileged over cognitive or emotional disabilities. There is also the perception that people with physical disabilities try to distance themselves from people with cognitive disabilities or people with mental illnesses.

People with cognitive disabilities have also benefited from institutional segregation. The switch from 'patient' to 'consumer' or 'customer' was forged by those diagnosed with mental illness who began to see that their treatment should privilege their position as a purveyor of goods. The term 'survivor' has been adopted as well and is generally used by people who oppose psychiatry (Riddell and Watson, 2003). Mentalism like ableism speaks to the discrimination of a marginalized group based on perceived

cognitive function. The Ex-patients Movement like the disabilities rights movement was borne out of the same moment and attempted to counteract the negative representations of people who were perceived to have mental illnesses. This included changing language and advocating for representation within the mental health administrative structure. Zines and support groups for survivors and consumers began to crop up and the communities created began to agitate, arguing that things like forced hospitalization were violations of peoples human rights and that 'madness' was socially constructed (Riddell and Watson, 2003). The anti-psychiatry movement is connected with the term survivor while the consumer movement is generally connected to a pro-psychiatry stance. These two movements are often lumped together because people have little familiarity with their claims. The transient nature of mental illness can present its own problems in organizing a sustained movement. Most comparable movements operate under the assumption of a stable identity category, i.e., physical disability, black identity, womanhood, etc. Mental illness is an unstable and contested state. Unlike the reclamation projects of re-appropriating terms like 'black', 'dyke', 'queer', or 'disabled', 'mentally ill' or 'insane' are not as easily divested of their problematic connotations (Riddell and Watson, 2003). As such, debates persist about the validity of their re-adoption.

People with cognitive disabilities are also tangentially located within the broad disability movement that often centers on physical impairments. Additionally people with physical disabilities may even try to distance themselves from this presumably even more stigma-producing categorization. Film and television often reinforce this problematic construction through the implementation of stereotypical roles and narratives that make the person with a cognitive disability the butt of a joke. The 2008 controversy over the Ben Stiller comedy *Tropic Thunder* illustrates this point well. In the film stiller plays a 'retard' who believes that his real life capture by the local people is part of the filming. The films' tag line 'once there was a retard' was pulled as a result of protests by various disability rights organizations within the US and abroad. The blatant use of this offensive term speaks to the invisibility of ableism within popular culture. Disability activists have even taken to using the construction 'the R-word' like black activists use of 'the N-word', further demonstrating that African-American activism around racial oppression continues to be a source of inspiration for the disability movement.

The Internet plays a large role in creating and sustaining disability community. From listservs to blogs and social networking sites, people with disabilities are able to stay connected in ways they never could before. This is especially useful for people with disabilities who have limited mobility or trouble with social interactions. Many people with autism spectrum disorders prefer the interactions created by online community rather than face to face interaction. The Internet allows for the creation of global community as well as global activism.

## Ascribed identity

Third, disability identity allows us to consider the central issue of legibility in ascribing identity categories. Identities, as Linda Alcoff (2006) has argued, play out in the arena of the visible. *Disabled* is an identity conferred from outside through social relations expressed attitudinally, institutionally, and materially. The ability/disability system creates identities referenced to embodied variations understood in the modern world as medical conditions or deficiencies of some sort; in this sense they are always visible or potentially visible, witnessed in body or behavior and depending for their enactment and meaning on some visible trace, either manifest or incipient. The specificity and acquisition of the widely varying characteristics we consider to be disabilities give shape to the development of disability identity.

To begin with, the traits that count as disability shift over history and across cultures so that certain populations or communities of people with disabilities wax and wane depending upon historical circumstances. For example, war creates disability in two ways. It makes disabled populations, often specific to the technologies of particular wars, through wounding; at the same time, it sustains populations of disabled people by producing new medical treatments applied to soldiers and civilians alike (Gerber, 2000). The population of people with paraplegia or quadriplegia, for example, increased after World War II in the US due to both the life-saving treatments developed for wounded soldiers and an increase of people with paralyzing conditions caused by war. The wars in Iraq produced the kinds of injuries requiring high-tech prosthetics that were part of the developing high-tech industry in the western world. Such prosthetics also accommodate athletes and have become fashion accessories displayed rather than hidden, which provide a compensatory status that traditional low-tech prosthetics such as crutches and canes do not. In another example, medicalization expands disability categories, such as pathologizing cognitive differences into learning disabilities, at the same time that it eliminates certain conditions, such as those associated with Down's syndrome, that count as disabilities.

Moreover, whether disabling conditions are acquired or inborn, incurred gradually or suddenly, perceptibly marked or associated with pain and illness – all affect the way disability identity is both assigned or achieved. As with racial or gender passing and denial – perhaps even more strongly – there is often a disparity between a person's being perceived as having a disability and self-identification with such a highly stigmatized category. In fact, the Americans with Disabilities Act of 1990 protects people against discrimination not only on the basis of having a condition that counts as a disability but also against discrimination based on the perception of disability identity. This aspect of the legal elaboration of disability firmly moves the significance of disability out of the body and into the social arena. Indeed, there are social costs and strong disincentives to identifying as disabled, even when a disabling trait is visibly present, that are reflected in the common denial of disability identity in which a person concedes impairment but denies the category 'disabled' as a descriptor or identity. Antidiscrimination legislation however has affected practices of disability identification by making it necessary for persons to be legally identified as disabled in order to seek reparations, accommodations, or claim discrimination. The legal definition of disabled, which in the US has been played out in a series of legal cases – several of which were decided by the Supreme Court – thus affects the social identification of disabled by forcing a closer alignment between the two in order for people to consider utilizing the legal protections against disability discrimination.

## Rationalization of the body

Fourth, disability identity allows us to address quite directly the issue of the rationalization of the body and modernity, both on an individual and collective level. Historians and cultural critics have observed that one of modernity's most prevalent forces is rationalization, which is the bureaucratic reduction of particularity and complexity in the social processing of people and things, as described by Max Weber in the beginning of his 1904 work *The Protestant Ethic and the Spirit of Capitalism* (Weber et al., 1930). Processes of rationalization along with the development of consumerism, technology, and medicalization of the body have contributed to a pervasive standardization of bodies during the twentieth century and beyond that forms the cultural context for disability and disability identity (Garland-Thomson, 2006). Disability increasingly emerges in opposition to a scientific-medical and statistical norm which pressures subjects to conform to a standard

bodily form and function both materially and ideologically that is a major part of one's social capital (Baynton, 1996; Davis, 1997). Failing to achieve this standard body merits punishment in the form of discrimination and exclusion (Elliott, 2003; Parens, 1998; Rothman and Rothman, 2003). According to the philosopher Ian Hacking: 'The normal stands indifferently for what is typical, the unenthusiastic objective average, but it also stands for what has been, good health, and what shall be, our chosen destiny. That is why the [...] word "normal" has become one of the most powerful ideological tools of the twentieth century' (Hacking, 1990, 169).

This neo-eugenic initiative against the human variations we name as disability occurs in several arenas (Hubbard, 1990; Kevles, 1985; Sandel, 2007). This eugenic reduction of human variation takes place through medical treatment of traits considered disability: first, as procedures performed on individuals to eliminate or normalize an increasingly wide range of characteristics defined as disabilities; second, as the selection and elimination through reproductive and genetic technologies of characteristics carried in early reproductive forms such as sperm, egg, embryo and fetus; third, as the elimination of people with disabilities through euthanasia, so-called physician-assisted suicide, or so-called mercy death of people with disabilities (Johnson et al., 2000; Somerville, 2001). While modern medical treatment of disability has in general improved quality of life and provided increased health for people, its ideology of normalization has at the same time enacted stigmatization and devaluation of people with disabilities (Scully, 2008; Shakespeare, 2006).

Here, then, is the paradox of disability identity in contemporary developed societies, in particular the US: a civil/human/rights and diversity based understanding of disability accommodates human variation and redresses inequalities, while at the same time a cultural mandate toward standardization through medical technology and consumerism attenuates and devalues that same human variation. Perhaps the most productive and radical critical conversations about the status of disability identity address just this paradox.

## MEDICAL GENOCIDE: A CASE STUDY

The persistent, modern cultural impulse to rationalize humanity through eliminating disability is a developing area of concern in what might be called disability cultural studies. Euthanizing disabled populations is the most discriminatory form of institutionalized stigmatization directed against disability and by extension people with disabilities. Garland-Thomson (2004) has argued that allegiance to the logic that justifies eugenic euthanasia is pervasive across western culture and that it has increased under the pressures of modernity in the contemporary era. The extreme yet instructive historical case study of Nazi medical genocide allows us to see in bold relief the rationale for eliminating disability in a way that is often muted in contemporary practices and assumptions shrouded in the language of improvement, enhancement, and choice. The program of medical genocide enacted by Germany between 1939 and 1946 illuminates how the progressive social and medical initiative in the contemporary developed world to supposedly improve health by eliminating disability cannot be extricated from eliminating people with disabilities. Nazi medicine's killing of targeted populations is an extreme and historically specific example of disability discrimination which allows us to trace the logic for reducing human variation as a virulent form of rationalization carried out by the modern nation-state.

The so-called science of eugenics emerged in the modernizing late nineteenth century world as a progressive idea that generated and legitimated officially sanctioned policies and practices aimed at ostensibly improving the human race. In fact, eugenics quickly moved from identifying supposedly inheritable forms of inferiority into identifying classes of people who were socially devalued and developing ways to eliminate them. The identity systems we think of as race, gender, class, sexuality, and disability all yielded narratives of biological inferiority taken up by the broad, popular eugenics initiatives that were intended to increase the population of valued people and reduce the population of devalued people. The US and most other modernizing countries used forced sterilization to accomplish eugenic cleansing (Nourse, 2008; Pernick, 1996). Because the totalitarian government of Nazi Germany could carry out eugenic elimination of devalued populations more fully than stable democratic societies, Hitler issued an order for September of 1939 that moved Germany from a surveillance and sterilization eugenic program to a eugenic euthanasia program.

In brief, the Nazi eugenic euthanasia program against people with disabilities, called Aktion T4 was carried out between 1939 and 1945. T4 was developed and implemented in six killing centers at inpatient medical care facilities within greater Germany. Genocide against medically identified groups expanded to ethnic genocide against Jews and most Sinti/Roma. In 1942, technology, practices, and staff from T4 were transferred to the death camps in the east (Aly et al., 1994; Friedlander and NetLibrary Inc. 1995; Kühl, 1994; Lifton, 1986; Müller-Hill, 1988; Proctor, 1988). It is important to note that while many groups, such as homosexuals, were targets of discrimination and incarceration, which was often synonymous with death, only disabled, Sinti/Roma, and Jewish populations were identified explicitly for extermination.

The point of bringing forward medical genocide as a case study here is that it illustrates how identification operates as a process of selection for discrimination. In other words the Nazi eugenics euthanasia program formed disability identity in a particular way at a particular moment to accomplish a particular national political goal. What is distinct about medical genocide as an identity formation political strategy is that it uses the authority and ideology of medical science to do the work of rationalizing human variation and instrumentalizing human value. The T4 program is a useful example because it took social stigmatizing and discrimination to its furthest logical conclusion: elimination. Medical genocide differs from traditional genocide, which murderers through military violence, in that it murders through medical violence. This modern means of genocide uses the logic, authority, practices, technology, and personnel of medical science to exterminate devalued populations. Medical genocide represents people with disabilities as 'life unworthy of life' in order to justify eugenic euthanasia (Hoche, 1920). According to this logic, disabled bodies become self-evident testimonies to their own essential and irredeemable inferiority through a four-part logic that employs rationalization, instrumentalism, medical authority, and scientific fact.

The bureaucracy and material institutions of the medical system offered an already existing opportunity for a Nazi government eager to redistribute economic and material resources. In other words, the Nazis had access to large disabled populations in hospitals and care facilities around Germany. In contrast, in order to exterminate Jews, Nazis had to extract them from communities and private living arrangements in order to round them up and concentrate them in camps before an extermination plan could be launched.

In medical genocide, identification functions as a form of selection, a way of marking human variation that is targeted for elimination. For example, the first step in medical genocide was to use the medical system to register people who were identified as disabled in certain categories, for example, people diagnosed as epileptic, deformed, stutterers, schizophrenic, as well as other selected diagnostic categories. This marking of diagnostic categories was summed up in a eugenics propaganda poster showing a depressed-looking, slumping, supposedly disabled man

explained by text saying, 'If this man had been sterilized, there would not have been born: one asocial female, four deaf and dumb, three stammerers, two epileptics, one mentally deficient female, one deformed abnormal female'. These diagnostic categories are, of course, not so much actual medical terms as they are ideological terms that appeal to scientific medical authority to do the work of stigmatizing and devaluing people with disabilities.

The material process of medical genocide was an enactment through established discourses, bureaucracies, and institutional facilities of both the rationalization of human variation and the instrumentalization of human value. The vocabulary of selection as identification of people targeted for medical genocide reveals the ideology of rationalization that drives eugenic euthanasia. The concept of health denotes valued populations. Terms such as *Rassenhygiene* (racial health) and *Erbhygiene* (genetic health) named systems of sorting people into categories such as *Gesundes Volk* (healthy people) and *Lebenunwert* (unworthy of life). Some were deemed *Hochwertig* (superior); others were deemed *Minderwertig* (inferior). Nazi eugenics has a particularly robust vocabulary that names its targeted devalued categories: *Entartet* (degenerate); *Unheilbar* (incurable); *Schwacher* (unfit); *Schwachsinnige* (feeble-minded); *Schizophrenie* (schizophrenia); *Arbeit Scheu* (work shy); *Mischlinge* (mixed race); *Nutzlos Essere* (useless eaters). Many of these terms discredit morally and diagnostically at the same time.

Moreover, the plentiful visual propaganda such as posters and films presented to the public and Nazi officials stressed an instrumental view of human value by constantly invoking the ostensible consumption to production ratio between disabled and non-disabled populations. For example, visual representations of people with disabilities show them not working, being fed, and living comfortably at the same time that it presented them as both suffering and causing suffering on the part of others through their supposed low quality of life and productiveness. Quantification and calculating were also a large part of the propaganda rationale that supported T4. Frequent statistical charts and comparisons appeared with statements such as, 'A Hereditarily Ill Person Costs 50,000 Reichsmarks on Average Up to the Age of 60', an illustration which appeared in high school biology textbook. Another 1938 Nazi propaganda poster offered a graph which showed the purported 'Qualitative Decline in the Population through Lower Reproduction Rates among Individuals of Higher Value: In the beginning, after 30 years, after 60 years, after 90 years, after 120 years [...].'

This explication of medical genocide as a historical, material phenomenon as well as a representation of disability illustrates the interdisciplinary critical intervention disability studies makes in the academic project of generating knowledge. Revealing the underlying logic of eugenic euthanasia centers this historical recuperation on issues of social justice, medical ethics, and the politics of representation. In this sense, the disability critique brought forward through the case of medical genocide described here gives a sense of the direction current work in disability studies is taking.

## DISABILITY STUDIES

Disability identity has been theorized over the last ten years or so in the academic fields of disability studies, bioethics, cultural studies, as well as in traditional disciplines such as sociology, anthropology, history, and literary studies. The formation of black and women's studies departments in academic institutions opened the door for disability studies starting in the 1980s. People with disabilities in the academy began to use the new framework of disability identity in groundbreaking scholarship.

Disability studies expands medicalized understandings of disability by critically considering disability as a representational system more than a medical problem, a social construction rather than a personal misfortune or a bodily flaw, an historical and culturally imagined community rather than a deviant social category, and a subject appropriate for wide-ranging intellectual inquiry that augments the medical, rehabilitation, or social work approach to disability. Extending a constructivist and materialist analysis that informs gender and race studies, disability studies embeds disability in the sociopolitical world by focusing on issues such as equal access for all, integration of institutions, and the historical exclusion of people with disabilities from the public sphere. The Ohio State University Disability Studies Program website offers this definition:

> Disability Studies seeks to study the nature, meaning, and consequences of disability in global culture from multiple perspectives in order to provide an enriched and coherent view of disability as part of universal human experience. By understanding and analyzing disability as a phenomenon that simultaneously manifests itself at the bodily, personal, and societal levels Disability Studies provides a context for understanding the meaning and experience of difference in society. (University, 2009)

One of the central tenants of disability studies is that society's prejudices towards people with disabilities are more disabling than impairment. Society discriminates against people with disabilities through architectural design, policy, and basic assumptions about what a normal body looks like and how it functions. The work of disabled writers such as Eli Clare, Nancy Mairs, and the late Lucy Grealy, offers insight into disability identity through the use of autobiography and memoir, a genre that highlights the complexity and often contradictory nature of disability experience.

Nancy Mairs's self-identification as a writer is an integral part of her ability to contribute to the world, something that counters the assumption that MS renders her a useless burden. Her book *Waist High in the World* (1996) asserts her right to exist free of 'normals' pity and her literal marginalization to the sidelines of life. Even though she is not able to do all the tasks that are traditionally associated with motherhood, she can write books. Her writing becomes her way of taking care, her 'means of taking the reader into [her] arms, holding a cup to her lips, stroking her forehead, whispering jokes in her ears [...]' (Mairs, 1996, 86). Mairs describes the nondisabled's tendency to admire her courage or perseverance simply because she uses a wheel chair.

Mairs, in contrast, sees her MS as something that has benefited her and the lives of others. She often feels a sense of adventure as though she 'is exploring uncharted territory' (Mairs, 1996, 145). Although she resists the prodigal disability narrative herself, she does advocate for greater diversity in the stories told because of its benefits for the whole of humanity. 'The more perspectives that can be brought to bear on the human experience, even from the slant of a wheelchair or hospital bed, or through the ears of a blind person, or the fingers of someone who is deaf, the richer that experience becomes' (Mairs, 1996, 106).

Eli Clare (1999) offers a revealing and complex narrative forged from the intersections of a rural, queer, disabled, working-class identity. Clare uses poetic prose to depict temporal, mutable truths that disrupt hegemonic dichotomies and craft more fluid conceptions of identity. Ambiguity and multiple right answers reign in *Exile and Pride* as the author charts her own evolution beyond binaries.

Clare discusses Michael Oliver's theoretical distinction between disability and impairment as inextricably connected within the context of her own lived experience. When explaining how the school rule that will not allow her more time to finish a test disables her, she experiences 'the problem on a very physical level', unable to control her pen as she tries to write faster; her muscles spasm as she tries to stop the tremors. In Clare's world, 'Oliver's model of disability makes theoretical and political sense but misses important emotional realities' (Clare, 1999, 7).

The politics of naming are central to how marginalized people manage the stigma. Naming is an elusive concept for Clare as she actively reclaims 'queer' and 'crip' but rejects 'freak' with its equally troubled history. For Clare (1999: 70), 'it doesn't feel good or liberating', causing her to interrogate the reasons some words are reappropriated and others are not.

The course of Clare's life illustrates the temporal and fluid nature of identity categories. While parts of his identity were formed in the dyke community, his relationship to that space has shifted now that he identifies as a transgendered man. Additionally, Clare is no longer living in the rural environment that informed so much of his relationship to place and political ideology. And though not completely at ease with the queer urban politic, he is not neatly ensconced in any one location (Clare, 1999).

Lucy Grealy's (1994) *Autobiography of a Face* locates her feelings about her appearance impairment in the reactions of others. She gradually internalizes others' reactions to her face and puts living on hold until she can have a surgery that will fix her perceived problem. It becomes clear that Grealy's disability has more to do with social stigma than any impairment, and she seeks refuge in the elusive cure that medicine can supposedly provide.

Despite disability identity's indebtedness to the civil rights struggle, issues of the intersections between race and disability are just coming to the fore. Christopher Bell, former president of the Society of Disability Studies, considers the intersections of black and disability identity and the lack of racial analysis in disability studies. Class as well remains an area that is severely under-investigated in disability studies scholarship and the academy at large. Scholar Angel Miles is exploring the intersections of race and class for disabled women of color. These are just a few of the people who are trying to expand conceptions of issues in disability.

Feminist disability studies has emerged productively as a comparative identity studies initiative which brings critical gender, sexuality, and race theories into conversation with an interrogation of disability identity and materiality. The robust theorization of intersectionality, the materiality of embodiment, and standpoint epistemology within feminist theory provides an expansive way to understand the social construction and material conditions of disability. According to a 2002 article by Garland-Thomson:

[T]he goal of feminist disability theory [...] is to augment the terms and confront the limits of the ways we understand human diversity, the materiality of the body, multiculturalism, and the social formations that interpret bodily differences. A feminist disability approach fosters more complex understandings of the cultural history of the body. By considering the ability/disability system, feminist disability theory goes beyond explicit disability topics such as illness, health, beauty, genetics, eugenics, aging, reproductive technologies, prosthetics, and access issues. Feminist disability theory addresses such broad feminist concerns as the unity of the category "woman," the status of the lived body, the politics of appearance, the medicalization of the body, the privilege of normalcy, multiculturalism, sexuality, the social construction of identity, and the commitment to integration. (2002, 4)

Susan Wendell (1996) also makes similar observations and asks folks to closely interrogate the invisible privileges akin to white and male privilege that are afforded to able-bodied people.

Queer theory and disability theory are forming a mutually beneficial alliance as well. Robert McRuer's (2006) seminal book, *Crip Theory*, lays out intersections between queer and disabled identity. Eli Clare's autobiography provides stunning testimonial. The similarities between queer and disability identity also make this an important collaborative project. Both queer and disability identity are marked with 'coming out' narratives, moments where minority subjects understand themselves as existing at odds with societal norms. Additionally this realization often happens in the context of isolation. Unlike people of color or women who may see themselves reflected in their immediate family, this is often not the case for queer

people and people with disabilities. Because of narrow constructions of masculinity and femininity that presume able-bodiedness, disability itself queers people. Disability is said to feminize men by making visible the interdependency of men with other people (McRuer, 2006). The autonomy myth is shattered. Women, held to rigorous standards of beauty are also queered through their supposed inability to meet these criteria. Women with disabilities have challenged this perception. Ellen Stohl's 1987 playboy pictorial was a way to show that women with disabilities are sexy too.

Transnational directions in disabilities include a 2008 call for an international registry of women working on disability theory by the Disability Studies in the Humanities organization. Disability scholar and activist Mia Mingus looks at the intersections of race, disability, transnationality, sexuality, and gender in her work. Intersectionality is a driving theoretical frame in disability scholarship.

Disability identity is also grappling with the transabled community. People who identify as transabled have no physical disability but feel as though they should be blind, use a wheel chair, etc. Most transabled people identify with physical disabilities as opposed to cognitive disabilities or mental illness. People who identify as transabled draw on the activism of transgender and transsexual individuals adopting similar narratives and strategies for advocating for recognition among the disability and medical communities (Transabled.org 2008).

How intersections of identity affect the lives of people with disabilities remains a site for more theoretical development. However, disability studies, like other identity derived scholarship, must carefully theorize identity formation and its attention to corporeality. Focusing on lived corporeal experience that centers the body's interaction with the world challenges the mind–body dualism common in western theorizing. This can challenge scholars in the field who must negotiate institutional demands and the needs of their research.

Embodiment theory seems to be opening up a new arena for these conversations.

# REFERENCES

Alcoff, L. (2006) *Identity Politics Reconsidered*. New York: Palgrave Macmillan.

Aly, G., P. Chroust, and C. Pross (1994) *Cleansing the Fatherland: Nazi Medicine and Racial Hygiene*. Baltimore: Johns Hopkins University Press.

Baynton, D.C. (1996) *Forbidden Signs: American Culture and the Campaign against Sign Language*. Chicago, IL: University of Chicago Press.

Clare, E. (1999) *Exile and Pride: Disability, Queerness, and Liberation*. Cambridge, MA: South End Press.

Davis, L.J. (1997) *The Disability Studies Reader*. New York: Routledge.

Disability, National Organization of (2009) 'Facts.'

Elliott, C. (2003) *Better than Well: American Medicine meets the American Dream*. New York: W.W. Norton.

Friedlander, H. and NetLibrary Inc. (1995) *The Origins of Nazi Genocide from Euthanasia to the Final Solution*. Chapel Hill, NC: University of North Carolina Press.

Garland-Thomson, R. (2004) 'The cultural logic of euthanasia: "Sad fancyings" in Herman Melville's "Bartleby",' *American Literature*, 76 (4): 777–806.

Garland-Thomson, R. (2006) 'Welcoming the unbidden: The case for conserving human biodiversity', in C.A. Schrager and Tichi (eds), *What Democracy Looks Like: A New Critical Realism for a Post-Seattle World*, 77–87. New Brunswick, NJ: Rutgers University Press.

Gerber, D. A. (2000). *Disabled Veterans in History*. Ann Arbor: University of Michigan Press

Gill, C.J. (2001) 'What is the "social model of disability" and why should you care?', *Alert: Newsletter of the Institute on Disability and Human Development*, 12 (2): 6–9.

Grealy, L. (1994) *Autobiography of a Face*. Boston, MA: Houghton Mifflin.

Hacking, I. (1990) *The Taming of Chance*. Cambridge: Cambridge University Press.

Hoche, A. a. K.B. (1920) *The Authorization for the Destruction of Life Unworthy of Life*. [Die Freigabe der Vernichtung lebensunwerten Lebens.] Leipzig: Verlag Von Felix Meiner.

Hubbard, R. (1990) 'Who should and should not inhabit the world', in R. Hubbard (ed.), *The Politics of Women's Biology.*, 179–208. New Brunswick, NJ: Rutgers University Press.

Johnson, H.M. (2003) 'The disability gulag', *New York Times Magazine*, November 23: 18.

Johnson, H.M. (2005) *Too Late to Die Young*. New York: Henry Holt and Co.

Kevles, D.J. (1985) *In the Name of Eugenics: Genetics and the Uses of Human Heredity*. New York: Knopf.

Kühl, S. (1994) *The Nazi Connection: Eugenics, American Racism, and German National Socialism*. New York: Oxford University Press.

Lifton, R.J. (1986) *The Nazi Doctors: Medical Killing and the Psychology of Genocide*. New York: Basic Books.

Linton, S. (2005) *My Body Politic: A Memoir*. Ann Arbor: University of Michigan Press.

Longmore, P.K. (2003) *Why I Burned My Book and Other Essays on Disability*. Philadelphia, PA: Temple University Press.

Longmore, P.K. and Umansky, L. (2001) *The New Disability History: American Perspectives*. New York: New York University Press.

Lorde, A., Rich, A.C. (1980) *The Cancer Journals*. Argyle, NY: Spinsters Ink.

Mairs, N. (1996) *Waist-High in the World: A Life Among the Nondisabled*. Boston, MA: Beacon Press.

McRuer, R. (2006) *Crip Theory: Cultural Signs of Queerness and Disability*. New York: New York University Press.

Müller-Hill, B. (1988) *Murderous Science: Elimination by Scientific Selection of Jews, Gypsies, and Others, Germany 1933–1945*. Oxford: Oxford University Press.

Murphy, Robert. *The Body Silent*. New York: W. W. Norton, 1987.

Nourse, V.F. (2008) *In Reckless Hands: Skinner v. Oklahoma and the Near Triumph of American Eugenics*. New York: W.W. Norton.

Parens, E. (1998) *Enhancing Human Traits: Ethical and Social Implications*. Washington, DC: Georgetown University Press.

Parens, E. and Asch, A. (2000) *Prenatal Testing and Disability Rights*. Washington, DC: Georgetown University Press.

Pernick, M.S. (1996) *The Black Stork: Eugenics and the Death of 'Defective' Babies in American Medicine and Motion Pictures Since 1915*. New York: Oxford University Press.

Proctor, R. (1988) *Racial Hygiene: Medicine Under the Nazis*. Cambridge, MA: Harvard University Press.

Riddell, S. and Watson, N. (2003) *Disability, Culture and Identity*. Harlow: Pearson/Prentice Hall.

Rothman, S.M. and Rothman, D.J. (2003) *The Pursuit of Perfection: The Promise and Perils of Medical Enhancement.* New York: Pantheon Books.

Sandel, M.J. (2007) *The Case Against Perfection: Ethics in the Age of Genetic Engineering.* Cambridge, MA: Belknap Press of Harvard University Press.

Scully, J.L. (2008) *Disability Bioethics: Moral Bodies, Moral Difference.* Lanham, MD: Rowman and Littlefield.

Shakespeare, T. (2006) *Disability Rights and Wrongs.* London: Routledge.

Shapiro, B.K. (1993) *No Pity: People With Disabilities Forging a New Civil Rights Movement.* New York: Random House.

Somerville, M.A. (2001) *Death Talk: The Case Against Euthanasia and Physician-Assisted Suicide.* Montreal: McGill-Queen's University Press.

Transabled.org. (2008) *Intersection: Disability, Transgender, & Intersex Experiences*: 90 min.

University, Disability Studies Program at Ohio State (2009) http://disabilitystudies.osu.edu/ (Accessed 1 November 2009).

Weber, M., Parsons, T. (1930) *The Protestant Ethic and the Spirit of Capitalism.* London: Allen & Unwin.

Wendell, S. (1996) *The Rejected Body: Feminist Philosophical Reflections on Disability.* New York: Routledge.

PART 4

# Sites and Contexts

# 21

# From This Bridge Called My Back[1] to This Bridge We Call Home: Collective Identities And Social Movements

Manisha Desai

Twenty-one years ago we struggled with the recognition of difference within the context of commonality. Today we grapple with the recognition of commonality within the context of difference. While This Bridge Called My Back displaced whiteness, this bridge we call home carries this displacement further [...] This book intends to change notions of identity, viewing it as part of a more complex system covering a larger terrain, and demonstrating that the politics of exclusion based on traditional categories diminishes our humanness. (Anzaldua, 2002: 2)

The shift articulated by Gloria Anazaldua for the US women's movement is also evident in the scholarship about collective identities in social movements more generally. In the past two decades there has been such a burgeoning of research on collective identities in social movements that some scholars have commented that it could be mistaken as the central concept in the field (Snow and McAdam, 2000). Few scholars, however, have defined collective identity. It is everything from a process, a thing, an outcome, a resource, or, as Polletta and Jasper (2001)

note, a residual category that is often used interchangeably to mean interests, ideology, and/or solidarity. Following Polletta and Jasper (2001: 285) I use collective identity to mean an individual's cognitive, moral, and emotional connection to a larger community (real or imagined), category, practice, or institution. While a collective identity may be defined by others/outsiders and in some instances by the state, it is accepted by people, is expressed in cultural materials, and leads to positive feelings for other members of the group. Despite the ubiquity of the concept in research on social movements, most scholarship about it and reviews of this scholarship are limited in two ways: the construction of the major perspectives in the field and the focus on movements within nation-states, primarily those in the US and Europe.

First, most scholarly writings and reviews of collective identities in social movements begin by differentiating collective identities in the resource mobilization, political process, and the new social movement perspectives even though today these distinctions are not as valid as the perspectives have changed in response to each other (Bernstein, 2005; Cohen, 1985; Larana et al., 1994; Polletta and Jasper, 2001; Stryker et al., 2000). Initially, in the resource mobilization and political process perspectives – both of which emerged in the 1970s in the US primarily to analyze the civil rights movement – collective identities were assumed and understood to be determined by one's race, gender, and/ or class. These identities were then seen as resources to be mobilized for collective action (McAdam, 1982; McCarthy and Zald, 1977; Tilly, 1978).

This structurally determined understanding began to change in response to the new social actors who were mobilizing as well as to the new social movement perspective that was emerging in western Europe. Now resource mobilization scholarship began to address how collective identities, like other resources, had to be first defined and framed by activists before they could be mobilized for action. As Polletta and Jasper (1997) note, scholarship on collective identities in social movements in the 1990s emerged to address the gap in the resource mobilization and political process models which were based on instrumental rationality and whose focus was explaining how marginalized groups mobilized resources and challenged the state to make legal and political changes rather than understanding why and how groups formed collective identities.

By contrast, the new social movement scholarship focused on explaining why and how new collective identities come into being. In part, this difference in the perspectives stems from their focus on different social movements in different parts of the world. In western Europe, the site of the new social movement scholarship, there was no civil rights movement challenging the state. Rather, the old labor movement was fragmented and new social movements were emerging whose focus was not the state and legal or political changes but the cultural understandings of self and society.[2] Hence, new social

movements scholars focused on the accomplishment of collective identities via self-reflexive processes of articulation, one of the practices that made social movements new. In this narrative, social movements are either strategic and instrumental (the resource mobilization perspective) or reflexive and articulators of identities (the new social movements perspective).

This narrative, however, erases the formulations of collective identities in the early work of radical feminists of color in the US who argued for both strategic and expressive understandings of identities in social movements. In fact, so entrenched is this construction of the field that feminists, including myself, re-inscribe this narrative even when we draw upon feminist movements and critique the mainstream's erasure of these voices. To destabilize this construction of the field, I begin by discussing how radical feminists of color understood collective identities and articulated what came to be called "identity politics" and show how they anticipated some of the debates and resolutions of the three mainstream perspectives that dominated the field in the 1980s and 1990s and continue to do so today in varied forms.[3] In other words, the collective identities theorized by US radical feminists of color transcend the usual dichotomies in social movement theorizing about identities namely: structural/contingent, class/culture, and solidarity/difference (Maiguashca, 2005).

Second, with few exceptions, most of the scholarship on collective identities is based on social movements within nation-states, primarily those in the Global North.[4] While there is a burgeoning literature on transnational social movements (Juris, 2008; Keck and Sikkink, 1998; Khagram et al., 2002; Smith et al., 1997; Tarrow, 2005; Tilly, 2004), most of it focuses on issues of scale, the role of technology in mobilizing transnational activism, and the strategic and instrumental rationality, i.e., the issues addressed by resource mobilization and political process perspectives, rather than collective identities. Here again, the geography of scholarly production seems to shape the focus of scholarly production. Scholars writing on transnational social movements outside the US are more likely to include issues of collective identities in their analysis than those writing in the US. Juris (2008) is an exception, as he is a US scholar who writes about collective identities in the anti-corporate globalization movements in Barcelona. Perhaps, his research sites in Europe might explain his focus on identities. To correct this myopia of the field, in the second part of the chapter I focus on collective identities in transnational social movements and show how transnational social movements have used the insights of identity politics to articulate a new conception of social movements and collective identities, namely social justice politics, in the context of contemporary globalizations.

## THIS BRIDGE CALLED MY BACK OR IDENTITY POLITICS[5]

I use *This Bridge Called my Back* to refer not just to the anthology edited by Cherrie Moraga and Gloria Anzaldua but also to the writings by women of color in the US who theorized a new conception of collective identities and social movements in the 1970s and 1980s (Davis, 1983; hooks, 1999; Hull et al., 2003; Lorde, 2007). The radical feminists of color focused on three important aspects of collective identities in social movements: (1) they demonstrated that collective and individual identities are not just a product of a single structural location, i.e., class, race, gender, or sexuality, but were a product of what later came to be called "a matrix of domination," or multiple, interacting axes of oppression; (2) feminists of color understood culture and class or material realities as mutually constitutive and hence did not privilege or differentiate one over the other; (3) finally, these multivalent identities were to be a source for a transformative politics through coalition building. These three issues – a

source of much debate among the three movement perspectives for over a decade – were anticipated and addressed by the early feminists in ways similar to that evident in contemporary scholarship.

## STRUCTURALLY SHAPED AND CONTINGENTLY ACCOMPLISHED

Radical women of color in the US were primarily writing against the feminism articulated by white, middle-class women who privileged gender as both the major source of oppression for all women and as a resource for solidarity among women, i.e., sisterhood is global or what came to be called an "essentialist" notion of gender. For feminists of color, gender oppression could not be separated from their class, racial, or sexual oppression.

> Although we are feminists and Lesbians, we feel solidarity with progressive Black men and do not advocate the fractionalization that white women who are separatists demand [...] We struggle together with Black men against racism, while we also struggle with Black men about sexism [...] We are socialists because we believe that work must be organized for the collective benefit of those who do the work and create the products, and not for the profit of the bosses. (Combahee River Collective Statement, 1986, http://www. buffalostate.edu/orgs/rspms/combahee.html)

Hence, radical feminists of color theorized collective identities away from, to use an erstwhile Marxist term, the primary contradiction of gender and focused on the intersecting axis of race, class, as well as sexualities that result in multivalent identities. And while these multivalent identities are experienced as a whole, based on specific historical and socio-political contexts one aspect of complex identities may have more salience than others. Hence, they moved away from a structural determination for collective movement identity to one that is shaped by multiple structures. Furthermore, these identities were not unchanging or uncontested, but had to be renegotiated in and for a political cause. This constant identity work was true for personal empowerment as well as for social change.

Such identity work was undertaken in some of the earliest black feminist organizations, namely the National Black Feminist Organization founded in 1973 in New York and the Black Women Organized for Action formed in San Francisco in 1973. These organizations included women of all classes and educational backgrounds and worked on intersectional issues such as forced sterilization, welfare rights, police brutality, labor organizing, as well as anti-nuclear issues (Hull et al., 2003).

The understanding of collective identities as contingent and fluid came to dominate the work of, the new social movement theorists a decade later (Habermas, 1987; Melucci 1989; Offe, 1985; Touraine, 1985). These theorists argued that European society beginning in the 1960s and 1970s was undergoing a profound transformation to a post-industrial age and in it class politics and identities of the "old," i.e., (labor movement) had been replaced by the identity politics of new movements such as the women's, students', environmental, and gay and lesbian movements. These theorists argued that the movements were new because they had new actors, new issues, and most importantly new identities.

The new actors were middle-class, educated men and women as opposed to the old actors, i.e., the proletariat; the new issues included gender and sexual equality, peace, and ecological justice as opposed to the old class issues; and the new politics was a new way of organizing based on participatory, non-hierarchical groups rather than bureaucratic and vanguardist parties and unions. Within the new movements, theorists argued, it was in the process of interaction, often in small groups – primarily homogenous ones as difference was not addressed either by the new social movements or by the theorists – that new movement identities of feminists, gays and lesbians, and radical students came into being. As such, these identities were contingent and fluid accomplishments and

not pre-determined by participants' structural location or brought into being by a vanguard. Or as Melucci noted:

> The freedom to have which characterized [...] industrial society has been replaced by the freedom to be. The right to property has been, and remains, the basis of both industrial capitalism and its competitor model, 'real socialism'. In post-material society, there emerges a further type of right, the right to existence, or rather, to a more meaningful existence (1989: 177–8)

The new social movement theorists made their case based on the women's, students, and gay and lesbian movements in Europe. Most of these movements in the 1970s and 1980s had come out of left movements but were organizing autonomously because of the lack of attention to issues of gender and sexuality in the new left. The new movements were composed primarily of many small groups working in many cities and towns with loose connections among them. There were no large movement organizations and with the exception of some large protest demonstrations most of the movement activity involved small groups of activists engaging in "consciousness raising," popularized by the women's movement groups and addressing what it meant to be feminist or gay or lesbian.

While articulating what these new identities meant was a major focus of most of these movement groups, it was not the sole focus as new social movement theorists claim. Most movements addressed local issues of gender and sexual equality, including their access to social and political institutions. Because most of these new movement groups did not work systematically with unions or the labor movements in most countries, the new social movement theorists argued that the new activists were not focused on class issues. But they were focused on economic issues, only this time it was not economic issues of the working class but their own economic interests. For example, issues like equal pay for equal work and pay for housework were some of the issues addressed by women's groups in Italy, Denmark and other countries.

In contrast to both the radical feminists of color and the new social movement theorists, the scholars of resource mobilization and the political process perspectives, which emerged in the US in 1970s and 1980s in the wake of the 1960s social movements understood collective identities as given or structurally determined based on a history of shared grievances emanating from race, gender, or sexuality (Gamson, 1975; McAdam, 1982; Tilly, 1978). The primary focus of both resource mobilization and political process perspectives was to understand how predetermined social groups gained access to institutions from which they were excluded. While resource mobilization scholars answered this question by examining how groups mobilized different kinds of resources, the political process analysts focused on the changing political opportunity structure and the role of elites and other groups. Hence, analysts working within both resource mobilization and political process perspectives initially ignored the question of collective identities, assuming them to be structurally determined.

For example, most analyses of the civil rights and women's movements in the US from this perspective rarely focused on how women and African Americans defined themselves. Rather the focus was on how movement organizations recruited members, how they mobilized resources to launch campaigns, how they convinced bystanders and ultimately, how they succeeded in making gains. McCarthy and Zald (1977), among the most influential scholars within this perspective, even saw social movements as another sector of the economy, the social movement industry. Hence, analyses of the civil rights, the women's, students, and anti-war movements focused on specific movement organizations such as the National Organization of Women or the Southern Christian Leadership Conference or the Students Non-Violent Coordinating Committee and their ideology and campaigns and how the state and the political elite responded to them. With the emergence of the Black Power movement and radical feminism, issues of collective identities became important but most analysts saw these in terms of movement strategies rather than collective identities.

However, this lack of attention to collective identities in resource mobilization and political process perspectives began to change, partly in response to the work of new social movement theorists whose focus was on the process of collective identity formation. It is this attention to collective identities in the 1990s in the US social movements that led to the proliferation of work on identities in social movements. As Polletta and Jasper (2001) note, they did so by studying the role of collective identities in different stages of social movements from making collective claims, to recruiting and sustaining members, to strategic and tactical decision making, and in movement outcomes.

For example, analysts have examined the role of macro factors such as industrialization and urbanization in facilitating the emergence of new identities such as that of homosexuals in the nineteenth century through expansion of personal and economic autonomy (D'Emilio, 1983) to the role of social networks and institutional spaces such as half way houses (Morris, 1984) in the emergence of the civil rights movements. Another dominant line of analysis has been around the efforts of activists to strategically 'frame' identities for recruiting and sustaining participation in social movements (Snow and Benford, 1988; Snow et al., 1986). Frames are interpretive materials that activists develop to establish the need for a movement, a clear sense of us and them, and potential strategies for addressing the needs. However, as within feminism, such identity constructions are often faced with challenges. So many movements juggle between the need to define a collective identity for mobilization and change and yet recognize the instability and exclusionary nature of such processes. Hence, many opt for what Gayatri Spivak (1993) has called "strategic essentialism" framing a 'we' for a political goal even as that 'we' is seen to be unstable and potentially exclusive.

Other analysts have examined the changing nature of identities within and outside movements as movements operate within a complex field of allies, competing and oppositional movements, media, authorities, and funders (Bernstein, 1997; Gamson, 1988; Hunt et al., 1994; Klandermans, 1997). Even the most strategic calculations are informed by collective identities such as feminist or peace groups using consensus to make decisions whether in the context of bureaucratic organization or in informally structured organizations or the decisions of movements such as ACT UP who are opposed to bureaucratic strategies and hence use disruptive street action to draw attention to their issues. Thus identity and strategy are not oppositional but activists use identity strategically and strategic options are shaped by the groups' identities, as women of color had demonstrated decades before this contemporary, consensus in the social movement literature.

## MATERIAL AND CULTURAL EMBODIMENTS OF IDENTITIES

The second way in which feminists of color anticipated and resolved another major issue about collective identities in movements was to break away from the material/cultural binary that was evident in much writing about collective identities in the new social movement and resource mobilization perspectives in the 1980s and 1990s. Feminists of color did not separate material from cultural issues and highlighted the role of both in the formation of collective identities as well as in how movements define their goals, strategies, and issues. For example, early Chicana feminist identities were constructed through the collectively imagined nation Aztlan as well as through rasquache cultural practices that are "fly-by night productions, cheap and economical" (Perez, 1999). Thus, in addition to organizing farm workers for fair wages, they were also engaging in cultural productions that were "tacky, lower

class" but which articulated a sense of belonging to *la raza* – the race, the people.

Similarly black feminists were organizing within the civil rights movement to demand equality but also forming cultural collectives and cooperatives that formulated new literary and musical productions and reexamined everything from dominant ideas of beauty to inventing cultural traditions such as Kwanza. Furthermore, their writings highlighted the discursive, symbolic and cultural nature of oppressions and identities in addition to the material dimensions. Thus, feminists of color wrote about the misogyny and homophobia in both the civil rights movement as well as in their communities. They also wrote about oppressive cultural representations of black women's sexuality as well as the color gradations within the communities of color, in addition to the crushing material inequalities.

Thus transforming oppressive into empowering identities, e.g., black is beautiful, was seen as life affirming and hence a political practice. Spiritual activism also played an important role in this transformative process as it did for radical white feminists and would for indigenous feminists and activists in the transnational movements a decade later. So while the collective identities were to serve as a mechanism for collective action, they also served as activism in themselves. But this recognition of the symbolic and discursive did not replace the importance of material inequalities and organizing for access to resources in different arenas. In this weaving together of the material and cultural, identity politics of radical feminists of color avoided the dichotomies of material/cultural that dominated the three perspectives on social movements in the 1980s and 1990s.

For example, because they focused on discursive and symbolic cultural elements that were used to fashion collective identities, new social movement theorists were seen as harbingers of the "cultural" turn in social movement theorizing about identities. Many scholars working from this perspective argued that for many activists, particularly radical feminists, environmentalists, and gay and lesbian groups coming together to define a new identity, organizing alternative spaces and questioning dominant cultural assumptions was itself activism. These groups did not seek to transform the existing political or economic structures, i.e., material issues. Or as Cerulo (1997) noted, new social movements were not about reacting to exclusion from the system and for emancipation but about acting to expand freedom and for more choice. Clearly new social movements analysts were looking through a very narrow range of movements to make such a case.

By contrast, scholars working within the resource mobilization and political process models, who for the most part saw collective identities as given, focused on how collective identities were deployed to achieve material goals. For example, in the writings of resource mobilization and political process analysts, the civil rights and then the Chicano and American Indian Movement as well as the women's movements, gay and lesbian movements, and disability rights movements used their new identities to demand access to power in the political arena, in corporations, and in the academy. In the academy, where these movements were often dubbed the "culture wars",[6] they were also about access to resources that were historically denied to groups based on gender, race, and ethnicity. They argue that identity politics has been successful not only because movements have constructed identities that resonate with people but also because the state recognizes these identities as a basis for access and equity.

While contemporary scholars within the dominant perspectives no longer make these distinctions between material and cultural goals of movements, what many still miss, as Armstrong and Berstein (2008) note, is how "material" issues and goals are culturally constituted and "cultural" issues have material ramifications. So what Armstrong and Bernstein recommend to get beyond the impasse of the three perspectives in social movements is a multi-institutional politics which recognizes multiple sources of power and hence inequalities that are both material and symbolic and that require empirical analysis rather than binary assumptions about material or cultural sources. Or as Sheila Benhabib notes, "(T)he time has come to move beyond identity politics, in the Hegelian sense of moving beyond—*Aufheben*—that is, by learning its lessons, rejecting its excesses, and moving to a new synthesis of collective solidarities with plurally constituted identities" (1994: 2). Work that feminists of color had been doing for over a decade as I show below.

## FROM DIFFERENCE TO SOLIDARITY

Feminists of color also contributed towards developing such solidarities by articulating a coalition politics that would enable groups to work together across their differing collective identities for common goals. Their identity politics did not collapse collective identity with solidarity or political action. Hence, defining oneself as a chicana lesbian did not preclude solidarity and action with either African American men or white women. While one might feel more comfortable with people who were like oneself, i.e., in what Bernice Johnson Reagon (1981) called "home", and there was need for such spaces for affirmation and rejuvenation, one could not be politically effective in that manner. For as Reagon noted:

> We've pretty much come to the end of a time when you can have a space that is 'yours only' – just for the people you want to be there. Even when we have our "women-only" festivals, there is no such thing. The fault is not necessarily with the organizers of the gathering. To a large extent it's because we have just finished with that kind of isolating. There is no hiding place. There is nowhere you can go and only be with people who are like you. It's over. Give it up. (1981)

What was necessary for our common survival and political action was coalition work.

> Coalition work is not work done in your home. Coalition work has to be done in the streets.

And it is some of the most dangerous work you can do. And you shouldn't look for comfort. Some people will come to a coalition and they rate the success of the coalition on whether or not they feel good when they get there. They're not looking for a coalition; they're looking for a home! [...] In a coalition you have to give and it is different from home. You can't stay there all the time. You go to the coalition for a few hours and then you go back and take your bottle wherever it is, and then you go back and coalesce some more. (Reagon, 1981)

Thus, feminists of color in the US theorized the importance of coalition work in identity politics. One example of this was their self-definition as Third World Within both to call attention to their treatment within the US but also to reach out to men and women in the Third World who were struggling against oppressions and seeking liberation. Their coalition efforts focused on women's movements and race and ethnic movements in the US as well as in the Third World.

Within resource mobilization and political process models, identity politics were initially seen as leading to greater fragmentation. As each collective identity is destabilized and new collective identities emerge they become the basis for further collective action leading to a "proliferation of identities". For example, many scholars have analyzed the fragmentation within women's, gay and lesbian, student, and environmental movements among others (e.g., Whittier, 1995). Most of this fragmentation, scholars argue, has been a result of policing boundaries of us and them and differences in strategies and tactics that emerge with new collective identities. The assumption of many early scholars within these two perspectives was that multiple collective identities, each based on difference, leads to a lack of solidarity. Such a charge leaves unanswered solidarity for what, as defined by whom, and at what costs?

As intersectional analysis has become the norm in feminist scholarship today, most analysts no longer pose difference and solidarity in opposition to each other and coalition building across differences has been embraced by most analysts as an important strategy, even as they recognize, like women

of color did several decades ago, that coalition building is hard work, fraught with tensions and contradictions, and not always productive. For most contemporary movements, coalition politics remains an instrumental strategy, as a means to a political goal, not an important part of one's collective identity or politics. Transnational social movements are among those for whom coalition politics is part of their collective identity, as I discuss in the next section.

As I have shown above, feminists of color in the US theorized collective identities and articulated identity politics in nuanced and complex ways much before the three dominant social movement perspectives did. Yet, their contributions while cited in specific scholarship on women's movements are neither acknowledged as path breaking nor seen as central to the scholarship on collective identities and social movements. I now move to another kind of myopia in mainstream movement scholarship, namely collective identities in transnational social movements.

## THIS BRIDGE WE CALL HOME OR SOCIAL JUSTICE POLITICS

While some contemporary transnational movements such as the women's movements and the environmental movements had begun to emerge in 1975 and were consolidated in the 1980s, and there was transnational activism around human rights issues in the 1980s in Latin America, the phenomenon of transnational social movements really took shape in the 1990s. And while northern movements still dominate transnational movements, there is not only more representation from southern countries, but the direction of flows of ideas, issues, and strategies is more multidirectional from the south to the north as well as from the north to the south.

Transnational movements transcend national boundaries either in terms of issues addressed, actors involved, strategies and methods used or the perspective of the activists. Most social movement scholars link the development of contemporary transnational movements to economic globalization (Keck and Sikkink, 1998; Khagram et al., 2002; Moghadam, 2005; Tarrow, 2003). In particular, economic globalization is seen both as a source of common grievances – such as rising inequality due to neoliberal trade policies which benefit the wealthy in both the Global North and the South at the expense of the poor in the north and the south – and a source of opportunities for activism via the information and communication technologies such as the Internet, which enable activists to connect rapidly with others across the globe.

While the scholarship on transnational social movements is burgeoning, that on identities in transnational movements is still rudimentary (Castells, 1997; Jung, 2003; Juris, 2008). This scholarship suggests that transnational social movement organizing has impacted the construction and deployment of collective identities. In particular, there have been two shifts in movement identities, one is from identities based on social status to those based on political goals, what Castells (1996) calls project identities; and second, what I call, the new global social justice regimes, are providing some of the frames for these project identities (Jung, 2003). Following Kardam's (2004) "global gender equality regime", I define global social justice regimes as norms, conventions, declarations, and legal mechanisms for equality and justice that have emerged from the various UN world conferences and are supported by the nearly 200 member nations of the UN.

To these two factors, I add the role of what I call the transnational activist class in shaping transnational movement identities. These shifts do not suggest that identity politics is no longer relevant to transnational social movements. In fact identity based transnational movements such as women's, dalit, and indigenous movements dominate the field. Rather, even identity based movements are organizing around project identities such as global justice or human rights as I show below.

## PROJECT IDENTITIES

Castells (1997) writing more generally about identities, in what he called "networked" societies, argued that networked societies lead to new forms of collective identities that are more important to people than those based on work and citizenship. He defined three kinds of identities, legitimizing identities – those which justify the existing social order such as religious or nationalist identities; resistance identities – those that resist contemporary globalizations and look to the past; and project identities – those that articulate new forms of democratic identities to further progressive social transformation. Project identities are hence hybrid identities that draw from identity politics of race, gender, and sexuality as well as the global social justice regimes and are based on creativity and diversity. For Castells these project identities emerge within movements and challenge both the commodification of the life world and also demand material equality across differences. The global justice and human rights frames are among these new project identities.

Similar articulations of project identities have also been made by feminist scholars who define collective identities as political constructions based on a common struggle for justice that is defined in alliance with others across differences. For example, Anzaldua (2002) talks of a new tribalism that is based on what we include rather than what we exclude. "El Mundo Zurdo" is a world in which differences are not oppositional but relational and lead to alliances. "I believe that by changing ourselves we change the world, that traveling El Mundo Zurdo path is the path of a two-way movement – a going deep into the self and expanding out into the world, a simultaneous recreation of the self and society" (cited in Keating, 2002: 522). Chandra Talpade Mohanty (2003) calls it feminisms across borders. Or as Cohen states: "I envision a politics where one's relation to power, and not some homogenized identity, is privileged in determining one's political comrades. I'm talking about a politics where the *non-normative and marginal* position of punks, bulldaggers, and welfare queens, for example, is the basis for progressive transformative coalition work" (cited in Harris, 2002: 375).

These new project identities have been most visible in the global justice movements which have been defined as the new, new social movements (McKenzie, 2000). The emergence of these project identities reflects both the limitations of identity politics but also the new realities of corporate globalizations that have furthered inequalities, drawing upon new racialized, gendered, and sexed subjects. Or, as Jung (2003) claims these new collective identities are themselves a product of politics of newly available discourses and regimes.

An excellent example of project identities in action is the World Social Forum (WSF) that began in 2001 in Porto Alegre, Brazil. Organized as an alternative to the World Economic Forum in Davos, where leaders of corporate globalization meet, the first WSF was organized in January 2001 in Brazil. It met in Brazil from 2001–2003, moved to India in 2004, back to Brazil in 2005, was organized as several polycentric forums around the world in 2006, was held in Nairobi, Kenya in 2007 and was again held in Belem, Brazil in January 2009 (http://www.world socialforum.org).[7] Today, the various regional, national, and even local World Social Forums that occur between the global ones are more important than the global gathering.

The first WSF in 2001 in Porto Alegre, Brazil was organized by the local Workers Party. It was a response to two contradictory tendencies in Latin America in the 1990s: increasing democratization and the spread of neoliberal globalization. The latter generated structural crises and inequalities while the former provided a space to address these growing crises. The protests against corporate globalization that began in Seattle in 1999 and continued through the end of the decade created new networks that led to the WSF.

The WSF was organized as a democratic space for movements, NGOs, and people from around the world to share their struggles and reflect on alternatives.

> The World Social Forum is an open meeting place where social movements, networks, NGOs and other civil society organizations opposed to neoliberalism and a world dominated by capital or by any form of imperialism come together to pursue their thinking, to debate ideas democratically, to formulate proposals, share experiences freely and network for effective action [...] it has taken the form of a permanent world process seeking and building alternatives to neoliberal policies. The World Social Forum is also characterized by plurality and diversity, is non-confessional, non-governmental and non-party. It proposes to facilitate decentralized coordination and networking among organizations. (http://www.wsf.org accessed 12 December 2008)

The language of the WSF stresses process and autonomy from state and parties, even though it was an initiative of a left party in Brazil. It has been a space for all kinds of movements and NGOs, including movements based on identities such as the women's, youth, dalit, and indigenous, to come together around the project identity best exemplified in its slogan: Another World is Possible. The focus is on developing collective alternatives to neoliberalism, sharing those formulations, and working together around the world to enact them. But as Bauman (2001) cautions, these new identities can just as easily "grease the wheels of globalization" as aid in social transformation. Hence, one of the tasks of the new transnational activist class has been to both critique their own interventions and to develop global social equality regimes that address such complicity with the neoliberal project. It is to these regimes that I now turn.

## GLOBAL SOCIAL EQUALITY REGIMES

Arguably, the United Nations Universal Declaration of Human Rights in 1948 was the first "global social equality regime." This declaration was followed by the International

Covenant on Civil and Political Rights and the International Covenant on Social, Economic, and Cultural Rights (1966), which in turn were followed by the establishment of various commissions and conventions.[8] While the declaration was important in shaping many of the postcolonial constitutions and policies, it were the United Nations World Conferences, accompanied by their Non Governmental (NGO) Forums,[9] beginning in the late 1960s and 1970s followed by a series of them in the 1990s that mobilized transnational activists to participate in shaping the global social justice regimes and not leave it to their governments. For example, elsewhere I have shown how the UN's International Decade for Women (1975–1985), with its four world conferences and NGO Forums – 1975 in Mexico city, 1980 in Copenhagen, 1985 in Nairobi, and, a decade later, a follow-up conference in Beijing in 1995 – and preparatory national and regional meetings shaped the gender global equality regime (Desai, 2008).

The four women's conferences,[10] and accompanying NGO Forums, were contentious events with women, not all of whom identified as feminists, from the south challenging northern women's conceptions of women's issues based solely on gender and sexuality and insisting on bringing in issues of development, nationalism, and neo-colonialism. These differences among women began to be acknowledged and "solidarities of difference" (Desai, 1997) were forged as they continued to meet over the decade and share experiences of inequalities and struggles for justice. Similarly, the World Conferences around the Environment, Social Development, Racism, Population, and Habitat were also contributing towards the multiple global social justice regimes.

I have argued (Desai, 1996) elsewhere that the human rights framework provided a way to bring together activists across differences that had become problematic for solidarities in the wake of identity politics discussed above. That, along with the effects of contemporary globalizations, meant that activists

in transnational movements had common grievances, and so needed a common framework to address these. But the insights of identity politics were not lost in this transnational phase. Activists are aware that issues manifest differently around the world and that identities have to be forged in struggle and not assumed. So global social justice regimes are translated and reconfigured in local contexts based on local histories of social justice.

For example, Jung (2003) argues that in the case of the indigenous movements, indigeneity as an identity replaced peasants as a political category in the 1990s in response to changes in the post-Cold War geopolitical configurations, as well neoliberal economic policies. Thus, for her identity is the basis of a political claims making and a way to engage the global dialogue. Collective identity, then, arises as a condition of politics itself. Thus, she argues that it develops to the extent that the state uses it as a category of inclusions and exclusion. While various identity markers of indigenous communities have been used to exclude and oppress minority groups, it is the confluence of neoliberal economic policies and the changing role of the state in protecting minorities that has led to claims making based on indigenous identity. This was facilitated by the role of the international human rights regime which expanded its ambit to include groups rights in the 1990s.

Similarly, Higgins (2005) argues that in the global justice movements new indigenous identities are being articulated that are rethinking political practices and imaginaries based on native poetics that are providing a new model for organizing. That is, Zapatismo is going global. But Hernández Castillo (Chapter 19, this volume) warns that indigenous movements in Latin America have yet to engage constructively with Afro-descendant and feminist movements as well as with the frames of diaspora and borderland that have a more complicated relationship with space and territory than is sometimes assumed by some indigenous movements. Marchand (2005) similarly argues that new regional identities are being articulated from old and new social equality regimes. For example, the Alternatives for America, is a hemispheric identity based on democracy and social justice as opposed to the Monroe doctrine and its notion of US hegemony. The Hemispheric Social Alliance (HAS) reinterprets the old Bolivarian doctrine to define a new "us", made up not of nation-states but more diffused actors that are movements, NGOs, and non-state actors. The "other" is not just the US but economic actors, corporations, and intergovernmental bodies. HAS regionalism is multidimensional, more democratic in decision-making, and links economic issues with those of rights and justice drawing upon global social justice regimes.

Such articulations are also true in other parts of the world where transnational environmental movements, dalit movements, youth movements, and media movements have all begun to frame some of their old issues and new realities around project identities that draw upon the new global regimes of social justice. The transnational activist class has been instrumental in making this happen and it is to them that I now turn.

## TRANSNATIONAL ACTIVIST CLASS

What I call the transnational activist class (Desai, 2008) has been instrumental in enabling the construction of these new project identities drawing upon the global social justice regimes. This class includes local and transnational activists, academics, bureaucrats, and journalists, who circulate and participate in local and transnational movement contexts such as UN conferences, World Social Forums, and other regional and transnational gatherings where they articulate and engage in various global justice movements.

Today's transnational activists are men and women from many parts of the world, though there is a domination of some countries in Africa, Asia, Europe, and Latin America and North America, such as South Africa, Kenya, and Ghana in Africa; India and the

Philippines in Asia; France and Italy in Europe; Brazil, Peru, Mexico in Latin America; and the US in North America.[11] The flow of ideas and political strategies, however, is multidirectional. Today there are structural mechanisms for on-going transnational articulations, facilitated by the information and communication technologies – such as Internet and web-based chat rooms, listservs, discussion boards, and instant messaging – and an expansive network of funding through private and public foundations that enables the maintenance and reproduction of this class. Finally, the processes of contemporary globalizations have reached many more parts of the world leading to both a "global consciousness" (Giddens, 2000), as well as the necessity for transnational response for local and global changes.

These men and women are recognized as providing a critique as well as alternatives to transnational politics dominated by inequalities of power between and within the north and the south. The class is internally differentiated between, what I call, the advocate-activists who are educated, urban, and middle class and the activist-advocates with low levels of formal education and who belong to the urban and rural working poor. The advocate-activists share many social and demographic characteristics of the transnational capitalist class (Sklair, 2002).[12] Many are highly educated professionals with some politicians, bureaucrats, and academics among them. Many of the advocate-activists circulate between international NGOs to the UN to the academy and/or running for political office. By contrast, the activist-advocates have low levels of education, are usually poor and have begun their transnational activism through local grass roots movements and NGOs. While they too circulate in some of the same circuits as the advocate activists, their sojourns are more temporary and their lack of education and professional training do not allow them the same kind of mobility.

For example, at the WSF the advocate activists are the ones who are members of the

International Council that organizes each forum, they are the ones who populate the plenaries, look after registration, logistics and media releases, blog and write. The activist-advocates may be in some plenaries but are more likely to be in organized workshops, in fair-trade and other cultural events, and in some local organizing. At other global gatherings such as NGO forums accompanying the United Nations conferences the activist-advocates have a larger voice. While class and educational differences within the transnational activist class does reproduce inequalities that exist among them at such global gatherings, there is a greater balance in participation at local levels. In recognition of such disparities many advocate-activists have started transnational organizing where the activist-advocates have an equal voice. Networks such as GROOTS, Grass Roots Organizations Operating Together in Sisterhood (http://www.groots.org), the Huairou Commission (http://www.huairou.org), Women in Informal Economy Organizing and Globalizing (http://www.weigo.org), among others, focus on providing voice and space to activist-advocates and forging more equal partnerships among activist-advocates and advocate-activists. They work with local activist-advocates and bring them together transnationally so they can share their knowledge and political expertise. For example, following the 2002 earthquake in Turkey, local activist-advocates from Gujarat, who had learned valuable lessons in getting rehabilitation and relief, went to Turkey through the Swayam Sikshan Prayog (http://www.sspindia.org) in Mumbai to share their successes with their Turkish counterparts.

Thus, this diverse transnational activist class works in varied ways. Some work to reform the system, others in anarchic tradition develop alternatives alongside the system, and still others work to develop counter-hegemonic politics. But all of them work within transnational networks and share a global consciousness and have been engaged in shaping global social justice regimes that have come to shape project identities in transnational movements.

## REWRITING COLLECTIVE IDENTITIES AND SOCIAL MOVEMENTS

As the above review shows, contemporary research on identities in social movements needs to be rewritten if it is to portray past contributions more accurately and reflect the changing realities of contemporary transnational social movements. In particular, I have argued for (1) foregrounding the contributions of US women of color and (2) attending to the insights of transnational social movements. First, the foregrounding is important to set the 'record straight' but more importantly to recognize that US feminists of color prefigured debates and provided valuable insights about issues that dominated the discussion in the resource mobilization, political process, and new social movement perspectives a decade later. I have addressed three specific debates in this chapter: whether collective identities are structurally determined or contingent; embody material or cultural dimensions; and finally the relationship between difference and solidarity. I've shown that US feminists of color in each case articulated positions that went beyond the binaries and argued that collective identities are shaped by multiple structural locations and contingently accomplished, that material and cultural dimensions of collective identities are mutually constitutive and need to be deployed strategically for material and symbolic transformation, and finally coalition building across differences is the way forward for social transformation that does not erase differences.

Second, attending to transnational social movements is important as they have brought to the forefront the ways in which identity politics continues to animate some of them as well as the emergence of new project identities. Furthermore, I have shown the importance of the differentiated transnational activist class in shaping the global social justice regimes and the new project identities in response to contemporary globalizations. These transnational movements focus on new issues of culture and democracy as well as old issues of access to economic and political resources. And finally, the new project identities are hybrid, interactive, and contingent accomplishments that are achieved in horizontally organized networks. The successes and limitations of the project identities will shape the future of identities in social movements yet to come.

## NOTES

1   *This Bridge Called My Back*, the book edited by Cherrie Moraga and Gloria Anzaldua, along with the Combahee River Collective Statement – developed by the Combahee River Collective based in Boston from 1974–1980 – are the classic statements of identity politics articulated by radical women of color in the US in the 1970s and 1980s.

2   There were movements in western Europe like the women's movement and the environmental movement that were challenging the state but the new social movement theorists focused on those parts of these movements that were focused on identities rather than challenging inequalities.

3   For good analyses and reviews of the three mainstream perspectives see, e.g., Armstrong and Bernstein (2008), Bernstein (2005), Cohen (1985), Larana et al. (1994), Polleta and Jasper (2001), and Stryker et al. (2000).

4   By north, I mean rich countries of Europe, North America, and East Asia and by the south I mean countries of Africa, Asia, and Latin America. Like Third World/First World, this categorization is also problematic as it fails to address, among other issues, the south within the north and vice versa. But I use it as it has become common usage now.

5   Identity politics, in both academic and popular discourse, is often used derogatively to denote anti-sexist, anti-racist, and anti-homophobic movements. My usage of the term does not share that view but rather describes movements around social statuses such as gender, race, sexuality, religion, disability, among others.

6   Because many women's, race, and ethnic movements challenged curricula that excluded their histories and contributions, many in the academy and in the popular media saw them as "cultural" movements.

7   I participated in three of the World Social Forums, the one in Bombay in 2004, Porto Alegre in 2005, and Nairobi in 2007.

8   For an insightful and thorough history of human rights through the ages see Ishay (2004).

9   The first NGO forum alongside a UN inter-governmental conference took place in 1972 at the Earth Summit. Following that, the women's conferences consolidated the presence of NGO Forums at each of the conferences. NGO Forums were organized simultaneously as the UN conferences to provide NGOs and social movements an opportunity to meet and discuss the issues being addressed at the UN conferences.

10   The UN conferences are for government delegations though increasingly many governments include activists and NGO members as part of their official delegation.

11   With the exception of Latin American, the rest of the countries are English speaking and that could partly explain their dominance. The political cultures in these countries also explain their prominence.

12   According to Sklair (2002), the transnational capitalist class is composed of four factions: one made up of corporate executives; another made up of state and inter-state bureaucrats and politicians; the third made up of professionals; and a consumerist faction made up of merchants and the media.

## REFERENCES

Anzaldúa, G. (2002) 'Preface', in G. Anzaldua and A. Keating (eds), *This Bridge We Call Home*. New York: Routledge, pp. 1–5.

Armstrong, E. and Bernstein, M. (2008) 'Culture, power, and institutions: A multi-institutional politics approach to social movements', *Sociological Theory*, 26 (1): 74–99.

Bauman, Z. (2001) *The Individualized Society*. London: Polity Press.

Benhabib, S. (1994) 'From identity politics to social feminism: A plea for the ninetes', *Philosophy of Education Society*. Downloaded 12 August 2008. file:///Users/manishadesai/Desktop/smidentity/Benhabib%20:%20FROM%20IDENTITY%20POLITICS%20TO%20SOCIAL%20FEMINISM:%20A%.

Bernstein, M. (1997) 'Celebration and suppression: The strategic uses of identity by the lesbian and gay movement', *American Journal of Sociology*, 103 (3): 531–65.

Bernstein, M. (2005) 'Identity politics', *Annual Review of Sociology*, 31: 47–74.

Castells, M. (1997) *The Power of Identities*. Malden, MA: Blackwell Publishers.

Cerulo, K. (1997) 'Identity construction: New issues, New directions', *Annual Review of Sociology*, 23: 385–409.

Cohen, J. (1985) 'Strategy or identity: New theoretical paradigms and contemporary social movements', *Social Research*, 52 (4): 663–716.

D'Emilio, J. (1983) *Sexual Politics Sexual Communities*. Chicago, IL: Chicago University Press.

Davis, A. (1983) *Women, Race, and Class*. Vintage Books.

Desai, M. (1996) 'From vienna to beijing: Women's human rights and the human rights community', *New Political Science*, 35: 107–20.

Desai, M. (1997) '"Constructing/deconstructing", Women: Reflections from the contemporary women's movement in India', in J. Dean (ed.), *Feminism and the New Democracies: Resiting the Political*. London: Sage, pp. 110–123.

Desai, M. (2008) *Gender and the Politics of Possibilities: Rethinking Globalization*. Langham, MD: Rowman and Littlefield.

Gamson, W. (1975) *The Strategy of Social Protest*. Homewood, IL: Dorsey.

Gamson, W. (1988) 'Political discourse and collective action', *International Social Movement Research*, 1: 219–44.

Giddens, A. (2000) *The Third Way and its Critics*. Cambridge: Polity Press.

Guidry, J., Kennedy, M. and Zald, M. (2000) 'Globalizations and social movements', in J. Guidry, M. Kennedy and M. Zald (eds), *Globalizations and Social Movements: Culture, Power, and the Transnational Public Sphere*. Ann Arbor, MI: University of Michigan Press, pp. 1–22.

Habermas, J. (1987) *The Theory of Communicative Action*. Vol. 2. Cambridge: Polity Press.

Hamel, P., Lustier-Thaler, H., Nederveen-Pieterse, J. and Roseneil, S. (eds) (2001) *Globalization and Social Movements*. Basingstoke: Palgrave.

Harris, L. (2002) 'Notes from a welfare queen in the ivory tower', in G. Anzaldua and A. Keating (ed.), *This Bridge We Call Home*. New York: Routledge, pp. 372–380.

Higgins, N. (2005) 'Lessons from the indigenous: Zapatista poetics and a cultural humanism for the 21st Century', in C. Eschle and B. Maiguashca (eds), *Critical Theories, International Relations and 'The Anti-Globalisation Movement': The Politics of Global Resistance*. London: Routledge, pp. 87–102.

hooks, B. (1999) *Talking Back: Thinking Feminist Thinking Black*. Boston, MA: South End Press.

Hull, G., Bell Scott, P. and Smith, B. (eds) (2003) *But Some of Us Are Brave: All the Women are White, All the Men Are Black. Black Women's Studies*. New York: The Feminist Press at CUNY.

Hunt, S., Benford, R., and Snow, D. (1994) 'Identity fields: Framing processes and the social construction of movement identities', in E. Larana, H. Johnston and J. Gusfield (eds), *New Social Movements: From Ideology to Identities*. Philadelphia, PA: Temple University Press, pp. 185–206.

Ishay, M. (2004) *The History of Human Rights: From Ancient Times to the Globalization Era*. Berkeley, CA: University of California Press.

Jung, C. (2003) 'The politics of indigenous identity: Neoliberalism, cultural rights, and the Mexican zapatistas', *Social Research*, 70 (2): 433–62.

Juris, J. (2008) *Networking Futures: The Movements Against Corporate Globalization*. Durham, NC: Duke University Press.

Kardam, N. (2004) 'The emerging global gender equality regime from neoliberal and constructivist perspectives', *International Feminist Journal of Politics*, 6 (1): 95–109.

Keating, Analouise. 2002. "Charting Pathways, Marking Thresholds . . . A Warning. An Introduction." Pp: 6–20 in Gloria Anzaldua and Analouise Keating, edited *This Bride We Call Home: Radical Visions for Transformation*. New York: Routledge.

Keck, M. and Sikkink, K. (1998) *Activists Beyond Borders: Advocacy Networks in International Politics*. Ithaca, NY: Cornell University Press.

Khagram, S., Riker, J.V. and Sikkink, K. (eds) (2002) *Restructuring World Politics: Transnational Social Movements, Networks, and Norms*. Minneapolis, MN: University of Minnesota Press.

Klandermans, B. (1997) *The Social Psychology of Protest*. Oxford: Blackwell.

Langman, L. (2005) 'From virtual public spheres to global justice: A critical theory of internetworked social movements', *Sociological Theory*, 23 (1): 42–74.

Larana, E., Johnston, H. and Gusfield, J. (eds) (1994) *New Social Movements: From Ideology to Identities*. Philadelphia, PA: Temple University Press.

Lorde, A. (2007) *Sister Outsider: Essays and Speeches*. Berkeley, CA: Crossing Press.

Maiguashca, B. (2005) 'Globalisation and the "politics of identity": IR theory through the looking glass of women's reproductive rights activism', in C. Eschle and B. Maiguashca (eds), *Critical Theories, International Relations and 'The Anti-Globalisation Movement': The Politics of Global Resistance*. London: Routledge, pp. 117–136.

Marchand, M. (2005) 'Contesting the free trade area of the Americas: Invoking a Bolivarian geopolitical imagination to construct an alternative regional power and identity', in C. Eschle and B. Maiguashca (eds), *Critical Theories, International Relations and 'The Anti-Globalisation Movement': The Politics of Global Resistance*. London: Routledge, pp. 103–116.

McCarthy, J. and Mayer Z. (1977) 'Resource mobilization: Towards a partial theory', *American Journal of Sociology*, 82 (6): 1212–40.

McAdam, D. (1982) *Political Process and the Development of Black Insurgency, 1930–1970*. Chicago, IL: University Chicago Press.

McAdam, D. (1988) *Freedom Summer*. New York: Oxford University Press.

Mackenzie, J. (2004) 'The continuing avalanche of historical mutations: The new "new social movement"', *Social Alternatives*, 23 (1): 50–5.

Melucci, A. (1985) 'The symbolic challenge of contemporary movements', *Social Research*, 52: 789–816.

Melucci, A. (1989) *Nomads of the Present*. London: Hutchinson Radius.

Moghadam, V. (2005) *Globalizing Women: Transnational Feminist Networks*. Baltimore, MD: Johns Hopkins University Press.

Mohanty, C.T. (2003) *Feminism Across Borders: Decolonizing Theory, Practicing Solidarity*. Durham, NC: Duke University Press.

Morris, A. (1984) *The Origins of the Civil Rights Movement*. New York: Free Press.

Offe, C. (1985) 'New social movements: Challenging the boundaries of institutional politics', *Social Research*, 52: 817–68.

Perez, L. (1999) 'El desorden, nationalism and chicana/o aesthetics', in C. Kaplan, N. Alarcon, and M. Moallem (eds), *Between Woman and Nation*. Durham, NC: Duke University Press, pp. 19–46.

Polletta, F. and Jasper, J.M. (2001) 'Collective identity and social movements', *Annual Review of Sociology*, 27: 283–305.

Reagon, B. (1981) 'Coalition politics: Turning the century'. Available at: http://www.shewhostumbles.wordpress.com/2008/01/12/bernice-johnson-reagon-coalition-politics-turning-the-century/ (accessed 20 August 2008).

Sklair, L. (2002) *Globalization: Capitalism and Its Alternatives*. Oxford: Oxford University Press.

Smith, J., Chatfield, C. and Pagnucco, R. (eds) (1997) *Transnational Social Movements and Global Politics*. Syracuse, NY: Syracuse University Press.

Snow, D. (2001) 'Collective identity', in N.J. Smelser and P.B. Bates (eds), *International Encyclopedia of the Social and Behavioral Sciences*. London: Elsevier.

Snow, D. and Benford, R. (1988) 'Ideology, frame resonance and participant mobilization', *International Social Movement Research*, 1: 197–217.

Snow, D. and McAdam, D. (2000) 'Identity work process in the context of social movements', in S. Stryker, T. Owens and R. White (eds), *Self, Identity, and Social Movements*. Minneapolis, MN: University Minnesota Press.

Snow, D., Rochford Jr, E.B., Worden, S.K. and Benford, R. (1986) 'Frame alignment processes, micromobilization and movement participation', *Annual Sociological Review*, 51: 464–81.

Spivak, G. (1993) *Outside in the Teaching Machine*. New York: Routledge.

Stryker, Sheldon, Timothy Owens, and Robert White, editors. 2000. *Self, Identity, and Social Movements*. Minneapolis, MN: University Minnesota Press.

Tarrow, S. (2003) 'Global movements, complex internationalism and North–South inequality'. Paper presented at Workshop on Contentious Politics, Columbia University, 27 October 2003 and Seminar on Inequality and Social Policy, Harvard University, 17 November.

Tarrow, S. (2005) *The New Transantional Activism*. Cambridge: Cambridge University Press.

Tilly, C. (1978) *From Mobilization to Revolution*. Reading, MA: Addison Wesley.

Tilly, C. (2004) *Social Movements: 1768–2004*. New York: Paradigm.

Touraine, A. (1985) 'An introduction to the study of social movements', *Social Research*, 52: 749–87.

Whittier, Nancy. 1995. *Feminist Generations: The Persistence of the Radical Women's Movement*. Philadelphia, PA: Temple University Press.

# 22

# Migrations, Diasporas, Nations: the Re-Making of Caribbean Identities

Carole Boyce Davies and Monica Jardine

The Caribbean is already the diaspora of Africa, Europe, China, Asia, India and this diaspora diasporized itself here. (Stuart Hall, 1992).
    [... After the Door of No Return, a map was only a set of impossibilities, a set of changing locations [...] A map, then, is only a life of conversations about a forgotten list of irretrievable selves. (Dionne Brand, 2001)

To think of diaspora and identity as these categories pertain to Caribbean people is to engage simultaneously issues of migration and nation from multiple disciplinary perspectives. Writing about Caribbean identity means engaging with a series of movements (and) coming to terms with the extent to which the relatively new Caribbean nation states and the Caribbean diaspora, in combination with global economic forces, have been fundamental sites for the creation of Caribbean cultural identities. The history of the Caribbean includes the destruction of native peoples, the wretchedness of enslavement, colonialism, and resulting subsequent struggles for self-possession and independence (Beckles and Shepherd, 1999; Hart, 1998; Knight and Palmer, 1989). The decolonization of the recent period has meant not

only the attempted dissolution of colonial political systems but also a reconfiguration of cultural institutions ranging from the academy to the everyday organizations of popular culture.

   In sections one and two of this chapter, we present the idea that Caribbean identities are unique. They are constructed of multiple tectonic layers which bear the various linguistic and cultural marks of prior indigenous ethnicities as well as multiple colonizers. We show the importance of the Caribbean diaspora in illustrating this 'identity layering' and the ways in which a history of multiple dispersals complicates identity formation. We introduce current theories that have tried to grapple with the evolution of the contemporary Caribbean diaspora through expanded definitions of transnationalism and cross-border im/migration, and we outline the historio-political context within which all of these developments are set.

   In section three, we illustrate the wealth of critical cultural cross-over found in literary representations of the Caribbean and of the diaspora on Caribbean identity. Written by what British cultural theorists call 'popular voices in diasporic nation space', the discussion of these texts offers a view of identity formation that is often obscured when only political and economic histories are used to describe diasporic experience. In section four we close by returning to the persistent questions this chapter raises: What is the relationship between identity, nation and migration? How has colonial and post-colonial domination indelibly marked the identities of the colonized? And how have diasporic actors mobilized their multiple constructed and inherited identities to decolonize – their lands, cultures, political and economic structures as well as their self-perceptions and their social, global identities?

## NATIONS, DIASPORAS AND CARIBBEAN IDENTITIES

The contemporary Caribbean still carries the linguistic, cultural and geographic separations instituted by the various colonizers – French, English, Spanish, Dutch and Danish – which have continued to stand in the way of any unified Caribbean nation. Colonially-imagined terms like 'West Indies/ West Indian' (a product of a Columbian error) still resound in the linguistic self-descriptors of those subjected by that same colonial misnaming, even as they proudly claim national identities created in the wake of political independence (e.g. Jamaican, Grenadian, Antiguan). In the meantime, Caribbean institutions like CARICOM struggle for an all-inclusive regional naming, and political and economic integration beyond these various separations.

For theorists of identity like Stuart Hall (1999), because 'migration has been a constant motif of the Caribbean story,' (p. 1), and because of the related creation of diaspora, 'identities become multiple' (p. 2), as a series of identifications and re-identifications create a pageantry of shifting and mutable, though enduring, Caribbean identities. Far from being permanently fixed to some originary point (even though this has had utility for political projects), Caribbean identities allow us to understand postmodern definitions of identity as fluid, constructed and shaped by history and by contemporary economic and global forces as much as by what happens in nation/home contexts.

Transnationalism has become a loaded term, initially signifying the movement of capital across nations, but it now also reflects a series of movements, including shifting cultures and socio-economic and political practices. Even though people hold dearly to national identities, we also know that these identities were shaped by the creation of colonially influenced flags, anthems and state apparatuses at the dawning of independence. Early tentative articulations of a 'Caribbean nation' were transformed into the possibility of a 'West Indian Federation,' itself signifying a partiality, limited to the Anglophone Caribbean, which preceded the newer nation-state instantiations. Thus, when many say they became 'West Indian' in migration, they enter into a particular constructed identity.

Global migratory processes have ushered in new identities as they create parallel histories, leaving a host of remaining identities – sexual, religious, ethnic, classed and gendered – which operate tectonically. These ongoing migrations consistently create new strata of identities as their actors struggle to hold on to older ones. The result is a host of hybrid identities in and outside of Caribbean space (Espinet, 2003; Puri, 2004). For example, in the United States, Caribbean-American identity was endorsed formally in 2006. In the United Kingdom, Afro-Caribbean identity has been accepted formally within and sometimes against a larger Black British formation. Within this logic of hybridity, finding an 'original' home from which one was exiled becomes increasingly complex.

Primary diasporas carry with them the logic of forced migration and thereby the now historic original home/exile dialectic.

Subsequent movements created the 're-diasporization' characteristic of the Caribbean diaspora which is more in keeping with twentieth and twenty-first century movements. There is an economic impetus behind these migrations, and they combine both the elements of the older African and Indian diaspora created through voluntary, forced, trade or induced migrations (Boyce Davies, 2008b, pp. xxxiii–xxxiv), and the more contemporary economic migrations. These have produced the contemporary diasporic communities of Caribbean peoples living in major world nations. According to Hall:

[I]dentities thought of as settled and stable are coming to grief on the rocks of proliferation and differentiation. Across the globe, the processes of so-called free and forced migrations are changing the composition, diversifying the cultures and pluralizing the cultural identities of the older dominant nation states, the old imperial powers, and indeed of the globe itself. The unregulated flows of peoples and cultures are as broad and as unstoppable as the sponsored flows of capital and technology. (Hall, 1999, p.16)

Still, in the wake of the theorizing of postcolonialism, we need new vocabularies that describe the various encounters between the different 'worlds' ushered in by international migration.

As the international migration of different peoples rises in the global system (Sassen, 1989; World Bank, 2008), theorists categorize the contemporary migrant subject/s as either a temporary or permanent economic immigrant: a new kind of political refugee belonging to communities of exiles emanating mainly, but not exclusively from ex-colonial countries, described as transnational, cross-border immigrants – or as Stuart Hall prefers, diasporans (Hall, 1996). In a timely intervention, Clifford (1994) contended that foundationally 'diasporas usually presuppose longer distances, a separation more like exile and a constitutive taboo on return or its postponement to a remote future'. This description may no longer fit the lived experience of contemporary diasporans, who now, because of information technology, interact in real time with their home communities. This is a diaspora/nation dynamic that is characteristically mobilized around frequent visits, maintenance of transnational family and social networks, flows of remittances to families back home, and reimagining homelands that are being transformed by capitalist modernity.

In an effort to bring together older and more contemporary versions of diasporas, Safran defines diasporas as:

[E]xpatriate communities that are dispersed from an original "center" to at least two "peripheral" spaces. People who live in diasporan communities maintain a memory vision or myth about their original homeland [...] diasporans believe they are not—and perhaps cannot be—fully accepted by their host country [...] diasporans see the ancestral home as a place of return when the time is right [...] diasporans are committed to the maintenance and restoration of this homeland [...] and finally the group's consciousness and solidarity are "importantly defined" by the continuing relation with an idea of a homeland. (Safran, 1991)

For Goulbourne (2002), transnationalism has to be unpacked to identify a 'popular transnationalism' which involves groups of ordinary people engaged in transnational experiences caused by migration as they create and maintain links across nation-states. Economic transnationalism has undermined the sovereignty of nation-states, as economic activities, banking, markets and their related structures demand a set of actions which may be in direct conflict with or enhance local interests. At the political level, developments necessitating 'regional integration' produce unions like CARICOM and CARIFTA, which sometimes transcend, but can also advance, individual nation-state decisions. They demand a set of actions and activities such as freedom of movement across nation-state borders, and in the process produce cultural festivals like CARIFESTA. Thus, points of cultural connection are more available through popular cultural links like music, dance, and festivals, and grass roots political and social movements. The strengthening of cultural, economic, and political ties across nation-states assists in the maintenance of multiple transnational identities.

The complex identity structures of the Caribbean diaspora offer an important understanding of how a history of multiple dispersals can shape the historical identity of a people. The long history of Western colonial rule in the Caribbean raises a number of fundamental questions about the present scope of Caribbean dispersal to the West. Should the post-war migration of the subaltern Caribbean subject into the imperial center be constructed as a search for jobs and economic opportunities, as immigration theorists in the U.S. maintain? (Palmer, 1990). Is it possible that after centuries of colonial rule, Caribbeans became willing accomplices in the Western colonial project? Are there other compelling explanations that combine these with conscious nation-state self-advocacy? A number of important Caribbean writers like Cesaire and Fanon have written extensively about the negative psychological effects of Western colonial rule on the racial and cultural identities of Caribbean peoples. More recent analyses of the 'practice of diaspora' (Edwards, 2003) have countered the focus on the psychopathology of Caribbean colonial identity with the West, by privileging the Afro-Caribbean's construction of the Pan Africanist movement over psycho-analytic theories.

The Pan Africanist movement's intention was to bring together Black political thinkers and actors from the New World and from Africa in common opposition to Western domination of Africa and her peoples. The Garvey-led U.N.I.A movement, for example, mobilized Black working class communities in the Caribbean, the U.S. and Latin America, Africa, and Australia in the inter-war conjuncture on the basis of restoring Black pride and racial consciousness through identification with Africa as the homeland of all expatriated African peoples. In tandem with Gandhi's instructions to Indian communities in Africa and the Caribbean to affiliate themselves to the national struggles of their new homelands, Dwarka Nath adds another critical dimension to the study of diasporic linkages in the modern field of Caribbean cultural

identities in his research on the development of Indian communities in Guyana. His research indicates that like Ghandi's adherents, viewing the Indian diaspora as a network of linkages could become the basis for implanting Indian culture into the spectrum of Caribbean ethnic identities in the post colonial era (Jagan, 1967; Nath, 1950).

Although Stuart Hall only hints at the possibility that the immigration of Caribbeans to the West is best conceptualized by the hybrid term, 'colonial diaspora' (Hall, 1996), it is clear that the scale of immigration from each colonial Caribbean periphery to a Western imperial center had created diasporas as representative of the Caribbean colonial condition in the postwar era. Stuart Hall in describing himself suggests 'dislocation and disjuncture' as the formative conditions of his identity as a Caribbean diasporan subject, even as he makes a clear decision to stay and participate as a resisting subject and support the establishment of second generation diasporans.

As the U.S. removed the legal and racial barriers to immigration after the passage of the U.S. Immigration Act of 1965, Caribbean migration was drawn into the military and economic structure of regional domination implanted by the US in the Caribbean region during the interwar conjuncture (Blanchard, 1949; Mintz, 1979). By the end of the 19th century, there was already evidence that U.S. capital would establish a new regional spatial mobility of labor, as Afro-Jamaican and Afro-Barbadian cane cutters migrated to U.S.-owned plantations in Cuba and Central America, and Jamaican, Barbadian and other Caribbean workers became the main labor force on the most important engineering project of the last century: the construction of the Panama Canal. A decade later, the military boundaries of U.S. hegemony became as important as the expansion of U.S. capital in explaining the direction of Caribbean migrations. As the U.S. took over the military and naval command of the Caribbean region in World War One, 'West Indians' still under colonization left the region to fight in the

British and European war theatres. The military presence of the U.S. in the Caribbean stimulated the expansion of U.S. cultural hegemony across the region (Blanchard, 1947).

As Bovenkerk has argued, each Western imperial power viewed the post-war migration of Caribbean labor to its imperial capital as an alternative to granting political independence to the Caribbean. Before current globalizing trends in labor flows, the U.S. launched a program of 'imperial development' (Levine, 1987) that moved Puerto Rican labor to the U.S. and U.S. capitalist industrialization to Puerto Rico. U.S. capital expanded in the Caribbean as decolonization politically separated the Anglophone Caribbean region from British imperial control. These early developments in the Caribbean anticipate Sassen's (1989) well known thesis that modern immigration to the U.S. developed fastest from regions in Asia and the Caribbean that were directly subordinated to U.S. imperial power.

After World War Two, Anglophone Caribbeans migrated to Britain on untested legal/cultural and racial grounds. They immigrated as legal subjects of an empire who were, in theory at least, entitled to formal citizenship in Britain in the same way that colonial Puerto Ricans who settled in the U.S. mainland were made legal citizens of the U.S. in 1917. Stuart Hall (1996) wryly observes that the U.S. has ethnicities whereas Britain has only races. This observation recognizes that the long history of institutionalized white racial superiority in Britain, as well as in the British colonial world, was bound to explode into racial clashes between white natives and black outsiders when Caribbeans and Asians began entering Britain at the moment when British imperial hegemony was collapsing (Mercer, 1994). Within a decade of the post *Windrush* (1948) push into Britain, the British state responded to these clashes by passing the Commonwealth Immigration Act of 1962, cutting off the inflow of Black colonials to the British nation space (Jones, 1964). After 1962, Caribbean immigration entered a new phase of expansion as Canada and the U.S. dismantled their racial barriers to immigration and Britain was consolidating hers. A decade later, the new Immigration Act of 1971 invented a 'patrial' clause that would make it possible for white South Africans, New Zealanders and Australians, etc. to enter Britain on the basis of the British ancestry of a father or grandfather (Freeman, 1987).

As the structure of U.S. control over Puerto Rico established a fundamental crisis of modern Caribbean nationhood vis-á-vis the power of the U.S. in the Caribbean, a new ruptural event, the modern Cuban revolution, broke through U.S. control of Caribbean space. Cubans declared that 'we too must have a national history' (Chatterjee, 1993). Since Cuba was the largest and economically the most important country to the project of U.S. hegemony in the Caribbean, the U.S./Cuban rupture quickly escalated into the dangerous, global dimension of the Cuban missile Crisis. After the threat of U.S. invasion had been negotiated around Soviet protection of Cuba, the U.S./Cuban rupture dominated the scope of modern politics in the Caribbean in general, and immigration relations between the Caribbean and the U.S. in particular. It is in this historio-political context that we analyze the impact of the diaspora/nation dualism in shaping the discourse of modern nationalist identities in the Anglophone Caribbean. Moving away from the better examined Cuban and Puerto Rican cases, we focus on the grouping of Anglophone territories stretching from Jamaica in the northern Caribbean to Guyana on the north east coast of South America that developed ties to each other during the time of British imperial rule in the Caribbean.

After the 1965 U.S. Immigration Act opened to modern Caribbean immigration, the increase in Anglophone Caribbean immigration to the U.S. was even more dramatic than the increase in immigration flows from poorer countries into this part of the Caribbean (Pastor, 1987). Like the fictive invention of 'commonwealth' status for colonial Puerto Rico, political 'independence' for territorial units, with populations as small as 45,000 people, tied the processes of development in the fragmented Anglophone Caribbean sub-region to exporting labor to the new imperial center: the U.S. While the first generation of Anglophile political scientists opted to shut down the discourse of nationalist identity around the creation of the small ethnically fractured nation state (Ryan, 1973), a newer generation of scholars raised the imperative of 'surviving small size' through the creation of Caribbean state collaboration against U.S. power in the region (Lewis, 2002). Even so, by the end of the decade, no Anglophone Caribbean theorist had confronted the impact of U.S. hegemony in 'displacing' (Mintz, 1974) the alignments of political and cultural identities in the Caribbean. The military intervention of the U.S. in Grenada in 1983 did, however, highlight the fact that the subalternity of the Anglophone Caribbean region was fully implanted within the axis of U.S. power in the region (Lewis, 2002).

What major cultural and political developments define the struggle for identity among Anglophone Caribbean diasporans in the U.S./Caribbean nation/diaspora? Among contemporary theorists of 'Black Identities' (Waters, 1999), an older discussion of the competition between African Americans and immigrant 'West Indians' for the status of 'a model Black minority' (Kasinitz, 1992) has been reframed as economic competition between working class black Caribbean immigrants and working class African Americans in blue collar labor processes, where young white supervisors barely disguised their contempt for both groups (Waters, 1999). However, the insistence of U.S. researchers that Caribbean identities should be exclusively framed as racial identities operating within U.S. nation space has been undermined by empirical studies showing the flows of remittances from the diaspora to the Caribbean, and the frequency of visits between the Caribbean diaspora and the Caribbean nation space.

Produced after political independence, the writings of Stuart Hall and the Black British cultural studies school capture the 'interspaces' between the struggles of the ex-colonial for citizenship in Western nation space and the cultural struggle in a neo-colonial Caribbean. While Black British cultural theorists see themselves as a minority responding to racial structures of domination in British nation space, Hall (1996) also writes as an anti-imperialist thinker interrogating the claim that a pure British nationalism exits in the Caribbean that has been uncontaminated by Britain's imperial past and present influence there. Fed less by explicit political coordination, and more by technological changes in the global system (Gilroy, 1999), the struggles of British Caribbean diasporans expose the stagnancy of state political cultures in Anglophone Caribbean space that continue to uphold British monarchical institutions in the Caribbean.

How far was the case for nationhood extended in the Anglophone Caribbean before setting up a powerless, mini, neo-colonial state? This is the question that we address in the second section of this chapter through the life and work of the less studied diasporic figure C. L. R. James. James was a political intellectual who inserted himself in nationalist Caribbean politics and for whom the diaspora became an important site for the production of ideas of nationalism and socialism that were so important to the post-war decolonization movement in the Caribbean.

## IMAGINING THE NATION AND CREATING THE CITIZEN IN THE CARIBBEAN DIASPORA

Although C. L. R. James played a distinctive role in attempts to reshape the political and intellectual discourse of decolonization of the Anglophone Caribbean, both V.S. Naipaul and Edward Said trivialized James's important international role in shaping the discourse of democracy and the state in socialist transitions (Worcester, 1996). For Said, James was 'an indigent and itinerant West Indian Black Marxist historian' (Worcester, 1996). Neither seemed unaware of, nor could explain, James's enduring intellectual importance in the discourse of post colonial identity in the Caribbean (Buhle and Henry, 1992). Born in Trinidad in 1901, James migrated to Britain in 1931 ahead of the grouping of well known Caribbean artists that included Edgar Mittleholzer, Una Marson, George Lamming, Sam Selvon, V.S. Naipaul, Wilson Harris, and Beryl Gilroy, the mother of the well-known contemporary cultural theorist, Paul Gilroy. The writings of this group were destined to fill high school and university curricula in the Caribbean. Distinctive among them, James developed a powerful historical and political consciousness, becoming the Caribbean diasporan intellectual with the greatest international political reach (Worcester, 1996). He also was the one who exercised the greatest influence on post independence Caribbean political and intellectual figures like the late Pan Africanist historian, Walter Rodney (Buhle and Henry, 1992). James died in England in 1989, and at his request, it was the Oilfield Workers Trade Union (OWTU) and not the Trinidadian state who took charge of his burial in Trinidad (Worcester, 1996).

Partha Chatterjee grounds the colonial diaspora as the setting where colonial students met to 're-imagine' the nation, to (re)-interrogate Western knowledges, and to map their return to the future nation space in the decolonization epoch (Chatterjee, 1993; 2003). C. L. R. James who had migrated to Britain a decade and a half before the University of the West Indies was established in Jamaica in 1948, became revered in Britain as a theorist of international revolution (Worcester, 1996). Before he left colonial Trinidad in the early 1930s, he had already published a novel, several short stories, and his first important political text: *The Case for West Indian Self Government*, republished in Britain in 1937. Within less than a decade, C. L. R. James made a second important leap

in the production of new Caribbean knowledge when he produced the classic historical study of the Caribbean's first national revolution: *The Black Jacobins: Toussaint L'Overture and the San Domingo Revolution* (1938), written first as a play and performed on the London Stage in 1937, with Paul Robeson in the title role of the Haitian leader.

Although *Toussaint L'Overture* was set in the specific historical conditions shaping the alignment between Haiti and France at the moment of the French revolution, James was making a larger point – a 150 years before the modern Cuban revolution put the Caribbean on the modern map of post-colonial transformation, a revolution of slaves had made the case for a Caribbean nationhood. As the Caribbean nation state emerged from the contemporary revolution, the West went out of its way to ensure that the world's 'first' Black anti-colonial revolution would become the world's first post-colonial failure (Mintz, 1979). While Anglophile Caribbean intellectuals defined the political transition to independence in terms of the preservation of British Westminster state institutions (Ryan, 1973), C. L. R. James positioned the Haitian revolution as the first signifying event in the rise of a modern Caribbean nationalist consciousness, and later publications of *Toussaint L'Ouverture* reinforced the theoretical linkage between Haiti of the past and the Caribbean in the present.

By the time James returned to the Caribbean in 1958, the British were firmly in control of the apparatus of the federal West Indian state, and political leaders like Alexander Bustamante of Jamaica and Cheddi Jagan of Guyana had already built a mass rural political following that threw aside the colonial federal apparatus in favor of localized conceptions of independence. James threw himself whole heartedly into nationalist politics in Trinidad in the belief that support for a transformative nationalist movement could be built among the popular classes (James, 1962). He joined with the development economist, Sir Arthur Lewis, in a desperate bid to save the federal structure of the state in 1961. As Henry recognizes, James's interventions were conceptually organized around his view that the establishment of a regional nation state and the creation of a democratic culture were the important priorities in the Anglophone Caribbean (Buhle and Henry, 1992).

Despite James's fidelity to the nationalist cause, the political scientist Selwyn Ryan (1973) claims that James was expelled from the dominant political party in Trinidad, the People's National Movement (PNM), in 1961 at the urging of the Americans. James's position in the PNM was too dependent on his personal relationship with the Trinidadian leader, Eric Williams, and when he returned to Trinidad to try his hand at a second round of oppositional electoral politics in 1965, the Trinidadian working class had already begun its move to the US, and the two-party Westminster system had institutionalized ethnic competitive politics between Africans and Indians in Trinidad and Tobago. Arguably, the quick and comprehensive shift from British to U.S. domination of the Anglophone Caribbean caught James by surprise. On his return to Britain in 1965, James became an older teacher, no longer generationally capable of the active political involvement that had marked his earlier life (Hall, 1992; Worcester, 1996).

James was one of several prominent actors in the revolutionizing of Caribbean thought, not all of whom were men. We now turn to one woman, Claudia Jones, who played a significant role in raising awareness of the struggle for independence in the Anglophone Caribbean.

By now we know that nationalist histories in the ex-colonial world have repeatedly disappointed the expectations of women (Chatterjee, 1993). At a time when men dominated the movement from the Caribbean to Britain, women like the Jamaican born Pan Africanist, Amy Ashwood Garvey, and the well known Trinidad-born international political activist Claudia Jones became central political figures in the early Caribbean

diaspora. Jones's life tells us much of the social circumstances that led women to activist lives in the diaspora when they would not have been allowed to pursue political careers in the colonial Caribbean. Placing herself at the center of the political and cultural events of her time, Jones became a prolific journalist who followed other Black American and Black Caribbean intellectuals into the Communist Party USA (James, 1998; Turner, 2005). She became the first Black woman to be appointed to the central committee of the Communist Party. U.S.A. Imprisoned in Ellis Island for her political activities, Jones was deported under the rules of British colonial citizenship to England in 1955. Once there, she became a key diasporan political figure who brought together anti-colonial leadership in the Anglophone Caribbean with leaders of the civil rights movement in the U.S. In Britain, Jones is memorialized for her political work in the Black community in East London (Hobsbawm, 2002), launching the first Caribbean newspaper in England, and establishing the first London Carnivals. She is buried in Highgate Cemetery, significantly 'to the left of Karl Marx' (Boyce Davies, 2008a).

The place of Claudia Jones in the Caribbean diaspora (Boyce Davies, 2008a) allows us to understand how Anglophone Caribbean women entered the diasporic space and became part of U.S. political culture as thinkers and actors. These activist women threw in their lot with the Caribbean and American working classes and absolutely identified with, and participated in, social movements to end racial oppression. We also see, in the Caribbean itself, that after the fragmented state system fell under the control of men who resisted critical gender transformations (Senior, 1990), another wave of migration began in the 1960s. Jones's early presence in the Caribbean diaspora speaks to its importance as a space for the greater political and economic autonomy of Caribbean women (Gordon, 1990; Pessar, 1990).

Stuart Hall would recognize C. L. R. James as an 'extremely important political and intellectual figure who is only just beginning to be recognized for his achievements' (Hall, 1992). Both James and Jones figured prominently in the colonial diaspora before the rise of independent states in Asia, Africa and the Caribbean. Hall himself has played a prominent role in more contemporary post-colonial diasporic activist intellectual projects. Hall entered Britain in 1951 as a young Oxford scholarship student who planned to return to the Caribbean for a political career in a federal West Indian nation state (Morley and Chen, 1996). Hall's break from the political choices of earlier generations was clearly rooted in the development of global decolonization that removed any credible Caribbean claim to speak on behalf of the liberation of Africa once decolonization had established a new generation of continental African leadership. In an interview with Kuan-Hsing Chen (Morley and Chen, 1996), Hall explained that like so many of his generation, he turned away from the international communist movement after the Soviet military intervention in Hungary. Instead of returning to the Caribbean, Hall became a central actor in the establishment of the British New Left movement as co-founder and editor of *New Left Review*. He was a political actor in various British labor/new left coalitions, an academic in the modern cultural studies movement, and according to Mercer (1994), the chief intellectual architect of the modern Black British cultural movement.

Hall attributes these important shifts in his political and intellectual development to the profound political and demographic transformation of a post-colonial Britain. While the first immigrant Caribbean generation had been willing to condone the racial responses of the British state in the fading grandeur of empire (Hall, 1996), younger British born Caribbeans, some of them students of Hall's, read their claim to British citizenship as a deep historical rejection of any imputed illegitimacy to their presence in Britain: 'we are here because you were there' (Mercer, 1994). By 1985, the population of the British Caribbean diaspora had grown to 850,000, and, in keeping with

new political attitudes that accompanied this transformation, Hall contended that the Black British were not simply 'Blacks of the West'. The cultural struggle in a post-colonial Britain was 'bound to the decolonization of the minds of the peoples of the Black diaspora' (Morley and Chen, 1996).

Even as Hall was willing to conceptualize the politics of a Black British identity within a global field of decolonization, he rejected the idea of meddling in Caribbean politics as a 'nomadic outsider' (Hall, 1996), believing that political action and theoretical debate are rooted in specific national political contexts. This decision marked the end of his earlier post-war conceptions of the British Caribbean diaspora as an 'exile community'. In contrast, the refusal of ruling elites in the Anglophone Caribbean to relinquish their links with the British monarchy while Diasporan political intellectuals like Hall (1996) developed critiques of the 'ancient high culture' of British imperial rule, marks an important turning point between critical cultural action in the diaspora and the political and cultural struggle against the rigidity of neo-colonial rule in the Caribbean.

In our view, the importance of this critical cultural 'cross-over' which the Black British has provided (Gilroy, 1993) has been overlooked in contemporary U.S./Caribbean discourses on transnational Caribbean identities (Glick, Schiller and Fouron, 2001; Levitt, 2001). We will address some of this in section three by looking at literary representations of diasporic culture. While contemporary U.S./Caribbean discourses on transnational Caribbean identity have tended to emphasize the political affiliation that exists between diasporans and this or that political or cultural faction in the Caribbean, Black British cultural theorists have advanced a concept of diasporic linkage resting on a realignment of popular voices in the diaspora and nation space, many of which are articulated through, and circulated by, global communication technologies (Gilroy, 1993). The expansion of what counts as a legitimate context for diaspora/nation linkage is fundamental.

Recent recognition of Hall's work in Jamaica (Meeks, 2007) is one among many examples suggesting that forging critical diaspora/nation linkages can re-invent the scope of what it means to be Caribbean in the global space (Jones, 1964; Gilroy, 1993; Hall, 1996; Mercer, 1994).

Turning to the U.S., after almost a century of migration northward, by 2001, the legal immigrant Caribbean population living in the U.S. was estimated to have almost doubled in size to 3,074,000. This number excluded the very high percentage of children of Caribbean immigrants who are born in the U.S. (Waters, 1990), increases in the size of the post-1986 illegal Caribbean population, and the population of mainland Puerto Ricans. Caribbean immigration continued to rise mainly due to increases in Haitian, Dominican and Guyanese flows to the U.S. after 1986. By 2009, only three countries, Cuba, the Dominican Republic and Haiti (despite its level of poverty), had national populations that were larger than the size of the regional Caribbean immigrant population in the U.S. (Jardine, 2008; Mitchell, 2004).

As Robert Bach (1989) predicted, the heightened political tensions between Cuba and the U.S. which rose to the surface during the unauthorized entry of 125,000 *Marielistas* into Florida in 1980 was an early sign that the U.S. would move to militarily contain Caribbean immigration. Within months of taking office, President Reagan entered negotiations with the Cuban government to control Cuban refugee movement, and ordered the U.S. Coast Guard into the Windward Passage between Haiti and Cuba to interdict Haitians intending to land in Florida (Mc Coy, 1987). Predictably, the drive of the U.S. to contain immigration movements from the Caribbean opened new interstate tensions. Jamaican and other Anglophone Caribbean states complained of the return of deportees who had no family connections to the region, and new ship rider and drug interdiction agreements gave an additional range of interventionist powers to the U.S. in the Caribbean (Griffith, 2004). Historically,

the Cuban leadership had battled several U.S. governments over the implementation of a regional immigration policy that would balance the interests of the U.S. and the interests of Caribbean countries (Bach, 1989).

When the Cuban Coast Guard successfully intercepted a hijacked Cuban steamer that was heading for Miami on March 11th 2003, President Fidel Castro ordered the execution of the ringleaders on the grounds that they had compromised the national security interests of Cuba in a dangerous era of U.S. preemptive intervention (Mitchell, 2004). The sharpness of the Cuban state reaction registered the effects of the tense atmosphere of September 11th, rising populist opposition in the U.S. against increases in illegal and legal cross-border immigration, and a new level of politicization of U.S./Caribbean immigration boundaries. As Isbister (1996) demonstrated, the fundamental turn away from the liberal premises in the 1965 Immigration Act was made with the passage of the Immigration Control and Reform Act of 1986. In the heightened atmosphere of national fear in the U.S. created by September 11th, a decade and a half of increasingly punitive anti-immigrant legislation became part of the broader framework of national security legislation established by the passage of laws like the Patriot Act (2001) and the Enhanced Border Security and Visa Entry Reform Act (EBSV-ERA) in 2002.

While Caribbean social scientists moved to place the costs and benefits of Caribbean emigration within the discourse of 'dependence and underdevelopment', legal immigration scholar, Robert Schuck described the passage of the Illegal Immigration and Immigration Responsibility Act (IIRIRA) in the U.S. in 1996 'as the most radical reform of immigration law in decades – or perhaps ever' (Shuck, 1998). According to Schuck, the new immigration law changed the rules of enforcing immigration convictions and extended restrictions adopted earlier in 1996 in ways that even many INS officials found 'arbitrary, unfair and unadministratable' (Shuck, 1998).

IIRIRA made claiming asylum more difficult in contexts where INS officials could exclude aliens at the border summarily and without judicial review if their papers were not in order. In 1999, 99% of Haitian applications for asylum that managed to reach U.S. courts were rejected out of hand (Finkel, 2000). More draconian shifts in U.S. immigration law allowed the INS to detain removable aliens, and equated the rights of aliens who had entered illegally and who had lived in the U.S. for many years with recent arrivals who had no ties at all to the U.S.

IIRIRA expanded the category of 'aggravated felon aliens' who could be deported even if they had been long-term residents of the United States (Schuck, 1998). The impact of IIRIRA extended beyond the powers of the state against criminal offenders to fundamental transformations in new citizenship rules. Whereas first generation European, Caribbean and immigrant others had settled for the constitutionally unprotected status of 'legal permanent residents of the U.S.', IIRIRA demanded that one had to be a citizen of the United States in order to collect earned social security earnings. This compelled Caribbeans and other new immigrants to join the queue of legal citizenship.

This shift to a greater interventionist role for the state in regulating immigration flows was bound to impact the size and the culture of the Caribbean immigration movement. Caribbeans of modest means had been able to manage their entry into major cities like New York through mobilizing autonomous family immigration networks, pooling family resources, sharing housing, and committing themselves to the authority of the family over the scrutiny of the host state. The passage of IIRIRA threatened to replace this culture of relative autonomy for the immigrant family with the subjection of family networks to the power of the state from the beginning of the immigration decision process. The second important area of transformation lay in the arena of political culture. While Black Caribbeans had historically thrown their lot in with the Black civil rights struggle in the U.S.,

the rise of more punitive post-1986 immigration legislation signaled passage to a post-civil rights era of immigration interest in which Caribbeans had to search for more independent modes of mobilization for their interests in U.S. political culture (Kasinitz, 1992).

We have provided only some key themes figures and movements in the historio-political formation of the Caribbean diaspora in the space provided. In the next section we will turn to some examples of literary renderings of the connections between migration, nation, and identity.

## NARRATIVES OF IDENTITY IN DIASPORA: RETHINKING MIGRATION AND NATION

The themes of migration, nation, and the meaning of identity in diaspora have been among the most dominant in Caribbean literature for several generations of writers. The literary imagination articulates at the experiential level a consciousness of diaspora and nation affected through various forms of migration. Each generation of writers has engaged the issues of home and exile, migration and diasporic identities, and the recreation of new identities in nation-state contexts pre- and post-political independence.

We begin with Claude McKay, of Jamaican origin who ended up a member of the Harlem Renaissance writers of the 1920s. McKay most represents the conflicted nature of navigating the space of migration, moving from Jamaica to the U.S., spending time in the United Kingdom and the Soviet Union (James and McKay, 2001). Penning the famous 'If We Must Die' poem in 1919, he expressed his absolute identification with U.S. African Americans as they battle racism. By his use of 'we', he saw himself as a resisting member of a global black movement and African diasporic community. Another of McKay's sonnets, 'America' captures well the sense of duality which African American, W. E. B. Du Bois, articulated in his notion of 'double consciousness', and also the resistance to state level terror which developed as it was unleashed on Third World and native peoples.

In a similar way, the writers of the Négritude generation, influenced by the Harlem Renaissance, created poetry and prose as they dealt with the French policy of deracination, having met its racism as young students in 1930s Paris. Aimé Césaire's *Cahier d'un Retour au Pays Natal* (1939) and Leon Damas's *Pigments* (2001) evoke the struggle to reclaim and define an independent identity in the onslaught of French colonialism. Here, migration figures substantially as the condition and the reality of living in Caribbean of colonies of France. These works usher in analysis and understanding of the conditions of migration and nation as it pertains to the French Caribbean. The unfinished nature of the Francophone decolonization process persists. Martinique and Guadeloupe are still technically French colonies, though named 'departments', and experience dire economic conditions. In the 2009 economic and political climate, these countries have experienced another wave of dissatisfaction and resistance in demonstrations and riots with predictable French military suppression.

Franz Fanon captures this tension well for the post-Negritude generation. Having experienced and articulated the emotions of colonial/racial separation, he finds he is unable to see himself fully in the gaze of others: 'I wait for me in the interval just before the film starts, I wait for me' (1967, p. 140). Fanon writes of the rupture between self-identification as a black Caribbean subject and as the interpellated racial subject constructed by French racism. In his chapter 'The Fact of Blackness' in *Black Skin*, *White Masks*, the confrontation with racism propels the black migrating subject into an engagement with self and the other, particularly with that all-encompassing 'gaze' which objectifies the black subject.

For the writers of the Anglophone Caribbean colonial period, going to Europe in the 1950s meant feeling a well-documented rejection from their colonial 'motherland'. The dynamic of this failed relationship is meticulously catalogued in texts like George Lamming's *The Emigrants* (1954), Samuel Selvon's *The Lonely Londoners* (1956), and Beryl Gilroy's *Frangipani House* (1982), written in an earlier time period but published in the 1980s when black women's writing became popular. As the 1980s and 1990s generation of writers articulate, in works such as Caryl Phillips's *The Atlantic Sound* (2001), the onward migration to Britain or the United States or Canada provide the material for the shifting discourses and a parallel sense of 'unbelonging' in any location.

Edwidge Danticat's autobiographical narrative *Brother I'm Dying* (2007) is an important illustration with specific reference to the Caribbean/USA migration. *Brother I'm Dying* can be taken as emblematic of a set of interrelated issues which center the migration/nation dialectic. In this case, the troubled nation-state, Haiti, violently propels the migrating subject outward, only to have him ensnared in and destroyed by the horror side of the U.S. immigration process. The dynamic core of this memoir rests on the lives of two brothers. One is Danticat's biological father who migrates, 'in search of a better life', but ends up sick, dying from his debilitating life of overwork as a gypsy cab driver in Brooklyn, New York. His frailness and difficult death represent the negative end of this aspect of migration. Ironically, both brothers end up being buried together in exile in Queens, New York: the one who migrates as well as the one who decided to stay at home determined to make life on the island. On the positive side, the family reunion outside of impoverished urban Port au Prince, produces Edwidge Danticat, the writer herself, who has the skills and access to write this narrative for which she received the American Book Award in 2008.

Writing migration and nation has been Danticat's forte, from *Breath Eyes Memory* (1994) to *The Dew Breaker* (2005), to

*Brother, I'm Dying* (2007). In her first novel, her concern is with women, raped and destroyed by the nation, living abroad now, still carrying that pain from generation to generation. *The Dew Breaker* deals with the idea that the violence wreaked by some state actors, like *tonton macoutes*, also lives among us and maintains its place even in our communities. Thus its central metaphor is the scar that the creative artist daughter carves in a representation of her father. It is the same scar that runs through the family, the nation, and visibly on his face as the product of his violence.

In between all of this, Danticat's *The Farming of Bones* (1999) captures intra Caribbean migration between the artificial boundaries of nation-states – Dominican Republic and Haiti – originally Hispaniola, the first place that Columbus made landfall. All of that history resides here, from the destruction of the native *Tainos*, to the Haitian Revolution and the seemingly perennial struggles of Haiti and the Haitian people. In the final analysis, migration and nation in the Danticat oeuvre is a perpetual encounter with history, a past of pain and a history of oppression which exemplifies Caribbean history in different ways.

Migrating to London, as we indicated above, produced a series of displacements, generationally articulated as a struggle for a Caribbean identity in diaspora. For the writers of the first generation who migrated to the colonial centers of Europe or the U.S., there were two critical subjects: what it means to migrate as a colonial subject, and the meaning of 'home'. The role of journalists like Una Marson in developing BBC's *Caribbean Voices* (Jarret-Macauley, 1998), and Claudia Jones's *The West Indian Gazette and Afro-Asian Caribbean News* (1958–1964) gave writers of the 1950s and 1960s access and audience. In the works of these writers, the narratives are marked by the reality of racism in the colonial center and the logic of rejection, the recreation of identity in a new place, and the relationship of home to exile.

Perhaps the most substantial writing of the epic of the long migration, is Kamau Brathwaite's *The Arrivants: A New World Trilogy* (1967). In this poetic trilogy made up of 'Rights of Passage', 'Islands' and 'Masks', the poet allows himself and the reader to ramble through the various movements which have doubly and triply diasporized the Caribbean subject. In this case, migration from Africa to the 'New World' – the Americas – with all the histories of being colonized and finally becoming semi-colonized in 'independence'. Donald Hinds captures well the desolation of London for the Caribbean migrant subject in his narrative *Journey to an Illusion: The West Indian in Britain* (2001). This articulates the theory of political un/belonging, which Alrick Cambridge develops in *Where You Belong: Government and Black Culture* (1992). A novel written seven years earlier by Joan Riley was actually entitled *The Unbelonging* (1985). The essays in *Where you Belong* seem in some ways an empirical social science response to these literary/experiential articulations of placelessness. These works of fiction prepare us well for the movement between migration destinations, often tracing the outlines of the Caribbean diaspora as Derek Walcott does in *Omeros* (2002). In Walcott's earlier articulated framing of the Caribbean, 'The Sea is History', he claims the hidden histories and movements for the Caribbean diaspora which often followed the path of the global economies, creating the push and pull migratory movements.

In the U.S. context, the women who preceded Edwidge Danticat, Paule Marshall and Rosa Guy, persuasively articulate the human dimensions of these movements in the 1950s and 1960s. Marshall's *Brown Girl, Brownstones* (1959) became the signature text of its generation. Marshall is of the same generation which produced the first black congresswoman from Brooklyn, Shirley Chisholm. Chisholm subsequently ran for president of the United States, and her story is documented in *Unbought and Unbossed* (1970). Marshall's book depicts the life of the Caribbean woman migrant in New York jostling with black and white Americans for resources and above all a home. The women captured so well in the essay 'The Bronx Slave Market' (1935) which describes how white women would come and select a domestic day labourer slave auction style, are clearly Marshall's women. These women comment wryly and poetically about making a way in this 'man's country' as the next generation is urged to seek the opportunities available here. In contrast, Jamaica Kincaid's *Lucy* represents another generation. Kincaid beginning to write in the 1970s is an independent actor who can think critically about the family with which she works, as she moves from au pair girl to becoming a published writer.

The familial contexts of these novels suggest the maintaining of transnational family links facilitated through a variety of common relations, such as 'shared heritage' and common assumptions. This is confirmed in some ways by *Leave to Stay: Stories of Exile and Belonging*, by Joan Riley (who also wrote *The Unbelonging*). In *Leave to Stay* one can identify three generations now in Britain: the first generation who came with the Windrush (1948) and throughout the 1950s, the second in the post-1960s influenced by Civil Rights and Black Power discourses and not willing to accept racism, and a third generation of Afro-Caribbean children growing up and assuming the rights of the state. Riley's subtitle and the introduction to *Leave to Stay* embody a genealogy of nation/migration movement as she notes that while her grandmother lived in the 'same house all her life', just as, say, Paule Marshall's grandmother 'Da-Duh' had done, her mother's generation 'had larger ambitions and more potential to realize these in the labour shortage of the post-war boom years' (p. 1).

In bringing this section to a close, it is useful to consider Dionne Brand's *A Map to the Door of No Return: Notes to Belonging* (2001). It navigates the intersection of the two diasporas – African and Caribbean.

The metaphor of the actual 'door of no return' at the exit of the slave castles to the New World and the imaginative door that exists once one leaves and enters 're-diasporization' is Brand's way of asking the question: 'How to describe this mix of utter, hopeless pain and elation leaning against this door?' (2001, p. 41). For Brand, as her epigraph at the beginning of this chapter indicates, selves are irrecoverable, memories are lost, families and histories scatter. Forgetting in this case becomes a gift as middle passage epistemologies give way to more complicated futures with the possibility of always beginning again. The Caribbean identity that she recuperates is one which has to be ready for continuous self-invention. Brand, in this semi-autobiographical/reflective work, offers a contemplation on the meaning of migration, loss, and recovery, moving skillfully between island and metropolitan center, rural and urban, sea and land. From this angle of roading history, these movements between always seem to generate a history of loss in an unhappy tension with im/possible recovery.

## CONCLUSION: RE-MAKING CARIBBEAN IDENTITIES

In engaging the question of Caribbean identities, we have considered migration, diaspora and nation as structures of contemporary Caribbean historical realities. These structures are also rooted in the crisis of modern Caribbean nationhood which the circumstances of Cuba, Puerto Rico, Haiti, the Dominican Republic and the Dutch, Francophone and Anglophone Caribbean variously demonstrate. The nation/diaspora rupture was articulated as a struggle between Caribbean nationhood and the contemporary force of U.S. hegemony in the Caribbean region. The diaspora/nation dualisms that have arisen in the rest of the Caribbean have been lifted into this principal rupture as U.S. capital has drawn immigrants from each

Caribbean territorial space into the American nation space.

In an earlier context, the map of the modern diaspora/colonial field was grounded in the ability of the U.S. to draw Britain and the European powers into its hegemonic domination of the Caribbean. This was when the U.S. was not so much interested in eliminating colonialism from the region as in using the existing colonial fragmentation of the region for a project of its imperial development. Key elements of a nationalist discourse were folded into the British Caribbean diaspora at the moment of decolonization of the Anglophone Caribbean from British imperial control. We have used the example of C. L. R. James to demonstrate how a discourse of decolonization already required the construction of a broader nationalist defense of the case for a Caribbean modernity. Thus, native Caribbean intellectual discourses of 'development and underdevelopment' within the tense interstate field of U.S./Caribbean relations developed as a result of the inability of the U.S. to sustain an unlimited supply of labor from the Caribbean south. This analysis allows us to identify a paradox: the larger the Caribbean immigration to the north, the greater the extent to which accounts of modern Caribbean identities have grown more critical of the extreme territorial fragmentation which the present political organization of the Caribbean sustains.

An interdisciplinary engagement with nation and diaspora enables an interrogation of modern Caribbean identities, as we have attempted to do here. In 1971, the well known Barbadian historian/poet, Edward Kamau Braithwaite, published *The Development of Creole Society in Jamaica: 1770–1820*, but despite his attempt to distinguish between the concepts of 'colonial' and 'creolization', the study ended up circularly proclaiming that 'creolization, then, was a cultural process that took place within a Creole society – that is, within a tropical colonial plantation polity based on slavery' (Braithwaite, 1971). It is in his poetic work that Braithwaite was able to articulate the various movements of Caribbean

migration which left Caribbeans imprisoned in the small spaces of the territorial fragmentation of the Caribbean world, while the Caribbean subject ended up pushing his/her way into imperial capitals that rejected the legitimacy of his/her presence. Braithwaite has more recently coined a term 'tidalectics' to describe these movements which for him mirror the ebb and flow of these movements (Bobb, 1998).

Edouard Glissant, from the Francophone Caribbean, made similar assertions in his *Caribbean Discourse* as he too came to terms with 'creolization' and the definitions around *Antillianite* or Caribbeanness:

> Caribbeanness, an intellectual dream, lived at the same time in an unconscious way by our peoples, tears us free from the intolerable alternative of the need for nationalism and introduces us to the cross-cultural process that modifies but does not undermine the latter. What is the Caribbean in fact? A multiple series of relationships [...] (1989, p. 139)

Cuban theorist, Antonio Benitez Rojo, also placed identities in movement in his work *The Repeating Island* (1992). He too eschewed the logic of stable identities in a culture born of chaos: '[...] the Peoples of the Sea proliferate incessantly while differentiating themselves from one another, traveling together toward the infinite. Certain dynamics of their culture also repeat and sail through the seas of time without reaching anywhere' (1992, p. 16). He gets, here, at the polyrhythmic movement which marks their formation. And 'the impossibility of being able to assume a stable identity' (Rojo, 1992, p. 27) takes us back to Hall where we began, reinforced now from a variety of Caribbean angles and interpretations.

The writing of migration and nation has been a substantial component, as we have shown in section three, of the definition and re-definition of Caribbean identity. Moving from a discourse in which identity was largely located in India or Africa in the first diaspora's dispersal, Caribbean writers have had to redefine their understanding of Caribbean identity. With this redefinition,

Kamau Brathwaite, for instance, had to move to *Middle Passages* (1992); pluralizing 'passages' capturing the re-definition of a Caribbean diaspora identity in migration.

A number of themes become relevant. The contradictions in identification on either side of the nation/migration movement indicated a dual allegiance to family in both locations so that it is impossible at times, as Dorothea Smartt shows us in *Ship Shape* (2008), to choose one familial grouping over the other. The only choice is to embrace both aspects of these identities, adjusting to each as appropriate with the recognition that living at home may become completely untenable. Dionne Brand captures another theme in this migration/nation/identity discourse. As the epigraph at the beginning of the chapter indicates, one is left with a series of continuing definitions, especially at the level of the imagination and through language.

One would imagine that for the children of Caribbean people, in succeeding generations, either born at home or in the host country, the determination to access the benefits of the state is accompanied by all the contemporary urban conflicts that one finds in youth culture in the United States, Paris or London, Kingston, Jamaica or Port-of-Spain, Trinidad. Major urban problems brought on by glaring social inequities and treatment by policing officials and educational systems alike remain unsolved. The permanence of transnational family links, though, remains constant. At once a declaration of will to stay in the host country or home nation, perhaps to go and then to return, perhaps never to have permanently migrated and with no desire to do so, perhaps to become instead an occasional traveler, it is also an acceptance of having to deal with disjuncture, or the 'discomfort of dislocation', or the sheer joy in finding comfort in one's own small place, resisting at times, re-shaping culture to meet needs as is necessary. The Caribbean experience is in this way a fitting articulation of the current human condition.

## REFERENCES

Baker, Ella and Marvel Cooke. (1935). "The Bronx Slave market." *The Crisis* 42 (November 1935): 340, 330–331.

Beckles, H. and Shepherd, V. (eds.) (1999) *Caribbean Slavery in the Atlantic World: A Student Reader.* Kingston, Jamaica: Ian Randle.

Benitez-Rojo, A. (1992) The *Repeating Island: The Caribbean and the Postmodern Perspective.* Durham and London: Duke University Press.

Bobb, J. B. (1998) 'Kamau Brathwaite'. *Encyclopedia of the African Diaspora.* Volume 1. Oxford and Santa Barbara: ABC-CLIO, Inc.

Boyce Davies, C. (1994) *Migrations of the Subject: Black Women, Writing and Identity.* London and New York: Routledge.

Boyce Davies, C. (2008a) *Left of Karl Marx: The Political Life of Black Communist Claudia Jones.* Durham and London: Duke University Press.

Boyce Davies, C. (2008b) 'Introduction'. In C. Boyce Davies (ed.) *Encyclopedia of the African Diaspora. Origins, Experiences and Culture.* Santa Barbara and Oxford: ABC-CLIO.

Boyce Davies, C. and Jardine, M. (2003) 'Imperial Geographies and Caribbean Nationalism: At the Border between "A Dying Colonialism" and U.S. Hegemony'. *The New Centennial Review,* 3 (3), pp. 151–74.

Braithwaite, E. (1971) *The Development of Creole Society in Jamaica, 1770–1820.* Oxford: Clarendon Press.

Brathwaite, E. (1967) *The Arrivants: A New World Trilogy.* London: Oxford University Press.

Brand, D. (2001) *A Map to the Door of No Return.* Toronto, Canada: Vintage (Random House).

Cambridge, A. and Feuchtwang, S. (eds.) (1992) *Where You Belong: Government and Black Culture.* Aldershot, England: Avebury Press.

Cesaire, A. (1939) *Cahier du'un Retour au Pays Natal.* In *Aime Cesaire: The Collected Poetry.* Translated by Clayton Eshleman and Annette Smith. Berkeley and Los Angeles: University of California Press.

Chatterjee, P. (1982/1986) *Nationalist Thought and the Colonial World: A Derivative Discourse.* Minneapolis, Minnesota: University of Minnesota Press.

Chatterjee, P. (1993) *The Nation and Its Fragments: Colonial and Post Colonial Histories.* Princeton, NJ: Princeton University Press.

Chisholm, S. (1970) *Unbought and Unbossed.* Houghton: Mifflin.

Clifford, J. (1994) 'Diasporas'. *Cultural Anthropology*, 9 (3), pp.302–38.

Damas, L-G. (2001) *Pigments/Nevralgies*. Paris: Presence Africaine.

Danticat, E. (1994) *Breath, Eyes, Memory*. New York and London: Random House Vintage.

Danticat, E. (1999) *The Farming of Bones*. London and New York: Penguin.

Danticat, E. (2005) *The Dew Breaker*. London and New York: Vintage.

Danticat, E. (2007) *Brother I'm Dying*. New York: Alfred A. Knopf.

Edwards, B. H. (2003) *The Practice of Diaspora: Literature, Translation and the Rise of Black Internationalism*. Cambridge: Harvard University Press.

Espinet, R. (2003) *The Swinging Bridge*. Canada: Harper Perennial.

Fanon, F. (1967) *Black Skins, White Masks*. New York: Grove Press.

Finkel M. (2000) 'America, or Death: At Sea with 44 Haitians Willing to Get Here at Any Cost'. *New York Times Magazine*, June 18th.

Gilroy, B. (1982) *Frangipani House*. London: Heinemann.

Gilroy, B. (1976/1994) *Black Teacher*. Bogle L'Ouverture Press.

Gilroy, P. (1993) *The Black Atlantic. Modernity and Double Consciousness*. Cambridge, MA: Harvard University Press.

Glick Schiller, N. and Fouron, G. E. (2001) *George Woke up Laughing: Long Dialism the Search for Home*. Raleigh Durham: Duke University Press.

Glissant, E. (1989) *Caribbean Discourse*. Charlottesville: University Press of Virginia.

Griffith, I. L. (2004) *Caribbean Security in the Age of Terror: Challenge and Change*. Mona, Jamaica: Ian Randle.

Gordon, M. (1990) 'Dependents or Independent Workers? The Status of Caribbean Immigrant Women in the United States'. In Ransford Palmer ed. *Search of a Better Life. Perspectives on Migration from the Caribbean*. New York: Praeger Publishers: 115–137.

Goulbourne, H. (2002) *Caribbean Transnational Experience*. London: Pluto Press.

Hall, S. (1992) 'Cultural Identity and Cinematic Representation'. In M. Cham (ed.) *Ex-Iles: Essays on Caribbean Cinema*. Trenton, NJ: Africa World Press.

Hall, S. (1999) 'Thinking the Diaspora: Home-Thoughts from Abroad'. *Small Axe*, 6 September, pp. 1–18.

Hall, S. (2006) 'Cultural Identity and Diaspora'. In J. Evans Braziel and A. Mannur (eds.) *Theorizing Diaspora*. Malden, MA. and Oxford: Blackwell.

Hall, S. (2007) 'Thinking about Thinking'. Afterword to B. Meeks (ed.) *Caribbean Reasonings. Culture, Politics, Race and Diaspora. The Thought of Stuart Hall*. Kingston, Jamaica: Ian Randle.

Hart, R. (1998) *From Occupation to Independence: A Short History of the Peoples of the English-Speaking Caribbean Region*. London and Jamaica: Pluto Press and University of the West Indies Canoe Press.

Henry, P. and Buhle, P. (1996) *C.L.R. James's Caribbean*. Durham: Duke University Press.

Hinds, D. (2001) *Journey to an Illusion: The West Indian in Britain*. London: Bogle L'Ouverture Press.

Hobsbawm, E. (2000) *Interesting Times. A Twentieth Century Life*. London: Allen Lane/Penguin.

Isbister, J. (2006) *Promises Not Kept: Poverty and The Betrayal of Third World Development*. Bloomfield, CT: Kumarian Press.

Jagan, C. (1967) *The West on Trial*. International Pub.

James, C.L.R. (1963) *The Black Jacobins*: New York: Vintage Books.

James, W. (1998) *Holding Aloft the Banner of Ethiopia: Caribbean Radicalism in EarlyTwentieth–Century America*. London and New York: Verso.

James, W. and Harris, C. (1993) *Inside Babylon: The Caribbean Diaspora in Britain*. London: Verso.

James W. and McKay, C. (2001) *A Fierce Hatred of Injustice: Claude McKay's Jamaican Poetry of Rebellion*. London: Verso.

Jarret-Macauley, Delia. (1998) *The Life of Una Marson, 1905–1965*. Manchester, UK: Manchester University Press.

Jones, C. (1964) 'The Caribbean Community in Britain'. *Freedomways*, (Summer), pp. 340–57.

Kasinitz, P. (1992) *Caribbean New York. Black Immigrants and the Politics of Race*. Ithaca, New York: Cornell University Press.

Kincaid, J. (2002) *Lucy. A Novel*. New York: Farrar, Straus and Giroux.

Knight, F. and Palmer, C. A. (1989) *The Modern Caribbean*. Chapel Hill and London: University of North Carolina Press.

Lamming, G. (1954) *The Emigrants*. London: M. Joseph. Reprinted, London: Allison and Busby, (1980).

Lamming, G. (1960) *The Pleasures of Exile*. London: M. Joseph, reprinted London: Allison & Busby, (1984).

Levitt, P. (2001) *The Transnational Villagers*. Berkeley University Press.

Lewis, P. (2002) *Surviving Small Size: Regional Integration in Caribbean Ministates*. Mona, Jamaica: University of the West Indies Press.

Lewis, R. C. (1998) *Walter Rodney's Intellectual and Political Thought.* Wayne State University Press, (1998).

Marshall, P. (1959) *Brown Girl Brownstones.* New York: The Feminist Press, (1981).

Marshall, P. (2009) *Triangular Road.* New York: Basic Civitas Books.

Meeks, B. Ed. (2007) *Caribbean Reasonings. Culture, Politics, Race and Diaspora. The Thought of Stuart Hall.* Kingston, Jamaica: Ian Randle.

Mercer, K. (1994) *Welcome to the Jungle. New Positions in Black Cultural Studies.* London and New York: Routledge.

Mintz, S. and Price S. (1985) *Caribbean Contours.* Baltimore, MD: Johns Hopkins University Press.

Mintz, S. W. (1974) *Caribbean Transformations.* Johns Hopkins.

Morley, D. and Chen, K-H. (1996) Introduction to *Stuart Hall: Critical Dialogues in Cultural Studies.* London and New York: Routledge.

Nath, D. (1950) *A History of Indians in British Guiana.* Thomas Nelson and Sons.

Ong, A. (1999) *Flexible Citizenship: The Cultural Logic of Transnationality.* Durham and London: Duke University Press.

Phillips, C. (2001) *The Atlantic Sound.* New York: Vintage.

Pessar, P. (1997) *Caribbean Circuits. New Directions in the Study of Caribbean Migration.* New York: Center for Migration Studies.

Puri, S. (2004) *The Caribbean Postcolonial: Social Equality, Post-Nationalism, and Cultural Hybridity.* Basingstoke: Palgrave, Macmillan.

Riley, J. (1985/1993) *The Unbelonging.* London: Trafalgar Square Publishing.

Riley, J and Wood, B. (eds.) (1996) *Leave to Stay. Stories of Exile and Belonging.* London: Virago.

Ryan, S. D. (1972) *Race and Nationalism in Trinidad and Tobago.* Toronto: University of Toronto Press.

Sassen, S. (1988) *The Mobility of Capital and Labor: A Study in International Investment and Labor Flows.* New York: Cambridge University Press.

Sasssen, S. (1992) *The Global City.* New York and London: Princeton University Press.

Schuck, R. 'Law and the Study of Migration'. In Brettell and Hollifield, *Migration Theory:* op cit: 187–204.

Senior, O. (1991) *Working Miracles: Women's Lives in the English-Speaking Caribbean.* Bloomington: Indiana University Press.

Selvon, S. (1956) *The Lonely Londoners.* London: Penguin, (2006).

Scott, D. (1999) *Refashioning Futures.* Princeton, NJ: Princeton University Press.

Smartt, D. (2008) *Ship Shape.* Leeds: Peepal Tree Press.

Turner, J. M. (2005) *Caribbean Crusaders and the Harlem Renaissance.* Urbana: University of Illinois Press.

Truillot, M-R. (2002) 'North Atlantic Universals: Analytical Fictions, 1492–1945' *The South Atlantic Quarterly*, 101 (4), pp. 839–57.

Walcott, D. (2002) *Omeros.* New York: Faber and Faber.

Watkins-Owens, I. (1996) *Blood Relations: Caribbean Immigrants and the Harlem Community, 1900–1930.* Bloomington, Indiana: Indiana University Press.

Waters, M. C. (2001) *Black Identities: West Indian Immigrant Dreams and American Realities.* Cambridge, MA: Harvard University Press

Worcester, K. (1996) *C.L.R. James. A Political Biography.* Albany: SUNY Press.

# 23

# Identities, Groups and Communities: The Case of Northern Ireland

Katharina Schmid, Miles Hewstone, Nicole Tausch,
Richard Jenkins, Joanne Hughes and Ed Cairns

Over and above the historical, political, and economic facets of ethno-political conflicts there exist distinct psychological and social components which underlie and can perpetuate intergroup tensions even after the initial causes of conflict have subsided (see Deutsch's [1973] notion of 'destructive conflicts' that are likely to continue after initiating causes have become irrelevant). Central to social-psychological explanations of such conflict is the notion that people characterize their social world into 'us' and 'them' and that these group identities may afford specific meaning to individuals. Social identification processes contribute uniquely to ethno-political conflicts, in that the intractability of such conflict is often mirrored in the contested group identities, which may become as important as contested territory, power or resources (Kelman, 2001).

Our primary aim in this chapter is to review pertinent social-scientific contributions that have aided understanding of the nature, extent and processes of social identification in one specific case of intergroup conflict, Northern Ireland. We will focus principally on the role of self-categorization and social identification processes in this context, but we will also discuss the broader identity-based issues at stake. Typically, the overarching aim of researchers studying the role of social identity and group-based processes in contexts of ethno-political conflict is to promote understanding and uncover ways in which intergroup tensions may be alleviated and positive intergroup relations fostered. Consequently, we also discuss the extent to which group-based processes are involved in shaping outgroup attitudes (for reasons of space, we exclude our related work on intergroup forgiveness and trust in Northern Ireland; for a review see Hewstone et al. [2008]). This chapter unfolds in five parts. First, we briefly describe the historical, political and social background to the Northern Ireland conflict. Second, we portray the nature of intragroup perceptions, that is self-categorization and social identification processes in Northern Ireland. Here we draw on research which focused explicitly on the interplay between the religious and national categories in the Northern Irish political and social arena. In addition, we discuss the critical role of category salience in shaping self-description and identification by reviewing some of the literature that has examined the situational variability of group identities in Northern Ireland (Waddell and Cairns, 1986). Third, we shift our focus to an exploration of intergroup phenomena, focusing on how self-categorization and social-identification processes contribute to shaping outgroup attitudes. In particular, we review how the study of multiple categories has aided understanding not only of the complexity of categorization per se, but also of the positive consequences of holding more complex and differentiated patterns of categorization and identification for intergroup relations. Such contributions include research into both experimentally-manipulated and naturally-occurring patterns of crossed categorization (Crisp et al., 2001; for a review see Crisp and Hewstone, 1999), social identity complexity (Roccas and Brewer, 2002), and the effects of identifying along a superordinate category or of endorsing both a subgroup and a superordinate category (see e.g. Gaertner and Dovidio, 2000).

Fourth, we move to an exploration of more general group-based processes and the consequences of these for outgroup attitudes. We emphasize that intergroup conflict typically entails some form of threat experienced by the respective parties to the conflict. Importantly, such threats need not only pertain to tangible, real-life issues but may also be of a more symbolic nature (Stephan and Stephan, 2000; Tausch et al., 2007), or may surround group identity per se, such as a threat to positive distinctiveness (for a review see Jetten and Spears, 2003). We also delineate how engaging in cross-group contact may have positive implications for group relations (for reviews see Brown and Hewstone, 2005; Hewstone and Brown, 1986). Fifth, we consider intra– and intergroup processes that go beyond religious and/or national categorization, by discussing the concept of social capital (e.g. Putnam, 2000), and the consequences of social capital in this context. We end by drawing general conclusions and making recommendations and suggestions for future work.

## HISTORICAL BACKGROUND

The conflict in Northern Ireland (colloquially known as 'The Troubles') is basically a conflict between those who wish to see Northern Ireland united with the Republic of Ireland (mainly Catholics), and those who want Northern Ireland to remain part of the UK (mainly Protestants; Moxon-Browne [1991]). The conflict itself dates back hundreds of years, yet escalated in the 1960s when conflict between the Stormont government and the local civil rights movement triggered a sustained period of violence, resulting in the deployment of British troops. Since then, Northern Ireland has witnessed periods of intense political violence, resulting in over 3,500 deaths, over 35,000 injuries, 16,000 people charged with terrorist offences, 34,000 shootings and 14,000 bombings (see, e.g. Fay et al., 1999). A series of ceasefires were negotiated in the 1990s, culminating in the 'Belfast' or 'Good Friday' Agreement and an attempt to establish a devolved government, embracing all major political parties. Although numerous attempts at installing this power-sharing government have faltered, it is once again in operation at the time of writing. Despite continuing efforts at peace-building, paramilitary violence continues, especially in so-called 'interface' areas, where Catholic and Protestant neighbourhoods are adjacent to each other (Jarman, 2004). As a consequence of both historical conflict and contemporary violence, Northern Irish society remains deeply segregated at many levels.

In fact it is the extent of segregation that helps explain many aspects of the conflict, above all its perpetuation (Cairns and Hewstone, 2002; Knox and Hughes, 1994; Murtagh, 2002; Whyte, 1990). Types of segregation include residential segregation (Poole and Doherty, 1996), personal and marital segregation (Gallagher and Dunn, 1991), educational segregation (McClenahan et al., 1996), and segregation at sport, work or leisure (Niens et al., 2003). Residential segregation between Catholics and Protestants has been in place since long before the outbreak of the Troubles (Smyth, 1995), but conflict has strengthened segregation. Ten years after the peace agreement was signed, segregated living is still commonplace and there appears to be an increased preference for segregated living in recent years (Robinson, 2003). Generally there is a strong covariance between levels of segregation and social class, with relatively disadvantaged working-class areas significantly more likely to be segregated than affluent middle-class areas (Shirlow, 2001).

Personal segregation also still exists, with the vast majority of people reporting that they have more friends from their own group than the outgroup, and indeed many have no outgroup friends at all (see Cairns and Hewstone, 2002). Similarly, mixed marriages or relationships still only account for a small proportion of all such relationships (estimated at 5–8 per cent). Educational segregation at primary and secondary level also persists (Cairns and Hewstone, 2002), despite generally widespread support for integrated schooling (see Hughes and Carmichael, 1998). There are a small number of integrated schools, but these only educate a small minority of the total pupil population (McGlynn et al., 2004). All these forms of segregation play a role in perpetuating conflict, not least by fostering mutual distrust, ignorance and suspicion (Gallagher, 1995).

In our recent work we have begun to focus extensively on the nature and consequences of segregation, comparing religiously mixed and segregated areas in Belfast and in several smaller Northern Irish towns. We make particular reference to this research throughout this chapter, to elucidate the effects of living in segregated versus mixed areas on self-categorization, social identification and general group-based processes in polarized societies.

## THE NATURE OF INTRAGROUP PERCEPTION: SELF-CATEGORIZATION AND SOCIAL IDENTIFICATION IN NORTHERN IRELAND

Social-scientific explanations of intergroup conflict recognize that individuals tend to categorize their social world into ingroups ('us') and outgroups ('them'), and that identification with social groups, along with the perceived functional relations between the ingroup and the outgroup, shapes attitudes and behaviours in intergroup contexts, and determines the nature of intergroup relations (see, e.g. Tausch et al., in press). In contexts of ethno-political conflict an understanding of *intra*group processes, that is, self-categorization and social-identification processes with reference to one's own membership group or the ingroup, is a prerequisite for understanding the nature of *inter*group processes, that is, the group-based processes involved in intergroup perception and behaviour.

Central to the social identity approach, encompassing both Social Identity Theory (SIT) (Tajfel, 1978; Tajfel and Turner, 1979) and Self-categorization Theory (SCT) (Turner et al., 1987), is the notion that there exists a distinction between personal and social identity (for a detailed description of SIT and SCT, see Reicher, Spears and Haslam, Chapter 2 this volume).[1] Moreover, self-description and behaviour is said to vary along a continuum from purely personal to purely social properties. Thus, individuals may come to think, act or even feel in terms of their social group memberships, often even to the exclusion of their personal identity (see e.g. Haslam et al., 1998).

The conflict in Northern Ireland is often described as a conflict between the Catholic and Protestant communities; hence the typical focal categories are those surrounding ethno-religious group membership. The groups and the corresponding identity are more accurately labelled 'ethno-religious' than 'religious' because Catholic–Protestant categorization in Northern Ireland does not only denote religious motivation or sentiment, but also holds ethnic and political connotations (Hewstone et al., 2005; Jenkins, 2008). Research has shown that the vast majority of people readily identity with being Catholic or Protestant (Cairns and Mercer, 1984), and that most children in Northern Ireland are able to categorize along the religious dimension by the age of nine (Cairns, 1987). Importantly, the religious categories are starkly divided, and it has been argued that there are few social categories in Northern Ireland that cross-cut this religious divide (Cairns and Mercer, 1984).

However, there also exists a range of national (British, Irish and more recently, Northern Irish) and political (Nationalist or Unionist) categories that are central to the conflict and that are also commonly endorsed as self-descriptive in this context. For example, Trew and Benson (1996) found that when individuals were offered a choice of religious, national and political categories the national identities, British, Irish and Northern Irish, were generally chosen over religious or political identities. National identities were also rated as more important to individuals than were religious categories (Trew and Benson, 1996). We observed a similar pattern in one of our recent studies (Schmid et al., 2009a) where respondents reported higher levels of identification with their national than their religious identities. Thus categorization processes in Northern Ireland are more complex than often initially assumed, in that multiple categories are central to intergroup conflict in Northern Ireland.

## Multiple categorization in Northern Ireland: Religious and national categorization

It is self-evident that individuals typically belong to many social groups and thus hold multiple social identities (see, e.g. Deaux et al., 1995). Moreover, the meaning subjectively ascribed to these different identities can vary across individuals and groups, and social category memberships can and often

do combine in different ways across varying contexts. Nonetheless, in Northern Ireland, where religious and national categories are both central to the conflict, the majority of Catholics in Northern Ireland have tended to describe their national identity as Irish, whereas Protestants have primarily chosen the British identity (McClenahan et al., 1991; Moxon-Browne, 1983, 1991; Rose, 1971; Trew, 1996). Noteworthy here is that categories are often correlated, with one category being functionally dominant over other associated categories (Eurich-Fulcer and Schofield, 1995).

At first glance, there appears to be a general divide between and essential unity among Catholic or Irish, on the one hand, and Protestant or British identities, on the other (Trew and Benson, 1996; Waddell and Cairns, 1991). However, it should be kept in mind that a sizeable minority of the Northern Irish population typically cross-cuts this more traditional pattern of religious and national categorization, instead claiming more unexpected category combinations, such as 'Catholic' and 'British' or 'Protestant' and 'Irish' (see, e.g. Fahey et al., 2005; Muldoon et al., 2005). Fahey et al. (2005) call these patterns of combined categorization 'incongruent' compared to more traditional, 'congruent' identity combinations (British-Protestant or Irish-Catholic). We have also observed such patterns of naturally occurring, cross-cutting religious and national categorization in our own recent work in this context (Schmid et al., 2009c). We found, on average, about seven per cent of Catholics self-categorizing as British, and about 5 per cent of Protestants self-categorizing as Irish in a population sample in Belfast ($N = 984$), and as many as 20 per cent of Catholics self-categorizing as British, yet only about one per cent of Protestants self-categorizing as Irish in a sample drawn from seven smaller towns ($N = 2000$). The number of Catholics self-categorizing as British tends to outweigh the number of Protestants self-categorizing as Irish. This may be because most people in Northern Ireland are legally British citizens (although Irish citizenship may be claimed, either as an alternative, or in addition, to British citizenship). Of interest is that respondents living in mixed neighbourhoods in Northern Ireland were more likely to choose these unexpected categorization patterns than individuals living in segregated areas.

In addition, a substantial number of Northern Irish residents now self-categorize as neither British nor Irish, but have started to embrace an emergent form of self-description, as 'Northern Irish'. Significantly, this identity can and has been embraced by both sides of the religious divide, Catholics and Protestants equally. This has been regarded by many commentators as a positive development which potentially defines a move towards transcending some existing group boundaries. This optimism may, however, be misplaced. Waddell and Cairns (1991) found that, when offering participants a number of forced choice national category combinations, participants generally only chose to describe themselves as Northern Irish when given a forced choice between two options, neither of which would have been their preferred choice. Thus, when Protestants were asked to choose between Irish or Northern Irish, they chose the latter; similarly, Catholics tended to describe themselves as Northern Irish only when offered a choice between that and 'British'.

In our most recent work we offered participants the option of self-categorizing as British, Irish or Northern Irish, and in our survey conducted in a number of smaller Northern Irish towns about 23 per cent of the overall sample self-categorized as Northern Irish, approximately 59 per cent of whom were Catholics and 41 per cent Protestants. An even higher per centage of people self-categorizing as Northern Irish (approximately 29 per cent) was observed in the Belfast sample; here substantially more Protestants (approximately 57 per cent) than Catholics (approximately 43 per cent) chose to do so. In both cases the number of respondents choosing the Northern Irish identity was higher in mixed than in segregated areas. A similar effect can be traced in the data from annual 'Northern Irish Life and Times' surveys of representative samples of adults (2003–2005) on which we conducted secondary analyses. We found that, overall, somewhat more respondents adopted a Northern Irish identity in mixed than segregated areas (30.6 per cent versus 23 per cent). This difference was, however, primarily witnessed for Catholics: almost twice as many Catholics adopted this identity in mixed than segregated areas (25.3 per cent versus 13.4 per cent), whereas the proportion of Protestants choosing this identity was almost identical in both types of area (37 per cent).

## The role of category salience

According to self-categorization theory (Turner et al., 1987) individuals will only categorize in terms of, and identify with, a collective category when group membership is salient[2] (Turner, 1999; Turner et al., 1987). This is also indicated by anthropological and sociological analyses of ethnicity (Jenkins, 2008). Although it is often assumed that in situations of conflict the social categories relevant to the conflict are chronically salient, research in Northern Ireland suggests that this is not always the case and that categorization is also context specific (see, e.g. Cassidy and Trew, 1998, 2004).

A key psychological study highlighting the context-dependence of social identity in Northern Ireland was carried out by Waddell and Cairns (1986). They presented participants with a range of scenarios (e.g. 'being amongst English/Irish people', 'living in part of Ireland/UK') and asked them to rate the extent to which they felt more British or more Irish, on a continuum from 'very British' to 'very Irish'. Results showed that, depending on the given situation, individuals' perceptions of 'Britishness' or 'Irishness' were more or less pronounced. For example, when presented with the scenario of 'watching Ireland play rugby' Protestants regarded themselves as slightly less British but more Irish (it should be noted that there are separate association football teams for Northern Ireland and the Republic of Ireland, but the Ireland rugby union team contains players from Northern Ireland and the Republic). Although the essential divide between the British and Irish categories remained (with Catholics self-categorizing as more Irish, and Protestants self-categorizing as more British, on the continuum), this research highlighted the context dependence of categorization and identification processes in Northern Ireland.

A recent, similar study (Schmid et al. 2009a) offered us the opportunity to add an additional identity category, Northern Irish (Waddell and Cairns (1986) reasonably enough, did not allow for this response option, because few respondents would have endorsed it at the time of their study). We asked respondents to complete three ratings for each scenario; they were asked to rate the degree to which they felt British, Irish *and* Northern Irish (order was counterbalanced) across 20 different imaginary scenarios, similar to those used by Waddell and Cairns (1986). Principal components analysis of these scenarios revealed that they were grouped into 'Irish' and 'British' situation types (e.g. 'living in part of Ireland', 'seeing the Irish Tricolour displayed', 'living in part of the UK' and 'seeing the Union Jack displayed in an area', respectively). We could thus compare respondents' self-ratings of the extent to which they would feel Irish, British and Northern Irish in either type of situations. As expected, respondents who had initially self-categorized as British or Irish generally reported feeling more British or Irish in 'British' and 'Irish' situation types, respectively. However, we observed variability in the extent to which respondents felt British or Irish. Specifically, Irish respondents reported feeling less Irish in 'British' than in 'Irish' situation types, and British respondents reported feeling less British in 'Irish' than in 'British' situation types. Interestingly, respondents who self-categorized as Northern Irish generally felt more Northern

Irish in 'British' than 'Irish' situation types, suggesting that the Northern Irish identity may be more akin to the British identity. However, it should be emphasized that the emergence of a Northern Irish identity is relatively recent and may be especially susceptible to future changes in the political and social context in Northern Ireland.

What is striking about this general set of findings is the fact that individuals reported variability in their identification processes, even for hypothetical situations, and even for identities they do not necessarily endorse as self-descriptive. These findings are even more notable given the protracted nature of negative intergroup relations in this situation of intergroup conflict, which one might have expected would lead to more consistent and exclusive self-categorization and identification patterns across situations.

## THE LINK BETWEEN INTRA– AND INTERGROUP PERCEPTION: CONSEQUENCES FOR OUTGROUP ATTITUDES

Much early research on social identity processes in Northern Ireland focused on intragroup processes, mainly examining self-categorization processes with respect to religion, nation and politics. Considerably less research has examined the nature of intergroup processes in this context, despite it being a long-established fact that social categorization and identification processes are central to intergroup conflict (see e.g. Cairns, 1982; Tausch et al., 2008). However, this gap between research into intra- and intergroup processes in the Northern Irish context has been bridged over the past few years, partly due to our own programme of research. Much of this research has examined the consequences of social identity as well as general group-based processes on both ingroup bias (i.e. the tendency to consistently evaluate the ingroup more favourably than the comparative outgroup) and general outgroup attitudes. One question that can be asked here is whether there exists a relationship between social identification and ingroup bias. It has been argued that identification with the ingroup should be positively related to intergroup bias (Hinkle and Brown, 1990; Turner and Reynolds, 2001), based on the assumption that identification determines intergroup attitudes, and not vice versa (Jetten et al., 1997). Although cross-sectional, correlational data does not provide strong support for this assumption (Hinkle and Brown, 1990; Mullen et al., 1992), experimental data does (Branscombe and Wann, 1994; Perreault and Bourhis, 1999).

In Northern Ireland, Cairns et al. (2006) carried out secondary analyses of 'Northern Ireland Life and Times' (2000–2001) data and showed that individuals who identified highly with their ethno-religious group tended to display more ingroup bias than individuals for whom their religious identity was less important,[3] a finding we consistently observe in our own cross-sectional data in this context. However, we need to keep in mind that ingroup favouritism cannot be equated with outgroup derogation (Brewer, 1999), to the extent that valuing one's own group highly, or more highly than a respective outgroup, does not automatically lead to prejudice or discrimination. This is of particular importance in the context of social-psychological and social-scientific research that tends to focus on the milder forms of intergroup prejudice, such as ingroup bias. In general, ingroup identification is more readily thought of as a moderator of the relationships between group-based processes and outgroup attitudes (we discuss this point at a later stage in this chapter).

Where a relationship between social identity and outgroup attitudes becomes more meaningful, and thus more interesting, is in the context of multiple categorization processes. In the following section we review research that has sought to understand how multiple categorization processes are involved in shaping outgroup attitudes and elucidating how negative intergroup relations may be alleviated in this, and other, contexts of ethno-political conflict when multiple rather than single categories are considered.

## Multiple categorization and outgroup attitudes

It has been argued that more complex societies, where loyalty structures cut across groups (e.g. through intermarriage), hold reduced potential for intergroup conflict compared with more polarized societies, characterized by a more singular hierarchical structure (see Brewer and Gaertner, 2001). Analogously it is assumed that the less individuals depend on a single ingroup to satisfy the psychological need of 'belonging' (see Brewer, 1993), the lower the potential for polarizing loyalties along any specific ingroup category and the lower the likelihood of intergroup tensions. Significant advances have been made in recent years in our understanding of multiple categorization processes and their role in intergroup perception.

Theoretical and empirical examinations of, for example, cross-cutting categories, or of categorizing along a superordinate versus a subordinate ingroup, have highlighted that multiple group identities can become salient at the same time, to the extent that individuals are able to attend to and process information along multiple categories simultaneously. Moreover, self-definition along multiple social categories more often than not is associated with more positive evaluation of outgroups (Crisp and Hewstone, 2000; Crisp et al., 2001; see also Brewer et al., 1987; Crisp and Hewstone, 2007, for a detailed review). The study of multiple categorization processes is also useful in the Northern Ireland context, given that categorization surrounding the religious and national categories tends to be much more complex than at first assumed. In the following sections we review research into crossed-categorization phenomena, naturally occurring patterns of crossed-categorization, common-ingroup identification processes and social identity complexity phenomena, all of which have proved fruitful to understanding not only the complexity of categorization in this context but also in highlighting the potential for fostering positive intergroup relations in this and other contexts of ethnopolitical conflict.

## Crossed categorization

The crossed categorization approach centres on the premise that individuals are able to process information along multiple category dimensions, and thus may perceive others as 'ingroup' or 'outgroup' members in a more differentiated and inclusive manner than implied by the single 'ingroup' versus 'outgroup' dichotomy (Brown and Turner, 1979; Deschamps and Doise, 1978; see also Brewer, 2000). To illustrate, if two horizontal categories are crossed, individuals may perceive others in terms of these multiple category combinations, that is, as *double ingroup members* (ingroup membership is fulfilled on both categories), *double outgroup members* (ingroup membership is not fulfilled on either of the two categories) or as members of one of two *partial* or *mixed* ingroup/ outgroup categories (ingroup membership fulfilled on one of the categories only). De-emphasizing a single polarized identity category is believed to lower the salience of any one category dimension and may therefore reduce intergroup bias and increase positive outgroup perception, as has been demonstrated using both artificial and real groups (Crisp and Hewstone, 1999; see Migdal et al., 1998; Urban and Miller, 1998, for meta-analytic reviews). However, bias reduction may only occur if certain moderating conditions are met (see Urban and Miller, 1998, for an overview of moderators).

Crossed-categorization processes have been studied experimentally in the Northern Irish context. Crisp et al. (2001) presented Catholic and Protestant student participants at a Northern Irish university with a fictitious newspaper article that included information on a person whose group membership was made salient on two categories, religion and gender, thus allowing for four crossed-category combinations (Catholic-male, Catholic-female, Protestant-female and Protestant-male). Later they gave them a surprise recall test concerning the information they had been presented with. Results demonstrated that religion influenced what was being remembered, but only in combination with gender. Recall was greater if the story character was a religion ingroup member, but only if the character also happened to be an ingroup member of the same sex. These findings highlight that even in a context as intractable as Northern Ireland, individuals are able to process information on outgroup members' multiple group identities, a phenomenon that can have important implications for intergroup relations. Important to keep in mind is that the crossed-categorization approach focuses on the perceived category memberships of comparative others and the extent to which these are functionally related to the ingroup. Self-chosen categorization patterns are not attended to in this model. The extent to which multiple self-categorization processes have consequences for intergroup relations in this, and other contexts, is discussed in the theoretical approaches and empirical findings below.

## Naturally occurring patterns of categorization

Much research into crossed-categorization phenomena rests upon experimental manipulations; considerably less research has focused on naturally-occurring patterns of crossed categorization or unexpected category combinations and the consequences of such self-descriptive categorization patterns. An exception to this is a recent line of research examining the effects of encountering familiar or unfamiliar category conjunctions on social perception (Hutter and Crisp, 2005, 2006). As mentioned above, a substantial minority of the Northern Irish population chooses what can be termed unexpected combinations of categories, self-categorizing as, for example, Catholic-British or Protestant-Irish. We have begun to examine these categorization patterns in our recent work (Schmid et al., 2009c) and have found that respondents choosing such unexpected or incongruent category combinations typically display significantly lower levels of ingroup bias than individuals endorsing the more commonly expected categorization patterns. This was a consistent finding in a number of student samples, as well as the two large population samples already referred to above. There is thus merit in exploring more extensively such naturally occurring crossed-categorization patterns, and we aim to continue doing so in our future work, given that individuals are able to combine their numerous group identities in complex and subjectively meaningful ways, a phenomenon that is more difficult to predict and thus lends itself less readily to experimental manipulation.

## Social identity complexity

Individuals may not only hold complex self-descriptive categorization patterns, which can be associated with more differentiated outgroup evaluations, but they are also able to subjectively combine their multiple ingroup identities in a more or less exclusive manner. Roccas and Brewer (2002) introduced the concept of social identity complexity to refer to an individual's subjective representation of the interrelationships among his or her multiple identities, where complexity can range on a continuum from high to low complexity (Roccas and Brewer, 2002). Individuals may thus perceive their range of social identities as largely overlapping, whereby only individuals who share membership on the sum of these identities are regarded as fellow ingroup members, and people who share none or only a few of these identities are regarded as outgroup members.

In this case, the individual's identity structure is relatively simplified and indicative of low identity complexity. Alternatively, however, individuals may be aware that their various ingroup identities, by necessity, do not overlap and that others do not always share ingroup membership on all of these self-descriptive categories (Brewer and Pierce, 2005; Roccas and Brewer, 2002). The latter case then is indicative of greater social identity complexity.

Thus whether another is perceived as an ingroup or outgroup member depends on the level of inclusiveness with which an individual cognitively conceptualizes ingroup status of his or her multiple group identities. Importantly, it has been advocated that social identity complexity ought to be positively related to tolerance and favourable outgroup attitudes. In two empirical investigations, Roccas and Brewer (2002) and Brewer and Pierce (2005) indeed reported that higher social identity complexity was associated with more positive outgroup attitudes. More specifically, higher social identity complexity was associated with greater tolerance, reduced intergroup bias and greater support for affirmative action and multiculturalism (Brewer and Pierce, 2005; Roccas and Brewer, 2002).

We have recently carried out a series of studies investigating the extent to which holding a complex representation of one's multiple ingroups may affect outgroup perception in Northern Ireland. We found an association between relative levels of social identity complexity and outgroup attitudes (Schmid et al., 2009b). Specifically we found that higher similarity and overlap complexity (i.e. less perceived similarity between the prototypical attributes surrounding, and lower perceived overlap between, individuals' religious and national identities) was associated with less ingroup bias and more tolerance towards outgroup members. Our results thus broadly mirrored the relationship observed by Brewer and colleagues (Brewer and Pierce, 2005; Roccas and Brewer, 2002), showing social identity complexity to be positively associated with outgroup perceptions.

## Common ingroup identification

The common ingroup identity model of recategorization (Gaertner and Dovidio, 2000; Gaertner et al., 1993) rests upon the notion that individuals can perceive others at different levels of inclusiveness. This model argues that subordinate categorizations ('us' and 'them') can be replaced with superordinate categorizations ('we'), an argument that is also common in sociological and anthropological analyses of ethnicity, which emphasise contextual variability (Jenkins, 2008). This may have positive consequences for intergroup perception. Thus recategorization (from former outgroup to ingroup member) may lead to a reduction in intergroup bias and prejudice. Extensive experimental data support this assertion (some support based on survey data also exists, but the evidence is generally weaker), demonstrating that, as predicted, bias is reduced primarily by improving attitudes towards former outgroup members, due to their recategorization from former outgroup to ingroup.

However, the common ingroup identity model has a number of limitations (Brewer and Gaertner, 2001). First, many categorizations are powerful and long-established, making recategorization an unrealistic possibility. Second, in contexts of intergroup conflict or in clearly defined minority–majority contexts, recategorization may be perceived as a threat, and may lead to increased, rather than reduced, ingroup bias. Thus the primary shortcoming of this model is that recategorization risks depriving individuals of valued social categories, making it a temporally unstable solution to the problem of intergroup discrimination (Brewer and Gaertner, 2001). In order to overcome some of these problems, Gaertner and Dovidio (2000) developed the dual identity model, which emphasizes a more complex form of common ingroup identity, recognizing both different and common group memberships. In this model, subgroups are allowed to maintain their original and distinctive identities while also sharing a common superordinate identity (Gaertner and Dovidio, 2000), and empirical findings confirmed that a dual identity led to more positive outgroup attitudes than did a superordinate identity alone (see Hewstone et al., 2007).

As mentioned earlier, Northern Ireland has witnessed the emergence of a novel identity, the 'Northern Irish' category, a label of self-description that has been embraced by both Protestants and Catholics equally. Data from the 'Northern Ireland Life and Times' survey (2003–2005) shows that respondents choosing a superordinate 'Northern Irish' identity showed less ingroup bias than individuals choosing an 'ingroup' ethno-religious identity (either Protestant or Catholic). However, ethno-religious categories (Catholic and Protestant) may not in essence be nested, as subgroups, within the superordinate Northern Irish identity, as would be the case with the national subgroup categories, 'British' and 'Irish', given that the 'Northern Irish' category is used as nationality label. We therefore also carried out comparisons between national subgroup categorizers (i.e. 'British' and 'Irish') and superordinate categorizers (i.e. 'Northern Irish'). In our two recent cross-sectional studies involving general population samples we found that respondents who self-categorized in terms of this superordinate Northern Irish identity tended to display lower levels of ingroup bias than did respondents choosing British or Irish categories. This suggests that the Northern Irish identity may actually be meaningfully perceived as a common, superordinate ingroup, bringing about positive effects on outgroup attitudes as argued by the common ingroup identity model. A further observation we made is that respondents who self-categorized as Northern Irish reported lower levels of ethno-religious identification than did those who self-categorized as British or Irish.

## GROUP-BASED PROCESSES AND OUTGROUP ATTITUDES: THE ROLE OF INTERGROUP THREAT AND INTERGROUP CONTACT

Social categorization and identification processes are central to intergroup conflict phenomena and form the basis for a range of intergroup processes that perpetuate intergroup conflict. Understanding these processes is therefore vital to understanding the dynamics of conflict per se, and is a prerequisite to alleviating negative intergroup relations. In the following, we review recent work on intergroup threat and intergroup contact, two group-based processes that are of particular relevance to understanding intergroup relations in the Northern Ireland context.

### Intergroup threat and outgroup attitudes

Threat perceptions play a central role in intergroup conflict, as group-based threats more often than not precede intergroup tensions and prejudice (see e.g. Tausch et al., 2008). One of the earliest theoretical accounts on the nature of group-based threats, realistic group conflict theory (Campbell, 1965; Sherif, 1966), asserts that intergroup tensions arise from and are perpetuated by conflicting group interests (see Esses et al., 1998; Sherif et al., 1961, for experimental support). It is now known, however, that perceptions of threat may not only surround real and tangible issues, but can also be of a more symbolic nature, such as threats to group values (Biernat et al., 1996), or threat to trust or morality (see Cottrell and Neuberg, 2005). In their integrated threat theory, Stephan and Stephan (2000) distinguish between realistic threats (surrounding tangible assets, resources or territory) and symbolic threats (surrounding differences in values or beliefs). Both realistic and symbolic threats are regarded as group-level threats, yet threats may also be felt at the level of the individual. As such

intergroup anxiety, defined as a personally felt threat or anxiety when encountering outgroup members, has also been found to be associated with intergroup bias (e.g. Voci and Hewstone, 2003). Research conducted in the Northern Irish context has shown both realistic and symbolic threats, as well as intergroup anxiety, to predict both ingroup bias and outgroup trust, confirming the predictions made by integrated threat theory (Tausch et al., 2007a, b). Moreover, research has found threat perceptions surrounding physical safety to be associated with more ingroup bias, as well as negative action tendencies (Schmid et al., 2008).

A different category of threat perceptions concerns threats to social identity. According to social identity theory (Tajfel and Turner, 1979), such threats occur when individuals no longer feel they compare favourably to a respective outgroup, thus compromising their need for positive distinctiveness. Moreover, situations in which a relevant outgroup is perceived as too similar to the ingroup may be perceived as threatening to one's sense of distinctiveness and, as a result, can lead to increased differentiation between groups (Jetten et al., 1997; see Branscombe et al., 1999) as well as an increase in self-stereotyping (Spears et al., 1997; for a detailed review see Jetten and Spears, 2003). Perceptions of distinctiveness threat also appear to play a role in Northern Ireland, with higher levels of distinctiveness threat predicting more ingroup bias and less outgroup tolerance. Higher perceived distinctiveness threat was also associated with reduced social identity complexity (Schmid et al., 2009b).

That identity-based threat plays a central role within the Northern Ireland social and political arena is alluded to in an early description of the conflict as one of threatened identities (Beloff, 1989). This description evokes notions of interdependence between the respective groups in Northern Ireland similar to those described by Kelman (1999) in his theoretical analysis of the Israeli–Palestinian conflict. In this argumentation Kelman (1999) speaks of a negative interdependence between the Israeli–Palestinian identities, where each group is said to perceive the other group as threatening to its own group identity. He argues that over and above the more direct or immediate threats experienced in situations of extreme conflict, each group perceives the mere existence of the outgroup, as well as the expression of outgroup identity, as highly threatening to own-group identity. These threat perceptions surrounding the respective out group are then believed to culminate in a negative interdependence of identities, in that each group can only thrive if the other fails (Kelman, 1999).

Kelman's reasoning suggests that negative interdependence of identities defines one of the primary obstacles for the resolution of intractable conflicts. This argumentation is readily applicable to the Northern Ireland problem, where identity expression is of prime importance and plays a unique role in everyday life, as evidenced in the strong adherence to divisive historical traditions and use of identity-related symbols (Cairns and Hewstone, 2005; Devine-Wright, 2001). Interestingly, Cairns and Darby (1998) observed that, with the resolution of realistic issues in Northern Ireland, such as economic inequalities between Catholics and Protestants, there has been a noticeable *increase* in sensitivity towards the symbols of cultural expression, such as the display of flags and symbols and the maintenance of traditional marching routes. An empirical examination into the role of threat perceptions surrounding the symbolic expression of identity in Northern Ireland, such as threat perceptions surrounding the display of flags or religious symbols representative of the outgroup, has uncovered a negative relationship with outgroup perceptions, with higher perceived levels of threat surrounding symbolic expression of identity being associated with more intergroup bias and more negative action tendencies (Schmid et al., 2008).

The typically observed link between threat and prejudice tends to occur primarily for individuals for whom the threatened ingroup identity is a valued one (e.g. Jetten et al., 2001; Roccas and Schwartz, 1993; Ullrich et al., 2006). This latter effect has also been observed in the Northern Irish context, and surrounding different types of threat. For example, research in this context has shown realistic and symbolic threats, as well as distinctiveness threat, to be more strongly associated with negative outgroup attitudes for high but not low ingroup identifiers in terms of ethno-political identities, but for these threats to be less associated with bias for respondents who endorse the Northern Irish identity (Schmid et al., 2009c; Tausch et al., 2007a, b).

Given the centrality of identity-based threat perceptions in intergroup conflict settings, social scientific approaches to intergroup conflict have aimed to uncover ways, both theoretically and empirically, by means of which not only more favourable outgroup attitudes may be encouraged, but also threat perceptions surrounding the outgroup may be reduced. One approach that has been found to be of particular merit in reducing threat and promoting more positive outgroup evaluation is that of intergroup contact.

## Intergroup contact and outgroup attitudes

The central tenet of the 'contact hypothesis' (Allport, 1954) is that frequent and positive intergroup contact can reduce prejudice and alleviate negative intergroup relations. There now exists extensive empirical support for this hypothesis in many different contexts and under many different conditions, even if not all of the optimal conditions as proposed by Allport (1954) are met (for meta-analytic evidence, see Pettigrew and Tropp, 2006). Significant advances have also been made in identifying the moderating and mediating conditions that aid understanding as to *when* and *how* contact works, respectively (for a detailed review of moderators and mediators see Brown and Hewstone, 2005).

Policymakers in Northern Ireland have long advocated the importance of cross-community contact, pursuing avenues by means of which meaningful encounters between Catholics and Protestants can be promoted in an attempt to foster a less conflictual society (see Cairns and Hewstone, 2002; Hughes, 1999; Hughes and Carmichael, 1998; Niens et al., 2003). Over the past few years research evidence has confirmed that contact is typically associated with reduced intergroup bias and more positive outgroup attitudes (Schmid et al., 2008; Tausch et al., 2007a, b; see also Hewstone et al., 2005). Most recently we have also confirmed the relationship between contact and improved intergroup attitudes in longitudinal research (Tausch et al., 2009).

We have also demonstrated that indirect intergroup contact with ethno-religious outgroup members can reduce ingroup bias. So-called indirect or extended contact, that is, by having a family member or close friend who has contact with an outgroup member, even if one has no direct contact oneself, is associated with reduced prejudice and increased perception of the outgroup as heterogeneous (Paolini et al., 2004; Wright et al., 1997). Paolini et al. (2004) showed that indirect contact exerted its effects both directly, and indirectly via reduced intergroup anxiety. And our recent longitudinal work has both identified additional mediators of the effect of indirect contact, and shown that indirect contact at time 1 promotes an increase in direct contact at time 2 (Tausch et al., 2009).

Intergroup contact theory has also been explicitly tested in the context of residential segregation and diverse ethnic and racial environments, generally providing support for the assertion that living in more diverse and integrated environments is associated with a higher degree of intergroup contact, and thus is associated with more positive outgroup perceptions (Bledsoe et al., 1995; Stein et al., 2000; Wagner et al., 2003, 2006). Given the extent to which Northern Irish society is segregated, we have recently begun to examine the effects of living in mixed and segregated neighbourhoods in Northern Ireland's capital, Belfast, as well as a number of smaller towns in Northern Ireland. We found that individuals living in mixed neighbourhoods in Northern Ireland reported more frequent and more positive intergroup contact with ethno-religious outgroup members and, as a consequence, tended to display less ingroup bias than individuals living in segregated neighbourhoods (Schmid et al., 2008; Tausch et al., 2009).

Notwithstanding the support we have accrued for intergroup contact in Northern Ireland, over many years and many studies, we emphasize that we are not proposing contact as a magical 'cure'. It should be noted that immediately before the conflict began, in 1968, many areas were 'mixed', and many remained so subsequently. Many 'mixed' public housing estates in the greater Belfast area rapidly became segregated in the early 1970s in response to conflict and fears over personal safety. Thus living side-by-side was not a bulwark against polarization and sectarianism, any more than long histories of co-residence were in some border areas. These facts emphasize that many factors other than contact are at work in conflict, and that we should not naively expect contact to 'inoculate' individuals against future rises in sectarianism, especially those in which close contacts with the other community are, at best, frowned upon, and at worst severely sanctioned.

## BEYOND RELIGIOUS AND NATIONAL IDENTITY: SOCIAL CAPITAL

Although religious and national categorization is central to the conflict in Northern Ireland, we do not expect the entirety of people's lives to be dominated by their ties to their religious and national groups. Individuals typically have available a wide range of social identities (Deaux, 1996), some of which may be considered more important than others, yet all of which are subject to situational, psychological activation. One particular line of research we have begun to pursue is the extent to which individuals build up and conceive their ties to and within their neighbourhood, and the extent to which social context becomes integral to people's lives. This is of particular interest in the Northern Ireland context, where, as mentioned above, religiously segregated living is still commonplace and many people tend to carry out the majority of their daily activities in their immediate neighbourhood. In our two recent studies we have focused explicitly on examining the role of social capital in mixed and segregated neighbourhoods in Northern Ireland, as well as the consequences of social capital for intra- and intergroup relations.

Social capital theory (Putnam, 2000) contends that social networks are an important resource for individuals, that they have value and that they are fundamental to the creation of a meaningful modern community. Social capital refers to the connections among individuals, including social networks, norms of reciprocity and trustworthiness (Putnam, 2007), and is thus said to have a range of positive implications (e.g. mutual support, co-operation, psychological well-being). However, social capital may also hold negative consequences such as sectarianism, own-group favouritism, and corruption. In diverse societies and situations of intergroup conflict, the goal is of course to maximize the positive and minimize the negative effects of social capital. Importantly, positive effects should be maximized between, and not just within, communities, for which reason Putnam (2000) drew a distinction between 'bridging' and 'bonding' forms of social capital.

Bridging social capital is inclusive, can generate broader identities and reciprocity; the 'weak ties' that link *between* networks (Granovetter, 1973) are, in fact, extraordinarily strong and important precisely because they link networks. Bonding social capital, in contrast, is exclusive, inward-looking and tends to reinforce exclusive identities and homogeneous groups. As it creates strong ingroup loyalty, it may also create outgroup antagonism, which can become particularly problematic in the context of ethnically homogeneous or segregated societies. Interestingly, research on conflict and diversity suggests that social capital may be lower in heterogeneous (more diverse) than homogeneous areas (Blokland, 2003; Vasta, 2000), and it has recently been argued that greater diversity may lower social capital and trust, not only for comparative outgroup, but also ingroup members (Putnam, 2007).

We have recently begun to explore the extent and role of social capital in the Northern Ireland context, and have explicitly focused on comparing mixed and segregated areas in Belfast, as well as in a number of smaller towns in Northern Ireland. Our research made use of in-depth interviews and focus groups, as well as large-scale cross-sectional surveys using a general population sample randomly selected from these areas. What generally emerged from the focus-groups and interviews was that bonding capital was higher in the segregated communities than in the mixed, to the extent that individuals displayed a greater sense of solidarity and cohesion in the segregated than the mixed areas, confirming strong social ties with family and neighbours. Individuals living in the segregated areas also participated more actively in social activities in those communities than did individuals living in mixed neighbourhoods. Interestingly, however, although levels of social capital were lower in the mixed than in the segregated communities, individuals living in mixed areas tended to display a greater preference for living in mixed environments than did respondents living in segregated environments. Furthermore, individuals living in the mixed communities reported less hostile sentiments towards ethnic minority group members.

Cross-sectional quantitative data from one of our neighbourhood surveys are in general alignment with this set of qualitative findings. In our sample drawn from several smaller towns in Northern Ireland we asked respondents to report how many of their family or friends lived in the area, to rate the extent to which people in the area could depend on each other, and to rate their general extent of 'belonging'. People living in segregated areas tended to report more and closer social ties in their neighbourhoods than did respondents living in mixed areas. Respondents in the segregated areas also felt more safe from crime, and reported greater levels of trust of their neighbours than did respondents in mixed areas. In our Belfast sample, however, we observed no difference in social capital between mixed and segregated areas. Respondents rated their area no less friendly, reported having no less trust in people, felt equally that people helped each other out, got along well, and rated the area a safe place, in which one could express one's identity. We also assessed the extent to which individuals identified with their neighbourhood. Interestingly, respondents from both segregated and mixed neighbourhoods reported comparable levels of identification with their neighbourhood, demonstrating that despite some of the differences in the aforementioned questions concerning social capital, the value placed on being a member of their own area was comparable for all respondents. Noteworthy also is that respondents in the mixed areas consistently expressed a stronger preference for inter-religious mixing and living in mixed areas.

We also assessed 'bridging social capital' by asking respondents to indicate how often they generally go outside their area to carry out everyday activities, visit people or socialize. Although we did not find an overall difference in the frequency with which individuals left their own area, there was a difference in the composition of the areas visited in terms of the number of ingroup and outgroup members also carrying out activities there. Respondents living in mixed areas showed a greater tendency to carry out their daily activities in areas in which both ingroup and outgroup members lived or carried out their daily activities than did individuals living in segregated areas. Conversely, when leaving their own area to carry out daily activities people from segregated areas were more likely to go to areas in which primarily ingroup members lived or carried out similar activities than were people from mixed neighbourhoods.

It is not easy to draw firm conclusions about social capital and the amelioration of intergroup conflict in Northern Ireland. Our research, and Leonard's (2004), suggests that social network effects ('social capital') do not 'operate' independently of long local histories of conflict and inter-ethnic distrust, and can only be understood in local context. This research also illustrates the interdependence of intergroup and intragroup identity processes and relations.

## CONCLUSION

Undoubtedly, the overarching objective of most, if not all, researchers studying intergroup conflict phenomena is to point out ways by means of which conflict may be reduced, intergroup tensions alleviated and conflict resolution becomes realizable. And although ethno-political conflicts are typically defined by their political, historical, social and economic components, phenomena relating to social identity also play an important role in perpetuating such conflicts. Research examining the role of self-categorization, social identification and general group-based processes thus adds to our understanding of the intricacies of intergroup dynamics.

In this chapter we have reviewed research, both quantitative and qualitative, that has examined the extent, role and consequences of social identity in one particular site of intergroup conflict, Northern Ireland. The growing body of research in this context yet again confirms the centrality of social identity processes in intergroup conflict, to the extent that social-identity based processes have consequences for intergroup attitudes and perceptions. Before examining these intergroup phenomena, however, we examined specifically the intragroup processes in this context. Importantly, we were able to highlight that self-categorization surrounding the involved parties in this context can be much more complex and differentiated than is commonly assumed, which in itself provides opportunities for depolarizing societies entrenched in intergroup conflict. We have shown that multiple categorization processes, such as crossed categorization, social identity complexity or common ingroup phenomena, are also meaningful in the Northern Irish context, being positively associated with outgroup perception. Thus the challenge, but also the opportunity, for conflict resolution lies, we believe, in de-emphasizing divisive and polarizing identities and encouraging more complex, differentiated and inclusive identities, without overriding valued social categorizations. Northern Irish society is, and has been for some time, undergoing significant changes, evolving from a situation of violent conflict to a post-conflict society approaching peaceful co-existence of its groups. At this time it is important not to forget how intricately linked social identity processes are to intergroup phenomena in this context, as they are in other situations of ethno-political conflict.

By further discussing the intergroup consequences of group-based processes we hope to have fostered understanding of the identity-based issues at stake in this context, over and above an understanding solely of categorization and identification processes. We have highlighted that threat perceptions emanating directly or indirectly from the outgroup can have adverse consequences for intergroup relations, while engaging in contact with outgroup members tends to have positive intergroup consequences, being typically associated with more positive outgroup attitudes as well as being an effective means for reducing intergroup threat perceptions. In fact, it is this extensive body of research on the consequences of intergroup contact that should be of particular interest to policymakers, as it provides consistent support for continuing contact schemes in educational and community settings in this context. Moreover, our own most recent work has focused explicitly on examining the consequences of segregation on self-categorization, social identification and intergroup processes, to which we have made continuous reference throughout this chapter. This research exemplifies the powerful effects that context can exert on intra- and intergroup phenomena, to the extent that individuals living in mixed areas in Northern Ireland tended to be more likely to endorse more differentiated categorization patterns and tended to display less ingroup bias than did individuals living in more homogenous, segregated environments.

## NOTES

1   Self-categorization can be defined as a person's membership, as well as a person's subjective choice of membership, in a collective group (Deaux, 1996), while social identification then pertains to the processes associated with and underlying such membership in a collective category. Social identification is multidimensional, encompassing interrelated but conceptually distinct elements, such as evaluation, importance, attachment or social embeddedness (see Ashmore et al., 2004, for a review). A shift in terminology from 'social identity' to 'collective identity' has been advocated (e.g. Simon and Klandermans, 2001), given that all identities, whether personal or social, are socially constructed and socially meaningful (e.g. Thoits and Virshup, 1997; see also Ashmore et al., 2004). We agree in principle with this argumentation, yet as 'social identity' remains widespread and commonly accepted terminology we retain the term in this chapter.

2   Salience is conceptualized as the degree to which a person self-defines as a member of a social category, based on the principle of meta-contrast (Turner et al., 1987). Thus, self-definition in terms of a collective category is context dependant and subject to psychological activation of the given category.

3   Ingroup bias was measured using a feeling thermometer, asking individuals to rate their feeling toward their own group as well as their respective outgroup on a scale ranging from 0 (extremely unfavourable) to 100 (extremely favourable). By subtracting outgroup from ingroup ratings, a discrepancy score of ingroup bias is obtained.

## REFERENCES

Allport, G.W. (1954) *The Nature of Prejudice.* Reading, MA: Addison-Wesley.

Ashmore, R.D., Deaux, K. and McLaughlin-Volpe, T. (2004) 'An organizing framework for collective identity: Articulation and significance of multidimensionality', *Psychological Bulletin,* 130: 80–114.

Beloff, H. (1989) 'A tradition of threatened identities', in J. Harbison (ed.), *Growing Up in Northern Ireland,* pp. 182–193. Belfast: Stranmillis College Resources Unit.

Biernat, M., Vescio, T. K. and Theno, S. A. (1996) 'Violating American values: A "value congruence" approach to understanding out-group attitudes', *Journal of Experimental Social Psychology,* 32: 387–410.

Bledsoe, T., Welch, S., Sigelman, L. and Combs, M. (1995) 'Residential context and racial solidarity among African Americans', *American Journal of Political Science,* 39: 434–58.

Blokland, T. (2003) 'Ethnic complexity: Routes to discriminatory repertoires in an inner-city neighbourhood', *Ethnic and Racial Studies,* 26: 1–24.

Branscombe, N.R. and Wann, D.L. (1994) 'Collective self-esteem consequences of outgroup derogation when a valued social identity is on trial', *European Journal of Social Psychology,* 24: 641–57.

Branscombe, N.R., Ellemers, N., Spears, R. and Doosje, B. (1999) 'The context and content of social identity threat', in N. Ellemers, R. Spears, and B. Doosje (eds), *Social Identity: Context, Commitment, Content,* pp. 35–58. Oxford: Blackwell.

Brewer, M.B. (1993) 'The role of distinctiveness in social identity and group behaviour', in M. Hogg and D. Abrams (eds), *Group Motivation: Social Psychological Perspectives,* pp. 1–16. London: Harvester Wheatsheaf.

Brewer, M. (1999) 'The psychology of prejudice: Ingroup love and outgroup hate', *Journal of Social Issues,* 55: 429–44.

Brewer, M. (2000) 'Reducing prejudice through cross-categorization: Effects of multiple social identities', in S. Oskamp (ed.), *Reducing Prejudice and Discrimination,* pp. 165-183. Hillsdale, NJ: Erlbaum.

Brewer, M.B. and Gaertner, S.L. (2001) 'Toward reduction of prejudice: Intergroup contact and social categorization', in R. Brown and S.L. Gaertner (eds), *Blackwell Handbook of Social Psychology: Intergroup Processes,* pp. 451–474. Oxford: Blackwell.

Brewer, M.B., Ho., Lee, J. and Miller, N. (1987) 'Social identity and social distance among Hong Kong school children', *Personality and Social Psychology Bulletin,* 13: 156–65.

Brewer, M. and Pierce, K. P. (2005). 'Social identity complexity and outgroup tolerance', *Personality and Social Psychology Bulletin,* 31: 428–437.

Brown, R.J. and Hewstone, M. (2005) 'An integrative theory of intergroup contact', in M. Zanna (ed.), *Advances in Experimental Social Psychology.* Vol. 37, pp. 255–331. San Diego, CA: Academic Press.

Brown, R. and Turner, J.C. (1979) 'The Criss-cross categorization effect in intergroup discrimination', *British Journal of Clinical and Social Psychology,* 18: 371–83.

Cairns, E. (1982) 'Intergroup conflict in Northern Ireland', in H. Tajfel (ed.), *Social Identity and Intergroup Relations,* pp. 277–297. London: Cambridge University Press.

Cairns, E. (1987) *Caught in Crossfire: Children and the Northern Ireland Conflict.* Belfast: Appletree.

Cairns, E. and Darby, J. (1998) 'che Conflict in Northern Ireland: Causes, consequences and controls', *American Psychologist,* 53: 757–60.

Cairns, E. and Hewstone, M. (2002) 'The impact of peacemaking in Northern Ireland on intergroup behaviour', in G. Salomon and B. Nevo (eds), *The Nature and Study of Peace Education,* pp. 217–28. Hillsdale, NJ: Erlbaum.

Cairns, E. and Hewstone, M. (2005) 'Northern Ireland: In-group pride and out-group prejudice', in I. Stewart and R. Vaitilingam (eds), *Seven Deadly Sins: A New Look at Society Through an Old Lens,* pp. 8–11. Swindon: Economic and Social Research Council.

Cairns, E. and Mercer, G.W. (1984) 'Social identity in Northern Ireland', *Human Relations,* 37: 1095–102.

Cairns, E., Kenworthy, J. B., Campbell, A. and Hewstone, M. (2006) 'The role of in-group identification, religious group membership, and intergroup conflict in moderating in-group and out-group affect', *British Journal of Social Psychology,* 45: 701–16.

Campbell, D.T. (1965) 'Ethnocentric and other altruistic motives', in D. Levine (ed.), *Nebraska Symposium on Motivation.* Vol. 13, pp. 283–311. Lincoln, NE: University of Nebraska Press.

Cassidy, C. and Trew, K. (1998) 'Identities in Northern Ireland: A multidimensional approach', *Journal of Social Issues,* 54: 725–40.

Cassidy, C. and Trew, K. (2004) 'Identity change in Northern Ireland: A longitudinal study of students' transition to university', *Journal of Social Issues,* 60: 523–40.

Cottrell, C.A. and Neuberg, S.L. (2005) 'Different emotional reactions to different groups: A sociofunctional threat-based approach to "prejudice"', *Journal of Personality and Social Psychology,* 88: 770–89.

Crisp, R.J. and Hewstone, M. (1999) 'Differential evaluation of crossed category groups: Patterns, processes, and reducing intergroup bias', *Group Processes and Intergroup Relations,* 2: 307–33.

Crisp, R.J. and Hewstone, M. (2000) 'Crossed categorization and intergroup bias: The moderating role of intergroup and affective context', *Journal of Experimental Social Psychology*, 36: 357–83.

Crisp, R.J. and Hewstone, M. (2007) 'Multiple social categorization', in M. Zanna (ed.), *Advances in Experimental Social Psychology*. Vol. 39, pp. 164–254. San Diego, CA: Academic Press.

Crisp, R.J., Hewstone, M. and Cairns, E. (2001) 'Multiple identities in Northern Ireland: Hierarchical ordering in the representation of group membership'. *British Journal of Social Psychology*, 40: 501–14.

Deaux, K. (1996) 'Social identification', in E.T. Higgins and A.W. Kruglanski (eds), *Social Psychology: Handbook of Basic Principles*, pp. 777–798. New York: Guildford Press.

Deaux, K., Reid, A., Mizrahi, K. and Ethier, K.A. (1995) 'Parameters of social identity', *Journal of Personality and Social Psychology*, 68: 280–91.

Deschamps, J.C. and Doise, W. (1978) 'Crossed-category membership in intergroup relations', in H. Tajfel (ed.), *Differentiation between Social Groups*, pp. 141–158. London: Academic Press.

Deutsch, M. (1973) *The Resolution of Conflict: Constructive and Destructive Processes*. Newhaven, CT: Yale University Press.

Devine-Wright, P. (2001) 'History and identity in Northern Ireland: An exploratory investigation of the role of historical commemorations in contexts of intergroup conflict', *Peace and Conflict: Journal of Peace Psychology*, 7: 297–315.

Esses, V.M., Jackson, L.M. and Armstrong, T.L. (1998) 'Intergroup competition and attitudes toward immigrants and immigration: An instrumental model of group conflict', *Journal of Social Issues*, 54: 699–724.

Eurich-Fulcer, R. and Schofield, J.W. (1995) 'Correlated versus uncorrelated social categorizations: The effect on intergroup bias', *Personality and Social Psychology Bulletin*, 21: 149–59.

Fahey, T., Hayes, B.C. and Sinnott, R. (2005) *Conflict and Consensus: A Study of Values and Attitudes in the Republic of Ireland and Northern Ireland*. Dublin: Institute of Public Administration.

Fay, M.T., Morrissey, M. and Smyth, M. (1999) *Northern Ireland's Troubles: The Human Costs*. London: Pluto Press.

Gaertner, S.L. and Dovidio, J.F. (2000) *Reducing Intergroup Bias: The Common Ingroup Identity Model*. Hove: Psychology Press.

Gaertner, S.L., Dovidio, J.F., Anastasio, P.A., Bachman, B.A. and Rust, M.C. (1993) 'The common ingroup identity model: Recategorization and the reduction of intergroup bias', in W. Stroebe and M. Hewstone (eds), *European Review of Social Psychology*. Vol. 4., pp. 1–26. Chichester: Wiley.

Gallagher, A.M. (1995) 'The approach of government: Community relations and equity', in S. Dunn (ed.), *Facets of the Conflict in Northern Ireland*, pp. 27–43. New York: St. Martin's Press.

Gallagher, A.M. and Dunn, S. (1991) 'Community relations in Northern Ireland: Attitudes to contact and integration', in P. Stringer and G. Robinson (eds), *Social Attitudes in Northern Ireland*, pp. 7–22. Belfast: Blackstaff Press.

Granovetter, M. (1973) 'Strength of weak ties', *American Journal of Sociology*, 78: 1360–80.

Haslam, S.A., Turner, J.C., Oakes, P.J., McGarty, C. and Reynolds, K.J. (1998) 'The group as a basis for emergent stereotype consensus', in W. Stroebe and M. Hewstone (eds), *European Review of Social Psychology*. Vol. 8., pp. 203–39. Chichester: Wiley.

Hewstone, M. and Brown, R. (1986) 'Contact is not enough: An intergroup perspective on the contact hypothesis', in M. Hewstone and R. Brown (eds), *Contact and Conflict in Intergroup Encounters*, pp. 3–44. Oxford: Basil Blackwell.

Hewstone, M., Cairns, E., Kenworthy, J., Hughes, J., Tausch, N., Voci, A., von Hecker, U., Tam, T. and Pinder, C. (2008) 'Stepping stones to reconciliation in Northern Ireland: Intergroup contact, forgiveness and trust', in A. Nadler, T. Malloy and J.D. Fisher (eds), *The Social Psychology of Inter-group Reconciliation*, pp. 199–226. New York: Oxford University Press.

Hewstone, M., Cairns, E., Voci, A., Paolini, S., McLernon, F., Crisp, R.J., Niens, U. and Craig, J. (2005) 'Intergroup contact in a divided society: Challenging segregation in Northern Ireland', in D. Abrams, J.M. Marques and M.A. Hogg (eds), *The Social Psychology of Inclusion and Exclusion*, pp. 265–92. Philadelphia, PA: Psychology Press.

Hewstone, M., Turner, R., Kenworthy, J. and Crisp, R.J. (2007) 'Multiple social categorization: Integrative themes and future research priorities', in R.J. Crisp and M. Hewstone (eds), *Multiple Social Categorization. Processes, Models and Applications*, pp. 271–310. Hove: Psychology Press.

Hinkle, S. and Brown, R.J. (1990) 'Intergroup comparisons and social identity: Some links and lacunae', in D. Abrams and M.A. Hogg (eds), *Social Identity Theory: Constructive and Critical Advances*. New York: Harvester Wheatsheaf.

Hughes, J. (1999) *Bridging the Gap: Community Relations Policy in Northern Ireland,* Papers in Public

Policy and Management, No. 87, Belfast: University of Ulster.

Hughes, J. and Carmichael, P. (1998) 'Community relations in Northern Ireland: Attitudes to contact and segregation', in G. Robinson, D. Heenan, A.M. Gray and K. Thompson (eds), *Social Attitudes in Northern Ireland: The Seventh Report*. Aldershot: Gower.

Hutter, R.R.C. and Crisp, R.J. (2005) 'The composition of category conjunctions', *Personality and Social Psychology Bulletin*, 31: 647–57.

Hutter, R.R.C. and Crisp, R.J. (2006) 'Implications of cognitive busyness for the perception of category conjunctions', *Journal of Social Psychology*, 146: 253–6.

Jarman, N. (2004) 'From war to peace? Changing patterns of violence in Northern Ireland, 1990–2003'. *Terrorism and Political Violence*, 16: 420–38.

Jenkins, R. (2008) *Rethinking Ethnicity: Arguments and Explorations*. 2nd edn. London: Sage.

Jetten, J. and Spears, R. (2003) 'The divisive potential of differences and similarities: The role of intergroup distinctiveness in intergroup differentiation', in W. Stroebe and M. Hewstone (eds), *European Review of Social Psychology*. Vol. 14. Hove: Psychology Press.

Jetten, J., Spears, R. and Manstead, A.S.R. (1997) 'Distinctiveness threat and prototypicality: Combined effects on intergroup discrimination and collective self-ssteem', *European Journal of Social Psychology*, 27: 635–57.

Jetten, J., Spears, R. and Manstead, A.S.R. (2001) 'Similarity as a source of differentiation: The role of ingroup identification', *European Journal of Social Psychology*, 31: 621–40.

Kelman, H. (1999) 'The interdependence of Israeli and Palestinian national identities: The role of the other in existential conflicts', *Journal of Social Issues*, 55: 581–600.

Kelman, H.C. (2001) 'The role of national identity in conflict resolution. Experience from Israeli–Palestinian problem-solving workshops', in R.D. Ashmore, L. Jussim and D. Wilder (eds), *Social Identity, Intergroup Conflict, and Conflict Reduction*, pp. 187–212. Oxford: Oxford University Press.

Knox, C. and Hughes, J. (1994) *Cross-Community Contact: Northern Ireland and Israel – a Comparative Perspective*. Ulster Papers in Public Policy and Management, Number 32.

Leonard, M. (2004) 'Bonding and bridging social capital: Reflections from Belfast', *Sociology*, 38: 927–44.

McClenahan, C., Cairns, E., Dunn, S. and Morgan, V. (1991) 'Preference for geographical location as a measure of ethnic/national identity in children in Northern Ireland', *Irish Journal of Psychology*, 12: 346–54.

McClenahan, C., Cairns, E., Dunn, S. and Morgan, V. (1996) 'Intergroup friendships: Integrated and desegregated schools in Northern Ireland', *The Journal of Social Psychology*, 136: 549–58.

McGlynn, C., Niens, U., Cairns, E. and Hewstone, M. (2004) 'Moving out of conflict: The contribution of integrated schools in Northern Ireland to identity, attitudes, forgiveness and reconciliation', *Journal of Peace Education*, 1: 147–63.

Migdal, M.J., Hewstone, M. and Mullen, B. (1998) 'The effects of crossed categorization on intergroup evaluations: A meta-analysis', *British Journal of Social Psychology*, 37: 303–24.

Moxon-Browne, E. (1983) *Nation, Class and Creed in Northern Ireland*. Aldershot: Gower.

Moxon-Browne, E. (1991) 'National identity in Northern Ireland', in P. Stringer and G. Robinson (eds), *Social Attitudes in Northern Ireland*, pp. 23–30. Belfast: Blackstaff Press.

Muldoon, O., Schmid, K., Downes, C., Kremer, J. and Trew, K. (2005) *The Legacy of the Troubles. Experience of the Troubles, Mental Health and Social Attitudes*. Belfast: Queen's University Belfast.

Mullen, B., Brown, R. and Smith, C. (1992) 'Ingroup bias as a function of salience, relevance, and status: An integration', *European Journal of Social Psychology*, 65: 469–85.

Murtagh, B. (2002) *The Politics of Territory: Policy and Segregation in Northern Ireland*. Basingstoke: Palgrave.

Niens, U., Cairns, E. and Hewstone, M.( 2003) 'Contact and conflict in Northern Ireland', in O. Hargie and D. Dickson (eds), *Researching The Troubles: Social Science Perspectives on the Northern Ireland Conflict*, pp. 123–40. Edinburgh: Mainstream Publishing.

Paolini, S., Hewstone, M., Cairns, E. and Voci, A. (2004) 'Effects of direct and indirect cross-group friendships on judgments of Catholics and Protestants in Northern Ireland: The mediating role of an anxiety-reduction mechanism', *Personality and Social Psychology Bulletin*, 30: 770–86.

Perreault, S. and Bourhis, R.Y. (1999) 'Ethnocentrism, social identification, and discrimination', *Personality and Social Psychology Bulletin*, 25: 92–103.

Pettigrew, T.F. and Tropp, L.T. (2006) 'A meta-analytic test of intergroup contact theory', *Journal of Personality and Social Psychology*, 90: 751–83.

Poole, M. and Doherty, P. (1996) *Ethnic Residential Segregation in Northern Ireland*. Coleraine: University of Ulster.

Putnam, R. (2000) *Bowling Alone: The Collapse and Revival of American Community*. New York: Simon and Schuster.

Putnam, R. (2007) 'E pluribus unum: Diversity and community in the twenty-first century. The 2006 Jonathan Skytte Prize Lecture', *Scandinavian Political Studies*, 30: 137–74.

Robinson, G. (2003) 'Northern Irish communities drifting apart', *University of Ulster Report*. Available at: http: //www.ulst.ac.uk/news/releases/2003/725. html (accessed 12th October 2009).

Roccas, S. and Brewer, M.B. (2002) 'Social identity complexity', *Personality and Social Psychology Review*, 6: 88–106.

Roccas, S. and Schwartz, S.H. (1993) 'Effects of intergroup similarity on intergroup relations', *European Journal of Social Psychology*, 23: 581–94.

Rose, R. (1971) *Governing without Consensus: An Irish Perspective*. London: Faber and Faber.

Schmid, K., Hewstone, M., Cairns, E. and Morgen, L. (2009a) 'The situational variability of social identification'. Manuscript in preparation.

Schmid, K., Hewstone, M., Tausch, N., Cairns, E., Hughes, J. and Jenkins, R. (2009b) 'Antecedents and consequences of social identity complexity: Intergroup contact, distinctiveness threat and outgroup attitudes', *Personality and Social Psychology Bulletin*, 35: 1085–1098.

Schmid, K., Tausch, N., Hewstone, M., Cairns, E., Hughes, J. and Jenkins, R. (2009c) 'Naturally occurring patterns of crossed-categorization: Implications for intergroup perception', Manuscript in preparation.

Schmid, K., Tausch, N., Hewstone, M., Hughes, J. and Cairns, E. (2008) 'The effects of living in segregated vs. mixed areas in Northern Ireland: A simultaneous analysis of contact and threat effects in the context of micro-level neighbourhoods', *International Journal of Conflict and Violence*, 2: 56–71.

Sherif, M. (1966) *Group Conflict and Cooperation: Their Social Psychology*. London: Routledge and Kegan Paul.

Sherif, M., Harvey, O.J., White, B.J., Hood, W.R. and Sherif, C.W. (1961) *Intergroup Conflict and Cooperation. The Robber's Cave Experiment*. Norman, OK: University of Oklahoma.

Shirlow, P. (2001) 'Fear and ethnic division', *Peace Review*, 13: 67–74.

Simon, B. and Klandermans, B. (2001) 'Politicized collective identity. A social psychological analysis', *American Psychologist*, 56: 319–31.

Smyth, M. (1995) 'Limitations on the capacity for citizenship in post-ceasefire Northern Ireland', in M. Smyth and R. Moore (eds), *Three Conference Papers on Aspects of Segregation and Sectarian Division: Researching Sectarianism; Borders within Borders; and the Capacity for Citizenship*, pp. 50–66. Derry/Londonderry: Templegrove Action Research.

Spears, R., Doosje, B. and Ellemers, N. (1997) 'Self-stereotyping in the face of threats to group status and distinctiveness: The role of group identification', *Personality and Social Psychology Bulletin*, 23: 538–53.

Stein, R.M., Post, S.S. and Rinden, A.L. (2000) 'Reconciling context and contact effects on racial attitudes', *Political Research Quarterly*, 53: 285–303.

Stephan, W.G. and Stephan, C.W. (2000) 'An integrated threat theory of prejudice', in S. Oskamp (ed.), *Reducing Prejudice and Discrimination*, pp. 23–46. Hillsdale, NJ: Erlbaum.

Tajfel, H. (1978) 'Interindividual behaviour and intergroup behaviour', in H. Tajfel (ed.), *Differentiation between Social Groups: Studies in the Social Psychology of Intergroup Relations*, pp. 27–60. London: Academic Press.

Tajfel, H. and Turner, J.C. (1979) 'An integrative theory of intergroup conflict', in W.G. Austin and S. Worchel (eds), *The Social Psychology of Intergroup Relations*, pp. 33-47. Monterey, CA: Brooks/Cole.

Tausch, N., Hewstone, M., Hughes, J. and Cairns, E. (2009) 'A longitudinal study of direct and indirect intergroup contact in mixed and segregated areas of Belfast', Manuscript in Preparation.

Tausch, N., Hewstone, M., Kenworthy, J., Cairns, E. and Christ, O. (2007a) 'Cross-community contact, perceived status differences and intergroup attitudes in Northern Ireland: The mediating roles of individual-level vs. group level threats and the moderating role of social identification', *Political Psychology*, 28: 53–68.

Tausch, N., Schmid, K. and Hewstone, M. (in press) 'The social psychology of intergroup relations', in G. Salomon and E. Cairns (eds), *Handbook of Peace Education*. Mahwah, NJ: Lawrence Erlbaum.

Tausch, N., Tam, T., Hewstone, M., Kenworthy, J. and Cairns, E. (2007b) 'Individual-level and group-level mediators of contact effects in Northern Ireland: The moderating role of social identification', *British Journal of Social Psychology*, 46: 541–56.

Thoits, P. and Virshup, L. (1997) 'Me's and we's: Forms and functions of social identities', in R.D. Ashmore and L. Jussim (eds), *Self and Identity: Fundamental Issues*, pp. 106–133. New York: Oxford University Press.

Trew, K. (1996) 'Complementary or conflicting identities?', *The Psychologist*, 9: 460–3.

Trew, K. and Benson, D.E. (1996) 'Dimensions of social identity in Northern Ireland', in G. M. Breakwell and

E. Lyons (eds), *Changing European Identities. Social Psychological Analyses of Social Change*, pp. 123–44. Oxford: Butterworth-Heinemann.

Turner, J.C. (1999) 'Some current issues in research on social identity and self-categorization Theories', in N. Ellemers, R. Spears and B. Doosje (eds), *Social Identity: Context, Commitment, Content*, pp. 6–34. Oxford: Blackwell.

Turner, J.C. and Reynolds, K. (2001) 'The social identity perspective in intergroup relations: Theories, themes, and controversies', in R. Brown and S. Gaertner (eds), *Blackwell Handbook of Social Psychology: Intergroup Processes*, pp.133–52. Malden, MA: Blackwell.

Turner, J.C., Hogg, M., Oakes, P., Reicher, S. and Wetherell, M. (1987) *Rediscovering the Social Group: A Self-Categorization Theory*. Oxford: Blackwell.

Ullrich, J., Christ, O. and Schlüter, E. (2006) 'Merging on mayday: Subgroup and superordinate identification as joint moderators of threat effects in the context of European Union's expansion', *European Journal of Social Psychology*, 36: 867–76.

Urban, L.M. and Miller, N. (1998) 'A theoretical analysis of crossed categorization effects: A Meta-analysis', *Journal of Personality and Social Psychology*, 74: 894–908.

Vasta, E. (ed.) (2000) *Citizenship, Community and Democracy*. London: Palgrave.

Voci, A. and Hewstone, M. (2003) 'Intergroup contact and prejudice toward immigrants in Italy: The mediational role of anxiety and the moderating role of group salience', *Group Processes and Intergroup Relations*, 6: 37–54.

Waddell, N. and Cairns, E. (1986) 'Situational perspectives on social identity in Northern Ireland', *British Journal of Social Psychology*, 25: 25–31.

Waddell, N. and Cairns, E. (1991) 'Identity preference in Northern Ireland', *Political Psychology*, 12: 205–13.

Wagner, U., Christ, O., Pettigrew, T.F., Stellmacher, J. and Wolf, C. (2006) 'Prejudice and minority proportion: Contact instead of threat effects', *Social Psychology Quarterly*, 69: 380–90.

Wagner, U., van Dick, R., Pettigrew, T.F. and Christ. O. (2003) 'Ethnic prejudice in East and West Germany: The explanatory power of intergroup contact', *Group Processes and Intergroup Relations*, 6: 22–36.

Whyte, J. (1990) *Interpreting Northern Ireland*. Oxford: Clarendon Press.

Wright, S.C., Aron, A., McLaughlin-Volpe, T. and Ropp, S.A. (1997) 'The extended contact effect: Knowledge of cross-group friendships and prejudice', *Journal of Personality and Social Psychology*, 73: 73–90.

# 24

# Families, Siblings and Identities

### Helen Lucey

One of the tensions that characterizes contemporary experience is that arising from the wish to be unique, special, autonomous and 'free' (freedom from dependence is seen as particularly desirable for many in westernized cultures these days) alongside an equally powerful wish to be seen as the same as, be part of a collective, recognized, understood and cared for by others: a typically human tendency to pull in opposite directions at the same time. Of all the contexts in which identities are shaped, it is in families and family-like groups that these tensions often work most effectively to pattern the frameworks through which we come to make sense of ourselves and the world in which we live. It is in these kinds of relationships that most of us first experience what it might mean to be an individual and to be a member of a group, to belong and to be an 'outsider', to feel connected as well as separate, to be dependent and independent, to love, to hate and to feel ambivalence. Focusing on families, kin and personal relationships can tell us something valuable about how we form ideas about ourselves and others in dynamic relation, that is, it provides a context in which to think about the *intersubjective* nature of identity formation.

My focus in this chapter is not on the functional role of identity in political action and social movements, nor the ways in which individuals explicitly understand themselves as members of particular groups with the emphasis on a shared identity, for example, connected to nation, social class, ethnicity and gender. What I am concerned with is the intimate and personal dimensions of identities and the ways in which they develop, in part, through close relationships with familial others who are situated in relation to history, location and social divisions.

There is a valuable and growing body of work in the social sciences that addresses a wide range of topics connected to identity, families and intimate relationships, including friendship, parenting, new family forms, divorce, migration, singleness, the domestic division of labour, sex and sexuality. I will not exhaustively review all of these burgeoning strands of work, although I will outline the main theories and debates in the field. I will also look critically at the assumptions about subjectivity and human experience that underlie this work to consider some of the absences and gaps that this leaves us with when considering the ways in which identity emerges in familial and intimate domains. These are the absences and gaps that typically fall between the dualisms between self–other, individual–society and private–public that pervade social science thinking, as well as understandings of subjectivity or identity that privilege rationality, visibility, objective reality and self knowledge.

In the second half of the chapter I will take a psychoanalytically informed psychosocial approach on families and identities with a specific focus on sibling relationships as a move towards thinking creatively about the permeability and fluidity of boundaries between individuals and groups, internal and external worlds, reality and fantasy, rationality and irrationality. This perspective takes as its starting point a notion of the self that is formed, from the earliest moments of life, through a continuous dynamic between conscious and unconscious, internal (individual) and external (social) realms. In this model, individuals and groups are mutually constituted, in that there is a constant, multi-directional flow between psychic 'states of mind' (emotions, feelings) (Froggett, 2002) and the social world of culture, politics and institutions. Rather than being distinct spheres of experience, both are represented in and shape the other and it is for precisely this reason that families are important spaces in which to examine the psychosocial dimensions of identity construction. Siblings in particular occupy a valuable position when attempting to transcend the traditional split between individual, psychological and group, social processes in social sciences thinking precisely because they are simultaneously the only one of their kind and one of a series: a characteristic that Juliet Mitchell refers to as their 'seriality' (Mitchell, 2003). With this in mind, in the last section of the chapter I present a case study of two young, white, working-class brothers from a psychosocial perspective to illuminate the simultaneity of psychic and social processes in the formation of identities in family relationships.

## IDENTITIES AND FAMILY STUDIES

It has become a conventional wisdom that familial roots which can locate a person emotionally, genetically and culturally are essential for ontological security and a sense of self. Yet at the same time, in a kind of parallel universe, it is argued that in postmodern conditions we make our own selves and biographies, and that we have become the authors (if not heroes) of our own lives. (Smart, 2007: 81)

The above quote captures the tensions that run through sociology's current interest in families and intimate relationships and which centre around questions of whether or not they have profoundly changed and what part they now play in the construction and realization of selfhood. It points to the kinds of dilemmas about identity that arise when considering the idea that 'traditional' families are in decline whilst simultaneously pointing to the possibility of a solution (at least a theoretical one) to this problem of instability and loss.

Early sociological debates focused on the structure and function of families paying little or no critical attention to the concept of family or of the construction of identities in them and promoting the idea of a gender-differentiated, heterosexual nuclear family as a successful and 'natural' adaptation to modern society. However, this complacent view was not to last; beginning in the 1970s, the second wave feminist movement was to mount the most comprehensive attack on the family as a success story so far. This work directly addressed the family as a site of identity construction by challenging the ideological supremacy of the heterosexual nuclear unit, nature and biology. Key critical feminist thinkers of the 1970s and 1980s (Barrett and McIntosh, 1982; Firestone, 1972; Millett, 1970; Oakley, 1972, amongst many others) tore apart reassuring stories about the family as a 'haven', painting it instead as a place which produced and reproduced patriarchal and capitalist power inequalities, and fostered the oppression of women and children. Feminist analyses also highlighted the identity constraints for women in the hegemonic operation of a public–private dualism which located women firmly in the private realm of home, children and family on the basis of their reproductive capacities and excluded them from the public domain of organisations, institutional life and politics (Rosaldo and Lamphere, 1974). There is no doubt that feminist work revolutionized ideas about family and gendered identities and added new theoretical dimensions to the study of intimacy, family and personal relationships.

Crossing over and emerging in tandem with feminist work of this period were critical approaches in the discipline of psychology. Discourse work in psychology grew from the broader movement of social constructionism and the 'turn to language' of this era. It explicitly critiqued the ontological and epistemological foundations of scientific social psychology which tends to reduce complex human experience to sets of variables that can be measured, to assume universal processes across all times, locations and cultures, and to obscure the influence of society by operating as though it were either invisible, static, or, could simply be switched off (Potter and Wetherell, 1987). In contrast, discursive approaches stress negotiation of meaning between people, with a view of 'the person' and 'their social context' as merged, where the boundaries of one cannot easily be separated from the boundaries of the other (Bruner, 1990; Harre, 1983). It puts the spotlight on language to focus on the part that everyday patterns of language and discourse play in constructing reality and views identity and a sense of self as being very much bound up with systems of meaning. Through this view of language as action, a social constructionist perspective pays attention to the discursive resources that are available to people and which they use in the course of their everyday lives. People draw upon interpretative repertoires in order to present and make sense of themselves according to the rhetorical demands of the immediate context and the subject positions made available through talk, in interaction and conversations. This approach allows for the operation of power and ideology in the everyday production and management of identity, and has been used and developed in relation to families and identities (Dixon and Wetherell, 2004).

In addition, the turn of this century has seen a lively resurgence of theoretical debate and empirical enquiry in the more sociologically inclined disciplines into a diverse array of questions about how people organize and live family, kin and close personal relationships and their significance in the construction, maintenance and re-construction of identities. Although identities are viewed in this broad field as fluid, changing, contingent, hybrid and as profoundly impacted upon by forces 'outside', there is a marked divide between small-scale, qualitative studies that focus on the micro practices of everyday family lives and work that focuses on large-scale, theoretical concerns about the extent and nature of the influence of social change. In particular, family sociology has recently been reinvigorated by the emergence of grand theories, such as the individualization thesis of Ulrich Beck and Elisabeth Beck-Gernsheim (2002) and Anthony Giddens' (1992) opus on intimacy, which seek to explain societal changes and their impact on the most private *and* public dimensions of contemporary relational lives (Smart, 2007: 17). The idea that economic and social change has resulted in de-traditionalization and the concomitant process of individualization has become generally accepted amongst sociologists. However, whether or not this has positive outcomes is widely debated. Some of this work challenges assumptions about what constitutes family, stressing diversity of relationships and questioning whether or not the very notion of families is even relevant anymore when thinking about the ways in which people construct self-identity (Budgeon and Roseneil, 2004: 128).

Beck and Beck-Gernsheim's (2002) 'individualisation' thesis suggests that the erosion of the old certainties of industrial society has presented both new risks and opportunities for the construction of identity. Changes such as the increased number of women in paid employment, higher rates of divorce, re-partnering, single-parent families and people living alone, have not only undermined the values and bonds that underpin family and contributed towards the loosening of obligatory ties in families, they have essentially transformed our experience of personal relationships, sexuality and family life. What would previously have been called primary relationships are now described in the concept of 'intimacy', signifying a shift in focus from the structure of such relationships to their quality (Jamieson, 1998). Love and intimacy are now seen to lie at the heart of detraditionalized life and are ever more important in countering the potential loneliness of these new, autonomous, individualized identities. 'Family relationships are rendered conditional, characterized by risk and fragility rather than rules and rituals, and individuals are caught in a paradox, as love and intimacy become ever more central, but ever more difficult to secure and maintain' (Holland et al., 2003: 16).

A more optimistic light on the effect of these changes is cast by Giddens (1991, 1992) who emphasizes a progressive move towards the emergence of a 'reflexive modernity' in the construction of self and the democratisation of personal relationships. This thesis emphasizes the liberating possibilities of a post-traditional society in which being freed from the constraints of conventional social ties means that men and women must reflexively create new, potentially more fulfilling relationships based on mutual satisfaction rather than contractual obligation (Giddens, 1991). For Giddens (1992), the twin notions of the 'pure relationship' and of 'confluent love' distinguish contemporary relationships from the highly

socially circumscribed heterosexual relationships of previous times. Here, the breaking up and transformation of intimate and family ties is conflated with liberation of choice for individuals: without the obligations that previously governed patterns of family relatedness and with roles no longer fixed, people are free to decide their identities for themselves.

With such a pronounced emphasis on change, what space is there to explore continuity in the construction of identity in family and intimate relationships? Can such an abstract, 'top-down' view ever meaningfully describe the lived experience of people's lives? Some maintain that the overplaying of new possibilities has resulted in an underplaying of old inequalities and differences in personal and family life, in particular those of gender, class and 'race' (Brannen and Nilsen, 2005; Duncan and Smith, 2006; Jamieson, 1998). The idea that we are now less drawn than we used to be to making serious and sustained commitments to family and kin is not born out by numerous studies which find that individuals continue to value family ties and obligations and see them as important in the construction of identity (Gillies et al., 2001; Ribbens McCarthy et al., 2003; Williams, 2004). There is evidence that this is also the case in families of choice. In her study of lesbian families Kathy Almack (2007) found that parents were heavily invested in their children being recognized and accepted by their families of origin despite the difficulties in pursuing, let alone achieving this.

When social psychologists and other social scientists conducted research on the family it was the norm to focus on parents' points of view: in terms of identity, children were viewed as 'becoming' rather than 'being'. In the 1990s an emergent 'sociology of childhood' (James et al., 1998) questioned many of the assumptions about contemporary notions of children and childhood that are prevalent in western societies, in particular of children as passive and naïve subjects. Subsequently, more attention has been paid to children as active agents in various aspects of family life. Importantly, much of this research has taken up the idea that rather than taking a 'top down', parental perspective, it is worth asking children directly about their experiences and understandings of families and relationships (Edwards et al., 2006; Smart et al., 2001).

Neil Gross goes some way to steer a middle course around change and stability, tradition and individualization arguing that while there is evidence of a decline in the kinds of 'regulative traditions' that reinforced patterns of heterosexual marriage, this does not mean that 'reflexivity, understood as unbounded agency and creativity, has rushed in to fill the void' (2005: 288). Threads of shared tradition are carried across and down generations and communities, as sense-making patterns or 'meaning-constitutive traditions'. This perspective stresses the historically and culturally situated elements of family and personal relationships as well as the power of everyday, deeply embedded habituality as the conduit of continuity. Furthermore, an emphasis on individualism and the weakening of family tradition is a particularly Western conceptualisation of identity that does not tally with those for whom socio-cultural and religious meaning systems are pivotal in the production and management of identity and social relations (Basit, 1997; Edwards et al., 2006). Research with British Muslims calls into question the 'extended reflexivity thesis' (Adams, 2003: 222), which rests on the notion of a self which is hyper-rational and calculating and above all, is unfettered by culture and tradition (Yip, 2004).

David Morgan's (1996) idea of family 'practices' has also represented an important conceptual development in the study of families and personal relationships. His argument that families must be defined by what they do rather than what they look like has challenged the orthodoxy that contemporary families can be objectively known (McKie et al., 2005). It has shifted sociological analyses of families away from structure and socio-legal

ties onto everyday activities, interactions and importantly, the negotiations and meanings that make up family experience (Finch and Mason, 1993).

Focusing on family as a set of interactional processes allows for more space to theoretically incorporate difference and diversity in family practices and throw light on the impact of 'race', culture, economic shifts, and migration on how people construct and experience individual and collective identities within different families. For example, Constance Sutton (2004) explored the importance of family reunion rituals of African-Caribbean transnational families, and looked at how internationally dispersed families build a sense of family identity across borders and sometimes vast spaces. Family reunions illuminate some of the complexities of contemporary processes of migration, the significance of family memory and narratives in constructing individual and family identities. They were an essential way of creating 'the knowledge that 'family' is your most basic (collective) identity' (Sutton, 2004: 245). Tracey Reynolds (2006) found that Caribbean young people in Britain developed models of group and individual ethnic identities that were both global, through participation in transnational family and kinship events, and local, through the building of cross-ethnic networks in the UK.

Some writers and researchers have engaged positively with ideas around individualization and the transformation of intimacy and have found them useful tools in wrestling the empirical gaze away from the heterosexual, parental couple in order to explore a range of counter-heteronormative personal relationships, including same-sex relationships (Stacey, 2004; Weeks et al., 2001), different kinds of friendships (Pahl and Prevalin, 2005) and couples who 'live apart together' (Levin, 2004). Some would maintain that a decentring of the notion of family, even 'families of choice', is called for because it can no longer 'contain the multiplicity of practices of intimacy and care which have traditionally been its prerogative and its raison d'etre' (Budgeon and Roseneil, 2004: 127). The idea that we are becoming increasingly reflexive creators of our identities has also been viewed positively. Jeffrey Weeks for example, explores the ways in which gay and lesbian identities are created through the telling of coherent life narratives. While they may fictions in that sense, they are agentic ones: 'the necessary ways we mobilize our energies in order to change things' (Weeks, 1991: 98).

Stephen Frosh in Chapter 1 in this volume refers to the 'relational turn' in psychoanalysis, a development that we can also see in kinship and family studies in sociology and anthropology (Carsten, 2004; Smart, 2007). Feminist writers have for a long time critiqued the concept of the 'autonomous ego' on which western social theory rests (Walkerdine, 1988). To counter this specifically masculine and ethno-centric way of understanding selfhood they have emphasized the idea of a 'relational self' which can only be understood because of and through formative and ongoing relationships with others, that is, intersubjectively (Gilligan, 1982). Although close kin ties are essential for the development of a sense of selfhood and individuality, these bonds do *not* have to be with people that are blood relatives. Carol Smart notes that the concept of relationality is important because it allows us to go beyond the notion of kin, which, however remodelled, still carries outmoded connotations with it (2007: 48). Together with Morgan's (1996) notion of 'practices', it is a way of thinking about families and identity that gives emphasis to the negotiated nature of affection, obligation and bonds between people.

The idea that one's subjective self-identity is entwined with others and cannot be understood as separate or individuated also underpins a psychosocial perspective. Where this approach departs from most social scientific work on family, personal relations and identity however, is on the inclusion of the psychoanalytic concept of the unconscious as a powerful force in the construction of selfhood and indeed, of reality. This adds an intra-psychic dimension to relationality that further blurs the lines between self and other, and posits the profound merging of internal, psychological and external, social realms of experience as the foundation for the development of subjectivity. It is this unconscious dimension that so deeply disrupts the privileging of and investment in rationality, reason and conscious intention and motivation in human subjectivity that we find across the social sciences.

In the following sections I will focus on a dimension of experience that is a familiar facet of family life for many people – sibling relationships – and consider the ways in which siblings enter into processes of individual and group identity formation from a psychosocial perspective. Looking at siblings through a psychosocial lens requires a shift in gaze away from the ascendancy of individualized, rational selves towards interdependent and variable identities and relational practices and meanings. It is politically important too: paying close attention to siblings forces us to think harder about sameness and difference and the difficulties of coping with both.

Being and having a sibling remains a common experience; in 2001, over half of UK children lived in households containing more than one child and 20 per cent of these contained three or more children (Office for National Statistics, 2001). Importantly, these figures do not include the number of siblings, half-siblings and step-siblings who live in separate households. As well as being a widespread experience, sibling relationships are far more important for our continuing social and emotional development and well-being than assumed in social science models that privilege parent–child dynamics (Dunn, 1993).[1] As children, siblings are apt to spend far more time with one another than with their parents (Kosonen, 1999). Relationships with sisters and brothers are likely to be the most long-standing that we have (Freeman, 1992; Mauthner, 2002) and whatever the quality of relationship between them, whether

we can ever dissolve psychological connections with brothers and sisters, as may be
possible with friends and partners, is open to
question (Lamb and Sutton-Smith, 1981).
As we become older they may become more
significant in terms of shared living and
care – although there is much evidence that
caring in families is also carried out by siblings as children (see for example, Aldridge
and Sharpe, 2007).

Now, I will turn to consider how psychoanalysis has viewed the development of identity in families and the part that siblings have
been understood to play in that process.

## SIBLINGS AND PSYCHOANALYSIS

Psychoanalysis tenders a compelling analysis of the drama of family life, painting a
picture of families as highly charged and
intense emotional environments, and putting
early relationships of care at the centre of the
development of the structures of the mind
and the growth of sexual and gender identity.
In all psychoanalytic models the most significant relationship is seen as that between
parent/primary carer and child. This, alongside the idea of a universal Oedipus complex,
has had consequences for how the specific
qualities of sibling relationships have been
perceived within traditional psychoanalytic
models of development.

Two main ideas about siblings dominated
Freud's thinking; first, that they represent a
'displacement' in the child's relationship
with the mother, and second, that they are
rivals in the Oedipal conflict. However, in the
last few years there has been vigorous debate
within psychoanalytic circles about the implications of Freud's legacy for theorising the
psychic significance of siblings and the continued usefulness and adequacy of these
ideas for clinical practice.

The feminist Freudian analyst and writer
Juliet Mitchell maintains that despite the
prevalence of siblings in the narratives of
analysands, 'psychoanalytic theory in all its
versions omits them from a structuring role
in the production of unconscious processes'
(2003: 7). She questions this omission by
remarking on the presence of siblings in case
histories where their central involvement in
patients' traumatic experiences are ignored
or viewed as insignificant, resulting in the
lack of an adequate framework through which
to more fully understand and work with sibling relationships therapeutically. Mitchell
is also critical of the emphasis on vertical
relationships at the expense of lateral (peer
and sibling) relationships (2000, 2003). As
mentioned earlier, this top–down approach,
which privileges the perspective of adults,
even when the focus of investigation is children, has until recently, been endemic in the
social sciences.

From an object-relations perspective,
Prophecy Coles (2003) looks to the testimony in her own and others' clinical case
studies, as well as in literature, to the importance of sibling love and attachment. She
argues that despite the evidence, the legacy
of Freud has meant that these experiences are
either ignored, or only understood as a transformation of the normal 'primal hatred' and
'unfathomably deep hostility' (Fliess, 1956:
8 cited in Coles, 2003: 29) that he insisted
must inevitably exist between siblings. Coles
highlights how sisters and brothers are therefore treated paradoxically; as significant
enough to evoke primal hatred and yet dismissed as not important to the development
of the inner world. In her interpretation of
Freud, siblings are consistently sidelined in
important developmental psychic processes
and thereby rendered irrelevant in discussions of mental health (Coles, 2003: 41).
Furthermore, sibling attachment is marginalized and rivalry posited as the norm with
sibling experience modelled on that of the
eldest.

Neither Mitchell nor Coles wish to dismiss
the difficult feelings we may have about our
siblings (including the wish for them not to
be there), nor the importance of parents in
our emotional development. But both, in different ways, insist that this is only half the

story of the development of the self. It is not enough to always understand relationships with siblings as a transfer from parental ones, when it is clear that children often 'create triangles among themselves that are independent of oedipal parental triangles and these triangles exert a powerful influence upon psychic development' (Coles, 2003: 2). The Oedipus complex forms only one constellation of the developmental processes that an individual goes through.

It is important to take siblings seriously (and, Mitchell would argue, other 'lateral', peer relationships) because it is with them that we are likely to have our first *social* relationship. At the very least, we need our siblings and peers to help us get away from our parents and teach us how to relate in a different way. That siblings are important in the infant's process of separation from the parent was an idea developed by Winnicott (1951) who used the concept of 'transitional spaces and objects' with regard to siblings' role in separation. And from a group psychoanalytic perspective Farhad Dalal argues that in order to move 'from the singular 'I' to the many varieties of 'us' we have to steer a course through two distinct developmental strands – learning that we are not our parents, and learning to cooperate with our siblings and peers' (1998: 226).

The weight given to the Oedipal drama has meant that even those psychoanalytic writers who study sibling relationships beyond dimensions of rivalry, assume that parent–child bonds constitute the core relationship for emotional development. For example, Bank and Kahn's (1982) fascinating analysis of the psychic complexity of sibling relationships from an object relations perspective, maintains the interpretation that intense sibling bonds can only be understood as a response to inadequate or unsatisfactory parenting. The idea that close bonds of affection in sibling or other lateral peer relationships only develop as a substitute for 'good enough' mothering, rather than being of intrinsic value, is thus reproduced.

The assertion that Freud neglected the importance of sisters and brothers in the structuring of internal worlds, or that the theoretical consideration of siblings and other lateral relationships has been severely hindered (Sanders, 2004) by adherence to Freud's thinking, has been strongly contested in other quarters. From her detailed review of material on siblings in Freud's writings, Susan Sherwin-White argues that he was astutely aware of the potential importance of sibling dynamics for the development of personhood, from childhood, to puberty and into adulthood, and that his observations are still relevant for therapeutic work today (2007: 5). Margaret Rustin concurs that siblings have tended to be overlooked in the fields of child development, family dynamics and psychoanalysis (2007: 21). However, she looks to child psychotherapy as a field of practice where the sibling dimension of a child's identity is apparent and valued in therapeutic work. This is partly because of the influence of family therapy on child psychotherapy, which explicitly lays emphasis on all of the relationships within a family, not just the parental ones. She would argue that this is the case, even when the child does not actually have brothers or sisters: 'The importance of imaginary siblings as a replacement for missing siblings is one thread in the world of imaginary companions' (2007: 22).

## A PSYCHOSOCIAL PERSPECTIVE ON SIBLINGS AND INTERSUBJECTIVITY

In this part of the chapter I take a psychoanalytically informed *psychosocial* perspective to explore the place that sisters and brothers have in the psychic life of children and young people and the ways in which they enter into processes of personal and group identity formation (Lucey, 2006; Lucey and Rogers, 2007). To do this I will draw on data from interviews with two young brothers which comes from a qualitative study of children and young people's sibling relationships carried out by myself, Ros Edwards, Lucy Hadfield and Melanie Mauthner (Edwards et al., 2006).

A psychosocial perspective holds that individual and group identities are constituted psychically and socially, with neither having an essence apart from the other (Frosh, 2003: 1555), and that we therefore need theoretical tools that can take account of both domains. Concepts from the object relations school of psychoanalysis such as identification and recognition (Benjamin, 1995 enable an exploration of the idea that selfhood is formed through unconscious identifications between siblings. However, attention also needs to be paid to the significance of social and cultural forces in the structuring of identities: the power of gender, ethnicity, class and age for example. There is a lively discussion in social psychology about the relationship between discourse work in psychology and psychoanalysis (Frosh et al., 2003), and the possibilities of developing a 'psychoanalytic discursive psychology' (Billig, 2006) or 'cultural psychoanalysis' (Wetherell, 2003). The work of discursive psychologists is valuable in examining the socio-cultural situatedness of subjects: what discourses are available to people at particular times and places, how are they positioned in those discourses, and what are their investments in discourse, that is, what room is there for taking up certain subject positions whilst refusing others?

The notion of identification as one of the processes involved in identity development is important in a psychosocial perspective because it is concerned with the ways in which people dynamically take on aspects of the outside world, and also how parts of themselves are experienced as existing out there, in other people and objects. Concepts such as identification, projection and projective identification help to shed light on the ways in which recurrent or habitual patterns, including individual roles within a group develop, and the complex and contradictory positions that individuals can occupy

in families. It allows for the possibility that what happens between people goes beyond conscious levels of awareness and conscious interests – unconscious emotions, desires and motivations – are also at play. Psychic reality cannot be directly correlated with events in the external world, but is profoundly subject to the (sometimes distorting) effects of anxiety and fantasy. It also ties in with a core premise of a psychosocial perspective, that identity construction, the self, including the self as sibling is a relational process. Identity is not something that an individual can do all by his 'Enlightened' self.

The children and young people who took part in the study reported here were recruited through numerous techniques including personal connections and subsequent 'snowballing' of contacts, advertising in youth projects, leisure centres and schools. The criteria for inclusion were that they were between 5 and 25 years old, all (or most) of their siblings would also take part and their parents or carers agreed to their participation. It is worth noting that psychoanalysts writing about siblings have most often based their work on material gathered in clinical contexts with clients who typically present because they are experiencing crisis in their emotional lives (Bank and Kahn, 1982; Kahn and Lewis, 1988; Lewin, 2004; Moser et al., 2005; Schacter, 1985). In contrast, we wanted to explore sibling dynamics in their 'ordinariness', although this is not equated with a one-dimensional view of happiness or harmony. While there were a few sibling groups in which destructive emotions dominated and where a sense of crisis prevailed, in the main, siblings illustrated a buoyant dynamism in their feelings and interactions with one another. Their narratives highlighted the constant social and emotional work, which could be as reparative as it was destructive, that children and young people 'ordinarily' undertake in trying to live with and make sense of the 'puzzle' of themselves in relation with their siblings.

In the following case study of two young brothers I will present only short extracts from the interviews that I conducted with them separately, but my reading of the data is from the whole range of material that I have available, as well as my fieldnotes. The extracts I have chosen are intended to illustrate themes that were recurrent in their narratives, in particular, the difficulties and complexities of connection and dependency for siblings.

## STEVEN AND ASHLEY: DEPENDENCY AND AMBIVALENCE

Steven (aged 13) and Ashley (aged 9) are white, British brothers, who lived with their biological parents on the outskirts of London. This is a family who were embedded in the locality and in their extended kin networks. Regular caring and leisure time was spent with maternal and paternal grandparents, who lived nearby, as well as aunts, uncles and cousins on both sides of the family and they enjoyed positive relationships with one another without (as their mother said) 'living in one another's pockets'. In their interviews with me the brothers talked lovingly about their paternal grandparents who lived across the road and their maternal grandparents who lived further away but who they also saw regularly. They also invoked warm relationships with specific uncles who made them feel 'special' and 'favoured'. This portrayal of wider kin relationships as harmonious and the source of pleasure was in stark contrast to Steven and Ashley's account of their *own* relationship, which they both described, in separate interviews, as full of conflict.

Ashley, the younger brother, was a slightly built, animated boy who loved to talk. There were few silences in his interview and Ashley responded to my questions in a tumble of thoughts, feelings and opinions, interspersed with lots of illustrative anecdotes. He came over as open, confident (at one point he told me that he thought he was good-looking!), sweet, articulate, witty and cheeky. At first he painted a rather rosy picture of brotherly

affection between himself and Steven, of sharing and mutual regard, but this was gradually eroded as the interview continued and stories of quarrels and clashes between them emerged.

In contrast, his older brother Steven seemed reserved. He spoke quietly, with care and quite slowly, often with long silences in-between. When he began to talk of his relationship with Ashley, alongside the thoughtfulness in his words, came a tide of angry feelings about him. He continued to choose his words (perhaps that is why he did not need so many of them) and there was a directness and candour that was striking.

The brothers had separate bedrooms, but Steven's was bigger than Ashley's and this became the site for much expression of envy, resentment and aggression between them. Because Ashley stored many of his toys and books in Steven's room, arguments about access were constant. Steven, who described himself as sometimes liking 'solitude' and being 'quiet' experienced Ashley as intolerably invasive of his 'private' space and highly manipulative of their parents to 'get his own way'. Ashley, in contrast, was furious that Steven wanted to literally and metaphorically shut him out – of his room and his life. He spoke with a keen awareness of his own power to get back at Steven by complaining vociferously to his parents who would exert pressure on Steven to include him.

> Well, my mum gets in a bad mood. She starts shouting. And my dad starts shouting [deep voice] 'You can come in here whenever you want' and everything. So, it gets me in a horrible mood and I just think… It's so that I can't go in his room whenever I want, and my dad says [deep voice] 'He can go in the room whenever you want and he can play the Play Station whenever he wants' and he goes 'Oh you always take his side don't you?'. And I go 'No that ain't true. Because it is true that I can play whenever I want'. (Ashley)
>
> If he comes in I let him come in, but I like, rush him and (…) if I say 'you've got 30 seconds to get whatever you want', I sort of, he goes downstairs and says to my dad 'oh he won't let me come in my room, his room, my room, yeah my room'. And then my dad says 'let him go in and get whatever he wants'. And then my brother starts taking

advantage, just sitting there and irritating me. (Steven)

A dominating idea in all fields that pay attention to siblings, not only psychoanalysis, is that of sibling rivalry. Freud maintained that the arrival of a new sibling can only be a traumatic experience for a child as the possibility of losing the primary carer, or of there not being enough of her to go around, stirs up hostile and destructively competitive feelings towards the newcomer. This was avidly taken up by subsequent Freudian theorists: Adler (1958) coined the term 'dethronement' to describe the intense experience of loss in the displacement of the older child by the incomer and Levy (1937, 1941) developed and popularized the concept of 'sibling rivalry'. But it was only later that psychoanalysts theorized the possibility that sibling rivalry could be a positive ingredient in processes of development (Neubauer, 1982). Mitchell argues that it is a commonplace experience to feel displaced by another and in that displacement to experience a feeling that there is no recognition for us anywhere. This is something that recurs throughout life, but may often be initially experienced at the arrival of a new sibling or by the 'sudden recognition of the meaning of [another sibling] who, as it were, intrudes dramatically on his consciousness. The one who is displaced refuses to recognize the new or new-found sibling – the other' (2003: 133).

This allows for the idea that aggression between siblings is not always motivated by rivalry, where one desires something that the other has. Bank and Kahn maintain that in many instances the payoff in aggression is 'internal, having to do with a forbidden satisfaction or the fulfilment of a deeper emotional need' (1982: 197) including the need to be recognized by others as subjects with our own desires worthy of fulfilment (Edwards et al., 2006: 90).

And what of the younger brother, who does not suffer the outrage of being pushed out by the new arrival, but rather is the one whose accident of birth causes the dethronement? Despite Ashley being the object of Steven's alternately and sometimes simultaneously aggressive, protective and envious feelings, he expressed a genuine desire to be close to and to be recognised by him. Across our siblings study we witnessed younger siblings tendency to 'look up' to older ones and their wish to connect with them, often in the face of older siblings seeking to establish distance from younger siblings. This process of identification and dis-identification is closely linked with status and power within the sibling group and of local normative positionings around age and status amongst other peers.

Steven's sense of being invaded and Ashley's of being pushed out – two perfectly interdependent positions – is enacted on a spatial level around his bedroom, but he also raises other metaphors of size to express his difficult feelings. He describes Ashley as 'acting big', 'acting like the big tough man' and having a 'big mouth'. Read through the lens of rivalry, we could view this as illustrating Steven's experience of Ashley taking up too much space in the family since his birth. But that he also denigrates this as a performance (as an 'act') may indicate awareness on a less conscious level that the physically diminutive Ashley takes up more psychic space than he does physical space. Seeming 'big and tough' is also key to performing a hegemonic version of masculinity that is comfortably distanced from anything feminine and may be especially salient for these working class boys (Connell, 1995; Frosh et al., 2003; Mac an Ghaill, 1994). That Ashley does this in front of Steven's friends may not only be a challenge to Steven's position as older brother, but is part of the necessary, ongoing construction and presentation of an acceptable masculine identity.

One of the challenges in sustaining emotional connection with another is recognising that they are like us – human at the very least. Across the study it was not unusual for ideas about similarity and difference to inform children and young people's understandings of what it means to be a sibling and how they are placed and viewed by others. Certainly, difference from one another was a driving sentiment in Steven and Ashley's narratives. They often compared themselves and were routinely compared by others in terms of similarities in personality, physical similarities (whether they looked the same or different), behavioural and attitudinal similarities (what they were 'good' at) and similarities of choice (what they liked doing) (Bank and Kahn, 1982). Ashley and Steven's parents had humorously told me when I arrived at their home 'you won't get a word out of Steven and you won't be able to shut Ashley up' and were surprised that the interview with Steven lasted for an hour and a half. The idea that they were in some way 'opposites' circulated in the family and both brothers were keen to deny their similarities and assert their difference from another.

> I see myself as completely different. I have a completely different attitude to him. I think I can act completely differently to how he does. I'm really quiet and he's the big-mouth one. Outgoing, sort of confident person. I can be, but not really. (Steven)
>
> Umm, I'm most different to Steven because I got different colour hair to him and I got different personality and we like different things and stuff.. Like I might like Harry Potter and he thinks it's stupid and I might like Lord of the Rings and he says it's boring and it's stupid. You know we have different hobbies and stuff. (Ashley)

However, there was less certainty about these differences than the boys might admit. Despite the antagonism between them, Steven included Ashley in play activities outside the home and tolerated his company even when Steven was with his older friends. He could be irritated by Ashley's confidence and his habit of challenging Steven's authority as the eldest: 'He tends to think he's older and bigger. And he back-chats when I say something to him.' But we may also detect envy in the 'quiet' Steven's comments of his 'big-mouth' little brother, perhaps a wish that he had some of Ashley's self-assurance.

> Because I'm not really outgoing and confident, I get a bit scared of doing something wrong, mucking up or something. (Steven)

Jessica Benjamin (1995) writes that the recognition of sameness may at times be painful to acknowledge, for instance because we see undesirable characteristics in another that we do not want to accept in ourselves. At these times we may draw back from, deny or reject our sameness or similarity to another person or group. In doing so, we may see 'them' as other to 'us'. In order to maintain those kinds of mental and spatial boundaries, a different order of psychological work is needed, such as projecting negative unwanted and disowned aspects of the self into another person or group. Equally, positive attributes of the self may also be defensively projected as they may need protection from the more destructive capacities of the self and so may be attributed to someone else so as to be kept safe. Siblings are handy repositories for such projections, although there may be a depletion of the self if vital qualities cannot be owned but instead are enviously viewed as belonging to another (Lucey and Rogers, 2007.

Bank and Kahn's (1982) typology of sibling identity processes describe as 'hostile dependent', those where there is a firm refusal of similarity, boundaries between self and sibling are rigidly demarcated and where competitiveness and gloating dominates. In these kinds of rigid relationships sisters and brothers are likely to be resistant to any change in dynamics that might alter the status quo. Although there are strong elements of this in Steven and Ashley's attitudes towards each other, we must keep in mind that the ambivalence that characterizes other intimate relationships is also evident between siblings. Though powerfully present between these boys, rivalry, resentment and disappointment between them was not so overwhelming that it destroyed all feelings of warmth, care and empathy. Ashley may have undermined Steven's authority at home but he needed him as his protector outside and while Steven enviously railed against Ashley's incursions, he was also invested in and took up the position of protector and mediator in certain situations.

Well, he can be, quite annoying to the neighbours, knocking on doors and running away. They come out and chase him, so I have to come out and tell them to leave him alone. Tell them he's only having a bit of fun. (Steven)

Yeah, mmm Cos my brother's in Year 8 and I'm in Year 5, and if some Year 7 or Year 6 picked on me yeah, I'll go 'I'll get my brother on you' and he's goes 'Try me'. And then I go and tell my brother and he goes 'Don't touch him' and 'Leave him alone because he ain't done nothing wrong'. (Ashley)

Woven through the brothers' narratives, with their stress on conflict, difference and Steven's desire for separation from his younger brother, are equally strong, though not always as explicitly articulated, themes of dependence. Rustin notes that although children with younger siblings have to deal with displacement and rivalry when they arrive, there is an upside to this intrusion:

The single child who has to share parents with a new arrival in the family does have to deal with rivalry, but at the same time gains a partner, and this mitigates the loneliness that a singleton can also experience. The sharing of what it is like to be at the centre of parental attention can also sometimes be a considerable relief. Not only does the child gain a companion, and one who will at times certainly be an ally in mischief and rebellious discontent with parental demands, as well as a playmate with whom a shared imaginary world can be created, but also it can lift a burden when one is not the only repository of the family's expectations and projections. (2007: 28)

Each boy entered the other's talk as a positive presence in connection with fears of being alone, and, significantly of being alone with their parents. At different times in his interview Ashley conjured up various scenarios in which Steven's presence becomes essential to guard against this.

Well, umm … We normally get um, if I wasn't, if I didn't a brother umm, I wouldn't really like, enjoy as much as I do because well, sometimes we don't get along like that good … sometimes we have arguments and stuff. But like, at Christmas and stuff you get toys that you like, have to have someone else to play with… and like, your dad and your mum um, might be like too old for it and like … […] How can I put it? You wouldn't, like, enjoy it so much. You wouldn't enjoy it. And if you

had something like, remote control car or something … and you just like, done it on your own … you wouldn't … Oh … Like, if you wanted, you had two remote controls and you wanted to like, have a little battle or something, you couldn't have a battle with yourself because it'd be a bit stupid … (Ashley)

Ashley struggled to finds words to express an aspect of his sense of identity and ontological security that was powerfully tied up with Steven. Interestingly, their parents were cast as too old here, heavily signifying their 'difference' and otherness to the youthful boys, whilst Steven was the 'same as'. Steven also expresses some of this in his comments below, though his aggression towards Ashley is, as always, closer to the surface:

When you are together you can play with someone. But I still think I was meant to be an only child. […] Cos I wouldn't call myself a recluse, but I like to be on my own. I don't like the intrusion of my little brother. But I'm not sure really, whether I'd like on or not, cos when he is away … I do like it. Then if none of my mates come round I tend to get bored. (Steven)

Steven invokes the cruel hand of fate in the thwarting of his true destiny to be an only child and his wish to wipe Ashley's existence out. We could certainly interpret his sentiment in the light of Freud's thoughts on the fathomless hostility that the usurped eldest child feels upon the arrival of the new baby. However, this would not do justice to the maelstrom of ambivalent identifications between the brothers. Moments after symbolically killing him off, Steven brings Ashley back to life in his narrative as an essential figure in his internal world and his fantasised version of the family constellation. No longer an intruder, now he needs Ashley to become his companion and to rescue him from the very aloneness that he craves.

The evidence of these brothers' aggression, envy and even hatred towards one another is indisputable. At the same time, their struggles for separation and difference cannot entirely extinguish their creative and generous impulses, towards the other, themselves and towards life (Winnicott, 1971). They demonstrate their capacity for imaginative agency (Hoggett, 2000) where internal representations of one another are not so frozen that they cannot take a break from attack to allow shared, pleasurable activities and feelings, including their deeply felt love for their grandparents. Perhaps Steven can envisage a future when they are 'grown up', in which he Ashley get on much better because they are embedded in a family in which they witness and experience the sustaining flows of affect and care between adults and between adults and children.

## CONCLUSION

While it may be possible to celebrate our potential as creators of our own lives and identities, putting sibling relationships centre-stage in a psychosocial perspective clearly conveys some of the limits as well as the possibilities of personal agency in families. For children and most young people, issues of power inequalities can be especially prominent; they cannot choose who their parents or carers are, in what family group they live, whether they have sisters or brothers or where the age-position they occupy in the sibling group. Like adults, they have no direct control over the social and structural forces of gender, race, class and culture that help shape all our lives.

Accounts of human agency also need to recognize that we are also subject to the power of *unconscious* forces. Rationalist models currently dominant in the field of family studies assume a composed, unitary and knowing self that negotiates, chooses and acts in her or his own interests. This framework leaves us little space to attend to why we act in ways which are destructive to our interests, get stuck, repeat damaging behaviours or relationships and destroy sense rather than make sense (Hoggett, 2000: 172) and is in contrast to a psychosocial perspective which views the human subject as fragmented. Although this divided subject can be its own worst enemy, moves towards reconciliation and integration are also powerful forces in subjectivity. The key to partially overcoming this fragmentation is not the reflexive agency of an autonomous subject (Giddens, 1992), but dependency and the difficulties and delights of connection to others and otherness (Butler, 2003). Here, the other is not necessarily exploitative, but can also respond to us with generosity. Much more than this, it is formative of the subject, not outside of it but 'right there at its unconscious core' (Frosh, 2002).

The narratives of the two young, white, working-class brothers presented here have revealed how a sense of self is constructed and felt through psychic, cultural and social connections that bind us to others in both positive and negative ways. These connections involve a profoundly relational version of the self: they constitute elements of our own dependence on others as well as independence from them, and conceptions of these others' reliance on or autonomy from us. These complex interdependencies invoke a sense of self, a subjectivity that, as we have seen, are replete with the contradictions of love and hate, pleasure and discomfort, connection and separation.

## NOTE

1 Robert Sanders (2004) provides a comprehensive overview of research and theorising on siblings.

## REFERENCES

Adams, M. (2003) 'The reflexive self and culture: A critique', *British Journal of Sociology*, 54 (2): 221–38.

Adler, A. (1958) *The Individual Psychology of Alfred Adler*. New York: Basic Books.

Aldridge, J. and Sharpe, D. (2007) 'Pictures of young caring'. Available at: http://www.lboro.ac.uk/departments/ss/centres/YCRG/current_research.html (accessed 20/3/2008).

Almack, K. (2007) 'Out and about: Negotiating the process of disclosure of lesbian parenthood',

*Sociological Research Online*, 12 (1). Available at: http://www.socresonline.org.uk/12/1/almack.html. Last accessed on 27.3.08.

Barratt, M. and McIntosh, M. (1982) *The Anti-Social Family*. London: Verso.

Bank, S. and Kahn, S. (1982) *The Sibling Bond*. New York: Basic Books.

Basit, T. (1997) '"I want more freedom, but not too much": British Muslim girls and the dynamics of family values', *Gender and Education*, 9 (4): 425–39.

Beck, U. and Beck-Gernsheim, E. (2002)*Individualization*. London: Sage.

Benjamin, J. (1995) *The Shadow of the Other: Intersubjectivity and Gender in Psychoanalysis*. London: Routledge.

Billig, M. (2006) 'A psychoanalytic discursive psychology: From consciousness to unconsciousness', *Discourse Studies*, 8 (1): 17–24.

Brannen, J. and Nilsen, A. (2005) 'Individualisation, choice and structure: A discussion of current trends in sociological analysis', *Sociological Review*, 53 (3): 412–28.

Bruner, J. (1990) *Acts of Meaning*. Cambridge, MA: Harvard University Press.

Budgeon, S. and Roseneil, S. (2004) 'Editor's introduction: Beyond the conventional family', *Current Sociology*, 52 (2): 128.

Butler, J. (2003) 'Violence, mourning, politics', *Studies in Gender and Sexuality*, 4: 9–37.

Carsten, J. (2004) *After Kinship*. Cambridge: Cambridge University Press.

Coles, P. (2003) *The Importance of Sibling Relationships in Psychoanalysis*. London: Karnac Books.

Connell, R. (1995) *Masculinities*. Cambridge: Polity.

Dalal, F. (1998) *Taking the Group Seriously*. London: Jessica Kingsley.

Dixon, J. and Wetherell, M. (2004) 'On discourse and dirty nappies: gender, the division of household labour and the social psychology of distributive justice', *Theory and Psychology*, 14(2): 167–89.

Duncan, D. and Smith, D. (2006) 'Individualisation versus the geography of 'new' families', *Twenty First Century Society*, 1 (2): 167–89.

Dunn, J. (1993) *Young Children's Close Relationships: Beyond Attachment*. Newbury, CA: Sage.

Edwards, R., Hadfield, L., Lucey, H. and Mauthner, M. (2006) *Sibling Identity and Relationships: Sisters and Brothers*. London: Routledge.

Finch, J. and Mason, J. (1993) *Negotiating Family Responsibilities*. London: Routledge.

Firestone, S. (1972) *The Dialectic of Sex*. London: Paladin.

Fliess, R. (1956) *Erogeneity and Libido*. New York: International Universities Press.

Freeman, D. (1992) *Multigenerational Family Therapy*. London: Haworth.

Froggett, L. (2002) *Love, Hate and Welfare*. Bristol: The Policy Press.

Frosh, S. (2002) The Other. *American Imago*, 59 (4): 389–408.

Frosh, S. (2003) 'Psychosocial studies and psychology: Is a critical approach emerging?', *Human Relations*, 56 (2), 1545–67.

Frosh, S., Phoenix, A. and Pattman, R. (2003) 'Taking a stand: Using psychoanalysis to explore the positioning of subjects in discourse', *British Journal of Social Psychology*, 42: 39–53.

Giddens, A. (1991) *Modernity and Self-Identity: Self and Society in the Late Modern Age*. Cambridge: Polity Press.

Giddens, A. (1992) *The Transformation of Intimacy: Sexuality, Love and Eroticism in Modern Societies*. Cambridge: Polity Press.

Gillies, V., Ribbens McCarthy, J. and Holland, J. (2001) *Pulling Together, Pulling Apart: the Family Lives of Young People*. London: Family Policy Studies Centre/ Joseph Rowntree Foundation.

Gilligan, C. (1982) *In a Different Voice*. Cambridge MA: Harvard Press.

Gross, N. (2005) 'The detraditionalization of intimacy reconsidered', *Sociological Theory*, 23 (3): 286–311.

Harre, R. (1983) *Personal Being*. Oxford: Blackwell.

Hoggett, P. (2000) *Emotional Life and the Politics of Welfare*. Basingstoke: Macmillan.

Holland, J., Weeks, J. and Gillies, V. (2003) 'Families, intimacy and social capital', *Social Policy and Society*, 2: 339–48.

James, A., Jenks, C. and Prout, A. (1998) *Theorising Childhood*. Cambridge: Polity Press.

Jamieson, L. (1998) *Intimacy: Personal Relationships in Modern Societies*. Cambridge: Polity Press.

Kahn, M.D. and Lewis, K.G. (1988) *Siblings in Therapy: Life Span and Clinical Issues*. Ontario: Penguin Books.

Kosonen, M. (1999) '"Core" and "kin" siblings: Foster children's changing families', in A. Mullender (ed.), *We are Family: Sibling Relationships in Placement and Beyond*. London: British Agencies for Adoption and Fostering (BAAF), pp: 28–49.

Lamb, M.E. and Sutton-Smith, B. (eds) (1981) *Sibling Relationships: Their Nature and Significance Across the Lifespan*. Hillsdale, NJ: Lawrence Erlbaum.

Levy, D.M. (1937) *Studies in Sibling Rivalry*. American Orthopsychiatry Research Monograph, no. 2.

Levy, D.M. (1941) 'The hostile act', *Psychological Review*, 48: 356–61.

Levin, I. (2004) 'Living apart together', *Current Sociology*, 52 (2): 181–97.

Lewin, V. (2004) *The Twin in the Transference*. London: Whurr.

Lucey, H. (2006) 'Families', in W. Hollway, H. Lucey and A. Phoenix (eds), *Social Psychology Matters*. London: Open University Press in association with The Open University, pp. 65–92.

Lucey, H. and Rogers, C. (2007) 'Power and the unconscious in doctoral student–supervisor relationships', in V. Gillies and H. Lucey (eds) *Power, Knowledge and the Academy: Exploring the Institutional and Personal Dynamics of Research*. London: Palgrave Macmillan, pp. 16–35.

Mac an Ghaill, M. (1994) *The Making of Men*. Buckingham: Open University Press.

McKie, L., Cunningham-Burley, S. and McKendrick, J. (2005) *Families in Society: Boundaries and Relationships*. Bristol: Policy Press.

Mauthner, M. (2002) *Sistering: Power and Change in Female Relationships*. Basingstoke: Palgrave.

Millett, K. (1970) *Sexual Politics*. New York: Doubleday.

Mitchell, J. (2003) *Siblings, Sex and Violence*. Cambridge: Polity Press.

Morgan, D. (1996) *Family Connections*. Cambridge: Polity Press.

Moser, C.J., Jones, R.A., Zaorski, D.M. and Mirsalimi, H. (2005) 'The impact of the sibling in clinical practice: Transference and countertransference dynamics', *Psychotherapy: Theory, Research, Practice*, 42 (3): 267–78.

Neubauer, P. (1982) 'The importance of the sibling experience', *Psychoanalytic Study of the Child*, 38: 325–36.

Oakley, A. (1972) *Sex, Gender and Society*. London: Temple Smith Gower.

Office for National Statistics (2001) *Census 2001*. Retrieved on-line: www.statistics.gov.uk.

Pahl, R. and Prevalin, D. (2005) 'Between family and friends. A longitudinal study of friendship choice', *British Journal of Sociology*, 56 (3): 433–50.

Potter, J. and Wetherell, M. (1987) *Discourse and Social Psychology: Beyond Attitudes and Behaviour*. London: Sage.

Rosaldo, M.Z. and Lamphere, L. (eds) (1974) *Women, Culture and Society*. Stanford: Stanford University Press.

Reynolds, T. (2006) 'Caribbean families, social capital and young people's diasporic identities', *Ethnic and Racial Studies*, 29 (6): 1087–103.

Ribbens McCarthy, J., Edwards, R. and Gillies, V. (2003) *Making Families: Moral Tales of Parenting and Step-Parenting*. York: Sociology Press.

Rustin, M. (2007) 'Taking account of siblings – A view from child psychotherapy', *Journal of Child Psychotherapy*, 33 (1): 21–35.

Sanders, R. (2004) *Sibling Relationships: Theory and Issues for Practice*. Basingstoke: Palgrave Macmillan.

Schacter (1985) 'Sibling deidentification in the clinic: Devil vs. angel', *Family Process*, 24: 415–27.

Sherwin-White, S. (2007) 'Freud on brothers and sisters: A neglected topic', *Journal of Child Psychotherapy*, 33 (1): 4–20.

Smart, C., Neale, B. and Wade, A. (2001) *The Changing Experience of Childhood*. Cambridge: Polity Press.

Smart, C. (2007) *Personal Life*. Cambridge: Polity Press.

Stacey, J. (2004) 'Cruising to familyland: Gay hypergamy and rainbow kinship', *Current Sociology*, 52 (2): 181–97.

Sutton, C. R. (2004) 'Celebrating ourselves: The family reunion rituals of African-Caribbean transnational families', *Global Networks*, 4 (3): 243–57.

Walkerdine, V. (1988) *The Mastery of Reason: Cognitive Development and the Production of Rationality*. London: Routledge.

Weeks, J. (1991) *Against Nature: Essays on History, Sexuality and Identity*. London: Rivers Oram Press.

Weeks, J., Heaphy, B. and Donovan, C. (2001) *Same Sex Intimacies*. London: Routledge.

Wetherell, M. (2003) 'Paranoia, ambivalence, and discursive practices: Concepts of position and positioning in psychoanalysis and discursive psychology', in R. Harre and F.M. Moghaddam (eds), *The Self and Others: Positioning Individuals and Groups in Personal, Political and Cultural Contexts*. Westport, CT: Praeger, pp. 99.

Williams, F. (2004) *Rethinking Families*. London: Calouste Gulbenkin Foundation.

Winnicott, D. (1951) 'Transitional objects and transitional phenomena', *Through Paediatrics to Psychoanalysis*. London: Karnac Books.

Winnicott, D. (1971) *Playing and Reality*. London: Tavistock.

Yip, A. (2004) 'Negotiating space with family and kin in identity construction: The narratives of British non-heterosexual muslims', *The Sociological Review*, 52 (3): 336–50.

# 25

# Neoliberalism, Work and Subjectivity: Towards a More Complex Account

Valerie Walkerdine and Peter Bansel

The aim of this chapter is to understand the making of the neoliberal subject in the context of global transformations in the workplace, in the meaning of work, and in the nature of identity projects. These changes are part and parcel of wider social and cultural shifts which have important and profound consequences both for our understanding of subjectivity and the world of work. In this chapter we will review major approaches to subjectivity and identity transformation under neoliberalism and globalization and discuss these in the light of research in two countries: Wales and Australia. Our research allows us to critically reflect upon the efficacy of sociological arguments about the 'subject' of neoliberalism and to point to the need for a more nuanced style of analysis which takes time and space seriously. Though understood as a regulatory regime, neoliberalism is not positioned in this chapter as hegemonic or deterministic, but rather as located in networks of emergent and intersecting conditions of possibility. We emphasize that there is no singular, stable 'neoliberalism' but rather a set of dispersed discourses, positions and practices inflected by the specificity of

the different contexts in which it emerges. It is something of this specificity and its effects for subjectivity and identity that we are attempting to articulate.

## NEOLIBERAL SOCIAL FORMATIONS

Much debate has emerged regarding the causes, reach and impacts of neoliberalism in recent years. Some find an oppressive regime that signals the erosion of democracy, the disappearance of civil society and other deleterious effects (Baudrillard, 1998; Bourdieu, 1998, 2003; Brown, 2003; Sennett, 1997). Others are enthusiastic about the emergence of a new politics beyond the limits of modernism, in which a new relation of the self to the state, and of the self to the self, has been made possible (Beck et al., 1994; Giddens, 1991). For Papadopoulos (2003) neoliberalism has resulted in a society which has more positive and negative qualities than before, and is hence at the same time both better and worse. That neoliberalism is a significant global capitalist enterprise is not disputed. Further we recognize that it has discernable features as a mode of liberal government, and is best understood as an intensification of liberalism, or as advanced liberalism (Burchell, 1996; Rose, 1989, 1999), rather than something entirely new. Change, in this sense, is understood not as the demise of welfare capitalism but as its augmentation by new techniques of political, social and economic regulation (Levi-Faur and Jordana, 2005).

Neoliberalism, despite its ambitions towards deregulation of markets and government intervention in both the social and the economic, is, Levi-Faur and Jordana (2005: 7) suggest, expanding and extending regulation. How might we understand this expanded and intensified regulation in terms of subjection and subjectivity? In thinking about this intensification of regulation we want, like Levi-Faur and Jordana, to take a position that does not assume neoliberal hegemony. In taking up ideas of diffusion and dispersal through networks of geographically dispersed sites and actors we propose a more nuanced reading of governmentality, neoliberalism and subjectivity. This address to diffusion and dispersal across time and space, across continents, cities, communities and subjects recognizes that 'while neoliberalism may well be the dominant discourse, it is not the only discourse available' (Levi-Faur and Jordana, 2005: 14). What we are signalling here is the endurance of other discourses, and positions within them, that exceed, defy, resist and intersect with dominant neoliberal discourses in ways that cannot be reduced to a deterministic hegemonic rationality. Historical changes in governance, subjection and subjectivity, simultaneously political, social, and personal, are understood as constituted within and by the networks of actors who are involved in the processes and practices through which these changes acquire meanings and are mobilized in action. We are concerned with the ways in which discourses and technologies of government are differently inflected at different times in different sites and in different subjects.

We foreground the discursive and material conditions that make certain kinds of subjects possible, recognizing that within and beside dominant discourses are other intersecting discourses situated within different power–knowledge relations. These locate subjects in different discursive networks that produce multiple subject positions that are always both more and less than the dominant discourse prescribes. Given our non-hegemonic account of neoliberalism we address subjectivity, and the particularity of embodied subjects, as constituted through neoliberal forms of governance in all their contradiction, incoherence and instability.

We attend to the relations among actors which proliferate and multiply across the whole network in ways that are simultaneously intentional and unplanned, rational and not. We think, then, about neoliberal policies and practices not simply as 'the consequences of legislation or as indicators of social structures, but as techniques possessing their own specificity in the more general field of other ways of exercising power' (Foucault, 1977: 23). In our account of neoliberalism, subjectivity and work as inflected by the specificities of time and place (and within variable constitutive and regulatory networks of power) we focus on relations between the state, the market and the subject within neoliberal modes of government. We address the fashioning of oneself as simultaneously consumer and commodity; as buyer of goods and services and as a seller of oneself in the market. This is accomplished through the articulation of oneself within a discourse of entrepreneurship.

## NEOLIBERALISM AS ENTREPRENEURSHIP

In preferring the term 'advanced liberalism' over neoliberalism, Rose (1989, 1999) signals the ways in which neoliberalism is not so much a 'new' form of liberal government, but rather a hybrid, refigured or intensified form. Rose's genealogical account of advanced liberalism avoids thinking in terms of a simple succession 'in which one style of government supersedes and effaces its predecessor' (1999: 142). Rather, he observes a complexification of forms of governance that open up new lines of power and truth, and the invention and hybridisation of techniques of government. Within advanced neoliberalism the 'social state' gives way to the 'enabling state', and is no longer responsible for providing all of society's needs for security, health, education and so on. Individuals, firms, organisations, schools, hospitals, parents and so on, must each and all take on a portion of the responsibility for their own well-being. The social and the economic are seen as antagonistic. Economic government is desocialized in order to maximise the entrepreneurial conduct of the individual: 'politics must actively intervene in order to create the organisational and subjective conditions for entrepreneurship' (Rose, 1999: 144).

This restructuring of the economy and the labour market constitutes a programmatic ambition of neoliberal government for the subject to self-actualize through their own labour. The terms of this self-actualisation are tautly strung between discourses of freedom and enterprise on one hand, and the regulatory and punitive practices of government on the other, with work positioned and promoted as the best way to improve one's situation. In this way, suggests Rose (1999), a new articulation of the relation between government, expertise and subjectivity takes shape. Government is restructured in the name of economic logic, and the goal of economic government is to create and sustain the central elements of economic well-being – such as the enterprise form and competition. All human actors to be governed are conceived of as individuals active in making choices in order to further their own interests and those of their family and are potentially active in their own government. The powers of the state are thus directed at

empowering entrepreneurial subjects in their quest for self-realization.

Neoliberalism constructs models of action based on economic enterprise and extends them to various areas of social life that were formerly excluded from it. Institutions previously constituting the welfare state (schools, public utilities, hospitals, charities, police and so forth) are increasingly required to operate according to a market logic of competition within newly invented systems of institutional re/forms and practices. Not only do neoliberal mentalities of government generalize an enterprise form to the conduct of organisations previously seen as non-economic, but also to the conduct of individuals themselves (Burchell, 1996).

As a result the concept of the citizen is transformed, or refigured. The passive citizen of the welfare state becomes the active citizen with rights, duties, obligations and expectations – becoming the citizen as active entrepreneur of the self. This is not, argues Rose, simply a re-activation of liberal values of self-reliance, autonomy and independence as the necessary conditions for self-respect, self-esteem, self-worth and self-advancement, but rather an emphasis on enterprise and the capitalization on existence itself through calculated acts and investments.

This is marked by the proliferation of new apparatuses, devices and mechanisms for the government of conduct and new forms of life: new forms of consumption, a public habitat of images, the regulation of habits, dispositions, styles of existence in the name of identity and lifestyle. In this new field, the citizen is to become a consumer, and his or her activity is to be understood in terms of the activation of rights of the consumer in the marketplace. (Rose, 1999: 164–5)

## NEOLIBERALISM AND SUBJECTIVITY

The British sociologist Anthony Giddens (1991), along with many other sociologists working on 'late modernity', describes the way in which the decline of traditional community ties, such as those based on social class and conventional gender relations, means that people have to live what he describes as a 'reflexive project of the self', deploying a succession of narratives through which they tell their life story. To sustain 'a self without ties which tells us who we are', Giddens (op cit) suggests a strong ego is required and resilience to withstand the lack of context and lack of traditional forms of belonging. 'You can be anything you choose', says Jane, one of our research participants, an 18-year-old Australian at university. Inside this apparently freeing statement lies the nub of her dilemma. So much is invested in choosing that she is terrified of making the wrong choice, which she explains by reference to a psychological discourse – 'she is indecisive'. Being indecisive is what comes to explain everything for Jane and those similarly positioned in neoliberal discourse. There is no sense that the need to choose who you want to be could prove to be in itself a huge and difficult imposition.

We could say that Jane, embarking on her life path, lacks resilience, lacks a clear sense of who she is, and is thus overwhelmed by this new freedom. We could then resolve that what Jane needs is resilience, so that we must find some way to assist her in strengthening her sense of self, enhance her possibility for making choices. But, as Nikolas Rose (1999) argues, the imperative to be free within liberalism, and developed within neoliberalism, demands that we live our life *as if* it were in furtherance of a biographical project of self-realization. Rather than choice and freedom being good per se, they are aspects of the governmental technologies of neoliberalism that demand that we take responsibility for managing and therefore regulating ourselves, so that we are, apparently, free. And this has to be achieved in a context in which jobs for life have disappeared for a large section of the workforce and so people are required to manage themselves in the context of short-term contracts, with constant shifts of work and with notions of 'life-long learning'

replacing 'jobs for life'. In this analysis, choice is not liberating but becomes what Rose calls 'a serious burden of liberty', in which freedom is an 'obligation'. The issue becomes one of how populations become governed and managed when traditional ties have been eroded by globalisation and neoliberalism, rather than being about a simple and positive opening up of choice.

In Rose's account, psychology has a special role to play in providing the discourse which props up the fiction of the autonomous subject of choice. So, for example, a person might invoke a psychological discourse to explain their own lack of success or as with Jane, her inability to choose – 'what is wrong with me that I can't succeed?' Or, 'why am I such an indecisive person?' The response to these questions is to look both to psychology as a form of explanation and as a restorative practice, using forms of counselling and therapy, for example.

In research which we carried out in Sydney, Australia between 2002 and 2004 this shift was obvious in the accounts presented to us in the interviews we conducted with a range of workers. A psychological narrative was central in these interviews. Indeed, the younger the participant, the less likely they were to mention social or external factors at all as having any bearing on their progress in work. So, for example, a secretary in her 30s talked about giving 150 per cent in her job, because 'she has very high standards'. She attributed these high standards to her feeling that her father expected high standards and that she felt never good enough. She described in the interview the way in which her bosses constantly gave her more and more work because, it appeared, she is capable of, and willing to give, that 150 per cent. As a result she is coping with amounts of work which are well beyond the bounds of a working week, but rather than talk about exploitation, the woman worker talks about her psychological history. This elides the exploitative aspects of the relation with her bosses, and by eliding and refiguring them inside a personal narrative no room is left for anything other than a personal and psychological response to the situation.

The issue, then, for studies of worker identities and subjectivities becomes the ways in which the breakdown of traditional communities, families, location and the introduction of what Beck and Beck-Gernsheim (2002) call reflexive modernisation come to figure and are understood. Public and private debates cohere around a subject, a person who is not located in a place, a job or a role but who is free to make constant choices and to make constant change. This is the classical subject of liberalism in the context of the global market. The role of psychology for Giddens and Rose (the two main commentators in this area) in these new figurings is rather different, however.

For Giddens (1991), the new kinds of markets introduced by liberalism bring the need for a psychological subject who is flexible and mutable, able to move across spheres and jobs, yet resilient, having an inner core of strength to withstand the need for constant adaptation. Giddens argues that the reflexive project of the self which accompanies these profound social changes involves a freedom from traditional positions and roles and therefore opens up new possibilities of being. The subject needs therefore to be both flexible and mutable, multiple and changing, but also have a strong resilience to withstand the loss of traditional supports.

Rose (1999), in contrast, acknowledges the central role of psychology within liberalism and neoliberalism, but unlike Giddens, he assumes that the management of the neoliberal subject demands self-management practices in which the subject has to live their life *as if* 'in furtherance of a biographical project of self-realisation'. Where Giddens sees a new freedom to which the subject has to adapt by developing new psychological characteristics and capacities, Rose understands this freedom as a form of regulation which is no more liberating than the traditional relations and ties that it replaced. Indeed, it could be argued that the subject who imagines themselves

free within the world of consumption and casualized contracts, is more stranded and fettered than the subject of jobs for life narratives characteristic of the welfare state of the post-war period. Within Rose's framework, psychology functions as a set of discourses and practices through which the subject has to live the new freedom and therefore has to learn to use psychology for practices of self-management.

In this sense psychology becomes *the* discourse to which subjects have recourse to explain what happens to them. Psychology is used to explain the career trajectory through theories of personality, motivation, skill, and so forth, and is there to pick up failure through discourses of pathology, and through practices such as counselling and therapy. The way in which we come to manage and regulate ourselves in terms of what Rose (1999) describes as a 'practice of freedom' forms a central component of how power works to produce docile neoliberal subjects who understand themselves as the agents of their own biography. We can understand psychology as implicated in providing the discursive organisation of the stories we tell ourselves to make sense of our lives in this new world of work.

Unlike earlier historical moments, we are understood, for example by Giddens (1991), no longer to be born into a role, a place with its own predefined stories, but as being constantly able to create our own unique stories presented to us by the myriad opportunities afforded by the market – opportunities to make and to spend money and thus to become free. So, for example, an old conception of having a place or a role within one's community, is taken to disappear. This, as we shall see, becomes very important with respect to our case study of a Welsh community which we will discuss later in the chapter. Indeed, we cannot only find psychological discourses within workers' narratives, we can also find its central location within recruitment literature for example, which refers much less to skills needed for a particular job and more to the type of person or personality needed. For example, the following ad appeared in the *Sydney Morning Herald* in 2004:

A leading international publisher and event organizer is looking for people with BIG IDEAS and BIGGER AMBITIONS. You'll be selling by telephone across our portfolio of products [...] Existing sales experience isn't necessary (full, recognized and ongoing training is provided) but a 'must win' attitude is. Can you succeed in a fast paced, dynamic sales environment? Do you feel you deserve the financial benefits that success will bring? Then call [...]

In this respect, we could argue that workers are no longer alienated from their labour as in the classic Marxist argument. Marx understood the factory worker as alienated from the craft of the production of an artefact. Now, workers do not even have a simple relation of alienation – it is something quite else because they often have to embody that which their company is selling, though it could be understood as a kind of super-alienation in which the worker can only approach the product of her or his labour through the position of the consumer, as we will explore later in the chapter.

Paul du Gay's (1996) research on workers in the retail sector argues that workers become part of lifestyle consumption because they have to become part of the 'personality' that the store sells. One of the interesting aspects of this is that this kind of work demands what we could describe as the more traditionally feminine. The much vaunted lifestyle – shopping for anything from fashion to houses to holidays – presents the relationship between production and consumption quite differently than for previous generations of workers. Although post-war workers were presented with the possibility of buying cars and fridges, they were not offered a variety of ways to make money in order to consume. If consumption is presented as the central locus of identity, work simply becomes one site for making money to consume, not the site of identity

itself. Because both shopping and looking good have traditionally been feminized concerns, it is not simply that the new worker is feminized but that the relationship between work and play, production and consumption has become feminized. We would expect to find, following Rose, narratives that become more psychologised the younger the worker, with the younger workers displaying a transformed relation to work.

This transformed relation may be evidenced in both Sydney and South Wales. In both places, young people under 21 are far more likely to express consumption as a primary goal for work and also more likely to use entrepreneurial discourse than older groups, as we shall see. Consider Helen, an 18-year-old, shop assistant, working in a small kiosk in the centre of Sydney:

Um, yeah. I buy a lot of clothes, a lot of going out clothes, casual clothes, sporty clothes, a lot of shoes, a lot of handbags, every colour sunnies. I've got two mobile phones, one with Vodafone, one with Optus, just for the fun of it because half my friends are Optus, half of them are Vodafone, yeah. The bill comes, not really a problem, I think sometimes $70 a month for Vodafone and $40 a month for Optus, that's nothing, just $110 dollars, so that's all right.

I just want what I want, I just get what I want. Yeah.

I'm normal but, um, I have everything I want and I get everything I want and I have everything my way all the time because I'm used to it. I'm never broke, I always have to have money on me, money in my keycard, um, if I see a top costs $100 I just buy it straight away, I wouldn't think twice. If it is nice I buy it, doesn't matter what the price is.

Her interview makes clear that she was out of work for some time, and the inability to consume the lifestyle she wanted was what propelled her into a precarious poorly paid job. This is quite common among young workers in both locations, with fantasies of consumption and 'being someone' sustaining them through difficult work conditions, though for many of the young in South Wales, the aim is simply to be able to have some work at all in an area of 33 per cent youth unemployment.

In the next section of the chapter, we will compare two Sydney workers in their thirties and fifties, to show key generational shifts at work.

## TWO SYDNEY CASE STUDIES

Sophia, is a 31-year-old woman who works in telesales, and Jim is a 55-year-old man who is out of work.

### *Sophia*

For Sophia selling bottled water, there is also a complex narrative. She has difficulty in finding work in telesales and has the fantasy of becoming a television presenter. This fantasy sustains her, but there are two other self-management techniques which Sophia presents as being central to her ability to cope with her poorly paid and insecure work. In this sense, we could say that her projection into the future is what allows her to withstand the exploitation of the present, which she tolerates as a temporary phenomenon. She presents success in sales as being an aspect of the personality. She has, she says, the personality to sell and is good at sales through believing in the product. This means that, as the recruitment literature suggests, if sales becomes an aspect of the personality, there are simply no skills to be learned and at the same time selling becomes an aspect of the person as though the salesperson were especially equipped to sell – there is then in this discourse a psychological niche for all of us. In this extract from the interview, Sophia explains her technique and her own relationship to selling the product, bottled water:

I think the building up of rapport is really important and a sense of humour over the phone. I try to mirror image the other person on the phone in their tone of voice. If their tone of voice is soft then I'm mirror image that soft tone of voice across to them and make sure I listen and see if I pick up anything that I may be able to reflect that back and include that in the conversation to make them feel comfortable with me in order to try and make them feel comfortable and not only really sell but to sell quality and to say that we are selling quality water and it is very good for our body brain system actually because we are made 80 percent out of water. And um, our normal tap water isn't as good as it used to be 15 years ago because even there is a lot of people drinking normal tap water out there I don't, maybe they are not educated enough to know with all the different chemicals stuff that are in the normal tap water what it can do to our life, later in life, what it can do to our body.

She explains that she undertook a detox programme, which helped her to understand the importance of water for the body:

Water is very important to our body to drink at least 2 litres a day because if flushes us out and um, water is important for the brain. To get the brain going and thinking clearly actually. I experienced that. So I've experienced the difference within my body when I don't drink water and when I do drink water.

In this discourse, the work so suffuses the worker that she is the product, she has to believe in the product. This is why we suggest that labour is no longer alienated in the traditional sense because work no longer embodies skills or craft, thus the psychological relation cannot be one of straightforward alienation, but is perhaps super-alienation. Sophia has to relate to her product, water, from the position of a consumer, not from the position of worker at all: indeed, as she says, she *is* water. In fact, a narrative of work is almost hidden in her stress that she has the personality to sell as though work were simply an aspect of the personality. She has to embody the consumer of water and then use her personality to sell to the consumer with whom she has identified. Perhaps the seller and the consumer are one. Any sense of her as a worker producing anything at all, any labour, seems to disappear under the weight of the shifts she is forced to make. She is water and she has the personality to sell it. What kind of fantasy, therefore, does this involve: a fantasy of a worker, who indeed is not really a worker (Guattari, 1984: 112).

Let us compare this with Jim, who refuses to do what Sophia does and is invested in.

### Jim

Jim is aged 55 and is out of work. He is in quite a different position, then, from Sophia. And, not only is he perfectly capable of talking about exploitation, but he has a historical discourse which allows him to understand that work and conditions have changed. Yet, this very discourse is what prevents him from finding work in the present. One of the things that is significant in his narrative is his clear reference to exploitation and his unwillingness to adopt the approach to work exemplified by Sophia. She sells a product, but in doing so she has to sell herself as possessing the personality to do it. He understands work as being able to do the job, as skills. He has been sent by the government's unemployment agency, Centrelink, to a number of training courses aimed at getting him to work as a self-employed contract cleaner:

> They told us ... how to wash a wall, but I've forgotten all about it now. In such a short time. And one of the practical things was window washing using a squeegee, which I already knew anyway. And um the floor polishing machine which I already knew anyway and there was a little bit of water blasting. Cleaning of cars without, but I wasn't interested in but um, I've had some cars previously and I've made an attempt to do it. I wasn't impressed by that, it's a chore rather than an occupation, but the was trying to tell us that it is an occupation now. Cleaners are service people, they are not trades people. The carpet extraction machine, we did a little bit of carpet cleaning. I've never used a carpet extraction machine, but it is just so straightforward without, you'd be thick if you couldn't pick it up in about three minutes.

He knows that he possesses the skills to be a cleaner but he argues that they demand that he present himself as *wanting* to clean, something he refuses to do, while being perfectly amenable to doing a good job of cleaning. The result of this is, according to him, that he never gets any work. His failure to accept neoliberal practices of self-management, which demand that he presents himself as a motivated cleaner (just as Sophia had to present herself as having the personality to sell), means that even for a low paid job like cleaning, he is not seen as a willing and motivated enough worker and fails to get work. Jim recognizes but does not value or embody the characteristics of self-promotion and short-termism that are necessary to succeed in even the most menial work. He explains to the interviewer that he has to 'sell' himself, make a sales pitch and be interested. These, of course are the qualities that Sophia embodied, but this older man finds them unpalatable and difficult:

> If I get the job I'll do it (but) I'm not really interested in cleaning to start. And if I was serious about a cleaning career well then they would be much more interested in putting me on, but from what I understand I have to sell myself which I am not very good at and one thing, you've got to believe in your product. Well if you don't really believe in your product how can you sell yourself, especially if you don't know how to sell. And it is more of an ability rather than an applied skill, I think.

Jim is painfully presented with the process of having to completely reconfigure his work identity in order to get work, a task that he finds demeaning and difficult. This demonstrates his different location within, and experience of, those changes in the labour market which accompany neoliberalism. Sophia and Helen embody a different relation to neoliberalism, which suggests a desire for a future which does not keep them locked in exploitative work, and which for Helen includes the idea of consumption, or work as something which has to be done in order to live. Work here becomes a solitary activity in which exploitation cannot be mentioned as there is no union or other support to make possible any different orientation to work. The worker has to rely on his/herself.

## SUBJECT POSITIONS UNDER NEOLIBERALISM

We have shown, through these case studies, the ways in which historical changes are lived through a set of narratives, informed by psychological discourses and underpinned by practices of self management through which new work identities are produced and lived. Those identities, by placing the burden of responsibility for work on the personality of the worker, sidestep and hide social and economic issues concerning exploitation and poor working conditions which would break apart many of the positive stories of the gains and benefits of neoliberalism. Our research suggests that the latter are maintained by recourse to:

- The benefits and pleasures of lifestyle and consumption.
- The ability to tolerate the present through a fantasy of a better future produced through the fantasy of 'being someone', supported by narratives of consumption, lifestyle and celebrity, which are relentlessly offered as the culmination of the hard work on the self.
- Narratives which stress personal qualities linked to practices of self management stressing personality and personal development.

What we are suggesting is a changed orientation to ideas about exploitation and alienation, which make the worker responsible for their own destiny and comportment. This for all workers, including Helen, Sophia and Jim, is lived through a complex relation to time and space. What we mean by this is that the younger workers (Helen and Sophia) tolerate the poor pay and conditions in the present by means of a dream of the future in which they have power, wealth and a sense of fulfilment. While Jim cannot cope with the present changes because of his relation to the past, in which he was formed as a worker through a different organization. We might well imagine that these are universal features of the production of work identities under the changes brought by neoliberalism and globalization.

These assumptions might be read as suggesting a stable relationship between stable subjects and stable practices of government. Given our concern with temporality and spatiality we are interested in the salience of these assumptions for subjects in another time and place. We are interested, then, not so much in what neoliberalism might tell us about those other subjects, times and places, but what attention to their differences and specificities might tell us about neoliberalism and our theorising of subjectivity.

## COMPLICATING THE PICTURE: SPECIFICITY, SPACE AND RELATIONALITY

Given this emphasis on movement (and the impossibility of stability) we ask: are identities ever still? Do they move through time and exist in temporally located spaces? What effect do these have? How does the history of an area as well as the temporal organisation of fantasy relate to it? This is the point at which we want to say that neoliberalism and globalisation are constituted within and by complex interlinking sets (or webs, Arendt, 1998; Studdert, 2006) of relations, through which subjectivity is constituted in specific times and places. It is through local as well as global processes and practices that these specificities take on meaning and are mobilized in action.

In the first part of the chapter, we could assume that all workers under neoliberalism would share the experiences of Helen, Sophia and Jim in Sydney. We showed how neoliberal discourses and practices permeated their working lives such that they came to understand their relation to work and identity as a worker in very specific ways. Using Rose's account, we would expect that neoliberal forms of governance would produce similar practices of subjectification. However, our work in Wales led to the necessity to rethink this position. While it could be argued that workers in Australia and Wales were both exposed to neoliberal modes of governance and quite similar shifts in employment – away from jobs for life, towards entrepreneurialism and so forth, there were local differences that made us recognize the need to complicate the picture. The work led us to conclude that we cannot simply read off from discourses but must see their effectivity in different locations.

We pursue these issues through comparing the Sydney case studies with those from a place we have called 'Steeltown', a town in South Wales in a formerly industrial area, which lost its central employer, a steel works in 2002. In the next section, we explore the narratives of redundant workers in Steeltown and Sydney (Walkerdine and Bansel, 2007). What this comparison allows us to see is the central importance of space/time for an understanding of how people in different locations and with different histories live neoliberal change. Moreover, because this section of the chapter deals with redundancy we are looking at immanence (Deleuze, 1991), at change. Rather than Rose's fixed subjects, outlined in the first part of the chapter, we begin to question not only how redundancy is experienced but also what is immanent in the changes forced upon the workers. We could understand this comparison as yielding a challenge to both Giddens and Rose: Giddens, because he assumes role, place and class become less important; Rose because he assumes too simple and fixed a relation of subject to governance.

## COMPARING SYDNEY AND STEELTOWN

We interviewed redundant steelworkers and others in the community in Steeltown, including women and young people. While the labour market changes which were applicable in each country were roughly similar, and indeed job shifts as far as they were comparable, were also similar, the responses to them were both similar and different. Our data suggests that subjectivities are produced specifically in relation, to the particularities of locations, with their own particular histories. This means that there are many conditions of possibility working together to produce particular responses among workers in any

location and that future accounts need to work with this specificity in order to understand both subjectivity and the changes taking place at this particular conjuncture.

In particular, we suggest that it is not possible simply to read off experience as governmentality theory would suggest. Rather, the very particular space/time locations of the two cohorts allows us to recognize that while the discursive shifts we have alluded to work in both countries, and the labour market changes are similar, the fact that these are experienced in different space/time locations does make for some differences in how these are lived. In this sense, we can say that subjectivity cannot simply be understood or read off from practices of governmentality, but suggest that the production of subjectivities is a complex accomplishment. In the past, we have understood this through an understanding that subjectivity 'is more than the sum total of positions in discourse since birth' (Henriques et al., 1998) in that positions may conflict with each other and are held together through complex relations of fantasy and desire (Walkerdine, 1991, 1997; Walkerdine et al., 2001). However, more recently, this position has felt too static and (has) not accounted for the complexities of time and space.

The idea that subjectivities are produced through a constellation of positions held together emotionally makes them seem both solid and static. Recent interest in affect (Clough and Halley, 2007) and the significance of time and movement (Deleuze, 1991), as well as social networks and associations (Latour, 2005), has emphasized the embodied movement and flow of action through which we are affected and in turn affect. This stresses the relational character of subjectivity as not simply a nexus of positions but constantly shifting sets of relations (Butler, 2004; Walkerdine, 2007), what we might call a relational matrix (Mitchell, 1988) or a web of relations (Arendt, 1998; Studdert, 2006). Add to this the current resurgence of interest in phenomenology (Merleau Ponty, 1962), and we see our attention turned less to stasis and fixity than movement and relations.

This focus allows us to think of the moment of neoliberalism in a different way. This is the moment at which, for example, in this case, steel production moves from the South Wales valleys to other parts of the world – India and Brazil. The consequences of this shift in the global movement of capital shifts relations and the ways in which a previous sense of solidity, place, belonging, is experienced. In addition, the complex networks and relations in a community and outside it (such as global relations facilitated by developments in travel, communications technology), make movement an important issue. But more than this, if subjectivity is constituted as one aspect of a web or matrix of relations, constantly shifting and developed in historically and temporally located spaces (Massey, 2005), our attention needs to be turned to those relations themselves. This is a move away from a direct relation between neoliberal governance and the production of governed subjects to one which is both more nuanced and local, on the one hand, and stresses movement and relationality, on the other. Although we cannot explore this idea fully in the space of this chapter, we want to demonstrate at least the complexity of relations which produce both global relations and specific local relations.

As we have seen in previous sections, aspiration and entrepreneurship are central to neoliberal discourses of work. We saw from the case studies of Sophia and Jim, that age makes a significant difference to the ways that neoliberal shifts in work identities are understood, accepted and taken on board. Jim's history as a worker formed at a different moment, with different work relations, made his transition to the new world of work difficult and painful. We found equally that the take-up of neoliberal discourse was age-related in South Wales, with young people demonstrating the clearest take up. Following our assumptions, we might have expected the older South Wales workers to show varying degrees of the take-up of this discourse as the

Sydney workers did. However, this was not the case. Quite simply, no redundant Steeltown steelworker used any aspirational discourse in their interview narratives. In order to understand why, we needed to understand local relationalities and histories.

The Steeltown steelworks closed in 2002. The steel works had given the inhabitants of the town a major employer. In the ways that many workers and others in the town describe their lives, it becomes clear that patterns of community have been largely based around the work practices of the steel works, with a strong gendered division of labour, a strong element of communal support and a strong political sensibility. Among the Sydney workers we studied, in their diverse forms of work and workplace, no such narrative emerged. Conversely, these workers are more likely to be defined by a discourse of aspiration and improvement. With this in mind, we can recognize that in the South Wales town, redundancy is managed as a collective experience and this is both in terms of a group of men from the same place all doing the same work and facing a mass closure, but also because of the intervention of the trade unions. The collective unions decided that it was impossible to fight the closure and adopted a strategy of supporting workers in finding other employment. In particular, they encouraged workers to think of ways in which they might build alternative work upon their interests and encouraged workers by paying for retraining. This act alone had an enormous impact upon the ways that the shift was experienced and the opportunities for employment that were opened up for the workers. While all the Sydney workers had experienced some form of redundancy or job change or restructure, it appeared from the narratives to have been experienced as a solitary and individual change with no mention of help, support or retraining opportunities.

In the space available, we will confine ourselves to making a comparison between the role of aspiration and entrepreneurship in worker identity. What we therefore wish to point to in this section is the ways in which the remaking into neoliberal workers in both locations is differently inflected, experienced and narrativized within different discursive repertoires and practices.

While the work changes among the Welsh workers are similar to those of the Sydney workers, these men do not talk about having an aspiration even though their new work practices may contain elements of entrepreneurialism. Indeed, it is the union which suggests workers think about their interests and hobbies as the basis for future jobs. This itself is of course a big shift, which blurs boundaries once made very rigid within working class manual work. However, for those workers who take up the union's suggestion successfully, the shift is experienced less as an aspiration than a revelation. Two men in their 40s became youth and community workers and both moved from leaving school with no qualifications to pursing a university degree while working to support the young people of their town. As one says eloquently 'I didn't realize there were jobs like this.' The phrase 'I didn't realise there were jobs like this' is not an entrepreneurial or aspirational statement. Rather, it signals the opening up of a world of work previously unknown, rather than any sense of wanting or needing to work towards a new or better form of work, or for upward class mobility. This shift happened for one of them because he mentioned the fact that he enjoyed coaching children at rugby and from a first interest in social work, youth and community work was suggested to him.

> Urm, there was I think up three thousand pound per employee, urm, to go in and use the training, basically anything you wanted to do ... but people from Careers Wales came in, urm, other agencies came in to try and find out exactly what your skills were, were there transferable skills you could use from inside so as you could use outside, urm, obviously what you wanted to do, urm, through coaching rugby and things like that, urm I sort of knew I had a bit of talent with working with kids and that, so my first choice was either, was teacher or social worker ... But the woman said to me, which is another girl that works here, she said have you ever thought of youth work, and I said what does that entail, and she's wrote down a lady's number,

she said phone her and make an appointment to go and see her. Found out then that she was the head of the youth service in (the local authority), so I went to see her, started doing a bit of the training, urm, after completing the initial first two sections of the training I enrolled for university, because I knew the money was there and it was only one day a week, so I enrolled for that, started doing a bit of voluntary work in the youth club, urm, two, I think it was, I got accepted for university in the October and started, I managed to get a job with the Prince's Trust, urm, in January, the start of January, urm, and I haven't looked back since then ... if somebody had told me like four and a half years ago that I'd be doing this now, managing people, I'd have told them they was bonkers, complete change but, urm, I'm lucky everything has worked out for me. I didn't realise, when I was still at the steel works, I didn't realise there were jobs like this, do you know what I mean? ... so I'm, I'm fortunate like that, that I've fallen into something that I really enjoy. Compared to the steel works this isn't like a job.

The phrase 'compared to the steel works, this isn't like a job' tells us how he understands the new world of work, not as aspiration but as a revelation in which the rigid boundaries between work and pleasure have been broken down. But what we see is that he had never sought these out. The history of steelwork in the area, often done by father and son for generations, produced class based modes of relationality in which aspiration may have been frowned upon or distanced from. We can glimpse it in phrases like 'class traitor', 'pencil pusher' – a term commonly used by working class men to describe non-manual workers. These serve to create sets of relations in which difference is othered, keeping the community solid. In this instance, however, othering has been forced onto the ex-steel worker and he is able to enter a world about which he knew nothing and which does not feel like work.

To take another example, John aged 49, was interested in music and this led him through the encouragement of the union, and by way of the union retraining fund, to train as a guitar maker. This involved weekly flights from Cardiff to Scotland for one year. He now works as a self-employed guitar maker from the living room of his family's small terraced house. This job move is clearly entrepreneurial. Before he took it, he suffered from depression which he attributed to poor relations with his boss at work in the steelworks. Now he presents himself as doing well, and as a 'minor celebrity' in the town.

His work relations, like those of Colin, have also blurred and shifted, challenging the separation of work and home. Having previously worked in a factory and to factory hours, he now works in his living room. This shifts not only his temporal relation to work: he now reports working as early as 5 a.m. or as late as midnight if he wants to:

> ... and it's more relaxed and if I want to, er, if I'm up here at 5 o'clock in the morning I can make a start and you just do it whenever you feel like doing it. Perhaps I might do it late in the night, perhaps it might be 12 o'clock when I'm doing something but at least I'm here.

However, his spatial relation – work and home are one. More than this, he has taken over the family living room, which means the family – his wife and two teenage children – are displaced to other rooms. Thus, the shift in family and work relations are profound to the extent of entirely redefining what work means in his life. If we imagine his work and his family previously as separate yet connected relational matrices or webs, they have now dramatically shifted, so that the overlap is more complete but with a dramatic shift in the inhabiting of relational space and the social relations of family in the home. So the shifts are clearly articulated as shifts towards entrepreneurialism which have had profound effects on the relationalities through which his subjectivity is produced and performed. John describes having been on incapacity benefit after the depression and recognized that he could simply have stayed on benefits: 'If the business wasn't successful, you'd just call it a day, shut the box up and stay on the sick, like. But it's not what I wanted to do, I wanted to work.' He acknowledges a painful past compared with a happy present, but the interview statements present a sense of relief that he has work he likes and a safe and secure financial future,

which allows him to go on foreign holidays to Turkey and to own an investment property with his redundancy money, rather than a sense of striving or aspiration.

> Just gone from strength to strength. So I got ... I do private lessons three days a week and a Saturday morning. Erm, and I've got a few days then that I'm in the workshop, you know, I do repairing, I do building, whatever. Er, at the moment I'm doing ... building like two guitars that I'm working on at the moment. So since the works have closed, my life has completely turned out, like. For when [Researcher] first came here, well I didn't have no plans or nothing I had. Started, I actually had started doing the guitar training but it was more as a hobby. I didn't think at the time that it was going to turn out into a business, you know, I didn't think it was going to go that way. But, er, that's the way it's gone and it is, well it's really successful from my point of view and to work from home as well. I pick my own hours, you know.
>
> Yeah, so I know, not this year maybe next year I want to take it to the next stage, I want to take it to schools and colleges and things like that, then. And, erm, maybe do some talks on it, about the construction of the guitar and just tell people how easy it is, you know, they can do it themselves, like, if they really put their mind to it ... 'Cause it's such an unusual job, people are interested in it, like. And, the kids that have come here, you know, for lessons, they tend to ... they do tend to look up to you, like. It's hard to explain in words, like, but it's ... it is like as if you're a celebrity.

John recognizes that had he not been depressed and made redundant, he would be commuting to another steel works a great distance away, whereas now he can work from home and he is happy. And it is happiness, not aspiration, which motivates him:

> Well (wife) will tell you like we've never been so well off like, we've never been so um not financial, well financially as well yeah, yeah even though we're not, we're not earning as much as I was down the works, it's just that we don't spend so much. You know what I mean, I used to change my car every two years well we're gonna change it this year now but we've had that car for years and years and years. I was due to change it when the works was closing and I thought I ain't and I just kept it you know. Watch what I spend it you know, Sky telly we got rid of that and just things like that you know. So really financially we're better but what it has taught us is that we wasted so much money like. Down the works like I was on

£26,000 a year no problem without working any overtime and if I'd gone to Port Talbot I would have been on £30,000 a year well it's good money but I ain't motivated by money like, money doesn't motivate me. Once we've got enough to pay the bills and everything. It's happiness that motivates me in that and I am happy. I am happy.

Indeed he sums up his position clearly: the difference now is that he can enjoy life, whereas the alternative faced by generations of steelworkers and their families, is a hard life and then death.

But otherwise you know. What's the saying? For some people life is hard and then you die. And that's what it's like sometimes. But that's what I felt for a long time. But um now I've got things to get up for like, things to get up in the morning to do and whether I've got a lesson or play the guitar.

So, like Colin, John's working life has changed dramatically. We can certainly recognize aspects of neoliberal discourse – the shift to celebrity, the sense of now being someone, are all aspects well understood within governmentality theory. His work practices have shifted in a clear neoliberal direction, but what we see form the abstracts is a relief that the entrepreneurialism has worked, that they have enough money, that he is happy and no longer faces a hard life and then death. These are signs of relief, not aspiration. While it is true that both men display enjoyment of their new work, and the positive benefits of neoliberalism, we could understand this shift as formed in complex relations in which the specificity of the history, of the location, of the previous practices of work, of family, of masculinity, are all significant.

If we simply look to governmentality, we miss this complexity and the ways that concepts, practices and discourses travel. We miss the complex relationalities in which neoliberal shifts are received and taken on board. Compare this with Justin in Sydney: 'I have a target to be comfortable, if I get filthy rich doing it well hey …' Like being comfortable, happiness as a work aspiration can be understood as new for such workers. Our point is that while these shifts are similar they are not identical and if we miss the specificities, we are missing something important.

## CONCLUSION

The first and most obvious point to conclude from the comparison we have presented between Sydney and Steeltown is that while globalized work practices and neoliberal modes of governance may be predominant in both Australia and Wales, local conditions mean that these are not experienced in the same ways at all. These local conditions must be understood to include the relationalities and meanings through which work is figured within any particular location. This includes not only historical issues of nation and community but also class, gender and how these enter the relations through which working lives are lived.

The intervention of the trade union in South Wales had a huge effect on the experience of redundancy and the refinding of work, for example, with this being understood as opportunity and a welcome change for some men. In contrast, in Sydney this was a lonely experience for the workers studied and seemed to produce a quite punitive narrative of the necessity of work on the self to be suitable to do the new kinds of work available. Neoliberal discourses as work on the self were experienced differently in the two locations. The emphasis on autonomy and agency produced by neoliberalism are not experienced directly but through the relations through which meaning and experience are created. Neoliberalism as a mode of governance provides ways of understanding ourselves and practices through which to produce ourselves, but these have to be understood in a context in which there are other competing claims for meaning.

In this sense then the practices of governance do not produce specific outcomes in subjects. Rather they provide the terrain through which the changes around the organisation of work and self are governed. There are complex conditions of possibility of which the introduction of neoliberalism is only one. We thus need to pay far more attention to the subtle experiences of subjectivity in particular locations than has been the practice in this tradition of scholarship. We could also infer that what we need here is an account of the relations through which space/time is experienced, that is, an account of relationality (Studdert, 2006; Walkerdine, 2007) and how things move across time and space, locally and globally.

We have emphasized the specific and local character of change. We are interested, therefore, in thinking through the recent work on experience which makes reference to the work of Bergson (Deleuze, 1991) and Deleuze (1991), as well as Guattari (Deleuze and Guattari, 1987), to understand that neo or advanced liberalism and globalisation are not monolithic forces that trample upon lives in such a way as to completely predict and specify the outcome. Rather, this work suggests that we cannot predict the complex, relational and rhizomatic activity which will develop and that we have to be prepared for things to develop in unexpected ways, ways which create something, new ways of being or the work of immanence of the constantly bringing into being of the new. Doreen Massey (2005) has understood this as a return to politics in that she argues that we cannot assume a certain historical march to any fixed or predetermined point.

The workers in our studies have not been completely defined by neoliberalism. Other practices of family, sociality, community, for example, come into play. There are complex histories and biographies which traverse the field of change. Neoliberalism and globalisation are simply two of those things and we cannot simply say that they cause the changes we witness. Some things sit comfortably with neoliberalism and other things do not, but the specificities of location unravel the idea that there is a stable neoliberalism that fixes a subject totally within its orbit. Rather, this body of work would suggest that we

cannot specify just exactly what will be the result in any time and place and that things may not indeed turn out as governments desire, and that new ways of being are created out of the juxtapositions of this change.

Most of the governmentality studies tend to look at what should happen according to the discourses of governance, but as the Latourian (2005) tradition of work has taught us, we cannot say that what should happen is what does happen. If we trace the particular and complex trajectories of any worker or community, it twists and turns and meets coincidences and unforeseen changes. It is produced in the complex and multidimensional tiny exchanges into which the workers enter. Thus we are suggesting that we cannot predict the outcome, even whether this will be shaped by neoliberalism and globalization in any simple causal sense, nor can we say what will be created out of what is immanent. For example, who knows what will happen to John the guitar maker and his new enterprise which takes over the home and differently organizes time and space of work. Who can say what effects the youth and community workers will have and whether the young men of Steeltown will manage to find positive and productive work. Who knows what the consequences are for an 18-year-old who refuses to work in a supermarket such as Tesco or who chooses to do it. To understand the production of the specificities of experience in this sense is one of the central tasks for work on identity.

## REFERENCES

Arendt, H. (1998) *The Human Condition*. Chicago, IL: University of Chicago Press.

Baudrillard, J. (1998) *Paroxysm: Interviews With Phillipe Petit*. London: Verso.

Beck, U. and Beck-Gernsheim E. (2002) *Individualization*. London: Sage.

Beck, U., Giddens, A. and Lasch, S. (1994) *Reflexive Modernisation*. Cambridge: Polity.

Bourdieu, P. (1998) *Acts of Resistance: Against the New Myths of Our Time*. Cambridge: Polity Press.

Bourdieu, P. (2003) *Firing Back: Against the Tyranny of the Market*. London: Verso.

Brown, W. (2003) 'Neo-liberalism and the end of liberal democracy', *Theory and Event*, 7: 1.

Burchell, D. (1996) 'Liberal government and techniques of the self', in A. Barry, T. Osborne and N. Rose (eds), *Foucault and Political Reason*. Chicago, IL: University of Chicago Press.

Butler, J. (2004) *Undoing Gender*. New York: Routledge.

Clough, P.T. and Halley, J. (eds) (2007) *The Affective Turn: Theorizing the Social*. Durham, NC: Duke University Press.

Deleuze, G. (1991) *Bergsonism*, translated by Hugh Tomlinson and Barbara Habberjam. New York: Zone Books.

Deleuze, G. and Guattari, F. (1987) *A Thousand Plateaus: Capitalism and Schizophrenia*. Trans. and Foreword Brian Massumi. Minneapolis, MN: University of Minnesota Press.

Du Gay, P. (1996) *Consumption and Identity at Work*. London: Sage.

Foucault, M. (1977) *Discipline and Punish*. London: Allen Lane.

Guattari, F. (1984) Molecular Revolution: Psychiatry and Politics. Trans. Rosemary Sheed. Harmondsworth: Penguin.

Giddens, A. (1991) *Modernity and Self-Identity: Self and Society in the Late Modern Age*. Oxford: Polity.

Henriques, J., Hollway, W., Urwin, C., Venn, C. and Walkerdine, V. (1998) *Changing the Subject: Psychology, Social Regulation and Subjectivity*, 2nd Edn, London: Routledge.

Latour, B. (2005) *Reassembling the Social: An Introduction to Actor-Network-Theory*. Oxford: Oxford University Press.

Levi-Faur, D. and Jordana, J. (2005) 'Globalizing regulatory capitalism', *The Annals of the American Academy of Political and Social Science*, 598: 6–9.

Massey, D. (2005) *For Space*. London: Sage.

Merleau Ponty, M. (1962) *Phenomenology of Perception*. London: Routledge and Kegan Paul.

Mitchell, S.A. (1988) *Relational Concepts in Psychoanalysis: An Integration*. Cambridge, MA: Harvard University Press.

Papadopoulos, D. (2003) 'The ordinary superstition of subjectivity: Liberalism and technostructural violence', *Theory and Psychology*, 13 (1): 73–93.

Rose, N. (1989) *Governing the Soul: The Shaping of the Private Self*. London: Routledge.

Rose, N. (1999) *The Powers of Freedom: Reframing Political*. Cambridge: Cambridge University Press.

Sennett (1997) *The Corrosion of Character*. New York: Norton.

Studdert, D. (2006) *Conceptualising Community: Beyond the State and the Individual*. Basingstoke: Palgrave Macmillan.

Walkerdine, V. (1991) *Schoolgirl Fictions*. London: Verso.

Walkerdine, V. (1997) *Daddy's Girl: Young Girls and Popular Culture*. London: Macmillan.

Walkerdine, V., Lucey, H. and Melody, J. (2001) *Growing up Girl: Psychosocial Explorations of Gender and Class*. London: Palgrave.

Walkerdine, V. (2007) *Children, Gender, Videogames: Towards a Relational Approach to Multimedia*. Basingstoke: Palgrave Macmillan.

# 26

# Legislating Identity: Colonialism, Land and Indigenous Legacies

Bonita Lawrence

For Indigenous peoples around the world, land and the web of relationships that the land sustains are at the heart of what it means to be 'the people' (as most Indigenous peoples conceptualize themselves, in their own languages). The land sustains the practices – fishing, hunting, planting, harvesting – through which people live. It also carries the stories, the songs and the ceremonies, which in turn sustains language and teaches the children who they are as part of 'the people'. And yet, centuries of colonization have persistently attacked and undermined these connections – a process that continues as globalization impoverishes land-based peoples, appropriates their lands, and forces profound changes on their communities. Indigenous peoples are facing these circumstances all over the world. As a result of such profound and forced changes, issues of Indigenous identity increasingly come to the forefront, as nations struggle with questions of belonging, tradition and continuity.

This chapter focuses on the relationship between Indigenous identity, nationhood and the categorization of peoples through legislation. It will focus mainly on the situation of

Indigenous peoples in Canada as the context for exploring the process of regulating Indigenous identity. Indigenous decolonization in Canada has, of necessity, focused on the question of identity – because Canada is one of only two settler states globally who maintain a system of formal, legally encoded identity regulation for Indigenous people. Understanding the violence contained in these acts of categorization, and the consequences – both in terms of individual lives and the collective survival of peoples as peoples – is crucial for identity scholarship. This chapter will explore the implementation of identity regulation, the land theft that it continues to enable, and the fragmentation and disempowerment it creates. The cultural genocide which has been crucial in enabling such an alien system of classification to be accepted by Indigenous peoples, will also be addressed, and the different forms of resistance engaged in by Indigenous peoples in Canada will be sketched out. The chapter begins, however, with identity theory and with Indigenous critiques of the contemporary understandings of identity found in postmodern and postcolonial discourses.

## INDIGENOUS PERSPECTIVES ON POSTMODERN AND POSTCOLONIAL THEORY

Current understandings of identity stress its multiple, fragmented and shifting nature. On the one hand, this reflects the critiques of essentialism found in postmodern theory. On the other hand, a focus on identity within contemporary postcolonial theory frequently includes critiques of racialized and gendered nationalist projects, an emphasis on histories of migration, and explorations of the ways in which concepts of hybridity utilized by diasporic subjects can potentially destabilize relationships of power by transgressing boundaries demarcating nation and diaspora, thereby disrupting the 'naturalness' of the nation-state. In general, while much of postcolonial theory addresses how the colonial project has constructed categories of 'race' which still structure contemporary social relations, there is a tendency to focus on colonialism as 'past', ignoring contemporary settler state colonization. For Indigenous theorists, a central concern is that postmodern and postcolonial discourses not only lack the theoretical tools to adequately address Indigenous identity, but can also marginalize and erase Indigenous presence.

A first concern for a number of Indigenous theorists is the tendency within postmodern writing to view indigeneity simply as a category to be deconstructed. While social constructionist approaches may be useful for peoples whose existence within modernity has never been questioned, it is quite a different matter for the peoples of stateless nations, who are already always assumed to exist in counterdistinction to modernity (and indeed, to have already vanished), to have their very existence as peoples deconstructed. For a number of Indigenous theorists (Grand, 2004; Weaver, 1998; Womack, 1999), the postmodern concern with deconstructing indigeneity and related aspects such as 'tradition', represents a closed system of thought that undermines their ability to speak as Indigenous peoples. This undermining is rendered all the more powerful by the manner in which western discourse remains privileged as 'true' knowledge, as compared to Indigenous knowledge, and by the fact that white academics are still referenced as authoritative voices when Indigenous issues are being discussed. Maori theorist Linda Tuhiwai Smith has addressed this in her work as follows:

> 'Authorities' and outside experts are often called in to verify, comment upon, and give judgements about the validity of Indigenous claims to cultural beliefs, values, ways of knowing and historical accounts [...] In Tasmania, where experts had already determined that Aborigines were 'extinct', the voices of those who still speak as Aboriginal Tasmanians are interpreted as some political invention of a people who no longer exist and who therefore no longer have claims. (1999: 72–3)

Postmodern deconstructions of nationhood are particularly problematic, in that they contribute to theoretically obscuring the reality of internal colonization in twenty-first century North America (Grand, 2004: 5). In Canada, where treaty-making has almost always violated the integrity of Indigenous territories by cutting treaty lines arbitrarily across them, and entirely bypassing the larger traditional governments in order to deal only at the village level with so-called 'bands', Indigenous scholars are forced to carefully re-trace concepts of nationhood from within the oral tradition, and to reconnect the lines of their territories back to traditional frameworks, despite the legal dismemberment of their nations by the Indian Act in 1876. In such a context, to face a discourse that insists that 'nationhood' is *always* only imagined undercuts the very real historic violations that Indigenous communities are seeking to redress – particularly as Indigenous perspectives on their own histories are seldom seen as authoritative. Postmodern discourse therefore, for the most part 'flattens' profoundly different worldviews, as if Indigenous epistemologies and the social complexity of Indigenous communities did not exist. The result is a fundamental erasure of the reality of Indigenous nationhood, thereby grossly misreading the nature of Indigenous liberation struggles.

More problematic still for Indigenous assertions of nationhood are those postcolonial
writings which deride any form of nationalism as representing only technologies of violence (McClintock, 1997), or as inevitably
degenerating into fundamentalism and 'ethnic
cleansing' (Nixon, 1997; Penrose, 1993). The
implication, within these writings, is that any
nationalist project is inherently flawed and
therefore highly problematic. None of these
perspectives enable Indigenous peoples colonized by settler states to envision any future
other than their ongoing erasure, since
Columbus, from global international political
relations (Venne, 1998). It is a small wonder
that, particularly in North America, Indigenous
decolonization, nationhood and sovereignty,
when seen through the lens of postmodern
and postcolonial theory, begins to appear not
only impossible and futile, but absolutely
irrelevant (Cook-Lynn, 1996: 88) for activist
agendas. It is for this reason that Linda
Tuhiwai Smith asserts the need for Indigenous
peoples to engage with theory on their own
terms, for their own empowerment:

> The development of theories by Indigenous schol-
> ars which attempt to explain our existence in con-
> temporary society (as opposed to the 'traditional'
> society constructed under modernism) has only just
> begun. Not all these theories claim to be derived
> from some 'pure' sense of what it means to be
> Indigenous, nor do they claim to be theories which
> have been developed in a vacuum separated from
> any association with civil and human rights move-
> ments, other nationalist struggles, or other theo-
> retical approaches. What is claimed, however, is
> that new ways of theorizing by Indigenous scholars
> are grounded in a real sense of, and sensitivity
> towards, what it means to be an Indigenous person
> [...] Contained within this imperative is a sense of
> being able to determine priorities, to bring to the
> centre those issues of our own choosing, and to
> discuss them amongst ourselves. (1999: 38)

In Canada, Indigenous scholars have begun
challenging the automatic equation of the
concept of 'nationhood' with European
modernity and the nation-state, by insisting
that within Indigenous epistemologies, one
can speak of 'nationhood' as well as 'people-
hood'. Lina Sunseri (2005), for example,
uses Oneida oral tradition to assert an Oneida

nationalism unconnected with notions of the
nation-state. Sakej Henderson (1997), meanwhile, in an extensive exploration of Mi'kmaq
oral tradition, has documented the seventeenth-
century concordat between the Mi'kmaq
Grand Council and the Holy Roman Empire,
as marked by the wampum belt currently
maintained at the Vatican. He has also written extensively about the larger geopolitical
organization of east coast nations in Canada
and the Northeastern US that existed prior
to military suppression – the Wabanaki
Confederacy – and its relationship to other
Indigenous confederacies of the time. Finally,
John Borrows clearly articulates Anishnabe
oral tradition as the means through which
Anishinabe customary law was maintained
(2002: 3–28). Through the work of these and
other theorists, we can see that concepts of
Indigenous nationhood in Canada reflect
carefully traced, researched and recollected
Indigenous orders of governance, forcibly
suppressed by British or Canadian colonialism, and that postmodern and postcolonial
arguments, with their blanket assumptions
of an erased or always imaginary past, and
their disregard for the complex histories of
that are currently being reclaimed, risk re-
primivitizing Indigenous peoples. As Craig
Womack has succinctly remarked, 'it is way
too premature for Native scholars to deconstruct history when we haven't yet constructed it' (1999: 3).

On a deeper level, attacks on Indigenous
nationhood come at many levels. Gail Guthrie
Valaskakis addresses the racist notions of
'the primitive' that underlie most aspects of
elite white culture, and how it denigrates oral
tradition as folklore and not history (2004: 76),
thereby undermining the epistemological
frameworks through which Indigenous perspectives on nationhood are understood.
Sandy Grande, meanwhile, speaks to the
prevalent assumption, maintained not only
within the mainstream but within some postcolonial theory, that pre-contact Indigenous
peoples were 'immature precursors to the
nation-state' (2005: 49), lacking both governments and law, and therefore nationhood.

On a still more basic everyday level are the sweeping assumptions of would-be cultural consumers who believe, as much as their openly racist ancestors did, that Native people have lost all cultural knowledge, and that a reclaimed, socially constructed and fairly two-dimensional 'pan-Indian' identity is all that remains of formerly distinct nations.

It is clear, of course, that a generic 'pan-Indian' identity *does* exist, the product of multiple levels of colonial violence, including forced relocation, being confined to reserves, and in particular, residential schooling which enforced a painful alienation while teaching a common language. However, it is equally clear that for a settler society, 'pan-Indian' identities are comfortable identities: lacking cultural specificity, they are capable of being moulded and appropriated into any image that the dominant culture requires, by all and sundry. Indeed, the widespread insistence on 'pan-Indianism', within the mainstream society and within some academic discourse, is simply another denial of Indigenous nationhood and cultural specificity. It is for this reason that a key concept in postcolonial discourse – the notion of hybridity – is viewed as quite problematic for many Indigenous scholars. A number of Indigenous theorists (Cook-Lynn, 1986; Deloria, 1998; Weaver et al., 2006; Womack, 1999) question the usefulness of the notion of 'hybridity', and point out the hazards of utilizing this concept in relation to Indigenous peoples.

There are two ways in which the term is utilized which are problematic in Indigenous contexts. The first way relates to the notion of hybrid identities, in the sense of being mixed-race – which, in postcolonial theory seems to inevitably involve an embracing of border identities and liminality. The second way relates to the notion of *cultural* hybridity, and related concepts of diasporic identity.

Any celebration of hybridity as mixed-bloodedness is highly problematic for Indigenous peoples in settler states. In the colonial discourse that still controls Indigenous identity, indigeneity is presumed to cease to exist with racial mixing (Garroutte,

2003; Lawrence, 2004; Sturm, 2002). In such a context, to embrace mixed-blood hybridity is to be asked to celebrate one's own extinction as a Native person. For many mixed-blood Native people, Indigenous empowerment means demanding the right to not be defined solely by their hybridity and instead identifying entirely with their Indigenous nations. At heart is an insistence that being Indigenous is a cultural/national identity, not a racial one; this strikes at the heart of the colonial definitions of identity by race enforced through identity legislation.

The second usage of 'hybridity' – the notion of cultural hybridity – closely related to concepts of diaspora, is in many respects even more problematic for Indigenous peoples in settler nations. Held firmly in the grip of colonialism for over 500 years, there has been little room for Indigenous peoples to challenge certain foundational racist myths that bind indigeneity firmly to notions of primordiality, in counter-distinction to modernity. Overwhelmingly, Indigenous peoples are 'not allowed' to change if they wish to remain Indigenous. This is particularly the case with respect to legal rights in Canada where cultural hybridity (as defined by the courts) can affect an individual's ability to assert Aboriginal title, and can interfere with their ability to practice Aboriginal harvesting rights.

For example, the Canadian Supreme Court decision *Van der Peet*[1] asserted that Aboriginal rights would be restricted to pre-contact practices (Mainville, 2001: 29). Meanwhile, the *Delgamuuk*[2] decision began the process of defining the content of Aboriginal title, in highly restrictive ways. One crucial restriction is that land covered by Aboriginal title can only be used for land-based activities that are part of the court's vision of a 'distinct' relationship between Aboriginal peoples and the land. Finding new (and hybridized) ways to survive in the face of ongoing colonization is not 'permitted' under the Canadian courts.

The prevalence of such legal opinions, of course, reflects biases that deeply penetrate western society, that cultural hybridity nullifies Indigenous cultural identity. Jace Weaver,

Robert Warrior and Craig Womack (2006), in their most recent work have strenuously argued the validity of tribally specific literary criticism – in face of strong opposition from those who see most Native American cultures as 'too hybrid' and impure to be distinct, because many of them have a written literature (much of it in English), a Christian tradition, and a diasporic existence.

Many of the difficulties that Indigenous peoples have with postcolonial discourse relates to there being little place in the discourse for land-based peoples. Chadwick Allen articulates this very clearly, below:

> Indigenous minority discourse poses a problem for those postcolonial theories that delegate 'essentialism', 'nativism', 'nationalism' and so forth as anachronistic politics, because Indigenous minority discourses often emphasize land and treaty rights and because they often insist on persistent racial, cultural, and linguistic distinctiveness despite other changes over time. They provoke charges of a retrograde 'essentialism' in particular, because orthodox postcolonial critics often fail to understand how the discourses that intersect with the controversial blood/land/memory complex, including the discourses of treaties, might appear cogent for Indigenous activists and writers. (2002: 30–1)

In examining Indigenous resistance to postmodern and postcolonial discourses, it is obvious that most criticism comes from Indigenous theorists situated within settler states. It might therefore be useful to consider the global parameters of indigeneity, in order for the international reader to have a better grasp of the particularities of Indigenous identities in Canada.

## CONTEXTUALIZING INDIGENEITY

As Maori theorist Roger Maaka has articulated, a global movement of 'Indigenous peoples', comprising approximately 350 million people, and representing 5000 cultures and languages across more than seventy countries is increasingly being recognized (2005: 29). While a number of Indigenous activists and theorists (LaDuke, 2003; Smith, 1999; Venne, 1998) recognize the commonality of Indigenous struggles for land and recovery of sovereignty globally, given the complexity and diversity of Indigenous experience, it may be useful to articulate some broad distinctions, particularly between Indigenous peoples marginalized with postcolonial states and those colonized by settler states.[3] This is not meant to be proscriptive – communities may have strong connections which will ignore such distinctions – it is merely suggested as a means of addressing our different positioning within global imperialism, historically and at present.

The situations of Indigenous peoples within postcolonial states are extremely varied. They are frequently targeted as a source of exploitable resources by local elites, who view them as expendable to 'development', as with the Borneo and Arang Asli peoples in Malaysia (Endicott, 2003: 156). They may have been designated as 'tribal people' by occupying Europeans, and then subsequently designated and controlled as such by the ascendant postcolonial state – like tribal peoples in Northeast India (Maitra and Maitra, 1995). Their homelands may frequently still bear the imprint of past European colonial occupation – some have been heavily affected by protracted wars of liberation, as with the !Kung San peoples of Angola and Namibia (Lee, 2003: 87), or by ongoing wars for profit and control waged by local elites on behalf of international oil corporations – as the Khanty people face in Northern Siberia (Balzer, 2003: 125). They may even be targeted for genocide by postcolonial nationalist regimes, as the people of East Timor are facing with Indonesia (Anderson, 2003: 174).

Indigenous peoples who are colonized by settler states may face many similar circumstances. Their lands are inevitably targeted as a source of exploitable resources, and they are too often viewed as expendable by ruling elites. Indigenous peoples who are situated within weaker settler states long dominated by American interests may have to deal with genocidal wars of repression waged by the state (as in Guatemala), by paramilitary groups (as in Columbia), or by left-wing fundamentalists (as in Peru). Indigenous peoples who are directly colonized by the larger western superpowers are usually subordinated internally through the police or occasionally by the national military. All Indigenous peoples within settler states face an ongoing colonial project that must be maintained in order for the settler state to continue to exist.

It is this aspect which may be unique to settler states – the hegemonic power, generally maintained over at least a century of nation-building, that is utilized to subjugate Indigenous peoples and remake their territories in the image of the settler nation. The process involves a focused, multifaceted and intergenerational process of genocide. Indeed, settler states must always be ready to suppress, sabotage and deny the nationhood of Indigenous peoples, regardless of the cost, not only to maintain control of the lands that are the source of their wealth, but to maintain settler nation-building myths. It is for this reason that settler states like Canada are willing to spend millions of dollars annually on police actions suppressing even the most basic assertions of sovereignty[4] – and for this reason that Indigenous theorists from settler states must focus their energies not on postmodern or postcolonial discourses but on resisting their erasure as peoples.

The power of settler states is only heightened by the fact that under current international law, despite the massive power they may have at their disposal to wield against Indigenous peoples, they cannot be considered colonial regimes. In 1960, the United Nations' General Assembly Resolution 1541 (XV) stated that colonialism could only be said to exist if at least 30 square miles of blue water existed between the homelands of the colonizer and the occupied territory of the colonized (Churchill, 1995: 2). Instead of international recognition of the need to decolonize settler nations (which would have demanded a fundamental reworking of every aspect of some of the most powerful nation-states in the world), Indigenous peoples

within settler states have had to fight within the United Nations for recognition of special rights *within* those states (Venne, 1998). In this, they have been joined by Indigenous peoples from postcolonial states who were marginalized *during* the decolonization process. So while Indigenous peoples around the world are in crisis because of globalization, and often have the same values, as land-based peoples, and have worked together to hammer out the Declaration of the Rights of Indigenous Peoples (Venne, 1998), they do so from distinctly different histories and regimes of struggle.

In white settler nation-states, land takes on an increasingly powerful symbolic and ideological force among settlers. It is therefore not surprising that the only nation-states who refused to sign the Declaration of the Rights of Indigenous Peoples are the four 'first world' white settler nations (Canada, the US, Australia and New Zealand) whose claims of sovereignty over the territories they occupy are most threatened by any recognition that the Indigenous nations whose territories they occupy are nations, with distinct land rights.

There are, of course, also broad differences in circumstances among Indigenous peoples colonized by settler states. Whether the colonizing settler state firmly holds to the concept of 'terra nullius', as in Australia or is faced with a sizeable Indigenous minority capable of forcing the renegotiation of treaties and the recognition of their language, as in New Zealand, or indeed, of forcing unpopular settler governments to fall, as in Bolivia – or whether Indigenous peoples are tiny minorities regulated through formal identity legislation, as in Canada and the US – myriad circumstances shape the expectations and possibilities of Indigenous communities in various settler states.

To narrow the focus of settler state colonialism to address Indigenous peoples' relationship to land in the Americas, it is immediately clear that that broad differences in circumstances exist between Indigenous peoples in 'Latin' and 'Anglo' America – to the extent that in some respects, south–south network-ing may be at least as important to the nations of South and Central America as rebuilding the connections between 'the condor and the eagle' (signifying the reconnecting of Indig-enous peoples from North and South America). Aside from the most obvious dif-ferences in levels of power of the different nation-states, a powerful difference lies in the area of self-representation. In those regions where Indigenous peoples are a significant percentage of national populations, they have managed to mobilize themselves, despite hunger, poverty and police or paramilitary brutality, to mount an open resistance to ruling powers in ways that are seldom under-taken in Canada where Indigenous peoples are approximately 5 percent of the population, or in the US, where Indigenous peoples rep-resent less than 1 percent of the population (St Germain, 2001: xix).

With mobilization comes tremendous net-working among Indigenous peoples and the demand to speak for themselves organiza-tionally, through their own political/cultural institutions. Indigenous peoples in some parts of Latin America therefore have unprece-dented powers of direct self-representation, compared to communities in Anglo America. However, when issues of poverty and lack of access to western education come into play, as well as lack of access to extensive publish-ing opportunities, it is obvious that most Indigenous peoples in Latin America have not acquired the means of self-representation intellectually. Most academic work is pro-duced 'about' Indigenous peoples in Latin America, rather than 'by' them.

In Anglo America, however, the relation-ship is reversed. Being such a tiny minority situated with the richest countries in the world, Indigenous peoples can seldom openly mobilize to challenge power in any direct sense without risking absolute destruction as peoples – although communities can and do take stands despite subsequent military occu-pation. However, resistance is weakened by government policies that forcibly supplanted the traditional leadership of most Indigenous communities with an elected leadership who, for the most part, espouse goals that are more closely aligned with those of settler govern-ments. As a result, Indigenous nations in Canada commonly experience a tremendous bifurcation between 'grassroots' or 'tradi-tional' leadership and the formal leadership recognized by the federal governments (Goodleaf, 1995: 20–1), which makes resist-ance much more difficult and facilitates ongoing land theft.

On the other hand, in Canada (and to an even greater extent in the US) a certain per-centage of Indigenous peoples now have had access to university education and therefore to publishing. As a result, in both Canada and the US, Indigenous theorists and academics increasingly are insisting on writing and speak for themselves and their communities (although non-Natives still speak for and about them). An accumulating body of Indig-enous theory – the source of considerable intellectual resistance – is the result.

The other significant difference that must be mentioned, across the Americas, are the distinctly different modes through which Indigenous peoples are controlled by settler governments in 'Latin' versus 'Anglo' America. Broadly speaking, in Latin America, nations with relatively small settler popula-tions and huge Indigenous populations, mes-tizaje has been a central aspect of the colonial project – the notion that the products of inter-marriage between the two groups would affiliate with the settler population rather than their *Indio/India* parents and grandpar-ents. In this framework, all citizens are assumed to be of Indigenous heritage, but only the poorest, darkest and least assimila-ble are considered to be Indian. It becomes a crucial part of the national mythologies of some of these nation-states that they have descended from the (past) glorious civiliza-tions of MesoAmerica or South America (thereby usurping the pasts of the Indigenous peoples that they continue to exploit and denigrate). It is also a highlight of these states that Indianness is not legally regulated. While a range of policies, from cultural genocide to loss of land to outright physical extermination, continue to be utilized in an attempt to control the peoples who in many cases constitute sizeable minority populations – little attempt is made to formally classify by law who is 'Indian' and who is not.

North of the Rio Grande, however, in the US and Canada (and only in these two nation-states), complex frameworks of formal identity legislation have been imposed to further fragment Indigenous identity, and to indelibly shape (and therefore distort) Indigenous relationship to land. Both systems grew from the unique circumstances present in Anglo America, where large numbers of white settlers were brought in and where Indigenous peoples have been reduced to between approximately 1 and 5 percent of the population. This approach has been characterized as 'miscegenationist', wherein absolute whiteness becomes the criterion for othering 'the Indian', and where possession of 'Indian blood'/descent therefore becomes the central criterion for defining indigeneity (while at the same time, constantly externalizing from Indianness those who, through intermarriage, begin to manifest lower blood quantum). Both Canada and the US rely extensively on formal regulation of Indigenous identity in a range of classifications based on 'blood' or descent, as a means of controlling Indigenous people, with economic benefits and restrictions attached to different categories of 'Indianness'. While there are land-based peoples who either reject or were excluded from formal recognition under identity legislation, who often assert more traditional values, for many federally recognized Indigenous peoples who have been forced to engage in an ongoing manner with settler governments, and rely on federal funding for their continued survival, legislation controlling 'Indianness' is central to their identities. To grasp what this means in Canada, it is important to understand the Indian Act, the history of its development, and the importance of its ongoing administration as a means of controlling Native identity.

## THE REGULATION OF NATIVE IDENTITY

For over a century, the *Indian* Act has controlled Native identity in Canada by creating a legal category, that of the 'status Indian', which is the only category of Indigenous person with whom an historic nation-to-nation relationship with Canada is recognized.[5] Without Indian status, and the band membership that goes along with it, an Indigenous person in Canada is not allowed to live on any land that is considered 'Indian land' (unless it is leased to them as an 'outsider').[6] They cannot take part in the life of their own community unless they have Indian status and hence band membership in that community. We can see, then, that the colonial act of establishing a legal definition of 'Indianness', which excluded vast numbers of Native people from obtaining or retaining status, has enabled the Canadian government to remove a significant number of Native people from the land. By 1985 there were twice as many non-status Indians and Metis as status Indians in Canada (Holmes, 1987: 13). In essence, by 1985, legislation ensconced in the *Indian Act* had already rendered two thirds of all Native people in Canada landless, and created tremendous fragmentation among Native people.

Indeed, Canada's definitions of Indianness from the start have controlled who was recognized as an Indian band, who could get any land under the treaties, and who could live on this land. These definitions are enshrined in a document known as the Indian Act, which has been in existence for over 150 years. While the Indian Act addresses every aspect of status Indian life in Canada, from the registering of the 'birth of a live Indian' to disposing of the property of 'deceased Indians', it has historically had two main areas of focus: defining 'the Indian', and maintaining social and political control of 'Indians' to facilitate the taking of Indigenous land.

## Defining the 'Indian'

The first pieces of legislation loosely defining who could be considered 'Indian', were passed in 1850, while 'Canada' was a small colony anxious to assume a nominal degree of self-government. Legislation aimed at assimilating individual 'Indians' into Canadian society was then implemented in 1857. This legislation was the first to suggest that 'Indianness' as a legal construct could be alienated from an individual, by authorizing the removal of 'Indian status' from selected individuals, with the goal of creating colonial citizens of Native heritage who had relinquished their collective ties to their community of origin, and any group claims to Native lands (including the right to live in their community or to be buried there). Through various changes in legislation over the years, Indigenous people could have their Indian status removed for acquiring an education, for serving in the armed forces, for working in a professional capacity or for leaving their reserves for any length of time to maintain employment. The legislation was openly aimed at the elimination of Indigenous peoples as a legal and social fact.

This process was facilitated tremendously by the Gradual Enfranchisement Act, passed in 1869, two years after Canada formally became a settler nation. The identity legislation created in the Gradual Enfranchisement Act, and later incorporated into the Indian Act, utilized notions of descent to limit Indianness (so that those with less than one-quarter Indian 'blood' were no longer eligible for annuities and funds designated for Indians). However, what has been most unique (and devastating) about identity legislation in Canada was the manner in which it utilized gender discrimination to eliminate Indianness. With this legislation, Indian women who married non-Indians lost their Indian status (as did their descendents). Along with their husbands these women were to be forcibly removed from reserve communities by Indian agents. For the next 116 years, the children, grandchildren, and great-grandchildren of the 125,000 women who lost their status over the years would continuously be excluded from Indianness; the result was that between half a million and two million descendants of these women were eliminated from Indianness. Indeed, only 350,000 individuals still held Indian status in 1985, when the 'marrying out' policy was terminated.

In 1876, all previous legislation pertaining to Indians was collected into a body of law comprising over a hundred sections, and known as *The Indian Act*. With these changes, Indianness became increasingly defined only along the male line, so that women could only acquire Indian status through their fathers or husbands (non-Native women married to Indian men became legally Indian). Perhaps even more crucially, a series of modifications were immediately introduced that differentiated between 'Indians' and 'half-breeds' and defined 'half-breeds' (now known as 'Metis') as non-Indian, thus creating one of the central divisions existing among Native people in Canada today – between those designated 'Indian' and those designated 'Metis'.

The creation of the category of 'Metis' in Canada – formally reclassifed as 'Aboriginal' in 1982 after over a century of liminal existence as legally not Native but socially not white – has involved the collapsing of multiple distinct historical processes. The first process is about cultural hybridity, due to the fur trade, which flourished across Canada for 250 years, and drew Native women into the process, initially as intermediaries – translators and diplomats, suppliers of the material goods that white men needed to survive in the bush – and ultimately, as wives of traders. The fur trade provided a niche for their mixed-blood offspring – as intermediaries, and as voyageurs who paddled huge canoes of furs on routes spanning half a continent. Eventually mixed-blood settlements, culturally hybrid and distinct, dotted the regions wherever the fur trade penetrated, resulting in a *cultural* group who self-identified as 'Metis'. Not all mixed-bloods self-identified as such; many simply remained part of their mothers' Indigenous nations.

The second historical process creating 'metisness' was the creation of a colonial *racial* category, the 'half-breed', and the forcing of all those who manifested any racial or cultural hybridity into that category during the treaty-making process. The British colonial administrators who were primarily involved with the Indian Department in Canada, with their theories about 'racial mixing' and 'pure' Indianness (and their desire to limit total numbers of 'Indians' on their lists) had no intentions of allowing mixed-bloods to be registered as 'Indian', whether they identified culturally as 'Metis' or not. Indeed, at treaty tables anybody manifesting any cultural hybridity (for example, the ability to speak English) were encouraged to sign on as 'half-breeds'. With the demise of the fur trade, and as numbers of white settlers multiplied many mixed-bloods might have rejoined their communities of origin, had the Indian Act not expressly forbidden it. Instead, a growing category of people excluded from treaties and yet racialized as 'not white' and therefore 'not settlers' grew. In 1870 and again in 1885, these individuals resisted white encroachment and were harshly suppressed. After 1885, forced to maintain separateness from 'Indians' through being classified within a separate racial category, living in a bifurcated world of 'settler' and 'Indian' with no place to call their own, and increasingly denigrated as "breeds', mixed-bloods 'went underground'. Those who could pass as whites did so; the rest retreated to marginal lands, fled to the US, and lived in the utmost poverty in urban slum settings.

A third trend that describes certain experiences of 'Metisness' were the 'half-breed settlements' that sprung up on the edges of most isolated reserves, where those who lost their Indian status due to intermarriage squatted. Prior to 1985, there was considerable two-way traffic in and out of Indianness as individuals from these 'Metis' villages and from reserves intermarried, and generations of families alternately gained or lost Indian status through their marriages.

In subsequent versions of the Indian Act, identity legislation was modified almost continuously. Although definitions of Indianness were frequently tightened in ways that restricted access to the reserves to increasing numbers of Indian people, the 1894 changes to the Indian Act created a much more simplified and inclusive definition of an Indian solely for the purpose of charging off-reserve Indians under the liquor section of the Act.[7] Judges could also use their discretion and punish non-status Indians according to Indian Act laws.

In 1951, the Indian Act was 'modernized', to reflect a global turn towards formal decolonization (at least in the '3rd world'). Indian organizations were consulted, and many of the more repressive laws were removed as were many of the more blatant discrepancies between the Criminal Code and the Indian Act. For example, the laws concerning intoxicants, the prohibition on Indian ceremonies and dances, and the requirement of obtaining permission from Indian agents to travel or sell produce were all removed from the books. Indian women finally regained the right to vote in band elections. Compulsory enfranchisement for Indian men was stopped.

And yet, in terms of identity legislation, the Indian Act 1951 was staggering in its implications. Indian women who married non-Indians had, in the past, been forced to leave their communities; under Section 12.1(b) they were now compulsorily enfranchised, thereby losing all vestiges of any connection to their territories of origin. This Act also contained two other means through which individuals lost status, Section 12.1(a) 4, the 'double mother' clause, whereby individuals whose mother and paternal grandmother gained status through marriage lost their status at 21; and Section 12.2, which formalized the processes for removing the illegitimate children of Indian mothers from the band list if the father was not known. Indeed, so complex was the identity legislation in the Indian Act 1951 that an Indian registrar was created simply to oversee band lists and ensure that the removal of names from band lists proceeded 'properly' (Lawrence, 2004: 50–4).

It was not until the Indian Act of 1985, also known as Bill C-31, that Indian women who married out, along with their children, were reinstated as Indians, although gender discrimination continues through the fragmenting of rules of descent, which specifically affect the offspring of women who intermarried. The fragmenting of Indian status (into 'full-status' [under Section 6.1] and 'half-status' [under Section 6.2]) is now applied to the offspring of all Indians (male or female) who marry non-Indians; it becomes correspondingly more difficult for any Indian to pass their status on to their children. The implications of this – where intermarriage for two generations can now mean the inexorable ending of Indian status for whole communities of people – are staggering. A number of reserves are now facing the prospect that within the next decades there will be no more status Indians left in their communities at all. In many respects, then, the current Indian Act is possibly the most destructive of all in terms of regulating Indigenous identity.

## Controlling the 'Indian' and taking Indigenous land

The Gradual Enfranchisement Act, imposed in 1869 on eastern nations drastically outnumbered by settlers and weakened by disease and years of warfare, provided the means for Canada to bypass and undermine existing traditional Indigenous governments at the level of the individual nation, as well as the larger geopolitical/spiritual alliances of nations known as Confederacies, which had

for centuries asserted their jurisdiction over different regions of what is now Canada (RCAP, 1996, Vol. 1: 275–6). Instead, after 1869, Canada dealt with Native people only at the 'band' level – which amounted to village-sized gatherings of families. A puppet 'chief and council' was installed for each 'band'; their responsibilities were for issues such as public health, property maintenance, and maintaining public order.

After 1869, Indian legislation became even more punitive, criminalizing the newly subjugated nations on the prairies as a means of controlling them. For example, an Indian found in a state of intoxication was to be jailed for up to one month, while any Native women found off-reserve could be labelled a prostitute and given a penalty of 100 dollars and up to six months in jail (Jamieson, 1978: 43).

As a result of the 1885 rebellion, extremely harsh measures were introduced to the Indian Act to suppress resistance in Indian communities, including mass hangings, imprisonment, the withholding of monies and rations, confiscation of horses, and in some cases the breaking up of bands and their forced integration into other bands (Stonechild and Waiser, 1997: 254–63). All reserves were declared off limits to anybody but band members after dark, and pass laws were implemented. This system, still in place formally until World War I, although difficult to enforce, prevented Indians from leaving their reserves without a pass from the local Indian agent. Indian agents were also given powers to enforce anti-vagrancy laws, providing them with the power to control Indian women through designating them as 'common prostitutes'.

In the process, legislation was continually introduced to weaken Indian control over reserve lands. The Department of Indian Affairs was granted the power to lease land to settlers, to sell off reserve lands near municipalities, to expropriate reserve lands for public works, or to allow mining operations on reserves, all without the band's consent. Other legislation was implemented to allow Native people to be forcibly removed from any reserves adjacent to or partly within towns of 8000 inhabitants or more; from sites where resources were to be developed, such a mining or hydro development, and eventually, from any region where land was wanted for settlers (Dickason, 1992: 323).

As the nineteenth century drew to a close, the Indian Act was increasingly being utilized to break the spirit of subjugated communities and criminalize any form of resistance. Most notable were the regulation which made it compulsory for children to attend residential schools, where they were forcibly removed from their parents and communities, in order to remove all knowledge of Native culture and language from them and to systematically negate the value of Native cultures (Grant, 1996: 23–4). The schools' goals were therefore *inherently* violent; it was therefore perhaps inevitable that they would attract as administrators and teachers those who were indifferent, insensitive, hostile and sadistic towards Indian children (Miller, 1989: 309).

The devastation residential schools wrought has been profound and intergenerational. In community after community, children returned home with their spirits broken (or never returned home at all), succumbing to alcoholism and acting out the self-hatred and abuse they had been taught at the schools, against their spouses and children and other loved ones, in a spiral of lateral violence that is intergenerational in scope. The children also returned with no idea of what family life meant, and therefore no notion, as adults, of how to parent their own children. Not knowing their own languages and unable to communicate with elders who spoke no English, there were no means of maintaining oral traditions, which had been the primary vehicle for intergenerational transmission of Native values, culture and identity (Grant, 1996: 193).

At the turn of the century, as the first generations to lose their children to residential school were resisting and challenging the process, Canada began its legal assault on Indigenous spirituality. Laws were passed which made it illegal for Indians to dance or

practice any of the ceremonies that maintained and strengthened communities (Backhouse, 1999: 65). For the most part, those who were jailed for dancing and practising the ceremonies were the powerful traditional leaders that people still relied on for guidance, despite the imposition of a 'chief and council' as formal government in their communities.

Prior to this assault on Indigenous spirituality, even those communities which had converted to Chrstianity due to missionary influence tended to imbue most aspects of life with the sacred, while for those communities who still practised traditional ways, all life was sacred. This provided communities with considerable strength in adversity. Ceremonies, dances, and other means of connecting communities to one another, to the sacred, and to the natural world were central to Indigenous life, creating interdependency and a cohesive sense of self in relation to land and life in all its forms (Pettipas, 1994: 43–61).

The suppression of ceremonies for almost 50 years was therefore crucial to the project of desacralizing Indigenous life. Intense pressures to Christianize accompanied these formal assaults on cultural integrity; the presence of the priest or minister as an absolute authority loomed large on most Indian reserves from this time onwards. Meanwhile, Indian agents systematically looted and sold the sacred objects of these communities as the practices that encompassed them were being driven underground (Crosby, 1991). This profound assault on Indigenous cultural autonomy facilitated the restrictions on political autonomy; with the imprisonment of spiritual leaders and the loss of the sacred objects that were central to ceremonial life, the potential for serious political resistance was severely hampered.

Despite this, the repressive legislation continued. The Indian Act was revised ten times between 1910 and 1930, primarily in an effort to suppress the growing political resistance by Indian communities by making it illegal to use band funds for land claim actions or to solicit or give money for pursuit of a land claim without permission from the Superintendent of Indian Affairs (RCAP, 1996, Vol. 1: 296). The cumulative effect of these restrictions was to make it extremely difficult for Indian people to hire lawyers or in any other ways engage in political organization to protect their lands.

## Implications of the Indian Act

Given this history of coercion, extortion and profound loss, perhaps it is not surprising how pervasive the influence of identity legislation has been in Canada. Categorizing who is 'Indian' and who is not, and on what basis, has been central to the project of acquiring control of Indian land, fragmenting resistance to land theft along gendered and racial lines, and ultimately distorting our ideas of what it means to be an Indigenous person in Canada. The Indian Act functions as a conceptual framework that governs ways of thinking about Native identity. In a sense, it produces a 'grammar', a way of thinking about Indianness that embeds itself even in attempt to change it (Lawrence, 2004). For example, at present, Native organizations, academics, and governments routinely speak of there being three *kinds* of Aboriginal people (Indians, Inuit and Metis, as defined by the 1982 Constitution), as if these are inherent, natural differences, as if these groups have no relationship to one another, and no common history that created these divisions.

'Indian Act' thinking hobbles possibilities of unity in a number of ways. It encourages status Indians to think of themselves as members of over 630 'First Nations' across Canada – each 'First Nation' actually the equivalent of a community, once known by the colonizers as an Indian 'band' – which ignores the reality that they are actually citizens of much larger Indigenous nations. It encourages parochial thinking with respect to land, so that even if Indigenous leaders speak of reclaiming their traditional territories, those territories are only reclaimed as

part of the territory of that community, not of the nation as a whole. Since the reserve, and not the entire Indigenous nation, is the primary object of concern, then the various boundaries which fragment the Indigenous nations – sometimes treaty boundaries, sometimes provincial boundaries, and sometimes national boundaries – are seldom challenged. Impelled by the very real struggles that communities are having with respect to survival, for many, the reserve appears to be the limit that 'decolonization' can reach. While contemporary First Nations network all the time, for the most part they do so as a loosely linked assembly of individual reserves, not as recreating Indigenous nations. And needless to say, those parts of Indigenous nations that are federally unrecognized – the communities not brought into treaty relationships, those whose traditional lands are on the wrong side of provincial boundaries from where they live, those that were never granted reserves, those designated 'half-breeds' and excluded, and those carved off, routinely, through gender discrimination and the relentless logic that racial purity defines Indigeneity – are simply externalized as not being 'Indian' at all (as if 'Indian' is equivalent to 'Indigenous').[8] And this seriously hinders Indigenous peoples' abilities to challenge colonialism in Canada. Indeed, Taiaiake Alfred suggests that too many First Nations people today see only the possibility of accommodating themselves to colonialism, rather than defeating it (2005: 26).

To speak of how pervasively the Indian Act has permeated the ways in which Native people understand their own identities is not to deny Native people the agency to move beyond its logic, or to suggest that traditional cultural ways of understanding the relationships between people, their communities, and the land are gone – far from it. Indeed, a tremendous decolonization process is underway, taking place largely at the grassroots or community levels, to addresses peoples' healing, traditional governance and reconnection to land.

## DECOLONIZATION

For Indigenous peoples from settler nations, each with different experiences of colonization, decolonization can never mean the eventual expulsion of Europeans from their territories, as was the goal during many 'third world' decolonization movements. Furthermore, many Indigenous people in Canada today are extremely cognizant that in the wake of such devastating policies of cultural genocide, to focus solely on the colonizer in Ottawa cannot remove the colonizer who was so brutally and forcibly introduced into Indigenous hearts and minds. On another level are the international corporate neo-colonizers attacking the land – so that Indigenous peoples need to be strong in order to protect the land. Nor can certain wounds be healed until language use – literally beaten out of generations of students – is regenerated.

Work on languages has been addressed nationally, through the Assembly of First Nations, but ultimately, in a country the size of Canada, must be undertaken regionally or provincially. Each region has taken different approaches, ranging from struggling for control over on-reserve language education, to bringing local languages into public schools, to forming language commissions to address the living civilizations of each region by focusing on development at the community level. Some universities have provided resources and some have focused specifically on language revitalization. Online resources have also been developed for specific languages.

And yet, as vital as this is, there is also a profound need to assert that Indigenous peoples have survived as distinct cultures despite the transition to English (or French, in Quebec, or Spanish, for that matter, elsewhere in the Americas). Acoma Pueblo poet Simon Ortiz, writes:

> Along with their Native languages, Indian women and men have carried on their lives and their expression through the use of the newer languages, particularly Spanish, French, and English, and they have used these languages on their own terms. This is the crucial item that has to be understood, that it is entirely possible for a people to retain and maintain their lives through the use of any language. (Ortiz, 1981: 10)

For many years, there has been a concern among many Indigenous women that while the formal leadership of communities, which under the Indian Act has been primarily male, continue to devote themselves to 'large-scale statist solutions' (Alfred, 1999: 31) such as self-government and land claims, the communities themselves are fracturing, and need to be healed from the cycles of abuse spawned by residential schools (Fernandez, 2003: 249; Lawrence and Anderson, 2005: 1). Work on healing is taking place 'on the ground' in Indigenous communities across Canada, as countless individuals, finding their own sobriety, begin to work in the alcohol and drug treatment programs set up on reserves and in urban centres. It is important to note that all this work, for the most part, is taking place across the barriers of identity legislation. The same holds true for family violence programs, and programs addressing youth suicide, which must all be set up separately for reserves or Inuit communities, Metis communities, and urban communities, due to the identity legislation that so totally divides Native people.

However, there have been powerful examples of communities resisting identity legislation – for example, implementing membership policies which enable non-status relatives to come home and be band members in their own communities, even if Canada will not provide funding for them. At other times it is those in the 'minority' position who must fight to challenge identity legislation, sometimes through the courts.[9] And finally, communities outside the Indian Act may struggle to protect the land, for example, the non-status Algonquin communities in Eastern Ontario who are resisting uranium mining and rebuilding land-based communities (Lovelace, 2007).

There are also nations who attempt to reclaim territory based entirely on their traditional rights to it, generally through the courts, largely because the phenomenal limitations of the 'business as usual' approach embedded in the comprehensive claims process, Canada's answer for 'settling the claims' of Indigenous nations who never signed treaties with the crown. Canada continues, relentlessly, year after year, to devise policies which involve more and more First Nations agreeing to schemes to allow private alienation of their land, as well as implementing 'self-government' plans which ensure that First Nations must continue to utilize the colonial policies set up by Canada, while responsibility devolves from the federal government to each community. Taiaiake Alfred has summed up the process most succinctly when he writes: 'The state has shown great skill in shedding the most onerous responsibility of its rule while holding fast to the lands and authorities that are the foundations of its power' (1999: xiii). Patricia Monture (1999), meanwhile, demonstrates how most legal venues for Indigenous empowerment within Canada remain heavily circumscribed by colonialist policies.

## CONCLUSION

While identity legislation, and the repressive framework that accompanied it, has significantly shaped Indigenous experience in Canada, Indigenous nationhood is far from vanquished. Perhaps the greatest legacy of identity legislation is the fragmentation that it has created. On the one hand are the divisions between on-reserve and off-reserve, between status and non-status, between status and Metis – divisions which have successfully derailed numerous attempts to redress land theft, and which continue to stymie efforts to define Indigenous citizenship. On the other hand is the legacy of cultural genocide – the generations whose families were shattered by residential schooling, and who are currently caught in a cycle of child welfare, prison and prostitution, for whom any sense of Indigenous identity may be tenuous and truncated and for whom basic survival continues to be an ongoing issue.

The repatriation of these citizens is fraught with the same divisions created by the Indian Act which makes healing much harder.

Possibly the deepest legacy, however, is the fragmenting of nations into bands, the resulting difficulty in unifying across provincial, treaty, and even national boundaries which run across some nations' territories, and the forced replacement of traditional governments with Indian Act governments – all of which are difficult to resist when a nation's citizenship is divided by questions of Indian status and reserve residency. The implications become even more profound when one takes into account the 'business-as-usual' assumptions within the circles of Indian Act governments that money can ultimately solve the deep-seated colonial condition of North American Indigenous peoples.

As Taiaiake Alfred (2005) notes, the means to Indigenous empowerment will be multi-levelled. Despite poverty, poor health, and the pressures of resource theft, Indigenous peoples at the grassroots level are engaging in cultural revitalization, seeking to engage in critical resistance, and sharing strategies for community empowerment. If the leadership once again becomes guided by the visionaries – not only the medicine people but the artists and the theorists – it may be capable to envision a future beyond the fragmentation of identity brought about by the Indian Act.

Um Sed Nogumak/All My Relations

## NOTES

1   In 1982, Canada repatriated her Constitution from Britain (where it had existed as part of the British North America Act which created Canada in 1867). At that time, Section 35 of the Constitution recognized and affirmed the pre-existence of Aboriginal rights in Canada (a legal concept, referring to unspecified rights which was only began to be defined by court cases in the 1990s. When Dorothy Van der Peet, a member of the Sto:lo Nation charged with violating the *Fisheries Act*, asserted that these restrictions violated her Aboriginal rights as defined by Section 35, the Supreme Court decision

*Van der Peet* began the process of defining how Aboriginal rights would be interpreted in the courts (Mainville, 2001: 26).

2   The Calder case in 1973 was a watershed case, whereby the Supreme Court asserted that something called 'Aboriginal title' to the land existed, and that Canada had a legal obligation to settle Aboriginal title, through treaties, in the many parts of Canada where no treaties had been signed. There was, however, no legal understanding of what this term meant in practice. In the next decade, the Gitksan and Wetsowe'ten traditional chiefs, on behalf of their respective houses, took Canada to court to ownership and jurisdiction over the entire 58,000 square kilometres of their traditional land base in central British Columbia. The case was dismissed by the BC court and subsequently appealed to the Supreme Court. The court decision began the process of defining Aboriginal title.

3   In this chapter, the author defines 'postcolonial states' as the regions where formerly colonized peoples successfully ended the European occupation of their territories and formed postcolonial states, and differentiates clearly between these states and the nation-states of the Americas, Australia, and New Zealand, where white settlers formed their own independent nations on top of colonized peoples' territories.

4   For example, in the wake of a Supreme Court decision recognizing Mi'kmaq rights to maintain their own Atlantic Fishery, the federal government's Fishery department spent CAN$13 million (Morrison, 2001) in police actions, involving high seas chases, and ramming Mi'kmaq boats, all to prevent Mi'kmaq fishermen from one tiny community, Burnt Church, from practicing this right, even though their fishery plan was for 2 percent of the CAN$160 million dollar fishery that non-Native commercial fishermen currently enjoy (Coates, 2000: 215). The police action was to force Burnt Church to enter into agreements with the DFO, simply so that the federal government would retain the right to control the fishery.

5   The three 'categories' of Aboriginal peoples in Canada are Indians (status and non-status), Metis, and Inuit. Inuit peoples, whose legal status as 'non-Indians' was addressed by the Canadian courts in re: Eskimo (Backhouse, 1999), were treated as wards of the state whenever Canada implemented policies that forced them off of the land. Legal definitions of 'Inuit', however, are the product of recent land claims policies whereby 'beneficiaries' have to be legally defined. While the Canadian government in recent years has also been forced to recognize Metis people, and non-status Indians as aboriginal people, it bases its policies on status Indians and only recognizes a formal fiduciary responsibility (and hence a historic relationship) towards this group.

6   A minor exception are the Metis settlements in northern Alberta, a handful of villages recognized provincially but not federally as 'Metis land' due to long-standing occupancy by northern Metis.

7   The definition of an Indian under the liquor section included any individual, male or female, with or without Indian status who was reputed to belong to a particular band, or who followed the Indian mode of life, or the child of such a person (Jamieson, 1978: 48).

8   For example, there are thirty Mi'kmaq 'First Nations' listed by the Atlantic chief's organization, rather than one Mi'kmaq nation; furthermore, there are nine non-status Mi'kmaq bands not even listed by the Atlantic chiefs' organization because they are non-status.

9   Sharon McIvor challenged gender bias in Bill C-31. The British Columbia Supreme Court ruled in her favor, finding that the federal government has a constitutional obligation to recognize, as full status, all Native women and their descendents previously deemed status through Bill C-31. The case is now going to the Supreme Court of Canada.

# REFERENCES

Alfred, T. (2005) *Wasase: Indigenous Pathways of Action and Freedom*. Peterborough, Ontario: Broadview Press.

Alfred, T. (1999) *Peace, Power and Righteousness: An Indigenous Manifesto*. Don Mills, Ontario: Oxford University Press.

Allen, C. (2002) *Blood Narrative: Indigenous Identity in American Indian and Maori Literary and Activist Texts*. Durham, NC: Duke University Press.

Anderson, B.R. (2003) 'Nationalism and cultural survival in our time: A sketch', in B. Dean and J.M. Levi (eds), At *the Risk of Being Heard: Identity, Indigenous Rights, and Postcolonial States*, pp. 165–190. Ann Arbor, MI: University of Michigan Press.

Backhouse, C. (1999) *Colour-Coded: A Legal History of Racism in Canada*, 1900–1950. Toronto, Canada: Osgoode Society for Canadian Legal History and University of Toronto Press.

Balzer, M.M. (2003) 'Hot and cold: Interethnic relations in Siberia', in B. Dean and J. M. Levi (eds), At *the Risk of Being Heard: Identity, Indigenous Rights, and Postcolonial States*, pp. 112–141. Ann Arbor, MI: University of Michigan Press.

Borrows, J. (2002) *Recovering Canada: The Resurgence of Indigenous Law*. Toronto: University of Toronto Press.

Churchill, W. (1995) *Since Predator Came: Notes from the Struggle for American Indian Liberation*. Littleton, CO: Aigis Publications.

Coates, K. (2000) *The Marshall Decision and Native Rights*. Montreal: McGill-Queen's University Press.

Cook-Lynn, E. (1996) *Why I Can't Read Wallace Stegner and Other Essays: A Tribal Voice*. Madison, WI: University of Wisconsin Press.

Crosby, M. (1991) 'Construction of the imaginary Indian', in S. Douglas (ed.), *Vancouver Anthology: The Institutional Politics of Art*, pp. 267–291. Vancouver: Talonbooks.

Deloria, P.J. (1998) *Playing Indian*. New Haven, CT: Yale University Press.

Dickason, O. (1992) *Canada's First Nations: A History of Founding Peoples from Earliest Times*. Toronto: McClelland and Stewart Inc.

Endicott, K. (2003) 'Indigenous rights issues in Malaysia', in B. Dean and J.M. Levi (eds), *At the Risk of Being Heard: Identity, Indigenous Rights, and Postcolonial States*, pp. 142–164. Ann Arbor, MI: University of Michigan Press.

Fernandez, C. (2003) 'Coming full circle: A young man's perspective on building gender equity in native communities', in K. Anderson and B. Lawrence (eds), *Strong Women Stories: Native Vision and Community Survival*, pp. 242–256. Toronto: Sumach Press.

Garroutte E.M. (2003) *Real Indians: Identity and the Survival of Native America*. Berkeley, CA: University of California Press.

Grande, S. (2004) *Red Pedagogy: Native American Social and Political Thought*. London: Rowman and Littlefield.

Grant, A. (1996) *No End of Grief: Indian Residential Schools in Canada*. Winnipeg: Pemmican Publications.

Goodleaf, D. (1995) *Entering the War Zone: A Mohawk Perspective on Resisting Invasions*. Penticton, BC: Theytus Press.

Henderson, S. and Youngblood, J. (1997) *The Mikmaw Concordat*. Halifax: Fernwood Publishing.

Holmes, J. (1987) *Bill C-31 – Equality or Disparity? The Effects of the New Indian Act on Native Women*. Background Paper, Canadian Advisory Council on the Status of Women.

Jamieson, K. (1978) *Indian Women and the Law in Canada: Citizens Minus*. Ottawa, Canada: Canadian Advisory Council on the Status of Women and Indian Rights for Indian Women.

LaDuke, W. (2003) 'Foreward', in B. Dean and J.M. Levi (eds), *At the Risk of Being Heard: Identity, Indigenous Rights, and Postcolonial States*. Ann Arbor, MI: University of Michigan Press, pp. ix–x.

Lawrence, B. (2004) *Real Indians and Others: Mixed-Blood Urban Native People and Indigenous Nationhood*. Vancouver: UBC Press.

Lawrence, B. and Anderson K. (2005) 'Introduction to "Indigenous women: the state of our nations"', *Atlantis*, 29 (2): 1–7.

Lee, R.B. (2003) 'Indigenous Rights and the Politics of Identity in Post-Apartheid Southern Africa', in B. Dean and J.M. Levi (eds), *At the Risk of Being Heard: Identity, Indigenous Rights, and Postcolonial States*, pp. 80–111. Ann Arbor, MI: University of Michigan Press.

Lovelace, B. (2007) 'An Algonquin history', Ardoch Algonquin First Nation website. Available at: http://www.aafna.ca/history.html. Accessed on July 8, 2008.

Maaka, R. and Fleras, A. (2005) *The Politics of Indigeneity: Challenging the State in Canada and Aotearoa New Zealand*. Dunedin: University of Otago Press.

Macklem, P. (2001) *Indigenous Difference and the Constitution of Canada*. Toronto: University of Toronto Press.

Mainville, R. (2001) *An Overview of Aboriginal and Treaty Rights and Compensation for their Breach*. Saskatoon, SK: Purich Publishing.

Maitra, R. and Maitra, S. (1995) 'Northeast India: Target of British apartheid', *Executive Intelligence Review*, 22 (41): 10–13.

McClintock, A. (1997) '"No longer in a future heaven": Gender, race, and nationalism', in A. McClintock, A. Mufti and E. Shohat (eds), *Dangerous Liaisons: Gender, Nation, and Postcolonial Perspectives*, pp. 89–112. Minneapolis, MN: University of Minnesota Press.

Miller, J.R. 1(989) *Skyscrapers Hide the Heavens: A History of Indian-White Relations in Canada*. Toronto: University of Toronto Press.

Monture-Angus, P. (1999) *Journeying Forward: Dreaming First Nations Independence*. Halifax: Fernwood Publishing.

Morrison, C. (2001) 'Dhaliwal says $13-M spent to control illegal fishing should have gone to natives', *St. John Evening Times Globe*, 5 April.

Nixon, R. (1997) 'Of Balkans and Bantustans: Ethnic cleansing and the crisis in national legitimation', in A. McClintock, A. Mufti and E. Shohat (eds), *Dangerous Liaisons: Gender, Nation, and Postcolonial Perspectives*, pp. 69–88. Minneapolis, MN: University of Minnesota Press.

Ortiz, S.J. (1981) 'Towards a national Indian literature: Cultural authenticity in nationalism', *Melus*, 8 (2): 7–12.

Penrose, J. (1993) 'Reification in the name of change: The impact of nationalism on social constructions of nation, people and place in Scotland and the United Kingdom', in P. Jackson and J. Penrose (eds),

*Constructions of Race, Place and Nation*, pp. 27–49. London: UCL Press.

Pettipas, K. (1994) *Severing the Ties that Bind: Government Repression of Indigenous Religious Ceremonies on the Prairies.* Winnipeg: University of Manitoba Press.

Royal Commission on Aboriginal Peoples (RCAP) (1996) *For Seven Generations: Report of the Royal Commission on Aboriginal Peoples.* Vols 1–5. Ottawa: Government of Canada.

Smith, L.T. (1999) *Decolonizing Methodologies: Research and Indigenous Peoples.* Dunedin: University of Otago Press and Zed Books.

St Germain, J. (2001) *Indian Treaty-Making Policy in the United States and Canada,* 1867–1877. Toronto: University of Toronto Press.

Stonechild, B. (Cree) and Waiser, B. (1997) *Loyal till Death: Indians and the North-West Rebellion.* Calgary: Fifth House Limited.

Sturm, C. (2002) *Blood Politics: Race, Culture and Identity in the Cherokee Nation of Oklahoma.* University of California Press.

Sunseri, M. (2005) 'Theorizing nationalisms: Intersections of gender, nation, culture and colonization in the case of Oneida's decolonizing nationalist movement'. Unpublished Ph.D. dissertation, Sociology Department, York University.

Valaskakis, G. (2005) *Indian Country: Essays on Contemporary Native Culture.* Waterloo, Ontario, Canada: Wilfrid Laurier University Press.

Venne, S.H. (1998) *Our Elders Understand Our Rights: Evolving International Law Regarding Indigenous Rights.* Penticton, BC: Theytus Press.

Weaver, J. (1998) *Native American Religious Identity: Unforgotten Gods.* Maryknoll, NY: Orbis Books.

Weaver, J. and Craig S. (2006) *Womack and Robert Warrior. American Indian Literary Nationalism.* Albuquerque: University of New Mexico.

Womack, C. (1999) *Red and Red: Native American Literary Separatism.* Minneapolis, MN: University of Minnesota Press.

# Reflections

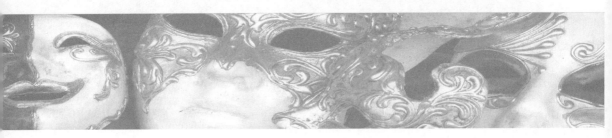

# Social Justice and the Politics of Identity

Chandra Talpade Mohanty

We began working on this book a number of years ago, at a time when Tony Blair and George W. Bush, collaborators in the imperial wars in Iraq and Afghanistan were busy mobilizing discourses of "us and them" and mapping similarly politicized, exclusionary identities in the UK and the US. It was clear to both of us then, a white New Zealander living in the UK, and a brown South Asian living in the US, that identities – those narratives and practices of self, and community that anchored our subjectivities and politics – had profound significance in the Blair/Bush moment that brought us together. Our own genealogies, our travels across the borders of cultures and nations, our commitments to social justice oriented scholarship, and our conviction that understanding the making and re-making of situated identities within the uneven geographies of place, and space all played a part in our collaboration.

In the UK and the US differently mobilized rhetorics of insiders and outsiders defined the terrain of identity politics[1] – through a supposedly benign but increasingly contested multiculturalist frame in the UK and an explicitly racist, militarist frame in the US. Thus, while at that time (2006) our respective governments consolidated militarist, hetero-masculinist, Eurocentric citizen-identities in the "war on terror," anti-war, anti-globalization, feminist, and social justice movements struggled to carve counter-hegemonic identities anchored in alternative understandings of citizenship and accountability.

We are now in a somewhat different historical moment in 2009/2010: the Gordon Brown/Barack Hussein Obama moment. Imperial wars, neo-liberal cultures, capitalist crises, global incarceration regimes, religious, ethnic and gendered violence continue to mark this geo-political landscape. But with the election of the first African American Head of State in the US, the politics of identity is once more propelled to the forefront in the public domain. While the continuities between the politics and economics of government of the previous Bush/Blair regime and the current one are evident, there has clearly been a shift in the meaning and perception of the salience of marginalized[2] identities not just in the US but across the Global North and South. As Harry J. Elam Jr and Michele Elam suggest in Chapter 9 and Rolland Munro in Chapter 10, discourses of racial identity, of Islam, and the performance of "blackness" dominated the election of Barack Obama. Debates, for instance, about whether Obama was "black enough" in terms of his behavior, attitudes, and personal genealogy provided endless hours of conversation for media pundits and scholars alike. Thus, the politics of identification (the Obama phenomenon), the histories and memories of civil rights and anti-racist struggles in the US, and the aspirations and hopes of marginalized communities across the globe were visible during this ground-breaking election process. It is this particular nexus of the politics of identity (identification, genealogies of oppression and resistance, and dreams and hopes for social justice) that animates my reflections here.

As Margaret Wetherell says in her Introduction to this volume, "Identity continues to be the place where collective action, social movements, and issues of inequality, rights and social justice come into focus and demand attention" (p. 4). It is this very focus that I take up here. The Handbook as a whole maps an enormously rich and generative terrain of scholarship on identity. No closure is possible, but in spite of the call to move "beyond identity" or embrace the politics of "post-identity," the category of identity continues to be important to think with. Here I want to "think with" identity in the ways in which it animates and is anchored in the current geopolitical landscape that engenders collective struggles for social and economic justice in the twenty-first century. I want to reflect then on identity politics and their horizons. Needless to say, this is a very partial, interested map of these questions, anchored in my own discontinuous intellectual and political projects.

Drawing on some of the rich formulations in the chapters in this Handbook, I attempt to map the politics of identity in the context of racialized and gendered colonial legacies, and global capitalist, neo liberal regimes of power and domination. I suggest that these regimes illustrate the contours of relations of rule (Smith, 1987) as well as collective resistance struggles, what Manisha Desai (Chapter 21) refers to as the current "global social justice regimes" within which we can map the politics of identity. The textures and interweaving of colonialism/race, gender/sexuality, nation/diaspora, faith/religion, and ethnicity/class are central to the discursive and material fabric of this cloth.

One way to think about the significance of these two frames (colonial legacies and capitalist/neoliberal processes) in addition to new settlements around faith and religion is to ask whether the paradigmatic figures that circulate in global social imaginaries can be understood *outside* of these frames. These figures include: the barbaric (male) terrorist, the imperial soldier, the trafficked woman, the third world immigrant, the civilized democratic citizen, the oppressed Muslim woman, the female domestic worker, the brown/black migrant worker, the IT professional, the refugee, the asylum seeker, the poverty stricken peasant, the indigenous revolutionary, etc. Every paradigmatic figure identified above is infused with gender, race, sexual, national, faith, and class particularities – and each can be understood in the context of the relational legacies of colonialism, capitalism, differentiated patriarchies, heterosexualities, and racialized institutions and ideologies. Any discussion of collective struggles and the politics of identity then needs to address these institutional and ideological frames.

## COLLECTIVE STRUGGLES AND THE POLITICS OF IDENTITY

Historically, identity politics has had both an activist and an academic existence. Activists involved in successful social movements, such as the civil rights movement, and the women's movement, who self-consciously invoked the concept of identity in their struggles for social justice held at least the following two beliefs: 1) that identities are often resources of knowledge especially relevant for social change, and that 2) oppressed groups need to be at the forefront of their own liberation. (Alcoff and Mohanty, 2006: 2)

In a discussion of the politics of identity in South Africa, Iris Berger (1992) states that the postmodernist emphasis on the fluidity and invention of identity categories, while useful, has also often erased the material significance of identity claims as the ground for political repression by nation states, as it has erased identity as the ground for resistance to such repression. Concepts of race, gender, class, and nation gain salience at particular historical moments, providing the basis for identities forged within collective action against domination. Berger states that "whether the meaning of being Black or being a woman may shift in another decade is of little import to people who perceive such an identity as fundamental to their personal and political consciousness. Indeed it is often through the strength of such identities in popular movements that changes in conceptual meaning occurs" (1992: 285). Thus, Berger draws our attention to the materiality and salience of identities as meaning-making, explanatory frames forged in collective struggles for social justice. Manisha Desai's discussion (Chapter 21) on collective identities and social movements suggests a similar trajectory, building instead on the theorization in the 1970s and 1980s of the complex and multiple identities of women of color in the US, as the source of engagement with a "matrix of domination" (rather than the result of discretely defined race, gender, or class hierarchies). It is this particular theorization of the politics of identity that came to be called "identity politics" in US feminist circles. What both Berger and Desai define as the politics of identity is anchored in an understanding of the epistemic significance of marginalized standpoints, not the collapsing of identity *into* politics.

Linda Alcoff (Chapter 7) suggests in her discussion of feminist standpoint theory, that standpoints are different from social location. Standpoints are the result of critical and self-conscious reflection on the social world and one's particular place within it, as informed by the everyday communal practices of living. Alcoff goes on to explain that post-positivist realist approaches to identity draw on both standpoints and social location to suggest that both the subjective self-reflexive interpretations and objective outward references of social identities have enormous explanatory value. Alcoff (Chapter 7) suggests that identities are "phenomenologically embodied and corporeal" and thus not open to any and all discursive meanings. Thus, she suggests, while we can re-signify the meanings attached to "black," or "queer," we cannot do the same for 'torture' or "rape" since these phenomena have objective meanings in the social world Alcoff's analysis draws attention to the epistemic significance of marginalized identities, thus providing a deeper philosophical theorization of the politics of identity in the context of collective struggles.

What Alcoff and other post-positivist realist theorists such as Mohanty (1998) and Moya (2001) suggest is that identities are like explanatory theories rather than "metaphysical posits." Thus, in this formulation, being "black" in the context of Berger's South Africa, or being a "woman of color" in the context of 1970s or 1980s US feminism, has unique explanatory potential in unraveling the intricacies of domination, reading "up" the ladder of power and forging politicized collective identities. These categories (black or women of color) can also be the basis of the construction of emancipatory knowledges about identity. Put another way, the above discussion of identity in the context of collective struggles draws attention to bodies and borders (social and geo-political) and the exercise of resistance on the basis of politicized group identities.

Some of the most radical liberation movements of the last century have drawn on politicized understandings of identity. From the mid and late twentieth-century anti-colonial movements in the Global South, to the women's, lesbian, gay, bisexual, transgender (LGBT), race and ethnic, and disability rights movements in the last few decades, politicized identity has served as the constitutive anchor for collective struggles against oppression and injustice. In fact it is these very identity-based struggles that gave birth to new interdisciplinary knowledge projects such as Women's and Gender Studies, Indigenous Studies, Disability Studies, Race and Ethnic Studies, LGBT Studies, and most recently, Postcolonial Studies. While these particular movements and knowledge projects have faced intense scrutiny from all sides of the political spectrum, they have not only survived, but have had a profound impact on multiple disciplines in the humanities, social and natural sciences (see chapters by Anne Fausto-Sterling [8], Lynne Segal [16], Harry J. Elam Jr and Michele Elam [9], R. Aída Hernández Castillo [19], and Rosemarie Garland-Thomson and Moya Bailey [20]). In the US and Canada, a number of Women's and Gender Studies programs and departments are celebrating 30- or 35-year anniversaries, while the College of Ethnic Studies at San Francisco State University celebrates its 40th anniversary in 2009. Conversely, the Arizona State Legislature is expected to pass a bill that prohibits ethnic studies being taught in Arizona public schools. Citing the teaching of "individualism" as preferable to ethnic studies, the bill essentially ensures that a Eurocentric, triumphalist national narrative of the US is written, once again, into the school curriculum. Needless to say, there is much organized opposition to this move (Rodriguez, 2009). Similarly, alongside the celebrations of Women's and Gender Studies there is also the experience in both the UK and the US of programs being closed down, amalgamated, or disappearing altogether from the architecture of higher education. Thus, the fight to maintain the radical, identity-based knowledge projects within Women's and Ethnic Studies remains a continuing struggle.

The fact that for instance, identity-based feminist and indigenous collective struggles continue to be waged globally, and that the politicized knowledges engendered by these struggles continue to transform subjective, scholarly, and political terrain is testimony to the centrality of identity politics in social justice movements. Cindy Patton's discussion of "Sexualities" (Chapter 18) highlights the interweaving of politics, epistemology, and collective struggle. Patton speaks of the global gay liberation movement being "as much an effect of the writing of its history as it is a product of history itself" (Patton, Chapter 18).

Thus, in spite of attacks on identity politics on the basis of "essentialist" or "special interest" agendas, politicized identity movements have clearly had enormous success, primarily because in the most complex and far-reaching of these movements, identity is not seen as just embodied (Avtar Brah's [1996] "names and looks"), but, as Brah also notes, is based on the creation of solidarities against particular injustices like heterosexism, racism, colonialism, etc. Hence, it is not just the fact of being an indigenous woman for instance that led to the formation of the Indigenous Women's Network (IWN) in North America, but the analysis of the systems of colonial and sexual oppression, and the solidarity generated through collective action to confront these oppressive systems and practices that constituted IWN as a group. Similarly, the transnational feminist group "Women Living under Muslim Law" (WLUML) traces its identity to a unity around the analysis of Muslim law in terms of its gendered impact on women in different Islamic nations (Moghadam, 2005). What unites the members of WLUML is not a reductive or essentialist construct of their identity as Muslim women (their victim status), but a common critique of the experience of living under and struggling against unjust patriarchal and religious fundamentalist regimes.

In my opinion, thinking with identity in struggles for social justice in the early twenty first century requires this philosophical formulation of the politics of identity (see also epigraph, Alcoff and Mohanty, 2006), specifically as it is located within the uneven geographies and economies of the present. How can we understand bodies and borders in subjective *and* communal terms? How do bodies move across geopolitical borders and how are they held in place? What is the salience of identity in confronting the regressive politics of global capitalism, racist and colonial legacies, heteronormative gender practices, religious and ethnic fundamentalisms? In what follows I try to answer some of these questions drawing on theorizations of the relationality of global capitalist and colonizing processes and cultures from the standpoints of marginalized communities (Hartsock, 2001; Mohanty, 2003), as well as on the contributions of feminist geographers on the intricacies of space, place, and scale in the analysis of power and difference (Mountz, 2001; Nagar et al., 2002).

As mentioned earlier, I suggest two broad maps or frames within which questions of identity and social justice can be analyzed in the present moment: (1) colonial, ethnic/racial legacies and practices and (2) capitalist/ neoliberal formations and processes. These frames also influence what many scholars believe to have been some of the oldest faith-based transnational communities – Sufi orders, Buddhist monks, and Catholic missionaries. As Susanne Rudolph argues, "religion has expanded explosively, stimulated as much by secular global processes – migration, multinational capital, the media revolution—as by proselytizing activity" (1997: 1). These two frames thus provide the context for understanding globalization and the collective struggles and social justice movements that confront it. These are partial, overlapping, profoundly gendered, intermeshed frames, and they operate through discursive/ideological as well as material/institutional processes and structures. Mapping them in this way, I draw attention to the persistent, albeit shifting, nature of power and domination along the axes of race, gender, class, religion, ability, and nation. Each frame draws on ideas presented in the chapters in this handbook, and together the frames suggest how we might think about, and collectively engage in envisioning "identity futures." In each frame, I move between various scales of analysis: subjective, communal/local, regional/ national, and transnational – i.e. from the subjective, individual body to local, regional and global embodied communities. As feminist geographer Richa Nagar suggests, "attention to processes at multiple geographical scales allows us to understand the nuanced ways in which neocolonial relations of power and political and economic structures of domination and subordination combine to shape gendered politics of inequalities, difference, and resistance" (2006: 685).

The Handbook as a whole represents different scales of thinking about identity: from the micro-politics of the construction of selves, psychosocial dynamics and the narration of identities (see for instance chapters by Stephen Frosh [1], Bethan Benwell and Elizabeth Stokoe [4], Wendy Hollway [11], and Helen Lucey [24]) to discussions of community identity practices, groups, institutions and performances (for example, chapters by Stephen Reicher, Russell Spears, and Alexander Haslam [2], Sarah E. Chinn [5], Diane Reay [14], Ann Phoenix [15], Rosemarie Garland-Thomson and Moya Bailey [20], Katharina Schmid, Miles Hewstone, Nicole Tausch, Richard Jenkins, Joanne Hughes and Ed Cairns [23], and Valerie Walkerdine and Peter Bansel [25]), to large-scale discussions of identities in the context of regions, cultures, nations, and diasporas (see, for example, chapters by R. Aída Hernández Castillo [19], Toon van Meijl [3], Pnina Werbner [12], Manisha Desai [21], and Carole Boyce Davies and Monica Jardine [22]). Scale as I am using it here then refers to one or more levels of experience, interpretation, and representation of identity. As feminist geographers use it to understand social and spatial difference, scale is produced by power relations and socio-economic processes, and in turn contributes to social inequalities (Smith, 1997).

## COLONIAL LEGACIES: IDENTITIES PAST AND PRESENT

Thus, we begin – rather than end – this discussion of race and racial formations with the recognition that "race" as we know it is both a lie and a truth. (Elam Jr and Elam, Chapter 9, this volume)

Held firmly in the grip of colonialism for over 500 years, there has been little room for Indigenous peoples to challenge certain foundational racist myths that bind Indigeneity firmly to notions of primordiality, in counterdistinction to modernity. Overwhelmingly, Indigenous peoples are "not allowed" to change if they wish to remain Indigenous. (Lawrence, Chapter 26, this volume)

Zapatism has provoked points of rupture in the State's hegemony, demanding the power to "name" and establish the terms of dialogue, by reorienting the debate on multiculturalism to a discussion on the autonomy and self-determination of indigenous peoples. (Hernández Castillo, Chapter 21, this volume)

The quotes above illustrate the profound, continuous impact of colonialism and anti-colonial struggles in the social imaginaries and institutions of rule in the early twenty-first century. I am referring here to the post-fifteenth-century institutions and ideologies of colonial rule that operated though the setting up of rigid, hierarchical distinctions between the colonizer and the colonized (Fanon, 1970; Memmi, 1965), actively creating the physical and symbolic separation of races to maintain control, transmuting the physical and spatial setting (for instance, of gender and racial segregation) to a moral plane of superiority and inferiority (Mohanty, 2003).

Colonial legacies and practices continue to traffic in the present, impacting the growth of global capitalism and neoliberal ideological and governance structures. At the same time, as in the case of Zapatism (Hernández Castillo, above) anti-colonial struggles for autonomy and self-determination, and struggles over questions of identity and social and economic justice also mark this terrain. In no geo-political context are these legacies and continuities so apparent as in the case of indigenous struggles globally. As Bonita Lawrence (Chapter 26) argues, the history of colonialism, and the systematic appropriation of land by European colonizers has led to the inevitable crafting of indigenous identities around questions of "belonging, tradition, and continuity." Drawing on an analysis of indigenous identity in Canada, Lawrence suggests that the legislation of identity on the basis of colonial definitions of race is challenged by indigenous movements that claim a cultural/national identity. Within indigenous epistemologies then, "one can speak of nationhood as well as people-hood" (Lawrence, Chapter 26). This is a place-based struggle and the very definition of

indigeneity is anchored in an understanding of the relationship of indigenous communities to land and sovereignty. Thus, in a number of ways, Lawrence's discussion of the collective struggles of indigenous peoples in Canada follows the contours of colonial rule suggested earlier: the setting up of rigid, hierarchical distinctions through the legislation of identity, the physical and symbolic separation of races, and the attendant ideologies of the primordiality and non-governmentality of indigenous people are all phenomena confronted by indigenous communities in their struggles for social justice.

In contrast, R. Aída Hernández Castillo's (Chapter 19) discussion of indigeneity as a field of power in Latin America, argues for a transnational construction of identity mobilized to engage anti-colonial struggles across Latin America. These are place-based struggles as well, but unlike Lawrence, Hernández Castillo focuses on the history of the struggles over the construction of an indigenous identity. Of course some of the differences between the two accounts of indigenous identity relate to the different histories of colonialism, as well as to the differences between the marginalization of large groups of indigenous peoples in postcolonial states and the colonization and genocide of considerably smaller indigenous nations by white settler nation-states. Thus, Hernández Castillo analyzes indigeneity and the social justice struggles that emerge in Latin America as the consolidation of power on the transnational stage, culminating in the passage in 2007 of the UN Declaration of the Rights of Indigenous Peoples, recognizing: "the right of indigenous peoples to self-determination, control over their lands and natural resources and the preservation of their culture and traditions" (Hernández Castillo, Chapter 19). She also points to the ways that Latin American neoliberal states move to "separate the policies of recognition from the policies of redistribution" thus co-opting indigenous demands and buttressing a domesticated discourse of multiculturalism. Desai (Chapter 19) echoes this suggestion claiming that the 1990s global human rights framework facilitates the crafting of indigeneity as the basis of claims-making, thus using indigeneity to replace peasants as a political category, in partial response to neoliberal economic policies and the changing role of the state in protecting minorities.

Perhaps the field of study that has had the most to say about colonial legacies in the formation of differentiated identities is post-colonial/subaltern studies. Citing the critical assessment and elaboration of colony and empire, history and community, and nation and modernity as central to the concerns of this field, Saurabh Dube (Chapter 6) presents an informative account of cultural and historical identities in the context of decolonization and nation-building projects. Dube suggests that the history and historiography of colonialism, nationalism, and imperialism in the crafting of modernity, and globalization, with its attendant cultural identities constitute the larger project of postcolonial and subaltern studies. Thus, for instance, studies of colonial practices and institutions have led to important insights into the centrality of gender and sexuality in the formation of national identities, just as it points to the formation of middle class identities in colonial centers at "home" as well as in postcolonial nations. Anti-colonial struggles for liberation as well as collective struggles for land and economic and political rights, environmental justice, and women's rights in the Global South bear the histories of these colonial landscapes.

Colonial legacies are a determining force in the re-making of Caribbean identities in the postcolonial world (Boyce Davies and Jardine, Chapter 22). Drawing on the histories of migration and the making of nations and diasporas as a result of the global movement of Caribbean peoples across oceans and continents, Boyce Davies and Jardine specify the "destruction of native peoples, the wretchedness of enslavement, colonialism, and the struggles for self-determination" as central to the making of Caribbean identity. The claim here is that

particular histories of colonialism, global economic forces, and struggles for liberation profoundly shape the contours of Caribbean identity. Boyce Davies and Jardine suggest that we need new vocabularies to describe the various geo-political and cultural encounters that constitute these migrations and diasporas. Thus, Dionne Brand speaks of "The Door Of No Return" as "that place where our ancestors departed one world for another, the Old World for the New. The place where all names were forgotten and all beginnings recast. In some desolate sense it was the creation place of Blacks in the New World Diaspora at the same time as it signified the end of terrible beginnings" (2001: 5). Here Brand is mapping a particular cartography of the postcolonial identities of black communities in the "New World." Brand's framing of the making of "black" in the crucible of enslavement, middle passage, and struggles for liberation in postcolonial and advanced capitalist nation-states, suggests the salience of the colonial legacies and marginalized epistemologies in the making of identity.

Complicating this diasporic narrative of "blackness," Elam Jr and Elam (Chapter 9) introduce the question of mixed race identity and of comparative racialization in the context of "Coloureds" in South Africa. They argue persuasively that "comparative racialization, then, relies on a relationality beyond the similarities and differences between two different racial contexts or races: rather it involves bringing submerged or displaced relationalities into view." The politics of racial identity within the context of colonial legacies and struggles of liberation take on a somewhat different valence here.

Pnina Werbner (Chapter 12) shows that religious encounters within and outside colonial contexts generate discourses of identities similar to those generated by racial/ethnic or national encounters. Werbner argues that faith based identities and movements have always been located within a "shifting social field of difference and differentiation." Thus, similar processes of the making of identity and social movements anchored in religious identity can be traced throughout history and continents (The Crusades and Militant Islam in the Middle Ages; Hindu fundamentalism and Liberation Theology in the twentieth century, etc.). Werbner defines religious identity as "above all, a discourse of boundaries, relatedness and otherness, on the one hand, and encompassment and inclusiveness, on the other – and of the powerful forces that are perceived to challenge, contest and preserve these distinctions and unities." In effect, the two frames (colonial legacies and capitalist/neoliberal projects) I discuss here exercise power by setting up of discourses of "boundaries, relatedness and otherness." The next section focuses on my second frame: capitalist/neoliberal processes.

## CAPITALIST/NEOLIBERAL IDENTITIES: CONFRONTING POWER

Capitalist dynamics infuse and traverse all struggles (such as sexuality, race, and gender) operating as the very background and terrain for their emergence of minority subjectivities. (Skeggs, Chapter 17, this volume)

Our practices of consumption are now more central to us than our roles associated with production in processes of identity: what we buy is more significant than what we do. (Wood, Chapter 13, this volume)

The border is a place where Spanglish is the lingua franca and where age-old Catholic shrines stand side-by-side with maquilas, the monuments of neoliberal capitalism, where el dia de los muertos and mariachis meet the electronicas [...] More than anything, the ambiguities within and between the notions of border and borderlands define religion's involvement in globalization. (Vasquez and Friedmann Marquardt, 2003: 62–63)

The constant, unevenly distributed flow of capital and labor across borders, and between nations, is not just an economic process – it impacts social identities and cultural relations across gender, race, ethnicity, religion, and sexuality. Unlike during the heyday of industrial expansion, the global working class today is primarily girls and women of color. It is migrant and displaced women and girls from the Global South who provide the labor for a transnational economy of care-giving, as domestic workers, nurses, and nannies (Rodriguez, 2008). And it is this very care-giving economy that underwrites the growth of the new middle classes. As Zillah Eisenstein (2009) argues, "these new workers are part of the continual migrant populations of displaced peoples, exiles, undocumented workers, traffickers, and so on." One hundred and seventy five million people live outside their country of birth and approximately 49 percent of these are women and girls. Of the 25 million persons internally displaced, 70 percent are women (Jones, 2008). The subjective and geo-political narratives of these particular groups of marginalized women (workers, migrants, refugees) suggest different contours of working class identities inflected through sexuality, gender, nation, and diaspora.

Working-class identity is also, of course crafted in collective struggles for economic justice, specifically in labor movements. Much of labor history over the last century attests to the collective mobilization of class, gender, and racial identities in the struggle against economic exploitation. For instance, Julie Guard (2004) analyzes how women strikers in 1964 Dunville, Ontario (Canada) claimed multiethnic identities as workers and authentic unionists, while Maria Mies (1986) maps self-employed, women worker's identities as entrepreneurs coping with the impact of global markets in Narsapur, India.

In her rich and provocative analysis of working-class identifications, Beverley Skeggs (Chapter 17) argues that class is a way of "narrating" oneself. Skeggs analyzes the ways in which discourses and figures of "the dangerous outcast, the urban mass, the revolutionary alien, the contagious women, and the dirty degenerate" produced working classness in the nineteenth century, and continue to do so today in modified form. Skeggs maintains that we need an analysis of an "economy of personhood" within capitalism to understand the process of class formation.

A somewhat different point of entry into thinking identity under neo liberal/capitalist social formations is suggested by Helen Wood (Chapter 13) in her discussion of the individualization of identity through the consumption of media and reality television. Wood suggests that media practices of consumption may be becoming more central than practices of production in identity construction (see above quote). While this argument is seemingly at odds with the earlier argument about the global diaspora of women of color caregivers, the two discussions operate at very different scales. Where Wood draws on the micro-practices of media consumption as central to the process of individualization of working-class identity in neo-liberal, capitalist cultures, Jones and Eisentein map the global flow of migrant women workers whose very labor makes neoliberal cultures of consumption possible. All three scholars, Wood, Jones and Eisenstein address questions of power, difference, and identity in the wake of global capitalism.

Valerie Walkerdine and Peter Bansel's (Chapter 25) work on neo-liberalism and workplace identities offers yet another layer of analysis in the construction of what they describe as "docile, neo-liberal subjectivities." Walkerdine and Bansel argue that neoliberal subjectivities produce their own individual biographies, anchored in the "boundless opportunities" offered by the market. The freedom to consume thus becomes the basis of identity. They also demonstrate, however, how specific neoliberal interpellations can be, reminding us again of the importance of space and time to the ways in which ideological apparatuses and material practices articulate in lived lives. Walkerdine and Bansel's discussion of identity and governmentality within neo liberal cultures is supported by Diane Reay's formulation in Chapter 14 of the way educational politics are grounded in "individualistic, entrepreneurial and aspirational conceptions of the self." Drawing on Basil Bernstein and Pierre Bourdieu's work, Reay discusses pedagogies of identity

formation in education – the production of appropriate attitudes, dispositions, and performances necessary for a market culture and a shrinking welfare state.

Thus, while Walkerdine and Bansel, Wood, and Reay map the processes of individualization, consumption, and instrumentalization of identities under global capitalist/neoliberal cultures in Britain, Wales, and Australia, Desai, Hernández-Castillo, and Boyce Davies and Jardine focus on collective identities in social movements within the same neoliberal capitalist landscape. Framing her arguments in terms of the theorization of identities and social movements by women of color in the USA in the 1970s and 1980s, Desai foregrounds the intersectionality of identities based on a matrix of domination, the experience of overlapping forms of difference and a particularized coalition politics that emerges from this understanding of identity. Thus, depending on the kind of capitalist/neoliberal processes and cultures specified by each of these scholars there is a shift in the scale of analysis. In each instance, individual, social, and geopolitical differences are produced within the frame of a relational understanding of power, individual and collective identities, and capitalist/neoliberal landscapes. Scale is fundamentally produced by capitalist, political economies, therefore, social actors can contest or challenge the politics of scale as it is played out in different sites: in households, communities, national, or global cultures. Thus, anti-globalization, anti-prison, and place-based labor movements as well as the white, working-class women in Skeggs' study all confront capitalist domination and neoliberal cultures suggesting the key significance of the politics of identity in social and economic justice work at the present time.

## IDENTITY FUTURES

The above discussion of colonial legacies and capitalist/neoliberal projects frames my central preoccupation in this reflection: how to think with identity in the context of collective struggles for justice in the geo-political landscape that we inherit and continue to exploit. I have been particularly concerned with the politics of identity mobilized by communities marginalized as a result of their gendered, racial, sexual, national, or class status and location. Identity based social movements have influenced political as well as academic arenas. And while understandings of the politics of identity have shifted in the last decades due to new epistemological and scholarly work as well as new cartographies of organized social movements, the salience of identity politics remains uncontested.

Given the geopolitical landscape described in this essay, anti-war, anti-globalization, prison abolitionist, labor, national liberation, women's and LGBT rights, indigenous, disability, and civil rights, environmental justice, and pro-democracy movements continue to mobilize complex formulations of identity in confronting power. While borders continue to be held in place to construct insiders and outsiders, and power is exercised at all scales transforming difference into hierarchy, identities will continue to matter in social justice work. Thus, for instance, while religion can provide the vision and energy for collective action in the service of social justice as in Liberation theology movements empowering the poor in Latin America, religious identities also become sources of great dilemmas, as, for example, when Muslims challenge compulsory dress codes in Marseilles or demand the enforcement of blasphemy laws in London (Rudolph, 1997).

I began with a narrative about the Bush/Blair and Brown/Obama moment. I want to end with a narrative about Sonia Sotomayor – the first Latina to be nominated to the US Supreme Court, and Meira Kumar, the first Dalit woman speaker of the Lok Sabha (the Indian parliament). Both women currently occupy center stage in the political identity narratives of the US and India. Both are poised to "represent" historically marginalized communities – and both are heralded as groundbreaking political events. Whether the "names and looks" (Brah, 1996) of Sotomayor and Kumar will translate into real meaningful political transformations for "women and minorities/minoritized women" remains an open question. Identities are about representation in the public arena as the above example suggests, but they also constitute the ground for deep challenges to power as illustrated by the Zapatistas in Mexico, Muslim feminists in North Africa, and environmental justice advocates in Syracuse, NY.

Let me end by re-iterating our hope that the chapters in this Handbook suggest identity futures not yet imagined. I have focused on two formative frames in contextualizing this reflection on social justice and the politics of identity, but I am well aware that as I write, the debate in Europe is being reconfigured by faith and new identity dilemmas and conjunctures. The future of identity politics lies open – after all, the achievement of justice and equality in racial terms, for instance, suggests the future irrelevance of racial identities. Similarly, gender identities are less important in a world where gender justice is no longer a necessary form of collective struggle. This is the world we seek in the future. But it is not the world we have inherited or occupy now. Scholarly and activist projects that mobilize politicized identities in the service of social justice point to new horizons, as well as mapping the limits of identity politics. I do believe that while a black man as US President does not erase legacies of racism, colonialism, and economic domination, it does perhaps mean that we can inhabit our histories and identities differently.

## NOTES

1   I am using the terms identity politics, politics of identity, and politicized identity somewhat interchangeably here to denote the significance of identity defined in relation to power and inequity in the public sphere.

2   Marginalization in this instance refers to a subjugated relationship to power.

# REFERENCES

Alexander, M.J. (2006) *Pedagogies of Crossing: Meditations on Feminism, Sexual Politics, Memory, and the Sacred*. Durham, NC: Duke University Press.

Alcoff, L.M. and Mohanty, S.P. (2006) 'Reconsidering identity politics: An introduction', in L.M. Alcoff, M. Hames-García, S.P. Mohanty and P.M.L. Moya (eds), *Identity Politics Reconsidered*. New York: Palgrave.

Berger, I. (1992) 'Categories and contexts: Reflections on the politics of identity in South Africa', *Feminist Studies*, 18 (2): 284–94.

Brah, A. (1996) *Cartographies of Diaspora*. London: Routledge.

Brand, D. (2001) *A Map to the Door of No Return, Notes to Belonging*. Canada: Vintage Books.

Eisenstein, Z. (2009) *The Audacity of Races and Genders*. London: Zed Books.

Fanon, F. (1970) *Black Skin, White Masks*. London: Paladin.

Guard, J. (2004) 'Authenticity on the line, women workers, native "scabs," and the multi-ethnic politics of identity in a left-led strike in Cold War Canada', *Journal of Women's History*, 15 (4): 117–40.

Hartsock, N. (2001) 'Domination, globalization: Towards a feminist analytic'. Paper presented at the Inkrit *Conference on Domination and Ideology in High Tech Capitalism*, Berlin, 24–27 May.

Jones, A. (2008) 'A silent but mighty river: The costs of women's economic migration', *Signs*, 33 (4): 761–9.

Memmi, A. (1965) *The Colonizer and the Colonized*. Boston, MA: Beacon Press.

Mies, M. (1986) *Patriarchy and Accumulation on a World Scale: Women in the International Division of Labor*. London: Zed Books.

Moghadam, V.M. (2005) *Globalizing Women: Transnational Feminist Networks*. Baltimore, MD: Johns Hopkins University Press.

Mohanty, C.T. (2003) *Feminism Without Borders: Decolonizing Theory, Practicing Solidarity*. Durham, NC: Duke University Press.

Mohanty, S.P. (1998) *Literary Theory and the Claims of History: Postmodernism, Objectivity, Multicultural Politics*. Ithaca, NY: Cornell University Press.

Mountz, A. (2001) 'Embodying the nation-state: Gendered narratives of human smuggling'. Paper presented at the annual meeting of the *Association of American Geographers*, New York, 27 February–3 March.

Moya, P.M.L. and Hames-García, M. (eds) (2001) *Reclaiming Identity: Realist Theory and the Predicament of Postmodernism*. Berkeley, CA: University of California Press.

Nagar, R. (2006) *Playing with Fire: Feminist Thought and Activism Through Seven Lives in India*. Minneapolis, MN: University of Minnesota Press.

Nagar, R., Lawson, V., McDowell, L. and Hanson, S. (2002) 'Locating globalization: Feminist (re)readings of the subjects and spaces of globalization', *Economic Geography*, 78 (3): 257–84.

Radcliffe, S.A., Laurie, N. and Andoline, R. (2003) 'The transnationalization of gender and re-imagining Andean indigenous development', *Signs*, 29 (2): 387–416.

Rodriguez, R.D.C. (2009) 'Tom Horne to ethnic studies: Drop dead!', *Arizona Watch, 19 June*. Available at: http://news.newamericamedia.org/news/

Rodriguez, R.M. (2008) 'The labor brokerage state and the globalization of Filipina care workers', *Signs*, 33 (4): 794–9.

Rudolph, S.H. (1997) 'Religion, states, and transnational civil society', in S.H. Rudolph and J. Piscatori (eds), *Transnational Religion and Fading States*. Boulder, CO: Westview Press.

Smith, D. (1987) *The Everyday World As Problematic: A Feminist Sociology*. Boston, MA: Northeastern University Press.

Smith, N. (1997) 'The satanic geographies of globalization: The uneven development in the 1990s', *Public Culture*, 10: 169–80.

Sudbury, J. (2005) *Global Lockdown: Race, Gender, and the Prison-Industrial Complex*. New York: Routledge.

Vasquez, M.A. and Friedmann Marquardt, M. (2003) 'Theorizing globalization and religion', in M.A. Vasquez and M. Friedmann Marquardt (eds), *Globalizing the Sacred: Religion Across the Americas*. New Jersey: Rutgers University Press.

# Index